D1034165

Ego Development:
Conceptions and Theories

Jane Loevinger
with the assistance of Augusto Blasi

EGO DEVELOPMENT

68105

OAKTON COMMUNITY COLLEGE
DES PLAINES CAMPUS
1600 EAST GOLF ROAD
DES PLAINES, IL 60016

Jossey-Bass Publishers

San Francisco • Washington • London • 1977

EGO DEVELOPMENT
Conceptions and Theories
        by Jane Loevinger with the assistance of Augusto Blasi

Copyright © 1976 by: Jossey-Bass, Inc., Publishers
                      615 Montgomery Street
                      San Francisco, California 94111
                            &
                      Jossey-Bass Limited
                      28 Banner Street
                      London EC1Y 8QE

Copyright under International, Pan American, and
Universal Copyright Conventions. All rights
reserved. No part of this book may be reproduced
in any form—except for brief quotation (not to
exceed 1,000 words) in a review or professional
work—without permission in writing from the publishers.

Library of Congress Catalogue Card Number LC 75-44880

International Standard Book Number ISBN 0-87589-275-2

Manufactured in the United States of America

JACKET DESIGN BY WILLI BAUM

OAKTON COMMUNITY COLLEGE
DES PLAINES CAMPUS
1600 EAST GOLF ROAD
DES PLAINES, IL 60016

FIRST EDITION
        First printing: March 1976
        Second printing: December 1977

Code 7603

The Jossey-Bass
Behavioral Science Series

Preface

Facing the complexity and diversity of human behavior, the mind seeks forms and order. This book endeavors to help, by sketching in Chapter Two a set of forms through which human behavior and thought develop. What is covered is not all of human behavior, for there are other aspects, like temperament, that seem relatively constant throughout long time spans or, like intelligence, that develop quite independently of those traced here. Our compass is large, however; many facets of thought, perception, motivation, valuation, and behavior are included.

The central claim of this book is that many diverse aspects of thought, interpersonal relations, impulse control, and character grow at once, in some more or less coherent way. As bold as this argument is, you might expect to find an array of psychological investigations marshalled in its support, but there is little of that. Nor do I claim support from the breadth of my own experience. I am no clinician, and my research has been almost entirely a paper-and-pencil exchange with my subjects. The empirical support for the conception of ego development presented is that it represents a common thread in the work of many authors: psychiatrists, psychoanalysts, sociologists, philosophers, psychologists, and others (Chapter Five). These authors have studied women and men, boys and girls, normal people, delinquents, neurotics, and psychotics. Their experience is not limited to one country or even to one century. Many of them have taken a single strand as their focus of interest, but they are invariably led to other facets of the conception. Nothing any of us can do by way of laboratory or psychometric research can compare with what emerges from the communality of their observations.

To conclude from that broad observational base that I am here putting together an eclectic view of human nature and its development is, however, a misconception. A central theme of the book is structure, as applied to personality (Chapter Three) and as applied to science as an endeavor (Chapter Twelve). While the book puts together what some will find a bewildering variety of themes, there is a coherence, not all of it evident on first reading. Coherence is the hallmark of ego; it is also the hallmark of science.

This book is intended for professionals and research workers in psychology, social work, education, counseling, psychiatry, psychoanalysis, sociology, anthropology, and related disciplines. In choosing topics to emphasize, I could not satisfy all their interests simultaneously; readers may feel I have not tried to satisfy any of them, and that in a way is true. I think of myself as the servant, not the master, of my topic. Writing has presented two minimax problems: how to maximize the logic of presentation while minimizing historical inversions and how to avoid boredom for those with considerable background in the field without mystifying those with less previous reading in it. I will state first what underlies the chosen order of topics and then offer some suggestions for those, like beginning graduate students, for whom this order presents difficulties.

In expounding the conception of ego development, Chapter One introduces the topic and provides a glimpse of its niche in psychology and its historical lineage. Chapter Two defines the conception by pointing to its stages. Chapter Three, by Augusto Blasi, deals with the conceptual issues differentiating development from other kinds of change as they pertain to personality and with the problem of reconciling a humanistic with a structural approach. Chapter Four deals with further conceptual issues relating to the ego and to ego development. Together, chapters Three and Four give the parameters of our conception and the terms used in comparing it with other related conceptions. Alternative formulations of what appear to me to be essentially the same concept are presented in Chapter Five; chapters Two, Three, and Four are the scaffolding on which chapters Five and Six are hung. Chapter Six is devoted to conceptions that are similar but view the underlying continuum directly rather than through its discrete stages; that topic is intertwined with description of the highest stage and of the relation to adjustment and mental health. The distinction between polar variables and milestone sequences also lays the groundwork for Chapter Nine on measurement techniques.

Part Two, on methodology, continues the topic of differential conception. Where Chapter Six differentiates ego development from adjustment, a nondevelopmental variable, Chapter Seven differentiates it from intellectual and psychosexual development. Chapter Eight, without looking at specific measuring instruments, asks why research cannot settle forthwith the differences in conceptions revealed in Chapter Five. Chapter Nine, on the other hand, ignores the differences in content of stages per different authors and examines the differences in assessment instruments and their logic. Chapter Ten puts ego development in the context of differential psychology; there I separate my position from that of trait theorists, among whom I once abided, and contrast my view with the specifist-nominalist current in American psychology.

Part Three concerns theories of ego stability and change. Most of the major contributions prove to come from Freud. Psychoanalysts, however, usually use the term *ego development* with different connotations, referring either to the earliest stage of ego formation or to the development of separate ego functions. Our discussion, by contrast, takes ego formation for granted and concerns itself with later transformations, and it neglects the several ego functions in favor of the organization underlying them. With the partial exception of Erikson's work, psychoanalysis has lacked a stage-type conception such as ours. Indeed, ego psychology and psychoanalysis were for long locked in a mutually stimulating opposition. Chapter Eleven shows how far early theories of ego development came before any appreciable influence from psychoanalysis was felt; this chapter fills a gap in other histories of psychology. Chapter Twelve asks how far we can go toward understanding theory of ego development by using general considerations of contemporary theories of development, such as those of Piaget on intellectual development and Kuhn on development of science. The early history of psychoanalysis, arising in opposition to and as a corrective to nineteenth-century ego psychology, is traced in Chapter Thirteen. Chapter Fourteen shows Freud's ego theory originating as a derivative of and a corrective to his drive theory, while Chapter Fifteen reviews some recent work recasting psychoanalysis as a theory of ego development. Chapter Sixteen, on origins of conscience, is not another review of superego theory; it takes from that literature only what is needed to tie the theory of Part Three to the stage conception of Part One. It brings our topic back to its source, the ethical nature of man. The final chapter reviews theories of ego development from a new perspective.

While I would be criticized had I left out the topic of chapters Thirteen through Sixteen, I expect to be criticized also for the audacity to write yet another history of psychoanalysis. My orientation is not to a literal reading of Freud, a topic on which others are more knowledgeable, nor to what most contemporary psychoanalysts assert about character development (assertions that Kohlberg frequently opposes); my orientation is to psychoanalysis as a structure of ideas, a system that I believe assimilates the conception developed in Part One without strain. T. S. Kuhn's book has helped me understand something about the structure of science, though Kuhn would not consider anything so controversial as the present book as mature science.

Thus, I begin by talking about a central core of personality development, but on another level I am also making a case for a view of human nature, and on another level I am making a case for a way of doing psychology as science.

The order of topics is not completely satisfactory logically, pedagogically or chronologically. In teaching a seminar based on these materials, I have tried about a dozen different orders, and I always find myself talking about topics that can only be clarified in terms of some later part of the course. Chapters are presented in the best order I can find from the point of view of a professional with considerable background or a graduate student in his second reading. Although this book is not a textbook, it may be used by instructors in graduate courses. They may prefer some different order, filling the gaps in the presentation by lecture or other readings. Since each chapter has its own unity and point, such rearrangement is facilitated. Other readers may wish to use this book as their portal of entry into a new field of study. Let me present one program for doing so.

Chapters One, Two, and the first half of Three need no further introduction and give the reader a fair taste of what is to come. At that point one should read *The Moral Judgment of the Child* (Piaget, 1932), then "Development of Moral Character and Moral Ideology" (Kohlberg, 1964) or some other writings of Kohlberg that present his scheme. *Forms of Intellectual and Ethical Development in the College Years* (Perry, 1970) is worth reading in its entirety. Finally, and most difficult, one should read *Interpersonal Theory of Psychiatry* (Sullivan, 1953). With that background, Chapters Five and Six follow without further difficulty. Those whose primary interest is in psychological research in this area should read the four chapters of Part Two next; some background in psychometrics is assumed in Chapter Nine.

Those whose interests are clinical or primarily conceptual can skip Part Two. Before beginning Chapter Eleven, some reading in original sources is helpful. A convenient source for brief excerpts from Baldwin, Mead, and Cooley is *The Self in Social Interaction* (Gordon and Gergen, 1968). "The Reflex Arc Concept in Psychology" (Dewey, 1896) has been reprinted by Dennis (1948). *The Structure of Scientific Revolutions* (Kuhn,

1970) may be read at any time but certainly before reading
Chapter Twelve.

What remains is psychoanalysis, and my suggestions are
addressed only to those whose knowledge of it has been obtained through secondary sources. That is not adequate. Some
reading of Freud is necessary to appreciate fully the psychoanalytic system. My argument depends on the fact that psychoanalysis was a workable therapeutic paradigm before introduction of the structural hypothesis of ego, superego, and id. A
brief, elegant version of the drive paradigm is found in the Clark
lectures, reprinted as "The Origin and Development of Psychoanalysis" or "Five Lectures on Psychoanalysis" (Freud, 1910).
Before reading the second half of Chapter Fourteen, one should
read the first part of *Beyond the Pleasure Principle* (Freud,
1920), *Inhibitions, Symptoms, and Anxiety* (Freud, 1926), and
Civilization and Its Discontents (Freud, 1930). Adequate excerpts from both the Clark lectures and Freud's writings on ego
psychology can be found in *A General Selection from the
Works of Sigmund Freud* (Rickman, 1975). Erikson's *Childhood and Society* (1963) should be read before Chapter Fifteen, and *Man, Morals and Society* (Flugel, 1945) before Chapter Sixteen. A valuable secondary source for psychoanalysis is
Basic Theory of Psychoanalysis (Waelder, 1960).

One of the considerations that led me to include so wide a
range of topics in one book is that students seem to tuck each
new set of ideas into a separate pocket, as if there were no more
problem in reconciling Walter Mischel's view of people with
Lawrence Kohlberg's than in appreciating both Dostoyevsky
and Jane Austen. Comprehensive examinations encourage such
compartmental thinking, but original and creative work usually
requires breaking down the divisions. Even if my integration of
the ideas is not convincing, bringing the many trains of thought
within one cover may stimulate others to integrative thinking.

To acknowledge all those who have helped me would take
an autobiography, so I shall mention only a few. Augusto Blasi's
influence extends beyond the chapters that he is credited with
as author or coauthor. For many years one of my most faithful
critics has been Robert R. Holt. William F. Shumate, Jr., has

helped particularly with syntax and style. William E. Henry
helped to transform an amorphous collection of essays into
something more like a book. In retrospect, the influence of my
first teachers at the University of California at Berkeley, particularly Egon Brunswik, Else Frenkel-Brunswik, and Erik Erikson, has not diminished.

Completion of this book has been possible thanks to Research Grant MH-05115 and Research Scientist Award K5
MH-657, both from the National Institute of Mental Health,
Public Health Service. Those grants have provided me with freedom to write, with secretarial help, and also with funds to do
research that, though much of it does not appear here, has
helped shape my ideas.

Acknowledgements

Some parts of this book have appeared previously in somewhat
different form. Parts of Chapters Four, Eleven, and Fifteen
appeared in "Theories of Ego Development" in *Clinical-Cogni-
tive Psychology: Models and Integrations,* edited by Louis
Breger, published by Prentice-Hall, 1969. Permission to reprint
has been granted by Prentice-Hall. The first part of Chapter
Seven appeared in "Models and Measures of Developmental
Variation," in the *Annals of the New York Academy of Sciences,* 1966, Volume 134, Article 2, pages 585-590. Figures 2, 3,
4, 5, and 7 appeared there. Permission to reprint has been
granted by the New York Academy of Sciences. Part of Chapter
Eight appeared in *Measuring Ego Development,* co-authored
with Ruth Wessler, published by Jossey-Bass, Inc. Part of Chapter Fifteen appeared as "Freud's Science," a book review of
Michael Sherwood's *The Logic of Explanation in Psychoanalysis,* published in *Science,* 12 December, 1969, Volume 166,
pages 1389-1390, copyright 1969 by the American Association
for Advancement of Science, by whom permission to reprint
has been granted. Most of Chapter Sixteen will appear as "Origins of Conscience" in "Psychology versus Metapsychology:
Psychoanalytic Essays in Memory of George S. Klein," *Psychological Issues,* 1976, Volume 9, number 4, Monograph 36,

edited by Merton M. Gill and Philip S. Holzman. Permission to reprint has been granted by Dr. Holzman and International Universities Press.

The poem by Ernest Kroll appearing as epigraph to Part One appeared originally in the *Virginia Quarterly Review*, 1953, Volume 29, page 383. Permission to reprint has been granted by the *Virginia Quarterly Review*.

Kenneth S. Isaacs has granted permission to reprint extensive passages from his doctoral dissertation, "Relatability, a Proposed Construct and an Approach to its Validation." Figure 1 is adapted from figures appearing there.

Washington University   Jane Loevinger
St. Louis, Missouri
January 1976

Contents

Tables and Figures

Ego Development:
Conceptions and Theories

PART I

CONCEPTIONS

The stream we did not know we lived upon the banks of
Proceeded nevertheless unto the sea.
It touched us in its effects, watering
The flowers in the field, which kept that one cause
      back.
The bloodroot clearly tapped a secret source,
Until we saw the surface shake
Its daytime diamonds in the windy brake,
And the thought occurred: of course.

So much within the scope of mind
Lay simply undivined
That even more without
Would, less than ever, be found out.

—Ernest Kroll

From *The Pauses of the Eye* by Ernest Kroll.
Copyright © 1955 by Ernest Kroll. Reprinted by permission
of the publisher, E. P. Dutton & Co., Inc.

Chapter One

The Domain: Ego and Character

Individual differences in character have interested men for centuries. Interest in how character is formed in childhood and youth is also ancient. But to see those two phenomena as manifestations of a single developmental continuum is a modern twist. That insight is the origin of ego development as a formal discipline. The term *ego development* can connote the course of character development within individuals, the history of the construct, or the increase in capacity for ego development that has occurred during man's history. This book will be devoted mainly to the first topic, but the present chapter will concern the second. The third will be touched on in Chapter Eleven.

I am here proposing a new use for an old term, but I am not just proposing an arbitrary redefinition. Although ego development has been dealt with in the field of ethics as *moral development,* the term usually used in child psychology for the most

3

closely related topic is *socialization*. Now, most approaches to socialization, like most of ethics, are irrelevant to our discussion, or, in some cases, even antithetical to our approach, as will be noted in Chapter Ten. Most child psychologists view socialization as the training of specific behaviors; but our topic is character *structure*. Its development, consequently, is seen as a transformation of structures, a formulation that suggests both the importance of the cognitive element and the influence of Jean Piaget (Chapter Three). Piaget's influence is felt not only through his seminal volume on *The Moral Judgment of the Child* (1932) but even more through his studies of cognitive development and the espousal of structuralism as a point of view. Thus our discussion of ego development includes some topics previously discussed under moral development, socialization, character structure, and even cognitive development. Indeed, the breadth of topics subsumed under *ego development* justifies the term, for nothing less than the ego has so wide a scope.

Although I shall take *ego development* to cover topics previously given other names, it is also true that the term has been used in ways quite different from mine, particularly by psychoanalysts. Indeed, many people believe that the term originated within psychoanalysis, or even that Freud originated the concept of the ego. On the contrary, psychoanalysis was originally a reaction to nineteenth-century ego psychology, and Freud rarely if ever used the term *ego*. His term was *das Ich*, literally, *the I*. Terms such as *the I, the me, self,* and *ego* were in wide though inconsistent usage in nineteenth-century philosophy, psychology, and psychiatry. Many pages could be spent tracing the definitions and usages of authors in different languages—but that would not prove anything about the people walking around in the real world with intact egos, who are the subject of this book. To give a formal definition of ego development would imply that the limits of the topic can be set arbitrarily, but that would belie the conception that ego development is something that occurs in the real world.

There are at least four meanings given to *ego development* in psychoanalysis, of which only one, Erikson's chronicle of psychosocial development, is at all compatible with the usage in this book. One usage current among psychoanalysts (for example, Spitz, 1959), confines development to the stage during which the ego is coming into existence. That usage, although logically correct, deprives the term of usefulness, for during ego formation one cannot distinguish ego development from psychosexual development or intellectual development (Chapter Seven) or even from adjustment (Chapter Six).

Another psychoanalytic usage takes *ego development* as referring to all development within the "conflict-free ego sphere" (Hartmann, 1939). But characteristics of the several stages of ego development are laden with connotations of conflict, as will be seen in Chapters Two and Five. Indeed, I will argue that coping with and accepting inner conflict are distinctive marks of high ego level.

Probably the most frequent psychoanalytic usage, a variant of the one just given, begins with a conception of the ego as the seat of many functions and defines ego development as comprising the development of any of those functions (for example, Bellak, Hurvich, and Gediman, 1973). That usage is inconsistent with mine: some, but not all, ego functions develop as an organic unity. That organic unity is my subject. Freud (1923) stated that the ego is an organization. Not long afterward, however, an eminent psychoanalyst discovered the "synthetic function of the ego" (Nunberg, 1931), as if the synthetic function were one among many, as if the ego were a little man with a bag of tricks, the ego functions. From my view, the organization or the synthetic function is not just another thing the ego does, it is what the ego is. (I return to this point in Chapter Four.)

Thus, the term *ego development* has been used too loosely by psychoanalysts, who seldom recognize that it has such diverse meanings or that it cannot have them and simultaneously be made to cover Erikson's (1950) sketch of psychosocial development. In none of the foregoing meanings, including the socialization of child psychology, is there a glimmer of the distinctive feature of the concept as I use it, namely, that ego development is a major dimension of individual differences in any age cohort, at least beyond the youngest.

Conception of the ego and the related conception of its development go back to the "axial age in human history" (Jaspers, 1948), the period when people became conscious of themselves as human, a period that occurred in various cultures more or less independently between 800 and 200 B.C. In Plato's *Apology,* Socrates says to Callias, "If your two sons were only colts or bullocks, we could have hired a trainer for them to make them beautiful and good and all that they should be; and our trainer would have been, I take it, a horseman or a farmer. But now that they are human beings, have you any trainer in your mind for them? Is there anyone who understands what a man and a citizen ought to be?"

The idea of the person as developing to fulfill his own best nature has, then, existed at least since the time of Socrates, and it has always coexisted with an alternative view of human nature as being elaborated entirely out of forces acting upon it, including instinctual drives and experience. One version of this alternative view has been called the Pleasure Principle: People act so as to maximize pleasure and minimize pain. The classic exposition of the person as a pleasure seeker is that of Bentham: "Nature has placed mankind under the governance of two sovereign masters, *pain* and *pleasure.* It is for them alone to point out what we ought to do, as well as to determine what we shall do. On the one hand the standard of right and wrong, on the other the chain of causes and effects, are fastened to their throne. They govern us in all we do, in all we say, in all we think: every effort we can make to throw off our subjection, will serve but to demonstrate and confirm it. In words a man may pretend to abjure their empire, but in reality he will remain subject to it all the while" ([1789] 1962, p. 33). Pleasures, according to Bentham, differ only in amount—that is, in intensity, duration, probability of occurring, and the like—what Skinner calls *schedules of reinforcement.* Pinball is as good as poetry, as long as it gives equal pleasure.

An answer to Bentham was written by John Stuart Mill, in an essay that requires little alteration to become the manifesto of contemporary ego psychology. Mill admired much of Bentham's work. Bentham, he said, introduced into philosophy the method of detail: he declined to reason about wholes until they were resolved into parts, about abstractions until they were reduced to things. But the writings of every philosopher who did not use his method Bentham dismissed as "vague generalities," forgetting, as Mill pointed out, that those vague generalities contain the "whole unanalyzed experience of the human race" ([1838] 1962, p. 94). Mill criticized the poverty of Bentham's view of human nature ([1838] 1962, pp. 99-101):

> Man is conceived by Bentham as a being susceptible of pleasures and pains, and governed in all his conduct partly by the different modifications of self-interest and the passions commonly classed as selfish, partly by sympathies or occasionally antipathies towards other beings. And here Bentham's conception of human nature stops. . . .
>
> Man is never recognized by him as a being capable of pursuing spiritual perfection as an end; of desiring, for its own sake, the conformity of his own character to his standard of excellence, without hope of good or fear of evil from other source than his own inward consciousness. . . .
>
> Nor is it only the moral part of man's nature, in the strict sense of the term—the desire of perfection or the feeling of an approving or of an accusing conscience—that he overlooks; he but faintly recognizes, as a fact in human nature, the pursuit of any other ideal end for its own sake. The sense of *honor* and personal dignity—that feeling of personal exaltation and degradation which acts independently of other people's opinion, or even in defiance of it; the love of *beauty*, the passion of the artist; the love of *order*, of congruity, of consistency in all things and conformity to their end; the love of *power*, not in the limited form of power over other human beings, but abstract power, the power of making our volitions effectual; the love of *action*, the thirst for movement and activity, a principle scarcely of less influence in human life than its opposite, the love of ease:—None of these powerful constituents of human nature are thought worthy of a place among the "Springs of Action"; and

though there is possibly no one of them of the existence of which an acknowledgment might not be
found in some corner of Bentham's writings, no conclusions are ever founded on the acknowledgment.
Man, that most complex being, is a very simple one in
his eyes.

Freud remarked of Mill that he was one of those rare people who rise above the prejudices of their time. Yet only in the
latter part of his life did Freud proceed "beyond the pleasure
principle," making integral to his theory those aspects of human
nature that Mill recognized and Bentham omitted. Freud's first
formulation of the origin of symptoms was as the outcome of
conflict between unconscious motives deriving from instinctual
drives and the consciously accepted standards of the ego, a conception far removed from the rational calculus of Bentham,
despite the fact that Freud also emphasized a version of the
pleasure principle.

Nineteenth-century philosophy was rife with speculations
concerning the nature and functions of the ego, but those speculations did not focus on development. Darwin's theory of evolution sparked a widespread interest in looking at many topics
in terms of development. Thus, although Freud's interest in
psychosexual development during the early years of the twentieth century and the interest of some psychologists in ego development in the same period were partly antagonistic to each
other, both drew inspiration from theory of evolution. For
example, James Mark Baldwin had sophisticated ideas about our
topic (Chapter Eleven) prior to and hence uninfluenced by
knowledge of psychoanalysis.

While psychoanalysis arose in opposition to ego psychology, opposition to Freud and the drive psychology of the early
years of psychoanalysis in turn gave new impetus to ego psychology. Among Freud's followers, Adler became spokesman
for the primacy of the ego over drives. That was a major factor
in the break between him and Freud in 1911. Psychoanalysts
such as Freud and Ferenczi did not deny the existence of the
ego, but they did hold that it was derived from drives through
processes of frustration and renunciation. Adler, by contrast,

believed in a spontaneous striving for self-realization as the moving force in ego development.

Adler's early ideas on the inferiority complex, overcompensation, and masculine protest have seeped into general knowledge, but his later work is of more systematic importance for our topic. Throughout he stressed the unity and coherence (*Einheit*) of personality. The drives, including the sex drive, are subordinated to a person's goal or purpose in life, his *guiding fiction*. The philosophical concept of the fiction was developed by Vaihinger (1911). Fictions are not fantasies but predictive schemes necessary to orient oneself in the world; they are subjective, created by the person, and unconscious in some sense. Adler's *guiding fiction* combined this idea of fiction with that of goal or purpose and adapted it to the field of development. According to Adler, by the time the child is four or five he has selected or constructed some purpose, only partly conscious, that guides the remainder of his life.

In his later years Adler's most characteristic concept was *style of life,* a term he used more or less interchangeably with *self* or *ego, unity of the personality, individuality, method of facing problems, opinion about oneself and the problems of life, whole attitude to life,* and *schema of life* (Ansbacher and Ansbacher, 1956, p. 174), a conception that can serve as a first approximation to the meaning of the term *ego* in the present book. By then Adler had relegated the striving for superiority to neurotic or otherwise failed persons. In normal people he saw the striving for personal power as supplanted or guided by social interest, a desire for the welfare of people in general. Throughout he retained the idea of spontaneous striving, the idea of self as creating self. The child, he wrote, is both the artist and the picture.

Some consequences of Adler's mature conception introduce topics that will be important later in this book. He understood that what one perceives and understands bears the imprint of the ego. Thus the person is protected against unwelcome or unassimilable observations. One term he used to cover that idea is *tendentious apperception.* This fact, that the ego provides the frame of reference that structures one's world and within which one perceives the world, provides the theoretical basis for current methods of assessing ego structure through projective techniques (Chapter Nine). Adler pointed out, too, that psychological theories are themselves aspects of one's view of the world and hence in part at least a function of one's style of life. That should forewarn us that there may be personal obstacles to understanding ego development comparable to the obstacles that many people feel when confronted with Freud's theory of the dynamic unconscious.

In the 1920s Freud returned to the field of ego psychology, making a number of contributions that cannot be subsumed under drive psychology (Chapter Fourteen). But most psychoanalysts had difficulty in assimilating those ideas and underemphasized their importance, at least until recently. The deficiencies of psychoanalytic drive psychology as a framework within which to understand ego psychology led Heinz Hartmann and his coworkers, Ernst Kris and Rudolph Loewenstein, to what has become known as the *new psychoanalytic ego psychology*. (Unhappily, some psychoanalysts, such as Blanck and Blanck [1974] abbreviate this to *ego psychology*, as if there were no other. This usage makes it impossible even to describe the history of psychoanalysis, much less the other contributions.) In postulating a conflict-free ego sphere, however, they abandoned a distinctive feature of Freud's early work, the idea that the same principles govern normal and pathological phenomena. How to incorporate Freud's ego and drive psychology into a coherent paradigm will be the topic of Chapter Fifteen.

So far as American psychology in the 1920s and 1930s was concerned, the differences between Freudian psychoanalysis and Adlerian ego psychology were entirely eclipsed by behaviorism (Hebb, 1960). Gordon Allport was one of the few American psychologists who even mentioned the ego in that period, and while he was universally respected, he was outside the mainstream. William McDougall defined *instincts* as *purposive behavior,* and Edward C. Tolman kept a cognitive and purposive approach alive even in animal psychology. In philosophy, George Herbert Mead made significant contributions to the

theory of ego development, but they had no immediate impact
in psychology.

Current interest in ego development has several sources.
Both drive psychoanalysis and behaviorism, when pursued as
monolithic reductionistic systems, are too simple to account for
behavior. Moreover, as therapies and as ideologies for child rearing they both have limitations. Despite the fact that psychoanalysis, properly understood, never claimed to be the cure for
everything from delinquency to schizophrenia, enthusiastic dis-
ciples were ready to use it so, and the failures of this over-
extended psychoanalytic psychotherapy led to renewed interest
in ego development. The greatest stimulus probably comes from
two factors, from the social importance of problems such as
character defect, delinquency, and psychosis, which can be construed at least in part as problems of ego development, and
from the intellectual challenge of a field with new conceptions.

A fully realized contemporary conception of ego development has the following four characteristics: firstly, stages are
potential fixation points and hence define types of children and
adults. Secondly, the stage conception is structural; that is,
there is an inner logic to the stages and to their progression
(Chapter Three). Thirdly, there are specific tests, experiments,
or research techniques that become the instruments for advancing knowledge in the domain (Chapter Nine). Fourthly, the conception is applicable to all ages and is particularly rich in its
description of the events of adolescence. Naturally, there is no
one year in which philosophical approaches are abandoned and
contemporary conceptions appear. Equating stages with adult
types is foreshadowed by Harry Stack Sullivan (Chapter Five).
The structural conception of stages may have begun with J. M.
Baldwin, but its contemporary impress is due largely to the
work of Piaget and his colleagues (Chapter Three), who also pioneered in the invention of appropriate research techniques
(Chapter Five). Erikson was one of the first to provide a rich
picture of adolescent development (Chapter Five). Some of the
most important contemporary conceptions will be discussed in
Chapter Five, together with enough history to show their evolution. Earlier versions, which are theoretical in a prescientific

sense and which do not have these four characteristics, will be discussed in Chapter Eleven. They were, by and large, more concerned with the dynamics of development than the modern conceptions have been.

In the next chapter the stages of ego development will be described in detail. The sources of those descriptions will be given in subsequent chapters, so that Chapter Two is in a sense a conclusion rather than an introduction. But it is needed now to give substance to the conception and a framework for the discussion. The changes it describes are the sort of thing that ego development denotes in this book; it is a pointing or denotative definition of our domain.

If every datum in the next chapter were a separate discovery, the mass of details would be overwhelming and incomprehensible. But most people do not find them so. Rather, readers experience a shock of recognition, remembering children or recognizing adults of their acquaintance. In describing the stages of ego development I seek, like Socrates, to call forth what you already almost know.

Chapter Two ══════════════════════

Stages
of Ego Development

Ego development is at once a developmental sequence and a dimension of individual differences in any age cohort, but this description does not suffice as a definition, for mental age can also be described so. In lieu of a logical definition, this chapter will present impressionistic descriptions of the stages, pieced together from many sources, as will be evident from Chapter Five, then refined and corrected by empirical work, to be sketched in Chapter Nine. A rigorous or final description of each stage is not possible, for methodological reasons that will be discussed in Chapter Eight.

The question most often asked—What age does each stage correspond to?—I shall not answer. For one thing, there are two different answers, since the average stage for a given age is not the same as the average age for a given stage. More importantly, to describe the progress of average children would be to slip back into a classical child psychology study of socialization. That would defeat the purpose of this book. In principle, I seek to describe every stage in a way that applies to a wide range of ages (granted, of course, that the earliest stages are rare after childhood and that the highest stages are impossible in childhood and rare even in adolescence). What I seek to describe is what persons of each stage have in common, whatever their age. This attempt requires excluding age-specific contingencies (such as, "This behavior pattern indicates Stage X if the subject is a small child, but not if he is over fifteen").

In describing the stages abstractly with minimal reference to age-specific elements such as entering school, puberty, courtship, marriage, and so on, a series of questions is opened up: What is the earliest possible age for transition to a given stage? The latest possible age? The optimal age? What conditions other than age are necessary for a given transition to take place? What conditions are favorable, though not necessary? What conditions inhibit or prohibit a given transition? Only a conception that is, in the first instance, independent of age permits asking such questions, which are more meaningful than the question of average ages.

A word about terminology: these stages should be referred to by name or by code symbol, not by a number. Several authors have numbered their stages. That practice invariably leads either to a terminological impasse when further stages are identified or to cutting off new insights arbitrarily. The conception presented here has grown during our research from a four-point to a ten-point scale, and I do not foreclose further evolution. Only confusion can result from referring to the "third stage," for example. That could mean any of several stages, since the first stage can be counted as one, as two, or not counted at all, since it does not enter our research. Moreover, what we call a *transition* someone else might call a *stage*. Even if such difficulties were arbitrarily resolved by a fixed numbering scheme in the present volume, others might assign a different numbering scheme to our stages.

While referring to stages by name avoids the difficulties of numbering them, it has its own hazards. Because I dislike neologisms, I have taken as the name for each stage a term from common speech, the name of some broad human function or characteristic. No such function arises all at once in one stage and perishes in the passage to the next. Impulsiveness, self-protection, conformity, and so on are terms that apply more or less to everyone. People differ with respect to such characteristics; those differences are related to but not identical with differences in ego level. Though stage names suggest characteristics that are usually at a maximum at that stage, nothing less than the total pattern defines a stage. An attempt to reason about ego development by a rigid interpretation of stage names can lead to disastrous errors. There is no substitute for grasping what Polanyi (1958, 1966) has called the "tacit component." While the tacit component cannot, by definition, be made fully explicit, and the possibilities for misunderstanding can therefore never be eliminated, progress lies in making as much explicit as possible.

In this book, capital letters will be used to distinguish the names of stages and types of people who can be classed in those stages. Where the same words are used for general human characteristics, whether of people at the corresponding stage or of people at other stages, lowercase letters will be used. (Arbitrary code symbols used in our research laboratory are given following the stage names in the next section.)

Descriptions of Stages

Presocial Stage (I-1). The baby at birth cannot be said to have an ego. His first task is to learn to differentiate himself from his surroundings, which becomes the "construction of reality," the realization that there is a stable world of objects. Aspects of the process have been referred to as achievement of *object constancy* and of *conservation of objects.* In the process, the baby constructs a self differentiated from the outer world. The child who remains at the stage where self is undifferentiated from the world of inanimate objects long past its appropriate time is referred to as *autistic.*

Symbiotic Stage (I-1). Even after he has a grasp of the

stability of the world of objects, the baby retains a symbiotic relation with his mother or whoever plays that part in his life (Mahler, 1968). The process of differentiating self from non-self is significantly advanced as the baby emerges from that symbiosis. Language plays a large part in consolidating the baby's sense of being a separate person. Partly for that reason, the remnants of the Presocial and Symbiotic stages do not appear to be accessible by means of language in later life, as remnants of all later stages are.

Impulsive Stage (I-2). The child's own impulses help him to affirm his separate identity. The emphatic "No!" and the later "Do it by self" are evidences. The child's impulses are curbed at first by constraint, later also by immediate rewards and punishments. Punishment is perceived as retaliatory or as immanent in things. The child's need for other people is strong but demanding and dependent; others are seen and valued in terms of what they can give him. He tends to class people as good or bad, not as a truly moral judgment but as a value judgment. Good and bad at times are confounded with "nice-to-me" versus "mean-to-me" or even with clean and pure versus dirty and nasty, reminiscent of what Ferenczi (1925) called "sphincter morality." The child is preoccupied with bodily impulses, particularly (age-appropriate) sexual and aggressive ones. Emotions may be intense, but they are almost physiological. The vocabulary of older children of this stage to describe their emotions is limited to terms like *mad, upset, sick, high, turned on,* and *hot.*

The child's orientation at this stage is almost exclusively to the present rather than to past or future. Although he may, if he is sufficiently intelligent, understand physical causation, he lacks a sense of psychological causation. Motive, cause, and logical justification are confounded.

A child who remains too long at the Impulsive Stage may be called *uncontrollable* or *incorrigible.* He himself is likely to see his troubles as located in a place rather than in a situation, much less in himself; thus he will often run away or run home. Superstitious ideas are probably common.

Self-Protective Stage (Delta Δ). The first step towards self-control of impulses is taken when the child learns to anticipate immediate, short-term rewards and punishments. Controls are at first fragile, and there is a corresponding vulnerability and guardedness, hence we term the stage Self-Protective. The child at this stage understands that there are rules, something not at all clear to the Impulsive child. His main rule is, however, "Don't get caught." While he uses rules for his own satisfaction and advantage, that is a step forward from the external constraint necessary to contain the impulsiveness of the previous stage.

The Self-Protective person has the notion of blame, but he externalizes it to other people or to circumstances. Somebody "gets into trouble" because he runs around with "the wrong people." Self-criticism is not characteristic. If he acknowledges responsibility for doing wrong, he is likely to blame it on some part of himself for which he disclaims responsibility, "my eyes" or "my figure." This tendency may help explain the imaginary companion some children have. Getting caught defines an action as wrong.

The small child's pleasure in rituals is an aspect of this stage. An older child or adult who remains here may become opportunistic, deceptive, and preoccupied with control and advantage in his relations with other people. For such a person, life is a zero-sum game; what one person gains, someone else has to lose. There is a more or less opportunistic hedonism. Work is perceived as onerous. The good life is the easy life with lots of money and nice things.

Conformist Stage (I-3). A momentous step is taken when the child starts to identify his own welfare with that of the group, usually his family for the small child and the peer group for an older child. In order for this step to take place or to be consolidated, there must be a strong element of trust. The child who feels that he lives among enemies lacks that trust. He may not become Conformist, taking instead the malignant version of the Self-Protective course, that is, opportunism, exploitativeness, deception, and ridicule of others. Perhaps that is one route to a more or less permanent "identification with the aggressor" (A. Freud, 1936).

The Conformist obeys the rules just because they are the group-accepted rules, not primarily because he fears punishment. Disapproval is a potent sanction for him. His moral code defines actions as right or wrong according to compliance with rules rather than according to consequences, which are crucial at higher stages. Conformists do not distinguish obligatory rules from norms of conduct, as we see when they condemn unusual dress or hair styles as immoral or as signs of immorality.

In addition to *being* conformist and to *approving* of conformity, the person at this stage tends to *perceive* himself and others as conforming to socially approved norms. While he observes group differences, he is insensitive to individual differences. The groups are defined in terms of obvious external characteristics, beginning with sex, age, race, nationality, and the like. Within groups so defined, he sees everyone as being pretty much alike, or at least he thinks they ought to be. Psychometricians call this phenomenon *social desirability*: people are what they ought to be, which is whatever is socially approved. The Conformist's views of people and of situations involving people are conceptually simple, admitting few contingencies or exceptions.

While the Conformist likes and trusts other people within his own group, he may define that group narrowly and reject any or all outgroups. He is particularly prone to stereotyped conception of sex roles; usually those will be conventional ones, but the same kind of rigid adherence to stereotyped norms can occur in unconventional groups. Conformity and conventionality are not the same. Outwardly conventional people can occur at any ego level except the lowest ones, just as outwardly unconventional people can be strict conformists in terms of the norms of their own group.

The Conformist values niceness, helpfulness, and cooperation with others, as compared to the more competitive orientation of the Self-Protective person. However, he sees behavior in terms of its externals rather than in terms of feelings, in contrast to persons at higher levels. Inner life he sees in banal terms such as *happy, sad, glad, joy, sorrow,* and *love and understanding.* He is given to clichés, particularly moralistic ones. His concern for the externals of life takes the form of interest in appearance, in social acceptance and reputation, and in material things. Belonging makes him feel secure.

Self-Aware Level: Transition from Conformist to Conscientious Stage (I-3/4). The transition from the Conformist to the Conscientious Stage is the easiest transition to study, since it is probably the modal level for adults in our society. Leaving open the question of whether this is a stage in itself or a transition between stages or whether there is no real difference between those two possibilities, we shall refer to it as a *level* rather than as a *stage.* Many characteristics of the Conformist Stage hold also for the transitional level; it can be called the Conscientious-Conformist Level. It is transitional only in a theoretical sense, for it appears to be a stable position in mature life.

Two salient differences from the Conformist Stage are an increase in self-awareness and the appreciation of multiple possibilities in situations. A factor in moving out of the Conformist Stage is awareness of oneself as not always living up to the idealized portrait set by social norms. The growing awareness of inner life is, however, still couched in banalities, often in terms of vague "feelings." Typically the feelings have some reference to the relation of the individual to other persons or to the group, such as *lonely, embarrassed, homesick, self-confident,* and most often, *self-conscious.* Consciousness of self is a prerequisite to the replacement of group standards by self-evaluated ones, characteristic of the next stage.

Where the Conformist lives in a conceptually simple world with the same thing right always and for everyone, the person in the Self-Aware Level sees alternatives. Exceptions and contingencies are allowed for, though still in terms of stereotypic and demographic categories like age, sex, marital status, and race, rather than in terms of individual differences in traits and needs. Perception of alternatives and exceptions paves the way for the true conceptual complexity of the next stage. For example, at this level a person might say that people should not have children unless they are married, or unless they are old enough. At the next stage, they are more likely to say unless they really want children, or unless the parents really love each other.

While the Conformist hardly perceives individual differences in traits, and the person at the Conscientious Stage may command a fairly elaborate catalogue of traits, in the transitional level one typically finds a kind of pseudotrait conception. Pseudotraits partake of the nature of moods, norms, or virtues, such as those mentioned in the Boy Scout oath. Norms are the most interesting, since they reveal the transitional nature of these conceptions, midway between the group stereotypes of the Conformist and the appreciation for individual differences at higher levels.

A trait adjective common at this level, at least among women, is "feminine." Different people cherish different connotations to the term: passive, seductive, manipulative, intraceptive, narcissistic, esthetic, and many others. Those alternatives are closer to being true trait terms, and they are concepts more characteristic of the next higher, or Conscientious, stage.

Conscientious Stage (I-4). Precisely where one first finds signs of conscience depends on what is called *conscience.* A child at the Impulsive Stage does more labeling of people as *good* and *bad* than do those at higher stages, but the connotations are not clearly moral. The notion of blame is evident at the Self-Protective Stage, but rarely does the person blame himself. Occasionally one will find total self-rejection at the lowest levels, but without a corresponding sense of responsibility for actions or their consequences. (Self-rejection may occur in depressed persons of any level; what is characteristic for low ego levels appears to be similar reactions without the overall depression.) A Conformist feels guilty if he breaks the rules; moreover, he classes actions, not just people, as right and wrong. Although self-criticism is not characteristic for the Conformist, one could say he has a conscience because he has guilt feelings. At the Conscientious Stage, the major elements of an adult conscience are present. They include long-term, self-evaluated goals and ideals, differentiated self-criticism, and a sense of responsibility. Only a few persons as young as thirteen or fourteen years reach this stage.

The internalization of rules is completed at the Conscientious Stage. Where the Self-Protective person obeys rules in order to avoid getting into trouble and the Conformist obeys rules because the group sanctions them, the Conscientious person evaluates and chooses the rules for himself. He may even feel compelled to break the law on account of his own code, a fact recognized in the status of the "conscientious objector." Thus rules are no longer absolutes, the same for everyone all the time; rather, exceptions and contingencies are recognized. A person at this stage is less likely than the Conformist to feel guilty for having broken a rule, but more likely to feel guilty if what he does hurts another person, even though it may conform to the rules.

At this stage a person is his brother's keeper; he feels responsible for other people, at times to the extent of feeling obliged to shape another's life or to prevent him from making errors. Along with the concepts of responsibility and obligations go the correlative concepts of privileges, rights, and fairness. All of them imply a sense of choice rather than being a pawn of fate. The Conscientious person sees himself as the origin of his own destiny.

He aspires to achievement, *ad astra per aspera,* in contrast to the feeling at lower stages that work is intrinsically onerous, but he may object to some work as being routine, boring, or trivial. Achievement for him is measured primarily by his own standards, rather than mainly by recognition or by competitive advantage, as at lower levels.

An aspect of the characteristic conceptual complexity is that distinctions are made between, say, moral standards and social manners or between moral and esthetic standards. Things are not just classed as "right" and "wrong." A Conscientious person thinks in terms of polarities, but more complex and differentiated ones: trivial versus important, love versus lust, dependent versus independent, inner life versus outward appearances.

A rich and differentiated inner life characterizes the Conscientious person. He experiences in himself and observes in others a variety of cognitively shaded emotions. Behavior is seen not just in terms of actions but in terms of patterns, hence of traits and motives. His descriptions of himself and others are more vivid and realistic than those of persons at lower levels. With the deepened understanding of other people's viewpoints, mutuality in interpersonal relations becomes possible. The ability to see matters from other people's view is a connecting link between his deeper interpersonal relations and his more mature conscience. Contributing to a more mature conscience are the longer time perspective and the tendency to look at things in a broader social context; these characteristics are even more salient at higher stages.

Individualistic Level: Transition from Conscientious to Autonomous Stages (I-4/5). The transition from the Conscientious to the Autonomous Stage is marked by a heightened sense of individuality and a concern for emotional dependence. The problem of dependence and independence is a recurrent one throughout development. What characterizes this level is the awareness that it is an emotional rather than a purely pragmatic problem, that one can remain emotionally dependent on others even when no longer physically or financially dependent. To proceed beyond the Conscientious Stage a person must become more tolerant of himself and of others. This toleration grows out of the recognition of individual differences and of complexities of circumstances at the Conscientious Stage. The next step, not only to accept but to cherish individuality, marks the Autonomous Stage.

Relations with other people, which become more intensive as the person grows from the Conformist to the Conscientious Stage, are now seen as partly antagonistic to the striving for achievement and the sometimes excessive moralism and responsibility for self and others at the Conscientious Stage. Moralism begins to be replaced by an awareness of inner conflict. At this level, however, the conflict, for example, over marriage versus career for a woman, is likely to be seen as only partly internal. If only society or one's husband were more helpful and accommodating, there need be no conflict. That conflict is part of the human condition is not recognized until the Autonomous Stage. Increased ability to tolerate paradox and contradiction leads to greater conceptual complexity, shown by awareness of the discrepancies between inner reality and outward appearances, between psychological and physiological responses, between process and outcome. Psychological causality and psychological development, which are notions that do not occur spontaneously below the Conscientious Stage, are natural modes of thought to persons in the Individualistic Level.

Autonomous Stage (I-5). A distinctive mark of the Autonomous Stage is the capacity to acknowledge and to cope with inner conflict, that is, conflicting needs, conflicting duties, and the conflict between needs and duties. Probably the Autonomous person does not have more conflict than others; rather he has the courage (and whatever other qualities it takes) to acknowledge and deal with conflict rather than ignoring it or projecting it onto the environment. Where the Conscientious person tends to construe the world in terms of polar opposites, the Autonomous person partly transcends those polarities, seeing reality as complex and multifaceted. He is able to unite and integrate ideas that appear as incompatible alternatives to those at lower stages; there is a high toleration for ambiguity (Frenkel-Brunswik, 1949). Conceptual complexity is an outstanding sign of both the Autonomous and the Integrated stages.

The Autonomous Stage is so named partly because the person at that point recognizes other people's need for autonomy, partly because it is marked by some freeing of the person from oppressive demands of conscience in the preceding stage. A crucial instance can be the willingness to let one's children make their own mistakes. The Autonomous person, however, typically recognizes the limitations to autonomy, that emotional interdependence is inevitable. He will often cherish personal ties as among his most precious values.

Where the Conscientious person is aware of others as having motives, the Autonomous person sees himself and others as having motives that have developed as a result of past experiences. The interest in development thus represents a further complication of psychological causation. Self-fulfillment becomes a frequent goal, partly supplanting achievement. Many persons have some conception of role or office at this stage, recognizing that they function differently in different roles or that different offices have different requirements. The person at this

Table 1. Some Milestones of Ego Development

Stage	Code	Impulse Control, Character Development	Interpersonal Style	Conscious Preoccupations	Cognitive Style
Presocial			Autistic		
Symbiotic			Symbiotic	Self vs. non-self	
Impulsive	I-1	Impulsive, fear of retaliation	Receiving, dependent, exploitative	Bodily feelings, especially sexual and aggressive	Stereotyping, conceptual confusion
Self-Protective	△	Fear of being caught, externalizing blame, opportunistic	Wary, manipulative, exploitative	Self-protection, trouble, wishes, things, advantage, control	
Conformist	I-3	Conformity to external rules, shame, guilt for breaking rules	Belonging, superficial niceness	Appearance, social acceptability, banal feelings, behavior	Conceptual simplicity, stereotypes, cliches
Conscientious-Conformist	I-3/4	Differentiation of norms, goals	Aware of self in relation to group, helping	Adjustment, problems, reasons, opportunities (vague)	Multiplicity
Conscientious	I-4	Self-evaluated standards, self-criticism, guilt for consequences, long-term goals and ideals	Intensive, responsible, mutual, concern for communication	Differentiated feelings, motives for behavior, self-respect, achievements, traits, expression	Conceptual complexity, idea of patterning
Individualistic	I-4/5	Add: Respect for individuality	Add: Dependence as an emotional problem	Add: Development, social problems, differentiation of inner life from outer	Add: Distinction of process and outcome

(continued on next page)

Autonomous	I-5	*Add:* Coping with conflicting inner needs, toleration	*Add:* Respect for autonomy, interdependence	Vividly conveyed feelings, integration of physiological and psychological causation of behavior, role conception, self-fulfillment, self in social context
Integrated	I-6	*Add:* Reconciling inner conflicts, renunciation of unattainable	*Add:* Cherishing of individuality	*Add:* Identity

NOTE: "*Add*" means in addition to the description applying to the previous level.

stage expresses his feelings vividly and convincingly, including sensual experiences, poignant sorrows, and existential humor, the humor intrinsic to the paradoxes of life. Sexual relations are enjoyed, or sometimes just accepted, as a physical experience in the context of a mutual relation. The Autonomous person takes a broad view of his life as a whole. He aspires to be realistic and objective about himself and others. He holds to broad, abstract social ideals, such as justice.

Integrated Stage (I-6). We call the highest stage Integrated, implying some transcending of the conflicts of the Autonomous Stage. It is the hardest stage to describe for several reasons. Because it is rare, one is hard put to find instances to study. Moreover, the psychologist trying to study this stage must acknowledge his own limitations as a potential hindrance to comprehension. The higher the stage studied, the more it is likely to exceed his own and thus to stretch his capacity. For the most part, the description of the Autonomous Stage holds also for the Integrated Stage. A new element is consolidation of a sense of identity. Probably the best description of this stage is that of Maslow's Self-Actualizing person (Chapter Six).

To telescope the whole sequence of ego development in terms of describing the lowest and highest levels is to miss the spirit of the exposition. Growth does not proceed by a straight line from one low level to another higher level. There are many way stations, and they are all important as stages of life and as illuminations of the conception. In some sense, moreover, there is no highest stage but only an opening to new possibilities.

Conclusions

What changes during the course of ego development is a complexly interwoven fabric of impulse control, character, interpersonal relations, conscious preoccupations, and cognitive complexity, among other things. Table 1 presents a somewhat arbitrary condensation of the preceding discussion. To interpret it as indicating four separate dimensions of ego development is a mistake. There is just one dimension. The four descriptive columns display four facets of a single coherent process. Such, at least, is the conception intended. Other authors have depicted essentially the same dimension with major stress on one or another facet (Chapter Five). Most have also implicated other facets in their exposition, but details differ. One might ask, why not get together and agree on a definition of ego development? Authors cannot be forced to adjudicate their differences, nor would a concept arrived at by committee be superior or more true to nature. Frequently it is suggested that differences would be settled by empirical research. To some extent this research is taking place, despite many methodological difficulties. What has not been done, what perhaps cannot be done, and what may not even be meaningful is what is most often suggested: to measure separately the four facets displayed in Table 1 and then correlate them, to prove that they are indeed aspects of a single process. The problems of measuring ego development and of discrepancies between general description and individual cases will be discussed in chapters Eight and Nine.

Discussion of facets reveals one reason this dimension should be called *ego development* rather than *moral development, development of cognitive complexity,* or *development of capacity for interpersonal relations.* All of those are involved. Nothing less than the ego encompasses so wide a scope.

Some critics assert that the description of stages of ego development is so ordered as to be a rationalization of society's scheme of values. That criticism does not hold. All societies are built on conformity and value conformity in the individual; perhaps that is how it must be. Persons driven to nonconformity by conscience are punished as harshly or more harshly by society as those incapable of conformity because of uncontrolled impulsiveness or those who choose nonconformity out of opportunism and self-interest. All nations appear to operate at the Self-Protective level. International relations are conducted as a zero-sum game, and perhaps no regime could survive that did not operate on that principle.

Another criticism is that the stages of ego development are ordered in accord with increasing approval by the writer. The answer to this charge will become evident gradually. There is, for one thing, substantial agreement among authors. Moreover, there are other lines of evidence to support the ordering. While I alone have written this chapter, the ordering of stages has come from work that has been intimately collaborative (Loevinger and Wessler, 1970). Ruthless mutual criticism by persons of diverse backgrounds and dispositions, many of them skilled clinicians, has helped to divest the conception of personal idiosyncrasies. Kohlberg (1971) has answered at length a similar criticism of his work.

Some persons believe that society ought to favor arrangements that will lead more people to stages above Conformity. Society, they may propose, should reward the Conscientious and Autonomous persons as it now rewards the Conformist and often the opportunist. But that proposal is, or leads to, paradox. For the essence of the Conscientious Stage is to be at least partially liberated from socially imposed rewards and punishments. How can one manipulate rewards so as to free a person from responding to them and being shaped by them? That, indeed, is the question a parent or teacher faces who aspires to encourage moral development. How people liberate themselves from the dominion of external rewards and punishments is a central mystery of human development and one of the lures that leads us to our subject matter.

While the criticisms that the sequence of stages merely encodes either my own values or those of society will not hold, two questions lie behind those criticisms. What determines the direction of growth? And how do we discover the sequence? We will return to those questions from various viewpoints. In the next chapter we will see how far we can get by examining the concept of development in relation to personality.

Chapter Three

Concept of Development in Personality Theory

by Augusto Blasi

The theory of ego development presented in this volume assumes a specific understanding of development, built on the metaphor of organism and using structure as a key concept. Over the past thirty years the organismic notion of development has been well defined, thanks mainly to Heinz Werner and Jean Piaget, and has gained increasing acceptance, especially among those studying cognitive processes. The structural approach to developmental psychology is the context for the remainder of this book. The first part of this chapter analyzes the structural conception of development, contrasting it with a conception that relies on an empiricist view of science and a mechanistic view of persons, familiar ground for those acquainted with current developmental psychology. The second part explores the limits of the structural concept of development when it is transferred from the cognitive domain to the domain of personality. The

29

metaphor of the organism is biological in origin, whereas the concept of structure, as it has been used in cognitive areas, is formal in nature, emphasizing the formal relations among objects rather than the content of the objects being related to each other. To what extent can concepts rooted in biology help us understand what is characteristically human? To what extent can structural concepts useful in understanding formal logic also be used in understanding personality?

There are two central aspects in human personality that seem to resist a structural treatment, namely, self-awareness and the experience of freedom, both implicit in our conception of ego development. While the metaphor of the organism constitutes an incalculable progress over the metaphor of the machine for the understanding of human development, it too leaves essential elements out and, if taken consistently to its last consequences, may have a reductive and alienating effect.

Development and Change

Development is a sort of change. Both concepts, development and change, refer to transformations, taking place in time and implying an element of continuity and stability. Can we say that every change is also development? The issue may seem trivial; yet its solutions are related to opposed theoretical and philosophical positions. Moreover, the *raison d'être* of developmental psychology as an autonomous discipline rests on this distinction. Necessary assumptions for the present argument are that the use of language corresponds to and depends on the understanding of reality, and that, consequently, linguistic distinctions are not capricious or arbitrary but reflect real differences.

In everyday language *change* and *development* are not used interchangeably. Consider purely spatial changes: a person walks from one room to another. His relations to his surroundings are not the same; yet we do not speak of development. Spatial change is too external to allow us to do so. This limitation holds true for change in nonspatial but external relations, for instance, relations of a social nature. When a woman has her first child, her mother becomes a grandmother. Again, we would not say she has developed. The word *development* seems to refer only to internal changes. The adjective *internal* is vague and needs to be specified and defined, but it points to a difference between changes that are developmental and others that are not.

Not all internal changes are called *developmental*. Consider such physiological changes as eye adaptation, metabolic changes, menstrual processes, and cyclic changes in general. In these examples, a series of events takes place *in* the individual, aimed at reestablishing the normal balance of the organism, which has been perturbed by internal or external factors. The end result of the sequence is return to the original state. Neither the organism nor any part of it has developed. The reversibility of the changes in these examples does not square with another important element of development, that is, a degree of stability and durability. This second characteristic appears to be as ill-defined as the first, internality. Absolute stability would preclude development. Between absolute stability and reversibility we recognize an area characteristic of development.

Are all internal and relatively stable changes developmental? Consider the following example: a three-year-old child is taught to say that three times six equals eighteen. Assume that this internal change (it obviously is one) is also permanent, thanks to a clever schedule of reinforcement. Is this a developmental change? Opinions here are more divided than for the earlier examples. Usually the child is not considered to have developed because he does not "understand" what the multiplicative statement means. We will accept such judgment, at least as a working hypothesis. Its validity, and also the value of the contrasting opinion—that rote learning is the beginning of development and that understanding is nothing but the accumulation of similar rote learning—will be clarified presently.

The three-year-old child, then, did not develop in learning his multiplication, because he does not "understand" it. To be sure, conscious understanding is not essential for development. People usually develop without understanding their development or even being aware of it. Understanding here means relating the object in question to a system and viewing that object in the context of the whole system. Understanding "3 × 6 = 18" means realizing why that equality is correct, makes sense, or is necessary. It means realizing, at least in principle, that that statement is equivalent to "3 + 3 + 3 + 3 + 3 + 3 = 18," and that, therefore, "6 × 3 = 18," "18/3 = 6," and "18/6 = 3." It implies the ability to relate that one equivalence to the whole system of numbers and to consider it from the point of view of the laws that constitute the system.

There is no development in the three-year-old child learning a multiplication statement, because the change does not consist in or lead to the acquisition of a new system or a new structure. The child understands the statement in some sense; he would not be able to learn it otherwise. But he understands it within the structures that he has available, which are not mathematical. To him "3 × 6 = 18" means a way for getting the desired reward. He understands punishment and reward; he has a system in which needs, satisfaction of needs, and his actions are related by certain rules. An arithmetical statement is spontaneously viewed in that framework and acted upon accordingly. Development, in his case, would consist in moving from the old punishment-reward system to a new system, perhaps a mathematical system. Thus development consists of the acquisition of a new structure or of the change from an old structure to a new one.

Structures and Organisms

Structure and similar terms (system, pattern, scheme or schema) are used in many different contexts, from architecture to biology, from management to poetry. They always imply (1) that there are many elements or parts, and (2) that these elements are not simply an aggregate, an assemblage, as in a heap of stones, but are related to each other so as to form a well-defined order. The nature of the relations may be spatial, temporal, causal, or something else, but in each case the structure consists of the set of relations among the elements. These relations provide the unity and give each element meaning as a part in the whole. When the basic relations change, the structure changes.

On the other hand, as Gestalt psychology has repeatedly demonstrated, all the elements may change without the structure changing. A melody is the same when transposed to a new key; the structure of a building can be the same, even though different materials are used.

In sum, structure is defined by relations, by the basic laws of totality, that is, by laws that are independent of the elements. Our three-year-old child may possess verbal elements for numbers; he may be able to count indefinitely, but this ability alone does not provide him with the structure of numbers. The conclusion of the previous section can thus be translated: Development consists of the acquisition or change of the basic rules governing the relations among the elements.

Structures not only possess wholeness and unity; they also appear to be in equilibrium, to have some sort of internal balance. Relations among the elements can be found in a heap of stones, but they simply happen to be there. They could be different, and we would not be surprised. There is nothing in the nature of stones or in the nature of any specific heap or of heaps in general that requires a certain order. Requiredness is what is meant by balance and is what distinguishes a structure from a heap. In the perceptual domain, Gestalt psychology referred to the same phenomenon by the concepts of "good form" and "Prägnanz" (pregnancy), which emphasize the completeness, the naturalness, and the stability of a structure. The circle is one such form. We tend to perceive circles even when there are none, and we tend to see them complete and perfect, even when the physical circles are only approximate, broken, and imperfect. Balance, in this sense, is recognized in scientific theories (Polanyi, 1958), in novels, and in psychological case histories. In each case, we recognize that the elements go together, they make sense, we understand them. The equilibrium of a structure depends on the same source from which unity and wholeness derive, namely, the rules governing the relations among the elements. Equilibrium stresses the "naturalness" of a structure, and, consequently, its tendency to resist changes or to maintain and recover the same form when for any reason it has been lost.

This train of thought brings us to the concept of organism.

An organism can be defined as a structure that is alive, that is, involved in an active exchange with the environment. This definition is an oversimplification but is useful in emphasizing some aspects of development. A piece of sculpture, once created, continues to exist in the environment, while remaining, as a structure, impenetrable by the environment. It is true that there is a sense in which the sculpture is "exposed" to the environment and "affected" by environmental events. But the environment is not needed for the piece to persist; the sculpture stolidly tolerates the external elements until it is inevitably destroyed by them. By contrast, an organism, such as a plant or an insect, needs the environment to survive in its present structure and is equipped to engage in exchanges with the environment.

The active exchanges assume two main forms: on one hand, organisms select what is environment to them; on the other, they possess flexibility, some repertory of responses, in accommodating to the varying demands of different environments. Both of these characteristics are results of the organisms being organisms; their structure determines the direction and the range of selectivity as well as the possible forms of flexibility. Environment is not an objective entity, the same for all organisms. Environment is what an organism is sensitive to and can use for itself, and that is determined by the basic laws of its internal balance.

Flexibility in the exchanges with the environment is no less an important property for survival. Because organisms are dependent on environments and open to them, and because environments can change, organisms need to adjust and accommodate, to substitute a new response for a once successful one. Such responses differ only superficially, since they proceed from the same organic structure and are expressions of the same equilibrating rules. The organism's internal equilibrium is a dynamic one. The degree of flexibility, as Piaget suggests, may be an indication of the organism's development and of its degree of perfection on the evolutionary scale.

Selectivity and flexibility, *assimilation* and *accommodation* in Piaget's terminology, derive from the organism's structural properties and lead to the organism's stability, to the permanence of its structural characteristics. Any organism's foremost tendency is to survive and to remain the same, and thus to oppose radical changes. There are limits, however, to the organism's stability. Sometimes structural changes (development, according to our definition) may depend on internal, even genetic, processes. Other times, they may depend on environmental pressures. When the range of its response repertory is inadequate to deal with a particular environment, the organism must die or change its structural laws to meet environmental demands. In psychological development, the alternatives are rarely so extreme. Here, the impulse to change one's structure is provided by the desire to satisfy one's needs more adequately, to become more competent, to grasp the world more fully, and similar motives. The dynamics, however, are basically the same and consist in the interplay of match and mismatch between a structure and its environment.

Defining development as changes of the structural laws of the organism helps us understand the other two characteristics, internality and stability. *Internal* does not mean taking place inside as opposed to outside; it refers to the relational laws of a structure. In this sense, anything is internal that is regulated by such laws and expresses them. Similarly, the concept of organism clarifies the nature and the limits of the permanence that is attributed to developmental changes. The internal balance of the organism implies a tendency to self-maintenance; on the other hand, the organism's openness to the environment and its limited flexibility exclude an absolute permanence.

The concept of biological organism has been our guiding metaphor, but not because only biological organisms can develop nor because the ultimate explanation of development is biological. The processes characteristic of live structures can be recognized in a variety of contexts, such as mathematical and logical ones. The functioning of societies, the domain of sociology, anthropology, and similar disciplines, can be described as being organismic, and organismiclike processes take place at the psychological level of the individual personality. Each person focuses on certain features of the environment, actively avoids some, and interprets others idiosyncratically, in ways that are congruent with his own internal rules, views, and prejudices. Nothing in the concepts of structure, selectivity, flexibility, and adaptation requires the notions of genetic code, maturation, and central nervous system. The analysis and the study of development, therefore, can be pursued in each case without prejudging its explanation.

Two Irreconcilable Approaches to Development

The metaphor of the organism has always been important in developmental psychology, sometimes implicitly, as in maturational theory, other times offering clear and articulated concepts and theoretical principles, as in Werner and Piaget. The dominant metaphor in psychology as a whole, however, has been that of the machine. The two metaphors are the foundations of irreconcilable views about man (Reese and Overton, 1970).

There are three assumptions at the foundation of the mechanistic view. First, that the human mind (not the body nor the brain) is like a *tabula rasa*, a blank page, infinitely malleable and open, whose only contribution to its own change lies in its state of readiness and receptivity. Second, that the human mind is affected by elementary sensations in such a way that its overall state could be described perfectly by the sum of the units of stimulation. What is a unit or an element has been defined variously, but in each case the whole is seen as the sum of its parts (elementarism), the exact opposite of the basic assumption of structuralism. The final mechanistic assumption states that the human mind changes in a more or less stable way by accumulating associations and "systems" of associations between elements. Which associations take place is determined by external conditions, the recurrent patterns of events, reinforcements, and so on.

While the organism actively selects its environment and interprets what is selected, the mechanistic mind, empty and receptive, is essentially passive. Not unlike a camera, it imprints what is offered to its eye, and all that is offered is imprinted. While the organism defines the environment, the environment defines the mind-machine.

An even more important difference between the two views lies in the source of intelligibility. Granted that human beings try to understand the world and that gathering systematic understanding is the task of science, one can still ask: What should one try to understand? Where should one focus his attention? What is there that can be understood? If the complete reason for what the mind is and for the changes that the mind undergoes ultimately lies in external stimulation, the only source of intelligibility is outside the mind and in the relations between external conditions. Understanding only means establishing causal connections: we know a mind when we know what produced it.

The situation is different if the source of intelligibility is internal, consisting in the relations that constitute a structure, independently of environmental conditions. This crucial difference between the mechanistic and the organismic view can be grasped only in terms of internal equilibrium. The mechanistic view does not deny that relations exist in the mind: associations are, after all, relations. It can even hypothesize, as some do (for example, Berlyne, 1965), that these relations may be complex and ordered in a hierarchic manner. But there is no reason why these and not other relations should exist, except in the history of environmental stimulation. Relations just happen to be the way they are, not unlike those existing between the stones of a heap. This view, in relation to personality and development, has been elaborated by Mischel (1969). Unlike the organismic approach, the mechanistic counterpart lacks the notion that certain forms or patterns are privileged, "good," or "natural." The organismic conception that a multiplicity of relations, all different from each other, are consistent with the same basic principle of equilibrium is foreign to the mechanistic approach.

Where the basic structural laws come from and how they are acquired are valid and important questions that aim at a more complete understanding of development. Intelligibility, however, is already present in the law that constitutes a structure. Genuine understanding is obtained in discovering that basic law or principle from the multiplicity of phenomena that it regulates. It is, therefore, wrong to consider Piaget's theory as being mainly descriptive because it focuses on the structural laws and their sequence and disregards almost completely the conditions under which the structures develop. Similarly, the conception of ego development in this book aims at isolating the basic structure or central meaning of each stage, neglecting the network of relations to social class, family antecedents, and similar external factors; it is not, however, merely descriptive on that account.

A third area of differences between the mechanistic and the organismic view consists in the way the succession of changes, the order between the structures, is conceptualized. Superficially, the mechanistic view looks at development as a neat and continuous succession of changes, while the organismic view looks at it as a series of upheavals and discontinuities. A more penetrating examination reveals that behind the continuity of mechanistic changes there is, in fact, lack of order, whereas a deeper continuity underlies the broken sequence of organismic development. When associations are all that can be acquired, and when the state of a mind consists of their sum, development can be represented in principle as the incremental addition of unrelated elements. The three-year-old child, learning a multiplicative equivalence without understanding it, is developing, and development continues for each new equivalence that he acquires. The reverse of the picture is that what he is acquiring now and the present state of his mind do not affect the direction of his changes. Depending on environmental conditions, he may acquire this or that equation, the correct ones equally well as the incorrect ones, or he may lose what he acquired and "regress" to an earlier state. Paradoxical though it may seem from a common sense of development, a frequent exercise for psychologists of a mechanistic persuasion consists first in changing a child by manipulating the environment, and then in bringing him back to his former state by changing again the conditioning situation.

However, if development consists in structural changes, any new structure constitutes a break from the old one. It cannot be obtained by adding and subtracting, but only by establishing a new principle governing the relations among the parts. At the same time, the selectivity by which an organism functions and the tendency always to integrate the available material guarantee a fundamental continuity between the successive organizations of a developmental sequence. There are restrictions in the direction development can proceed. While the environment may determine the nature of the specific change, the structure of the organism determines the range of possibilities within which it must occur. Piaget, studying intelligence, summarized these principles in a set of rules characterizing any true developmental sequence. A sequence of stages is hierarchical, proceeds by gradual step-wise integrations, and is irreversible.

Ultimately, the differences between the mechanistic and the organismic approach are grounded in the refusal of the mechanistic approach to see anything special in development that would differentiate it from other changes, the first theme of this chapter. Baer (1970) concludes a paper: "Learning procedures, in their considerable variety, are exactly behavior-changing processes. But they need not be called developmental processes for two reasons. One is that they already have names which are considerably more precise than 'learning' and tremendously more precise than 'development,' . . . patterns of reinforcement, punishment, extinction, differentiation, and discrimination" (p. 243). According to this view, changes do differ from each other in duration, consistency (if the notion of consistency makes any sense), orderliness, and so on, but the differences depend simply on what is offered by the environment.

The proponents of the organismic view, on the contrary, postulate some sort of "natural" order that accounts for intra-organismic consistencies, for the laws of development, and for the universality of some developmental sequences. The word "natural" has been placed in quotation marks to acknowledge its unclear meaning and to express the sense of awkwardness that "nature" arouses in us. It reminds us of metaphysical ghosts and of the suspiciousness towards them inculcated by decades of logical positivism and of empiricisms of all sorts. Developmental psychology as an autonomous discipline must look those ghosts in the face. Are statements such as "2 + 3 = 5," "If $A > B$, and $B > C$, then $A > C$," and "Nothing can be in two different places at once," believed to be true only because the culture around us agrees in considering them true and has conditioned us to accept them? Or does our culture believe them to be true because of a necessity and order, intrinsic in those statements, which transcends cultures and individuals and to which cultures and individuals have to submit?

Personality Development and Cognitive Structures

The organismic approach to psychological development has been so successful as to revolutionize child psychology. Its search for the structures that underlie developmental phases directed observations at the same time that it brought unity to the diversity of behaviors. The construction, at least hypothetical, of intelligible units made it possible, in turn, to look for abstract sequences, that is, for sequences that are independent of specific ages and of environmental conditions, and thus to study the laws of the developmental process *per se*. Such progress took place originally in cognitive domains (perception, concept formation, language) because of the affinity between structuralism and cognition. In extending structuralism to other areas, in particular to personality and social development, the same conceptions and insights have been used. The most ambitious and the best articulated among such attempts has come to be known as *cognitive developmentalism,* an approach that is not a single coherent theory but includes researchers of varying backgrounds. They share two general tendencies: first, to adopt the most general developmental concepts advanced by Piaget, such as assimilation, accommodation, stage, and hierarchical and universal sequence; second, to hypothesize that the development of cognitive structures is the fundamental factor in psychological development as a whole, affecting in particular the acquisition of personality structures. The rest of this chapter will be concerned with cognitive developmentalism, with its attempt to explain the development of personality organizations by resorting to conceptual and logical structures, and with the limitations and the dangers of this enterprise.

The discussion will revolve around three fundamental characteristics of the human personality. The first is that personality is specific; it has a content, a number of more or less well-defined traits, which may be universal within the species but which differentiate the human species from other species and objects. The other two characteristics are consciousness and freedom. Since these seem to be essential human traits, at least as ideals to be pursued, any approach to the explanation of human personality should be able to integrate them without distortions. Can structuralism, particularly a structuralism relying on logical-cognitive categories, accomplish this task?

These issues are central to theory of ego development. Ego development is presented as the "master trait" in personality, as the frame that provides more specific traits with their meaning and around which the whole edifice of personality is constructed. This theory shares with cognitive developmentalism the Piagetian notion of stage: ego stages are conceptualized as equilibrated structures, related to each other in an invariant hierarchical sequence. Finally, autonomy and consciousness are the hallmarks of mature ego stages. Thus in the first part of this chapter we have discussed characteristics that differentiate the approach of the present book from its polar opposites, mechanistic and behavioristic approaches to development; in the second half we will discuss characteristics that differentiate it from its nearest relative, the cognitive-developmental approach.

The Forms of Cognition and the Content of Personality

Cognitive developmentalism looks at the vicissitudes of cognitive development for an understanding of the development of personality. For instance, the development of the infant's attachment to his mother is explained by the acquisition of the concept of the permanent object; the rise of social values in adolescence is explained by the development of formal operations. No doubt cognitive development affects personality, because what affects an individual at the psychological level has to be known by him in some sense. The question is whether cognitive development provides us with principles that are internal and specific to personality development.

Cognitive development is the cornerstone of human development as a whole, because cognitive principles constitute the broadest and the most encompassing structures that one can imagine. That insight is at the base of cognitive developmentalism. But precisely because cognition is so general, so open to everything, it cannot contain the principles of its specific realizations. What is principle of generality cannot be at the same time principle of determination. Thus, the understanding of logical categories cannot provide us with an adequate basis for understanding personality. Personality is specific in its constituents; it does not consist of a concrete exemplification of a logical principle or of a set of logical categories.

In Piaget's theory, cognition has the characteristics of generality and openness for two interdependent reasons. First, Piaget focuses on what he calls the *operational,* that is, the characteristics of the action, the "style" by which individuals handle, literally and figuratively, the objects, rather than on the characteristics of the objects. Styles and action patterns are much more general than the contents to which they are applied. The second reason is that Piaget is interested in objects as objects, that is, for their most abstract and general characteristic of being things. He focuses on those action patterns that are common in the handling of all things, and from which the universal characteristics of things, or at least of physical things, derive—for example, extension in space, mobility and reversibility in space and time, and permanence. The explanation for the universality of Piagetian sequences lies here, and not in any genetic-maturational mechanisms.

Given the nature of cognition in Piaget's theory, one may ask: How does the acquisition of the concept of the permanent object by a baby explain his attachment to his mother? The question is relevant to our inquiry, since attachment, tying the individual affectively to the members of his species, is the foundation of social development. In a group of babies, Bell (1970) found that those attached to their mothers had developed object permanence for people ("person permanence") before permanence for things, while the reverse was true of those not yet attached to their mothers. She also found that attached babies tended to develop the cognitive concept a bit earlier than the nonattached babies, but that all went through the same cognitive sequence. Thus the concept of the permanent object does not affect attachment intrinsically, since it was possessed by babies who were not attached and who did not differ cognitively from the attached babies. The "permanent object" does not tell us why some individuals prefer things and other individuals prefer people, or why human individuals prefer humans and monkeys (who also develop the "permanent object") prefer monkeys. It does not even tell us why there should be any preference. Attachment or similar concepts seem to be essential for the understanding of personality, but they remain unclear when approached from a cognitive viewpoint.

A concept analogous to attachment but more central to ego development is value. When one considers values in general and moral values in particular from a cognitive viewpoint, one is faced with the same problem. Cognition does not offer the principle of determination, of preference, of value.

In recent years, Kohlberg (1964, 1969, 1971) has formulated a theory of moral development in which the central role is played by sequential structures of moral judgment (Chapter Five). In this theory, qualitatively different modes of role taking, the cognitive abilities to take into account the others' perspective in order to solve moral dilemmas, are considered the determining factor in the unfolding of moral structures. Though role-taking structures are less broad than logical structures and assume certain content distinctions (for instance, between physical and psychological reality, between subject and object), like logic they are forms of reasoning. They prescind from any content, are applicable to every content, and constitute, thus, a hierarchy of increasing differentiation and increasing adequacy.

Because of these characteristics, Kohlberg concludes that moral development not only proceeds along a specified series of stages but ought to proceed in that direction, and, in a critical and unwarranted step, he extends the increasing universality and prescriptiveness from the forms of moral reasoning to the content of moral values. That later and more mature moral stages are characterized by a greater universality of values may be correct as a fact. But the explanation of the fact need not lie where Kohlberg puts it, without supporting argument, in the universality of cognitive forms. From the fact that taking my fellow's views and feelings into account is a more adequate form of knowing than not doing so, I can conclude that I ought to prefer that form of knowledge. However, knowing my neighbor's feelings through role taking does not tell me whether I ought to respect those feelings or hurt them.

The transition from the form of knowledge to the content of values is not immediate or direct. Some other premise is required, directly related to the nature of human personality. Kohlberg recognizes that one can ask: Why should I be moral? But he considers facing and answering this question as another stage, in the same sequence with and, one can assume, of the same nature as the forms of moral reasoning. This question, however, needs to be answered in some way at each stage to translate moral judgment into action. The criteria that an individual resorts to in his search for an answer (not necessarily explicitly and consciously) cannot be strictly formal but must refer to the content of his personality.

The issue concerning logic as an adequate source of values is exemplified in Wittgenstein's* philosophical development. In an early period he assumed a thoroughly structural mathematical-propositional model in his approach to logic and science; he then proceeded to separate art and ethics from the domain of logic. It is impossible, he thought, to have propositions about ethics; thus, we must be silent about what really matters in human life (Janik and Toulmin, 1973, pp. 190-191). The only way we can speak about these topics, Wittgenstein felt, is through the imprecise and emotive connotations of poetic metaphors.

At a later stage, however, he realized that a formal model, such as a logical-linguistic system is, does not immediately give us what is real, even in the domain of science. It only provides

---

*Much of the material reported here, as well as the quotations from Wittgenstein's writings, are taken from *Wittgenstein's Vienna* (Janik and Toulmin, 1973).

us with an ensemble of possibilities in a "logical space." Logical relations hold only within the formal system. In order to apply them to what is real, as opposed to what is simply possible, we need a special set of rules, which are neither propositional nor purely formal. These rules, on which the meaning (in contrast to the structure) of logic and language depends, are based on the ways language is used, which, in turn, are based on broader forms of life (Spranger's *Lebensformen*). Wittgenstein wrote: "Language is *our* language" (p. 224), logic is part of the "natural history of man" (p. 223), and "It's a question of who's to be master, you or the words" (p. 227).

We need not follow Wittgenstein in depth to recognize and accept two valid points: first, the limitations of a formal system when we deal with concrete determinations rather than with possibilities, and second, the subordination of logic and language to more encompassing structures, those forms of life that constitute human personality.

What is inadequate in the attempts to explain personality development by resorting to formal cognitive structures is that the latter represent systems of possibilities. More adequate and developmentally more mature cognitive structures widen the range of possibilities, without moving from the domain of what is possible to the domain of what is, whereas in relation to cognition, personality is factual and determined. (In relation to behavior, however, personality is structure and behavior is specific content.) Moreover, since logical systems exist in concrete personalities, the attempt to explain the second by the first is a reversal of a basic structural axiom, that the part is explained by the whole, and not vice versa. Personalities are structures—*forms* of life, as Spranger and Wittgenstein called them—but structures of a different nature from cognitive structures. That human beings, developing, go though an ordered sequence of such structures is the premise of this book. In this context, cognitive structures are important as providing the individual with a more or less wide range of alternatives. Where within that range personality in fact develops is determined by different factors and different rules.

Subjectivity, Freedom, and Structuralism

That consciousness and freedom are part of the human experience needs no demonstration, at least at a nonanalytical level.
As Dubos (1974) writes, "I shall accept free will as a needed
and useful belief, even though I do not know how to account
for it—simply because I consider the experience of freedom
more impressive than the failure to prove its existence" (p.
224). Not surprisingly, this is also the strongest argument
among philosophers.

Self-consciousness and freedom constitute for at least a
few people the central aspect of personality, which gives meaning to their life. Many recent theorists have recognized self-
awareness and concern with autonomy as characteristic of the
mature personality (Chapter Six). The Autonomous Stage of
Chapter Two, Kohlberg's postconventional level, Riesman's
autonomous orientation, Maslow's self-actualization, and Kelman's (1958) internalization, among other constructs, seem to
point to the same reality, rediscovering what was probably self-
evident to the generation of Baldwin, McDougall, and Dewey,
that personality develops by acquiring successive freedoms.
There is, first, freedom from impulses through the assimilation
of culture, social expectations, and conventions. Later, there
starts a continuing struggle to secure some freedom from conventions and social pressures. If subjectivity and freedom are
not simply the achievement of a few individuals but are also the
universal orientation and goal, then a theory of personality
development must be able at least to approach an explanation
of them.

How well can structuralism guide us in this enterprise? On
the face of it structuralism seems to be of little help. Indeed,
there appears to be an intrinsic opposition between the structural method and its underlying philosophy, on one side, and
the reality of subjectivity and freedom, on the other. This statement can be supported by two lines of reasoning.

Structuralism aims to establish a system of categories and
of relations among categories isomorphic with the organizations
existing in reality. Even when a set of categories concerns the

subject and the object, the relations are looked at in purely objective terms, as elements that a person differentiates whether he consciously experiences them or not. Thus a system of relations, however complex, can be in principle translated into mathematical formulas and represented in the functioning of a cybernetic machine.

The proponents of artificial intelligence generally do not believe that everything that is present in the human mind can be replicated by a computer, but they believe that the mind's formal properties, its structure, can. Subjectivity and consciousness are not denied, but they are deemed to be unnecessary to the understanding of the mind's structural properties. The machine can solve problems and follow rules similar to those handled by the human mind, without being aware that it is doing so, that *it* exists, and that *it* is different from *non-it*. Thus, if subjectivity and consciousness exist in human beings and if the mind's structures can be divorced completely from them, then structures and structuralism give us no help in understanding subjectivity and its development.

The second argument is grounded on what could be called the problem of the units in structuralism. Within the structural approach, the units of analysis are always abstractions, no matter how internally coherent. They contain, at one end, subordinated units, also internally coherent, and, at the other end, they are always contained in larger units. Thus, the structuralist's units, while being wholes at one level are also parts at another. Phonological structures are part of morphological structures, which are part of grammatical structures, which are part of semantic structures.

That this situation is problematic for human freedom becomes evident when one considers structuralism's basic axiom, that the whole regulates the parts. The parts receive their meaning, their role, and their function only in the whole and by the whole. If, therefore, the person is looked at exclusively through structural glasses, as part of an ecological system and, more importantly, as a member of a society and of a culture, labels such as "autonomous," "postconventional," and "independent" retain little meaning. Human beings could be exhaustively conceptualized as "roles" or sets of roles, depending on the complexities of the social environments.

The solution to the dilemma requires finding a source of unity that is not structural. Consciousness offers such a source, provided that consciousness is not simply a reflection of structures but at least partially a creator of them. Consciousness sets the individual apart from, and opposed to, the environment, while giving an internal unity that has a different kind of coherence from the structural unit. Freedom and consciousness are inextricably tied, partners of the same developmental vicissitudes.

The organismic approach in biology and its more general version, structuralism, were not devised to protect freedom from the mechanistic threats. Their aim was to explain the internal coherence and spontaneous activity of living units. Internal coherence and spontaneous activity are essential prerequisites for freedom; they do not necessarily imply freedom. The organismic approach can be, and usually is, as deterministic as the mechanistic approach, though in a different way.

Many proponents of the organismic approach, under any of its names (structuralism, general systems theory), do not agree with this conclusion and believe that freedom is not eliminated but, on the contrary, is made understandable. They point out the organism's spontaneous activity, the interaction and reciprocal causation between organisms and environments, and the presence of a certain degree of indeterminacy among equivalent alternatives. They point out, in particular, that more complex organisms arrive at action through a "decision-making" procedure, namely, by processing multifarious information through a set of rules that inevitably leads the organisms to the right alternative, the one that maximizes gains and minimizes losses.

But freedom is neither spontaneity or indeterminacy: freedom may be present even when only one alternative is available. Reciprocal causation can be perfectly determined and determining, especially when the organism's historical antecedents are also considered. Decision-making procedures, as defined, for instance, by the thoroughly structural approach of game theory, do not go beyond a "rational" adjustment to the environment. One wonders what the "rational" decision would have been in Nazi Germany, or how "rational" Solzhenitsyn's decisions have been.

The results of a rigid but consistent application of the methodological and philosophical principles of the structural approach are evident in the French school of structuralism. Authors such as the anthropologist Lévi-Strauss, the philosopher-psychologist Foucault, the literary critic Barthes, the psychoanalyst Lacan, and the philosopher Althusser are considered members of this movement. In spite of their protestations of individuality, they share a number of traits. Besides applying the structural method, they all depend on the ideas of the linguist de Saussure and resort to language not only as a model for structures but also as the matrix from which all other human structures derive.

They also share, in various degrees, an attitude of anti-humanism and a tendency to negate the individual person as a reality. Foucault (1973) stated: "In our day . . . it is not so much the absence or the death of God that is affirmed as the end of man. . . . Man will disappear" (p. 385). Even the moderate Lévi-Strauss (1968) wrote at the end of *Triste Tropiques*: "And yet I exist. Not in any way, admittedly, as an individual: for what am I, in that respect, but a constantly renewed stake in the struggle between the society, formed by several million nerve-cells which take shelter in the anthill of the brain, and my body, which serves that society as a robot? . . . Not merely is the first person singular detestable: there is no room for it between 'ourselves' and 'nothing' " (pp. 397-398). In the end, the message conveyed by French structuralism as a whole is not very different from that in Skinner's *Beyond Freedom and Dignity,* only more sophisticated and subtle.

The antihumanistic conclusions of French structuralists do not represent their idiosyncratic attitudes but reflect real hazards in their principles. De Saussure's approach, on which the French school depends, was characterized by a triple abstraction: language, considered as the ideal set of rules, was abstracted from its concrete expressions, namely from speech and from the speaker; language was also abstracted from its history; and it was, finally, abstracted from its object, from what it represents and signifies. Language, de Saussure argued, can be understood only in its universal aspects, and these are above the individual users and determine the individual use. Moreover, language can be understood, has meaning, not from the relations to the world outside itself, but exclusively from its internal relations. The meaning of the word *tree,* for instance, does not consist in its relation to the thing tree, but in its opposition to all other words in the vocabulary. In order to understand a word, we only need to relate it to other words, as any entry in the dictionary demonstrates; and vice versa, we cannot understand words and language without ultimately resorting to words and language. De Saussure's abstractions contain some of the emphases that are characteristic of structuralism: first, the emphasis on the formal and the relational rather than on substances and contents; then, the emphasis on the closedness and autonomy of systems, that closedness that allows the organism to operate by internal laws of equilibrium.

After these premises, one more assumption is needed to arrive at the dogmatic conclusion of the French school, the assumption that language is the inescapable matrix out of which the person as person is born and functions. It follows, then, that the person does not speak in any real sense, but that the impersonal and objectified "culture" speaks through him. It speaks, moreover, not what the individual understands of the world, but the meaning intrinsic in the closed structure of language. As Foucault proclaimed in an interview, "The 'I' is destroyed . . . the issue now is to discover the 'there is.' There is an 'impersonal they' (*on*) . . . we do not put man in the place of God but we start with anonymous thinking, knowledge without a subject, a theoretical [entity] without identity. . . . It is our task finally to get rid of humanism" (*La Quinzaine Littéraire,* 1966, no. 5; quoted by G. Schiwy, 1971, pp. 18-19).

Parenthetically, these examples show that the controversy as to whether language is subordinated to a conceptual understanding of the world, as Piaget asserts, or is autonomous and determines one's conceptual understanding, as some linguists and anthropologists (Sapir, Whorf, and Chomsky) assert, is not idle or mere pedantry. In the field of ego development, particularly in psychoanalysis, the central terms are most difficult to translate (Chapter Fourteen). Thus the question (to which we revert in Chapter Eight) of whether the conception of ego development is a universal one, applying across linguistic-cultural boundaries, requires the assumption of a reality not wholly created by the words with which it is described.

Conclusions

This chapter may seem to follow a Sysiphean pattern, with the second part undoing what was built in the first. In reality, nothing has been retracted. In spite of reservations about the structural approach, I believe that the only way to understand development consists in conceptualizing it as a sequence of structural changes, often stimulated by the interaction of an organism with its environment.

The problems that structuralism encounters when it deals with the development of personality do not lie in the notions of structure and organism, but in the background of those two concepts. *Structure* and *organism* came to personality theory from biology and the logical-mathematical sciences. These disciplines share two characteristics, the necessity that is indigenous to the subject matter itself and the formalization of their approach. Logic is naturally fit for a purely formal treatment, and biology has been moving in the same direction. This movement was facilitated by broadening biological inquiry from the organism to its environment considered as a unit (*Umwelt*) and by realizing the advantages that mathematical formulations and computer analogues bring. A similar progression is also evident in Piaget's work. Formalization and inflexible necessity are the source of the difficulties that arise when the concepts of structure and organism are applied to personality. Its domain, within which ego development lies, requires a concept of structure that can deal with the intrinsic characteristics of objects (a term that is used here for both people and things) and not only with the relations between objects or with the styles by which a knower relates objects to each other. To use a linguistic analogy, it is as necessary or more necessary to attend to what a person says as to how he says it; one must attend to what statements signify as well as to their formal meaning.

What the extremists within structuralism tend to forget, disregard, or deny is that objects have a sense that does not consist exclusively of the relations they have with other objects. Objects are not like mathematical points, defined by the intersection of lines.

Piaget avoids many of the problems of the French school of structuralism, because he conceives of structures as being open and in contact with the world. This conception allows him to account for development and history, which French structuralists have to bracket out. It also allows him to maintain abstract structures in contact with the concrete ground out of which they develop. But Piaget's interest lies in the patterns of action by which knowers relate objects to each other, such as ordering, dividing and grouping, and numbering. As a result, things are reduced to being points at the intersection of actions and can be replaced by numbers or other abstract symbols, while people are reduced to the action of relating.

Such an approach is legitimate when one is interested in logical and mathematical development. It becomes inadequate when the intrinsic nature of objects is significant. Piaget's approach cannot help in understanding even the basic distinction on which all personality theories ought to be grounded, the distinction between object and subject. The farthest one can go, within his theory, is to recognize that a distinction exists, that there are two categories that can be labeled *1* and *2*. Even so, what is common and not what is different between the two categories is emphasized, such as permanence, spatial and temporal order, classifiability, and existence in a field of logical possibilities.

The study of personality, though related to the development of logic, lies elsewhere, in the consideration of the nature of that special object that is the person and of its functional (as opposed to operational) relations to other objects. Persons and objects are considered for their content characteristics, not as terms in relations, except insofar as relations become internally constitutive of the individual. A purely formal notion of structure as well as Piaget's logical operationalism, with their focus on external relations, do not suffice for the understanding of contents and of internal constituents. A type of structuralism is needed that is more contemplative than pragmatic and that tries to capture the "essences" rather than the external relations. The notion of structure that underlies the Gestalt approach to visual forms, Werner and Kaplan's approach to symbols, Erikson's analogical approach to zones and modes, the traditional study of myths, and other kinds of thematic analyses, is more appropriate than logical-mathematical structures* to the task of this book, discerning ego types and stages.

If the intrinsic properties of personality become the object of inquiry, then consciousness and freedom, their different modalities, their role in the overall functioning and their importance to the individual, will also become manifest. These characteristics are lost to a purely relational and operational structuralism, since they are more a quality of being than of action. Human consciousness is always influenced by external, cultural structures; sometimes also it directs and constructs them.

*A distinction is sometimes made between structure-form and structure-model (Parain-Vial, 1969), which seems to capture the difference between these two kinds of structuralism.

Chapter Four ══════════════════════

Fundamental
Characteristics

The subject of ego development cannot be encompassed by a formal definition, since ego development is something that occurs in the real world. The stages (Chapter Two) give an approximate notion of what is denoted by the term. There may be errors of detail, but the scope and arena are defined. In Chapter Three implications of the concept of development were explored. Analysis of terms continues in the present chapter with some implications of the conception of ego development and of ego.

Attributes of Ego Development

Stages. Describing ego development in terms of stages implies, firstly, that there is not a smooth transition from very low to very high ego level; instead, there are discontinuities. But what appear to be discontinuous variables can, on analysis, be shown to contain underlying continuities, whereas what appear to be continuous variables may harbor discontinuities; so the difference is not absolute.

A second implication is that there are qualitative differences in the transition points along the way. Variables that differ only in amount as one goes from low to high can be called *polar variables*. Those that are characterized by a succession of qualitatively different turning points can be called *milestone sequences* (Loevinger, 1965). The difference between polar variables and milestone sequences is an extension and elaboration of the difference between continuous and discontinuous variables.

Abilities have long been considered perfect examples of polar variables—the difference in an ability between any two persons can always be thought of as a difference in amount. In accord with the polar model, tests of ability are scored simply by counting the number of right answers. They are thus cumulative tests (Loevinger, 1948). Piaget has shown, however, that what had been classed simply as wrong answers in fact embody a certain logic. A particular style of thought, such as preoperational or concrete-operational logic, becomes increasingly frequent up to some point in a child's development and then decreases in favor of a succeeding style of logic. Thus Piaget has shown that some fundamental abilities also grow in terms of milestone sequences.

In the complexities of polar variables and milestone sequence lies the explanation of why earnest and arduous work can go on with reference to behaviors in this domain without revealing the major outline of the variable. In the area of abilities the obvious and most easily measured aspects were just the polar aspects, so that while Binet did not see the succession of children's logics, he caught a significant and useful aspect of ability. The sequence of qualitatively different stages that Piaget and his coworkers uncovered is more abstract and inferential.

With ego development the situation is reversed. If one sticks to observables, he will be forever concerned with the several stages, which are more obvious than the continuity that underlies them. A psychologist determined to be behavioristic and psychometric-operational is bound to treat the several stages as polar variables. Thus many have studied conformity as a polar variable. A person high on a conformity scale can be assumed to be at the Conformist Stage, but a person low on such a scale may be preconformist or postconformist, as recent research has confirmed (Hoppe, 1972). There is no statistical technique that can construct the variable of ego development out of a set of measures of the several stages or aspects of the stages. There are polar aspects of ego development (Chapter Six), but they are more abstract and inferential than the aspects displayed in Table 1.

Some other implications of the concept of stages have been brought out by Piaget and Inhelder (Tanner and Inhelder, 1956, 1960). Although their work has been chiefly with stages of logic, Piaget and Inhelder have abstracted the general features of the stage concept: (1) there is an invariable sequence; no stage can be skipped; (2) each stage builds on, incorporates, and transmutes the previous one and prepares for the next one; and (3) there is an inner logic to each stage that accounts for its equilibrium and stability. As a consequence of those three characteristics, the succession of stages also has an inner logic. These researchers see the logic of the developmental sequence as being of equal importance with hereditary, situational, and environmental determinants of behavior.

Our conception necessarily entails the difference between polar variables and milestones. The Piaget-Inhelder notion of stages is not necessarily entailed, however, and many people who work with the concept prefer to think of gradations along a qualitative continuum rather than discrete stages.

Typology. Our conception is typological, that is, within each age cohort it provides a characterology. In this sense typology is not opposed to continuous variation but to unidimensionality or univocality. Since the existence of only two types is formally equivalent to existence of a single dimension, three or more types must be proposed. Even if differences in ego development within an age group are graded continuously, they are qualitative and are not completely reducible to quantitative differences.

That the stages of ego development also constitute a typology is hardly a received opinion, since the best-known ego theorists do not make the point. Allport (1961) sees stages of ego development similar to ours, but when he talks of typologies, he refers to humoral and other typologies that appear to have no connection with ego development. His emphasis on an idiographic approach, with every individual to be understood in his own unique terms, is also somewhat antagonistic to the idea of a typology.

Abstraction. A conception that has ego development both as a typology and as a developmental sequence implies that it is an abstraction. It cannot be reduced to concrete, observable performances of average children, as one might infer from child psychology texts. Ego development is related to and based on observation, but it is not directly observable. Thus it is simply unavailable or nonexistent to a rigorously behavioristic approach. In Chapter Two the descriptions were chosen to emphasize what is common between children passing through the stages at the normal time and adolescent or adult types at that stage. Age-specific aspects are excluded from the definitive descriptions, in contrast to most other expositions, such as that of psychoanalysts or of child psychology texts.

A precedent for that kind of abstraction exists in the concept of mental age. Its value is that it reveals and differentiates a series of questions about the relations of age and stage, questions that encompass the theory of change. Moreover, it encourages distinguishing the inner logic of ego development from the matrix of physical development, intellectual development, psychosexual development, and social expectations in which it is embedded and from which it gains some of its form and impetus.

That development is itself an abstract concept has been shown in Chapter Three. Werner who was primarily concerned with cognitive development, made a similar point ([1940] 1964). One must not expect identity among children, primitive peoples, and pathological cases but simply certain parallels, Werner wrote, since the circumstances are different for primitive man living in a society where he is master and well adjusted, the sick person living in a society to which he is maladjusted, and the child living in a world of culturally advanced adults. What applies to all three is the abstract concept of development. Werner's statement of the orthogenetic law of development applies as well to ego as to cognitive development: "The development of biological forms is expressed in an *increasing differentiation* of parts and an *increasing subordination,* or *hierarchization.* Such a process of hierarchization means for any organic structure the organization of the differentiated parts for a closed totality, an ordering and grouping of parts in terms of the whole organism" (Werner, [1940] 1964, p. 41). That Werner's is not the only model applicable to ego development will be shown in Part III.

Attributes of the Ego

Our concept of ego development contains by implication a conception of the ego that in some ways resembles and in other ways differs from that of other writers. Knowledgeable readers will want a bridge particularly to the conception prevalent in psychoanalytic writings.*

Process. Defining the ego is difficult in the same way that defining life is. Air and water are not living beings. When one drinks water or breathes air, at what point does it become part of a living object? (This illustration is borrowed from an informal lecture by James Franck at Woods Hole in 1962. He used the question to show how misguided are attempts to define life rigorously.) If we think of life as being a process of interchange with the environment, the question loses point. There is no problem. Similarly, the ego is above all a process, not a thing. The ego is in a way like a gyroscope, whose upright position is maintained by its rotation. To use another metaphor, the ego resembles an arch; there is an architectural saying that "the arch never sleeps." This saying means that the thrusts and counterthrusts of the arch maintain its shape as well as support the

---

*Those not familiar with psychoanalytic literature can proceed to the next chapter, leaving the remainder of this chapter to read later or not at all.

building. Piaget (1967) uses the term *mobile equilibrium*—the more mobile, the more stable. The striving to master, to integrate, to make sense of experience is not one ego function among many but the essence of the ego.

Freud originally used the concept of the ego (*das Ich*) as a term taken from the public domain. His elaboration of consciousness (more correctly, the preconscious) as a system distinct from the unconscious as a system took the place of the ego in *The Interpretation of Dreams* (1900). A major difficulty that led Freud to return to the concept of the ego and to replace the concept of the unconscious as a system by the concept of the id was the question of where repression took place. If the repressing force is in the unconscious, then the notion of psychic systems, proposed as a means of portraying inner conflict, loses point, for both parties to the conflict, the repressed idea and the repressing force, are in the same system. If it is consciousness that represses unconscious ideas, why are we not conscious of repression? Must there be a repression of the fact of repression, and so on in infinite regress? Use of the term *ego* permits a kind of solution of the problem by definition. To say that there is an unconscious part of the ego is less awkward than to say that there is an unconscious part of consciousness.

Many psychologists may find acceptable Freud's final position on the ego, as formulated by Waelder (1960, p. 177):

> The boundary [between ego and id] is the boundary between instinctual and purposive processes, between blind propulsion on the one hand and the choice of suitable means for particular purposes on the other hand . . . . Psychoanalysis includes in the id everything by which man appears to be impelled to function, all the inner tendencies which influence him, each *vis a tergo*. The ego, on the other hand, represents the considered direction of man, all purposeful activity . . . . Psychoanalysis, in so viewing the id and the ego, thus perceives man's being both impulsively driven and his being purposefully directed . . . . The scheme of processes in the id would then be, in short: instinct—instinctual expression; those of

the ego, however, are: task—task-solving, or attempted solution.

Would a thoroughgoing process conception of the ego ob-
viate the necessity for assuming an unconscious part of the ego?
Repression, as Freud pointed out, is something that occurs between systems. Is not the question of whether repression is in
the ego analogous to the question of whether air in the lungs or
water in the stomach is part of the living body? Or, to put the
matter another way, will it suffice to say that noninclusion in
the ego is what repression is? We must drop the question, for it
leads to technical questions beyond our scope.

Structure. As we saw in Chapter Three, the concept of
structure is embedded in that of development; it is also embedded in that of ego. Most ego theories are structural, that is,
the ego is seen as striving (or as the striving) for self-consistency
and meaning. (Obviously this formulation is not Titchener's
kind of structural psychology; in fact, it is close to what was
then called *functional psychology*.) Although the idea appeared
earlier in some philosophers, it is especially characteristic of
Adler. Freud also spoke of the ego as being or having organization, though he assigned the ego a smaller place in life and
behavior than Adler did.

For Sullivan (1953) the self-system tends to preserve self-
consistency by means of selective inattention to facts inconsistent with the current level of development. Since these ideas
are central to Sullivan's conception and seminal for ours, they
will be presented in detail in the next chapter. Allport (1943
and elsewhere) has always stressed the organization of the ego,
which accounts for or at least is related to the functional autonomy of motives. Lecky (1945) was chiefly preoccupied with the
striving for self-consistency, much as Festinger (1957) has been
preoccupied with the other side of the coin, cognitive dissonance. Structure was the essence of the conception of Merleau-
Ponty (1942), whose views on selective inattention as resulting
from and preserving ego structure are similar to those of Sullivan.

A radical version of the structural conception of the ego is that of Fingarette (1963). He begins by accepting the observations and the essential theory underlying psychoanalysis as therapy but points out that Freud's visual metaphor, which depicts the task of psychoanalysis as uncovering hidden realities, has become an implicit ontology for many psychoanalysts, at times including Freud. The same observations and the same theories are compatible with an alternative ontology that depicts the major task of psychoanalysis as helping the patient to see new meanings in events already known to him. Successful therapy is not so much a matter of finding a rabbit hidden in the bushes as discerning the shape of a rabbit in a cloud, according to the meaning-reorganization view. The striving to make experience meaningful is for Fingarette not something that a thing called *ego* does; the striving for meaning is what ego is. Meaning is not an afterthought to behavior and experience; meaning is constitutive of experience, an idea also developed by Mead (1934). (The meaning-reorganization view of psychoanalytic therapy can also be found in Ricoeur, 1970, and Loewald, 1960).

Fingarette defines anxiety also in structural terms, as a hypothetical construct rather than as an affect. Failure of the striving for meaning is itself what constitutes anxiety. Just as meaning is not so much what the ego seeks as what it is, so anxiety is not what the ego experiences but is the opposite of ego: disorganization or meaninglessness. If one thinks of anxiety as an affect, then unconscious anxiety and the substitution of symptom for anxiety become anomalies. If anxiety is interpreted as a hypothetical concept, these difficulties do not exist. The term *neurotic anxiety* is a misnomer. What is neurotic is not the anxiety but how the ego responds to it, whether creatively and reparatively or by restricting itself and making its own fragmentation into a permanent structure.

The striving for consistency seems to be absent from some conceptions, such as Peck and Havinghurst's (1960) conception of moral development. The difference does not result from their emphasis on moral as compared to ego development—Kohlberg, who is also concerned with moral development, has a strongly structural orientation.

Gergen (1968) believes that the tendency toward personal

consistency has been exaggerated in psychological theory. Here we touch one aspect of the long opposition to the concept of ego. For years the predominant strain in American psychology has been a doctrine of specificity, a denial that there are consistent individual differences. We will examine this view in Chapter Ten.

The use of the term *structure* in the received version of psychoanalysis represents a different usage. The structural view has come to stand for the division of the personality, or person, into ego, id, and superego. Those are the structures. The ego, as Freud said, is an organization. The id and the superego, on the other hand, to the extent that they are unconscious, cannot be said to be organized, for the unconscious admits of no contradiction. If contradiction is meaningless, so is consistency. (This argument does not exclude the possibility of organized ideas within the superego or the id; the idea is that the superego and the id are not self-consistent or organized wholes. Similarly, the ego may contain inconsistencies, even though as a whole it represents the striving for consistency.) Of course, the word *structure* is not uniquely attached to striving for consistency. Gill (1963), using the term to connote degree of organization, concludes that ego and id are two extremes of a continuum. In a more common usage, structure connotes stability or semipermanence rather than organization. But the reason for stability of the id and superego is more or less opposite to the reason for stability of the ego. Accounting for the stability of the ego is a theoretical problem, and the striving for coherence is an element of the solution, as the gyroscope and arch metaphors are meant to suggest; the relation of stability to coherence has been discussed in Chapter Three. The id and the unconscious component of the superego, on the other hand, owe their stability to being unconscious, hence impervious to the influence of experience as well as to the requirement of consistency. This is the principle of the dynamic unconscious (Chapter Thirteen).

Holism. Most contemporary theories of the ego are holistic, as opposed to dualistic or elementaristic. The primary datum is the person. While his ideas and sensations (in another era) or his traits or sensorimotor functions may be studied, he himself is the unit of study. Moreover, the ego is not a spirit animating a machine or a pilot in a ship; the Cartesian dichotomy of mind and body is currently rejected.

In a witty essay, Jung (1933) argued that scientific reductionism, expressing mind in terms of body, is logically no different from the creed of an earlier, theological era that believed that the physical world was no more than a manifestation of the spiritual one. Mind is no more reducible to body than body to mind. Although not incompatible with Jung's thesis, modern arguments have a different ring. Strawson (1959) and Polanyi (1958) maintain that "person" is a primitive notion; Strawson points out that there are no disembodied minds known to us. Ryle (1949) and Chein (1972) argue that there are not two series of events, say, in playing chess or taking a test, one that of the bodily movements, the other of the mind that tells the body what movements to make. The person is not thus divisible. "Neural processes cannot produce ideas, and thoughts cannot make the muscles contract, but the total organism, the person, can do both" (Angyal, 1965, p. 31).

These arguments are, in part at least, ontological. Ego development is an empirical and theoretical topic of psychology rather than an ontology. As such, it is concerned with functioning persons, not with mind as opposed to body. The holistic view permeates writings of many psychologists and psychiatrists—for example, William Stern, Adolf Meyer, Kurt Goldstein, Gordon Allport, and Donald O. Hebb. If opponents of the holistic view still exist, they are presumably the psychologists for whom our topic is not a clear and present concern. Most major research programs of present-day psychology are not, however, based on holistic paradigms.

The question of whether ego functioning (or should one say psychic functioning?) is best conceived holistically remains a major unresolved issue in contemporary psychoanalytic theory. In Freud's formulation inner conflict alone occasions neurosis; therefore, any truly psychoanalytic view must allow for inner conflict. Hartmann and Rapaport treat the ego as an omnibus of functions or "apparatuses," some autonomous with respect to drives and (hence?) conflict-free, others derived from neutralized drive energies. This view seems to be incompatible with a holistic assumption. At the same time, Rapaport asserted, "All behavior is that of the integral and indivisible personality" (1960, p. 42).

How can we reconcile the possibility of inner conflict with a holistic conception of personality? One can say that while the ego functions as a whole, some memories or experiences are retained by the person outside that frame of reference. Freud spoke of repression and the unconscious, while Sullivan and Merleau-Ponty spoke of *dissociation,* a term Freud had used in his early writings. In either case, the juxtaposition provides one way of describing inner conflict without hypostatizing any of the variety of additional entities whose nature and functions are disputed in current psychoanalytic literature. That solution is Merleau-Ponty's (1942) description of psychic pathology. Freud's conception of the dynamic unconscious is a modification of the holistic assumption, but one which most ego theorists today accept in some version. It is, however, a modification and not an abrogation of the holistic assumption, as Merleau-Ponty has shown. For it is the person as a whole who refuses to recognize or assume responsibility for the repressed complex of ideas. If it were not so, if the person as a whole were not involved, how would one account for the force of resistance (Vergote, 1957)?

Social Origin. Most theories of ego development see the ego as intrinsically social in character—the person is a social animal—a view as old as the early Greeks. Sullivan made central to his psychiatry the view that one is constituted in and by his interpersonal relations (Chapter Five). (He might, in place of interpersonal, have said human or social relations, but the fact that the substitution can so easily be made testifies to the truth of the view.) Baldwin, also an extremist on this issue, argued that there is hardly anything in ego other than what is in one's alter or "socius." G. H. Mead argued that while a man might maintain his ego in isolation, the ego would never come into being for a person raised in isolation (Chapter Eleven).

The issue is one of the oldest ones in philosophy. Socrates, Plato, and Aristotle expressed in various ways that man is by nature a social animal, that he achieves his true estate in and through the community. The Sophists, the Cynics, and other post-Socratic philosophers expressed in various ways that man is by nature selfish and a creature of impulse, that society must be imposed on him against his will. Sartre is a contemporary advocate of this position. The initial thrust of psychoanalysis strengthened the view of socialization as forcibly thrust on the selfish, instinctual child, and on that point Freud agreed with behaviorists such as John B. Watson. But the practice of psychoanalysis was interpersonal from the beginning, and with increasing recognition of the importance of transference and identification, theory too became interpersonal (Chapter Fourteen).

Allport (1943) seems to straddle this issue, with his insistence that personality be defined entirely within the skin. Chein (1972), on the other hand, insists that even traits cannot be defined without invoking the social and physical environment.

Purpose and Meanings. Finally, most ego theories are purposive, not in the sense of declaring a purpose in the universe but in the sense of being concerned with purposes as phenomena of human life. One might speak alternatively of behavior as meaningful or of meanings as determinative of behavior. The opposite view, programmatically mechanistic, but as Allport and others have noted, never more than quasi-mechanistic or naturalistic in practice, sees the causes of behavior as lying entirely in the past. But ego phenomena can hardly be formulated in such terms. The belief that all behaviorism ignores purposes is false, however. Both McDougall (1908) and Tolman (1922) had systems of purposive behaviorism. A mechanistic view, which sees instincts or drives as compounds of reflex arcs, is false, they said; such instincts exist neither in man nor in other animals. The reconciliation of a mechanistic and deterministic view with the view that the ego acts in terms of purposes and meanings is accomplished in terms of levels of organization in Merleau-Ponty's philosophy (1942).

Psychoanalysis remains a special case. Freud avowed an allegiance to physiological reductionism from his earliest to his latest period, and his writings on psychic energy are hard to construe as anything but reductionism, even when psychic energy is differentiated from physical energy. On the other hand, much of Freud's best writing and all of psychoanalysis as therapy are phrased in terms of meanings, purposes, intentions, wishes, and so on. Indeed, Flew (1956) has pointed out that the essence of the psychoanalytic contribution is to extend the meaning of such terms to phenomena, such as dreams, symptoms, and mistakes, that had previously seemed meaningless. A similar point has been made by other philosophers, E. B. Holt (1915), Fisher (1961), and Fingarette (1963), and by Home (1966), a psychoanalyst.

Defective as cathexis theory may be, if it were nothing more than a mistake, one would be hard put to account for its long tenure. Ricoeur (1970) has accounted for it more satisfactorily than other philosophers. The ground of psychoanalysis, he writes, is precisely the juncture of an energetics and a hermeneutics. Many of the key concepts of psychoanalysis bear witness to that mixture of discourses, the discourse of force and that of meaning: resistance, repression, displacement, condensation, and dream work. All have connotations of force and of meaning. The force is displayed only in alteration of meaning, and the meanings are altered only at the behest of psychic forces. The psychic forces involved are knowable only through their effects on meanings and meaningful discourse. While recognizing the validity of the energy metaphor, Ricoeur is also unsympathetic to the bizarre algebra of cathexis, countercathexis, hypercathexis, and so forth.

As Allport often pointed out, there is a cleavage between those psychologists who see man as he sees himself, as searching for meaning and carrying on purposes, even if sometimes unconscious ones, and those who see his behavior as determined by meaningless forces outside his ken. Despite the assertions of some critics, this cleavage does not separate psychoanalysis from humanistic approaches to psychology. On the contrary, the cleavage goes right down the middle of psychoanalysis, indeed, down the middle of Freud's writings. On the whole, psychoanalysis must be ranked among the psychologies concerned with meanings, for without interpretation there is no psychoanalysis.

Conclusions

The conception of ego development as a sequence of *stages* that also constitutes a set of personality *types* is necessarily an *abstraction*. The fundamental characteristics of the ego are that it is a *process*, a *structure, social* in origin, functioning as a *whole*, and guided by *purpose* and *meaning*. Development implies *structural change*, but the mechanistic philosophy of some structuralists forecloses our topic of study (Chapter Three). We acknowledge both *consciousness* and the possibility of freedom and the validity of the *dynamic unconscious*; so the ego is not the same as the whole personality. It is close to what the person thinks of as his self.

These are the parameters of our conception; the terms serve as further definition of our domain. The conceptions and theories within our purview share most of them, but not always the same ones. The same terms will be used to describe theoretical differences within the domain.

Chapter Five

Alternative Conceptions

Versions of the sequence of stages and types of people that ego development comprises can be found in literature, philosophy, psychology, psychiatry, and elsewhere. When many people operating from different assumptions and different kinds of data have convergent conceptions, that convergence confirms the common elements. In terms of building a scientific discipline, however, the result is chaotic, with numerous workers cultivating separate schools of thought, each with its small cadre of followers, often out of touch with the theory or empirical findings of others working on essentially the same problems, often with vocabularies so different as to make connections hard to establish. To be a scientist one must assume some fixity in nature, some limitation to its variety; whatever one's personal beliefs, that is the only way to do scientific work. Different kinds of development proceed simultaneously in children, but one cannot be comfortable with a dozen or two dozen versions of personality development. The various accounts are too different to be collapsed into one account, yet too much alike to refer to altogether different aspects of human nature. In reviewing some of the major conceptions, one aim must be to establish connections.

The expositions can be divided into those that depict only the developmental sequence, those that depict only the typological dimension, and those, like ours, that include both. Exclusive emphasis on developmental process leads to concentration on age-specific aspects, while to define the dimension requires just that one note the aspects that are not age-specific. On the other hand, exclusive emphasis on dimension leads to neglecting the dialectics of growth, which supplies the ordering of types. In the latter case the ordinal variable may be construed as a nominal one or the milestones treated as if they were polar variables; that is, each type may seem to be independently defined, with the ordering more or less arbitrary.

Sullivan's Interpersonal Psychiatry

If one person is the ancestor of our concept, it is Harry Stack Sullivan.* Sullivan was deeply influenced by Freud but sought to differentiate his own thinking where he thought Freud's was philosophically untenable. He found the psychoanalytic usage of *ego, superego,* and *id* unacceptable; the term *self-system* was the closest equivalent to Freud's *das Ich* in his psychology. Psychiatry for Sullivan is the study of interpersonal relations; it "cannot be concerned with that which is inviolably private" (1953, p. 19). The idea of human instincts is preposterous, he said, taking issue with the instinct-derivative view of the personality in early psychoanalytic writings: "Personality is the rela-

---

*The most complete version of Sullivan's views is given in *Interpersonal Theory of Psychiatry,* assembled from his last series of lectures prior to his death in 1949, published posthumously in 1953. All quotations in the following account refer to that volume. An earlier version, *Conceptions of Modern Psychiatry* (1939), was widely circulated, so one can hardly set a date on his conception.

tively enduring pattern of recurrent interpersonal situations which characterize a human life" (pp. 110-111).

Sullivan was impressed with how much more human beings are like each other than they are different from each other. Individual differences he held to be different stages of essentially a single developmental sequence. With what he called the "one-genus postulate," Sullivan laid the basis for developmental characterology: "Everyone is much more simply human than otherwise, and . . . anomalous interpersonal situations, insofar as they do not arise from differences in language or custom, are a function of differences in relative maturity of the persons concerned" (pp. 32-33).

Sullivan made anxiety a key element in his theory: it is the most unpleasant experience that an infant has, the opposite of euphoria; hence avoiding it is a major motive. The infant's earliest learning is guided by the anxiety gradient; he moves toward whatever decreases anxiety and away from whatever increases it. The infant becomes anxious by means of empathy with (that is, contagion from) an anxious mother; this link in the reasoning is admittedly obscure. There are two major categories of needs, the need for interpersonal security, which at first is simply tenderness, and physiological needs. Anxiety is aroused when security needs are not satisfied. The infant can learn to cope with his other needs and discomforts by means of trial and success, by reward and punishment, and later by imitation of human models. He has no way of coping with anxiety. None of his actions are appropriate to remove it, and it interferes with gratification of all other needs. The self-system arises as a means for avoiding and managing anxiety.

The infant's earliest self-concept is split into three elements: the *good-me* is whatever leads to or is associated with reward or interpersonal security; the *bad-me* is whatever leads to or is associated with mild or moderate anxiety; and the *not-me* is associated with sudden access of overwhelming anxiety, which cannot be integrated by the infant as a learning experience. The not-me corresponds approximately to what Freud called *traumatic* events subsequently repressed into the unconscious. Nightmares and psychotic processes testify to their continued existence.

At first the significant other is not distinguished according to person; mother and mother surrogate are the same. The infant distinguishes only *good-mother* from *bad-mother*. Sullivan's foremost example of the bad-mother is the anxious mother, but it may also be, for example, the resentful older sister pressed into baby-sitting duties. For the young infant, all good ones are the same person, all bad ones the same person.

By means of experiences such as thumb sucking, where the infant experiences not only sucking but being sucked, he integrates the good-me and the bad-me into *my body*, as opposed to environment. Language helps fuse the personifications of the good mother and the bad mother into *my mother,* no longer interchangeable with surrogates. These constructs characterize childhood, the second stage in the sequence. Much of the child's interpersonal learning of this period is based on human models and can be called *dramatization.* The child plays at *acting-like* and *sounding-like* his parents, and then at *acting as if one were.* The transition from childhood to the juvenile era is marked by increasingly clear distinction between reality and fantasy. In large part this distinction takes place by means of *consensual validation,* a term with which Sullivan called attention to the importance of others in consolidating our perceptions of reality.

In the juvenile era, roughly the early school years, mother declines as the significant other in favor of compeers. This change is developmental, not just an artifact of experience, since a similar change occurs in the fantasies of youngsters without schoolmates. Popularity and approval are positive motives, with ostracism the corresponding sanction. There is a "shocking insensitivity to feelings of personal worth in others" (p. 230). Formation of social stereotypes, especially those differentiated according to gender, is characteristic. The juvenile learns social subordination and accommodation; his modes of interaction are competition, compromise, and cooperation. A favorable outcome of this period is an orientation in living, that is, long-term goals and values, as well as insight into his interpersonal needs and how they can be satisfied without too much anxiety. One alternative is to go on permanently living for approval, to be liked or to amuse.

The self-system for Sullivan arises and develops to meet

the needs of interpersonal relations. In infancy the need is for tenderness, later for approval and self-esteem; the opposite of these satisfactions is anxiety. Thus the self-system operates to avoid and minimize anxiety. It incorporates a person's frame of reference or view of the universe (a statement explicit in Adler and possibly only implicit in Sullivan). Since discordant observations create anxiety, the self-system screens them out or distorts them. Thus it tends to escape influence by experiences incongruous with its current organization and functioning. The screening process is called *selective inattention,* and it is an active vigilance. Events and processes that are selectively inattended to are approximately ones Freud referred to as *preconscious* processes; under some circumstances they can be brought into focal awareness.

"Because of the general effect on personality which accompanies every newly matured need or capacity in the early stages of each developmental phase, the functional activity of the self-system invariably does change somewhat in direction and characteristics; and it is at those times that the self-system is peculiarly open to fortunate change" (p. 192). Thus it is the developmental timetable that initiates change, and when change is anyhow imminent, unfortunate aspects of previous adjustments can often be more or less spontaneously corrected.

An unfortunate turn that Sullivan discusses is the "malevolent transformation," the attitude that one is living among enemies. It can be adopted as a self-protective device by a child who is made fun of or made anxious or hurt when he is manifesting a need for tenderness. The malevolent transformation constitutes or brings about a partial arrest of development, since that attitude insulates a child from the favorable experiences that normally result in further development. Another kind of developmental arrest is for the child to cling to dramatizations and "as if" performances or to obsessional preoccupations to ward off anxiety or punishment. Arrest of development is never absolute; experiences go on being assimilated, but the rate is slower and the possibility of further development and other favorable change is much reduced. Because of the screening effect of anxiety, ordinary trial-and-success or reward-and-punishment training is not effective in changing the self-system in the way it is effective in training geared to other needs. Unsuccessful and nonrewarding aspects of the self-system can persist for a lifetime.

Sullivan saw in the relation of the preadolescent youngster to a chum of the same sex a unique opportunity to advance from the egocentricity of the juvenile era to a truly social state. In an exclusive relation to a chum the preadolescent learns for the first time to value another as he values himself, to experience love in its true depth. The need for intimacy propels a youngster into such a relation; the corresponding sanction is loneliness, which rivals anxiety as an unpleasant experience. True collaboration originates in this period. In Sullivan's usage, collaboration implies mutuality, going beyond the cooperation of the juvenile era, which he saw as motivated by self-interest. Sullivan saw the gangs of the preadolescent period as extensions of the chumship and as often benign in their effects. The achievements of the preadolescent era are not inevitable. Many persons go through life in the juvenile mode of competition or compromise. An adult who remains at the juvenile level may become a Don Juan or a "teaser."

Early adolescence begins at puberty. The significant other normally shifts from a chum to a member of the other sex. Major needs are security, intimacy, and lust. A difficulty is that puberty comes at widely varying ages to individuals in a given social group or even to two members of a chumship. Early adolescence ends with achievement of a pattern of preferred genital activity. Late adolescence extends till "the establishment of a fully human or mature repertory of interpersonal relations, as permitted by available opportunity, personal and cultural" (p. 297). Sullivan's discussion of early and late adolescence is chiefly concerned with the age-specific problem of integrating lust with various personality patterns under varying circumstances.

Sullivan's conception of the self-system, his version of the ego, is a process, it is social, and it is a structure; that is given in his very terminology. It is also purposive and concerned with meanings. It operates holistically to the same extent that the

ego does in much of psychoanalytic theory; that is, the problem
of the dynamic unconscious or dissociated aspects of personality is allowed for. Sullivan wrote of the developmental sequence and developmental arrest in a way that at least anticipated a typology. What is lacking in his exposition is ego development as an abstraction; his choice of titles for the stages,
always in age-specific terms, proves that.

The stability of the ego is movingly and cogently described
by Sullivan, but that intensifies the perplexity of accounting for
its development. Here Sullivan has recourse to maturing needs
and capacities, but the argument is not elaborated or made convincing. Indeed, the capacities and needs to which he refers can
be separated into two groups, those that are themselves an integral part of ego development, which cannot then also be explanations of it, and those whose origins are partly or wholly
independent of ego development. The need for compeers and
the need for intimates obviously have their driving aspects, but
the appearance of such needs is too closely tied to ego development for them to serve also as independent accounts of its
dynamics. Sexual maturity, which Sullivan refers to as the *lust
dynamism,* arises largely in independence of psychological
forces. Lust can be integrated into immature personalities, and
thus does not account for the dynamics of development, though
it may lead to advance where other conditions are favorable.
Language is an intermediate phenomenon. It is important in the
earliest stage of ego formation, but it cannot account for later
dynamics (Chapter Three). Thus Sullivan has supplied a keen
theory of ego stability and some sense of the dialectics or inner
logic of development, but he has not contributed much to
understanding its dynamics or motive power.

Developmental Sequences

Conceptions of ego development must have originated in observation of developmental sequences. Characterologies are also
ancient; some go back 2,000 years. Developmental characterologies are probably of recent origin. One aim of the discussion
will be to establish connections and correspondences between
studies that have not been juxtaposed.

Ferenczi. A classic psychoanalytic paper is Ferenczi's "Stages in the Development of the Sense of Reality," first published in 1913, hence having priority both as a contribution and in its concern with the formation of the ego. We shall summarize and excerpt relevant parts. The restriction of the term *ego development* to cover only the earliest stages is clear: "The replacement (to which we are compelled by experience) of the childhood megalomania by the recognition of the power of natural forces composes the essential content of the development of the ego" (Ferenczi, [1913] 1956, p. 185). An aspect of the megalomania, or perhaps the chief clue to its existence, is a feeling of omnipotence. "Psychoanalytic experience has made it clear to me that this symptom, the feeling of omnipotence, is a projection of the observation that one has slavishly to obey certain irresistible instincts" (p. 183). The period in the womb is the period of unconditional omnipotence when the infant's needs are continually gratified. Immediately after birth there follows the period of magical-hallucinatory omnipotence. As he learns that crying and other expressions of needs will bring satisfactions, the child enters the period of omnipotence by the help of magic gestures. When the child first learns to distinguish ego from non-ego, he "seeks to find again in every object his own organs and their activities" (p. 193); this is the animistic period. Ferenczi comments ([1913] 1956, pp. 193-194):

> The derisive remark was once made against psychoanalysis that, according to this doctrine, the unconscious sees a penis in every convex object and a vagina or anus in every concave one. I find that this sentence well characterises the facts. The child's mind (and the tendency of the unconscious in adults that survives from it) is at first concerned exclusively with his own body, and later on chiefly with the satisfying of his instincts, with the pleasurable satisfactions that sucking, eating, contact with the genital regions, and the functions of excretion procure for him; what wonder, then, if also his attention is arrested above all by those objects and processes of the outer world that on the ground of ever so distant a resemblance remind him of his dearest experiences.

Thus arise those intimate connections, which remain throughout life, between the human body and the objective world that we call *symbolic*. On the one hand the child in this stage sees in the world nothing but images of his corporeality, on the other he learns to represent by means of his body the whole multifariousness of the outer world. This capacity for symbolic representation is an important completion of the gesture-language; it enables the child not only to signalise such wishes as immediately concern his body, but also to express wishes that relate to the changing of the outer world, now recognised as such. If the child is surrounded by loving care, he need not even in this stage of his existence give up the illusion of his omnipotence. He still only needs to represent an object symbolically and the thing, believed to be alive, often really "comes" to him; for the animistically thinking child must have this impression at the satisfaction of his wishes. From the uncertainty regarding the arrival of the satisfaction it gradually dawns on him, to be sure, that there are also higher, "divine" powers (mother or nurse), whose favour he must possess if the satisfaction is to follow closely on the magic gesture. Still this satisfaction also is not hard to obtain, especially with indulgent surroundings.

As this passage shows, the psychoanalytic conception of symbolic representation contains an early version of schemes and their transposition. Speech begins as a symbolic gesture, Ferenczi continues, but quickly assumes special significance. It accelerates conscious thinking and the consequent capacity for delay of motor discharge. Since the child's wishes at this time are still few and simple, his entourage easily guesses them and often hastens to fulfill them. The child comes to believe that it was the thought or word that brought gratification to his wishes. This period is the basis for superstition, magic, and some religious cults. It is also the period to which obsessional patients seem to regress. At this point Ferenczi's account of ego development stops. The approximate correspondence between Ferenczi's stages and those of Chapter Two is shown in Table 2.

Table 2. Ego Stages of Ferenczi, Erikson, and Ausubel

Approximate ego level	Author		
	Ferenczi (1913)	Erikson (1950)	Ausubel (1952)
Autistic	Magical-hallucinatory omnipotence	Trust	
Symbiotic	Omnipotence by magic gestures Animism	vs. mistrust	Ego omnipotence
Impulsive	Magic words and thoughts		Crisis of ego devaluation
Self-Protective		Autonomy vs. shame and doubt	Beginning of satellization
Conformist		Initiative vs. guilt Industry vs. inferiority	Satellization
Conscientious-Conformist			Crisis of desatellization
Conscientious		Identity vs. role diffusion	Desatellization
Individualistic		Intimacy vs. isolation	
Autonomous		Generativity vs. stagnation Ego integrity vs. despair	

That Ferenczi distinguished ego development from psychosexual development is shown in the following passage: "We suspect that the wish-constituent of the neurosis, i.e. the varieties and aims of the erotism that the symptoms present as fulfilled, depends on where the fixation-point is in the phase of the development of the sexual hunger, while the mechanism of the neuroses is probably decided by what stage in the development of the ego the individual is in at the time of the determining inhibition" (p. 199).

Ferenczi anticipated the problem of defining what the moving force in ego development is, and he sketched one psychoanalytic position on it, though it is no longer the only one. "In general the development of the reality-sense is represented by a succession of repressions, to which mankind was compelled, not through spontaneous 'strivings towards development,' but through necessity, through adjustment to a demanded renunciation" (pp. 200-201). Evidently this essay stated exactly the position that Adler had opposed.

Erikson. Since Erikson's (1950, 1963) *Childhood and Society* is well known, I need only show its connection with our topic. His observations are based on his psychoanalytic practice, anthropological studies, and research with normal children. He defines the stages of psychosocial or ego development in terms of a series of tasks, each of which comes to a crisis, described with an antinomy. At times the antinomies are spoken of as if they represent achievements; at other times the reader is cautioned against that. Rather, at the conclusion of each period a certain balance or ratio of the positive to the negative pole is attained; but this ratio can be changed by later experiences. This model, although complex and (as he complains) often oversimplified by those who quote Erikson, has the advantage of clearly differentiating developmental level, that is, the particular crisis, from one aspect of adjustment, the ratio of the favorable to the unfavorable alternative.

The first task is achieving a measure of basic trust as opposed to mistrust with respect to three areas: the continuity of the world of objects, the difference between self and others, and control of one's own impulses. These are problems of the Presocial, the Symbiotic, and the Impulsive Stages. The next problem in Erikson's scheme, autonomy versus shame and doubt, characterizes the Self-Protective Stage in ours. The problems of the next two periods, initiative versus guilt and industry versus inferiority, seem to fit the Conformist Stage. Erikson discusses the next problem, identity versus role diffusion, in terms of ideals and ideologies, thus making it correspond to what we have called the Conscientious Stage, though the problems of role conception and identity are located at later stages in Table 1. The next task, intimacy versus isolation, is discussed in terms of deepening interpersonal relations and development of an ethical sense; hence this also is an aspect of the Conscientious Stage. The problems of generativity versus stagnation and ego integrity versus despair are probably Erikson's version of the Autonomous and Integrated Stages (Table 2). Erikson's exposition of the crises ties them to age-specific problems such as

courtship, marriage, child rearing, and aging, thus foreclosing
questions of the outside limits of the age range during which the
transition from one stage to another can take place. Ego development as an abstraction or as a typological dimension of adult
life seems foreign to him.

Erikson's use of the term *autonomy* to denote one of the
earliest stages differs from our use to denote one of the highest
stages. The self-conscious assertion of independence that he is
talking about is one of the criteria used in differentiating Self-
Protective subjects from Impulsive, dependent subjects. The
explanation of the discrepant usage lies in the dialectics of
growth rather than in semantic carelessness. There is an access
of autonomy at both periods and also at other times. The meaning of stages cannot be extracted from the titles alone.

Erikson is talking primarily about ego rather than psychosexual development, but in parts of his exposition the two
topics are intertwined. His emphasis on age-specific tasks encourages confusion, since the two kinds of development overlap
in time. Optimal delineation of the relations between ego and
psychosexual development will follow only after they have been
separately characterized (Chapter Seven).

Piaget. Although Piaget's contributions to developmental
psychology have occupied dozens of volumes, only one is directly concerned with the phenomena of ego development, *The
Moral Judgment of the Child* (1932). It has been an important
influence on many authors reviewed here. Whereas in Sullivan's
exposition ego growth is somewhat confounded with adjustment and in Erikson's with psychosexual development, in Piaget's exposition there is some confounding with purely cognitive development, which has been his chief interest. Some
criticisms of Piaget's work are inapropos, since they have con-
tested the particular age to which Piaget assigns a given type of
thinking. Piaget's interest is in the sequence and its dialectics,
not in establishing age norms. Unlike American psychologists,
he has little interest in individual differences as such, and speeding development is not his mission.

Piaget explored the moral judgment of children by asking
them (or having his collaborators ask them) what a lie is and

why it is bad; which of several misdemeanors is worst and why; which of several punishments is fairest and why; and above all, where the rules of the game of marbles acquire their sanction. Moreover, Piaget asks his readers to do a thought experiment (1932, pp. 348-349):

> Let us imagine a community of which the members had always been each other's contemporaries, and had lived their lives without experiencing either the constraint of the generations preceding them, or the education of the generations following them. . . . All the elementary social phenomena would be radically different from what they are. . . . The younger child feels respect for the older, and for its parents— and the more simply constituted the society in which he lives, the more durable a part does this unilateral respect play in the life of an individual, as the respect for age and elders in the more primitive communities seems to show. Without this unilateral respect one simply does not see how the ethics and the logic peculiar to social constraint and conformity could ever have come into being. In the moral sphere, it may very well be that such facts as ritual obligations and prohibitions, moral realism and objective responsibility would not exist without the respect which the child feels for the adult. But one can go a step farther and surmise that the outstanding features of "primitive mentality" can be explained by a conjunction of the childish mentality with the effects of the constraint exercised by one generation upon the other. Primitive mentality would therefore be due to social constraint being refracted through the childish mind. In our civilization, on the contrary, with its foundation of cooperation and individual differentiation, the egocentric mentality of the child hardly enters into fundamental social phenomena.

Piaget sees moral judgment in terms of a polarity, with heteronomous morality at one extreme and autonomous morality at the other. He recognizes, however, a prior stage of anomy.

The infant in the beginning has no conception of rules; he simply follows his own wishes. As soon as his musculature is capable of controlled movements, he plays with toys such as marbles according to repetitive motor schemas, largely dictated by the nature of the materials. These motor schemas are the forerunner of rituals, hence of rules.

As he grows a little older, the child tries to imitate his parents and older children. When first playing games, he does not understand that the point is to win; his point of view is egocentric, with everything interpreted in terms of his own interest. Moreover, physical and moral laws are not distinguished. Things are as they should be and as powerful persons like father decree that they shall be. What is bad is what is punished. At first punishment for misdeeds seems not so much exacted by individuals as immanent in things; later, it appears as arbitrary revenge, which in turn gives way to the notion of expiation. Since the child does not see anything wrong about speaking his fantasies aloud, he cannot comprehend what a lie is, except that it is spoken and punished; hence a lie is at first just a "naughty word."

This heteronomous morality rises from unilateral respect of the child for his parents and is enforced by constraint. The child regards the rules of the game as sacred and given for all time or decreed by adults. A change of rules would be a transgression. The very exteriority of the rules, however, means that he does not obey them dependably. Responsibility for accidents and transgressions is "objective"; that is, the greater the palpable damage, the greater the fault, regardless of intent. A big exaggeration is a worse lie than a little exaggeration, even though it deceives no one. Hence what matters is not consequences, but what is real to the child.

Another term used by Piaget to describe the thinking of this stage is *moral realism,* meaning that morality is thought of as subsisting outside of and independently of the child's own mind. Its three features are that the good is defined entirely by obedience, that the letter rather than the spirit of the law must be observed, and that actions are evaluated not in terms of motive but "objectively" in terms of exact conformity to rules.

It is caused by egocentrism, which implies a confusion of the subjective with the objective, and by intellectual constraint by adults.

As the child grows older, he cooperates more with other children. The game of marbles is particularly valuable for judging the child's development, since boys of about twelve or thirteen years are the oldest players. They understand that they can change rules by mutual consent, that the rules originate with children, not with adults, and that the rules vary with the time and place. Between children of the same age there arises mutual respect, as opposed to unilateral respect, and thus reciprocity and cooperation based on reciprocity. Reciprocity is the essence of autonomous morality. The child accepts the rules of the game on the basis of mutual agreement; this acceptance results in the interiorization of the rules. The paradoxical result is that the child becomes dependably faithful to the rules when he no longer believes they are sacred and immutable.

A child at the stage of autonomous morality believes in subjective responsibility—that is, the intent behind the transgression is what makes it reprehensible. A lie is wrong because it deceives; a real whopper, since it deceives no one, is hardly reprehensible. Retributive justice gives way to distributive justice. When there is a choice between treating everyone equally or punishing wrongdoers, the child may choose equality. Punishment is not motivated by a need for expiation; rather, it restores reciprocity. Correspondingly, older children choose less harsh punishments than younger ones or opt for no punishment beyond disapproval or mere explanation of why something is wrong.

An interest in the codification of rules is the final stage of the game of marbles. Some of the oldest children, in their conception of distributive justice, go beyond equality to equity; that is, rather than treating everyone strictly the same, one should make allowances for special circumstances. Punishment may be dispensed with entirely.

On all of these points Piaget presents examples of the reasoning of the older and younger children. What he does not do or permit his readers to do is to examine the connections of these topics empirically in the answers of the children. There is of course some overlap of age groups; some of the younger children give answers typical for the older ones and vice versa. According to Piaget, there is no invariable sequence of stages. At the same time he does talk of a striving for coherence and equilibrium as part of the dynamics of development. The reciprocity that is the basis for autonomous morality is, he believes, more compatible with equilibrium than is unilateral respect for authority. Piaget denies that it is the greater intellectual capacity of the older child that accounts for his moral development; rather, he prefers to believe that the rise of cooperation as a social mode accounts for the child's intellectual advance. For example, the need to communicate can lead to formulation of reasons.

As Piaget does not describe stages but studies separately the evolution of moral reasoning with regard to several topics, setting up correspondence with the scheme of Chapter Two is

Table 3. Piaget's Developmental Sequences of Moral Judgment

Approximate ego level	Practice of rules	Consciousness of rules	Type of morality	Conception of punishment
Presocial	Motor schemes	No conception of obligation	Anomy	Immanent in things
Impulsive	Egocentric rules Imitation of seniors Noncompetitive			Arbitrary revenge
Self-Protective		Rules sacred, unchangeable, given by adults	Heteronomy	Expiatory
Conformist	Cooperative rules Interest in winning			
Conscientious-Conformist		Rules changeable by mutual agreement, founded on mutual respect	Autonomy	Restoring reciprocity
Conscientious	Codification of rules	Interest in rules per se		

not easy. Table 3 is an attempt to align the trends described by Piaget with each other and with our stages. He points out that the practice of rules is about a year ahead of the consciousness of rules. Such discrepancies naturally lead to difficulties and inconsistencies in describing and matching stages (see Chapter Eight).

Piaget's account has a tendentious tone. He seems to want to prove the moral superiority of children to adults. There is a lower kind of morality, heteronomy, based on authority and constraint, and a higher kind of morality, autonomy, based on cooperation and reciprocity. The inequality of ages must give rise initially to heteronomous morality, but parents and teachers, by demanding obedience and conformity and sometimes even punishing cooperation between children, discourage normal progress toward autonomy, which is the appropriate form of morality in adults in a democracy. "If one thinks of the systematic resistance offered by pupils to the authoritarian method, and the admirable ingenuity employed by children the world over to evade disciplinarian constraint, one cannot help regarding as defective a system which allows so much effort to be wasted instead of using it in cooperation" (Piaget, 1932, pp. 366-367).

Using the game of marbles as paradigm is elegant. Marbles seem to the adult as hardly having anything to do with morality at all. That is why the game suits Piaget's purpose, since there adults leave children to their own society. Thus it is a natural experiment showing how children run things when removed from adult constraint. But what happens to the sophisticated virtue of twelve-year-olds when they become parents and teachers? How do they lose their insight into the value of mutuality and reciprocity and lapse back into heteronomous morality? Piaget would not have it so. He would have parents and teachers be egalitarian companions from the beginning.

At the same time, Piaget recognizes that even under the most benign regime children will go through the heteronomous stage before achieving the autonomous one. Moral realism reflects the small child's intellectual realism, that is, his tendency to see things in concrete and simplified form. One could fault

Piaget for redundancy; if the cognitive capacities of the child limit him at first to moral realism, we need not then seek an additional explanation in the behavior of parents and teachers. Even worse, Piaget is not faithful to his own developmental logic in demanding that parents and teachers from the earliest years treat the child as equal. That would not be comprehensible to a small child still struggling to come to terms with palpable inequalities of size, age, and power.

Ausubel. Ausubel objects to the confusion of ego and psychosexual development in psychoanalysis. (His views on psychoanalysis are not altogether fair or accurate. They are presented to trace his thought in his own terms, rather than as an endorsement.) The ego, Ausubel says, is not just an outer layer differentiated out of the id. He objects to the doctrine of childhood sexuality, which he interprets as preformationism or homunculism. "Ego development is the outcome of continuous biosocial interaction. There is no predetermined course or sequence of events which reflects the unfolding of a detailed blueprint designed by inner impulses" (Ausubel, 1952, p. 44).

Those points are reminiscent of Sullivan's account; however, Ausubel's sketch of early ego stages resembles that of Ferenczi, who emphasized infantile omnipotence, more than that of Sullivan, who emphasized early consciousness of helplessness. Contradicting Sullivan's emphasis on maternal anxiety as an early influence, Ausubel says: "The level of overt parent behavior is far more crucial than its underlying attitudinal substrate in early infancy, since it is only the former which is actually communicable and relevant in terms of the child's perceptual capacity and psychosocial needs at this stage of development" (p. 250).

Ausubel objects to Ferenczi's two earliest stages of omnipotence, since feelings of omnipotence cannot precede a sense of self. The preverbal empirical self develops by correlation of sense impressions and by delays in need gratification. The mother is the scaffolding of the first self-image. The empirical distinction between self and environment is reinforced by the sense of volition. Normally a period of ego omnipotence develops after the first distinction between self and environment

has been achieved. The infant misinterprets his parents' solici-
tude to satisfy his needs immediately as proof of his own "volitional omnipotence" even when he recognizes his "executive
dependence." That is, he believes his wishes are all-powerful,
though he recognizes that others have to carry them out.

Possessiveness towards toys is a first step in the emergence
of the ego; then there is objective awareness of his own doings
and third person references to himself; and finally there is use
of the personal pronoun "I." Thus language helps consolidate
the ego.

The parents begin to make demands on the child, who for
the first time "realizes that his dependence is volitional as well
as executive in nature and that his parents are not *obliged* to
serve him just because he is helpless. Helplessness is no longer a
regal badge of volitional omnipotence, but a perceived condition for impotent dependence on the will of others" (p. 56). At
this point the child faces the crisis of ego devaluation, which
poses two unacceptable alternatives. If he maintains notions of
his own omnipotence, he will face constant frustration. On the
other hand, a realistic recognition of his own complete dependence would be an almost intolerably painful devaluation of
himself. Normally, the child escapes these alternatives by assigning his own omnipotence to his parents; he becomes their satellite; and his self-esteem is preserved by shining in reflected
glory.

Ausubel comments (pp. 57-58):

> The great advantage inherent in satellization as a
> solution to the crisis in ego organization is its capac-
> ity for providing the child with intrinsic feelings of
> security and adequacy. He is relieved of the burden of
> justifying his adequacy on the basis of actual per-
> formance ability, which in fact could be meager at
> best. Instead, he acquires an indirect status which has
> nothing to do with his own ability to manipulate real-
> ity, but is vicariously derived from the fact of his
> dependent identification with his parents who are
> omnipotent in this respect. As a result of this identifi-
> cation, he does not vicariously become possessed of

their powers, but shares (in a highly diluted form) in their magnificence—in the same way as the retainers of a powerful potentate would revel in the glory of their liege.

In most children the tendency to satellize is so strong that satellization is difficult to prevent, even with such child-rearing errors as overpermissiveness. Two parental patterns that can prevent satellization are rejection of the child and extrinsic valuation. The intrinsically valued child is valued just because he is the parents' child, while the extrinsically valued child is valued for his great and good traits and the glory he sheds on the parents. Failure to satellize sets limits on the kind of person one can ultimately become, with the consequences, such as anxiety neurosis, delinquency, selfishness, and so on, depending on various contingencies in the parent-child relation.

Ultimately, successful maturation depends on desatellization, on the child reacquiring autonomy along with newly matured realistic abilities. The dethronement of parents is begun with entry into school, for at that time there is already a second set of authorities. Transfer of satellizing tendencies to new authorities outside the family is a first stage; some people never go further, and this halt represents another failure of maturation.

Desatellization includes return to extrinsic valuation. The child whose sense of personal worth was derived from reflection of parental glory must find his worth in what he himself can do. In favorable instances, the work becomes its own reward. In late childhood when desatellization appropriately takes place, the nonsatellizer may have a temporary advantage over the satellizer; because of his competitiveness, as contrasted with the satellizer's being content with personal approval, he achieves more. In the long run, however, optimal ego development is achieved by those who have, at least to some extent, become satellites and have then desatellized.

Thus the two crises in ego development are ego devaluation in early childhood and ego maturation in late childhood and adolescence. Each carries the possibility of failure with distinctive consequences. Being rejected is more unpleasant than being extrinsically valued, and hence more likely to be reversible. If parental attitudes change or a surrogate can be found, the rejected child is usually eager to satellize. If rejection is accompanied by neglect rather than by hostility, the child's ego may become completely devalued. The child's own stubbornness or submissiveness has some bearing on the outcome. If rejection and neglect are severe enough early enough, omnipotent fantasies may not develop in the first place, and severe emotional impoverishment will result.

Unlike the satellizer, the extrinsically valued child need not give up his volitional omnipotence. It is confirmed by the continued gratification of his wishes in the face of his visible executive dependence. While the self-esteem of the satellizer is maintained by being valued by his parents, the self-esteem of the nonsatellizer can be maintained only by his own achievements. He is thus driven prematurely into an achievement orientation, distorted, however, by constant reference to his own ego enhancement.

Satellization is one of three life orientations. The other two are incorporation and exploration. *Satellization* is a form of identification in which status is gained through dependence, subservience, and conformity. *Incorporation,* as Ausubel uses the term, is a form of identification involving accepting the values of another person and using him as a model in order to enhance one's own ego status, without an accompanying emotional dependence. *Exploration* is oriented toward mastery of the task for its own sake. To some extent it exists from the earliest years. Normally it becomes predominant at maturity, but various maturational failures can prevent this step from taking place. Incorporation occurs prior to satellization and is important to nonsatellizers. Ausubel sometimes speaks of these as three types of children and at other times as three potentialities in everyone.

Satellization and desatellization are the mechanism of ego development; its substance is the attenuation of hedonistic motivation, increased capacity for delay of gratification, increased executive independence, and growth of moral responsibility. Each of these is something like a polar variable (see Chapter Six).

In adult life a person must find his security on the basis of his real achievements. One who has had a period of satellization has a lasting residue of inner security. The nonsatellizer must strive for extrinsic security based on power, position, wealth, and prestige. Neurotic anxiety, which is always due to threats to self-esteem, according to Ausubel, is a major hazard for the nonsatellizer but much less likely for the adult who has gone through a period of satellization.

Ausubel's depiction of stages in the development of conscience recapitulates his discussion of satellization in a way that permits collation with our scheme (Table 2). In the presatellizing period, inhibition and control of behavior are based on anticipating and avoiding punishment. There is no sense of guilt. During the early stage of satellization the child assimilates his parents' values. True conscience begins in this period, because the child accepts the values rather than just fearing punishment, but his sense of obligation to conform is rudimentary. Guilt, which requires accurate self-perception to perceive the disparity between behavior and internalized standards, is also rudimentary or absent. In the latter part of the satellizing period there is internalization not only of parental standards but also of the moral obligation to conform to them. Self-critical ability increases. Guilt becomes important as a sanction and regulator of behavior. It is aroused by parental reproof, which makes the child automatically assume he has done wrong. The prime offense is rebellion. Satellization peaks at about age eight, at which time the child begins to think about right and wrong in somewhat general terms. At earlier ages, right and wrong refer to specific situations. Piaget's notion of moral absolutism applies in this period, that is, moral obligation is unilateral rather than reciprocal, and rules have self-evident rightness.

During the desatellizing period the child acquires all the essential ingredients of a rational conscience. He becomes less egocentric and more self-critical; thus he judges his own behavior in the same framework as that of others. Moral absolutism declines. His conscience becomes less authoritarian and more reciprocal. Moral principles acquire greater generality and abstractness. Moral accountability is placed on a societal instead of parent-child basis. During adolescence the changes of the desatellizing period are carried further. The incorporative and exploratory orientations are strong. The incorporative orientation results from the greater need for achieving extrinsic status. The exploratory orientation is related to needs for independence, equality, and self-assertion. The peer group is the source of extrinsic feelings of adequacy, but it also is the chief moral authority and the object of residual satellizing tendencies. Compared with those of the preadolescent, the moral beliefs of the adolescent show more expedience and conformity, greater concern with extrinsic status, more cynicism and aggression towards adults, but also more tolerance and flexibility. And there Ausubel's account of the development of conscience ends.

Ausubel, like Sullivan, sees ego maturation as a sequence of tasks and crises that are fateful for adult personality. Unlike Piaget, he is concerned with individual differences. Yet Ausubel's view of ego development is primarily developmental rather than dimensional, though the point is arguable. He does not present ego development as an abstraction, with common terms for stages and types, nor does he view it as a structure. While the elements he describes are similar to those of our scheme, he gives a separate account of the growth in the various elements.

Ausubel gives the impression of being able to see through walls; he knows the causes and the consequences of every childhood deviation, as well as of the normal developmental sequence. Occasionally he admits that constitutional differences may be an element determining the outcome, hence, that the outcome is not completely determined by parents' practices and attitudes. Data are rarely cited and only in relation to minor points. One must assume that Ausubel drew on his experience as clinician, as parent, as teacher, as scholar, and as observer of the scene. He draws ideas from many scholarly sources, but he does not always do justice to them. Erikson, for example, having labeled his scheme of psychosexual development as *epigenetic,* would hardly agree with Ausubel's labeling of it as *preformationist.* Childhood sexuality never meant, as Ausubel says it does, that sexuality is the same in children and adults. One could ignore Ausubel because he misunderstands psychoanalysis, borrows and misinterprets its terms and ideas, and does not contend with the dynamic unconscious, but his blindness to some phenomena may sharpen his insight into others. The idea of satellization helps us understand the dynamics of conformity.

Characterologies

Some authors have described the major aspects of ego development taking as their starting point types of character in a given age cohort, usually adults. The question of the developmental course that generates the differences may be ignored, or the author may postulate complex contingencies to account for the different outcomes. Our purpose in using a term like *typology* or *characterology* is to mark the break with the factorial logic of the mainstream psychometric approach to intelligence and personality. A well-trained psychologist, looking at the scheme of Table 1, immediately imagines the columns as more or less independent factors that can be measured separately. They are, on the contrary, diverse signs and manifestations of a single underlying entity, itself not directly measurable.

Fromm. Erich Fromm and, following him, David Riesman, have been primarily concerned with social character, the predominant character structure in different societies. This concern leads them to emphasize social and economic determinants of character more than other writers do.

In *Escape from Freedom,* Fromm (1941) presented the basic problem of character development in terms of freedom and spontaneity. As the child emerges from his symbiotic dependence on his mother, he achieves *freedom from* imposed restraint. Then he is faced with a choice between slipping into an automatic conformity or becoming a truly autonomous person. In the former case he becomes an authoritarian character or a potential one. In the latter case, becoming autonomous, he achieves *freedom to* choose his style of life. Approximate correspondence with ego stages is shown in Table 4. Fromm's con-

Table 4. Ego Types of Fromm, Riesman, and Graves

Approximate ego level	Author		
	Fromm (1941)	Riesman (1950)	Graves (1966)
Autistic			Autistic behavior
Symbiotic	Symbiosis		
Impulsive		Anomy	Animistic existence
Self-Protective		Tradition-directed conformity	Awakening and fright Aggression and power
Conformist	Conformity	Other-directed conformity	Sociocentric attitudes
Conscientious		Inner-directed conformity	Aggressive individualism
Individualistic	Autonomy		Pacifistic individualism
Autonomous		Autonomy	

ception is a typology rather than a developmental sequence because the crucial difference, that between the authoritarian and the autonomous character, is seen as a kind of moral or existential choice made in childhood under social influence. Authoritarian conformity is not seen as a necessary developmental step on the road to autonomy.

There is an echo of Rousseau in Fromm's reasoning, as also in that of many others, such as Rogers (1959). The child is seen as bringing into the world a spontaneity that is unnecessarily crushed by maternal or parental harshness. There is also an assumption that everyone is in principle capable of attaining the highest ego stages. The hypothesis in our scheme of ego development implies, by contrast, that a rule-bound impulse control is a necessary stage in the evolution of personality from impulsiveness to autonomy. The increase in spontaneity, in being at home with one's impulses, is indeed a mark of the highest stages of ego development, as many expositions agree. That does not justify the conclusion that intermediate stages of rigid controls can be bypassed.

Riesman. In *The Lonely Crowd* Riesman and his collaborators (1950) primarily aimed to describe the predominant character types in several kinds of society. Riesman's anomic and autonomous persons are easily matched with stages of ego development (Table 4). The chief emphasis in his exposition, however, is on three modes of insuring conformity, which relate to stages of population growth. In primitive societies, characterized by high birth and death rates, the predominant character type is tradition-directed. This mode of conformity is of diminishing relevance in a highly industrialized society. The death rate falls first, resulting in a rapid population growth, during which time inner-directed characters predominate. In the most highly developed periods, when the birth rate also declines, the predominant type of conformity is other-directed.

Among tradition-directed people, conformity is insured by their tendency to follow tradition; shame is the emotional sanction; emphasis is on behavior and custom. Among inner-directed people, conformity is insured by a tendency to acquire early in life internalized goals, which act like an implanted gyroscope; guilt is the chief emotional sanction; emphasis is on conscience, character, and self-improvement. Among other-directed people, conformity is insured by their tendency to be sensitized to expectations and preferences of others; anxiety is their radar or emotional sanction; fashion supplants conscience, and personality supplants character. "Approval itself, irrespective of content, becomes almost the only unequivocal good in this situation; one makes good when one is approved of" (Riesman, 1950, p. 66). "The tradition-directed child propitiates his parents; the inner-directed child fights or succumbs to them; the other-directed child manipulates them and is in turn manipulated" (p. 70).

Riesman's hypothesis that inner-directedness characterizes an earlier stage of social evolution than other-directedness does not directly contradict our hypothesis that the Conformist is at an earlier stage of his personal development than the Conscientious person. There need be no ontogenetic law here. In some respects, however, Riesman's picture contradicts our scheme enough to require resolution. He finds large numbers of both inner-directed and other-directed types in contemporary American society, as we find both Conformist and Conscientious types. Riesman asserts that inner-directed persons are more interested in material things and other-directed persons more concerned with feelings, whereas we find that Conformists are more interested in material things and Conscientious people more interested in inner feelings. However, the feelings that Riesman refers to are primarily those of approval and disapproval, which do indeed preoccupy the Conformist, rather than the differentiated experiences of the Conscientious person.

Riesman's concept of the tradition-directed man has been one of several influences which led to modification of our scheme. When a stage between the Impulsive and the Conformist ones was first postulated, it was called the Opportunistic Stage. While hedonism and calculation of short-term gains remain as characteristics, *opportunism* is too pejorative a term when applied to the normal child passing through this phase at the appropriate age. Our data with older children and adults lend support to the alternative characterization as the Self-Protective Stage. Even this, however, is too narrow to apply to the age-appropriate version. Small children normally display a ritualism on the road to conformity that is easily seen as the counterpart of Riesman's portrait of a tradition-directed person. Piaget's observations on children learning the rules of the game also show ritualism as a way station between impulsivity and conformity.

Adorno, Frenkel-Brunswik, Levinson, and Sanford. One of the first studies to capture the full range of interrelated ego functions that constitute the core of ego development is *The Authoritarian Personality* (Adorno and others, 1950). The California research group constructed tests for ethnocentrism and anti-Semitism, by methods that we need not examine, and administered them to men and women in various organizations, institutions, and schools. Subjects in the highest and lowest quartiles of the total population were contacted for extended interviews. Under the direction of Else Frenkel-Brunswik, interview data for the two groups of subjects, those highly prejudiced and those low in prejudice, were encoded and rated. The highs turned out to be more distinctive in their responses, that is, they were more like each other than were the lows.

The greatest differences between the groups occurred in attitudes toward current self and in cognitive structure. Those scoring high in prejudice tend to be conventional, conformist, stereotyped in their thinking, given to use of clichés, intolerant of ambiguities, and given to moralistic condemnation of those who do not adhere to conventional mores. Their interpersonal relations are often exploitative or manipulative, concerned with things rather than with feelings. They describe themselves and their parents in idealized but stereotyped terms. Their conception of sex role differences is conventional. They think of their work in terms of competition, power, and status. There is sometimes an opportunistic dependence on parents.

Those scoring low on prejudice are often unconventional or nonconformist. They are tolerant of or even cherish individual differences. Their interpersonal relations are dominated by a search for companionship and affection, the latter at times insatiably strong. They admit or even dwell excessively on unfavorable traits and conflicts in themselves, including conflicts over sex roles. Their parents are described as real people with good and bad traits, and there is often open admission of conflict with them or ambivalence towards them with consequent conscious guilt feelings. Low scorers describe other people and their own inner experiences more vividly than do high scorers. Lows tend to think of work in terms of achievement or in terms of social values and ideals. The high scorer, while glorifying his present self, sees a discontinuity with childhood; he makes few spontaneous references to his childhood. The low scorer makes spontaneous comments on his childhood and explains his present self in terms of development, and in general explains human behavior in social and psychological terms. Low scoring women may develop a conflict between emotional dependence on a man and striving for independence that leads to competition with men.

Major interview findings were based on a sample of eighty cases, forty men and forty women. The men were evenly divided between high- and low-prejudice groups, but there were twenty-five women in the high-prejudice group, fifteen in the low. There was an attempt to balance the high- and low-scoring subjects according to age, political and religious affiliation, and national or regional background.

The California investigators began with some psychodynamic theories about origins of prejudice. The interview schedule was drawn with emphasis on theoretically derived "underlying questions" and only suggestions as to the direct questions. The scoring manual was drawn up after reading over the interviews, so as to encompass and formalize the findings obtained by scanning them. The scoring categories were inferential. For example, under self-estimate of traits for men, alternatives are: "Pseudo-masculinity. Determination, energy, industry, independence, decisiveness, will power. No admission of passivity," for the presumably high variant. "Ego-accepted admission of passivity, softness, weakness, etc." was the presumably low variant (p. 422). As another example, the rater was asked to judge whether the subject's self-estimate and his ego ideal are the same or separate.

The above account of their findings is somewhat filtered in order to make it more comparable with ours (Chapter Nine). They aimed to extract maximum inference from each observation, as many clinicians do, in contrast to our attempt to state observations at a minimal inferential level. The difference is not merely one of reporting findings; in encoding interview data their raters were instructed to consider unacknowledged, unconscious, and repressed trends. Regardless of whether such inferences are correct, the methodology is different. The findings summarized above are those that are plausibly related to observations rather than remote inferences concerning manner of resolving the Oedipus complex or relations between ego, superego, and id. In general, those high in prejudice have the traits of Conformists and Self-Protective persons by our scheme. Those low in prejudice have the traits of those at the Conscientious and higher levels.

Adorno reported "types and syndromes" within both the high and low prejudice groups; however, in contrast to the previous findings, nothing is said about method for deriving or confirming these pictures. The terms *type* and *syndrome* seem to be used loosely and interchangeably.

Among the highly prejudiced the first syndrome he presents is that of surface resentment. This type of person accepts his prejudices from outside as ready-made formulas to rationalize or to overcome his own difficulties. He is, for example, happy to have someone else to blame for his own economic failure. For him prejudice is not too libidinized, however.

The second type is the conventional syndrome. For this type also the tendency to stereotype comes from outside, but it is integrated as part of a general conformity. Discontent is less important than in the previous type, acceptance of prevailing standards more important. Adherence to conventional sex norms is prominent. Such persons are not vicious or violent.

The third type is the authoritarian, described as sado-masochistic, compulsive, and ambivalent. For him the tendency to stereotype is highly libidinized. He takes pleasure in obedience and in being obeyed. He has an overly-rigid but external superego; one subject said that adultery is wrong only if found out, for example. There is great concern for authority and control. The authoritarian and the conventional types are the two most common among the highly prejudiced.

The next type is described as "the rebel and the psychopath" but is better rendered as the psychopathic rebel. Persons in this group are prone to insurrection in place of identification with authority. They have a penchant for tolerated excesses, such as heavy drinking and overt homosexuality. They are not rigid nor are they terribly prejudiced, but they are infantile and asocial, hence capable of crude sadism. Included are the "tough guys," the hoodlums and rowdies who do the dirty work of fascist movements. Naturally, the interview situation did not reveal samples of such conduct, but it did draw forth references to bodily violence.

The crank is a paranoid and isolated type of person. Prejudice is important for him as a means of escaping mental disease. Sharing of his prejudices with others provides a kind of social validation of aggression against out-groups. Some mysticism and superstition may be found in this type.

Finally, there is the manipulative type, a pattern found in numerous persons in business, managerial, and technological groups. Such persons are concerned with efficient carrying out of tasks without regard to the justifiability of the purposes. In comparison with the authoritarian type, they are more narcissistic and more empty and shallow. For one such person, loy-alty was the only moral quality he was much concerned with, and he objected to Jewish refugees from Hitler's Germany for not having been loyal to Germany.

Among those low in prejudice, the first type described is the rigid low. He is described as the counterpart of the surface-resentment type of prejudiced person, though the basis for that comparison is not made plain. The rigidly low person is as prone to clichés as his opponents. His opposition to prejudice is stated in terms of broad, categorical principles, such as being a "true Christian." His similarity to some prejudiced types is shown by his aggressive intolerance of other people's characteristics (in one case cited, smoking and drinking).

The exemplar of the next syndrome, the protesting type, is thoroughly guided by conscience. He wants to make good the injustices wrought by prejudice. He regards everyone as guilty. He may be constricted, neurotic, shy, or tormented by self-doubts.

The impulsive type of low-prejudice person has strong im-pulses but not destructive ones. He is attracted by whatever is different; therefore the in-group versus out-group difference does not mean anything to him. This group includes libertines and addicts, some prostitutes and nonviolent criminals, and some psychotics. These people do not think in stereotypes, but it is doubtful if they conceptualize clearly at all.

The easy-going low syndrome is said to be the opposite of the highly prejudiced manipulative syndrome. A person of this type just lets things go, on a live-and-let-live basis. He is non-acquisitive, nondestructive, but also uncommitted. He does not harbor stereotypes, but he is also reluctant to make decisions. He is open to experience. The two types most common among the unprejudiced are the easy-going and the protestor types.

Finally, there is the genuine liberal. This person has a strong sense of personal autonomy and independence. He can-not stand to have others interfere with his beliefs, and he does not want to interfere with others' beliefs. He is individualized himself and sees others as individuals. Like the impulsive low, he is emotional, but he is compassionate and values the other as a person. He is characterized by moral courage.

In Table 5 each of these subtypes is matched as closely as the limited information permits to a stage described in Chapter Two. The crank is put at the Self-Protective stage more or less *faute de mieux*. Information relevant to classifying as to ego level is not given; possibly persons of various ego levels may become cranks. The person characterized by surface resentment is also not clearly assignable; he may be of the Conformist Stage, though his tendency to blame others suggests a lower level. At low ego levels one can find both prejudiced and unprejudiced types, while at high ego levels there are only unprejudiced syndromes. The two most common types of highly prejudiced persons apparently represent the Self-Protective and the Conformist stages. The two most common types of unprejudiced persons apparently represent the Conscientious-Conformist level and the Conscientious Stage. The presence of markedly different syndromes within a stage raises the problem of subtypes (see Chapter Eight).

Table 5. Adorno's Types of Prejudiced and Unprejudiced Persons

Hypothetical ego level	High prejudice types	Low prejudice types
Impulsive	Psychopathic rebel	Impulsive
Self-Protective	Crank	
	Manipulator	
	*Authoritarian	
Conformist	Surface resentment	Rigidily unprejudiced
	*Conventional	
Conscientious-Conformist		*Easy-going
Conscientious		*Protestor
Individualistic		
Autonomous		Genuine liberal

*Frequent types

SOURCE: Chapter 19 of *The Authoritarian Personality* (Adorno, Frenkel-Brunswik, Levinson, and Sanford, 1950).

In rendering Adorno's types and syndromes, I have omitted his comments on the family constellations that gave rise to the syndromes and on the Oedipus complex, id, and superego. The family members and their relationships are known only through the eyes of the subject; therefore they do not seem to provide additional data. The objections to the inferences about intrapsychic forces and structures are more serious. The terms *id* and *superego* are ambiguous, and nothing in the studies reported serves to anchor them in behavior.

There is another reason for omitting from our summary the psychodynamic explanations that the authors may have felt were their most important discoveries. The thrust of the present book is that constellations that others have explained in psychodynamic terms are stages in a universal development sequence. An explanation is needed for why someone failed to develop further than he did, but granted that he has become fixed at a given stage, many aspects of his character follow without further explanation. That a person of low ego level will not differentiate his notion of self from his ego ideal does not require a dynamic explanation; persons of low level simply do not have that degree of conceptual complexity. They did not repress the differentiation; they never had it. Clearly, ego level does not explain why some persons of the Conformist or lower stages become prejudiced and some do not, nor does it explain why some Self-Protective persons become cranks, some become authoritarian, and some become manipulative. Many psychodynamic explanations were, however, directed to the aspects of the constellation that are given by the developmental sequence. Table 5 clarifies schematically what must be accounted for. Granted there are many factors other than ego level and psychodynamics determining whether a person will become prejudiced. There are parental prejudices, group influences, his own abilities, economic self-interest, and so on. But the major group differences between those high and low in prejudice involve aspects of character that are involved in ego development, and the most frequent syndromes are plausibly ordered to different ego stages.

In *The Authoritarian Personality* Adorno and his colleagues explicitly denied that the prejudiced were in any way less mature than the unprejudice subjects. Frenkel-Brunswik (1951), however, in studying rigidity in the personality of prejudiced and unprejudiced children, noted that the personality test items that correlated with prejudice were the same as those that differentiated younger from older children. She also noted similarities between tendencies of prejudiced children and those described by Piaget (1926, 1932) as characterizing younger children. "Some of the trends which are connected with ethnocentrism are thus natural stages of development which have to be overcome if maturity is to be reached" (Frenkel-Brunswik, 1951, p. 406). She foretold that a most promising direction for research in personality would combine a developmental approach with simultaneous interest in motivational and cognitive aspects of personality.

Graves. Most business executives who are concerned with deteriorating work standards propose solutions that involve changing either the managers or the workers. Graves (1966), in an article that attracted much popular attention, suggested that the solution lies in more appropriately matching worker, manager, and job specifications. His proposal is made as an alternative to other widely known approaches, such as the Blake-Mouton grid of managerial strategies and the formulation of Douglas McGregor.

McGregor, according to Graves, believed that much managerial strategy is based on the assumption that the average man dislikes work and will avoid it if possible. He has little ambition, seeks only security, and prefers to be directed. Therefore he must be controlled and forced to work. McGregor believed that production would be improved if management were based on the alternative assumption that effortful work is natural. External control and threat are not optimal conditions for work. If a man's ego needs and actualization needs are met, he will exercise self-control and self-direction and display imagination and ingenuity. He will seek responsibility when it is appropriate. In our terms, McGregor was urging management to give up the assumption that workers operate below the Conformist level in favor of the assumption that they operate above the Conformist level.

Graves describes his alternative view as based on fourteen years of research, but he does not give his data or research methods. He describes his point of view as follows (1966, p. 120):

> The psychology of the mature human organism
> is an unfolding or emergent process marked by the

progressive subordination of older behavioral systems
to newer, higher order behavior systems. The mature
human being tends, normally, to change his psychology as the conditions of his existence change. Each
successive stage or level is a state of equilibrium
through which people pass on the way to other states
of equilibrium . . . . His acts, feelings, motivations,
ethics and values, thoughts, and preferences for management all are appropriate to that state . . . .

A person may not be genetically or constitution-
ally equipped to change in the normal upward direction if the conditions of his existence change. He *may*
move, given certain conditions, through a hierarchically ordered series of behavior systems to some end,
or he *may* stabilize and live out his lifetime at any
one or a combination of the levels in the hierarchy.
Again, he may show the behavior of a level in a predominantly positive or negative manner, or he may
under certain stressful circumstances regress to a behavior system lower in the hierarchy . . . .

In this conception of man, an employee is not
something to be managed by a general set of managerial principles. He should be managed by principles
which are appropriate to his level of behavior . . . .
Therefore, when deteriorating work standards are
present, we should look primarily for incongruency
between the psychological level of the producer and
the managerial style of the manager.

Graves outlines seven "levels of human existence," but
states that there are probably higher levels. The first level is
called *autistic behavior*. Men at this level are only vaguely aware
of their existence, being absorbed by staying alive, illness, reproduction, and disputes. They cannot be expected to be very productive, and they respond only to giving and to care. There are
few employees of this type in advanced economies, but they are
more frequent in underdeveloped areas.

The second level is that of animistic existence. The person
has magical beliefs, superstitions, and taboos. Concepts such as
time, space, and quantity are poorly developed. Hence the per-

son works only under close supervision. Work is spotty and sporadic. These employees also do not do well in a country like the United States but may play a part in, say, Peace Corps work. Force and threats of force may serve to motivate persons at this level so long as their taboos are not violated. Force is ineffective with persons at the autistic level.

The third level is called "awakening and fright." People at this level are aware of frightening impulses in themselves and of bewildering forces in the world. They crave an orderly, predictable, unchanging world in which everyone has a predestined place. They live in a moralistically prescribed world and respond to rigidly prescribed and rigidly enforced rules. Such persons do not respond well to autonomy and participation. Given a choice between autocracy and democracy, they will choose autocracy.

The fourth level is described in terms of aggression and power. The person at this level does not see himself as having to fit into a prescribed organizational design. It is his right to change things if he can. Production can be maintained by sufficient incentives, but the real struggle is for power rather than for material gain.

The fifth level is described in terms of sociocentric attitudes. As a person achieves a certain basic physical and material security, his concerns turn to social rather than physiological or material things. He wants a congenial atmosphere and a comfortable work pace, hence he may be less productive than those at the third or fourth levels. He no longer believes, as do those at third level, that work is his moral duty. However, group effort can keep productivity up, particularly if the group is encouraged to participate and to substitute new ideas for the loss in sheer effort. If management reacts to this attitude on the part of workers by emphasis on increased productivity, neglecting the workers' human needs, the results are disastrous. Still worse are the results if the managers are fifth-level people while the workers are at the third or fourth level. Then managers try to woo the workers because of their own desire to be liked. To the fourth-level worker this is an invitation to "take" management for as much as possible, and third-level workers are disgusted.

The sixth level is described as aggressive individualism. The person at this level is not motivated by man's common fears, as those at lower levels are motivated by fear about survival, fear of God, of the boss, or of social disapproval. He is responsible and creative. He is willing to have management set goals, but he does not want to be told when, how, or where to get his work done. He will not follow standard operating procedures. He is an excellent producer so long as management provides the wherewithal to do the job and does not plan or organize his work methods without consulting him. Most business men do not understand this type of person. He is threatening to their frame of reference if they are fourth-level authoritarian types or fifth-level social leaders. Thus a person of this level may be fired or put in a position where his talents are lost.

The seventh-level person, described in terms of pacifistic individualism, is similar to the sixth-level man but less oppositional. His work is important to him; he resists domination, coercion, and restriction; and he thrives under trust and respect.

This typology is proposed as applying to adults. While it is hierarchical, Graves does not compare his levels with normal development in childhood. Different as they are, his third and fourth levels could both be rated as equivalent to the Self-Protective Stage in our scheme (Table 4). Adjustment in terms of aggression and power, while more effective, probably precludes further advance more decisively than does "awakening and fright"; however, in adult life neither is likely to lead much further up the scale. The sixth and seventh levels differ largely with respect to aggressiveness. Pacifistic individualism could include some persons at the Conscientious stage and would most likely include all persons at higher stages.

While Graves has skimped aspects of ego development stressed by others, he has given more detail on work adjustment. In applying the same dimension to management and workers, he opens up a series of topics that have not yet been explored. What will be revealed when we use a common scale of ego level to look at teachers and their students, social workers and their clients, psychiatrists and their patients, parents and their children?

Developmental Characterologies

Many authors describing ego development as a sequence saw that its course has fateful consequences in adult life. Those describing characterologies knew that each type must have some history. Sullivan elevated the point to a postulate, that individual differences in character are largely differences in relative maturity. The expositions in the present section take the point further, identifying types with stages.

Sullivan, Grant, and Grant. Our scheme has evolved out of that of Sullivan, Grant, and Grant (1957), who call it levels of interpersonal integration but also "psychological development in general." They and their collaborators have been interested in problems of delinquency.*

Sullivan, Grant, and Grant postulate a core structure of personality, comprising experience, needs, expectations, and perceptions, in some more or less integrated cognitive scheme. This central core of personality grows by spurts, with intervening periods of relative stability: "However important learning may be in cultural transmission, it cannot by itself account for the character and style of what is transmitted, nor for the integrative character of the human mind in so far as the emotional relationship of the person to his environment is concerned. Thus, we believe that in addition to acculturation and direct learning processes, a person builds within himself an integrative system of goals, values, and aspirations which are uniquely satisfying to him and manageable by him. Without such simplification and integration the complexity of stimuli impinging on him would be overwhelming" (Sullivan, Grant, and Grant, 1957, p. 374).

Development proceeds in the direction of increasing in-

---

*For some years their base of operations was Camp Elliott Naval Retraining Command in San Diego, where they worked with delinquent young men, most of them in late adolescence. More recently the work of some members of the group has been sponsored by the California Youth Authority, which has jurisdiction over delinquent boys and girls in the state of California. Key persons have been Marguerite Warren (formerly Grant) and Ted Palmer.

volvement with others, increasing perceptual and cognitive discrimination, increasingly accurate perception, and more effective operation. At each of the successive development levels, they describe the core problem, the characteristics of children passing through the stage in normal time, the characteristics of adults fixated at that stage, typical anxieties, and potentialities for delinquency.

At Level 1 the central problem is the integration of separateness. The infant must first master the differentiation of self from non-self. There is poor comprehension of reality, magical thinking, superstition, and a need for symbiotic relationships in which needs are instantly satisfied. There is little attempt to achieve or to solve problems. Adults at this level are always in difficulty; sometimes they are in mental hospitals or in fringe groups, such as hobo camps, but not all psychotics or vagrants are at this level.

At Level 2 the central problem is the integration of non-self differences. There is beginning differentiation of people from objects, but both are seen merely as means to the person's own gratification. The person in this stage makes constant demands. "In his need to master objects, situations, and people, he will frequently fall into a pattern of *crude* manipulation, tending to use people as tools without awareness of their feelings and without regard for consequences to them or himself" (p. 378). Failure to meet his demands results in anger, anxiety, leaving the field, or superficially compliant behavior hiding a smoldering resentment, but no realistic commerce or give-and-take with others. Laws, rules, and punishments are interpreted simply as denials of gratification. Delinquency and nomadism are common when this level persists into adult life.

At Level 3 the central problem is the integration of rules. The child at this level has discovered that the world is governed by rules, but the rules are arbitrary, specific, all-or-nothing, and magic talismans of control. An adult at this level "understands the behavior of others purely as a reflection of his own manipulations and seeks for final and absolute social rules which will define *exactly* what is expected of him and what he must avoid so that he may later invoke the rule to get what he wants, thus controlling others as he feels controlled" (p. 379).

There are two types of adults at this level, the cons, that is, the confidence-man personality types, and the conformists. Both are interested in quick and easy gratification of their own needs. While they are afraid of being caught in transgression of rules, they do not experience genuine guilt feelings, though they may say they do. Thus persons at this level have an externalized superego. They deny having problems or emotions, and they are superficially mentally healthy, without classical neurotic symptoms. Interpersonal relations are conceived in terms of persons trying to make suckers out of each other, at least by the level 3 cons. They tend to see people and events in terms of power, reacting either by surface compliance (Conformists) or by challenging, fighting, and usurping power (cons) (Warren, 1969).

The central problem of Level 4 is the individuation of response. The person at this level, rather than identifying himself with the norm, characterizes himself as different from it and from specific people (Warren, 1969). The earlier characterization of the Level 4 person as "tense, suspicious, bewildered, sometimes hostile, and always anxious" (Sullivan, Grant, and Grant, 1957, p. 382) now is reserved for the neurotic subtypes (see Chapter Eight).

At Level 5 the core problem is the integration of continuity. The person perceives his own behavior and that of others in terms of patterns. He has a capacity for empathy and for differentiated role conceptualization. As he begins to free himself from over-intense identifications, he can understand and enjoy other people more, responding to them as complex individuals. "However, role ambiguities in himself may still arouse his anxieties. He may be bothered by the incompatibility of the roles he plays; he may feel diffuse, wondering which of his roles is basic, which is 'the real me' " (p. 384).

At Level 6 the core problem is the integration of self-consistency. The person has a sense of self-consistency despite changes in roles, that is, changes in his relations with others. The separation of self from role makes possible mature, long-term goals and relations with others.

At Level 7 the core problem is integration of relativity, movement, and change. The person perceives integration processes in himself and others, which increases his capacity for understanding and dealing with those functioning at lower levels. The most likely matching of these stages to ours is presented in Table 6.

A way of accounting for a number of differences between these levels and the work of others is that the work of Sullivan, Grant, and Grant led them to the maladapted persons at each level, whereas some other research, including ours, is concerned mainly with well-adjusted persons. They do not provide adequately for the cheerful, good-natured, trusting, salt-of-the-earth Conformist nor for the well-adjusted, responsible, achievement-oriented Conscientious person who lacks the kind of insight into himself that would raise him to Level 5 or higher; yet these may be the two most common types in the general adult population. Recent work of Warren and Palmer has been based on subtypes, which we will examine in Chapter Eight.

Isaacs. The central term in the formulation of Isaacs is *relatability.* (Isaacs, 1956; Isaacs and Haggard, 1956). It refers to the development of the capacity for interpersonal relations, but to potentiality, not to current level of functioning. Although behavior is not assumed to reflect the level of relatability accurately, a prerequisite for behavior of a given level is that signs of it should appear in fantasy in relation to oneself or another. On this reasoning Isaacs has used the Thematic Apperception Test (TAT) as his chief measuring instrument. Most of his subjects have been college students or psychotherapy patients or both.

Relatability is not the same as psychosexual development, as cognitive development, as emotional health, or as ego strength. (At one time Isaacs also said that it is not the same as maturity of ego development, but currently [personal communication] he agrees that they are closely related concepts, though he uses the term *ego development* for a broader set of components.) "The relatability scale is a sequence of levels of increasing differentiation of the self from others, and the increasing affective appreciation of the delineation of others" (Isaacs, 1956, p. 12). People vary in the extent to which they are aware of others as existing separately and in the complexity of their conception of others. This delineation of other people

Table 6. Ego Stage-Types of Sullivan, Grant, Grant, Peck, Kohlberg, Bull, and Perry

| Approximate ego level | Sullivan, Grant, and Grant | Peck | Kohlberg | Bull | Perry |
	Levels of integration	Character type	Basis for morality	Type of morality	Intellectual-ethical paradigm
Presocial	1. Separateness				
Impulsive	2. Non-self differences	Amoral	Punishment and obedience	Anomy	Duality
Self-Protective	3. Rules ("Cons")	Expedient	Naïve instrumental hedonism	Heteronomy	Multiplicity prelegitimate
Conformist	3. Rules (Conformists)	Conformist	Good relations and approval	Socionomy	Multiplicity
Conscientious-Conformist	4. Conflict and response		Law and order		Relativism
Conscientious		Irrational-conscientious	Democratic contract	Autonomy	
Individualistic	5. Continuity	Rational-altruistic	Individual principles of conscience		
Autonomous	6. Self-consistency				Commitment
Integrated	7. Relativity				

occurs first perceptually, then intellectually, and finally emotionally. Relatability is concerned with emotional awareness of others. At each level of relatability there are many manifestations. There can be variability in the level of the manifestations, but at any given time there is relative stability of the characteristic level, that is, of the highest potential. Development continues longer than for other growth sequences, probably into the fourth decade of life.

At the lowest or Zeta level, the person is affectively at the level of the neonate. Few adults operate at this level except during illness or severe stress. The person at this level may distinguish self from others perceptually and intellectually but not affectively. Fantasies show no distinction between self and other objects, between human and nonhuman, nor even between animate and inanimate. "Fantasies at this level tend to be barren, lifeless, and impersonal. They are devoid of awareness of own feelings, or affects of personal needs and wants . . . . There are few 'rules of life' at this level, and these few are inadequate to the real complexity of the world . . . . The affective blindness is so limiting that confusion, bafflement, and chaos result from attempts of persons at this level to understand and predict events in their environment. In some ways what is part of the environment for the more developed persons does not exist for these people" (p. 16).

At the Epsilon level there is an appreciation of self as separate from others but not of the possibility of interaction, though in daily life interaction occurs. The person perceives his own needs and difficulties, but not the possibility of gratification or help from others. Feelings may be as intense as at higher levels, but "they tend to be automatic, accepted, without a specific human object, although part-object relations do occur. Satisfactions and gratifications are all within the self, rather than to, from, or with the other. Thus the other person's part is not meaningful . . . . In the fantasies, even physical interaction is absent" (p. 18).

At the Delta level interpersonal effects are recognized, but they are of the form of one person acting on another rather than true interaction. Response is not perceived. Rather than merely wishing for things, as the Epsilon person does, the Delta person actively seeks what he wants. Identification with others and true social participation are other new elements. Fantasies include (pp. 19-20):

> Receiving from others or being deprived by others; controlling others or being controlled by others; making efforts to insure further receiving; struggling to gain satisfactions through attempts to snare, trap, capture, outwit, outdo; or avoiding being caught while taking advantage of others. There is stubbornness and resistiveness, yet there may be obedience, mainly in reaction to fear.
>
> The affects which are evidenced are highly personal, rather than interpersonal. The affects include shame, disgust, fear, anxiety, grief, rage, or any others which require interaction with but do not require understanding or consideration of another person. When there are two or more persons perceived as having affects, they all tend to be perceived as one person: there is a generalization rather than individuation. When a group is perceived, it is looked upon as having a unitary mind, and a unitary affective reaction. There is a tendency to think of people as belonging to groups, for uniqueness is not yet perceived . . . .
>
> Teasing, playing tricks, punishing, or doing violence are methods of control . . . . Competition with others seems to represent a gaining of control, or gaining of power. It is sometimes a way of making one's self safe from harm, or to assure supply of food or other gratification. Competition may take the form of struggle against forces of nature or general trends of economic cycle, but even in these, there is the element of a struggle to keep from being overcome and controlled . . . . Some tenderness and giving may be manifested when the recipient is identified with, so that a symbolic tenderness to self, or giving to self is carried on.

At the Gamma level there is perception of two-way interpersonal relations. Formality and rules are important in impulse control. Where the Delta person experiences identification with or pity for others, the Gamma person is capable of true sympathy. The Gamma level is probably the most numerous and the predominant level in society, according to Isaacs, who describes this level in the following terms (p. 21-22):

> The fact that the other is taken into account as a person also having needs, and also having personal feelings, both of which may be different from one's own, gives the basis for tenderness, giving, and loving someone different from one's self. Giving becomes of as much importance as receiving, although receiving remains an important aspect behind the giving, and one can often discern the underlying motive as giving now to receive later. Capacity to wait to receive has developed. Indications of Gamma level of relatability are: beginning of considerateness, niceness, thoughtfulness, charity, helpfulness, caring for or taking care of, cooperating, sharing. Other signals of attainment of Gamma level are guilt over Delta tendencies, and disapproval of Delta tendencies in one's self and others.

At the Beta level there is a "transcendence of orientation from that of giving and receiving, to a more objective state of being able to stand off from one's self and view the activity around one's self, including one's own activity, with some perspective" (p. 23). The person has a more differentiated and complex perception of his own and other people's feelings, and he perceives more complex patterns of interpersonal interaction. There is less concern for guilt, perhaps because of "working through of guilt feelings about receiving" (p. 23). "The focus at this level is with a final intra-psychic separation of self from others. In the process of attempting to disidentify with and rearrange the various aspects of earlier identifications, there may be a struggling against others who may temporarily personify the forces fighting within the self" (p. 24). The Beta struggle for freedom from internal restrictions may seem to

resemble the Delta struggle against encroachment of ego boundaries, but it is only superficially similar. As a result of the increasingly realistic perception of self and others, there is more
genuine consideration for others and also more freedom for
genuine long-term self-interest than at lower levels.

At the level of interpersonal maturity, the Alpha level,
"the struggle toward individuality is over, since one's own and
others' individuality is recognized . . . . There is no longer the
Beta struggle for freedom, the Gamma struggle from guilt, the
Delta struggle for control and definition of ego-boundaries" (p.
26). "There is no longer the Beta tendency to be trapped by
feelings for others, nor the Gamma need to help others, or the
Delta need to master others" (p. 28). Freedom from the struggles and needs of earlier levels leaves the Alpha with "a greater
amount of affective warmth available and there is the ability to
extend it with full appreciation for the individuality of the
other person and with awareness of varying dimensions of the
other's personality" (p. 27).

Isaacs's assertion that his concept is not a behavioristic one
harbors a confusion. He does not distinguish behavior as sign
and as sample of the trait intended. Current interpersonal relations do not index relatability, because his target is preconscious affective attitudes. There is no means of access other
than behavior, however. Responses to the TAT are behavior,
but behavior used as a sign rather than as a sample of the trait at
issue. Many of Isaacs's assertions that have been omitted here
are in terms that do not reveal what kinds of behavior (including reported fantasies) could have conveyed the information to
him.

In Table 7 Isaacs's stages are compared with ours. He
allows more self-insight to his Beta level than is characteristic of
the Conscientious Stage; his version of the Beta level corresponds rather closely to the transition from the Conscientious
to the Autonomous Stage. His portrayal of the Alpha level is,
like the highest stage in many formulations, too idealized, too
much all good things. The sturdy Conformist is represented in
the Gamma level, but the Conscientious person without much
insight into himself is not represented in the system, an omis-

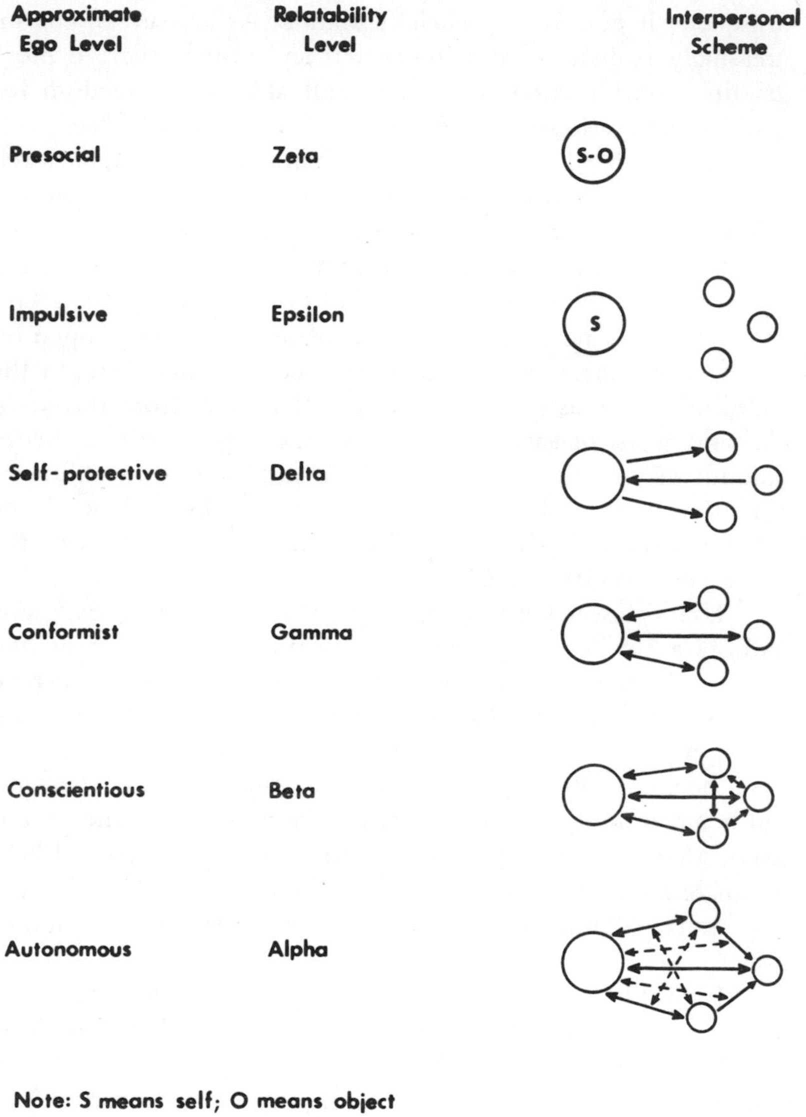

Approximate Ego Level	Relatability Level	Interpersonal Scheme
Presocial	Zeta	
Impulsive	Epsilon	
Self-protective	Delta	
Conformist	Gamma	
Conscientious	Beta	
Autonomous	Alpha	

Note: S means self; O means object

Figure 1. Development of relatability, after Isaacs

Table 7. Characteristics of Isaacs's Levels of Relatability

Approximate ego level	Isaacs level	Basis for self-control	Concern for others	Method of understanding others	Object-relation capacity
Presocial	Zeta	Not internally based			No object relations
Impulsive	Epsilon	Fear of punishment			Part object
Self-Protective	Delta	Fear of punishment	Fear of others; demand from others	Identification	Whole object attempted
Conformist	Gamma	For mutual satisfaction	Reaction-formation, sympathy	Sympathy	Resolved whole object
Conscientious	Beta	Appreciation of sensibilities of others	Recognition of freedom	Empathy	Disidentification from object
Autonomous	Alpha	Respect for individuality in terms of self-concept	Respect for individuality	A capacity superordinate to empathy	Introjects no longer important

SOURCE: *Relatability, a Proposed Construct and an Approach to its Validation* (Isaacs, 1956).

sion we noted also in Sullivan, Grant, and Grant. Table 7 and Figure 1, adapted from his tables and figures, show something of the inner logic of the development.

Peck. In connection with a longitudinal study of normal adolescents, Peck (Peck and Havighurst, 1960) has developed a motivational concept of moral character. His thinking has been influenced by Freud, Jung, Sullivan, Horney, and Fromm. Peck sketches five types of people, each representing a stage of psychosocial development. The five types are intended to be exhaustive of possible modes of adaptation. He collates the five types with stages of psychosexual development (a correlation Isaacs argues against), raising a topic deferred to Chapter Seven. Peck's conception emphasizes mode of control and motivation as expressed in behavior, which seems to contrast with Isaacs's nonbehavioristic emphasis; however, Peck and Havighurst's raters were encouraged to include "motivations which are not quite strong enough to have resulted in actual overt expression to date" (Peck and Havighurst, 1960, p. 228).

Since everyone's behavior contains variability, the five motivation patterns are also components of everyone's character. Persons can be classed into types according to the dominant component. Not all of the cases in their study had a single dominant component, however; they were therefore classed according to the pattern of components. Remembering that no one is all of one type, let us follow Peck's description of each stage as pure or ideal type.

The Amoral type corresponds to the psychopathic personality. He is impulsive, uncontrolled, and self-centered. He has no internalized moral principles or conscience. Other people are seen as a means to his own gratification. If an adult at the Amoral level is basically hostile, he may become delinquent or criminal; if he is nonhostile, he may be known as charming but irresponsible. This pattern is normal for the first year of life.

The Expedient type is also self-centered and also has no internalized moral principles or conscience. He considers the reactions and welfare of others only as they further his personal ends. When his personal aims include an advantageous reputation or social approval, his behavior may resemble that of higher levels, showing outward conformity to moral principles. In contrast to the Amoral person, he sees the advantage of conforming to social rules, but he may lapse in a situation where breaking the rules is to his advantage and he is not likely to be caught. This pattern is characteristic of many young children, whose behavior must therefore be controlled by rewards and punishments.

For the Conforming type the one general internalized principle is to do what the others in his group do. He follows specific rules of conduct literally. When he breaks a rule, he suffers not guilt but shame, defined as fear of disapproval by others. He has a crude conscience, since he is uncomfortable about breaking rules, but he has no abstract moral principles, nor is he concerned with the effects of his behavior on others. If abiding by the rules hurts others, he feels no guilt or responsibility. He may be kind to some people and cruel to others. This pattern occurs in middle and late childhood and resembles Piaget's heteronomous morality.

The Irrational-Conscientious type has internalized and abstract moral principles. When he violates them, he suffers guilt. It is not the effects of his acts nor the disapproval of others that causes him suffering but the violation of his rigid superego. The Irrational-Conscientious type is judged to be of the same developmental level as the Conformist.

The Rational-Altruistic type has stable moral principles, assesses the effects of his actions realistically, and acts in accord with the welfare of others as much as of himself. His conscience or superego is firm, but he is flexible in applying rules. He is able to recognize other people's feelings, but he does not lose perspective by completely identifying himself with them. He is insightful and candid with himself. He has a constructive attitude towards work and views social life as cooperative effort towards mutual goals. He is able to judge a person's particular actions without approving or condemning the person as a whole. He respects the integrity of every person and is kind to all. He is spontaneous and rational, his emotions are appropriate, and he does not have irrational anxiety or guilt. "He is also mature, emotionally 'well-adjusted,' and using his constructive capacities to the fullest" (p. 9). Peck and Havighurst admit that the characterization of the Rational-Altruistic type is idealized to the point where probably no one fully reaches it and unfalteringly maintains it. Table 6 presents the approximate ego level for each of Peck's types.

Peck's conception includes neither the lowest nor the highest stage. While the Rational-Altruistic person has some of the characteristics of the highest ego levels, he has only the virtues, not the problems. The problems of coping with inner conflict (as distinct from suffering conflict), of role conception, and of consolidating a sense of identity do not appear in this scheme. Since the problems of the lowest and highest ego levels need not be construed as moral issues, however, this limitation can be justified.

If one takes the Rational-Altruistic pattern as an ideal, one can maintain that the Irrational-Conscientious and the Conforming patterns fall short of it to an equal extent, but to assert that they represent parallel developmental stages is another matter. Peck seems to have decided the issue on logical grounds. Other psychologists have regularly considered the Conscientious type as representing a higher developmental level than the Conformist type. One can look at Peck's two top levels as dividing the Conscientious Stage according to another quite different variable, something like neurotic tendency, neurotic character deformation, or adjustment.

The Peck and Havighurst approach is marginal as a developmental characterology, because these researchers see each type as a component of every person. One can logically maintain that everyone retains a component of stages that he has outgrown but not that he has a component of stages much beyond his current level. Further, Peck and Havighurst state that their adolescent subjects "were appraised for the proportion of their character that resembled this pattern, in ways one could reasonably expect of boys and girls their age" (pp. 9-10). This statement implies age-contingent scoring, which violates the logic of a developmental characterology.

Kohlberg. The sophisticated theoretical writings of Kohlberg (1963, 1964, 1969, 1971), have provided the focal conception for a wide range of research. Since his own version is widely available, our summary is brief. Kohlberg's concern is the development of moral character. Unlike Peck, he stresses ideology rather than behavior as the core of the construct. While criticizing details of Piaget's exposition, Kohlberg acknowledges his influence, as well as that of Baldwin, McDougall, and Mead (Chapter Eleven). The child's moral judgments evolve as a function of cognitive and emotional restructuring in a fore-ordained sequence, Kohlberg asserts. He contrasts his view with that of social learning theory, which represents different moral styles as directly stamped in by training rather than, as he views it, evolved by an inner logic partly independent of what parents and other authorities desire to teach.

All investigators must somehow establish the thingness or generality of their construct, and those studying moral development must contend with the long-known findings of Hartshorne and May (1928) that cheating and dishonesty in children are partly specific to the situation and are not related to the child's expressed opinions about their wrongness. Kohlberg addresses this problem by shifting emphasis from the content of the moral judgment to its form. What evolves and becomes increasingly moral with age is not the specific actions condemned or approved but the child's reasons, his structuring of the situation. Kohlberg documents that ego variables are implicated in this maturational process. (At times he correctly describes this process as *ego development*, at other times as *ego strength,* an unfortunate term, since, as Erikson and others have warned, ego strength is not primarily a maturational variable. The child has his own age-appropriate kind of ego strength.)

Kohlberg's chief instrument has been incomplete stories presenting classical moral dilemmas. For example, a man's wife will die without a certain drug he does not have money to buy. Should he steal it? Stories are presented in individual interviews. The children are asked to complete the stories and then questioned as to their reasons. Only the reasons are scored. The original formulation of stages or types came from a study of seventy-two normal boys of ten, thirteen, and sixteen years of age; subsequent studies have been done on a variety of subjects in various cultures.

Kohlberg begins with McDougall's stages of moral development (Chapter Eleven), which he summarizes as the premoral level, the level of conventional role conformity, and the level of self-accepted moral principles. Within each of these levels Kohlberg discerns two types. Those six types of moral orientation represent his stages.

He distinguishes some thirty aspects of morality, such as motivation for moral action, basis of moral worth of a human life, and basis of respect for authority. Sometimes he calls them "dimensions," but he is postulating a single dimension of which these are but manifestations. Each of the six stages has a characteristic stance on each aspect of morality. Verbatim illustrations of responses scored at each stage are given in his scoring manuals.

For Type 1, punishment and obedience orientation, there is no concept of duty or morality except in terms of concrete rules enforced by external constraint. Punishment is conceived as impersonal retaliation. People of high status or authority are not bound by rules. Authority is seen in terms of age, size, and power; respect for authority simply means obedience. There is no concern for the welfare of others beyond avoiding taboo acts. The value of human life may be confused with the value of physical possessions, or it may be based on status or physical attributes of the person.

For Type 2, naive instrumental hedonism, rules are followed in order to obtain rewards and favors. There is a beginning of reciprocity, but strictly on a tit-for-tat basis. It is all right to take advantage of other people's mistakes; one is not responsible for any harm that they suffer. Rights are based on ownership; there is no concern for how exercise of one's rights may interfere with rights of another. Punishment is not needed if physical restitution or other undoing has occurred; expiative punishment is interpreted as the victim's revenge.

For Type 3, good-boy morality of maintaining good relations with and approval of others, one conforms in order to avoid disapproval or being disliked. There is genuine sympathy and liking for others and concern for maintaining loyalty. Duty is defined in terms of what is customary or "natural," but deviations from rules are permitted for the sake of loyalty. No one has a right to do evil. Moral reciprocity is based on gratitude rather than a one-to-one exchange. Authorities are idealized.

For Type 4, authority-maintaining morality, one conforms to avoid censure by authority and resultant guilt. The law demands invariant obedience because it is the basis of the social order, which maintains distributive justice. Deviations from the rules are unfair to those who conform. There is a rational appraisal of what is best for the whole community. Exceptions to moral and legal rules are not justified on the basis of status but may be justified by the situation. Punishment is seen as expiation, paying one's debt to society. It teaches the culprit he did wrong and makes him feel remorse. Persons at this level deny the possibility of moral conflict, as do those at lower levels, and they do not feel responsible for the effects of their behavior beyond their defined role responsibilities. A right is a claim, a legitimate expectation, usually earned. Life is seen as sacred in terms of its place in a categorical moral or religious order of rights and duties.

For Type 5, morality of contract and democratically accepted law, one conforms to maintain the respect of an impartial spectator judging in terms of the community welfare. Laws command obedience because they are the product of democratic process. Reciprocity fulfills the social compact. Distributive justice is conceived in terms of equality of opportunity rather than of outcome. Positions of authority are differentiated from the particular persons holding the positions; respect for authority is based on the qualities necessary to be chosen rather than on status as such. Punishment serves rehabilitation; it is the contractual obligation of the judge to administer it. In addition to the rights adhering to one's role and status, there are universal human rights, including the right to life.

For Type 6, morality of individual principles of conscience, one conforms to avoid self-condemnation. Duty is an inner compulsion of conscience. One is responsible for the consequences of what he has done but also for not having done what he might. Moral principles are universal axioms from which concrete rules can be derived. Reciprocity is based not on contract but on the need to maintain personal trust as a condi-

tion for an ideal society. The sacredness of human life represents a universal value of respect for the individual.

Concentration on moral issues blurs the outlines of the
highest ego stages, which are not differentiated from the Conscientious Stage by moral stance. Conscious coping with moral
conflict as an inner problem, typical for our Autonomous Stage,
is not stressed in the description of Type 6, but it does appear
in illustrations of that level of thinking. Approximate correspondence between Kohlberg's stages and ours is given in
Table 6.

Kohlberg presents evidence relevant to such methodological issues as the ordering of stages and the invariance of the
sequence. His subjects are classified as belonging in the stage
that corresponds to the modal level of their thinking. Most of
the thoughts scored outside the modal stage occurred in the two
adjacent stages for his subjects (Kohlberg, 1969). A longitudinal
study showed that within the limits of error of the test, subjects
either stay the same or advance in level. However, some modification in definition of stages was necessary to maintain this pattern (Kohlberg and others, 1973). His method of measuring
moral development will be considered further in Chapters Eight
and Nine.

Bull. The idea of moral development is largely a twentieth-
century one, Bull (1969) reminds us. In previous centuries conscience was believed to be inborn in children, and their misbehavior was consequently judged harshly. Bull divides moral
development into four stages, Anomy, Heteronomy, Socionomy, and Autonomy. There are types of people who remain at
each stage into adult life, and each stage persists as a pattern of
moral judgment after it is outgrown. Thus this conception is a
true developmental characterology. Bull sees conscience as
being social in origin and as being a function of the whole person. What is lacking in his conception is any notion of structure.

Bull's subjects were 360 school boys and girls of ages seven
through seventeen. He gave them a series of tests, mostly presented as individual interviews but supplemented by some paper
and pencil tests. Many of the moral problems presented in the
interviews resemble those of Piaget. They included problems of

stealing, cheating, lying, and the value of life. Bull shows that the child's level depends partly on the situation or problem. He presents no way to integrate the findings in the subtests to get the person's characteristic level of functioning.

Anomy is a premoral stage. Behavior is instinctive, with pleasure and pain as sanctions. Some learning and adaptation occur at this stage, guided by pleasure and pain. At one point he refers to this stage as *expedient*, but this label fits more logically with the description of the next stage, or perhaps of the transition between stages.

Bull reminds us that Kant proposed the term *heteronomy* for morality imposed from outside and *autonomy* for morality freely accepted, hence arising within. Heteronomy is external morality. Its sanctions are reward and punishment and fear of detection. Its purpose is to train the child in control of his natural impulses. In its initial phase, offences are identified solely by punishment. Where the offence is undetected or unpunished, there is no sense of wrongdoing. As the original specific prohibition is generalized into a universal rule, Heteronomy develops in the direction of the next stage, Socionomy.

Socionomy is external-internal morality. It covers the era when moral judgments are shaped by relations with others, especially peers. Since cooperation is involved, there is decreased egocentricity, and the person becomes conscious of himself as a member of a group. There is a beginning of a sense of obligation and responsibility. Self-respect begins to replace fear as a motive for moral conduct. Sanctions are praise and blame, with public opinion replacing parents and other authorities. Other motives include dread of social isolation, sympathy, and altruism founded on reciprocal affection. Inner development takes place during the stage of Socionomy with respect to awareness of others, relations with others, responsibility to them, and mutual codes of behavior. Socionomy is the stage of social conformity. Much of what Piaget calls *reciprocity* belongs here, though the term itself is ambiguous. Reciprocity can also apply to strict vengeance, an eye for an eye, as well as to cooperation. Guilt partly replaces fear as a sanction in this stage, in turn giving way to a more developed conscience at the next stage.

The highest stage is that of Autonomy or internal morality. Emotional autonomy means breaking away from family bonds. Value autonomy involves criticism of conventional rules. Behavioral autonomy means making one's own decisions. Self-judgment, self-criticism, and self-control are all aspects of autonomy. The growth of conscience in this period comprises both the irrational superego, with its repression and suppression of impulses, and the conscious ego ideal, rooted in love rather than fear.

Bull objects to Piaget's view of heteronomy as a hindrance to the development of autonomy; heteronomy, he says, is a necessary predecessor of autonomy. Piaget, Bull asserts, over-emphasizes mutual respect and underemphasizes self-respect as basis for moral autonomy. Bull's insistence that autonomy is grounded on heteronomy rather than on reciprocity, as Piaget maintains, seems inconsistent with admitting that reciprocity or socionomy is an inevitable intermediate stage. Bull's "Up with parents, teachers, and preachers" seems as tendentious as Piaget's "Down with parents, teachers, and preachers."

Approximate correspondence between Bull's stages and ours is shown in Table 6. Bull does not concern himself with problems that characterize our highest stages; indeed, he suggests that moral development does not progress much beyond age seventeen.

Of Bull's empirical findings, probably the most interesting is that girls advance to maturity more quickly than boys in the ages thirteen to fifteen. He confirms Piaget's finding that children do not consider cheating much of a moral offense. This confirmation is significant, since much theorizing about moral development is based on the studies of Hartshorne and May, which took cheating as the prototypic moral situation.

Howe. A developmental characterology that antedates some of the better-known ones but remains largely unpublished is that of Howe (Holt, 1948; Howe, 1955, 1970). She is one of the few and may have been the first to note the parallels in the contributions of Mead and Freud to theory of ego development, to which we will return. Like Peck, she sets up a tentative correspondence between ego stages and psychosexual stages, but we shall omit that as being probably erroneous and certainly without empirical basis.

Howe's first ego stage is called Physical, and its moving principle is the passive-dependent infant's primitive empathic identification with its active, nurturing mother. In respect to this stage, as to all others, she recognizes some residue throughout life. Interactions between persons continue to have active-passive aspects, leading to assistance, support, and protection. The pathological form of this stage is manifest as basic irresponsibility. Although Howe is not explicit on the point, one may assume that what she calls the pathological form is related both to the malevolent transformation of Sullivan and to persistence of a stage past its age-appropriate time. The Physical Stage corresponds to the Presocial and Impulsive stages of our scheme.

Howe's second stage is Power-Dependent. Interest in possessions, controlling, being controlled, and rebelling are important aspects of this stage. Social manifestations include master-disciple relations and respect for great figures and tradition. Pathological forms include authoritarianism, preoccupation with status and power as threats, and compulsive ritualism. This stage corresponds to our Self-Protective Stage.

Howe's third ego stage is called Equality-Seeking. Obeisance to powerful persons is partly supplanted by respect for rules, to which everyone is equally subject. Social manifestations include respect for truth, justice, and fair play and a sense of group solidarity. Pathological forms include ethnocentrism, overconformity, anticonformity, prejudice, and jealous rivalry. This stage corresponds to the Conformist Stage of our scheme.

The fourth stage is Goal-Oriented. Goals partially supplant rules as the basis for both personal and social organization. Social manifestations include collaboration and technical progress toward democratically agreed-on goals. In the Equality-Seeking and even more in the Goal-Oriented Stage, identification with another person is based on functionally relevant aspects of the relation rather than on a personal and emotional tie, as is the case in the first two stages. Howe ties the two kinds of identification to Freud's distinction between primary and secondary process thinking, the earlier form being predominantly irrational, the later form predominantly rational. The Goal-Oriented Stage corresponds approximately to the transition to the Conscientious Stage, possibly also including it.

The highest stage in Howe's scheme is called Value-Oriented. It is characterized by ideals, perspective, commitment, a capacity for intimate relations, and the possibility of ever-expanding interests and values. This stage corresponds to all levels above the Conscientious Stage in our scheme.

Perry. Of all the schemes of ego development, the one with greatest poignancy for most college students is that of Perry (1970). He reports a study in which counsellors at Harvard's Bureau of Study Counsel interviewed seventeen students of the class of 1957 at the end of each of their four years, and, similarly, sixty-seven members of the classes of 1962 and 1963. The interviews were unstructured, beginning with a question like, "Would you like to say what has stood out for you during the year?" A second general question was, "As you speak of that, do any particular instances come to mind?" Further remarks by the interviewer were clued to the topics presented by the student and were attempts to clarify his train of thought.

Perry's scheme is a chronicle of the succession of forms through which the students construe their experience, particularly as it pertains to the nature and origins of knowledge, of value, and of responsibility, that is, the development of meta-thinking. Influenced by the California studies of the authoritarian personality, Perry and his colleagues began by looking for the range of student types or outlooks, from those most dualistic and absolutistic to those most relativistic and contingent in their thinking. In studying the completed protocols from the class of 1957, Perry detected a limited set of positions from which the students viewed their common world. There was, moreover, a developmental sequence, defined both by the inner logic of the positions and their sequence in the successive interviews of the students. The scheme was then applied to the replication of the study with the classes of 1962 and 1963, with satisfactory fit.

Perry introduces his topic in capsule as follows (1970, pp. 1-2):

Let us suppose that a lecturer announces that today he will consider three theories explanatory of ____ (whatever his topic may be). Student A has always taken it for granted that knowledge consists of correct answers, that there is one right answer per problem, and that teachers explain these answers for students to learn. He therefore listens for the lecturer to state which theory he is to learn.

Student B makes the same general assumptions but with an elaboration to the effect that teachers sometimes present problems and procedures, rather than answers, "so that we can learn to find the right answer on our own." He therefore perceives the lecture as a kind of guessing game in which he is to "figure out" which theory is correct, a game that is fair enough if the lecturer does not carry it so far as to hide things too obscurely.

Student C assumes that an answer can be called "right" only in the light of its context, and that contexts or "frames of reference" differ. He assumes that several interpretations of a poem, explanations of a historical development, or even theories of a class of events in physics may be legitimate "depending on how you look at it." Though he feels a little uneasy in such a kaleidoscopic world, he nonetheless supposes that the lecturer may be about to present three legitimate theories which can be examined for their internal coherence, their scope, their fit with various data, their predictive power, etc.

Whatever the lecturer then proceeds to do (in terms of his own assumptions and intent) these three students will make meaning of the experience in different ways which will involve different assessments of their own choices and responsibilities . . . .

B's assumptions are of a form which includes the form of A's; and C's assumptions include, in a different and broader form, the forms of both A's and B's. This is evident in the different predicament of each student in the event that what the lecturer proceeds to do conforms to the expectations of one of the other students. For instance, student C, faced with the lecture expected by either A or B, would have little difficulty in interpreting the experience accurately without revising his basic assumptions about the nature of knowledge. His assumptions logically extend to the possibility that a given lecturer might "have the point of view that" there was but one correct answer. Student A, however, faced with the kind of lecture expected by B or by C, must either revise his basic assumptions or interpret the experience in some such way as, "The lecturer is talking all over the place" or "This just doesn't have anything to do with the course."

Thus the ordering of the stages is not arbitrary nor is it chosen just to accord with Perry's personal value system, but it is dictated by the logic of the situation. Individual students, moreover, tend to move from the position of A to that of B to that of C. Another and subtler confirmation of the ordering of stages appeared later in connection with deviations from that order.

In Position 1, Basic Duality, the world is seen in dualistic terms, right versus wrong, good versus bad, we versus others. There are absolute Right Answers, known to Authority, whose job is to teach them. Knowledge and goodness are accumulated bit by bit, through obedience and hard work. Diversity is not perceived.

In Position 2, Multiplicity Pre-Legitimate, the student perceives diversity of opinion but not as sign of legitimate uncertainty. He may perceive the multiple opinions as an exercise given by Authority "so we can learn how to find the Answer," or the diversity may be interpreted as a sign of confusion and error in the others, who are wrong. Those of conformist bent at this position identify themselves with an Authority seen as right and possessed of absolute truth; others, they think, are confused and wrong. Those of oppositional bent may see Authority as wrong and needlessly confused; "we," who are right, are opposed to Authority.

In Position 3, Multiplicity Subordinate, the student perceives diversity of opinion and uncertainty as legitimate in some

areas; perhaps Authority itself "hasn't found The Answer yet."
He is puzzled by standards of grading in such areas; perhaps it is
"good expression," or glibness, or pull.

Position 4 has two alternatives, Multiplicity Correlate and
Relativism Subordinate. In Multiplicity Correlate the student
perceives two realms, one in which there is an absolutely correct
Authority, as in the previous positions, and another extensive
realm where diversity of opinion is legitimate and uncertainty
prevails—"anyone has a right to his own opinion." This area of
multiplicity is relevant to the self, being experienced as confusing, liberating, or intriguing. An oppositional student may strive
to expand the area of multiplicity, because in that area "They"
have no right to make us feel guilty. In Relativism Subordinate
the student has discovered something about contextual and relativistic reasoning, that is, data can be shown to be congruent
with a proposition, propositions can be shown to be coherent
with each other or with a theoretical position. This is perceived
as "how They want us to think," rather than as how things are,
the nature of knowledge.

In Position 5, the alternatives are Relativism Correlate,
Relativism Competing, and Relativism Diffuse. Here relativism
is a way of perceiving, analyzing, and evaluating, not because
"They want us to think this way," but because all knowledge is
contextual and relativistic. Dualistic, right-versus-wrong thinking is a subordinate special case. In Relativism Correlate the
world is divided into areas where Authority has the answers,
like physics, and those where relativism must be used, like
English. In Relativism Competing, relativism applies to the
whole world, with binary answers as a subclass, but this view
alternates with the view of earlier positions. The most fully
developed structure is that of Relativism Diffuse, in which relativism is accepted generally, but there is no implication for commitment. There are no absolutes; authority as well as the rest of
us are subject to the same relativistic universe, in which things
differ in degree and according to the frame of reference.

Position 6 is labeled Commitment Foreseen. In this position simple belief in absolute certainties is no longer possible.
Relativism is accepted as part of the nature of knowledge. In

order to orient himself in a relativistic universe, the student perceives that personal commitment is a logical necessity or a felt need. This realization may bring eagerness, dismay, turmoil, or acceptance.

Position 7 is called Initial Commitment, The student makes a commitment or affirmation in some area, accepting its origin in his own experience or choice, and deciding how much he will seek continuity with his past values and how much he will break away from them. Commitment "refers to an affirmation made in a world perceived as relativistic, that is, *after* detachment, doubt, and awareness of alternatives have made the experience of personal choice a possibility. It is an act in an examined, not in an unexamined, life" (p. 136). With regard to religion, the loss of unquestioning belief may be the beginning of a more profound faith. The crucial criterion for distinguishing unquestioning belief from a faith following doubt and acceptance of relativism is the person's attitude towards and acceptance of those having other religious beliefs or none at all.

Position 8 is called Orientation in Implications of Commitment. Position 9 is referred to as Developing Commitments. These positions are not clearly distinguished in qualitative terms but include further development with respect to the issues of Position 7 and a sense of identity growing out of commitments.

Development along this sequence is not inexorable. Perry describes three alternatives to growth, Temporizing, Retreat, and Escape. Temporizing means pausing for more than a year in any one position, typically with awareness of the step ahead. Retreat occurs after some glimpse of multiplicity and involves an active denial of the legitimacy of the opinions of others. Variations include the dedicated reactionary, the dogmatic rebel, and a negativistic, passive resistance to authority without espousing any cause. While Retreat typically takes one back to an extremely dualistic position, Escape typically entrenches the student in one of the middle positions. Here relativity or multiplicity is used in the service of alienation or cynicism, or it may be permanently encapsulated and exploited to serve Authority's purposes.

While these possibilities seem to negate the evidence for

sequence, a closer look reveals a confirmation: "Those students whom we saw as 'progressing' made their own awareness of maturation clear, explicitly or implicitly, and conveyed a sense of satisfaction in it. Those whom we perceived as standing still, or stepping to one side, or reaching back, acknowledged that they were avoiding something or denying something or fighting something, and they regularly remarked on an uneasiness or dissatisfaction akin to shame. Some others referred to periods in which they felt they had 'moved too fast' and had become alarmingly confused. In short, the students experienced quite consciously an urge toward maturation, congruent with that progression of forms we were learning to see in their reports" (p. 50).

In other times and places the normal adolescent urge to rebel against authority has the effect of encouraging progress in the sequence. At Harvard and other liberal arts colleges with a similar atmosphere an anomaly occurs. The school lends its authority to a relativistic, antiauthoritarian outlook, in part as a consequence of the commitment of individual professors and the institution itself, in part as a consequence of the diversity of views among professors. This atmosphere makes overcoming authoritarian tendencies easier for those inclined to conformity, since they can assimilate toleration for diversity to "what They want us to do." For some oppositional young people, rebellion in those circumstances takes the anomalous course of return to an authoritarian, dualistic outlook, just because that is clearly not what the university is trying to encourage.

Perry discerned in his protocols something of the dynamics of the developmental course (pp. 51-52):

> The impetus [to growth] seemed compounded of many "motives": sheer curiosity; a striving for the competence that can emerge only from an understanding of one's relation to the environment; an urge to make order out of incongruities, dissonances, and anomalies of experience; a wish for a community with men looked upon as mature; a wish for authenticity in personal relationships; a wish to develop and affirm an identity, and so on. It was the convergence

of all such motives into an urge toward maturation that brought them under that encompassing inner standard to which each man held himself accountable.

If the motives making up this urge to progress were the only forces operative in the students' development, there would of course have been no problematic balance, no drama calling for courage, and no meaning in a standard. Maturation did indeed have its joys of discovery and expansion, but its moral significances derived from its challenge by countervailing forces. At every step, the movement required the students to "face up" to limits, uncertainties, and the dissolution of established beliefs, while simultaneously it demanded new decisions and the undertaking of new forms of responsibility.

This constellation of countervailing forces appeared to consist of such tendencies as the wish to retain earlier satisfactions or securities, the wish to maintain community in family or hometown values and ways of thinking, the reluctance to admit one has been in error, the doubt of one's competence to take on new uncertainties and responsibilities, and, most importantly, the wish to maintain a self one has felt oneself to be (Angyal, 1965). Pervading all such motives of conservation lay the apprehension that one change might lead to another in a rapidity which might result in catastrophic disorganization.

One difference between theories of the physical universe and psychological theories is that psychological theories are reflexive; indeed, one way to judge psychological theories is to ask how well they account for the behavior of the theorist himself. On this criterion theories of ego development do better than reductionistic theories. Perry deals with the point in these terms (p. 203):

As contextualistic pragmatists, we see our philosophical assumptions to be doubly reflexive. For one thing, at the highest point of development in our scheme, the majority of our students are portrayed as addressing the world in the very same general terms of our scheme's own philosophical outlook. For another, we apply the same general assumptions to our own relation, as investigators, to the data of the study. But since within our contextualistic-pragmatic and existential framework we see reasoning to be circular by ultimate necessity, we look upon this double reflexiveness as a manifestation of the virtue of coherence without looking upon circularity as necessarily a vice. We have cared only that the circle be of sufficient scope to illuminate more than its own return upon itself. That is to say, we have cared that the circle make a sufficient sweep to generate propositions which integrate a variety of experience and which may be susceptible, in some instances at least, to test.

Table 6 shows approximate correspondence of our stages and an abbreviated version of Perry's stages. Nothing in his account corresponds to the Impulsive Stage, nor would one expect persons of that stage to arrive at Harvard. Perry's finding that the average Harvard graduate is likely to be in some stage of making a commitment makes a chilling contrast with Graves's finding that the average business manager, for whom he may soon be working, is likely to be authoritarian in his thinking.

Conclusions

Every classification is an injustice, someone has said. That holds true for classifying a person into any ego level. The injustice is compounded in lining up the stages of one psychologist's system with those of another. The authors whose schemes have been reviewed are not all talking about the same variable all the time, but in all the expositions there are some common elements, common phenomena to which they give varying access. The cumulative effect, in part owing to the differences in outlook, presuppositions, samples, problems, and means of access to the subjects, is that there is some underlying reality. More-over, having found as many versions as we have in as many places, we cannot doubt that there are many more.

Some authors have taken interpersonal relations as their central or primary topic, some moral judgment or character, and some cognitive aspects. Among those for whom interpersonal relations are the primary topic, H. S. Sullivan, Erikson, and Ausubel are developmentalists, Graves is a characterologist, and Isaacs and C. Sullivan, Grant, and Grant are developmental characterologists. Among those for whom moral character or judgment is the primary topic, Piaget is a developmentalist, and Bull and Kohlberg are developmental characterologists. Characterologies can be found in classical sources not examined here, such as the Bhagavad-Gita. Among those primarily concerned with cognitive aspects, Ferenczi was a developmentalist, Riesman and Adorno, Frenkel-Brunswik, Levinson, and Sanford have been characterologists, and Perry is a developmental characterologist.

Tables 2 through 7, summarizing the correspondence of stages and types, may do more harm than good, since they encourage premature closure on complex issues. There is no way to say exactly what stage or type in one system corresponds with that of another, for the same reasons that it is impossible to say exactly what are the characteristics of each stage or type; we will examine those reasons in Chapter Eight. Obviously, key words alone will not suffice for matching stages; "autonomy" occurs up and down the scale, for example.

Many versions have been omitted. Harvey, Hunt, and Schroder (1961) sometimes call their variable *cognitive complexity,* sometimes *ego development;* however, connections between their types and our stages are too complex to be useful. Several researchers are basing current work on much of that reviewed here, such as that of Kohlberg and ours. Van den Daele (in press) has proceeded towards a theoretical reconstruction, introducing many new parameters. Selman (1974; Selman and Byrne, 1974) and Broughton (1975) both seek continua that are in some sense fundamental sources or prerequisite for ego and moral development. Selman reasons that ability to take the other's role is fundamental to interpersonal development, hence has sought stages in that ability. Broughton reasons that epistemology, particularly conceptions of self, mind, and knowledge, are prerequisite. He has drawn ideas from a little known work of Baldwin, *Thought and Things* (1906-1915). Blasi (1971, 1976) has presented stages in the development of responsibility. He contends that what makes a variable fundamental also makes it in some sense not crucial. What is crucial is whether the person adopts as his own the higher mode of responsibility that his abilities make available to him (see Chapter Three).

A number of issues have been skirted in this chapter. For example, what is the relation of ego development to adjustment and psychopathology? How can it be differentiated from other kinds of development? How can it be measured? These will be among the topics of succeeding chapters.

Chapter Six

Optimum Growth and Mental Health

Having reviewed conceptions of ego development as a series of qualitative stage changes, we turn now to complementary conceptions of it in terms of polar variables, that is, aspects of ego that constantly increase during the period of development. Stage conceptions are most illuminating in midrange, tending to fade into vagueness at the upper extreme, whereas polar variables are by definition anchored at their two extremes. Any measurable trait can be considered a polar variable, but only a few of those are polar aspects of ego development. Conformity, for example, is a trait that many have found ways of measuring that peaks at a middle range of ego development (Hoppe, 1972; Harakal, 1971). The beginnings of ego development obviously are found in infancy. Identification of the high extreme is more problematic. Different authors may differ even on which individuals exemplify the optimum. The confusion between ego development and other variables such as adjustment and psychosexual development is greatest at the high extreme.

The topics of polar aspects of ego development, characteristics of the highest stage, and the relation between ego development and mental health are thus intertwined. The purpose of the present chapter is both to enrich the conception of ego development by bringing out new aspects and to delineate its limits. Further delineation of limits with respect to cognitive development and psychosexual development is deferred to the next chapter.

Polar Aspects

Flugel (1945) combined insights from psychologists such as Baldwin, McDougall, and Piaget, with those of Freud, Adler, and others to arrive at a broadly developmental conception of "moral progress." He did not have stages nor did he draw detailed analogy with periods of childhood. He described moral progress in terms of eight general tendencies: firstly, moral progress proceeds from egocentricity to sociality, from exclusive concern with one's own wishes and needs to increasing awareness of the claims of others. The circle of the others constantly enlarges until it includes ever widening classes within the community, many of whom are not personally known. Secondly, moral progress proceeds from unconscious to conscious, that is, towards bringing an increasingly large proportion of life into the person's awareness and control. Thirdly, moral progress proceeds from autism to realistic thinking. Fourthly, moral progress proceeds from moral inhibition to spontaneous goodness. There is, however, spontaneous goodness in small children; psychoanalysis in particular stresses the harm of excessive inhibition and repression. In middle age, as Frenkel (later, Frenkel-Brunswik) and Weisskopf (later, Weisskopf-Joelson) (1937) showed, wishes and duties tend to coalesce, thus leading to spontaneous goodness. Fifthly, Flugel said, moral progress proceeds from aggression to tolerance and love. Sixthly, moral progress proceeds from fear to security. Anxiety, he pointed out, is characteristic of all forms of mental illness and neurosis. He did not maintain, nor is it clearly true, that there is normally a progress with age from fear to security. Seventhly, moral progress proceeds from heteronomy to autonomy. Finally, moral progress proceeds from moral judgment to cognitive or psychological judgment; that tendency can be translated as progress from aggression to understanding. Flugel stated clearly that these are not independent dimensions but eight aspects or ways of looking at a single dimension.

So obvious is the growth in the child's capacity for realistic thinking that many authors have discussed it. Freud's terms were *primary process* thinking and *secondary process* thinking. Primary process characterizes the thought of young children; it is governed by wishes and fears rather than by realistic considerations. This mode lives on in the unconscious mind of the adult, being evident in dreams and demonstrable during psychoanalytic treatment in neurotic symptoms and slips of the tongue. Thus Freud did not construe children's thinking as just a failure to achieve adult reasoning but saw it as having its own sense. Bleuler (1912, 1916) distinguished realistic thinking from *autistic* thinking, which he later called *dereistic*. Sullivan distinguished thinking in the *prototaxic mode,* the *parataxic mode,* and the *syntaxic mode.* The most primitive mode of thinking and experiencing is prototaxic; in it the infant does not distinguish himself from the environment and he is aware only of the situation of the moment, without what comes before or after. Thinking in the parataxic mode is illogical, characteristic of young children and of symptom formation; it corresponds approximately to what Freud called primary process thought. Thinking in the syntaxic mode is consensually validated thought, approximately what Freud called secondary process thought. Piaget, who is studying intellectual development per se, traces thinking from sensorimotor schemes through preoperational and concrete operational thought to formal operational thought. These distinctions are probably not exactly comparable to those of Freud, Bleuler, and Sullivan, but one should keep in mind the limits of the child's intellectual capacities at each stage before assessing the significance of the limits in psychiatric terms.

A key term that many authors have found useful is *internalization*; often it is used to describe a basic polar aspect of ego development. It is the central term in Kahler's *Inward Turn of Narrative* (1957, 1959), a synoptic view of literature from the earliest epic poems through eighteenth century novels. Kahler viewed the arts as records simultaneously of man's consciousness of himself and of the reality in which he lives. Over the centuries, men have increasingly turned from writing exclusively about external events (at first not even human doings but those of the gods) to writing about their own inner world and reactions to outer events. The expansion of inner consciousness is simultaneously an expansion and objectification of the world in which we live and of our selves. Kahler's book is thus explicitly about ego development in our sense as reflected in the development of world literature.

Maslow: Self-Actualization and Peak Experiences

Maslow's (1954, 1962) subject has been motivation. The motives of all men, he has said, can be described in terms of a hierarchy of instinctoid needs, namely, physiological needs, the need for safety, need for love, belonging, and identification, and need for respect and self-esteem. All of these are deficiency needs. The crowning need is of a different type; it is the need for growth and self-actualization. Since these needs constitute a hierarchy, the ordering is significant. Lower ones are prepotent when they are unsatisfied; higher ones are prepotent when the lower ones are satisfied. The characteristics of basic or instinctoid needs are (Maslow, 1962, p. 20):

> 1. its absence breeds illness, 2. its presence prevents illness, 3. its restoration cures illness, 4. under certain (very complex) free choice situations, it is preferred by the deprived person over other satisfactions, 5. it is found to be inactive, at a low ebb, or functionally absent in the healthy person. Two additional characteristics are subjective ones, namely conscious or unconscious yearning and desire, and feeling of lack or deficiency, as of something missing on the one hand, and, on the other palatability . . . . The original

criterion of motivation and the one that is still used
by all human beings except behavioral psychologists
is the subjective one.

A number of Maslow's followers use his hierarchy of needs
as a basis for a typology. Looked at this way, the correspondence with stages of ego development is fairly clear. The physiological needs correspond to the Presocial and Impulsive Stages;
the need for safety corresponds to the Self-Protective Stage;
needs for love and belonging correspond to the Conformist
Stage; needs for respect and self-esteem correspond to the Conscientious Stage; self-actualization corresponds to the Autonomous and Integrated stages. With Maslow the emphasis remained on the presence of all the needs in everyone. That most
of us function most of the time on a level lower than that of
self-actualization he called the *psychopathology of normality.*
At one time Maslow set out to find and to study as many
self-actualizing persons as possible. Since they occur at the rate
of about one per 1,000 college students, case finding by survey
methods was impractical, so he picked cases among friends and
acquaintances. Because many of them were embarrassed by his
request to study them, he finally studied public figures and literary characters from open records. The characteristics of self-
actualization are, according to Maslow: not a fixed state but a
changing process, thus, openness to development; more efficient
perception of reality, that is, "lesser blindness"; availability of
inner life; vivid perception of the outer world; capacity for both
abstractness and concreteness; tolerance for ambiguity; capacity
for guilt and sense of responsibility; capacity for spontaneity, as
opposed to intensive striving; existential as opposed to hostile
humor; gaiety, particularly in sexual and other love relations;
transcending of contradictions and polarities; acceptance of
reality; greater integration, autonomy, and sense of identity;
increased objectivity, detachment, and transcendence of self;
democratic character structure. At one time he thought that
oceanic, mystic, and profound esthetic experiences were universal in this group, but that proved not to be true. Since his
description could serve for the highest or Integrated Stage of

ego development, Maslow's assertion that this represents the highest state of psychological health is somewhat contradictory to our view. Health and ego development are not the same. The contradiction is somewhat blunted by Maslow's own reservations about psychological illness as the opposite pole; he preferred the term *human diminution.*

Later Maslow became interested in what he called *peak experiences,* the most wonderful experiences or ecstatic moments the person could remember. In part his interest was in the characteristics of those experiences per se, in part his premise was that what ordinary people experience in such moments is akin to what self-actualizing people experience much more of the time.

Psychologists almost unanimously accept the premise that all behavior is motivated, Maslow pointed out; yet man is most truly human precisely when he is not motivated but enjoying an experience for its own sake, as during peak experiences. There may indeed be consequences of such experiences, but such experiences are sought for themselves rather than for any other end they may serve. These are the moments of Being rather than Becoming. Cognition at such times has a different character from ordinary, deficiency-motivated cognition (D-cognition). In B-cognition, the cognition of Being or of peak moments, persons set aside the usual tendency to classify objects into categories according to the uses that can be made of them. Things are appreciated for themselves as unique objects rather than as members of a class. Perception is richer; the object is fully attended to. Perception is passive and receptive at such moments. There may be a suspension of orientation in time and space. There is a temporary dropping away of anxieties and inhibitions. Thus peak experiences may be considered part of what Kris (1934) has called "regression in the service of the ego." At such moments boundaries between ego, id, and superego and the distinction between primary and secondary processes seem to disappear.

Maslow's exposition, emphasizing the continuing presence in all persons of the motivations of all stages, at least as potentialities, is a valuable corrective to those expositions that pres-

ent stages of ego development as a ladder of irreversible achievements, like a series of courses in mathematics. At the same time,
Maslow's point of view and his methods of study are such as to
obscure the achievementlike elements in the progression. By
failing to coordinate his ideas with any developmental scheme,
Maslow has left us with substantial problems. His self-actualizing person is the acme of maturity, but he also embodies one
definition of good adjustment or optimal psychic health. Good
adjustment or good psychic health can characterize persons of
any age, as maturity cannot. Maslow, indeed, implies that most
of his exemplars of self-actualizing persons were over fifty.
What is needed is a concept of good adjustment or of psychic
health that applies irrespective of age in order to clarify the relation of maturity to psychic health.

Maslow's distinction between deficiency motivation, seeking only relief, and growth motivation, seeking exercise and fulfillment, is both illuminating and perplexing. We recognize at
once, as we are meant to, that most of experimental psychology
has been built around studies powered by deficiency motivation. Learning theory, like early psychoanalytic theory, tends to
ignore growth motivation. Yet growth motivation is present
from the beginning of life, while the hierarchy of motives develops in time. The infant displays strivings to develop before
such concepts as self-esteem or identification can meaningfully
be applied. Who is to say that infants and children lack peak
experiences? In relation to infants and children, at least, Maslow's assertion that growth motivation comes into play when
deficiency motives are satisfied requires some modification or
revision. We shall have to look beyond Maslow to coordinate his
insights into the conception and theory of ego development.

Schachtel: Metamorphosis of Perception

As the title of his book, *Metamorphosis*, announces, Schachtel's
(1959) primary topic is development; he has particular reference to emotion, perception, focal attention, and memory. Let
us follow his argument. The exposition must be somewhat intricate, since Schachtel first interprets, then rebuts some of
Freud's arguments.

The earliest conflict of life, according to Schachtel, is that between the urge toward growth and the anxiety of separation from primal embeddedness. The tension-reduction model of pleasure, common to Freud's writings and much of learning theory, derives from exclusive emphasis on embeddedness affect. The new psychoanalytic ego psychology, although putting greater stress on the ego's autonomy from the id than did earlier psychoanalysis, retains the tension-reduction model as its basis. The Hartmann school maintains that to the extent the ego is autonomous, that is, that its development is not the outcome of conflict between id and reality, there must be a conflict-free ego sphere. Schachtel maintains, on the contrary, that people are open to and enjoy the world; pleasure cannot be reduced to abolition of excitation; nor do all of one's strivings derive from sexual and aggressive ones. On the other hand, the exercise of one's faculties is never free from conflict.

Freud viewed affects both as disturbances and as alternatives to action. In contrast, Schachtel believes there is no action without affect. Eagerness and zest are examples of activity affects. The affects associated with diffuse discharge of tension Schachtel calls *embeddedness affects*; for such states pleasure can be defined as relief from tension. Prototypes of pure embeddedness are fetal life and sleep; in those conditions all stimuli are indeed disturbing. Activity affects are observable in the eagerness of the nursing infant, in the infant's staring at bright objects, later in his reaching for objects and in learning to walk.

Schachtel distinguishes two modes of perception. In the *autocentric mode,* the emphasis is on the sensory quality and on the pleasure or lack of pleasure of what the person feels. In the *allocentric mode,* the emphasis is on what the object is like. In infancy all perception is at first autocentric; with age, it shifts largely to the allocentric mode. The lower senses, such as smell and taste, lend themselves almost exclusively to autocentric perception. Vision is the prototype of the allocentric sense; hearing is also largely allocentric; sense of touch is adaptable to both. Since autocentric perception tells the perceiver relatively little about the world and allocentric perception is not closely linked to pleasure, perception of pleasure and of reality are quite separate, which weighs against Freud's assertion that the reality principle arises as a detour of the pleasure principle.

Pleasure in muscular and tactile experiences is not inherently sexual or aggressive. Such experiences are steps in the evolution of play, which is at first objectless. Later the object emerges from play. Thus the infant proceeds from experiencing in an autocentric mode, in which stimuli are at first mostly unpleasurable, to a state where they are predominantly pleasurable. Then gradually an allocentric interest in objects dominates the autocentric interest of stimulation. At the same time, there is a growth in the capacity for focal attention. The feeling of pleasure in sensory contact is a tie to reality, not an attempt to get rid of the stimulus, as Freud's model of the pleasure principle implies.

There is an affect of familiarity, a pleasure in resensing something already seen, that precedes the development of conscious recognition. The infant smiling at mother's face is an example. The division of experiences into the familiar and the new is an important element in the conflict between desire for embeddedness and desire for encounter and exploration. Perception in the allocentric mode is more readily recalled voluntarily than autocentric perception, because of its greater objectification, that is, because it is couched in terms of familiar categories of thought.

Much of perception in adult life is dominated by what Schachtel calls *secondary autocentricity*. In primary autocentricity perception is colored by pleasure and unpleasure and, at least at first, new stimuli are reacted to negatively. The parallel in secondary autocentricity is that perception is limited to the way the object serves the person's needs and purposes; such perception helps the person to avoid encountering new aspects of reality. Science that takes as its goal prediction and the power to manipulate is typically of this nature. In relation to perception of other people, secondary autocentricity can take the form of seeing people in terms of status or functions, such as servants or customers. The most usual form of secondary autocentricity is seeing everything in terms of labels and stereotypes. Corresponding to secondary autocentricity there is a secondary embeddedness in the person's own subculture.

Thus the child's allocentric openness to the world is lost in most adults. Schachtel uses the term *sociocentric perception* for shared autocentric perception. As secondary autocentricity and sociocentric perception become predominant, they interfere both with allocentric perception and also with appropriate primary autocentric perception at the adult level. In everyday language, thinking and perceiving in terms of stereotypes and labels interferes both with realistic perception of the objective world and with full enjoyment of the sensuous encounter with the world.

Man's interest in the world differs from an animal's appetite by its enormous range as well as by its fullness and richness. In what Schachtel calls the *allocentric attitude,* there is an interest in and turning toward the object; it involves the whole object and the whole being of the observer. Allocentric interest in an object leads to global perception of it, but it is a different kind of globality from that of infancy, which fuses subject and object, or of early childhood, in which the distinct features of the object are not perceived. Rather, it presupposes full objectification, that is, appreciation of the object as an object.

Creativity is inhibited not so much by repression, as some psychoanalysts have maintained, as by encroachment of labels and stereotypes on our openness to the world. Schachtel disputes Kris's conception of creativity as resulting from "regression in the service of the ego." The drive content of creative activities varies and is not decisive. What is decisive is the openness in the encounter with the object, something very different from drive discharge.

Development of the idea of an object depends on development of focal awareness. When the infant attends to an object, the unattended-to background has some resemblance to repressed ideas. The difference, of course, is the possibility of quick and voluntary shift of attention. The capacity for thought and interest in the real world do not develop merely as a detour on the way to gratifying instinctive needs, as Freud assumed. Rather (here Schachtel accepts the additions of Hartmann, Kris, and Loewenstein), thought develops under the impetus both of needs and of autonomous interest in objects. Optimal development cannot take place where needs are too urgent. Freud's assumption that in early infancy unsatisfied impulses result in hallucinatory satisfaction is contrary to what we now know about infant development. The infant could not hallucinate mother's breast or bottle, because it does not have such percepts yet. What the infant longs for or hallucinates is the total experience of satisfaction; that may be the ancestor of hallucination in later life, but it is not the ancestor of secondary process thinking. Playful exploration of objects, freed from driving needs, is the basis for development of secondary process thought.

Freud explained the universal amnesia for most memories of infancy and childhood in terms of repression of childhood sexuality, but it is not clear why repression of sexual memories would entail repression of other autobiographical events. Schachtel places greater emphasis on a different factor. The categories or schemata of adult thought are not suitable to preserve the experiences of childhood nor to facilitate their recall, an explanatory mechanism that shades into that of classical Freudian repression, without directly contradicting it. The amnesia of childhood is for autobiographical events, not for words or skills, which are used continuously. A similar difficulty in memory can be observed when one tries to recall dreams or children's speech with unusual grammatical errors. Each successive recall makes it sound more like normal adult thought or speech. Taboo and repression as instruments for suppression of sexual and pleasurable experiences are crude by comparison with the subtle erosion of faculties accomplished by the quasi-educational means of imposing society's labels and categories on the child's mind. "Memory cannot be entirely extinguished in man, his capacity for experience cannot be entirely suppressed by schematization. It is in those experiences which transcend the cultural schemata, in those memories of experience which transcend the conventional memory schemata, that every new insight and every true work of art has its origin, and that the hope of progress, of a widening of the scope of human endeavor and human life, is founded" (Schachtel, 1959, p. 322).

Schachtel's book enriches the conception of ego development by relating it to perception. One element of what Maslow calls peak experiences is the openness to encounter that Schachtel describes. We can assume that adults who retain or recapture a high level of allocentric perception are those at high ego levels, since vivid descriptions of people and of sensory experience are found at those levels. Thus Schachtel is documenting a dialectical aspect of ego development—that is, attitudes with respect to which the most mature people are in some way more like children than are persons of intermediate ego level.

Again we are left with questions. Is the openness to experience something that certain people retain through childhood and adolescence and into adult life, or is it necessarily lost, then regained by some people? Is openness to experience a consequence of attaining a high ego level, or is it associated with high ego level because it is a condition that happens to favor ego growth? These questions lead beyond the topic of conceptions of ego development and into the theory of its dynamics.

Jahoda: Conceptions of Positive Mental Health

For many years "psychology of adjustment" and "mental hygiene" were mainstays of the academic psychology curriculum. In recent years there has been disenchantment with traditional approaches to those topics. Adjustment more or less necessarily means adjustment to the world in its present imperfection. Psychologists have increasingly questioned whether conformity represents man's highest estate. Schachtel and Maslow are only two of the many authors who have discussed alternative views of optimal growth and "positive mental health." Jahoda (1958) has summarized the views on this topic of a large number of authors.

She begins by establishing the unsuitability of three criteria for mental health: absence of mental disease, normality, and adjustment or well-being. (We will follow her argument, including her references to other authors, except for some changes in phraseology and in illustrative examples. Interpolations will be in parentheses.) Normality in the sense of a statistical average has many pitfalls as a definition of mental health. In setting the limits of the population over which the average is taken or of the traits with respect to which one takes an average, one has implicitly built in certain meanings of mental health, so that the appearance of objectivity is spurious. Moreover, in some cases it offends common sense. If the average man over a certain age has high blood pressure, that does not make high blood pressure healthy. The difficulty in taking well-being or adjustment as a definition of mental health is that there are circumstances of oppression, deprivation, or misery to which a mentally healthy person could not adjust himself. An enduring disposition to personal happiness and well-being is a possible element of mental health, however. Most problematic is the question whether positive mental health should be defined as absence of mental disease. Indeed, Barton (1958), a psychiatrist, appended to Jahoda's monograph a dissenting opinion, to the effect that *positive mental health* is a term better reserved for the absence of disease. Jahoda prefers to think of absence of mental disease as a necessary but not sufficient condition for positive mental health.

Jahoda summarizes the criteria for positive mental health under six headings, chosen to reflect the spirit of the original authors rather than logically distinct rubrics.

The attitudes of the person toward his self is her first heading; under it she includes the accessibility of the self to consciousness, correctness of the self-concept, acceptance of the self, and a sense of identity. She raises the question in relation to Maslow's discussion of this point whether the healthy person fails to experience ego-alien impulses or whether he accepts them as such. Evidently it is the total configuration of self that is to be accepted under this criterion. Erikson's discussion of ego identity belongs here, as does McDougall's self-regarding sentiment (see Chapter Eleven). In relation to achieving a sense of identity more or less autonomous from transient environmental influences, White (1952) points out that this achievement is a suitable criterion only in maturity, not in childhood, a pervasive problem in discussing positive mental health.

Jahoda's second set of criteria refers to growth, development, and self-actualization. She includes in that topic investment in work and in social values beyond what yields immediate personal gain. She attributes the term *self-actualization* to Goldstein (1939), who saw in it the sole motive of the organism. (It is not clear, however, how self-actualization differs from Dewey's term *self-realization,* whose ancestry extends to Aristotle. Would the difference between the terms survive in translation to another language?) Allport, Rogers, and Fromm, who credits Spinoza, are others for whom this concept is central. The inclusion of commitment to values outside oneself keeps this criterion from being interpreted as an egocentric one. She brings out one of the logical difficulties in some of the theorists: "Sometimes the term is used as implying a general principle of life, holding for every organism; at other times it is applied specifically to mentally healthy functioning" (Jahoda, 1958, p. 31). If everyone obeys the principle of self-actualization, it adds nothing to say that the mentally healthy do.

Integration, Jahoda's third category, is sometimes included as part of the self-concept or as part of self-actualization; other times it is given as a separate criterion. Among recent psychoanalysts, such ideas as balance of psychic forces and flexibility are included here. In a different vein, Allport (1937) saw a unifying philosophy of life as a sign of maturity. A task of the unifying philosophy is reconciliation of two conflicting tendencies, that toward self-extension or commitment to the world and that toward self-objectification or detachment in respect to oneself. A final aspect of integration is resistance to stress. Recent authors have emphasized not the absence of anxiety but the capacity to cope with it as a criterion for mental health.

The criterion of autonomy, the fourth category, includes regulation of behavior from within and a trend towards independence from the pressures of the immediate environment, a point emphasized by Hartmann (1939) and Maslow. There is a connotation, Jahoda points out, of being partially safeguarded from the badness of the world by autonomy. The capacity for autonomy includes the capacity for conformity when appropriate; indeed, some authors make a point in this connection also of balance as a criterion, that is, maximum autonomy may not represent optimal adjustment any more than maximum conformity does.

Jahoda's fifth set of criteria relates to perception of reality; under this heading she includes empathy or social sensitivity and freedom of perception from distortion by the person's own needs. Perception of reality in the mental health literature always has interpersonal connotations, she points out; it always concerns the reality provided by other people. Jahoda is aware of the difficulty in defining mental health in terms of veridical perception, for who is to say what is reality? The majority of people may dismiss the most farsighted and original minds as unrealistic or unbalanced, from Columbus to Semmelweis to Solzhenitsyn.

The sixth criterion, environmental mastery, includes adequacy in interpersonal relations; capacity for and adequacy in love, work, and play; and capacity for adaptation, adjustment, and problem solving. The problem of what constitutes a healthy adaptation to bad circumstances, such as prison, is a difficulty for this criterion. Another problem is to avoid identifying mental health with success in life.

There is no necessary contradiction in these several criteria, though under some circumstances an extreme of one may be incompatible with that of another. In prison one cannot be both autonomous and adjusted; the person committed to an idealistic but lost cause may need to guard his illusions; and so on. One way of reconciling the different criteria is to allow for different types of people, each type finding its optimum of mental health in its own way. Another way to reconcile them is by some kind of multifaceted criterion. Different authors have conceived the multiple criterion different ways. Erikson, for example, sees the different elements as maturing in different periods. The several elements can also be construed as a kind of syndrome, with different elements being most prominent in different cases.

With respect to one after another of Jahoda's criteria, it is clear that they do not apply to children in any useful way without modification; yet the mental health of children is as meaningful and as important as that of adults. A second persistent problem is that positive mental health in Jahoda's sense is not the opposite of mental disease. Both of these problems are solved by recognizing that the syndrome that Jahoda and the authors she summarizes are aiming at is to a large extent the highest level of ego development. The richness of the conception is lost when one sees only the extremes, and the nature of its course is implicitly distorted.

Rogers: The Process of Psychotherapy as a Scale

The problem to which Rogers (1961) addresses himself is discerning the common elements in the process of psychological change, particularly with reference to psychotherapy. He found the study of outcomes to be unsatisfactory. The effect of therapy is not moving from fixity through change to a new fixity but rather moving from fixity to changingness. How the client discusses his feelings and problems is the clue to where he stands on a continuum characterized at one extreme by rigidity, remoteness from and lack of awareness of feelings, and at the other extreme by fluidity, closeness to feelings and immediate awareness of them. While a client may function at somewhat different stages with respect to different areas of his life, on the whole his behaviors cluster within a narrow range.

Rogers describes the continuum in terms of seven stages, but the stages are not sharply demarked, and the conception appears to be more that of a polar variable than a true stage conception. At the first stage, personal constructs in Kelly's sense (Chapter Twelve) are rigid and fixed. At the second stage feelings are unowned or described in the past. At the third stage there is some conceptualization of self, and personal choices of conduct are often seen as difficult to enforce on oneself. Feelings not currently present are talked about; feelings mostly are not accepted but considered shameful, bad, or abnormal. Personal constructs are rigid but may be recognized as constructs rather than as external facts. Roger's fourth stage has current feelings experienced but often not accepted; there is recognition of personal constructs and beginning of questioning of their validity. In the fifth stage, present feelings are expressed freely, but the immediacy of feelings is surprising and frightening rather than pleasant. There is interest in self-discovery. At the sixth stage there is greater acceptance of immediate, intense feelings, and meanings are sharply differentiated. The incongruence between experience and awareness is vividly experienced as it disappears into congruence, and the relevant personal construct simultaneously disappears. The seventh stage is described in terms similar to those of the sixth stage, but it represents a more advanced state; in addition, the choice of courses of conduct becomes real and effective because the elements of experience are available to the person.

In Table 8 passages in which Rogers describes the stages in the process of therapy are compared with passages in which Loevinger and Wessler (Chapter 4, 1970) summarize manifestations of ego level in sentence completions (see Chapter Nine). Passages are chosen to emphasize the similarities and parallels, rather than to convey the full flavor of the two continua being compared. With Rogers relying entirely on spoken communication between client and therapist and Loevinger and Wessler relying on written sentence completion protocols of normal (non-client) women, greater similarity could not be expected.

Most of psychotherapy, according to Rogers, is concerned with his fourth and fifth stages. Cases judged to be successful by other criteria show more movement on this scale than do less successful cases; moreover, the more successful cases begin higher on the scale. How to help those at the lowest stages is not yet fully understood.

Isaacs (1956; see Chapter Five) reported that in several hundred cases known to him, almost none showed a rise in level of relatability following psychotherapy, even successful, extensive, psychoanalytically-oriented therapy. Since Isaacs's scale of relatability, like Rogers's scale for psychotherapy, is either a version of ego development or a closely related variable, his assertion of no change in therapy appears to conflict with Rogers's assertion that this is the very dimension in which there is a change in therapy. The contradiction is blunted by noting that Rogers specifically disclaims that any single patient goes from the low stages to the highest stages in the course of psychotherapy and by his acknowledgement that more successful patients begin higher on the scale. The latter observation corresponds to the observation by Isaacs that the more success-

Table 8. Comparison of Rogers's Process of Psychotherapy with Ego Development

	Ego Development	Process of Psychotherapy	
Stage	Description	Description	Stage
I-2	S tends to dichotomize the world; stereotyping is the most conspicuous sign.	Personal constructs are rigid.	1
	Affects are seen as bodily states or impulses rather than as differentiated inner feelings.	Feelings and personal meanings are not recognized or owned. Communication is about externals only.	
	There is a limited emotional range.		
	Trouble is located in a place rather than a situation.	No problems are recognized or perceived; there is no desire to change.	
△	S does not see himself as responsible for trouble or failure; you are lucky or unlucky, or other people are to blame; or blame is external and impersonal.	Problems are perceived as external to self; S has no sense of personal responsibility for problems.	2
△/3	Obedience and conformity to norms are simple, absolute rules. Emotions are seen as quasi-physiological.	Personal constructs are rigid and thought of as facts, not recognized as constructs.	
I-3	Inner life is mentioned in generalities; feelings are denied or mentioned in a vague, evasive, or noncommittal way.	Differentiation of personal meanings and feelings is limited and global.	
	Inner conflict may be manifest, but it is not acknowledged.	Contradictions may be expressed but without recognition as contradictions.	
I-3/4	Self-consciousness and rudimentary self-awareness and self-criticism are characteristic.	There is freer flow of expression about self, self-related experiences, and self as reflected in others.	3
	There is stronger awareness of feelings than before. S is more aware of individual differences in attitudes, interests, and abilities, but still in global and banal terms.	Differentiation of feelings and meanings is slightly sharper and less global than before.	
	S sees multiple possibilities and alternatives in situations; there are contingencies, exceptions, and comparisons, though global and banal ones.	There is recognition of contradictions in experience.	

(continued on next page)

Table 8 (continued)

Stage	Ego Development — Description	Process of Psychotherapy — Description	Stage
I-4	S has a richly differentiated inner life; experiences are savored and appreciated. S is aware of the problem of impulse and control.	Past feelings are described as intense; present feelings are still distrusted and feared.	4
I-4	Interpersonal interaction is intensive. S sees patterns in behavior and has a vivid sense of individual differences in behavior and in the long-term dispositions that underlie behavior. Descriptions of people are more realistic because S perceives more complexities. S is aware of self, reflects on self, and describes self and others in terms of reflexive traits. S sees intentions and motives as well as consequences of behavior. S distinguishes appearances from underlying feelings. S has a strong sense of responsibility. S sees life as presenting choices; he holds the origin of his own destiny.	There is an increased differentiation of feelings, constructs, and personal meanings, seeking exactness of symbolization. S is concerned about contradictions and incongruities between experience and self. There are feelings of self-responsibility in problems, though such feelings vacillate.	
I-4/5	Where the I-4 S sees polar, incompatible opposites, the I-4/5 S is more likely to see a paradox, a quasi-contradiction in nature rather than a forced choice. S becomes aware of conflicting or constrasting emotions. There is greater complexity in conception of interpersonal interaction. The idea of communication and expression of feelings is deepened and made more complex. Psychological causality replaces vague statements of "reasons" and "problems" at lower levels. S gives vivid and personal versions of ideas presented as clichés at lower levels. S distinguishes inner life from outer, appearances from reality. Maintaining one's own individuality is perceived as a problem.	There is increasingly clear facing of contradictions and incongruities in experience. Feelings are close to being fully experienced. There are fresh discoveries of personal constructs and a critical examination of them. There is a strong tendency towards exactness in differentiation of feelings and meanings. There is increased acceptance of self-responsibility for problems and freer internal communication. There is increasing ownership of self-feelings and a desire to be the "real me."	5

I-5		6
S feels the full force of inner conflict and tries to cope with it or transcend it.		New feelings are experienced with immediacy and richness of detail.
S is concerned with communicating feelings.		Differentiation of experiencing is sharp and basic.
Emotions are differentiated and vividly conveyed. Sensual experiences come through vividly. S displays spontaneity, genuineness, intensity.		7
S has a high tolerance for ambiguity; conflicting alternatives are construed as aspects of many-faceted life situations.		There is acceptant ownership of changing feelings, a basic trust in his own process.
		Personal constructs are tentatively formulated and loosely held.

NOTE: Descriptions of stages of ego development are excerpted from Loevinger and Wessler, 1970, Chapter Four, pp. 54-109. Descriptions of stages of psychotherapy are excerpted from Rogers, 1961, Chapter Seven, pp. 125-159.

ful patients are the ones who begin with vivid and differentiated descriptions of themselves and others; that, indeed, was one of Isaacs's initial clues to the dimension. Isaacs uses the maximum level to characterize a protocol or a patient, while Rogers presumably is talking about the level of core functioning. Isaacs acknowledges (personal communication) that after psychotherapy a person may behave at his maximum level far more of the time than before psychotherapy. Thus his assertion that the maximum level to be found in a person's protocol does not change in therapy is not incompatible with the assertion of Rogers that the level of core functioning does change in successful therapy.

A vulnerable aspect of Rogers's position is the equation in some of his writings of maturity with adjustment and of both with congruence between self and experience (Rogers, 1959, p. 207). Lack of congruence between self and experience would seem to be only one kind of maladjustment, perhaps the only kind that client-centered therapy can cope with or that Rogers is interested in. In the first instance *maladjustment* has some simpler, more phenotypic reference; it was a common term before there was a client-centered therapy. Regarding all maladjustment to be of that form requires proof; the only way to prove it is to begin with a different definition of maladjustment.

Conclusions

In this chapter we have scanned a variety of topics having in common the format of polar variables, defined by their extremes, in constrast to the variables defined by multiple stages or types that we have surveyed in the previous chapter. In part the purpose has been substantive, to further enrich understanding of ego growth. In part the purpose has been to aid differential definition, that is, to acknowledge frequently raised questions as to the similarities and differences between the proposed construct of ego development and other well-known lines of theory and research. Differential definition will be continued in the next chapter. In part the purpose has been methodological, to sharpen the distinction between polar and milestone variables in preparation for discussing problems of measurement in chapters Eight and Nine. Relation of ego development to psychotherapy came up almost incidentally, chiefly because of the repeated confusion of ego maturity with good adjustment and positive mental health in the literature. There are other conceptual threads linking the field of ego development with theory and practice of psychotherapy, to which we will return in later chapters.

PART II

METHODOLOGY

Truth is no empty dream. She is a phantom only when we think that we grasp her. She is real when, recognizing that she is a being enthroned above us, we are content to touch the hem of her robe.

—Leonard T. Hobhouse
Morals in Evolution

Chapter Seven

Intellectual, Psychosexual, and Ego Development

Ego development is the same thing as or has much in common with developmental sequences described in terms of morality and character, interpersonal relations, and cognitive complexity and dimensions of individual differences described in terms of authoritarianism, intraception, and other variables. But it is not the whole of personality development. If we think of it as encompassing all of personality development, we will be back at the status quo ante, an amorphous and undifferentiated concept. In the last chapter we drew a boundary with adjustment; in the present one we will draw boundaries with intellectual and psychosexual development. The conceptual distinction must precede study of correlations or causal relation.

161

Consider height and weight. Not only does a child normally gain weight as he grows taller, but also among adults height and weight are appreciably correlated. Nonetheless, the conceptual distinction is clear. In fact, there is no difficulty in measuring one entirely uncontaminated by the effects of the other. In measuring ego level, one can be much less sure that there is no contamination from other associated variables, as discussion of methodological difficulties (Chapter Eight) will show, but we will strive for as clear a conceptual distinction as that between height and weight. Naturally the difficulties in distinguishing abstract variables like ego development from related ones are greater than those in distinguishing concrete variables like height and weight.

Models of Developmental Variation

The term *development* covers processes that differ not only in content but also in form (Loevinger, 1966b). Five formal models will be discussed; combinations of them can yield additional possibilities. The five models differ in whether rate, terminal achievement, and terminal age of change are the same for all persons or not. Effects of nonlethal growth disturbances also differ in the several models. Another difference is whether the growth is assumed to be monotonic, that is, a nondecreasing function of age.

For the first four models, age is represented on the abscissa (x-axis) and the scale of growth on the ordinate (y-axis). Psychology does not, in general, have scales that permit direct comparison of gains in one function with gains in another function during the same period nor direct comparison of gains early in the growth period with those later on. Scammon (1930) demonstrated the marked difference between the postnatal growth curves of brain, which grows most rapidly in the first two years, and sex organs, which grow most rapidly during puberty. A comparison of that sort has no counterpart or representation in the models presented here. Stretching or shrinking the scale on the y-axis, the measure of development, does not change anything, because the scale is arbitrary to start with. For this reason arbitrarily simplified curves, such as straight lines, will be used to represent the course of growth. Translation of these "curves" into algebraic equations is not permissible.

In Model 1 (Figure 2) the growth rates differ but the final growth achieved is the same for everyone, although it is

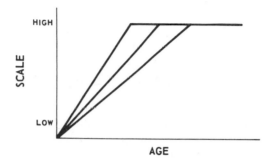

Figure 2. Model 1 for development

achieved at different ages. Skeletal age, that is, ossification of the epiphyses, takes this form. For everyone the epiphyses ultimately are completely ossified, but the age at which the process is completed differs for different people. When one knows the extent to which it has taken place for a given child, one knows how much of his adult height he has achieved. Popular speech, referring to a child as "slow," implies that this pattern may hold for some psychological characteristics. There are a few instances of the pattern: a steep developmental gradient, wide differences in the age of completion of development, perhaps also wide differences in the age of starting the developmental climb, but essentially no differences in the final accomplishment. Walking, elimination of bedwetting, and the like follow such curves. In the case of walking, such differences as there are in adult life almost certainly have nothing to do with differences in the age of first walking.

In Model 2 (Figure 3) growth rates differ, but the terminal age for growth is constant. A person tends to hold a constant place with respect to his own age cohort throughout childhood

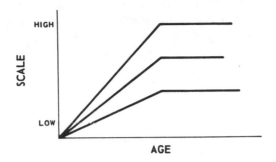

Figure 3. Model 2 for development

and adult life, and individual differences in childhood thus become predictive of adult differences. In computing the IQ,
dividing mental age (MA) by chronological age (CA), one implicitly uses Model 2. For the 1937 Stanford-Binet test, sixteen
years was taken as the maximum CA for all cases; thus, by
implication, sixteen was assumed to be the terminal age of intellectual growth. In fact, the assumption is known not to hold
precisely. There have been demonstrations of slight continued
growth in subsequent years, especially in individuals of superior
intelligence. The evidence as to whether feebleminded persons
end their growth earlier is mixed. To escape the assumptions of
Model 2, intelligence tests usually express scores in terms of per-
centile rank or standard score within the individual's own age
group. But if status within one's own age cohort is taken as predictive of later status and particularly of adult status, as it commonly is, then Model 2 is still implied.

  In Model 3 (Figure 4) the rates for different people are the
same but the terminal age for growth differs. Adult differences
thus reflect the age that growth stopped. To the extent that this
model holds, early childhood differences for a given age are
small and not predictive of adult differences. This model has a
special virtue. When it can be combined with a Model 1 process,
giving essentially the percentage of adult growth achieved, then
it again becomes possible to predict adult status. Height differences in childhood are predictive of adult height differences

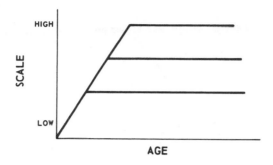

Figure 4. Model 3 for development

(Model 2), but the prediction can be improved by taking skeletal age into account and thus predicting age of growth termination (combining Model 1 with Model 3).

A clear, pure case of a Model 3 process is not easy to show. Model 3 implies that the developmental sequence is the same for all people, the rate is about the same, but the end points differ. A given developmental transition either takes place at its appointed time in the sequence, or it is fated never to take place, and development ceases. Educational attainment, as measured by highest school grade reached, can be represented this way to a first approximation.

In Model 4 (Figure 5) we arbitrarily group all those growth curves for which the final adult status is not the maximum value. The thymus gland, which reaches its greatest size about age twelve, is an example from physical development. Many psychological functions are of this form. Most physical and cognitive measures peak at maturity, but noncognitive aspects of personality, for example, interests, typically follow a nonmonotone course (Model 4). Figure 5 does not depict individual differences in Model 4 functions. They may be of several types. The curves can differ with respect to the peak age, the scale value at peak age, the rate of growth or decline, or the scale value at maturity. A special case is depicted in Figure 6.

Underlying almost all measurement of intelligence has been a subtle bias in favor of construing abilities as nondecreas-

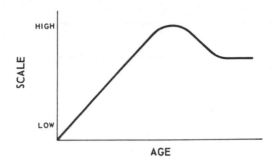

Figure 5. Model 4 for development

ing functions (Model 1, 2, or 3) rather than as nonmonotone functions (Model 4). This bias is built into the concept of mental age (MA); the scale of measurement is defined in terms of the achievements of average children at various ages. Thus the growth curve of average children must be a straight line to maturity.

Piaget's studies of cognitive development have revealed a more complex picture, one that can be looked at in other terms. Piaget traces intellectual development through the following stages: six stages in the sensorimotor period, the preoperational stage, the stage of concrete operations, and the stage of formal operations. One way of looking at this sequence is to say that it defines a developmental scale, so that it would constitute the ordinate in Model 1, 2, or 3. Piaget never quite tells us which of those models applies. Do all adults eventually reach the stage of formal operations, even though at different ages (Model 1)? Do children progress at different rates and all level off at about the same time during adolescence (Model 2)? Do children progress at about the same rate until they hit their own highest potential, then level off (Model 3)? These questions could be answered by research. Recent research has, in fact, suggested that some people never acquire formal operational thinking (Blasi and Hoeffel, 1974); so Model 1 can be ruled out.

Obviously, definition of successive points on such a scale bears no resemblance to a yardstick but is an intricate inferential process, more intricate than the definition of MA. This type of scale cannot be arrived at simply by observing the development of normal children.

Another way to look at Piaget's sequence of stages of cognitive growth is to see them as a set of separable Model 4 processes. Each stage is a kind of reasoning that increases up to some age and then decreases in favor of the next type of reasoning. A hypothetical picture of a succession of stages, each indexed by a particular sign, is shown in Figure 6. Note that the

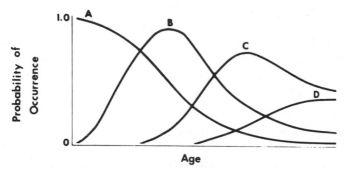

Note: A, B, C, and D are signs of successive stages.

Figure 6. Model for a milestone sequence

maximum probability for successive signs decreases, on the premise that fewer persons reach successively higher stages. The earliest stage characterizes all infants and is a decreasing function of age, though it does not necessarily decrease to zero. Signs of the highest stage are increasing functions of age but never reach high probability, since most persons never reach the highest stage. There is a possibility that some signs fluctuate irregularly from stage to stage; such signs have been omitted partly to simplify the diagram but chiefly because they would be omitted from any measuring instrument because of their equivocality.

Models 1, 2, 3, and 4 have some elements in common. Development in each case is described in terms of progression and regression along a single scale, though the units of the scale are not in general equal nor need they be defined in any simple way. Moreover, the scale must be defined independently of age. If the scoring standards are themselves specific to (that is, variable with) age, there remains no means for comparing one age with another. Two children of differing CA but the same MA have been asked the same questions on the Stanford-Binet and may have given the same pattern of right answers. An answer is always scored right or wrong independently of the CA of the child on all intelligence tests. There are no age-contingent scores. Thus the scales of development that appear as ordinates for models 1 through 4 are abstractions. Age-specific signs, anything that defines a given stage at a particular age, must not be used for definition of the points (or stages) of the ordinate if these models are to make any sense. Rather, the points on the scale must be defined in just such terms as apply regardless of age. Thus an MA of five is just what an average five-year-old, a bright three-year-old, and a dull eight-year-old have in common.

An interesting and not altogether obvious aspect of kinds of growth depicted in models 1 through 4 is that moderately severe growth disturbances are, in general, compensated without disturbing the pattern of growth or affecting final adult status. This observation is well established for growth in height (Tanner, 1963), and similar effects probably account for some of the variation in IQ and similar measures. This finding suggests a symmetrical hypothesis that crash programs to stimulate cognitive growth will not have long-term effects.

For Model 5 (Figure 7), by contrast with the preceding models, growth disturbances affect the pattern permanently. In this model successive stages are defined by the predominance of different organs, organ-systems, or functions. When a growth disturbance of any kind occurs, it affects predominantly the organ or function in ascendance at that period. The organ may hypertrophy or hypotrophy, and the change will, in general, be permanent and affect all subsequent patterns. This model applies to embryonic development, which tends to be protected effectively against sublethal growth disturbances, however. Monstrosities are rare. Thus a description of embryonic development is at once a description of what ought to take place and what almost always does.

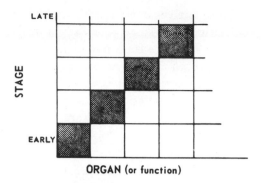

Figure 7. Model 5 for development

Erikson has used an adaptation of Model 5 for depicting psychosexual development (1950, p. 84). He represents it in terms of a matrix, with rows representing zones in the order of their predominance, that is, oral, anal, and genital zones (with elaborations not germane here), clearly analogous to the organ-systems of embryonic development. The predominance of a given zone is used to define the corresponding stage. The columns represent modes, so ordered that the mode appropriate to each zone falls in the diagonal, so far as possible. Examples are incorporation as the appropriate mode for the oral zone and retention and elimination as the appropriate modes for the anal zone. Deviations in development may take the form of clinging to the old zone while progressing to the new mode, or premature advance to a new mode.

The disanalogies between psychosexual development and embryonic development are as striking as the analogies and seem not to have been dealt with by Erikson. One obvious contrast between prenatal and postnatal development is that the uniformity of prenatal environment is lost at birth. Moreover, psychosexual development is far more responsive to environmental influence than physical development. Viable variations in the pattern of development are the rule rather than the exception in psychosexual development. Psychosexually, we are all more or less monstrous. Erikson does not clarify whether his description applies to what development ought to be, what it usually is, or what it usually approximates.

Model 5 is prescriptive as well as descriptive, and the description is age-specific. Each stage is described in terms of what is appropriate or inappropriate for a particular age. There is not, in general, a possibility of having at one age a pattern exactly appropriate for another age, which is the basis of all the other models. Appreciable acceleration or retardation in a Model 5 process always means alteration of pattern. Thus, there is no scale of measurement built into Model 5 processes. If one speaks of measuring such development, it must be in terms of a different scale for each stage. Attempts to measure psychosexual development have, indeed, taken the form of a series of scales. But this is not measurement in the sense of the preceding models.

To summarize, developmental sequences can be divided into those where variations consist primarily in acceleration and retardation along a single continuum (Models 1, 2, 3, 4) and those where every alteration from the norm is a deformation (Model 5); into those where variability at maturity is a minimum (Model 1) or a maximum (Models 2, 3, 4, and 5); into monotone (Models 1, 2, and 3) and nonmonotone (Model 4) functions of age; and into those where status at maturity is primarily a function of rate (Model 2) or of terminal age (Model 3) of growth.

Wohlwill (1973) has taken the topic of models for development much further. His chief interest is in development of functions for which there is a scale of measurement sufficiently exact so that individual differences in the growth function can be plotted. Our interest here is more limited. In the foreseeable future no such precision in measurement of ego development or related variables will be achieved; in Chapter Eight we will examine some of the reasons why precision is unattainable. Our concern with models for development is limited to what light they can shed on conception and measurement of ego development.

Models for Ego Development

Erikson has been a pioneer among psychoanalysts in calling attention to and elucidating the special characteristics of ego development. In doing so, he has relied chiefly on another version of Model 5 (Erikson, 1963, p. 273). The successive stages of ego development he characterizes, or perhaps defines, by successive "nuclear conflicts" (Table 2). Each of these conflicts is represented in the diagonal cell of a matrix like Figure 7 with the rows again representing successive stages. But what do the columns represent? In principle, each column contains the precursors in earlier periods of the nuclear conflict and the consequences in later periods of its solution. This model, however, bears the air of being contrived to match the somewhat more appropriate model for psychosexual development, where different organs or body zones are indeed involved in successive periods. The ego, however, is like a single organ. The predecessor of each nuclear problem can be thought of as the nuclear problem of the preceding period. Erikson has in fact presented off-diagonal entries only for the identity crisis of adolescence.

Application of Model 5 to ego development involves all of the difficulties of its application to psychosexual development. The model is prescriptive as well as descriptive. It makes no clear allowance for comparison between stages, thus no allowance that a person at one age might have a pattern appropriate for another age. There is no systematic way to express the relation between what happens at one stage or age and what happens at the next. There is an additional difficulty in applying Model 5 to ego development, for one is hard put to say what in ego development corresponds to the difference between modes and zones. Thus the one link between embryonic development and psychosexual development is lacking for ego development.

Erikson, of course, makes no pretense to mathematical precision in his formulations. The virtues of his expositions are literary and philosophical. Not surprisingly, he has also written of ego development in quite different terms: "It is . . . as true for adolescence as it is for childhood that man's way stations to maturity can become fixed, can become premature end stations, or stations for future regression" (1964, pp. 225-226). This seems to be a verbal formulation of Model 3, quite different in its implications from Model 5.

Sullivan's description of the development of the self-system clearly follows Model 3. Each transition has an appropriate period. When it fails to occur, the person meets the problems of later periods with one or another type of immaturity. He acknowledges circumstances favorable for resumption of growth, including long-term psychotherapy, but the resumption of interrupted growth is rarer and more problematic than normal growth.

The question of the form of the growth curve for the ego is an appropriate one for empirical research. A definitive answer will depend on adequate measuring instruments (Chapter Nine). Such evidence as is currently available suggests a combination of Model 2 and Model 3 processes—that is, people differ in their rate of growth, and they also differ in the age at which growth stops.

There is another way of applying the foregoing discussion to our variable. The scale of ego development can be thought of as similar to Piaget's scale of cognitive development, with qualitatively different points whose ordering is given by age. The signs of each stage can then be thought of as a series of Model 4 processes, as in Figure 6. Each sign increases in its probability of occurrence up to some point and decreases thereafter. These signs then become a milestone sequence. The abscissa in such a graph can be thought of either as age or stage. The curves will be more sharply peaked for a graph using stage as abscissa, since persons at the same age will be of various stages. To measure ego development we then turn this reasoning around, using the signs exhibited by the subject as an indication of his probable stage of development.

Distinction of Psychosexual and Ego Development

The phenomena of ego development have been the basis in recent years for a kind of tug of war. On the one side are those who seek to discount the Freudian emphasis on psychosexual development as exaggeration of a subsidiary aspect of ego development; on the other side are those who seek to assimilate the facts of ego development to the stages of psychosexual development, which they regard as firmly established. The former group, who feel that the ego phenomena are the overarching ones and psychosexual phenomena are in the domain of the ego, include Alfred Adler, Kurt Goldstein, and Carl Rogers. A recent version can be found in Sullivan, Grant, and Grant (1957).

Persons whose first profound glimpse of personality occurs through the eyes of psychoanalysis may be so imprinted with the conception of psychosexual development that they find it hard to cope with ego development as something separate. Both Freud and Ferenczi, however, even in the early years, spoke of ego development as separate from psychosexual development. Nonetheless, when faced with the complexities of ego development and particularly with its abstract and intangible aspects, many psychologists find comfort in assimilating it to the concrete sequence of bodily zones. So strong was this tendency that Hartmann created a virtual revolution in psychoanalysis by insisting that there were ego functions autonomous of drives (see Chapter Fourteen).* However, this psychoanalytic ego psychology did not work out a conception of stages.

Although to Erikson the conceptual distinction between psychosexual and ego development is clear, his writings may have encouraged confusion in his readers. For one thing, he does not stress the extent to which the sequences are separable and independently variable. Secondly, he takes the formal features of his model of psychosexual development as the framework for his model of ego or psychosocial development. Finally, because his exposition is a normative one, whether in the sense of describing average growth trends or of ideal ones not being clear, a spurious interpenetration of the timetables is implied. Erikson's expositions are couched in age-specific terms. Each developmental crisis is described with reference to age-appropriate problems, such as going to kindergarten, dating, marriage, and so on. The abstract aspects, those shared by persons of different ages but the same stage, are not stressed. Since all kinds of development necessarily take place simultaneously,

---

*The usefulness of the drive concept has been questioned in recent years. Holding that problem in abeyance till Chapter Fourteen, here we take the term as pointing to an aspect of life and experience.

describing the normal course of events in average children does not lead to clear separation of the several strands of development.

At this point Sullivan's description is useful. However much it may be true that his basic concepts are renamed adaptations of Freud's concepts (and it is only partly true), his conception of the development of the self-system is sharply and clearly differentiated from the development of zonal needs and satisfactions. He may indeed underestimate the influence on the total personality of zonal needs and their gratification.

We start then from these premises: both ego development and psychosexual development contribute decisively to personality. They are conceptually distinct lines, differing not only in substance but also in formal properties. There is an inner logic to ego development; each stage is built on the preceding one. The sequence of drives is determined by the organic substrate rather than by logical connections. If the problems of some stage of ego development are insurmountable for a child, by reason of trauma, deprivation, indulgence, environmental restriction, or whatever, he will cease to develop at that point or develop very slowly thereafter. Future problems will be met and construed in terms of the ego structure appropriate to the earlier age. In the psychosexual sphere, however fixated a child may be at some stage, he is nonetheless precipitated into coping with the drives of the next stage at the appointed time. He may be handicapped, but he is not spared the necessity to try.

The question of the correlation of ego and psychosexual development is meaningless. Psychosexual development does not constitute a continuum such that evidence of functioning at one level contraindicates functioning at another level. In some sense everyone beyond a certain age bears the mark of functioning at every level. This aspect contrasts with ego and intellectual development. There are various ways of looking at ego development, none of which totally exhausts the phenomenon; one of them is to look at it as a series of achievements, or as a succession of increasingly complex views of the world. There does not seem to be any corresponding aspect of psychosexual development. It is therefore meaningless to talk about measuring psychosexual development in any way comparable to the measurement of ego or intellectual development.

There are, however, many possible relations between ego and psychosexual development, construing the term relation more broadly than correlation. The many accounts of child development that encompass aspects of both, such as are to be found in the writings of Hartmann and his collaborators, Erikson, and others, show numerous interconnections. A vast human wisdom is to be found in these accounts, and no attempt will be made to summarize them. We seek here only the theoretical skeleton, not the flesh and blood.

From one point of view, drives are the impetus for all behavior, hence for all of ego development. From another point of view, the ego is the antagonist of the drives; again, however, it would be in part structured by drives. These views are quasi-philosophical or metapsychological and do not have much content. On a more specific level, a change in drives can trigger a new phase of ego development by disturbing a previously achieved equilibrium. Other possibilities include drive changes facilitating or inhibiting ego changes, depending, for example, on whether the person is in phase or out of phase with social expectations.

What has happened in the past has been that all of these possibilities have been confused and obscured in fine writing. One of the most pervasive errors has been to meld the highest ego stage with all good attributes, and particularly with good sexual adjustment and psychosexual maturity. Whether the highest stage of ego development requires full psychosexual maturity is an unsettled empirical question.

The Relation of Intelligence to Ego Development

Since increase in cognitive complexity is one aspect of ego development, the conceptual distinction between cognitive and ego development is not simple and obvious. Intuitively, we understand ego level to be something not altogether identical with intellectual level. More convincing is to recall a few exceptionally brilliant people who are low in ego level and some intellectually limited people with unusual wisdom about human relations. Anecdotal as such accounts may be, they are not trivial as evidence. A single case can establish the possibility of a discrepancy in levels for the two sequences.

That does not mean that everyone, regardless of his intellectual endowment or achievement, has an equal chance to achieve high level. Nature does not promise us an orthogonal universe, a world arranged in rows and columns, where every distinguishable trait is statistically independent of all others. On the average one may suppose that high intelligence conduces to at least fairly high ego level, and intellectual defect severely limits ego level. A question frequently asked is: What is the correlation between intelligence and ego development? Although some coefficients have been obtained in particular and limited studies, on the whole the question is meaningless, though not for the reasons given for psychosexual development.

Consider MA and CA. What is the correlation between them? If you ask a sixth-grade teacher, she will most likely report a negative correlation in her own classroom; the school principal will report a positive correlation for the whole grade school. (I owe this illustration to Warren Norman.) If we remove the effect of age by expressing intelligence in terms of IQ or some equivalent age-corrected score, we will still find a discrepancy; the sixth-grade teacher will report a negative correlation and the principal a zero correlation. That illustrates the arbitrary nature of correlations. Different values can be obtained by a suitable choice of samples.

Correlations between our sentence completion test of ego development (Chapter Nine) and IQ have ranged from about .1 to .5 in a series of unpublished studies, the value depending on heterogeneity and the mode of sampling. One naturally thinks of intelligence as an independent variable in such a situation and ego level as a dependent variable, but a particular measure of intelligence may be influenced by ego level. For example, a person of low ego level may be uncooperative on the test. Most educators must hope that their efforts foster ego development, but what is more obvious is that ego level determines whether a young person will stay in school, particularly during the high school years. An Opportunist can make it at the secondary or college level, but he is less likely to try than a person at the Conformist or higher level, since delay of gratification is necessary for education to take place. Unmodulated impulsiveness is likely to lead either to dropping out or to being expelled from school during high school. Few persons at the Impulsive Stage ever enter college. Thus disentangling the causal factors in the correlation may be difficult.

A potential area of research is the microanalysis of the relation between different kinds of development, that is, investigation of more specific question than the statistical correlation between developmental sequences. One such specific question is the minimum intellectual equipment for achieving each ego level. The question is not one of probabilities or correlation but of necessary prerequisite. The speculations that follow are meant as preparatory to such empirical study rather than as substitute for them.

The progress out of the Autistic Stage appears to require confidence in the stability of the world of objects. Even symbiotic interpersonal relations imply the existence of another person. The construction of the world of objects has been the subject of a long series of experiments by Piaget (1937). Particularly relevant are the phenomena of the fourth, fifth, and sixth stages of sensorimotor development. The fourth stage occupies about the eighth to twelfth month, the fifth stage about the twelfth to sixteenth month in Piaget's observations. At the fourth stage the child will search at point A for an object that he has seen hidden there; but if the object is subsequently hidden at point B, he will still continue to search at point A. At the fifth stage the child follows the visible displacements of the object, and will search at point B for an object he has seen hidden there, despite the fact that it has previously been found at point A. He cannot, however, follow invisible displacements. At the sixth stage the child conceives of invisible displacements and searches for lost objects in accordance with where they might be, rather than merely where he last saw them put. Through many such experiments and observations Piaget showed how the world of objects becomes constituted for the infant as independent of his own actions and perceptions. The gradualness of the transition from a world constituted by the act of perception, the world of the Autistic Stage, to the world of permanent objects suggests a continuous rather than a discrete development. Further, at the level of sensorimotor intelligence, intellectual and ego development are probably indistinguishable.

The construction or apprehension of mother as an object distinct from the entire environmental matrix is perhaps a condition for the full-fledged symbiotic position. Yet with continued and increasing perception of mother's independent movements, symbiosis normally declines. Knowledge of invisible displacements may be the beginning of the end of symbiosis in normal instances; also required would appear to be the concept of negation—what is me is not mother; what is mother is not me. Spitz (1957) locates the beginning of negation at about sixteen months, at which time the child shakes his head to avoid food that he rejects.

As *no* may be the key word for the transition from Symbiosis to the Impulsive Stage, so does *why* seem to be the key word for the transition from the Impulsive to the Self-Protective Stage. The child making this transition must conceive that things have causes or reasons, that the impulse is separate from the action, hence that one can delay and control action, however briefly. Piaget (1926) has described the child's earliest questions in terms of the concept of precausality, which is an undifferentiated combination of physical causality, logical justification, and psychological motivation. The *whys* of psychological motivation predominate up to about the age of seven, but because of the child's egocentric and animistic modes of thought, intention and physical causality are not clearly separate until about that age.

Piaget (1932) has found that the Conformist attitude, the belief that rules are sacred and unchangeable and given from above, is characteristic at about the ages of six and seven. The transition to more differentiated ideas about causality that occurs at around seven does not, however, account for the child's increased ability to conform to rules, for Conformity is characterized exactly by lack of logical justification. Of all the changes in child thought occurring at that age, the one that seems most relevant as an intellectual prerequisite for Conformity would seem to be the idea of logical subordination. One cannot accommodate oneself to the rules unless one knows which rules apply. This requirement entails classifying oneself properly, as child or adult, as boy or girl, and so on. Similarly, one must be able to classify situations; company manners are as nonconformist on the playground as playground manners are at mother's party. The single word that seems best to indicate the understanding of the logic of rules is the word *but* when used as a conjunction of discordance. For as Piaget (1928) points out, the existence of exceptions implies the existence of rules. Among Piaget's subjects *but* rarely appears as a conjunction of discordance prior to seven years.

To be a truly Conscientious person requires giving up some of one's childish egocentricity, seeing the world and one's own actions from the view of another. But the modification of the egocentric sentiment can hardly precede the modification of intellectual or cognitive egocentricity. Piaget (1928) has studied the child's understanding of reciprocal relations in terms of the word *brother,* among others. So long as the child uses *brother* as representing membership in a class, most often as synonymous with *boy,* he has not the capacity to understand reciprocal relations. Proper use of *brother* as representing a reciprocal relation appears at about age ten in Piaget's subjects. The crucial test is not whether a child knows how many brothers and sisters he has, but whether he knows how many his brother has, which requires the shift in viewpoint. Some reciprocity in interpersonal relations and some genuine cooperation is compatible with a Conformist stance in adolescence and maturity, that is, with continued emphasis on external rules rather than internal obligations. Since all normal adults understand the word *brother* properly, crucial instances would be retarded persons. Do they reach the Conscientious Stage without learning the meaning of *brother?*

A characteristic of the highest ego levels is coping with contradiction, including contradictory roles and duties. The small child, as Piaget shows repeatedly, has no need to cope with contradictions. Instead, he is quite comfortable with juxta-position or with syncretistic amalgamation of unrelated or con-tradictory ideas. Around the age of seven or eight there is a decline in mental egocentrism and a correspondingly increased sensitivity to contradiction. But it is only at about the age of eleven or twelve that the child becomes capable of formal reasoning and therewith capable of discerning and concerned to reconcile contradictory ideas (Piaget, 1928). Among the charac-teristics of this stage that Piaget discusses are the reversibility of formal reasoning, the ability to perform logical addition and multiplication, and the ability to reason from hypothesis con-trary to one's own beliefs. All of these characteristics are more or less missing from previous stages. A word such as *although,* which is an explicit conjunction of discordance, as compared to the vaguer word *but,* partly typifies the intellectual capacities of this stage. Thus the conditional clause may be taken as one of the intellectual prerequisites of the Autonomous Stage.

The foregoing speculations, although based on the work of Piaget, are contrary to the spirit of some of his own thinking even if not directly contradictory. Piaget repeatedly writes that it is social pressures that drive the child up the scale of intellec-tual achievement, in contrast to the foregoing argument that ego level and social responsiveness are limited by intellectual level. In Piaget's view the child becomes aware of the need to explain his ideas from another's point of view in arguing with his companions. Convincing as Piaget's arguments are, common as well as clinical observation shows many instances of people whose intellectual development is far in advance of their ego development. Most adults who are at the Conformist or Self-Protective Stage have perfectly adequate understanding of recip-rocal relations and conditional clauses. Kohlberg (1969) has also been concerned with intellectual prerequisites for the several stages of moral judgment.

Conclusions

In order to take a fresh look at the relation of ego development to other kinds of development, particularly intellectual develop-ment and the development of drives, this chapter has stressed methodological issues and the formal properties of different kinds of conceptions. Statistical correlations are hardly worth doing, except perhaps as base rates in a particular study, since they are arbitrary in magnitude and uninterpretable due to cross-currents of causation. The logic of conventional construct validation, with its emphasis on the network of correlations as the definition of what a test measures, is too crude in the context of developmental variables. It becomes a form of psychometric know-nothingism. Numerous questions remain to be studied by a theoretically informed empiricism.

Chapter Eight

Issues in Defining Stages and Types

with Augusto Blasi

A sensible psychologist must become exasperated reading the many versions in Chapter Five of what is patently the same developmental sequence or, at worst, a set of closely related sequences. Why not settle the disputed issues by empirical research? If the stages really exist and constitute a developmental sequence, prove it. If there are differences as to the ordering of the stages, resolve them by evidence. Where the authors differ as to the content of the stages or the time of appearance of a given sign, observe children and decide who is right. While some pertinent studies have been carried out, there are numerous difficulties involved in empirical research. We will begin with some specific and concrete difficulties and move to more abstract, philosophical issues. Indeed, the conflict between the intuitive appeal of concrete descriptions and the need for abstraction to achieve universality will be the theme of this chapter.

182

Methodological Difficulties in Defining Stages

First, there is not a one-to-one correspondence between particular behaviors and underlying traits or dispositions. Any observable behavior can be arrived at by many routes, can be undertaken or given in to for a variety of reasons. While there may be exceptions, one cannot assume any behavior to be unequivocally related to ego level. There are no absolutely certain signs of any level, only probabilistic ones. Some signs, of course, have a higher probability of being displayed by a given ego level than others, and such signs are used for measuring devices. This point is the cornerstone of Brunswik's conception of psychology (Tolman and Brunswik, 1935; Hammond, 1966).

Second, no task can be set that is sure to call forth just what one wants to know about ego level. Neither a structured nor an unstructured test guarantees the most revealing signs. If the test is structured, it projects the test constructor's frame of reference rather than that of the subject. But the subject's frame of reference is what reveals his ego level. Given a choice of responses, most subjects prefer the one given spontaneously by those of highest ego levels (Rest, Turiel, and Kohlberg, 1969). Since such responses are rarely produced in a free-response situation but are commonly chosen in a multiple-choice situation, the two types of test are not equivalent. In the case of an unstructured test, however, one cannot control what the person will choose to reveal. The tester can become adept at interpreting minimal signs, but there is always a chance that a subject will conceal all, by choice or by accident, or that he will for some reason respond in a way characteristic of those of a different ego level. A frequent instance is administration of the test under circumstances that arouse hostility in a group of subjects; many of them will give responses under those circumstances that would ordinarily occur only on protocols of subjects of lower ego level.

Third, all kinds of development occur in children simultaneously. A behavior may reflect more than one kind of development; indeed one must assume as the general case that every bit of behavior in some way reflects the whole person. No completely error-free method exists to separate the several kinds of development, either in theory or in behavior. Ego development is bound to be correlated with intellectual and psychosexual development during childhood and adolescence. There may not even be what psychometricians call "local independence"; that is, even for a group all of whom have the same chronological age, there may be a correlation between ego development and intellectual or psychosexual development. If such correlation exists, it will result in a confounding of variance that no amount of data will resolve into its component sources. If we depend entirely on empirical methods, we are at the mercy of such confounded variance. Theory must guide data gathering at the same time that data straighten out theory.

Fourth, there is no error-free method of distinguishing probable signs of ego level from signs of probable correlates. As point 1 asserted, there are only probable signs, not absolutely certain ones. With respect to another developmental variable that correlates with ego development, point 4 only repeats point 3. There are correlates that are not developmental, such as socioeconomic status or perhaps adjustment. There seem to be more persons of low ego level at the lowest socioeconomic levels than at middle or upper levels. Consider, for example, test behaviors such as vulgar and obscene responses. These responses occur more often on protocols of subjects of low ego level than those of middle and high ego level, but the same subjects tend also to be of low economic and social level. How shall we decide whether such responses should be considered signs of low ego level? If the responses occur only because those subjects are members of lower-class groups, regardless of their ego level, then in fact it is erroneous to use those responses as a sign of ego level. That is what is meant by confounding of variance, and it is the general rule rather than an exceptional case. The pragmatist, who wishes only to predict or identify those of low ego level, can ignore point 4, since it only means slightly lower probabilities. To understand the essential characteristics of those levels, however, these considerations are crucial.

Fifth, as a rule, everyone displays behavior at more than one level. Every behavior sample—and a test is a behavior sample—must be assumed to show more than one level. There is no unique psychometric strategy to translate that diversity into a single score. Different pictures of the successive stages may result from different psychometric strategies. However, the different behavior samples chosen for different tests probably matter more than psychometric differences.

Sixth, there are intrinsic difficulties in assigning a behavioral sign to any developmental level just because the underlying continuum is developing. A sign that appears at one level in tentative or embryonic version appears at higher levels in increasingly clear and elaborated versions. When should we say that a child has learned to walk? When he takes his first steps with help or his first steps alone? When he toddles in preference to crawling? Or when he walks confidently and skillfully? There is a similar progression with respect to the more intangible accomplishments of moral and interpersonal life.

Seventh, a behavioral sign may be discriminating in one direction only. In that case, there is an intrinsic ambiguity in assigning it to any particular level, though one can say unambiguously that there are some levels where it is ordinarily absent. Walking is again a useful analogy. Skill in walking is an index of physical development in early childhood, but it is nondiscriminating beyond the age of four or five years. Suppose we have a scale of physical achievements. Where shall we put the item "walks skillfully"? If we put it at the three-year-old level, every fifteen-year-old is at the three-year level with respect to that item. Shall we compromise and put the item at the eight-year level? Then normal three-year-olds score at the eight-year level on that item. This kind of difficulty is inevitable in a scale built on developmental milestones. Binet met the psychometric difficulties by constructing an age scale, but an age scale of ego development would present difficulties that the MA scale does not. At any rate, no one has constructed an age scale of ego development or any related variable. No psychometric device has been proposed to cope with the problem.

Eighth, when we locate a sign at a given level, there are two sets of probabilities with respect to which we may compute our probability of error. The two sets generally dictate that a sign be placed at different levels. The first set is based on just those subjects showing the given sign; the second set is based on the distribution of subjects in the sample. In the first case we ask: Given this sign, what is the probability that the subject comes from a given level? Or, to say it a different way: Given this sign, what is the expected level of the subject who so responds? With respect to a given sample, this question is easily answered, but the answer is heavily dependent on the composition of the sample. Most samples contain only small numbers of cases at extreme levels. Thus, one might find no sign that could be placed at the extreme levels by following this set of probabilities.

One can make a strong case for placing signs only with respect to the alternate set of probabilities: Given a particular ego level, what is the probability of showing this sign? Following this set of probabilities exclusively builds in much error, since extreme cases will be rare in most subsequent samples. Moreover, since extreme cases are rare in any case, and since there is always the likelihood that they will differ from other cases in respects other than ego level, decisions about the characteristic signs of extreme levels will inevitably be based on small numbers. Even if there were not a danger of systematic error due to other associated variables, we would be at the mercy of the idiosyncrasies of a few people. An example of the kind of systematic error is the following. In order to get a sizeable number of adults below the Conformist Stage, one must go to places like prisons, reform schools, and welfare offices where they will constitute perhaps a quarter or a half rather than the small percentage found in other settings. They are, however, those who have in some sense failed or been caught. Are they characteristic of the persons of low ego level who avoid such agencies? The question is almost unanswerable. Thus we come again to the conclusion that, particularly at the extremes, theory is indispensable as a supplement to data.

And ninth, most of the authors of the schemes of Chapter Five are clinicians. For most clinicians the probabilistic considerations of points 1 through 8 are more or less foreign. A clinician relies on his own insights, and he tends to think of every bit of behavior as completely determined by the patient's particular constellation of traits and circumstances. A probabilistic sign of a given ego level he might see as unrelated to ego level, and he would be right by his lights, since it is not an unequivocal sign. Or he might see it as a direct sign, with all negative instances accounted for by special circumstances. A clinician, of course, can avoid facing the negative instances, as a research worker cannot. The research-psychometric frame of reference is radically different from the clinical frame of reference (Loevinger, 1963).

There is a deeper reason why the clinician's intuitive perceptions may be misleading. Every developmental level builds on and transmutes the achievements of the previous one. The unconscious or preconscious components of the attitudes of any level are the corresponding attitudes of earlier levels. Precisely because the clinician has a deeper knowledge of his patient than is available to a research worker or to everyday companions, he may misjudge the level of a person or of a particular sign. Characteristically, the clinician sees through to the level of our common humanity, the level where individual differences are minimal. But the dimension of ego development is just the one where individual differences are maximal. Hence clinical observation fails as a court of last appeal, though with proper precautions it is a valuable line of evidence additional to theory and tests and experimental data.

The Postulate of Just One Source

All of the foregoing points are concerned with a single issue: suppose that all the authors whose stage schemes are presented in Chapter Five are indeed giving their versions of a single developmental sequence. Why do they differ as to details? The assumption is that there is just one source for all the hypothesized developmental sequences and typologies. The considerations that account for differences between one author and another, the above nine points, also account for differences that would appear if a single investigator constructed two types of tests to measure his own variable.

There is, of course, no crucial evidence to support the postulate of one source. The same considerations that account for the discrepancies in the several accounts also show how difficult it would be to disprove it. It cannot be defended as a scientific conclusion, and it would be foolish to adopt it as an unshakeable view of a complex area of psychology. It is, however, a point to start from, a serviceable working assumption.

If the postulate has any substance, there must be some alternative assertions. Most of the authors whose schemes have been presented are presumably to be counted among its opponents, else why would they have given their dimension such names as *moral development, interpersonal integration, cognitive complexity,* and so on? The issue, of course, is not the name, but whether moral character or capacity for interpersonal relations develops separately from ego development as a whole.

One alternative is that there are several more or less independently variable dimensions encompassed in ego development, a hypothesis encouraged by the format of Table 1, which has been circulated for many years in earlier versions (Loevinger, 1966*b*; Loevinger and Wessler, 1970). A number of unpublished attempts at discovering those dimensions by different researchers have been unsuccessful (for example, Lambert, 1972), but that is not conclusive evidence against some new resolution into dimensions.

Kohlberg (1971) and Selman (1971) also have an alternative hypothesis. They believe that there are several related lines of development, cognitive, interpersonal, and moral at a minimum, and that they stand in asymmetrical relation to each other. A given stage of cognitive development is a necessary but not sufficient condition for the corresponding stage of interpersonal development, and the latter stands in the same relation to moral development. Ego development is either an intermediate term or perhaps less tightly organized or less clear in what it refers to than the other terms. It is not clear how many such developmental lines Kohlberg would discern in the expositions of Chapter Five. There is a problem in how to define corresponding stages. What are construed as corresponding stages of two sequences of development will depend on whether one assumes that stages in one sequence correspond to stages in the other sequence as necessary but not sufficient or whether one assumes that they are alternative measures of the same thing or measures of closely related sequences, hence correlated symmetrically. There is thus a circularity between the definition of corresponding stages and the rule of correspondence.

The Problem of Types

A radical alternative to the postulate of one source is to say that stages or types of ego development, moralization, and all the others are chimerical, or a statistical artifact, or an artifact of age differences. According to the Doctrine of Specificity (Chapter Ten), there are only particular behaviors, with no underlying dispositions. Typologies and dimensions of individual differences are the work of psychologists, not of nature. The nine points listed above show how easy it is to assemble evidence in support of this view. Indeed, they are evidence that there is some truth to the specifist view. But the Doctrine of Specificity puts us back to viewing child development as an amorphous sequence of events and contingencies, and the subject matter of this book comes to nothing.

On the other hand, one of the oldest endeavors of psychology is to find a typology to express in some simplified form the diversity of human character. A trait is a single dimension with respect to which everyone can be placed or measured; the differences between people usually can be expressed completely as quantitative differences. Typologies, by contrast, place everyone into one of a limited number of patterns, with each pattern defined in terms of several associated qualitative terms. We shall take the essential element to be not the distinction between quantitative and qualitative or between continuous and discontinuous differences but that between single traits and patterns of traits. Patterning implies that several traits or other characteristics are associated.

Dahlstrom (1972) has discussed typologies and their implications for personality theory. Part of the difficulty with the concept of types, he points out, is that the word *type* is used in a variety of senses, sometimes meaning something like the mode of a distribution and in other cases meaning the extreme values. Currently acceptable statistical methodologies are so thoroughly oriented toward measurable, one-dimensional traits as to run the risk of excluding the variables that may be crucial in defining types.

Type conceptions are built on analogies with powerful conceptions from two neighboring disciplines, the species concept from biology and the syndrome concept from medicine, Dahlstrom continues. A biological species is identified by intra-group fertility and cross-group sterility, but knowing what species an individual belongs to conveys an indefinitely large amount of additional information about size, shape, developmental course, interactions with environment, and so on. A syndrome covers a pattern of patient complaints, physical signs, and clinical findings, such as those of laboratory tests or autopsy. Where there is an identifiable etiology, such as a pathogenic organism or specific chemical imbalance, the equivalence of superficially dissimilar signs can be established. The syndrome concept also carries additional information, such as prognosis and probable response to therapies. An organism can belong to just one species, and that is unchangeable, but a person can have more than one syndrome ("complications"), and a syndrome runs a typical course, ordinarily not being permanent or unchanging.

Personality types can be constructed after either the species or the syndrome model. The classical typologies of Galen, Kretschmer, or Sheldon, postulating an association between psychological and constitutional or somatic traits, are close to the species conception. The nosological typologies are close to the syndrome conception. The Minnesota Multiphasic Personality Inventory (MMPI) was originally based on an implied nosological typology; each of its original pathology scales was so constructed as to maximize the discrimination between persons in one diagnostic category and the general population. To the extent that a person can be described as being of one somatotype, he is less of another; however, having a high score on one of the MMPI pathological scales does not make any less likely a high score on another scale. A nosological typology describes people in terms of an n-space, while a somatotypology locates people on the surface of an n-sphere. The issue is not continuity versus discontinuity. To the extent that conceptions are structural, there would appear to be an implication of discontinuity, since structures do not ordinarily blend into one another. There is, however, no evidence for discontinuity with respect to any personality types. To the extent that any types are measurable, they are a matter of degree. Superficially similar behaviors, such as delinquency, may indicate either a character type of the species sort or a pathological syndrome. The appropriate mode of treatment may differ in those cases; so the distinction that Dahlstrom has drawn is not trivial.

Some of the typologies in Chapter Five are built on the syndrome model, some on the species model. Many of the authors have set out to provide exhaustive and mutually exclusive categories into which everyone must fall, though few are explicit on the point. Fromm, coming up with new typologies from time to time, must be presenting clinical types, that is, syndromes. Shapiro's (1965) "neurotic styles" are excellent examples of syndromes that embody much of what we have included within the sphere of ego development.

Some typologies are "degenerate" in the mathematical sense, including authoritarian versus nonauthoritarian and biophilic versus necrophilic (Fromm, 1973). Degenerate typologies are defined in terms of the two extremes, though there may be many or even predominantly intermediate cases. Formally, degenerate typologies are identical to traits, even if they are conceptualized as complex structures.

We will look now at some philosophical aspects of the problem of types and then turn to the problems posed by postulating subtypes, as some authors have done.

Types and Stages as an Epistemological Problem

That there are difficulties in the use of types and stages is obvious. How should one define a type? What sets of types are most useful in understanding psychological reality? What is the range of objects to which a specific type can be applied? These and similar questions can be answered only slowly and tentatively by scientists. There are questions, however, that are so general and so fundamental as to exceed the domain of any specific scientific discipline, questions that cannot be answered by science but that belong properly to the domain of philosophy. One such question is: Are types or stages statistical artifacts, arbitrary creations of the theoretician, or are they valid representations of the psychological world? Pointing to the nature of a question is not the same as answering it. By doing so, however, the issue is inserted in the right context and the debate is clarified, the assumptions implicit in each solution are uncovered, and the consistencies and inconsistencies that each set of assumptions has with the scientific enterprise can be analyzed.

There is a basic affinity between types and stages, on one hand, and concepts on the other. The objections traditionally raised against the former are essentially the same as those raised against the latter. Firstly, things are concrete and individual while stages and types are abstract. What is concrete is not represented and things that are simply different are considered equivalent. Secondly, reality is continuous, in the sense that all degrees of variation can be observed among objects, and also in the sense that changes from one state to another are imperceptible. Types and stages transform this continuity and flux by imposing on it arbitrary categories and breaks. Types and stages, finally, distort reality in yet another way, namely, by reading into it what cannot be obtained simply through sense perception. Types and stages, to the extent that they are based on structural definitions, are not readily open to the kind of empirical verification that is dear to empiricist and positivist approaches.

These objections are general; they are shared by all sciences. They are also old, as the issues underlying them, the problem of the one and the many and the problem of universals, have been debated by philosophers for at least twenty-five centuries.

The ontological problem of the one and the many, of

whether there is a basic unity underlying the diversity of things, occupied a central position among pre-Socratic thinkers and marked the dawn of Western philosophical inquiry. The solutions ranged from the monism of Parmenides, who argued that only one Being exists, as there is no intermediate between being and nonbeing, to the dialectics of Heraclitus, who believed that no two things are alike and that one thing is not like itself at two different moments. The pre-Socratics were not directly concerned with epistemological issues. Epistemological and ontological problems, however, are intertwined. If the world we live in is Heraclitean in nature, if things are simply different and in continuous flux, our knowledge is either of particulars, that is, nonconceptual, or else it is radically inadequate.

The problem of universals, almost as old as the problem of the one and the many, starts with the observation that many of our words are class words and are predicated in the same way for an indefinite variety of objects. There seems to be a gap between the abstract and the concrete, the universal and the individual, that calls in question the validity of the predication and of our conceptual knowledge. The solutions suggested are many and range from Plato's extreme realism, for which universal ideal objects actually exist, to Hume's extreme nominalism, for which there is nothing universal either in the world or in our mind corresponding to the predication of the same word for different objects. Nevertheless, philosophers generally agree on some points. Firstly, there are no universal things; things are concrete and individual. Secondly, predications and scientific laws are universal and have universal value; there is no science of the individual. Thirdly, such predications are not arbitrary but are based either on the nature of things or on the nature of our minds.

Returning to the validity of types and stages as bases for understanding personality, we recognize that scientific knowledge is by necessity conceptual, that is, abstract and general. That is the only kind of science available to us. Attempts to deny or challenge its validity can only be self-contradictory and arbitrary and ultimately doomed to silence, the fate of radical relativisms and skepticisms. This line of reasoning concerns only concepts directly and, as such, does not justify positively the use of types. It does, however, dispose of the objections to types and stages that are the same as objections to all conceptual thinking.

The radical source of the objections is a sense-based positivist view of knowledge. Greek philosophers, precisely in the context of their debate on the one and the many and on universals, had already realized this much. Parmenides's distinction between truth and opinion, Plato's distinction between knowledge and opinion, and similar ones conveyed the recognition and acceptance of sense impressions, appearances, surface diversities, as well as the belief that reality can only be reached by going beyond this level to the level of forms, structures, and ideas.

Subtypes and Universality

All of the schemes discussed in Chapter Five have descriptions that fit some persons closely, others not so well. Is the solution to our problem there, that some people do not fit the categories of certain authors but are adequately described by a category of another? None of the authors advocate this solution or put limits on the applicability of their conceptions. All probably believe they have found a conception of more or less universal validity; "more or less," because some would be reluctant to claim universality beyond Western culture. Kohlberg (1969, 1971) discusses the problem directly and presents evidence for the cross-cultural validity of his scheme. (Osamu Kusatsu and Harry Lasker [personal communications] have found cross-cultural validity for our scheme in Japan and Curaçao). Our conception of ego development explicitly aims at more or less universal validity, though we would not feel that we had to retract anything if modifications were necessary for radically different cultures. Some people will be more typical of a given stage than others, but there is no room for exceptional cases, for people that cannot in principle be classified anywhere on the scale. A person may withhold information, or we may make mistaken inferences from the information we have, but whether we can discover it or not, there is just one scale position that properly classifies each person. Difficult cases, cases that do not quite fit, have been handled different ways by different authors. Some have broadened the definition of stages; some have postulated subtypes. Most have ignored the problem. Let us look at some ways of handling difficult cases.

The most universally recognized type is the Conformist; one of the most problematic types is the hippie (in previous generations one would have said Beatnik or Bohemian). A study by Haan, Stroud, and Holstein (1973) found hippies to be predominantly in Kohlberg's Stage 3 or in the transition into or out of Stage 3. With respect to ego stages, the hippies tested distinctly higher than the Self-Protective Stage but lower than the Conscientious Stage. Although their responses were not typical of any group previously tested, the place they fitted best in our scheme was at the Conscientious-Conformist transitional level. In this connection it is important that that is still fundamentally a Conformist position. Thus, with regard to these persons whose life-style is nonconformity, we arrive at the paradoxical conclusion that they are classed as Conformist by the ego development scheme and as Conventional by Kohlberg's scheme. Many people have noted that hippies conform to their own sometimes rigid code of anticonformity. That observation, however, does not dispel the paradox unless we are willing to have words lose their meanings. Nonconformity or anticonformity is not the same as conformity or conventionality, even when it becomes a rigid code, at least in terms of concrete, observable behaviors ordinarily termed *conformist*. At some abstract level these behaviors may merge, but that becomes a different, more abstract meaning of the word *conformity*.

That is precisely the point: to turn the dimension into one on which everyone, without exception, can be assigned just one characteristic level requires that the points on the dimension be given an abstract, not specific, meaning. To make the solution to the hippie-conformist paradox concrete, one could define the Conformist Stage as including all those for whom conformity-nonconformity-anticonformity is the central issue of life. Once we make that broad a definition, a kind of metaconformity is defined. The typical, conventional person is only one of the possible types or realizations of the stage.

An alternative way to meet the problem of difficult cases is to break down each stage or type into substages or subtypes. Kohlberg has added detail to his original six stages in several ways, both by assigning mixed or intermediate scores, presumably to persons in transition, and by postulating substages. Substages represent a specification of the continuum that has no necessary relation to variability within the protocol or to transition. According to Kohlberg, persons at each stage can be divided into those at substage A, who are oriented in terms of rules or utilitarian consequences, and substage B, who are oriented in terms of fairness or justice. The latter group includes those with a role-taking orientation or an orientation in terms of an ideal self. Substage B is more complex, more internal, and more universalized than substage A. Everyone at B has gone through A but not vice versa; one may go from substage A either to substage B or to substage A of the next stage.

On Perry's scale of intellectual and ethical development, going from basic duality through relativity to commitment, some of the nine positions are defined in terms of alternative subtypes. For example, in Position 5 the alternatives are Relativism Correlate, Relativism Competing, and Relativism Diffuse. One might reasonably ask of Perry that he carry the abstraction a bit further and describe what those three possibilities have in common that characterizes them as constituting the same position. But Perry goes in the other direction, recognizing the problem of difficult cases more directly than any other investigator. To his nine positions he adds the three possibilities of temporizing, escape, and retreat (regression). While presumably every student can be assigned to some position on the original scale, the latter three categories apply only to certain students and carry negative connotations. Thus what Perry has done is to sketch a species-type concept, including alternative subtypes for some of the positions, and then superimpose a set of three syndrome-types.

The major example of a research program built around ego subtypes is that of Warren, Palmer, and their associates. Warren

(1976) points out that the principle on which I-level is based is the person's way of *perceiving* the world, whereas the principle on which subtypes within I-level are based is the individual's typical mode of *response* to his view of the world. The subtypes were derived not from theory but from observation of frequent patterns among delinquents. The two types among I-2 delinquents (corresponding to our Impulsive Stage) are the Asocial Aggressive type and the Asocial Passive type. The former reacts to frustration with demands and hostility, the latter with whining, complaints, and withdrawal. The three types they discern among their I-3 delinquents (corresponding to our Self-Protective and early Conformist stages) are the Immature Conformist, the Cultural Conformist and the Manipulator. The Immature Conformist reacts with compliance to whoever has power. The Cultural Conformist responds similarly to the delinquent peer group. The Manipulator tries to undermine authorities or to usurp power. The four types they discern among their I-4 delinquents (who would probably be predominantly Conscientious-Conformists in our scheme) are the Neurotic Acting-Out type, the Neurotic Anxious type, the Situational Emotional Reaction type, and the Cultural Identifier. The two neurotic subtypes are reacting to underlying guilt. The Situational Emotional type is responding to a personal or family crisis, whereas the Cultural Identifier is identifying himself with a deviant value system. Although Warren's conception of interpersonal maturity has a logical coherence and universal applicability, the subtypes are ad hoc and specific to the field of delinquency. The abstract quality of the original conception is lost in the subtypes, for there are no clues given as to how those of one level connect with those of the next. For example, are there no neurotics at the I-2 and I-3 levels?

Kohlberg's substages are intradimensional and asymmetrical. Perry's subtypes are intradimensional and symmetrical, and he also has symptomlike subtypes. Warren's subtypes are extradimensional and symmetrical. They seem to be intended as exhaustive of the delinquents at each level, but we are not told what relation, if any, they have to the types of normal people at corresponding stages. Kohlberg and Perry apparently arrived at their substages and subtypes by longitudinal study of small samples. Warren and Palmer have studied masses of cases, but the definition of subtypes has not changed while data have accumulated, and they do not describe the original data bases for the subtypes.

Using the method of Kohlberg and Perry one may fashion neat theories that fit the small number of cases at hand but that are of no more value than the original broadly defined scale for people in general. Kohlberg, moreover, depends heavily on his own ability to reason out the inner logic of each position. Warren (1969) and Palmer (1971, 1974) are empiricists, collecting data of the form: for this subtype under this experimental condition, results are more favorable than for a matched control group when measured by the criterion of subsequent arrests, but not when measured by the criterion of subsequent conviction. The hazard of Kohlberg's method is that it may become a mantle of papal infallibility that facts do not easily penetrate. The hazard of the Warren-Palmer method is that a stupefying mass of facts may be accumulated that do not always lend themselves to scientific generalization. Beyond those methodological problems is the question to what extent substages or subtypes help solve the problem of difficult cases.

How were the conceptions of Chapter Five discovered? Probably every author began by noting a few instances in which people resembled each other in whole patterns of seemingly diverse traits. Different authors probably began with somewhat different coincidences of that form. Gradually each noticed several alternative patterns and that the patterns were both logically and empirically mutually exclusive. Then he observed the power and wide applicability of the conception to which his thinking was moving. If he was responsive to data or to criticism, however, he must have come across cases that did not easily fit his types. If he was still operating with a syndrome model, that problem did not bother him. If he had already turned to a species model, he had the alternative of broadening definitions of types or stages, adding new ones, or defining subtypes or substages. We are not arguing against using feedback from data to revise the dimension. On the contrary, in the next chapter we will present our own program for doing so. The question being raised is to what extent substages or subtypes solve the methodological problems posed by stage and type conceptions.

The question of the reality of subtypes is exactly the same as the question of the reality of types. There will always be difficult cases, no matter how detailed the typology. Substages such as those of Kohlberg are addressed to the problem of the discontinuity of stages and amount to a detailed exposition of the dimension. Inevitably, they heighten the problem Piaget has termed *décalage*, the tendency for a person to be at different stages with respect to different issues or even at different moments. Intradimensional subtypes such as those of Perry open up many problems, such as the relation of subtypes of one stage to those of the next, that would require large numbers of cases to answer. Extradimensional subtypes such as those of Warren and Palmer address the fact that ego development does not comprise every important trait, but the fact is better approached by adding new dimensions defined independently of the original one. Thus substages and subtypes are either stopgaps or diversionary.

The complexity and diversity that have driven some of the most active research groups to resort to substages and subtypes are the same complexity and diversity that gave rise to the many conceptions of Chapter Five. Only an abstraction holds together the stages, types, and subtypes. Such abstractions are the stuff of science.

Special Cases

There are two kinds of special cases often brought up in discussions of the validity of our conception, persons with special gifts or training and persons who are clinical cases. The question is raised with respect to both whether there will be a disparity between the person's level of functioning in one area, that of his speciality or his pathology, and his functioning in all other areas. If so, does the conception of ego structure break down or need to be modified at least for those cases? By way of answer, we must remember that ego structure is not predictive of specific, concrete behaviors. It is a structure, an abstraction. At the same time, if it has no connections with behavior, it would not hold our interest for long.

Particularly in cases of people who have serious emotional or psychiatric problems there may be gross and apparent discrepancies between level of functioning in some areas and that in others. In such cases, however, only by chance would the lines of cleavage correspond with the columns of Table 1. What is more likely than different levels with respect to impulse control, interpersonal relations, and conscious preoccupations is different levels in different specific circumstances, such as sex life versus work, or relations with men versus relations with women, or relations with bosses and relations with employees, or even more specific and idiosyncratic patterns. Regression under stress probably takes place with respect to all facets defined in Table 1. Classifying a person at a given stage means, approximately, that that is the highest level at which he is capable of functioning consistently. The capability may be more a potentiality than an actuality in some cases (see the discussion of Isaacs, Chapter Five), but normally the correspondence should be reasonably close. Thus the conception of ego structure does not need to be modified to accommodate the case of lower functioning in an area of vulnerability, nor does it contradict the possibility of peremptory ideation or impulsive action at any stage.

What of gifted persons? Would a moral philosopher not function higher on Kohlberg's test than he functions in other areas of life? Might not a poet test higher on the sentence completion test, where the highest responses are often poetic, than he functions in his family relations? Might not an untutored but warm and intuitive woman function higher in her actual relations with others than in her responses on a paper-and-pencil test? There are no research results bearing on these issues, but suppose we acknowledge these possibilities in every case. Has anything vital been given up? We have admitted no more than that tests of ego or moral development are not error-free, that in some particular kinds of cases the error may be larger than in the average case.

But those objections are, after all, only guesses. Those who make them can be assumed to be reporting correctly that persons behave differently in areas of special vulnerability or expertise than in other areas of life, but that is obvious. What they do not know definitely, however, is that those differences correspond to different measurable ego levels. Perhaps their informal impressions are more easily deceived than standardized tests are.

Even if the differences apparently take the form of different ego levels, there is still the possibility that the behavior at issue, whether regressed and symptomatic or expert performance, may bear in some way the telltale mark of the person's most characteristic level. In that case, correct inference of the level may depend on the perspicacity of the test scorer.

Conclusions

We have speculated that the authors of schemes summarized in Chapter Five began with observations guided by the syndrome model and, as they became convinced of the universality of the conception, changed toward something like a species model. Few of them were explicit in their thinking on the point; hence confusion of models has resulted. Moreover, the specific details that make a portrait come alive reduce its universality. There is always the temptation to resort to subtypes in order to retain the vitality of concrete detail without sacrificing breadth of coverage. Substages increase the décalage, while diverting attention from the underlying continuum, and they only postpone momentarily without overcoming the problem of difficult cases. The question of the reality of subtypes or substages is not different from the reality of the original types.

We are operating on the postulate that most of the developmental and typological variability described springs from a single source imperfectly captured by any of the schemes. Remedying the deficiencies of the various schemes and reconciling their differences are the same thing. Obstacles abound. Some obstacles may be looked at, in Brunswik's fashion, as matters of the inherently probabilistic connection between dispositions and actions. Some may be looked at epistemologically as manifestations of the necessarily imperfect fit between abstractions and concrete reality, between concepts and things.

Without conceptions and abstractions science is a poor thing, or nothing. The differences between our conception of ego development and the other schemes reviewed are not negligible, but they are all negotiable. What is distinctive for our approach and not negotiable is our conception of the mission and the method of science. That will become clearer in the next chapter as we sketch some of our studies, which are directed towards constructing a measure of ego development and at the same time towards refining the conception.

Some individuals, we are admitting, are well described by one author, others by another. Those differences account for the multiplicity of descriptions, but they do not justify a multiplicity of conceptions. Perhaps the final question is Why? Why do people form character structure at all? Not many children aspire to chairs of moral philosophy, but all must find their way in a difficult and confusing world. Character structure is formed for that purpose and in that process. A person's character may be inchoate or unformed, his character structure may fluctuate, his actions at times will be out of character, but there can only be one character structure per person. The navigator, so to speak, (or the compass or the map) is the ego, nothing less. Structure is its primary task. In that sense, all the conceptions, in so far as they are structural, must be conceptions of ego development. There may be indefinitely many mental substructures, some (such as conceptions of fairness and justice) intimately related to ego structure, others (such as the structure of rational numbers) hardly at all. Those substructures may be more tightly coherent than the ego structure in a particular person or even in people in general. But if we are talking about character structure, we are talking about ego structure.

Chapter Nine

Issues and Strategies of Measurement

The psychometric approach to differential psychology has cast a long shadow over developmental psychology. Until the Piagetian revolution, developmental psychologists were largely content to evaluate children in terms of the proportion of adult status achieved. The prevailing ideology of differential psychology for many years was epitomized in a slogan originating with Thorndike, that "if a thing exists, it exists in some amount; and if it exists in some amount, it can be measured" (1914, p. 141). An unfortunate consequence of this view has been the proliferation of trait names and tests to a number beyond the compass of any reasonably parsimonious view of human nature. Perhaps nobody said that anything that could be named had to exist in a meaningful sense, but neither was there a clear defense against such an assumption. The factorial problem became the central problem of differential psychology, absorbing its best energies and talents. Factor analysis became a one-way street, however, leading into technical concerns, producing a literature virtually unintelligible to most psychologists, and returning little substance to psychology.

A radically developmental view is partly antagonistic to the classical psychometric view. Stated in the form of a counter-slogan, it is that anything existing in human nature must have developed, and that development can be traced. This slogan implies that the logical polarities on which trait theory and trait measurement have traditionally been based only rarely or superficially correspond to the developmental trace. Moreover, the developmental course has an interest and importance aside from measurement. To measure how far persons have proceeded in some developmental sequence, we must first determine the course of development. Presumably the arbitrary element of differential psychology, that anything nameable is measurable, will be removed by this approach, not by statistical analyses but by grounding in the realities of development. A radically developmental approach to differential psychology could conceivably winnow the number of measurable dimensions to the point where the factorial problem, insoluble as it presently appears to be, will cease to be the central focus of the field of individual differences.

A new problem arises, however. If we abandon logical polarities in favor of tracing developmental sequences, how do we get back to measurement in any nonarbitrary meaning of the term? That is the topic of this chapter. First we will discuss some fundamental psychometric issues that ought to be discussed in relation to every proposed psychological measure but seldom are. These issues turn out to connect with substantive issues in the conception of ego development. Next we will be concerned with current attempts to measure ego level and related dimensions that pose the same psychometric problems. In that section the validity of the basic construct is assumed and concern is with the tactics of measurement. The discussion will be hampered somewhat, since most of the work is fragmentary and unpublished.

Fundamental Psychometric Issues

If one is content to say that any way of assigning numbers to people or their effects can be called *psychological measurement,* the problems of psychometric strategy can be solved in any arbitrary way, but then there is no answer to those who choose a different mode of measurement. The alternative view I take is that for measurement in a strict sense, no step in the process of assigning numbers to people or their effects can be arbitrary. Removal of arbitrary elements is not something that can be accomplished once for all but requires constant renewal of insight. The issues with which we are concerned can be stated as a series of questions. Granted the diversity of people and their effects, is there a discernible pattern or syndrome corresponding to the proposed variable? Granted that the proposed syndrome is discernible, is it more salient than alternative ways of construing the behaviors at issue? Are the steps, stages, or points along the dimension correctly or optimally ordered? Is the dimension continuous or discontinuous? Are the objectively available signs monotonically related to the dimension?

Syndrome. The convergence shown in Chapter Five among descriptions by authors starting with primary interest in a variety of problems signals a syndrome or rather a series of syndromes corresponding to the various stages or types. Measurement should help define and clarify the syndromes.

Salience. The fundamental variables in any discipline are those in terms of which functional relations and laws can be most simply stated. Conventional evaluation of tests in terms of their reliability and validity is trivial beside such claims; many more variables can be measured reliably and validly than can be fundamental or salient. To write a book or monograph or to devote a program of research to a dimension of individual differences implies a belief in its salience and importance. This book stakes out a claim for the salience of ego development. No one who recognizes ego as construct disputes the salience of the ego as part of the person, but ego development as here defined is explicitly not a chronicle of the development of all ego functions. Hence claims for the salience of ego development cannot rest simply on the importance of the ego. What establishes the salience of a variable is a survey of all evidence in some broadly defined field. Just because nothing can be excluded, nothing can be crucial. Evidence as yet fragmentary suggests that ego level increases monotonically with age at least through early years of maturity, with education, with intelligence, and possibly with social level. This is one kind of evidence having relevance to its claim as a fundamental variable.

Order. The proposed scale of ego development is an ordinal scale. The question of whether there might be found a corresponding interval scale is hardly meaningful, since no operations correspond to adding or subtracting ego levels. Among those investigators who believe that there are stages and that they constitute an ordinal scale and who agree approximately on the descriptions of the stages, there are still disagreements on their order. Sullivan, Grant, and Grant divide their I-3 stage into Cons and Conformists. Their I-3 Cons closely resemble either the entirety or a substantial fraction of the Expedient Stage of Peck, the Delta Stage of Isaacs, and the Self-Protective Stage of Table 1. In each of the last three cases the Conformist Stage is the next higher one. On the other hand, Peck and Havighurst are reluctant to consider the Irrational-Conscientious Stage as higher than the Conforming Stage. The description of the Irrational-Conscientious group tallies closely with that of the I-4 group of Sullivan, Grant, and Grant, hence is definitely higher than Conformity for the latter investigators. These persons most closely match the Conscientious-Conformist transition in our scheme, probably including also some persons at our Conscientious Stage.

The order shown in Table 1 has been derived both by reasoning from theory and by empirical data. For example, in the sentence completion test the typical Conformist Stage protocol will not resemble that of the Autonomous subject as much as the typical Conscientious Stage protocol will. Similarly, the typical Self-Protective Stage protocol will resemble that of the Impulsive subject more than will the Conformist Stage protocol.

The most convincing determination of order comes from developmental studies, either longitudinal psychometric ones or experimental ones. Kohlberg (1969) claims sanction for his ordering from several longitudinal and experimental studies whose data have not yet been fully published, but Holstein (1973) has raised questions on the basis of her own longitudinal study. Longitudinal studies are hampered by a variety of psychometric difficulties, including unreliability of measures and effects of retesting per se (Redmore and Waldman, 1975). Evidently there are differences of opinion on the order of stages, and the differences are neither trivial nor easily resolved.

Continuity. Granted that there are stages, and that the order of stages is known, is the transition from one stage to the next saltatory or continuous? Because each stage embodies its own "cognitive map" of the universe, to use E. C. Tolman's term, one could make out a case for the necessity to exchange one for another all at once. At present no measuring instrument is sufficiently refined to decide whether development proceeds by jumps or by continuous gradations. A process that according to one way of measuring reveals discontinuity can, on further analysis, be shown to proceed by continuous steps. Further analysis may reveal the apparent continuity as a summation of a series of discontinuous changes (Tanner and Inhelder, 1960). Speaking of his work with Inhelder on cognitive stages, Piaget said, "On the one hand we find stages which characterize a certain proportion of individuals at any given age. On the other hand we always find sub- or intermediary stages, but as soon as we try to pin these intermediary stages down we enter a sort of cloud-dust of sub-intermediaries because of their instability. Other organizational steps are relatively more stable and it is these that one can consequently consider as 'stages' " (Tanner and Inhelder, 1960, p. 122). Lack of agreement on substages and subtypes (Chapter Eight) confirms Piaget's point.

When one puts together the various schemes of Chapter Five, it appears that what for one scheme is a stage is for another a transition between recognizable stages. Thus, taken all together the differences among the conceptions may argue for continuity, though there are other possible explanations of the differences in terms of special characteristics of populations studied or biases of the investigators.

Monotonicity. Personality traits must be assumed to have

both polar and milestone manifestations. What is a polar aspect or variable in respect to one way of construing the personality domain is a milestone if different variables are seen as the fundamental or organizing constructs. Conformity, a favorite variable for research, is curvilinear with respect to ego development, that is, a milestone. Such variables as spontaneity (Peck and Havighurst, 1960, p. 88) and impulse expression (Sanford, Webster, and Freedman, 1957) follow a complementary curve, being high at the low and high ends of the ego scale and low among those whose conformity is high.

The distinction between milestone sequence and polar variable is essential to our conception of ego development and a link with the measuring process. Since ego development has both polar and milestone aspects, test technology, to be even minimally adequate, must distinguish between such aspects and use appropriate techniques. That psychology should choose polar variables as its major ones hardly needs to be argued. I contend that while ego development is by definition a polar variable, its most easily observed manifestations are milestones. Just those milestones are construed as polar variables and made into major concepts by the predominant trend in personality research. Unfortunately there is no scheme, formula, or computer to take the place of a psychologist in determining what the major variables are and what their subsidiary manifestations are. There is a popular school of psychometric thought that advocates factorial methods to separate and define the major variables. But factor analysis is of no avail in this instance, since it can only treat all variables like polar variables. Thus if the items or subtests put into a factorial pool include many milestones rather than polar functions of ego development, ego development cannot emerge as a factor. Indeed, one cannot expect to get sensible or clearly interpretable results (Loevinger, 1965).

Although no statistical method can determine what are the milestones and what are the polar variables, probably there are or could be methods to test hypotheses about these matters, once a psychologist has made clear proposals and gathered appropriate data. The harder we look for manifestations of ego level observable at a minimal inferential level and hence suitable for test items, whether of self-report or rating of others, the more we are driven towards milestones rather than polar aspects. The more we try to search out or construct indices of ego level that are polar variables, the more we will find ourselves with inferred rather than observable variables. The bedrock of psychometrics is observation, whether observation of oneself or others. Hence psychometric techniques appropriate to handling milestone sequences are required.

Assessment Techniques

Two central problems of psychological measurement are those of the quantification strategy and the scoring algorithm. The quantification strategy is the method for converting qualitative observations into quantitative differences. Since no single observation is reliable as a means of classifying anything so undependable as people, and since a set of observations is bound to contain variability, there must be some rule for reducing a set of quantitative differences to a single score, rating, or category; that is the scoring algorithm.

In addition to the substantive differences among the several investigators of ego level and related conceptions, there are formal differences in their constructs. Those formal differences map into different scoring algorithms. One concept type has ego level akin to a latent ability; consistent with that concept type, the scoring algorithm is the highest scored sign. The idea is that to reach a given ego level, one must have passed through all lower levels. Those lower levels may be exhibited or even predominant in behavior, including fantasy as behavior, but behavior cannot reflect levels not yet reached. Isaacs's work exemplifies this viewpoint.

A second concept type is the profile of dispositions. In this view, which is not so starkly hierarchical in its implications for ego growth as the previous one, each ego type exemplifies a set of dispositions or motivations more or less present in all people. What characterizes each person is his profile of scores, reflecting each of the separate levels. Maslow's conception of kinds of motivation lends itself to this format, and Peck and Havighurst's approach to measurement follows this model.

The third concept type sees ego level in terms of the core

functioning of a structured or organized whole. Many authors appear to conceive ego level this way, Sullivan, Grant, and Grant specifically using the term *core function*. This conception is bolstered by the psychoanalytic conception of the ego as an organization (which I share), by structural conceptions of Merleau-Ponty, Sullivan, and others, and by the Piagetian idea of equilibration. Some dispersion of observable signs above and below the level of core functioning is consistent with this conception. Unfortunately, the concept of core function does not translate into a unique scoring algorithm. The modal level of functioning is one possible form; it is espoused by Kohlberg.

In looking at ways of measuring ego level and related variables, we orient our discussion about the solutions to the problems of the type of concept, the quantification strategy, and the scoring algorithm. I shall discuss briefly a number of measures used by other investigators and at greater length two lines of research on measurement pursued by my colleagues and me. The greater emphasis on our work is partly because we have been more explicit about psychometric issues than others have and partly because by now the reader may wonder what train of thought led to so long a book. The order is arbitrary, as each investigator or group seems to have worked out its assessment techniques uninfluenced by the others, with the exception of the influence of the Grant-Warren group on ours.

Isaacs: Rating TATs for Relatability. Isaacs (1956) sees his construct of interpersonal relatability as a latent ability, a capacity for a given degree of complexity of interpersonal relations. That level may not be expressed in current functioning because of lack of opportunity, emotional blocks, or other reasons. He assumes that before the capacity can appear in behavior it must appear in fantasy; hence he uses the TAT as an instrument appropriate to draw out fantasies concerning interpersonal relations. The story for each TAT card is assigned one rating, corresponding to the highest level of relatability displayed in it. The person is then assigned the highest level assigned to any of his stories. The reasoning is that a person does not understand a level of interpersonal interaction above his own, hence cannot display at any time a higher level than characterizes his own relatability. A person cannot receive too high a rating except as a result of rating error, but he can receive too low a rating by not displaying his highest level on a given occasion.

Isaacs's method leads to some difficulties. Changing the score of a single story can change the total protocol rating; yet psychologists have long known that the problem of unreliability, both of subject variability and rater error, is best met by increasing the number of observations on which a person's score is based. In practice Isaacs has met this problem by using the second highest score rather than the highest to determine the total protocol rating. Ordinarily the two highest scores will be the same. Another difficulty is that maximum rating is biased with respect to length, that is, whatever rating a person has after a five-picture TAT, his rating after five more pictures must be at least as high and may be higher. In the clinic an examiner may be tempted to add more pictures for patients who he feels have not displayed their full potential but to stop with a short test for less appealing patients.

The conception of relatability is a broad one, referring to many facets of ego functioning, but the scoring scheme relies on a single facet, the complexity of interpersonal relations described. A story concerned with achievement as measured by an internalized standard of excellence would, if no other persons happen to be mentioned, arbitrarily rate lower than one in which success was indicated by approval of other people, though by our scheme of ego development the former would be a Conscientious level response, the latter a Conformist level response. Every test, or at least every one that endures, must have a "saving circularity." The saving circularity of Isaacs's test is here—using the highest rating as the scoring algorithm requires that only the most diagnostic and unequivocal indicators be rated, regardless of how many aspects of personality are implicated in the conception. Presumably Isaacs has found that level of complexity of interpersonal relations is a valid and reliable indicator, though he has not provided evidence for such an assertion. Systematic downgrading of stories of the type indicated, ones that happen not to mention more than one person, even though other aspects of the response may indicate high ego level, will not affect the total protocol rating so long as a single story appears with a high level of relatability (or two stories, if the highest-rating algorithm is modified to be second highest rating). Isaacs's scoring manual has not been published. A mimeographed one that was circulated among some colleagues was an exemplar manual, giving illustrations of ratings at various levels. Lack of an adequate scoring manual undoubtedly has limited the value of Isaacs's contribution, but it is the clearest example of the latent-ability concept type.

Peck and Havighurst: The Motivational Profile. Peck and Havighurst organized their study (1960) around five character types; each represents a mode of adaptation, a motivational pattern, and a stage in psychosocial development, in short, an "ideal type." At the same time, each pattern is a component in the character of every person. While, like most investigators other than Isaacs, they assume that the dominant pattern is what best characterizes the person, and they use it in all correlations with other variables, their fundamental quantification strategy is based on the profile of motives. They studied normal adolescents, using the TAT, sentence completion tests, interviews, and sociometric and other instruments and ratings, but ratings based on single instruments were not made. Their reported results are based mainly on global evaluations made by members of their staff after examining all relevant materials. Differences among staff members were compromised in order to arrive at a single set of ratings for each case.

The basic quantification strategy of their study is to treat each character type as a polar variable; each rater then estimates, on a ten-point scale, how much of that motivational pattern the subject has. In effect, the rater takes all data into account and then constructs the individual's profile of motivational patterns (essentially, ego levels) directly on the basis of his intuitive weighting of different tests, observations, interviews, and so on. That equivocal data result from treating a milestone sequence as a set of polar variables is apparent in their own instructions to raters. While a high rating on Expediency is unequivocal, they describe a subject who is rated low on Expediency as "Tendency either to gratify impulse immediately without considering ultimate effect on self or others, or to behave in conformity with the moral code . . . because of internalized principles or concern with the welfare of others as well as self" (Peck and Havighurst, 1960, p. 231). In other words, low on this variable can mean either very low or very high in moral level. Differences among the staff raters were compromised in case conference. The result of this step is that each subject has five ratings, representing how much of each of the motivational patterns he is judged to display in his behavior or his potential behavior.

The problem of the scoring algorithm is to reduce those five ratings to a single score or rating. Their method of doing so involved translating the set of five scores per person back into a single score that places the person on an eight-point scale based on his modal rating, if there is one, or where there are two or more approximately equal high scores, on a compromise, not necessarily a numerical averaging. Five of the eight points are the same five character types with which the study began, in the original order; the remaining three points are interpolated between them. Thus they began with an a priori developmental scale, turned each scale point into a polar variable, and then summarized the set of polar scores by returning to a slightly expanded version of the original scale.

This procedure raises the question whether their raters generate a profile, as Peck and Havighurst intend, or a distribution. To have a true profile, the several ratings must be experimentally independent. In a true distribution, the number of ratings is fixed, so that the more that fall at one level, the fewer can fall at another. The latter case applies to the thirty-six item sentence completion test to be described; there are always thirty-six item ratings distributed among the possible rating levels. One way that has been used to achieve a true profile is to have subjects answer a separate set of items to evaluate how much each level is characteristic of them. In their study there is only one set of observations, however complex and diverse they may be. All of the data are taken into account in estimating each motivational level for each subject. In principle, every observation has a possibility for error; when two ratings or scores are based on the same observations, their errors are correlated, and it becomes logically impossible to assert any relation between the variables. To assert that this study produced motivational profiles is to assert that one knows something about the relations between the strength of one motivational level as compared to another, and that claim is not legitimate with these data. While the data do not constitute a true profile, they also do not constitute a true distribution. If the raters had been constrained to make the sum total of all ratings for a subject a constant, the ratings would have constituted a kind of distribution, intuitively arrived at, to be sure. The sum of all ratings for one subject was seventeen, for another, twenty-six. This discrepancy raises the question: Do some people have more motivation altogether, irrespective of kind, than others?

The use of the profile encodes an important fact, that the behavior of all older children and adults displays variability in ego level. There is no evidence in this or other studies where a profile is used that the profile contains valid information other than some measure of central tendency. No one has correlated the profile (or distribution or variability) as measured by one technique with that measured by another. Peck and Havighurst themselves used the profile only as a means to ascertain the dominant character type, which they used in all correlations with other variables.

Warren, Grant, Palmer, and Others: Estimating the Ego Level of Delinquents. The article of Sullivan, Grant, and Grant (1957), one of the first and clearest expositions of a developmental typology (Chapter Five), has been the origin for many years' work in the field of delinquency, involving many investigators (Warren, 1969, 1976; Palmer, 1974). At least four different kinds of measuring instruments have been used, including interviews, sentence completion tests, objective (self-report) tests, and behavioral rating scales.

The basic quantification strategy of the interview is to elicit by open-ended questions the frame of reference within which the person perceives and integrates interpersonal relationships. Anything in the interview can contribute to the assessment, depending on the perspicacity of the rater in drawing inferences from it. The rater, who may be the interviewer or another person working from a tape recording, takes account of the variability subjectively and integrates a picture of how the person functions. The concept type is the core function; the rater assigns a single I-level rating to the interview and hence to the subject. Since only one rating is assigned, there is no scoring algorithm.

In using the sentence completion test, they apparently assign an I-level rating only to the total protocol. The only scoring manual available (Jesness and Wedge, 1970) describes characteristic responses to each stem for persons of each type. They do not appear to have codified rules for going from the item responses to a total protocol rating. Thus they have a reverse manual. It lists the responses to be expected if the rater already knows the ego type. But the rater's task is the reverse, to estimate the ego type from the responses. A reverse manual assists the rater in an intuitive rating of the total protocol, but it is not adaptable to psychometric study.

At one time Eric Gunderson, Warren, and others constructed separate objective tests, where the subject needed only to check his response, for assessing the strength of each I-level for each subject. The items were of the single-stimulus type. In constructing different tests for each level, the researchers perforce treated each level as a polar variable. Each individual's score on a particular level is the number of items scored plus on the corresponding test. In this format, with different items and different responses, the score for each level is experimentally independent of the others, and the set of scores can be interpreted as a profile of I-level. However, their express commitment is to a core-functioning concept type rather than to a profile concept type. Probably the peak score was interpreted as the subject's characteristic level, but that is not clear. The fundamental difficulties are two. Can any objective tests serve in place of free-response tests to ascertain the subject's frame of reference? And does it not result in a fundamentally meaningless measure to turn a stage in a developmental sequence into a polar variable? The problem is the same one we met in Peck and

Havighurst's ratings: while a high score may be meaningful, low scores are ambiguous, representing either higher or lower ego stages. Throw in a bit of measurement error, and you have a bowl of porridge. Jesness, as we shall see, has refined this method without changing the logical difficulties.

Another assessment instrument they devised was behavioral rating scales for use by persons acquainted with their subjects but not necessarily with their conception. The scales present descriptions of observable or easily inferrable behavior presumably characteristic of the several levels. There is no clear account of the scoring algorithm, but again some modal or peak score can be assumed. Behavior rating scales have an immediate appeal for most psychologists, who are comfortable talking about observable behaviors and are suspicious of abstract conceptions such as ego development. Even those interested in ego development demand verification of the construct and of such thought-sample instruments as sentence completions and TAT in terms of directly observable behaviors. Behavior rating scales are obvious devices for this purpose. Jesness has adapted that method also. There are three difficulties, in part apparent from theoretical considerations (but brought home to my colleagues and me by an attempt to adapt this instrument to a study of graduate students in social work). The first difficulty is that what the raters perceive is to an unknown degree dictated by their own ego level rather than that of the person being rated. The second difficulty is that there is no one-to-one correspondence between any behavior and any ego level, with the possible exception of impulsivity. Even probabilistic connections between particular behaviors and other ego levels are hard to specify. The third difficulty is the tendency of raters to use socially desirable terms in describing almost anyone of whom they approve generally.

Jesness: Actuarial Classification. Jesness (1974; Jesness and Wedge, 1970) has set about to codify and improve classification of delinquent youths into Warren's nine subtypes (see Chapter Eight), using the Jesness Inventory, which is a self-report checklist, and two forms of the Jesness Behavior Checklist, the self-appraisal and the observer forms. Although he worked on scoring manuals for the interview and the sentence completion test (Jesness and Wedge, 1970), both instruments were dropped as being too time-consuming. The Jesness Inventory has 155 true-false items, which yield scores on 10 personality characteristics, the scales having been derived by item or cluster analysis. (Items are keyed in more than one scale.) In addition, keys were derived empirically for each Warren subtype. Thus Jesness is committed to a profile concept type. Beginning with almost 2,000 wards of the courts who had already been classified as to subtype, a multiple discriminant analysis was performed for I-level and subtype. The outcome of that analysis was used to set up a computer program that is used as follows. The boy is given the Jesness Inventory and the self-appraisal form of the Jesness Behavior Checklist. His responses are fed into the computer, which calculates his scores on the several scoring keys, and from the latter calculates his relative distance from the centroids of the three I-levels and of the subtypes within each I-level. In using the output, one first assigns I-level according to whichever probability is highest, then one selects the subtype with the highest probability within that I-level. Additional large samples have been used to refine the probabilities.

One validational study was as follows. The behavior of a group of boys was rated on the observer form of the Jesness Behavior Checklist, by counselors, social workers, or teachers. This rating was used as a measure of observed behavior. The expected behavior was obtained by having seven I-level experts sort the eighty Behavior Checklist items according to the expected frequency of occurrence for each of the nine subtypes, using a Q-sort technique. For seven of the subtypes, substantial validity coefficients were obtained, ranging from .54 to .80. However, for the Immature Conformist and the Neurotic Acting-out subtypes, validity coefficients were about zero. The difficulty is that there seems to be no way of using these data to change or improve the method. Discriminations with no validity and those with high validity seem to be treated the same in subsequent work. Thus this extremely actuarial approach, like an extremely a priori approach, leaves no room for modification of the conception or theory by means of the data. For Jesness's purposes, which are more practical than scientific, that may be satisfactory, but from the point of view of theory, the result is unsatisfactory.

Kohlberg: Modal Moral Reasoning. Kohlberg and his associates have several different methods for measuring moral maturity. There have been three successive scoring manuals for Kohlberg's test of moral reasoning, and at least two additional tests drawn up by James Rest, a former student of Kohlberg's. The latter will be discussed in the next section. Kohlberg's conception of a personally achieved integration aligns itself with the core-function type of conception, and his basic scoring algorithm, the modal scored level, is compatible with the idea of a core function. His chief instrument has been incomplete stories followed by an inquiry. As in the clinical inquiries of Piaget and coworkers, the specific questions may be altered in order to bring out the subject's reasoning; however, currently a standard form is being worked out with set questions. The standard form is sometimes presented as a written form. Several of the stories used by Kohlberg have been published in his articles, but details of the scoring technique are available only in mimeographed form, and expertise is said to be acquired only by long, supervised practice. Whatever is conveyed in such personal contacts is for the time being lost to the scientific literature.

The fundamental quantification strategy is to match each scored unit against a rating scale with six qualitatively defined stages. Corresponding to each stage there is a position on each of several moral issues; the number of issues or "issue systems" varies in different versions but is about nine. The three most important issues currently are punishment and sanctions, contracts and obligations, and the value of life. The reasoning by which a position on a given issue is related to a particular stage is in principle a priori, though one may assume that experience with the reasoning of many boys helped shape the ideas to start with. In the past there has been no systematic program for altering the scoring scheme with further data, nor is it easy to suggest such a scheme. However, some versions postulate substages that are attempts to cope with experience that does not fit neatly into the original stages (Chapter Eight).

The original scoring scheme had as its scored unit the "unit of thought," more or less equivalent to a sentence or a relevant sentence, since a remark about the weather, for example, would not have been scored. The method allows for scoring only what can be construed as aspects of moralization, as distinct from adherence to a particular moral code and as distinct from other aspects of ego development. Since each subject completes several stories and may make a number of scorable remarks about each of them, the problem of the scoring algorithm is acute. For the most part Kohlberg assumes that the person's level of core functioning will be represented by the mode of the distribution of his ratings. In some analyses, however, he has classified subjects according to whether any responses occur at his two highest stages; at that point, in effect, he is using a maximum rule, which corresponds to a latent-ability concept type.

The second version of the scoring manual took as its scored unit the story or dilemma. The score was in the form of a predominant stage representing the stage of reasoning most used in the story and if necessary a minor score, representing a stage used but less often than the predominant stage. Something like a unit of thought must have been used with that manual too.

For the current version of the scoring manual (Kohlberg, Colby, Lieberman, and Speicher-Dubin, 1973) the unit of analysis is the "point" or "idea elaborated by the subject" in discussing an issue. There are two forms of the test, Form A and Form B. Each contains three stories, each of which is intended to cover two issues. The stories and the inquiry are so arranged that each scored issue occurs in two stories; forms A and B are parallel in this respect, covering the same issues. Usually a subject will give a single point or idea in response to a single question, but it is possible for him to give two points for one question and to make a single point in response to more than one question. An idea or point is considered scorable only if it appears in the scoring manual for that story.

The scoring procedure is approximately as follows. One begins by looking for signs of Stage 2 reasoning with regard to a particular issue. If it occurs, it may be in one point, scored 1, two points, scored 2, or an ambiguous point, scored one-half.

More than two points are scored the same as two. Then one looks for signs of Stage 3 reasoning, and so on till reaching the subject's maximum level, or if necessary falling back to look for Stage 1 reasoning. Each issue is then assigned a stage-score; that will be the modal form of reasoning for that issue. A secondary mode will be assigned only if the secondary form of reasoning accounts for more than 25 percent of the reasoning on that issue; these two modes are referred to as *major* and *minor* scores. The number of issues scored appears to be somewhat variable and optional.

The Moral Maturity Score is a way of averaging scores on two or more issues to make a total protocol score for that person. An issue that has been given a pure score is weighted three, a major score is weighted two, and a minor score is weighted one. The numerator of the Moral Maturity Score is the weighted sum of the issue scores, the denominator is the sum of the weights, thus bringing the protocol score into the same terms as the scale of stages, though usually expressed as 100 times the stage number; that is, a person whose stage is exactly three would have a Moral Maturity Score of 300. The reason for so intricate a scoring algorithm is not presented. What it amounts to is the use of the mode for issue scores and a weighted mean of issue scores for the total protocol score.

There are several difficulties in Kohlberg's psychometrics. For one thing, he is not committed to any single concept type, or rather, while he is committed to core function, he sometimes uses methods appropriate to latent ability and profile concept types. Use of the mode as the essential algorithm is consistent with the idea of core function, as is also the averaging involved in the computation of the Moral Maturity Score. His claim (1969, p. 387) that persons tend to use reasoning of their dominant stage about half the time and reasoning one stage higher or lower more than half of the remaining time must be taken with reservations. Is he talking about the dispersion of units of thought around the total protocol rating? Or of point ratings around the issue rating? Or of issue ratings around total protocol ratings?

At times Kohlberg treats the distribution of scores (one

cannot always be sure whether issue scores or "point" scores) as if it were a profile, with the frequency of scores at each stage treated as a score giving the strength of that tendency. Thus he labels one figure (1969, p. 387) as "profile of stage usage." Further evidence that in the past he has confused distribution with profile is that at times he has intercorrelated the frequencies of different stages, thus treating frequencies like scores. However, currently the Moral Maturity Score has replaced reasoning in terms of a profile in that research group. Carrying the quantitative logic further, Lieberman (1973) has worked out a method for treating moral maturity as a latent ability to be estimated by several stories or issues. He is exploring possible refinements of scoring parameters on this basis.

There is an ambiguity in the current scoring manual over whether or to what extent the separate issue scores are experimentally independent. Some raters may go over a given passage in an interview and rate it more than once in relation to different issues. Repeated scoring of a passage would produce artifactual coherence and homogeneity. The accepted method appears to be to score an issue only in relation to a question designed for it; hence the same passage is not scored twice. However, there are complex and not fully formulated contingencies for taking context into account in scoring, so that some halo effect may occur intentionally.

Rest: An Objective Test of Moral Judgment. Rest (1973, 1974) has devised some alternative measures of moralization of judgment. His first alternative test was a comprehension test, drawing out the latent ability implications of the Kohlberg conception (Rest, Turiel, and Kohlberg, 1969). He argued that a person should be able to understand the reasoning of his own stage, that of all lower stages, and to some extent that of one stage higher; he judged the person's own stage by spontaneous usage of that stage in Kohlberg's test. As test of moral comprehension, he presented some Kohlberg moral-dilemma stories followed by possible solutions, with the subject asked to restate the arguments in his own words. For each stage arguments were presented that supported each of the possible choices, for example, a poor man must either steal a drug to save his wife's life or let her die. For a given story, the arguments at different stages referred to the same issues, such as motivation, rules, or the value of life. The score of a subject for a stage was the proportion of arguments in which he correctly restated the reasoning for that stage. An advantage of this format over Kohlberg's test is that each response can be scored blindly, without reference to any other responses by that subject, and Rest did so. In general, the logic of Kohlberg's stages was confirmed, that is, subjects tended to get more than 50 percent of their answers right for stages below their own and less than 50 percent right for higher stages.

Rest has recognized some of the psychometric weaknesses of Kohlberg's test, such as the subjectivity and unreliability of scoring, difficulty of learning how to score, and the relatively long time it takes to give and score the test. The comprehension test retains the free-response format and hence is plagued by the same difficulties. To meet these problems, Rest (Rest and others, 1974) devised an objective test, the Defining Issues Test, whose format is as follows. The subject is given a moral-dilemma story, ending with a binary choice, such as stealing the drug or letting his wife die for lack of it. The subject is asked which choice he would make or whether he is undecided. Then he turns the page and reads twelve questions or issues that bear on the decision. For each issue he records the degree of importance for him on a five-point scale. At the bottom of the page he records the four most important issues in order of their importance. In scoring the test, only the last set of data is used. Each of the issues is intended to represent a prominent concern of one of Kohlberg's stages, beginning with Stage 2, and including two substages of Stage 5, morality based on social contract. Stage 1 reasoning was considered too primitive for the groups involved in Rest's study, students in ninth grade through college and graduate school. Two questions or issues keyed to a given stage would be slanted toward opposite choices to the original dilemma, for example, one slanted toward stealing the drug, one slanted toward not stealing. Rest arrives at four scores, representing stages 2, 3, 4, and all principled stages, since the principled stages proved to be more or less indistinguishable, plus a composite score. The score for a stage is the average percentage of rank order of importance given to issues representing that stage; a rank of one is weighted four, a rank of two is weighted three, and so on, so that issues not ranked are weighted zero. The scores for stages 2, 3, 4, and principled must add to 100 percent. The composite score weights the score for Stage 2 by one, that for Stage 3 by two, that for Stage 4 by four, and that for principled stages by eight; apparently the sum is divided by eight as a normalizing factor. The rationale of that series of weights is not presented. The score assigned to principled stages, a score whose values range from zero to ninety-five, works about as well as the composite score as an overall measure, despite the lack of intuitive appeal in omitting all effect of use of the first four stages. In one sample, heterogeneous with respect to age, a global score on Kohlberg's test correlated .68 with the principled score on the Defining Issues Test. The latter correlated .52 with Rest's comprehension test of moral judgment in an adult sample; somewhat higher correlations in younger samples may be inflated by large variance in both variables due to age (Rest, 1974).

The fundamental assumption of the Defining Issues Test is that persons will assign greatest importance to issues stated at their own level. Exactly what their own level is is an ambiguous idea, however. Rest (1976) expects that a person will adopt a stage of moral judgment first in terms of preference, then in terms of comprehension, and finally in terms of spontaneous production. Preference and comprehension may be as consequential as spontaneous use, for example in voting.

Rest (1976) has discussed a variety of scoring algorithms. His preferred algorithm is frequency of use of principled reasoning. He has also explored assignment to a stage type according to highest stage of substantial use, rejection of low stages, and exceptional use. The first is of course a modification of the maximum algorithm. The second is not explicitly worked out. The third assumes that reasoning of some stages will never be predominant. A person is assumed to be in a stage when his reasoning or preference falls more in that stage than in others relative to the preferences of others. Thus this procedure is a modification of the mode as algorithm. Rest's experiments with a variety of quantification strategies and scoring algorithms should encourage novel methods and more rigorous thinking about measures in this area.

Loevinger, Sweet, and Ernhart: An Objective Test of Authoritarian Family Attitudes. Initially I sought, like many others, to map out the domain of personality traits generally, looking specifically for traits that follow the lines of some predictions from psychoanalytic theory. My purview was mothers' attitudes towards problems of everyday family life (Loevinger, 1962; Loevinger and Sweet, 1961). Blanche Sweet and I assembled a set of items tapping those attitudes as broadly as possible, items whose content referred to a wide variety of activities of all ages. We kept in mind the supposed character types corresponding to psychosexual stages, as well as common-sense or eclectic clinical hypotheses about punitiveness-permissiveness and other traits.

Among the findings of previous research that guided our research was the pervasiveness of various forms of response bias in psychological tests (Loevinger, 1959, 1965). Our items were carefully formulated to control response bias. Each item expresses two opposed opinions about some problem of family life, so far as possible in the language of the person who holds the opinion, thus not always logically or grammatically contradictory. The subject's task is to choose the opinion closer to his. Since every subject chooses the same number of statements, the problem of acquiescence as a response bias is eliminated. The subjects do not express their degree of agreement; the assumption is that extreme attitudes will be displayed in a greater number of items marked in the given direction. Many clinicians mistrust this probabilistic reasoning and cannot bear to discard the potentially relevant information of strength of feeling; however, the "information" registered as degree of agreement contains as much error as information, since it is contaminated by response bias. We attempted to minimize "social desirability," that is, self-description in terms of a socially acceptable facade, by sympathetic phrasing of both alternatives of the item and by seeking items of median popularity, ones where the two alternatives are chosen about equally often. Despite these precautions, initial results seemed to reflect the subjects' social facade. The care we had exercised in constructing the test meant that what we were seeing was not just an artifact of the test situation but represented something real about the persons responding. Moreover, included among the first groups tested were student nurses, members of public school mothers' groups, and Vassar graduates. Large group differences appeared; that was another reason for believing that we were getting at some traits that were not merely artifacts.

Responses of a heterogenous sample of 202 women were analyzed using the method of homogeneous keying (Loevinger, Gleser, and DuBois, 1953). This method is basically a factorial method, but it yields homogeneous clusters of items with maximum discriminating power rather than hypothetical factors. Although homogeneous keying is designed to yield several independent clusters of items of about equal weight or importance, of the five clusters that emerged one was essentially a general factor. Analysis of the content of the items included and excluded suggested the title, Authoritarian Family Ideology (AFI). It was shown that a test of punitiveness-permissiveness would have a high correlation with AFI. However, some items having direct reference to punishment do not correlate with AFI, while other items having authoritarian connotations but no direct reference to punishment are part of the cluster.

LaPerriere (1963; Loevinger, 1962), in a cross-validational study with a new sample, verified the homogeneity of AFI. The KR 20 (Kuder-Richardson formula 20) coefficient of homogeneity was .83 for a twenty-nine-item version of AFI in the original sample; using the same scoring key in the cross-validation sample, the KR 20 coefficient was .85, the increase in homogeneity probably due to greater variability. Three other clusters had a smaller coefficient of homogeneity in the cross-validational sample, an expected regression effect, while a final cluster had no homogeneity on cross-validation.

In a later study with over 1,000 women, including about 20 percent black women, Ernhart (Ernhart and Loevinger, 1969) demonstrated the robustness of AFI in another, important sense. With homogeneous keying used on a revised pool of items, AFI again emerged as the central cluster with substantially the same content and a majority of the same items as before. In the keying sample of 934 cases, AFI had forty-nine items and a KR 20 coefficient of .89. For an independent cross-validation sample of 104 cases, the coefficient was .88. Four additional but smaller clusters also were found. Ernhart was able to find psychologically plausible descriptions and explanations of their content and their correlations with other variables, as we did in the previous study of the Family Problems Scale, but the four minor clusters do not replicate any of the clusters of the previous study. Only AFI is convincingly replicated.

The syndrome captured in the items of AFI is complex but convincing; it resists being reduced to any single word or phrase. An individual rating high on AFI "has a punitive and controlling attitude towards many areas of child rearing; she has little ability to conceptualize the child's inner life; and she has a view of family life at once hierarchical and sentimental. If we assume this mother also scores high on the correlated clusters, the following characteristics can be added: she has a rigidly conventional conception of woman's social role; some mistrust of other people and corresponding anxiety; an orderly, scheduled approach to daily life; and perhaps a somewhat [unfavorable] view of woman's biological functions" (Loevinger, 1962, p. 113). The salience of this cluster in the data belies its characterization in terms of punitiveness-permissiveness; however, authors of other studies of child-rearing ideology have usually so characterized a similar trait that invariably turns up as the salient one in their research. The concepts of punitiveness and permissiveness do not account for the salience of items referring to the child's inner life nor to the affinity for banal expressions of sentiment. This syndrome resembles the authoritarian personality, despite the fact that our study included no mention of political or religious beliefs or ethnic prejudices, which was the jumping-off point for Adorno, Frenkel-Brunswik, Levinson, and Sanford; our study was based entirely on women, theirs largely on men; and we had avoided two kinds of response bias that bedeviled their results, that due to degree of agreement and that due to acquiescence.

These considerations led LaPerrierre, Abel Ossorio, and me to hypothesize that AFI measures ego development. From LaPerriere and Ossorio, I learned that the immature end of the continuum is not marked by extreme authoritarianism, though immature persons may endorse extremely authoritarian remarks. The low extreme is characterized by a chaotic, impulsive, and extremely self-centered style of life. A truly authoritarian character, one who respects and conforms to an authoritarian order, represents a considerable advance; the conceptual extreme point is a developmental midpoint.

To test the developmental hypothesis concerning AFI, LaPerriere tested post partum a sample of women stratified with respect to parity (first versus second or third child), religion (Catholic, Protestant, Jewish), and education (grade school, part high school, finished high school, some college). There were five cases per cell, except that no Jewish women who had not finished high school could be found; the total number of cases was 100. The AFI score varied significantly with parity, education, and age but not with religion. Authoritarianism decreases among women as they grow older, raise children, and have more education. In LaPerriere's sample, AFI correlated $-.28$ with age, which is confounded with parity and education. Therefore an analysis of covariance, holding age constant, was performed. Highly significant effects for education and parity remained even with age partialled out.

Ernhart (Ernhart and Loevinger, 1969) repeated the analysis of variance study, expanding the parity to four levels (one, two, three, or four children), education to five levels (grade school, part high school, finished high school, part college, finished college), discarding religion as a basis for stratification though continuing to seek variability with respect to it, and adding white versus black as a stratifying variable. Ernhart demonstrated again that AFI decreases significantly with age and education; she confirmed LaPerriere's finding of a decrease with parity for a white sample, but there was no effect of parity for the black sample. Correlation of AFI with age was again $-.28$.

All effects, including the race by parity interaction effect, remained significant with age held constant in a covariance analysis. For the white subsample of her analysis of variance sample,
which partly overlapped her homogeneous keying sample, Ernhart found that AFI had a homogeneity coefficient of .87; for
the corresponding subsample of black women, the coefficient
was .82. Ernhart devised a method for ascertaining either homogeneity or correlation holding constant stratifying variables, in
this case race, education, parity, or any combination of them.
The coefficient of homogeneity, .88 for the entire sample computed by the conventional method, is .80 within groups, holding all stratifying variables constant. This finding demonstrates
further the robustness of AFI.

The statistical techniques devised by Ernhart enabled her
to test an hypothesis latent in all factor analytic studies though
rarely acknowledged, namely, the hypothesis that there are no
item by subject or test by subject interaction effects. Factor
analysis depends for its force and value on the assumption that
the same factors will emerge regardless of what sample of persons is chosen within wide limits. Rotation of axes is supposed
to free the factors from the contingencies of the sample tested,
but that is an article of faith, not a proven proposition. The factors are determined from the pattern of correlations between
tests. If one can show that not just the magnitude but the pattern of correlations depends sharply on the choice of subgroups
within a broad and fairly typical sample, then this underlying
assumption of factor analysis is proved untenable. That is precisely what Ernhart did. The item by subject and test by subject
interaction effects cannot be tested directly, but Ernhart
showed that there are significant interaction effects between
subgroup and item or test; a fortiori, there must be interaction
effects with subjects. This result brings into question the whole
trait-factorial approach to personality measurement and individual differences (Chapter Ten).

Considering AFI as a measure of ego development, let us
note its characteristics. The basic quantification strategy is to
find a set of binary or dichotomous items such that the higher
the ego level, the fewer will be marked in a specified direction.

The scored response is the choice of a designated one of the two statements. The scored unit is the binary item. The scoring algorithm is the number of items scored plus. The content of the items refers to authoritarian family ideology and other problems of family life that empirically are highly correlated with patently authoritarian items. In order to provide an independent validation of the test as a measure of ego level, Elizabeth Nettles studied the correlation between AFI and a sentence completion test scored intuitively for ego level, finding a modest coefficient, .39 (unpublished study, Washington University, 1963). That study led to a line of work that will be described in the next section.

Some general conclusions can be drawn from the foregoing studies. First, the belief that some guidance for differential psychology can come from the psychoanalytic theory of psychosexual stages appears to have been in error. No tests of psychosexual stages have demonstrated much success; in the studies with the Family Problems Scale, no subsets of items confirmed hypotheses about psychosexual stages. Probably psychosexual stages are not the sort of thing for which tests are appropriate. Psychoanalysis is, in the first instance, a study of ways in which we are all alike despite whatever superficial differences we may have. Psychometrics, on the other hand, is a way of codifying our differences. While we were thinking of psychoanalysis as a study of sexuality, the analysts themselves were turning to ego psychology, as our own data compelled us to do also.

A second error that we made was to assume that factorial methods, which, broadly interpreted, include homogeneous keying, could serve to map out the personality domain. Factorial methods have value in test construction, in testing for homogeneity, and in other problems, but they cannot serve in place of a psychologist in the context of discovery. Only a psychologist can integrate the many lines of evidence to construct a novel hypothesis or to discover a new trait or syndrome. In particular, no factorial method can cope with the problem of nonmonotone relations between variables, a problem that is the nub of measuring personality development.

Loevinger, Wessler, Redmore, and Others: Rating Sentence Completions for Ego Development. Once the broad outlines of the conception of ego development came into focus, we recognized it as a conception that others had already discerned, but there was no accepted measure of it. The sentence completion test had been used, but without a scoring manual. The construction of our scoring manual* has gone hand in hand with the evolution of our conception. That has been our distinctive contribution. Details of our psychometric methodology are not, therefore, digressions from the topic of this book. The rules that have guided our enterprise include putting everything in writing, rating every response, and justifying every rating theoretically and empirically.

The first rule is to put everything in writing, so far as possible. We wish to avoid building a staff of expert raters who leave in the scientific literature no adequate trace of the skill they have acquired, as happened with the highly trained cadre of raters for *The Authoritarian Personality*. There is, of course, a tacit component in every judgment, and any set of instructions can be taken literally in such a way as to defeat its purpose. Literal adherence to rules may even be encouraged by writing them down rather than communicating them orally. On the other hand, there are many advantages to writing down rules and instructions to raters. In the first place, the person giving the instructions is forced to clarify his own thinking in putting it on paper; contradictions that are not evident in speaking may jump out from a written record. In the second place, the rater or typist to whom the directions are given always has a

---

*Over the years those holding major responsibility for evolving and codifying our rules for scoring sentence completions included Nettles, LaPerriere, and Hana Gach deCharms, assisted by Virginia Ives Word, in addition to the authors of the published version (Loevinger, Ruth Wessler, Carolyn Redmore). Many other persons participated as raters, including men and women, black and white, single, married, and divorced, young and old, Catholic, Protestant, Jew, and atheist, recent immigrants and old-line Americans, and persons of varied socioeconomic and geographical origins. Almost all of them have left their mark on our conception at some point; the variety of backgrounds has contributed to the catholicity of our conception.

record to go back to in case he becomes confused or meets marginal cases. In the third place, a dated, signed record is invaluable when writing reports and articles. Finally, there are fewer misunderstandings of written than of oral instructions.

Another ground rule has been that every response must be scored. To our surprise, no two raters agreed exactly on how many subjects had provided no response, which they had tallied item by item for 200 cases. Omissions were clear, but there were differences of opinion on how fragmentary a response could be and still be scorable; some raters, in fact, were prepared to score outright omissions in terms of what topic was omitted. We have not found that omissions can be assigned any score usefully, and we have codified how fragmentary a response can be and still be assigned some score. Where a stem is omitted or the response is too fragmentary or is unscorable for some other reason, we arbitrarily score it at the Conformist level; that is in part, therefore, a "wastebasket category." One of our "saving circularities" is that we expect scores at the Conformist level on every protocol; presence of some responses scored at that level does not contraindicate any other score for the total protocol. Therefore the total protocol rating is not unduly affected by arbitrarily giving a Conformist rating to omissions and unratable responses.

We have been criticized for the rule of rating every response, on the grounds that some responses carry no information about ego level. Many kinds of response in which we saw no a priori relation to ego level proved as good as or better than categories of response we expected to be diagnostic. Had we permitted ourselves the option of not rating what we thought were irrelevant responses, we might never have made many small discoveries that have enriched our conception. Another advantage of rating every response is that every protocol has the same number of item ratings, thirty-six, since we always use thirty-six sentence stems.

Our scoring manual has evolved through three types, the exemplar manual, the categorized manual, and the rationalized category manual. When we started working on a manual, we used four scoring levels, I-2, I-3, I-4, and I-5, taken from the

Sullivan, Grant, and Grant system, about the same as what we now call the Impulsive, the Conformist, the Conscientious, and the Autonomous stages. Each rater sorted the responses intuitively into those four categories, and then we compromised our disagreements. The *exemplar manual* consisted of lists of responses at each I-level, but it was never used. Instead, examples at each level were grouped together in categories with obvious or unnecessary examples deleted. This format helps to draw the rater's attention to the feature of the response that determines its placement on the scale. The categories are not an end in themselves; they do not encode usable information. They serve to assist the rating task. They are also essential to manual revision, which is the core operation of our enterprise. This *categorized manual* was used in several studies. As we moved towards clarifying and explaining the categories, we evolved a *rationalized category manual,* trying to justify every scoring decision both empirically and theoretically. While that aim is unattainable, it gives shape to the enterprise. It is an unattainable aim because every sample of responses to a stem will contain some unique ones. Some will be replicated when the sample is enlarged, but then there will be new unique responses. Only when a response is replicated or is a member of a replicated category can one study empirically whether it is correctly scored. When a response is given by only one person, we cannot be sure that the level of his total protocol is the one to which that response should be assigned; it may be uncharacteristically high or low for him, for every person shows variability. In the published manual there is a blurb for almost every scored level of every stem, giving what we can discern of the rationale of the content included at that level for that stem. Most scoring manuals for other sentence completion tests and for other projective tests are of the exemplar type.

When we began constructing the manual, we believed that there would be clear-cut differences in the kind of content discussed at different levels, but that turned out to be only partly true. People at different levels often discuss the same things with different emphasis and with finely different shades of meaning. Moreover, as our skill increased, we learned to discriminate many more levels than the original four. Because the difference in response between one level and the adjacent ones is slight, a careful accounting operation is needed. This operation is our manual revision scheme. With minor variations it takes the following form.

We begin by giving a form of the test to a large, heterogeneous sample of persons, all of one sex. Originally we used all women and girls, recently we have worked with samples of men and boys, and in a few instances with mixed samples. After some experimentation with tests of different lengths, we settled on thirty-six items for most uses, that proving to be long enough to give a reasonable portrait of the respondent and short enough not to try his patience. The original protocols are read only by typists, who remove all identifying information as they type the protocol, if necessary deleting parts of some responses and so indicating. If in a particular study age differences are of interest, for example, all references to the subject's age must be deleted. The only identification is an arbitrary code number. If there are subsamples, they are randomly distributed throughout the sample. That is essential where comparison of subsamples will be made, as with pretests and posttests or experimental and control groups. Next, all responses to a single item are typed on a list, again with no information but the sample designation and the code number. This procedure is repeated for each of the thirty-six items. Two raters rate each response to the item, recording the category as well as the level at which the response is rated. After completing all ratings for one item, they discuss and compromise any differences, again for each of the thirty-six items. After all responses to items have been rated, total protocols are rated by three expert raters, each recording his own rating, then compromising their differences. The resultant agreed-on total protocol rating is the criterion rating for the protocol.

The typist now constructs what we call *decoding sheets*. For each item separately all the responses in the sample are typed, not in the arbitrary order of the code number but in order of their place in the manual. That is, for each scored level the category titles are listed, and under each category title, instead of the examples given in the manual, there will appear the responses in this particular sample that the raters placed in that category, together with the code number of the subject giving the response and the subject's total protocol rating. Within a category, responses are typed in order of increasing protocol rating. Thus one can see at a glance how well the criterion ratings of the people who gave responses in a given category correspond to the level at which the category has been placed. The manual constructor is now in business. For each category the following decisions must be made: Should it stay at the level where it is now placed, or should it be moved to a higher or lower level? Should it be split into two or more categories? Splitting is justified where there are detectable differences in content corresponding to differences in subjects' criterion rating. The reverse operation is also possible; fine shades of meaning that supposedly discriminate ego levels may not stand up to the cross-validation of the new sample. In such cases, categories can be combined, thus reducing the number of discriminations the rater is asked to make. Occasionally raters may misunderstand a category title, particularly at the higher levels; this will be evident to the manual constructor when he sees inappropriate responses classed in the category. Then the blurb may have to be changed or the title clarified. Finally, new categories may be discerned in previously unclassified responses.

This procedure is a bootstrap operation. Provided that we can do any better than chance to start with, by repeated use of this process we can discover signs of the various levels we had not previously suspected, and we can improve our classification of signs previously noted. Granted improved item ratings, we will be better at rating total protocols next time around. More accurate protocol ratings then provide a better criterion for improving our item ratings.

Just prior to completing the scoring manual, Blasi and I independently surveyed category titles for all thirty-six items, level by level, in order to draw up a revised portrait of each stage and each transitional level. The major changes necessary were evident to both of us. For example, the stage we had been calling Opportunistic showed in fact relatively few blatantly opportunistic responses (as many of our raters had been warning) and more self-protective and naively hedonistic ones. Thus the conception of that level was broadened. Many changes have crept into the conception at other times, and the version presented in Chapter Two is the result of that extended process of microvalidation. This process for using data to refine and clarify the basic conception constitutes the claim our conception has to authority in regard to disputed details of the stages.

The basic quantification strategy is to match each rated item against a rating scale composed of several points, each defined in qualitative terms. In principle, the same quantification strategy can be applied to other thought or behavior samples or to a case history. Any behavior sample qualifies if it is sufficiently unstructured to permit the subject to project and the rater to discern the subject's frame of reference. Each point along the scale represents at once a character type and a perceptual style, arranged in what is believed to be the developmental order. The fact that in practice most raters will find most responses in the scoring manual does not affect the underlying logic; when a response deviates in any way from the ones recorded in the manual, an understanding of the logic is required to judge whether that deviation affects the rating to be given. Not the specific content but the thought structure it reveals is decisive.

Because of the rule to rate every response, the scoring algorithm becomes a rule for translating thirty-six item ratings into a single total protocol rating. Originally we read the total protocol and tried to reconstruct intuitively what kind of a person would have written it. For this exercise, the item ratings served only as loose guides. Following the rule to make everything explicit, however, we could not rest there. The next set of rules were descriptions of typical cases at the several stages. They worked well for typical cases but provided too little guidance for cases that did not exactly match the description of any stage.

One obvious alternative algorithm is to translate each scored level into a number corresponding to its ordinal position. A numerical score is assigned to each item rating, and the total protocol rating is the sum of item ratings. The problem that remains is assigning a cutting score for each scored level; that should be done so as to maximize the fit to intuitive protocol ratings. Item-sum scores have proved valuable in many studies, and for some purposes, such as studying interrater agreement or test-retest reliability, the cutting scores are not needed. There are intuitive and logical objections to the item-sum algorithm, despite its usefulness. It implicitly assumes not just an ordinal but an interval scale of measurement, a claim for the ego scale not only gratuitous but probably meaningless. The logical difficulty is that the presence of a certain amount of primitive material in a protocol is not necessarily incompatible with a high-level rating, in part because the person must have passed through all earlier stages to arrive at his present one, in part because flexibility and availability of all kinds of impulses are possible indications of high ego level. In practice, presence of low-level responses on high-level protocols does not happen to a sufficient extent to distort high scores. What seems to happen is that impulse expression takes such modulated form as to reflect the person's ego level, or else the rare low-level response is outweighed by the many responses scored at higher level.

An algorithm has been devised that, like item-sum, uses the whole distribution of responses, but it does not assume an interval scale. It is called the *ogive rules* (Loevinger and Wessler, 1970), since it uses cumulative distributions. Cutting scores rather than typical cases are used to characterize the different levels, so that every case is classified. Some studies show better results for the ogive rules, some for the item-sum algorithm.

Finally, how we met one recurrent problem will illustrate the relation between method and theory. The question is, how should composite responses be rated, that is, responses that have two or more parts, each of which is a ratable response? We have always had rules for this common contingency, and we have always believed that we understood and agreed with each other about the rules after each discussion of them. A graduate assistant was asked to write the rules down after one such discussion, and he spent many weeks at the task. As we were not satisfied with what he wrote, the following year another staff member attempted the task. This process was repeated several times over a period of years. The rules finally formulated show both why the process of making them explicit was difficult and why it was valuable.

The rater must first distinguish pseudo-compound responses that are either clichés or repetitions. Examples of clichés are "A woman feels good when—she is dressed neat and clean" and "A good mother—has love and understanding." Such responses are rated at the Conformist level unless there is a specific category for them at another level. A repetitious pseudo-compound response is "My main problem is—I am sometimes too shy and self-conscious." Such responses often combine two responses that are rated in the same category, as this one does, and they should be rated accordingly. True compound responses contain two or more contrasting ideas or refer to two or more alternative aspects of a situation. When the combination generates a more complex level of conception, the response is rated one-half step higher than the highest element, where the transition between two stages is considered a half step. This rule applies only above the Conformist Stage. Occasionally there may be two contrasting ideas at the Conformist level that generate a Conscientious-Conformist (Self-Aware) level response, but that is not frequent. Two contrasting ideas at the Conscientious-Conformist level frequently generate a Conscientious level response. Three contrasting ideas, at least one at the level of the Conscientious-Autonomous transition, generate an Autonomous stage response. An example is "I am—a happy person but discouraged at times," rated at the Conscientious Stage. "I am—a happy person" is a common response at the Conscientious-Conformist transition. "I am—discouraged at times" would be rated at the same level but in a different category, "Thoughts, worries about life, the future (vague and general)." The idea that a person can be basically happy but also discouraged at times raises the response to a higher level of complexity than either response alone. An example of a compound response classed at the Conscientious-Autonomous transition is "If I can't get what I want—I either try to forget about it, rationalize by saying I can do without it, or find some way to get it without hurting anyone." The first clause ("try to forget about it") by itself would be classed at the Conscientious-Conformist level, the other two clauses at the Conscientious level. When the combination of ideas in a compound response does not generate a higher level of conceptual complexity, the response is rated in terms of the less frequent alternative or in terms of the higher level alternative. Usually the two considerations agree. If the higher level is above the Conformist level, that one is always used. Where one element is rated at the Conformist level and the other at a lower level, the element at the Conformist level will often be the more frequently occurring one, and the lower rating would be given. (Popular categories are indicated in the manual.) The justification for letting the less frequent response prevail is that in principle it contains more information. In case of doubt, the higher rating is used. (For further details, see Chapter Five of Loevinger and Wessler, 1970.)

This discussion illustrates the complexity of the rating task and the importance of the metarule to make every rule explicit in writing. The insight that combining two differing responses from one level generates a response at the next higher level was forced on us by frequently encountering such categories in the manual-construction process. Writing down in coherent fashion the rules for rating compound responses proved enormously difficult, but in laboring to make them explicit, we were alerted to new categories. The final rules are not arbitrary nor based solely on a priori reasoning; they reflect experience with large amounts of data, and they improve the test's discriminating power. Finally, the data suggest a possible theory of how the person advances from one level to the next higher one. Beginning at the Conformist Stage, the capacity to hold in mind two contrary or contrasting ideas, each compatible with one's own current level, may be one way in which a person acquires the ability to see the next more complex level.

Conclusions

Our conception is that underlying the qualitative changes in ego development there is an ordered quasi-quantitative variable or dimension. The problem of measuring ego development is to ascertain how far a person has come along that dimension. Logically, the major quantification strategies appear to be seeking the number of signs corresponding to the lowest levels (or, what is logically equivalent, the highest levels) and matching responses qualitatively to qualitative descriptions of all discernible points along the scale. The first strategy leads to cumulative tests and translates directly into an item-sum scoring algorithm. Examples are the Family Problems Scale scored for Authoritarian Family Ideology and Rest's use of principled responses as a measure of moral maturity on his Defining Issues Test.

When the quantification strategy matches responses against a scale with qualitatively defined points, the problem of scoring algorithm becomes central. The major outlines of the scale must be provided in advance as the framework for the observations. No one has proposed an objective technique for arriving at such a conceptual framework. While our method for constructing a sentence-completion scoring manual is a codified, quasi-objective method for refining the scale, it could not work unless the broad outline was available first.

Consider a sample of responses from each subject, each response assigned to some point along the ego scale. How shall we best characterize the person's position? The main possibilities seem to be the mode of the distribution, the maximum value, or some parameter of the total distribution such as the median. Isaacs has used a modification of the maximum-value algorithm. Kohlberg uses a modification of the mode as his principal algorithm. The ogive rules for the sentence-completion test appear to provide a new algorithm. This algorithm uses the subject's distribution of responses but rather than the median being taken as its representative value, there is a different cutting score for each level.

Treating the distribution of scores within a protocol as if it represented a characteristic profile for that person's ego structure appears to be erroneous. The only parameter of the distribution that anyone has attempted to validate is some measure of central or maximum tendency. No one has sought independent verification beyond his own instrument for the profile or variability of a person. Probably variability is more a function of the instrument than of the person. There is in any case a "saving circularity" between the rules for scoring responses and the rules for inferring total protocol ratings from the distribution of response ratings.

Despite the intuitive appeal of the ogive algorithm, experience has shown that about the same results are obtained by item-sum scores. They build in an assumption of an interval scale, as does Kohlberg's Moral Maturity Score. In justification of this assumption, it seems to give as satisfactory scores as any other method, and it probably does not introduce gross distortions. Sources of systematic error variance, such as social class and verbal fluency, are more likely to bias research results.

There may be methods of measuring development of character that have not been reviewed here, but probably they are variants or combinations of the foregoing techniques. Granted that measurement of developmental variation has many difficulties, many of the methods reviewed are excessively flawed. They do not coordinate concept type with scoring algorithm, they confuse distributions with profiles, and they use rules and parameters that are arbitrary to the point of caprice. For measurement to serve as the leading edge of a scientific discipline, it must be informed by theory, and there must be clear lines for results to feed back as corrections to theory. Most of the approaches have inadequate articulation of theory, method, and data.

I have bypassed the problem of validity, despite its interest. The question of what constitutes evidence for validity of a measure of ego development or related variables raises further methodological issues, such as the relative importance of sequentiality, correlational studies of construct validity, and practical predictions. Consideration of specific studies would lead into a maze of issues such as reliability, randomness and heterogeneity of samples, motivation, and so on. Thus this chapter should not be read as a claim for or critique of the validity of the tests mentioned.

As a summary judgment, none of the tests is as convincing as the underlying construct. They have proved useful, however, as means for probing the construct and for doing research on the network of relations to which it is tied.

Chapter Ten

Alternatives to the Structural Model

The distinctive claim for our conception of ego development is that it is both a developmental sequence and a dimension of individual differences. Most of this book relates it to developmental psychology, but the last chapter and the present one relate it to differential psychology. Looking at our topic as a subfield of individual differences permits contrasting our approach with measures of moral and ego development based on other models. Here, as in the contrasting approaches to development, the different approaches represent different views of human nature and of the nature of science. To some extent, therefore, the models and the data they generate are not commensurate. One can consider, however, whether the alternative models provide consistent and parsimonious descriptions of their own data.

The field of individual differences began by studying intelligence. Though that may sound like a straightforward, non-controversial topic to personality theorists, there have been lively disputes over alternative models (Loevinger, 1951). When attention turned to individual differences in personality, the methods used in studying intelligence were imported, some-times without considering whether the subject matter differ-ences might require methodological differences.

The Thorndike doctrine, that whatever exists in human nature exists in some amount, and that amount can be mea-sured (Chapter Nine), leads to difficulties, for it implies indefi-nitely many measurable traits. To find the most parsimonious set that can account for the scores of a sample of persons on a set of tests, various methods of factor analysis have been de-vised. Some methods lean towards construing data so as to find several group factors of about equal importance; others tend to find hierarchically ordered factors, with more general ones encompassing more specific ones.

Factor analysts have differed from each other also on the interpretation of factors. Some see them as no more than con-venient rubrics to summarize inconvenient masses of test scores, the latter being the real things. Others stress the arbitrary nature of test scores and view factors as explanatory variables and hence as more real. Efforts expended on rotation of factorial solutions imply a search for real, nonarbitrary forms; the prob-lem of the reality of factors is essentially the same as the reality of types, stages, and concepts in general (Chapter Eight).

Thorndike, with his doctrine of specificity, took an ex-treme position with respect to the unreality of factors. When he constructed an intelligence test, he called it "Intellect CAVD," specifying the tasks it called for: completions, arithmetic prob-lems, vocabulary, and following directions (Thorndike and others, 1927). The measurement of an ability is no more than an inventory of products or tasks achieved, he asserted. Some psychologists still advocate positions like that of Thorndike, which philosophers call *nominalistic*. Lord, for example, be-lieves that the overall validity of a test is not a basic psycho-metric concept. "The discriminating power of the test for a spe-cified decision problem regarding a specified examinee is the truly basic concept" (Lord, 1955, p. 509).

The specifist hypothesis was given a different twist by Thomson (1939) and Tryon (1935). They were deeply invested in factorial statistical methods, hence somewhat committed to a view of dispositions covering diverse behavior manifestations. The general or group factors, in their view, are artifacts of the statistical method employed. The explanatory constructs they find acceptable are not hypothetical traits but specific elements, such as genes, neural arcs, or segments of experience, psychological components rather than mathematical components, as Tryon (1935) put it. Every test samples a large number of elements, according to this theory, and the correlations between tests reflect the number of overlapping elements. Factors are accounted for by chance or by assuming that the elementary determinants are organized into more or less overlapping "subpools of the mind" (Thomson, 1939, p. 50). No connection has ever been established between any gene or neural arc and test performance in humans, so that such explanations are as hypothetical as any postulated ability; indeed, modern neurology makes such hypotheses unacceptable.

The foregoing ideas have applied to measurement of intelligence in the first instance and measurement of personality by extension. Measurement of ego development seems to be a recent idea. Pittel and Mendelsohn (1966) have reviewed earlier measures of moral values. They found three periods. In the first period, moral values were measured by paper-and-pencil tests, mostly designed to differentiate normal children and adolescents from delinquents. They tended to be tests of moral knowledge; the keyed or right answers were supplied a priori. The best of these studies was that of Hartshorne and May. The second period was characterized by a broader and more theoretical approach, setting moral problems in larger behavioral and personality contexts, whether cognitive, behavioristic, or psychoanalytic in viewpoint. Piaget's *Moral Judgment of the Child* they class in this period. In the third period, projective tests, often story completions, have been used. However, the examples cited by Pittel and Mendelsohn were interpreted primarily in terms of superego strength, strength of projected guilt feelings, and the like; they do not include Kohlberg's cognitive developmental approach. Thus their account provides the historical background for the measures discussed in Chapter Nine.

The remainder of this chapter will discuss measures and research programs based on two psychometric models: the specifist model of Thorndike, currently exemplified in the work of Mischel, and the resolution of moral or ego development into a set of more or less independent traits. Our purpose is to highlight structural conceptions by contrast, not to make a complete survey of alternative models.

Specifist Models

The first major empirical study of moral development was that of Hartshorne, May, and their collaborators (1928, 1929, 1930). Their studies continue to be of importance because they were carefully done on large numbers of children. They set out to find whether there is a single factor underlying measures of moral behavior among school children in grades five through eight. Their first and most often quoted set of studies (Hartshorne and May, 1928) concerned the resistance to temptations to cheat, lie, and steal in a variety of situations in school, home, and parties. In general, they found low positive correlations between the measures of cheating, with the size of the correlation depending on the similarity of the task, the mode by which cheating was permitted, and the setting in school or home. For somewhat similar situations in the same setting, the correlation ran about .3, with lower values the more the situation and the setting differed. These correlations, they noted, are of the same order of magnitude as the correlations between specific tests of intellectual ability, which also vary in accord with degree of similarity of the tasks. Similar results were obtained in their second set of studies on measures of service and self-control (Hartshorne, May, and Maller, 1929).

In their final set of studies, concerning the organization of character (Hartshorne, May, and Shuttleworth, 1930), they found a high correlation that is not often cited. To measure deceit, they gave a test twice, once with opportunity for surreptitious cheating, for example, letting the children score their own papers, then without opportunity to cheat. The assumption was that if the child had a lower score on retest, he must have cheated when grading his own paper the first time. The excess of the first over the second score was considered a measure of cheating. The scores were standardized and normalized so that the scale was the same from one test and situation to another. Each child who had taken the entire battery of tests for honesty had a distribution of honesty scores. Its standard deviation was his integration score. Overall, their estimate of the correlation between honesty and integration, corrected for attenuation, was .78. (They give an uncorrected value for one population of .52.) They examined various possible sources of artifact and concluded that the association was real and substantial. Honesty, they concluded, is often an integrated character trait, but dishonesty is usually specific to the situation.

These studies have almost always been cited as support for the doctrine of specificity. The authors were aware of this interpretation—Thorndike was their immediate supervisor—but they also had a notion of the difference between specific behaviors and the organization of character in some larger sense. The primary target of their studies, as the overall title, "Character Education Inquiry," suggests, was the methods of teaching moral character then in vogue. Attendance at Sunday School and membership in boys' or girls' groups supposed to teach character had no consistent influence on the children's honesty scores. They concluded that teaching honesty or morality as a set of precepts had no influence on conduct.

Among those who have replied to the specifist interpretation of the studies are Allport (1943) and Kohlberg (1971). Allport pointed to the minimal ego involvement of the youngsters in many of the little games and tests of these and similar studies that have been cited in support of the specifist view. Allport, in fact, argued for the importance of the concept of ego in psychology on exactly that basis: people behave more consistently when they are deeply ego-involved, as shown in a study of Klein and Schoenfeld (1941). Hartshorne, May, and Maller (1929, p. 446) made a similar point. Kohlberg states that there is no such thing as moral or immoral behavior, but only behavior that is more or less in accord with the actor's moral principles. Some of his own experiments, he points out, could be interpreted in terms of Kohlberg lying to and cheating his subjects, since he deceives them about the real purpose of the experiment. Yet most people would not conclude from that that his moral character is deficient. Similarly, not paying one's income taxes can be an attempt to cheat the government or a matter of high moral principle, as in the case of Edmund Wilson or Thoreau doing so as a matter of conscience.

A recent advocate of the specifist view is Mischel (1966, 1968), whose paradigmatic moral or prosocial act is the ability to resist a small immediate reward in anticipation of a larger postponed reward. His favorite topic is the effect of experimental circumstances on percentage choice of the larger, delayed reward. Mischel specifically disclaims a desire to set up another trait or typology of individual differences. His interest is in demonstrating the importance of specific situational contingencies. He interprets his data, along with previous findings of others, as supporting "specificity of different aspects of self-control behavior . . . without any underlying unitary moral agency" (1966, p. 115). Why, then, would Mischel and his students spend a couple of decades studying such specifics? On the next page he justifies the work by its presumed importance in relation to the development of psychopathy, masochism, depression, and sadism, all of which he construes as inappropriate regulation of rewards and punishments to self and others, which he evidently equates with inappropriate self-control. Mischel seems to justify his research in terms of enduring dispositions whose existence the research is intended to disprove. A recent finding (Mischel and Ebbesen, 1970), that nursery school children tolerate delay for reward better if they are distracted than if they are reminded constantly of the reward, contradicts neither common sense nor, as Mischel supposes, psychoanalytic theory. (It may, however, contradict an element of Hull's learning theory, the "anticipatory goal response.") Should we conclude that moral development is encouraged by having children watch television while waiting for meals?

Mischel calls his opponents "state-trait theorists." He means by trait theory essentially what has been called that in this chapter; by state theories he means psychodynamic and psychoanalytic ones. The advocates of traits and of psychoanalysis do not ordinarily consider themselves allies. What they have in common, and hence the real target of Mischel's animus, is the use of observable responses as signs rather than solely as samples of inferred behavioral tendencies. Is the mark of science to avoid all but the most obvious and low-level theoretical inferences? That is a view alien to contemporary physical sciences and directly contrary to the one that animates this book.

In answer to the situation-specific view, Bowers (1973) points out that the experimental approach in its nature emphasizes situational effects, just as the correlational approach emphasizes individual differences. He cites smoking, homosexuality, and autism as kinds of behavior not easily modified by situational manipulation. Where subjects are similar and situations differ widely, behavior will be a function of the situation, and vice versa. Bowers tabulated a set of studies using analysis of variance to evaluate relative effects of situations and person variables; they showed a slightly greater effect of individual differences, but still greater effects due to the interaction of persons and situations. In discussing theoretical implications of the large interaction effects, Bowers points out that the person to some extent creates his own environment, in part by how he construes it (as we have seen in this book), but also because he creates an environment for others and they respond accordingly. Bowers cites several empirical sources for the last statement, as an example, a study by Kelley and Stahelski (1970) using a prisoner's dilemma game. Cooperators adopt a cooperative strategy when their partners do but a competitive strategy when faced with a competitive partner. Competitors adopt a competitive strategy no matter what their partner does. Moreover, competitors view themselves as realistic, since they find only competitive partners. Thus, people not only maintain their behavior by how they perceive others, they also really evoke behavior consistent with their own character, a point made by Wachtel (1973). Thus environment contributes to the consistency and stability of character structure, a topic to which we return in Chapter Twelve.

Mischel (1973) has been modifying his position to acknowledge the influence of cognitive factors in response, and of course he never denied the existence of individual differences, just as those whom he criticized never denied that behavior is largely determined by situations. Mischel, however, is still a specifist, as shown by his liberal quotations from his own earlier work and by the following: "Rather than talk about 'behavior,' it may be more useful to conceptualize *behavior-contingency units* that link specific patterns of behavior to the conditions in which they may be expected" (Mischel, 1973, p. 278). Implicit personality theories about self and others may be among the most stable and situation-free constructions, he allows. The burden of the present book is that moral development is intimately tied to such factors; so that admission largely undermines his attack on the dispositional approach to moral development.

Trait Models

A dimensionalized view of moral development is proposed by Hogan (1973); for him moral maturity comprises the maturation or optimization of five independent traits. Three of these traits, socialization, empathy, and autonomy, are essentially developmental, he believes, but not the last two, moral knowledge and a dimension unique with him, ethics of conscience versus ethics of responsibility. Hogan believes that socialization develops before empathy, which in turn precedes autonomy; but the outcome of one developmental sequence is not tied to the initiation of the next, as in a Piagetian sequence of stages. What are for Kohlberg stages of moral development are for Hogan independent events. Hogan's preferred instrument is an objective test or a semi-projective test scored in the manner of objective tests, that is, by counting specific signs. His test of moral maturity is scored by counting how many items contain reference to concern for the sanctity of the individual, the spirit rather than the letter of the law, the welfare of society, or seeing both sides of an issue. His subjects are often college students, and the data are often correlations between tests.

Particular interest attaches to the conscience-versus-responsibility dimension, for which Hogan has devised a test, the Survey of Ethical Attitudes. Hogan sees two main types of ethical theory, those that posit a higher law to which appeal can be made against the laws of a given society and those for which the rule of law and the authority of society are beyond appeal; the former he refers to as the ethics of conscience and the latter (somewhat prejudicially) as the ethics of responsibility. The Survey of Ethical Attitudes consists of a set of statements deemed to be consistent with each of these ethical theories; to each statement the subject expresses his degree of agreement on a five-point scale. Hogan cites the following items as representative: "(a) All civil laws should be judged against a higher moral law; (b) right and wrong can be meaningfully defined only by the law; (c) an unjust law should not be obeyed; (d) without law the life of man would be nasty, brutish, and short" (1973, p. 225). Although Hogan scores the ethics of responsibility as the high end of his scale, his own data support an interpretation of the ethics of conscience as more mature. He reports a correlation of the Survey of Ethical Attitudes with empathy as $-.2$, with autonomy as $-.3$, and with maturity of moral judgment as $-.4$. Only socialization, another measure of social conformity, correlates positively with it. The problem appears to be a small one that can be met by merely reversing the scoring of the Survey of Ethical Attitudes. I believe, on the contrary, that at this point his whole model falls.

Issues of conscience versus law are the kind that preoccupy persons at the highest stages of Kohlberg's dimension and our dimension of ego development; our schemes would both put the ethics of conscience at a higher stage than the law-and-order ethics that Hogan terms "responsibility." Indeed, his opposition to seeing the ethics of conscience as more mature than the ethics of conformity is deeply embedded in the rationale of his endeavor, which begins with "a conception of man as a rule-formulating and rule-following animal" (1973, p. 217). Hogan acknowledges that the morally most mature find some intermediate or compromise position on issues of conscience versus responsibility. But his model, resolving moral maturity into a set of traits, is badly weakened if one of the traits is not univocally related to moral maturity. Precisely here the structural model comes into its own: adherence to law for its own sake and intuitive rebellion against injustice are integrated finally and optimally into a more complex structure, adherence to abstract principles of justice tempered by realistic assessment of consequences. Hogan's model neither conceptualizes nor permits the assessment of such complex integrations.

Another dimensional approach has come from a group at John Hopkins University who have been working on a measure of psychosocial maturity (Greenberger and others, 1974, 1975). They reasoned that psychosocial maturity in all societies includes the capacity to function effectively, to interact adequately with others, and to contribute to society, thus, Individual Adequacy, Interpersonal Adequacy, and Social Adequacy. Under Individual Adequacy they include self-reliance, work orientation, and identity; Interpersonal Adequacy includes communication skills, enlightened trust, and knowledge of major roles; Social Adequacy includes social commitment, openness to sociopolitical change, and tolerance of individual and cultural differences. Each of those topics is further subdivided and separate sets of items composed for each; however, the subscales as scored correspond to the nine traits named above. Items are in the degree-of-agreement form, and the subject answers on a four-point scale. An example from the identity subscale is: "I change the way I feel and act so often that I sometimes wonder who the 'real' me is," scored negatively. Most of their analyses are based on the nine subscales.

They also performed a hierarchical factor analysis on the 188 items of Form B of their test. Had their model been completely confirmed, the analysis would have yielded one first-order factor for each subscale and a higher-order factor corresponding to each of the three major categories, Individual, Interpersonal, and Social Adequacy. The first such analysis, constrained to yield nine first-order factors, was discarded because it did not fit their structure; so was the second analysis, constrained to six first-order factors. The third analysis was performed without constraint on the number of first-order factors except for a technical requirement related to the maximum residual variance. That analysis yielded a good fit to the model only for Social Adequacy. No first-order factors supported the postulated subscales of Individual Adequacy, and the second-order factor most closely corresponding to Individual Adequacy included items from the communication subscale. Interpersonal Adequacy did not appear as a factor (Greenberger and others, 1974). These results are not as favorable for their model as they claim, particularly since the first two analyses were discarded for no apparent reason but not fitting the model. As in the case of some authors reviewed in chapters Eight and Nine, they do not seem to have any program for revising their model in the light of their data.

Josselson, Greenberger, and McConochie (1975) interviewed a group of eleventh-grade boys and girls selected to represent the extremes of psychosocial maturity as measured by the scales for Individual and Social Adequacy. The source was a high school that drew from a stable, white, blue-collar neighborhood. Their intention was to take the highest and lowest twenty-five students, but most of the highest were girls, the lowest, boys. So they chose separately the twelve highest and lowest boys and girls. Data are presented for a total of forty-one subjects. They remark on the similarity of their low-maturity girls to our sketches of Self-Protective and Conformist stages and of the high-maturity girls to our Conscientious Stage. Since they make no such remark concerning the boys, let us look at their findings with the boys.

The low-maturity boys are nonintrospective and focused on the present, concerned with sports, cars, motorcycles, girls, adults who yell at them, and staying out of trouble, particularly with respect to drink, dope, and reckless driving. They make many allusions to fights, being tough, and getting mad, yet these boys also are passive, depending on others for decisions about going to college or jobs. In their free time, too, they just wait for something to happen. They are preoccupied with being liked, and most have or have had steady girl friends. They value self-control and are grateful for controlling agents. Their fathers they tend to see as weak or as tyrants (which is probably as much a reflection of their own conceptual structure as of their fathers' characters, a point the authors fail to make). Most feel they have disappointed one or both parents. Friends are valued because "they help you." Their goal is to have a good job, a family, a house, a car, and lots of money; they are not concerned with what they will become.

For the high-maturity boys, school is relatively more important, as well as individual hobbies and religious interests; they are less focused on hypermasculine pursuits and popularity. They are oriented to the future and are more concerned with what they will be than with what they will have. Their self-esteem is derived more from what they do and hope to do than from peer approval. They appraise themselves more realistically than do the low-maturity boys, and they are more open to self-doubt. They recognize and tolerate individual differences. Most have not gone steady. A friend for them is someone to talk to, who understands you, who helps you out emotionally. They have little concern over impulse control, though some describe past struggles over it. They see themselves as changing and developing. They have differentiated conceptions of their parents, including speculations about psychological causation of their parents' behavior, something the authors report as never occurring with low-maturity boys. There is, however, a lack of rebellion in these boys and an excessive focus on being good, according to the authors.

Thus the low-maturity boys appear to be predominantly at the Self-Protective Stage, with unmistakable remnants of the Impulsive Stage, and the high-maturity boys appear to be predominantly at the Conscientious-Conformist level, with a clear potential for moving to the Conscientious Stage. One result that contradicted their expectations is that low-maturity boys are more involved in heterosexual relations than high-maturity boys; the two groups of girls did not differ in this regard. This finding cannot be predicted from their assumption that psychosexual maturity and psychosocial maturity occur together, nor from ours that they are largely independent, though it is closer to our view. It is probably best accounted for in terms of the relatively stringent impulse control characteristic of the Conformist and Conscientious stages.

On the whole, the results of the Greenberger group do not

confirm their own dimensional model. Their pictures of high- and low-maturity adolescents conform well to our stage descriptions. Thus, even though they begin with nine dimensions, they do not gain anything beyond our one-dimensional conception. That supports the major claim of this book, that the single variable of ego development gives a parsimonious account of a wide variety of data.

Another set of dimensions within which to view ego development is provided by Bellak, Hurvich, and Gediman (1973). Their list of twelve ego functions includes reality testing, judgment, sense of reality of the world and of the self, regulation and control of drives, affects, and impulses, object relations, thought processes, adaptive regression in the service of the ego, defensive functioning, stimulus barrier, autonomous functioning, synthetic-integrative functioning, and mastery-competence. They provide an interview schedule and a coding scheme for rating each of them on a seven-point scale. That their emphasis is on detecting and measuring pathology is shown by their scale: a rating of one for extreme pathology, six for normal or average, and seven for optimal functioning. Despite their primary interest in degrees of pathology, particularly schizophrenia, their list of functions overlaps that of Greenberger and coworkers and to some extend that of Hogan; however, one would have to go behind the labels to specific content and quoted examples to establish correspondences. For our purposes it suffices to note that this is a psychoanalytic approach in which ego development is conceived of as twelve more or less independent dimensions.

Among the other attempts to dimensionalize ego development are those of Prelinger and Zimet (1964), which is, like Bellak's, based on psychoanalytic theory, and Heath (1965), whose major dimensions are schemata, skills, and motives. The question is whether any of the proposed sets of dimensions adds appreciably to the explanatory or predictive power of our single dimension of ego development.

Conclusions

Suppose we look at individual differences from the point of view of Brunswik's lens model, his summary representation of the common format of his approach to perception and Tolman's to behavior (Hammond, 1966; Tolman and Brunswik, 1935). For Tolman, the behavioral means by which an organism achieves its purposes are multiple and substitutable, like Hull's habit-family hierarchy. For Brunswik, the perceptual clues by which an organism reconstructs the objective world are also multiple and mutually substitutable, a cue-family hierarchy. By making use of probabilistic cues and by behaving probabilistically, the organism adapts itself to the probabilistic texture of its environment, particularly the environment provided by other organisms. Because of the facts that behavior is a function of the whole organism and that a given disposition has many, diverse, mutually substitutable manifestations, only in the rarest circumstances will a particular behavior be an unequivocal index of a particular disposition or purpose. The equivocal significance of particular behaviors and of particular perceptual cues is the heart of the Brunswikian lens model. The lens of the model is the envelope of alternative behaviors or alternative perceptual cues. The foci of the lens are, for perception, the objects in the environment and the perception as apprehended. For behavior, the purpose and the person's dispositions are aspects of the focus within the organism, while achievements are the other focus of the lens. Brunswik (1952) argued that the foci of psychological theory should lie where the foci of psychological events do, within the organism and in the environment.

The specifist theories of individual differences look at the lens of the lens model, that is, at the multiple alternative behaviors, which cannot be other than equivocal cues to dispositions. Finding only low correlations among the alternative manifestations of the dispositions, the specifist wrongly concludes that there are only negligible dispositional factors, rather than seeing that the relations between a particular disposition and a particular indicator is only probabilistic. Thus the specifist view of individual differences differs from trait theories and from structural theories such as ours and Kohlberg's by focusing on a different layer, as Brunswik would call it. One may consider the specifist approach an example of what Brunswik, following Whitehead, called "the fallacy of misplaced concreteness." It seems to represent not a real theory but a point of view that precludes theory.

The Mischels' critique (Mischel and Mischel, 1976) of Kohlberg's work is that Kohlberg's sequential development of forms of moral reasoning is parsimoniously explained by the sequentiality of the related cognitive capacities interacting with socialization practices. The Mischels denigrate Kohlberg's evidence of a highly significant relation between cheating and moral maturity, because half those of low stage did not cheat. (Evidently they attribute to Kohlberg a belief in Original Sin.) Some moral behaviors can be predicted from Kohlberg's test with coefficients of about .3, they say, just about the value found with other measures that aim to predict such behavior. Thus Mischel, punctuating almost every paragraph of his articles and books with reference to empirical studies, appears to be asserting that the difference between his view and that of the structural and trait views is an empirical one. A closer look, however, often shows the research to bear on only minor points, with the major claims, such as that maturity of moral reasoning can be explained by cognitive maturity plus socialization, unsupported by data. Kohlberg's claim for the construct validity of his measure does not depend on high correlation with any particular behaviors; his focus is on moral judgment, not behavior. Situational specificity of behavior is consistent with Kohlberg's theory. If moral behavior can be predicted about as well by Kohlberg's test as by other tests that aim explicitly and solely to predict, that is a remarkable confirmation of the saliency and power of the conception of moral judgment.

On another plane, Mischel and Mischel criticize Kohlberg's reasoning as follows: a twelve-year-old juvenile delinquent from a lower socioeconomic stratum and an Ivy League professor no doubt would be scored differently on the test. In part that is because the professor's superior cognitive and linguistic maturity permits him to formulate his reasons more articulately. In addition, "For the professor, moral reasoning oriented explicitly towards approval from others, and adherence to conventional authority, is unlikely to be rewarding, unlikely to be valued, and thus unlikely to be used" (1976). Thus it is precisely because he is dependent on social approval that the professor makes it sound as if he is not! The transformation of motives is ruled out by definition. No matter what the professor's motivation may look like, it must be at bottom a matter of social approval. That is an illustration of what I shall call the Ontological Fallacy (Chapter Seventeen).

The decomposition of moral or ego development into a set of more or less independent traits, functions, or dimensions, as in the work of Hogan, Bellak, and Greenberger, is in effect a denial of the holistic or organismic view of our topic. Thus again more is at stake than issues of fact. In comparing the trait models with structural models, we must return to the distinction between polar variables and milestone sequences. Traits are ipso facto polar variables, defined in terms of their extremes. The developmental progression of structures is a milestone sequence. In the structural view, traits are reinterpreted as clues to structure rather than as the fundamental entities of individual differences. Some traits, such as spontaneity and conformity, can be shown to bear a curvilinear relation to the dimension of structural change. Once we admit the possibility of a multivalued curvilinear relation between some trait scores and the dimension of ego development, whose meaning and nature we are investigating, we see why factor analysis cannot discover such dimensions. The whole of classical psychometric theory is based on the assumption that the observed test scores are linearly related to the fundamental underlying determinants. That assumption is incompatible with the demonstrated curvilinear relationships. Thus the received psychometric approach to trait theory, with its General Linear Hypothesis (Cohen, 1968) and paraphernalia of linear decomposition, must be discarded or modified in this field. Trait models cannot represent adequately the complex integration of higher stages.

In conclusion, in viewing our topic in terms of structural transformations, I am in effect opposing its view in terms of a small set of traits or in terms of a larger set of environment-organism contingencies. To the extent that these are differences in scientific paradigms (Chapter Twelve), the issues are unlikely to be resolved by further research, for the proponents of different paradigms acknowledge different kinds of data. The measuring instruments proposed for structural conceptions have deficiencies (Chapter Nine), in part because of difficulties intrinsic to the field (Chapter Eight), but those deficiencies of particular instruments should not be interpreted as disproof of the structural model. The different models reflect different views of human nature, different scientific philosophies, and perhaps differences in personal temperament.

PART III

THEORIES

Unless it can be asserted that mankind did not know anything until logicians taught it to them . . . it must be allowed, that even the originality which can, and the courage which dares, think for itself, is not a more necessary part of the philosophical character than a thoughtful regard for previous thinkers, and for the collective mind of the human race. What has been the opinion of mankind, has been the opinion of persons of all tempers and dispositions, of all partialities and prepossessions, of all varieties in position, in education, in opportunities of observation and inquiry. No one inquirer is all this; every inquirer is either young or old, rich or poor, sickly or healthy, married or unmarried, meditative or active, a poet or a logician,

an ancient or a modern, a man or a woman; and if a thinking
person, has, in addition, the accidental peculiarities of his
individual modes of thought. Every circumstance which gives a
character to the life of a human being, carries with it its
peculiar biasses; its peculiar facilities for perceiving some things,
and for missing or forgetting others. But, from points of view
different from his, different things are perceptible; and none are
more likely to have seen what he does not see, than those who
do not see what he sees.

John Stuart Mill
Bentham

Chapter Eleven ═══════════════════

Early Theories:
Before Psychoanalysis

═══════════════════════

There major questions for a theory of the dynamics of ego development are: How does the ego function? How does it remain stable? How does it change? Within each question there are subsidiary issues; change, for example, poses the problems of both direction and impetus. The problem of ego functioning seems to be assimilated either to stability or to change, and no author has made a major contribution to both problems.

As a first approximation, the formal requirements for a theory of ego development are that the successive events of the sequence not all be formally identical, and that the postulated sequence of events be connected by an inner logic. These requirements differentiate the conception from the theory, while at the same time relating them. That the successive events of the sequence not be identical implies some idea of stages, though

without specifying how strictly the term *stage* must be construed. That the sequence of events be connected by an inner
logic is a statement that the conception of stages by itself does
not constitute a theory. A theory must have subject and predi-
cate; the sequence of stages is just the subject.

One purpose of this chapter is to reconstruct the history
that preceded the conceptions presented in Chapter Five. Perhaps because the subject has not been seen as having its own
history, many ideas have been rediscovered and presented as
new in generation after generation. A second purpose is to
sketch part of the background for psychoanalysis, a major
source of contemporary ego theory.

Psychology in Nineteenth-Century Philosophy

Before psychology became separated from philosophy as a discipline at the end of the nineteenth and the beginning of the
twentieth century, our topic was harbored chiefly within ethics,
where it appeared as moral development. There were two great
schools of ethical thought in the nineteenth century, the intuitionists and the utilitarians. The utilitarians had their source in
the British school of associationism. Roughly, the associationists believed that there is nothing in the mind except what
comes to it through the senses and what is evolved by a quasi-
mechanical association of sense data, the latter including information about both the environment and feelings.

Our concern is with the psychology, express or implied,
rather than with the ethics of utilitarianism. Bentham was the
arch-utilitarian, and in Chapter One we saw a bit of his doctrine,
that the "springs of action" can be described entirely in terms
of pleasure and pain. Bentham's "hedonic calculus" remains
alive today in psychologies based on reward-punishment and
stimulus-response, to which our view is an alternative.

The best known of the intuitionists is Immanuel Kant.
Kant differentiated hypothetical imperatives from the categorical imperative. Hypothetical imperatives tell us what we have to
do to satisfy our desires; they are the domain of science. The
categorical imperative, the domain of ethics, tells us what we

must do as moral beings; it is, essentially, conscience. The one categorical imperative is that each should act so that he could will his action to become a universal law. That is the whole content of morality. Not the consequences of the action but the goodwill with which it is undertaken determines its morality. Goodwill is like a jewel that shines by its own light even when wholly incapable of bringing about the good ends for which it aims. The utility of the deed cannot add to or subtract from its moral value. Whatever else one may say about the philosophy and psychology of Kant, one must admit that he was restoring to the conception of man a sense of agency, a sense that he was not merely the pawn of environmental forces but in some measure the origin of his own choices. Let us now turn to some developmental views of moral behavior.

Adam Smith, a Scot best known as an economist, wrote a book on moral philosophy in 1759, *The Theory of Moral Sentiments.* The first stage in evolution of conscience or the moral sense, he wrote, is the ability to put oneself in the place of another and to feel what he feels. When one reacts as the other does, one approves of or sympathizes with him. Having had this experience, one then realizes that the other is reacting the same way to oneself. Thus one learns to see oneself as others see one. Finally one forms a true social standard or "impartial spectator" within one's own breast, that is, a conscience. If a person could be raised outside society, he could no more judge the beauty or deformity of his character than he could judge the beauty or deformity of his own face without a mirror. Society holds for him the mirror of how he is seen by others. In passing judgment on himself, a person is divided into the judge and the judged, or the spectator and the agent (Smith, 1759).

Alexander Bain (1818-1903) was the author of the first standard text in psychology, widely used in the second half of the nineteenth century. His views on development of a sense of duty therefore must have been widely known at the time. The first stage for Bain (1859) was one where the child obeys in response only to direct, immediately imposed pleasures and pains. In the next stage the child obeys not only to protect his own interests but also to protect the interests of those he loves, such as his parents. In the third stage the child appreciates the reason for the command, and his sense of duty is thereby transformed into an autonomous conscience. It is an internal and idealized authority, the government within in imitation of the government outside. This transformation also generalizes the sense of obligation, so that it pertains to the intent and meaning of the law rather than merely doing or not doing specific deeds.

John Stuart Mill classed himself as a utilitarian, but he meant utility in a large sense, grounded upon the long-term interests of one developing towards his own best self. In Chapter One we saw his critique of the hedonic calculus of Bentham; conscience and a desire for excellence by one's own lights are among the elements that he found missing in Bentham's springs of action. In his essay on liberty, Mill added ([1859] 1962, p. 188):

> Among the works of man, which human life is rightly employed in perfecting and beautifying, the first in importance surely is man himself. Supposing it were possible to get houses built, corn grown, battles fought, causes tried, and even churches erected and prayers said, by machinery—by automatons in human form—it would be a considerable loss to exchange for these automatons even the men and women who at present inhabit the more civilised parts of the world, and who assuredly are but starved specimens of what nature can and will produce. Human nature is not a machine to be built after a model, and set to do exactly the work prescribed for it, but a tree, which requires to grow and develop itself on all sides, according to the tendency of the inward forces which make it a living thing.

Mill regarded individuality as a positive good and the pressure of custom as a form of despotism. Most people, he said, are conformist; they do not ask themselves what they prefer, even in private matters and things they do for pleasure. They ask themselves only what is suitable to their station and circumstances. "I do not mean that they choose what is customary in preference to what suits their own inclination. It does not occur

to them to have any inclination, except for what is customary . . . . Peculiarity of taste, eccentricity of conduct, are
shunned equally with crimes: until by dint of not following
their own nature they have no nature to follow: their human
capacities are withered and starved" (p. 190).

As between ethics based on conscience and one based on
the greatest happiness of the greatest number, Mill saw no contradiction. Conscience is the internal sanction for the sense of
duty, whatever its content. Conscience is associated with and
derived from sympathy, love, fear, religious feelings, childhood
recollections, self-esteem, desire for the esteem of others, and
self-abasement; this complexity gives rise to the mystical character that the intuitionists ascribe to conscience. While conscience, Mill believed, is acquired rather than innate, it is nonetheless natural, not in the sense of being present in everyone,
which it surely is not, but in being a natural outgrowth of human
faculties. The social feelings of mankind, the desire to be one
with other people, are one strong basis for conscience, Mill said,
though he did not reduce conscience to sympathy.

An element of the sense of justice noted by Mill is a desire
for retaliation or vengeance against those who have harmed
those with whom we sympathize. There is nothing moral about
the desire for vengeance, however. Only to the extent that it
becomes subordinate to the interests of society does it become
a part of the sentiment of justice and hence of the moral sense.

Much of the impact of evolution on philosophy and
psychology was due to Herbert Spencer (1820-1903) rather
than to Charles Darwin, or perhaps rather to the coincidence of
Spencer's and Darwin's contributions. Spencer came upon the
idea of development early in his life, long prior to the publication of the *Origin of Species.* The idea of evolution or development was compelling to him as a universal principle of life at all
levels. He saw evolution as a continuous change from indefinite,
incoherent homogeneity, to definite, coherent heterogeneity of
structure and function, through successive differentiations and
integrations. This principle he applied or found exemplified in
the fields of biology, psychology, sociology, and ethics. Only
his ethics is germane to our discussion.

Dewey and Tufts (1908, pp. 358-359) summarized Spencer's ethics as follows: "The consciousness of duty—the distinctively moral consciousness—is the control of proximate ends by remote ones, of simple by complex aims, of the sensory or presentative by the ideal or representative. An undeveloped individual or race lives and acts in the present; the mature is controlled by foresight of an indefinitely distant future. . . . Each step of the development of intelligence, of culture, whether in the individual or the race, is dependent upon ability to *subordinate* the immediate, simple, physically present tendency and aim to the remote, compound, and only ideally present intention." Moral restraint develops out of forms of restraint that are not distinctively moral. Originally the person is forced by outside authority to pay heed to remote consequences. The long-term, intrinsic effects of a given course, originally only associated with the immediate extrinsic restraints, ultimately predominate in determining his behavior. At this point the person is acting morally. Finally, moralization proceeds even further, so that duty itself becomes pleasure. For Spencer all this takes place by natural law. For him evolution was itself a kind of force.

While Spencer was the philosopher of evolutionary development, the nineteenth century also had philosophers of revolutionary development, preeminently G. W. F. Hegel (1770-1831). Hegel's formula for development was a dialectical one: to every thesis there is an antithesis, with the contradiction resolved by achieving a higher synthesis. This synthesis in turn becomes a thesis, is opposed by an antithesis, and the contradiction resolved by a new synthesis. This formula was his logic, an alternative to Aristotle's syllogistic reasoning, but it was also a kind of metaphysics and a theory of history: Each stage in history destroys, preserves, and improves the previous one. Passages in Hegel can be read as if he was describing something akin to ego development. His style is too obscure, however, for the description to provide much nourishment for us.

Auguste Comte (1798-1857) proposed a theory or law of three stages of human intellectual development. It is meant to be both an historical account and a law of intellectual progress. The three stages are the theological, the metaphysical, and the positive or scientific. In the first or theological stage natural phenomena are conceived by analogy with the human mind, animistically and anthropomorphically. Phenomena are personified; things are seen as having spirit or will that animates them to behave as they do. Within the theological stage the first substage is fetishistic. In it physical objects are supposed to be alive, with their own purposes and feelings. The second substage is polytheistic, with more or less invisible gods presiding over classes of phenomena. The third substage is monotheistic, with a single god creating and governing the universe. In the second great stage, the metaphysical, in place of spirits the universe is populated and animated by essences, tendencies, or potentialities. God, "Reason," or "Nature" provides the ultimate account of things, operating both as cause of and as reason for natural phenomena. With the dispute between realists and nominalists over the status of abstract concepts, this stage is brought to an end. In the final or positive stage the metaphysical search for absolute causes is given up, and men search instead for laws describing regularities of occurrence. This final stage is a fixed stage. All sciences, even the most advanced, bear marks of having passed through the earlier stages. The phases of development of the individual correspond to the same stages. "Each of us is aware, if he looks back upon his own history, that he was a theologian in his childhood, a metaphysician in his youth, and a natural philosopher in his manhood" (Comte, [1842] 1956, p. 126).

American Psychology at the Turn of the Century

E. B. Titchener, British by birth and Wundtian by training, was a major figure in American psychology at the beginning of this century. His school of thought was called *structuralism*; it was concerned with the generalized, adult human mind. Its method was introspective; it sought to find the contents of mind. Analysis of mind in terms of sensations and images connected by associations continued the elementarism of the British school of associationistic psychology and the German tradition of introspective analysis. The psychologists whose work forms the historical antecedents of the theory of ego development all stood in opposition to Titchenerian structuralism.

The typically American school of thought around the turn

of the century was called *functionalism,* by contrast with Titchener's structuralism. William James was the best known member of the functionalist school. Although he wrote several chapters in his *Principles of Psychology* (1890) on the self and closely related topics, he only skirted our subject matter. At the closest he wrote of the hierarchy of selves: the material self, the social self or selves, and the spiritual self. His description of the stream of consciousness, in which no idea ever returns exactly as a reinstatement of a previous one, was an argument against the elements of structuralism.

The school of functionalism can be summed up and defined by Angell's (1907) presidential address to the American Psychological Association. There are, according to Angell, three conceptions of functionalism as a school of psychology. It may be considered as the psychology concerned with mental operations rather than with mental elements; in this view it is contrasted with structuralism. Secondly, functionalism may be considered as the psychology concerned with the utility of consciousness; in this view mind or consciousness accommodates the organism to the environment, particularly to novel aspects of it. Thirdly, the broadest view of functionalism is as the psychology of the total mind-body organism. Angell argued against confining functional psychology to any one of these definitions; rather, the three domains are interdependent.

The most important single paper in establishing the functionalist point of view was Dewey's "The Reflex Arc Concept in Psychology" (1896). To understand the paper we must first reconstruct its topic, the reflex arc. The elementarist tradition encouraged the resolution of behavior into fragmentary constituents; the newer evolutionary movement encouraged the tracing of behavior to primitive origins, often ones shared with animals. While reflex action had long been known, the view of the reflex arc as both the model for the instigation of behavior and the basic unit out of which complex behaviors were compounded apparently arose in the latter half of the nineteenth century. The neurone theory, enunciated around 1890, permitted schematic representation of the reflex arc by three nerve cells, an afferent one, a central one, and an efferent one. According to this scheme, the stimulus excited the sense organ, which excited the afferent neurone or neurones; the excitement was centrally transmitted by another neurone; and the efferent neurone or neurones then elicited an appropriate response of muscle or gland.

That picture, said Dewey, is false. The elements of behavior are not stimuli and responses united by a reflex arc; from the beginning there are coordinations rather than separable stimuli and responses. Responses help constitute and thus create "stimuli." Moreover, reflex acts are not separable; the end of one is already the beginning of the next. What really happens is a circular response. Breaking acts into sensations and responses ignores the function of the act; the function is the clue to and source of the act's unity.

Dewey's coordinations have become Piaget's sensorimotor schemes (Chapter Twelve). Piaget has elaborated Dewey's insight that stimuli are constituted by responses and do not exist for the organism prior to and independently of response, as well as the concept of circular reactions. Oddly, Dewey's functionalism is an ancestor of a contemporary viewpoint that calls itself structuralist (Piaget, 1970; Merleau-Ponty, [1942] 1963). By the time Dewey's coordinations are reinterpreted as structures of behavior, however, much has been added (see Chapter Three). Despite the brilliance and the immediate impact of Dewey's paper, psychology based on the reduction of behavior to reflexes continued to grow. The whole conditioned reflex school of thought lay ahead, and even Freud paid obeisance to reflexes as the basic unit of behavior. Going from knowledge that reflex actions occur to taking them as the model of behavior involves a leap. The corresponding psychological assumption, coming from the British school of associationists, was that mind or consciousness is the passive spectator of behavior, which must originate in sensations. The subject matter of the present book thus lies in direct line of descent from Dewey's paper. The contemporary descendants of reflexology describe the mind as the passive recipient of inputs or as the processor of other people's programs.

Baldwin: The Dialectic of Personal Growth

James Mark Baldwin (1861-1934), one of psychology's great theorists, exemplified the evolutionary point of view in his books on mental development and on social and ethical development, published before the turn of the century. Baldwin (1897) made central to his theory of ego development the "dialectic of personal growth." The infant first learns to distinguish persons from other objects, which Baldwin called (in a usage different from the current one) the *projective* stage. Next a child learns to see himself as a person among persons but possessed of special feelings he cannot observe in others; this Baldwin termed the *subjective* stage in the development of the sense of self. Then the child learns to think of others as having those feelings he can discern in himself; this Baldwin termed the *ejective* stage. By continual repetition of these processes, seeing himself in the light of what he can observe in others and inferring in others what he can feel within himself, his ego development proceeds into childhood and adolescence. As a result, the content of the ego and of the alter are almost identical; one thinks of himself very much as he thinks of others.

The young child's behavior exhibits a polarity; he imitates those more powerful and practices on those less powerful. Towards those in authority he appears altruistic; this aspect is his accommodating self. But toward younger siblings he is apt to be aggressive and selfish; this aspect is his self of habit. Gradually, however, he builds an ideal self, at first modeled after persons in the environment, especially parents, but gradually, through operation of intelligence, generalized into principles to which even his models are required to adhere. Imitation, a kind of instinct, is the moving force in development. Baldwin noted (1897, p. 42):

> Here, in this dawning sense of the larger limits which set barriers to personal freedom, is the "copy" forming which is his personal authority, or law. It is "projective" because he cannot understand it, cannot anticipate it, cannot find it in himself. And it is only

by imitation that he is to reproduce it, and so arrive at a knowledge of what he is to understand it to be. So it is a "copy for imitation" . . . . It is not I, but I am to become it. Here is my ideal self, my final pattern, my "ought" set before me. My parents and teachers are good because, with all their differences from one another, they yet seem to be alike in their acquiescence in this law. Only in so far as I get into the habit of being and doing like them in reference to it, get my character moulded into conformity with it, only so far am I good. And so, like all other imitative functions, it teaches its lesson only by stimulating to action . . . . But as I thus progress in doing, I forever find new patterns set for me; and so my ethical insight must always find its profoundest expression in that yearning which anticipates but does not overtake the ideal.

When the child is able to see himself as bipolar—now the aggressive egoist, now the unselfish and accommodating pupil— he then sees the same two possibilities in others. With that he learns to classify actions rather than persons and then to adapt himself appropriately to occasions. One cannot say that either the egoistic self or the altruistic one is more real; the real self is the bipolar self, the social self, in all its complexity. With the rise of an ideal self, something new is added. The child learns to obey commands even when he does not want to. This aspect is not the same as the accommodating self that gladly imitates. The new self sets laws for both of the old selves; thus arises the self of conformity and the beginning of conscience. Although the child learns always and only by imitation, his attempt to reproduce a copy has an element of invention and interpretation. The child needs to have others agree with his inventions and interpretations. Children differ in the relative strength of their needs for social confirmation and for a sense of agency, the former leading to adaptability, the latter to originality.

Social judgment and private judgment are virtually equated in Baldwin. Under the heading of "selective thinking" he wrote, "The organization of the personal self is the ground of the selection of the particular thought as true" (p. 130) whenever personal attitude is involved in a judgment. Social factors influence this selection; the need for social confirmation follows from the dialectic of personal growth. (These ideas reappear in Sullivan as *selective inattention* and *consensual validation*.)

The ethical sense remains throughout life largely social. Social approval induces self-approval, social disapproval induces self-disapproval, regardless of whether they are justified. This reaction is not simply a reflection of public judgment. Rather, the judgment of another is necessary to call forth the full ethical sense because of the similarity of ego and alter.

The detailed instincts of animal life do not exist in man, according to Baldwin. Man's hereditary constitution is plastic, and social heredity takes the place of hereditary instincts. He insisted, however, on continuity in animals and man. Sympathy and even jealousy are observable in dogs, for example. The organic sympathy observable in dogs and babies differs from the reflective sympathy that arises with the sense of self, deriving from the similarity of ego and alter. Nonetheless, there is a continuity in the development of sympathy from organic to reflective.

Baldwin said that the intuitionist schools of ethics are based on psychologically false assumptions because they ignore the continuity of man and animal. The utilitarian schools of ethics, whose logic depends on reduction of sympathetic impulses to egoistic ones, are also false, since both sympathetic and egoistic impulses extend down to animals. Moreover, the ethical sense is based not on sympathy but justice; the two need not coincide. The ethical or ideal sense overcomes the antithesis between reflective sympathy and intelligent self-seeking. Ethical intelligence finds it unnatural and unreasonable to be either purely self-seeking or purely altruistic, because of the equivalence of ego and alter, but natural and reasonable to be dutiful.

Baldwin discerned much of the sequence here called *ego development*. There are, he stated, three great epochs of behavior, the spontaneous, the intelligent, and the ideal or ethical. The sanctions of behavior in those epochs arc, successively, impulse, desire, and right. The first departure from the sanction of impulse is toward the hedonic sanction of pleasure and pain, operating as an inhibition on pure impulse. In the epoch of desire, motive and sanction of behavior are equated; the sanction of intelligent action inhibits that of impulse. Objectively, the sanction of behavior is its success in this epoch. In the period of about two to four years, actions are governed or sanctioned by the aggressive self. When the child first learns that he has intelligence and can use it to his advantage, "he hoodwinks his juniors, circumvents his attendants, attempts to deceive his elders" (p. 395). Some grown men are of this type, using their social environment for personal advantage. But for the normal child in this epoch, the other side of his nature also continues to govern his conduct, resulting in sympathetic, disinterested conduct, which is also sanctioned by its success. As this epoch develops, the child becomes aware of the distinction between things as facts and things as objects of desire. Then pleasure itself becomes an object of desire. Thus for this period there is a real "hedonic calculus." Imitative accommodation and growth towards unity and organization of thought lead on towards the ethical epoch, during which the sanction becomes the categorical imperative of conscience, which is quasi-impulsive, as Baldwin astutely noted, anticipating Freud's conception of superego.

Since he leaned so heavily on imitation as the moving principle, one can guess that Baldwin would have greater difficulty dealing with stages of ego development beyond the Conformist Stage than in discussing earlier stages. He did acknowledge the possibility that an individual may evolve an ethical sentiment that conflicts with the actual opinion of his society, but in principle, conscience remains an internalized version of a social judgment. "The ethical in man represents the essential and highest outcome of his individual nature. . . . The socially established represents the highest outcome of the collective activities of man. . . . What then can be done, in the case of conflict between these two? *Nothing! . . . This is the final and irreducible antinomy of society*" (pp. 566-567). Later, however, in a little-known epistemological study, Baldwin (1906-1915) showed a profound understanding of some aspects of more mature stages.

Cooley: The Reflected Self

The origins of the self in social relations is a topic associated with Cooley, who used the term "the looking-glass self" in *Human Nature and the Social Order* (1902). There is, Cooley said, no sense of *myself* without a correlative sense of *you.* Moreover, there is a large class of cases in which one's self-feeling is determined by how he imagines he appears to another particular person. This kind of self-idea has three main elements: "the imagination of our appearance to the other person; the imagination of his judgment of that appearance; and some sort of self-feeling, such as pride or mortification. The comparison with a looking-glass hardly suggests the second element, the imagined judgment, which is quite essential" ([1902] 1968, p. 90).

Moreover, "As social beings we live with our eyes upon our reflection, but have no assurance of the tranquility of the waters in which we see it. In the days of witchcraft it used to be believed that if one person secretly made a waxen image of another and stuck pins into the image, its counterpart would suffer tortures, and that if the image was melted the person would die. This superstition is almost realized in the relation between the private self and its social reflection. They seem separate but are darkly united, and what is done to the one is done to the other" ([1902] 1968, p. 141).

Self-respect implies a higher or ideal self to which one always aspires. The ideal self is built up in social intercourse by imagining how one would look to admired people. These people need not be actual companions but may themselves be idealized heroes. It is easier to enjoy someone else's garden than one's own, where one always thinks of needed improvements; so it is with the self. This kind of self-respect Cooley equated with Goethe's term *self-reverence* and Emerson's term *self-reliance.* Evidently conceptions of the ideal self were part of the public domain.

Evolution of Morals

In the early years of the twentieth century there was great interest in moral development, culminating in the publication of

Hobhouse's two volumes, *Morals in Evolution* (1906), and the two volumes of Westermarck, *The Origin and Development of the Moral Ideas* (1906, 1908). The works drew on many of the same sources; neither would have been possible except as the result of an interest pursued by many others. These books came out of the then-new field of cultural anthropology, largely a post-Darwin development. While the idea of inevitable progress in human institutions was characteristic for the eighteenth and nineteenth centuries, viewing morals as a natural phenomenon to be investigated historically was new. Modern anthropology has retreated somewhat from this interest, which was in part at least speculative and anecdotal, in favor of topics that can be treated with more methodological rigor. The analogy between the development of the child and the race, summarized in the nineteenth-century slogan, "Ontogeny recapitulates phylogeny," has been discredited. Moreover, viewing primitive peoples as childlike has been stigmatized as ethnocentric. From our point of view, however, something important has been lost in dropping this line of thought. At any rate, it can be included for its historical importance.

As representative of this point of view we will take the *Ethics* of Dewey and Tufts (1908), a popular textbook in a time that most college students took a course in ethics. It drew on Baldwin, Hobhouse, and the first volume of Westermarck. Let us follow their discussion.

The terms *ethos* and *mores,* referring to customs, are the roots of the words *ethics* and *morals.* In primitive communities there are no distinctions between customs and moral standards. Conduct in primitive societies is largely determined by group customs and by one's place in the group. When someone transgresses, the whole group may be held responsible. There are three levels of conduct. The first level arises from instincts and fundamental needs. It may lead to action in accord with moral laws, but this level is not directed by moral judgment. Its motives are external to moral ends. The second level is regulated by the standards of society. This is the level of custom and of social motives. No society exists where behavior consists of conduct of the first level only. Even in savage life, social motives prevail. Use of physical coercion to enforce standards is the exception in primitive societies. Taboos, rituals, and public opinion suffice. The third level is the level of conscience. Conduct on this level is social and rational; it is examined and criticized. The things we have to do to satisfy our needs lead to rationalizing and socializing endeavors; they are not necessarily moral, but they are necessary predecessors. Foresight, control of impulses, continuity of purpose, organized habits all are developed to fulfill nonmoral needs and then form the groundwork for morality.

With the evolution of more complex social forms, there are many factors requiring and leading to social cooperation, such as differentiation of labor, arts and crafts, and even war. War develops courage, efficiency, and a sense of power and achievement. Arts and crafts give visible and audible embodiment to the idea of order or form. Division of labor makes for mutual cooperation, to which family life adds sympathy and kindness. Certain conditions bring out the importance of group standards and make group control conscious. They include the education of the young, adjustment of conflicting interests, restraint of refractory members of the group, and occasions of crisis and danger.

Moral progress occurs as a result of collision of the authority and interests of the group with the independence and private interests of the individual. The occasion for moral growth is the tension between order and progress, between habit and reformation. The first results of the growth of individualism may seem like a breakdown of standards, but individualism is the condition for moral progress. Among the forces leading to growth of individualism are economic ones. The farmer, unlike the hunter, must plant for a distant future; hence foresight and planning are required. Trading with other groups leads to exchange of ideas as well as goods, expanding the range of possibilities open to persons in the group. Science leads to growth of individualism by discrediting some beliefs on which customs are based. The arts and technologies not only create useful artifacts that may lead to change but by encouraging craftsmanship may further promote individualism. Among the psychological forces leading to individualism are the demands and interests of sexual life, the demand for possessions and private property, the desire for honor and social esteem, and the struggle for either mastery or liberty. While religion is often conservative in its effect, the struggle for religious liberty is carried on by religious persons.

Both the Hebrew and the Greek cultures contributed to moral development of the modern world. In the Hebrew culture conscience was associated with the will of God, in the Greek culture with rational standards. The Jewish prophets extolled righteousness, while the Greek philosophers extolled measure and harmony. Wisdom or insight was the chief virtue for Plato and Socrates, while in the Jewish Bible the fear of the Lord is the beginning of wisdom.

The covenant between God and Israel represents a moral advance over custom as the source of moral rules. Religious laws became the personal commands of a personal deity; thus offenses were also personal disobedience, not bad luck nor the responsibility of the family or group. God's commands were not arbitrary but righteous. The idea of atonement and reconciliation introduces a new element: righteousness is not mere conformity to a set of rules but is a matter of the spirit. There is constant reconstruction of the spirit and possibility for renewal. Justice, love, and peace became social ideals among the Jews. Seeing greed, oppression, and land monopoly practiced by their rulers, who were zealous observers of ritual and defenders of traditional religion, led to a more abstract and examined morality, transcending ritual and custom.

Among the things leading to conflict and moral growth in the Greeks were the stories of the gods, embodying various human vices from infidelity to murder. Seeing the despots governing many Greek cities also led to a questioning of secular authority. Once the question is raised of what is good or just, the merely conventional ceases to be an answer.

Let us, following Dewey and Tufts, look at Plato's *Republic*. We find there an early version of a theme, the personification of forces within the individual, that reappears in Mead and in Freud. Plato continually compared the individual with the state. In the ideal state there should be three classes: the guardians or magistrates, the auxiliary (including soldiers), and the producers. Corresponding to these three classes, the soul of man contains three principles, the appetitive principle or love of gain, the spirited principle or love of honor, and the rational principle or love of wisdom. The just state is achieved by harmony of the three classes, and the just man models himself on the just state, striving for harmony of appetite, spirit, and reason. While appetites represent the largest part and reason the smallest part in the soul of any man, yet in the just man reason must prevail. The ideal state may never be achieved, but it exists as a form in the mind of God, and thus may serve as a model even though it does not exist.

When we discard convention as the ultimate test of truth and set against it the natural, the question arises, What is natural? Some Greek philosophers, the Cynics and the Cyrenaics or hedonists, felt that society is artificial. This view was of course a form of individualism. For the hedonists the good is pleasure, and a wise man aims to find the purest and most intense pleasure. For Aristotle, however, the true nature of anything, including man, is not to be found in its crude beginnings but rather in its complete development. The political state exists to make life good; so the state is a natural institution. Man is a political animal whose highest and true nature is achieved within society.

The contrast in both Plato and Aristotle between the real and the ideal represents a contribution to moral thinking, Dewey and Tufts continue. This contrast was indelibly stamped on them by the official execution of Socrates, Plato's teacher, making it impossible for them to equate the existing state with an ideal one. Both Plato and Aristotle had an idea of human development towards an ideal and thought that the state should foster this development but that the actual state might not do so.

In the Greek poets conscience at first was seen as largely compounded of Nemesis, an external symbol of divine penalty, and Aidos, respect for public opinion and reverence for the authority of the gods. Later poets added notions akin to character and responsibility, that a man should not desert his true self nor do that which is not meet.

Modern society evolved out of other elements in addition to the Greek and Hebrew traditions. Roman civilization contributed conceptions of government, law, and rights. Christianity grew out of and reflected other traditions as well, such as the German and Celtic. The rise of universities, even though they were at first dominated by religious studies, led to an interest in dialectical discourse that contributed to the growth of individualistic conscience. The battle for civil and political liberties has been fought by various elements of society at various times; what is morally significant has been development of the conception of natural rights as an explicit moral principle to appeal to.

Both commerce and art have the effect of raising the question of values to an explicit plane, requiring people to search themselves as to what is worth most for them. During the Reformation the conflict of authorities led to a questioning of dogma, as did the growth of science in the Renaissance. The thrust of the eighteenth-century Enlightenment was directed against ignorance, superstition, and dogma. In the seventeenth, eighteenth, and nineteenth centuries philosophy took a reflexive turn, concerning itself with human understanding and thus with man's own contribution to knowledge. Widespread education, the invention of the printing press, and translation of the Bible into the Vulgate all had the effect of elevating a sense of choice and judgment among people generally. Knowledge and wisdom are indispensable elements of conscience; in Greek and Latin, as in French, the word for *conscience* is not distinguished from the word for *consciousness,* they point out.

As conscious morality evolves out of customary morality, there is a deepening of meaning. In the economic sphere men not only weigh values, but they see themselves as the measure of values and as giving value. This perception leads to the idea of each man as himself worth more than the things that gratify him and hence to a valuing of character itself. A similar deepening of meaning occurs in the juridical sphere. As Dewey and Tufts note (1908, pp. 182-183):

It is in the school of government and courts that man has learned to talk and think of right and law, of

responsibility and justice. To make these moral instead of jural terms, the first thing that is needed is
that we make the whole process an inward one. The
person must himself set up a standard, recognize it as
"law," judge his conduct by it, hold himself responsible to himself, and seek to do justice . . . . That a
single person can be himself lawgiver, judge, and jury,
as well as claimant or defendant, shows that he is
himself a complex being. He is a being of passions,
appetites, and individual interests, but he is also a
being who has a rational and social nature. As a
member of society he not only feels his individual
interest but recognizes social interests. As a rational
being he not only feels the thrill of passion but responds to the authority of a law and obeys the voice
of duty. Like a member of a democratic State, he
finds himself in the sphere of conduct not only a subject but a sovereign, and feels the dignity of a *person*.

With the growth of reflective morality out of customary
morality, individual differences in moral level are greatly increased. Because the moral element of life is separated from
fashion, business, politics, and other spheres, because morality
requires reflection on deeper meanings, because reflective
morality potentially leads to conflict with society, and because
these factors operate together, not only are prophets created
but also dissolute men and women. The latter feel justified in
flouting the moral laws that bind the Philistines, to whom they
feel superior. Thus the effect of individualism and moral progress is to raise some men above the generality and to lower
others.

The vice of the criminal and the coarsely selfish man is to
act contrary to the purposes and wishes of others; the vice of
the egoist and of every man on his egoistic side is to neglect the
interest of others; the vice of the reformer and philanthropist is
to try to "promote the social welfare in ways which fail to engage the active interest and cooperation of others" (p. 303).
Only in modern times has this kind of spiritual selfishness been
recognized, as, for example, in some of Ibsen's later plays.

Dewey and Tufts criticized both the intuitionist type of ethics, judging morality only in terms of good will or motive and not at all in terms of consequences, and the utilitarian type, judging only in terms of consequences, not motive. Neither view can be held consistently, they asserted. Truly good intentions require consideration for consequences, and actions that bring good consequences will only rarely occur by accident without an intention to produce them, that is, without goodwill. Each of the traditional schools thus embodies but a part of the highest ethical ideal. The highest ethical good they defined in terms of self-realization, "that which is harmonious with all the capacities and desires of the self, that which expands them into a cooperative whole" (p. 314), an ideal going back to Aristotle. Self-realization is not a static condition but a continual reconstruction of character. There remains always a tension between what the person has accomplished and what is possible. Neither self-assertion nor self-sacrifice for its own sake constitutes self-realization, but rather self discovered in the moral act and at the same time self lost via identification of self with the purposes of the moral act.

Hobhouse (1906), more than Dewey and Tufts, brought out the structure of thought and of social institutions and of their relationships. He traced moral evolution in terms of ethical conceptions, character, and social institutions. Institutions cannot rise too far above nor fall too far below the character of the people subject to them. For primitive people who believe in magic and evil spirits, only a morality of retaliatory vengeance is possible. With the growth of clearer conceptions of causality, the gods first become another human community with human foibles, then evolve towards more idealized figures. The development from concrete images to abstract entities paves the way for abstract ethical principles, or rather, the same mental capacities are needed for both. The contradictions to which the spiritual religions lead —such as, how can an all-powerful Deity countenance evil?—then encourage the growth of critical and philosophical thinking, which prepares for the highest, most universalized ethical thinking. Hobhouse left open the possibility of ethical evolution beyond what he himself had achieved or could foresee.

Because he was concerned with the structure of society and ideas, Hobhouse brought out a paradox of social evolution: development from primitive to civilized society proceeds towards a greater differentiation and integration of functions within ever-wider social groups. One effect of the progression is to bring about the institution of slavery, the subjugation of women, and other distinctions of class and caste that are more onerous to the victims and more morally repugnant to us than the egalitarianism of primitive societies. At the highest ethical stages a key concept for Hobhouse was personality, in which he included rights that inhere in the individual by virtue of being a person. Recognition of personality in that sense is incompatible with subjugation of individuals by virtue of their membership in an unprivileged class. The conception of personality is unknown among primitive groups governed by custom and taboo. Hobhouse's conception is developmental in a double sense. He not only viewed morality as developing, he saw the highest ideal in terms of self-development. Thus Hobhouse, like Dewey and Tufts, saw as the highest stage of ethics something akin to our highest stage of ego development.

McDougall: Psychology of Instincts

William McDougall was trained as a physician, worked for a time as an anthropologist, established an experimental laboratory, and contributed to experimental psychology. Those of his contributions that enter our story are, however, theoretical in a philosophical rather than an experimental tradition. Connections between his data and experience and his theories are not obvious, in contrast with Freud, as we shall see.

His account of the growth of character McDougall considered to be the most novel and original albeit neglected part of his *Social Psychology,* originally published in 1908 but later revised and added to. The fundamental problem of social psychology, he stated, is moralization. Ethics, along with the social sciences, has been based on false psychological assumptions of two main types. One of these is that conscience is a special faculty, instinct, or intuition, such as Kant's categorical imperative. The other is psychological hedonism, the doctrine that the desire for pleasure and aversion to pain is the sole and universal motive, the basis for utilitarianism. There are at least three different types of psychological hedonism, which are often confused. If past pleasures and pains provide the motive, the theory can be a mechanistic one. If future pleasures and pains provide the motive, the theory encompasses purpose. Another alternative depends entirely on current pleasures and pains. McDougall rejected all forms of hedonism. The hungry man desires a steak, the lover desires his beloved. Neither wishes for pleasure per se; rather, pleasure is the byproduct of achieving his desires, just as pain results from frustration of desire. Moreover, hedonism confuses happiness with pleasure or with the sum of pleasures. Only children and less developed and poorly unified personalities are wholly dominated by the pleasure and pain of the moment. The more highly developed and the more integrated the personality, the more the person can sustain happiness despite intercurrent pains, that are as ripples on the surface of the tide. Among the objections to the doctrine of conscience as a special faculty are that it hardly allows for development and that it introduces a type of explanation for conduct that has no counterpart in animal behavior. McDougall, like Freud, turned to instincts or instinctual impulses (*Triebe*) for a class of explanations that allows for continuity between animal and human behavior.

McDougall considered instincts in both animals and men to be purposive behavior (a definition akin to that of some modern ethologists). Each instinct includes a propensity for a certain perception, a characteristic emotion, and a pattern of reaction. The emotion and the goal are relatively fixed, but other elements are plastic in the service of the goal and hence subject to learning and alteration. His list of instincts varied from time to time but included reproduction, flight, the gregarious instinct, curiosity, pugnacity, the instinct of acquisition, and so on—all, he said, species-specific goal-directed behavior. Men do such things because it is in their nature. There is thus a circularity in invoking instincts as explanation of behavior, but perhaps no more than in hedonic explanations. McDougall criticized Baldwin's explanation in terms of an instinct of imitation. Actions being imitated can be almost anything; hence imitation, having no specific goal, cannot be an instinct. McDougall approved of Freud for making instincts the prime movers of behavior and also for seeing purpose in all behavior, even dreams and neurotic symptoms. He complained, however, that Freud confused the sex instinct with the sentiment of love. For McDougall sentiments were separate from instincts. He defined a sentiment, following Shand, as "an organised system of emotional tendencies centred about some object" (McDougall, [1908] 1928, p. 105). A complex is the pathological counterpart. A sentiment is thus a structured, semipermanent part of the personality.

McDougall sketched moral behavior as proceeding through the following stages (p. 156):

> (1) the stage of instinctive behaviour modified only by the influence of the pains and pleasures that are incidentally experienced in the course of instinctive activities; (2) the stage in which the operation of the instinctive impulses is modified by the influence of rewards and punishments administered more or less systematically by the social environment; (3) the stage in which conduct is controlled in the main by the anticipation of social praise and blame; (4) the highest stage, in which conduct is regulated by an ideal of conduct that enables a man to act in the way that seems to him right regardless of the praise or blame of his immediate social environment.

That the development of the individual more or less recapitulates the evolution of human society he made plain. McDougall also allowed for the developmental sequence generating a dimension of individual differences, though he did not stress that fact. Even of the lowest stage he said (p. 154):

> There are, no doubt, even in civilised communities, individuals of low type, brought up under unfavourable circumstances, whose behavior hardly rises above this level. Whatever power of conceptual

thought such a being attains is exercised merely in the immediate service of desire springing directly from some one or other of the primary instinctive impulses; he may display a certain cunning in the pursuit of his ends and may form certain habits in the service of these impulses, perhaps an habitual caution in the presence of strangers, an habitual brutality towards those of whom he has no fear. He has no sense of responsibility or duty or obligation, no ideal of self; he has but rudimentary sentiments in regard to himself or others, has no character, whether good or bad, in the proper sense of the word, and, therefore, is incapable of true volition.

McDougall saw the genesis of higher levels out of the lower ones as one of the central mysteries of life. How is it that the immensely strong instinctual impulses come to be governed by the much weaker rational and moral ideals? Having discarded solutions in terms of a special faculty of conscience or of learning what gives pleasure and pain, he proceeded to work out his solution in terms of instinctual impulses and organized sentiments.

Among the elements that enter into the moralization of conduct are the idea of the self and several instincts. The instinct of self-abasement and the corresponding emotion of subjection are necessary to account for shame and bashfulness, which can be observed in children and even in dogs. The parental instinct with its emotion of tenderness is the root of all altruism. Tender emotion is not to be confused with sympathy, which is a desire for sharing of sentiments. Active sympathy is thus basically egoistic, a seeking of one's own satisfaction. It is not the root of altruism, as Bain and others have asserted, but it is a valuable adjunct to tender emotion in formation of altruism and in stimulating social cooperation. Moreover, sympathy, along with the influence of authority, accounts for the transition from the stage governed by reward and punishment to that governed by approval and disapproval; no doubt self-abasement and the gregarious instinct contribute.

The parent aroused in defense of his child is the prototype

of that alliance of tender emotion and the emotion of anger, deriving from the instinct of pugnacity, that is the germ of all moral indignation. Moral indignation in turn is, along with the emotion of revenge, the root of justice and the public law.

For a person to advance to the highest moral plane requires that his predominant sentiment be the self-regarding sentiment, which derives originally from the self-assertive instinct and the corresponding emotion of positive self-feeling. Self-respect always contains a strong mixture of desire for the approval of others, in part because our idea of self always develops in a social context. The extension of the self-regarding sentiment to one's family and to wider social groups with which one identifies himself, such as the community or nation, leads to a quasi-altruism that is an important part of the moral equipment of the person. It leads to enrichment of emotional life and subjection of immediately personal motives.

Once a child moves beyond the limits of his own home, he is subject to conflicting standards of approval and disapproval, something that does not take place in primitive societies governed by rigid customs. McDougall, like Dewey and Tufts, found in this circumstance the occasion both for moral progress for the elite and for the possibility of some moral retrogression for the mass of men. At its highest level, moral character is based not on approval or disapproval of those in whose company we live but on allegiance to abstract moral principles, to which we are wedded by our own self-regard. Altruism does not suffice; self-criticism is also an indispensable component of the highest level of character. Altruistic and egoistic emotions and sentiments are reconciled in the highest moral estate, that of striving for the realization of abstract ideals such as justice.

The infant's actions are caused by instincts in some almost mechanical sense. Only as he becomes able to represent purposes to himself is a child's behavior guided by those ends. At first the purposes are immediate ones and often at variance with each other. "With the development of a unified personality (*i.e.* of clear self-consciousness, a consistent ideal of conduct and a strong sentiment for the self and for that ideal), these are more and more superseded and controlled by a single all-powerful final cause, the ideal of the self" (p. 226). Thus the highest types of human character are shown to develop from instinctive dispositions shared with animals.

Mead: Social Behaviorism

George Herbert Mead was a philosopher at the University of Chicago, having gone there with John Dewey in 1896. His continuing influence on psychology has come largely via his influence on sociology. Directly or indirectly, his thinking seems also to have influenced H. S. Sullivan, who was a medical student at the University of Chicago during Mead's tenure. Since Mead's work, like Sullivan's, was published largely posthumously, his influence is not always easy to trace.

Although he was influenced by Baldwin, particularly in regarding the genesis of the self as the central problem of social psychology, Mead did not accept Baldwin's explanation in terms of an instinct of imitation. It is absurd to suppose that we have a ready-made response to act the way other people act, with each such response triggered by sight of exactly the same behavior in the other person, Mead (1934) said. He also rejected the view of the central nervous system as analogous to a telephone switchboard; here he was following the argument of Dewey's paper on the reflex arc. The nervous system acts as a unity, even though we do not know where the integration lies. Moreover, the organism to a considerable extent selects its own environment, that is, its "stimuli," by virtue of its sensitivities. The chief thrust of Mead's exposition was to oppose the view of each man as imprisoned in the cell of his own consciousness, tapping on the walls to communicate with other such prisoners.

Mead's explanation of imitative behavior was based on the idea of circular reaction. Social behavior is antecedent to mind, self, or consciousness. The social act can be analyzed into a gesture on the part of one person (or animal), an accommodation on the part of another, all relevant to some outcome that gives the meaning of the act. A gesture is a significant symbol when the sender responds to it, at least implicitly, the same way the receiver does. Vocal gestures are uniquely suited to become significant symbols because we hear our own voice much as others do, whereas we do not see ourselves as others do. Imitation is particularly characteristic of vocal gestures, which are naturally suited to circular reactions.

Mind and consciousness arise when we learn to represent ourselves to ourselves by taking the view of others. Thus behavior, the social act, is both logically and temporally prior to consciousness. Meaning is not an idea or state of consciousness separate from the social act but is constituted in the experience. Symbolization constitutes objects; language does not simply represent things already there. An outcome of symbolization is the self, which arises just at the point where one becomes self-conscious.

One can watch the evolution of the self in children. In play, the young child at times takes several roles alternately; some children have imaginary playmates. In either case, the child is carrying on a "conversation of gestures" with himself. In an organized game, characteristic of a later stage, the child must implicitly take the attitude of everyone in it. The different roles must have a definite relation to one another. Rules are part of the enjoyment of the game. Thus, in the evolution of self, one first takes the view of particular others, later that of the "generalized other." The social process or community enters behavior as a controlling factor in the form of the generalized other. "What goes on in the game goes on in the life of the child all the time. He is continually taking the attitudes of those about him, especially the roles of those who in some sense control him and on whom he depends" (Mead, 1934, p. 160).

The child, of course, cannot incorporate the whole personality of the parent. He assumes only the corresponding role, for the personality of the parent has become more complex, having evolved on the basis of just such play, as well as later social interactions, so that it incorporates the various roles within itself. The young child as yet has no such complexity in himself, nor does he understand its existence in his parent. When a child behaves in a parental fashion towards dolls, his nascent and incipient parental attitudes are being stimulated by his own dependent needs, just as his parents' responses are stimulated by his needs. Thus, what is called *imitation* is, in this and some other instances, rather, self-stimulation.

Mead used the term the *me* to stand for the conventional, habitual self embodying the view of the generalized other and hence largely similar to the selves of other members of the near community. The *I* or ego always remains somewhat unpredictable and spontaneous. For this reason, and also because each person formulates the generalized other from his own standpoint, Mead allowed for individual differences more effectively than did Baldwin.

It is inconceivable from Mead's view that there be a self prior to social experience, since selfhood arises in taking the view of others to oneself. Mead said (p. 223):

> In defending a social theory of mind we are defending a functional, as opposed to any form of substantive or entitive, view .... We are opposing all intra-cranial or intra-epidermal views as to its character and locus. For it follows from our social theory of mind that the field of mind must be co-extensive with ... the matrix of social relations and interactions among individuals, which is pre-supposed by it, and out of which it arises or comes into being. If mind is socially constituted, then the field or locus of any given individual mind must extend as far as the social activity or apparatus of social relations which constitutes it extends; and hence that field cannot be bounded by the skin of the individual organism to which it belongs.

Conclusions

While a conception of ego development as the characterological trace of a developmental sequence is modern, the elements are old. The generality of the ideas is such that one would be foolhardy to say who was first with many of them. Characterologies go back at least as far as Plato; the concepts of moral growth and of the ideal self to Plato and Aristotle; stages of moral growth to Adam Smith, Alexander Bain, Baldwin, Hobhouse,

Dewey and Tufts, and McDougall. Specific stage-types were tellingly described by various authors: Conformity by John Stuart Mill, the Self-Protective Stage by Baldwin, and the Impulsive type by McDougall.

Sympathy, in Adam Smith and Bain, and imitation, in Baldwin, were proposed as moving principles to account for ego growth. Later authors disputed those accounts as oversimplified or wrong. Mill acknowledged some role for sympathy but recognized, as did McDougall and Hobhouse, the complexity of the sources of conscience, including elements as disparate as the desire for vengeance. Thus conscience originates in part from elements that are antithetical to itself.

The model for development comes out of nineteenth-century philosophy and biology, influenced by Darwin's discoveries. Evolution of social and psychological phenomena was anticipated by Spencer, indeed by the eighteenth-century idea of inevitable progress. Hegel's dialectical model of development applies specifically to psychological and social evolution and is entirely different from the biological model. To what extent ego development is best thought of in terms of an evolutionary model of differentiation and integration, to what extent in a revolutionary or dialectical model of growth by opposites remains an issue today.

The idea of circular reaction can be found in Baldwin, Dewey, and Mead. Baldwin's dialectic of personal growth was anticipated by Adam Smith and elaborated by Mead. The social origin of the self goes back at least to Aristotle; Smith, Baldwin, Cooley, and Mead are major sources for the conception. Since Cooley and Mead both influenced Sullivan, who specifically mentioned McDougall's self-regarding sentiment as the origin of his conception of the self-system (Sullivan, 1925), the history in the present chapter leads directly to the conceptions of Chapter Five.

The analogy between the person and the state, and by implication personification of functions within the individual, begins with Plato; Dewey and Tufts explicitly saw it as a source for personal complexity. In Mead personification of functions coalesced with Baldwin's dialectic of personal growth to become the dialogue of roles. In Chapter Fourteen another version of personification of functions turns up in Freud's later writings, an aspect of psychoanalysis that has been criticized as particularly unscientific. Historical perspective reveals this aspect of Freud's theory as less original, more profound, and more legitimate than his critics assert. The same line of thought will show psychoanalysis as more interpersonal than Sullivan was willing to acknowledge.

In the early twentieth century, McDougall spoke for the influence of instinctual drives on behavior, Dewey and Mead spoke for environmental influences. Dewey and Tufts and Hobhouse presented the influence of large historical forces, influences that are not much spoken of today, even by those who represent the environmentalist or situationalist point of view.

The period from 1900 to 1920 included at least four schools of psychology relevant to our topic: self theory, instinct theory, reflexology, and learning theory based on pleasure or reward. Baldwin, Dewey, and Mead represented self theory. McDougall represented instinct theory. Reflexology was represented by I. P. Pavlov and J. B. Watson, among others. Kuo (1921), one of Pavlov's and Watson's partisans, argued that the concept of instinct was superfluous because instincts are merely concatenations of reflexes. E. L. Thorndike, with his Law of Effect, was representative of associationist learning theory based on pleasure-pain and reward-punishment. Hedonistic associationism and reflexology were elementaristic and reductionistic, while both self theory and instinct theory were nonreductionistic.

Each of the foregoing schools of thought was concerned to differentiate itself from the others, although McDougall discussed character development, as did the self theorists, and Baldwin assumed one instinct, imitation. McDougall, for example, criticized Kuo, saying that instincts as concatenations of reflexes do not exist even in lower animals; instincts are always purposive behavior. The rigidity of behavior in lower animals results from their lack of intelligence, not their domination by instincts. McDougall criticized Freud for assuming the existence of instincts and simultaneously postulating a pleasure principle.

If there are instincts, their satisfaction naturally produces pleasure, which need not then be postulated as an additional principle.

What shall we think of a school of thought that starts with
the assumption that the reflex arc is the basic unit of behavior,
adds a pleasure principle, says that all behavior is motivated by
instincts, and says that the ego governs access to motility? All
these elements, drawn from four mutually antagonistic approaches, can be found in Freud's writings, though he never
seriously tried to weave them into a coherent account. Rapaport (1960) tried to construct a system using them all as elements, but neither he nor anyone else was completely satisfied.
Such inconsistencies led Sullivan, who was much influenced by
Freud, to create a new vocabulary and new footings for his
psychiatric theory.

Unlike American behaviorists, Freud and his colleagues
never passed through a period when terms such as *ego* and *self*
were taboo, when there was no such concept. The initial thrust
of psychoanalysis, however, was to dethrone the ego and give
new emphasis to instincts and the unconscious as determinants
of behavior. At the time of the split with Adler, Freud declared
that Adler was just an ego psychologist, that to return to that
view would be to give up the hard-won gains of the psychology
of the unconscious. Later, Freud gave greater emphasis to the
ego and propounded an original theory of ego functioning and
ego growth, but his followers were slow to accommodate themselves to the change in emphasis, and many of them have never
given his theory of ego development full recognition. There
were always divergent strands in Freud's thought and hence
sanction for alternative views.

In comparison with Freud, McDougall was a rigorous
theorist with a logically coherent system. While Freud of course
was more profound and more inventive, he was also closer to
the spirit of modern science in ways his detractors do not always acknowledge. McDougall built his social psychology in
separation from his extensive laboratory research. The basic elements of psychoanalysis are, or can be construed as, a scientific
paradigm in some important aspects comparable to the best of

modern scientific theories. Freud never integrated his theory tightly, and he hung on to absurd vestigial postulates of rival theories. On the other hand, there is a sense in which Freud integrated his theories with his laboratory studies and with his clinical practice in ways that lifted psychology and psychiatry to a new plane of sophistication. One must, however, look beneath the surface to discern this sense.

Before reviewing psychoanalysis from this point of view, we will discuss some theories of development in general and in so doing look at the idea of paradigm in modern science.

In choosing the bits of philosophical psychology for this chapter, I have selected those authors and passages that anticipate or lay the groundwork for contemporary problems of ego development. While some authors wrote of stages or even of an adult type that preserved a normal stage of childhood, the fully developed stage-type conception is not found, nor did any of the authors contribute a research technique. Early authors were more concerned with the dynamics of development than are many contemporary stage theorists. This concern comes to us most directly from psychoanalysis. We need not accept as gospel all the insights of our philosophical predecessors to acknowledge how much our own sources borrowed from them and to see how much more insightful they were than some of our contemporaries are even now.

Chapter Twelve

Paradigms: The Problem of Stability

If the laws of development in general suffice to explain ego development, then it would be parsimonious to invent no new laws. Therefore, before tackling theoretical approaches to our topic, let us glean what we can elsewhere, specifically, from Piaget's ideas about development in general and development of intelligence in particular and Kuhn's ideas about scientific development.

Piaget on Development

We have already drawn bits from the psychological contributions of Piaget, a glimpse of his conception of stages in Chapter Four, fragmentary observations of cognitive development in Chapter Seven, and his conception of moral development in

294

Chapter Five. Here we shall follow his view of development of intelligence.

The behavior of the infant is elaborated by practice from a few rudimentary reflex patterns, according to Piaget (1936). The well-formed patterns of movements that one thinks of as the sucking and grasping reflexes are not present immediately after birth but arise during the next days or weeks. In this they are distinguished from reflexes such as sneezing and yawning that remain hardly changed over long periods. Sucking and grasping are examples of what Piaget calls *schemes of action* or simply *schemes*. The infant applies each scheme to everything he can; everything suckable within reach is sucked, everything graspable that comes to hand is grasped, everything within sight is looked at, and so on. Every time a scheme is applied to a new object, the scheme itself is slightly affected, becoming more general.

Just as reflexes elaborate into sensorimotor schemes, so schemes gradually elaborate into intelligence. The sum total of the baby's sensorimotor coordinations is the origin and core of his intelligence. It constitutes an organ of adaptation, operating in two complementary ways, by assimilation and by accommodation. Piaget's term for use of a scheme is *assimilation,* whether simply repeated or used in relation to new objects or materials. His term for modification of a scheme to fit new objects is *accommodation.* In a sense they are opposite; yet every time a scheme comes into play, both assimilation and accommodation take place. Assimilation and accommodation describe the relation of the scheme to the world; the internal aspect of the scheme is its organization. Assimilation has three types: reproductive, generalizing, and recognitory. Pure or *reproductive assimilation* consists of the repetition of the same scheme with the same objects. The term *generalizing assimilation* refers to broadening the range of application of the scheme, such as sucking finger or toy. The term *recognitory assimilation* refers to discrimination aligned with repetition, as, for example, when the hungry baby rejects a finger to suck.

By exercise, schemes regularly become more abstract and are interiorized. As the infant sucks or grasps more and different things, he acquires the sensorimotor equivalent of a concept of suckability or graspability. There is no room in this concept for stimulus and response as separate entities; the sensorimotor scheme operates as a unity. There is no environment or stimulus except as the organism has a structure prepared to react to it. Thus at the first there is for the infant no such thing as a new object; there are only objects for which he has a scheme.* Other objects do not exist for him.

For Piaget the existence of schemes accounts for their repetition; when a scheme unrolls, it leaves in its wake a kind of vacuum to be filled by its own repetition. Since repetition cannot be exactly the same, the child is always changing. Each scheme seeks to assimilate to itself everything around it. Thus schemes tend to occur simultaneously; moving objects may elicit sucking and grasping as well as looking. At first these remain merely simultaneous exercises of different schemes, but gradually, at first perhaps entirely by chance, the simultaneously operating schemes become reciprocally assimilated and then coordinated. From such coordination of disparate schemes the child gradually constructs for himself the world of objects, which he learns are independent of his actions on them. The child in Piaget's experiments who searches for a toy hidden by a handkerchief is demonstrating his knowledge that the toy continues to exist even when he is not seeing or touching it.

Somewhere around the middle of his first year, during the period Piaget terms the *third sensorimotor stage,* children adopt what he calls "procedures to make interesting spectacles last." Prior to that time the child does not seem to evince interest in novelty. At this stage, however, something that is novel, but not too novel, is attractive to the child, and he wishes to prolong it. Initially his reaction to it is simply to exercise schemes he already has for other things, that is, whatever it may be, he grasps, sucks, kicks, looks, hits, and so on. This reaction shows

*I am following Furth (1969) in translating Piaget's *schème* as *scheme* rather than the more usual English translation of *schema.* Furth does so in order to preserve a distinction Piaget makes between the *scheme* and the *schema,* the latter term being used for (approximately) the figurative (that is, configurational) aspect of the particular situation to which the scheme is accommodating itself in a particular instance.

the beginning of intentional action. What Piaget calls *true intelligence* requires one more step towards intentionality, namely, the gradual separation of means and ends. Thus, during the fourth stage, the child will employ one scheme in order to activate another one, for example, removing one object in order to obtain another one that can be shaken or sucked.

An essential element in the evolution from the sensorimotor period to that of practical intelligence is the child's capacity to represent to himself absent objects (Piaget, 1937). The typical experiment goes this way. The child sees a toy or other object hidden in a box, the box is put behind a screen, then brought out empty. He removes the screen to obtain the object, already an achievement, since the youngest babies will not look for absent objects. Now the child sees the box into which the toy was put removed from screen A to screen B to screen C, let us say from under a beret to under a pillow to under a handkerchief. Will he look behind screen A, where he previously found it, or behind screen C, where it was last put? When he has learned to look behind screen C, Piaget says he has learned of the constancy of the object despite spatial translation, remembering that the child has not seen the toy move but only the box that he saw the toy put into.

The prototype of accommodation is imitation; the prototype of assimilation is play (Piaget, 1951). As imitation evolves from imitation of present models to imitation of remembered models, it gradually gives rise to the mental image. In play the child uses whatever is easily available in line with his current schemes; thus a box may be assimilated to the scheme of bed or that of truck. Thus play gives rise to symbols. In purposeful activity, there is an equilibration of accommodation and assimilation, with neither predominating.

Construction of the world of objects is only a first step in the objectification of the world and the corresponding knowledge of self or ego. Later invariances include space, time, conservation of matter and weight, and so on. Corresponding to those achievements there is a decentration or decrease of the child's egocentrism, that is, he learns to see things from points of view detached from his own.

Intelligence for Piaget is the total of coordinated schemes, and it grows by its own exercise. While sensorimotor schemes are in a broad sense operations, in another sense they precede and prepare for true operations. Practical intelligence is preoperational, and gradually it evolves through concrete operations to formal operations. A word is required about Piaget's terms. In one sense, sensorimotor schemes are one end of a continuum of which formal operations are the other extreme. In a broader sense of the term *scheme,* however, operations are subsumed as schemes. It is also true the other way, that *operation* can be used as the generic term, with sensorimotor schemes as the primitive exemplars.

Most of what the child knows is acquired incidentally to exercise of his intelligence rather than by direct tuition. The name of the capital of his state or country can be learned by rote, but that is a trivial piece of knowledge compared to the whole structure of knowing what a state is and that it has a capital, the general scheme or operation that is accommodated to the fact that Albany is the capital of New York or Paris is the capital of France. Rarely is a child taught that today will be called yesterday tomorrow, but he knows it when he has mastered the structure of time. The words are acquired long before the corresponding invariances. A child of three knows the meaning of *same* and *different* yet for several years cannot respond correctly to questions of conservation of quantity. Present him, for example, with two equal balls of plasticene. Then roll one out long and thin. He will declare they are no longer the same amount. He may say the rolled-out one is bigger because it is longer or smaller because it is thinner. Only when he can hold those two factors in mind simultaneously to constitute a more complex operation does he perceive the conservation involved.

Piaget's term *equilibration* corresponds approximately to homeostatis in physiological systems; it is the internal regulatory factor. The term *equilibration* refers to the inner logic or deep structure of the stages as well as to the logic of their stability and evolution. The implication of the term is that certain periods of development contain an inner coherence that is self-sustaining; those periods can be labeled properly as stages. Other periods are intrinsically unstable and can only be transitions. A degree of equilibration occurs towards the end of the sensorimotor period and again at the end of the period of concrete operations; however, complete equilibration does not come about until adolescence, when the child becomes capable of formal reasoning. At that point his thinking takes the form of operations on operations. He is able to take a hypothetical standpoint, whereas a younger child cannot reason from premises he believes to be untrue.

Through Piaget's eyes we have now identified several progressive factors in the development of intelligence. Schemes by their nature demand to be exercised, and in being exercised they are generalized by assimilation and altered by accommodation. New schemes are also generated by coordination of two different schemes. Novelty itself becomes attractive after the first few months. Novelty, however, must be of optimal level. If something is too novel, it does not exist for the child because he cannot assimilate it to any scheme that he has. The conservation of schemes by assimilation and their gradual evolution through generalizing, through combination, and through accommodation are clear in Piaget. That a scheme leaves in its wake a vacuum that demands it to be exercised must perhaps be accepted as a given but is not altogether clear. At any rate, for Piaget, as for Freud, there is some kind of "repetition compulsion." When accommodation results in the formation of a new scheme (as compared to when the discrepancy is so great that no accommodation can take place) is not something for which Piaget gives us a general answer, and there may be none. Learning and growth mostly take place by imperceptible steps. Are there also distinct jumps?

Kuhn on Scientific Development

Let us look at a different realm of thought, Kuhn's (1962) discussion of the development of scientific theories. Kuhn disputes the conception of science widely held, perhaps particularly among those psychologists most anxious to view themselves as scientists. This view of science has it being erected from observed and experimentally demonstrated facts as a building is constructed from bricks and boards. Kuhn also does not present a hypothetico-deductive model, in which an abstract theory is verified by checking deductions from it against the facts of nature. The model of science he presents has puzzle solving as its central occupation.

Scientists in mature sciences constitute themselves as cohorts united in the theory they accept and united also in what they perceive as problems, as acceptable classes of solutions, as appropriate methods, and as suitable data. Often a great scientific classic, such as Newton's *Principia,* Franklin's *Electricity,* Lavoisier's *Chemistry,* and Lyell's *Geology,* created such a scientific paradigm. Such volumes were achievements that attracted many scientists as adherents and yet left sufficient problems unsolved and presumably soluble as to constitute a new field of study.

Kuhn uses the term *paradigm* in two senses, as disciplinary matrix and as exemplary experiment (1970*b*). The disciplinary matrix is the whole complex of theory, data, method, and values that guides the work of the cohort. The exemplar is the typical or original experiment or set of observations, of which many subsequent ones are variations, extensions, or new applications. The experimental exemplar typically becomes the laboratory exercise that is used to teach new scientists in the discipline. Much of their advanced training is learning more ways to apply the exemplar or more areas to assimilate to it.

Now, *normal science,* as Kuhn calls it, does not expect and is not able to deal with any results that are radically new, contrary to popular opinion. As the paradigm is applied to solving more and newer puzzles, it becomes elaborated. There are always some puzzles that are not solved or not completely so. Normally either the paradigm is stretched and altered to fit the anomalous results, or the problem is put aside for later consideration. However, a paradigm is never given up for such reasons alone. A paradigm is only given up in favor of an alternative, presumbly better one.

Ultimately, anomalous results and unsolved problems accumulate to the extent that more and more members of the community become uneasy. This pervasive mental tension constitutes a state of crisis. During such a crisis, the way is open to new possible paradigms. Characteristic of crisis is concern for fundamental assumptions of the paradigm that are simply taken for granted when it is in full bloom. When competing paradigms are offered, however, there is no clear superordinate set of rules by which one can choose. Each paradigm makes its own rules. Proponents of competing paradigms talk different languages or at least quite literally mean different things by the words they use.

Originally each proposed paradigm is most effective at accounting for the experiments that gave rise to it and less successful than competitors at accounting for the data that gave rise to them. There is thus no absolute standard for choosing between them. Indeed, what constitutes data within one paradigm may not be construed as data within another. A stone swinging on a string was a pendulum for Galileo, but for earlier scientists there were no laws of pendulums because they did not perceive pendulums as a class of things. A stone swinging on a string would have been classed as a falling object whose fall was constrained. The data for one paradigm are regularly reconstrued in different categories by other paradigms, but they may also be reclassified as simply not scientific observations.

At the beginning a paradigm is often concerned with data interesting for their own sake, but most scientific research concerns data not intrinsically interesting but made so because of their relation to the paradigm. Instruments such as cloud chambers and x-ray tubes are invented by scientists; the data they generate are not facts of everyday life that must be accounted for.

In mature sciences the period of competing paradigms does not last long; one paradigm does win out and gain the allegiance of all the qualified practitioners. In a sense, this formulation is a tautology on Kuhn's part, since he does not consider an individual doing scientific work enough to make a science. Rather, creation of a science requires also a community to receive, cross-reference, and elaborate that work. To what extent Kuhn has made a valid sociological observation about physics, chemistry, astronomy, and other contemporary sciences, to what extent unanimity of paradigm is not properly a criterion for science is a point on which his view has been disputed (Lakatos and Musgrave, 1970).

The exchange of paradigms constitutes a scientific revolution, as distinguished from normal science. While Kuhn's view of normal science differs from the usual model of science, his view of scientific revolutions is even more removed from the Baconian empirical model. How, he asks, has the Baconian building-block view of science attained such wide circulation if his alternative view is correct or more nearly so? Textbooks, which now take the place formerly filled by classical monographs in inducting new members into the cohort, are almost invariably written within a paradigm. To the extent that they present historical materials, they do so not in the terms in which those studies were conceived at the time but as they are conceived in terms of the prevailing paradigm. That the guiding ideas of early work came from a quite different paradigm is commonly lost, as are the mental and interpersonal struggles that exchange of one paradigm for another cost. Most scientists bitterly resist any proposal to change paradigms. This resistance is in one sense unfortunate, since it is an obstacle to progress when a better paradigm is offered. On the other hand, the resistance to change is also necessary, since science requires relatively stable paradigms for its pursuit, and many seeming anomalies are ultimately shown compatible with the paradigm. Kuhn regards the Baconian ideal of no paradigm as incompatible with science; moreover, observations untainted by theoretical preconceptions are psychologically impossible.

Kuhn sees the ideas of paradigm and of revolution as applicable both to large aspects of the scientific enterprise, such as to thermodynamics or quantum mechanics, and to small-scale aspects engaging cohorts of perhaps as few as twenty-five people working on a common problem by common methods. The latter groups, sometimes referred to as "invisible colleges," stay in touch with each other and constitute themselves a cohort by correspondence, exchange of reprints, and so on. Kuhn's illustrations add much to his exposition, but they have been largely omitted here because they are drawn from physics, chemistry, and related fields that are far from our own concerns.

In the next two chapters I will argue that Freud's *Interpretation of Dreams* (1900) is a great scientific classic that created a paradigm. Kuhn disagrees, for he considers one criterion of a mature science to be that sooner or later all qualified persons come to accept such a paradigm. That acceptance will surely not occur for psychoanalysis nor probably for any large-scale psychological theories, for reasons implicit in the subject matter of this book, a topic to which we return in the final chapter.

Other philosophers of science, while acknowledging that Kuhn has illuminated the history of science, have disagreed on a number of details (Lakatos and Musgrave, 1970). The niceties of philosophical theory are outside our purview, but some of the issues raised are doubly important to us, both with respect to application of his paradigm of science within psychology and its subfields and with respect to the analogy I will draw between scientific development and ego development. The major issue raised is whether the difference between normal science and extraordinary or revolutionary science is as great as Kuhn has drawn. There are many microrevolutions in science, generating a sequence of conceptual modifications differing in degree (Toulmin, 1970). Scientists cannot normally be as closed to alternative frameworks as Kuhn sometimes seems to suggest, so committed to unquestioning loyalty to their paradigm, or there would be no revolutions. New paradigms take time to form, and rather than a situation in which a crisis generates new paradigms, it may be the new paradigm that generates the crisis (Watkins, 1970). Instead of normal periods alternating with revolutionary periods during which fundamental philosophical commitments are questioned, there are normal and philosophical components to science generally (Feyerabend, 1970). Long periods of competing paradigms are more characteristic of developed sciences than Kuhn acknowledges (Popper, 1970). While Kuhn has added to our understanding of science by going back to its early history, he merges three distinguishable phases, those of no paradigm, of multiple paradigms, and of two competing paradigms. Multiple-paradigm science, which exists in disciplines like psychology, is full-fledged science except that each subfield must be treated as a separate field. Kuhn has proposed many definitions of paradigms, which fall into three types, the philosophical or metaphysical, the sociological, and the artifactual or instrumental paradigm. If we ask not what a paradigm is but what it does, it becomes clear that the fundamental meaning is that of artifact, for only by means of an artifact can one solve puzzles (Masterman, 1970).

Some social scientists have adopted Kuhn's conception of a paradigm but misread his book (Kuhn, 1970a). One misinterpretation takes any shared commitments, model, or frame of reference as a paradigm, neglecting the original emphasis on an achievement as the basis for a paradigm. An even more bizarre misinterpretation takes unanimous agreement on mature paradigms as something that can be achieved by arbitrary agreement or persuasion. Kuhn proposes that the essential criterion for mature science is replacing problem solving by puzzle solving. A problem is generally understandable, such as inflation or housing shortages, but has no single, clear-cut, and final solution. A puzzle is of more limited scope and may be meaningful and understandable only for a limited coterie, such as chess players or contract-bridge players. The solution to a puzzle, like the solution to a problem in mathematics, can be complete, final, and fully convincing to all qualified persons. Contemporary physical sciences operate in the puzzle-solving mode; the cohorts communicate their most significant findings by journal articles. Social scientists operate in the problem-solving mode, and significant contributions tend to be books proposing new conceptual frameworks.

Kuhn (1974) would now cede the conception of paradigm to the social scientists, at the expense of reducing it to any shared commitment, such as that of the Dadaists or composers who write for a twelve-tone scale. I believe, however, that the shared commitments that hold together a group of artists are different from the shared commitments that hold together Kohlberg and his associates studying moralization of judgment or those of the contemporary psychoanalytic movement, each of which has an artifact and a puzzle-solving mode. In taking such lessons as I can from Kuhn's picture of scientific revolutions, I expect to have the indulgence of at least some philosophers of science.

Science as a Branch of Knowledge

Piaget's theory of the growth of intelligence and knowledge, closely allied as they are for him, is based originally on observations of infants and small children. He maintains, in fact, that his earlier work in biology slanted his thinking in the direction of assimilation and accommodation as the two fundamental modes of adaptation, and he freely applies his concepts to animals as well as infants. Kuhn's essay, by contrast, aims to describe the functioning of the most highly developed manifestation of human intelligence. Yet if we interpret Kuhn's model for the structure of scientific revolutions in terms of Piaget's model for the origin of intelligence, the fit is surprisingly good.

For Piaget knowledge and intelligence are hardly different concepts; both imply a system of operations behind which lies an implicit logic. Only a relatively small part of knowledge, which he calls *figurative*, refers to specific circumstances. The great bulk of what we know consists of rules and patterns of operations. Science also does not consist of a static collection of facts, or only minimally so; the bulk of science is also a set of rules and patterns of operations, the paradigm and exemplar of Kuhn. Normal science, in Kuhn's terms, consists of applying the operations of the exemplary experiment to ever-new problems; in Piaget's terms, normal science assimilates new problems to an old operational scheme. Scientific paradigms develop by means of normal science, just as a baby's sensorimotor schemes enlarge by exercise, mutual assimilation, and so on.

Scientific revolutions are big changes that occur when an old paradigm no longer fits nor can be made to fit new facts developed under the old paradigm. In Piaget's terms, a major accommodation may eventuate in development of a fundamentally new set of operations, that is, a new paradigm. The new paradigm will again be applied over and over again, assimilate most problems, accommodate itself somewhat to new problems, and finally break down when the accommodations called for are repeatedly too large.

For Kuhn the core of a paradigm is its experimental exemplar, thus a set of operations, just as for Piaget operations are the core of intelligence. Kuhn, like Piaget, does not separate method from product. Science for Kuhn, like intelligence for Piaget, cannot stand still. In functioning at all it necessarily brings about its own evolution.

Piaget's notion of equilibration leads to the postulation of self-sustaining stages. Such stages can only be glimpsed in intellectual development, whose continuity is impressive. Kuhn's conception of a scientific paradigm in fact is a more convincing example of equilibration. Scientists operating within a given scientific paradigm construe as much of the universe as possible in terms dictated by their paradigm. What does not fit is, when possible, ruled out as not part of the data of science, just as, for the child, stimuli for which he has no scheme of operations are not part of his environment.

Of course it is no accident that scientific development and the behavior of scientists conform to the structures of intellectual development sketched by Piaget. Piaget did not in any way limit his scope and intends to encompass the highest intellectual activities within his theory. Kuhn, in turn, must be gratified to have the implicit testimony of an eminent psychologist (or *genetic epistemologist*, as Piaget calls himself) to the psychological plausibility of his version of scientific history; more, Kuhn lists familiarity with some of Piaget's writings, though not the ones we have drawn on here, as influential in the development of his thinking. Kuhn, however, does not see himself as originating a model of wide applicability in other fields. On the contrary, the idea of tradition-bound periods broken by periods of radical change has always been current in fields such as art, politics, and literature, and his application of that model to the area of science is what is new. Usually a contrast is made between science and other such fields, with science depicted as cumulative and progressive in contrast to literature, art, and politics. Thus Kuhn (1970b) has a lengthy discussion of how we can still rescue some conception of progress for science within his model.

Kelly on People as Scientists

We have looked at the development of intelligence through Piaget's eyes, at the development of science through Kuhn's eyes, then at science as an exercise of intelligence. One more theme will be presented before returning to the topic of ego development—the person as a scientist. That is the theme of the "psychology of personal constructs" of George Kelly (1955, 1970). Kelly noted that psychologists talk about their subjects differently from the way they talk about themselves as scientists. Suppose we pay our subjects the compliment of considering them like ourselves, he suggested, rather than seeing them merely as objects of study. Suppose, in his words, we take "scientific behavior as a paradigm of human behavior" (Kelly, 1970, p. 7).

Kelly's basic postulate is, "A person's processes are psychologically channelized by the ways in which he anticipates events" (p. 9). Thus he begins, like Piaget, with person in process. Therefore he does not need a concept of drive or motivation without which a person would be inert. "A person anticipates events by construing their replications" (p. 11). Granted that the same event cannot by definition occur twice, what is construed as a replication depends on how the person construes the situation. The sum total of all such constructions is his system of *personal constructs*. Everyone evolves a system of such constructs for himself, and it will never be exactly the same as another person's. A person's constructs are organized hierarchically, though that is not to say that everyone resolves all the contradictions within his own construct system.

According to Kelly, the choices people make are such as to develop and extend their system of constructs. Rather than rewards and punishments or drive reduction, what governs the direction in which a person's behavior develops is the confirmation and disconfirmation of his predictions. The unit of experience for Kelly is "anticipation, investment, encounter, confirmation or disconfirmation, and constructive revision" (p. 18). People differ, however, in their ability to profit from experience in altering their constructs. This difference he labels *permeability*. This term refers not just to plasticity of constructs but also to their adaptability to novel events and to their hierarchization.

Kelly maintained that each person's constructs are dichotomous; for example, at any given moment one person might be

seen as good and another as bad, even though in a later comparison the good one may turn up as bad. This postulate of his
system has often been disputed and does not seem necessary to
his basic logic. Further, it does not seem necessary to say that
the *only* basis for one's choices is to extend his system of constructs in order to accept Kelly's insight that that is one important basis. Kelly's view is completely process-oriented, but it
lacks developmental footing. Some of his formulations might
have been altered by giving close attention to infancy and childhood.

Kelly goes on to a wide range of theoretical and clinical
applications, in which a key conception is his version of role:
"To the extent that one person construes the construction processes of another, he may play a role in a social process involving the other person" (p. 22). One need not be accurate in
construing the other person's processes to play a role relative to
him, but one must see the other as having his own point of
view, not simply as being a behaving organism.

Our purpose here is not to give a complete review or critique of Kelly's theory, but to fit it into a frame with the contributions of Piaget and Kuhn. One can easily place assimilation
and accommodation into Kelly's system. His conception of hierarchy is much less than Piaget's concept of stage or Kuhn's of
paradigm. Permeability has to do with change, and Kelly saw the
problem posed for a person by the need to change his core constructs. He did not, however, have ideas exactly like equilibration or paradigm.

Pacers

Dember (1965) has summarized and interpreted some recent experimental work on motivation in many species of laboratory
animals including humans. These studies have proved incompatible with viewing motivation in terms of reduction of physiological need states. Indeed, they resist being conceived in terms
of responses. Rather, animals and especially people are motivated, at least in part, by the novelty and complexity of stimulus objects. As objects vary in their complexity so people vary

in their ability to cope with complexity. For each person there is some ideal level, neither too simple nor too complex. When a person can, he chooses stimulus objects of a level of complexity that matches his own. He selects such objects, seeks them out, works for them, and learns what he must do to obtain them. Those activities are classic indicators of rewarding objects; thus the appropriate stimulus is itself the reward. While his own capacity determines the level of complexity he seeks, a person tends to sample stimulus objects above and below his own ideal level. Indeed, the modal amount of time goes to stimuli just a little more complex than the person's ideal. These objects are called *pacers*. As the person maintains contact with and thus masters a pacer, his own level of complexity grows and he is ready for a new, more complex pacer.

The conception of pacer is almost identical with Piaget's idea of optimal novelty, though of course the experiments summarized by Dember are of quite a different type from those of Piaget. The conception of pacer is also intimately related to Kelly's idea that the choices men make are such as to develop and extend their system of constructs.

The pacer appears to be the formula or model for nonrevolutionary growth. Its importance in relation to ego development and particularly the growth of conscience will appear in later chapters.

Implications for Ego Theory

How much can we glean for a theory of ego development just from these considerations, a theory of intellectual development and of the development of scientific theories, without even looking at considerations specific to our own field? The problem of stability, of how the ego functions so as to remain effectively the same from minute to minute, hour to hour, and day to day, despite big shifts in circumstance and mood, is aptly described in terms of assimilation. That in fact is what the theory of Sullivan and that of Merleau-Ponty do. The self-system of Sullivan and the structures of behavior of Merleau-Ponty are compatible with Piaget's model of the constancies of behavior residing in operations. The idea of ego as process rather than as a finished or quasi-tangible thing is essential to the view advanced in Chapter Four. Fingarette's discussion of the ego as the search for meaning is also apposite here, though anything as real and as complex as the human ego is not exhaustively described by a single characterization, accurate as it may be. If we take seriously the view of ego as search for meaning, then what Nunberg called the synthetic function of the ego is not something the ego does but the essence of what it is. (Alternatively, we may follow Masterman's remark about the Kuhnian paradigm and say the *proper question* is not what the ego is but what it does.)

Thus the ego remains stable because the operations by which the person perceives his environment effectively admit only those data that can be comprehended already, hence are compatible with current ego structure. Incompatible situations are either distorted to conform to prior expectations, that is, assimilated, or else ignored. In Piaget's terms, the latter case implies that parts of the objective situation effectively do not exist for the person. Baldwin's *selective thinking*, Adler's *tendentious apperception*, and Sullivan's *selective inattention* are similar ideas, and a subset of Piaget's *assimilation*.

Following Kelly in viewing scientific behavior as the model of human behavior, we can ask to what extent ego development takes place as a succession of paradigms whose exchange is the occasion for mental turmoil, as is true of science. Alternatively, it may be a continuous process, where qualitative changes result from the gradual accretion of quantitative or at least small changes, as appears to be true of intelligence. This question remains one of the unsolved problems of the field. Still, one should not exaggerate its content. Real growth, as opposed to religious conversion, must take place gradually over time. The qualitative nature of the changes occurring during the course of ego development is beyond question. Perhaps the only question is whether growth hurts while it happens.

Prima facie evidence for a more discontinuous or paradigmlike model for ego development arises from the patent fact that in adult life every stage is represented. While there are many degrees of intelligence in adult life, a large proportion of adults arrive at what Piaget considers the highest stage, the stage of formal, reversible operations. There is some equilibration at lower stages, but complete equilibration requires achievement of formal operations. Hence normally development proceeds to that stage. With regard to ego development, however, the vast majority of the population stabilizes at some stage far below the maximum compatible with their intellectual and other development. This fact implies equilibration to hold them steady at that stage. The greater the extent of equilibration at a stage, presumably the more disruptive would be a breakout to a higher stage. Moreover, the very fact that people do not indeed proceed to higher stages or perceive the need or possibility to do so suggests that it would be costly for them to change further.

The question of why apparently normal people stabilize in their ego level far below their hypothetical maximum level, as contrasted with the tendency to approach the maximum in cognitive level, has been insufficiently researched or even discussed. The conceptions of pacer and equilibration suggest the following hypothesis: natural phenomena act as pacer for cognitive growth, constantly disconfirming expectations based on false hypotheses. Hence maximal equilibration requires attainment of formal operations. The ego is a structure of expectations not about natural phenomena but primarily about interpersonal ones. As long as the child is operating in an environment that does not conform to his expectations and that disconfirms them in a way to pace his growth, he has the potential for further growth. When the child's view of his interpersonal surroundings conforms to what really exists, when his expectations match the conduct of those around him, equilibration is achieved and the likelihood of change is small. For example, a Self-Protective child living in a dog-eat-dog environment can hardly afford to change. As long as the child's environment is chiefly his family, they will provide the upper limit of ego development for him. As he moves out into the community, he may equilibrate at a higher stage if higher models are provided for him there. Going away to school or job may in some cases provide a higher ego paradigm as pacer. The institutional atmosphere of dormitory or army can provide a powerful force for equilibration at some level, often, unfortunately, at a level lower than the young person has already achieved. That may account for the apparent regression observed by Kohlberg and others in early college years as well as the notorious behavior of some young soldiers. Such regression is ordinarily reversible, according to both theory and such observations as are available. According to the hypothesis being put forward, the effect of parental personality patterns and ego level on the child's potentialities occurs not by direct tuition, modeling per se, reinforcement, identification, nor "introjection," whatever that may mean. The force of the parents' personality patterns on the child is greatest when they confirm the child's expectations based on his own autochthonous development. The parent is then no longer pacer but a factor of equilibrium. The point made by Bowers (1973) and Wachtel (1973) (see Chapter Ten), that personality remains consistent in part because each of us elicits behavior in accord with his own, adds another factor favoring equilibration below one's highest potential. The unique place of the family in fostering ego growth is highlighted again. Where others are likely to treat the young person according to his deserts and thus encourage stabilization, good parents are altruistic and thus, at best, encourage change both by providing a pacer model and by their expectations for their child. The relative rarity of ego change in adult life follows from these considerations, and one sees why the teacher or therapist who stands in loco parentis can provide the exceptional circumstances for growth in mature life. Carl Rogers's idea that "unconditional positive regard" is the condition for therapy has theoretical justification as the equivalent of parental intrinsic valuation, with its potential pacer effect. Further, the rationale for Kohlberg's (Kohlberg, Scharf, and Hickey, 1972) approach to moral development in schools and prisons, creating a "just community," lies in the concepts of equilibration and pacer.

Finally, the conception of selective inattention can be applied to other psychological theories of personality to account for their obliviousness to many of the phenomena that have preoccupied us in this book. Lacking categories for understanding or even perceiving the phenomena, they do not see them as part of the field of psychology.

Scientists, particularly when they are deeply and personally committed to their work, virtually incorporate their scientific paradigm into their ego structure. Hence at least some of Kuhn's observations on scientific revolutions can be classed as a consequence and a subset of the phenomena of ego development, even though we have used them the other way around, as a model for ego development. Kuhn's observation is that new paradigms usually come from either young scientists or scientists new to the field. Old scientists sometimes decline to give up their accustomed paradigm even when the community as a whole has moved on. Thus while science may be hospitable to revolution, the individual scientist is not, and he is as unlikely to change in mature life as the average adult is to advance in ego level.

Chapter Thirteen

Psychoanalysis: From Hypnotism to the Oedipus Complex

The major part of the theory of ego development derives from psychoanalysis, particularly the writings of Freud. One cannot simply plunge into psychoanalytic ego theory, however, without first coping with the many misconceptions that prevail regarding psychoanalysis. At the same time, even an elementary introduction to psychoanalysis is a major enterprise, beyond the scope of this book.*

Freud has never been assured of a hearing both fair and

*The sources for this chapter, where not otherwise indicated, are the writings of Freud, the history of dynamic psychiatry by Ellenberger (1970), and the first volume of the life of Freud by Jones (1953).

critical. There are those who espouse everything he has said as the deepest of truths. Show them an absurdity or a contradiction and, like true believers, they will only be more convinced of his profundity. Then there are those who come to Freud with a litigious attitude: if they can find one flawed or ridiculous argument, everything Freud said can be thrown out of court, as if it were a case at law or one gigantic, logically coherent syllogism. Another kind of reader is the eclectic, who takes from Freud whatever appeals to him and combines it with whatever he likes in other systems and theories. To do so, however, violates the coherent core of Freud's contribution.

Scholarly writing about Freud contains additional pitfalls. Among those who acknowledge that Freud espoused contradictory ideas, there are many who claim to be privy to what he really meant. They are divided among those who find that what he really meant is the truth they themselves wish to promulgate and those who find that what Freud really meant was the error that they feel called upon to battle. Another approach finds in his important discoveries nothing but a new edition of some work that he read, from the Cabala to the writings of Pierre Janet. Most elements in his system were drawn from the public domain, far more than is understood by some devotees. As Jones pointed out, however, the ideas he took from others were a constraint as well as a help, since he had to go beyond his sources to create psychoanalysis.

Psychoanalysis contains theories of all ranges of generality; hardly any of them have escaped attack, even by persons who consider themselves psychoanalysts. Some things that Freud believed are either irrelevant or contradictory to the mainstream of his thought. What matters is the logical structure of psychoanalysis as a system of thought. To find that, we must proceed historically, looking for the origins and the development of his ideas.

I shall argue that Freud introduced a scientific paradigm in something close to Kuhn's sense, combining a method of investigation, a family of theories, and a set of data in interrelationship. No psychiatrist before had done that. Even here, Freud was not consistent, for some of his speculative writings, such as

Totem and Taboo (1913), *Moses and Monotheism* (1939) and the latter half of *Beyond the Pleasure Principle* (1920), are at the other extreme, at worst almost treating his own speculations as if they were observational data. Psychoanalysts do not treat their patients by such lights, and the foundations of psycho-analysis are more solid than that kind of speculation. At the same time, one of the keys to Freud's greatness was his ability to tolerate such contradictions. The Oedipus complex would not have been discovered by a man who rejected an idea because it was manifestly absurd.

Freud as Neurologist

Freud reported that hearing Goethe's essay on nature determined his choice of medicine as a career; this is a clue to a lifelong paradox in his thinking, his simultaneous allegiance to and propensity for both a romantic and a hardheaded approach to science (Holt, 1972). He began his medical studies in 1873, prolonging them in order to continue his research in Ernst Brücke's laboratory of physiology. He published a number of papers on topics in physiology and neuroanatomy. His greater interest in and success in observational than in experimental research foreshadowed the emphasis he would later place on passive observation rather than manipulation of patients. He turned from research to clinical medicine only because he needed to earn a living.

Brücke, the teacher to whom Freud apprenticed himself and whose laboratory he left with reluctance, was among the young physicists and physiologists, mostly students of Johannes Müller, who formed the Berlin Society of Physicists, aiming to destroy the doctrine of vitalism, which Müller advocated. Within a generation this group, including Hermann Helmholtz, Emil DuBois-Reymond, and Carl Ludwig, became the predominant school in German physiology and medicine. The spirit of the school is exemplified by the following statement, to which Brücke and DuBois pledged themselves: "No other forces than the common physical-chemical ones are active within the organism. In those cases which cannot at the time be explained by these forces one has either to find the specific way or form of their action by means of the physical-mathematical method or to assume new forces equal in dignity to the chemical-physical forces inherent in matter, reducible to the force of attraction and repulsion" (Jones, 1953, pp. 40-41). Thus, while reductionistic determinism was the spirit of the times, there was an ambiguity in the notion of "forces equal in dignity" that left Freud free to become a psychologist.

Freud's contributions to physiology and neurology were sufficient for a respectable scientific career. He wrote a monograph on cocaine and did a number of studies on the histology of the nervous system in various species at various stages of development. The fundamental structure of the nervous system was not known at that time, and Freud's studies contributed to knowledge of its evolution and development. He discovered some of the essential elements of the neurone theory, which was formulated shortly thereafter. In his book *On Aphasia* (1891) Freud took issue with the then-prevailing theory that different kinds of aphasia were to be explained by minute differences in the localization of the lesions. In its place, he proposed a functional theory, which was basically an application of Hughlings Jackson's doctrine that more recently acquired and less important capacities are disrupted by injuries before the more fundamental ones are. Freud's views on aphasia were closer to modern views than were the more widely accepted doctrines of his time. Finally, Freud published several monographs or long articles on paralyses in children that are still considered valuable.

The contributions Freud made to neurology are a measure of his solidity as a scientist; our concern, however, is with the effect of his studies in neurology on psychoanalysis. The developmental approach exemplified in his laboratory studies of the nervous system became a permanent and valuable feature of his thinking. The Hughlings Jackson neurological model, with hierarchic layering of functions and injury leading to regression, profoundly influenced Freud's psychiatric theory.

On a different plane, the determinism of the Helmholtz school was impressed on him by Brücke and Theodore Meynert, another of his teachers. As Amacher (1965) has shown, both of them believed the reflex arc to be the basic unit of behavior. This belief was not a purely neurological hypothesis but was based on a psychological assumption derived from association psychology, that the mind is the passive spectator to reception and association of sensations and their conversion to responses. Such beliefs fit well with the pledge of the Berlin Society of Physicists. Freud often referred to the doctrine that the reflex arc is the basic unit of behavior as if it were an uncontested finding (compare Dewey's paper, Chapter Eleven). Having himself come close to discovery of the neurone theory, he probably saw it as reinforcing the reflexive view of mental functioning.

Another aspect of the neurological views of Brücke and Meynert that Amacher documents apparently also influenced Freud's later theorizing. They believed, in line with the reflexive view but prior to the discovery of the neurone as the basic unit of the nervous system, that the function of the nervous system is to convey excitation from the sensory periphery to the central nervous system and out to the muscular periphery. The quantity of excitation was believed to be unchanged by this process. Mind or consciousness does not determine the course of excitation or alter its quantity. Excitation can accumulate at certain junctures until it is sufficient to follow particular pathways. The nervous system thus acts like a set of hollow interconnecting pipes, as Descartes indeed believed it to be, and the laws of association are analogous to hydrodynamics. Long after Freud turned from neurology to psychology, he continued to believe that the nervous system operates so as to rid itself of excitation and that psychic energy operates by a kind of hydrodynamics.

Hysteria, Hypnotism, and Suggestion: Some Background

When Freud began the practice of medicine, many of his patients were neurotic, particularly hysterical, women. To understand the direction his work took, we need to know something of the background of the psychotherapy of hysteria. Two seemingly different topics, hypnotism and suggestion or suggestibility, are historically interwoven with hysteria, because hysterical and other neurotic illnesses have long been cured by means that one would today classify as suggestion or as hypnotism.

In the early part of the eighteenth century psychotherapy took the form of faith healing, and cure was predicated on belief in the Savior. Those cured were mostly persons whom we would call *hysterics*; at the time the diagnosis of "vapors" was a common one for women, presumably another term for hysteria. Johan Josef Gassner (1727-1779), one of the last and greatest of the faith healers, was a priest and an exorcist. He began a treatment by precipitating a crisis, which was an acute form of the symptom. He would then suggest that the symptom disappear, which it often did. Thus his therapy was cathartic; "implosion therapy" is a contemporary relative.

Franz Anton Mesmer (1734-1815) opposed faith healing as unscientific; for him the scientific alternative was "magnetism," a theory based on analogy with then-recent discoveries of electricity and magnetism. He was a physician; other physicians at the time also were treating ailments with magnets. Mesmer had patients swallow fluids containing iron, then applied magnets to create an "artificial tide" in their bodies. He soon understood that the effects were not entirely the result of the magnets but were in some way emanating from his person; so he called them "animal magnetism." He believed that there is a subtle fluid within everyone and indeed throughout the universe. A faulty distribution of the fluid within the body causes disease; restoring equilibrium produces recovery. Using techniques to channel or convey the fluid from one person to another, he provoked crises and effected cures. The term *rapport*, still used for the relation between therapist and patient, originally meant physical touching. Mesmer assumed that Gassner, like himself, possessed a high degree of animal magnetism, which was the real means of the faith cures. Some patients observed no effects from his treatment, but others had a convulsion or "crisis" of some sort, and many declared themselves healed of a variety of disorders. How much was charlatanism, how much a benign use of suggestion operating on pathologically suggestible patients was disputed. At times Mesmer was lionized, at times rejected and ostracized by the medical profession.

In 1784 a royal commission was appointed to investigate and evaluate Mesmer's methods. They did not question whether Mesmer cured his patients but sought to evaluate his claim that he had discovered a new physical fluid. In the absence of any evidence for a magnetic fluid, they ascribed his therapeutic results to "imagination." There was concern over the dangers of an erotic attraction between a magnetized young woman and man magnetizer. Among other things, Mesmer has left us with the term *mesmerism* and the notion of a magnetic personality. Two features of the history are already evident. The power of the relation of therapist to patient has long been known, and each new conception proclaimed itself to be scientific and its predecessor to be unscientific.

One of Mesmer's pupils, Amand-Marie-Jacques de Chastenet, Marquis de Puységur (1751-1825), was an aristocrat and an army officer who did experiments in electricity. Some of his discoveries are associated with a patient, Victor Race, a peasant whose family had worked for that of Puységur for many generations. That the hypnotized subject was socially subordinate to the hypnotizer is another recurrent feature of this history. Victor was easily magnetized, but Puységur noticed some peculiar features in his crisis. Rather than convulsive movements, he fell into a kind of sleep in which he was brighter and more aware than in his waking state. He was receptive to suggestions from the magnetizer, and on awakening he was amnesic for these occurrences. Puységur called these states the "perfect crisis"; soon the resemblance to somnambulism was recognized, and it was called "artificial somnambulism." Puységur learned from Victor that the patient could talk freely during hypnosis of things he was reluctant to talk about during his normal state, even though they were accessible to consciousness. The therapist could make practical suggestions for handling life problems by this means. Puységur believed that the agency of the treatment was the magnetizer's will, not a physical fluid.

James Braid (ca 1795-1860) coined the term *hypnotism*. He was opposed to mesmerism and sought to expose it as fraudulent, but, though rejecting the implied explanation of animal magnetism, he became convinced of the reality of the phenomena. At first Braid stressed physiological concomitants of sensory fixation as the cause of hypnotic sleep; later he recognized the effects of suggestion in inducing hypnotic phenomena. Interest in hypnotism declined after the work of Braid, but revived, particularly in France, in the 1870s and 1880s. Important to Freud's development were the school at Salpêtrière, under Charcot, and the smaller group at Nancy, under Bernheim. Freud obtained a traveling fellowship to study with Charcot for a few months in 1886 and 1887, then returned to Vienna and used hypnosis in his psychiatric practice. Finding that many patients could not be hypnotized at all or not deeply enough, he spent a couple of months studying with Bernheim in 1889.

The hospital and clinic at the Sâlpetrière near Paris was the most important center for psychiatry in France. Its chief teacher was Jean-Martin Charcot (1835-1893), the leading neurologist of France before he turned to psychiatry and hypnotism. Charcot investigated hysteria as he had investigated organic neurological diseases, by beginning with a minute description of the symptoms. The symptoms of hysteria, he showed, were similar in different times and places and resembled the symptoms reported in the Middle Ages of demoniac possession, which he believed to be a form of hysteria. Like most psychiatrists of the time, Charcot believed that "mental degeneration" was the basis for hysteria. He regarded hypnosis as an abnormal phenomenon indicative of an hysterical constitution. The mental degeneration was not visible on autopsy but was evidenced by relatives with various kinds of pathology.

The advent of railroads led to a large number of accidents and an increase in the number of traumatic paralyses, which followed accidents but could not be shown to have an organic basis. They were believed to be based on lesions of the nervous system, though not demonstrable ones. Charcot showed that the symptoms of such paralyses differed from organic ones but resembled hysterical ones. Also, he could suggest such symptoms to patients under hypnosis; the symptoms that appeared were like those of traumatic and hysterical paralyses. The symptoms could be made to disappear by similar means. Thus the hysterical, hypnotic, and posttraumatic paralyses constituted a group of "dynamic paralyses" that he contrasted with organic paralyses. Following trauma, Charcot postulated, there was a kind of hypnoid state that favored the development of neurotic disturbances by autosuggestion.

On a suggestion from Charcot, Freud (1893) studied the distinction between hysterical and organic paralyses. They differ in three ways, he showed. Firstly, an hysterical paralysis can be complete in one limb or one part of the body without affecting other parts. An organic paralysis, by contrast, if intense is also extensive. Secondly, sensory changes (anesthesia) are more conspicuous than motor changes (paralysis) in hysteria. The opposite is true of organically based effects. Thirdly, and most important, the distribution of organic paralyses corresponds to tracts of the nervous system, while hysterical symptoms are delimited according to popular ideas of organs. This paper became the definitive discussion of the topic.

Auguste Ambroise Liébeault (1823-1904), a country doctor in Nancy, was among the few physicians who dared to hypnotize his patients during one of the long periods when hypnosis was in official disrepute. He treated his patients with hypnosis apparently regardless of the nature of their symptoms; the therapy consisted in assuring the hypnotized patient that his symptoms would go away.

Hippolyte Bernheim (1840-1919), a university professor and a fashionable physician, became converted to Liébeault's ideas and joined him at Nancy in 1882. Bernheim was more discriminating in his practice of hypnosis and more sophisticated in his theorizing about it. He recognized that hypnotism was effective largely with people used to obeying passively, such as soldiers and factory workers, rather than with upper-class patients. For Bernheim hypnosis was a normal phenomenon; the effects, he believed, were largely the same as those that could be obtained by direct suggestion in the waking state. Bernheim did experiments on posthypnotic suggestion: A hypnotized subject would be told to perform a certain action a specified time after being waked from his trance. The subject would carry out the act at the suggested time, awake and fully conscious of what he was doing, but without memory of the hypnotizer having made the suggestion to him. These experiments impressed Freud with the strength of ideas of which one is not conscious. Freud was also impressed with Bernheim's demonstration that the demarcation between the hypnotic and the normal state is not as complete as had been assumed, since skillful questioning by Bernheim and concentration by the patient could bring the patient to remember what he had experienced under hypnosis; thus posthypnotic amnesia was not absolute. Bernheim used hypnosis less and less and came to rely more on suggestions given to the patient in the waking state. He disputed Charcot's theories of hysteria and hypnosis. Many of the supposed symptoms of hysteria, Bernheim believed, were artifacts. Charcot's prestige as a neurologist plus the open disagreement between him and Bernheim, also a respected physician, elevated the topic of hypnosis into a respectable scientific field.

Pierre Janet (1859-1947) was in some respects Freud's predecessor; in some respects he went beyond Freud; in some ways they were rivals. Janet was probably the better-known man at midpoint in their lives, which were contemporaneous. Today Janet is hardly known to the general public, some of his major works unavailable in English; his followers have never been more than a handful. He began as a philosopher and psychologist. His first book was *Psychological Automatism* (1889). The phenomena of automatism are related to those of hypnotism; they include automatic writing, automatic speaking, crystal gazing, and so on. In a typical instance, the subject's attention is occupied in some way; meanwhile a pencil is slipped into his hand and a whispered suggestion made that he write on some topic or a whispered question asked him. Many subjects are able to answer, often producing answers not available to their conscious mind or writings superior to what they can produce when concentrating their full attention. This "method of distraction," often used by Janet with persons who could not be hypnotized, can be compared with Freud's use of free association.

In view of the importance of patients as subjects and of the therapeutic implications of his work, Janet began studying for a medical degree in 1889. In the same period that Breuer and Freud were treating the cases reported in *Studies On Hysteria* (1895), Janet was treating and writing up several similar cases. Janet's theory of hysteria centered on a "narrowing of the field of consciousness," caused by the patient's psychological weakness (*insufficance psychologique*). Psychological weakness was a version of the then-prevailing French notion of "mental degeneration," which included constitutional weakness and effects of physical traumas and physical illnesses. According to Janet, hysterical symptoms can be traced back to subconscious fixed ideas, which are autonomous parts of the personality having their own life and development, a course favored by the narrowed field of consciousness. They originate in traumatic events. When they are discovered, brought to consciousness, and dissolved, hysterical symptoms may be cured. In other cases, however, the treatment may only transform a subconscious fixed idea into a conscious one, an obsession. Janet used suggestion, induced dissociation, and reeducation as measures to deal with the fixed ideas once discovered. He might suggest to the patient under hypnosis that the traumatic event did not occur or that some unpleasant feature of the event was false. Subconscious fixed ideas, similar to what Jung later called *complexes*, Janet saw as resulting from mental weakness but then causing further mental weakness.

Janet understood the importance of rapport in hypnotism and described its electivity, that is, that the patient became permanently suggestible towards one person, the hypnotist. Since this suggestibility is a distortion in the perception of the world, Janet considered it a form of anesthesia. The most highly suggestible patients might display the quickest cures but also the greatest dependence on or addiction to the therapist or to hypnotism. With such patients, possessing an inherent mental weakness, the therapist should first take charge of the patient's mind and then gradually increase the intervals between sessions.

As a scholar, Janet dug up much of the history of hypnotism and hysteria, showing that the new phenomena being discovered by Charcot and Bernheim had in fact been known to a number of earlier investigators. There are two quite different kinds of behavior that can be elicited under hypnotism, he showed, those roles the subject plays to please the hypnotist and an unknown side of the personality that can also be displayed spontaneously. The name Janet gave to his method was *psychological analysis*; he intended it to be followed by synthesis. The latter was a form of education in which the patient undertook a task he could carry through to a successful completion, then followed it with a little harder task, and so on.

Two sets of ideas in Janet's later work, *The Major Symptoms of Hysteria* (1907) and *Psychological Healing* (1925), parallel some ideas of Freud's, though the men do not seem to have influenced each other, particularly with respect to ego psychology.

The symptoms of hysteria are protean, Janet pointed out; they can simulate many other diseases. Monoideic somnambulism is spontaneous somnambulism that always concerns a particular complex of ideas. During the episode the patient is completely absorbed in the reproduction of the memory of some traumatic event and oblivious to his real circumstances. He may have hallucinations and remarkable powers, such as an acting ability not available to him in ordinary life. On awakening, the patient is restored to awareness of his real life and is amnesic for the somnambulic episode, including the traumatic memory that he has reenacted. Janet postulated that the complex of ideas and memories involved is dissociated from the rest of the conscious personality. He took this dissociated complex as the prototype of all hysterical phenomena.

Proceeding up the scale of complexity, polyideic somnambulisms are similar to monoideic somnambulisms but involve more than one complex of ideas. In fugues the patients may take off, assume a new identity, and begin a new life. They are amnesic for their former identity though usually not for their native language and other everyday skills. Eventually something happens that reminds them of family, home, or the like, and they return to their former identity and are amnesic for the period of the fugue. In the case of double or multiple personalities, the person may go back and forth between the identities repeatedly. A peculiar feature of multiple personalities is that the amnesia might be just one way, personality A being unaware of personality B but B being fully aware of both. All of the phenomena of somnambulism can be reproduced by means of hypnotism. In dual personalities the second personality is often the more apparently normal. Janet assumed that the patient once had a normal personality, that his present state is the sick one, and that hypnotism restores him to his true, healthy state. The purpose of hypnotic treatment in such cases is to prolong the second state and minimize the first. Optimally, all amnesias are removed and the patient has access to all memories.

Janet described hysterical symptoms limited to particular parts of the body, such as limitation of the field of vision to a region around the fovea, evidently the model for his explanatory concept of narrowing of the field of consciousness. The stigmata of hysteria, he pointed out, could mean two quite different things, the usual diagnostic signs or the invariable features. Suggestibility in the strict sense, not in the popular, vague meaning, is the invariable stigma of hysteria: the immediate translation of an idea into an action, without intervention of consciousness and without willful participation. This meaning of suggestion is allied to dissociation of fixed ideas and to the correlative weakness of the synthetic function of consciousness. Such suggestibility disappears with the cure of hysteria, he asserted.

In later writings Janet estimated that the traumatic event was a sexual one in about three-fourths of cases and that Freud erred in saying it was so in all cases. However, Janet construed the word *sexual* in a narrower sense than Freud did. Janet rejected Freud's concept of repression, evidently because his patients were not conscious of any such thing, and he saw it as a gratuitous inference.

Throughout Janet retained a place for various adjunct therapies that Freud ultimately discarded. Towards the end of his life Janet was developing ideas that resemble those of ego development, and they are related to the place in therapy of rest and exercise of functions. Human behavior can be described in terms of a hierarchy of tendencies, ranging from primitive impulsions to the most complex and thoughtful acts. The higher tendencies Janet described as requiring higher tension, a somewhat confusing terminology, since what everyday speech calls *anxious tension* pertains to or reduces a person to what he called the *lower tendencies*.

Another concept in Janet's mental economics is that of force or mental energy. (Janet, like Freud, did not distinguish force, a concept from Newtonian physics, from energy, a thermodynamic concept. Force is a vector, having direction and amount; energy is a scalar, having amount but not direction. [See Holt, 1967]). Where the force is large and the person is restricted to the lower tendencies, behavior tends to be chaotic and confused. Great mental energy belongs with high tension, that is, with the capacity to act according to the higher tendencies. When a person with high tension has insufficient force, he experiences exhaustion, and rest might be called for. In other cases, stimulation is appropriate. Permanent restriction of the stimulation value of the environment can be important for some people, he thought, even to the extent that they might need permanently to forego any hope of joy or triumph. Such prescriptions followed from his view of therapy as a kind of budget balancing.

A traumatic fixed idea was conceived of as an uncompleted act, or as an unpaid debt that requires liquidation. The completion consists in establishing the associative connections between the traumatic event and the rest of the conscious personality, thus rendering it available for free recall and at the same time rendering it unable to unroll as a somnambulistic episode. This view has more in common with Freud's ideas of abreaction and working through than Janet seemed to recognize.

In summary, the fact that ideas can create and can remove hysterical symptoms such as anesthesias and paralyses was demonstrated directly in experiments with hypnosis by Charcot. Further support came in the study of the distinction between hysterical and organic paralyses. Experiments by Bernheim on posthypnotic suggestion showed that patterns of action can be motivated by unconscious ideas, and that unconscious memories can in principle be recovered to consciousness. Charcot argued for trauma as the predisposing cause of neurosis. Where Charcot linked hypnosis with hysteria as pathological and Bernheim linked hypnosis with suggestion as normal, Freud cast a single umbrella over all with his rejection of mental degeneration and his belief that there is one set of psychological laws for the normal and the neurotic alike. The importance of the relation of the hypnotizer to his patient, long known, must have alerted Freud to the key issue of transference. Janet has shown us what a gifted but not revolutionary mind would do with these data.

Studies on Hysteria

With publication of *Studies on Hysteria* (Breuer and Freud, 1895) Freud can be seen working towards something resembling a scientific paradigm or protoparadigm. The first case in the book is that of Anna O., treated about 1890 to 1892 by Josef Breuer (1842-1925), a distinguished Viennese physician who was Freud's teacher and friend. When Breuer was treating Anna O., Freud was still studying neuroanatomy, but he learned about the case not long afterward. The case remained in his mind when he was struggling with the difficulties of treating hysterical patients. The revival and elaboration of Breuer's method and the eventual publication of the case were on Freud's initiative.

During a long, severely incapacitating illness, Anna O. fell easily into somnambulistic states, during which she recalled the times the various symptoms had occurred, tracing each back to an original traumatic event. When such an event had been recalled, accompanied by the original strong emotion, she was relieved of the corresponding symptom. During his daily or even twice daily visits, Breuer often induced deep somnambulism to aid Anna in recalling these events.

Many psychiatrists were using hypnotism during the 1880s and 1890s. Typically, hypnosis was used to make the patient receptive to the suggestion that his or her symptoms would disappear. The hypnotic state itself, particularly when prolonged, was believed to have some therapeutic effect, a kind of rest cure. Breuer's use was different; it was a medium for inducing a cathartic reliving or *abreaction* of a traumatic event. Hysterics suffer from reminiscences, Breuer and Freud wrote. A single major trauma or a succession of minor traumas generates a symptom when the strong affect aroused is not adequately expressed in action or words. This situation may occur because the trauma is one to which no response suffices, such as a death in the family, or because the trauma itself arouses a paralyzing affect, such as fright, that precludes reaction. The pathogenic memories become dissociated from the remainder of consciousness and hence are not subject to normal erosion of memory.

Most psychiatrists of the time, having an organic orientation, were impatient with or contemptuous of hysterical women patients who, they knew, had no visible organic lesions and would not die of their ailments. Since the symptoms might remit spontaneously, they could be dismissed as due to "imagination." Breuer, Charcot, Bernheim, Janet, and Freud differed from most of their colleagues in their willingness to listen in detail to their patients' complaints, as the frequency of Breuer's visits to Anna O. illustrates. With the exception of inducing deep somnambulism, Breuer appears to have played a passive and receptive role in this therapy, anticipating the physician's role in psychoanalysis.

Comparing the Breuer-Freud theory of hysteria with that of their predecessors, we can trace connections with Bernheim, Charcot, and Janet, as did the authors themselves. Where Charcot believed that one kind of hysteria was the direct result of a physical trauma, Freud believed that all hysteria was the indirect result of a psychic, specifically a sexual, trauma; Breuer did not commit himself to the universality of this formula, though he endorsed it for many cases. This theory was similar to that of Janet. Since Breuer had treated Anna O. before Janet began his medical training, he undoubtedly came to his theory independently. So did Janet, who had some priority in publication of the theory. A common element in the two theories was seeing the traumatic events as like uncompleted acts.

The major difference was that Freud early became interested in what prevented the patient from recovering the traumatic memories. He observed the patient's behavior when the train of associations led to this area; the patient might become tense or restless, he might say he could think of nothing, he might quickly change the subject, and so on. The patient behaved as if he were defending himself against the pathogenic memory or as if something in him were resisting the memory. Here Freud made an important leap: he guessed that the same force that repressed the memory in the first place was now responsible for keeping it out of conscious memory. (The terms *defense* and *resistance* were used interchangeably, and *repression* was a related term.) Janet ridiculed Freud's idea of repression.

The idea of psychological weakness or mental degeneracy, stressed variously by Janet and Charcot, was attacked by Freud and Breuer. They called attention to the intellectual achievements, the refinement, and the moral sensibilities of their hysterical patients, which are incompatible with mental degeneracy or psychological weakness. They joined Charcot in postulating hypnoid states as the condition for the genesis of an hysterical symptom, but in his later writing Freud dropped that idea, attributing it to Breuer.

Since Breuer discovered the cathartic method and Freud originated psychoanalytic theory, one might be surprised that the chapter on theory was written by Breuer and that on therapy was written by Freud. On second thought, however, it was precisely this distribution of effort that foretold the future. Breuer's chapter included speculations about hypnoid states and bound versus free energy, the former a concept quickly discarded, the latter one that still haunts psychoanalysis. Freud's chapter describes the method he used, a preoccupation that led both to the substance of psychoanalysis and to a quasi-scientific paradigm.

In the five case histories that Freud recounted and in his chapter on therapy, he mentioned using a variety of adjunct therapies, including mild electric shock, diet, rest, hydrotherapy, and massage. Hypnosis was used extensively, though not in every case. Freud concluded that hypnosis was not harmful, but he withdrew that view in a few years. His main tool had become free association, practiced according to the basic rule, that nothing could be withheld because it was too embarrassing, too irrelevant, or too trivial. Freud would press the forehead of the patient, assuring her that when he did so, something significant would come to mind; if necessary, he did so more than once. If the meaning of the association was not evident, it became so when the train of thought it initiated was followed.

The chapter on psychotherapy, and the book, end with Freud's discussion of resistance and transference, a specially difficult form of resistance that attaches itself to the person of the physician. What turn out to be memories directly connected with the patient's chronicle often intrude into consciousness first as impulses directed towards the physician. These new symptoms are obstacles to therapy and must be analyzed just as the patient's presenting symptoms are.

Freud's chapter on psychotherapy captures the method at a point of transition. He had dropped electrotherapy as ineffective. Suggestions to the patient that he did not suffer from certain symptoms, when in fact both physician and patient knew he did, Freud found intolerable. Freud's intellectual integrity, which became the instrument of his self-analysis, precluded using a method that depended on pretense and self-deception.

By now Freud's theoretical understanding showed the relation between resistance in treatment and the original repression of traumatic memories; free association was a means to overcome resistance and recover the lost memories. Because there was no connection between the adjunct therapies and theory, they were dropped. Suggestion, pressure on the forehead to induce memories, and hypnosis were apparently the last to go. Objections to hypnosis included the fact that Freud was not a gifted hypnotist and that many patients could not be hypnotized. Moreover, even where hypnosis yielded the forgotten trauma, the therapeutic effect was often disappointing, for the patient in his normal waking state had to accept and assimilate this rejected, pathogenic piece of his past. Hypnosis bypassed the resistances, but the patient was not relieved of his symptoms until the resistances themselves were gradually overcome. In place of other techniques, Freud leaned increasingly on free association and analysis of dreams, accompanied by showing the patient gaps, discrepancies, and implausible details that he would not himself have noticed in his narrative. Those gaps and discrepancies, Freud pointed out, indicate the operation of unconscious forces. Just that coordination of theory and therapeutic method was crucial to the evolution of psychoanalysis.

Freud's Two Projects

In 1895 Freud wrote and sent to his friend Wilhelm Fliess an untitled manuscript, later called by Kris *Project for a Scientific Psychology* (1954), an attempt to construct a neurophysiological and neuroanatomical model that would accommodate the major facts both of normal psychology and of psychopathology. Freud decided not to publish the manuscript and soon turned decisively to psychology and away from neurology, despite the fact that he had better credentials as a neurologist. The chief interest of the *Project* is that it enables us to trace the origins of some of Freud's later ideas. One can see the limitations and errors of that early period of neuroanatomy; for example, at times Freud identified each idea with a single neurone.

The thesis argued by Holt (1965), following the research of Amacher (1965), is that many of the most obscure and flawed parts of Freud's later theorizing have their origins in the model of the *Project*. In Chapter Seven of the *Interpretation of Dreams* the model reappears, this time however with a specific disclaimer, that it does not refer to anatomical locations or structures. The physical-physiological language is exchanged for a psychological language, but otherwise there is not much change. In the *Project* the nervous system disposes of physical energy, consistent with the reflex-arc model; in Chapter Seven that has become psychic energy. When advances in neurophysiology decisively refuted the reflex-arc model, psychoanalysis was for long unchanged, in part because neurological ideas had been translated into psychological terms that disguised their origin. Thus *cathexis*, Freud's term for a charge of psychic energy, and its derivatives, countercathexis, bound and free cathexis, and so on, remained in Freud's theorizing to the end, though always eluding clear definition (Holt, 1962).

At about the time he completed the *Project*, Freud began another project, his self-analysis, accomplished largely by analysis of his dreams. Since both theory and practice of psychoanalysis require that every psychoanalyst first submit himself as a patient to another analyst, one may ask how anyone could be the first. The role of the psychoanalyst includes three functions: to serve as a target or object person for the patient as he replays the traumatic and problematic events of his childhood; to point out the gaps and discrepancies in his stories and associations as places to look for the operation of unconscious resistances; and to supply interpretations of his associations and memories. For Freud the first of these functions was fulfilled by the physician Fliess, with whom he maintained an active and affectionate correspondence during the period of his self-analysis. Fliess does not seem to have served at all in the latter two capacities. For them Freud had no outside help that we know of during the most crucial years. His self-analysis was doubly remarkable, for he criticized his own thinking and saw through his own unconscious subterfuges and self-deceptions, going a way that no one had ever gone before, without even a general guide as to what might lie ahead in the analysis or behind in his infancy.

During his self-analysis, Freud became convinced that many of the stories of sexual seduction in childhood that he believed true when told to him by his patients (who did not always themselves accept them as true) had been fantasies, not actual occurrences. The reasons Freud gave for doubting the reality of the childhood sexual traumas were disappointment in the therapeutic results, his astonishment at being asked to believe that all fathers were given to perversions, that there was no criterion of reality in the unconscious, and that such memories do not emerge in the deliria of psychotics. Jones believed, however, that Freud's self-analysis may have been the decisive factor.

Freud's first reaction to discovering that one of the essential points of the trauma theory had been destroyed was to believe that psychoanalysis was totally discredited. He quickly came to realize that most of it could be salvaged and that it would now rest on a firmer foundation. If the seductions did not take place in most cases, then they were fantasies. Thus fantasies appear to have the same force as reality in determining traumatic experiences for a child. If the seduction had not been initiated by the adult but had arisen in the fantasy of the child, then the child must have sexual impulses. Herein lies one of Freud's major discoveries, infantile sexuality. While it may be true, as Ellenberger (1970) points out, that an occasional pediatrician had anticipated this discovery, and, as Freud said, that every nursemaid knew it, Freud himself certainly did not know it in 1895, and the idea aroused much opposition.

The Trauma Paradigm

Let us now recapitulate the position of Freud during the first period of psychoanalysis. There is, in fact, no publication of his that puts forth exactly the set of ideas I wish to identify as "the trauma paradigm." Rather it is my reconstruction of the logical structure to which his thinking was converging up to the time that he ceased to believe in the reality of the infantile seductions.

Freud's basic assumption is that behavior and thought are lawful. There is only one kind of person; the laws of psychology hold for neurotic and normal, psychiatrist and patient. The explanation of neurosis is not to be found in degeneracy. Freud's self-analysis stems from this assumption, as does his effort to decipher symptoms and other apparently senseless acts.

Freud's first big discovery, originally a conclusion but a postulate in relation to later work, is psychic determinism: ideas can cause physical symptoms, and hence ideas can cure them. This was not an armchair discovery but came from years of scientific and clinical work. Breuer's therapy with Anna O. showed that symptoms could be dissipated by recovery of traumatic memories, a finding confirmed in many cases by both Freud and Janet. Using hypnotism, Charcot both created and removed symptoms by means of ideas. Bernheim's experiments on post-hypnotic suggestion reinforced the conclusion. Freud's own work on hysterical versus organic paralyses showed that ideas can cause symptoms that mimic physical afflictions.

A related principle is that of the dynamic unconscious, the best known of Freud's discoveries, but perhaps not uniquely his, for Janet had a similar conception. It states that unconscious ideas influence behavior in somewhat the way that conscious ideas do—but this formulation is too weak. That the most important determinants of behavior are unconscious is too strong, though it is a popular version. One version is that a given idea influences behavior more strongly when it is unconscious than after it is made conscious. The most elegant version, though it must be qualified to be strictly true, is that both conscious and unconscious ideas affect behavior, but the consequences of behavior affect only its conscious sources. Not encompassed are the conscious appearance of derivatives of unconscious wishes, censorship, and other complications. If the statement held exactly, therapy would be impossible. It is a schematic version of the short-run relation of conscious and unconscious determinants to behavior. Behavior of unconscious origin is not stamped out by ordinary rewards or consequences; hence, this is the "law of no effect" (Loevinger, 1966).

The precipitating cause of hysteria, according to Freud, is always inner conflict; parties to the conflict are a sexual wish and the person's moral standards or ego. That inner conflict causes neurosis has been an enduring tenet, but more attention at the time was paid to the predisposition to neurosis, which Freud believed always to be a psychic trauma, specifically, a sexual seduction in childhood. Since children, as Freud then believed, have no capacity for sexual feelings, it was the reactivation at puberty of the memory of the seduction that proved pathogenic. What made an event traumatic was that the person did not have an adequate and appropriate emotional response at the time; repression of the memory made it pathogenic. The aim of therapy was to recover repressed memories of traumatic events, to abreact fully the aborted emotions, and to establish connections between those memories and the rest of the conscious ego.

The method of therapy was free association and in particular analysis of dreams. Data consisted of associations, dreams, forgetting, symptoms, and so on, which had not been conceptualized as data by previous psychologists. The chief obstacle to therapeutic progress was resistance on the part of the patient to recollecting the repressed memories, evidenced by pauses and other signs visible to the therapist though often not apparent to the patient. This concept was new; it connected observations during therapy with the pathogenic repression. One form consisted in the transference of the patient's symptoms to his relation to the therapist. Thus resistance and transference appeared in the system as processes that interfere with recovery of repressed, traumatic memories.

Another significant finding was that of displacement of affect. That an affect appropriate to one idea can become associated to another idea seems to be an original finding of Freud's though the raw materials for it must have been available to Aristotle. Displacement of affect is a necessary premise in the deciphering of symptoms or dreams.

The concept of ego is used as a term from the public domain. The terms *primary* and *secondary process* appear in the *Project,* but the ideas are worked out differently later. One direction of theorizing was towards connecting particular kinds of sexual traumas with particular kinds of psychoneuroses; that proved fruitless. Freud realized, however, that he had found a therapeutic method that was not specific to hysteria but of more general applicability.

When the common element in the memories of neurotics, traumatic sexual seductions, turned out to be not common experiences but common fantasies, the paradigm collapsed. However, the postulate of lawfulness, the dynamic unconscious, free association, resistance, transference, and displacement of affect were all unscathed. Psychic determinism was more impressive than ever, since fantasies had the same force as reality in determining pathogenic memories. The case for inner conflict as the cause of neurosis was also strengthened; the child felt himself responsible for his wishes and fantasies, hence the case for repression became more intelligible (Jones, 1953, p. 285). In place of the false hypothesis of traumatic seduction, Freud discovered the Oedipus complex, a central feature of the next period.

Freud's Sources

Freud was an immensely learned man, and one can easily miss important sources of his ideas. How shall we weigh the sources of his errors as compared to those of his great discoveries? His sources, moreover, were of three kinds. Firstly, there were full-fledged, mature sciences. Secondly, there were philosophical and literary writings that bear resemblance to some aspect of his thinking. Thirdly, there were his own experimental and clinical researches and those of his teachers.

In the first category there are the scientific discoveries of thermodynamics, theory of evolution, and Hughlings Jackson's neurology. These paradigms could have influenced his thinking only by way of analogy; none was directly germane to his work. The influence of thermodynamics has been misunderstood often. The pledge of the Helmholtz group, to find no other forces in living matter than those in physics and chemistry or ones of equal dignity, may have predisposed Freud to the doctrine of psychic determinism, but there is no logical connection between that pledge and thermodynamic theory. Energy and its conservation are basic conceptions of thermodynamics, and they became for psychologists and psychiatrists around the turn of the century the very model of a scientific construct. Charles Spearman, for example, postulated that "g," the general factor in tests of ability, was best conceived as mental energy. Janet's concept of psychic energy came close to being an ego concept. For Freud psychic energy or "charge of affect" was something that arose prior to and outside of ego. As Erikson has remarked, even the greatest minds are caught in the myths of their times. Energy was the myth of Freud's time. The solid observations that lay behind Freud's postulate of a displaceable charge of energy or "cathexis," as it is usually translated, relate to displacement of affect, an enduring finding.

The most important source for psychoanalytic psychology lies in the work of Freud and others with whom he was associated in laboratory and clinic. Although Freud ultimately abandoned hypnosis, it played an indispensable part in his early discoveries. Thus even the most valuable sources may turn into obstacles. Freud's research in physiology and neuroanatomy contributed to his great discoveries but also left an impress that still hobbles psychoanalysis in complicated and unfruitful aspects of the metapsychology. Another evident result of this background was Freud's theory of anxiety neurosis as resulting from unsatisfactory sexual practices such as masturbation and coitus interruptus. There are various versions of Freud's original theory of anxiety neurosis (Freud, 1895). At times he seemed almost to be saying that anxiety results from an accumulation of sexual toxins. At other times he spoke of the source of anxiety in terms of the dissociation of the physical and psychic elements of sexuality, a quite different idea. In any case, the theory was later supplanted.

Many passages in the writings of philosophers, particularly on the subject of the unconscious, anticipate those of Freud. Helmholtz wrote about perception in terms of unconscious inference. Herbart had a concept of repression, but in his version the strong, conscious ideas repressed the weaker, unconscious ideas, whereas Freud had to account for the strength of the unconscious ideas. Although Eduard von Hartmann published the *Philosophy of the Unconscious* in 1869, Schopenhauer's earlier conception of the Will was closer to Freud's conception of the unconscious. For Schopenhauer the Will was a blind, unconscious, driving force governing the universe, of which the phenomenal world was only a representation (or idea). The human being in particular is an irrational being in whom the force of will takes the form of two instincts, an instinct of conservation and the sexual instinct, serving procreation; the latter is far more important. From the metaphysical speculations of Schopenhauer and other philosophers, Freud could have gotten only fragmentary glimpses, hypotheses, analogies, far removed from his task of curing neuroses.

Ernest Jones emphasized that Freud's exploration of the unconscious was bound up with his description of two types of mental functioning, primary process and secondary process, that obey differing laws, a conception new with Freud. "If anyone were to say that he [Freud] got the idea of the unconscious from someone else, the crass ignorance implied in the remark would not be redeemed by the tiny atom of truth in it" (Jones, 1953, p. 379). Ellenberger, on the other hand, devotes hundreds of pages to Freud's predecessors in the "discovery of the unconscious." Both men are scholars and provide solid backing for their views.

Freud was the most creative and original thinker psychology has ever had, but there is no way for anyone to invent whole systems of thought without any background. The mind must have something to work with. Psychoanalysts and psychiatrists have credited Freud not only with discovery of the unconscious but with discovery of the ego, the pleasure principle, the pathogenic effect of psychic trauma, and the importance of the patient's attachment to the therapist. All of those ideas have a long history. What filters into the popular mind, into most psychology texts, and perhaps even into the psychoanalytic catechism as "Freud's discoveries" is a version almost as primitivized as a dream: concrete, quasi-pictorial, and lacking in connections between the elements. The primitivized version represents about what Freud took from the public domain. What he added that was original was detail, nuance, and, above all, the relations between the elements, just what establishes the claim of psychoanalysis as a quasi-scientific paradigm, just what most people never learn of psychoanalysis.

Conclusions

If this chapter seems to have strayed from our topic, that is because ego development has been presented earlier as if it concerned an almost disembodied soul. The ego is the locus of personhood, but the whole person is involved—physical, physiological, instinctual, and social. Psychotherapy can be thought of as aiming to reconcile the ego with the drives; in those terms psychoanalysis is the heir of faith healing and hypnotism, not of organic psychiatry. But Freud was a neurologist, not a faith healer, and the fundamental principles of psychoanalysis were evolved in years of medical research.

The drives and the unconscious that are the ego's antagonist in the pathogenic conflict, *non-ego*, drew Freud's interest at first. The common-sense meaning of *ego* that he adopted was later replaced by a technical conception that has roots equally in the conceptions of defense, repression, and resistance, at the heart of the paradigm. Without psychoanalysis our conception of *person* remains thin and overly rational. Without its history the psychoanalytic conception of ego is an arbitrary, even baffling, construction. In the next two chapters we will trace how, as Freud and other analysts sought to remedy their one-sided preoccupation with drives, conflict, and the unconscious, they returned to our topic, bringing to it a richer, deeper, and more original theory than any preceding one.

Chapter Fourteen

Psychoanalysis: From Drive Theory to Ego Theory

The history of psychoanalysis can be divided into three eras. A different view of human nature is implied in each: man as subject of his environment (contrasting with the earlier doctrine of "mental degeneration"), man as subject of his drives, and man as subject and master of his drives and his environment (Higgins, 1961). The first period has been discussed in the last chapter as leading to the trauma paradigm. In this chapter we will show the chief features of the second period, outlining the drive paradigm. The third period consists of two overlapping movements. In the first one, the drive paradigm is stretched to cover ego development and related aspects of ego psychology; that will be described in the latter part of this chapter. A second movement within the third period proposes a new or ego paradigm to cover the major features of drive psychology and ego psychology simultaneously; that will be the topic of the next chapter. Such terminology invites a comparison with if not a literal application of Kuhn's model for a scientific paradigm. How far and in what ways psychoanalysis conforms to the criteria of a science will be touched on in the next chapter, though not exhaustively or definitively.

The trauma paradigm was discarded by Freud before he fully consolidated it and before he acquired cohorts. In the present chapter the drive paradigm will be presented with emphasis on its relation to our topic. We shall follow Freud closely, but invoking the idea of paradigm is a commitment to seek the logical realization rather than the literal expression.

In 1900 Freud's greatest book, *The Interpretation of Dreams*, was published. Drawing on his own analysis of his own dreams, on the analysis of the dreams of some patients, and on the dreams of other normal people, some drawn from literary sources, Freud established the fundamentals of psychoanalytic theory. Three books followed that further established psychoanalysis as a general psychology of normal life, *The Psychopathology of Everyday Life* (1901), *Three Essays on Theory of Sexuality* (1905b), and *Jokes and their Relation to the Unconscious* (1905a). During this period, the clinical theory of psychoanalysis was developed further, and Freud wrote all of his classical case histories. He acquired many followers and lost some. The *Introductory Lectures on Psychoanalysis* (1916-1917), coming toward the end of the period, contain a fully realized version of the drive paradigm. In the next section I will confine myself to following its argument.

The Drive Paradigm

"The interpretation of dreams is the royal road to a knowledge of the unconscious activities of the mind" (Freud, [1900] 1953 p. 608). However bizarre dreams seem, they make sense. To decipher them one must look beyond the manifest content to the latent content; that can be determined by the person's free associations to the elements of the dream. The meaning invariably turns out to be the fulfillment of a wish. In small children it may be an unfulfilled wish of the dream day, but in adults, some small unnoticed happening of the dream day arouses an infantile wish, long repressed. Seeing the disguises that cloak the dream thoughts, one learns about the laws of unconscious thought, that is, *primary process*. Primary process includes *condensation* of several elements into a single dream image and *displacement* of the affect appropriate to one element onto another one. In the dream, abstract ideas are represented pictorially and concretely as in a rebus or pictogram. Elements of the dream thoughts may be omitted in the manifest dream, particularly those expressing connections between elements. The mental processes by which the latent content is disguised is called the *dream work*; the work of psychoanalysis is to undo those disguises.

Everyone dreams; hence the application of psychoanalysis to normal life and to the normal mind is established. The psychopathology of everyday life includes the small slips, errors, and forgetting that plague us all. Mistakes, like dreams, have meaning, revealing either something the person chooses not to reveal or some motive that he himself is not conscious of. The term *parapraxes* (*Fehlleistungen*) to represent slips of the tongue or pen, errors, forgetting of recent and important things, and so on, was a concept new with Freud. Such things had not been conceptualized as data for psychology and psychiatry previously. Jokes and parapraxes are constructed by processes similar to the dream work.

The symptoms of psychoneuroses are constructed on a similar model; they appear to be pointless actions, senseless ideas, or both, but in some past situation the idea was justified and the action served a purpose. Past experiences must once have been conscious, but the original purpose of the symptomatic act may or may not have been conscious at first. Hysterics typically are amnesic both for the experience and the purpose. With obsessive neurotics, the experiences on which the symptom is grounded may have remained accessible to memory, but the connection to the symptom, that is, the purpose of the symptom, is repressed. In either case, therapy consists in lifting the repressions, restoring the memories and the connections; then the problems, often trivial from an adult view, are dealt with by the conscious ego, and the symptoms disappear. The experiences that form the basis of symptoms are traumatic ones to which the patient has become fixated. The definition of trauma is quantitative, or, as Freud said, "economic." A trauma is an experience during which the increase in the stimulus in a short time is too powerful to be dealt with or worked off adequately.

In the transference neuroses, that is, anxiety hysteria, conversion hysteria, and obsessional neurosis, symptoms are substitute satisfactions for sexual wishes. Transference neuroses constitute the realm in which psychoanalysis as therapy is effective, as contrasted with the realm of narcissistic neuroses, which include paranoia, dementia praecox, and melancholia. The former patients fall ill because, for one reason or another, their sexual wishes are frustrated in reality. The symptoms are compromises expressing both the repressed sexual wish and the ego's defensive measures against it.

Calling the wishes *sexual* implies a broadening of the concept of sexuality, including all kinds of perversions and childish form of sensuality, such as the sensual sucking observable in babies. Only the broadened version is tenable to account for the facts of normal life. Sexuality does not spring full blown at puberty. Various component elements are present in childhood. Normally at puberty they become subordinate to reproduction, though not entirely so in many cases and not at all in sexual perversions, universally recognized as sexual, though not aiming at reproduction and in some cases not even involving genital organs. The sexual fears, fantasies, and wishes of children, particularly the fear of castration in boys and the wish to be a man in girls, play a great part in character formation in normal people, in symptom formation in neurosis, and in resistance in psychoanalytic treatment. The perverse, incestuous, and murderous dreams of normal people show us that the Oedipus complex of the neurotic is only a magnified version of universal characteristics of normal development.

The concept of repression has no intrinsic link to sexuality, Freud continued. It is a dynamic or topographic concept, where *topography* refers to the different mental systems, the unconscious and the conscious-preconscious system. Repression must be distinguished from regression, a term for turning from a higher to a lower stage of development. In sexual development there regularly occurs more or less fixation at the several stages (oral, anal, and phallic). Under frustration, the libido—that is, the sexual drive—may regress to earlier stages, particularly those at which fixation is strong. There are many ways of tolerating deprivation without falling ill. Regression without repression leads to perversion rather than to neurosis. Moreover, the sexual impulses are plastic, amenable to substitution of aims and objects. *Sublimation* is the name for substitution of valued social goals for unattainable sexual ones. For frustration to result in neurosis there must be conflict between the sexual drives and the ego drives, or between the ego and sexuality.

Childhood episodes that lead to neurosis and symptom formation include observation of parental intercourse, seduction by an adult, and threat of castration. Those things happen, but, for example, intercourse may be described in more detail than could have been observed. For a small child fantasy has as much psychic reality as what really happens. (The recurrence of these primal fantasies with a common content led Freud to guess that they are part of a phylogenetic endowment. He always believed in the false doctrine of the inheritance of acquired characteristics.)

The symptoms of hysteria are modeled on the patient's fantasies. In obsessional neuroses, the reaction formations become the symptoms. In paranoia, delusions are formed on the model of the "secondary revision" of dream theory, that is, they are rationalizations invented to surround a core of unconscious motivation so as to present it in a plausible context. In traumatic neuroses, particularly those of wartime, the ego is seeking protection and advantage, and there is little hope of cure until the threatening situation of real life is lifted. The latter motivation, the gain from falling ill and the secondary gain from remaining ill, is also present in all other neuroses, but to a far lesser extent than in traumatic war neuroses; correspondingly, the other unconscious and infantile sources of illness are present in war neuroses but to a lesser extent than in other situations.

Anxiety is a central problem of psychopathology, Freud pointed out; at the time of writing the *Introductory Lectures* he continued to believe that unconsummated sexual excitation becomes transformed into anxiety. This theory, however, was part of a broader conception. When a memory is repressed, the content of the idea remains the same when it is unconscious as it was when conscious. Freud did not feel that the idea of an unconscious affect was tenable. The affect that belonged to the repressed idea, whatever its nature might have been (anxiety, shame, rage, or positive libidinal excitation), becomes transformed into and discharged as anxiety. Anxiety, in turn, leads to the formation of symptoms. Repression is an attempt at flight by the ego from libido felt as a danger. In phobias, inner danger is converted into outer danger.

Psychoanalytic therapy evokes intense feelings in the patient. Positive feelings produce a desire to please the analyst and to a point can assist the therapy. Sooner or later, however, the patient's feelings toward the analyst pose an obstacle to the treatment, whether as negative feelings or as demands for intense affection; in either case they betray their origin in instinctual life. To continue therapy requires that this relationship itself be analyzed. The patient must be shown that it is a transference onto the analyst of feelings and ideas that originated much earlier in his life. Thus in place of repeating the patterns, he is enabled to remember their sources. This process is the core of psychoanalysis as a therapeutic enterprise. Thus transference is turned from being an obstacle to being the chief instrument of therapy.

The psychotherapy of Bernheim, Janet, and others who used suggestion and hypnosis, Freud said, made minimal demands on patient and therapist, whereas analysis of resistances and transference is lengthy and laborious for both parties. But there is no reason to hope that large effects for the patient can be achieved at low price. Where hypnosis leaves the patient inert and basically unchanged, even when particular symptoms are removed, psychoanalysis aims to help him overcome resistances and thus be strengthened against falling ill again.

That, in outline, is psychoanalysis of the early twentieth century, the drive paradigm. Drive (*Trieb*) is the connecting thread in the theory of symptoms, dreams, parapraxes, jokes, free association, and transference. The principles that account for normal life, for neurosis, and for therapy are interrelated.

Let us look first at the most prominent dissenters of this period, then at the direction of Freud's own thinking that provided both a triumphant extension into ego psychology and the undermining of the drive paradigm.

Dissenters: Adler and Jung

In 1911 Alfred Adler and several other Viennese psychoanalysts broke with Freud's group. In 1913 Carl Gustav Jung and a group of Swiss psychoanalysts and psychiatrists followed suit. Both Adler and Jung had been prominent in the small and beleaguered circle of psychoanalysts. What I seek to discern in their writings is not necessarily what others consider most important but a coherent structure of ideas covering pathology, therapy, and ego development, to compare with the ideas of Freud and Janet.

Adler and the other analysts who decamped when he did were socialists. His thinking put a greater emphasis on the importance of the social milieu than did Freud's. As Ansbacher and Ansbacher (1956) point out, many recent dissenters from psychoanalysis, such as Erich Fromm and Karen Horney, who also emphasize environmental and situational factors, should be called neo-Adlerians rather than neo-Freudians, as they usually are.

Adler published no extensive case histories; so it is hard to reconstruct his therapeutic methods. He called his theory *individual psychology* and the method of treatment *individual psychotherapy*, referring to the unity and coherence of the individual, in contrast with the emphasis on inner conflict in psychoanalysis. Adler sat facing his patient and insisted that their two chairs be alike in size and shape; the physician must not make the patient feel inferior. (By contrast, Freud's patients lay down, and Freud sat behind them, where he could observe without being observed.)

The first step in individual therapy is brief; its aim is for the therapist to understand the patient, his life-style, and his fictitious life goal. Adler used the terms *life-style* and *fictitious life goal* for normal persons as well. The patient, however, has a mistake, central to his thinking and aims, that must be discovered. Like normal people, he strives for unity and coherence. Thus he will use his illness to excuse himself from whatever life task he seeks to avoid. Ask the patient what he would do if he were completely well, and his answer will tell you the life task or social demand that he most wants to avoid.

In the second stage, which lasts longer, perhaps several months, the therapist helps the patient to become aware of his life-style and his fictitious life goal and of the contrast between them and the realities of his situation, in specific, concrete terms. In the final stage the patient must work out for himself whether he will change in those respects. In Freud's terms, Adlerian therapy consists of exploration of the preconscious; much the same territory is routinely covered in early stages of psychoanalytic therapy, though the theoretical justification is different.

Adler had alternative explanations for resistance and transference. Resistance is the way the patient shows his superiority over and deprecatory tendency toward the therapist. Such tendencies are an invariable part of a neurotic's approach to other people; they are part of the neurotic's mistaken life-style and must be pointed out as such. Positive transference is artificially created by the therapist by pointing to repressed sexual factors. Patients lack courage and have insufficient social interest. They need a good human relationship to encourage them and arouse their potential social interest.

This summary, too brief to be just to Adler, shows that from Freud's point of view, Adler had abandoned the psychology and analysis of the unconscious, even though he retained the word in his writings. Adler's "individual psychology" cannot be called a school of psychoanalysis, for it departs from the essentials, particularly analysis of resistance and transference.

Where Adler retreated from the unconscious toward a psychology of common sense, Jung (1943, 1945) plunged into the depths, finding a pantheon—or stable—of characters there. The *persona* is defined as something like a facade or mask, as the sum of the conscious ego and the unconscious self, and as part of the collective psyche. It is the face the person presents to the world, appropriate to his office and station in life, largely defined by society rather than by his own individuality but accepted by him as himself. Contrasting with the persona is the *shadow*, his negative personal traits, more or less unknown to and unaccepted by his conscious ego. His unconscious has two quite different components, the personal and the collective unconscious. The *personal unconscious* relates to his own history and contains elements that can in principle be conscious. Since no amount of psychoanalysis and repression lifting exhausts the unconscious, there must be something more, and that is the *collective unconscious*. It contains the inherited archetypes, preeminently the *anima* in men and the *animus* in women, as well as figures such as wise old men, magicians, and demons that recur in the myths and religions of all societies.

Even before he became associated with Freud, Jung was working with the word-association technique as a means of exploring unconscious, emotionally charged complexes of ideas. The term *complex* he adopted from Theodor Ziehen, but he knew of the similar ideas of Janet (with whom he had studied) and Freud and of the implications of unconscious complexes for therapy of hysteria.

Jung disagreed with Freud on the topics of infantile sexuality in general and the Oedipus complex in particular. He identified libido with *psychic energy*, not necessarily sexual in connotation. Moreover, he sometimes took energy to mean magic power. Energy, he said, requires a tension of opposites; thus Jung's psychic energy, unlike Freud's, has no overtones of thermodynamics. Jung saw the beginnings of sexuality in what Freud labeled the *latency period*.

Neurosis breaks out in the face of a task a patient wishes

to avoid or a difficulty he wishes to escape; this view of Jung's resembles those of Janet and Adler. Freud recognized the importance of such factors in war neuroses but believed that in most cases the gains through illness were minor factors, though probably always present. Jung treated most patients without recourse to analysis of the unconscious; much of his theory, however, pertains to the smaller proportion of cases in which he did so.

Jung's method of analyzing the unconscious, which he called *analytical psychology*, proceeded by analysis of dreams to an even larger extent than does psychoanalysis. The dreams are interpreted primarily in terms of universal symbolism rather than in terms of the individual associations stressed by Freud. The ideas of repression and censorship are not essential to Jungian dream interpretation. When deeper analysis is undertaken, it proceeds in three stages. The first stage is occupied with analysis of the persona and the shadow. The patient needs to dissolve his persona and recognize, accept, and assimilate the negative aspects of his personality. The second stage is concerned with the problem of the anima or animus. The man has an ideal image of a woman, derived from his mother; that is his anima. The woman ordinarily has many ideal images of men combined in the animus. In addition to being ideals, the anima and animus are also a kind of second self; thus they both distort one's perception of the other sex and dominate one's behavior. They must be understood and absorbed as psychological functions. In the final stage archetypes such as those of the wise old man or the great mother emerge in dreams and must be dealt with.

Jung's best-known work (1921) was published subsequent to his break with Freud in 1913 and concerns his typology. His major distinction is that between *introverts* and *extraverts*, terms that have passed into common speech, though not always in Jung's precise definitions. The term *introversion* refers to finding one's motivations in inner or subjective factors, *extraversion* to deriving motivation from external factors. A person may shift from one attitude to another, but if he remains fixed at one pole, he can be described as a person of that type. Jung fancied that Freud was extraverted, since he ascribed major importance to a person's past experiences and to objective causes, while Adler, ascribing major importance to goals and purposes, was subjective and hence introverted. Jung saw his "analytical psychology" as integrating and profiting from the theories of Freud and Adler. He did not disdain their methods, but saw them of about equal importance and primarily of value for the problems of the young.

In Jungian therapy the persona, which comprises the conscious ego and the unconscious self, is dissolved and the person comes to grips with his unconscious. To the extent that the personal unconscious is absorbed, the person's horizons are widened, and he approaches the ideal of self-realization or attainment of individuality. The hazard is that the analysis will continue further into the collective unconscious. Then the person may retreat to his starting point, or he may identify himself with the archetypes and become inflated, perhaps seeing himself as a prophet or possibly becoming psychotic. The problem is to avoid these hazards of the collective unconscious.

In young persons therapy may consist in coming to terms with sexual impulses or with the will to power, as in Freudian or Adlerian therapy. For persons in middle and later life, philosophical and religious issues are unavoidable; ordinarily older patients have already overcome the parental transferences and youthful illusions that must be dealt with in therapy of young patients.

Although Jung's conception of self-realization would seem to imply ego development, his typology was constructed along different lines. The conscious psyche has four fundamental functions, thinking, feeling, sensation, and intuition. A person tends toward one or the other. These functions characterize both extraverts and introverts, so that eight psychological types are generated. Patients are likely to choose consciously to emphasize whatever function they are already overcommitted to; therefore, to achieve psychic balance, the therapist may urge him to take up activities that emphasize some other function. A mathematician (thinking) might be encouraged to read poetry (feeling) or to paint (sensation). Thus although in some respects

Jungian analysis is not so diametrically opposed to psychoanalysis as is Adlerian therapy, the Jungian analyst plays a more
active and directive role than the psychoanalyst.

The conceptions of resistance and transference are blurred
in Jung's theory. He does not appear to discuss resistance,
though he must have dealt with it, perhaps under the heading of
the persona. While he discusses transference, he belittles Freud's
emphasis upon it. In some cases transference is best left to play
itself out rather than being subject to analysis, he states. The
mark of psychoanalysis is not, however, mere recognition of
transference. The hypnotists and the magnetists often recognized the erotic nature of the rapport between the hypnotist
and his patient. For Freud transference was the therapeutic
arena, in which the old conflicts were reenacted for a new outcome. That idea does not appear to be present in Jung. Finally,
while Freud believed in the inheritance of acquired characteristics, it was not an essential part of his paradigm; subsequent
psychoanalysts have not shared that belief. The conception of
the collective unconscious is at the center of Jung's paradigm; if
there is any way to make sense out of the collective unconscious, it must be in terms of the false doctrine of the inheritance of acquired characteristics.

Ego Development within the Drive Paradigm

The drive paradigm was a revolutionary achievement, bringing
within the scope of psychology areas of life that had not previously been encompassed. With much of psychology accounted
for in terms of drives, the problem became how to integrate
drive psychology with ego psychology. Are they two separate
disciplines, or does one include the other? Jung and Adler continued to be interested in dreams and parapraxes; to that extent
their psychologies are drive psychologies. Adler thought Freud
overemphasized drives, and his own explanations were in terms
of ego aspects. Jung desexualized the drives, but for him the
personal and collective unconscious developed almost independently of the conscious ego. Because their premises were so
different, Jung and Adler did not affect the direction in which

Freud and his followers moved. Although originally Freud took as given the opposition between ego (or moral impulses) and sexual drives, later he undertook to show that the ego is derived from the drives. Thus drives account even for their own antagonist, and the drive paradigm absorbs ego psychology.

Ferenczi (see Chapter Five) argued that the child accommodates himself to reality and hence his ego develops, not because of a spontaneous striving toward development but because his surroundings demand that he renounce complete instinctual gratification. Ferenczi's account stopped with the earliest stages, those of ego formation.

Freud's ([1914] 1957) essay on narcissism carried the drive-derivative view of ego development an important step forward. In it he advanced diverse lines of evidence for postulating a narcissistic disposition as a regular part of psychosexual development. The perversion of narcissism represents only an extreme and atypical case. Freud postulated a stage of *primary narcissism* in infancy, preceding any true love of objects. The central argument for his conception of narcissism is that when later object love is frustrated, the libido returns regressively to the narcissistic position. Such return is called *secondary narcissism*. In this broadened sense narcissism is not a perversion but "the libidinal complement to the egoism of the instinct of self-preservation" (p. 74). In schizophrenics the withdrawal of interest from the world and the megalomania can be construed in terms of the libido withdrawn from the world being invested in self. A person suffering organic disease withdraws interest from the outside world and is concerned only with himself. Hypochondria is like organic disease in being characterized by distressing bodily signs and withdrawal of libido from the world.

The belief in omnipotence of thoughts and wishes to be found in the mental life of children and primitive men is narcissistic. "The charm of a child lies to a great extent in his narcissism, his self-contentment and inaccessibility" (p. 89). Parents overestimate their children, overlook their shortcomings, demand privileges on their behalf, and expect rules to be suspended for them. They expect their children to fulfill the dreams and wishes which reality has forced them to relinquish for themselves. "Parental love, which is so moving and at bottom so childish, is nothing but the parents' narcissism born again, which, transformed into object-love, unmistakably reveals its former nature" (p. 91).

Freud continued the argument of Ferenczi's paper on early ego development as follows. The self-love of the small child, who believes himself the possessor of all perfections, must be surrendered as he accommodates himself to the demands of family and society. It is saved by being transferred to his ideal ego, to which he assigns the perfection he can no longer claim for himself. The creation of the *ego ideal* (a term used interchangeably with *ideal ego* and *conscience* in this essay) is at bottom also a regression to narcissism. Thus a major step forward, the creation of the ego ideal, is simultaneously a regression.

The concept of the ego ideal, often attributed to Freud, was part of the public domain, appearing in writings of Dewey, James, Baldwin, and McDougall (Chapter Eleven) before the essay on narcissism; we may forego tracing its ancestry to Plato and Aristotle. What was original was postulating a regression to narcissism as the dynamics of its origin, seeing progression as taking place through regression. This was a *tour de force* for the drive-derivative view of ego development.

Psychoanalysts of the time were disturbed by what the essay did to the dual instinct theory. Freud had repeatedly stated that there were two classes of instincts, the self-preservative instincts and the sexual instincts, patterned after hunger and love; sometimes he called them *the ego instincts* and *the sexual instincts*. Now he was contrasting object-libido with ego-libido, and the theory depended on the conversion of one to the other. This elaboration would seem to be a classical case of a scientific theory being followed out to consequences that undermine its original assumptions. The reaction of analysts corresponded to that state of affairs. In retrospect we may ask whether the dual instinct theory, that is, the separation of sexual from ego drives, had any real grounding in psychoanalytic observation and whether it was in any way related to psychoanalysis as method. Freud discussed these questions in the essay on narcissism. The distinction between sexual and ego instincts is biological, not psychological, he said. So far as the psycho-analytic method is concerned, instinctual wishes are not clearly distinguishable according to their origin in the postulated dual instincts. Thus what was relinquished was not an essential part of the paradigm.

The essay on narcissism began a line of thought that ulti-mately undermined the drive paradigm in a fundamental way. If a drive can be gratified by setting up an ideal or conscience within oneself, can the nature of that drive ever have been a "demand of the body on the mind" as Freud (1915) defined instincts? Does not the envelope of possible gratifications define the drive? In this sense the spectacular success of the drive-derivative view of ego development was the beginning of the downfall of the drive paradigm.

In "Mourning and Melancholia" Freud (1917) initiated a theme that later became a major contribution to ego theory. In this essay, as in many others, he went back and forth between the phenomena of psychopathology and those of normal life. Melancholia, he stated, in many respects resembles normal grief, with its dejection, loss of interest in the world, loss of capacity to love, lowering of activity, poor appetite, and sleeplessness. An important difference is that in melancholia there is a debase-ment of self-esteem that does not characterize normal mourn-ing. The reproaches of the depressed person against himself depart in one respect from those of a person who feels normal remorse or self-reproach, namely, he lacks shame before others. On the contrary, he talks about himself too much and enjoys exposing his defects. Thus, on the one hand, the melancholic seems to have lost a love object; on the other hand, he reports a loss within himself. Moreover, his self-reproaches usually fit someone else he loves or has loved. Putting these indications together, Freud reconstructed a model somewhat as follows. First the person loved someone, then he lost that person, then he mastered the loss by identifying himself with the lost person. The conflict between the ego and the lost love is now internal-ized by a kind of narcissistic regression. So the reproaches directed against the self are by proxy directed against a former love object. Often the very person is a member of his immediate environment and one of those who suffer from the depressed person's behavior. In *The Ego and the Id* (1923) and *Civilization and Its Discontents* (1930) Freud took the same basic scheme and applied it to the identification of the child with his parents and thus to normal ego development.

Another essay of this period, "Instincts and Their Vicissitudes" (1915), has two features germane to the present topic: first, the discussion of love and hate, and second, a gap in the essay. Freud remarked that love and hate are not as directly opposed to each other as they seem at first. Even though one often sees a love-relation turn to hate and vice versa, the hate-relation is not derived primarily from sexual life but from the struggle of the ego for self-preservation. For that matter, neither love nor hate can be said to characterize the relation of drives to objects but only the relations of the ego as a whole to its objects. Properly, the component sexual instincts cannot be said to love their objects; the applicability of the term *love* begins with genital primacy. Evidently Freud in this essay was giving some ground to an Adlerian view of the drives as subordinated to the ego.

The vicissitudes of the drives that give the essay its title are enumerated as reversal into its opposite, turning round on the subject, repression, and sublimation. Under the heading of the reversal of a drive Freud mentioned only two possibilities, reversal of content, that is, change from love to hate, and a change from active to passive. In an essay that specifically attempts to list possibilities exhaustively, there is a curious omission, that is, the possibility of reversal from passive to active. The subsequent history of psychoanalysis suggests the following explanation. Consideration of the reversal from passive to active opened the door to a new psychoanalytic paradigm. In the midst of the hardships of World War I, when he was almost sixty years old, Freud must have hesitated to set forth on a course that would lead to radical changes in his system of thought. Yet five years later he did so.

Freud's Ego Psychology

In 1920, Freud inaugurated a new direction in psychoanalytic theory. The book in which the new principle of ego functioning is first propounded is well titled *Beyond the Pleasure Principle*.

That man seeks to maximize pleasure and minimize unpleasure and pain Freud regarded as clinically incontrovertible; he identified that principle with Fechner's principle that man seeks to maintain psychic tension at a constant low level. Rise in tension was construed as unpleasurable. One can argue that these principles are not identical; that they are not necessary to or even consistent with the body of psychoanalytic theory; and that they are not consistent with the facts of psychology, even less so today than in Freud's time. All of those arguments have been made in rebuttal to the essay. None of them, however, are germane to the thrust of Freud's argument. Why is not life more pleasurable, then? Freud answered that the real difficulties of life require the replacement of the pleasure principle by the reality principle. Moreover, the partial instincts and the parts of the personality have different and conflicting wishes, so that satisfaction of a wish can cause remorse or guilt. But the pleasure or constancy principle cannot account for some striking observations. Persons suffering from traumatic neuroses return in their dreams constantly to the occasion of the trauma, the most painful of their life experiences. This pattern is not simply a matter of fixation, for in their waking life they do not dwell on the event. It also goes contrary to the character of dreams, which are wish fulfillments.

The decisive observations related to Freud's grandson, who repeatedly threw away his best-loved toys, calling out "Gone." On one occasion he threw out of sight a toy attached to a string, then drew it back with a delighted exclamation, "There." Thus the game was disappearance and return; indeed, it was the child's only game. Freud deciphered its meaning as a reproduction under his own power of the most painful of his experiences, that of his mother's coming and going, which he could not control. The universal problem of mother's disappearance is reflected in the universal game of peek-a-boo. The formula is that painful experiences are mastered by the child's actively repeating what he has passively suffered. Similarly, the child who has visited the dentist plays dentist when he comes home, using younger children as the victims. In addition to mastering experience by active repetition of what he has passively undergone, Freud saw in the latter example two other motives, re-

venging oneself on a substitute and also expressing "a wish that
dominates them the whole time—the wish to be grown-up and
to be able to do what grown-up people do" ([1920] 1955, p.
17). Apparently Freud meant that mastery through reversal of
voice and the pleasure principle, expressed in terms of the wish
to be grown-up and the wish for revenge, are partially competing explanations but that both are required to account for play.

I would argue, contrary to Freud, that to speak of a child's
wishes to be grown-up and to take revenge is to reveal the
vacuity of the pleasure principle. The operative principles are
those that account for the origin of such wishes, not for the fact
that they seek gratification, which says no more than that they
exist. Are not both these wishes expressions of desire for mastery through changing from a passive to an active role? If so, the
two interpretations, that in terms of pleasure principle and that
in terms of reversal of voice, reduce to aspects of a single one;
the impulse to master operates like a drive and seeks gratification in many alternative ways.

There is, Freud concluded, a drivelike compulsion to
repeat that is more primitive and more elementary than the
pleasure principle that it overrides. In addition to the dreams of
traumatic neuroses and the play of children, he adduced two
other lines of evidence. One was the tendency of some people
to bring the same unhappy fate upon themselves repeatedly, as
some women marry one alcoholic after another. More important for psychoanalysis, however, its therapy depends entirely
on the fact that patients invariably repeat in their transference
reactions to the analyst exactly the most unpleasant and frustrating experiences of their early relations with their parents.
Thus the causes of their problems are certain to be presented in
the treatment, even though the patients themselves are unaware
of those causes.

Some other important ideas are included in the same essay.
Since resistances are at first unconscious during treatment, one
should contrast not so much conscious versus unconscious as
the coherent ego versus the repressed. Resistance arises from the
ego, and much of the ego is unconscious. This passage presages
the replacement of the topographic model (conscious, precon-

scious, unconscious) by the structural model (ego, superego, and id). One of the problems that led to the shift appears here: If repression takes place at the behest of the conscious system, why are we not conscious of it? If the fact of repression is itself repressed into the unconscious, must there then be a repression of that repression, and so on in infinite regress? That, to be sure, is not how Freud stated the problem. Whether the postulation of an ego that is coherent but largely unconscious solves the problem or merely bypasses it is a question.

Another line of thought in the essay continues one from Freud's earliest period and presages his later essay on anxiety. A function of the nervous system is to shield the organism from excessive stimulation. Where that shield is breached and the organism is flooded with more stimulation than it can assimilate in a short period of time, trauma occurs. The state of the organism at the moment of trauma is fright; anxiety immunizes against fright. The repetition of the trauma in dreams is an attempt at retroactive mastery of the traumatic event and the fright that was not attenuated by anticipatory anxiety.

Beyond the Pleasure Principle is best known for postulating two new instincts, the life instinct and the death instinct. Psychoanalysts generally have rejected the idea of a death instinct; in their embarrassment over the unacceptable parts of the essay, they have at times neglected the foregoing contributions to ego psychology. The difficulties and contradictions in the idea of a death instinct have been discussed by others (for example, Ricoeur, 1970; Loewald, 1971b). Suffice it to note that these primal urges are miles removed from Freud's original model instincts of sex and hunger, another indication of the unraveling of the drive paradigm.

In *The Ego and the Id* (Freud, 1923) the thesis is presented that the task of the ego is mastery. The ego is a coherent organization, beset from three directions, the real environment, the id, and the superego, each of which it must strive to master. Two new terms are used here, *superego*, equivalent to the *ego ideal*, and *id*, a term taken from Groddeck (1923), signifying the feeling of the impersonal force of unconscious drives. Despite its title, *The Ego and the Id* is in some respects more closely aligned with the drive paradigm than with the ego paradigm. Most of the book is occupied with cathexis theory and with accounting for the growth of the ego in terms of psychic energy and its disposition.

In *Inhibitions, Symptoms and Anxiety* Freud ([1926] 1959) turned to the problem of anxiety, for which he offered a different solution in each of his three paradigms. In the trauma paradigm, anxiety was virtually a toxic reaction to undischarged sexual tensions. In the drive paradigm, anxiety was seen as a means of discharging any affect belonging to a repressed idea. Thus repression caused anxiety. In the new version the causal sequence is reversed, with anxiety causing repression.

Although Freud did not ascribe to the trauma of birth the importance that one of his followers, Otto Rank, did, he saw in the physical signs of anxiety much the same pattern that occurs at birth as a result of the physiological experience. Thus birth may be a prototype for later anxiety experiences. In infancy trauma is caused by excessive stimulation in short time without adequate opportunity for reaction, leading to fright. There is (always or usually?) also an element of instinctual need-tension present. The weakness of the ego in infancy leads it to be easily overwhelmed. "The situation [an infant] regards as a 'danger' and against which it wants to be safeguarded is that of non-satisfaction, of a *growing tension due to need*, against which it is helpless" ([1926] 1959, p. 137). The infant comes to fear loss of mother—since he does not know of the permanence of objects, her temporary disappearance is experienced as loss—in advance of being overcome by excess stimulation. "This change constitutes a first great step forward in the provision made by the infant for its self-preservation, and at the same time represents a transition from the automatic and involuntary fresh appearance of anxiety to the intentional reproduction of anxiety as a signal of danger" (p. 138). "Let us call a situation of helplessness of this kind that has been actually experienced a *traumatic situation* . . . . A danger-situation is a recognized, remembered, expected situation of helplessness. Anxiety is the original reaction to helplessness in the trauma and is reproduced later on in the danger-situation as a signal for help. The ego, which experienced the trauma passively, now repeats it actively in a weakened version, in the hope of being able itself to direct its course" (pp. 166-167).

Anxiety thus serves a double purpose. By preparing himself, the infant avoids being overcome by fright and experiencing a trauma, and by reproducing the situation under his own impetus, he masters it. This theory has become known as the *signal theory of anxiety*. Anxiety is an activity of the ego under pressure from drives and for the purpose of forestalling trauma. The central concepts from all three paradigms, trauma, drive, and ego, are united in this theory.

The situations that typically elicit anxiety are different in different periods of life, and each grows out of the preceding one. The child progresses from fearing separation from mother to fearing loss of her love, an anxiety typical for girls. From this fear there grows castration anxiety, a form typical for boys. Animal phobias in boys, such as the fear of horses in little Hans (Freud, 1909*a*) or the fear of wolves in the Wolf-man (Freud, 1918), are disguised representations of castration fear. The little boy fears that if his father knew the strength of his desires, both the affectionate ones toward his mother and the (typically) hostile ones toward his father, the latter would take his vengeance by way of castration. All of this is repressed, and what appears in consciousness is only the fear of the animal, presumably capable of castrating the boy by biting. The child in his fantasies lacks one vital piece of information, namely, that parents do not punish their sons by castrating them. With the dissolution of the Oedipus complex, the danger that the ego seeks to avoid and whose imminence creates anxiety is disapproval by its own superego. The manner in which Freud justified his often-quoted statement that the superego is heir to the Oedipus complex is further explained in *Civilization and its Discontents* (Freud, 1930).

Freud often expressed the view that one day, when scientific understanding had progressed far enough, qualitative or meaningful descriptions would be replaced by purely quantitative ones, known in psychoanalysis as the *economic* point of view. This is the program of reductionism; Freud never disavowed it, though by the time of *The Interpretation of Dreams* he recognized that his own efforts lay entirely within the arena of meaning. What happened in the essay on anxiety contradicted the supposed direction of progress: "At one time I attached some importance to the view that what was used as a discharge of anxiety was the cathexis which had been withdrawn in the process of repression. Today this seems to me of scarcely any interest. The reason for this is that whereas I formerly believed that anxiety invariably arose automatically by an economic process, my present conception of anxiety as a signal given by the ego in order to affect the pleasure-unpleasure agency does away with the necessity of considering the economic factor. Of course there is nothing to be said against the idea that it is precisely the energy that has been liberated by being withdrawn through repression which is used by the ego to arouse the affect; but it is no longer of any importance which portion of energy is employed for this purpose" (Freud, 1926, p. 140). When anxiety was understood as a signal, as meaningful, the economic version was no longer of interest, exactly the reverse of the sequence anticipated by programmatic reductionism (which Freud nonetheless continued to advocate).

Development of conscience is a central problem in the institution of culture, Freud stated in *Civilization and its Discontents.* In place of the lofty death instinct of *Beyond the Pleasure Principle*, Freud here was concerned with the aggressive drive, a simpler and less inferential construct though also controversial. He accounts for it as a manifestation of the death instinct, but this explanation does not appear to be an essential part of his argument. Tendencies to aggression and destruction are primitive and instinctual, he said; he also noted his own reluctance to admit this fact when it was urged on him in earlier years, no doubt referring to his dispute with Adler. A new twist is given to psychoanalytic theory in Freud's proposal that the institution of conscience derives entirely from transformations of the aggressive drive rather than from libido. Let us follow his argument.

The child is restrained in expression of his earliest and most passionate impulses by his father. The child wishes to take vengeance on his parent for imposing restraint, but that is not permitted; besides, it would endanger the parent's love, which he needs. He therefore masters the situation by taking the vengeance on a part of himself, namely, the errant impulses, that he would like to have taken on the parent. Moreover, by means of identification he assumes the role of the parent, treating part of himself, that is, his impulses, as his parent treated him or them. By both of these means he establishes control of his impulses. The former particularly accounts for the observation that the child may be much harsher with himself than his parents would have him be. The child thus reproduces within himself the relation of obedience to authority, as a means of mastering an otherwise frustrating situation. The internalized authority is the superego, which watches over the ego as the parent watched over the child.

In this explanation Freud was making use of the principle that experience is mastered by actively repeating what one has passively suffered. Another principle implied in the argument is that one's relations with other people become at once the model and the impetus for internal differentiation. In "Mourning and Melancholia" Freud seemed to be applying the principle to adults; here the application to the child's earliest relations with his parents is both more plausible and more theoretically powerful. Here is the link between the Oedipus complex and at least the beginnings of conscience. In this formulation, however, it is the aggressive element in the Oedipus complex, projected onto the father and then identified with, that gives rise to conscience.

"The New Psychoanalytic Ego Psychology"

While the label of the "new psychoanalytic ego psychology" is usually attached to the writings of Hartmann, Kris, Loewenstein, and Rapaport, and the initial date given as 1939, the year of Freud's death and of publication of Hartmann's *Ego Psychology and the Problem of Adaptation*, we have seen that many contributions to ego psychology are to be found in Freud's later work. During Freud's lifetime contributions of Wilhelm Reich,

Ernst Kris, and Anna Freud added essential elements to psycho-analytic ego psychology.

An extension of the theory of psychoanalytic technique is contained in *Character Analysis* by Reich (1933). Symptoms are relatively easy to analyze, he said, since they are experienced by the ego as foreign. Resistances, however, are compatible with and incorporated into the ego structure and therefore hard to analyze, since the ego does not ally itself with the analyst in their pursuit. Moreover, symptomatic neuroses are invariably based on neurotic character structure, though the neurotic character does not necessarily result in overt symptoms. In some patients the character armor makes psychoanalysis very difficult, for example: the good patients, who are too obedient, friendly, and trusting; the patients who are always conventional and correct; patients who are affect-lame; and patients who complain of a lack of genuineness in their feelings and expressions, that is, who suffer from depersonalization, constant play-acting, or a perpetual "inward smile." The appropriate technique, according to Reich, is for the analyst consistently to analyze not the content of what the patient does but his manner of doing it. If the analyst constantly calls attention to the character armor, it becomes somewhat alien and to that extent like a symptom. Thus Reich was a pioneer in adapting psychoanalytic technique to the new insights of ego psychology.

In *The Ego and the Mechanisms of Defense* Anna Freud (1936) stated that psychoanalysis is not merely a depth psychology, nor is the value of an analysis only to explore the unconscious. Ego, id, and superego are all worthy of attention in psychoanalysis. The ego is preeminent both as a medium for observation of the other psychic institutions and also as the agency whose adaptive capacity the analysis aims to restore. Hypnosis used as a technique in Freud's preanalytic period was valued because it bypassed the ego in order to reveal the unconscious. But precisely for this reason its therapeutic results were not permanent, and it was given up. To a lesser extent free association, dream analysis, and interpretation of symbols and parapraxes are subject to the same objection. The ego is not immobilized as in hypnosis, but the basic rule, for the patient to say everything that occurs to him without censorship, is equivalent to a temporary silencing of the patient's ego. In analysis of transference, however, the analyst obtains access not only to id contents but also to ego defenses. Recognition in theory that much of the ego is unconscious has increased the importance of analysis of the ego. But the ego by its nature resists the work of the analysis. While the analysis aims to make the unconscious conscious, the ego aims always to master the instinctual life, and in the short run these aims conflict.

Two types of defense are given special attention in the book, and both illustrate the operation of the principle of mastery through reversal from passive to active; these defenses are identification with the aggressor and a type of altruism. In children one can observe identification with the aggressor in process of formation; the child may impersonate the aggressor, or assume his attributes, or simply imitate the aggressive act. An example of the latter is the child who had a painful visit to the dentist and played it out by sharpening pencils repeatedly, each time breaking off the points. Identification with the aggressor is frequently a normal way station in the development of the superego. The child perceives some infraction of his own and anticipates punishment. At that point he projects his own guilt onto someone else, often the person from whom he expects punishment, and turns against that person the very outrage that he expected to receive himself. The child has internalized the criticism but he has dissociated it from his guilt. True conscience begins only when the internalized criticism becomes self-criticism, a stage that some people never reach. Such people become more harsh and indignant against their victims the more guilty they feel.

In altruism, or at least in one form of it, the person signs over to someone else his own desires, for which he has come to expect frustration. This is the story of Cyrano de Bergerac and of the legendary unmarried woman who enjoys being matchmaker. Passionate interest in securing satisfactions for one's surrogates will betray the selfish origin of altruism. The explanation of this form of altruism is two-fold: by identification one substitutes gratification for frustration, and one exchanges the passive role of the rejected one for the active role of benefactor.

The concept of "regression in the service of the ego" comes from Kris (1934). In dreams, during intoxication, and in psychosis the ego surrenders its supremacy, and primary process takes over. By contrast, in wit, humor, and caricature primary process is used by the ego for its own purposes. The cover of humor permits the expression of aggressive tendencies that would otherwise be socially unacceptable. Regression to primary process modes of thinking in service of ego purposes is not exclusive to humor but pervades many aspects of life, such as esthetic experiences, myths, and rituals.

Despite the earlier appearance of all the foregoing and related contributions to psychoanalytic ego psychology (for example, Waelder, 1930), publication of Hartmann's essay in 1939 created a sensation. Psychoanalysis, he wrote, being originally concerned with pathology, had begun by preoccupation with conflicts. In broadening to become a general psychology, it must now also encompass the conflict-free ego sphere. Instead of seeing ego as differentiated out of the id, Hartmann proposed that ego and id were differentiated out of a primal matrix. We are born with the potentiality to adapt to an average expectable environment. Functions such as perception, thought, and motor skills have their own course of learning and maturation; they are *apparatuses of primary autonomy*, because they have no clear dependence on drives nor are they born of conflict. They are precursors and then functions of the ego. An ego function, such as curiosity or rationalization, may arise as a defense against drives but come to serve adaptation or even become a goal in its own right; then it is said to have *secondary autonomy*. Freud had bridged the gap between normal psychology and psychopathology, but even when he was concerned with normal persons, he looked for manifestations of drives, conflicts, and the unconscious. Hartmann was staking out a claim for psychoanalysis as a general psychology in a broader sense, asserting that adaptation to reality and hence apparatuses of learning, perception, and intelligence are also within the purview of psychoanalysis. Whether this essay had direct implications for psychoanalysis as therapy is not clear. At any rate, psychoanalysis was no longer unequivocally committed to a drive-derivative view of ego development.

Hartmann's approach was continued in a series of collaborative papers with Kris and Loewenstein (1945-1962). The ego, they said, operates not only with energies from drives but also with neutralized energy. *Neutralization* is a generalization of Freud's concept of sublimation to refer to the aggressive as well as the sexual drive. Part of the impact of these papers, besides the fact that they contain much clinical wisdom with respect to ego development and related topics, has come from the reluctance of most psychoanalysts to give up the idea of their discipline as a psychology of drives.

A scholarly and definitive systematization of psychoanalysis was undertaken by Rapaport (1960). He placed central importance on a tension-reduction conception of drives, deducing many elements of the theory from that model. In particular, ego structure was depicted as a kind of dike system, damming the flow of drives. The ego is a structure created by countercathexis of drives; countercathexis is an energy distribution opposed to the cathexes or energy charges of the drives. Many of the ideas that Rapaport elevated to the status of major principles of psychoanalysis are not in fact specific to psychoanalysis: "The subject matter of psychoanalysis is behavior" (p. 39), "All behavior is that of the integral and indivisible personality" (p. 42), and "The ultimate determiners of all behavior are the drives" (p. 47). Such principles are at best shared with other schools of psychology, at worst vacuous. The principles of ego development worked out by Freud from 1920 onwards are scarcely mentioned.

All of the psychoanalysts whose work has been presented in this section as that of the new psychoanalytic ego psychology saw it as an expansion of the scope of psychoanalysis to new fields. In none of them is there explicit recognition that the trend of Freud's thinking on ego psychology in his later years required for its consolidation an entirely new paradigm, in which some elements of the drive paradigm had to be dropped or radically changed. Others said exactly that. In the next chapter we shall look at contributions of two psychoanalysts and a philosopher to psychoanalysis as an ego paradigm.

Fundamental Terms

A difficulty in understanding psychoanalytic theory is that the fundamental terms cannot be defined once and for all. In some cases Freud's usage was inconsistent or changed with his paradigm. In some cases translation has altered the connotations drastically (Brandt, 1961). We will consider four terms, *drive, id, ego,* and *cathexis.*

The central concept of the drive paradigm is *Trieb,* officially translated as *instinct* in the *Standard Edition* of Freud's work in English. Many scholars prefer the term *drive* or *instinctual drive,* since Freud used the German word *Instinkt* differently. (I have used both, believing that fixing on a single usage simulates a precision that is not there.) Freud at different times had different descriptions of what the basic drives are: sexual drives contrasted with ego or moral values, sexual drives contrasted with ego drives, life instinct contrasted with death instinct, sex contrasted with aggression. But these changes run far deeper than simply changes in the catalogue of drives; they involve changes in the conception of what kind of a thing a drive or instinct is. Contemporary usage has tended to settle on sex and aggression as the fundamental drives. Holt (1976) argues for discarding the term *drive* and returning to Freud's early usage of *wish* as less ambiguous. Loewald (1971*b*), defending the term *instinct*, points out that it need not have biological connotations, since it is a term that biology took over from everyday speech.

The term *ego,* from the Latin, was seldom if ever used by Freud. He intentionally took his terms from common speech. Where *ego* appears in English, he used *ich* or *das Ich*, terms with the same connotations as *I* or *the I* or *the me*, as in the French *le moi.* Thus Freud used a word that is in the vocabulary of all but the youngest children, while his translators have chosen a sophisticated word of adult life. Where *ego* suggests a hypothetical entity that one must justify and define, *the I* is the most salient and immediate experience. That contrast suggests what has been lost in translating Freud, something that must be admitted even if one maintains that no better translation could have been made. (The topic of this book, for example, could not easily be called *I development*, nor could conscience be called *super-I*.)

The term *id* is also from the Latin and lacks English connotations apart from its psychoanalytic usage even more completely than does *ego*. Freud's term was *das Es, the It*. Brandt (1966) points out that patients sometimes use expressions where *it* stands for the id, but that more often id derivatives appear in their speech as the passive voice, as something that happened to them without a sense of agency. The formula Freud proposed for psychoanalytic therapy, to replace the original formula of making the unconscious conscious, is usually translated, "Where id was, there ego shall be" (Freud, [1933] 1964, p. 80). A closer translation would be, "Where It was, I ought to become" (Brandt, 1966, p. 374), retaining the flavor of process and the emotional immediacy of Freud's sentence (*"Wo Es war, soll Ich werden"*), according to Brandt. The changes introduced in translation encourage reification of what are after all invariably processes.

All of the foregoing terms, while presenting difficulties for the novice, can be deciphered by those sympathetic to psychoanalysis as a system of ideas. Disagreements over translation and usage, even differences as great as Holt's use of *wish* and Loewald's use of *instinct*, do not prevent mutual understanding when the terms are used in context. Such arguments, while not the most fruitful kind of theorizing, prevent psychoanalysis from becoming a lifeless catechism, reminding us always to look behind the words to the things signified. I cannot say as much for *cathexis* or *psychic energy*.

Cathexis has no English connotations, being an ad hoc word of Greek derivation for Freud's term *Besetzung*. In military usage *Besetzung* stands for occupation of a position or country, but it has many other connotations, its most general meaning being to put something into some place (Brandt, 1961). One of the few theories of ego development intentionally omitted from this book is the one in terms of cathexis theory, since I do not understand its principal term, *cathexis*, nor have I found a quotable version of how countercathexis accounts for ego development.

Cathexis has been defined as a charge of *psychic energy*, but while this formulation introduces recognizable English words, the phrase remains elusive. Physical energy is a meaningful concept, but what is psychic energy? Critics from E. B. Holt (1915) to Lashley (1957) have attacked the concept of psychic energy as a contradiction in terms. Lashley declared that psychoanalytic theory is demolished if the concept of psychic energy is destroyed, but an increasing number of authorities within psychoanalysis have criticized the concepts of cathexis and psychic energy and find them irrelevant to psychoanalysis as therapy or as theory (Gill, 1975). Kubie (1947) was one of the first to do so. R. R. Holt (1962) traced more than a dozen different usages of the terms *bound* and *free energy* in Freud's writings alone.

Moreover, as we have seen, the same or a similar term has been used by other authors with different meanings: for Spearman, mental energy was the hypothetical nature of the g factor of general intelligence; for Jung psychic energy was desexualized libido, a magical force or tension; for Janet psychic energy represented something akin to ego development. That diversity of usage alone is enough to make one suspicious of the theoretical value of the concept.

Reviewing the origins of psychoanalytic theory in Freud's neurology, it appears that conceiving motives or drives in terms of investments of psychic energy is a remnant of the reflex-arc model of mental functioning, now decisively disproved and never as compelling as Freud believed. The tension-reduction model of motivation that pervaded much of Freud's theorizing is another aspect of the same structure of ideas (Amacher, 1965; Holt, 1965). Whether tension reduction as a motivational model is necessarily implied by or even compatible with the psychoanalytic drive paradigm is doubtful; historically, however, they were intertwined. When the drive paradigm is replaced by the ego paradigm, there is no question that cathexis theory and the tension-reduction model are obsolete. Energy, psychic energy if you will, becomes what it must have been originally, a description of human feelings without pretension of quantitative meaning or high-level explanatory power.

Conclusions

The Interpretation of Dreams created a scientific revolution in Kuhn's sense. It recorded one of the great achievements of the human spirit, Freud's self-analysis. It was made possible by the trauma protoparadigm, following out the premises of psychic determinism and universal psychological laws, which led Freud to analyze himself in the same terms as he did his patients. His analysis of dreams used the principles of the earlier paradigm, such as condensation and displacement, but led him to reject the importance of seduction in childhood as the invariable basis for neurosis. Childhood sexuality, in particular the Oedipus complex, became the basis for neurosis but also for normal development. The formula for interpreting dreams, that they are disguised representations of repressed wishes, was extended to symptoms and to many aspects of everyday life. Freud found data for his paradigm where his predecessors found no meaning encoded, in dreams, symptoms, and mistakes. Psychoanalysis as therapy is of a piece with psychoanalysis as theory. The same principles apply. Analysis of resistance and transference, the essential method, is based on analysis of dreams, symptoms, mistakes, gestures, free associations, and so on. Many elements of what Kuhn calls a *scientific paradigm* are thus present.

The achievements of Freud's teachers and predecessors are reinterpreted within the drive paradigm. The phenomenon of hypnosis is accounted for in terms of regression and transference (Ferenczi, 1909). Cures effected by hypnosis are transference cures, more easily obtained but more transient than psychoanalytic cures, which require not just the induction but the analysis of transference.

The extension of psychoanalytic theory to cover the phenomena of ego development led to discovery of new principles that at first seemed to be a brilliant extension of the drive paradigm. Then it became apparent that new conceptions would be required; the ego cannot be conceived as simply derived from drives.

I have tried to present the ideas of Janet, Adler, and Jung with regard for the interrelations of the method of treatment and the theory of normal and pathological development. None of them began with a major achievement comparable to Freud's self-analysis, so far as I can discover. They did not bring whole realms of experience into the purview of science as new kinds of data. Freud's central conceptions of resistance and transference, tying together the genesis and treatment of neurosis, are more powerful and elegant than any corresponding ideas of Janet, Jung, or Adler. In the next chapter we will see how those conceptions can be related to normal ego development.

Chapter Fifteen

Psychoanalysis: The Ego Paradigm

The new psychoanalytic ego psychology extended the drive paradigm to cover many of the phenomena of ego development by means of concepts such as ego functions of primary and secondary autonomy, but the price for extending the purview was to sacrifice elegance. The strength and intellectual appeal of the drive paradigm is that with a single formula—that what seems nonsensical is meaningful when interpreted as the disguised expression of unconscious wishes—many previously inexplicable aspects of behavior are brought within the purview of psychology. What characterizes autonomous ego functions is precisely that they are not encompassed in that formula, nor, indeed are many of Freud's later discoveries.

An immense literature that we cannot review has grown up around the problem of reconciling the insights of psychoanalytic ego psychology with the drive paradigm. Among the high spots are Hendrick's (1942) essay on the instinct for mastery in infancy, White's (1963) argument for independent ego energies and for the importance of competence as motivation, and Schafer's (1968) discussion of introjection, incorporation, identification, and internalization.

Loewald has expressed an alternative point of view: "Modern psychoanalytic ego psychology represents far more than an addition to the psychoanalytic theory of instinctual drives. In my opinion, it is the elaboration of a more comprehensive theory of the dynamic organization of the psychic apparatus, and psychoanalysis is in the process of integrating our knowledge of instinctual drives, gained during earlier stages of its history, into such a psychological theory . . . . Ego psychology is not concerned with just another part of the psychic apparatus, but is giving a new dimension to the conception of the psychic apparatus as a whole" (1960, pp. 16-17). I propose to call what Loewald is talking about the *psychoanalytic ego paradigm* to distinguish it from psychoanalytic ego psychology within the drive paradigm. Three representatives of this point of view, Erik Erikson, Hans Loewald, and Paul Ricoeur, have made separate but I believe fundamentally compatible contributions to this branch of psychoanalytic theory.

Erikson: Play and Identity

Erikson is best known for his diagrammatic representations of psychosexual and psychosocial development (discussed in Chapter Seven). These concrete and pictorial aspects of his writings are less germane to ego development than the more abstract and systematic ones. Not only is his model for psychosocial development patterned after his model for psychosexual development, but he also states (1956) that the two schedules are dovetailed and essentially inseparable. Nonetheless, his discussion makes clear that he distinguishes ego and psychosexual development conceptually.

Using Freud's principle of mastery through active repetition of what one has passively experienced, Erikson (1950) has formalized a theoretical basis for play as a technique of psycho-analytic therapy with children. In doing so, he has made explicit another idea implicit in Freud's writings from the beginning, namely, that schemes are transposed from one realm to another. The three realms of the child's life are those of play and toys, of real relations with others, and of his own body. A problem in any of the realms can be reenacted in the others via a transposition of the scheme. Optimally, this is the child's means for planning, experimenting, and growing. Under pressure of a repressed, traumatic experience, it becomes a stereotyped or symptomatic repetition. With skillful interpretation, it can be turned into therapy.

A major principle of ego development that Erikson adopts from Freud is an extension of the idea of transposition of schemes: the child becomes internally differentiated as a means of mastering loss or frustration in his relations with other people; interpersonal schemes serve as model and as impetus for intrapersonal schemes. The third principle that he culls from Freud's ego theory is that of progression through regression (see Chapter Fourteen).

Erikson (1956) has introduced the concept of *ego identity* to cover much the same ground that the present book does. It is an evolving configuration, he says, sometimes referring to the person's conscious sense of individual identity, sometimes to his unconscious striving for continuity of personal character, sometimes to silent working of ego synthesis, sometimes to inner solidarity with a group's ideals and identity. Ego development takes place at first by the process of introjection and projection, then by identification, and then by identity formation. These are not stages of ego development but rather modalities of ego formation and transformation. The incorporation of parental commands and images in early childhood, called *introjection*, and the identifications of later childhood and early adolescence do not add up to a mature identity. That must be forged by the adolescent himself, incorporating among other things the way he is seen by others and the place he finds for himself in the world of work.

A long study of Gandhi by Erikson (1969) dwells on one

of the major unsolved problems of psychoanalytic ego psychology, the dialectic of pathology and creative identity. How did
Gandhi make himself a world leader, beginning with traits that
were potentially psychoneurotic? Gandhi's term for his political
method of passive resistance or militant nonviolence, *Satya-
graha*, Erikson translates literally as "truth force." That term
itself suggests the comparison with psychoanalysis as therapy,
which also operates with truth as its force, Erikson points out.

Ricoeur: The Archaeology and Teleology of the Subject

Psychoanalysis as method and the theory it generates are
uniquely suited to revealing the archaic origins of our conduct
and our nature, Ricoeur (1970) points out; that is the archaeology of the subject. Creative development, including artistic
creating and also ego development, cannot in principle be reduced to archaic causes; such achievements constitute the teleology of the subject. Freud recognized that infantile sources fail
to explain precisely what is valuable in artistic achievement. In
Ricoeur's terms, the archaeology of the subject does not exhaustively explain the teleology of the subject. How then are
they related? We follow his argument. (In this section I seek
only to transmit Ricoeur's argument, reserving my own comments until after I expound Loewald's argument in the next
section.)

   Psychoanalytic interpretation refers only to language that
has double or multiple meanings. Interpretation in Freud, as in
Marx and Nietzsche, is a decoding or demystification, contrasting with the religious or aesthetic vision, which is an encoding, a
restoration or enrichment of meaning. Freud saw desire, or
instinct, manifest everywhere. At first he deciphered symptoms,
dreams, and failed or distorted acts, but almost from the beginning he included works of art, wit, myths, and religion. Symbols
in psychoanalysis are distortions, but in religion or poetry they
are revelations. To what extent are these different hermeneutics
in opposition? Is the revealing-hiding of double meaning always
dissimulation of what is desired, or can it sometimes be revelation?

Freud's *Project for a Scientific Psychology* was his most mechanistic picture of the psychic apparatus. Successive revisions moved away from the physical model to one that is a scene of the debate of roles and masks, a place of coding and decoding. The *Project* bears the mark of his erroneous belief that neurosis originates in childhood trauma; hence there was emphasis on place for storage of memories rather than for elaboration of fantasies, which later experience proved to be more pathogenic than memories per se. The metapsychology of Chapter Seven of *The Interpretation of Dreams* still bears the traces of the false belief in the traumatic potential of memory traces of real perceptions. What he was trying to create there and in the *Project* was a model of an isolated psychic apparatus regulated by tension seeking discharge. Neither the Oedipus complex nor the transference of psychoanalytic therapy can be represented in such a model. The Freudian wish is not a tension that can be discharged; it is insatiable.

The interpretation of dreams is the paradigm of all interpretation because the dream is the paradigm of all the artifices of desire. The desire represented in the dream is always infantile; thus the interpretation is not only a decoding but also a revelation of the archaism of our nature. The language of desire is symbolic, and sexuality is the stuff of that symbolism.

A work of art is both the symptom and the cure, as Freud showed in his essay on Leonardo (1910*a*). In interpreting the works of Michaelangelo and Leonardo as if they were dreams, Freud was comparing a durable creation of the day with a fugitive and sterile product of the night. Psychoanalysis calls the difference *sublimation,* but that only names the problem. A work of art is esteemed as a creation in proportion as it is not simply a projection of the conflicts of the artist but a sketch of their solution.

In his essay on narcissism Freud proposed one path to superego formation that has not been absorbed or replaced by later formulations. The formation of the ego ideal is a way both to retain infantile narcissism and to replace it. The narcissistic basis of the ideal self provides a base for identification and explains how what is borrowed from the parents can become oneself. Perhaps it is necessary that the fragments of other people that form the ego ideal collect around a core rooted in narcissism in order that identification succeed.

Ricoeur asks: How is the regressive character of narcissistic identification brought into accord with the structural, hence progressive, effect of identification that sets up the superego? The foundation of the superego in the Oedipus complex shows its close relation to the id, farther from consciousness than the ego. The superego is the inheritor of the Oedipus complex in the double sense that it is derived from it and it represses it. The Oedipus complex must decline because its aims are unattainable, and also because the phallic stage, to which it corresponds, is ended by fear of castration, which receives quasi-empirical support from the discovery of sex differences. These facts explain how the turning away from the Oedipus complex saves narcissism, and they show also that the superego is the expression of the most powerful drives.

The daily bread of psychoanalysis is the lost or absent or substitute object. The Oedipal drama would not be possible unless the child wished for too much, for what he could not obtain. Wish fulfillment is basic to primary process, and it is essential to wish fulfillment that the fantasy be a substitute for a lost object of desire. The idea of derivatives that are displaced or distorted implies a relation to something lost. The dream, all symbols, all works of art are representations of lost or absent objects. Reality testing is the comparison of a mental representation, always the reproduction of an absent object, with the outside world. There is here a common element underlying the disappearing-reappearing Freud noted in children's play; the disavowing-surmounting of fantasy in artistic creation, as analyzed in Freud's essay on Leonardo; and the loss and finding again involved in perceptual judgment. Freud stated that the ego is the precipitate of abandoned objects. Thus the idea of absence is introduced into the constitution of the ego. Reality is the correlate of that internalized absence. Thus the psychoanalytic conception of the ego is inseparable from the lost or absent object.

The problem of the ego is domination. It is menaced by

reality, by instincts, and by conscience, and it must dominate the situation to defend itself. That is the theme of the three masters in *The Ego and the Id*. The interior agency of morality is an exterior menace internalized. Thus moral man is at first *aliéné*, submitting to the law of a foreign master as he submits to that of desire and as he submits to the law of reality. Interpretation, in exploring hidden desires that disguise themselves in dreams and the like, unmasks all sources not original and primitive, all sources foreign and alien to the self. Because the superego remains my alter in myself, it must be deciphered; foreigner, it remains foreign.

The superego is a construction, not an observation, though it is based on such discoveries as unconscious guilt observed as obstacle to cure. It includes three functions: the ego ideal, self-observation, and conscience. Self-observation denotes the doubling of self, an idea derived from Hegel, Ricoeur points out. Psychoanalysis is always concerned with a doubling of consciousness, beginning with the pre-Oedipal desire to be like the father. Identification is never adequately represented in the metapsychology, which sees it only in its regressive aspect. Since desire is from the beginning interpersonal, identification is not something added on from outside; it is the dialectic of desire itself. Desire is always a desire that another should desire. The profound and constructive significance of the Oedipus complex is not captured in the economic version, where it is spoken of as abandoned or as libidinal investment renounced.

Freud never explained the mechanism of sublimation or its epigenesis. Economically it is regression to narcissism, hence progression by means of regression. The innovation of meaning in sublimation requires another hermeneutics than that of libido. The task that "Where id was, there shall ego be" cannot in principle be reduced to the economics of desire.

Freud explicitly created an analysis, not a synthesis. But, writes Ricoeur, in reading Freud I do not understand myself except by forming the notion of an archaeology of the subject, and I do not understand the notion of an archaeology except in relation to a teleology. Returning to Freud, I find that dialectic in his work.

Loewald: Psychoanalysis as Ego Development

Loewald* asserts that Freud did not fully or consistently carry through the implications of the ego theory of his later years; psychoanalytic theory has tended to remain under the sway of the older version of instinct theory. Some deviation from the text of Freud's writings is necessary to carry out the spirit of the new approach.

The way instincts are conceived of in psychoanalysis changed with the development of ego psychology, Loewald continues. The out-of-date reflex-arc model did not dominate Freud's later writings; instincts became strivings for objects rather than strivings for contentless satisfaction. Thus in Freud's later writings, instinct implies a relation to the environment as much as does ego, but the relation is integrated on a more primitive level. To see the child as born into a reality-world from which he is separate and with which he then establishes relations is not to see from the point of view of the child or even the mother. Rather, infant and mother are originally a unity, first biologically and increasingly psychologically. Each step of the increasing differentiation between them leads to and is accompanied by a corresponding integration. Reality is necessarily constituted for the child in the same stages as his ego develops, for they are differentiated out of a common matrix. Differentiation of mother and child gives rise to the striving for reunification found at all later stages, an urge that is the origin of the child's libidinal tie to the mother as well as the origin of the synthetic function of the ego.

The primal unity between mother and child is gratifying, but the strong early tie to mother, and particularly regression to

---

*This summary is based on a number of Loewald's papers (1951, 1960, 1962a, 1962b, 1970, 1971a, 1971b, 1971c). Loewald elects to retain the terms *instinct* and *psychic energy*, in the former case because it has become the official translation of *Trieb*, in both cases because the term originally referred to human feelings. The biological and thermodynamic connotations to which theoretical objection has been raised are recent changes in meaning; originally, it was biology and chemistry that borrowed the terms from phenomenology. Loewald believes (wrongly, I think) that the terms can revert to their original prescientific connotations.

it from later stages, is also threatening, since it implies return also to an earlier, less differentiated stage of ego development. To the young child, father serves not only as a rival for mother's affection, but also as an identification figure needed as a defense against ego regression. The Oedipus complex is thus given an extended meaning, including both positive and negative feelings toward both parents and occurring over an extended period rather than in a few traumatic events. Indeed, ambivalence toward both parents plays an essential part in ego growth. Freud overstressed the aspect of the castrating father as representative of external reality opposing and interfering with the libidinal tie of mother and child, Loewald asserts. But in the pre-ego of primary narcissism, reality is not something outside. Genetically, reality and ego are one. Since instinct and environment are mutually structured, in Loewald's view, instinct is no longer conceived as something inside and hostile to the ego, nor is reality something outside and hostile to the ego.

The regressive phenomena of neurosis and particularly of psychosis are understood differently in these terms. The schizophrenic does not so much withdraw from reality as lose the boundaries between ego and reality. For the infant and the regressed psychotic, magical qualities are experienced as both in the ego and in the outer world, hence as threatening and overpowering. (Here Loewald is reconciling Ferenczi's concept of infantile omnipotence and Sullivan's concept of infantile helplessness. See Chapter Five.)

Ego development occurs by progressive restructuring of the child's relation to his environment and correlative internal restructuring of the child, not by changing the relation to fixed objects. The reality to which the child adjusts and the love objects to which he is attached are also changing for him as he becomes different. In the pre-Oedipal period, ego formation proceeds via introjection and projection to establish internality and externality as such. True attachment to external objects, which presupposes a clear external and internal sense, first takes place in the Oedipal period. Its optimal outcome is formation of the superego, that is, internal differentiation of the psychic structure, or ego. That is not adequately described in terms of internalization of parents or of images of the parents. Rather, the *relation* is reestablished internally to the child's psychic structure. That implies that the old relation is destroyed, not repressed, and the elements are reintegrated into something new, making the child different and thus giving him a different view of his parents. Repression differs from formation of psychic structure, for it precludes development by making the constituents unavailable for a new integration.

The internalized image of the mother includes her attitude to, perception of, and relation with the child. Ideally, she perceives the child not only as he is but as he will be at later stages. This is conveyed to the child and internalized by him, helping establish his feeling of identity. There is a tension between the stage of the child's present level of functioning and the more mature stage represented by the mother and the mother's hopes for his future. There is a similar tension between the level of the patient's ego functioning and that of the analyst and the analyst's appreciation of the patient's potential growth. The tension between what one might be at best in the future and what one is at present exists not only between parent and child, between analyst and patient, but also between superego and ego. Thus the condition for psychic growth is itself internalized. Internalization means the process by which the relations between the person and his environment become transformed into intrapsychic relations. The inner world thus constituted establishes new and more complex relations with the environment.

The death instinct, the tendency to abolish stimulation, reduce tension, and seek rest, is not what is "beyond the pleasure principle," for it turns out to be another version of Freud's earliest assumption of the constancy or pleasure principle, based on nineteenth-century mechanistic physics. What is truly beyond the constancy principle is Eros, the life instinct, the tendency to integrate or create structure. Satisfaction for Eros is not reduction of stimulation leading back to a previous level of equilibrium but absorbing and integrating stimuli, leading to a higher level of equilibrium. Only the latter is compatible with Freud's formula for psychoanalysis, that "where id was, there shall ego become."

The term *transference* has three usages in Freud. It refers to the transfer of libido to objects, as when one speaks of transference neuroses; this sense is virtually synonymous with object cathexis. The second meaning is that of transferring relations with infantile objects onto later objects, especially the analyst during psychoanalysis. This usage is currently predominant. The third meaning is the transferring of intensity from an unconscious idea to a preconscious one. In the connections of these three meanings lies the nature of psychoanalytic therapy and of normal growth.

The mechanisms of neurosis are, after all, distortions of normal processes. Transfer of libido to objects and of infantile object relations to contemporary figures is normal; life draws its vitality from it. Only by such transference does the ego integrate the instinctual life with reality and thus achieve maturity. The difference between the conscious-preconscious psychic system and the unconscious is another version of the differential between more maturely organized and more primitive psychic apparatus that is the condition for psychic development.

The id is the past as represented in the present. The superego is the future as anticipated and aimed for in the present. The ego as organizing agent integrates and presents them. Precursors of the superego include the recapturing of the primary narcissistic, omnipotent perfection of infancy by identifying oneself with parents seen as omnipotent. The term *ego ideal* indicates a later realization that perfection is something to strive for. In these notions the parents' idealization of the child is involved as well as the child's idealization of the parents. Some disillusionments and modifications in the direction of more realistic understanding of potentialities foster growth of the superego. The superego is a "differentiating grade in the ego," as Freud (1921) called it, recognizable when there is a clearly internal authority, differentiated from external authorities and from ideal images.

Elements of the superego Loewald describes as being at varying distance from the ego core or internalized to different degrees. Although the superego endures as a structure, its constituent elements change; for example, toilet rules cease to be experienced as aspirations or demands and become automatic. Normally superego elements become assimilated as ego elements when an aspiration becomes an actuality, but the process can be reversed in ego disorganization, growth crises, or psychotherapy.

Repetition is basic to psychic life. All psychic functioning is in some way repetition; yet in being repeated, it becomes different. Repetitive behavior that is a reenacting of repressed, unconscious experiences has a compulsive, unchanging character and does not contribute to development; this is passive repetition. The person is not conscious of its repetitive aspect. To become conscious of experience as repetitive of one's past is to assume an active role. In doing so, one lifts the experience to a new plane and puts it within the scope of the ego as integrating agent. In active repetition the old is mastered, not eliminated or abolished but dissolved and reconstructed. "Where id was, there ego shall become" means change from passive to active repetition. It is not only the formula of psychoanalytic therapy but an aspect of all of ego development.

Basic Principles

Ego development is a central topic for Erikson, Ricoeur, and Loewald, and they integrate it with drive psychology in different but compatible ways. Erikson's discussion of psychosexual development in terms of modes and zones is well known, as is his discussion of the tasks and crises of normal ego development (Chapter Five). For him these are complementary processes, intertwined in life history. Further, he has been concerned with how the ingredients that in one person's life lead to neurosis will lead another to great achievement. Perhaps more than any other analyst, he has divided his attention equally between drives, ego, and environment. For Ricoeur, a philosopher, drive psychology and ego psychology are complementary in a different sense, one looking backward toward origins, the other forward toward purposes and achievements. For Loewald ego development in childhood is a model for psychoanalysis as therapy, and analysis reopens and continues ego development.

All three, though differing in terminology, select the same principles from Freud's later writings and reject the same vestiges of earlier paradigms. In particular, the reflex-arc tension-reduction model is rejected as not only unnecessary but as incompatible with the principle that the child masters experience by actively repeating what he has passively undergone. The principle of mastery cannot be reduced to economy in expenditure of energy; activity cannot be construed as requiring less energy than passivity. The principle of mastery becomes the pivotal one in all versions of the psychoanalytic ego paradigm, replacing the constancy or pleasure principle as the central explanatory principle. No one denies that people seek pleasure, that they often follow the path of least resistance, or that growing up involves postponing near pleasures for more distant ones. None of those is a specifically psychoanalytic discovery; they are all part of the public domain. Thus they can be assimilated by the ego paradigm as given.

Among the elements of the drive paradigm that are retained in the ego paradigm are the presupposition of universal psychological laws and explanations, and Freud's discoveries of the dynamic unconscious, displacement of affect, primary and secondary process, the plasticity of the interpersonal drives, and childhood sexuality and the Oedipus complex. Internal conflict as the universal basis for neurosis is probably also retained by all psychoanalytic ego theorists, but that doctrine is in a different category from the preceding ones. I am looking for general psychological principles that govern neurosis, treatment, and ego development, rather than principles specific to one realm alone.

Transference, which was seen as an obstacle to treatment in the trauma paradigm and as the method of treatment in the drive paradigm, is reconceived as being also the core of normal development by Loewald. Resistance likewise changed from being obstacle in the trauma paradigm to being a central focus of treatment in the drive paradigm. To the extent that it is the same as or an aspect of the synthetic function of the ego, it also is tied to normal growth.

The principle of progression through regression stands as

pivot between drive paradigm and ego paradigm. Ricoeur's account has shown the depth of meaning contained in the dialectic of progression and regression, of encoding and decoding, of enrichment and deciphering. Ekstein (1965) shows the application of this principle to psychoanalysis as therapy. The very position of the patient, prone, being observed by someone alert, is an invitation to regression. Regression in the form of disorganization is required to make reorganization possible (Loewald, 1971c).

All the accounts stress what might be called Freud's *structural principle*, that interpersonal schemes serve as model and as impetus for intrapersonal schemes. I call it the *structural principle* because it is the major theoretical basis for internal differentiation, that is, for ego development. (In terms of Rapaport and Gill's five metapsychological points of view [1959], this principle could also be called *genetic, adaptive,* and *dynamic*; that illustrates their redundancy and why I do not find them an instructive way of looking at explanations of behavior.)

Underlying this transposition of schemes is a principle that is hard to state clearly or rigorously because of its great generality. It is also a structural principle, but in a different sense, not in the sense of building psychic structure but in the sense of structuralism as a mode of thought (see Chapter Three). Erikson's discussion of the transposition of schemes among the realms of body, toys, and people is, after all, only the application to the child of Freud's observation that schemes transpose from interpersonal relations to bodily symptoms and vice versa and that schemes from both sources are represented in dreams. This observation was both a discovery and the means for further investigation, both the method of decoding and the substance of what was decoded, as Ricoeur showed. Loewald's discussion of transference of relations also falls within the scope of this broad principle.

Granted that interpersonal schemes give rise to intrapersonal ones, where do the interpersonal ones come from? In part, that is the wrong question, as Loewald points out. The child and mother are originally one, and their relation is constituted simultaneously with their separation. That is not, however, the whole story. The principle of mastery states a simple interpersonal scheme: what someone has done to me, I must do to him. This principle operates like a drive (hence Freud called it the *repetition compulsion*, but that term I have avoided because it blurs the line between the operation of the principle in the normal and the neurotic course.) It has the plasticity of drives, and permits the substitution of a wide range of victims. An enormous theoretical simplification is effected if we take the principle of mastery as the origin of the aggressive drive (granting that the topic of aggression is complex and leads outside our purview). Freud's statement that ego development is born of transformation of the aggressive drive is compatible with that formulation.

Can we push back any further the question of where this fundamental interpersonal scheme comes from? I would like to speculate on the matter. The principle asserts that the child must do to someone or something more or less what has been done to him; this principle is formally similar to saying that action and reaction must be equal and opposite. Newton's third law bears an abstract resemblance to this most fundamental principle of ego functioning. Every child from the moment of birth, indeed from before birth, is surrounded by instances of the workings of Newton's third law. If he hits his bed or the floor, the bed or floor hits him with equal and opposite force. If he is playing under a table and stands up, the table hits his head with the same force that his head hits the table. Some sort of appreciation of this physical principle is bound to impress itself on the child about as soon as anything does.

For the small child, even at a much older age than what we are now concerned with, physical principles, psychological principles, and moral necessity are simply indistinguishable. Thus it is at least conceivable that the (inchoate) observation that action and reaction are equal and opposite would generate some obscure sense that events require to be balanced or undone. The primitive law of the talion of which Mill wrote (Chapter Sixteen) may originate in this way. There is no way to bring up a child in a non-Newtonian world to see what would change, nor is there any obvious way to watch in more detail how such primitive mechanisms develop. That intrapersonal schemes are given shape and impetus by interpersonal schemes is clear and traceable. That interpersonal schemes in turn owe their shape to sensorimotor schemes and physical principles is logical but not easy to render compelling.

Is It Science?

Psychoanalysis with its schools and schisms is the sort of thing Kuhn does not want to call science. As we have seen (Chapter Twelve), however, he may exaggerate the unanimity of paradigm in the physical sciences, and other philosophers do not all accept that criterion for science. Many leading philosophers, psychologists, and psychoanalysts have discussed the status of psychoanalysis as science, and a review of that broad problem is not in our domain. This discussion will only tie up some loose threads of topics already introduced.

Lewin (1931) wrote that while modern science is often represented as substituting mathematical, functional relationships for qualitative statements, that characteristic is incidental to more fundamental aspects of the change from the Aristotelian to the Galileian mode of thought. In the Aristotelian mode the individual case is considered subject to chance; only frequently recurring instances are considered lawful or needing explanation. Exceptions do not serve as counterarguments so long as they are not numerous. Explanation in Aristotle consisted in classification, with the common characteristics of the class constituting a kind of essence that was then used as explanation. Many of the classifications are dichotomies, with one extreme representing the positively valued alternative. Examples of the reasoning of contemporary psychology that represent Aristotelian modes of thought are: explaining two-year-old negativism by the fact that two-year-olds are usually negativistic, explaining behavior in terms of drives that are postulated on the basis of the same kind of behavior, and categorizing behavior as "normal" or "pathological."

One of Freud's greatest contributions was to abolish the boundary between the ordinary and the unusual and between normal and pathological, Lewin asserted. Freud's homogenization of psychology, seeking one set of laws for his patients and himself, was comparable to Galileo seeking a common set of laws for the movement of the stars, the flight of birds, and falling stones. Moreover, as we have seen, Freud brought within the realm of law many behaviors that psychologists before him, and many even today, regarded as senseless or due to chance. Thus Freud's fundamental assumptions of universal psychological laws and of psychic determinism are scientific ones in an important sense.

Is psychoanalytic reasoning comparable to reasoning in other sciences? Can there be a science of human behavior at all? Granted that there can be, does it constitute a separate domain to which the reasoning and standards of the physical sciences do not apply? These are the questions that Sherwood (1969) has addressed.

Sherwood begins by asking, What is explanation, anyhow? We must begin with a frame of reference that specifies what interests us and what we take for granted by virtue of common sense and other knowledge. Then there must be some puzzle or incongruity, something we cannot make fit. A satisfactory explanation must solve the puzzle in the proper frame of reference at the proper level of complexity. That, he says, is precisely what the psychoanalytic narrative attempts to do. Psychoanalytic reasoning is best seen in a case history, the psychoanalytic narrative. The psychoanalyst looks for common themes in the patient's life, manifest in alternative ways and not necessarily exhaustively accounting for any single manifestation. The explanatory power of his reconstruction is clearer in relation to a life history than in relation to isolated dreams, symptoms, or acts. To suppose that he explains this symptom, that dream, then another act, and that the case history is the sum of such explanations is to miss the force of the psychoanalytic narrative.

Sherwood shows that Freud had a sophisticated analysis of causation in his early writings. In the case that Sherwood takes as exemplary, that of Paul Lorenz, the "rat man," Freud (1909b) used explanation of symptoms, wishes, and behaviors in terms of their origin, their genesis, their current function, and in terms of prediction, in addition to the explanations in terms of symbolic significance that are usually called "Freudian."

The thesis that human behavior constitutes a domain separate from that of all other sciences in relation to its standards of reasoning may be justified in terms of a distinction between movements and actions or between causes and reasons, with reasons distinguished from other causal factors by the element of human awareness, he continues. But it was just Freud's mission to show that these are not two different sorts of things. Unconscious motives, which must be causes since they are by definition excluded from awareness, affect behavior in a manner closely similar to that of the corresponding conscious motives or reasons. Causes and reasons are not distinguished in the event but in the explanatory context. Thus Sherwood argues for the possibility of a science of human behavior and against the thesis of a separate domain.

In evaluating the adequacy of psychoanalytic explanations, Sherwood suggests the usual criteria of self-consistency, coherence, and comprehensiveness. He recognizes difficulty in applying the criterion of self-consistency. The existence of opposite motives or trends in a person is not evidence for inconsistency of explanation, since this is a patent feature of human nature. Indeed, he might have stressed more strongly that psychoanalysis postulates inner conflict as the core of every neurosis. Since there are few diseases, neurotic or otherwise, that protect the person against other diseases, the criterion of consistency is of limited value in assessing psychoanalytic explanations. Perhaps coherence and comprehensiveness can suffice.

While the distinction between causes and reasons is bypassed in the drive paradigm, we have seen that it is revived by Ricoeur as the distinction between the archaeology and teleology of the subject. Ricoeur concludes that to understand the person one must understand both causes and reasons, and this dialectic can be found in Freud's later writings, which Sherwood does not discuss. Perhaps philosophers will look at this issue once more for further clarification.

One respect in which psychoanalysis appears to be most

unlike the paradigmatic sciences of Kuhn's account is in its method of teaching new members of the profession, depending largely on classical case histories. (Indeed, those who teach analysts may underestimate the extent to which the art of interpretation is teachable by exercises with fixed answers, but of course problems of interpretation can never be reduced to mathematical certainty.) But let us look at how physics is taught, a topic that Kuhn himself has discussed (1974). The classical formulas of physics must be transformed by being given specific meaning to apply to textbook problems, he asserts. The step of adapting the general laws to apply to a particular situation is the hardest task for the student. That is the step that is learned by watching others do it in case after case, Kuhn states; in general, there are no rules to assist the process. Thus, by Kuhn's own testimony, the hardest step in becoming a physicist is most like the training of a psychoanalyst.

From "It" to "I"

For many psychologists the concepts of the ego, the id, and the superego, now central for most psychoanalytic theorists, are so remote from their experience and so abstract as to be unconvincing. Leaving the superego for discussion in the next chapter, let us look again at the concepts of the ego and the id in terms of their relation to direct observation. As Brandt points out (1966), Freud's terms, *das Ich* and *das Es,* had a more immediate and personal impact (see Chapter Fourteen).

Brandt cites the case of a patient who described her feeling of being trapped by some part of herself over which she had no control by "I'm up here and *it's* down there." Brandt continues: "After repeatedly stating 'I am trapped,' then 'I am trapped by my emotions' and a little later, 'I am trapped by myself'—all passive voice statements which, transformed into the active voice, say 'It traps me'—this patient arrived at the insight 'I trap myself.' The replacement of 'it' by 'I' as subject of the sentence corresponds to the process of 'it' becoming 'I' . . . . Finally, this person could recognize her interactions with others and state with an unequivocal 'I': 'I suppose I'm letting you trap me ... like I let everybody else' " (1966, p. 377).

Bruch (1961, 1973) has observed that distortions of body image and ego boundaries, characteristic of schizophrenics and patients with severe eating disorders, may be due to misinterpretation of stimuli from inside the body, which she shows in some cases originated in inappropriate responses by the patient's mother dating from the patient's infancy. "If the falsification of body awareness is severe, a person may feel that he *neither owns* his body *nor is in control* of its functions. Patients suffering from eating compulsion will say: '*It* just happens to me—*I* do not want to eat.*' There is an overall lack of awareness of living one's own life, a conviction of the ineffectiveness of all efforts and strivings" (Bruch, 1961, p. 475; italics in original).

Horowitz (in press) described an adult patient who had no words for genitals or bodily functions, all of which she referred to as "it." In the course of her treatment the analyst helped this exceptionally intelligent patient find words for parts and functions she had previously not been able to describe. In doing so, her sense of her self also gradually expanded to encompass the previously unnamable parts and functions. Correspondingly, her capacity for sexual pleasure and gratification grew, and her interpersonal relations improved.

A group therapy technique has been built around a similar insight (Enright, 1972). Each person in the group is asked to look around the room and pick out an object that stands out vividly for him. He is asked to spend a couple of minutes identifying himself with the object, and then to make statements about it as if he were the object, "describing it, but saying 'I' instead of 'it' " (p. 153). When the person stops, he is asked to say one or two more things, on the assumption that he has stopped when he got close to something important. "The object provides a recurrent 'nudge' into areas that might not emerge in pure fantasy. As person B observes A working with his object, it is obvious to B that A is selecting quite idiosyncratically from the possibilities of the object, missing some 'obvious' features, and choosing very peculiar ones that B would never have dreamed of. Person A, however, experiences himself not as

choosing, but as being compelled and pulled by what truly seem
to him the objective features of the object" (p. 154).

While my knowledge of my *ego* may be problematic, my
sense of what *I* am is immediate, not a remote or abstract inference. One thing to be considered is whether everything in
psychoanalysis—and also everything in this book—that is said
about the ego applies to or can be coordinated with the conception variously called *I, me*, and *myself*. Further, the clinical observations just quoted suggest a number of research projects. Is
the change from speaking in terms of "it" to "I" discernable in
all cases of successful psychoanalysis? Is there always a shift
from passive to active voice in describing the self by patients
treated successfully? Does the same process occur in other kinds
of psychotherapy?

Conclusions

The psychoanalytic ego paradigm reveals common principles
underlying neurosis, therapy, and ego development. Thus it
recaptures the elegance that the drive paradigm lost when it had
to be stretched to accommodate ego phenomena by ad hoc conceptions and amendments. Erikson, Ricoeur, and Loewald have
all taken the same principles from the ego psychology of
Freud's later writings and constructed essentially compatible
versions of the ego paradigm, despite some terminological differences. In many respects the ego paradigm resembles other
scientific paradigms: a method of investigation, the psychoanalytic case study, is united by a theory to a body of findings.
Major discoveries serve as exemplars: the interpretation of
dreams as disguised expressions of repressed wishes and the
interpretation of children's play as the active repetition of passive experience. The patient's behavior or symptoms can be construed as a puzzle that the treatment, at its best, solves. (Strictly
speaking, comparison with other sciences is closer when some
class of cases is found to reveal common elements.) To compare
the psychoanalytic paradigm at its best to more exact sciences is
not to condone vague, poorly reasoned studies or blind appeals
to the authority of Freud or other senior analysts. The concept

of paradigm has been used to signal an interest in the structure of ideas rather than the letter of the literature. Psychoanalysis has as much or more claim to comparison with rigorous sciences as some of its rivals, not only with respect to coordination of theory, method, and data, but also with respect to the fundamental assumptions of universal laws and psychic determinism.

Psychoanalysis has been discussed to the exclusion of other schools of psychiatry not as a judgment on its efficacy as therapy but because it has contributed to theory of ego development. Although sophisticated discussion of ego functions can be found in psychiatry as early as Griesinger's textbook (excerpted in Altschule, 1965), first published in 1845, I know of no substantial contributions to theory of ego development from other schools, nor any other attempts to find principles common to ego development, neurosis, and treatment. The school of psychiatry that takes as its mission the diagnosis, classification, and enumeration of symptoms of the various nosological entities represents a vestige of Aristotelian reasoning, however much its journal articles may contain modern-looking tables of numbers.

A recurrent issue is the extent to which cognitive or structural explanations may replace psychodynamic ones. That issue was raised in Chapter Twelve with respect to limits on ego development in individuals. It will surface again in Chapter Sixteen with respect to Sullivan's and Piaget's account of development of conscience in adolescence. Kohlberg (1966) has raised the issue often, particularly with respect to sex-role identification. The child, he says, first learns to identify himself as being permanently of one gender, much as he learns of the permanence of other objects. Then he identifies himself with other children and adults of the same gender and tends to prefer the same-sex parent because he perceives him as like himself. This view contrasts with the psychoanalytic hypothesis that identification with the same-sex parent is a way out of the Oedipus complex. Horowitz's (1974a, 1974b) cognitive approach to psychotherapy raises the problem again. Neither Kohlberg nor Horowitz acknowledges the full extent of the issue. Kohlberg often states the issue as the choice between the cognitive-developmental and the psychoanalytic explanation. Horowitz absorbs the cognitive explanation as a special case of the structural point of view within the psychoanalytic metapsychology. Closer examination is needed to the ways in which they are complementary or mutually alternative. If I hypothesize that little girls envy the little boy's penis because they assume that pleasure is proportional to visible size, is that a Freudian or a Piagetian hypothesis? Or does the distinction become obsolete? Bruch (1973), who has apparently been criticized for mixing cognitive explanations with psychoanalytic ones, argues for their integration on clinical grounds.

Whether, finally, psychoanalysis is classed as a science does not matter. The flag is not worth fighting for. The idea of a paradigm has served our purposes. We are left, as we should be, with questions: Can the criterion of self-consistency be applied to psychoanalytic reasoning? How far can cognitive and structural explanation replace psychodynamic ones? Is successful therapy marked by transition from passive to active voice? Does "It" literally become "I"?

Chapter Sixteen

Origins
of Conscience

The question of the origins of conscience has woven its way through our chronicle. How is it that people, some of them at least, are induced to assume a debt that can never be paid, to shoulder a burden that can never be delivered, to accept a punishment that can never be escaped? The complexity and diversity of the sources of conscience have been described in various ways by Mill, Hobhouse, Dewey and Tufts, and McDougall (Chapter Eleven). The purpose of this chapter is to examine the origins of conscience reflectively and theoretically.

What are the experiences to which we assign the name *conscience,* according to common sense and common speech? Since conscience may, empirically, mean different things to persons at different ages, the developmental course cannot be excluded completely from consideration even in the first instance; a guiding idea must be some conception of a mature conscience. At the same time, we must allow for the possibility that among the necessary antecedents of a mature conscience are some behaviors or attitudes that appear antithetical to a mature conscience. At what point in development one says, "Here conscience begins," may prove to be arbitrary.

The Phenomena of Conscience

The elements of conscience include a sense of accountability, including both responsibility for past actions and feelings and obligation in regard to future ones, a capacity for self-criticism, and standards and ideals. All of these ideas seem directly implied by the notion of conscience. They may have different developmental origins even though not logically independent.

There is no meaning to conscience unless the person is accountable for his behavior, which may include thoughts or feelings. Perhaps the closest term for accountability in common speech is *blame*. Of the vocabulary of conscience, it is one of the first words acquired. Blame has reference to the past and to responsibility for it. It has connotations of blaming others, but blaming oneself is not excluded. Accountability also implies present and future obligations. Accountability, responsibility, and obligation have both cognitive and motivational aspects. A set of concepts is involved, that of rights, duties, privileges, and the like. In addition there must be some pull, call, or commitment. Whether one can have a clear conception of rights and duties without feeling obligated to fulfill one's duties and to allow others their rights is not clear a priori.

Conscience is above all a reflexive concept. It implies self-criticism and hence self-observation—in common speech, *self-consciousness*. Perhaps self-consciousness is an early, unfocused version of self-observation. All such reflexive terms apply only to a person with some articulated sense of self. Differentiation of self from non-self, the earliest problem in ego development, is thus the forerunner of all reflexive aspects of conscience. Even if we include in the realm of conscience the fear of punishment for disobeying rules, there would still be implied some sense of self.

One reflexive trait that may be included in conscience in careless usage but cannot be integral to its definition is self-control. Some minimal self-control is prerequisite to the sequence of development that culminates in mature conscience, but lapses may occur at any stage. What is essential is the ability to distinguish impulse from control. Infallible control is good conduct, a different matter from conscience. (The topic of over-control will be omitted from this discussion.)

Perhaps the most essential aspects of conscience are the emotional components of self-criticism, including shame, being ashamed, and guilt. Erikson (1950) has described the feeling of being shamed, of feeling naked, exposed, and "put down" by rivals or by hostile critics. Although the distinction is not a usual one, one can distinguish being shamed from being ashamed. To be ashamed implies a more self-administered put-down than to be shamed. One is ashamed typically before those one loves. Thinking in terms of the small child, what changes as he progresses from being shamed to being ashamed is not the persons before whom he stands, who are likely to be parents in either case, but rather his ability to integrate them as loved persons at the same moment he feels himself blamed or shamed.

One can be ashamed not only of actions for which one is responsible but also of characteristics such as clubfoot or illegitimacy for which one is not responsible. One feels guilty for actions one might have done differently and often enough also for thoughts or feelings that one rejects. Guilt is very different from being shamed, but not so different from being ashamed; it is one step further in the internalization and evolution of conscience. The presence of an audience or of onlookers, actual or potential, is essential to the idea of being ashamed, but it is absent or less important to the feeling of guilt. The judgment of others is the core of being ashamed; self-judgment is the core of guilt feelings.

A different element of conscience is involved in upholding standards and striving for ideals. Here the emphasis is on the "ought" rather than on the "ought not," on striving rather than

on constraint. There is no sharp divide, for one may criticize
oneself for not upholding standards or for not living up to
ideals. The origins of self-criticism and of ideals are different,
however. The ultimate ideal to which a mature conscience gives
its allegiance is the ideal of justice; so Kohlberg asserts (Chapter
Five). The term *sense of justice* implies both an ideal of justice
and a feeling that justice must be made to prevail, thus both a
standard and a commitment.

A complete account of so rich and varied an experience as
conscience may be impossible. There is, however, one additional
element that must be added: that is disinterestedness. A person
with a truly mature conscience has the possibility, even the pro-
clivity, if not to love others exactly as he loves himself, at least
to take their standpoint into equal account with his own. This
stance involves treating others as ends rather than as means, but
more than that. It involves transcending both egocentrism and
the orientation in which conscience can be satisfied by mere
obedience.

Superego and Ego Ideal

In turning to some related psychoanalytic ideas, the more or
less phenomenological approach adopted to define our purview
must be abandoned. There are conflicting usages of the terms
conscience, superego, and *ego ideal* in contemporary psychoanalytic writing, as a result of Freud having used the terms at
times interchangeably and at other times with a variety of connotations. The term *conscience* here is taken primarily in terms
of its connotations from common speech, with only such alteration as is required by fidelity to things as they are. The terms
superego and *ego ideal* will be used in what I take to be their
most usual contemporary meanings. Since the purpose is insight
into developmental origins, neither originality nor a comprehensive review of the literature is needed.

Chein (1972) summarizes his version of the psychoanalytic
structural theory: the ego and the superego are moral; ego and
id seek gratification of wishes; and the superego and id are
archaic and primitive. This formulation shows why none of the

three concepts, id, ego, and superego, can be dispensed with. Let us leave open for now whether the development of the superego is an aspect of ego development or pursues an independent course. For the moment it suffices that the concept of the superego cannot be dispensed with.

Flugel (1945) in a comprehensive discussion of the varied origins of a mature conscience, delineated four essentially independent sources, though granting that specific behaviors reflect the influence of several sources simultaneously. One source is the ideal self or ego ideal. A second source is the incorporation of moral attitudes and precepts of others, particularly one's parents. These two sources he called the *ego ideal*, in contradistinction to the superego; both sources were known before Freud, particularly to Baldwin and McDougall. The third source is aggression turned against the self. The fourth source Flugel described primarily in terms of sadomasochism, but at times in terms of the need for mastery; the latter will be emphasized here. The last two sources Flugel termed the *superego*; they represent unique contributions of psychoanalysis. These four sources will be discussed presently in terms similar to but not limited to those of Flugel, in what I take to be their developmental order. (Other psychoanalysts differ in what functions they ascribe to ego ideal and superego and in whether they see ego ideal as precursor of superego or vice versa.)

In a brief but pithy essay, Lampl-de Groot (1962), who has been influenced by Flugel (Lampl-de Groot, 1949), traces the origins of the superego and the ego ideal. The ego ideal begins with the infant's "hallucinatory wish fulfillment" in the stage of primary narcissism. As the infant becomes aware of the distinction between inside and outside, hallucinatory wish fulfillment is replaced by fantasies of omnipotence and grandeur. Following experience of his relative powerlessness, these fantasies are replaced by fantasies of his parents' omnipotence. After he is disillusioned in this regard also, he forms ideals and ethics. For Lampl-de Groot the entire sequence remains one primarily of wish fulfillment.

Equating conscience with superego, Lampl-de Groot traces the origin of superego in a separate sequence, beginning with

the experience of unpleasure. Some of the experiences of unpleasure later become structured as restrictions and demands of
the parents, which the child obeys to retain the parents' love.
At the next stage some of these demands are internalized via
identification. Finally the child accepts the restrictions and
forms a conscience in order to safeguard his social relations with
parents and the wider group that by now he finds himself in.
The superego throughout remains primarily an agency of restriction.

Lampl-de Groot asks: As different as these two sequences
are, how were they ever seen as one sequence, establishing a single agency or substructure within the ego? Her answer includes
the observation that parental images are crucial in both sequences, though in different ways; the ego ideal is related to
being like parents, whereas the superego is related to living up
to their demands. Moreover, although their aims are opposite,
wish fulfillment served by the ego ideal and restriction and prohibition served by the superego, in practice both agencies unite
into one substructure and influence each other's function. Thus,
ultimately ideals can be experienced as demands.

Lampl-de Groot apologizes for speaking of ego ideal both
as an ego function and as a substructure within the ego. This
duality is a problem that has troubled other writers. Surely the
solution is that the course of ego development must always lie
in the direction of structuralization, which entails the creation
of substructures within the ego. Formally, what else can ego
development mean? Differentiation of functions and formation
of structures are two ways of describing the same set of phenomena; only concrete habits of thought make them sound like
different things.

One difficulty with all expositions of early development is
that the words of adult life do not fit. "Hallucinatory wish fulfillment" seems to imply three elements: a wish, perception of
its nonfulfillment, and then the false perception of its fulfillment. In early infancy such a sequence is unbelievable. Rather,
wish and perception must be merged; to wish for the breast is at
first not different from imagining it there. The disappointment
of the merged wish and fulfillment is what structures the wish

as separate from the perception of its fulfillment (see Schachtel, 1959, and Shapiro, 1970).

Psychoanalysis is a developmental theory through and through. Flugel made the point that nothing so complicated as the superego can arise at one fell swoop, as may seem to be implied by Freud's statement that the superego is heir to the Oedipus complex. In the light of the more detailed tracing of developmental origins by Lampl-de Groot, the truth of Flugel's assertion is emphasized. Is it any more valid to set the origin of conscience at the beginning of latency than to set the origin of sexuality at the beginning of puberty?

Evolution of Conscience

To reconstruct the evolution of conscience, I draw on the foregoing and other sources, including my own reflection. The growth of conscience is not available to direct observation; one cannot discuss it without at least low-level inference. I shall try to use only concepts with specifiable and fairly obvious observational referents.

The infant at first has the ability to wish only by imagining his wish as fulfilled. Failure of gratification to ensue leads to the distinction between wish and perception and between the inner world and the outer. For long thereafter, however, primary process thinking largely prevails, in the talking child taking the form of fantasy fulfillment of grandiose and other wishes. He does not have side by side a correct perception of himself and a fantasied omnipotent and grandiose self, as some accounts of the idealized self might seem to suggest. His thoughts are more fluid and less structured than that. He does not distinguish reality and fantasy, his real self and his idealized or wished-for self. To establish the distinction is the same as to recognize the unreality of his idealized or wishful picture of himself.

Similarly, as he consoles himself for his own perceived smallness and weakness by ascribing all power to his parents, he does not entertain simultaneously an idealized and a realistic image of them. To make the distinction between parents as they are and parents as they ought to be is more or less the same thing as forming rules and standards to which parents (and others) must subordinate themselves. Before the child has some abstract standards of conduct, it is power itself that confers rightness (Kohlberg, 1971). Granting always that archaic forms persist and continue to have some influence, true ideals and ethics are founded on the demise—that is, take the place of— idealization of self and parents.

The foregoing is the structural or formal aspect. The content of the child's standards continues to change long after the structural aspect of his ethics is fairly well established. Beginning at first with what Ferenczi (1925) called "sphincter morality," the child proceeds to a morality of authoritarian conformity, then, in favorable instances, to self-evaluated standards, and in unusual cases, to disinterested standards of justice, an evolution that has been traced in greater detail by Kohlberg (1971).

Narcissism. Freud proposed a psychodynamic explanation of crucial steps in the foregoing sequence. The child transfers some of his self-love from his real self to his ego ideal, which can retain the perfection that reality forces him to admit he does not have (Chapter Fourteen). Another dynamic explanation comes from Ausubel (Chapter Five). The child, facing disastrous loss of self-esteem when he learns to recognize his own smallness and dependence, becomes a satellite of his all-powerful parents, shining in their reflected glory. One can, in fact, accept both Freud's and Ausubel's explanations; they do not seem to be contradictory, nor do they contradict the purely cognitive explanation that is implied in the exposition of the formal aspects of the sequence. Is not the self-esteem that Ausubel writes of itself a version of narcissism?

Aggression. Nonfulfillment of wishes is the starting point for another contributory line of development, turning aggression against the self. We can speak of a neonate as having wishes or impulses only if we do not impute too much meaning to the terms. The frustration of those wishes, even though temporary, must lead to something akin to aggression. By the time one can speak appropriately of an aggressive impulse, the infant has gone beyond the first inchoate state of merged impulse and fulfillment, though what appears to be rage can be observed in babies. As Flugel observes, the one target of baby's aggression that is always present and within reach is himself. Control of impulses, even control motivated by self-interest, comes later than the structuring of impulse as such. So long as expression of impulse, per se, is experienced as more compelling than any calculated self-interest requiring control, directing aggression against the self is likely to occur. Since impulse predominates over control for a long time into childhood, the path back to aggression against the self may remain open for a long time. Indeed, self-rejection and naked aggression against the self are useful as signs of low ego levels (Loevinger and Wessler, 1970). Control of impulse is in part the heir of aggression directed against the self. Differentiation of impulse from control implies a split or doubling of self, a higher degree of structure. Impulse control remains the most important transmutation of aggression turned against the self. Later versions of aggression against self are shame, being ashamed, and guilt feelings, sensibilities acquired in that order over a period of years, none totally lost. A mature conscience is likely to be robust with respect to all of those negative emotions, however, and thus is tolerant of self as well as of others.

Mastery. Whether the drive for mastery is closely allied to or derived from the aggressive drive or, alternatively, a drive for mastery exists separate from an aggressive drive, each capable of being turned inward, need not be decided to pursue our interest in the origins of conscience. The specifically psychoanalytic version of the need for mastery is that one must do what one has suffered, that experience is mastered by actively repeating what one has passively undergone (chapters Fourteen and Fifteen). Freud used this principle to explain children's play, the repetition of unpleasant experiences in the transference and of traumatic events in dreams, anxiety, and aspects of impulse control and superego formation. In various ways, Anna Freud, Flugel, Erikson, Loewald, and Ricoeur, no doubt among many others, have made similar points. Let me say how it seems to me after having profited from the contributions of those writers and others.

It makes no sense to speak of mastering experience by

actively repeating what one has passively undergone at the time of the so-to-speak "hallucinatory wish fulfillment," that is, of the inchoate impulse-gratification image. Even such structuring of impulses as to permit a definite perception of nongratification followed by aggression or anger does not suffice. Experience must be structured in some more coherent way for one to speak meaningfully of mastering it. Thus we are not talking of the neonate at this point.

What experiences does the baby or young child feel the need to master? Freud's examples are the trip to the doctor and the temporary or permanent loss of a beloved person or thing. According to Fenichel, whenever the child is "flooded with a very large quantity of excitation," (1945, p. 44) the situation is one that he will attempt to master by actively reproducing it in his play. The child also endlessly repeats newly acquired but not wholly automatic skills, in what appears to be a related need (drive? instinct?), as Hendrick (1942) has pointed out. Whatever may be the limits of its application, this principle is a central mode of ego functioning.

It is also a driving force in the evolution of conscience. The child's impulses are such that he must be restrained by his parents. The child would like to restrain and control his parents, as they restrain and control him, but he cannot and dare not. This situation is doubly frustrating, in that the child is both controlled and then prevented from making the natural response to being controlled. But the needs involved are plastic, and the child substitutes a new victim for the ones whose use he is denied. This victim may be at times a younger sibling or playmate, but usually he is restrained in this direction also, and the ultimate victim must be the child himself. He masters the situation by taking the role of the parents towards himself or a part of himself. This role play is the origin of self-control and of the distinction between impulse and control, and part of the dynamics of ego structuring and of superego formation (chapters Fourteen and Fifteen).

Doing to others what one has suffered from others is formally similar to the primitive mechanism of undoing. More than similarity, what is involved is an evolution of more or less reflexive undoing in the direction of active and often constructive mastery of experience. One outcome of these impulses is a sense that accounts must be balanced. At first this sense takes the form of revenge and of the law of the talion. The part that the law of the talion plays in the development of conscience has been recognized by Mill, Westermarck (1906), Hobhouse (1906) and Odier (1943).

Mill ([1861] 1965) pointed out that the desire to punish those who have done harm is a natural sentiment that derives from two impulses that "either are or resemble instincts; the impulse of self-defense, and the feeling of sympathy" (p. 306). Our desire for revenge or retaliation against those who have harmed us or those we sympathize with we share with lower animals, who try to hurt those who have hurt them or their young. By virtue of our intelligence our range of sympathy may be broader, extending not merely to our children but to tribe, country, or mankind. Thus what Mill calls the "sentiment of justice," which includes the desire to punish, he sees as not in itself moral; what is moral is its exclusive subordination to the social interest. The law of the talion is a favored principle of a primitive and spontaneous sentiment of justice and remains a secret hankering in most minds: "When retribution accidentally falls on an offender in that precise shape, the general feeling of satisfaction evinced bears witness how natural is the sentiment to which this repayment in kind is acceptable" (Mill, [1861] 1965, p. 313).

Parental Standards. The fourth element of conscience identified by Flugel is the incorporation or acceptance as one's own of the prohibitions, standards, and ideals of the parents. A child about whom one can speak in such terms has again taken a large step forward in the organization of his experience. He needs a rudimentary notion of rules, and that requires a degree of mental development going beyond that required for mastery through activity. It is not easy to put an age on this achievement, not only because there are conspicuous individual differences but also because there is an inherent ambiguity in putting a date on a slowly evolving conception (Chapter Eight). To pursue further the meaning and mechanism of the adoption or incorporation of parental standards would lead us back over ground already covered here and in many other places in terms similar to A. Freud's (1936) discussion of identification with the aggressor.

Mutual Love. The fifth element of conscience has been expressed in various ways: valuing another person equally with oneself; valuing another person as an end in himself rather than as a means towards one's own ends; the ability to see from another person's point of view. At its highest and rarest reach, this element becomes disinterestedness, the opposite pole from the egocentricity of childhood and youth, achieving what lawyers call the "judicial temperament."

The origin of this fifth contributor to conscience lies in love, or, if you will, the human bond. In explaining altruism, love and conscience are alternatives. Sacrificing one's own interests so as to further the interests of one's own children or spouse is a less decisive evidence for conscience than doing so for some person more remote. At the same time, it is hard to believe that a person would develop much if any conscience without love for other people. The child's love for his parents is involved in acceptance of their standards and ideals, and it is involved somewhat less directly in other aspects of the previous account of formation of conscience.

The love of a child for his parents is, however, intrinsically an asymmetrical relation. Symmetrical love, the love for a peer, appears to be essential for a mature conscience to develop. This is truly a new element in late childhood and early adolescence, and by no means inevitable.

Freud's account (1921) postulates the following sequence: the child is jealous of his parents' love for his siblings. Under influence of their common tender tie to their parents, the hostile feeling towards his siblings is reversed into identification. The demand for equality of treatment arises in this manner as a reaction formation to jealousy, and in turn becomes the root of social conscience and a sense of duty.

Harry Stack Sullivan's contribution lies in his observations on the role of the chum in the preadolescent era (Chapter Five). In the chumship the youngster learns for the first time to value another as he values himself, to cherish his triumphs and happiness as if they were his own. To rejoice in the happiness of one's chum is not disinterestedness, but it is an essential precursor. Through the affective tie to another person seen as one's equal the capacity to take another's point of view matures; such experiences open the way for a few to achieve disinterestedness. The highest altruism and idealism have their origins in these or comparable experiences; they are less likely to develop in a sexual relationship not preceded by a relation with a chum of the same sex, according to Sullivan.

In *Moral Judgment of the Child,* Piaget is concerned with the same pivotal point of development in different terms (Chapter Five). Piaget sees the key to the change from heteronomous morality to autonomous morality in the transition from the unilateral respect of the child for parent to the mutual and egalitarian respect of the child for other children.

Sullivan stresses the emotional impetus of loneliness as driving the youngster into an exclusive relation with a chum; Piaget stresses the cognitive aspects and the need to communicate with a group of equals. Both authors locate the transition in preadolescence, or at about twelve years of age. As different as their reasoning is, they bring us to the same point; it is essential to maturity of conscience to advance beyond authoritarian conformity to seeing and feeling oneself a member of a society of equals.

By itself, mutuality does not suffice to create the "judicial temperament"; it is but a step or prerequisite. The point is rather that the morality of obedience cannot, failing such transformation to mutuality, lead to the highest estate of conscience. One of the paradoxes of the growth of conscience is exposed at this point. We may desire to create or encourage maturity of conscience in our charges, but in the nature of things there is no direct way to lead them beyond the morality of obedience. Disinterestedness, even more than responsibility, can only grow; it remains radically unreachable by tuition, with or without sanctions.

Sources and Stages

We have noted five more or less independent sources that contribute to the evolution of a mature conscience. These sources are, in their developmental order, (1) the formation of a sense of self, (2) turning of aggression against the self, (3) the need for mastery, (4) adoption of parental precepts and standards, and (5) mutual love and respect. Each source has its origin in one of the stages of ego development:

1. The ideal self, originally better called an *idealized self*, has its origin in the sense of self that dates back to the earliest narcissistic period; ultimately this strand of development becomes the ego ideal. This developmental strand originates in the Presocial Stage's differentiation of self from non-self.
2. Turning of aggression against the self is observable in many infants and is characteristic of the Impulsive Stage; the inability to delay acting on impulse long enough to calculate advantage is precisely one of the marks of the Impulsive Stage. Impulse control gets at least some of its force from aggression turned against the self, as do, later, shame and a sense of guilt.
3. The need for mastery, including self-mastery as a protection against inner and outer dangers, is characteristic for the Self-Protective Stage.
4. Adoption of and identification with parental and other rules and standards obviously characterize the Conformist Stage.
5. Finally, mutual love and respect are characteristic potentialities of the Conscientious Stage. From them develop the toleration of individual differences and devotion to disinterested justice that mark the highest estate of conscience and the Autonomous and Integrated stages of ego development.

While these several strands make quasi-independent contributions to the formation of conscience, they are not independent lines of development. On the contrary, the growth of conscience and ego development are so intimately intertwined that they constitute a single complex sequence of events. This is not to say that ego and conscience are one, or that either term is dispensable; indeed, they are terms from different universes of discourse. Stages in the development of conscience, however, closely parallel stages of ego development, and the dynamic principles that one needs to account for the development of conscience are the same as or overlap those needed to account for ego development.

Conscience as Pacer

There is one final turn to the argument, and that is to show that conscience, or perhaps the ego ideal, is itself a moving principle in ego development. The operative word is *pacer*, a topic discussed in Chapter Twelve. "It is the pacer, if one is available, that enables the individual to change . . . . As he maintains active contact with the pacer and eventually masters it, his own level of complexity grows, and he is ready for a new pacer" (Dember, 1965, p. 421).

To construe conscience as pacer goes back at least to Baldwin (Chapter Eleven). In contrasting the young child's accommodating self that seeks to learn from older persons and his habitual self that practices on younger ones, Baldwin anticipated the principle that Freud later clarified in terms of mastery through transition from passive to active. Ultimately the child evolves an ideal self, originally representing the standards set up by parents and teachers. With growth, the child incorporates the ideal self into his habitual self, but as he progresses, new patterns are set for him. Thus his "ethical insight must always find its profoundest expression in that yearning which anticipates but does not overtake the ideal" (Baldwin, 1897, p. 42).

A similar but more sophisticated view has been worked out within the framework of psychoanalytic theory by Loewald (Chapter Fifteen). For Loewald, the condition for psychological growth is the tension between a more organized or more mature psychic structure and a less organized, less mature one. Originally the mother fulfills the function of creating this condition. As the child grows, this tension between the less organized structure and the more organized one becomes internalized as the tension between the (unconscious) id and the (conscious and preconscious) ego or as the tension between the ego and the ego ideal or superego. The superego embodies hopes, ideals, and aspirations for the future; this is not only its function but its nature. As those aspirations are realized and become habitual, they become part of the ego, and the child or adult has new aspirations. Thus the superego does not present a fixed program of aspirations and injunctions, constant throughout life. Rather, *superego* is a name for the function of formulating ideals and aspirations. The superego is the future as embodied in the present. Loewald writes of the conscience as the "voice" of the superego. On the whole, his usage of the term *superego* approximates that of the term *conscience* in the present chapter.

The parallel is striking between Dember's conception of pacer, arising out of laboratory experiments in cognitive psychology, Baldwin's conception of the ideal self as pacer, and Loewald's conception of superego as pacer of ego development.

Conclusions

Distinguishable elements of conscience originate in different stages of ego development. Seen from the viewpoint of man as animal, conscience is a sickness, as Nietzsche and Ricoeur have noted; yet it is also a sublime achievement and the beginning of all culture, as Freud noted. The sources of conscience lie in both conscious and unconscious mental life. Conscience is grounded on narcissism and on interpersonal relations. Conscience has its origins in love and in aggression. Conscience in its nature reproduces and memorializes the inequality of station of parent and child; yet in its fullest and rarest reach conscience transcends all inequalities of station.

The question often raised, to what extent our whole chronicle is the chronicle of superego development rather than that of ego development, can now be answered. The domain of the ego is defined by experience and by its own coherence. Its moral, interpersonal, and cognitive elements are too intertwined to be separated conceptually or developmentally. Development of conscience is an integral part of that sequence. Whether one considers *superego* as another term for *conscience* or as a distinctive set of functions partly subordinate to and partly inde-

pendent of conscience or ego, its development is normally subordinate to that of the ego. To the extent that *superego* has
another meaning, it refers to archaic and rigid sources of conscience (Schafer, 1974). That makes it all the plainer that to
whatever extent the development of the ego and of the superego are two separate topics, the topic of this book is the development of the ego.

Chapter Seventeen ═══════════════════════

Toward an Articulated
Conception and Theory

Scientists are like lovers—they see reminders of their beloved everywhere. We have found intimations of our subject in many places and as far past as Plato's *Republic*. In Figure 8, some of the interrelations of topics covered in this book are presented schematically. Ego development is an emerging area of study, a discipline having distinctive conceptions, problems, methods of measurement, theories, and practical applications. One book cannot do justice to it. Many authors have enriched our understanding of different stages and types, often with unique observations. Probably the most vivid and interesting descriptions are subtypes rather than universally applicable descriptions. Let us review the stages, emphasizing dynamic, motivational, more or less theoretical accounts of the stages and transitions, then turn to theories that apply across all or several stages.

413

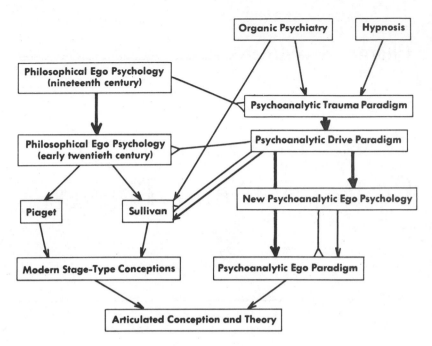

Note: A→ B means B is a direct outgrowth of A
       C→ D means C influences D
       E—<F means F develops in opposition to E

Figure 8. Schematic history of conceptions and theories
of ego development

The neonate cannot be described as having an ego. Its actions can be described as instigated by instinctual drives and guided at first by reflexes, but from the first those drives and reflexes are shaped by the environment they meet (Piaget; Loewald).* As the infant's reactions gradually evolve towards meaningful behavior, the infant simultaneously works out a correlative construction of reality. At every step his reality and his evolving self or ego are mutually structured (Fenichel, 1945; Loewald; Kahler). This period of ego formation is represented

*In this chapter, where the topics have been covered in earlier chapters, reference will be made to the author's name only.

in our scheme as the Autistic or Presocial Stage. There is almost no chance that a person operating in the Presocial mode beyond childhood will pass for normal in our society. Probably most such adults are institutionalized or live on the fringe of society, such as in hobo camps. This period has been covered more fully in the clinical literature.

The Impulsive Stage is taken by many authors as the lower limit of ego development. Its pathological exemplars are the impulse-ridden personalities and what have been called *hot psychopaths*, by contrast with *cool psychopaths*, the latter being a subtype of the Self-Protective Stage. Many children remain at the Impulsive Stage into early adolescence, apparently without being seen as markedly abnormal, though that may depend on the social milieu. Adults of this type may make marginally normal adjustments, often as vagrants or in menial positions. The sketch of the Impulsive character type has much in common with Lewis's (1966) description of the "culture of poverty," but that surely is within the range of normal.

One kind of transition from the Impulsive to the Self-Protective Stage is suggested by Graves's term for an intermediate stage, "awakening and fright." The person is aware of frightening impulses in himself and bewildering forces in the world; hence he craves a morally prescribed, rigidly enforced, unchanging order. Autonomy and democracy do not suit him; he prefers autocracy, and, if permitted, will choose it rather than democracy. Evidently Graves has located one dynamic of the frequent alliance of low ego level and fascistic tendencies.

The definitive description of the Self-Protective stage-type is that of Isaacs's Delta stage. The prototypic authoritarian personality belongs here; such a person enjoys obedience and being obeyed (Adorno). Sullivan's description of the "malevolent transformation" of some children, the conviction that they are living among enemies, can account for how the sweetness of the normal child takes this turn. The essence of the stage, the traits that are shared by the normal child and the embittered adult, are summed up by Kohlberg's term, *naive instrumental hedonism*. Behavior is governed by pleasure and pain, rewards and punishments, hence *hedonism*. The term *instrumental* refers to expedient or opportunistic relations to other people and to social rules. The term *naive* refers to the concrete nature of the rewards sought and the short term over which personal advantage is calculated. Concentration on concrete gain and short-term advantage characterizes not only normal children but also intelligent adults of this type, frequently leading to their exposure and undoing.

Self-interest may guide the child from impulsivity to self-protective opportunism, but the transition to conformity requires some further explanation. That the child's long-term self-interest is thereby served does not suffice, for it is the surrender of self-interest in favor of a shared interest and identity that is at issue. The most vivid evocation of this transition is Ausubel's description of satellization. Freud's somewhat similar description uses the term *narcissism* where Ausubel refers to *self-esteem*, and in Freud's original version the outcome was the acquisition by the child of an ego ideal, omitting the stage stressed by Ausubel where that ideal is represented by omnipotent parents.

The Conformist type has been recognized and described by more authors than any other type. Mill understood that pressure for conformity arises from need to subordinate men of strong impulses to social control, but his primary concern in his essay *On Liberty* was the hazard conformity presents to full development of individuality. The time is not long past when "adjustment" was assumed by psychologists to be an obviously desirable state, and it easily became equated with conformity to social norms. Dissatisfaction with that equation is one of the forces within psychology that led to interest in our topic.

There are differences in the many descriptions of the Conformist type. Sullivan spoke of insensitivity to feelings of personal worth in others, while Isaacs describes the beginnings of niceness, considerateness, helpfulness, and sharing. Peck attributes to the Conformist a capacity for shame but not for guilt, where others see guilt for breaking rules. Such differences may represent different subtypes of Conformity or differences with respect to where the line is drawn between Conformity and the preceding and succeeding stages. C. Sullivan, Grant, and Grant seem to locate the beginnings of identification at the stage following the Conformist one; Isaacs sees the origins of identification in the stage prior to Conformity. This disagreement is of consequence, since identification is an important element in theoretical explanations of the dynamics. The term *identification,* however, is a name given to a variety of processes changing with ego stage. Some psychoanalysts prefer other terms, such as *internalization* or *introjection,* to demarcate the evolution of the process (Loewald; Erikson; Sanford, 1955; Schafer), but usage is not uniform.

Most of the late adolescent and adult population in urban United States are at the Conformist Stage or the Conscientious Stage or squarely between them, at what we have called the Self-Aware or Conscientious-Conformist level, according to research results (Loevinger; Kohlberg). For Sullivan, the transition from Conformity to the Conscientious Stage is achieved during preadolescence via the chumship, which fosters mutuality. For Perry, a similar transition during the college years takes the student from a dualistic outlook, to multiplicity, then to relativism, and finally to commitment.

Differences among authors increase with respect to the higher stages, whether because of the greater richness and diversity of mature personalities or the tendency for the authors to project their own limitations and aspirations onto their image of the optimum.

Psychologists who have some insights into directions and dynamics of ego development above the Conscientious Stage include Isaacs, C. Sullivan, Grant, and Grant (Warren), Kohlberg, Perry, Maslow, and probably Rogers. For Isaacs, the transition from the Beta to the Alpha level is marked by a struggle to recognize individuality in one's self and others and by recognition of increasingly complex interpersonal interactions and effects. For Sullivan, Grant, and Grant, the transitions to the sixth and seventh levels are marked by growth in self-perception as much as by changes in interpersonal relations. At the sixth level the person perceives self as distinct from the role he plays, at the seventh level he perceives integrating processes in self and others. Rogers calls attention to the greater immediacy of feelings and fluidity of personal constructs at the upper end of his continuum. The latter point particularly is related to increase in realistic perception at the highest stages, "lesser blindness," as Maslow terms it. Perry emphasizes change towards commitment and affirmation in a relativistically conceived universe; developmentally mature commitment is distinguished from immature uncritical belief by acceptance of and respect for alternative beliefs of others. Toleration for ambiguity (Frenkel-Brunswik) and ability to live intensely in the present (Rogers; Schachtel) are aspects of the highest stages.

Turning now to trans-stage theories (that is, theories of change) which apply in principle to all or to a wide range of stages, five kinds emerge: the monolithic or single-motive theories, the time-and-tide theories, the dialectical theories, the structural theories, and psychoanalytic theories.

Monolithic theories take the motivation of a single stage and make of it the explanation of all stages and of the transition between stages. A careful search would probably reveal for each stage some theorist who has taken one of its salient motives and made it the explanation for all of human behavior; indeed, there may be several such theories for a given stage. All such theories commit the ontological fallacy: they take the motivation of one stage of human development and assert that deep down, really and truly, all human conduct is so motivated, no matter how differently motivated it may appear or claim to be. I label that view a fallacy not because it is untrue, though the single-motive theories cannot *all* be true, but because that view denies the subject matter of this book, which is, among other things, transformation of motives.

Goldstein (1939) and Rogers see the striving for self-actualization as the master motive. Goldstein's argument for a single master motive is that if there are two such motives, the person must at times choose between them, and the principle on which he makes his choice would then be the master motive. Where Rogers and Goldstein concentrated on self-actualization, a motive characteristic of the highest stage, Bentham made the single motive the search for pleasure and avoidance of pain, thus making something like the Self-Protective Stage the model for all stages. Similarly, E. L. Thorndike with his law of effect made the search for reward and avoidance of punishment the motive, and B. F. Skinner's schedules of reinforcement bring hedonism up-to-date. Some reductionist theories even make their explanations dependent on reflexes, instinctual drives, or nerve networks; we have not been concerned with them, because our topic is largely beyond their purview. Among the old-fashioned theories of the master motive are imitation in Baldwin and sympathy in Adam Smith and in Bain; such theories have a Conformist ring.

Among the authors we have reviewed, there has often been a preference for a single dominant motive, though not necessarily to the exclusion of recognizing other motives. For Sullivan the avoidance of anxiety was the predominant motive in formation and maintenance of the self-system. Ausubel emphasizes the importance of self-esteem, which seems to be a new version of what McDougall called the *self-regarding sentiment.* In order that self-esteem, as distinct from esteem in the eyes of others, be the dominant motive, one almost has to be at the Conscientious Stage; that is not so far from McDougall's version, for he saw self-esteem as the key to the higher stages. Perhaps the closest McDougall's ideas could be translated to our terms would be to say that McDougall saw self-esteem as what brings a person to the Conscientious Stage. Ausubel, however, utilizes self-esteem as the motive power to explain transformations very early in life, ones for which psychoanalysts would use the term *narcissism,* whose connotations are more compatible with early ego development. For Adler striving for superiority was at one time the master motive, but when he later added social interest, it became essentially a two-stage theory with the striving for superiority corresponding to the Self-Protective Stage and social interest compatible with Conformist and Conscientious stages.

In Freud's ego theory the master motive is mastery. That does not make it a new version of Adler's striving for superiority, however. The imagery is that of the Self-Protective period, but the ego in Freud's theory must strive to master not only the impinging world but also its own instinctual impulses and internal prohibitions. In Freud far more than in Adler mastery means as much self-mastery as domination; moreover, the person must above all master his own experience. Thus mastery as an ego motive is too broad and complex a conception to be ordered to any particular stage. It has some affinity with Fingarette's characterization of the ego as the search for meaning. Self-actualization may be thought of as the highest form of the search for meaning. Kelly denied the need for a concept of motivation; in his system, the nearest equivalent was the way the person anticipates events, surely close to the search for meaning. If there is a master motive in Piaget, it must be adaptation, a conception that many more or less Conformist persons gravitate to, though it would shock Piaget to be so classified, and he means something broader than conformity. If Kohlberg has a master motive, it must be equilibration. Equilibration and search for meaning are both akin to Adler's *Einheit*, that is, unity and coherence.

Quite a few theorists are wedded to a pluralistic view of motive so completely that they do not present a master motive: Mill, Peck, Maslow, and probably Isaacs and Sullivan, Grant, and Grant. All of them recognized the transformation of motives, but lacking a trans-stage motive, they do not tell much about how a person changes from one stage to the next.

In contrast with the monolithic theories, the time-and-tide theories do not select any distinctive or distinguishable motives. They are the theories that account for human development in terms of the interplay of a multitude of diverse influences; Arnold Gesell's writing is typical. Some put primary emphasis on maturation within the individual, others on changing environmental demands. Time and tide of course enter most theories, as they enter all lives, but as auxiliary explanations rather than as the principal force. Much of the motive power for the development of the self-system in Sullivan's theory is provided by maturation of a variety of physical and emotional needs, presumably on the basis of an inner timetable. Piaget says nothing of maturing physical needs but writes about social interaction as source of the need for developing higher stages of moral reasoning. Social learning theorists, whom we have largely neglected because of their minimal concern for our topic, put major emphasis on environmental demands and rewards, quite a different environmental emphasis from that of Piaget. Erikson grants strong effect to all elements of time and tide. Other authors who give a wide reading to social and maturational influences on ego development include Ausubel and Hartmann, Kris, and Loewenstein.

Perhaps the oldest clearly articulated theme in theory of ego development is that it proceeds dialectically. Baldwin's term was the *dialectic of personal growth*; for him the parties to the dialogue were ego and alter, each perceiving and construing the other and being progressively altered by that perception, so that ultimately one's conception of others and of oneself are intimately related. An earlier version came from Adam Smith, for whom sympathy guided the process and for whom the impartial spectator within the breast was the outcome. Cooley added the term the *looking-glass self* for the self reflected through the eyes of others. This line of thinking culminated in Mead's theory of the internalized dialogue of roles as the social origin of self, presided over by the generalized other. What is absent in these classical dialectical theories but present in their recent descendants is the concept of structure. Baldwin's epistemological study (1906-1915) was one of the origins of structural theory.

The outcome of the dialogue of roles is not merely a static inner representation of society's view, however, but adoption of the dialectic itself. This aspect of ego development is hard to describe without seeming to endorse philosophically objectionable ideas, such as *inner forces* or *inner elements*. That terms such as *force* and *element* have objectionable connotations is obvious, but Schafer (1972) also objects to the use of the term *internalization* or the adjective *inner*. Such terms, he says, are based on a spatial metaphor that adds nothing to our understanding and lends itself to a concrete type of thinking that detracts from accurate conceptualization. Description of psychic structure relies implicitly on a metaphor that turns mind or ego into a place, he says, but strict definition of structure is in terms of stable functioning, slow change, and grouping of functions by their similarities; here Schafer is following the definition of Hartmann, Kris, Loewenstein, and Rapaport. Thus he brings out the difference between our view and that of the Hartmann-Rapaport school. Structure for us is defined by organization; it is explicitly not spatial; stability and slow change are consequences, not defining aspects; and similarity of function is not essential (Blasi). Thus our use of the terms *internalization* or *inner* hinges on our conception of structure. To Schafer's question, "Inside what?" our answer is, inside the structure. The hazards Schafer describes are real and worthy of concern. Nonetheless, understanding personal experience in terms of observation of the world and understanding the world in terms of personal experience are the stuff of ego development, and metaphors provide some grasp of a difficult subject. Therefore, disavowing all spatial and mechanical connotations, I shall describe a form of the dialectical theory as the *personification of inner forces*. This is the theory that the relations between people serve as model for internal psychic differentiation.

The analogy in Plato's *Republic* between governance and harmony within the person and governance and harmony in the state anticipates the theory of the personification of inner forces. Dewey and Tufts explicitly saw the division of labor in society and particularly in the courtroom as model and source for development of personal complexity, particularly the growth of conscience. The best-known version of the personification of inner forces is Freud's conception of the ego, the superego, and the id, commonly called the *structural theory* in psychoanalysis. It is almost universally accepted among psychoanalysts. That the ego, the superego, and the id sometimes have the character of three homunculi within the person has been one of the most bitterly criticized aspects of psychoanalytic theory among those who want to guard the scientific respectability of psychology, even among psychoanalysts themselves, as Grossman and Simon (1969) show. Freud rejected the idea that psychoanalysis must outgrow its anthropomorphism, saying, "Our understanding reaches as far as our anthropomorphism" (Nunberg and Federn, 1962, p. 136).

The dialectic of ego and instinctual impulse, a central theme of psychoanalysis, merges with the dialectic of roles in ego theorists such as Baldwin and Mead, for the child's role is originally embodied in his impulses, and his ego at first is borrowed from the role of parents. The thrust of our argument is, therefore, to support Freud. The anthropomorphism of the psychoanalytic dialectic is firmly grounded in the history of philosophy, in the psychology of Baldwin, Dewey, and Mead, and, most important of all, in what we know or surmise of the developmental history of children.

The most conspicuous fact about ego structure is its comparative stability. Most theories take ego stability for granted without any mention of it; all theories of it appear to be variations of a single one, whose chief proponent was Sullivan. Anticipations of the theory can be found in Adler and even in Herbart. According to this theory, each stage of ego development embodies a view of human motivation and interpersonal interaction consonant with its own mode of functioning. The ego or self-system screens out observations of interpersonal interactions that do not fit with its frame of reference. The purpose of the self-system is, among other things, to guard against anxiety, and motives beyond its own ken or compass cause anxiety (Sullivan). Hence by misperceiving or selectively inattending to such motives or interactions, the person is protected against the painful necessity of revising his frame of reference. At bottom this theory is the same as the theory of stability of any mental structure, whether that of a cognitive structure (Piaget; Merleau-Ponty) or the structure of a scientific system (Kuhn). A structure or system of thought tends to admit as data only observations compatible with its own basic premises. Hence its stability, which is necessary for its functioning. By a slight extension, the synthetic function of the ego (Nunberg) and resistance in psychoanalysis (Vergote) are assimilated to this theory.

Kohlberg derives a theory of change strictly from structural premises: "A cognitive-developmental theory of moralization holds that there is a sequence of moral stages for the same basic reasons that there are cognitive or logico-mathematical stages, that is, because cognitive structural reorganizations toward the more equilibrated occur in the course of interaction between the organism and the environment" (Kohlberg, 1971, p. 183). He characterizes the common elements of all cognitive-developmental theories as follows (pp. 183-184):

> All have postulated (a) *stages* of moral development representing (b) *cognitive-structural transformations* in conception of self and society. All have assumed (c) that these stages represent successive modes of *"taking the role of others"* in social situations, and hence that (d) the social-environmental determinants of development are *its opportunities for role-taking.* More generally, all have assumed (e) an *active* child who structures his perceived environment, and hence, have assumed (f) that moral stages and their development represent the *interaction* of the child's structuring tendencies and the structural features of the environment, leading to (g) successive forms of equilibrium in interaction. This equilibrium is conceived as (h) a level of *justice,* with (i) change being caused by disequilibrium, where (j) some optimal level of match or discrepancy is necessary for change between the child and the environment.

Kohlberg stretches a bit to include Baldwin, Dewey and Tufts, Mead, and Piaget among those theorists who share all of those assumptions with him. Piaget, for example, denies that there are structural stages of moral development, Mead has only a minimal conception of stages, and structural equilibrium is not a prominent element in Dewey and Tufts. Although Kohlberg classes all psychoanalysts along with learning theorists and sociological role theorists as believing in the direct internalization of cultural norms, the conceptions of disequilibrium and optimal mismatch are as explicit in Loewald as anywhere. There is a question, moreover, as to how far structural equilibrium can suffice to cover both stability and change, both fixation and progression.

The idea of pacer has the firmest confirmation in laboratory psychology (Dember) of any part of the theory of ego development. For Baldwin, the ideal self originating in the parents' standards serves as pacer. For Loewald the superego serves as pacer; his conception is similar to Baldwin's but more developed and articulated with psychoanalysis. For Kohlberg the arguments and reasoning of the next stage of moral reasoning serve as pacer. Thus Kohlberg apparently sees only the external pacer, while Baldwin and Loewald postulate the internalization of what was originally an external pacer.

By now it must be apparent that the five kinds of trans-stage theories are really five theoretical topics for discussion, not mutually exclusive theories or logically coordinate headings. Returning to our fifth heading, psychoanalytic theory, the dialectic of ego and instinct is a central theme through all three periods or paradigms of psychoanalysis, though the vocabulary and the details of the conceptions change. The central task and motive of the ego is mastery of its instinctual drives, of the environment, of its own moral imperatives. Indeed, experience is what must be mastered, by actively repeating what has been passively suffered; that is the ultimate momentum.

The dialogue of roles is child versus parent, impulse versus control, dependence versus mastery, all at once. Each time the role of alter or object is appropriated, the child's ego and hence his alter or object is correspondingly complicated. Ego development proceeds towards bringing more of life within the scope of ego at the expense of unconscious impulse. But this direction of growth cannot be consummated; life will always draw its vitality from impulsive sources. Moreover, sometimes or perhaps always there is a regressive element in developmental advance, for example, the formation and adoption of an ego ideal guards and preserves the child's narcissism. This formulation is approximately Loewald's version of ego theory; many others have an essentially similar reading of Freud, though differing on the exact mode of expression.

Historically, psychoanalysis developed in opposition to ego psychology, and ego psychology was stimulated by opposition to psychoanalysis. Indeed, the dialectic of psychoanalysis and ego psychology mirrors the long debate of authority and desire that Ricoeur identifies as a central theme of psychoanalysis, turning up on the one hand in the pleasure principle versus the reality principle, and on the other hand in the fictitious ethno-history of *Totem and Taboo*. The contemporary psychoanalytic ego paradigm, as found in such authors as Erikson, Loewald, and Ricoeur, appears to embody a way of surmounting the opposition of this dialectic and bringing psychoanalysis and ego psychology into a common frame of reference.

The focus of this book has been on conceptions and theories rather than on research, and still less on practical applications. But research and applications are always on the periphery and potentially shape the field of study. Rather than review recent empirical research, which is only a fragment of the possibilities provided by this approach and framework, let us look at some of those possibilities, with an eye to the heuristic value of the ideas of this book.

The most frequently proposed research design, particularly by newcomers to the field, is to test some suitable group, then interpose an experiment or wait for a life experience such as parturition, then retest, looking for ego changes. Nothing in the theory justifies the hope that changes can be wrought in short time or by brief laboratory, classroom, or even life experiences. Some measures of ego level may change as an artifact of instructions or of the testing experience per se, but that cannot be taken as indication of change in ego structure, which is in any case not easily measured reliably. There are some ethical limitations to devising experiments with excessive impact on subjects. On the whole, however, fewer ethical problems arise in devising programs to encourage ego development than in alternative programs, such as behavior modification. Ego development is growth, and there is no way to force it. One can only try to open doors. It will always be the person's own choice whether he will walk through the door. Favorable changes have been obtained by some research workers, however. The contexts in which change has been sought include prison (Kohlberg), psychotherapy (Isaacs), work situation (Lasker), and school (Kohlberg; Blasi).

The problem of practical applications is not limited to producing change in ego level. Wherever one works with people, in classroom, in prison, in mental hospital, in outpatient psychotherapy, or in work settings, one must reach them through their egos, so to speak. Thus whatever our educational, therapeutic, rehabilitative, or administrative aims may be, knowledge of ego development is in principle germane. How much practical advantage it brings remains to be demonstrated; no one maintains that ego level is the only significant variable.

One direction that use of the conception can take is sorting persons into groups of similar ego level for purposes of instruction or treatment. That has been tried by Warren and Palmer, Blasi, and others. The importance of the pacer in leading to change at least partly negates the advantage, however, for members of higher ego level can provide an appropriate pacer point of view for those less advanced, ordinarily without danger of losing ground themselves. Thus natural group diversity has its own advantages.

Let us focus more narrowly on the interests of the clinician, whether trained as psychologist, social worker, psychiatrist, or psychoanalyst. He should keep his patient's problems and adjustment conceptually distinct from ego level; a person of any ego level may become a patient, though there may be differences in the kind of pathology or presenting symptoms characteristic for different levels. In principle, the process of psychotherapy may reopen the ego to new growth. That is central to the theories of Sullivan, Rogers, and Loewald, though for different reasons. There is, in fact, little proof that such growth occurs, but the evidence either way is scanty. An entirely different point is that the amenability of a person to psychotherapy may be related to his ego level; that can be supported both theoretically and empirically. Carrying that point further, the appropriate kind of therapy may be related to the patient's ego level, with organic and manipulative therapies more appropriate at lower levels, insight therapies at higher levels (a topic being studied by Clifford Swensen, personal communication).

While research on therapists encounters many problems, it too should be done. What is the relation between the therapist's ego level and his therapeutic ideology? A difficulty in researching this question is the large number of therapeutic ideologies, the variety of dimensions they differ on, and the different inter-

pretations within each ideology. (Consider the difference between my interpretation of psychoanalysis and the received
opinion.) What is the relation between the therapist's ego level
and the success of therapy? All the problems of studying effectiveness of therapy would be obstacles here. An important variant of this topic concerns the relation of therapist's ego level to
patient's ego level as a factor in therapy. Is the best therapist
always the one with highest ego level, or should therapist's ego
level be matched to that of patient? Grant and Grant (1959)
have studied the effectiveness of different supervisory teams in
treating young delinquents in the Navy. The criterion was successful return to duty. Their subjects were classified according
to high and low ego level; supervisory teams were classed according to predicted effectiveness, without specification of
what entered the prediction. Ego level was presumably one
component in predicting effectiveness. Subjects with high ego
level responded best to teams of highest predicted efficiency,
but the relation was reversed for offenders of low ego level. This
finding confirms differential effectiveness of different kinds of
therapists according to the offender's ego level. Related research
on differential treatment of juvenile delinquents according to
their ego level by Warren (1969) and Palmer (1974) is continuing in the California Youth Authority and elsewhere. Optimal
relation of therapist's to patient's ego level presumably connects
with the theory of the pacer.

Even more embarrassing than research on therapists is
examination of the therapists' supervisors. Suppose a Conformist or a Self-Protective person is a training analyst, a member of
a committee to select candidates for training, or a social work
supervisor. An issue might arise that the person in subordinate
position, whether patient or candidate, saw as a matter of conscience. If the therapist or supervisor was of lower ego level, he
might interpret guilt feelings or scruples as symptoms to be removed. The result would be an impasse in which the patient or
candidate would rarely be given the benefit of the doubt. The
considerations in this book give no solutions to such problems,
but they do provide ways of looking at them. Some persons in a
position to match patients and therapists or supervisors and
trainees might find such considerations useful.

One arena that has been neglected in this book is application to politics and large social issues. A frequent student comment runs as follows: "Since the world is in so much trouble nowadays, are you not obligated to devote yourself to raising the general ego level?" By way of answer, first we must admit that the nature of relations between ego development and social institutions broader than the family is a theme that has been relatively neglected. Hobhouse, Dewey and Tufts, Riesman, Fromm, and Erikson are exceptions, but of that group, only Erikson has had a conception of ego development at all close to ours. As to the pressing question of social reform or even social survival, there is no proof that a modest rise in the general ego level will accomplish that. Moreover, one can hardly undertake to raise the ego level of an elected or appointed official while he is in office, and raising a man's ego level before he assumes office might prevent him from being chosen. There are, after all, a wide variety of candidates of all ego levels who aspire to public office. Furthermore, no one knows how to assist ego development effectively, nor do the advocates of higher ego level have a means of access to formative institutions. The world could be incinerated or its resources exhausted in less time than it would take to learn how to foster ego development through the public school system and to have such a program accepted over the protests of those who would consider it radical and subversive.

The only major way the conception can be applied usefully in the political arena appears to be by calculating how one can appeal to different segments of the population without offending others. While this application may have a manipulative ring, it is not necessarily so. There are in every generation politicians gifted at appealing to their fellow citizens' basest and most self-serving instincts, and they are often successful both at being elected to office and in stirring up destructive social unrest. The question is, can one ever be both right and President? The possibility is raised that a sophisticated knowledge of the conceptual, moral, and ego structure of large segments of the population may be helpful. Studies such as those of Tapp and Kohlberg (1971), Adelson (1971), and Hess and Torney (1967), directed specifically to political and legal ideologies, can be of assistance. Theory postulates a certain ethical safeguard, for in principle persons of higher ego level have access to the mode of reasoning of those of lower ego level, while those of lower ego level can only translate the motives of persons of high ego level into their own terms, thus misunderstanding them. Hence dissemination of theory of ego development in principle ought to assist candidates of high ego level, but not those of low ego level.

Standing back and painting with a broad brush, one can discern and sketch four main schools in contemporary psychology: behaviorist-psychometric, psychoanalytic, cognitive-structural, and humanistic. The enterprise projected in this book is impossible without drawing from all of them. By the same fact, we cannot commit ourselves to the program of any of them, at least as interpreted by purists or devotees.

Like the behaviorists, I strive to be clear about the difference between what is observed and what is inferred; empirical research should be conducted at a minimal inferential level. I part company with behaviorists when they turn from methodological precision to a doctrine that only specific stimuli and specific responses are real, or are proper topics for scientific investigation. The behavioristic ideology, which is nominalistic and antitheoretical (Chapter Ten), is not a scientific conclusion from evidence but a philosophical presupposition, and one that is incompatible with our enterprise. What we are talking about in this book is within the organism, where pure behaviorists would forbid us to look.

The psychometric approach is closely related to the behavioristic one (though behavioristic therapists join psychoanalytic ones in insisting on the importance of single-case reports, which is uncongenial to the statistical mind). A rigorous approach to assessment of ego development and related variables has been sufficiently stressed (chapters Eight and Nine). Perhaps my most distinctive contribution has been devising a means for the mutual feedback of theory and measurement. But the typically psychometric approach, measuring polar traits and analyzing them through methods based on the general linear hypothesis, eclipses the topic of this book. Our central conception would never emerge from such studies (Chapter Ten).

Our conception of ego development is that of a transformation of structures. To that extent it would appear to be part of the cognitive-structural school of psychology, particularly in the Piagetian tradition. But as Chapter Three shows, structuralism, when pursued to its logical extreme, is antihumanistic, leading to a denial of human freedom and having no place for consciousness and choice. We part company with the structuralists at that point. As Freud noted, to deny consciousness is to deny the one thing we are surest of, our original observation, our portal of entry.

The humanistic school of psychology has in recent years been presented as an alternative to the behavioristic-psychometric school on the one hand and the psychoanalytic school on the other. I may not agree with all of their objections to those schools, from which I have drawn and to which I have ties. At the same time, ego development is not ultimately intelligible without some locus of choice or agency within the person, a spontaneous striving for development (Adler), a proactive tendency (Allport, 1960), a teleology of the subject (Ricoeur). Psychoanalysis has shown that we often deceive ourselves about the extent of our freedom and about the determinants of our choices. Nonetheless, neither psychoanalysis nor other psychotherapies would work if consciousness did not matter or if there were no truth to our feelings of self-determination.

My thesis in relation to psychoanalysis is complex. What was original in Freud's contribution, I have shown, is what is usually missed, not only by the lay public but also by professionals who learn psychoanalytic theory by rote. Virtually all the elements often called Freud's discoveries came from the public domain, and most of them are to be found in far less consequential work, such as that of Janet. Freud supplied the articulation of a paradigm, a theory that united present with past, diagnosis with treatment, pathogenesis with normal development, the trivial and senseless with the most meaningful aspects of life, all accounted for with the same few principles. Each paradigm began with a great discovery. Central to the trauma paradigm was psychic determinism and the dynamic unconscious. The drive paradigm began with the formula for the interpretation of dreams and with infantile sexuality. The discovery of mastery through reversal from passive to active is central for the ego paradigm. Curiously, the most central terms of the drive paradigm are the most difficult to translate, raising the question touched on in Chapter Three, to what extent language shapes our conceptions, as opposed to merely naming them. With the changes in paradigm, not only theory but also therapeutic method have evolved. Relations between psychoanalysis as therapy and theoretical problems of ego development have been investigated from various angles by theorists such as Erikson, Loewald, and Ricoeur. Pivotal to all of Freud's work is the assumption that a single paradigm covers normal and abnormal mental life and behavior. To the extent that the concepts and principles of the Hartmann-Rapaport school sacrifice that position, I reject them. Our stage conception of ego development is, like psychoanalysis, in principle universally applicable (Chapter Eight). What psychoanalysts call their structural theory lacks an essential element of what psychologists call *structuralism*, namely, equilibration (Chapter Three). Importation of cognitive principles into psychoanalytic theory can enrich and deepen its therapy (chapters Twelve and Fifteen).

Conceptions of ego development within contemporary psychology that are built around an experimental or psychometric research method lack the explanatory theoretical power of psychoanalysis. Therapy, of course, is itself an investigatory tool—many would say a more powerful one than is available in the laboratory, though limited by its narrow sampling base. Whether or in what ways psychological research can benefit from psychoanalytic theory is not clear. If, however, psychological research is not an end in itself but a means to a greater understanding of persons, then psychological and psychoanalytic currents can both contribute to our knowledge of ego development. Indeed, even the vein of philosophical theorizing (Chapter Eleven) may not have been mined of all its riches yet.

What then has been presented in this book? It is not an eclectic amalgam, for it has a logic and a structure of its own. Is it another school of psychology, to compete with those just named? To the extent that "ego development" becomes a school, I should count this book a failure. What I have tried to present and to help create is something like a paradigm, a disciplinary matrix, having distinctive methods, its own history, schematized in Figure 8, a body of theory, gradually accumulating bodies of data, and growing possibilities for practical uses. What I find missing in the work of my fellow-laborers in this vineyard is a well-articulated feedback loop between theory and data.* The techniques for that feedback embodied in our sentence completion manual construction may not be directly usable for those working with other assessment devices; at least the problem should be recognized. One can hardly call oneself a scientist if there is no way to alter theory in response to data.

There is, I acknowledge, a tension in our conception of science. A scientific paradigm is shaped by its data and in turn shapes them. No simple Baconian program for data accumulation nor hypothetico-deductive program for disconfirmation of hypotheses encompasses that dialectic, still less a program based on factor analysis, multiple discriminant analysis, or random computer searches of data. There is a corresponding tension in our conception of people, not surprisingly, since scientists are people. Much as we have learned about how the structure of character evolves and is maintained, there will always be more. I do not count as failure but as an act of courage to admit that the heart of the matter is and always will be a mystery, opaque to the scientific glance.

Here, then, is what I aspire to do: to help establish a subdiscipline within psychology that inherits some of the wisdom of philosophical psychology, that unites the discoveries of psychoanalytic ego psychology with contemporary stage-type conceptions of personality, and that has its own research methods and sphere of applications. This book is meant to help create a paradigm by giving it a local habitation and a name.

---

*Rest (1975) quotes Kohlberg as labeling Rest's work as part of the Minnesota tradition of "dust-bowl empiricism," comparing it to the atheoretical derivation of the MMPI. But even in Rest's case, as I think he would agree, the scoring scheme is entirely a priori. Thus neither Rest nor Kohlberg has made any provision for letting data alter theory.

Appendix

Current Research and Some Prospects

with Augusto Blasi

A field of psychology is shaped not by official pronounce-ments nor even by abstract logic but by the interests and activi-ties of its most vigorous research workers. Several research pro-grams now under way have been undertaken within a frame of reference similar to the one of this book, but they lead in new directions not yet fully integrated with the point of view pre-sented herein. Research in this field is intrinsically a long-term endeavor, and some important work may not eventuate in pub-lications for quite awhile. The primary intent of this appendix is to give a glimpse of the conceptual content of some ongoing activities.*

*We wish to thank John Broughton, Lawrence Kohlberg, Harry Lasker, and Robert Selman for many stimulating discussions and for permis-sion to refer to their unpublished work.

435

Selman on Interpersonal Perspective Taking

The chief aim in the research of Robert Selman and his colleagues in the Harvard-Judge Baker Social Reasoning project is
to delineate growth in reasoning about interpersonal relations,
particularly in terms of the capacity to take the perspective of
others in interpersonal situations. Selman sees this capacity as
the crucial element of what this book has called ego development. The chief elements in Selman's conception of development of interpersonal relations are subjectivity (that is, an
understanding of covert thoughts and feelings), self-awareness,
personality, and the nature of interpersonal ties per se. Although originally he put great emphasis on the importance of
the cognitive capacity to take the perspective of another, currently he appears to be putting more stress on content, with
perspective taking as just one element. Let us look at Selman's
stages, then examine his method of assessment.

The youngest children have no clear conception of subjectivity as characteristic of persons. Thus they are puzzled and
worried about clowns or puppets, who they know are not people but who are objectively present. This is the presubjective
period, not represented in Selman's research but included for
completeness.

Selman's level zero is the level of egocentric perspective
taking. Here the child, typically of preschool age, knows that
others have thoughts and feelings as he does, but he does not
clearly differentiate theirs from his. The physical self and the
psychological or subjective self are not clearly differentiated,
and questions about thoughts and feelings are responded to in
terms of actions or appearances. Interpersonal relations are defined either in physical terms or in terms of egocentric wishes:
A friend is someone who lives near you, or who has nice toys.

Level one, subjective perspective taking, is typical for early
elementary school age. Here the child sees people as interpreting
social events, and he differentiates the perspective of self from
other. However, he perceives only one perspective at a time, and
that is specific to the context. Thus, while he understands that
someone else may have a different view of an event than his

own, he does not allow for mixed feelings, which would imply two perspectives within a person, nor for reciprocal interactions. One person acts, the other evaluates; they do not take each other's feelings into account. Generalized traits or attitudes are not formulated; questions calling for them are answered in terms of responses to specific situations. A friend may be defined as someone that you play with.

Level two, self-reflective perspective taking, is characteristic for children in the upper elementary grades. At this level the child can entertain more than one subjective perspective at a time. In consequence, he understands reciprocity. Not only do each person's actions affect the other's feelings, two people may react to each other's intentions and feelings. That makes it possible to see the self from the perspective of another, hence a growth in self-awareness. Further, one person can have more than one perspective on an event, hence one may experience inner conflict. The self one shows to others may not be one's real or true self. Typically, friends are people who like each other.

Level three, third-person perspective taking, characterizes the preadolescent child. After multiple perspectives, the next step is to take the view of a disinterested spectator or "generalized other," in Mead's term. By taking an outside perspective, the child can see himself as responding to the other's subjective feelings simultaneously with seeing the other's reaction to his subjective perspective. This opens the way to moving from reciprocity to mutual interests. There is a growth in distance from self and in reflection on one's own social actions. People, the child now sees, are more than a succession of specific actions; there is a continuing self or personality with generalized traits, underlying and accounting for behavior. These traits are, however, conceived in stereotyped terms. A friendship is a continuing relation, not broken because of one small fight.

At level four, the adolescent moves to qualitative systems in conceptions of persons and their relations. Personality and interpersonal relations are seen as having depth and complexity. People are seen as having differentiated traits, attitudes, and values. Interpersonal relations differ qualitatively, being deep or superficial, for example. Moreover, a person operates at different levels of awareness, so that, for example, he may be unaware of how he affects others or even of some aspects of his own personality. Going beyond multiple perspectives, the person may assume an abstract or hypothetical perspective, such as that of society or of the legal system. Close friendship may mean sharing intimate secrets.

Selman's highest level is that of symbolic interaction. Here conceptions of persons and of interpersonal relations merge in a complex process. A relationship can be seen as part of a personality structure, and a person's subjective sense of himself may be seen as tied to his relationship with others.

Thus subjectivity of thoughts, feelings, and motives emerges clearly at level one, awareness of self at level two, and a conception of personality at level three. At each level beyond that at which it first emerges clearly, there is a further delineation of the conceptions of subjectivity, self-awareness, and personality, the three characteristics uniquely attaching to persons. At each level there is also a characteristic view of the relations between persons.

Selman's chief instrument is a set of six interpersonal dilemmas, suitable for a younger age than Kohlberg's test, preferably presented on an audiovisual tape, then followed with a structured interview. The following story is an example (Selman, 1974, p. 10):

> Tom has just saved some money to buy Mike Hunter a birthday present. He and his friend Greg go downtown to try to decide what Mike will like. Tom tells Greg that Mike is sad these days because Mike's dog Pepper ran away. They see Mike and decide to try to find out what Mike wants without asking him right off. After talking to Mike for a while the kids realize that Mike is really sad because of his lost dog. When Greg suggests he get a new dog, Mike says *he can't just get a new dog and have things be the same.* Then Mike leaves to run some errands. As Mike's friends shop some more they see a puppy for sale in the pet store. It is the last one left. The owner says

that the puppy will probably be sold by tomorrow. Tom and Greg discuss whether to get Mike the puppy. Tom has to decide right away. What do you think Tom will do?

The child, who is interviewed individually, is first asked what he thinks Tom, the boy who is buying the birthday present, will do, and why. Then there follows a set of standard questions, relating to conceptions of persons and their subjectivity, to self-awareness, to personality, and to relations between persons. The questions are graded in difficulty in order to bring out the successive stages. Thus, in the puppy story, the child is asked about Mike's feelings, whether he could feel both happy and sad, how people can know other people's feelings, and so on. As in Piaget's *methode clinique*, the interviewer is charged with probing further when the import of the subject's response is not clear. The intent is not to measure memory or understanding per se, and parts of the story are repeated if necessary.

The primary emphasis in Selman's group has been on developing the foregoing scheme of stages together with a scoring manual for the test. The project is now also studying the development of interpersonal perspective taking longitudinally in normal and disturbed children between the ages of six and fourteen years, relating it to development of logical reasoning as measured by Piagetian tasks and moral judgment as measured by Kohlberg's test. Finally, they are interested in evolving intervention strategies to encourage development in moral and social reasoning in normal children and those with learning disabilities.

Selman views logical reasoning as deep structure with respect to which interpersonal perspective taking is content; interpersonal perspective taking is deep structure with respect to moral judgment as content. However, those theoretical relationships do not predict empirical results with respect to tests of those capacities with any certainty, because tasks designated at a particular level may vary in difficulty. Nonetheless, Selman has constructed hypothesized relations between the domains he has measured in his studies and then examined the data obtained with normal and disturbed children in relation to those hypotheses.[1] Stages of interpersonal perspective and of moral reasoning, he has shown, do indeed lag behind the stage of cognitive reasoning, more so in the case of the disturbed children than of a matched normal group. However, the hypothesis that interpersonal relations are the structure or groundwork for moral stages receives no support in his data; indeed, appreciably more cases appear to be advanced in moral reasoning with respect to their own interpersonal perspective taking than the other way around, the discrepancy again being more marked with clinic children. Some, though by no means all, clinic children lag behind their age-mates in development of interpersonal perspective taking. Thus, these data suggest that in some cases the behavioral disturbance may be a result of faulty development of the specific capacity that Selman is measuring. That finding provides a rationale for the development of intervention strategies to encourage growth in those capacities.

Evidently Selman's conception of interpersonal perspective taking has much in common with the conception of ego development in this book; it would be of interest to us even if it did no more than trace aspects of ego development in greater detail than other conceptions have done. Selman's conception is richer than ours or Kohlberg's in its delineation of early stages. Moreover, Selman has an excellent technique for obtaining a sample of behavior from young children, with whom neither the sentence completion test nor Kohlberg's test is usable without modification. At the same time, Selman's test can be used with adults and provides a measure of individual differences among them.

Selman's conception appears to be closer to that of ego development than to that of moral development; his test, however, is more similar to Kohlberg's than to the sentence completion test. Because of its hybrid nature, it may provide an especially valuable link between moral and ego development as

[1]R. L. Selman, "Toward a Structural Analysis of Developing Interpersonal Relationship Concepts: Research with Normal and Disturbed Preadolescent Boys," in A. Pick (Ed.), *Minnesota Symposia on Child Psychology*, Vol. 10 (Minneapolis: University of Minnesota Press, in press).

represented in current research. One of the central themes of this book has been our contention that there is but one major source for all of the conceptions of moral and ego development, one thread of reality to which all of the conceptions give varying access. Kohlberg, on the other hand, sees ego development as prior to moral development. Although Selman has appeared to side with Kohlberg on this issue, his own data now appear to support our view. His data provide no evidence that interpersonal perspective taking leads moral development. Some data suggest the opposite relation, but because results are mixed, the hypothesis that they are both aspects of a single variable cannot be rejected.

Broughton on Natural Epistemologies

John Broughton's chief interest is in the development of what he calls *natural epistemologies*. Just as Kohlberg sees the child as a moral philosopher, so Broughton sees the child as a metaphysician, a psychologist, and above all an epistemologist. The major aim of Broughton's work is to trace the stages in the development of that natural epistemology. His work has drawn on that of Baldwin, particularly the four-volume work on "genetic logic" (1906-1915), on that of Piaget, particularly his early books, and on that of Perry (1970). Broughton's interviews are lengthy, two to four hours. He presents each child with a set of questions followed by standard follow-up or probe questions, adapted as necessary to clarify the subject's meaning. We will look first at his final formulation of stages, then examine the format of his research.

At the lowest level, level zero, children of preschool age think of self as "inside" and reality as "outside." Thoughts are not distinguished from their objects.

At level one, about five or six years of age, the self is the physical body, and bodily movement changes the self. Active and passive movements are not differentiated. Thinking, however, changes the self without moving the body. Thoughts are invisible but distinct from their objects. What is real must be visible or tangible, so thoughts are intrinsically paradoxical.

Mind (or brain) controls the self, telling the body what to do. But the body also moves itself; so mind's control of body is equivalent to self-control. Broughton explicitly points out that at this level the relation of mind or brain to body is that of authority; he invokes (presumably following his subjects) a metaphor of a big person and a little person. (Compare the discussion of the *personification of inner forces* in Chapter Seventeen.) There is no distinction between reality and appearance, so that people are assumed to see and feel things alike. Differences in perception can only be mistakes. This is the stage of naive realism.

Level two, naive subjectivism, occurs at about ages seven to twelve years. Mind and body are differentiated at this level; the self is an individual person, including both mind and body. The self or mind includes the person's reactions to and ideas about things. Individuality resides in the uniqueness of those reactions and opinions. Knowledge is personal, so that the distinction between facts and opinions or hypotheses is blurred.

At level three, occurring at about ages eleven through seventeen, and characterized as divided or spiritual, appearances are differentiated from reality. The social personality or role is seen as a false outer appearance, different from the true inner self. The conscious mind is distinguished from subconscious mental processes. Social corroboration or consensus is seen as the means of finding the reality behind appearances, but that leaves reality and truth quite arbitrary. While hypothesis is distinguished from fact, abstractions tend to be reified. The self is what the person's nature normally is; it is a kind of essence and remains itself over changes in mental contents. The normal person is seen as conscious and controlled, contrasting with abnormal and unconscious. The self is not assumed to be automatically aware of itself, as at earlier levels; one can surprise or scare oneself. Thus reflective self-awareness appears at this level.

At level four, which appears in late adolescence and is characterized as dualist or positivist, the person becomes capable of logical systems of thought, of hypothesis and deductions from hypotheses. The self or mind is seen as a construct postulated to explain patterns of behavior. On the other hand, mind at this level may be conceived of in terms of its physico-chemical basis. Thus mind may be a caused effect or an uncaused cause.

In another version of level four, which Broughton calls level four and a half to preserve a parallel with Kohlberg's levels, thought takes a skeptical or even cynical turn. The self, rather than being an abstract postulate lending unity and integrity to personality, experience, and behavior, is simply identified with the experience and the behavior. The person is a cybernetic system guided to fulfillment of its material wants. At this level, radical emphasis on seeing everything within a relativistic or subjective frame of reference leaves the person close to a solipsistic position. Following Kohlberg, Broughton leans toward considering this level as following level four, but he leaves open the possibility that it may be an alternative version of four, occupying the same place in the developmental sequence. Even if it is an outgrowth of level four, the question is unsettled as to whether it is a necessary step in the progress from level four to level five.

At level five the self as observer is distinguished from the self-concept as known; the inner self as chooser is distinguished from the inner self as impulse or desire. The physiological body is recognized as a conceptual construction just as mind is. Problems of reality and knowledge are conceived in terms of method and perspective. Reality is defined by the coherence or utility of the interpretive framework.

At Broughton's highest level, level six, mind and body are both experiences of an integrated self. What is true is a judgment, a construction of what may be universally experienced under properly controlled conditions.

For his pilot study, Broughton interviewed ten persons between the ages of ten and twenty-four. Beginning with Baldwin's conceptions, he outlined a preliminary set of questions about self, mind, reality, and knowledge. Some examples of his questions are: "What is the self?" "What is the mind?" "Is the mind part of the body?" "What parts of the body are parts of the self?" "Does the self control the body or the body control the self?" "What is a thought?" "How do you know things?"

"Is there a real world?" "How do you know the world is real?" Using data from his pilot study, he revised both his interview and his definition of the stages. The outline for the questionnaire for the main study included about 100 such questions. Subjects were four boys and four girls in each of grades four, eight, and twelve, plus six college undergraduates and six graduate students. Following the main study, definitions of levels were again revised on the basis of the data collected. The above summary is far from giving the flavor of Broughton's sketches of the levels; he devotes many pages to delineating the thinking of each level.

Broughton has been more explicit than most authors about the process by which he arrived at his sketches of stage-types. He sought self-consistent clusters of related ideas in the interviews. The description within each stage-type draws upon ideas at the same level of abstraction; all types are concerned with the same topics; and each type can be seen in a logical sequence with the others. Thus each type is sketched in relation to all the others. To advance from these ideal types to a structure of true stages, Broughton requires that there be shown a single formal principle from whose transformations each type and the ideas in each subdomain can be derived.

Broughton has validated his scheme as follows: Within the interviews there are three subdomains—self, mind and body, and epistemology and ontology—that can be scored separately. He has shown that scores on the subdomains are highly correlated. Moreover, scores advance with age, and relations with other domains that are theoretically reasonable have been demonstrated. Level of epistemology tends to lag behind the level of logical thinking as measured by a Piagetian test but to run in advance of level of moral judgment as measured by Kohlberg's test. While these relations are not perfect, Broughton showed that the hypothesis that the domains are independent and the hypothesis that they develop synchronously must be rejected, thus establishing that there is some form of asynchrony.

Summarizing, Broughton has validated his construct in terms of logical coherence within level, logical sequentiality of levels, empirical confirmation of internal consistency within levels, correlation with age, and empirical confirmation of logical relations with other domains. The final criterion, he recognizes, is empirical confirmation of sequentiality of levels by means of a longitudinal study. That is one direction of his future research.

Broughton has criticized our conception of ego development for confusing the self with the ego, or, more concretely, for confusing reflecting on objects with reflecting on the self. For him, certain aspects of our Conscientious Stage and of higher stages, such as interest in reflexive traits and in the distinction between appearance and reality, are set apart from the other traits of those stages. Our method of stage definition, growing out of the sentence completion test, did not constrain the elements of the definition to be in the same domain or of the same level of abstraction, as his method does. Although both his method and ours use data and although both use the criterion of logical coherence, our method is heavily weighted toward data, his toward logic. More evidence is needed than he has yet presented to establish that the epistemological subdomain develops asynchronously with respect to the rest of the domain of ego development.

In a sense Broughton and Selman are competing for the same niche, namely, that of a fundamental, more or less cognitive capacity that provides the deep structure for which moralization of judgment is the surface structure or content. Both have oriented their work primarily with reference to Kohlberg's, though in neither case is the value of the work contingent on its relation to Kohlberg's. (In Selman's case, he has even adopted some of the arbitrary facets of Kohlberg's scoring algorithm.) Both have adapted Piaget's *methode clinique*. So far they do not appear to have tried relating their work to each other's. Judging by the excessive length of his interviews, which must be trying for some subjects, Broughton has not yet accepted the conventional psychometric logic that a domain can be assessed without exhaustive exploration of it, by drawing a suitable sample of behaviors. The logic of sampling has served well in heterogeneous domains; it must hold with even greater force in domains as structured as these are.

Blasi on Responsibility

Augusto Blasi's central interest has been the development of responsibility. Like Selman and Broughton he has adapted Piaget's method of structured interview, and like them he has explored a domain more narrowly defined and more coherently structured than the whole of ego development. In a sense his work lies on the other side of Kohlberg's from that of Selman's and Broughton's. Moral judgment can be looked at as structure, within which what the person feels responsible for becomes content.

Blasi originally saw the connection between ego development and development of responsibility in terms of a dimension of internality-externality. Ego development can be summarily described as proceeding from an external approach to oneself and the world (dependence on external sources of reinforcement, being subject to external stimulation and immediate impulses, lack of insight into oneself, projection of blame onto others and onto the world in general) to a progressive interiorization of one's experience, interests, and control (for example, awareness of and focus on thoughts, desires, and motives; emphasis on self-reliance, competence, and autonomy). Responsibility, as commonly understood, is an aspect of this inclusive dimension. Moreover, evidence obtained with the sentence completion test shows that persons at different ego stages tend to approach responsibility differently: at the preconformist stages responsibility is either externalized or not recognized at all; at the Conformist Stage it is accepted but rigidly focused on rules and authority; at the Conscientious Stage and above it is oriented toward the self.

Reflecting on the concept of responsibility in relation to philosophical traditions, Blasi has now refined his definition of it. Responsibility is that relation of necessity that an individual establishes or recognizes between himself and his own action, before the action takes place as well as after it has been performed. The relation between the person and the action before it is performed corresponds to the notion of obligation and is an answer to the question, "Do I have to act in such and such a way?" The relation between the person and the action already performed involves ownership and corresponds to the notion of accountability. The question is, "Is this action necessarily mine?" The key element in the definition is necessity. There are other kinds of relations between an individual and his action, such as seemliness, desirability for him, or simple physical causality. Only when the action is recognized by the person as necessarily his, either in the sense that he must perform it or in the sense that the performed action is forever part of his moral experience, is there responsibility.

Since responsibility, by definition, consists in establishing relations of consistency between self and actions, the structure of responsibility must be related logically to the basic rules presiding over the definition of oneself as a person and determining the meaning that one has for himself and that the world has for him. Those rules correspond to what this book has called ego structure. Because a person understands himself to be essentially and unequivocally thus and so—his self-definition, he also understands the actions that are related to his essential characteristics to be necessarily his—his responsibility. The obligation to act may come from different sources, such as authority, social pressure, his conscience, or the person himself; responsibility, nonetheless, is ultimately always a response of the ego (or of the person) that defines him as necessarily related to that source of obligation. Research on responsibility should help to clarify two aspects of ego development: first, the definition of the central element or structural core of ego stages; second, the manner in which the ego extends into and is expressed by action.

In the approach of Kohlberg, Selman, and Broughton is an implicit criticism of the conception of ego development presented in this book—that the structural properties of the stages and the inner logic of the developmental sequence have not been specified. A consequence of this vagueness is that at times it may be difficult to decide whether certain characteristics are part of the ego or simply happen to be correlated with it (a topic discussed in Chapter Eight). In part, this vagueness is a consequence of the fact that the structural properties of the ego are not the same as those of logical or mathematical structures (Chapter Three), but it also results from treating the ego as all-inclusive and as like a single organ, as well as from the empirical approach to its measurement. That approach has uncovered the richness of the ego and its transformations; it may now be time to focus on a single aspect to help isolate the logical properties and the essential structure of the stages. The self-concept or self-definition is a candidate for that role; search for stage-characteristic rules of responsibility is one way of studying self-definition.

In the long run, the importance of and interest in ego development will depend on understanding how ego stages are expressed in action, as opposed to how they are expressed in sentence completions or other verbal statements. Predicting action from personality has always constituted a problem for psychology, whether approached from the angle of attitudes and values or from that of moral judgment. Relations between the domain of mental structures and that of behavior are not immediate or simple. A theory of the links between the domains and their articulation is needed. Study of responsibility and its development may provide such a theory, though actions determined by responsibility are not the only category of actions affected by ego stages.

A by-product to look for in such a study is a better understanding of the relations between Loevinger's conception of ego development and Kohlberg's domain of moral judgment. The nature of those relations is not clarified by the empirical correlations between measures, nor by Loevinger's hypothesis of a one-organ system, nor by Kohlberg's hypothesis of a necessary-but-insufficient relation. What is needed is an analysis of functional relations both in concrete instances, such as performance of moral actions, and in development.

In Blasi's first study (1971, 1976) groups of sixth-grade children were sorted according to their ego level as measured by the sentence completion test. Each group was presented with stories giving dilemmas that had to be acted out, with different children playing different roles. Each story aimed at a particular ego level. For children at the Impulsive Stage, training toward parent-independent responsibility was considered appropriate; for those at the Self-Protective Stage, training toward rule-oriented responsibility; for those at the Conformist Stage, training toward spirit-of-the-law responsibility; for those beyond the Conformist Stage, training toward self-oriented responsibility. The experimental design called for some groups to receive appropriate training; others were to receive training that was too high or too low for their own level. The hypothesis was that only training at the appropriate level would be effective. However, the experiment only lasted two weeks, and in that time not enough change occurred to provide an adequate test of the hypothesis. (We return below to some results of this study.) In addition to acting out the dilemmas, the children were asked to soliloquize on the reasons for the hero's actions and to exchange roles, with those who played the hero on one occasion asked to play the authority on another, and so on. Thus, although the experiment did not succeed in its original purpose, it provided a good deal of insight into the structure of children's thinking about responsibility.

Current work takes the following form: The Responsibility Story Test consists of a number of stories, each accompanied by a semi-standardized interview schedule, administered to each child individually. A story is presented in three sections. In the first, the hero is confronted with a dilemma, say between obedience and altruism, or between personal desire and keeping a promise. The subject is asked what the hero should do and why, and particularly whether the hero really has to do something and why. Thus, responsibility here is studied as influencing judgments of strict obligation for an action yet to be performed. In sections two and three accountability, the other side of responsibility, is studied by describing first the hero's negative or bad action and its risk of being discovered, and by presenting then the negative consequences of the action, such as punishment or loss of friendship. Questions here aim at discovering the subject's thinking about accepting one's actions and their consequences and about the referent of accountabil-

ity, such as authority, law, others in general, or oneself. The
following illustrative story is taken from Form A, intended for
early elementary school children:

> Part 1: One day mother had gone out to buy
> some groceries and had left John and his little brother
> David alone at home. John was watching his favorite
> show on TV, while David was playing by himself with
> a chair. At one point John saw that David was trying
> to climb on the chair: he was very little and might
> have fallen. Perhaps John should go and take him
> away; but he did not want to miss any of the show,
> especially now. John did not know what to do: help
> his brother or keep watching the show.

> Part 2: John wanted to see the end of the show
> and decided to stay in front of the TV set. But before
> the end David fell, and the chair fell with him. He was
> still crying when their mother came back. She then
> asked John what had happened.

> Part 3: Mother was not happy with what John
> had done, and she told him that he could not watch
> TV for two days. John did not like that and told his
> mother that she was not being fair and that she did
> not like him.

The dilemmas in Form A concern desire versus obedience,
desire versus responsibility, desire versus altruism, obedience
versus altruism, and desire versus keeping a promise. In Form B,
intended for grades three through eight, a dilemma is added,
altruism versus the law, and the specific content is adapted to
be age-appropriate. In Form C, intended for high school and
college, the same dilemmas as Form B are presented with the
specific content again changed, and a dilemma is added on altruism versus personal development. From this instrument the following information is obtained: (a) what the hero of the stories
should do and why, (b) what, if anything, the hero really must
do and why, (c) how the hero should handle his misbehavior,

and (d) how the relation between action and sanction is perceived, or whether blame is accepted or rejected.

In order of increasing maturity, the reasons children give for a necessary action have been found to be: punishment or physical consequences; social relations and social motives, such as reciprocity or friendship; and considerations based on contract or commitment. The following are some examples of how various orientations toward responsibility are expressed in the interviews:

Punishment: "A mother really has to cook or else my father yells at her."

Physical consequences: "You must go to school or you won't get a job—you'll have no money and no food."

Social reciprocity: "I would want someone to help me if I were in trouble; you have a responsibility since you may be in the same position." "My mother must make my father happy, because he makes her happy."

Authority: "It's an authoritative atmosphere, this man knows his business; you must do what the boss asked: he's the holy divine."

Contract: "Her job has specifications which she's paid to follow; she has to do what is precisely and clearly stated in the job: a contract has to be followed."

Self-consistency, self-orientation: "The teacher chooses to be a teacher, therefore she must teach the best she can." "One has an obligation to oneself, one is driven to follow one's principles."

These categories of responsibility can easily be related on the one hand to stages of ego development and on the other to stages of moral reasoning. In many people, however, there is a gap between the criteria they apply in decisions about right and wrong and the application of the same criteria to decisions about responsibility. For example, in a group of first graders it was found that 95 percent understood and on occasion used social motives such as compassion and friendship as criteria for moral judgments, what one should do and why. Further, for 65 percent of them social motives were their dominant criteria.

However, only 30 percent of the children understood that an action may be necessary for reasons other than punishment. Blasi's research aims to explain this gap between moral judgment and responsibility.

Cross-Cultural Applications

The question of the universality of the ego development continuum is handled most convincingly by cross-cultural research. Considerable cross-cultural research, which has not been reported in detail, has been done with Kohlberg's test. However, some salient findings, and in particular the general applicability of the construct and the method, are apparent from the fragments reported in various of Kohlberg's articles (1969, 1971).

Two researchers have been using the sentence completion test of ego development in widely different cultures. Osamu Kusatsu has tested a number of Japanese groups. He has found wide and statistically significant differences in ego level characteristic of different occupational groups.

Harry Lasker began by studying the achievement motive using the Thematic Apperception Test, first in India, then in Curaçao in the Netherlands Antilles; the intent of this work was to find ways to stimulate achievement orientation. He found that treating all achievement themes alike, as the standard scoring system he was using dictated, obscured some interesting aspects of his data. There was, he found, a hierarchy of achievement themes, roughly paralleling the stages of ego development. Further, in Curaçao he found statistically significant differences in mean ego level corresponding to socioeconomic class differences. His attention thus turned to stimulating ego development. We will return to Lasker's Curaçao studies below.

The Process of Change

Probably the most powerful and convincing way to investigate any psychological phenomenon is to try to change it. Currently there is widespread interest in methods of intervention aimed at raising ego or moral level; indeed, not all such studies come within our purview, since they do not always have a research aim, nor do they always focus on conceptual issues.

Many studies have been done with the following format: A class, often of high school students, is pretested with one or more measures of ego or moral development. An experimental curriculum designed to increase ego or moral level is then used for one class period over a semester or a year. Then the tests are readministered. Studies of this type have been done by students of Ralph Mosher at Boston University and students of Norman Sprinthall and others at the University of Minnesota, among others. (Edwin Fenton of Carnegie-Mellon University is also active in curriculum development.) Often a significant rise in comparison with a control group has been demonstrated. In fact, so many curricula or programs have been validated by such studies that there is now a need to summarize and coordinate the results.

Kohlberg's paradigm for producing change was originally to have a class discuss moral dilemmas at regular intervals over a period of months.[2] The teacher or leader was instructed to lead the discussion so that arguments of the developmentally more advanced children were called to the attention of those putting forth more immature arguments, where possible confronting each stage with the next more advanced stage. Thus the more mature children served as pacers for the others. The leader presumably provided the pacer effect for the more mature children, but it is questionable whether the process is as effective for those ahead of the group as it is for the laggards.

When Kohlberg and his colleagues attempted to set up a moral discussion group in a prison (Kohlberg, Scharf, and Hickey, 1972), he found that the setting defeated his purpose. Generally, the men viewed themselves as operating at Kohlberg's level two, instrumental hedonism, but they viewed the institutional atmosphere as being at level one, punishment and obedience orientation. They concluded that it was impossible to stimulate moral growth under such unfavorable circumstances.

[2]M. Blatt, "The Effects of Classroom Discussion on the Development of Moral Judgment" (Ph.D. diss., University of Chicago, 1969).

Kohlberg calls the formula for change that he has now adopted the *just community* approach. In order to create a community that will be perceived as just by all its participants, control must be granted to the participants not just for a block of time but for the whole of the institutional arrangements. In a prison setting this means that inmates share with guards and supervisors the creation of the disciplinary and other rules and the responsibility for administering discipline. The first step is creating a constitution for the community, followed by deciding on specific rules, punishments for infractions, setting up disciplinary procedures, and so on. Discussion of moral dilemmas does not need to be introduced as an arbitrary exercise, since it comes about naturally in community meetings. For example, when there has been a serious breach of rules, such as stealing, destruction of property, or selling drugs, those who know the culprit may experience a conflict between their loyalty to their friend and their loyalty to the community or to its goals. The just community approach is now being tried in alternative schools as well as in prisons.

The disadvantage of this approach is that it requires an inordinate amount of time on the part of the staff as well as much time on the part of the participants. For example, in setting up the constitution, guidance is needed to keep it from becoming a set of specific rules. Later, in community meetings, guidance is needed to keep the group focused on genuine moral issues rather than being diverted to procedural issues. The balancing advantage is that the real-life conflicts and dilemmas continue to engage the participants when made-up stories begin to pall. Above all, the advantage of this approach is that a just community is a desirable thing, regardless of its relation to moral growth.

From a theoretical point of view, the interest in the just community lies in a kind of embodiment of the idea of equilibration. Particularly among those close to the Conformist Stage, as many inmates and many junior and senior high school students are, the weight of the community feeling generated by the institutional arrangements should be effective. For example, the frequent community meetings and group pressure to maintain the advantages of the community without offending higher authorities or the wider community in which the school or prison is situated must facilitate development to the Conformist Stage. The guiding idea of fairness or justice may serve as a pacer, facilitating the growth of those at the Conformist Stage in the direction of the Conscientious Stage. Opportunity to consider the feelings and points of view of others, to observe cognitive-moral conflict, and to participate in group decisions about moral issues should benefit various levels. However, participants who begin at the Conscientious Stage or higher probably benefit little in terms of moral or ego growth.

Blasi's experiment, referred to above, was designed to encourage growth in responsibility level, but it lasted only about ten hours for each group over a two week period. Thus, particularly as contrasted with the total change in institutional arrangement which Kohlberg now finds necessary, it was disproportionate to the task of changing ego level. However, some minimal changes that were observed are instructive. The most effective kind of training appeared to be that for independent responsibility. The first step is to move away from a literal interpretation of rules and orders, which requires the ability to distinguish between words and mind. Substeps include seeing laws in terms of their purposes rather than their form, identifying with the authority's mind and understanding the impossibility of foreseeing every eventuality, and comparing the relative importance of the purpose and the letter of the law. The next major step is to accept responsibility for acting against the letter of the law. Substeps include seeing that the subordinate may have to follow considerations more important than obedience, that the authority should accept that decision, and finally, accepting responsibility for negative consequences of an act of obedience. In moving toward a self-oriented responsibility, the major steps appear to be acquisition of a trait orientation, acquisition of self-standards, and orientation to the self as the main referent of responsibility.

Lasker found in his studies in Curaçao that a large proportion of the adult population, perhaps as much as one third, can be classed at the ego stage transitional between the Self-Protective and the Conformist stages. In collaboration with Victor Pinedo, under the auspices of the Humanas Foundation, Lasker has organized training courses designed to produce stage change. These courses, like Blasi's, are set up so that all participants in one group are of about the same stage, and they are recruited from a single work setting, which may be anything from a very large to a relatively small company. The training courses begin with an intensive session of a couple of days, then taper off, continuing at lengthening intervals for about six months. The activities of the course are adapted from many group therapy and group training techniques. What is of interest here is that Pinedo has traced the chain of conscious or preconscious convictions that accompany stage changes on the basis of far more extensive data than Blasi had available.

Pinedo's observations are most extensive and his training most effective in fostering transition into the Conformist Stage of persons at the Self-Protective-Conformist transitional level. In recognition of the still self-protective nature of the participants, the atmosphere created at first is one of safety and rewards. The person is encouraged to recognize his own strengths. Greater self-awareness and awareness of other people's feelings lead through exercises in role reversal to an understanding of reciprocity and hence to greater group feeling. Starting in another direction, Lasker has traced a succession of feelings that goes somewhat as follows: "I am important," "I am like other people," "I can be more like other people," "I want others to like me," "I want others to accept me," and finally, "I want to be part of a group."

Concentration on a single level, negotiating one particular transition, as Lasker has done, may bring out the essential structure of beliefs more sharply than other techniques. One limitation on his approach is that it is more suited to some transitions than others. The transition to the Conformist Stage may be its prime point of use because of the inherent fit or equilibrium between the group technique and the rewards of group approval. The other limitation of Lasker's method, when viewed as a research technique, lies in Broughton's observation that every stage must be defined in relation to every other one, which is difficult to combine with Lasker's approach. Whereas Broughton clearly, and to a lesser extent Selman and Blasi, attempt to reduce ego development to the transformations of a single coherent principle, Lasker uses himself simply as a transducer of other people's life-scripts. Thus Lasker's research is weighted more toward the empirical than toward the rational side. Perhaps the vagueness and irrationality for which the concept of ego development has been criticized will prove to be true to life. (All the work of the Humanas Foundation has been a close collaboration of Lasker and Pinedo. Pinedo has had primary responsibility for developing and using the training techniques.)

References

Adelson, J. "The Political Imagination of the Young Adolescent." *Daedulus,* 1971, *100,* 1013-1050.

Adorno, T. W., Frenkel-Brunswik, E., Levinson, D. J., and Sanford, R. N. *The Authoritarian Personality.* New York: Harper & Row, 1950.

Allport, G. W. *Personality: A Psychological Interpretation.* New York: Holt, Rinehart and Winston, 1937.

Allport, G. W. "The Ego in Contemporary Psychology." *Psychological Review,* 1943, *50,* 451-478.

Allport, G. W. "The Open System in Personality Theory." *Journal of Abnormal and Social Psychology,* 1960, *60,* 301-310.

Allport, G. W. *Pattern and Growth in Personality.* New York: Holt, Rinehart and Winston, 1961.

Altschule, M. D. *Roots of Modern Psychiatry.* New York: Grune and Stratton, 1965.

Amacher, P. "Freud's Neurological Education and its Influence on Psychoanalytic Theory." *Psychological Issues,* 1965, *4* (4, Whole No. 16).

Angell, J. R. "The Province of Functional Psychology." *Psychological Review,* 1907, *14,* 61-91.

Angyal, A. *Neurosis and Treatment: A Holistic Theory.* New York: Wiley, 1965.

Ansbacher, H. L., and Ansbacher, R. R. (Eds.) *The Individual Psychology of Alfred Adler.* New York: Basic Books, 1956.

Ausubel, D. P. *Ego Development and the Personality Disorders.* New York: Grune and Stratton, 1952.

Baer, D. M. "An Age-Irrelevant Concept of Development." *Merrill-Palmer Quarterly,* 1970, *16,* 238-245.

Bain, A. *The Emotions and the Will.* London: Longmans, 1859.

Baldwin, J. M. *Social and Ethical Interpretations in Mental Development.* New York: Macmillan, 1902. (Originally published in 1897.)

Baldwin, J. M. *Thought and Things: A Study of the Development and Meaning of Thought, or Genetic Logic.* New York: Arno Press, 1975. (Originally published 1906-1915.)

Barton, W. E. "Viewpoint of a Clinician." In M. Jahoda, *Current Concepts of Positive Mental Health.* New York: Basic Books, 1958.

Bell, S. M. "The Development of the Concept of Object as Related to Infant-Mother Attachment." *Child Development,* 1970, *41,* 291-311.

Bellak, L., Hurvich, M., and Gediman, H. K. *Ego Functions in Schizophrenics, Neurotics, and Normals: A Systematic Study of Conceptual, Diagnostic, and Therapeutic Aspects.* New York: Wiley, 1973.

Bentham, J. *Introduction to the Principles of Morals and Legislation.* Excerpts in M. Warnock (Ed.), *John Stuart Mill: Utilitarianism, On Liberty, Essay on Bentham, Together with Selected Writings of Jeremy Bentham and John Austin.* Cleveland: World Publishing, 1962. (Originally published in 1789.)

Berlyne, D. E. *Structure and Direction in Thinking.* New York: Wiley, 1965.

Blanck, G., and Blanck, R. *Ego Psychology: Theory and Practice.* New York: Columbia University Press, 1974.

Blasi, A. "A Development Approach to Responsibility Training." Unpublished doctoral dissertation, Washington University, 1971.

Blasi, A. "Role-Taking and the Development of Social Cognition." Paper presented at the American Psychological Association Convention, Chicago, Illinois, September 1975.

Blasi, A. "Personal Responsibility and Ego Development." In R. deCharms, *They Need Not Be Pawns: Toward Self-Direction in the Urban Classroom.* New York: Irvington Publishers, 1976.

Blasi, A., and Hoeffel, E. C. "Adolescence and Formal Operations." *Human Development,* 1974, *17,* 344-363.

Bleuler, E. "Das autistische Denken." *Jahrbuch für psychoanalytische und psychopathologische Forschungen,* 1912, *4,* 1-39.

Bleuler, E. *Textbook of Psychiatry.* New York: Macmillan, 1924. (Originally published in 1916.)

Bowers, K. S. "Situationism in Psychology: An Analysis and a Critique." *Psychological Review,* 1973, *80,* 307-336.

Brandt, L. W. "Some Notes on English Freudian Terminology." *Journal of the American Psychoanalytic Association,* 1961, *9,* 331-339.

Brandt, L. W. "Process or Structure?" *Psychoanalytic Review,* 1966, *53,* 374-378.

Breuer, J., and Freud, S. *Studies on Hysteria: Standard Edition.* Vol. 2. London: Hogarth Press, 1955. (Originally published in 1895.)

Broughton, J. M. "The Development of Natural Epistemology in Adolescence and Early Adulthood." Unpublished doctoral dissertation, Harvard University, 1975.

Bruch, H. "Transformation of Oral Impulses in Eating Disorders: A Conceptual Approach." *Psychiatric Quarterly,* 1961, *35,* 458-481.

Bruch, H. *Eating Disorders: Obesity, Anorexia Nervosa and the Person Within.* New York: Basic Books, 1973.

Brunswik, E. "The Conceptual Framework of Psychology." In *International Encyclopedia of Unified Science.* Vol. 1, Part 2. Chicago: University of Chicago Press, 1952.

Bull, N. J. *Moral Judgement from Childhood to Adolescence.* Beverly Hills, Calif.: Sage Publications, 1969.

Chein, I. *The Science of Behavior and the Image of Man.* New York: Basic Books, 1972.

Cohen, J. "Multiple Regression as a General Data-Analytic System." *Psychological Bulletin,* 1968, *70,* 426-443.

Comte, A. *Cours de philosophie positive.* Excerpts in H. D. Aiken (Ed.), *The Age of Ideology.* New York: Mentor, 1956. (Originally published in 1842.)

Cooley, C. H. *Human Nature and the Social Order.* Excerpts in C. Gordon and K. J. Gergen (Eds.), *The Self in Social Interaction.* Vol. 1. *Classic and Contemporary Perspectives.* New York: Wiley, 1968. (Originally published in 1902.)

Dahlstrom, W. G. *Personality Systematics and the Problem of Types.* Morristown, N.J.: General Learning Press, 1972.

Dember, W. N. "The New Look in Motivation." *American Scientist,* 1965, *53,* 409-427.

Dennis, W. *Readings in the History of Psychology.* New York: Appleton-Century-Crofts, 1948.

Dewey, J. "The Reflex Arc Concept in Psychology." *Psychological Review,* 1896, *3,* 357-370.

Dewey, J., and Tufts, J. H. *Ethics.* New York: Holt, Rinehart and Winston, 1908.

Dubos, R. "Biological Determinants of Individuality." In H. V. Kraemer (Ed.), *Youth and Culture: A Human-Development Approach.* Monterey, Calif.: Brooks/Cole, 1974.

Ekstein, R. "Psychoanalytic Techniques." In D. Brower and L. E. Abt (Eds.), *Progress in Clinical Psychology.* Vol. II. New York: Grune and Stratton, 1965.

Ellenberger, H. F. *The Discovery of the Unconscious.* New York: Basic Books, 1970.

Enright, J. B. "Thou Art That: Projection and Play in Therapy and Growth." *Psychotherapy: Theory, Research and Practice,* 1972, *9,* 153-156.

Erikson, E. H. *Childhood and Society*. New York: Norton, 1950.

Erikson, E. H. "The Problem of Ego Identity." *Journal of the American Psychoanalytic Association*, 1956, *4*, 56-121.

Erikson, E. H. *Childhood and Society*. (2nd ed.) New York: Norton, 1963.

Erikson, E. H. *Insight and Responsibility*. New York: Norton, 1964.

Erikson, E. H. *Gandhi's Truth*. New York: Norton, 1969.

Ernhart, C. B., and Loevinger, J. "Authoritarian Family Ideology: A Measure, Its Correlates, and Its Robustness." *Multivariate Behavioral Research Monographs*, 1969, No. 69-1.

Fenichel, O. *The Psychoanalytic Theory of Neurosis*. New York: Norton, 1945.

Ferenczi, S. "Introjection and Transference." In *Sex in Psychoanalysis*. Boston: Gorham Press, 1916. (Originally published in 1909.)

Ferenczi, S. "Stages in the Development of the Sense of Reality." In *Sex in Psychoanalysis*. Boston: Gorham Press, 1916. (Originally published in 1913.)

Ferenczi, S. "Psycho-Analysis of Sexual Habits." *International Journal of Psycho-Analysis*, 1925, *6*, 372-404.

Festinger, L. *A Theory of Cognitive Dissonance*. Stanford, Calif.: Stanford University Press, 1957.

Feyerabend, P. "Consolations for the Specialist." In I. Lakatos and A. Musgrave (Eds.), *Criticism and the Growth of Knowledge*. Cambridge, England: Cambridge University Press, 1970.

Fingarette, H. *The Self in Transformation*. New York: Basic Books, 1963.

Fisher, A. L. "Freud and the Image of Man." *Proceedings, American Catholic Philosophical Association*, 1961, *35*, 45-77.

Flew, A. "Motives and the Unconscious." In H. Feigl and M. Scriven (Eds.), *Minnesota Studies in the Philosophy of Science*. Vol. 1: *The Foundations of Science and the Concepts of Psychology and Psychoanalysis*. Minneapolis: University of Minnesota Press, 1956.

Flugel, J. C. *Man, Morals and Society*. New York: International Universities Press, 1945.

Foucault, M. *The Order of Things: An Archeology of the Human Sciences*. New York: Random House, 1973.

Frenkel, E., and Weisskopf, E. *Wunsch und Plicht im Aufbau des menschlichen Lebens*. Vienna: Gerold, 1937.

Frenkel-Brunswik, E. "Intolerance of Ambiguity as an Emotional and Perceptual Personality Variable." *Journal of Personality,* 1949, *18,* 108-143.

Frenkel-Brunswik, E. "Personality Theory and Perception." In R. R. Blake and G. V. Ramsey (Eds.), *Perception: An Approach to Personality*. New York: Ronald Press, 1951.

Freud, A. *The Ego and the Mechanisms of Defence*. New York: International Universities Press, 1946. (Originally published in 1936.)

Freud, S. "Project for a Scientific Psychology." In M. Bonaparte, A. Freud, and E. Kris (Eds.), *The Origins of Psycho-Analysis: Letters to Wilhelm Fliess, Drafts and Notes: 1887-1902*. New York: Basic Books, 1954.

Freud, S. *On Aphasia*. New York: International Universities Press, 1953. (Originally published in 1891.)

Freud, S. "Some Points for a Comparative Study of Organic and Hysterical Motor Paralyses." *Standard Edition*. Vol. 1. London: Hogarth Press, 1966. (Originally published in 1893.)

Freud, S. "On the Grounds for Detaching a Particular Syndrome from Neurasthenia Under the Description 'Anxiety Neurosis.' " *Standard Edition*. Vol. 3. London: Hogarth Press, 1962. (Originally published in 1895.)

Freud, S. *The Interpretation of Dreams: Standard Edition*. Vols. 4 and 5. London: Hogarth Press, 1958. (Originally published in 1900.)

Freud, S. *The Psychopathology of Everyday Life: Standard Edition*. Vol. 6. London: Hogarth Press, 1960. (Originally published in 1901.)

Freud, S. *Jokes and Their Relation to the Unconscious: Standard Edition*. Vol. 8. London: Hogarth Press, 1960. (Originally published in 1905a.)

Freud, S. *Three Essays on the Theory of Sexuality: Standard Edition.* Vol. 7. London: Hogarth Press, 1953. (Originally published in 1905*b*.)

Freud, S. "Analysis of a Phobia in a Five-Year-Old Boy." *Standard Edition.* Vol. 10. London: Hogarth Press, 1955. (Originally published in 1909*a*.)

Freud, S. "Notes on a Case of Obsessional Neurosis." *Standard Edition.* Vol. 10. London: Hogarth Press, 1955. (Originally published in 1909*b*.)

Freud, S. *Leonardo da Vinci and a Memory of His Childhood: Standard Edition.* Vol. 11. London: Hogarth Press, 1957. (Originally published in 1910*a*.)

Freud, S. "Five Lectures on Psychoanalysis." *Standard Edition.* Vol. 11. London: Hogarth Press, 1957. (Originally published in 1910*b*.)

Freud, S. *Totem and Taboo: Standard Edition.* Vol. 13. London: Hogarth Press, 1955. (Originally published in 1913.)

Freud, S. "On Narcissism: An Introduction." *Standard Edition.* Vol. 14. London: Hogarth Press, 1957. (Originally published in 1914.)

Freud, S. "Instincts and Their Vicissitudes." *Standard Edition.* Vol. 14. London: Hogarth Press, 1957. (Originally published in 1915.)

Freud, S. *Introductory Lectures on Psychoanalysis: Standard Edition.* Vols. 15 and 16. London: Hogarth Press, 1963. (Originally published in 1916-1917.)

Freud, S. "Mourning and Melancholia." *Standard Edition.* Vol. 14. London: Hogarth Press, 1957. (Originally published in 1917.)

Freud, S. "From the History of an Infantile Neurosis." *Standard Edition.* Vol. 17. London: Hogarth Press, 1955. (Originally published in 1918.)

Freud, S. *Beyond the Pleasure Principle: Standard Edition.* Vol. 18. London: Hogarth Press, 1955. (Originally published in 1920.)

Freud, S. *Group Psychology and the Analysis of the Ego: Standard Edition.* Vol. 18. London: Hogarth Press, 1955. (Originally published in 1921.)

Freud, S. *The Ego and the Id: Standard Edition.* Vol. 19. London: Hogarth Press, 1961. (Originally published in 1923.)

Freud, S. *Inhibitions, Symptoms and Anxiety: Standard Edition.* Vol. 21. London: Hogarth Press, 1959. (Originally published in 1926.)

Freud, S. *Civilization and Its Discontents: Standard Edition.* Vol. 20. London: Hogarth Press, 1961. (Originally published in 1930.)

Freud, S. *New Introductory Lectures on Psychoanalysis: Standard Edition.* Vol. 22. London: Hogarth Press, 1964. (Originally published in 1933.)

Freud, S. *Moses and Monotheism: Standard Edition.* Vol. 23. London: Hogarth Press, 1964. (Originally published in 1939.)

Fromm, E. *Escape from Freedom.* New York: Farrar, Straus & Giroux, 1941.

Fromm, E. *The Anatomy of Human Destructiveness.* New York: Holt, Rinehart and Winston, 1973.

Furth, H. G. *Piaget and Knowledge: Theoretical Foundations.* Englewood Cliffs, N.J.: Prentice-Hall, 1969.

Gergen, K. J. "Personal Consistency and the Presentation of the Self." In C. Gordon and K. J. Gergen (Eds.), *The Self in Social Interaction.* Vol. 1: *Classic and Contemporary Perspectives.* New York: Wiley, 1968.

Gill, M. M. "Topography and Systems in Psychoanalytic Theory." *Psychological Issues,* 1963, *3* (2, Whole No. 10).

Gill, M. M. "Metapsychology Is Irrelevant to Psychoanalysis." Paper presented at the convention of the Psychologists Interested in the Study of Psychoanalysis, Chicago, August 1975.

Goldstein, K. *The Organism.* New York: American Book, 1939.

Gordon, C., and Gergen, K. J. (Eds.) *The Self in Social Interaction.* Vol. 1: *Classic and Contemporary Perspectives.* New York: Wiley, 1968.

Grant, J. D., and Grant, M. Q. "A Group Dynamics Approach to the Treatment of Nonconformists in the Navy." *Annals of the American Academy of Political and Social Science,* 1959, *322,* 126-135.

References   467

Graves, C. W. "Deterioration of Work Standards." *Harvard Business Review,* 1966, *44,* 117-128.

Greenberger, E., Josselson, R., Knerr, C., and Knerr, B. "The Measurement and Structure of Psychosocial Maturity." *Journal of Youth and Adolescence,* 1975, *4,* 127-143.

Greenberger, E., Knerr, C., Knerr, B., and Brown, J. B. "The Measurement and Structure of Psychosocial Maturity." Mimeographed. Baltimore: Report No. 170, Center for Social Organization of Schools, Johns Hopkins University, 1974.

Groddeck, G. *The Book of the It.* London: Vision Press, 1950. (Originally published in 1923.)

Grossman, W. I., and Simon, B. "Anthropomorphism: Motive, Meaning and Causality in Psychoanalytic Theory." *Psychoanalytic Study of the Child,* 1969, *24,* 78-111.

Haan, N., Stroud, J., and Holstein, C. "Moral and Ego Stages in Relationship to Ego Processes: A Study of 'Hippies.'" *Journal of Personality,* 1973, *41,* 596-612.

Hammond, K. R. (Ed.) *The Psychology of Egon Brunswik.* New York: Holt, Rinehart and Winston, 1966.

Harakal, C. M. "Ego Maturity and Interpersonal Style: A Multivariate Study of Loevinger's Theory." Unpublished doctoral dissertation, Catholic University, 1971.

Hartmann, H. *Ego Psychology and the Problem of Adaptation.* New York: International Universities Press, 1958. (Originally published in 1939.)

Hartmann, H., Kris, E., and Loewenstein, R. M. "Papers on Psychoanalytic Psychology." *Psychological Issues,* 1964, *4* (2, Whole no. 14). (Originally published 1945-1962.)

Hartshorne, H., and May, M. A. *Studies in the Nature of Character.* Vol. 1: *Studies in Deceit.* New York: Macmillan, 1928.

Hartshorne, H., May, M. A., and Maller, J. B. *Studies in the Nature of Character.* Vol. 2: *Studies in Service and Self-Control.* New York: Macmillan, 1929.

Hartshorne, H., May, M. A., and Shuttleworth, F. K. *Studies in the Nature of Character.* Vol. 3: *Studies in the Organization of Character.* New York: Macmillan, 1930.

Harvey, O. J., Hunt, D. E., and Schroder, H. M. *Conceptual*

Systems and Personality Organization. New York: Wiley, 1961.

Heath, D. H. *Explorations of Maturity: Studies of Mature and Immature College Men.* New York: Appleton-Century-Crofts, 1965.

Hebb, D. O. "The American Revolution." *American Psychologist,* 1960, *15,* 735-745.

Hendrick, I. "Instinct and the Ego During Infancy." *Psychoanalytic Quarterly,* 1942, *11,* 33-58.

Hess, R. D., and Torney, J. V. *The Development of Political Attitudes in Children.* Chicago: Aldine, 1967.

Higgins, J. W. "Some Considerations of Psychoanalytic Theory Preliminary to a Philosophical Inquiry." *Proceedings, American Catholic Philosophical Association,* 1961, *35,* 21-44.

Hobhouse, L. T. *Morals in Evolution.* New York: Holt, Rinehart and Winston, 1906.

Hogan, R. "Moral Conduct and Moral Character: A Psychological Perspective." *Psychological Bulletin,* 1973, *79,* 217-232.

Holstein, C. B. "Moral Judgment Change in Early Adolescence and Middle Age: A Longitudinal Study." Paper presented at the convention of the Society for Research in Child Development, Philadelphia, March 1973.

Holt, E. B. *The Freudian Wish and Its Place in Ethics.* New York: Holt, Rinehart and Winston, 1915.

Holt, L. P. "Psychoanalysis and the Social Process: An Examination of Freudian Theory with Reference to Some of Its Sociological Implications and Counterparts." Unpublished doctoral dissertation, Radcliffe College, 1948.

Holt, R. R. "A Critical Examination of Freud's Concept of Bound vs. Free Cathexis." *Journal of the American Psychoanalytic Association,* 1962, *10,* 475-525.

Holt, R. R. "A Review of Some of Freud's Biological Assumptions and Their Influence on His Theories." In N. S. Greenfield and W. C. Lewis (Eds.), *Psychoanalysis and Current Biological Thought.* Madison: University of Wisconsin Press, 1965.

Holt, R. R. "Beyond Vitalism and Mechanism: Freud's Concept of Psychic Energy." In J. H. Masserman (Ed.), *Science and Psychoanalysis*. Vol. 11: *Concepts of Ego*. New York: Grune and Stratton, 1967.

Holt, R. R. "Freud's Mechanistic and Humanistic Images of Man." In R. R. Holt and E. Peterfreund (Eds.), *Psychoanalysis and Contemporary Science*, 1972, *1*, 3-24.

Holt, R. R. "Drive or Wish? A Reconsideration of the Psychoanalytic Theory of Motivation." In M. M. Gill and P. S. Holzman (Eds.), *Psychology Versus Metapsychology: Psychoanalytic Essays in Memory of George S. Klein. Psychological Issues*, 1976, *9* (4, Whole no. 36).

Home, H. J. "The Concept of Mind." *International Journal of Psycho-Analysis*, 1966, *47*, 42-49.

Hoppe, C. F. "Ego Development and Conformity Behaviors." Unpublished doctoral dissertation, Washington University, 1972.

Horowitz, M. J. "Microanalysis of Working Through in Psychotherapy." *American Journal of Psychiatry*, 1974a, *131*, 1208-1212.

Horowitz, M. J. "Stress Response Syndromes: Character Style and Dynamic Psychotherapy." *Archives of General Psychiatry*, 1974b, *31*, 768-781.

Horowitz, M. J. "Hysterical Personality: Cognitive Structure and the Process of Change." *International Journal of Psycho-Analysis*, in press.

Howe, L. P. "Some Sociological Aspects of Identification." *Psychoanalysis and the Social Sciences*, 1955, *4*, 61-79.

Howe, L. P. "The Application of Community Psychiatry to College Settings." *International Psychiatry Clinics*, 1970, *7*, 263-291.

Isaacs, K. S. "Relatability, a Proposed Construct and an Approach to Its Validation." Unpublished doctoral dissertation, University of Chicago, 1956.

Isaacs, K. S., and Haggard, E. A. "Some Methods Used in the Study of Affect in Psychotherapy." In L. A. Gottschalk and S. H. Auerbach (Eds.), *Methods of Research in Psychotherapy*. New York: Appleton-Century-Crofts, 1956.

Jahoda, M. *Current Concepts of Positive Mental Health.* New York: Basic Books, 1958.

James, W. *Principles of Psychology.* New York: Holt, Rinehart and Winston, 1890.

Janet, P. *L'automatisme psychologique.* Paris: Alcan, 1889.

Janet, P. *The Major Symptoms of Hysteria.* New York: Hafner, 1929. (Originally published in 1907.)

Janet, P. *Psychological Healing: A Historical and Clinical Study.* Vol. 1. New York: Macmillan, 1925.

Janik, A., and Toulmin, S. *Wittgenstein's Vienna.* New York: Simon and Schuster, 1973.

Jaspers, K. "The Axial Age in Human History." In M. R. Stein, A. J. Vidich, and D. M. White (Eds.), *Identity and Anxiety.* New York: Free Press, 1960. (Originally published in 1948.)

Jesness, C. F. "Sequential I-Level Classification Manual." Mimeographed. Sacramento, Calif.: American Justice Institute, 1974.

Jesness, C. F., and Wedge, R. F. "Sequential I-Level Classification Manual." Mimeographed. Sacramento, Calif.: Department of Youth Authority, Division of Research, 1970.

Jones, E. *The Life and Work of Sigmund Freud.* Vol. 1: *The Formative Years and the Great Discoveries.* New York: Basic Books, 1953.

Josselson, R., Greenberger, E., and McConochie, D. "Phenomenological Aspects of Psychosocial Maturity in Adolescence." Mimeographed. Baltimore: Report No. 198, Center for Social Organization of Schools, Johns Hopkins University, 1975.

Jung, C. G. *Psychological Types.* Princeton, N.J.: Princeton University Press, 1971. (Originally published in 1921.)

Jung, C. G. "The Basic Postulates of Analytic Psychology." In H. M. Ruitenbeek (Ed.), *Varieties of Personality Theory.* New York: Dutton, 1964. (Originally published in 1933.)

Jung, C. G. *Two Essays on Analytic Psychology.* New York: Meridian, 1956. (Originally published in 1943, 1945.)

Kahler, E. *The Inward Turn of Narrative.* R. and C. Winston, Trans. Princeton: Princeton University Press, 1970. (Originally published in 1957, 1959.)

Kelley, H. H., and Stahelski, A. J. "Social Interaction Basis of Cooperators' and Competitors' Beliefs About Others." *Journal of Personality and Social Psychology,* 1970, *16,* 66-91.

Kelly, G. A. *The Psychology of Personal Constructs.* New York: Norton, 1955.

Kelly, G. A. "A Brief Introduction to Personal Construct Theory." In D. Bannister (Ed.), *Perspectives in Personal Construct Theory.* New York: Academic Press, 1970.

Kelman, H. C. "Compliance, Identification and Internalization: Three Processes of Attitude Change." *Journal of Conflict Resolution,* 1958, *2,* 51-60.

Klein, G. S., and Schoenfeld, N. "The Influence of Ego-Involvement on Confidence." *Journal of Abnormal and Social Psychology,* 1941, *36,* 249-258.

Kohlberg, L. "The Development of Children's Orientations Towards a Moral Order. I: Sequence in the Development of Moral Thought." *Vita Humana,* 1963, *6,* 11-33.

Kohlberg, L. "Development of Moral Character and Moral Ideology." In M. L. Hoffman and L. W. Hoffman (Eds.), *Review of Child Development Research.* Vol. 1. New York: Russell Sage Foundation, 1964.

Kohlberg, L. "A Cognitive Developmental Analysis of Children's Sex-Role Concepts and Attitudes." In E. Maccoby (Ed.), *The Development of Sex Differences.* Stanford, Calif.: Stanford University Press, 1966.

Kohlberg, L. "Stage and Sequence: The Cognitive-Developmental Approach to Socialization." In D. A. Goslin (Ed.), *Handbook of Socialization Theory and Research.* Chicago: Rand McNally, 1969.

Kohlberg, L. "From Is to Ought: How to Commit the Naturalistic Fallacy and Get Away with It in the Study of Moral Development." In T. Mischel (Ed.), *Cognitive Development and Epistemology.* New York: Academic Press, 1971.

Kohlberg, L., Colby, A., Lieberman, M., and Speicher-Dubin, B. "Standard Form Scoring Manual." Mimeographed. Cambridge, Mass.: Harvard University, 1973.

Kohlberg, L., Scharf, P., and Hickey, J. "The Justice Structure of the Prison—A Theory and an Intervention." *Prison Journal,* 1972, *51,* 18-31.

Kris, E. "The Psychology of Caricature." *Psychoanalytic Explorations in Art.* New York: International Universities Press, 1952. (Originally published in 1934.)

Kubie, L. S. "The Fallacious Use of Quantitative Concepts in Dynamic Psychology." *Psychiatric Quarterly,* 1947, *16,* 507-518.

Kuhn, T. S. *The Structure of Scientific Revolutions.* Chicago: University of Chicago Press, 1962.

Kuhn, T. S. "Reflections on My Critics." In I. Lakatos and A. Musgrave (Eds.), *Criticism and the Growth of Knowledge.* Cambridge, England: Cambridge University Press, 1970*a.*

Kuhn, T. S. *The Structure of Scientific Revolutions.* (2nd ed.) Chicago: University of Chicago Press, 1970*b.*

Kuhn, T. S. "Second Thoughts on Paradigms." In F. Suppe (Ed.), *The Structure of Scientific Theories.* Urbana, Ill.: University of Illinois Press, 1974.

Kuo, Z. Y. "Giving Up Instincts in Psychology." *Journal of Philosophy,* 1921, *18,* 645-664.

Lakatos, I., and Musgrave, A. (Eds.) *Criticism and the Growth of Knowledge.* Cambridge, England: Cambridge University Press, 1970.

Lambert, H. V. "A Comparison of Jane Loevinger's Theory of Ego Development and Lawrence Kohlberg's Theory of Moral Development." Unpublished doctoral dissertation, University of Chicago, 1972.

Lampl-de Groot, J. "Neurotics, Delinquents and Ideal-Formation." In K. R. Eissler (Ed.), *Searchlights on Delinquency.* New York: International Universities Press, 1949.

Lampl-de Groot, J. "Ego Ideal and Superego." *Psychoanalytic Study of the Child,* 1962, *27,* 94-106.

LaPerriere, K. "Maternal Attitudes in Different Subcultural Groups." (Doctoral dissertation, Washington University, 1962.) Ann Arbor, Mich.: University Microfilms, No. 63-4850.

Lashley, K. S., and Colby, K. M. "An Exchange of Views on Psychic Energy and Psychoanalysis." *Behavioral Science,* 1957, *2,* 231-240.

Lecky, P. *Self-Consistency: A Theory of Personality.* New York: Island Press, 1945.

Lévi-Strauss, C. *Tristes tropiques.* New York: Atheneum, 1968.

Lewin, K. "The Conflict Between Aristotelean and Galileian Modes of Thought in Contemporary Psychology." In *A Dynamic Theory of Personality.* New York: McGraw-Hill, 1935. (Originally published in 1931.)

Lewis, O. "The Culture of Poverty." In *La Vida.* New York: Random House, 1966.

Lieberman, M. "Psychometric Analysis of Developmental Stage Data." Paper presented at the American Psychological Association Convention, Montreal, Canada, August 1973.

Loevinger, J. "The Technic of Homogeneous Tests Compared with Some Aspects of 'Scale Analysis' and Factor Analysis." *Psychological Bulletin,* 1948, *45,* 507-529.

Loevinger, J. "Intelligence." In H. Helson (Ed.), *Theoretical Foundations of Psychology.* New York: Van Nostrand, 1951.

Loevinger, J. "A Theory of Test Response." In *Proceedings, 1958 Invitational Conference on Testing Problems.* Princeton: Educational Testing Service, 1959.

Loevinger, J. "Measuring Personality Patterns of Women." *Genetic Psychology Monographs,* 1962, *65,* 53-136.

Loevinger, J. "Conflict of Commitment in Clinical Research." *American Psychologist,* 1963, *18,* 241-251.

Loevinger, J. "Measurement in Clinical Research." In B. B. Wolman (Ed.), *Handbook of Clinical Psychology.* New York: McGraw-Hill, 1965.

Loevinger, J. "The Meaning and Measurement of Ego Development." *American Psychologist,* 1966a, *21,* 195-206.

Loevinger, J. "Models and Measures of Developmental Variation." In J. Brozek (Ed.), *Biology of Human Variation. Annals of the New York Academy of Sciences,* 1966b, *134,* art. 2, 585-590.

Loevinger, J. "Three Principles for a Psychoanalytic Psychology." *Journal of Abnormal Psychology,* 1966c, *71,* 432-443.

Loevinger, J., Gleser, G. C., and DuBois, P. H. "Maximizing the Discriminating Power of a Multiple Score Test." *Psychometrika,* 1953, *18,* 309-317.

Loevinger, J., and Sweet, B. "Construction of a Test of Mothers' Attitudes." In J. C. Glidewell (Ed.), *Parental Attitudes and Child Behavior.* Springfield, Ill.: Thomas, 1961.

Loevinger, J., and Wessler, R. *Measuring Ego Development I: Construction and Use of a Sentence Completion Test.* San Francisco: Jossey-Bass, 1970.

Loewald, H. W. "Ego and Reality." *International Journal of Psycho-Analysis,* 1951, *32,* 10-18.

Loewald, H. W. "On the Therapeutic Action of Psycho-Analysis." *International Journal of Psycho-Analysis,* 1960, *41,* 16-33.

Loewald, H. W. "Internalization, Separation, Mourning, and the Superego." *Psychoanalytic Quarterly,* 1962a, *31,* 483-504.

Loewald, H. W. "The Superego and the Ego-Ideal. II: Superego and Time." *International Journal of Psycho-Analysis,* 1962b, *43,* 264-268.

Loewald, H. W. "Psychoanalytic Theory and the Psychoanalytic Process." *Psychoanalytic Study of the Child,* 1970, *25,* 45-68.

Loewald, H. W. "Some Considerations on Repetition and Repetition Compulsion." *International Journal of Psycho-Analysis,* 1971a, *52,* 59-66.

Loewald, H. W. "On Motivation and Instinct Theory." *Psychoanalytic Study of the Child,* 1971b, *26,* 91-128.

Loewald, H. W. "The Transference Neurosis: Comments on the Concept and the Phenomenon." *Journal of the American Psychoanalytic Association,* 1971c, *19,* 54-66.

Lord, F. M. "Sampling Fluctuations Resulting from the Sampling of Test Items." *Psychometrika,* 1955, *20,* 1-22.

Mahler, M. S. *On Human Symbiosis and the Vicissitudes of Individuation.* Vol. 1: *Infantile Psychosis.* New York: International Universities Press, 1968.

Maslow, A. H. *Motivation and Personality.* New York: Harper & Row, 1954.

Maslow, A. H. *Toward a Psychology of Being.* New York: Van Nostrand, 1962.

Masterman, M. "The Nature of a Paradigm." In I. Lakatos and A. Musgrave (Eds.), *Criticism and the Growth of Knowl-*

edge. Cambridge, England: Cambridge University Press, 1970.

McDougall, W. *An Introduction to Social Psychology.* Enlarged Edition. London: Methuen, 1928. (Originally published in 1908.)

Mead, G. H. *Mind, Self and Society.* Chicago: University of Chicago Press, 1934.

Merleau-Ponty, M. *The Structure of Behavior.* Boston: Beacon Press, 1963. (Originally published in 1942.)

Mill, J. S. "Bentham." In M. Warnock (Ed.), *John Stuart Mill: Utilitarianism, On Liberty, Essay on Bentham, Together with Selected Writings of Jeremy Bentham and John Austin.* Cleveland: World Publishing Company, 1962. (Originally published in 1838.)

Mill, J. S. "On Liberty." In M. Warnock (Ed.), *John Stuart Mill: Utilitarianism, On Liberty, Essay on Bentham, Together with Selected Writings of Jeremy Bentham and John Austin.* Cleveland: World Publishing Company, 1962. (Originally published in 1859.)

Mill, J. S. *Utilitarianism.* In M. Warnock (Ed.), *John Stuart Mill: Utilitarianism, On Liberty, Essay on Bentham, Together with Selected Writings of Jeremy Bentham and John Austin.* Cleveland: World Publishing Company, 1962. (Originally published in 1861.)

Mischel, W. "Theory and Research on the Antecedents of Self-Imposed Delay of Reward." In B. A. Maher (Ed.), *Progress in Experimental Personality Research.* Vol. 3. New York: Academic Press, 1966.

Mischel, W. *Personality and Assessment.* New York: Wiley, 1968.

Mischel, W. "Continuity and Change in Personality." *American Psychologist,* 1969, *24,* 1012-1018.

Mischel, W. "Toward a Cognitive Social Learning Reconceptualization of Personality." *Psychological Review,* 1973, *80,* 252-283.

Mischel, W., and Ebbesen, E. B. "Attention in Delay of Gratification." *Journal of Personality and Social Psychology,* 1970, *16,* 329-337.

Mischel, W., and Mischel, H. "A Cognitive Social Learning Approach to Morality and Self-Regulation." In T. Lickona (Ed.), *Morality: Theory, Research, and Social Issues.* New York: Holt, Rinehart and Winston, 1976.

Nunberg, H. "The Synthetic Function of the Ego." In *Practice and Theory of Psychoanalysis.* New York: International Universities Press, 1948. (Originally published in 1931.)

Nunberg, H., and Federn, E. (Eds.) *Minutes of the Vienna Psychoanalytic Society.* Vol. 1: 1906-1908. New York: International Universities Press, 1962.

Odier, C. *Les deux sources, consciente et inconsciente, de la vie morale.* Neuchâtel, Switzerland: De La Baconnière, 1943.

Palmer, T. B. "California's Community Treatment Program for Delinquent Adolescents." *Journal of Research in Crime and Delinquency,* 1971, *8,* 74-92.

Palmer, T. B. "The Youth Authority's Community Treatment Project." *Federal Probation,* 1974, *38,* 3-14.

Parain-Vial, J. *Analyses structurales et ideologies structuralistes.* Toulouse, France: Privat, 1969.

Paterson, D. G. *Physique and Intellect.* New York: Century, 1930.

Peck, R. F., and Havighurst, R. J. *The Psychology of Character Development.* New York: Wiley, 1960.

Perry, W. G., Jr. *Forms of Intellectual and Ethical Development in the College Years.* New York: Holt, Rinehart and Winston, 1970.

Piaget, J. *The Language and Thought of the Child.* New York: Harcourt Brace Jovanovich, 1926.

Piaget, J. *Judgment and Reasoning in the Child.* New York: Harcourt Brace Jovanovich, 1928.

Piaget, J. *The Moral Judgment of the Child.* New York: Free Press, 1932.

Piaget, J. *The Origins of Intelligence in Children.* New York: International Universities Press, 1952. (Originally published in 1936.)

Piaget, J. *The Construction of Reality in the Child.* New York, Basic Books, 1954. (Originally published in 1937.)

Piaget, J. *Play, Dreams and Imitation in Childhood.* New York: Norton, 1951.

Piaget, J. *Six Psychological Studies.* New York: Random House, 1967.

Piaget, J. *Structuralism.* New York: Basic Books, 1970.

Pittel, S. M., and Mendelsohn, G. A. "Measurement of Moral Values: A Review and Critique." *Psychological Bulletin,* 1966, *66,* 22-35.

Polanyi, M. *Personal Knowledge.* Chicago: University of Chicago Press, 1958.

Polanyi, M. *The Tacit Dimension.* Garden City, New York: Doubleday, 1966.

Popper, K. R. "Normal Science and Its Dangers." In I. Lakatos and A. Musgrave (Eds.), *Criticism and the Growth of Knowledge.* Cambridge, England: Cambridge University Press, 1970.

Prelinger, E., and Zimet, C. N. *An Ego-Psychological Approach to Character Assessment.* New York: Free Press, 1964.

Rapaport, D. "The Structure of Psychoanalytic Theory." *Psychological Issues,* 1960, *2* (2, Whole No. 6).

Rapaport, D., and Gill, M. M. "The Points of View and Assumptions of Metapsychology." *International Journal of Psycho-Analysis,* 1959, *40,* 153-162.

Redmore, C., and Waldman, K. "Reliability of a Sentence Completion Measure of Ego Development." *Journal of Personality Assessment,* 1975, *39,* 236-243.

Reese, H. W., and Overton, W. F. "Models of Development and Theories of Development." In L. R. Goulet and P. B. Baltes (Eds.), *Life-Span Developmental Psychology: Research and Theory.* New York: Academic Press, 1970.

Reich, W. *Character Analysis.* New York: Farrar, Straus & Giroux, 1949. (Originally published in 1933.)

Rest, J. R. "The Hierarchical Nature of Stages of Moral Judgment." *Journal of Personality,* 1973, *41,* 86-109.

Rest, J. R. "Manual for the Defining Issues Test." Mimeographed. Minneapolis: University of Minnesota, 1974.

Rest, J. R. "New Options in Assessing Moral Judgment and Criteria for Evaluating Validity." Paper presented at the convention of the Society for Research in Child Development, Denver, Colorado, April 1975.

Rest, J. R. "New Approaches in the Assessment of Moral Judgment." In T. Lickona (Ed.), *Morality: Theory, Research, and Social Issues.* New York: Holt, Rinehart and Winston, 1976.

Rest, J. R., and others. "Judging the Important Issues in Moral Dilemmas—An Objective Measure of Development." *Developmental Psychology,* 1974, *10,* 491-501.

Rest, J., Turiel, E., and Kohlberg, L. "Level of Moral Development as a Determinant of Preference and Comprehension of Moral Judgments Made by Others." *Journal of Personality,* 1969, *37,* 225-252.

Rickman, J. (Ed.) *A General Selection from the Works of Sigmund Freud.* Garden City, N.Y.: Doubleday, 1975.

Ricoeur, P. *Freud and Philosophy: An Essay on Interpretation.* New Haven, Conn.: Yale University Press, 1970.

Riesman, D., Glazer, N., and Denney, R. *The Lonely Crowd.* Garden City, New York: Doubleday, 1954. (Originally published in 1950.)

Rogers, C. R. "A Theory of Therapy, Personality, and Interpersonal Relationships, as Developed in the Client-Centered Framework." In S. Koch (Ed.), *Psychology: A Study of a Science.* Vol. 3: *Formulations of the Person and the Social Context.* New York: McGraw-Hill, 1959.

Rogers, C. R. *On Becoming a Person.* Boston: Houghton Mifflin, 1961.

Ryle, G. *The Concept of Mind.* New York: Barnes and Noble, 1964. (Originally published in 1949.)

Sanford, N. "The Dynamics of Identification." *Psychological Review,* 1955, *62,* 106-118.

Sanford, N., Webster, H., and Freedman, M. "Impulse Expression as a Variable of Personality." *Psychological Monographs,* 1957, *72,* No. 11 (Whole No. 440).

Scammon, R. E. "The Measurement of the Body in Childhood." In J. A. Harris, C. M. Jackson, D. G. Paterson, and R. E. Scammon (Eds.), *The Measurement of Man.* Minneapolis: University of Minnesota Press, 1930.

Schachtel, E. G. *Metamorphosis*. New York: Basic Books, 1959.

Schafer, R. *Aspects of Internalization*. New York: International Universities Press, 1968.

Schafer, R. "Internalization: Process or Fantasy?" *Psychoanalytic Study of the Child*, 1972, *27*, 411-436.

Schafer, R. "Problems in Freud's Psychology of Women." *Journal of the American Psychoanalytic Association*, 1974, *22*, 459-485.

Schiwy, G. *Structuralism and Christianity*. Pittsburgh, Penn.: Duquesne University Press, 1971.

Selman, R. "The Relation of Role-Taking to the Development of Moral Judgment in Children." *Child Development*, 1971, *42*, 79-92.

Selman, R. "The Development of Conceptions of Interpersonal Relations: A Structural Analysis and Procedures for the Assessment of Levels of Interpersonal Reasoning Based on Levels of Social Perspective-Taking." Mimeographed. Cambridge, Mass.: Harvard-Judge Baker Social Reasoning Project, 1974.

Selman, R., and Byrne, D. "A Structural Analysis of Levels of Role-Taking in Middle Childhood." *Child Development*, 1974, *45*, 803-807.

Shapiro, D. *Neurotic Styles*. New York: Basic Books, 1965.

Shapiro, D. "Motivation and Action in Psychoanalytic Psychiatry." *Psychiatry*, 1970, *33*, 329-343.

Sherwood, M. *The Logic of Explanation in Psychoanalysis*. New York: Academic Press, 1969.

Smith, A. *The Theory of Moral Sentiments*. New Rochelle, N.Y.: Arlington House, 1969. (Originally published in 1759.)

Spitz, R. A. *No and Yes: On the Beginnings of Human Communication*. New York: International Universities Press, 1957.

Spitz, R. A. *A Genetic Field Theory of Ego Formation*. New York: International Universities Press, 1959.

Strawson, P. F. *Individuals: An Essay in Descriptive Metaphysics*. London: Methuen, 1959.

Sullivan, C., Grant, M. Q., and Grant, J. D. "The Development of

Interpersonal Maturity: Applications to Delinquency." *Psychiatry,* 1957, *20,* 373-385.

Sullivan, H. S. "Schizophrenia: Its Conservative and Malignant Features." In *Schizophrenia as a Human Process.* New York: Norton, 1962. (Originally published in 1925.)

Sullivan, H. S. *The Interpersonal Theory of Psychiatry.* New York: Norton, 1953.

Tanner, J. M. "The Regulation of Human Growth." *Child Development,* 1963, *34,* 817-847.

Tanner, J. M., and Inhelder, B. (Eds.) *Discussions on Child Development.* Vol. 1. New York: International Universities Press, 1956.

Tanner, J. M., and Inhelder, B. (Eds.) *Discussions on Child Development.* Vol. 4. New York: International Universities Press, 1960.

Tapp, J. L., and Kohlberg, L. "Developing Senses of Law and Legal Justice." *Journal of Social Issues,* 1971, *2,* 65-91.

Thomson, G. H. *The Factorial Analysis of Human Ability.* Cambridge, England: Houghton Mifflin, 1939.

Thorndike, E. L. "Units and Scales for Measuring Educational Products." In *Proceedings of a Conference on Educational Measurements. Indiana University Bulletin,* 1914, *12,* No. 10.

Thorndike, E. L., and others. *The Measurement of Intelligence.* New York: Teachers College, Columbia University, 1927.

Tolman, E. C. "Can Instincts Be Given Up in Psychology?" *Journal of Abnormal and Social Psychology,* 1922, *17,* 139-152.

Tolman, E. C., and Brunswik, E. "The Organism and the Causal Texture of the Environment." *Psychological Review,* 1935, *42,* 43-77.

Toulmin, S. E. "Does the Distinction Between Normal and Revolutionary Science Hold Water?" In I. Lakatos and A. Musgrave (Eds.), *Criticism and the Growth of Knowledge.* Cambridge, England: Cambridge University Press, 1970.

Tryon, R. C. "A Theory of *Psychological* Components—An Alternative to 'Mathematical Factors.' " *Psychological Review,* 1935, *42,* 425-454.

Vaihinger, H. *The Philosophy of "As If": A System of the The-oretical, Practical, and Religious Fictions of Mankind.* New York: Harcourt Brace Jovanovich, 1925. (Originally published in 1911.)

Van den Daele, L. D. "Ego Development and Preferential Judgment in Life-Span Perspective." In N. Datan and L. H. Ginsberg (Eds.), *Life-Span Development Psychology: Normative Life Crises.* New York: Academic Press, 1975.

Vergote, A. "Psychanalyse et phénoménology." *Recherche et débats,* 1957, *21,* 125-144.

Wachtel, P. L. "Psychodynamics, Behavior Therapy, and the Implacable Experimenter: An Inquiry into the Consistency of Personality." *Journal of Abnormal Psychology,* 1973, *82,* 324-334.

Waelder, R. "The Principle of Multiple Function: Observations on Over-Determination." *Psychoanalytic Quarterly,* 1936, *5,* 45-62.

Waelder, R. *Basic Theory of Psychoanalysis.* New York: International Universities Press, 1960.

Warren, M. Q. "The Case for Differential Treatment of Delinquents." *Annals of the American Academy of Political and Social Science,* 1969, *381,* 47-59.

Warren, M. Q. "Intervention with Juvenile Delinquents." In M. Rosenheim (Ed.), *Pursuing Justice for the Child.* Chicago: University of Chicago Press, 1976.

Watkins, J. W. N. "Against 'Normal Science.' " In I. Lakatos and A. Musgrave (Eds.), *Criticism and the Growth of Knowledge.* Cambridge, England: Cambridge University Press, 1970.

Werner, H. *Comparative Psychology of Mental Development.* New York: International Universities Press, 1964. (Originally published in 1940.)

Westermarck, E. *The Origin and Development of the Moral Ideas.* Vol. 1. London: Macmillan, 1906.

Westermarck, E. *The Origin and Development of the Moral Ideas.* Vol. 2. London: Macmillan, 1908.

White, R. W. *Lives in Progress.* New York: Dryden Press, 1952.

White, R. W. "Ego and Reality in Psychoanalytic Theory." *Psychological Issues,* 1963, *3* (3, Whole No. 11).

Wohlwill, J. *The Study of Behavioral Development.* New York: Academic Press, 1973.

Name Index

Subject Index

489

D1031742

HANDBOOK OF PLASMA PROCESSING TECHNOLOGY

MATERIALS SCIENCE AND PROCESS TECHNOLOGY SERIES

Editors

Rointan F. Bunshah, University of California, Los Angeles *(Materials Science and Technology)*

Gary E. McGuire, Microelectronics Center of North Carolina *(Electronic Materials and Processing)*

DEPOSITION TECHNOLOGIES FOR FILMS AND COATINGS: by *Rointan F. Bunshah et al*

CHEMICAL VAPOR DEPOSITION IN MICROELECTRONICS: by *Arthur Sherman*

SEMICONDUCTOR MATERIALS AND PROCESS TECHNOLOGY HANDBOOK: edited by *Gary E. McGuire*

SOL-GEL TECHNOLOGY FOR THIN FILMS, FIBERS, PREFORMS, ELECTRONICS AND SPECIALTY SHAPES: edited by *Lisa A. Klein*

HYBRID MICROCIRCUIT TECHNOLOGY HANDBOOK: by *James J. Licari* and *Leonard R. Enlow*

HANDBOOK OF THIN FILM DEPOSITION PROCESSES AND TECHNIQUES: edited by *Klaus K. Schuegraf*

IONIZED-CLUSTER BEAM DEPOSITION AND EPITAXY: by *Toshinori Takagi*

DIFFUSION PHENOMENA IN THIN FILMS AND MICROELECTRONIC MATERIALS: edited by *Devendra Gupta* and *Paul S. Ho*

SHOCK WAVES FOR INDUSTRIAL APPLICATIONS: edited by *Lawrence E. Murr*

HANDBOOK OF CONTAMINATION CONTROL IN MICROELECTRONICS: edited by *Donald L. Tolliver*

HANDBOOK OF ION BEAM PROCESSING TECHNOLOGY: edited by *Jerome J. Cuomo, Stephen M. Rossnagel,* and *Harold R. Kaufman*

FRICTION AND WEAR TRANSITIONS OF MATERIALS: by *Peter J. Blau*

CHARACTERIZATION OF SEMICONDUCTOR MATERIALS—Volume 1: edited by *Gary E. McGuire*

SPECIAL MELTING AND PROCESSING TECHNOLOGIES: edited by *G.K. Bhat*

HANDBOOK OF PLASMA PROCESSING TECHNOLOGY: edited by *Stephen M. Rossnagel, Jerome J. Cuomo,* and *William D. Westwood*

Related Titles

ADHESIVES TECHNOLOGY HANDBOOK: by *Arthur H. Landrock*

HANDBOOK OF THERMOSET PLASTICS: edited by *Sidney H. Goodman*

SURFACE PREPARATION TECHNIQUES FOR ADHESIVE BONDING: by *Raymond F. Wegman*

2 0265048 \ 5935838

Ta
2020
H3. ₵
1990
c. 1

HANDBOOK OF
PLASMA PROCESSING
TECHNOLOGY

Fundamentals, Etching, Deposition, and Surface Interactions

NORMANDALE COMMUNITY COLLEGE
LIBRARY AVENUE SOUTH
9700 FRANCE AVENUE SOUTH
BLOOMINGTON, MN 55431-4399

Edited by

Stephen M. Rossnagel

IBM Thomas J. Watson Research Center
Yorktown Heights, New York

Jerome J. Cuomo

IBM Thomas J. Watson Research Center
Yorktown Heights, New York

William D. Westwood

Bell-Northern Research
Ottawa, Canada

DISCARDED

 NOYES PUBLICATIONS
Westwood, New Jersey, U.S.A.

Copyright © 1990 by Noyes Publications
    No part of this book may be reproduced or utilized in
any form or by any means, electronic or mechanical,
including photocopying, recording or by any information storage and retrieval system, without permission
in writing from the Publisher.
Library of Congress Catalog Card Number: 89-22834
ISBN: 0-8155-1220-1
Printed in the United States

Published in the United States of America by
Noyes Publications
Fairview Avenue, Westwood, New Jersey 07675

10 9 8

Library of Congress Cataloging-in-Publication Data

Handbook of plasma processing technology : fundamentals, etching,
    deposition, and surface interactions / edited by Stephen M.
    Rossnagel, Jerome J. Cuomo, William D. Westwood.
            p.   cm.
        Includes bibliographical references.
        ISBN 0-8155-1220-1 :
            1. Plasma engineering. 2. Semiconductors--Etching. 3. Plasma
    etching. I. Rossnagel, Stephen M. II. Cuomo, J.J.
    III. Westwood, William D. (William Dickson), 1937-
    TA2020.H37   1989
    621.044--dc19   89-22834
                                                  CIP

This book is dedicated to the memory of Professor John Thornton of the University of Illinois, and formerly of Telic Corporation. John was a pioneer, an innovator, and a tireless teacher in the fields of sputtering and thin film technology. He was a colleague and friend of each of the editors and the majority of contributing authors to this book. His intelligence, integrity, and dedication have touched many of us.

Preface

The field of plasma-based thin film processing has grown rapidly over the past two decades. The technologies discussed in this book are the basis for the revolutionary increase in computer capabilities, as well as for such applications as tool coatings, food packaging and architectural coatings on skyscraper windows.

Plasma processing technology has a number of manifestations, from simple dc discharges up to the complicated electron cyclotron resonance (ECR) plasmas intended for single wafer processing. Films are deposited and etched by a range of devices, including rf diodes, magnetrons, broad beam ion sources, hollow cathode sources and more. Each of these techniques can operate in primarily non-chemical modes with inert gases, or can easily be switched to reactive modes, where a surface can be chemically eroded or a specific chemical compound deposited. A number of hybrid technologies have emerged, such as ion plating, ion cluster beam and activated, reactive evaporation deposition techniques.

In addition to simply the plasma process, a wealth of knowledge has been generated on ion-surface interactions. The impact of ions at many times the thermal energy of the surface can strongly change the structure as well as the chemistry of the surface. Techniques such as these allow one to explore materials not available in bulk form, and to produce new compounds, phases or structures.

Much remains to be accomplished in terms of plasma-based processing technologies. The fundamental understanding of the plasma itself is still at a crude level; the most sophisticated models are making progress in understanding the operation of simple rf diode plasmas. Classical plasma physics, as it applies to, perhaps, high temperature fusion plasmas, is beginning to make some sense of processing plasmas. However, the application of magnetic fields and the practical situation of using reactive, molecular species in the plasmas dramatically complicates the level of understanding.

This book is intended to provide a perspective look at a range of thin film plasma processing technologies. The authors were selected to represent the state-of-the-art understanding. The chapters are not just the classical review-type chapter found in many texts, but provide a more concise view of the level of understanding of the field today, without wading through the entire history of each field.

Yorktown Heights, NY   Stephen M. Rossnagel
October, 1989

About the Editors

Stephen M. Rossnagel is presently a research staff member at the IBM T.J. Watson Research Center, Yorktown Heights, New York. His current research is in plasma-based processing, particularly in ion beam and magnetron areas. He received his doctorate in physics from Colorado State University, and has held positions at Princeton University and at the Max Planck Institute in Garching, West Germany. Dr. Rossnagel has published extensively in areas of magnetron sputtering and also film modification by ion bombardment. He has published over 58 research papers and book chapters, and co-edited two books. He is the author of 6 patents, and is chairman of the Plasma Science Technology Division of the American Vacuum Society.

Jerome J. Cuomo is presently Manager of the Materials Processing Laboratory at the IBM T.J. Watson Research Center, Yorktown Heights, New York. Dr. Cuomo received his Ph.D. at Odense University and is particularly involved in the study of materials and the processing of materials by sputtering, ion beam and plasma processes. He has made important contributions to the development of LaB_6 electron emitters and Si_3N_4 as dielectric layers, and also pioneered work in chemical vapor deposition, dendritic solar thermal absorbers, sputtered amorphous silicon, amorphous magnetic bubble domain materials, ion beam modification and synthesis of materials, enhanced plasma processes, and high T_c superconductors. Dr. Cuomo has been active in various capacities in the American Vacuum Society and the Materials Research Society. He is a member of the Advisory Committee to the Materials Science Department of North Carolina State University and Pennsylvania State University and is an Adjunct Professor at Cornell University. He is the author or co-author of 56 patents, 197 patent publications and 85 research papers, chapters in several books and is co-editor of two books. He is distinguished by having the highest patent level in the IBM Corporation.

William D. Westwood is presently Manager of Advanced Materials and Devices at Bell-Northern Research's Advanced Technology Laboratory, Ottawa, Canada. He received his Ph.D. from the University of Aberdeen, Scotland in solid state physics. He then joined Northern Electric R&D Laboratory to work on magnetic oxide ceramics, and developed sputtering methods for fabricating thin films of these oxides. His research interests have centered on this technique since then. From 1966 to 1968, he was a faculty member at Flinders University in Australia. In 1969, he headed a group at Bell-Northern Research studying thin films for hybrid circuits, and from the sputtering aspects of this work evolved research on integrated optics. He has also been involved in technology research for electronic office applications, such as facsimile and displays. Since 1982, he has been involved in III-V semiconductor device technology for high speed electronics and optoelectronics. He has co-authored over 100 technical papers, co-edited a book, and has more than 20 patents. He has served the American Vacuum Society as a director, and is presently the Clerk of the society.

Contributors

Jes Asmussen
Michigan State University
East Lansing, MI

Soren Berg
University of Uppsala
Uppsala, Sweden

Rointan F. Bunshah
University of California, Los Angeles
Los Angeles, CA

Joseph L. Cecchi
Princeton University
Princeton, NJ

Chandra V. Deshpandey
University of California, Los Angeles
Los Angeles, CA

David B. Fraser
Intel Corporation
Santa Clara, CA

David W. Hoffman
Ford Research Center
Dearborn, MI

Chris M. Horwitz
University of New South Wales
Kennsington, Australia

Harold R. Kaufman
Front Range Research
Fort Collins, CO

Roger Kelly
IBM, Thomas J. Watson Research
   Center
Yorktown Heights, NY

Joseph S. Logan
IBM, Thomas J. Watson Research
   Center
Yorktown Heights, NY

Gerald Lucovsky
North Carolina State University
Raleigh, NC

Robert J. Markunas
Research Triangle Institute
Research Triangle Park, NC

Donald M. Mattox
Sandia National Laboratories
Albuquerque, NM

Robert C. McCune
Ford Research Center
Dearborn, MI

James J. McNally
U.S. Air Force Academy
U.S. Air Force Academy, CO

Russell Messier
Pennsylvania State University
University Park, PA

Claes Nender
University of Uppsala
Uppsala, Sweden

Gottlieb S. Oehrlein
IBM, Thomas J. Watson Research
  Center
Yorktown Heights, NY

Lawrence J. Pilione
Pennsylvania State University
University Park, PA

Rafael Reif
Massachusetts Institute of Technology
Cambridge, MA

Raymond S. Robinson
Colorado State University
Fort Collins, CO

Stephen M. Rossnagel
IBM, Thomas J. Watson Research
  Center
Yorktown Heights, NY

David N. Ruzic
University of Illinois
Urbana, IL

David Sanders
Lawrence Livermore National
  Laboratory
Livermore, CA

David V. Tsu
North Carolina State University
Raleigh, NC

William D. Westwood
Bell-Northern Research
Ottawa, Canada

Isao Yamada
Kyoto University
Sakyo, Kyoto, Japan

Joseph E. Yehoda
Pennsylvania State University
University Park, PA

NOTICE

To the best of the Publisher's knowledge the information contained in this book is accurate; however, the
Publisher assumes no responsibility nor liability for
errors or any consequences arising from the use of the
information contained herein. Final determination of
the suitability of any information, procedure, or product for use contemplated by any user, and the manner of
that use, is the sole responsibility of the user. The book
is intended for informational purposes only. Expert ad-
vice should be obtained at all times before implementation of any procedure described or implied in the book,
and caution should be exercised in the use of any materials or procedures for plasma processing which could be
potentially hazardous.

Contents

Part I
General Information

1

Techniques for IC Processing

David B. Fraser and William D. Westwood

1.1 INTRODUCTION

The driving force for the rapid development of plasma based processing over the past 15 years has been the microelectronics industry and in particular, the fabrication of silicon integrated circuits. There has been a consistent annual doubling of the complexity of these circuits: today, memory chips containing over 1 million transistors have been in production for a few years, chips with 4 million transistors are beginning production, chips comprising over 16 million transistors are being developed, and plans are being developed for circuits with 4 times that number of active devices. This increased complexity is driven by the need to provide more functionality and to reduce the cost of providing it. If the automobile industry had been able to do the same over this time period, a racing car would cost less than \$10. The large increase in the number of transistors has been accomplished primarily by reducing their size; whereas feature sizes (e.g. transistor gate length) were 20μm in the early 1970's, they are now 0.7μm or less.

These very high transistor count chips utilize CMOS (Complementary Metal Oxide Semiconductor) technology, because of its low power dissipation. However, other technologies for circuit fabrication have also developed rapidly. Bipolar silicon technology provides higher clock speeds than CMOS (400 MHz VS 40 MHz) and has also evolved from larger to smaller feature sizes to provide higher performance. Gallium arsenide MESFET (Metal Semiconductor Field Effect Transistor) circuits have developed in the past few years; 1μm features are standard but 0.5μm and even 0.25μm transistor gate lengths are in production for microwave integrated circuits.

In all these technologies, circuit fabrication involves a number of process steps carried out sequentially. The precise nature of the steps and the sequence in which they are performed may vary, but they are generically similar. They may involve:

(i) Epitaxial growth of doped Si or GaAs layers on a Si or GaAs substrate respectively.

2

(ii)   Ion implantation of dopants (B and P into Si, Si into GaAs) selectively in depth and location. The implant damage must then be annealed out.

(iii)   Ion implantation of non-dopants (e.g. protons) to deliberately cause damage and thus lower conductivity to provide electrical isolation of devices.

(iv)   Deposition of dielectric layers to isolate conducting layers. In MOS technology, the gate oxide is thermally grown on the silicon, thus consuming some of the silicon: the thermal oxide provides a lower density of interface states (i.e. states within the electron energy band gap of the semiconductor) which affect transistor performance. However. dielectric films are required in other stages of the process to provide electrical isolation between conducting interconnects as well as for other functions, such as passivation, scratch protection, etc. Silicon nitride is usually deposited, as well as various form of silicon dioxide, sometimes doped with B,P, etc.

(v)   Patterning a mask to define specific features. This usually involves covering the wafer with photosensitive material (resist), exposing it to energy (ultra-violet or X-ray photons, electron or ion beams) to change its structure locally so that the pattern can be developed. Once the pattern is established in the photosensitive material. it provides the mask for the next step in patterning.

(vi)   Etching the pattern in the semiconductor (e.g. GaAs) in one of the dielectric layers (e.g. Si_3N_4), or in a metal film (e.g. Al).

(vii)   Planarization of the surface to allow for the next process stage. For example, it is very difficult to carry out the patterning step on non-planar surfaces. For optical lithography, the depth of focus may be only $1\mu m$ whereas the wafer surface may have larger height variations after several processing steps. Planarization may involve the deposition of an organic layer, such as polyimide, which fills the depressions coupled with some etching process to remove material from the high points.

(viii)   Deposition of a polycrystalline semiconductor, particularly Si, for transistor gates.

(ix)   Cleaning between process steps. Many process steps depend on starting with a clean surface: for example. epitaxial growth of Si on Si, ohmic contact formation between GaAs and Ni-Ge-Au. In fabrication of a typical circuit, there may be 10-12 mask levels, each requiring a different process step and a clean surface for the process. Since each mask level involves photolithography, removal of residual resist at each stage is vital.

Twenty years ago, all of these steps, except metallization, involved a chemical process carried out in either liquid or gas phase. Chemical vapor deposition was used to deposit semiconductor and dielectric films. These are relatively high temperature processes; poly-silicon is obtained by cracking silane at $625°C$. Etching was carried out using acid or alkaline solutions and sometimes required slightly elevated temperatures. Etching SiO_2 required hydrogen fluoride acid baths, for example. Similar solutions, such as Garo's acid or organic solvents or several combinations of chemicals were used to provide clean surfaces between process steps.

Today, many of these deposition and etching process steps are instead based on the chemistry and physics of plasmas. This book deals with these processes over a broad range of deposition and etching technologies. In general, plasma processes are often quite complex, difficult to understand and usually require significantly more equipment than the wet chemical processes which they replace. A plasma can be thought of as a special state of matter in which the number densities of positive and negative (usually electron) charges are equal, on average, but these individual densities may be quite high (10^9 to 10^{14}cm^{-3} , see Chap. 2). Typically only a small percentage ($<$ 1%) of the gas is ionized. However, the properties of transistors are very sensitive functions of the electronic charge carrier density in the transistor channel. Many years of research were required to control the charges in MOS transistors and reduce them to an acceptable level of 10^{10}cm^{-2} . It therefore seems contradictory to expose these structures, during processing, to the energetic environment of a plasma of any kind. Yet, plasmas now provide the most practical way to carry out many of the process steps involved. Some of these steps, and the advantages provided by the plasma, are discussed briefly below while the rest of the book will examine in more detail a broad range of plasma processes which are relevant to the deposition and etching of films, both for microelectronics, and for other fields.

1.2 PLASMA PROCESSING IN MICROELECTRONICS

A cross section of one cell of a CMOS circuit is shown schematically in Fig. 1. This is just one of the many complex microelectronic structures now being fabricated. It provides a good example of the different process steps discussed above. We will concentrate here on these steps which directly involve the use of plasmas. Although ion implantation is a very important step, it utilizes plasmas only indirectly. The ions for implantation are generated by a plasma in the source. However, they are extracted from this plasma, analyzed and accelerated through a high vacuum region to the substrate to be implanted. While the efficient extraction of high ion current densities is an important topic in the design of implanters, since it affects wafer capacity, there is no direct affect of the plasma on wafer processes. Therefore, ion implantation will not be discussed here.

There are two aspects of plasmas which are important in processes: physical and chemical. Any plasma contains positive and negative charges in equal number densities. Because electrons have a much higher mobility, any surface in contact with the plasma will develop a negative potential with respect to the plasma. The resulting electric field reduces the electron current density to the surface until it equals the ion current density and the electrical neutrality of the plasma is thus maintained. The ions are accelerated to the surface by the electrical field; they arrive with an energy up to a maximum value of eV_f, where $-V_f$ is the floating potential of the surface relative to the plasma. In dc discharge plasmas, V_f is normally a few volts, and the effect of these low energy Ar$^+$ ions, for example, may be insignificant. However, the ion energy can easily be increased by applying a potential $-V_b$ (relative to ground) to the surface; the ion energy is then $e(V_b + V_f)$ and this may have a significant effect on the surface. For example, sputtering will take place when this energy exceeds about 20eV. In rf discharges, floating surfaces may develop even higher negative potentials, so that sputtering may occur even without supplying a bias to the sample deliberately. The actual potential depends on the geometry of the system and the frequency of the supply voltage. This topic will be discussed in more detail in Chap. 2.

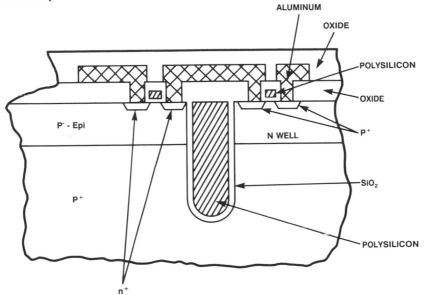

Figure 1: Schematic cross section of a basic cell of a CMOS circuit with a transistor gate width of 1 μm.

Many of the physical effects resulting from the plasma are due to the arrival at the sample of photons, electrons and ions. If the charged particles have sufficient energy, they may cause significant effects on the substrate, such as sputtering or stress generation. In most plasma systems, the electric field will be normal to the substrate and ions therefore reach the sample at normal incidence. Thus, some parts of a surface may be affected much less, or remain unaffected, by ions because of the substrate geometry. An example is shown in Fig. 2(a); no physical sputtering can occur in the region which is essentially masked by the mask overhang.

The chemical effect of plasmas results from the chemical activity of species which can be generated by mechanisms within the plasma, such as ionization by electron collision with molecules. For example, N_2^+ ions are very easily produced in the plasma. When N_2^+ impinges on a substrate, it may dissociate into N atoms, which are very reactive. While molecular N_2 is a very stable molecule which is unlikely to react with any substrate material, the addition of the same gas to a discharge produces highly reactive N atoms. For example, refractory materials such as AlN and TiN are readily formed when N_2^+ ions impinge on Al or Ti surfaces whereas N_2 does not react with Al even at elevated temperatures and even then only incompletely with Ti. More complex gases, such as CF_4, may be introduced into a plasma, producing different molecular ions (CF_3^+, CF_2^+ and CF^+) each of which will have different reactivities. In addition to ions, uncharged radicals may be generated which are extremely reactive: e.g. atomic oxygen in an O_2 plasma or CF_x in a CF_4 plasma. These radicals reach surfaces isotropically from any direction and cause reactions there. For example, In Fig. 2(b). the sidewall of the mask is eroded by reaction with a radical, the result being a gaseous species.

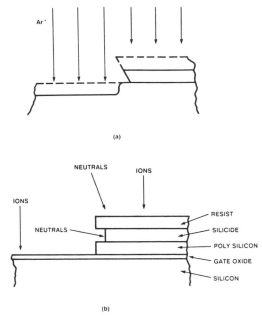

Figure 2: (a) Physical effects caused by the plasma. The substrate is sputtered by energetic (>20eV) ions, except in the region protected by the mask overhang because the ions are at normal incidence on the substrate. (b) Removal of material from under the mask due to chemical reaction with a neutral radical generated in the plasma. Since they are uncharged, they can reach all surfaces.

Care must be taken to ensure that no unexpected reactions take place. For example, water vapor is the most common constituent of the background gas in most vacuum systems after pumpdown. It is absorbed on the chamber walls, when a system is open, or on the surfaces introduced into the system (e.g. substrates and holders): the water vapor then desorbs from the surface in the vacuum system; the desorption rate may be increased by substrate heating or by ion bombardment from the plasma. Water vapor is then dissociated within the plasma into O, OH and H fragments. Both O and OH are very reactive with many metals to form oxides: the remaining hydrogen is not efficiently pumped in many vacuum systems, and is easily incorporated in many film materials.

In most plasma situations, both the physical and chemical effects may be important and should be considered carefully. Thus, combined effects of the situations shown in Fig. 2 can occur. The relative importance of the physical and chemical effects will, of course, depend on the circumstances of each case: the reactivities, the substrate potential, and the ion species in the plasma are the important parameters. However, these depend in turn on the plasma volume, gas flows, excitation volume, etc. These are considered in following chapters.

With these two effects of plasmas in mind, we may consider their application in microelectronics processing. Here we briefly review the various process steps required in fabricating the device in Fig. 1 and the plasma requirements.

1.2.1 Cleaning

Successful fabrication of complex ICs requires many lithography steps in which each mask is accurately aligned with the previous patterns on the wafer. A sequence of 9-13 individual masks may be required to complete the process. For each stage, the wafer is covered with a layer of photoresist which is exposed using the mask and the resulting pattern developed, producing areas which are free from photoresist. This pattern is used in the next process step. For example, the remaining resist may prevent etching of a SiO_2 layer from the Si wafer in these areas. After etching, the photoresist is removed, leaving the SiO_2 layer in selected areas, as required for the next process step. Alternatively, the mask may be used to selectively deposit films in unmasked areas: when the photoresist is removed, the excess metal is removed.

It is clearly required that following the etching or deposition step the photoresist is thoroughly removed, both before etching the SiO_2 and before proceeding to the next process step. If it is not thoroughly removed in the first case, regions of SiO_2 will remain, after etching, in additional uncontrolled areas.

Photoresists are hydrocarbon-based polymers, with the cross-linking being determined by the exposure and development. All traces of polymer should be removed by the developer or the photoresist stripper. However, this is often not the case, particularly when the photoresist has been subjected to extreme conditions. The last traces of hydrocarbon can be removed in a suitable oxidizing atmosphere, by conversion to CO_2 and H_2O. The process for this should ideally not require high temperatures nor produce damage to either the Si or SiO_2.

An oxygen plasma supplies atomic oxygen which reacts rapidly with the hydrocarbon to form volatile CO_2 and H_2O. Although any O_2 plasma would provide the necessary reactive oxygen substrate damage is minimized by ensuring that O_2^+ ions do not reach the surface being etched.

1.2.2 Deposition

The fabrication of a CMOS circuit involves the deposition of a variety of films, including polycrystalline silicon, Si_3N_4, and SiO_2 which may be doped with B and P, Al-Si alloys and possibly diffusion barriers such as TiN. Other microelectronic devices require different materials to be deposited: for example, epitaxial GaAs, Au/Ge/Ni and WSi_x for GaAs integrated circuits. Some of these films (e.g. Al-Si, WSi_x) can he deposited by a purely physical method, such as sputtering or evaporation, while others require a chemical method, such as plasma enhanced chemical vapor deposition (PECVD); reactive sputtering, which is widely used to deposit TiN, combines both chemical and physical aspects. Evaporation is preferred for lift-off processes because of the line-of-sight deposition. However, it is difficult to control alloy composition, and the adhesion of the film is often low, requiring the use of additional adhesion layers.

1.2.2.1 Sputtering. Evaporation was the first method used to deposit metals for microelectronics, such as Al, for interconnect conductors. With the increased complexity of integrated circuits came the need for different materials. Alloys of Al-Si or Al-Si-Cu have been widely used to obtain smaller line widths and to decrease electromigration in the conductors. However, the elemental constituents of alloys evaporate independently and the individual evaporation rates are proportional to the respective vapor pressures at the source temperature.

It is difficult to obtain from an alloy source an evaporated flux ratio which represents the original alloy composition and the source composition changes with time. Initially, the more volatile component evaporates from the charge and the flux is enriched in this component but the flux will eventually become rich in the other component as the source nears exhaustion. The scarcity of alloys which evaporate congruently (i.e. without change in composition) makes evaporation unattractive for alloy deposition.

The situation for sputtering is quite different because of the momentum transfer processes responsible for ejecting atoms from the alloy target. The sputtering yields S_A and S_B for the two elements in the binary alloy target AB represent the probabilities of these atoms being ejected. The numbers which are ejected are, therefore, proportional to the product of these probabilities and the numbers of A and B atoms which are present within the sputtering depth. In equilibrium, the surface composition of the target changes such that the composition of the elements in the sputtered flux is the same as the original alloy composition.

The sputtering mechanism is therefore, clearly advantageous for the deposition of alloys. Two points must be emphasized, however. First, the sputter mechanism alone is responsible for producing the correct flux ratio and other target effects will change this ratio. If the target temperature is too high, diffusion will occur and will modify the surface composition, so that the sputtered flux has a different composition from the alloy target.

Second, the sputtering process responsible for the correct equilibrium flux requires that the target be a homogeneous alloy and not simply a mixture of the two components. Sintered powder composite targets do not satisfy this requirement although they are sometimes used for deposition of silicides. If the target used to deposit $TaSi_2$ contains grains of Ta and Si, even if they are extremely small ($<5nm$), the alloy sputtering mechanism does not apply because sputtering occurs within individual Ta and Si grains rather than from an alloy in which atoms are homogeneously mixed. Then, the relative fluxes of Ta and Si will depend on the area ratio of Ta and Si grains and the elemental sputter yields for Ta and Si. Although the resulting film is a Ta-Si alloy, the sputtering process does not make use of the inherent advantage of the alloy sputtering process and there is no reason to expect the film to have the desired $TaSi_2$ composition. However, a constant composition (i.e. Ta/Si ratio) may be obtained if the relative areas of Ta and Si in the target are constant.

Since the vapor pressure of metals is very low except at elevated temperatures, the sticking coefficient for the different species in the sputtered fluxes is effectively unity and the film composition will be the same as the composition of the flux. However, the film composition may differ from the incident flux if energetic ions and neutrals reach the substrate and cause sputtering there.

The sputtering process is basically simple, although practical systems are actually quite complex because substrates must be transported, and gases and pressures controlled. A plasma is generated by applying either dc or rf power in a suitable geometry and the target is biased to accelerate ions of the sputtering gas to it. At present, most systems use a magnetron target arrangement; a magnetic field constrains the electrons to generate ions within a few millimeters of the target surface (Chap. 6).

1.2.2.2 Reactive Sputtering.   By adding a gas which reacts with a sputtered metal in the presence of the plasma, compound films can be deposited using basically the same sputtering system as that used for metals. This topic is treated in detail in Chap. 9. As an example, TiN is often used as a diffusion barrier because it is refractory and has high conductivity. It is deposited quite easily by adding N_2 while sputtering a Ti target provided a sufficient N_2 supply is maintained. N_2^+ ions are formed in the plasma and bombard both the target and substrate: the N atoms resulting from the impact dissociation react with the Ti. The energy and flux of the N_2^+ ions are determined by the sputtering parameters such as bias potentials and power.

1.2.2.3 Step Coverage.   In microelectronics, the films are often deposited onto a patterned wafer on which there are many steps which must be covered. For conductors. for example, the alloy must be continuous over each step and it is desirable that the film thickness be the same on the vertical wall of the step as on the flat surface since this will minimize high resistance regions at each step. However, this is obviously difficult because it would require that the sputtered flux normal to the side wall be the same as the flux to the wafer surface. In the usual system geometry, the substrate is parallel to the target and the sputtered atom flux is predominantly normal to the substrate surface so that the flux to the side wall is quite small (Fig. 3).

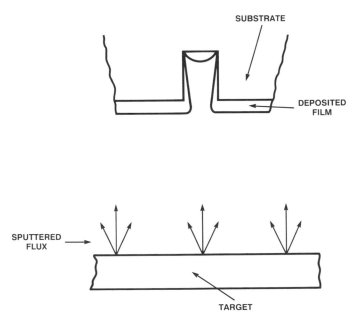

Figure 3: Schematic of the problem of step coverage during sputtering.

By applying bias to the substrate, ions are accelerated to the substrate and cause sputtering (usually termed resputtering) of the film. If the resputtering ratio is high (i.e. the thickness removed from the flat surface is comparable to the thickness deposited), the film thickness on the side walls will be increased by collecting the resputtered atoms, while the thickness on the top wafer surface is reduced. However, the alloy composition can be changed significantly by the resputtering. In fact, the step coverage by Al-Si alloys is greatly improved by applying substrate bias even when the resputtering ratio is negligible. This is most likely due to ion bombardment enhanced diffusion, which may be the most important mechanism for Al alloys but is probably insignificant for refractory metals.

The ability to improve step coverage is a significant advantage and is easily implemented because of the plasma environment in which the sputter deposition is carried out. It should be noted, however, that the enhancement of step coverage by bias sputter deposition may be incompatible with some masking techniques.

1.2.2.4 PECVD.   Chemical vapor deposition has been used in IC fabrication almost since it began, and is still used in many cases. In its simplest form, it requires increasing the temperature of the substrate to a value at which the required chemical reaction takes place at a useful rate in a controlled manner. Perhaps the simplest case is the deposition of silicon from SiH_4 and N_2 and silicon nitride from SiH_4 and NH_3 at 625°C.

While these are well understood reactions, they do require quite high temperatures. In PECVD, the chemical effects of the plasma allow the reactions to proceed at much lower temperatures (See Chap. 10). Lower temperatures are desirable to prevent diffusion of dopants during these subsequent processes.

Films deposited by PECVD have increased in importance for IC processing as device dimensions have decreased and imposed the requirement for much tighter tolerances on the dopant location. In depositing these films, it is the chemical aspects of the plasma which are usually of prime importance. However, physical effects of the plasma may be important in determining the film properties. For example, Si_3N_4 films may have high compressive stress when deposited in plasma conditions where substantial ion bombardment of the substrate occurs.

There are two basic plasma arrangements in which the physical effects may be quite different. These are shown schematically in Fig. 4. In the downstream arrangement (Fig. 4(a)), the plasma generation is remote from the substrate, so that physical effects are minimized. The gas reactants may be introduced either into the plasma region or near the substrate. In the parallel plate reactor (Fig. 4(b)), the substrate is immersed in the plasma and is therefore subject to physical effects such as ion bombardment.

Films can be deposited at temperatures determined by the plasma environment and the heat generated by the reactions. While no elevated temperatures are required for the chemical reaction, the film properties may be improved by heating. For example, silicon films deposited from SiH_4 will be amorphous and will contain a significant fraction of hydrogen, in the form SiH_x, unless the substrate temperature is above 600°C. SiO_2 films are deposited from SiH_4 and N_2O, just as in the CVD case. However, silicon nitride can be deposited using either NH_3 or N_2. Whereas N_2 cannot he used in CVD because of its low reactivity, (due to the stability of the molecule), its reactivity in the plasma is high due to dissociation processes. There are advantages to using N_2 in reducing NH bonding in the Si_3N_4 films as well as being more convenient.

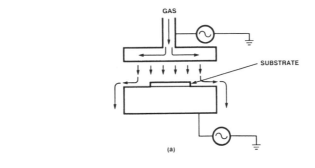

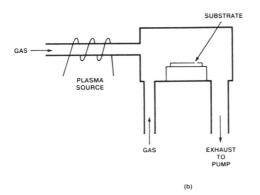

Figure 4: Schematic of (a) downstream and (b) parallel plate plasma deposition systems.

1.2.2.5 Etching.   The selective removal of one material from another is an important part of IC processing (Chap. 8). In the example already discussed in (a), the SiO_2 has to be removed from the underlying silicon but it is important that no significant amount of silicon be removed. Typically the dopants necessary for device operation are within 100 nm of the wafer surface and must remain there throughout processing. Thus, while it is possible to remove the SiO_2 by a physical method, such as sputtering, this is not acceptable for a process step since sputtering will etch the silicon at a faster rate than it removes the SiO_2 and may also introduce damage or impurities into the exposed Si.

For selectivity, a chemical reaction is required which etches one layer (e.g. SiO_2) but not the other (e.g. Si). For wet chemical etching, this often involves mixtures of several chemicals with competing interactions with the exposed surfaces. Just as chemical reactions for depositing films are made possible by injecting suitable gases into a plasma, so are chemical reactions for etching. The arrangements to do this are similar to these in Fig. 4. The chemical reaction must, in this case, convert the material to be removed into a volatile gas which will thus desorb from the surface within the plasma environment and be pumped out of the system.

A wide variety of gases are used in reactive plasma etching to etch different materials. For example, BCl_3, $SiCl_4$, Cl_2 and CCl_4 are all used to etch Al alloys and CF_4, C_2F_6, CHF_3, NF_3, SF_6, SiF_4, $CFCl_3$, CF_2Cl_2 and CF_3Cl are used to etch SiO_2. Mixtures of gases, such as $CF_4 + O_2$ are also used. Due to the variety of reactions that may occur, a large number of species may exist in the plasma.

As discussed with reference to Fig. 2, the type of etching which takes place will depend on the balance between the physical and chemical effects in the plasma. One effect not considered was the deposition onto a side wall of a non-volatile product, such as a polymer or C. If this polymer or carbon compound does not react chemically with the etch gas species, it will remain on the wall, preventing any further reaction because it cannot be sputtered away since the ions do not reach the side wall. This can be used to the advantage of the operation in that it inhibits undercutting of masks and results in a more anisotropic etch. The technique is known as "sidewall blocking" (Chap 8).

1.3 SUMMARY

Despite the apparent anomaly of subjecting an IC, during processing, to an environment containing charged species, plasmas obviously play an important role in IC fabrication. The two aspects, physical and chemical, are important although their relative importance will change with the application, the plasma equipment and the gases being used. A plasma is, however, a very complex environment in which to carry out these processes. Only an improved understanding of the plasma environment will make it possible to fully utilize the various process methods and to develop new methods.

Part II
Plasma Fundamentals

2

Introduction to Plasma Concepts and Discharge Configurations

Joseph L. Cecchi

2.1 INTRODUCTION

2.1.1 The Plasma State

A plasma is a gas containing charged and neutral species, including some or all of the following: electrons, positive ions, negative ions, atoms, and molecules. On average a plasma is electrically neutral, because any charge imbalance would result in electric fields that would tend to move the charges in such a way as to eliminate the imbalance. As a result, the density of electrons plus the density of negative ions will be equal to the density of positively charged ions (1). An important parameter of a plasma is the *degree of ionization*, which is the fraction of the original neutral species (atoms and/or molecules) which have become ionized. Plasmas with a degree of ionization much less than unity are referred to as *weakly ionized*. The presence of a relatively large population of neutral species will dominate the behavior of this type of plasma. In *fully ionized* plasmas, the degree of ionization approaches unity, and neutral particles play little or no role.

To form and sustain a plasma requires some energy source to produce the required ionization. In steady state, the rate of ionization must balance the losses of ions and electrons from the plasma volume by recombination and diffusion or convection to the boundary. Plasma is often referred to as the *fourth state of matter*, since it occurs by adding energy (heat) to a gas. There is not, however, a distinct phase change in going from a neutral gas to a plasma; the process is more continuous.

The plasmas we will consider here are initiated and sustained by electric fields which are produced by either direct current (dc) or alternating current (ac) power supplies. Typical ac frequencies of excitation are 100 kHz, at the low end of the spectrum, 13.56 MHz in the radio frequency (rf) portion of the spectrum, and 2.45 GHz in the microwave region. These plasmas are also referred to as *electric discharges, gaseous discharges, or glow discharges* (the latter because they emit light). In fact, there is a slight distinction between the terms *plasma* and *discharge*. Strictly speaking, there are regions of a dis-

14

charge (such as cathode sheaths) which do not actually fulfill the definition of a plasma (which will be presented below). As a practical matter, however, this distinction is not usually significant. Since the plasmas of interest here are always part of an electric discharge, we will tend to use the various terms interchangeably.

2.1.2 Brief Survey of Plasmas

Although plasmas are not common terrestrially, they do represent the most ubiquitous form of matter in the universe. Because electrons play such an important role in plasmas, it is useful to categorize plasmas by electron densities and electron energies. As we shall see, the electrons in a plasma have a distribution of energies, so we will typically use an average electron energy. In a number of cases, the electrons will have a Maxwellian distribution (2), which can be described in terms of the electron energy ε as,

$$f(\varepsilon) = 2(\varepsilon)^{1/2}/((\pi)^{1/2}(kT)^{3/2}) \exp(-\varepsilon/kT) \tag{1}$$

where $f(\varepsilon)$, the electron energy distribution function, is proportional to the number of electrons having an energy between ε and $\varepsilon + d\varepsilon$, k is Boltzmann's constant, and T is the electron temperature. The electron energy is given by

$$\varepsilon = (1/2)mv^2 \tag{2}$$

where m is the electron mass and v is the magnitude of the electron velocity. The constants in Eq. (1) are such that if we integrate over all energies, we get:

$$\int f(\varepsilon)d\varepsilon = 1 \tag{3}$$

The average energy can be obtained by the integral:

$$\int \varepsilon f(\varepsilon)d\varepsilon = (3/2)kT \tag{4}$$

Thus, the electron temperature T for a Maxwellian electron energy distribution is a measure of the average energy of the electrons.

The Maxwellian distribution is also called the *equilibrium* distribution, because it represents a case where the electrons are in thermodynamic equilibrium. In a number of cases, especially weakly ionized plasmas, $f(\varepsilon)$ will not be Maxwellian; however, it is quite common to still speak of an electron temperature T when referring to the average electron energy.

A convenient unit for the electron temperature is the electron volt (eV) which is equivalent to a temperature of approximately 11600 K. In Fig. 1, typical values of electron densities and temperatures are shown for a variety of plasmas. They range from the very rarified and cold interstellar plasmas up to the dense and hot plasmas used for controlled fusion. The plasmas of interest here are the process plasmas, which have electron densities in the range of $1x10^9$ to $1x10^{12}$ cm^{-3}, and average   electron energies between 1 and 10 eV. The degree of ionization for these plasmas varies from about 10^{-6} to as high as 0.3. At the lower end of the density, energy, and ionization scale are the discharges that are formed between planar electrodes, while the upper end of this scale applies to discharges sustained at a frequency that corresponds to some natural frequency for the plasma (such as electron cyclotron resonance (ECR) plasmas).

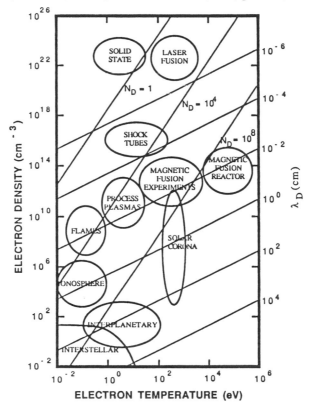

Figure 1: Electron density and temperature ranges for a variety of natural and man-made plasmas. Lines of constant Debye length (λ_D) are shown, along with lines of constant number of electrons in a Debye sphere (N_D). The region labelled **PROCESS PLASMAS** delineates the parameter ranges for the plasmas used for thin film deposition and etching.

2.1.3 Plasmas for Thin Film Deposition and Etching

The extensive use of plasmas for the deposition and etching of thin films derives from two salient features. Firstly, plasmas are capable of efficiently generating chemically active species. Examples of this include atomic chlorine for the etching of silicon and CH_x (x = 0-3) for the deposition of amorphous hydrogenated carbon. The generation of chemically active species in a plasma is initiated by the bombardment of molecules and atoms by the plasma electron, which have sufficient energy to break chemical bonds. The products of the electron bombardment processes, which include radicals and ions, can undergo further reactions, often at high rates, to form additional chemically reactive species.

As a generator of reactive species, a plasma reactor is similar to more conventional chemical reactors (3) which utilize thermal activation of chemical reactions that typically proceed with Arrhenius rates κ of the form.

$$\kappa = A \exp(-B/RT), \tag{5}$$

where A is the pre-exponential factor, B the activation energy for the reaction, R the universal gas constant, and T the absolute temperature. For a given reaction, which fixes A and B, the rate depends only on temperature. In actual practice, other factors, such as fluid flow, heat transfer, and mass transfer will play important roles. Nevertheless, the conventional reactor, with its Arrhenius rates, will be comparatively simpler than a plasma reactor, in which the chemistry is governed by many elementary processes that depend in very complicated ways on the plasma parameters. The additional complications of a plasma reactor are generally offset by greater process efficacy (e.g., higher rates or unique capability). It is clear that the design and operation of plasma reactors requires an understanding of the plasma and the processes that occur within it, and this is one of the major objectives of this chapter.

The second feature that makes plasma discharges so useful is their ability to generate ions and to accelerate the ions to energies of 50 - 1000 eV in the vicinity of the deposition or etching substrate. Energetic ions are useful for sputtering, as in the sputter deposition of metals. Energetic ions can also play a synergistic role in the deposition or etching of thin films. A prominent example of this is the anisotropic etching of semiconductor devices (4,5), where the etch rate perpendicular to the substrate (the direction of the energetic ion impingement), can be enhanced over that lateral to the substrate surface by a variety of ion bombardment-activated processes.

Ions are formed in a plasma principally by electron bombardment ionization. The ions can then be accelerated in relatively strong electric fields which, in certain discharge configurations, exist outside the main plasma volume near the substrate. The formation of such strong electric fields in the so-called sheath region of the discharge follow quite naturally, as we shall see.

In this section, we have taken a *process* point of view of a plasma, which is certainly appropriate in the context of this book. It is clear, however, that for any process, we need a stable equilibrium plasma discharge in the "background" of the process of interest. This will involve a number of elementary collisional interactions (including ones responsible for the process of interest), as well as the interaction of plasma electrons and ions with electric and possibly magnetic fields. In this chapter we will examine these topics, also.

2.1.4 An Elementary View of Plasma Reactors

Although we will consider a number of aspects of plasmas and discharges in this chapter, we are primarily interested in these topics as they relate to the plasma reactors that are used for thin film processes. Therefore to provide some general framework for what is to follow, we will consider here some general characteristics of the most common types of reactors.

2.1.4.1 Planar Reactors Perhaps the most ubiquitous class of plasma reactor is one in which the plasma is formed between planar parallel electrodes (6,7), which are attached to the power source. This includes configurations with a single electrode in a metallic containment vessel, the latter comprising the second electrode.

The importance of the plasma electrons in generating chemically active species in the plasma volume, and the edge electric fields accelerating ions into the substrate suggests a schematic picture in which a reactor is decomposed into two regions. The embodiment of this for a planar geometry is shown in Fig. 2. Here, we see the plasma volume where chemically reactive species (and/or ions) are generated, in which there is only a small electric field. Adjacent to this is a "plasma free" sheath region of strong electric field. Although this picture is only approximate, it is represents a useful framework for examining relevant plasma and sheath phenomena. It also underlies the approach to many of the advanced plasma deposition and etch tools which are constructed to afford independent or nearly independent control of the two regions.

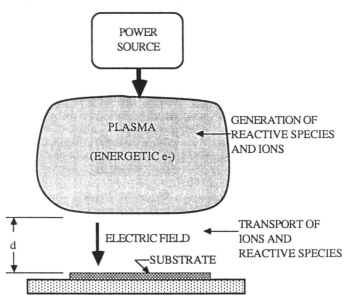

Figure 2: Generic plasma reactor for thin film deposition and etching. A power source supplies energy to the main plasma discharge where reactive species and ions are generated. These species are transported to the substrate or wafer for deposition or etching. In many configurations, there is an electric field in the vicinity of the substrate which accelerates the ions.

In many types of plasma reactors, the electrodes between which the plasma is sustained are not simply planar, an example being the hollow cathode discharge (see Chap. 11). Even in such cases, the discharge will still exhibit the bulk plasma/sheath dichotomy, though the geometry of the regions will be more complicated.

The operation of planar reactors can be enhanced by the addition of magnetic fields. This is usually accomplished by introducing a magnetic field that is nominally parallel to an electrode, as in a magnetron sputter source (see Chap. 6) or a magnetically enhanced reactive ion etcher (8). As we shall see, the magnetic field will increase the ionization efficiency of the electrons. This results in higher density plasmas with decreased sheath voltage.

2.1.4.2 Barrel Reactors. A barrel reactor (9) is a tubular-shaped structure, in which a plasma is sustained either by inductively coupling an ac power supply through a coil which surrounds the reactor (Fig. 3(a)), or by capacitatively coupling via external rings (Fig. 3(b)). For this configuration, the electric field is established inside the non-conducting vacuum vessel without internal electrodes. Consequently, this reactor does not develop the larger sheath electric fields that a planar reactor does, so that ion bombardment usually plays little or no role. The main application of barrel reactors is for isotropic etching, including the removal of organic materials as in resist stripping.

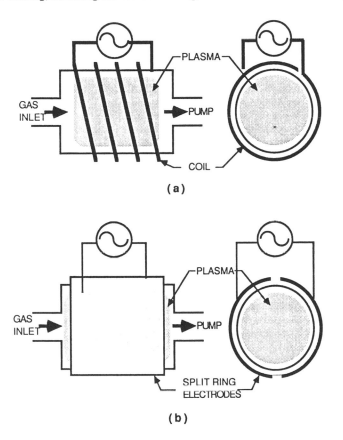

Figure 3: (a) Inductively coupled plasma reactor. An alternating current power source creates a time varying current, the magnetic field from which generates a voltage that sustains the discharge. (b) Capacitively coupled plasma reactor. Similar to (a), except the two plates are used to create an electric field to sustain the discharge.

2.1.4.3 Downstream Plasma Reactors Another class of plasma reactor is the *downstream* reactor (10-12), in which the region of the bulk plasma is separated by a large distance (i.e., much more than a cathode sheath thickness) from the substrate. Such plasmas are usually electrodeless, being sustained by microwaves introduced by some radiation launching structure. An important example of the downstream plasma reactor is the electron cyclotron resonance (ECR) plasma reactor (11,12). This apparatus includes a magnetic field. Electrons are heated by a microwave source which is applied at a frequency that corresponds to that of the electrons circulating in the magnetic field. The processes that are involved in ECR apparatus will be considered in detail below.

Oftentimes in the downstream geometry, ion bombardment of the substrate is not wanted. Owing to the separation of the plasma from the substrate, this is easily accomplished. In situations where ion bombardment of the substrate is essential to a process, it is possible to provide this by substrate bias and/or by taking advantage of the behavior of particles in magnetic field gradients.

The downstream configuration represents an even further emphasis on separating the bulk plasma from the environment of the substrate. For this reason, the downstream configuration is an important approach to advanced deposition and etch tools.

2.2 FUNDAMENTAL PLASMA DISCHARGE CONCEPTS

In this section, we will consider the fundamental plasma discharge concepts which underlie the operation of plasma reactors for deposition and etching. The concepts discussed here are covered extensively in a number of excellent plasma physics texts (13-17) and therefore, in some cases, we will present results with only limited derivations.

In presenting formulae, there is always the question of appropriate units. In general, we will use the International System (SI) nomenclature (previously referred to as rationalized MKS units). However, in some cases, we will deviate from this standard either for convenience, or to follow convention.

2.2.1 Debye Shielding

In general, the characteristics of plasmas will differ greatly depending on things like the constituent atoms and molecules, densities, energies, and degree of ionization. There is, however, one universal plasma characteristic which was noted earlier: the free charges in the plasma will move in response to any electric field in such a way to decrease the effect of the field. In particular, it is usually the lighter and more mobile electrons that respond to electric fields, and in what follows we will adopt a simplified, but reasonably accurate, picture of a discharge in which the ions are assumed stationary, and the electrons are free to move in response to any electric fields.

We have already noted one implication of this tendency of plasma electrons to decrease electric fields. There will not be regions of a plasma with excess positive or negative charge, because if there were, an electric field would arise that would move electrons to effectively eliminate any charge imbalance. This feature is called *quasineutrality*.

In addition, if a "test" charge is inserted in a plasma or an electric field is imposed on a plasma, the plasma electrons will move in such a way as to diminish the effects. This is the phenomena of Debye shielding, which we will examine more quantitatively by assuming that we place a positive test charge Q in a plasma. We further assume that before inserting the test charge, the plasma was quasineutral, with equal electron and ion densities given by n. In free space the charge would give rise to an electric potential V_0 given by (18)

$$V_0 = Q/(4\pi\varepsilon_0 r) \tag{6}$$

where r is the distance from the charge, and ε_0 is the permittivity of free space and is equal to 8.85×10^{-12} farad/m. The total potential V will include the effects of the plasma electrons and ions, along with the test charge, and is given by Poisson's equation,

$$\nabla^2 V = -\rho/\varepsilon_0 \tag{7}$$

where ρ is the total charge density in the plasma. The charge density is

$$\rho = e(n_i - n_e) + Q\delta(r) \tag{8}$$

where $\delta(r)$ is the Dirac delta function (18), which specifies that Q is a point charge, and n_i is the ion density, which, since the ions are assumed to be immobile, may be taken as equal to n. For simplicity, we have assumed that there are only positive ions in the plasma.

The existence of the potential V will cause the electron density to be altered. If we assume that the electrons are in thermodynamic equilibrium at temperature T, then we can write

$$n_e = n \exp(eV/kT). \tag{9}$$

If we now assume that

$$eV/kT << 1 \tag{10}$$

we can expand the exponential term and rewrite Poisson's equation as

$$\nabla^2 V = -(en/\varepsilon_0)(1 - 1 - (eV/kT)) + Q\delta(r) \tag{11}$$

or

$$\nabla^2 V = V/\lambda_D + Q\delta(r), \tag{12}$$

where the quantity λ_D is called the Debye length and is given by

$$\lambda_D = ((\varepsilon_0 kT)/(ne^2))^{1/2} \tag{13}$$

$$= 743(T_e(eV)/n(cm^{-3}))^{1/2}.$$

The solution to Eq. (12) is

$$V(r) = (Q/4\pi r\varepsilon_0) \exp(-r/\lambda_D). \tag{14}$$

The plasma thus modifies V_0 from its free space value (Eq. (6)) by attenuating it exponentially with a characteristic decay length of λ_D. This effect is called Debye shielding, and quite generally describes how a plasma will respond to an electric field.   Plasma electrons will collect in the vicinity of the test charge to screen its effect. Fig. 4 shows this effect schematically.

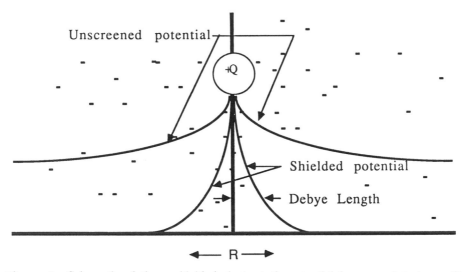

Figure 4: Schematic of the unshielded electrostatic potential from a point charge Q compared to the Debye shielded potential that occurs when the charge is immersed in a plasma. The electron density increases in the vicinity of the charge, creating the exponential fall-off in the potential.

The solution (Eq. 14) makes sense only if many electrons are involved in the shielding process. Since the shielding falls off exponentially, we can quantify this by calculating the number of electrons N_D in a sphere of radius λ_D, called a Debye sphere,

$$N_D = (4\pi/3)\lambda_D^3 n. \tag{15}$$

In fact, the criterion that $N_D \gg 1$ is generally taken as the definition of a plasma. Lines of constant N_D are plotted in Fig. 1. Clearly, the dependence of N_D on n and T_e is such that for T_e above 1 eV, any plasma with a density less than 1×10^{18} cm^{-3}, will easily satisfy the large N_D criterion. Implicit in our definition of a plasma is the criterion that the *size* of the plasma is large compared to λ_D, since, otherwise, the shielding would not be complete.

If we were to use (Eq. 14) to calculate the potential energy associated with the *shielding* (i.e., subtract out the contribution from the test charge with $Q = e$), we would find that N_D was proportional to the ratio of the particle kinetic energy, kT, to the Debye shielding potential energy. It may seem somewhat paradoxical that the Debye shielding potential energy *decreases* relative to the kinetic energy for an increasing number of particles in a Debye sphere; however, we can understand this in terms of a reduced "shielding" requirement on a individual electron as N_D increases.

For the plasmas of interest here, the relevant range of λ_D is from 0.01 to 1 mm, with 0.1 mm being a good average for weakly ionized planar discharges. The value of N_D varies from about 1×10^4 to 1×10^7, which easily satisfies the definition of a plasma.

2.2.2 Plasma Oscillations

If a charge imbalance does occur in a plasma, we have seen how the electrons will move to shield out its effects. This does not happen instantaneously, however. A reasonable estimate of the time it takes for the shielding to "get in place," would be the time required for an electron to move a Debye length. This time t_p is

$$t_p = \lambda_D/v = ((\varepsilon_o me)/(ne^2))^{1/2}. \tag{16}$$

Furthermore, we might imagine that the electrons, moving under the force of the electric field from the charge imbalance, may "overshoot" and execute an oscillatory motion. A more rigorous treatment of this problem (19) reveals that this is the case. The electrons will oscillate at a frequency which is just the inverse of t_p called the *plasma frequency* ω_p,

$$\omega_p = t_p^{-1} = 5.64 \times 10^4 \cdot (n(cm^{-3}))^{1/2} \tag{17}$$

Collisions will damp out this oscillatory motion, so that the shielding electrons will eventually assume the static distribution in Eq. (14).

In the absence of magnetic fields, this is the only "normal mode" of a plasma. In the presence of magnetic fields, however, plasmas display a number of additional oscillatory modes. Detailed discussion of these, which is beyond the scope of this chapter, can be found in a number of excellent references (20,21). We will, however, consider the important case of electron cyclotron oscillations in Sect. 2.2.5.3.

The oscillatory modes of a plasma establish its response to externally applied electromagnetic radiation. A discussion of the dielectric properties of plasmas is given in Sect. 2.2.5.2. We note here the general observation that the plasma will screen out an oscillating field with a frequency below ω_p, but above this frequency, the electrons cannot respond fast enough to accomplish the shielding.

2.2.3 Particle Orbits

The charged particles in a plasma will move in response to electric and magnetic fields. These fields may arise from external sources (such as a power supply or an electromagnet) or from collisional interactions among the particles. In the next section, (2.2.4) we will consider the effects of collisions. In this section, we will look at how charged particles move in electric and magnetic fields of various kinds and in various combinations. We will confine our discussion to fields that do not change in time and will generalize to time varying fields in Sect. 2.2.5. We know from Sect. 2.2.1 that the plasma will modify external fields we attempt to put on. We will deal with this complication in Sect. 2.2.7, where we will consider plasma sheaths, and again in our discussion of glow discharges (Sect. 2.4).

2.2.3.1 Effects of Electric and Magnetic Fields. In the presence of an electric field $\mathbf{E}$ and magnetic field $\mathbf{B}$, a particle of charge q and velocity $\mathbf{v}$ will experience a force $\mathbf{F}$ given by:

$$\mathbf{F} = q\mathbf{E} + q\mathbf{v} \times \mathbf{B}. \tag{18}$$

The quantities $\mathbf{F, E, v}$, and $\mathbf{B}$ are all vectors, and $\times$ denotes the vector cross product. Particle orbits are calculated by using Newton's second law to relate the particle acceleration a to the force:

$$\mathbf{F} = m\,\mathbf{a}, \tag{19}$$

where m is the particle mass. We will now consider a number of cases to illustrate typical particle motions.

$\underline{\mathbf{E} = \text{constant}, \mathbf{B} = 0}$

In this case, a particle will experience a constant acceleration in the direction of $\mathbf{F}$ given by

$$\mathbf{a} = q\mathbf{E}/m. \tag{20}$$

$\underline{\mathbf{E} = 0, \mathbf{B} = \text{constant}}$

The magnetic force acts in a direction perpendicular to the velocity of the charged particle. If a particle is at rest ($\mathbf{v} = 0$), then there is no force and the particle remains at rest. For a nonzero velocity, let us define the component of velocity of the particle parallel to $\mathbf{B}$ to be $v_{\parallel}$ and the velocity component perpendicular to $\mathbf{B}$ to be $v_{\perp}$. For the case of $v_{\parallel} = 0$, the particle will move in a circular orbit perpendicular to the direction of $\mathbf{B}$. The radius of the orbit is call the gyro radius ρ and is given by

$$\rho = mv_{\perp}/qB, \tag{21}$$

where B is the magnitude of **B** . Noting that the kinetic energy W of the particle is given by

$$W = mv_\perp^2/2. \tag{22}$$

we can write the gyro radius as

$$\rho = (2mW)^{1/2}/qB \tag{23}$$

Thus, for particles of the same energy, the heavier species will have larger circular orbits.

As a particular example, let us consider an electron in a 100 G (0.01 T) magnetic field. If the electron energy is 100 eV, then the gyro radius would be 2.4 mm. At 1000 eV, the gyro radius would increase to 7.5 mm. If we now consider a Cl$^-$ ion at 100 eV and 1000 eV, we find that its gyro radii are 62 cm and 197 cm respectively.

These parameters are typical of the cathode region of a magnetron discharge. Thus, the electrons will tend to execute circular orbits near the cathode (though, as we will see, this will be modified by field gradients and collisions). This will have the effect of "confining" the electrons in a region there they can efficiently ionize, with attendant improvement in plasma performance. The ions, with gyro radii much larger than the reactor, will be largely unaffected. Processes such as anisotropic etching, which rely on ion orbits being perpendicular to the wafer, will not be disturbed by the magnetic field.

The frequency of rotation of a particle in a magnetic field is called the gyro frequency or cyclotron frequency ω and is given by

$$\omega = qB/m. \tag{24}$$

Here, ω is given in units of radians/s, and is related to f the frequency in Hz by

$$\omega = 2\pi f. \tag{25}$$

We note that, although the gyro radius will increase with particle energy, ω is independent of the particle energy. As we will see below, this fact underlies our ability to couple energy efficiently to plasma electrons by using an ac power source with a frequency that matches the natural rotational frequency of the electron in a magnetic field. In particular, if B = 875 G, then f = 2.45 GHz. This is a typical combination for electron cyclotron resonance plasma reactors.

The component of the particle velocity parallel to the magnetic field, $v_\parallel$, is not affected by **B** . Thus, the general orbit of a charged particle in a magnetic field is a helix, as shown in Fig. 5. The sign of the charge will determine the sense of the helix; electrons and ions will have opposite directions of rotation.

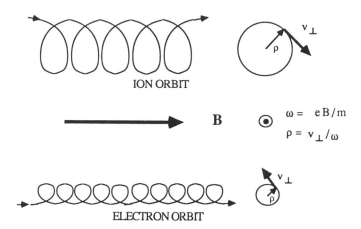

ION ORBIT

B   ⊙ $\omega = eB/m$
$\rho = v_\perp/\omega$

ELECTRON ORBIT

Figure 5: Orbits of ions and electrons in a homogeneous static magnetic field B. A particle follows a helical orbit, with a gyro frequency omeqa that is independent of the particle energy. The gyro radius depends on ω and the perpendicular velocity as noted.

E = constant, B = constant

If **E** is parallel to **B** , then it acts on the particle just as in Eq. (20), i.e., **B** has no effect on the component of velocity parallel to itself. If **E** is perpendicular to **B** , then the particles will undergo a drift motion which is perpendicular to both **E** and **B** and has a magnitude given by v_{ExB}:

$$v_{ExB} = E/B. \tag{26}$$

This drift velocity is independent of the particle charge and mass, although implicit in the derivation of Eq. (26) is the assumption that the particles are free to undergo gyro motion. Collisions may interrupt the gyro motion, in which case Eq. (26) will not be valid. This drift will operate on electrons in the cathode region of a magnetron, where the cathode electric field has a component perpendicular to the magnetic field, and the electron gyro radius is small. It will not affect the ions, because their gyro radii are larger than the reactor.

Nonuniform Fields

A nonuniform electric field will result in an acceleration which changes in space. It is difficult to generalize about the results of this. The main implication is that Eq. (20) will be more difficult to solve.

A nonuniform magnetic field will result in additional drift motion. In particular, a field gradient will produce a drift velocity v_g, which is perpendicular to both the field and the gradient, given by

$$v_g = (v_\perp^2/\omega)(\mathbf{B} \times \nabla\mathbf{B}/2B^2). \tag{27}$$

Unlike the $\mathbf{E} \times \mathbf{B}$ drift, a gradient drift will depend upon the particle mass, charge, and velocity. If the magnetic field is curved, the particle will experience a drift velocity v_c, which is perpendicular to both the field and its direction of curvature, given by

$$v_c = (v_\parallel^2/\omega)(\mathbf{R}_c \times \mathbf{B})/(BR_c^2). \tag{28}$$

Here $\mathbf{R}_c$ is the radius of curvature of the field. As in the gradient drift, v_c depends upon the particle mass, charge, and velocity. As in the case of the $\mathbf{E} \times \mathbf{B}$ drifts, it is implicit in the above two formulae that the particles undergo full gyro radii. If we again consider a magnetron discharge, the magnetic field will usually have both curvature and a gradient, so that the drifts in Eqs (27) and (28) will affect the electrons in the discharge (22), providing the rate of collisions is low enough to permit the electrons to execute their gyro motion.

2.2.3.2 Adiabatic Invariants

In general, the effects of a nonuniform magnetic field are complicated to predict. Under certain circumstances, however, we can take advantage of quantities which are invariant with changes in B. One example of this is the magnetic moment μ which is defined as (23)

$$\mu = W_\perp/B, \tag{29}$$

where $W_\perp$ is the perpendicular energy of the particle given by

$$W_\perp = mv_\perp^2/2. \tag{30}$$

If a particle passes through a changing field slowly, then μ is constant., and is referred to as an adiabatic invariant. "Slowly" in this case means that from the particle's point of view, the field is changing at a rate less than the gyro frequency. This is a bit difficult to calculate exactly, but for most cases of interest this condition is met.

One application of the constancy of μ is in a magnetic mirror, which is a configuration, shown schematically in Fig. 6(a), where the magnetic field gets stronger at the ends. Let us assume that the strength of the field is B_0 and B_M at its minimum and maximum respectively. Let us also assume that the particle has velocity components at the point where $B = B_0$ of $v_\parallel$ and $v_\perp$. Then, if the particle does not undergo collisions in the time it take to traverse the mirror, total energy W is also conserved and given by

$$W = mv_\parallel^2/2 + mv_\perp^2/2. \tag{31}$$

Using Eqs. (30) and (31), we can write an expression for $v_\parallel$

$$v_\parallel = (2(W - (mv_\perp^2)/2))^{1/2}.$$

$$= (2(W - \mu B)/2)^{1/2}. \tag{32}$$

Now, if the particle moves into a region of stronger magnetic field, it will gain perpendicular energy at the expense of parallel energy. If B increases to the point that $W = \mu B$, then $v_\parallel$ will go to zero and the particle will reverse its direction and thus be "reflected" by the magnetic mirror. For this to happen, the particle must start out with sufficient perpendicular velocity. We can quantify this in terms of the pitch angle Θ, shown in Fig. 6(b), which is the angle the velocity vector $\vec{v}$ makes with $v_\parallel$. At B_0 the magnetic moment is given by

$$\mu = W_\perp/B_0 \tag{33}$$

and at the maximum field, if mirroring is to occur, $W_\perp = W$, so we can write

$$\mu = W/B_M. \tag{34}$$

Thus from Eqs. (33) and (34), we have that

$$B_0/B_M = W_\perp/W, \tag{35}$$

or

$$B_0/B_M = v_\perp^2/(v_\perp^2 + v_\parallel^2). \tag{36}$$

Now $\sin \Theta = v_\perp/v$, so we can write

$$\sin^2 \Theta = R_M^{-1}, \tag{37}$$

where R_M is the mirror ratio defined by

$$R_M = B_M/B_0. \tag{38}$$

Particles with pitch angles greater than Θ given in Eq.(37) will be reflected in the mirror, while particles with smaller pitch angle have too much parallel velocity to undergo reflection.

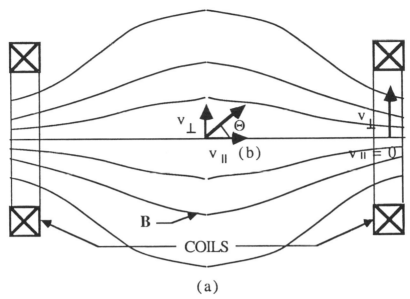

(a)

Figure 6: (a) Magnetic mirror field configuration produced by a pair of Helmholtz coils. Mirroring takes place as a result of conservation of the particle magnetic moment when the parallel velocity goes to zero. (b) Parallel and perpendicular components of the velocity, showing the pitch angle Θ.

In many magnetron configurations, the field gradients will be such as to provide some mirroring of electrons (22). Clearly, at some point, the electrons will undergo collisions, thus disrupting the conservation of μ, but at low pressures, their confinement is increased by this effect. Also, it is possible to utilize mirror confinement in an electron cyclotron resonance (ECR) reactor to increase the confinement of the electrons.

Some ECR reactors make use of a sort of "reverse" mirror in which electrons can *gain* parallel energy by moving into a magnetic field which is *decreasing* (24). In a downstream configuration, if the magnetic field at the substrate is B_0 and the maximum field in the ECR region is B_M, then the electrons which leave the discharge and stream to towards the substrate will increase their parallel energy at the expense of perpendicular energy. Let us assume that in the resonance region, since the electrons are being accelerated by the resonant electric field, the energy of the electron is totally perpendicular, $W = W_\perp$. Then the parallel energy at the substrate is

$$W_{\parallel s} = W - W_{\perp s} = \mu B_M - \mu B_0. \tag{39}$$

This can be rewritten as

$$W_{\parallel s}/W = (1 - B_0/B_M). \tag{40}$$

If the magnetic field at the substrate is 1/4 times the field in the resonance region, then 75% of the electron energy will be converted to parallel energy. The electrons streaming rapidly from the discharge will set up an electric field which will accelerate the ions into the substrate.

2.2.4 Collisional Processes

Collisions are generally characterized by a cross section σ which has the dimensions of area. If an electron collided with a "hard sphere" of radius a, then $\sigma = \pi a^2$ (see Fig. 7).

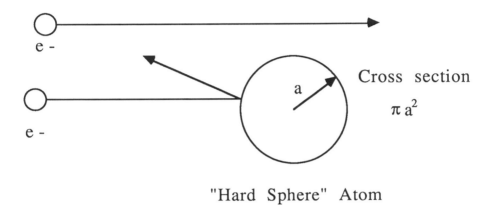

$$e -$$

Cross section

$$\pi a^2$$

$$e -$$

"Hard Sphere" Atom

Figure 7: Hard sphere atom cross section. Electrons that approach within a distance a of the center will undergo a collision, while those that have a larger impact parameter will not collide.

The cross section is a measure of the probability that a given process will occur. For some complicated processes there may not be a corresponding physical picture as above, although σ still will have units of area. If we are considering electron - neutral collisions where N is the neutral density, then the quantity,

$$\lambda = (N\sigma)^{-1}, \tag{41}$$

is the collision *mean free path*. This is the average distance travelled by the electron between collisions or processes.

Another important quantity which is related to the cross section is the *collision frequency*. If v is the electron velocity, then the collision frequency ν is defined by

$$\nu = N\sigma v \tag{42}$$

and has units of sec^{-1}. The time between collisions is just ν^{-1}.

Collisions fall into two general categories: *elastic collisions*, which are those for which the internal energy of the colliding partners is unchanged by the collision, and *inelastic collisions*, in which internal energy changes.   Internal energy refers to electronic excitations in atoms or electronic, vibrational, and rotational excitations in molecules. Ions will, in general, have different states of internal energy, however, an electron does not.

In weakly ionized plasmas $(n_e/N < 10^{-4})$, collisions between electrons and neutrals will be very important in establishing the electron energy distribution function. In fact, the dominance of electron-neutral collisions is responsible for the general character of these glow discharges, which behave very differently from plasmas with higher degrees of ionization, where electron-electron collisions dominate.

In what follows we will consider example of some important collisions processes. Additional information can be found in the references (25,26).

2.2.4.1 Electron-Neutral Elastic Collisions   The elastic cross section for electron-neutral collisions σ_N will depend on the electron velocity. Examples of σ_N for the rare gases is shown in Fig. 8. For rare gases heavier than He, the cross section has a minimum at low electron velocities, rises to a peak which increases with mass, and then falls off at higher velocities. The minimum is called the Ramsauer effect and arises from the quantum mechanical wave nature of the electron. The increase in the maximum cross section with mass is related to the increased size of the atom. At higher electron velocities, the interaction time is shortened, so that the collision has less effect on the electron.

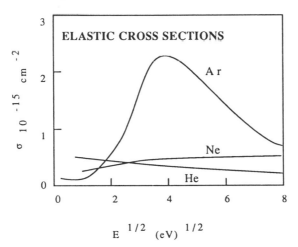

Figure 8: Elastic scattering cross sections for electrons of energy E incident on He, Ne, and Ar.

The average amount of energy transferred from the electron to the neutral is E_t, given by (27)

$$E_t = \delta E. \tag{43}$$

E is the electron energy and δ is given by

$$\delta = (2m/M)E, \tag{44}$$

and m and M are the electron and neutral mass respectively. Since the neutral mass is much larger than the electron mass (e.g., for Ar, $(2m/M) = 1/40,000$), very little energy is transferred to the neutral in an elastic collision. However, the electron will experience a large change in the direction of its velocity, and hence its momentum is changed. We will see why this is important when we consider how an electron moves in an electric field.

From Eq. (42), we can write the collision frequency for electron-neutral elastic collisions ν_N, as

$$\nu_N = N\sigma_N v \tag{45}$$

where v is the electron velocity. From Eq. (45) we can see that ν_N will depend on the neutral gas pressure. As noted previously, collisions will affect the behavior of electrons in a magnetic field. At higher pressures, where $\nu_N > > \omega_c$, electrons will be unable to execute a full cyclotron orbit, and their drift motion will be interrupted.

2.2.4.2 Electron–Electron Collisions   Electron-electron collisions are characterized by a cross section σ_{e-e} which is given by

$$\sigma_{e-e} = e^4 \ln \Lambda / (4\pi\varepsilon_0^2(mv^2)^2) \tag{46}$$

where

$$\Lambda = 12\pi(\varepsilon kT/e^2)^{3/2}/n^{1/2}. \tag{47}$$

and m, e, v, n, T are the mass, charge, velocity, density and temperature of the electrons, respectively. The term $\ln \Lambda$ is called the Coloumb logarithm. The collision frequency for electron-electron elastic collision will be given, from Eq. (42) as

$$\nu_{e-e} = n\sigma_{e-e}v. \tag{48}$$

In electron-electron collisions, since the masses are equal, the electrons can exchange energy very effectively, unlike an electron-neutral collision, where there is a large mass difference. Hence, electron-electron collisions will become important even at low degrees of ionization. We quantify this in terms of the parameter P, defined by Eq. (28)

$$P = \nu_{e-e}(v_0)/\delta\nu_m(v_0) \tag{49}$$

where we evaluate the electron-electron and electron-neutral collision frequencies at a velocity v_0 given by

$$v_0 = (2kT/m)^{1/2}, \tag{50}$$

with T the electron temperature. P is the ratio of the rate of electron energy loss by electron-electron collisions to that for electron-neutral collisions. When $P > 1$, electron-electron collisions will become important. Due to the factor δ, this condition will occurs for degrees of ionization around 10^{-4} or 10^{-3}. In ECR discharges, where the degree of ionization is above this, electron-electron collisions will dominate, while in planar reactors, with lower degrees of ionization, electron-neutral collisions will be most important. This will have important implications for the electron energy distribution function, as we shall see in the next section.

2.2.4.3 Electron Impact Inelastic Collisions   Though the inelastic cross sections are often much smaller than the elastic ones, the electron can lose a much larger fraction of its energy given by (29)

$$(M/(m + M))E. \tag{51}$$

Since $M \gg m$, virtually all of the electron energy is available for inelastic processes.

As a first example, we will consider the inelastic processes that result when an electron impacts an atom like He. In the He atom, the electrons occupy certain discrete states, as in Fig. 9.

There are a number of important processes shown here. The first is ionization,

$$e + He \rightarrow He^+ + 2e,$$

where ions and additional electrons are created. Another process is electronic excitation,

$$e + He \rightarrow He^* + e$$

where the electrons in the He atom are promoted to excited states. The lifetime of many of the He excited states is very short (typically 100 ns or less), so that excitation is frequently followed by radiative decay,

$$He^* \rightarrow He + h\nu$$

where a photon of frequency ν is emitted. Certain states in He have much longer lifetimes. These *metastable* states, which are shown in Fig. 9, can have lifetimes of 1 ms or longer. The metastable states also have considerable energy (e.g., 20 eV for He) and if they collide with ground state neutrals, they may cause excitation or ionization. These are the *Penning* processes, which, for metastable species A* colliding with species B look like

A* + B → A + B* (Penning excitation)

A* + B → A + B⁺ (Penning ionization).

These processes will increase the ionization rates and excitation rates in plasmas, and this is one reasons why rare gases like He and Ar are added to process plasma discharges.

He Atomic Energy Levels

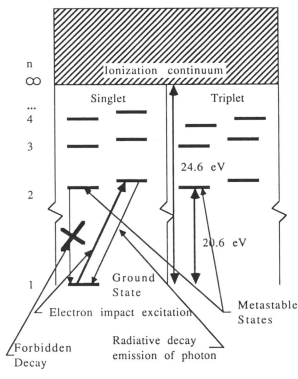

Figure 9: Atomic energy levels for He, showing the singlet and triplet series. The energy necessary to ionize is 24.6 eV, while the energy for the first electronic excitation is 20.6 eV. States which are forbidden to decay to the ground state have long lifetimes and are called metastable states.

The inverse processes, where electrons are lost by recombination can also be important. One example is three body recombination,

He⁺ + 2e⁻ → He + e,

where two electrons are necessary to conserve momentum. Another recombination process is *radiative recombination*,

He⁺ + e⁻ → He + hν,

where energy and momentum are balanced by emission of a photon after recombination.

An important process for electron loss that can occur in a plasma where the neutral species has a high electron affinity (such as halogen discharges) is electron capture, shown here for fluorine

$$F + e^- \rightarrow F^-.$$

Each process will have a cross section associated with it. In all of these processes, the incident electron will lose an amount of energy equal to that required for the inelastic process. For the electron loss processes, the entire energy of the electron is lost.

In rare gas atoms, electron excitation requires an amount of energy which is very close to that for ionization, and therefore, the cross sections are quite similar. Owing to this, for rare gas plasmas, we can reasonably assume that where light is emitted (radiative decay following electron excitation), ionization is probably also occurring. Note that the excitation process represents an important energy loss mechanism for the electrons.

Atoms other than the rare gases will generally have lower lying levels for excitation, as will molecules, which have rotational and vibrational states which require much less energy than excited electronic states. Electron energy losses will therefore be greater than in non-rare gas plasmas. When an electron collides with a molecule (which we will represent as AB), a number of processes may occur. *Dissociation*, such as

$$e + AB \rightarrow A + B + e$$

can result in the formation of chemically reactive radicals. Another important process is *dissociative ionization*,

$$e + AB \rightarrow A^+ + B + 2e,$$

where ions and radicals may be formed. The dissociation products of molecules may react to form additional species. The chemically active species may also undergo surface reactions, as in etching or deposition.

Some electron loss processes associated with molecules are *associative recombination*

$$e + A^+(+B) \rightarrow A(B)$$

and *dissociative attachment*

$$e + A(B) \rightarrow A^- (+ B).$$

2.2.4.4 Ion Collision Processes   There are a few ion impact processes which are crucial to the discharge. The first is secondary electron emission from a surface bombarded by an energetic ion. This process is usually characterized by a coefficient γ which is the ratio of the number of electrons emitted for each incident ion. Typically $1/10 > \gamma > 1/20$.

Another important ion process is that of charge transfer:

$$A^+ + B \rightarrow A + B^+$$

where A and B can be the same species. This process is an important loss mechanism for energetic ions in the sheath region of discharges.

2.2.5 Diffusion and Particle Losses

At the pressures typical of deposition and etching ($10^{-4} - 10^{-1}$Torr) , the loss of charged particles by the volume processes discussed in Sect. 2.2.4 are relatively small. The dominant charged particle loss mechanism is diffusion and convection to the reactor boundaries (walls or electrodes), where recombination will occur rapidly on the solid surfaces. In Sect. 2.3.1, we will introduce the concept of mobility, and will consider how electrons move convectively due to an electric field. In this section, we will consider diffusion, which can be described by the equation of conservation of particles,

$$\delta n/\delta t + \nabla \bullet \Gamma = S, \tag{52}$$

where n is the particle density, S is the net volume production rate, and Γ is the particle flux given by Fick's Law

$$\Gamma = = D\nabla n, \tag{53}$$

with D the diffusion coefficient. The choice for the diffusion coefficient is depends on a number of things. At low enough densities, the diffusion coefficient is given by (30)

$$D = (v^2/3\nu), \tag{54}$$

where v is the particle velocity and ν is the collision frequency for momentum transfer. This means that electrons would tend to diffuse much faster than ions. However, as the electron and ion densities become greater, electric fields will arise because of this disparity in diffusion rates, and this will tend to equalize the rates. This latter type of diffusion is called *ambipolar*, and in the extreme limit, which occurs for electron densities above 10^9cm^{-3} , both electrons and ions diffuse at two times the slower ion rate (31-33).

2.2.6 Sheaths

2.2.6.1 Non-conducting or Isolated Surfaces   We have already examined the effects of Debye shielding which occurs inside the plasma volume. We will now explore the manifestation of this effect at the plasma edge. At the boundary, electrons and ions will diffuse out of the plasma, as noted previously, owing to their thermal energies. From simple kinetic theory, the flux j is

$$j = (nv/4), \tag{55}$$

where, n is the particle density and v the thermal velocity which is given by

$$v = (3kT/m)^{1/2} \tag{56}$$

with T the (ion or electron) temperature and m the mass.   In the absence of any sheath effects, and for electron temperatures equal to or greater than the ion temperature, the electron velocity will be much greater than the ion velocity.

Let's consider what happens near a non-conducting wall (or an isolated conducting wall). The electron flux to the wall will be higher initially, owing to their greater thermal velocities. However, this will cause the plasma to become more positive, since there is an excess of positive ions left behind. An electric field will develop which will retard the electrons and accelerate the ions, in such a way to make the net current zero.   The magnitude of the potential which the plasma acquires is about $(3kT_e/e)$, where T_e is the electron temperature. As we might guess, this potential falls off from the wall into the plasma over a distance of the Debye length λ_D (Eq. (13)), as shown in Fig. 10.

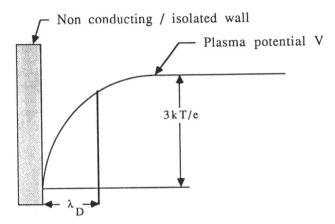

Figure 10: Behavior of the plasma potential in the vicinity of a non- conducting or isolated wall. The characteristic fall-off for the sheath potential is the Debye length (Eq. (13)).

2.2.6.2   Sheath Near a Conducting Electrode.   Let us now consider the case of a surface across which current flows (e.g., the cathode in a dc glow). The form of the potential in this region can be found from Poisson's equation. We will assume that the potential on the electrode is negative and large, which will have the effect of attracting ions and repelling electrons. We will take the electron density in the sheath region to be zero. The current density J is then given by

$$J = nev, \tag{57}$$

where n is the ion density, e is the electronic charge, and v is the ion velocity. The potential $V(x)$ obeys

$$(d^2V/dx^2) = -ne/\varepsilon_0. \tag{58}$$

The ion velocity is related to the potential V by conservation of energy

$$mv^2/2 = eV. \tag{59}$$

From these two equations, we have

$$(d^2V/dx^2) = (1/\varepsilon_o)(m/2e)^{1/2}(1/V)^{1/2}. \tag{60}$$

Multiplying this equation by (dV/dx) and integrating,

$$(dV/dx)^2 = (4/\varepsilon_o)(m/2e)^{1/2}(1/V)^{1/2}. \tag{61}$$

Taking the square root of both sides and integrating,

$$J(x) = (4\varepsilon_o/9)(2e/m)^{1/2}(V^{3/2}/x^2), \tag{62}$$

which is the Child-Langmuir Law for space charge-limited current flow. The resulting sheath thickness will be many times the Debye length.

In addition to this "free fall" sort of sheath, in which we assumed that the ions did not make any collisions, it is also possible to have a mobility-limited sheath, where the ion velocity is determined by its mobility (34).

2.3 ELECTRON HEATING AND ENERGY DISTRIBUTION

The discharges of interest here are sustained by some dc or ac power source which establishes an electric field in the plasma. As we shall see, plasma electrons will gain energy from being accelerated in the electric field. In steady state, a balance is established between the energy which the electrons gain from the electric field and the energy which they lose through collisional and other loss processes described above. The energetic electrons are responsible for most of the ionization, which produces additional electrons and ions to sustain the discharge against the various loss processes. There is clearly a very complicated interplay among the many processes which work to establish the energy balance and particle balance which is necessary for maintaining a discharge. In this section, we will examine how the electrons are "heated" by the external power source and how the electron energy distribution function is established.

2.3.1 Interaction of Electrons with a Static Electric Field

An electric field will accelerate all charged particles, however, the electrons with their smaller mass will be accelerated more (35), and we will now consider the result. From Eqs. (10) and (18), when an electron is subjected to an electric field $\mathbf{E}$, it experiences a force given by

$$\mathbf{F} = -e\mathbf{E}, \tag{63}$$

and an acceleration

$$\mathbf{a} = - e\mathbf{E}/m. \tag{64}$$

We will assume that electron-neutral collisions dominate, as is the case for planar or barrel reactors. Let us consider the effect of elastic collisions, assuming, as an example, that electrons are moving in Ar at a pressure of 30 mTorr ($N = 1 \times 10^{15} \text{cm}^{-3}$). Then, since the average elastic collision cross section is about $1 \times 10^{-15} \text{cm}^2$, we note that from Eq. (41) the mean free path λ is about 1 cm. If the angle between the electron velocity and the electric field is θ, then the electron will gain an average amount of energy

$$e E \lambda \cos \theta, \tag{65}$$

between collisions.

The electron will loose only a relatively small amount of energy during each elastic collision. If W is the electron energy, then the amount lost, ΔW, is from Eqs. (43) and (44)

$$\Delta W = (2m/M)W, \tag{66}$$

which for Ar (M=40 AMU) is

$$\Delta W = 2 \times 10^{-4} W. \tag{67}$$

Although little *energy* is exchanged in this elastic collision, it does have a profound effect on the electron *velocity*, i.e., there is a large *momentum* change. The electron velocity will be redirected after the elastic collision, as shown schematically in Fig. 11. Thus, the elastic collisions effectively transforms the *directed* energy which the electrons acquire from the electric field into *random* energy. This begins to establish the electron energy distribution function, and the electrons "heat up."

Eventually a steady state is reached where the energy gained by the electrons between collisions is equal to the energy lost during the collision. Since the energy lost is a small fraction of the total energy, the electrons will heat up to a sufficiently high energy to establish this balance. This means that the random velocity will be much greater than the directed velocity which the electron gains from acceleration in the electric field.

We can examine this more quantitatively by writing Newton's second law including the effect of collisions. The electrons will attain an average directed velocity, or drift velocity, u, due to the electric field. Collisions will cause the electrons to lose their directed momentum, μ, at the rate given by ν_m, where ν_m is the collision frequency for momentum loss. Though all types of electron collisions will contribute to the momentum loss, it is usually the elastic collisions that dominate, so we will take $\nu_m = \nu_N$. Newton's second law is then

$$(d/dt)(mu) = -eE - mu\nu_N. \tag{68}$$

In Eq. (68) we are ignoring the random thermal motion. However, writing the equation is justified because the average random velocity is zero. Equation (68) is called the Langevin equation (36).

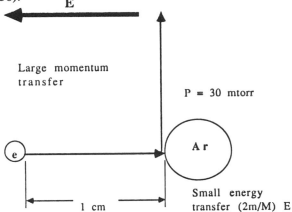

Figure 11: Elastic collisions between electrons and Ar transform the directed energy which the electrons gain from acceleration in the electric field to random thermal energy, thus causing heating of the electrons. There is very little energy transfer in an electron-neutral elastic collision, owing to the large mass difference between the electron and neutral; however, the electron will have its momentum randomized by the collision.

In steady state, the solution to Eq. (68) is

$$u = \mu E \tag{69}$$

where μ is the electron mobility defined as

$$\mu = e/(m\nu_N). \tag{70}$$

From Eqs. (69) and (70), we can see that the drift velocity is proportional to the quantity (E/N). This ratio of the electric field to the neutral density (or pressure) will arise in many of the formula we will derive here.

The current density J due to the directed motion of the electrons is given by

$$J = -enu, \tag{71}$$

where e is the electron charge and n is the electron density. From Eq. (69) we can write

$$J = \sigma E, \tag{72}$$

where σ is the electrical conductivity given by

$$\sigma = ne^2/(m\nu_N). \tag{73}$$

We will now consider the energy balance. The rate at which the external power source puts energy into the electrons is

$$P_{in} = JE = \sigma E^2. \tag{74}$$

The rate at which energy is lost due to collisions is

$$P_{out} = n \, \delta W \nu_N + n \sum_i W_i \nu_i, \tag{75}$$

where the first term is the energy loss rate due to elastic collisions and the second term is the sum over all inelastic processes, with energy loss W_i and collision frequency ν_i. To simplify the present discussion, we will assume that the elastic loss term dominates. In steady state, $P_{in} = P_{out}$, so that from Eqs. (74) and (75), we get

$$n\delta W \nu_N = \sigma E^2 = ne^2 E^2/(m\nu_N). \tag{76}$$

Solving Eq. (76) for W we get

$$W = e^2 E^2/(\delta m \nu_N^2). \tag{77}$$

As an example, let us consider He at 0.5 torr pressure in a typical electric field of 1 V/cm (100 V/m). Then Eq. (77) would predict an electron energy of approximately 5 eV. The energy lost per collision (δW) is 0.00125 eV, which, in steady state, is just equal to the energy which an electron gains from the electric field between collisions. Since such a small fraction of the electron's energy is lost in a collision, the electrons must heat up to 5 eV to provide the energy balance. The small energy transfer results in negligible heating of the neutrals, which therefore usually remain at room temperature (37).

From Eqs. (77) and (42) we can write ν_N as

$$\nu_N = N\sigma_n v. \tag{78}$$

Then, if we take v to be the average thermal velocity, we have

$$W = mv^2/2, \tag{79}$$

and from Eqs. (42), (78) and (79) we can write

$$W = (e/\sigma_N(2\delta)^{1/2})(E/N).\tag{80}$$

This shows that electron energy depends linearly on the quantity (E/N). From Eqs. (69-70) and (77-79) we can derive the ratio of the drift velocity u to the average thermal velocity v,

$$u/v = (\delta/2)^{1/2}.\tag{81}$$

For Ar, this ratio is 3.5×10^{-3}. Thus, the drift velocity is a small fraction of the average thermal velocity which the electrons attain by virtue of the collisions, which transform the directed energy the electron gains from the electric field to thermal energy.

The inclusion of inelastic processes will modify the energy balance because, in those processes, an electron can lose a large fraction of its energy. This will result in a lower electron energy than that predicted by Eq. (77). It will also result in a larger ratio of u/v. However, the cross sections for inelastic processes are usually smaller than for elastic processes, so that the electrons will still be hotter than the neutrals.

Thus far we have considered only the steady state. If we were to solve the time dependent equation, we would find that, to achieve steady state, an electron would have to undergo approximately δ^{-1} collisions (38). In a dc electric field, the electron would have to move a distance d in the field given by

$$d = u/(\delta\nu) = eE/(m\delta\nu^2).\tag{82}$$

Using the previous example of He at 0.5 torr, we find that the drift distance is 5 cm.

In what we have derived above, we have not invoked the existence of a plasma. The derivations would be entirely appropriate for a beam of electrons going through a neutral gas. One important aspect of a plasma is Debye shielding. Which raises the question of how do we actually get an electric field into a plasma? In fact, we cannot introduce just any arbitrary value of the electric field into a plasma. The limiting criterion is that the potential across a Debye sphere must be less than the thermal energy:

$$e E \lambda_D < W.\tag{83}$$

Now from Eq. (80), we can write W as

$$W = e E \lambda / (2\delta)^{1/2}\tag{84}$$

Where λ is the collision mean free path,

$$\lambda = (N\sigma)^{-1}\tag{85}$$

Therefore, our criterion Eq. (83) is just

$$\lambda_D < \lambda/(2\delta)^{1/2}. \tag{86}$$

Taking Ar at 30 mTorr as an example, we find that the right hand side is 200cm. This is clearly much larger than the Debye length, so we are well within the limits of our criterion.

2.3.2 Interaction of Electrons with a Time Dependent Electric Field and Magnetic Field

We will now consider the particle motion that results from using an ac power source at frequency ω, with no magnetic field present. It is convenient to write the electric field as a complex quantity (18)

$$\vec{E} = \vec{E}_0 \exp(j\omega t), \tag{87}$$

where $j = \sqrt{-1}$, and E_0 is the amplitude of the field which is independent of time. Since the electric field changes direction, the resulting motion of the particles will be oscillatory, as will be the particle drift velocity. We can solve the Langevin equation Eq. (68) to derive a mobility and conductivity given by

$$\mu = e/m(\nu + j\omega), \tag{88}$$

and

$$\sigma = ne^2/m(\nu + j\omega). \tag{89}$$

Let us now examine the power input to the electrons in this case. It will be given by

$$P_{in} = Re(JE), \tag{90}$$

where Re denotes the real part of the complex quantity. From Eqs. (72), (87) and (89) we get

$$P_{in} = ne^2 E_0^2/(m\nu_{eff}), \tag{91}$$

where ν_{eff} is an "effective" collision frequency given by

$$\nu_{eff} = \nu(1 + (\omega/\nu)^2). \tag{92}$$

Let us examine some special cases. If $\omega = 0$, we recover the dc case. If there were no collisions (i.e., $\nu = 0$), we find from Eqs. (89) and (90) that P_{in} averages to zero. The reason for this is that the drift velocity and electric field would be 90° out of phase, and thus no power could be transferred. As in the dc field case, the collisions transform the directed energy that the electrons gain from the oscillating electric field to the random energy that represents electron heating.

If $\omega >> \nu$, then the mobility and conductivity are similar to the dc case with n replaced by ω^2/ν. The power input would therefore decrease with increasing frequency.

Although it is not obvious from our derivations here, a more detailed calculation would reveal the fact that the maximum power input occurs when $\omega = \nu$ (33). This can be seen qualitatively by the following argument. If the ac power frequency is much lower than the collision frequency, then the particles make numerous collisions during each ac cycle which prevents the particles from reaching the maximum energy during the ac oscillations. On the other hand, if $\omega >> \nu$, then the particles undergo many oscillations between collisions, but this does not increase their energy. When $\omega = \nu$, the electrons make approximately one collision for every cycle of the ac power, and that represents the optimum for transforming energy from the electric field to the electron energy distribution.

We noted in Sect. 2.2.2 that if the frequency of an ac electric field were above the plasma frequency, it would not be shielded, because the plasma electrons are incapable of responding on such a fast time scale. If ω is below ω_p, we would like to know how far the field would penetrate into the plasma. We will consider a number of cases.

For a typical planar reactor with an electron density of 10^{10} cm^{-3}, the plasma frequency is around 1 GHz. Most commercial planar equipment utilize 13.56 MHz power, which seems to contradict the discussion above. This is easily resolved by noting that in a planar reactor, we are not really launching rf radiation, because the wavelength of the 13.56 MHz source is over 20 m, which is much larger than the reactor. We are in what is called the *near zone* (18). In this sense, the plasma will respond much as it would to a dc field, and the criterion noted in the last section apply.

If we wanted to use an oscillating electric field with a wavelength short compared to the plasma size, then the associated field would be attenuated if its frequency were below the plasma frequency. In particular, if this radiation were such that the electric field it produced in the plasma pointed in the direction of propagation, then it would be attenuated in a Debye length.

If, on the other hand, we introduced radiation where the electric field was perpendicular to the direction of propagation, the wave would penetrate a distance δ_s called a skin depth, given by

$$\delta_s = c/\omega_p. \tag{93}$$

Notice this is like the Debye length, except that the speed of light replaces the average thermal velocity of the electrons. Thus, the "fast" electromagnetic wave can penetrate deeper by a factor of typically 1000 times the Debye length. For a process plasma with a typical λ_D of 0.01cm, the radiation may penetrate to a distance of about 10 cm.

Radiation at frequencies higher than the plasma frequency will be phase shifted by the plasma, with the amount of phase shift depending on ω_p. Since ω_p depends on density, the phase shift can be used to deduce the plasma electron density (39).

2.3.3 Interaction of Electrons with a Time Dependent Electric Field in the Presence of a Static Magnetic Field

A quantitative discussion of this case, which is beyond the scope of this chapter, can be found in the references (40). We will consider this problem heuristically, utilizing a number of our previous derivations. We know from Sect. 2.2.3 that in a magnetic field, the particles undergo a natural circular motion in a plane perpendicular to the magnetic field (we can neglect motion along the field for this discussion). The angular frequency of this electron cyclotron motion is from Eq. (24)

$$\omega_c = eB/m, \tag{94}$$

and is independent of the particle energy. If we introduce an electric field of frequency ω which is resonant with ω_c, then we will be able to accelerate electrons synchronously. As the electron's perpendicular energy increases, the gyro radius will increase, but the cyclotron frequency will remain constant, and therefore the particles will remain in phase with the applied field. As in all the previous cases, if we want to heat the electrons, we will need collisions to transform this directed energy to random thermal energy. However, one big difference here is that the electron energy is increasing with each ac cycle, so that there is no need to have the collision frequency equal to the applied frequency. This facilitates operation at lower pressures.

Let us look more closely at the resonance condition, and assume that there is some difference $\Delta\omega$ given by

$$\Delta\omega = \omega - \omega_c. \tag{95}$$

Then, after a time given by approximately $(\Delta\omega)^{-1}$, the applied electric field will start to get out of phase with the electron's natural cyclotron motion and begin to slow it down. If, however, the electron were to undergo a collision within this time, then the directed energy gained from the oscillating electric field will be transferred to the electron's thermal distribution. Thus, the criterion for optimum power coupling is

$$\nu = \Delta\omega. \tag{96}$$

In practice, there will be a number of effects that can cause a deviation between the electron cyclotron and the applied frequencies, including things like magnetic inhomogeneities.

If the collision frequency becomes of the order of ω_c or larger, then the electrons will not be able to undergo the complete cyclotron orbit. In this case, from arguments analogous to those given above, the collisions will broaden the cyclotron resonance by an amount given in Eqs.(95) and (96). If the resonance is sufficiently broad, then there is little advantage to having a magnetic field at all.

As noted previously, the presence of a magnetic field will give rise to additional oscillatory modes in addition to that discussed in Sect. 2.2.2. One consequence of this is that radiation which is below the electron cyclotron frequency can propagate in a plasma, regardless of its relationship to the plasma frequency. This means that in an electron cyclotron reactor, the incident radiation can propagate through regions of higher magnetic field to reach an interior resonance region.

2.3.4 The Electron Energy Distribution Function

In Sec. 2.1.1, we defined the electron energy distribution function, $f(\varepsilon)$, which is proportional to the number of electrons having an energy between ε and $\varepsilon + \delta\varepsilon$. In particular, we looked at the Maxwellian, or equilibrium form for f. The electron energy distribution function is a very important quantity, because the rates k_i of all electron-induced processes, such as ionization and dissociation, will depend on it through the expression

$$k_i = \int \sigma_i v f(\varepsilon) d\varepsilon \tag{97}$$

where σ_i is the cross section for the particular process and v is the electron velocity.

The electron energy distribution function f will be determined by the energy input to the electrons via the electric field and the energy lost through elastic and inelastic processes, through the Boltzmann Equation (41). The solution of the Boltzmann equation is beyond the scope of this chapter; however, we will consider a few special cases.

For a dc electric field where the electron kinetics are dominated by elastic collisions between electrons and neutrals and the collision frequency is independent of electron velocity (i.e., $\sigma \simeq v^{-1}$), the solution to the Boltzmann equation is a Maxwellian. If, however, the collision frequency is linear in v (i.e., $\sigma \simeq$ constant), then the result is the Druyvesteyn distribution, which has a form like

$$f(\varepsilon) = A\varepsilon^{1/2} \exp(-B\varepsilon^2), \tag{98}$$

where A and B are constants. This distribution falls off faster with energy than does a Maxwellian, and arises because the collision frequency is greater for higher energy electrons.

The inclusion of inelastic processes will drastically alter the form of f. In particular, above the thresholds for the various inelastic processes, f will usually decrease rapidly. Many examples can be found in the literature (42).

In cases where electron-electron collisions are important, $f(\varepsilon)$ will tend towards a Maxwellian (43). As noted before, due to the fact that electrons can exchange energy much more efficiently than will electrons and neutrals, electron-electron collisions can become dominant at even relatively low ionization fractions. The quantity P, defined in Eq. (49), gives a more quantitative measure. The distribution will become Maxwellian for $P > 5$. Such conditions are commonly met in an electron cyclotron resonance reactor.

2.4 BREAKDOWN

In this section we will consider the breakdown processes that precede the formation of dc and rf glow discharges.

2.4.1 DC Breakdown

We will examine dc breakdown by considering, as an example, Ar at 30 mTorr in a system, shown in Fig. 12, comprising two electrodes connected to a dc power supply with voltage V_{ps} through a ballast resistor R.

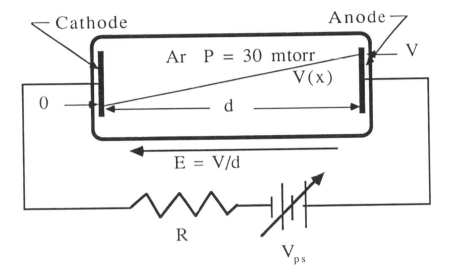

Figure 12: Schematic of an Ar discharge prior to breakdown. The resistance of the Ar is much greater than that of the ballast resistor R, so the entire voltage is dropped across the discharge tube.

Initially, the resistance of the neutral gas will be much greater than that of R, so the voltage across the discharge $V = V_{ps}$. Let us assume that there is one free electron, formed perhaps by a cosmic ray or some UV photon, near the cathode. The electric field will accelerate the electron towards the anode. Let α be the probability per unit length that ionization will occur. The quantity α is called Townsend's first ionization coefficient, and represents the net ionization probability, including losses. As a result of the acceleration by the electric field, the electron will gain energy (see Sect. 2.3.1) and produce ionization. This will lead to a multiplication of the number of electrons as shown in Fig. 13.

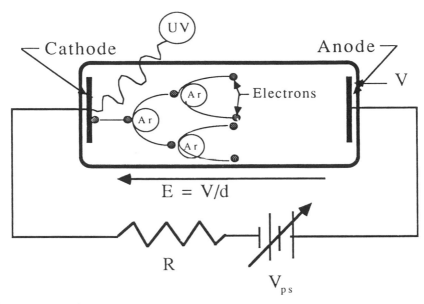

Figure 13: Behavior of the discharge at breakdown. An electron is created by photodesorption at the cathode. The electron is accelerated by the electric field and causes ionization, creating ions and additional electrons.

The current at the anode arising from an electron current I_o emitted from the cathode is given by

$$I_{(d)} = I_o \exp(\alpha d). \tag{99}$$

The electric field will also accelerate ions, and when ions strike the cathode, electrons will be emitted by ion impact secondary electron emission with a probability γ. The total number of ions created by the first electron multiplication is $I_o(\exp(\alpha d) - 1)$. This will give rise to $\gamma I_o(\exp(\alpha d) - 1)$ secondary electrons, which will also be accelerated by the electric field and cause more ionization and consequently more ions. If we add up this sequence of successive generation of secondary electrons giving rise to more ions giving rise to more secondaries, etc., we find that the total current arriving at the anode is

$$I(d) = I_o \exp(\alpha d)/[1 - \gamma(\exp(\alpha d) - 1)] \tag{100}$$

If $\exp(\alpha d) >> 1$, we can write Eq. (100) as

$$I(d) = I_o \exp(\alpha d)/[1 - \gamma \exp(\alpha d)]. \tag{101}$$

When

$$1 - \gamma \exp(\alpha d) = 0 \qquad\qquad (102)$$

the current I(d) tends to increase rapidly, a condition referred to as breakdown. Let us look a little more closely at the form of the breakdown condition. The ionization probability per unit length α will be proportional to the number of collisions per unit length, multiplied by the probability that the collision will cause ionization. Thus we can write α as (43)

$$\alpha = (1/\lambda) \exp(-V_i/eE\lambda), \qquad\qquad (103)$$

where λ is the collision mean free path, and $eE\lambda$ is just the energy gained by the electron between collisions. V_i is an *effective* ionization potential, i.e., it takes into account the effect of losses. The exponential term thus expresses the probability that the electron will cause ionization. Now, from Eq. (41), the mean free path will be inversely proportional to the neutral density or pressure P as

$$\lambda = \lambda_1/P, \qquad\qquad (104)$$

where λ_1 is a constant. Then from Eqs. (102-104) we find that the breakdown electric field E_B is given by

$$E_B = AP/(C + \ln(Pd)) \qquad\qquad (105)$$

where A and C are constants which depend on the gas. We can therefore write an expression for the breakdown voltage $V_B = E_B/d$ as

$$V_B = A(Pd)/(C + \ln(Pd)). \qquad\qquad (106)$$

For large Pd, the breakdown voltage will be proportional to Pd. This is equivalent to the breakdown condition being a constant value of E_B/P for a given gas, and is consistent with E/P being a measure of the average energy gain of an electron between collisions (see Eq. 80). For this case electrons make many collisions, and therefore the breakdown condition is equivalent to a constant value of the energy gained by an electron between collisions. This means that the electric field must scale linearly with the pressure, or V_B is linear in Pd. At very small values of Pd, there are very few collisions, and therefore, V_B, the breakdown voltage rises to increase the probability of breakdown per collision. A graph of the breakdown condition for Ar is shown in Fig. 14. The minimum breakdown voltage is called the Paschen minimum.

One important application of the breakdown formalism is the design of ground shields (also called dark space shields) for the discharge electrodes. These shields are intended to prevent the formation of a plasma at the edges and behind the electrodes. For a dc discharge, they must be placed within a distance d_s such that the maximum discharge voltage V_M satisfies the condition (44)

$$V_M < V_B(Pd_s) \tag{107}$$

where V_B is the breakdown voltage for the particular gas used in the discharge evaluated at the product of pressure and distance using the shield-electrode spacing. Similar results apply to ground shields for rf discharges, although the complexity of the particle oscillation in the rf field must be considered.

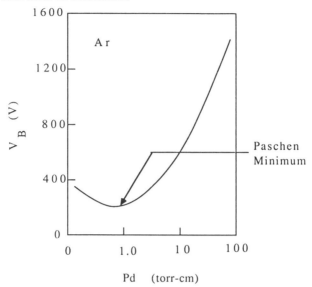

Figure 14: Plot of the minimum breakdown voltage for Ar as a function of the product of the Ar pressure and spacing of the electrodes.

2.4.2 RF Breakdown

Breakdown in an rf field is actually somewhat simpler than that for dc, if most of the electrons are able to undergo their oscillatory motion without colliding with a wall. In this case, the alternating electric field can heat the electrons sufficiently to produce the required amount of ionization, and it is not necessary to invoke secondary electron emission processes. What is required is that the rate of ionization balance the losses due to diffusion to the walls, volume recombination, electron attachment, etc. We will consider the case which is typical of the process plasmas of interest, where diffusion losses dominate.

As we saw in Sect. 2.2.5.2, the oscillating electric field will put directed energy into the electrons, which will then heat up by undergoing collisions with neutrals. The electrons will cause ionization which must balance the diffusive losses. We assume for simplicity that the diffusion coefficient and ionization rate are independent of position. From Eq. (52) we can write the steady state diffusion equation as

$$\nabla^2 n = (\nu_i/D)/n, \tag{108}$$

where ν_i is the ionization rate. Taking n = 0 at the boundary of the plasma region, the solutions require that (53)

$$\nu_i/D = 1/\Lambda^2, \tag{109}$$

where the constant Λ depends on the geometry of the plasma. If the discharge is cylindrical with the radius of the cylinder R_D much larger than the length h_D (a typical planar configuration), then

$$\Lambda = h_D/\pi \tag{110}$$

If the cylinder is long and has a small radius then

$$\Lambda = R_D/2.405. \tag{111}$$

The ionization rate and D will depend on the parameter (E/N). Then Eq. (109) in conjunction with Eq. (110) or (111) will determine the breakdown condition on (E/N) as a function of the product of NΛ.

2.5 GLOW DISCHARGES

Prior to breakdown, we started with a homogenous neutral gas with a constant electric field and a linear voltage drop. Following breakdown, a discharge forms, and rearranges itself into characteristic regions to provide optimally for particle generation and energy input to balance losses. For a dc discharge, just at breakdown, the current will increase with little increase in the voltage. This is called the Townsend discharge (46) and precedes the avalanche that signifies "full" breakdown. The first "state" after breakdown is a glow discharge. Initially, the glow will not completely cover the cathode surface. It operates at near constant voltage in this regime (called the *normal discharge*), with the current increasing as the cathode coverage increases. Eventually, the glow expands to fill the cathode surface, and subsequently, further increases in power result in increases in both voltage and current. This is called the *abnormal glow*. The salient characteristics of a glow discharge is that electrons are created by ionization and secondary electron generation from ion impact of surfaces. If the power is increased further, the cathode will begin to heat. Eventually, thermionic emission will occur, and become the dominant electron creation process. At this point the discharge voltage will decrease and the glow has evolved into an arc.

In the following sections, we will consider the main characteristics of dc and rf glow discharges. In particular, we will look at those features which pertain to our application of glow discharges to the deposition and etching of thin films.

2.5.1 DC Glow Discharge

It is convenient (and traditional) (47) to picture the glow discharge as comprising a number of distinct regions. Of course, this is an artificial construct; in reality the discharge is a continuous entity. We can, however, associate particular processes and functionality with the various regions, and in this sense, the picture of the glow discharge presented here is useful. We will also consider some recent numerical modeling of the dc glow in this section, the results of which largely substantiate the simplified view presented here. Fig. 15 shows the dc glow schematically. We will now consider each region.

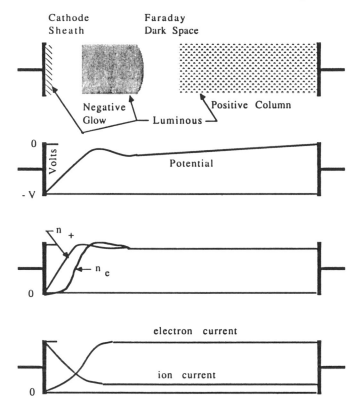

Figure 15: Classical picture of the architecture of a dc glow discharge. After breakdown, the discharge arranges itself into characteristic regions to provide for particle and energy input. Most of the potential is dropped across the cathode sheath region, which contains ions but very few electrons. There are approximately equal ions and electrons in the negative glow, Faraday dark space and positive column.

    2.5.1.1 The Cathode Region. A narrow luminous layer is often observed adjacent to the cathode. The light emitted from this region is thought to be due to excitation of the neutral gas and surface bombardment by ions. Beyond this luminous region is the cathode (or Crookes) dark space, which extends to the next luminous region, the negative glow.

    Whereas originally the voltage was dropped uniformly across the entire discharge tube, in the glow phase, almost the entire voltage appears across the cathode dark space. This voltage will accelerate ions from the negative glow region to the cathode where they will cause secondary electron emission with a probability of approximately 0.1 to 0.05.

The secondary electrons will be accelerated back through the cathode region by the potential and enter the negative glow.

Owing to the large electric field that exists in the cathode dark space region, the electron density is small, and the ion current is determined by space charge-limited flow or mobility-limited flow as described in Sect. 2.2.6. Assuming that we have a free fall condition (i.e., the ions do not suffer collisions in the sheath), we can use Eq. (62) to write the Child-Langmuir expression for the ion current density at the cathode, j_c

$$j_c = (4\varepsilon_0/9)(2e/M)^{1/2}(V_c^{3/2}/x_c^2), \tag{112}$$

where V_c and x_c are the potential drop across the cathode sheath and the sheath width respectively.

2.5.1.2 Secondary Electron Generation. Ion bombardment of the cathode will cause secondary electron generation. The secondary electron yield, which is the ratio of secondary electrons emitted per incident ion will depend upon the material and the ion energy. It will also depends critically on the condition of the surface, including both the crystal orientation and the degree of surface contamination. Some materials can have secondary electron coefficients which exceed unity. The energy of the secondary electrons is generally quite low, typically peaking around 2 - 5 eV (56).

2.5.1.3 Ionization in the Cathode Sheath. One of the greatest debates in the area of low-temperature plasma behavior is whether there is signification ionization in the cathode sheath. Much of the older literature has assumed that virtually all of the ionization needed to supply the ions which are accelerated to the cathode (and therefore lost at the cathode) occurs in the sheath (49). One observation that supports this position is that the product of the dark space thickness and the neutral pressure are constant for a given supply voltage. This behavior of Pd = constant is reminiscent of the condition for breakdown that we discussed earlier. On the other hand, for species like Ar, excitation will accompany ionization, since the energy threshold for the first excited state is similar to that for ionization (11.5eV and 15.6 eV respectively). Thus, if there is no emission, there will be little or no ionization. This point of view is consistent with that of Chapman, who uses simple calculation of ionization rates to conclude that ionization in the sheath cannot account for the observed electron density (50).

This apparent conflict may be resolved by the numerical modeling of the dc glow performed by Graves and Jensen (51). They developed a continuum model which they applied to a dc Ar discharge at 500 mTorr. While the identification of their results does not exactly follow the schematic description of the dc glow given above, they do show a sheath region of high electric field and a bulk region which seems to be identified with the negative glow region (see next section). The ionization does occur in the sheath region; however, upon close inspection, the high electric field extends beyond the sheath region into the negative glow, as does the ionization source. From their results, it would appear that ionization does occur in the sheath and in the region of the sheath-glow interface. In general, in a dc discharge sufficient ionization must occur due to the secondary electrons to sustain the plasma.

2.5.1.4 Ion Charge Exchange in the Cathode Sheath. Ions which are being accelerated through the sheath will, in general, undergo charge exchange collisions with the neutral species. This will alter their energy distribution at the cathode, since an ion produced by charge exchange somewhere in the sheath will not receive the full acceleration of the sheath drop. This problem has been studied both theoretically and experimentally by Davis and Vanderslice (52). They put an energy analyzer behind a small hole in the cathode to determine the energy distribution of ions arriving at the cathode. They assumed that all ions originated near the start of the sheath and that no ionization occurred in the sheath. The dominant process considered was symmetric charge exchange, given by

$$Ar^+ + Ar \rightarrow Ar + Ar^+. \tag{113}$$

They assumed that the electric field was linear in the sheath. For a mean free path much shorter than the sheath thickness, Eq. (113) can be written as

$$(V_c/N_o)(dN/dV) = (1/2\lambda_{cx}) \exp(-LV/(2\lambda_{cx}V_c)), \tag{114}$$

where V_c is the cathode voltage, dN is the number of ions arriving with an energy between V and V+dV, L is the dark space thickness, and λ_{cx} is the charge exchange mean free path, given by

$$\lambda_{cx} = (N\sigma_{cx})^{-1}, \tag{115}$$

with σ_{cx} the charge exchange cross section. Their experimental measurements were in reasonable agreement with the above expressions.

2.5.1.5 The Anode Sheath. Before considering the negative glow and positive column regions of the discharge, let us consider the anode sheath region (see Fig. 16). The anode sheath is, more or less, a Debye sheath. That means that there will be a voltage drop of typically $3kT_e/e$ (see Sect. 2.2.6). For a typical discharge with $T_e = 3$-4 eV, the plasma will be at a potential of about 9-12 V above the anode. Since there is a current flowing through the plasma, which for the dc case must be constant everywhere, then there must be a net electron current at the anode equal to the ion current at the cathode. We note, however, that there will also be an ion current at the anode, given the fact that the discharge is at +10V with respect to the anode. From the numerical calculations (51), the ion current is about 10% of the electron current at the anode. In any case, the energy of the ions bombarding the anode is sufficiently low as to not cause secondary emission. Some of the secondary electrons created at the cathode and accelerated by the cathode sheath may pass through the discharge and strike the anode with enough energy to emit additional secondary electrons. This can be an important process at low pressures.

2.5.1.6 The Negative Glow Region. The luminous negative glow is a plasma region characterized by nearly equal electron and ion densities, typically in the range of $10^9 - 10^{11} cm^{-3}$. Electron temperature measurements within the glow show typical values of 2 - 10 eV, although there is considerable question whether there is any semblance of a Maxwellian distribution in this region. Also, there is considerable non-uniformity of the temperatures and densities in the axial direction. Since this region is a plasma, the electric field is small. The sources of energy input to the glow include the energetic secondary electrons emitted from the cathode and accelerated across the sheath, and direct acceleration of the electrons in the glow by the electric field.

The strong electric field in the cathode region is responsible for energy input to the negative glow, both through acceleration of secondary electrons, and by acceleration of glow electrons near the glow edge. Thus, the magnitude of this field will be determined self-consistently by the plasma's requirements for ionization to sustain itself.

As we saw in Sect. 2.2.3, a magnetic field nominally parallel to the cathode, as found in a magnetron configuration, will cause the electrons to undergo gryo orbits, providing the collision frequency is below the cyclotron frequency. As a consequence, the electrons will spend more time in the vicinity of the cathode and their ionization efficiency will be increased. This will result in a decrease in the sheath field and potential, and will also produce a higher density discharge.

The continuum model for the dc glow (51) displays a negative glow region adjacent to the sheath and extending to the anode. The calculated temperature for this region is about 0.7 eV, which is considerably less than is typically measured.

The negative glow region, along with the cathode and associated dark space comprise a self-sustaining discharge configuration as shown in Fig. 16. The sheath field will accelerate ions formed in the negative glow. These ions will cause secondary electrons to be emitted at the cathode. The secondary electrons will be accelerated across the sheath and represent the main energy input to the plasma. A discharge will operate with the anode at the negative glow, in which case it is call an obstructed glow.

2.5.1.7 Beyond the Negative Glow. Although a dc glow discharge may end with the negative glow, in general it does not. Beyond the negative glow is another dark space, called the Faraday dark space, followed by the positive column and the anode sheath, which we have already discussed. Although the positive column is not typically found in processing plasma discharges, we will now consider briefly the so-called Faraday dark space and the positive column.

Regardless of whether the energetic secondary electrons formed at the cathode and accelerated through the (Crooke-Hittorf) dark space directly cause ionization or whether they transfer their energy to the electrons in the negative glow which then cause ionization (or whether it is a combination of both types of processes), it is clear that the energetic electrons represent the main source of energy input to the glow. The extent of the negative glow is determined by the range over which the energetic electrons lose their energy. This determines the location of the cathode end of the Faraday dark space. There is, however, a small electric field in the plasma regions of the discharge, and this electric field will increase the temperature of the electrons by acceleration and subsequent scattering, as in the Langevin model discussed in Sect. 2.5.1. We noted there that it will take a certain distance before the electrons reach their equilibrium energy as a result of the electric field acceleration. Where the electrons have not yet equilibrated, we would expect no light. As the electron distribution gains energy, the inelastic processes will come into play. In order to determine the distance over which the electrons will equilibrate, let us return to the Langevin model for a moment to recall that the distance for electrons to equilibrate with an electric field d is given by Eq. (82)

$$d = u/(\delta \nu).\tag{116}$$

where δ is the energy transfer fraction (2m/M) and ν is the collision frequency. We can rewrite (116) as

$$d = \lambda/(2\delta)^{1/2},\tag{117}$$

where λ is the collision mean free path. This says that the distance for the electrons to come into equilibrium with an electric field is equal to the collisional mean free path multiplied by $(M/4m)^{1/2}$. Let us consider as an example, Ar at a pressure of 50 mTorr ($N = 1.8 \times 10^{15} \text{cm}^{-3}$). The collision cross section is about $4 \times 10^{-15} \text{cm}^2$, so that $\lambda = 0.1$ cm and d = 14 cm.

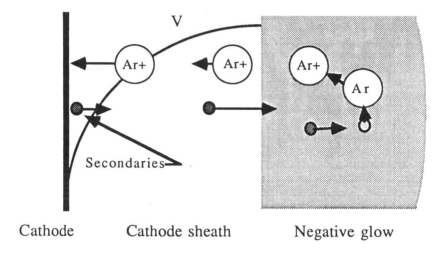

Cathode   Cathode sheath   Negative glow

Figure 16: Schematic of the discharge behavior in the cathode sheath - negative glow regions. Ions from the negative glow fall through the cathode sheath causing secondary electron emission. The secondaries are accelerated back through the sheath and comprise the main energy input to the negative glow which supports the ionization process, both through direct ionization and through ionization by the high energy tail of the electron distribution. These regions comprise a self-sustaining combination.

Thus the electrons would have to drift 14 cm in the electric field to come into equilibrium. Until they have drifted that far, the electron energy will be below that necessary to excite inelastic processes, such as excitation. Since this distance is longer than the negative glow, there is another dark space, namely the Faraday dark space. As noted previously, this distance is not necessarily equal to the thickness of the Faraday dark space, because we might expect that Ar emission would occur even before the electrons have fully equilibrated.

2.5.1.8 The Positive Column. In the positive column, the electrons have equilibrated with the electric field. The local electric field accelerates the electrons and represents the main energy input source. The main losses are diffusion to the walls and radiation from line emission. In electro-negative discharges, electron attachment may be an additional important loss mechanism. Since many plasma processes involve halide-containing gases, this is an important consideration. We will not consider this in the present case, however.

We will examine the positive column using the diffusion equations developed in Sect. 2.2.5. We will assume that a steady state is reached in which ionization in the positive column is balanced by diffusion of particles to the wall. If we write the source term for ionization in Eq. (52) as

$$S = n\nu_i \tag{118}$$

where n is the electron density and ν_i is the ionization rate, then the steady state form of Eq. (52) can be written as

$$\nabla^2 n = -(\nu_i/D)n \tag{119}$$

where we have used Eq. (53) and assumed that D is independent of position. We will assume that the length of the positive column is much greater than its radius R_D . The solution (53) of Eq. (119) can be written in terms of a diffusion length Λ where

$$\Lambda^2 = D/\nu_i. \tag{120}$$

To satisfy the boundary conditions that n= 0 at R_D (recombination at the surface), we require that

$$\Lambda = R_D/2.405 \tag{121}$$

From Eq. (120), we get that

$$\nu_1 = D(2.405/R_D)^2. \tag{122}$$

Then, from Sect. 2.2.4, we can write

$$\nu_1 = N\sigma v = N A(T_e), \tag{123}$$

where $A(T_e)$ is a function of the electron temperature, and from Sect. 2.2.5,

$$D = CT_e/N, \tag{124}$$

where C is a constant, and we have used the form of the ambipolar diffusion coefficient. Then, from the last three equations we get that

$$T_e/A(T_e) = (NR_D)^2/(2.405)^2 C, \tag{125}$$

From Eq. (125) we see that the electron temperature is determined by the square of the product of the neutral density and the radius of the discharge.

The positive column and other features beyond the negative glow do not usually play an important role in plasma processing (although they are very important for discharges used as light sources). One reason for studying the positive column here is that the general behavior is similar to what occurs in as rf powered discharge, as we shall see in the next section.

2.5.1.9 Summary of the dc Glow Discharge

To recapitulate, the dc discharge comprises, firstly, a self consistent combination of a cathode surface, cathode dark space region, with associated large electric field, and the negative glow region. Ions, formed in the dark space and negative glow regions are accelerated by the cathode electric field into the cathode surface, where they cause secondary electron emission and sputtering. The secondary electrons are accelerated back across the dark space and cause ionization, either directly or by transferring their energy to electrons in the plasma. Other types of discharges, such as the hollow cathode discharge, (see Chap. 12) rely on the formation of secondary electrons, which are accelerated by sheath voltages and are the primary source of ionization which sustains the discharge.

Additionally, a dc glow discharge may have another dark space beyond the negative glow and a positive column. In these regions, electrons are heated by the local electric field, which results in a balance between ionization and losses of charged particles. The plasma in the positive column follows the Langevin model. The positive column may be arbitrarily long (54), or absent entirely, and serves to connect the anode electrically to the remainder of the discharge.

2.5.2 RF Glow

In a dc glow discharge, most of the input power is used to accelerate the ions through the sheath, and appears as heat when the ions strike the cathode. If the secondary electron coefficient were 0.1, then, to a good approximation, only 10% of the power will end up in the negative glow from the secondary electrons which are accelerated in the sheath. In this sense, the dc glow is a rather inefficient plasma generator, though for processes which depend on ion bombardment, such as sputtering, this is not a problem.

An even more serious limitation of a dc glow discharge is the necessity of conducting net current to sustain the discharge. This requirement generally precludes the use of insulating materials in sputtering targets, substrates, or deposited films, because the insulators would prevent dc current conduction. If the insulators did not cover the entire electrode surface, it may be possible to sustain a dc discharge, but the insulators will build up a charge, making processes difficult to control.

The use of an ac power source can alleviate both these shortcomings of the dc glow discharge. Let us start by considering a very low frequency ac power source, with a period which is long compared to the time it takes for the plasma particles to come to equilibrium with the electric field. We will further assume that there are no insulators present. In this case, the ac discharge will be very similar to the dc discharge, except that the current will reverse every half cycle. A sheath will form at the electrode which is negative during the particular half cycle of the ac power, and ions will be accelerated across this sheath. The ions, which are able to cross the sheath in a short time compared to the ac period, will gain an amount of energy roughly equal to the instantaneous ac voltage. Thus, the ions striking the electrodes will have a distribution of energies, which will extend to approximately the peak ac voltage.

If we now consider what happens if we have an insulating electrode, we would find that current would flow until the insulator charged up and terminates the discharge. On the next half cycle, however, the insulator would discharge, and current would flow in the opposite direction until the insulator charged up again. The insulator behaves like a capacitor that is charged in alternate directions by the plasma. If the ac frequency is increased to the point where the charging time is much longer than the ac period, current will flow in the plasma for the entire ac cycle. A frequency of about 50 - 100 kHz is usually sufficient to achieve this condition. In this case, also, we would find that sheaths would form and ions would be accelerated by the instantaneous field, and arrive at the electrodes with a distribution of energies up to approximately the peak ac voltage.

As the frequency of the ac source is increased, new phenomena begin to appear. The details of the various frequency-dependant effects have been reviewed by Flamm (55), and have been reported for a few specific processes (56-58). However, due to the fact that most commercial rf plasma equipment is designed to work at the FCC assigned frequency of 13.56 MHz, the use of different frequencies has not been exploited and remains an untapped opportunity for optimizing processes. We will not consider this topic further here, but will instead explore the salient features of plasma operation at 13.56 MHz. At this frequency, the massive ions have too much inertia to respond to the instantaneous electric field in the sheath regions, while the lighter electrons will. Owing to the differences in mobilities of the ions and the electrons, however, a time-average bias will arise for certain configurations.

2.5.2.1 Self Bias and Plasma Potential. To see how this comes about, let us consider a discharge system with one small electrode connected to an rf power source through a coupling capacitor shown in Fig. 17. The characteristic response of the plasma to a voltage V is given by the curve in Fig. 18. Owing to the much greater mobility of the electrons compared to the ions, a given positive voltage will result in a much larger electron current than the ion current which flows for the same negative voltage. In effect, the plasma behaves like a leaky diode, showing a much larger effective resistance for ion current than for electron current.

Let us now apply a square wave with peak amplitude V_1 (See Fig. 19). Initially, when the applied voltage goes to V_1, the potential across the plasma is V_1. The capacitor will be charged through the effective resistance of the plasma for electron current flow, and will drop as shown in Fig. 20. When the power supply changes sign, the voltage across the plasma drops instantaneously by $-2V_1$, after which the voltage decays with the longer time constant associated with the higher effective resistance ion current flow. As shown in Fig. 20, this continues until the time average electron and ion currents are equal, a condition which results in a time-average negative bias on the electrode (59). Although the derivation was presented with a square wave power source, a similar effect holds for a sine wave, as in Fig. 21.

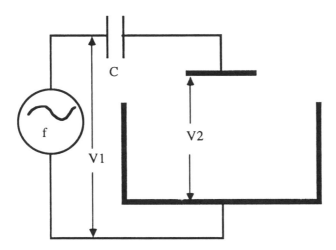

Figure 17: Schematic of electrode configuration for an rf glow discharge. An rf power supply is capacitively coupled to the electrodes.

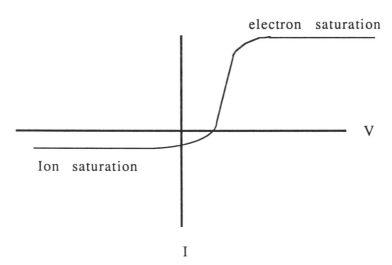

Figure 18: Electron and ion current as functions of the applied potential. The greater mobility of the electrons compared to the ions results in a larger electron current for a given positive voltage than the ion current which flows for an equal negative voltage.

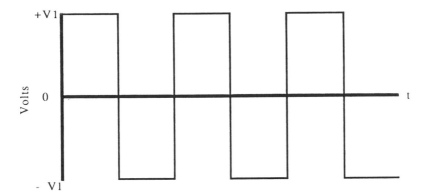

Figure 19: Output square wave of peak voltage V_1 which is used for the circuit shown in Fig. 17.

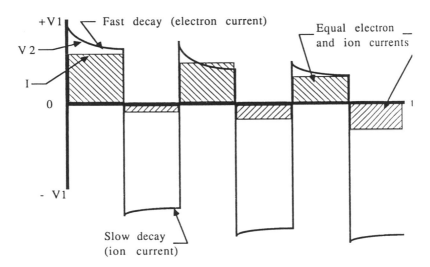

Figure 20: Behavior of the discharge voltage V_2, as the self bias develops to produce equal electron and ion currents. On each half cycle, the current decays as the capacitor charges from the plasma. On the half cycle where electron current flows, the decay is faster, because the plasma has an effectively lower impedance owing to the greater mobility of the electrons.

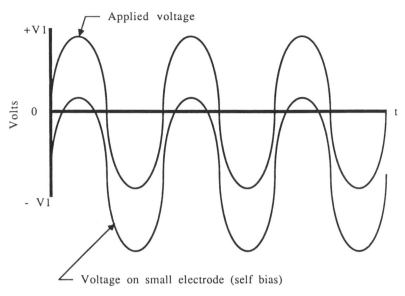

Figure 21: Self bias for a sine wave driven system.

Implicit in this derivation is the fact that the area of the large electrode was sufficient to permit all of the necessary currents to flow during each cycle. In other words, the limiting impedance for current flow on both half cycles occurs at the small area electrode. It is important to note that the features of the rf discharge which resulted in the self bias were the presence of the coupling capacitor (which ensures a time-average zero current), and the fact that one of the electrodes was much smaller than the other. The driven electrode is not necessarily the one where the bias occurs. The location of the capacitor is similarly irrelevant in determining the bias. In fact, if the apparatus were symmetric and totally decoupled from ground, there would be no self bias. The grounded electrode can have a bias if there is a coupling capacitor somewhere in the circuit and the grounded electrode is smaller than the driven electrode.

We noted in Sect. 2.2.6 that the plasma prefers to be more positive that the most positive surface. Then, for the case of a large bias, we would expect the plasma potential to behave as shown in Fig. 22. Even with the self bias, the small electrode is positive for some fraction of a cycle, so the time average plasma potential is usually higher than for the dc case. Ions, which cannot respond on the fast rf time scale will bombard the small electrode with an energy given by the difference between the time-average plasma potential and the time-average self bias.

Although not obvious from our simplified derivation, the magnitude of the bias will depend on the neutral pressure (4). As the pressure is increased with constant power into the discharge, the bias will decrease. This is due in part to decreases in the rf voltage, because the plasma impedance decreases as the neutral density increases. Another way of looking at this phenomenon is that at high densities, the discharge does not require as high a sheath field to sustain itself, because it is able to put energy directly into the glow electrons as we will discuss below.

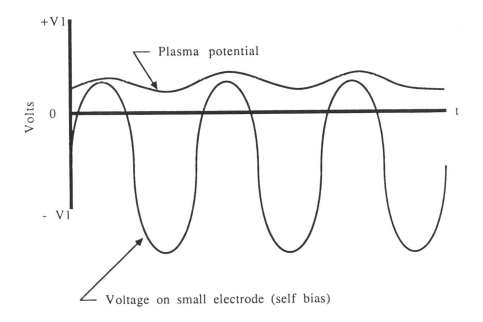

Figure 22: Time variation of the plasma potential shown with the self bias voltage on the small electrode. In the absence of collisions in the sheath, the ion energy at the small electrode will be the difference between the average potential and average self bias.

The asymmetric rf discharge configuration, which results in high bias, is the chosen configuration for reactive ion etching (60), where ion bombardment produces anisotropic etching. The highest bombardment energies are obtained as the pressure is lowered. Since excessive ion energy can result in damage to a wafer, however, some reactive ion etch processes are operated at higher pressures (200-300 mTorr), to reduce the ion energy both through a lower bias and collisions in the sheath. The latter effect, however, tends to destroy the directionality of the bombarding ions, which reduces their utility for anisotropic etching.

For the case of a symmetric discharge (equal area electrodes), where there is no self bias, the plasma potential appears as in Fig. 23. Here we see that the time average bias will be much greater than for the dc case, and, even though there is no bias, there will be energetic ion bombardment which will occur at both electrodes. An example of the near-symmetric etch reactor is the Reinberg etch reactor (5). In this apparatus, energetic ion bombardment occurs primarily due to the large plasma potential. An excellent summary of the self bias and plasma potential behavior has been given by Kohler, et al (61).

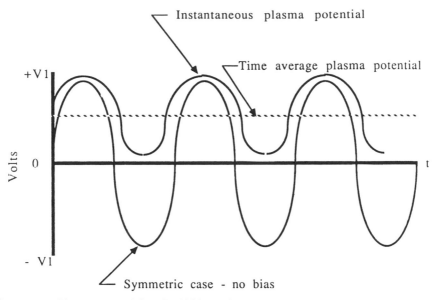

Figure 23: Plasma potential and self bias voltage for a symmetric discharge configuration. There is no self bias in this case, but the plasma potential is higher than for the asymmetric case. Energetic ion bombardment will occur at both electrodes. In the absence of collisions in the sheath, the ion energy at the small electrode will be the difference between the average potential and average self bias.

The sheaths in an rf discharge have large rf displacement currents flowing through them, but rather small conduction currents. The sheaths will behave like capacitors with some leakage current. The main part of the rf glow will be resistive, much as the negative glow and positive column in a dc discharge. Based on this picture, Koenig and Maissel (59) evolved an equivalent circuit of an rf discharge which provides a simple and quite useful model of the discharge.

One application of this model is the calculation of the self bias voltage division. The self bias voltage will divide between the two electrodes inversely proportional to the capacitance of the sheath regions

$$(V_a/V_b) = (C_b/C_a), \tag{126}$$

where a and b denote the two electrodes. The capacitance of the sheath regions is *roughly* given by:

$$C = \varepsilon_o A/D_s, \tag{127}$$

where A is the area of the sheath and D_s is the sheath thickness. There are two effects which make this expression difficult to use in practice: (1) the effective area of the sheath will depend on (unavoidable) stray coupling from the electrode to other surfaces, and (2)

D_s will depend in a complicated way on the discharge parameters. Koenig and Maissel attempt to relate D_s to the voltage by requiring that the Child-Langmuir space charge-limited currents at each electrode be equal:

$$V_a^{3/2}/D_a^2 = V_b^{3/2}/D_b. \tag{128}$$

Using this expression in conjunction with the capacitive voltage division leads to the conclusion that the bias divides between the electrodes inversely proportional to the fourth power of the ratio of the electrode areas. The caveats noted above, however, conspire to render this simplistic derivation much less than adequate. More sophisticated models have been presented by Horwitz (62) and Kohler et al (61).

2.5.2.2 Discharge Characteristics Owing to the self bias, there will be energetic ion bombardment of the smaller electrode, with attendant secondary electron emission. (In addition, there will also be some bombardment of the larger electrode.) In this respect, an rf discharge can be similar to the dc discharge: there will be a cathode sheath and a quasi-negative glow which is energized by the accelerated secondaries. There are differences, however. Although the ions are typically going slowly enough that they will respond only to the time average potential, the electrons will generally cross the sheath region in a fraction of the rf period. This can give rise to time dependent phenomena. In particular the edge of the sheath will generally oscillate. Some researchers believe that this mechanism can put energy directly into the electrons by a "surf riding" effect (63).

One characteristic which distinguishes the rf discharge from the dc discharge is that, because the rf field is changing direction in time, it can put energy into the electron energy distribution function more readily than the dc field. In the dc case, as we saw, an electron had to drift a considerable distance in the field to come into equilibrium with it. This is the reason that the positive column is separated from the negative glow. In the rf case, however, the electrons will not experience a net drift, since the field is changing direction. They will equilibrate after a characteristic time. Owing to this, the rf discharge is more efficient than the dc discharge. In a sense, the negative glow and positive column regions overlap.

2.5.2.3 RF Discharge Modeling Recently, the rf discharge has been studied numerically by a number of groups using the continuum model (57,64-66). The results of the models are consistent with the qualitative description given above on the three energy input mechanisms for an rf discharge. For electro-negative discharges, where electrons may not be the dominant negative charge, the discharge characteristics are very different from that predicted by the self bias picture above. The case of SF_6 discharge has been modeled and compared to experimental results by Gogolides, Nicolai and Sawin (67).

While the continuum models are very powerful, the underlying assumption is that the electron mean free path is short compared to the sheath size. It is questionable whether this assumption is valid below 50-100 mTorr, where many of the current etch processes operates. Low pressure discharges have been modelled using a Monte Carlo approach (63). In this calculation, an rf electric field profile was assumed, including an oscillating sheath boundary. While the results are not self-consistent, they do show clearly the increasing importance of the "surf-riding" acceleration mechanism as the pressure is lowered.

2.5.2.4 Summary of the rf Glow Discharge The rf glow discharge embodies many of the same qualitative features of the dc glow discharge, with the formation of sheaths in which strong electric fields will accelerate ions and electrons. At low frequencies, where ions can follow the changing electric fields, the discharge will behave similarly to the dc case. As the frequency increases, the ions will no longer be able to follow the instantaneous electric field, but will instead respond to the time averaged fields. Here, for discharge configurations with unequal electrode areas and where the electrons are the dominant negative charge carriers, a self-bias will arise which will produce a time-average negative voltage on the smaller electrode. Ions will be accelerated by the difference between the time-average plasma potential and the time-average bias. In general, the energy of the bombarding ions in an rf discharge will increase as the driving frequency is decreased and/or the neutral pressure is decreased.

Energy input to the rf discharge occurs through three mechanisms. Energetic ions striking the electrode will cause the formation of secondary electrons. These electrons can be accelerated through the sheath and cause ionization as in the sheath and negative glow regions of the dc discharge. The oscillating electric fields in the glow can input energy directly into the electrons, much in the same way as the positive column of the dc discharge. Finally, the oscillating sheath electric field will accelerate electrons in the glow. This "surf-riding" mechanism has no direct analog in the dc discharge.

Several enhancement schemes for the rf discharge are possible. The addition of a magnetic field nominally parallel to the electrode surface will result in confinement of the electrons as described in Sects. 2.1.4 and 2.2.3. Such schemes are used for magnetically enhanced reactive ion etching (8). Their principle advantage is that the presence of the magnetic field increases the electron ionization efficiency. This results in a lowering of the sheath potential and concomitant lowering of the bombarding ion energy, with no degradation of plasma performance.

It is also possible to use microwave power, typically at 2.45 GHz, to operate a discharge. In these schemes, the power can be coupled in radiatively, obviating the need for electrodes as described in Sect 2.1.4. One very important such configuration is the electron cyclotron resonance reactor (12), which includes a magnetic field and microwave at a frequency which is matched to the cyclotron frequency of the electrons as described in Sect 2.3.3.

2.6 REFERENCES

1. In cases where the positively charged ions have a charge greater than unity, this equality holds with the density of positive charges multiplied by their respective charge. In the plasmas used for thin film deposition and etching, it is rare to have multiply charged ions.

2. N.A. Krall and A.W. Trivelpiece, Principles of Plasma Physics (McGraw-Hill, New York, 1973) p5.

3. J.M. Coulson and J.F. Richardson, Chemical Engineering, Vol. 3 (Pergammon Press, Oxford, 1979).

4. D.L. Flamm and V.M. Donnelly, Plasma Chemistry and Plasma Processing 1: 317 (1981).

5. L.M. Ephrath, in ULSI Science and Technology 1989 ed. by M. Osburn (The Electrochemical Society, Pennington NJ, 1989).

6. A.R. Reinberg, US Patent 3,757,733.

7. R.A. Heinecke, Sol. State Electron. 18: 1146 (1975).

8. I.Lin, D.C. Hinson, W.H. Class, and R.L. Sandstrom, Appl. Phys. Lett. 44: 185 (1984).

9. J.M. Moran and D. Maydan, Bell System Tech. J. 58: 1027 (1979).

10. D.E. Rosner and H.D. Allendorf, J. Chem. Phys. 75: 308 (1971).

11. K. Suzuki, S. Okudairi, N. Sakudo and I. Kanomata, Jpn. J. Appl. Phys. 16: 1979 (1977).

12. S. Matatsuo and Y. Adachi, Jpn. J. Appl. Phys. 21: L4 (1982).

13. Sanborn C. Brown Introduction to Electrical Discharges in Gases (John Wiley and Sons, New York, 1966).

14. Frances F. Chen, Introduction to Plasma Physics and Controlled Fusion (Plenum Press, New York, 1983).

15. V.E. Golant, A.P. Zhilinsky, I.E. Sakharov and S.C. Brown, Fundamentals of Plasma Physics (John Wiley and Sons, New York, 1977).

16. E.W. Holt and R.E. Haskell, Foundations of Plasma Dynamics (Macmillian, New York, 1965).

17. N.A. Krall and A.W. Trivelpiece, *op cit.*

18. J.D. Jackson, Classical Electrodynamics (John Wiley and Sons, New York, 1975).

19. Sanborn C. Brown, *op cit.*

20. T.H. Stix, The Theory of Plasma Waves, (McGraw-Hill, New York, 1962).

21. Frances F. Chen *op cit.*

22. J.A. Thornton and A.S. Penfold, in Thin Film Processes, ed. by J.L. Vossen and W. Kern (Academic, Orlando, 1978), p75.

23. N.A. Krall and A.W. Trivelpiece, *op cit.* p. 627.

24. T. Ono, M. Oda, C. Takahashi and S. Matsuo, J. Vac. Sci. Technol. B4: 696 (1986).

25. Sanborn C. Brown, Basic Data of Plasma Physics (John Wiley and Sons, New York, 1959).

26. B.E. Cherrington, Gaseous Electronics and Gas Lasers (Pergammon, Oxford, 1979).

27. B. Chapman, Glow Discharge Processes (John Wiley and Sons, New York, 1980) p. 12.

28. B.E. Cherrington, *op cit.* , p. 68.

29. B. Chapman, *op cit.* , p. 24.

30. Sanborn C. Brown, *op cit.* , p. 28.

31. Sanborn C. Brown, *op cit.* , p. 60.

32. Frances F. Chen, *op cit.* , p. 159.

33. C.M. Ferreira and J. Loureiro, J. Phys D: Appl. Phys. 17: 1175 (1984).

34. Sanborn C. Brown, *op cit.*, p. 204.

35. One exception to this is the sheath region of a glow discharge, where there are very few electrons and we must consider the effect of the electric field on the electrons.

36. B.E. Cherrington, *op cit.* , p. 11.

37. An exception to this is the case of a reactor with hot walls or electrodes, in which the neutral species can heat up. Also neutrals can heat by collisions with sputtered species (Chap. 6).

38. B.E. Cherrington *op cit.* , p. 18.

39. H. Meuth and E. Sevillano, in Plasma Diagnostics, Vol 1, Discharge Parameters and Chemistry ed. by O. Auciello and D.L. Flamm (Academic Press, Boston, 1989), p. 239.

40. Sanborn C. Brown, *op cit.* p. 166.

41. B.E. Cherrington, *op cit.* p. 49.

42. B.E. Cherrington, *op cit.* p. 64.

43. A. von Engel, Ionized Gases (Oxford University Press, London, 1965) p. 180.

44. Sanborn C. Brown, *op cit.* , p. 183.

45. Sanborn c. Brown, *op cit.* , p. 169.

46. J.L. Vossen and J.J. Cuomo, in Thin Film Processes, ed. by J.L Vossen and W. Kern (Academic, Orlando, 1978), p. 24.

47. Sanborn C. Brown, *op cit.* , p. 211.

48. E.N. Sickafus, Phys. Rev. B 16: 1436 (1977).

49. A. von Engel, *op cit.* , p. 234.

50. B. Chapman, *op cit.* , p. 96.

51. David B. Graves and Klavs F. Jensen, IEEE Trans on Plasma Sci. PS-14: 78 (1986)

52. W.D. Davis and T.A. Vanderslice Phys. Rev. 131: 219 (1963).

53. Sanborn C. Brown, *op cit.* , p. 29.

54. Sanborn C. Brown, *op cit.* , p 213.

55. D.L. Flamm, J. Vac. Sci. Technol. A4: 729 (1986).

56. V.M. Donnelly, D.L. Flamm and G. Collins, J. Vac. Sci. Technol. 21: 817 (1982).

57. M.R. Werrtheimer, J. Vac. Sci. Technol. A3: 2643 (1985).

58. H. Curtins, N. Wyrsch and A.V. Shah, Electron. Lett. 23: 228 (1987).

59. H.R. Koenig and L.I. Maissel, IBM J. Res. Dev. 14: 168 (1970).

60. J.D. Chin, I. Adeside, E.D. Wolf and R.C. Tiberio, J. Vac. Sci. Technol. 19: 1418 (1981)

61. K. Kohler, J.W. Coburn, D.E. Horne, E. Kay and J.H. Keller, J. Appl Phys. 57: 59 (1985).

62. C.M. Horwitz, J. Vac. Sci. Technol. A1: 60 (1983).

63. Mark J. Kushner, IEEE Trans. Plas. Sci. PS-14: 188 (1986)

64. M.S. Barnes, T.J. Colter and M.E. Elta, J. Appl Phys. 61: 81 (1987)

65. A.D. Richards, B.E. Thompson and H.H. Sawin, Appl. Phys. Lett. 50: 492 (1987).

66. J-P. Boeuf, Phys. Rev. A 36: 2782 (1987).

67. E. Gogolides, J-P. Nicolai and H.H. Sawin, J. Vac. Sci. Technol. A7: (in press).

3

Fundamentals of Sputtering and Reflection

David N. Ruzic

3.1 INTRODUCTION

Sputtering and reflection of ions and neutral atoms from solid surfaces are closely related complex phenomenon. The behavior of the surface and the incident projectile depend greatly on the relative masses and energies of the atoms involved, the structure of the solid, and other factors. A model or semi-empirical expression that fits one behavioral regime such as linear-cascade response may be quite inappropriate for another response region. This chapter looks closest <u>not</u> at the linear-cascade, where theoretical and empirical models are well developed, but at the non-isotropic-cascade in-need-of-surface-corrections response, where both data and modeling effects are sparse. It is this low-energy surface regime that is of most interest to the plasma-processing community.

3.1.1 Sputtering Regimes

When an atom or ion strikes a solid surface the collective response of the atoms in the target can be grouped into five distinct categories. Which phenomena dominates depends on the mass and atomic number, Z_i , of the incident projectile; the mass and atomic number, Z_t , of the target; and the incident energy, E. Figure 1 (1) shows these regions mapped onto two cuts through the Z_i, Z_t, E space. Though the boundaries are drawn as sharp lines, the types of collective surface behavior gradually meld into one another in reality. There is not a 50% chance of either phenomenon at one of the boundaries---instead the surface behavior incorporates features of both types of interactions.

The response that is typically described is not shaded in Fig. 1. It primarily occurs at intermediate energies (5 to 100 keV). A <u>cascade</u> of recoil atoms is produced along the path of the incident ion. The number of recoil atoms produced at any point depends linearly on the amount of energy lost by the incident ion at that point. At these intermediate energies, energy loss is due to electron drag from the free electrons in the solid, and screened Coulomb interactions from the nuclei. Analytic expressions for the energy loss exist, so the density and energy of the recoil cascade can be calculated. Assuming that the energy lost to the recoil atoms is isotropic, transport theory can be used to determine the number of recoil atoms that will reach the surface, overcome the potential barrier of the work function and become sputtered atoms. The energy distribution and angular distributions of these sputtered atoms can also be determined. The sputtering yields and distributions that result fit the known data well. This transport theory approach forms the basis for most of the analytic sputtering yield, angular distribution and energy distribution expressions in the literature (1-5).

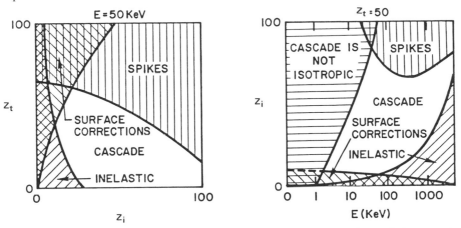

Figure 1: The five collective responses of a target with atomic number Z_t being struck by an atom or ion of atomic number Z_i and energy E. Two cuts through (Z_t, Z_i, E) space are shown.

If the ion energy is high (greater than about 50 keV) and the incident ion is heavier than the target atoms an entire block of atoms located along the initial path of the projectile can be set into a violent motion. This is known as the spike regime and transport theory breaks down because of non-linear effects: the next target atom for the incident projectile may well be an atom that is in motion due to the collision.

At very large energies (greater than 1000 keV) for any projectile-target pair, and at somewhat lower energies when the projectile is lighter than the target, inelastic energy loss channels must be considered. For example, energy could be lost by the ionization of inner core electrons in the solid. Transport theory can still be used, but a more complicated energy loss expression is needed.

Going to lower energies than the most-understood cascade region (ion energy is less than 5 keV, certainly less than 1 keV) the energy lost to the recoil atoms in the cascade is not isotropic. The first target atom struck by the projectile will absorb most of the lost energy and respond in an individual manner. It becomes the primary knock-on and may in turn generate additional knock-on atoms. In this regime transport theory and the analytic sputtering expressions based upon that theory cannot be used. However, empirical fits (5) to the known experimental data have been made for H and He ions.

At even lower energies (hundreds of eVs), or when the projectile mass is much less than the target, the cascade is not only anisotropic, but corrections due to the surface topology must be included. The atomic-scale roughness on the surface must be considered since the range of the particle may only be a few Å.

The sputtering interactions that are of importance to the plasma-processing community primarily fall in this last low-energy non-isotropic-cascade in-need-of-surface-correction regime. Bombardment energies are kept fairly low in plasma processing to minimize damage and contamination of the wafers: if the difference between the plasma potential and the bias potential of the sputtering target is too high, ions will be accelerated to such great energies that cluster emission and high energy reflections (which can then cause damage to the substrate) are likely to result. Therefore most sputtering systems are run such that the incident ions are less than one thousand eV. In an etching system the sheath drop, and thus the energy of the incident ions, is also kept low to avoid the damage and indiscriminate physical sputtering that could result. However, even at these lower energics some damage to the surface is inevitable and the surface of both sputtering targets and etched substrates is not atomically smooth.

Due to the relative inefficiency of the sputtering process in terms of energy, most sputtering targets or cathodes must be actively cooled. In some cases, such as magnetron sputtering, the limiting factor to high power, high rate operation is the ability to cool the cathode. The most energy-efficient range for sputtering is in the 300-800 eV ion energy range. This can be found by differentiating the sputter yield-as-a-function of energy (see Figs. 9, 10 below). There are other practical reasons for keeping the energy low as well, related to operator safety, vacuum feedthroughs, shielding, high-power supply stability and cost.

Since most of the phenomena of interest occur on atomically rough surfaces at low energies (less than 1000 eV), this regime will be examined in detail. In this regime Monte-Carlo computer simulations form the basis for analytic treatment and physical understanding. They are discussed in the next section along with new techniques to model surface roughness (6). Section 3.3 contains a review of the experimental sputtering data for H+ and Ar+ on Si, Al, Cu, Ni and C. Section 3.4 points out the numerous effects that can further influence sputtering yields such as substrate temperature, single crystal channeling, chemical reactions, preferential sputtering of alloys, cluster formation, fluence dependence and topology evolution. A brief discussion of review articles is also included.

3.2 MODELING

3.2.1 TRIM

The entire non-isotropic-cascade or primary-knock-on regimes of sputtering is well suited to a Monte-Carlo binary collision approach. In the TRansport of Ions in Matter (TRIM) program (7,8) the target is considered to be amorphous or polycrystalline. Incident projectiles are followed until a collision occurs. The location of a collision is determined by a random variation of the particles mean-free-path for a nuclear stopping result. Electron energy loss is subtracted for the particles entire path length inside the surface. A random impact parameter and azimuthal scattering angle are chosen and the energy and momentum transfer are calculated classically. This allows the new velocity (speed and direction) and location of both the incident projectile and primary knock-on atom to be determined. They are then treated in the same manner as the incident projectile and create a new generation of knock-on atoms.

Both the original projectile and all of the atoms it collides with are followed by the program. Often the primary knock-on will create an entire cascade of its own. Atoms are followed until their energy falls below the energy needed to escape from the lattice.

When either the initial projectile or a recoil atom reaches the surface, the perpendicular-energy of the particle is compared to the surface binding energy of the target. If the particle can escape, its energy is reduced by the surface binding energy and its emission angle is refracted. If the energy is not great enough to escape, the particle is specularly reflected into the bulk and the process continues.

On the way into the target TRIM does not consider the surface to be atomically flat. Effectively, the initial starting position of the projectile is randomly distributed over a measure of its perpendicular mean free path. This surface model is quite important at low energies and has allowed TRIM to predict experimental results at <u>normal</u> incidence with a high degree of accuracy. At higher angles of incidence a more accurate surface model is needed.

3.2.2 Fractals

Real surfaces of amorphous and polycrystalline material are not flat or smoothly varying; they are approximate fractals (9,10). Figure 2 (10) shows a log-log plot of the radius of adsorbed gas atoms vs the number of those atoms it takes to completely cover an Al_2O_3 surface. If the alumina were perfectly flat the slope of the line would be -2.00, since area is proportional to radius squared. Al_2O_3 is not perfectly flat, however. In fact its surface is quite convoluted. It takes many more small gas atoms to cover all the surface sites than large gas atoms because the small atoms can fit into all the nooks and crannies that the large adsorbate simply plasters over. Surprisingly the points on the curve fall on a straight line. That means that the roughness is self-similar; the surface looks the same independent of the magnification with which it is viewed. The slope of the line and the fractal dimension of the surface is 2.79 + 0.03.

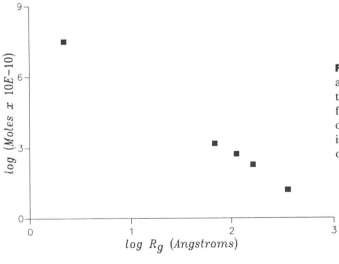

Figure 2: Gas adsorption as a function of adsorbate size for Al_2O_3. The slope of the line, 2.79 $\pm$ 0.03 is the fractal dimension of the surface (10).

Of course, any real object can only be fractal to some finite magnification. Ultimately the atomic diameter is reached. At the other extreme, the macroscopic character of the material is realized. Fractal geometry becomes a useful construct for sputtering and reflection calculation because the mean free path for collisions within the target and the ultimate range of the projectiles fall within the range over which the targets surface is fractal. The alumina described in Fig. 2 is fractal at least over the range of 4 Å to 210 Å. Many materials have been shown to have fractal surfaces over the range of interest (11). For instance carbon black has a fractal dimension of 2.25 ± 0.09 and Vulcan 3G graphite has a fractal dimension of 2.07 ± 0.01.

3.2.3 Fractal TRIM

The self-similar properties of fractal geometry have been utilized to add a more realistic surface model to the TRIM computer code (6,12). Basically the Fractal TRIM code calculates the distance to the first surface and the distance through the fractal in the scattering plane. If the random selection of the next path step would predict the next collision to occur beyond the first surface but still within the surface feature, the simulation is restarted using the particle's energy and incident angle on entering that surface feature. Since fractal self-similarity implies an equivalence of angular orientation as well as magnification, a three dimensional surface structure does not have to be carried through the simulation. Since a cut through an object with fractal dimension D produces a new object with dimension D - 1.00, only the individual scattering plane is modeled and the simulation becomes tractable.

Figure 3 shows the pronounced effect of surface roughness on sputtering yields. The sputtering yield of target material for 100 eV C on C is shown as a function of fractal dimension for a variety of incident angles. Also shown on this figure is the effect of the surface model in the planar TRIM code. Planar TRIM with no surface model gives exactly the same results as Fractal TRIM with D = 2.00. An effective approximate fractal dimension can be calculated for Planar TRIM which varies with incident angle of the projectile (12). These surface-corrected planar TRIM results are also shown in Fig. 3. Note that Fig. 3 does not give the self sputtering yield for C on C; reflection must be included. It does show the general dependance for the sputtering of many materials at low energy.

A striking result from Fig. 3 is that a small amount of surface roughness can lead to a large change in the sputtering yield. Yet, as surface roughness is increased the sputtering yield drops off for high angles of incidence. This effect can be explained by the schematic drawing in Fig. 4. In Fig. 4(a) a projectile is incident on a perfectly flat surface. The primary knock-on atom will be struck in a downward direction. Since at low energies the first collision is likely to have the highest chance of producing a sputtering event, sputtering is unlikely for a planar surface. This is especially true for normally incident projectiles.

A small amount of roughness (Fig. 4 (b)), allows some primary knock-ons to have a directed energy out of the plane. Thus the sputtering yield increases. Higher angles of incidence promote this effect even more. However, if the surface becomes too rough the sputtered atoms may collide with other surface features (Fig. 4 (c)) and the sputtering yield decreases.

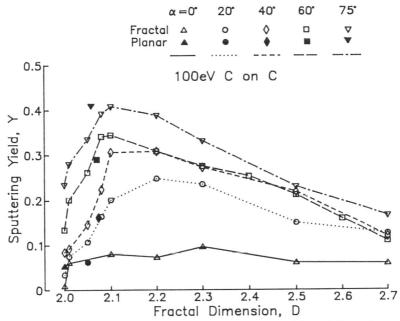

Figure 3: Sputtering yield of target material as a function of fractal dimension and angle of incidence for 100 eV C incident on a C target. Normal incidence is 0 degrees. Statistical errors in the yield are generally less than 5%.

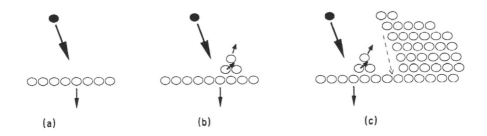

Figure 4: (a) On a flat surface the primary knock-on is always directed downward. (b) With some roughness, a primary knock-on could be directed out of the surface, this effect increases as angle of incidence increases. (c) For a very rough surface, sputtered atoms may be recaptured by other surface features.

At higher energies, these detailed surface effects become less important, but a realistic model of the surface remains essential to accurately portray grazing incidence events. Figure 5 shows the sputtering yield for 300 eV H on C as a function of fractal dimension for normal and 60 degree incident angles. Planar TRIM (13) overestimates the sputtering yield at 60 degrees by a factor of two compared to experiments (14). The slight variation with fractal dimension can also explain why different types of graphite targets gave different experimental results.

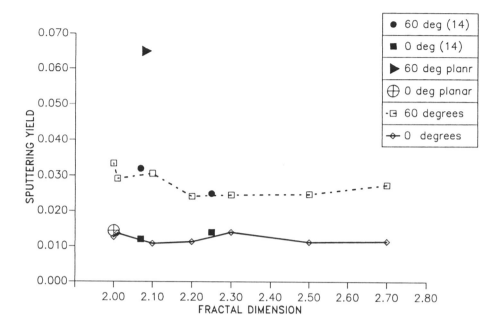

Figure 5: Sputtering yield as a function of fractal dimension for 300 eV H on C at normal and 60 degree incidence. Experimental points (14) are shown for a smooth and rough graphite. The fractal dimensions assigned are based on Avnir (11) and are only approximate. Planar TRIM overestimates the sputtering yield by a factor of 2-3 for the 60 degree case. Statistical errors in the yield for the simulation are less than 5%.

3.2.4 Reflection

Sputtering is only one of the phenomena that can occur when an ion strikes a surface. At these low energies simple reflection is often more likely. When ions reflect they almost invariably reflect as neutral atoms in their ground states (15,16). An excellent review of reflection data and computer simulations through 1984 can be found in (3). Surface roughness has a profound effect on the reflection of low-energy particles, especially at high angles of incidence (6).

Reflection from fractal surfaces shows a complimentary effect to that of sputtering. Figure 6 shows the number R_n and energy reflection R_e coefficients for 50 eV H incident on Ni as a function of fractal dimension for normal and 75 degree incident angles (6). Note how the reflection coefficients drop precipitously for the grazing incident case as soon as some surface roughness is added. This effect is not unusual to anyone who has tried to skip a rock on a choppy lake.

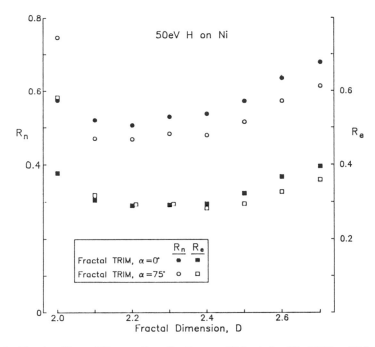

Figure 6: Number R_n and Energy R_e reflection coefficients for 50 eV H on Ni for normal ($\alpha = 0°$) and grazing ($\alpha = 75°$) incidence as a function of the fractal dimension of the Ni surface. Statistical error in the coefficients are generally less than 5 %. Note the dramatic drop in reflection at grazing incidence when a small amount of surface roughness is added.

At higher energies, above 100 eV, the reflection curves for normal incidence mimic the shape of the sputtering yield (Y) curves. Figure 7 shows R_n and Y as a function of fractal dimension for 200 eV Ar on Cu. The number reflected and sputter yield jump with a small amount of roughness, reach a maximum and then decrease. When a projectile is incident normally and has a moderate amount of energy it is very unlikely to reflect in one collision. Therefore if the projectile is to escape at all, its geometrical interactions with the surface are very similar to the interactions produced in the collision cascade. Therefore reflection and sputtering have a similar behavior as a function of roughness.

3.2.5 Molecular Dynamics

At the lowest energies, the binary collision model should break down. While the physics is quite different, Fig. 8 shows that, for at least one case, a full blown molecular dynamics treatment (17) utilizing a rough fractal-like surface (18) gives nearly the same result as Fractal TRIM. Molecular dynamics codes treat all the interactions of the atoms in the target on an equal basis. At each time step, the forces on all of the atoms in the simulation are simultaneously computed. The extreme computer resources demanded by such routines make them unsuitable for most sputtering and reflection calculations, but they make tremendous learning tools for obtaining a physical feel for low-energy interactions.

This physical feel is best comprehended visually. We have created a movie (19) of a molecular-dynamics simulation of a 10 eV hydrogen atom interacting with a rough Ni surface. To produce the same sense of the interaction through the written word requires some degree of imagination:

Imagine yourself as a hydrogen ion speeding toward a nickel surface. You are moving at 450 angstroms per picosecond (10 eV) and the gentle tug of the protruding electron cloud whose effect is known as the work function is accelerating your progress. A mountain range is coming into view---the surface is not a single crystal, there are hills and valleys below. If you could stop and look closely you'd see a surface alive with random motion. The surface is at room temperature. The mountain peaks almost seem to be swaying in the breeze. Their restoring forces are less and those atoms make larger displacements before being pulled back. The peaks may travel a whole tenth of an Angstrom.

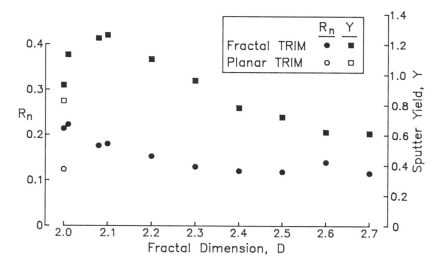

Figure 7: Sputtering yield and reflection as a function of fractal dimension for 200 eV Ar normally incident on Cu. Statistical errors for the sputtering yield and reflection coefficients are generally less than 5% and 10% respectively.

A look at the overall topology reminds you of a fractal. If you were twice as close everything would look the same. Of course there is a limit to this self-similar geography---the diameter of a nickel atom is 2.1 Å! The material is basically in a FCC structure with a lattice constant of 3.52 Å . So each plane of atoms is about 1.76 Å apart. The surface roughness is only fractal-like in the range of about 2 to 15 Å. In this range the surface area is proportional to the length of a side of the unit cell to the 2.3 power, i.e. the fractal dimension is 2.3.

Of course, you can't really stop. Compared to your motion the thermal motion is 400 times smaller. You whiz by apparently motionless objects. In this flight you are normally incident to the surface heading almost directly into a valley. The electron cloud reaches up and envelopes you when you are a few Angstroms above the highest peak. Now you've become an atom. When you are still 7 Å above the floor of the valley and just 1 Å or so below the mountain tops your presence begins to be felt by the atoms in the lattice. The atom directly beneath you and the one closest to your side have their potential energy greatly increased and they are accelerated away from you. The reaction force gradually gives you a component of velocity away from the mountain side. By the time you are even with the floor of the valley you have an angle of 20 degrees with respect to the normal.

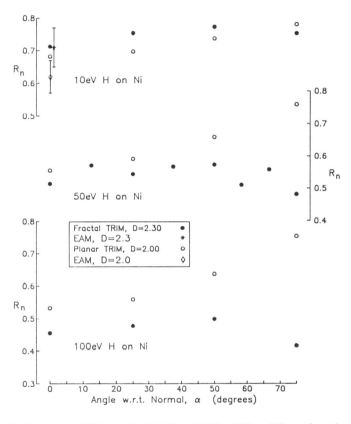

Figure 8: Reflection coefficients for 10, 50 and 100 eV H on Ni as a function of incident angle for a fractal Ni surface with dimension 2.30. Planar TRIM results and a molecular dynamics calculation using the Embedded Atom Method (EAM) are also shown. Note that planar TRIM predicts reflection at grazing incidence to be 2-3 times more likely than the fractal TRIM results. Statistical errors in the fractal and planar TRIM reflection coefficients are generally less than 5%.

The news of your arrival travels faster than you do. The neighbors of the atoms initially perturbed have their potentials increased, and a disturbance in the potential of the atoms travels out in waves. This potential shock wave extends about 3 or 4 atoms deep in a rough hemisphere pointing in the direction of the initial push. If the surface were at absolute zero the disturbance would undoubtedly travel much much further, but the collective effect quickly becomes indistinguishable from the thermal noise.

By the time the first potential wave has damped itself out you have moved less than an Angstrom. New waves are made as you move closer, but a given atom can generally only initiate a wave once. It is not that these initial progenitors disappear. They have effectively not moved at all---it is that their acceleration is now constant so their potential remains the same:

$$ma = dV/dx \tag{1}$$

The velocity vectors of the initial surface were pointing in all directions. The atoms in the potential wave experience a force that slowly bends those velocity vectors around so that they point away from the incident hydrogen atom. However, due to the inertia and restoring forces of the lattice, only the nearest atoms completely turn their velocity vectors in this grazing type of collision. Even this first layer won't have turned completely until the H atom is long gone from the scene.

As you pass into the surface the potential wave effect which slowly produces displacement from your path continues until something dramatic occurs. At about 3 layers in you hit an atom head on and go careening off 135 degrees away now traversing parallel to the surface about 5 Å below the valley floor. In this type of almost binary collision the struck atom changes potential dramatically and its velocity vector immediately swings to the direction it was pushed. However, the speed only builds up to three or four times thermal velocity before its acceleration is slowed by its neighbors. Again the propagation extends only 3 or 4 layers, but the effect is more localized.

On average you make another collision every 4 Å or so. Each of these violently change your direction but effect your speed very little. Sometimes the collisions are not binary. Two or more atoms can seemingly be struck simultaneously, effecting them all fairly evenly. In each collision the energy transferred away from you is small. It will take 30 collisions or so to come to rest. About half the time you will pop back out of the surface instead. To get out you have to have enough energy to escape that electron cloud, i.e. you have to overcome the work function. If you have almost enough energy you will be drawn to just an Å or so above the surface and travel over the surface like a hover craft until you run into some relief.

So how does sputtering work? Each violent collision or gentle brush leaves a ripple of disturbed atoms with somewhat directed velocities and at least at some point in time a raised potential energy. These ripples of velocity could overlap since the hydrogen is moving much faster than the atoms in the lattice. If the interference happens just right, and one wave of disturbance pushed an atom outward toward the surface at the same time that another wave pushes the same atom outward, an atom on the surface could have a potential great enough the work function. Long (10^{-13} seconds) after the hydrogen atom hits, a sputtered nickel atom is released. It happens once for every 50,000 hydrogen atoms that strike at 10 eV at normal incidence or so.

3.3 EXPERIMENTAL YIELDS

The determination of the sputtering yield of a material can be done in many ways (1). As with most experiments, a large amount of effort is required for each reproducible data point. Without these experiments, however, modelling would be futile. A model should not be whole-hearted subscribed to unless it fits at least some of the experimental data. In this section most of the experimental data from the era of clean vacuum conditions is assembled for some of the cases of interest to the plasma processing community. The total sputtering yield (sputtered atoms per incident ion) for H^+ and Ar^+ ions incident normal to the surface as a function of energy, up to energies of 1000 eV, are shown next.

Figure 9(a) shows that the yield for H on C decreases with energy, while Fig. 9(b) shows the yield for H on Al, Si, and Ni increasing with energy. H on C is a peculiar case because of the rampant chemical effects (see Sect. 3.4), though the data in Fig. 9(a) were performed on non-heated samples and are believed to represent physical sputtering.

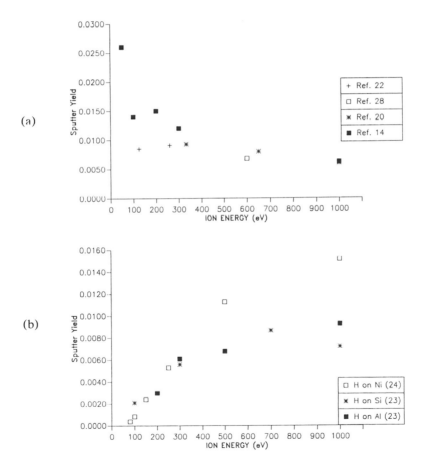

Figure 9: Experimental sputtering yield of H^+ on (a) C, and on (b) Al, Si, and Ni.

Figure 10(a) through (e) show the yield for Ar bombarding C, Al, Si, Ni, and Cu at normal incidence. The yield increases with energy. Figure 10(a) shows experimental data for two types of carbon (diamond vs turbostratic) to differ markedly in their sputtering yield. The difference can easily be explained in terms of surface roughness. The diamond surface is likely to have a fractal dimension near 2.00 while the layered turbostatic will have some degree of roughness. As seen in Fig. 3, these difference between very flat and somewhat rough surfaces can give appreciable differences in sputtering yields.

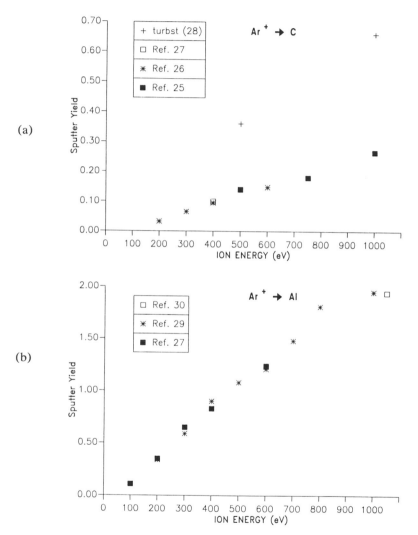

(a)

(b)

Figure 10: Experimental sputtering yields of Ar+ on (a) C, and (b) Al. In (a) the rougher turbostatic carbon has a higher yield than diamond as expected from the model results in Fig. 3.

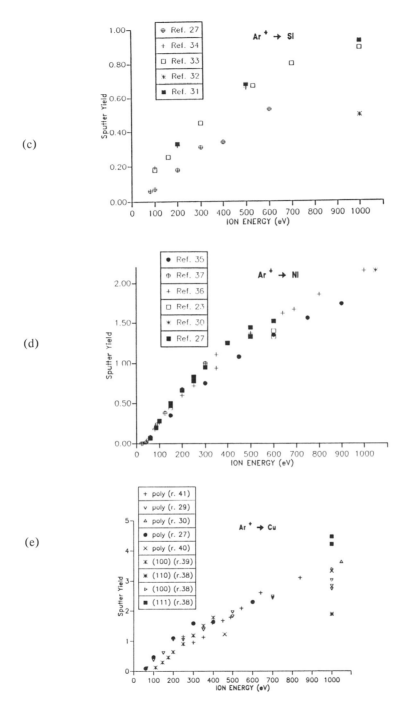

Figure 10: continued, (c) Si, (d) Ni and (e) Cu. In (e) the effects of crystal orientation are seen at higher energies.

In Fig. 10(e) the effect of crystalline structure is apparent (see Sect. 3.4). These effects are most pronounced at higher energies (1000eV). At lower energies the long-range order of the crystallite does not matter as seen by comparing the (39) data to the spread of the other data in Fig 10(e).

Though normal incident sputtering is often the typical situation for plasma processing, substrate masks, non-normal ion beams and some magnetic configurations may introduce more glancing incident events. In the cascade region the total sputtering yield as a function of incident angle with respect to the normal, θ, is predicted to follow a $1/\cos \theta$ dependence. For Ar ions incident on Al, Ni and Cu at 1050 eV (Fig. 11) and H ions incident on Ni and C at 1000 eV (Fig. 12) this prediction is close to the observed values. Note however, that as the mass of the target increases, the shift is below the cosine prediction. As the incident energy is lowered the shift to a "under-cosine" distribution is quite pronounced as seen in Fig. 12. Here the total sputtering yield as a function of angle for H on C is seen as a function of energy.

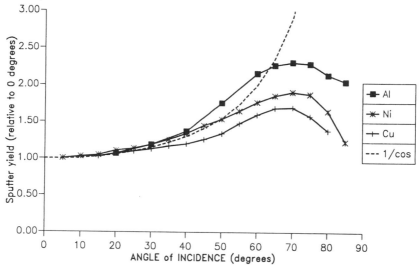

Figure 11: Experimental sputtering yield normalized to the yield at normal incidence as a function of angle for Ar+ on Al, Ni and Cu from Ref. (30) compared to a 1/cosine function.

Both Figs. 11 and 12 show another remarkable feature. At the highest angles of incidence the sputtering yield drops. This is due to an increased number of reflections of the projectile at the grazing incident angles. In the collision with the the first atom struck---the primary knock-on---very little energy is transferred since the path of the projectile is only deflected by a small amount. At higher energies the rounding-over effect is less pronounced since the first collision is less likely to deplete a large fraction of the projectile's energy, and further interactions can take place with higher energy transfer. In these cases, many atoms along the projectile's path are set into motion and cascade theory fits well. If the surface is rough, Fractal TRIM tells us to expect an even lower sputtering yield at high angle of incidence. This is seen in Fig. 12 when comparing V800 and EK98 (rough industrial graphites) to highly oriented graphite. The sputtering yield is a factor of 2 to 3 times lower as was the prediction in Fig. 5.

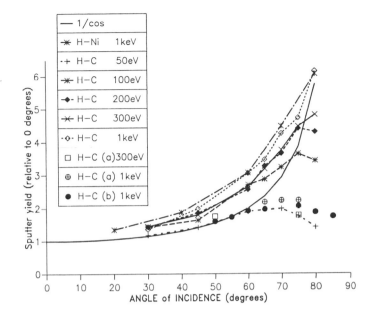

Figure 12: Normalized to normal incidence, experimental sputtering yields as a function of angle and energy for H on Ni and H on C. Results for a variety of graphites are also shown. The rougher technical grades of graphite, V800 and ek98, give lower sputtering yields as predicted by the fractal model. Data for H-Ni from Ref. 42, all other data from Ref. 14. NOTE: (a) V800 grade graphite, (b) ek98 grade graphite.

Linear cascade theory also predicts energy and angular distributions of the sputtered flux. For light ions at most energies, and all ions at very low energies, a cascade will not develop. Figure 13 shows a measurement (42) of the emission angle of sputtered Ni as a function of incident angle for a 1000 ev H ion beam. For lower energies and rougher surfaces, simulations (12) show that the angular distribution of sputtered atoms does not show the forward peaking seen in Fig. 13 . Instead the emission is almost isotropic.

The energy of the sputtered atoms can also be predicted, but again at low energies some correction is needed (44). Figure 14 shows the energy of the sputtered atoms for Ar bombardment of Cu at a variety of energies.

3.4 EXCEPTIONS

Of the events that lead to sputtering only physical sputtering has been examined in this chapter. For particular pairs of atoms, chemical sputtering (the formation of volatile compounds on the target surface) can be very important. For these chemical systems the temperature of the substrate is often the yield determining factor (3,45,46). The chemical environment can be even more complicated by the presence of other reactive gases such as oxygen (47) even in very small quantities.

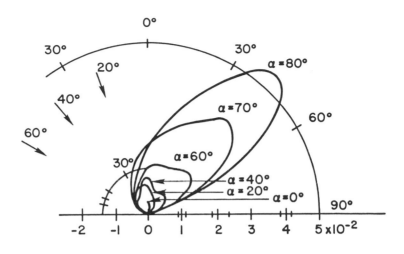

DIFFERENTIAL SPUTTERING YIELDS
(ATOM/ION x STERA D)

Figure 13: Measured angular distribution of sputtered atoms for 1 keV H on Ni at a variety of incident angles (42).

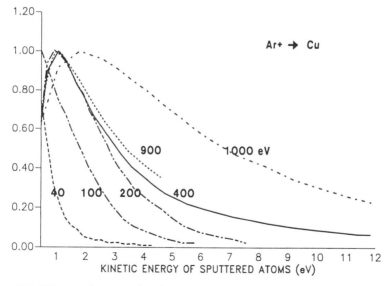

Figure 14: Measured energy distributions of sputtered Cu atoms from Ar bombardment at normal incidence. The curves have been scaled to all have a maximum at 1.0. 900 eV is from ref. 61. The other energies are from ref. 43.

The addition of the projectiles which become embedded in the lattice can also alter the sputtering yields (48,49). This fluence effect is due to two factors. The composition of the target is being changed and the surface topology has been altered. In fact, at high fluence the original surface completely erodes away. Some studies have been carried out on the topography evolution (50-52) due to ion fluence, and more work utilizing fractal geometry is planned by the author.

It is because of this erosion and deposition in the first few atomic layers that channeling by single crystal targets is not a significant effect in this low-energy, surface-dominated regime (53). An excellent Monte-Carlo code, MARLOWE (54), exists to calculate the effects of a single crystal environment, but its greatest utility is simulation of much higher energy sputtering and reflection phenomena.

The changing surface morphology does not just occur due to the addition of some of the incident beam ions. When alloys are sputtered, one of the components is likely to have a higher sputtering yield than the others (55,56). Not only will the yields differ but the angular emission of species can also change (57-59). Sometimes entire clusters of atoms can be knocked loose (60). All considered, sputtering remains one of the most complicated and intriguing branches of particle-surface interactions.

In this chapter I have tried to focus on the types of sputtering phenomena that are of most interest to the plasma processing community. In this low-energy regime surface corrections play a major role, yet with their inclusion modelling can be fairly accurate in determining yields, energy and angular information. Several excellent reviews (1,3,4,61,62) of the larger picture of sputtering exist which contain many analytic and empirical formulas along with a wide variety of experimental data and modelling results.

3.5 REFERENCES

1. Sputtering by Particle Bombardment ed by R. Behrisch, Springer-Verlag, Berlin, 1981.

2. P. Sigmund, Theory of sputtering. I.   Sputtering yield of amorphous and polycrystalline targets, Phys. Rev. 184: 383 (1969).

3. R. A. Langley, J. Bohdansky, W. Eckstein, P. Mioduszewski, J. Roth, E. Taglauer, E. W. Thomas, H. Verbeek, K. L. Wilson, Data compendium for plasma-surface interactions, Nucl. Fusion special issue: (1984).

4. P. C. Zalm, Handbook of Ion Beam Processing Technology Chap. 6, ed. by J. J. Cuomo, S.M. Rossnagel, H.R. Kaufman, Noyes, Park Ridge, NJ, 1989.

5. H. L. Bay, An analytical formula and important parameters for low-energy ion sputtering, J. Appl. Phys. 51: 2861 (1980).

6. D. N. Ruzic, and H. K. Chiu, Modeling of particle-surface reflections including surface roughness characterized by fractal geometry, J. Nucl. Mater. 162-164: 904 (1989).

7. J. P. Biersack, L. G. Haggmark, A Monte-Carlo computer program for the transport of energetic ions in amorphous targets Nucl. Instrum. Meth. 174: 257 (1980).

8. J. P. Biersack and W. Eckstein, Sputtering studies with the Monte Carlo program TRIM.SP, App. Phys. A34: 73 (1984).

9. B. B. Mandelbrot, The Fractal Geometry of Nature, Freeman, San Fransisco, 1982.

10. D. Avnir, D. Farin, and P. Pfeifer, Molecular fractal surfaces, Nature 308: 261-263 (1984).

11. D. Avnir, D. Farin, and P. Pfeifer, Chemistry in non-integer dimensions between two and three, II. Fractal surfaces of adsorbents J. Chem. Phys. 79: 3566 (1983).

12. D. N. Ruzic, The effects of surface roughness characterized by fractal geometry on sputtering, accepted in Nucl. Instr. and Meth. in Phys. Res. B (1989).

13. W. Eckstein and J. P. Biersack, Self-sputtering and reflection, Z. Phys. B63: 109 (1986).

14. A. A. Haasz, J. W. Davis, C. H. Wu, Angle of incidence dependence of light ion physical sputtering of carbon, J. Nucl. Mater. 162-164: 915 (1989).

15. W. Eckstein, F. E. P. Matschke and H. Verbeek, Reflection of hydrogen from stainless steel and Nb, J. Nucl. Mater. 63: 199 (1976).

16. J. Weng and E. Veje, Absence of excited molecules in sputtering processes, Phys. Rev. 31: 1600 (1985).

17. M. S. Daw, M. I. Baskes, Dynamical calculation of low energy Hydrogen Reflection, J. Nucl. Mater. 128-129: 676 (1984).

18. H. K. Chiu, The reflection of hydrogen off nickel surfaces as a function of fractal dimension, MS Dissertation, Univ. of Illinois, 1988.

19. D. N. Ruzic, H. K. Chiu, C. A. Hoyer, Molecular dynamics on a rough surface, a scientific video, published and available from the National Center for Supercomputing Applications, Scientific Media Services, University of Illinois, 605 E. Springfield Ave, Champaign, IL 61820 (1990).

20. J. Bohdansky, J. Roth, and M. K. Sinha, Erosion of different first wall and limiter materials by low energy hydrogen ions, Proc. 9th Symp. on Fusion Technology (Pergamon, London 1976) 541.

21. J. N. Smith, Jr., C. H. Meyer, Jr. and J. K. Layton, Hydrogen sputtering of carbon thin films deposited on platinum, J. of Nucl. Mater. 67: 234 (1977).

22. J. Bohdansky, H. L. Bay and W. Ottenberger, Sputtering yields of graphite and carbides and their potential use as first wall materials, J. of Nucl. Mater. 76 & 77: 163 (1978).

23. J. Roth, J. Bohdansky and W. Ottenberger, Data on low energy light ion sputtering, Max-Planck-Institut fur Plasmaphysik Report, IPP 9/26, May 1979.

24. J. Bohdansky, H. L. Bay and J. Roth, Erosion of iron and nickel based alloys by mono- and multi-energetic light ion bombardment in the energy range from 0.1 - 8 keV, Proc. 7th Int. Vac. Congr. & 3rd. Int. Conf. Solid Surfaces p.1509 (Vienna 1977).

25. T. J. Whetten, A. A. Armstead, T. A. Grzybowski and Arthur L. Ruoff, Etching of diamond with argon and oxygen ion beams, J. Vac. Sci. Technol. A2: 477 (1984).

26. G. K. Wehner, General Mills Report No. 2309 (1962), in reference 1, Chapter 4.

27. N. Laegreid and G. K. Wehner, Sputtering yields of metals for Ar^+ and Ne^+ ions with energies from 50 to 600 eV, J. Appl. Phys. 32: 365 (1961).

28. J. N. Smith, Jr., C. H. Meyer, Jr. and J. K. Layton, Sputtering measurements on controlled thermonuclear reactor materials using auger electron spectroscopy, Nucl. Technol. 29: 318 (1976).

29. C. H. Weijsenfeld, Yield, energy and angular distributions of sputtered atoms, Thesis, University of Utrecht, (1966).

30. H. Oechsner, Sputtering of polycrystalline metal surfaces at oblique ion bombardment in the 1 keV range, Z. Physick 261: 37 (1973).

31. P. C. Zalm, Energy dependence of the sputtering yield of silicon bombarded with neon, argon, krypton, and xenon ions, J. Appl. Phys. 54: 2660 (1983).

32. A. L. Southern, W. R. Willis and Mark T. Robinson, Sputtering experiments with 1- to 5-keV Ar+ ions, J. Appl Phys. 34: 153 (1963).

33. S. Tachi, K. Miyake, T. Tokuyama, Proc. of Symp. on Dry Process, Oct. 26-27, 1981, Tokyo, p. 17 (Institute of Elec. Engr. Tokyo, 1981).

34. J. M. E. Harper, J. J. Cuomo, P. A. Leary, G. M. Summa, H. R. Kaufman, and F. J. Bresnock, Low energy ion beam etching, J. Electrochem. Soc. 28: 1077 (1981).

35. H. Fetz and H. Oechsner, Proc. 6th Int. Conf. Phenomenes d'Ionization les Gaz Vol. II p. 39 (Paris, 1963).

36. C. H. Weijsenfeld, Sputtering of polycrystalline metals by inert gas ions of low energy (100-1000 eV), J. Physica 27: 763 (1961).

37. R. V. Stuart and G. K. Wehner, Sputtering yields at very low bombarding ion energies, J. of Appl. Phys. 33: 2345 (1962).

38. G. D. Magnuson and C. E. Carlsson, Sputtering yields of single crystals bombarded by 1- to 10-keV Ar+ ions, J. Appl. Phys. 34: 3267 (1963).

39. A. Van Veen and J. M. Fluit, Low yield sputtering of monocrystalline metals, Nucl. Inst. and Meth. 170: 341 (1980).

40. F. Keywell, Measurements and collision-radiation damage theory of high-vacuum sputtering, Phys. Rev. 97: 1611 (1955).

41. K. Akaishi, A. Miyahara, Z. Kabeya, M. Komizo and T. Gotch, Sputtering yields of graphite, copper, using torsion microbalance technique with keV region H+, He+ and Ar+ Proc. 7th Int. Vac. Congr. & 3rd Int. Conf. Solid Surfaces (Vienna 1977).

42. H. L. Bay, J. Bohdansky, W. O. Hofer, and J. Roth, Angular distribution and differential sputtering yields for low-energy light-ion irradiation of polycrystalline nickel and tungsten, J. of Appl. Phys. 21: 327 (1980).

43. R. A. Brizzolara, C. B. Cooper, and T. K. Olson, Energy distributions of neutral atoms sputtered by very low energy heavy ions, Nucl. Instr. and Meth. in Phys. Res. B35: 36 (1988).

44. W. Eckstein, Energy distributions of sputtered particles, Nucl. Instr. and Meth. in Phys. Res. B18: 344 (1987).

45. C. E. Carlston, G. D. Magnuson, A. Comeaux, and P. Mahadevan, Effect of elevated temperatures on sputtering yields, Phys. Rev. 138: 759 (1965).

46. G. S. Anderson, Low-energy sputtering yields of Ge single crystals as a Function of Temperature, J. of Appl. Phys. 38: 1607 (1967).

47. K. S. Kim, W. E. Baitinger, J. W. Amy and W. Winograd, ESCA studies of metal-oxygen surfaces using argon and oxygen ion-bombardment, J. of Electron Spect. and Rel. Phen. 5: 351 (1974).

48. P. Blank and K. Wittmaack, Energy and fluence dependence of the sputtering yield of silicon bombarded with argon and xenon, J. Appl. Phys. 50: 1519 (1979)

49. J. Kirsfchner and H. W. Etzkorn, On the fluence dependence of the sputtering yield for low-energy noble gas ions, J. Appl. Phys. A29: 133 (1982).

50. G. Carter, M. J. Nobles, I. V. Katardjiev, J. L. Whitton, and G. Kiriakidis, The effect of ion species on topography evolution, Nucl. Instr. and Meth. in Phys. Res. B18: 529 (1987).

51. I. V. Katardjiev, Simulation of surface evolution during ion bombardment, J. Vac. Sci. Technol. A6: 2434 (1988). 2434-2442.

52. S. Valkealahti and R. M. Nieminen, Molecular dynamics simulation of the damage production in Al (110) surface with slow argon ions, Nucl. Instr. and Meth. in Phys. Res B18: 365 (1987).

53. M. Hou and M. T. Robinson, Computer simulation of low-energy sputtering in the binary collision approximation, Appl. Phys. 18: 381 (1979).

54. M. T. Robinson, I. M. Torrens, Computer simulations of atomic-displacement cascades in solids in the binary-collision approximation, Phys. Rev. B9: 5008 (1974).

55. R. Shimizu, Preferential sputtering, Nucl Instr. and Meth. in Phys. Res. B18: 486 (1987).

56. P. Sigmund, Preferential sputtering from isotopic mixtures and alloys of near-neighbor elements, Nucl. Instr. and Meth. in Phys. Res. B18: 375 (1987).

57. R. R. Olson and G. K. Wehner, Composition variations as a function of ejection angle in sputtering of alloys, J. Vac. Sci. Technol. 14: 319 (1977).

58. R. R. Olson, M. E. King, and G. K. Wehner, Mass effects on angular distribution of sputtered atoms, J. Appl. Phys. 50: 3677 (1979).

59. E. Dullni, Velocity distributions of the metal atoms sputtered from oxygen and nitrogen covered Ti- and Al- surfaces, Nuclear Instr. and Meth. in Phys. Res B2: 610 (1984).

60. G. P. Konnen, A. Tip and A. E. de Vries, On the energy distribution of sputtered clusters, Rad. Eff. 26: 23 (1975).

61. H. Oechsner, Sputtering-a review of some recent experimental and theoretical aspects, Appl. Phys. 8: 185 (1975).

62. H. H. Andersen, Computer simulations of atomic collisions in solids with special emphasis on sputtering, Nucl. Instr. and Meth. in Phys. Res B18: 321 (1987).

4

Bombardment-Induced Compositional Change With Alloys, Oxides, Oxysalts, and Halides

---

Roger Kelly

4.1 INTRODUCTION

4.1.1 The Early Situation

Bombardment-induced compositional change with alloys, oxides, oxysalts, and halides has been the subject of both experimental and theoretical study for the past two decades. Concerning theoretical work, it is worth pointing out that the emphasis has changed to a remarkable extent as the experimental base has grown. Work written before 1980 tended to emphasize preferential sputtering as triggered by differences of mass, chemical binding, or volatility. Mass and chemical binding were envisaged as governing collisional sputtering, volatility as governing thermal sputtering.

Mass is now regarded to be an important factor in preferential sputtering, thence in compositional change, only under near-threshold conditions, as when Ta_2O_5 is bombarded with 1 keV H^+ or He^+ and loses O (whereas it is largely unchanged with 1 keV Ar and Xe) (Fig. 1)(1), and in isotope sputtering, as when lighter isotopes are lost preferentially with Li, Ti, Ga, and Mo (2). With alloys the role claimed for mass other than near the threshold or with isotopes (3) was subsequently shown (4) to be largely irrelevant: this was not because the theory (3) was wrong but because bombardment-induced Gibbsian segregation (4) had been neglected and the latter can cause either a light or heavy species to be lost. (A simplified restatement of the argument of (3) about the role of mass is given in (5).) Whether or not mass plays a role with oxides and halides is less easily settled. For example, MoO_3 is reduced mainly to Mo^{IV}, as expected thermodynamically, but the reduction products of WO_3 include W^0 (Table 8, to follow): is this an effect of mass? Also, Malherbe et al. (6) advocate a more general role for mass with oxides, equivalent to that of Ref. 3. We will in general not discuss mass except for a brief reference in Sect. 4.4.4.1. A review in the context of near-threshold effects is given elsewhere (7).

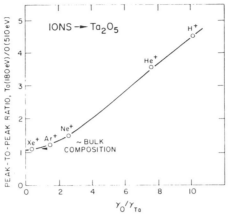

Figure 1: Steady-state composition ratio, Ta/O in arbitrary units, for Ta_2O_5 as a function of the ratio of the energy transfer factors, γ_O/γ_{Ta}, for bombardment with various 1 keV ions at $\theta_1 = 30°$. As usual, γ is given by $4M_1M_2/(M_1+M_2)^2$, "1" refers to the incident particle, and "2" refers to the target. Compositions were obtained with AES. Due to Taglauer (1).

Chemical binding, reflected explicitly in the surface binding energy and ideally proportional to ΔH^a, the heat of atomization (8), was at one time the most popular framework for explaining preferential sputtering, thence compositional change, with alloys. It had the advantage, one lacked by the mass argument, that it gave a nearly perfect correlation: e.g. Au is known to be lost from near the surface of Au-Pd (Figs. 2 (9) and 3) and, at the same time, although it is heavier, it has a slightly lower ΔH^a: $\Delta H^a_{Au} = 3.82$ eV, $\Delta H^a_{Pd} = 3.90$ eV. It is easily shown, however, that chemical binding as manifested in the surface binding energy should, at least with alloys, normally lead to significantly smaller composition changes than are observed, for example the evolution of $Au_{0.50}Pd_{0.50}$ to $Au_{0.498}Pd_{0.502}$ (Sects. 4.2.3 and 4.2.4). But as manifested in segregation, chemical binding can lead to very large effects indeed, for example the evolution of $Au_{0.50}Pd_{0.50}$ to $Au_{0.76}Pd_{0.24}$ (Fig. 3, curve labeled "annealed"; see also Refs. (5,10)). On the other hand, there is a hint that with oxides and halides the surface binding energy may play an unsuspected role. This is because energies calculated for atom removal from undisturbed surfaces can differ markedly depending on whether one considers an anion or cation, e.g. 12 eV for O in Al_2O_3 and 30 eV for Al in Al_2O_3 (11). The topic is pursued further below in Sect. 4.1.6 and then in Sects. 4.2.5 and 4.2.6.

The role of volatility, i.e. of thermal sputtering, is more problematical than that of mass or chemical binding. After being alternately accepted and rejected for 130 years (12), it was in a phase of acceptance in the decade 1970-1980. This was because the experiments of Nelson (13) had not yet been re-interpreted (14,15), since physically correct theories had just appeared (16,17), and since thermal effects were being widely advocated to justify the presence of ions and excited states amongst sputtered particles and to explain O loss (18,19). For example, differences in volatility (relevant if thermal sputtering occurs) were found to explain many examples of O loss from oxides, with both the correlation ("yes" or "no") and the required magnitude of the volatility ($10^{2\pm1}$ atm at

~4000 K) being reasonably correct for the systems then known (19). Since then, many additional oxides have been shown to lose oxygen, including some like HfO_2, Nb_2O_5, SnO_2, Ta_2O_5, WO_3, and ZrO_2 which (unlike the systems known when Ref. (19) was prepared) have very low volatility, at least for the observed extent of O loss. With alloys the best evidence for thermal sputtering relates to energy distributions, as for $Xe^+ \rightarrow Ag$ (20,21), which showed departures from the form expected for cascade sputtering as if a thermal distribution were superimposed. Temperatures of 20,000 to 30,000 K were implied, however, and this contradicts the idea that a condensed phase cannot exceed its critical temperature, 5100 K for Ag (22), because of a "phase explosion" (23,24). There is an important qualification, namely that a phase explosion may have a natural delay time, possibly as much as 10^{-7} to 10^{-9} s although possibly much less (23).

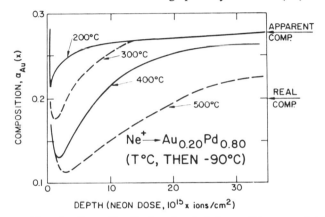

Figure 2: Composition-depth profiles for bombarded $Au_{0.20}Pd_{0.80}$ as obtained by first bombarding to steady state with normally incident 2 keV Ne^+ at the indicated temperatures, then quenching to $-90°C$, and finally profiling with 2 keV Ne^+. Compositions were obtained with ISS, using the same 2 keV Ne^+ as the probe ion. The reason that the bulk composition implied by the Figure, $Au_{0.28}Pd_{0.72}$, disagrees with the stated composition, $Au_{0.20}Pd_{0.80}$, is that the system is subject to on-going Pd loss as a mass effect (cf. Fig. 1). For notation, see Sect. 4.1.7. Due to Swartzfager, Ziemecki, and Kelley (9).

4.1.2 Bombardment-Induced (Gibbsian) Segregation, BIS

We have been emphasizing the inadequacies of the older theoretical works, those before 1980, on the subject of what causes bombardment-induced compositional change, with their emphasis on a more or less universal role for preferential sputtering as triggered by differences of mass, chemical binding, or volatility. The first new feature was the realization of a pervading role for BIS in causing changes with alloys (4,5). Such segregation occurs in nearly all cases in the same sense as equilibrium segregation (Figs. 2 and 3), though always has a smaller numerical extent for ambient temperature (5,10). It is demonstrated in characteristic composition-depth profiles (Fig. 2), formally equivalent to those found with equilibrium segregation when there is a moving surface; in conflicts between ISS and AES or XPS analysis of bombarded surfaces (Fig. 3), which follow naturally from the profiles; conflicts between the sense of equilibrium segregation and the sense of composition change (also shown in Fig. 3); in characteristic results for yield-vs.-angle (25,26), such that the non-segregating species is emitted more nearly normal to the surface; in delayed segregation; and in suppressed sputtering. Delayed segregation relates to such systems as a bilayer of Ni on Ag (27) or homogeneous Au-Cu (Fig. 4 (28)), where segregation was found to continue evolving for a few minutes after bombardment ceased. Such experiments show in an explicit way that chemical effects can occur during the prolonged relaxation that occurs subsequent to particle impact, a subject that was anticipated also in computer simulation (29), in work with alkali halides (30), and, particularly relevant here, in work on the decomposition of oxysalts (31-34) such as the delayed relaxation of randomized $BaSO_4$ (containing BaO) to true $BaSO_4$ (33). Suppressed sputtering (e.g. 35) is to be expected if segregation is sufficiently strong to exclude one component from the outer surface.

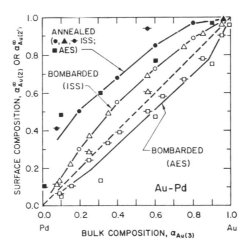

Figure 3: Comparison of surface or subsurface compositions with bulk compositions for Au-Pd specimens which have been either annealed or bombarded. The segregating element is seen to be Au and, in addition, the outermost atom layer of a bombarded surface is also Au rich ("ISS"); in agreement with Fig. 2, however, the subsurface region of a bombarded specimen is deficient in Au ("AES"). This example is generic of many others in which the species which segregates on annealing shows a composition spike followed by severe depletion when the specimen is bombarded. Details are as follows: ● (600°C, Ne ISS (9)); ▲ (500°C, Ne ISS (58)); ◆ (400°C, He ISS (59)); ■ (600°C, AES (60)); ○ (bombarded, Ne ISS (9)); △ (bombarded, He ISS (61)); ⊿ (bombarded, He ISS (59)); □ (bombarded, AES (60)); ⊡ (bombarded, AES (62)). A further point "●" which lies in the upper left under the "E" of "bombarded" is not shown.

Segregation is, we would emphasize, not a type of sputtering, so invoking it to explain composition change constitutes a major change. We treat BIS with alloys in Sect. 4.3.

Oxides also show segregation but the evidence for it playing a role in composition change was slow to come. In such a case as Na^+ on SiO_2, the movement of the Na^+ was a response to the charge of the incident particle (36), an effect that can occur only under conditions of ultra-high diffusivity and that is here classified as a form of redistribution (Sect. 4.1.5). In the case of CaO in MgO, the loss of Ca during bombardment at 1250°C probably involved equilibrium segregation, the onset temperature for which is ~900°C (37). The first straightforward example, with behavior like that of an alloy, relates to Na loss from Na_2O-SiO_2 (38). We will not further treat BIS with oxides in what follows.

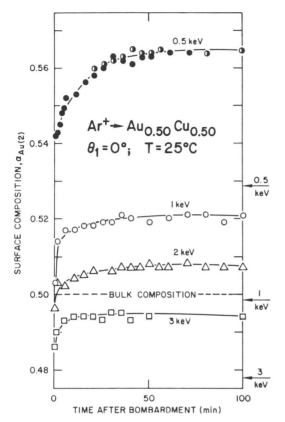

Figure 4: Changes in surface composition with time after stopping bombardment of $Au_{0.50}Cu_{0.50}$ at $25°C$ with normally incident Ar^+ having energies of 0.5-3 keV. Compositions were obtained with low-energy (60-69 eV) AES. The arrows mark the <u>average</u> steady-state compositions achieved during bombardment and differ from what is shown in the figure for t = 0 only because of being averages (63). The composition changes are seen to involve an increase in the amount of Au at the surface and are in accordance with what is found with heated specimens (64). The relevant mass transport is not regarded as thermally activated diffusion but rather the post-bombardment analog of bombardment-enhanced diffusion (65). Due to Li, Tu, and Sun (28).

4.1.3 Bombardment-Induced Mixing

Mixing and BIS are not the same but have such close similarities that it is worth comparing them. Furthermore, the existence of the one supports the existence of the other.

An important aspect of BIS is that, assuming it to resemble equilibrium segregation, then the driving force is only 0.06 to 0.52 eV, values which are very much less than the energies characterizing particle bombardment, $\gtrsim 1$ keV, or recoil motion, $\gtrsim 10$ eV (columns 2 and 3 of Table 1). Historically, mixing was described as a purely collisional (ballistic) effect, though with recognition of random and directed parts (e.g. 39). It was recently shown (40,41), however, that binary metallic systems show mixing rates which correlate with the heats of mixing (Fig. 5 (41)). Apparently a significant part of the driving force for the mixing is based on chemical energy differences and we note that the magnitude, ≤ 1.3 eV, is again small compared with incident particle or recoil energies (column 4 of Table 1). It is clear that there is an extreme disparity between the chemical energy differences relevant to BIS or mixing and typical bombardment or recoil energies.

When we consider BIS in Sect. 4.3 one objective will therefore be to show a way out of the paradox.

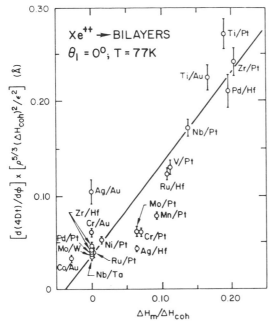

Figure 5: Correlation suggesting that ion-beam mixing of metallic bilayers using 600 keV Xe^{++} at 77 K scales as the heat of mixing, ΔH_m. $d(4Dt)/d\phi$ is the experimentally observed mixing rate, ϕ is the fluence (dose), ρ is the target number density (cm^{-3}), ΔH_{coh} is the cohesive energy for $A_{0.50}B_{0.50}$, and ε is the density per unit length of deposited energy. Due to Cheng et al. (41).

A further similarity is that both mixing and BIS persist to very low temperatures, at least to 20 K in the former case (42) and at least to $-120°$C in the latter (43).

4.1.4 Bombardment-Induced Decomposition

The third new feature in the post-1980 period originated with four separate groups of authors, Christie et al. (e.g. 31), Hofmann et al. (e.g. 32), Rabalais et al. (e.g. 33), and Marletta et al. (e.g. 34). They suggested what is effectively an alternative to thermal sputtering. Basically, the traditional (thermal) point of view emphasizes transient vaporization subject to the laws of equilibrium thermodynamics. When several components are present, compositional changes arise due to the loss of the more volatile species. Although this is a strictly surface process, it could influence greater depths if the surface composition change served as a diffusion boundary condition, as when a surface of Ti_2O_3 triggers bombardment-enhanced out-diffusion of O from TiO_2 (44). The point of view of the authors indicated above is that the cascade itself should be regarded as a source of new stoichiometries as the initially disrupted lattice relaxes (cf. Fig. 4) and various alternative stoichiometries compete. In effect, a species of chemical driving occurs similar to what is postulated to govern BIS and mixing. The laws of equilibrium thermodynamics, especially the relevance of the <u>free</u> energy, probably do not apply. For example, bombarded $Ca(NO_3)_2$ (31) could return to $Ca(NO_3)_2$ itself, but as an alternative could evolve to CaO or Ca_3N_2. The argument goes that $Ca(NO_3)_2$ is unfavored because of a combination of point-defect accumulation, amorphization, volatility, diffusional transport, and BIS; whereas between CaO and Ca_3N_2 the former is favored <u>energetically</u> (Fig. 6 (31)). We treat bombardment-induced decomposition in Sect. 4.4.

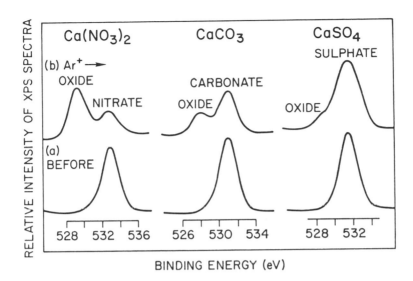

Figure 6:   XPS spectra of the oxygen ls photoelectron peaks from $Ca(NO_3)_2$, $CaCO_3$, and $CaSO_4$: (a) before Ar^+ bombardment; (b) after 3 keV Ar^+ bombardment to a fluence of 7.5×10^{16} ions/cm^2 at an angle of incidence of 50°. The targets were in the form of anhydrous powders. Similar results were obtained for compounds of Ca, Sr, and Ba, with the fractional conversion to oxide being 0.92-0.94 for nitrates, 0.53-0.57 for carbonates, and 0.40-0.45 for sulfates. We agree with the authors that what is being observed is more nearly a chemical re-arrangement of atoms displaced within each cascade than, for example, a process related to the thermal spike. Whether the re-arrangement occurs on a short time scale (as envisaged by Johnson (66)) or on the rather long time scale evident in Fig. 4 is unclear. Due to Christie et al. (31).

4.1.5 Redistribution

The fourth new feature in the post-1980 period was the general acceptance that composition change can be caused by point-defect fluxes or electric fields, whether or not sputtering occurs (45). We have termed this "redistribution" (46). The effect has no inherent thickness limitation, i.e. it is not confined to the outermost atom layer like BIS. A component which is transported preferentially by vacancies is depleted at the surface, while one transported as an interstitial is enriched at the surface (47). Similarly, transport due to electric fields can be in either sense (48). Transport by point defects or electric fields will be additive to BIS and, although it is really the combination which controls composition change, it is usually obvious in individual cases which effect dominates. The subject is reviewed elsewhere by Lam and Wiedersich (45).

We would note in passing that, to some extent, the terminology has been a problem, as the word "segregation" is frequently used to mean "redistribution", just as "adsorption" is used to mean "segregation". We also note, in order to forestall misunderstanding, that redistribution is normally regarded as a kinetic effect. By contrast, BIS and decomposition as developed here are essentially thermodynamic effects. The only purely collisional effect of any significance to compositional change is the role played by mass near the threshold and with isotopes (1,2,7), as well as possible roles played by the surface binding energy.

4.1.6 Surface Binding Energies of Oxides and Halides

It is clear from Sect. 4.1.2-4.1.5 that the role of preferential sputtering (in the formal sense of the term) in causing compositional change is much less important than had once been thought. Exceptions occur in the near-threshold regime (1) and with isotopes (2), while another exception relates to the surface binding energy of oxides and halides. Thus, there is recent evidence that the anions and cations in some oxides may have significantly different binding energies. That oxides have somewhat lower <u>overall</u> yields has long been known (Fig. 7, "total Cr" (49)) but that <u>cation atoms</u> are particularly reluctant to be emitted was realized only when laser-induced fluorescence was applied to the sputter products of systems such as $Cr + O_2$. The yield of Cr^0 fell by over a factor of 100 as the ratio flux(O_2)/flux(ions) increased (Fig. 7). Behavior as in Fig. 7 was subsequently rationalized by calculations in which energies were deduced using parameters appropriate to point defects in perfect oxide (11) or halide (50) surfaces. The cation binding energy was found to be unusually high for oxides of group III and beyond (11), while a similar effect was shown for halides of group II and beyond (50).

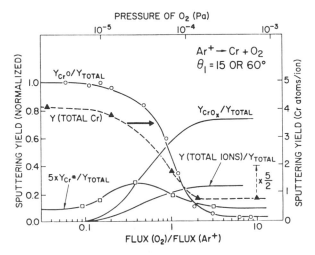

Figure 7: Composition of the sputtered flux as a function of the ratio of the O_2 to Ar^+ fluxes or of the O_2 partial pressure for 15 keV Ar^+ bombardment of polycrystalline Cr. All curves except that for Y(TOTAL Cr) refer to the left-hand scale and give the fractional composition of the sputtered flux. Cr^0 is the Cr ground state, a^7S_3, Cr^* is the 425.4 nm transition of the state $z^7P_4^0$, while CrO_x denotes neutral molecules in general, of which CrO can be expected to be the dominant component. The relative yields other than that for Cr^* were obtained by LIF, "laser-induced fluorescence", at $\theta_1 = 60°$, the Cr^* yield was obtained by light emission at $\theta_1 = 15°$, while the total Cr yield was obtained by use of a quartz-crystal microbalance and $\theta_1 = 15°$. The unexpected feature is the factor of 130 fall in the Cr^0, a result that has been explained (11) in terms of the surface binding energy for Cr^0 being significantly higher than that for O^0. Due to Betz and Husinsky (49).

Table 1: Examples of chemical energy differences which can act as driving forces for changes in bombarded solids. The heat of segregation, ΔH^{seg}, leads to BIS, while the heat of mixing, ΔH_m, contributes to bombardment-induced mixing. ΔH^{seg} is taken from Ref. 67; ΔH_m is taken mainly from Ref. 68, and applies to systems with 1:1 proportions. The entries AES, FIM, ISS, and XPS are the usual acronyms referring to the methods of surface analysis.

System	ΔH^{seg} (eV) (experimental from Arrhenius plots)	ΔH^{seg} (eV) (experimental from individual data points using Eq. (10) with $\Delta S^{seg} = 0$)	ΔH_m (eV)
Ag-Au	...	0.04-0.07 ISS	-0.048
Ag-Pd	0.09-0.13 AES	0.02-0.04; 0.098 AES	-0.052
Au-Cu	0.13 AES; 0.13 ISS	0.03-0.06 AES; 0.04-0.10 ISS	-0.053
Au-Ni	0.52 AES; 0.45 ISS	~0.4 AES[a]	+0.078
Au-Pd	...	0.05-0.13 AES; 0.09-0.11 ISS	-0.081
Cr-Mo	...	~0.02 AES[b]	+0.075
Cu-Ni	0.42 ISS	0.21 FIM; 0.2-0.3 ISS	+0.018
Cu-Pd	0.059 AES	0.02-0.07 AES	-0.111
Cu-Pt	...	0.1-0.2 AES, XPS; 0.09-0.2 ISS	-0.115
Mg-Al	...	0.1 AES	-0.034
Mo-W	...	~0.4 AES	+0.021
Ni-Co	0.069; 0.18 AES	0.04-0.09 AES	0.000
Ni-Mo	...	...	-0.011
Ni-Pt	0.15; 0.25 AES; 0.11 0.24 ISS	...	-0.096
Pd-Ni	0.31 AES	0.06 AES	-0.006

[a] This information is all for dilute Au. For concentrated Au, ΔH^{seg} is much lower, ~0.07 (58).

[b] The information on the surface composition is not fully self-consistent (69).

Malherbe et al. (6) advocate a similar but less extreme effect in a treatment which is somewhat empirical. The binding energy is also believed to play a role in such cases as the sputtering of Si by a combined flux of gaseous Cl_2 or XeF_2 and inert-gas ions (51,52). Mo shows a similar response with respect to O_2, especially at elevated temperatures (53), while in still other cases effects involving binding occur due to the incident beam, as in the sputtering of Mo (54) or W (55) by O^+. We treat surface binding energies of oxides and halides in Sects. 4.2.5 and 4.2.6.

4.1.7 General Comments

It is worth commenting further on what should already be clear: the concepts of preferential sputtering and compositional change may or may not coincide. The former relates to changes in the outermost atom layers and is correctly attributed to differences of mass, chemical binding, or volatility. Refs. (1,2,3,6,11), for example, relate to preferential sputtering. Preferential sputtering is, by its nature, an essentially universal effect but it will contribute significantly towards compositional change only (a) if the change is defined by a method of analysis which is, like ISS, a true surface probe, or (b) when the system, for whatever reason, fails to show segregation, decomposition, or redistribution. Reasons include near-threshold behavior (1) and the sputtering of isotopes (2). Table 2 is an attempt to clarify the difference between preferential sputtering and compositional change.

We will use in what follows the notation of (5,56). Subscript "o" will designate a property of a cascade particle, "1" a property of the incident particle, "2" a property of a surface atom (atom layer one), "2'" a property of a subsurface atom (atom layer two), and "3" a property of a bulk atom. In Sect. 4.3.2 we will also use "2'" to represent an atom in atom layer three, which is justified if the profile is extended like those in Fig. 2. "α" denotes atom fraction, subscript A, B, or (in general) i a component, and superscript "∞" steady state, whence the use of such forms as $\alpha_{A(2)}^{\infty}$. M designates a metal, O oxygen, X a halogen, U the surface binding energy, Y the sputtering yield, Z the coordination number, and λ the mean atomic spacing. The acronyms AES, FIM, ISS, and XPS refer to the well-known methods of surface analysis.

Atoms and point defects will be designated (as is usual (57)) with the entity as the main symbol, the location as subscript, and the charge as superscript. Thus, Mg_{Mg}^{2+} is a normal Mg ion in such a compound as MgO, V_{Mg} is an Mg vacancy without associated electrons, Mg_i^+ is an Mg^+ interstitial, e^- is an electron, and h^+ is a hole. (The charge convention of Ref. 57 is actually slightly different, being the so-called relative charge.)

It will sometimes be necessary to distinguish "s", i.e., solid or crystalline, "ℓ", i.e., liquid or amorphous, and "g", i.e., gaseous or sputtered. For example, when $TiO_2(s)$ is bombarded, it evolves first to $TiO_{2-x}(\ell)$ and then to $Ti_2O_3(s)$ by loss of O(g) or $O_2(g)$.

4.2. THE ROLE OF THE SURFACE BINDING ENERGY

4.2.1 The Surface Binding Energy in Cascade Sputtering

Let us consider briefly the recoil-density derivation (70) of the standard relation for slow collisional (i.e. cascade) sputtering. This approach has the advantage of being

Table 2: Mechanisms for compositional change.

Effect	Systems where the effect is important	Role in compositional change
Preferential sputtering due to mass differences	(a) The outermost atom layer of nearly all alloys.	Normally overwhelmed by segregation or redistribution.
	(b) Near-threshold conditions.	Loss of lighter species.
	(c) Isotope sputtering.	Loss of lighter species.
Preferential sputtering due to differences in chemical binding	(a) The outermost atom layer of nearly all alloys.	Normally overwhelmed by segregation or redistribution.
	(b) Oxides of group III and beyond.	Loss of O; reduction of the cation (tentative).
	(c) Systems like Si exposed to Cl_2 plus inert-gas ions.	Loss of the species with the most altered binding.
Preferential sputtering due to differences in volatility	(a) Alloys with a very volatile component.	(Untested)
	(b) Alloys in general.	Normally overwhelmed by other effects.
	(c) Oxides with high decomposition pressures.	Loss of O; reduction of the cation (tentative).
Bombardment-induced segregation	(a) Almost all alloys.	Massive subsurface loss of the segregating species.
	(b) The system Na_2O-SiO_2.	Subsurface loss of Na.
Bombardment-induced decomposition	(a) Oxides and oxysalts in general.	Loss of O,C,N,S; reduction of the cation.
Redistribution	(a) Alloys containing Si.	Massive subsurface loss of Si.
	(b) Alloys in general.	Subsurface loss of whichever species is redistributed.

somewhat more transparent than that based on transport theory (71) but is otherwise equivalent. An ion is regarded as starting from the reference plane x = 0, which is equivalent to the surface. During the penetration of the ion into the target, assumed to be random, a "linear" collision cascade is generated. Let E_1 be the incident energy and $C_n(x)dx$ be the differential depth-distribution function for energy deposited in elastic (nuclear, "n") events. The deposited energy creates recoiling target atoms with energy E_0 and an assumed isotropic motion. If we accept the result that the recoil density has the form appropriate to the value m = 0 for the power-law parameter,

$$F(E_1, E_0)dE_0 \sim (\Gamma E_1/E_0^2)dE_0; \quad \Gamma = 6/\pi^2 = 0.608,\tag{1}$$

then it follows that the total number of recoils at the surface which would be able to overcome an energy barrier U is just

$$\int_0^{\pi/2} (1/2)d\theta_0 \sin \theta_0 \times \int_{U/\cos^2\theta_0} dE_0 \times \Gamma E_1 E_0^{-2} \times C_n(0)L_0$$

$$= (1/6)\Gamma E_1 C_n(0)L_0/U,$$

where θ_0 is the polar angle of a sputtered atom, $C_n(0)dx$ has been replaced with $C_n(0)L_0$, and L_0 is the characteristic depth of origin of sputtered particles. L_0 has been evaluated both theoretically (71) and experimentally (10,72), though unfortunately with somewhat different results (10). It is conventional to reduce L_0 to $3L_0/4$, which is a sort of angle averaging, and this gives for the cascade sputtering yield, $Y_{cascade}$, the usual (70,71) form:

$$Y_{cascade} = (1/8)\Gamma E_1 C_n(0)L_0/U.\tag{2a}$$

For a binary target, $C_n(0)$ will not partition quite stoichiometrically (3,5) but will depend on the masses. This leads to the further general result:

$$Y_{cascade} \propto 1/M^{2m}U.\tag{2b}$$

The important quantity in Eq. (2), in the context of this Section, is U. If it differs for different components of a target, then sputtering will cause a compositional change, though the change will be significant only if the difference in U is sufficient.

4.2.2 The Bulk Binding Energy, W

Eq. (1) for the recoil density assumes, amongst other things, that the bulk binding energy, W, is zero. The possibility of a non-zero W was discussed first by Sigmund (73), where the result obtained was stated to be valid only for $E_1 >> E_d >> W$. We have obtained a very similar result and were able to show that it is more generally valid, namely for $E_1 >> E_d$ or W (74). The form appropriate to m = 0 is

$$F(E_1, E_0, W) \, dE_0 \sim \frac{\Gamma(E_1 + W)}{(E_0 + W) E_0} \, dE_0,\tag{3}$$

where Γ is as before. We are still studying the significance of Eq. (3) to compositional change, the main reason for introducing it here being to show that the problem of W being non-zero is tractable and that W should not be perfunctorily overlooked. We also note that, for a binary target, important compositional changes can arise if the components have different values of W (75).

4.2.3 The Surface Binding Energy for Alloys

Attempts to define U for metals and alloys showing miscibility have been made repeatedly. With metals, it has been usual to identify U with the cohesive energy, i.e. the heat of atomization ΔH^a. We would point out that, if U_{AA} is the A-A "bond strength" and if Z_3 is the bulk ("3") coordination number, then we have the well-known result (76):

$$\Delta H^a = -(1/2)Z_3 U_{AA}, \tag{4}$$

which means, effectively, that the use of ΔH^a is equivalent to regarding the sputtered atom as occupying a half-space site (A in Fig. 8). Since half-space atoms are atypical of an undisturbed surface as compared with in-surface atoms (B in Fig. 8), it follows that ΔH^a underestimates U.

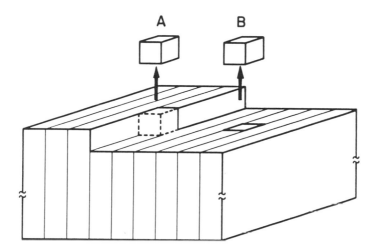

Figure 8: (A) Sketch of a half-space atom with coordination number $Z_3/2$ which has been emitted by vaporization. Such an atom, which is bound by the cohesive energy or heat of atomization, ΔH^a, is <u>not</u> characteristic of the sputtering process because it is atypical of an undisturbed surface. When a half-space atom is removed, there is no resulting surface vacancy but rather the jog is displaced. (B) Sketch of an in-surface atom with coordination number Z_2 which, being more nearly typical of an undisturbed surface, is here assumed to be relevant to sputtering. If the expulsion is sufficiently <u>rapid</u>, such an atom is bound by $(2Z_2/Z_3)\Delta H^a$, thence by a quantity somewhat greater than ΔH^a. A surface vacancy is always formed, i.e. whether the expulsion is rapid or slow.

Similar in spirit to the use of ΔH^a with metals, is to describe binding in miscible alloys in terms of the cohesive energies of the pure substances (e.g. 62). However, not only is the wrong type of atom being dealt with, but such an approach neglects the fact that binding in an alloy is governed in all cases by the statistics of site occupancy (e.g. random, ordered, segregated) and in some cases (as when species such as B or Si are involved) by changes in the character of the binding.

An approach which avoids the twin problems of ΔH^a underestimating U and of ΔH^a not being correct in any sense for an alloy, is based on the "quasichemical" variant of thermodynamics (5,56). It is easily applied to both metals and binary alloys as it requires knowledge only of nearest-neighbor "bond strengths", U_{AA}, U_{BB}, and U_{AB}.* Self-consistency is achieved if U_{AA} and U_{BB} are defined as in Eq. (4). Similarly, U_{AB} is defined in terms of the heat of mixing, ΔH_m (76):

$$\Delta H_m \equiv \alpha_{A(3)}\alpha_{B(3)}h_m = \alpha_{A(3)}\alpha_{B(3)}Z_3[U_{AB} - (1/2)(U_{AA} + U_{BB})],$$

where $\alpha_{i(3)}$ is the atom fraction of component i in the bulk. The surface binding energy U now follows as the sum of nearest neighbor energies under the assumption that the typical atom expelled is an in-surface atom (reasonable if L_o in Eq. (2a) is about 0.80λ (10,72)) with atom fraction $\alpha_{i(2)}$ and coordination number Z_2:

$$U_A = (Z_2/Z_3)[(1 + \alpha_{A(2)})\Delta H_A^a + \alpha_{B(2)}(\Delta H_B^a - h_m)] \qquad (5a)$$

for a binary alloy and

$$U = (2Z_2/Z_3)\Delta H^a = (1.42 \pm 0.08)\Delta H^a \qquad (5b)$$

for a unitary system, i.e. $\alpha_{A(2)} = 1$. The numerical factor 1.42 ± 0.08 applies to the more densely packed surfaces of fcc, hcp, and bcc. In practice, the term h_m is normally unimportant (5,56), with Si-containing systems being a marked exception (e.g. Fe-Si (68)). Nevertheless, we take it into account (Table 4, to follow).

Equation (5) should be acceptable whenever two conditions are met: U describes atom removal from an undisturbed surface and the act of removal is sufficiently rapid that the relaxation of the lattice around the surface vacancy can be neglected. If the act of removal is slow, the relaxation around the vacancy cannot be neglected. As discussed in Ref. 8, U is then somewhat smaller than in Eq. (5).

Examples of U as given by Eq. (5b), as well as experimental values where known, are given in Table 3. The agreement between theory and experiment is moderately good, though with experiment typically more similar to ΔH^a than to Eq. (5b). The obvious problem is that atom ejection from real systems does not involve undisturbed surfaces as in Fig. 8 and as assumed in Eq. (5b). Nevertheless, we conclude that it is realistic to assume a proportionality, $U \propto \Delta H^a$, and this will be done in what follows.

4.2.4 Application to Compositional Change with Alloys

It follows from the requirement that matter be conserved that the steady-state sputtered flux ratio for a binary alloy is, to lowest approximation,

---

*We would note that the U_{ii} are not "bond strengths" in the formal sense but rather parameters derived from observable thermodynamic quantities.

Table 3: Examples of calculated and observed surface binding energies for metals.

Metal	ΔH^a (eV)	$U \approx 1.42\Delta H^a$ (Eq. (5b)) (eV)	U from experiment (eV)	Ref.
Al	3.41	4.8	3.6	(83)
Au	3.82	5.4	...	
Ba	1.89	2.7	$2.1^{(b)}$	(84)
Ca	1.85	2.6	1.3	(85)
Ce	4.38	6.2	...	
Cr	4.12	5.9	4.2 ± 0.2	(86)
			4.4 ± 0.2	(87)
$Cr^{(a)}$	>4.12	>5.9	5.1 ± 0.2	(87)
Cu	3.49	5.0	...	
Fe	4.31	6.1	$4.3; 5.0^{(b)}$	(88,89)
Ge	3.88	5.5	...	
In	2.52	3.6	4.0	(90)
Mg	1.52	2.2	...	
Mo	6.82	9.7	...	
Ni	4.46	6.3	...	
Pt	5.85	8.3	...	
Rh	5.73	8.1	$8.0; 11 \pm 1$	(90,91)
Si	4.72	6.7	...	
Sn	3.12	4.4	...	
Th	5.96	8.5	...	
Ti	4.87	6.9	4.6	(83)
U	5.42	7.7	5.4	(92)
W	8.80	12.5	...	
Zn	1.35	1.9	...	
Zr	6.31	9.0	6 ± 2	(93,94)
			6.3	(95)

[a] Stainless steel with 17% Cr and the remainder dominantly Fe.
[b] Corrected by Garrison et al. (96) for geometrical effects (97).

Table 4: Examples of calculated and observed surface compositions for alloys with 1:1 proportions.

System, A-B	ΔH_A^a (eV)	ΔH_B^a (eV)	h_m [a] (eV)	$\Delta H_B^a/\Delta H_A^a$	$U_B/U_A = \alpha_{B(2)}^\infty/\alpha_{A(2)}^\infty$ from Eqs. (5a,7)	$\alpha_{B(2)}^\infty/\alpha_{A(2)}^\infty$ from experiment using AES or XPS [b]
$Ag_{0.50}Au_{0.50}$	2.94	3.82	-0.193	1.30	1.14	2.0
$Ag_{0.50}Pd_{0.50}$	2.94	3.90	-0.216	1.33	1.15	2.2
$Au_{0.50}Cu_{0.50}$	3.82	3.49	-0.197	0.91	0.96	1.0
$Au_{0.50}Ni_{0.50}$	3.82	4.46	+0.295	1.17	1.08	~2.7
$Au_{0.50}Pd_{0.50}$	3.82	3.90	-0.320	1.021	1.010	1.4
$Cr_{0.50}Mo_{0.50}$	4.12	6.82	+0.229	1.66	1.29	1.7
$Cu_{0.50}Ni_{0.50}$	3.49	4.46	+0.074	1.28	1.13	1.8
$Cu_{0.50}Pd_{0.50}$	3.49	3.90	-0.461	1.12	1.054	1.6
$Cu_{0.50}Pt_{0.50}$	3.49	5.85	-0.461	1.68	1.27	2.1
$Mg_{0.50}Al_{0.50}$	1.52	3.41	-0.135	2.24	1.44	3.6
$Mo_{0.50}W_{0.50}$	6.82	8.80	+0.084	1.29	1.14	1.4
$Ni_{0.50}Co_{0.50}$	4.46	4.44	~0	0.9955	0.998	1.2
$Ni_{0.50}Pt_{0.50}$	4.46	5.85	-0.362	1.31	1.14	1.6
$Pd_{0.50}Ni_{0.50}$	3.90	4.46	~0	1.14	1.069	1.3

[a] Most entries for h_m were obtained by averaging values deduced from integral ΔH_m for solid alloys (68) using $h_m = \Delta H_m/\alpha_{A(3)}\alpha_{B(3)}$. The value for Mo-W is from (77).

[b] See Table 7 for the references.

$$\frac{\text{surface flux}_A}{\text{surface flux}_B} = \frac{\alpha^\infty_{A(2)} Y_A}{\alpha^\infty_{B(2)} Y_B} = \frac{\alpha_{A(3)}}{\alpha_{B(3)}} , \tag{6a}$$

but to higher approximation,

$$\frac{\text{surface flux}_A}{\text{surface flux}_B} = \frac{\alpha^\infty_{A(2)}(1-\beta) + \alpha^\infty_{A(2')}\beta}{\alpha^\infty_{B(2)}(1-\beta) + \alpha^\infty_{B(2')}\beta} \times \frac{Y_A}{Y_B} = \frac{\alpha_{A(3)}}{\alpha_{B(3)}} , \tag{6b}$$

where "2'" refers to atom layer two and β is the fraction of sputtering from beyond atom layer one. Values of β (the notation $f(\lambda)$ is also used) range from 0.11 to 0.30 with an average of 0.19 (10). In both cases Y_A/Y_B, the yield ratio, can also be written $Y_A/Y_B = M_B^{2m} U_B / M_A^{2m} U_A$ (Eq. 2b). Eq. (6b) is most useful when BIS occurs and $\alpha^\infty_{A(2)}$ and $\alpha^\infty_{A(2')}$ therefore differ strongly. The overall result is that the value of $\alpha^\infty_{A(2)}$ is controlled by 3 parameters: the power-law scattering parameter m (a rather weak dependence since $m \approx 0$, cf. p. 390 of Ref. 72), the subsurface sputtering fraction β (10), and the BIS ratio K^b (Table 7, to follow).

Using the lower approximation of Eq. (6a) it follows that the compositions will change until they obey the relation

$$\frac{\text{surface flux}_A}{\text{surface flux}_B} = \frac{\alpha^\infty_{A(2)} M_B^{2m} U_B}{\alpha^\infty_{B(2)} M_A^{2m} U_A} = \frac{\alpha_{A(3)}}{\alpha_{B(3)}} . \tag{7}$$

If U_B/U_A is taken as defined by Eq. (5a), then the latter expression and Eq. (7) can be solved iteratively for $\alpha^\infty_{B(2)}/\alpha^\infty_{A(2)}$ (column 6 of Table 4).

Table 4 (final column) also contains observed values for $\alpha^\infty_{B(2)}/\alpha^\infty_{A(2)}$, in all cases taken from work using AES or XPS. The outstanding feature is that the predicted compositional changes due to bond-strength effects are without exception very much less than what is observed with AES or XPS. There are two reasons for such a trend:
(i) One relates to the mathematical form of the expression for U_B/U_A. As seen in Table 4, the ratio U_B/U_A is significantly closer to unity than $\Delta H_B^a/\Delta H_A^a$, and it is the former which governs $\alpha^\infty_{B(2)}/\alpha^\infty_{A(2)}$.
(ii) The other reason is a practical problem. Systems such as Ag-Mo or Au-W, which might be expected to show a large compositional change in view of the highly dissimilar values of ΔH^a, are not miscible.

Nevertheless, the conclusion is inescapable: compositional changes with alloys as measured by AES or XPS are not governed by bond-strength effects.

We note in passing that, even if the numerical value $U \simeq 1.4 \Delta H^a$ was not fully in agreement with experiment (Table 3), at least the proportionality $U \propto \Delta H^a$ was acceptable. This is a sufficient condition for the arguments made here to be valid.

4.2.5 The Surface Binding Energy for Oxides and Halides

Oxides and halides do not permit quite as straightforward a definition of U as do metals and alloys: ionized species and diatomics are emitted to an important extent and, due mainly to the major role of polarization, oxides and halides cannot be described in simplistic terms such as pair-wise interactions (78) or quasichemical thermodynamics (5,56).

We have proposed (11) that a possible description of binding at undisturbed surfaces with oxides and halides is in terms of processes in which individual surface atoms are removed slowly to infinity, using as the basis defect theory of the type pioneered by Norgett and Lidiard and recently further refined by, amongst others, Mackrodt (57). Slow removal was suggested on the grounds that the characteristic time for <u>electronic</u> relaxation is of order 10^{-15} s and thus distinctly shorter than the sputtering time (e.g. 9×10^{-14} s for a 5 eV Al atom or 22×10^{-14} s for a 5 eV W atom (8)). In evaluating the energies, it is convenient to take advantage of the result that, for an oxide or halide, most bulk defects have similar energies to surface defects, the divacancy binding energy apparently being the only exception (11).

4.2.5.1 Cation Atom Binding. Using MgO as the example, we consider the process in which a neutral Mg atom is removed slowly to infinity:

$$Mg_{Mg}^{2+} = Mg(g) + V_{Mg} + 2h^+ .$$

The energy change is

$$U_{Mg} = E(V_{Mg}) - I_1(Mg) - I_2(Mg) + 2E(h^+), \qquad (8)$$

where $E(V_i)$ is the lattice energy for vacancies of type i, i.e. the energy to slowly remove a lattice <u>ion</u> to infinity, $I_n(M)$ is the nth ionization potential of the cation M, and $E(h^+)$ is the formation energy of a hole inclusive of electronic and ionic relaxation.

4.2.5.2 Anion Atom Binding. We next consider the process in which a neutral O atom is removed slowly to infinity:

$$O_O^{2-} = O(g) + V_O + 2e^- ,$$

where e^- is a <u>lattice</u> electron and the energy change is

$$U_O = E(V_O) + I_1(O^{2-}) + I_2(O^{2-}) + 2E(e^-) . \qquad (9)$$

Here $I_n(O^{2-})$ is the nth ionization potential of O^{2-} and $E(e^-)$ is the formation energy of a lattice electron. In those instances where $E(e^-)$ is the energy of an electron at the bottom of the conduction band, we have $E(e^-) = - \mid E_c \mid$, $\mid E_c \mid$ being the conduction band width.

Input parameters for calculating U for oxides, as collected from a variety of sources, are given in (11), while evaluations of Eqs. (8) and (9) as well as corresponding equations for MO diatomics and M^+ ions (11) are given in Table 5. The results show that, if U for an <u>ionic</u> oxide is taken as the lower of that for the metal atom or O atom, then ionic oxides are more tightly bound than the corresponding metals (Table 3) by factors of 1 to 5. This result, which should be manifested in low total yields, is not surprising in view of what has long been known experimentally. What is somewhat unexpected is that, for ionic oxides of group III and beyond, O atoms as well as MO diatomics are predicted to be far more easily removed than metal atoms, so that one can expect abnormally low metal-atom yields in appropriate circumstances as well as essentially universal preferential loss of O for group III and beyond.

Table 5: Examples of calculated surface binding energies in eV for oxides as in Eqs. (8) and (9). The input parameters are given in Ref. (11).

Type of binding energy, U_i	CaO	MgO	NiO	ZnO	Al_2O_3	ThO_2	ZrO_2
Metal atom, U_M	12.3	13.5	7.7	8.0	29.8	~29.7	32.2
Oxygen atom, U_O	~12.2	~13.1	10.9	4.8	~11.8	8.5	<7.1
MO diatomic, U_{MO}	~8.4	~8.2	~6.8	...	~18.2	~18.1	~19.0
Metal ion, U_M	14.1	15.8	10.8	10.8	28.5	~33.5	35.6

4.2.6 Application to Compositional Change with Oxides

4.2.6.1 Metal Atom Yields from Oxides. Before considering compositional changes with oxides, we will digress in order to discuss metal-atom yields because of the light which is shed on binding energies. While it has been known for some time that total yields were generally somewhat lower for <u>ionic</u> oxides than for metals, whereas partial yields for ions, excited states, and MO diatomics were greatly enhanced, almost nothing was known about neutral, ground state atoms because of the difficulty in detecting them explicitly. This problem was recently overcome by using either laser-induced fluorescence (49) or secondary neutral mass-spectroscopy (79). The example of Cr, Fig. 7, reveals that metal-atom yields can fall drastically as the oxygenation of the surface increases. This in turn tentatively supports the newly proposed oxide binding energies as in Table 5.

4.2.6.2 Preferential Effects. Oxygen loss from oxides is well documented, leading either to well-defined changes in composition (Fig. 9 (80)) or else to an ill-defined state of understoichiometry (Fig. 10 (32)). We first note that considerations of mass are not useful for understanding such O loss, since it would follow that all oxides (except, e.g., BeO) would behave similarly and reduce to pure metal, at least at the outer surface. (Near-threshold processes as in Fig. 1 are a well-defined exception: see Sect. 4.4.4.1.) This leaves considerations of binding, with which this section is concerned, together with arguments based on bombardment-induced decomposition (Sect. 4.4).

Figure 9: Reflection electron diffraction patterns taken at 80 kV for TiO_2: (a) before bombardment; (b) after exposure to 5×10^{15} ions/cm^2 of 30 keV Kr^+ at normal incidence; and (c) after exposure to 6×10^{16} ions/cm^2 of 30 keV Kr^+. The patterns, respectively those of rutile $TiO_2(s)$, amorphous TiO_{2-x}, and $Ti_2O_3(s)$, are an explicit indication of preferential O loss which leads to a well-defined change of composition. Due to Parker and Kelly (80).

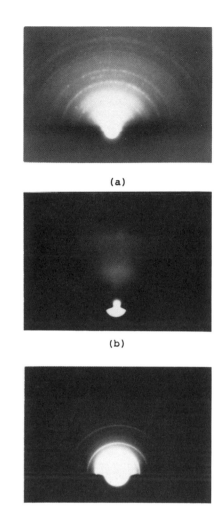

(a)

(b)

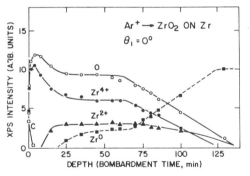

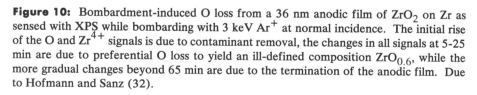

(c)

Figure 10: Bombardment-induced O loss from a 36 nm anodic film of ZrO_2 on Zr as sensed with XPS while bombarding with 3 keV Ar^+ at normal incidence. The initial rise of the O and Zr^{4+} signals is due to contaminant removal, the changes in all signals at 5-25 min are due to preferential O loss to yield an ill-defined composition $ZrO_{0.6}$, while the more gradual changes beyond 65 min are due to the termination of the anodic film. Due to Hofmann and Sanz (32).

What has not been generally appreciated is that a properly defined U leads naturally to preferential effects with oxides and halides: as borne out in Table 5 for ionic oxides of group III and beyond, the O atom binding at an undisturbed surface is distinctly (up to a factor of 4) smaller than the metal-atom binding. This is the result of the cations, with their greater charge, sitting in a deeper potential well. There should therefore be a universal tendency for O to be lost from appropriate oxides, as when ZrO_2 evolves to $ZrO_{0.6}$ (Fig. 10). (The latter probably consists mainly of a saturated solid solution of O in α-Zr, namely $ZrO_{0.41}$.) Similar comments apply to TiO_2 but with an important difference: O deficiency is accommodated when sufficiently slight as V_O plus Ti_{Ti}^{3+}, then for greater loss as shear planes, and finally as a lower stoichiometry. Experimentally, bombarded $TiO_2(s)$ shows a well-defined surface layer of $Ti_2O_3(s)$, seen both by electron diffraction (Fig. 9) and electron spectroscopy (81), or, alternatively, Ti^{II} plus Ti^{III}, seen by XPS (82).

The same argument also explains why TiO_2 evolved to Ti_2O_3 rather than Ti: Ti_2O_3 is metallic (44) and there is therefore no longer the large difference between U_{Ti} and U_O as for the more nearly ionic TiO_2. This leads to the rule that, if an ionic system has a metallic lower stoichiometry, then this stoichiometry forms under bombardment. Otherwise, there is an ill-defined state of understoichiometry as with ZrO_2.

Nevertheless, we still maintain firm reservation about whether the binding energy is the sole reason for composition change with oxides. The problem is the same as with mass: the lack of universality. Specifically, binding energy would account nicely for O loss from the highly stable HfO_2, SnO_2, and ZrO_2, and for the greater than expected loss from Nb_2O_5, Ta_2O_5, and WO_3 (Sect. 4.4). It fails, however, to account for the stability of Al_2O_3, Cr_2O_3, and SiO_2. Moreover, a final decision cannot yet be made owing to the lack of appropriate experiments. For example, although the highly powerful XPS approach was indeed used with Al_2O_3, Cr_2O_3, and SiO_2, the apparent lack of O loss could have been due to the lack of diffusional deepening, with the O loss confined to the outer surface and therefore undetected.

4.3. THE ROLE OF SEGREGATION

4.3.1 Equilibrium Segregation

One of the most difficult effects to study in thermodynamics is equilibrium segregation. With Cu-Ni, for example, it is manifested in the tendency, with specimens heated to above 400-500°C, for the outermost atom layer to be enriched by up to a factor of 40-100 in Cu since Cu has the lower bond strength (98). With Au-Cu the outermost atom layer is enriched by up to a factor of about 4 in Au since the Au atom is oversized (99). The driving force for equilibrium segregation lies in the interval 0.06 to 0.52 eV (Table 1).

It is now known that segregation occurs also when alloys are bombarded, even at very low temperatures (43). BIS is almost always in the same sense as equilibrium segregation and can be therefore assumed to have the same low driving force, 0.06 to 0.52 eV. Since sputtered atoms come mainly (70-90%) from atom layer one (10), it follows that BIS must lead to important perturbations of the sputtering process. In the case of Cu-Ni or Au-Cu this involves major Cu or Au loss variously from near the surface (as in Fig. 2) or from orders of magnitude greater depths (100). The reason for the loss is that BIS serves to "pump" Cu or Au into the outer atom layer, where it is preferentially sputtered away so as to leave the <u>subsurface</u> depleted. Corresponding work with bombarded oxides is very limited even though equilibrium segregation is well known (101) and well understood (102). Examples include Ca loss from MgO during bombardment at 1250°C (37), a tentative example as it probably involved equilibrium segregation; segregation-related perturbations to composition-depth profiles in Si (103); and Na loss from $Na_2O\text{-}SiO_2$ during bombardment at ambient temperature (38). The latter work is particularly important since alloy-like profiles as in Fig. 2 were inferred.

Returning to equilibrium segregation, a standard argument (4) based on minimizing the free energy of the system (surface plus bulk) suggests that the magnitude of the composition spike at equilibrium, $\alpha_{A(2)}^{\infty}$, is related to the bulk composition, $\alpha_{A(3)}$, by the relation:

$$
\begin{aligned}
\frac{\alpha_{A(2)}^{\infty}}{\alpha_{B(2)}^{\infty}} &= \frac{\alpha_{A(3)}}{\alpha_{B(3)}} \exp\left\{ \frac{\Delta H^{seg}}{kT} \right\} \times \exp\left\{ \frac{-\Delta S^{seg}}{k} \right\} \\
&= \frac{\alpha_{A(3)}}{\alpha_{B(3)}} \exp\left\{ \frac{\Delta G^{seg}}{kT} \right\} \equiv \frac{\alpha_{A(3)}}{\alpha_{B(3)}} K^{eq} ,
\end{aligned}
\tag{10}
$$

where ΔH^{seg} and ΔS^{seg}, the heat and entropy of segregation, are given in very general form by relations discussed by Wynblatt and Ku (104), K^{eq} will be here termed the <u>equilibrium segregation ratio,</u> and the sign convention used for ΔG^{seg} is appropriate for $\Delta G^{seg} > 0$. (The opposite convention is also used (98).) To lowest approximation, ΔH^{seg} is the total energy difference when an A atom in the bulk is exchanged with a B atom at the surface and ΔS^{seg} is zero (4,105). Neglecting the heat of mixing this energy difference is

$$
\Delta H^{seg} \approx (Z_v/Z_3)(\Delta H_B^a - \Delta H_A^a) \approx (1/4)(\Delta H_B^a - \Delta H_A^a) ,
$$

where Z_v is the "vertical" coordination number, e.g. $Z_v = 3$ for (111) of f.c.c. To higher approximation, both "bond strength" and size must be taken into account, the trends being that the segregating species has either the weaker bonds (e.g. Cu in Cu-Ni) or is oversize (e.g. Au in Au-Cu).

4.3.2 Bombardment-Induced Segregation, BIS

Values of ΔH^{seg} were given in Table 1 and we note that they are numerically small, 0.06-0.52 eV. Estimates of the onset temperatures for atomic-scale thermally activated diffusion are given in Table 6 and we note that, for systems other than Mg-Al, they are all well above ambient temperature, $\geq 250°C$.

The information in Tables 1 and 6 might suggest that a bombardment-induced analog to equilibrium segregation, i.e. BIS, would not occur, as the driving force is too small and the required temperature too high. It is therefore important to accept that, as already discussed in Sect. 4.1.2, there is overwhelming empirical evidence that it does occur.

A further objection to BIS is that a composition spike in the first atom layer would not be stable with respect to ion-beam mixing. We cannot answer this problem explicitly but would note that segregation could well develop subsequent to the maximum activity in each cascade, e.g. after ~0.5 ps, when a persisting tail in the Frenkel-pair population can be expected (106). Alternatively, it could involve what we will term "chemically guided final steps" (see after Eq. (11)). In any event, we are not surprised that it has a a small magnitude.

Because sputtered atoms originate mainly from the outermost atom layer (10,72), this layer must have a steady-state composition, $\alpha^{\infty}_{A(2)}$, governed by the conservation relations of Eq. (6a) or (6b).

The second atom layer, with steady-state composition $\alpha^{\infty}_{A(2')}$, bears a relation to the first governed by the kinetics of atom movement as treated first in Refs. 9,56,107,108. We here restate the argument of (56,108) in a form which differs mainly by avoiding the simplification that only atom layer one contributes to sputtering ($\beta = 0$). (This is, how-ever, not an important change.) Sites are conserved in a bombardment-induced relocation process if the lattice relaxes appropriately following each elementary jump (109,110). For example, let A tend to segregate. Then a transfer of A from (2') to (2), with a rate per second $k_+\alpha_{A(2')}$, triggers a relaxation in which a converse transfer occurs. For ho-mogeneous (i.e. stoichiometric) relaxation, the converse transfer could involve either A or B so that a net change in the system occurs only at a reduced rate $k_+\alpha_{A(2')}\alpha_{B(2)}$. Concurrent with the radiation-enhanced jumps, A is added to (2) at a rate the first term of which is $(1 - \beta)(v_B/\lambda)\alpha_{B(2)}\alpha_{A(2')}$, where $v_B = IY_B/N$ is the velocity of surface recession at a B site, I is the ion flux, and the factor $\alpha_{A(2')}$ recognizes that a net change occurs in (2) only if an A is exposed in (2').* A second term also exists, $\sim \gamma\beta(v_B/\lambda)\alpha_{B(2)}\alpha_{A(2')}$, where $\gamma\beta$ with $\gamma < 1$ is the fraction of atoms emitted simul-taneously from (2) and (2'), and $\alpha_{A(2')}$ is intended to describe atom layer three. Con-sidering also the inverse terms by which A is lost from (2), the following rate equation is obtained:

$$d\alpha_{A(2)}/dt = [k_+ + (1 - \beta + \gamma\beta)v_B/\lambda]\alpha_{A(2')}\alpha_{B(2)} -$$
$$- [k_- + (1 - \beta + \gamma\beta)v_A/\lambda]\alpha_{A(2)}\alpha_{B(2')},$$

so that at steady state one has (Eq. 11):

$$\frac{\alpha^{\prime\prime}_{A(2)}}{\alpha^{\infty}_{B(2)}} = \frac{\alpha^{\prime\prime}_{A(2')}}{\alpha^{\infty}_{B(2')}} \times \frac{k_+ + (1 - \beta + \gamma\beta)v_B/\lambda}{k_- + (1 - \beta + \gamma\beta)v_A/\lambda} \equiv \frac{\alpha^{\prime}_{A(2')}}{\alpha^{\infty}_{B(2')}} \times K^b,$$

where k_- is the rate constant for a jump unfavorable to segregation and K^b is the BIS ratio (the analog of K^{eq} in Eq. (10)).

We have suggested (111) that the rate constant k_+ be attributed to a low-energy, chemically guided final step appended to a fraction f (probably near unity) of the ballistic trajectories ending in either of the outer two atom layers. Thus if the ballistic trajectories have a rate constant k^b then BIS is governed by

$$k_\pm \simeq fk^b.$$

---

*The use of a factor such as $\alpha_{A(2')}$ agrees with Ref. 56 and Eq. (33) of Ref. 108 but not with Ref. 9.

This identification is necessary to avoid the paradox (Sect. 4.1.3) of requiring a driving force of only 0.06 to 0.52 eV to have meaning amongst the violent motions of a cascade.

The expression for BIS, Eq. (11), is thus of similar form to that for equilibrium segregation, Eq. (10). This result differs from both Ref. 9 (their Eq. (14)) and Ref. 108 (their Eq. (34) but not (33)), where the proposed expressions can be written, in the present notation,

$$\alpha_{A(2)}^{\infty} \approx \alpha_{A(2')}^{\infty} \times K^{b}. \tag{12}$$

The difference between Eqs. (11) and (12) is brought out in Fig. 11, with Eq. (12) seen to be unsatisfactory. A further point of comparison is that, owing to the presence of v_i in K^b, one can expect the inequality $K^b << K^{eq}$.

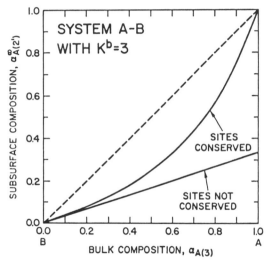

Figure 11: The role of site conservation in BIS shown by comparing the subsurface composition with the bulk composition, here approximated by $\alpha_{A(2)}^{\infty}$, for a system with $K^b = 3$. The two curves show the result when sites are either conserved (Eq. (11)) or not conserved (Eq. (12)). Agreement with experiment as in Fig. 3 is obtained only when sites are conserved.

The altered second atom layer acts as a boundary condition for the diffusion-like motion which accompanies all particle bombardments, and induces a composition profile such as that seen in Fig. 2 to develop extending to roughly ($<x> + \Delta x$), i.e. the sum of the projected range and the projected straggling. The transport in question can be assumed to be the <u>ballistic step</u> of the same process as that which leads to BIS and to ion-beam mixing. It follows that the effective diffusion coefficient, D^b, is just

$$D^b = (1/6)k^b m^2 \lambda^2 \simeq (1/6)(k_{\pm}/f)m^2 \lambda^2, \tag{13}$$

where $m\lambda$ is the average length of a ballistic trajectory. At sufficient depths the bulk composition is normally resumed unless (trivially) the system is at a sufficiently high temperature that self-diffusion can contribute (100). An approach to the high-temperature situation is seen in Fig. 2.

The simplest treatment of the region depleted by the diffusion-like motion is to assume a species-independent diffusion coefficient as in Eq. (13), to assume surface recession at average velocity, v, and either to terminate the motion abruptly at depth, L^b, or to introduce an appropriate spatially decreasing factor. The diffusion equation appropriate to the first case (diffusional freezing at depth L^b) is

$$\partial\alpha_i(x, \phi)/\partial\phi = D^b(\partial^2\alpha_i(x, \phi)/\partial x^2) + v(\partial\alpha_i(x, \phi)/\partial x),$$

where ϕ is fluence (dose) and x is depth beneath the surface. The steady-state boundary conditions are $\alpha_A(x) = \alpha_{A(2')}^\infty$ for $x = 0$ and

$$D^b(\partial\alpha_A^\infty(x)/\partial x)_{L^b} + v\alpha_A^\infty(L^b) = v\alpha_{A(3)}$$

for $x = L^b$ (112), leading to the well-known solution

$$\alpha_i^\infty(x) = \alpha_{i(3)} - (\alpha_{i(3)} - \alpha_{i(2')}^\infty)\exp(-vx/D^b) \quad \text{for } 0 < x < L^b; \tag{14}$$
$$\alpha_i^\infty(x) = \alpha_{i(3)} \quad \text{for } x > L^b.$$

Eq. (14) is easily fitted to profiles as in Fig. 2 and one thereby obtains explicit values of v/D^b (56).

4.3.3 Evaluation of K^b

K^b can be evaluated in 3 ways: from profiles as in Fig. 2, from AES or XPS (but not ISS) analysis of bombarded surfaces as in Fig. 3, and by analyzing information on angular distributions (10,25,26).

The use of profiles is straightforward, as they enable Eq. (11) to be evaluated explicitly. Owing to the profiling process being imperfect, however, $\alpha_{A(2')}^\infty$ will normally be overestimated so that K^b will be too small. AES and XPS tend to have significant subsurface sensitivity so that, to a greater or lesser extent, they sense $\alpha_{i(2')}^\infty$ rather than $\alpha_{i(2)}^\infty$. This suggests that $\alpha_{i(2)}^\infty$ be eliminated between Eqs. (6a) and (11), yielding

$$\frac{\alpha_{A(2')}^\infty}{\alpha_{B(2')}^\infty} = \frac{\alpha_{A(3)}}{\alpha_{B(3)}} \times \frac{Y_B/Y_A}{K^b} \approx \frac{\alpha_{A(3)}}{\alpha_{B(3)}} \times \frac{1}{K^b}. \tag{15}$$

The approximation is justified whenever U_B/U_A (Table 4) and M_B^{2m}/M_A^{2m} are of order unity. Since the presence of the composition spike at the surface will always cause $\alpha_{A(2')}^\infty$ to be overestimated, K^b will again tend to be too small. Finally, one can analyze angular distributions. This method avoids the problem of estimating $\alpha_{A(2')}^\infty$ precisely but introduces a new problem in that it depends totally on the underlying theory (109), conceived for an infinite continuous medium, being valid immediately next to the surface of a semi-infinite crystalline medium.*

---

*For example, the theory assumes straight-line motion for the sputtered particles (109).

Table 6: Onset temperatures for atomic-scale thermally activated diffusion with the alloys considered in Tables 1 and 4. The second column gives temperatures deduced from the knees in Arrhenius plots which separate the regions of radiation-enhanced and thermally activated diffusion. The third column is based on information either as in Fig. 16, where surface composition is measured during bombardment at an elevated temperature and the approximate temperature interval for the transition from BIS to equilibrium segregation can be inferred, or as in Fig. 2, where profiles deepen at a sufficiently high bombardment temperature. The final column gives experimental values for the onset temperature of equilibrium segregation, a quantity which is definable only if the time scale is restricted to "reasonable values". Systems noticeably absent are Cu-Pd and Cu-Pt, where the information was not consistent.

System	Onset temperatures from the knees in Arrhenius plots ($^\circ$C)	Onset temperatures from information as in Figs. 16 or 2 ($^\circ$C)	Approximate onset temperatures for equilibrium segregation ($^\circ$C)
Ag-Au	350 (9)	350 (120) 250-335 (9)	300 (120)
Ag-Pd	...	...	400 (126)
Au-Cu	250-350 (43)	400 (113) 300-350 (113)	300 (117)
Au-Ni	650-750 (127)	>600 (127)	700 (128)
Au-Pd	...	400-500 (9)	400-500 (129)
Cr-Mo	...	...	~650 (69)
Cu-Ni	500-600 (9,98)	400-500 (120-122)	500 (98)
Mg-Al	...	...	125 (131)
Mo-W	...	...	~1550 (132)
Ni-Co	...	...	~525 (133)
Ni-Pt	...	...	~450 (134)
Pd-Ni	...	...	~550 (135)

Table 7 gives values of K^b as deduced in the first two ways discussed, i.e. from information as in Figs. 2 and 3. In connection with Fig. 3, Eq. (15) was used in its truncated form with $Y_B/Y_A \approx 1$. Figs. 12 and 13 compare values of K^b and K^{eq} for Au-Cu and Cu-Ni, which are amongst the most well studied of all alloy systems; similar information for Ag-Au is given elsewhere (111). What is striking is that K^b and K^{eq} are always in the same sense except for Ni-Pt, that K^b lies in the interval $1.25 \leq K^b \leq 5.4$ for 14 out of 16 different systems, and that for ambient temperature the inequality $K^b << K^{eq}$ holds. The fact that K^b and K^{eq} are almost always in the same sense suggests that bombardment leads to true chemically driven segregation rather than the closely similar phenomenon redistribution (Sect. 4.1.5). The inequality found for ambient temperature, $K^b << K^{eq}$, shows, however, that the role of the bombardment is not simply one of bringing the system to equilibrium at a normally inaccessible temperature (here ambient). We have suggested (67) that what is happening is that BIS is not an equilibrium process but depends on the interplay between chemically guided steps (rate k_+) and the somewhat more numerous surface-recession steps (rate v_i/λ). This is clear from the presence of v_i in K^b (Eq. (11)).

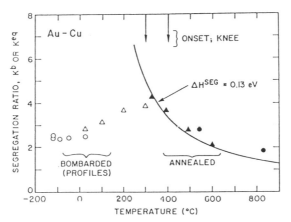

Figure 12: The equilibrium segregation ratio, K^{eq}, and the BIS ratio, K^b, for Au-Cu as a function of temperature. It is clear that, for ambient temperature, the inequality $K^b << K^{cq}$ holds, suggesting that the role of the bombardment is not simply one of bringing the system to equilibrium at a normally inaccessible temperature (here ambient). Details are as follows: o, $\triangle$ (BIS evaluated from profiles by combined AES (43,113) and ISS (115,116)); •, ▲ (equilibrium segregation studied by ISS (117,118)).

Also shown in Figs. 12 and 13 are the onset temperatures for atomic-scale thermally activated diffusion as surveyed in Table 6 and based on information such as that in Fig. 14 (113). These temperatures serve to demarcate the domains in which the two types of segregation can be studied separately. The temperature dependence of BIS, like that of mixing (42), is seen to be relatively slight.

Values of K^b deduced from angular distributions are given in (10). They tend to be erratic but, in general, rather larger than the values in Table 7.

It is important to realize that the interpretation given here to AES or XPS analysis of bombarded surfaces conflicts strongly with most other work, whether from 10 years ago

Table 7: Experimental values of the segregation ratios, K^b and K^{eq}, for the alloys considered in Tables 1, 4, and 6. The second column gives K^b as deduced from profiles as in Fig. 2 using Eq. (11). The third column gives the temperature range for the profiles. The fourth column gives K^b as deduced from AES or XPS analysis of bombarded surfaces as in Fig. 3 using the truncated form of Eq. (15) (but see notes (a) and (b)). The final column gives K^{eq} for the temperature range of onset as summarized in Table 6.

System	K^b from profiles as in Fig. 2	Temperature range for the profiles (°C)	K^b from AES or XPS information as in Fig. 3	K^{eq} for the temperature range of onset as in Table 6
Ag-Au	1.3-2.7 (9)	200-335	2.2 (120, 136 - 138)	3.0-3.2 (139,140)
Ag-Pd	...	...	2.5 (62, 123,141-143)	1.9 126)
Au-Cu[(a)]	2.4-3.9 (43, 113,115,116)	−120-300	...	3.4-5.1 (117,144)
Au-Ni	1.2-4.1 (127)	100-400	2.4 (145)	55-96 (127)
Au-Pd[(b)]	1.4-3.1 (9)	200-500	4.3,2.4 (129,146)	~10 (147)
Cr-Mo	...	...	1.7 (69)	(Cr segregates (69))
Cu-Ni	2.5 (119); 1.7 (9)	ambient; 200	1.9 (100, 120-123)	41-104 (98)
Cu-Pd	...	...	1.5 (62)	~2 (148,149)
Cu-Pt	...	...	2.2 (62)	~6 (140,150, 151)
Mg-Al	...	...	5.4 (152)	13-19 (131)
Mo-W	...	...	1.5 (153)	(Mo segregates (132))
Ni-Co	...	...	1.25 (114)	2.8 (133)
Ni-Mo	4.5-15 (154)	ambient	...	(would expect segreg. of Ni)
Ni-Pt[(c)]	...	...	1.8 (62)	(Pt segregates (134,155))
Ni-W	1.0-14 (119)	ambient	...	(would expect segreg. of Ni)
Pd-Ni[(d)]	...	...	1.25 (123,142)	~50 (135)

[(a)] K^b was deduced by combining ISS measurements of $\alpha_{Au(2)}$ (115,116) with $\alpha_{Au(2')}$ inferred from profiles based on AES (43,113). An example is shown as Fig. 2 of Ref. 67. K^b

cannot be deduced from AES or XPS analysis alone since such analysis implies that there is no compositional change, i.e. $\alpha_{Au(2')} \approx \alpha_{Au(3)}$.

(b) K^b was deduced by combining ISS measurements of $\alpha_{Au(2)}$ (9,156) with $\alpha_{Au(2')}$ inferred from AES information (129,146). The various data points are included in Fig. 3. Effectively we have used Eq. (11) instead of (15).

(c) We note that in all cases but Ni-Pt it is the first designated species which shows equilibrium segregation and which is, at the same time, lost preferentially from the subsurface. Quite surprisingly Ni-Pt shows equilibrium segregation of Pt (134,155) and bombardment-induced loss of Ni (62).

(d) A significantly lower value of K^{eq} is also reported (130).

(62) or contemporary (114). In this work the conservation relation of Eq. (6a) is used to deduce what is supposedly Y_A/Y_B. Our contention is that what is in every case deduced is an approximation to the product $(Y_A/Y_B)K^b$ and that in many cases the product is close to K^b itself as in the truncated form of Eq. (15).

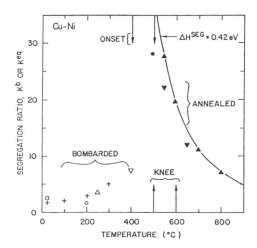

Figure 13: The equilibrium segregation ratio, K^{eq}, and the BIS ratio, K^b, for Cu-Ni as a function of temperature. Details are as follows: o, □ (BIS evaluated from profiles by ISS (9) or multiple energy AES (119)); Δ, ▽, + (BIS evaluated using AES (120,121) and the truncated form of Eq. (15). Each point "+" is the average of at least 3 (100, 120-123)); •, ▲, ▼ (equilibrium segregation studied by ISS (98, 124) or FIM (125)).

4.3.4 Application to Compositional Change with Alloys

It was emphasized in Sect. 4.1.1 that compositional changes with alloys, for example Au-Pd, cannot be explained in terms of differences in the surface binding energy. The lack of effect is inherent in the scaling $Y_{cascade} \propto 1/M^{2m}U$ seen in Eq. (2b), together with the recognition that U must be evaluated for a mixture and not for a pure substance (Sect. 4.2.3).

If thermal sputtering were to occur then the above scaling would be replaced with $Y_{thermal} \propto (\Delta H^a)^{-2} \exp(-\Delta H^a/k\hat{T})$, where $\hat{T}$ is the "thermal-spike", i.e. maximum, temperature (16,17). It is true that, because of its exponential form, this relation leads to a much stronger effect. However, the evidence for thermal sputtering, at least with metals, is still troubled (Sect. 4.1.1).

This was the situation in 1980 when the proposal was first made that the origin of compositional change with alloys was predominantly BIS. There was at the time no explicit evidence for such an effect as in Figs. 2 to 4. This information is now available and, as already noted in Sect. 4.1.2, the wide-spread occurrence of BIS, at least with alloys, must now be regarded as fully established.

In practice the following guides can be used to predict compositional changes with alloys:

(a) The compositional change consists in subsurface loss of the component showing BIS. As discussed in Sect. 4.1.7, such loss should not be termed "preferential sputtering".

(b) The sense of BIS is normally the same as that of equilibrium segregation. However, the magnitude tends to lie within a narrow interval for most systems, $1.25 < K^b < 5.4$, and in addition, for ambient temperature, the inequality $K^b < < K^{eq}$ holds.

(c) The composition profile is as in Fig. 2, with the atom layer one composition given by Eq. (6a) or (6b) and the atom layer two composition given by Eq. (15). Because of the nature of the profile, there tends nearly always to be a conflict between ISS and AES or XPS, as well as between the sense of equilibrium segregation and the sense of compositional change. These conflicts are both apparent in Fig. 3.

(d) Beyond atom layer two a deeply penetrating diffusion-limited profile forms which is governed to lowest approximation by Eq. (14). This profile causes the compositional change to be far more extensive than what would occur for true preferential sputtering.

4.4 THE ROLE OF BOMBARDMENT-INDUCED DECOMPOSITION

4.4.1 General Comments

Four separate groups of authors (31-34) have examined a long series of oxides and oxysalts by alternately bombarding them and studying the surfaces with XPS. The latter serves to detect different valence states, especially of cations and even when the states do not give stable bulk compounds. Typical results are reproduced in Figs. 6 (31) and 15 (33), Table 8 summarizes most of the results of Rabalais et al. (33,157-159) together with information on TiO_2 and V_2O_5, while Table 9 summarizes various group II compounds. We note that in earlier work it was more usual to use either electron diffraction (160) or AES (1), but neither conveys as much information as XPS as far as valence states are concerned.

Table 9 includes values for the enthalpy increase (eV/atom) corresponding to the evolution of the initial substance to oxide. For example, for $PbSO_4$ we have $PbSO_4(s) = PbO(s) + SO_3(s)$, whence $2.55/6 = 0.42$.

The trends in Tables 8 and 9 are clear. Fixed valence systems lose a volatile component (O, C, N, S) and at the same time evolve mainly to oxides rather than to carbides, nitrides, or sulfides. Variable valence systems lose oxygen and alkali metal or Ba or Ag (as is the case) and at the same time evolve towards lower valence states. Table 9 shows in addition that the ordering of the extents of decomposition, especially for a given author, are similar to the ordering of the enthalpy increases. We also see that increases up to about 0.8 eV/atom are tolerated.

Table 8: Summary of compositional changes as observed by Rabalais et al. (33,157-159) when oxides and oxysalts are bombarded with 4 keV Ar+. The surfaces were analysed by XPS. Because of its importance, information on TiO_2 and V_2O_5 as studied mainly with XPS by other authors is included.

Substance	Loss deduced by assuming that one cation is fixed[a]	Fractional loss	Ref.
Li_2CO_3	$0.62CO_2 + 0.38CO$	0.82 (C)	(33)
$BaCO_3$	$0.78CO + 0.22CO_2$	0.84 (C)	(33)
TiO_2[b]	$Ti^{IV} \rightarrow Ti^{II}, Ti^{III}$	...	(32,82)
$LiNO_3$	$0.72O_2 + 0.28N_2$	0.95 (N)	(157)
$NaNO_3$	$0.64O_2 + 0.36N_2$	0.82 (N)	(157)
$NaVO_3$[c]	$V^V \rightarrow V^{IV}, V^{III}$	0.79 (Na), 0.46 (O)	(158)
V_2O_5[d]	$V^V \rightarrow V^{III}$	...	...
$NaNbO_3$	$Nb^V \rightarrow Nb^{II}, Nb^{IV}$	0.84 (Na), 0.53 (O)	(158)
Nb_2O_5[e]	$Nb^V \rightarrow Nb^{II}, Nb^{IV}$	0.43 (O)	(158)
$NaTaO_3$	$Ta^V \rightarrow Ta^0$ etc.	0.54 (Na), 0.48 (O)	(158)
Ta_2O_5[f]	$Ta^V \rightarrow Ta^{II}, Ta^I, Ta^{IV}$	0.43 (O)	(158)
Li_2SO_4	$0.74SO_3 + 0.26O_2$	0.67 (S)	(33)
$BaSO_4$	$0.66SO_2 + 0.34SO_3$	0.62 (S)	(33)
Li_2CrO_4	$Cr^{VI} \rightarrow Cr^{III}$	0.22 (Li), 0.51 (O)	(159)
Na_2CrO_4	$Cr^{VI} \rightarrow Cr^{III}$	0.61 (Na), 0.48 (O)	(159)
K_2CrO_4	$Cr^{VI}, Cr^{III} \rightarrow Cr^{III}$	0.69 (K), 0.45 (O)	(159)
$BaCrO_4$	$Cr^{VI} \rightarrow Cr^{III}$	0.13 (Ba), 0.32 (O)	(159)
Cr_2O_3[g]	unestablished $\rightarrow Cr^{III}$	none	(159)
Na_2MoO_4	$Mo^{VI} \rightarrow Mo^{IV}, Mo^0$	0.35 (Na), 0.38 (O)	(158)
MoO_3[h]	$Mo^{VI} \rightarrow Mo^{IV}$	0.56 (O)	(158)
Li_2WO_4	$W^{VI} \rightarrow W^0$ etc.	0.69 (Li), 0.49 (O)	(158)
Na_2WO_4	$W^{VI} \rightarrow W^0$ etc.	0.68 (Na), 0.53 (O)	(158)
Ag_2WO_4	$W^{VI} \rightarrow W^0$ etc.	0.75 (Ag), 0.54 (O)	(158)
WO_3	$W^{VI} \rightarrow W^0$ etc.	0.55 (O)	(158)

[a] For example, with Li_2CO_3 Li was taken as fixed, but with Li_2CrO_4 Cr was taken as fixed.
[b] Only Ti^{III} is seen by electron diffraction (44).
[c] As in Fig. 8 and not Table 3 of Ref. (158).
[d] Electron diffraction (176).

(e) Supported by other XPS studies (32,82). Only Nb^{II} is seen by electron diffraction, as if any NbO_2 present were amorphous (160).

(f) Or else Ta^0 instead of Ta^I (32).

(g) Described as "$(NH_4)_2CrO_4$" but in fact evolved to Cr_2O_3 in the targe chamber vacuum.

(h) Described as "MoO_2" but "MoO_3" is more accurate. Supported by electron diffraction (176).

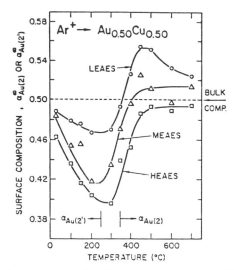

Figure 14: Surface ($\alpha_{Au(2)}$) or subsurface ($\alpha_{Au(2')}$) composition vs. bombardment temperature for $Au_{0.50}Cu_{0.50}$ bombarded with 2 keV Ar^+ and then studied with low, medium, and high-energy AES. The use of LEAES reveals that up to about 250°C there is a net subsurface loss of Au due to BIS, whereas over about 350°C there is an overall gain of Au due to equilibrium segregation. Since MEAES and HEAES are less sensitive to $\alpha_{Au(2)}$, they show a greater extent of loss at the lower temperatures but nearly fail to demonstrate the gain at higher temperatures. Due to Li (113).

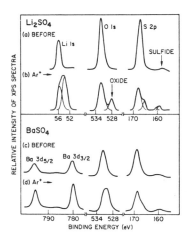

Figure 15: XPS spectra of metal, O, and S photoelectron peaks from Li_2SO_4 and $BaSO_4$: (a) and (c) are before Ar^+ bombardment; (b) and (d) are after 4 keV Ar^+ bombardment to a fluence of $2 - 8 \times 10^{17}$ ions/cm². The targets were in the form of compressed powders. We agree with the authors that what is being observed is more nearly a chemical rearrangement of atoms displaced within each cascade than, for example, a process related to the thermal spike. Due to Contarini and Rabalais (33).

Table 9: Comparison of the extent of chemical alteration with the enthalpy increase per atom for divalent nitrates, carbonates, and sulfates bombarded with 3-8 keV Ar⁺. The surfaces were analyzed by XPS.

Substance	Fractional evolution to oxide due to Christie et al. (31)	Fractional evolution to oxide from other work	Enthalpy increase per atom[a] (eV/atom)
$Ca(NO_3)_2$	0.92-0.94	...	0.30
$CaCO_3$	0.53-0.57	0.49 (177)	0.37
	...	0.59 (34)	
$CaSO_4$	0.40-0.45	...	0.60
$Sr(NO_3)_2$	as above	...	0.40
$SrCO_3$		0.41 (177)	0.49
$SrSO_4$		...	0.69
$Ba(NO_3)_2$	as above	...	0.46
$BaCO_3$		0.35 (177)	0.56
		0.76 (33)	
$BaSO_4$		0.38 (33)	0.80
$Pb(NO_3)_2$	0.99	...	0.22
$PbCO_3$	0.93	...	0.18
$PbSO_4$	0.83	...	0.42
$CoCO_3$, $MnCO_3$, $NiCO_3$, $ZnCO_3$		0.80-0.83 (34)	0.09-0.24

[a] Obtained by dividing the enthalpy change for oxide formation, e.g. for $PbSO_4(s)$ = $PbO(s) + SO_3(s)$, by the number of atoms in the formula of the starting substance.

The results for various oxides, this time of a wider group of authors, are summarized in a different way in Fig. 16, which shows the enthalpy increases (eV/atom) for the observed changes vs. the number of atoms in the formula of the starting substance, i.e. the "complexity" of the substance. The trend here is that a system will tolerate enthalpy increases up to about 0.7 eV/atom (marked with arrow), this result being independent of the "complexity"; the systems HfO_2, Nb_2O_5, SnO_2, Ta_2O_5, WO_3, and ZrO_2, however, constitute exceptions. We will overlook the stability found for Cu_2O (161), as this substance lies near the limit of 0.7-0.8 eV/atom. We will also overlook the instances in which Al_2O_3 (1) and PbO (162) were claimed to lose O, as well as certain instances with Ta_2O_5 (1), as the work in question was carried out under near-threshold conditions as in Fig. 1.

There are at least four ways to rationalize results as in Table 8, Table 9, and Fig. 16. The first concerns the surface binding energy, while the remaining three are different aspects of bombardment-induced decomposition.

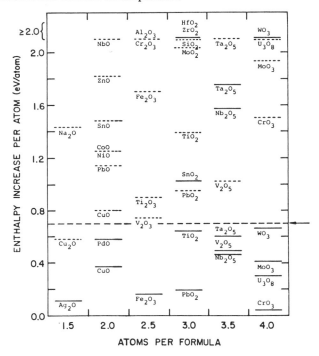

Figure 16: Diagram of enthalpy increase per atom (eV/atom) vs. atoms in the formula, i.e. the "complexity", for various bombarded oxides. A solid line indicates that the oxide reduced, a dashed line that it did not, with the two categories separated at about 0.7 eV/atom (arrow). This figure constitutes a trend analysis appropriate to energy-limited rearrangement as discussed in Sect. 4.4.4. Details are as follows: column 1.5 (reduction to metal), column 2.0 (reduction to Cu, Pd, Cu_2O, Pb, Ni, Co, Sn, Zn, Nb), column 2.5 (reduction to Fe_3O_4, VO, TiO, Fe, Cr, Al), column 3.0 (reduction to PbO, Ti_2O_3, Pb, SnO, TiO, Mo, Si, Zr, Hf), column 3.5 (reduction to NbO_2, V_2O_3, interpolated TaO_2, VO, NbO, interpolated TaO, Ta), column 4.0 (reduction to Cr_2O_3, UO_2, MoO_2, WO_2, Cr, Mo, U, W).

4.4.2 Surface Binding Energy

We have already discussed in detail in Sect. 4.2.6 the possible role of the surface binding energy in governing compositional changes with oxides and oxysalts. In brief, for oxides of group III and beyond and which are reasonably ionic, the anion binding energy at an undisturbed surface should be distinctly lower than the cation binding energy, an effect which is tentatively supported by experiment (Fig. 7). The binding energy argument would be particularly relevant to the exceptions noted above: HfO_2, Nb_2O_5, etc. The problem, as with the role of mass (Sect. 4.2.6.2), is the lack of universality: e.g. why do Al_2O_3, Cr_2O_3, and SiO_2 not show extensive O loss?

4.4.3 Stochastic Rearrangement

Suppose that during the active phase of a cascade the atoms of, for example, $PbSO_4$ become interchanged or otherwise uncoordinated. Then in the cooling phase of the cascade the system would tend to re-establish local order and one possibility is that the new order, thence stoichiometry, would form randomly. To some extent this would be guided by partial loss of a volatile species, by diffusional transport, or by BIS (Sect. 4.4.4.4, to follow). One would then expect a wide range of products, with $PbSO_4$, for example, evolving to a mixture of PbO, Pb, and PbS. Since this is contrary to what is observed as the dominant process ((31; Table 9), stochastic rearrangement is evidently not the most important process. Nevertheless, an element of such rearrangement is probably relevant with most systems, as follows from these examples. CoO is largely stable but evolves to a small extent to Co^0 either at ambient temperature (82) or at ≥ 550 K (163). NiO yields Ni^0 at ≥ 400 K (163). Fe_2O_3 evolves mainly to Fe^{II} but with some Fe^0 also present (82).

4.4.4 Energy-Limited Rearrangement

We again suppose that a bombarded system tends to first become uncoordinated but finally to re-establish local order. Then another possibility is that this change is energy (enthalpy) limited, i.e. constitutes what is effectively a bombardment-induced phase change. For example, $PbSO_4$, known to evolve mainly to PbO rather than Pb or PbS (31), will be assumed to do so because the energy increase is 0.42 eV/atom in the first case, 0.80 in the second, and 1.42 in the third. One is thus again dealing with energy differences which, in units of eV/atom, are similar to those involved in BIS and mixing (Table 1).

The argument at this stage is imperfect, as it does not explain why the system did not return to $PbSO_4$, given that $PbSO_4$ constitutes the lowest energy state. By contrast, in BIS and mixing the final state that is observed is that of lowest energy. One can propose a number of reasons why the system might tend to avoid the state $PbSO_4$ (or whatever was the ground state), although, as will be clear, no one explanation appears to cover all systems.

4.4.4.1. Mass Differences. Mass is most clearly relevant under near-threshold conditions, including with Al_2O_3 (1), PbO (162), and Ta_2O_5 (1). Nevertheless, even at higher energies near-threshold behavior might be expected for large enough mass differences, and this would explain why WO_3 reduced to products including W^0 but MoO_3 mainly to Mo^{IV}, or why Ta_2O_5 yielded products including Ta^0 or Ta^I but Nb_2O_5 stopped at Nb^{II} (Table 8). A still more general role for mass is suggested by the relation $Y_{cascade} \propto 1/M^{2m}U$ (Eq. (2b)) and was in fact advocated by Malherbe et al. (6). As noted previously (Sect. 4.2.6.2), however, this general role would suggest that all oxides (except, e.g., BeO) would behave similarly and reduce to pure metal, at least at the outer surface. We therefore tend to discount it.

4.4.4.2   Bombardment–Induced Amorphization. If the amorphization process is taken as being equivalent to fusion, then with $PbSO_4$ one can expect a ground-state energy increase of 0.07 eV/atom, whence a decrease in the energy needed for formation of PbO from 0.42 to 0.35 eV/atom. This is an unimportant change, though with some systems the change is larger, e.g. about 0.26 eV/atom (average from (164)) for oxides of the type MO_2. Indeed, as seen in Fig. 18, the latter change is sufficient to justify the recent claim that bombarded SnO_2 evolves to SnO (165).

4.4.4.3   Point–Defect Accumulation. Fecht and Johnson (166) have argued that point-defect accumulation can cause a phase to become unstable. For example, they show that Al would amorphize if it acquired 5% vacancies, a number that is obtained by comparing the vacancy formation energy (0.7 eV (8)) with the heat of fusion (<0.11 eV for temperatures below the glass transition temperature (166)). Considering now $PbSO_4$, then a possible (though simplistic) description of a high oxygen vacancy concentration is the formation of $PbSO_3$, leading to a ground-state energy increase of ≤ 0.43 eV/atom. With such an increase, together with amorphization, it is possible that $PbSO_4$ would become unstable.

4.4.4.4   Volatility, Diffusional Transport, BIS. To some extent the evolution of $PbSO_4$ to PbO will be conditioned by the volatility of O_2, SO_2, and SO_3. This effect is clearly not as important as it might seem, however, as it would be expected to lead to a universal decomposition of all oxides and oxysalts, for example Al_2O_3, Cr_2O_3, and SiO_2. Ease of diffusional transport is somewhat different and, in principle, plays a role with selected systems. From a thermodynamic point of view these should either not lose O at all (HfO_2, SnO_2, ZrO_2) or should lose less O than is observed (Nb_2O_5, Ta_2O_5, WO_3). The key may lie in the fact that in most cases the diffusion coefficient for O transport in understoichiometric material is unusually large. For example, $(4Dt)^{1/2}$ is about 1 nm for O transport in 10 min at 450 K with ZrO_{2-x} (167,168), while the corresponding distance for Nb_2O_{5-x} is about 10 nm (167,169) and for MoO_3 (MoO_{3-x}?) about 2 nm (170). (We give results for MoO_3 since there is a lack of information on WO_3.)

An intriguing example is that of CoO and NiO, which in one AES study showed bombardment-induced decomposition only at elevated temperatures (163). MnO was stable up to 900 K. Are these to be considered examples involving diffusional transport or stochastic rearrangement (Sect. 4.4.3)?

Finally there is BIS. Very little is known about this effect with oxides or oxysalts except for the unique example of Na_2O-SiO_2 (38). Here bombardment led to a profile like that of an alloy as in Fig. 2, thence to Na loss.

4.4.5 Equilibrium Rearrangement

If the system underwent equilibrium decomposition at the transient high temperature ("thermal spike") which is conventionally assumed to exist during the cooling phase of a cascade, then changes essentially as observed could be expected. This was the point of view taken to explain O loss from oxides (19) and the loss of both alkali metals and other volatile species from oxysalts (Fig. 15 (158)). We note, first of all, that this mechanism does not avoid the problematical cases such as HfO_2, Nb_2O_5, etc.: i.e. just as they lie at the top of Fig. 16, they also lack volatility.

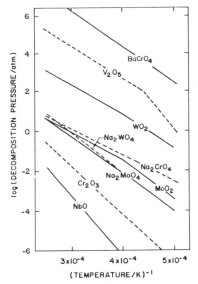

Figure 17: Decomposition pressure vs. $1/T$ for oxides and oxysalts at very high temperatures. Those lying above MoO_2 (including, for high enough temperatures, Na_2WO_4 and Na_2MoO_4) show a bombardment-induced loss of O, whereas the others do not. The separation between the two groups occurs at about 10^1 atm for a temperature of ~4000 K. This is a similar kind of trend analysis as that shown in Fig. 16 except that it presupposes the validity of equilibrium rearrangement as discussed in Sect. 4.4.5. Due to Ho et al. (158).

The mechanism has never been properly tested, the current situation being that most tests are either a trend analysis as in Fig. 17 or Ref. 19, or are based on experiments (20,21) which are inconclusive. Our position is the same as that taken elsewhere (111) with BIS and mixing. Although we cannot disprove a thermal-spike interpretation we can propose an alternative in which chemical energy differences are important (a) without regard to the inequality (111 171),

$$\text{(driving force)} \gtrsim kT , \tag{17}$$

and (b) without violating the problem of a phase explosion (Sect. 4.1.1). The alternative was given in Sect. 4.4.4.

A further general objection also exists in that the mechanism requires chemical changes to occur in an assumed equilibrium during a time interval similar to 10^{-12} to 10^{-9} s. By contrast the process discussed in Sect. 4.4.4 is essentially open ended in time. For example, with $BaSO_4$ a change in the O XPS peak was reported to take place over ~3 hours (33), while bombarded alloys have been shown to undergo BIS for up to 10 minutes after the end of the bombardment (Fig. 4).

SnO_2 presents a novel sort of objection. It is known to evolve to SnO (165), but since the latter is not stable above $\sim 270°C$ (172) equilibrium rearrangement can be excluded.

4.5. OVERVIEW

The main theme of this Chapter is that compositional changes with bombarded alloys, oxides, oxysalts, and halides are normally <u>not</u> due to preferential sputtering but rather to surprisingly weak chemical driving forces (Table 1). Preferential sputtering enters in two ways: (a) It occurs as a mass-related preferential loss under near-threshold conditions (Fig. 1), possibly under not-quite-threshold conditions if the mass difference is large enough (WO_3 vs MoO_3), and with isotopes. (b) It occurs tentatively due to the surface binding energy in the case of reasonably ionic oxides of group III and beyond (Sects. 4.2.5 and 4.2.6). In a formal sense, preferential loss based on differences of volatility (thermal sputtering) would also constitute preferential sputtering but the evidence for it is problematical (Sects. 4.1.1 and 4.4.5).

Rather, we have emphasized that weak chemical driving forces play a major role role in bombarded targets even when, for reasons of the extreme energy disparity, it might be difficult to understand why this should be so. With BIS the basic result is that bombarded alloys show segregation in the same sense, although to a factor of 10-100 lesser extent, than equilibrated alloys (Fig. 12, Fig. 13, Table 7). The driving force is 0.06 to 0.52 eV/atom (Table 1) and we have suggested (see after Eq. (11)) that the result becomes understandable if a fraction f of ballistic trajectories ending in either of the outer two atom layers is followed by a low-energy, chemically guided step, while BIS thus resembles mixing. We have further suggested that BIS is the single most important reason for compositional change with alloys (Sect. 4.3.4).

Finally we have considered what has been termed bombardment-induced decomposition. This is a multifaceted phenomenon in which bombarded oxides lose O, sulfates lose S and O, and other systems lose, as is appropriate, alkali metal, Ba, Ag, C, N, etc., the result being an energy increase of ≤ 0.8 eV/atom (Fig. 16). The idea of a chemical driving force is here at first sight unfavorable in that the "ground state" (e.g. $PbSO_4$) has a lower energy than the observed product (e.g. PbO). The point of view of Fecht and Johnson (166) is relevant, however, which is that if there are sufficient bombardment-induced vacancies (simplistically, conversion of $PbSO_4$ to $PbSO_3$) then the ground state will be unstable. This is how Fecht and Johnson described bombardment-induced amorphization and other phase changes, processes which we see now to be related to those that are discussed here. Besides point-defect accumulation, the changes will also be aided by amorphization, volatility, diffusional transport, and BIS.

We have shown that the alternative of a stochastic loss of components is not as viable: $PbSO_4$ does not evolve significantly to Pb or PbS. Nor, however, can it be excluded as playing at least a minor role in view of such systems as CoO, NiO, and Fe_2O_3, which yield small amounts of Co^0, Ni^0, and Fe^0 inspite of the large energy increases (Fig. 16). Likewise, equilibrium loss at a transient high temperature runs into the various problems associated with thermal-spike descriptions. These are (a) Eq. (17), (b) phase explosion, (c) the severely proscribed time-scale, and (d) the evolution of SnO_2 to SnO, which is stable only at low temperatures (Sect. 4.4.5).

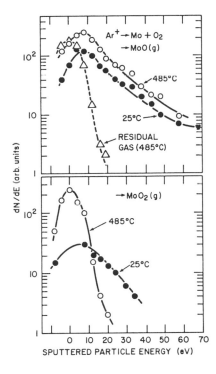

Figure 18: Energy distributions of neutral MoO(g) and MoO$_2$(g) sputtered from polycrystalline Mo exposed to 1×10^{-3} Pa O$_2$. The bombardments were carried out with 8 keV Ar$^+$ at an angle of incidence of 70°. The energy scale was set to zero at the maximum of the residual gas distribution and negative energies were attributed to poor resolution. Of particular interest here is the thermal form of the MoO$_2$(g) distribution at 485°C, as if the MoO$_2$ was released by either a stochastic or energy-limited rearrangement (a distinction is not possible) at the particular ambient temperature. Due to Saidoh et al. (173).

An important source of information has not yet been considered, namely sputtered particle energy distributions as in Fig. 18 (173). They have apparently never been obtained for the various oxysalts dealt with here and only rarely for oxides, but if the results of Fig. 18 are accepted at face value they imply that ar 485°C the MoO$_2$(g) was released by either a stochastic or energy-limited rearrangement (a distinction is not possible) at the particular ambient temperature but in no case by an equilibrium rearrangement at a very high temperature. Related examples are known from work on laser-pulse sputtering, as when the species P and P$_2$ are released from GaP and give time-of-flight spectra appropriate to the ambient temperature (174,175).

4.6 REFERENCES

1. E. Taglauer, Appl. Surf. Sci. 13: 80 (1982).

2. H. Gnaser and I. D. Hutcheon, Surf. Sci. 195: 499 (1988).

3. N. Andersen and P. Sigmund, Mat. Fys. Medd. Dan. Vid. Selsk. 39: No. 3 (1974).

4. R. Kelly, in Proc. Symp. on Sputtering, eds. P. Varga et al. (Inst. für Allgem. Physik, T. U. Wien, Austria, 1980) p. 390.

5. R. Kelly and D. E. Harrison, Mat. Sci. Engin. 69: 449 (1985).

6. J.B. Malherbe, S. Hofmann, and J.M. Sanz, <u>Appl. Surf. Sci.</u> 27: 355 (1986).

7. R. Kelly, in <u>Ion Beam Modification of Insulators,</u> eds. P. Mazzoldi and G. W. Arnold (Elsevier, Amsterdam, 1987) ch. 2.

8. A. Oliva, R. Kelly, and G. Falcone, <u>Nucl. Instr. Meth.</u> B19/20: 101 (1987).

9. D. G. Swartzfager, S. B. Ziemecki, and M. J. Kelley, <u>J. Vac. Sci. Technol.</u> 19: 185 (1981).

10. R. Kelly and A. Oliva, <u>Nucl. Instr. Meth.</u> B13: 283 (1986).

11. R. Kelly, <u>Nucl. Instr. Meth.</u> B18: 388 (1987).

12. W. O. Hofer, in <u>Erosion and Growth of Solids Stimulated by Atom and Ion Beams,</u> eds. G. Kiriakidis et al. (Nijhoff, Dordrecht, Netherlands, 1986) p. 1.

13. R. S. Nelson, <u>Phil. Mag.</u> 11: 291 (1965).

14. R. Kelly, <u>Surf. Sci.</u> 90: 280 (1979).

15. K. Besocke, S. Berger, W. O. Hofer, and U. Littmark, <u>Rad. Eff.</u> 66: 35 (1982).

16. R. Kelly, <u>Rad. Eff.</u> 32: 91 (1977).

17. P. Sigmund, <u>Appl. Phys. Lett.</u> 25: 169 (1974).

18. A. E. Morgan and H. W. Werner, <u>Anal. Chem.</u> 49: 927 (1977).

19. C. J. Good-Zamin, M. T. Shehata, D. B. Squires, and R. Kelly, <u>Rad. Eff.</u> 35: 139 (1978).

20. M. Szymonski, R.S. Bhattacharya, H. Overeijnder, and A.E. de Vries, <u>J. Phys. D</u> 751 (1978).

21. D.J. Oostra, R.P. van Ingen, A. Haring, A.E. de Vries, and F.W. Saris, <u>Phys. Rev. Lett.</u> 61: 1392 (1988).

22. M.M. Martynyuk, <u>Russ. J. Phys. Chem.</u> 57: 494 (1983).

23. M.M. Martynyuk, <u>Phys. of Combustion and Explosions</u> 13: 178 (1977).

24. H.M. Urbassek, <u>Nucl. Instr. Meth.</u> B31: 541 (1988).

25. H. H. Andersen, B. Stenum, T. Sorensen, and H. J. Whitlow, <u>Nucl. Instr. Meth.</u> 209/210: 487 (1983).

26. S. Ichimura, H. Shimizu, H. Murakami, and Y. Ishida, <u>J. Nucl. Mat.</u> 128/129: 601 (1984).

27. J. Fine, T. D. Andreadis, and F. Davarya, <u>Nucl. Instr. Meth.</u> 209/210: 521 (1983).

28. R. S. Li, L. X. Tu, and Y. Z. Sun, <u>Appl. Surf. Sci.</u> 26: 77 (1986).

29. D. E. Harrison and R. P. Webb, <u>Nucl. Instr. Meth.</u> 218: 727 (1983).

30. H. Overeijnder, R. R. Tol, and A. E de Vries, <u>Surf. Sci.</u> 90: 265 (1979).

31. A. B. Christie, J. Lee, I. Sutherland, and J. M. Walls, <u>Appl. Surf. Sci.</u> 15: 224 (1983).

32. S. Hofmann and J. M. Sanz, <u>J. Trace and Microprobe Tech.</u> 1: 213 (1982-1983).

33. S. Contarini and J. W. Rabalais, <u>J. Electron Spect. and Related Phenom.</u> 35: 191 (1985).

34. G. Marletta, <u>Nucl. Instr. Meth.</u> B32: 204 (1988).

35. P. J. Rudeck, J.M.E. Harper, and P. M. Fryer, <u>Appl. Phys. Lett.</u> 53: 845 (1988).

36. R. A. Kushner, D. V. McCaughan, V. T. Murphy, and J. A. Heilig, Phys. Rev. B10: 2632 (1974).

37. R. C. McCune and P. Wynblatt, J. Am. Cer. Soc. 66: 111 (1983).

38. A. Torrisi, G. Marletta, A. Licciardello, and O. Puglisi, Nucl. Instr. Meth. B32: 283 (1988).

39. U. Littmark, Nucl. Instr. Meth. B7/8: 684 (1985), and preceding articles.

40. Y-T. Cheng, M. van Rossum, M-A. Nicolet, and W. L. Johnson, Appl. Phys. Lett. 45: 185 (1984).

41. Y-T. Cheng, T. W. Workman, M-A. Nicolet, and W. L. Johnson, Mat. Res. Soc. Symp. Proc. 74: 419 (1987).

42. J. Bottiger, S. K. Nielsen, and P. T. Thorsen, Proc. Mat. Res. Soc. (Europe) (Strasbourg, France, 1984) p. 111.

43. R. S. Li and T. Koshikawa, Surf. Sci. 151: 459 (1985).

44. T. E. Parker and R. Kelly, J. Phys. Chem. Sol. 36: 377 (1975).

45. N. Q. Lam and H. Wiedersich, Nucl. Inst. Meth. B18: 471 (1987).

46. R. Kelly, Nucl. Instr. Meth. 182/183: 351 (1981).

47. R. C. Piller and A. D. Marwick, J. Nucl. Mat. 71: 309 (1978).

48. H. L. Hughes, R. D. Baxter, and B. Phillips, IEEE Trans. Nucl. Sci. NS-19: 256 (1972).

49. G. Betz and W. Husinsky, Nucl. Instr. Meth. B13: 343 (1986).

50. N. Itoh and A.M. Stoneham; also R. Kelly: work in progress.

51. J. van Zwol, A. W. Kolfschoten, J. van Laar, and J. Dieleman, in Materials Modification by High-fluence Ion Beams, eds. R. Kelly and M.F. da Silva (Kluwer, Dordrecht, Netherlands, 1988) p. 117.

52. R. A. Haring, A. Haring, F. W. Saris, and A. E. de Vries, Appl. Phys. Lett. 41: 174 (1982).

53. M. Saidoh, J. Nucl. Mat. 128/129: 540 (1984).

54. J. Bohdansky and J. Roth, Rad. Eff. 89: 49 (1985).

55. E. Hechtl, J. Bohdansky, and J. Roth, J. Nucl. Mat. 103/104: 333 (1981).

56. R. Kelly and A. Oliva, see Ref. 12, p. 41.

57. W. C. Mackrodt, Sol. State Ionics 12: 175 (1984).

58. P. Biloen, R. Bouwman, R. A. van Santen, and H. H. Brongersma, Appl. Surf. Sci. 2: 523 (1979).

59. G. Hetzendorf and P. Varga, Nucl. Instr. Meth. B18: 501 (1987).

60. A. Jablonski, S. H. Overbury, and G. A. Somorjai, Surf. Sci. 65: 578 (1977).

61. P. Varga and G. Hetzendorf, Surf. Sci. 162: 544 (1985).

62. G. Betz, Surf. Sci. 92: 283 (1980).

63. R. S. Li (Institute of Metal Research, Shenyang), private communication (1988).

64. G. C. Nelson, J. Vac. Sci. Technol. A1: 1037 (1983).

65. R. S. Li, in <u>Diffusion and Defect Data,</u> ed. F. H. Wohlbier (Trans Tech S. A., Aedermannsdorf, Switzerland) (in press).

66. W. L. Johnson, see Ref. 51, p. 405.

67. R. Kelly, <u>Nucl. Instr. Meth.</u> B39: 43 (1989).

68. R. Hultgren, P. D. Desai, D. T. Hawkins, M. Gleiser, and K. K. Kelley, <u>Selected Values of the Thermodynamic Properties of Binary Alloys</u> (Am. Soc. for Metals, Metals Park, OH, U.S.A., 1973).

69. P. T. Dawson and S. A. Petrone, <u>Surf. Sci.</u> 152/153: 925 (1985).

70. G. Falcone, R. Kelly, and A. Oliva, <u>Nucl. Instr. Meth.</u> B18: 399 (1987).

71. P. Sigmund, <u>Phys. Rev.</u> 184: 383 (1969).

72. B. Jorgensen, M. J. Pellin, C. E. Young, W. F. Calaway, E. L. Schweitzer, D. M. Gruen, J. W. Burnett, and J. T. Yates, see Ref. 51, p. 83.

73. P. Sigmund, <u>Rev. Roum. Phys.</u> 17: 969 (1972). See in particular p. 974.

74. R. Kelly and A. Oliva, in preparation.

75. D.M. Parkin, in <u>Structure-property Relationships in Surface-modified Ceramics</u> (Kluwer, Dordrecht, Netherlands, 1989).

76. R. A. Swalin, <u>Thermodynamics of Solids,</u> 2nd. ed. (Wiley, New York, 1972), p. 144.

77. S. V. Nagender Naidu, A. M. Sriramamurthy, and P. Rama Rao, <u>Bull. Alloy Phase Diagrams</u> 5: 177 (1984).

78. D. P. Jackson, <u>Rad. Eff.</u> 18: 185 (1973).

79. H. Oechsner, H. Schoof, and E. Stumpe, <u>Surf. Sci.</u> 76: 343 (1978).

80. T. E. Parker and R. Kelly, in <u>Ion Implantation in Semiconductors and Other Materials,</u> ed. by B. L. Crowder (Plenum, New York, NY, 1973) p. 551.

81. V. E. Henrich, G. Dresselhaus, and H. J. Zeiger, <u>Phys. Rev. Lett.</u> 36: 1335 (1976).

82. T. Choudhury, S.O. Saied, J.L. Sullivan, and A. Abbot, <u>J. Phys. D</u> (in press).

83. E. Dullni, <u>Nucl. Instr. Meth.</u> B2: 610 (1984).

84. D. Grischkowsky, M. L. Yu, and A. C. Balant, <u>Surf. Sci.</u> 127: 315 (1983).

85. W. Husinsky, G. Betz, and I. Girgis, <u>J. Vac. Sci. Technol.</u> A2: 698 (1984).

86. W. Husinsky and G. Betz, <u>Nucl. Instr. Meth.</u> B15: 165 (1986).

87. W. Husinsky, P. Wurz, B. Strehl. and G. Betz, <u>Nucl. Instr. Meth.</u> B18: 452 (1987).

88. C. E. Young, W. F. Calaway, M. J. Pellin, and D. M. Gruen, <u>J. Vac. Sci. Technol.</u> A2: 693 (1984).

89. B. Schweer and H. L. Bay, <u>Appl. Phys.</u> A29: 53 (1982).

90. J. P. Baxter, J. Singh, G. A Schick, P. H. Kobrin, and N. Winograd, <u>Nucl. Instr. Meth.</u> B17: 300 (1986).

91. J. P. Baxter, G. A. Schick, J. Singh, P. H. Kobrin, and N. Winograd, <u>J. Vac. Sci. Tech.</u> A4: 1218 (1986).

92. R. B. Wright, M. J. Pellin, and D. M. Gruen, <u>Nucl. Instr. Meth.</u> 182/183: 167 (1981).

93. W. Berres and H. L. Bay, <u>Appl. Phys.</u> A33: 235 (1984).

94. W. Husinsky, J. Vac. Sci. Technol. B3: 1546 (1985).

95. M. J. Pellin, R. B. Wright, and D. M. Gruen, J. Chem. Phys. 74: 6448 (1981).

96. B. J. Garrison, N. Winograd, D. Lo, T. A. Tombrello, M. H. Shapiro, and D. E. Harrison, Surf. Sci. Lett. 180: L129 (1987).

97. H. L. Bay, W. Berres, and E. Hintz, Nucl. Instr. Meth. 194: 555 (1982).

98. N. Q. Lam, H. A. Hoff, H. Wiedersich, and L. E. Rehn, Surf. Sci. 149: 517 (1985).

99. M. J. Sparnaay and G. E. Thomas, Surf. Sci. 135: 184 (1983).

100. M. Shikata and R. Shimizu, Surf. Sci. 97: L363 (1980).

101. Y. M. Chiang, A. P. Henriksen, W. D. Kingery, and D. Finello, J. Am. Cer. Soc. 64: 385 (1981).

102. E. A. Colbourn, W. C. Mackrodt, and P. W. Tasker, J. Mat. Sci. 18: 1917 (1983).

103. V. R. Deline, W. Reuter, and R. Kelly, in Sec. Ion Mass Spectrometry, SIMS V, eds. A. Benninghoven et al. (Springer-Verlag, Berlin, 1986) p. 299.

104. P. Wynblatt and R. C. Ku, Surf. Sci. 65: 511 (1977).

105. R. A. van Santen and M.A.M. Boersma, J. Catal. 34: 13 (1974).

106. L. E. Rehn and P. R. Okamoto, Nucl. Instr. Meth. B39: 104 (1989).

107. N. Q. Lam and H. Wiedersich, J. Nucl. Mat. 103/104: 433 (1981).

108. N. Itoh and K. Morita, Rad. Eff. 80: 163 (1984).

109. P. Sigmund, A. Oliva, and G. Falcone, Nucl. Instr. Meth. 194: 541 (1982).

110. A. Oliva, R. Kelly, and G. Falcone, Surf. Sci. 166: 403 (1986).

111. R. Kelly, Mat. Sci. Eng. A114: (1989).

112. R. Kelly, Surf. and Interface Anal. 7: 1 (1985).

113. R-S. Li, Surf. Sci. 193: 373 (1988).

114. E. E. Hajcsar, P. T. Dawson, and W. W. Smeltzer, Surf. and Interface Anal. 10: 343 (1987).

115. H. J. Kang, R. Shimizu, and T. Okutani, Surf. Sci. 116: L173 (1982).

116. H. J. Kang, E. Kawatoh, and R. Shimizu, Surf. Sci. 144: 541 (1984).

117. G. C. Nelson, J. Vac. Sci. Technol. A1: 1037 (1983).

118. T. M. Buck, G. H. Wheatley, and L. Marchut, Phys. Rev. Lett. 51: 43 (1983).

119. J. Bartella and H. Oechsner, unpublished.

120. M. Yabumoto, H. Kakibayashi, M. Mohri, K. Watanabe, and T. Yamashina, Thin Sol. Films 63: 263 (1979).

121. H. Shimizu, M. Ono, and K. Nakayama, J. Appl. Phys. 46: 460 (1975).

122. L. E. Rehn and H. Wiedersich, Thin Sol. Films 73: 139 (1980).

123. M. L. Yu and W. Reuter, Appl. Phys. Lett. 38: 525 (1981).

124. H. H. Brongersma, M. J. Sparnaay, and T. M. Buck, Surf. Sci. 71: 657 (1978).

125. Y. S. Ng, S. B. McLane, and T. T. Tsong, J. Vac. Sci. Technol. 17: 154 (1980).

126. G. P. Schwartz, Surf. Sci. 76: 113 (1978).

127. N. Q. Lam, H. A. Hoff, and P. G. Regnier, J. Vac. Sci. Technol. A3 : 2152 (1985).

128. J. J. Burton, C. R. Helms, and R. S. Polizzotti, J. Vac. Sci. Technol. 13: 204 (1976).

129. A. Jablonski, S. H. Overbury, and G. A. Somorjai, Surf. Sci. 65: 578 (1977).

130. K. Wandelt and G. Ertl, Z. Naturforsch. 31a: 205 (1976).

131. C. Lea and C. Molinari, J. Mat. Sci. 19: 2336 (1984).

132. P. T. Dawson and N. A. Burke, J. Electron Spect. and Related Phenom. 31: 355 (1983).

133. E. E. Hajcsar, P. R. Underhill, W. W. Smeltzer, and P. T. Dawson, Surf. Sci. 191: 249 (1987).

134. L. de Temmerman, C. Creemers, H. van Hove, and A. Neyens, Surf. Sci. 183: 565 (1987).

135. D. A. Mervyn, R. J. Baird, and P. Wynblatt, Surf. Sci. 82: 79 (1979).

136. W. Färber, G. Betz, and P. Braun, Nucl. Instr. Meth. 132: 351 (1976).

137. M. Yabumoto, K. Watanabe, and T. Yamashina, Surf. Sci. 77: 615 (1978).

138. P. H. Holloway and S. K. Hofmeister, Surf. and Interface Anal. 4: 181 (1982).

139. G. C. Nelson, Surf. Sci. 59: 310 (1976).

140. M. J. Kelley, D. G. Swartzfager, and V. S. Sundaram, J. Vac. Sci. Technol. 16: 664 (1979).

141. S. Dong, Y. Pang, J. Deng, and X. Zhu, Acta Metall. Sinica 20: B110 (1984).

142. H. J. Mathieu and D. Landolt, Surf. Sci. 53: 228 (1975).

143. F. Garbassi and G. Parravano, Surf. Sci. 71: 42 (1978).

144. W. Losch and J. Kirschner, J. Vac. Sci. Technol. 15: 1541 (1978).

145. H. G. Tompkins, J. Vac. Sci. Technol. 16: 778 (1979).

146. G. Betz, J. Marton, and P. Braun, Nucl. Instr. Meth. 168: 541 (1980).

147. G. Hetzendorf and P. Varga, Nucl. Instr. Meth. B18: 501 (1987).

148. A. D. van Langeveld, H.A.C.M. Hendrickx, and B. E. Nieuwenhuys, Thin Sol. Films 109: 179 (1983).

149. T. S. Sampath Kumar and M. S. Hegde, Appl. Surf. Sci. 20: 290 (1985).

150. A. D. van Langeveld and V. Ponec, Appl. Surf. Sci. 16: 405 (1983).

151. C. R. Barreto, R. C. Gragnani, R. A. Douglas, and V. S. Sundaram, Rev. Brasileira de Fisica 9: 217 (1979).

152. P. Braun, M. Arias, H. Stori, and F.P. Viehbock, Surf. Sci. 126: 714 (1983).

153. P. T. Dawson and S. A. Petrone, J. Vac. Sci. Technol. 18: 259 (1981).

154. J. Bartella and H. Oechsner, Surf. Sci. 126: 581 (1983).

155. D. C. Peacock, Appl. Surf. Sci. 26: 306 (1986).

156. P. Varga and G. Hetzendorf, Surf. Sci. 162: 544 (1985).

157. S. Aduru, S. Contarini, and J.W. Rabalais, J. Phys. Chem. 90: 1683 (1986).

158. S.F. Ho, S. Contarini, and J.W. Rabalais, J. Phys. Chem. 91: 4779 (1987).

159. S. Contarini, S. Aduru, and J.W. Rabalais, J. Phys. Chem. 90: 3202 (1986).

160. D.K. Murti and R. Kelly, Thin Sol. Films 33: 149 (1976).

161. J. Herion, G. Scharl, and M. Tapiero, Appl. Surf. Sci. 14: 233 (1982-83).

162. K.S. Kim, W.E. Baitinger, and N. Winograd, Surf. Sci. 55: 285 (1976).

163. M.A. Langell, Surf. Sci. 186: 323 (1987).

164. M.W. Chase, C.A. Davies, J.R. Downey, D.J. Frurip, R.A. McDonald, and A.N. Syverud, "JANAF Thermochemical Tables, 3rd ed.", J. Phys. Chem. Ref. Data 14: (1985) Suppl. 1.

165. G. Marletta (Univ. di Catania, Catania, Italy), work in progress.

166. H.J. Fecht and W.L. Johnson, Nature 334: 50 (1988).

167. D.L. Douglass, in Corrosion of Reactor Materials (Intern. Atomic Energy Agency, Vienna, 1962) p. 223.

168. T. Smith, J. Electrochem. Soc. 112: 560 (1965).

169. W.K. Chen and R.A. Swalin, J. Phys. Chcm. Sol. 27: 57 (1966).

170. V.P. Elyutin, T.G. Lenskaya, Yu. A. Pavlov, and V.P. Polyakov, Sov. Phys.-Doklady 16: 581 (1972).

171. T.W. Workman, Y.T. Cheng, W.L. Johnson, and M-A. Nicolet, Appl. Phys. Lett. 50: 1485 (1987).

172. G.H. Noh, Chem. Erde 33: 243 (1974). See also Phase diagrams for ceramists, vol. IV, no. 5017 (The Am. Cer. Soc., Columbus, OH, 1981).

173. M. Saidoh, H. Gnaser, and W.O. Hofer, Appl. Phys. A40: 197 (1986).

174. T. Nakayama and N. Itoh, in Desorption Induced by Electronic Transitions, DIET II, eds. W. Brenig and D. Menzel (Springer Verlag, Berlin, 1985) p.237.

175. A. Namiki, S. Cho, and K. Ichige, Jap. J. Appl. Phys. 26: 39 (1987).

176. H.M. Naguib and R. Kelly, J. Phys. Chem. Sol. 33: 1751 (1972).

177. A.B. Christie, I. Sutherland, and J.M. Walls, Vacuum 31: 513 (1981).

Part III
Non-Reactive Plasma Processes

5

RF Diode Sputter Etching and Deposition

Joseph S. Logan

5.1 INTRODUCTION

5.1.1 History

The process of sputtering and sputter-etching has been studied and used for over 100 years. Sputtering of insulating materials was difficult, using dc, due to the problem of neutralization of the charge carried to the surface of the insulator by the gas ions, with the consequent difficulty of maintaining an accelerating voltage between the surface of the insulator and the plasma. Methods of dealing with this problem include the use of neutralized ion beams and the use of independently supported discharges, both of which involve a degree of complexity greater than conventional dc discharges, and sometimes cannot be applied over large areas. In 1962, Anderson, Mayer, and Wehner (1) following an earlier proposal by Wehner (2) reported the successful use of capacitively coupled high frequency potential to sputter-etch insulating materials.

In 1965, Davidse and Maissel (3) reported the use of a simple parallel-plate diode apparatus using rf power at 13.56 MHz, to sputter-deposit insulating films. Since then, many other variations of electrode geometries, frequencies, and power control methods have been demonstrated in the sputter-deposition or sputter-etching of insulating materials and substrates. All of these applications make use of the large mobility difference between electrons and ions to provide a negative bias between insulator surface and plasma, as explained in section 5-2.

RF sputter-etching has proved to be extremely useful in the semiconductor industry for cleaning of integrated circuit metallization via contact holes, because of the insulating nature of the substrates, and because of the relatively low pressure discharge which minimizes backscattered material. It has also been very useful as a pretreatment to insulating surfaces prior to film deposition, to improve adhesion of the deposited film. Many evaporation and sputter-deposition systems (dc or rf) are provided with the ability to rf sputter-etch prior to deposition. Sputter etching is often used for pattern transfer, but because sputter-etching (dc or rf) is a high-energy process, it is rarely used for patterning thick films, except when the energy requirements can be lowered by using chemical re-action (RIE) (see later chapter).

The major usefulness of rf sputtering is for the deposition and etching of insulators which cannot easily be done with dc because of substrate and target charging. RF sputter deposition is widely used for insulators such as silicon oxide, aluminum oxide, and other oxides where the substrate temperature limits preclude other techniques, or where compositional control is easier to achieve than for alternate methods and the films or targets are insulating. Large deposition areas can be coated uniformly without the need for substrate motion, and films can be sumultaneously ion- bombarded during deposition to improve properties (bias sputtering) as has been done with conductive films/substrates and dc sputtering. Deposition by reactive rf sputtering has the advantage over dc sputtering that the oxides formed on the cathode surface do not charge up and break down in destructive arcs.

Rf sputtering has been reviewed before by several authors; in 1970 by Maissel and Glang (4), in 1971 by Vossen (5), and in 1980 by Chapman (6). This article again reviews the subject in brief, adding more detail on the practical aspects and developments since 1980.

5.2 RF DISCHARGES

5.2.1 Breakdown

Breakdown of a gas by rf electric fields has been studied in the past by many re-searchers. An extensive discussion of rf discharges is given by Jackson (7) in his review article. In general, rf capacitively coupled discharges can be started and maintained at lower pressures than dc discharges. The minimum pressure at which discharges can be maintained decreases with increasing frequency. The reason for this is that additional ionizing collisions can be induced by the rf field acting on electrons within the plasma to increase their energy.

5.2.2 RF Self-bias

At each boundary of a capacitively coupled rf discharge, a depletion, or space-charge layer is induced by the rf field, similar to the sheath observed around a probe or at the cathode of a dc discharge. Electrons are repelled from this layer over most of the rf cycle, resulting in a positive time- averaged space charge. To preserve charge neutrality overall, a time-averaged negative charge accumulates on the surface of the insulating boundary. The buildup of this negative charge on the surface of an insulated electrode connected to a high frequency voltage, and in contact with a plasma was first explained simply in a paper by Butler and Kino (8). The key principle is that with no dc path through the insulated electrode, the average flow of ions and electrons to the electrode surface during each cycle must be equal to preserve charge neutrality. The electrons, being highly mobile, can easily provide enough charge over a small fraction of the cycle to neutralize the positive ion charge which flows during the majority of the cycle. Thus, within the first rf cycle, a large electron flow establishes a negative charge at the insulator surface in response to the first positive voltage swing. Subsequently, a nearly steady saturated ion current flows during most of the rf cycle, except during a brief period near the positive maximum, when a pulse of electron current restores the negative charge lost during the rest of the cycle. The insulator potential relative to the plasma must be positive only a few volts to draw saturation electron current. This means that the average (dc) sheath voltage is normally negative and within a few volts of the peak rf voltage after transients have decayed. This is illustrated in Fig. 1, for a typical plasma density. The two particle currents, ionic and electronic, are plotted vs time, in Fig. 2. Not shown is a large displacement current which corresponds to the oscillation of the sheath-plasma boundary as the sheath field fluctuates. This displacement current is not sinusoidal, due to the non-linear charge- voltage characteristic of the sheath, but is approximately 90 degrees ahead of the sheath voltage.

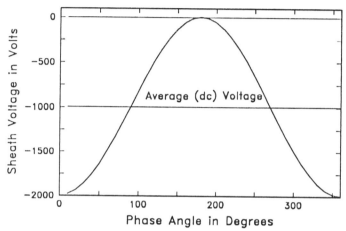

Fig.2.2.1 Voltage at an rf Plasma Boundary

Figure 1: Voltage at an rf plasma boundary

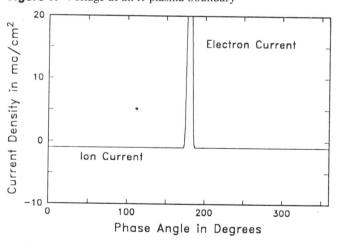

Fig.2.2.2 Current Flow at a rf Plasma Boundary

Figure 2: Current flow at an rf plasma boundary

5.2.3 Frequency Effect

At low frequencies, most of the applied voltage at the cathode appears across the dielectric target plate, and the remainder of the voltage is easily screened from the plasma by the resultant flow of either electrons or ions during the relatively long cycle time, so that the average potential between insulator surface and plasma is nearly zero. At higher frequency, less of the applied rf voltage appears across the insulator and there is insufficient time for the ion flow to completely neutralize induced charge at the insulator surface during the negative excursions. The large electron flow during positive excursions easily prevents large positive potentials from forming with respect to the plasma. The "crossover" frequency for the self-bias effect is usually estimated to be about 1 MHz, but in fact is somewhat dependent on the target capacitance and external circuit capacitance as well as on the gas composition.

5.2.4 Electrical Models

The simplest electrical model of a diode-type system shown in Fig. 3 was first proposed by Koenig and Maissel (9), based on the representation of each sheath boundary as a simple capacitor in parallel with a diode and a resistor. The diode carries the large electron current flow during positive excursions, the resistor represents the energy consumed by the ions falling through the boundary potential, and the capacitor represents the storage of charge (unscreened positive ions) at the boundary in response to the rf voltage difference.

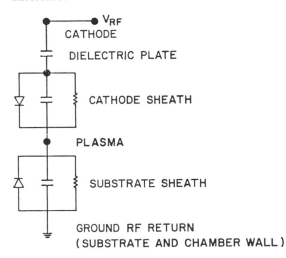

Figure 3: Simple model of an rf diode discharge

For most gases at frequencies above 1 MHz, this is a reasonable representation. The largest rf current is the capacitive component. The resistive component is usually less than 20% of the capacitive component, except for electronegative gases, where the discharge can become nearly resistive, with little sheath charge storage.

Koenig estimated the value of the capacitance by using the familiar Child Langmuir equation for a dc sheath to calculate the sheath thickness, and assumed that the capacitance value is that of a vacuum capacitor with the sheath thickness and area. This simple model was used to show that the dc (and rf) voltage ratio between cathode and substrate sheaths was inversely proportional to the 4th power of the cathode to substrate area ratio in a simple diode system. Coburn (10) tried to verify the area-ratio/voltage-ratio relationship, and found that it was not valid for area-ratios far from unity. Horwitz (11) made detailed measurements in a stainless steel electrode system which showed the complex relationship in Fig. 4. Godyak (12,13) has analyzed a diode system for a restricted range of conditions (frequency, pressure), and developed integral equations for the voltage ratio which must be evaluated numerically. Others (14-16) have recently attempted to model the voltage ratio relationship, with qualitative experimental agreement, but no comprehensive model has evolved as yet which can accurately predict the voltages or voltage ratios for a wide range of system geometries. Nevertheless, the simple model of Fig. 3 is still useful for qualitative understanding of multi-electrode rf discharge systems if one recognizes that 1) the capacitances determine the rf voltage division, and 2) the capacitances are proportional to electrode area and inversely proportional to the square root of peak rf sheath voltage (approximately). Figure 5 is a model of a 3-electrode system (cathode, substrate, and wall) which is applicable to most parallel-plate systems in use today. RF power is normally applied between cathode and wall electrodes, and the resulting discharge carries rf current from the cathode and divides it between the wall and substrate in some ratio, depending on the relative areas of each, and on the return path impedance from the substrate to the wall (which is usually ground). If the substrate is powered from a second generator as in Fig. 6, then the resulting current through the substrate and into the wall can be adjusted to any value depending on the relative phase and power applied, assuming that a common exciter frequency is used. If the applied substrate voltage is in phase with the cathode voltage, then the resulting rf currents will add in the plasma and flow to the wall, giving a larger wall-to-plasma voltage. If the voltage is out of phase with the cathode, then the rf current will subtract in the plasma giving a small wall-to-plasma voltage.

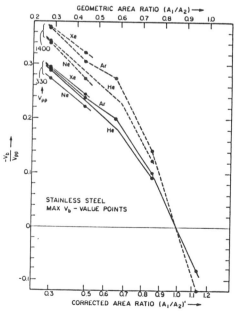

Figure 4: Electrode Voltage Ratio vs Electrode Area Ratio (Horwitz, ref. 11)

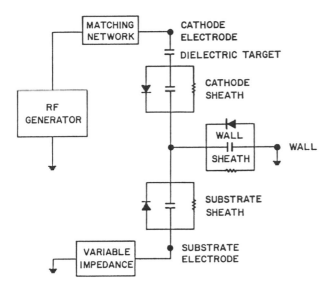

Figure 5: Model of a 3-electrode rf discharge (single generator)

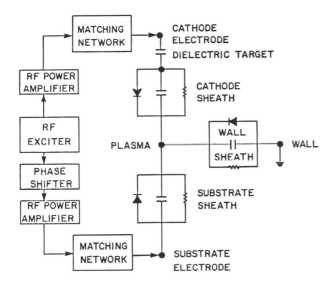

Figure 6: Model of a 3-electrode rf system (2 generators)

The important thing to understand about rf sputtering systems operating at frequencies above 1 MHz is that the voltage developed at any boundary with the plasma depends on the rf current density flowing through the boundary and on the plasma density. This rf current flows through the boundary capacitance creating a boundary rf voltage drop to the plasma. This rf voltage is rectified by the highly mobile electrons so that the average (dc) value developed is approximately equal to the peak rf voltage. Thus, the sputtering (dc) voltage is intimately related to the rf voltage at each electrode or boundary. The sputtering ions respond primarily to the dc field at the boundary, and only very weakly to the rf field. Ions gain sputtering energy up to the average dc voltage at each sheath. At higher pressures (> 50 mTorr), charge exchange collisions in the sheath cause the energy distribution to spread to lower energies, which can lower the total yield of sputtered material.

5.3 EQUIPMENT

5.3.1 System Designs

The earliest rf deposition systems in practical use were simple diode parallel-plate systems, as shown schematically in Fig. 7. Use is sometimes made of axial magnetic field to enhance the plasma density, and a frequency of 13.56 MHz is widely used for excitation because of the ease of compliance with FCC rules and ready availability of equipment. The rf power is typically connected to the cathode electrode through a cable and a matching network which serves to maximize power transfer from the rf generator.

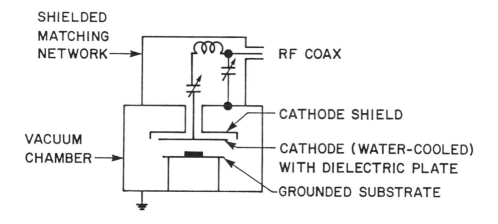

Figure 7: Early diode rf sputtering system

In a deposition system, the substrate may be placed on a grounded surface, typically at a spacing of 2 to 5 cm from the dielectric source. For some applications, it is desirable to bias (sputter-etch) the substrate during deposition, so the substrate support is constructed like a second cathode, as in Fig. 8. Cooling is often required, because of the ion and electron bombardment at the substrate, and heat transfer between the substrate and its support can be a problem.

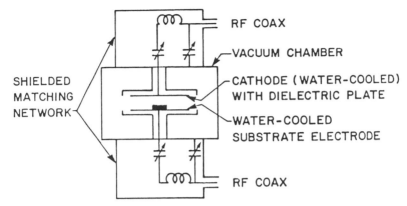

Figure 8: Substrate bias added to diode system

For rf etching purposes, rf power is applied to the substrate electrode, usually a water-cooled cathode on the bottom as in Fig. 9.   Additionally, a counter-electrode, sometimes called a "catcher" (17) is often used in close proximity opposite the substrate to be etched, in order to minimize backscattered material. The "catcher" may contain a pattern of deep holes or annular rings in which to trap sputtered material.

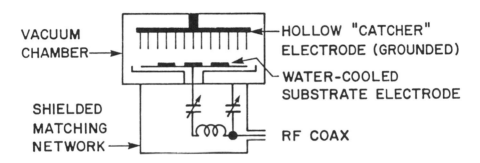

Figure 9: Sputter-etch system

As with dc sputtering systems, other geometries can be used, such as cylindrical or rectangular cathodes, but as system size increases, there is the possibility that non-uniformities in sputtering will be experienced due to either inductive voltage drops, or due to standing waves in the plasma itself. The author has had experience with a small parallel plate system at a frequency of 40 MHz, in which a non-symmetrical rf connection to the cathode resulted in a deposition profile which was non-symmetric (higher rate closer to the point of rf attachment). Also, a large cylindrical rf sputtering system with a cathode diameter of 20 cm and length 1 m was found to have a significant sputtering rate variation along the axis when used with an axial magnetic field at 13 MHz. In the case of the small parallel-plate system, the non-uniformity could be attributed to an inductive voltage drop, and in the coaxial case at lower frequency, standing waves in the plasma is the more likely reason.

An unusual rf system design was reported by Holland (18) in which the target is attached to a split cathode. The cathode is then driven by a balanced rf drive (i.e. ungrounded but equal amplitude, opposite phase) as shown schematically in Fig. 10. This arrangement allows a grounded substrate to be biased with respect to the plasma by unbalancing the drive.

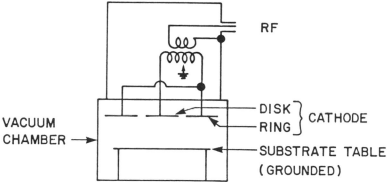

Figure 10: Balanced rf drive system

5.3.2 Cathode Design

In most systems, the target material is a plate which is thermally bonded to a water-cooled metal electrode. The bonding agent may be indium or indium-tin solder, or it may be a conductive epoxy. In some applications, a thermal grease may be used. A grounded metal shield surrounds the metal electrode at a close spacing, typically 3 mm, to prevent sputtering of the metal electrode. Often, the target plate is allowed to extend beyond the edge of the metal electrode to better shield the metal from sputtering. Alternatively, shielding can be accomplished by burying the metal electrode in a dielectric cavity as in Fig. 11 which minimizes stray capacitance. Another alternative is to incorporate the metal electrode as part of the chamber wall, as in Fig. 12. This last alternative substantially reduces stray capacitance-induced losses, especially for large diameters.

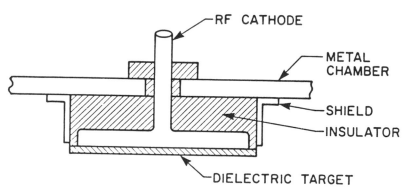

Figure 11: Dielectrically shielded cathode

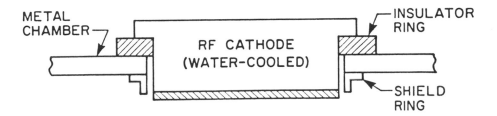

Figure 12: Drop-in rf cathode

A large amount of heat may be deposited at the target surface by the bombarding ions, so it is important to have adequate cooling. In extreme cases of high power operation, the target surface temperature may exceed the sublimation temperature (19), and material may be evaporated as well as sputtered. For this reason, with poor thermal conductors it is preferable to use a thin target, although there must be a practical compromise with the useful life of the target plate, and with the need for mechanical strength. Dielectric glasses such as SiO_2 are typically used in thicknesses of about 6 mm. Lossy materials may be destroyed by self-heating when used as an rf cathode, if not thin enough to allow adequate cooling.

5.3.3 RF Power Supply

In most modern equipment, rf power is supplied by a physically separate commercial generator, crystal-controlled, which is coupled to the vacuum deposition or etching apparatus by a coaxial cable. Since the electrical impedance of the discharge is usually much lower than the cable impedance (typically 50 ohm cable), a matching network must be provided to transform the discharge impedance to the cable impedance. This matching network is normally constructed or mounted in intimate contact with the vacuum chamber cover or plate which contains the rf electrode to allow proper shielding from stray radiation. Thus, the coaxial cable is connected to a bulkhead fitting in the shield box covering the matching network/system cover.

In the case of a separately biased substrate electrode, rf power can be supplied in a number of different ways. The most common way is to provide a separate power amplifier, driven by a common exciter, which is then coupled by rf coaxial cable to a matching network at the substrate electrode mounting plate and shielded in a manner similar to the cathode matching network (Fig. 13). This provides the ability to adjust the phase of substrate voltage relative to cathode voltage by introducing an adjustable delay-line between exciter and power amplifer, and an independent control of substrate power. It also adds a degree of rf isolation between the substrate circuit and the cathode circuit, but the two are usually coupled anyway by a common plasma.

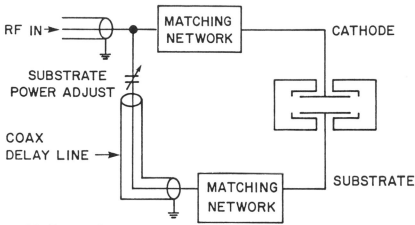

Figure 13: Power-splitting rf drive

Less expensive passive power-splitting networks such as the one shown in Fig. 13 can be used, but may result in regions of instability and very sensitive tuning due to the interdependence of cathode and substrate power. A simpler method for substrate bias adjustment which does not require a separate cable and full matching network is the tuned substrate (20) method of Fig. 14. Here there is no independent phase and magnitude adjustment, but a useful range of magnitude of substrate bias can be obtained simply by adjusting the impedance between substrate and ground. It is important to minimize the stray capacitance in the substrate assembly and to minimize wall area to get the greatest possible range of substrate bias.

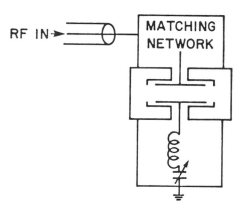

Figure 14: Tuned substrate bias adjustment

5.3.4 Matching Networks

In order to deliver rf power effectively through a coaxial transmission line, it is necessary to transform the load impedance to match the coaxial line impedance (usually 50 ohms resistive). A very commonly used network for this purpose is shown in Fig. 15. Over a wide range of frequencies, the load impedance is capacitive, dominated by the cathode sheath charge storage, and by the stray capacitances of the electrode structure itself.

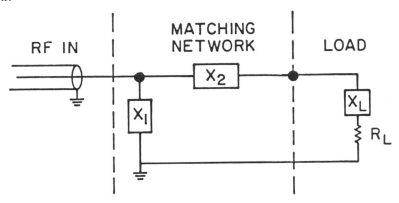

Figure 15: Common L-type matching network

The equations that predict the appropriate series and shunt elements for this matching network to transform a load whose series equivalent representation is R_L and X_L, are given as follows:

$$X_2 = -X_L + \sqrt{(R_L R_0 - R_L^2)}$$

$$X_1 = \frac{-R_0}{\sqrt{(\frac{R_0}{R_L}) - 1}}$$

R_o is the coaxial line impedance, usually 50 ohms. The elements X_1 and X_2 are as shown in Fig. 15 and are usually capacitive and inductive, respectively. The signs associated with these reactances are positive for inductive and negative for capacitive elements. It is important to note that the network cannot transform loads with resistive (series) parts which are in excess of the coaxial line impedance. This is not usually the case, but if it should be, the L-network can be reversed.

Values for the discharge load impedance have been measured by various researchers (21,22). These values can be used to predict values for the matching network, by adapting them to a specific system geometry (electrode areas, stray capacitances and inductances), and using the equations given above.

5.4 RF SPUTTER-DEPOSITION

5.4.1 Direct rf Sputter-Deposition

The widest use of rf sputter deposition has been the direct sputtering of insulating compounds, such as SiO_2, Al_2O_3, BN, Si_3N_4, Ta_2O_5, HfO_2, and other oxides and glasses. These have been studied for a variety of uses. The high dielectric constant materials are attractive for capacitors (23) and the low dielectric constant materials are useful for thin film circuit applications on silicon integrated circuits as well as on other substrates. Another common use is for protective coatings.

In many cases the target materials can be obtained in reasonably pure form as a glassy or sintered disk, which may be attached to a metal electrode as described in section 5.3.2. This is the case with SiO_2, Al_2O_3, Cr_2O_3, and glasses such as Pyrex ®, which are easily joined to a metal backing plate. In other cases, the brittleness of the target material may create mechanical problems either initially, or during use. These problems are not unique to rf sputtered materials. However, one problem that is unique to rf sputtering is the problem of dielectric heating by the rf current in the target. If the material is inherently lossy at the rf frequency used, then heat will be developed which can cause destructive failure of the target itself or of the joint to the backing plate. Materials which have been rf sputtered successfully in spite of their relatively high loss factor at 13.56 MHz are Pyrex ®, graphite, and silicon.

As with dc sputtering, argon is most frequently used as the sputtering gas for the same reasons. The mass of argon is high enough so that there is little interaction of the rf field with argon ions at 13.56 MHz. Tsui (24) has calculated this interaction and shown that light gases such as helium will interact with the rf field at 13 MHz sufficiently to cause a significant spread in the arrival energies of the ions, but not much for argon. Xenon, Neon, and Krypton have all been used by experimenters, but do not appear to have sufficiently higher sputtering yields to justify the higher costs in some cases, nor even a higher yield in others.

5.4.2 Film Composition

Since there are practically no elemental insulators of interest, most insulator sputter-deposition applications involve compounds, usually oxides or nitrides, and occasionally carbides or high resistivity semiconductor compounds where there may be significant difficulty in carrying out dc sputtering, or where the lower pressure discharge is attractive to enhance film purity and reduce backscattering. Complex compounds are rarely transferred from the target to the substrate in exactly the original composition. Nevertheless, the film composition in many cases is sufficiently close to that of the target that no adjustment is necessary for useful properties. This is the case with SiO_2 and Al_2O_3. In other cases where one component is particulary unstable, eg. glasses containing lead oxides, a significant loss of one component may be found, requiring either that the substrate be cooled, or that excess material be introduced either in the target or in the gas stream. Often, the addition of oxygen to correct stoichiometry, or for other reasons results in a reduction of the target removal rate. This is evident in the sputtering of SiO_2, Al_2O_3, and other materials. Figure 16 shows the effect of oxygen additions on the deposition rate of SiO_2 (25). This depression of deposition rate has been observed for other compounds as well (26). The mechanism has not been confirmed, but it has been suggested that the oxygen restores surface stoichiometry of the target, thereby increasing the binding energy of surface atoms compared to that of a disturbed surface.

5.4.3 Substrate Bias Effects

Bombardment of growing films is well known from dc sputtering work to be useful in controlling film properties (27), so it is no surprise that the same is true of rf sputtered films. In the case of dc sputtering, one can easily control the resputtering bias down to the floating potential (usually a few volts) with the dc power supply. In the case of rf sputtering, the actual bias between film and plasma is not easily measurable directly, and is very dependent on the chamber geometry as discussed in section 5.2.4. With a simple diode system using a large area ratio between "anode" (substrate + wall) and cathode, there will be a minimum dc bias developed providing that the substrate connection to ground (wall) is a low-inductance connection. This is not always the case. Many commercial systems have a rather long stem connection to the substrate table, and simple external "grounding" of this stem with a wire or strap does not produce the desired electrical condition. Indeed, it is sometimes possible to increase the bias by such action, because the inductance represented by the ground strap and stem actually resonates with the sheath capacitance in series to produce a large rf current flow, resulting in a large sheath voltage. Even if the substrate is dc-grounded, the plasma potential will be forced up to satisfy equilibrium conditions. For this reason, it is difficult to guarantee near-zero bombardment of the substrate in an rf sputter-deposition system, as might be desirable for depositing crystalline materials.

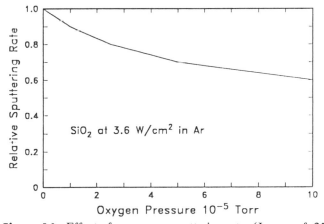

Figure 16: Effect of oxygen on sputtering rate (Jones, ref. 25)

More often, however, it is desirable to increase the bias at the substrate, which can be done by the methods mentioned in section 3.1. In the case of rf sputtered SiO_2, substrate bias has been found to improve dielectric breakdown (28), decrease chemical etch rate (26), and can be used for planarization (29). Also, bias has been found to relate to stress (30), and to trapped gas (31).

5.4.4 Material Transport and Uniformity

The physics governing the emission and transport of material is the same for both rf and dc sputtering. With rf sputtering, however, the lower pressure range which is normally used reduces the number of collisions in transit, so that the efficiency of transport is usually higher than for dc diode sputtering and the energy of arrival of species is higher because of the fewer collisions.

The use of an axial magnetic field to enhance the plasma density has been found to increase the rate of deposition (3) for a fixed rf power input. This is due to operating at a more energy-efficient point of the sputter yield vs energy curve (lower voltage). However, the axial magnetic field has been observed to create a radially non-uniform plasma density, which results in more intense plasma near the perimeter of a circular target. The target becomes more like a ring source as a result, and the deposition pattern reflects that change, rising toward the edge. The pattern can be flattened by increasing the separation between target and substrate, which creates more edge loss. If the system is scaled to a larger diameter, then the required spacing for best uniformity is increased. This is not true of the case without axial magnetic field, where the optimum spacing is almost independent of target diameter.

5.5 SPUTTER ETCHING APPLICATIONS

5.5.1 Comparison to dc Sputter-Etching

Sputter-etching using rf power removes material by the same fundamental mechanisms as with dc sputter-etching. However, rf sputter-etching can be used with insulators as well as with metals, and as with rf sputter-deposition, lower pressures can be used, allowing easier transport of material (less backscattering (32)). The equipment used is different only in that the cathode should be adequately shielded and stray capacitance should be minimized. For minimum backscattering, a "catcher" plate (17) may be used, spaced as closely as possible. The "catcher" should have many deep cavities, such as a honeycomb structure, and should be well grounded with low-inductance wide straps or foils to prevent self-bias.

5.5.2 Surface Cleaning

Probably the simplest and earliest applications of rf sputter-cleaning is the removal of surface oxides on metals for contact purposes. This has been shown to be exceptionally effective for making low-resistance contact between successive aluminum thin-film wiring layers on semiconductor devices. Bauer (33) showed that the measured distribution of contact resistances shifted dramatically downward when rf sputter-cleaning was done in-situ prior to evaporation of the next aluminum contact film. This has been shown to be due to the removal of a native oxide layer of 2 to 3 nm thickness. The residual gas level present during the sputter-cleaning and immediately after is critical, as the water-vapor or oxygen can quickly re-form the native oxide.

There are many other examples of the use of rf sputter-cleaning for both oxide removal and for adhesion of subsequent layers. Since the treatment is usually for a short time, cooling of the substrate is not necessary, but can be a problem in some cases of temperature-sensitive substrates. The author has found that a temperature of 200 °C is reached in a time of 3 minutes for silicon substrates 0.38 mm thick subjected to an input rf power density of 0.4 W/cm^2 in 8 mT Ar.

5.5.3 Patterning

The sputter-yield of most materials is not widely different, so that it is necessary usually to use a masking material that has a thickness comparable to the thickness of the material being etched, or greater. Sputter-yields of a number of materials of interest is shown in Table 1 (34). Some of the material will be re-deposited on the mask edges, and can remain when the mask is removed if it is sufficiently thick and survives the mask removal process. For this reason, patterning of thick layers by sputter-etching is not usually practical and is better accomplished by reactive ion etching. In addition, heat developed by the sputter-etching can harden the mask material and make it difficult to remove.

Table 1: Relative sputtering rates of some materials (34).

Material	Sputter Etch Rate $(Ar^+, 500\ eV, 1\ mA/cm^2)$ $\mathring{A}/\min$
Al_2O_3	80-130
Cr_2O_3	50
FeO	450-490
SiO_2	260-400
Y_2O_3	75
AZ1350 resist	200-250
In_2O_3/SnO_2	80-200
Si_3N_4	250
$LiNbO_3$	390-420
Si	200-380

5.5.4 Uniformity

In general, uniform removal across the diameter of a parallel-plate diode etcher is readily obtained, provided that the pressure-spacing product is not too low. The usual problem is near the edge of the electrode, where the ground shield configuration can increase the etch rate by "focussing" the ion flux. Extending the ground shield above the planc of the electrode by a few mm usually improves the situation. This cuts off the "focussed" ions.

5.6 PRACTICAL MATTERS

5.6.1 Power Measurements and Power Loss

Power is usually measured with coaxial line elements in the coaxial feed to the matching network. Of necessity, the power measurement includes losses in the matching network which can sometimes be significant. Excessive power loss can occur in rf sputtering equipment, usually due to poor matching network design, possibly aggravated by high stray capacitance in the cathode design. Loss is almost always concentrated in the matching network inductance, although connecting straps and associated hardware may also be a problem. It is common practice to water-cool the inductor in high power applications. In general, one should avoid the use of stainless steel screws in any rf current-carrying path. Brass screws are usually quite adequate. The inductor carries not only the discharge rf current, but also the rf current to the electrode shield. The shield current is often much greater than the discharge current.

A reasonable measurement of the loss can be made using an rf voltage probe on the cathode connection and plotting power input vs rf voltage with the discharge on and without a discharge. A discharge can be suppressed by working at atmospheric pressure or at very low pressure, although it is sometimes difficult to completely stop the discharge at the chamber base pressure. An example of such a measurement is shown in Fig. 17 for a small sputtering system. The difference between the curves at constant voltage is (approximately) the net power delivered to the discharge, and the lower curve represents the power loss at a given voltage.

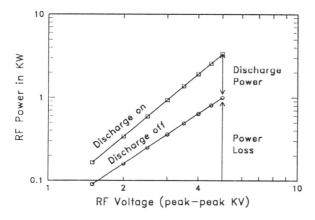

Figure 17: Measurement of rf Power Losses

5.6.2 Current Measurement

It is not possible to measure the ion current in an rf discharge directly in the cathode circuit, since the dielectric target is insulating and it is masked by displacement current and electron current. Langmuir probes have been used by many investigators, but it is difficult to prevent rf current flow in the probe circuit. A small probe area and effective decoupling of the discharge from the wires are essential. To this end, thick glass tubing can be used for shielding the wires. Equally important are a very low capacitance feedthrough and a good rf inductor in series to prevent rf current flow to ground in the probe circuit.

The ion current density can be estimated from the power delivered to the discharge and the sheath voltages, assuming a simple diode system of unequal areas. A rf probe in the plasma can sense the rf plasma potential. Power can be apportioned to each sheath according to the sheath rf voltage and the sheath area, correcting for voltage drop in the dielectric target. Then ion current should be approximately the ratio of sheath power density divided by sheath peak voltage.

RF current transformers can be obtained to measure rf current flowing into the cathode or substrate electrode terminals. Using this current, and subtracting stray capacitance currents (from discharge-off measurements) gives the net rf current into the electrode. RF current into the cathode sheath can be used to calculate the rf voltage drop in the dielectric target plate.

5.6.3 Voltage Measurement

Sometimes a dc voltmeter is connected to the cathode circuit through a suitable rf isolation inductor. This voltage may indicate the target surface potential through surface leakage at the target edge, but it is often unreliable for small shield gaps.

RF voltage is usually measured with a capacitance divider probe located as close as possible to the rf feedthrough. The voltage so measured has two principal errors; first the rf drop in the target plate and second the inductive voltage drop in the conductor between the measuring point and the cathode electrode. The voltage drop in the target plate is a capacitive drop and therefore normally adds to the target surface potential, and the voltage drop in the conductor is an inductive drop which normally reduces the rf voltage. If the conductor is long enough, then it can actually reduce the voltage to zero, or even reverse the phase. Calibration for these errors can be done but involves making internal rf voltage measurements. Many applications do not require absolute calibration, so that the rf voltage measurement is used as a control monitor to reproduce conditions.

5.6.4 Rate Measurement

Deposition rates are usually not possible to measure in an rf system with a conventional crystal rate monitor, unless the monitor can be closely coupled to ground and provided with special shielding. If the substrate is biased, such a monitor does not represent the net flux of material, but can be proportional to the incident flux. Another method useful for transparent films on reflective substrates is to measure reflectance variation to sense the optical thickness, such as is commonly done in the optical coating industry. This method is non-intrusive and can be quite accurate.

5.6.5 RF Leakage

All rf sputtering or etching equipment should be provided with complete electrostatic confinement of the discharge and its electrical connections to prevent unauthorized or unsafe leakage of rf energy. This usually means that the vacuum chamber should be metal, or surrounded by metal screen, and that the matching network components be contained in a metal box in intimate contact with the chamber walls or electrode plate. A low-inductance path must be provided for rf return currents within the discharge chamber. If, for example, a substrate electrode is attached to a chamber bottom plate, which is prevented by an O-ring from making metal-to-metal contact with the chamber, then rf currents cannot return inside the vacuum chamber to the cathode plate, and will seek alternative paths externally, usually resulting in instrument rf noise as well as perceptible rf voltage differences at the gap.

5.7 REFERENCES

1. G.S.Anderson, W.N.Mayer and G.K.Wehner J. Appl. Phys. 33: 2291 (1962). J. Vac. Sci. Tech. 4: 33 (1967).

2. G.K.Wehner Advances in Electronics and Electron Physics, vol. 7 (Academic Press Inc., New York) p. 239 (1955).

3. P.D.Davidse and L.I.Maissel Trans. 3rd Int. Vac. Cong. 3: (1965).

4.   L.I. Maissel and R. Glang, Handbook of Thin Film Technology (McGraw Hill, New York, 1970).

5.   J.L. Vossen "Control of Film Properties by rf-Sputtering Techniques" J. Vac. Sci. Tech. 8: 5 (1971)

6.   B.N. Chapman, Glow Discharge Processes; Sputtering and Plasma Etching (John Wiley & Sons, New York, 1980).

7.   G.N. Jackson, "R.F. Sputtering" Thin Solid Films 5: 209-246 (1970).

8.   H.S.Butler and G.S.Kino Phys. Fluids 67: 1346-1355 (1963).

9.   H.R. Koenig and L.I. Maissel, "Application of RF Discharges to Sputtering" IBM J. Res. Dev. 14: 168-171 (1970).

10. J.W. Coburn and E. Kay, J. Appl. Phys. 43: 4965 (1972).

11. C.M. Horwitz "Rf Sputtering-Voltage Division Between Two Electrodes" J. Vac. Sci. Technol. A1: 60-68 (1983).

12. V.A. Godyak and A.A. Kuzovnikov, Sov. J. Plasma Phys. 1: 276-280 (1975).

13. V.A. Godyak, "Steady-State Low Pressure RF Discharge" Sov. J. Plasma Physics 2: 78-85 (1976).

14. S.E.Savas, "Estimation of Ion Impact Energies and Electrode Self-bias Voltage in Capacitive rf Discharges" MRS Symposium, Anaheim (1987).

15. M.S. Barnes, T.J. Colter and M.E. Elta, "Large-signal Time Domain Modelling of Low-pressure rf Glow Dischages" J. Appl. Phys. 61: 81-89 (1987).

16. K. Suzuki, K. Ninomiya, S. Nishimatsu, J.W. Thoman Jr. and J.I.Steinfeld "Analytical Investigation of Plasma and Electrode Potentials in a Diode Type rf Discharge" Jap.J.Appl.Phys. 25: 1569-1574 (1986).

17. L.I. Maissel, C.L. Standley and L.V. Gregor, "Sputter Etching of Heterogeneous Surfaces" IBM J. Res. and Dev. 16: 67 (1972).

18. L. Holland, T.I.Putner and G.N.Jackson J. Sci. Instruments 1: 32 (1968).

19. D.H. Grantham, E.L. Pradis and D.J. Quinn, "High-Rate rf Sputtering System" J. Vac. Sci. Tech. 7: 343-346 (1970).

20. J.S. Logan, "Control of rf Sputtered Film Properties Through Substrate Tuning" IBM J. Res. Develop. 14: 172-175 (1970).

21. J.S. Logan, N.M. Mazza and P.D. Davidse, "Electrical Characterization of Radio-Frequency Sputtering Gas Discharge" J. Vac. Sci. Tech. 6: 120-123 (1969).

22. A.J. van Roosmalen, W.G.M. van den Hoek and H. Kalter, "Electrical Properties of Planar rf Discharges for Dry Etching" J. Appl. Phys. 58: 653-658 (1985).

23. W.B. Pennebaker, "RF Sputtered Strontium Titanate Films" IBM J. Res. Dev. 13: 686-695 (1969).

24. R.T.C. Tsui, "Calculation of Ion Bombarding Energy and Its Distribution in rf Sputtering" Phys. Rev. 168: 107-113 (1968).

25. R.E. Jones, H.F. Winters and L.I. Maissel, "Effect of Oxygen on the rf Sputtering Rate of SiO_2" J. Vac. Sci. Tech. 5: 84 (1968).

26. D.M. Mattox and G.J. Kominiak "Physical Properties of Thick Sputter-Deposited Glass Films" J. Electrochem. Soc. 120: 1535-1539 (1973).

27. L.I. Maissel and P.M. Schaible, "Thin Films Deposited by Bias Sputtering" J. Appl. Phys. 36: 237-242 (1965).

28. H.-U. Schreiber and E. Froschle, "High Quality RF-Sputtered Silicon Dioxide Layers" J. Electrochem. Soc. 123: 30-33 (1976).

29. C.Y. Ting, V.J. Vivalda and H.G. Schaeffer, "Study of Planarized Sputter-deposited SiO_2" J. Vac. Sci. Tech. 15: (1978).

30. J.S. Logan, F. Jones, J. Costable and J.E. Lucy, "Radio Frequency Sputter Deposition of SiO_2 Films at High Rate" J. Vac. Sci. Technol. A5: 1879-1882 (1987).

31. W. Hoffmeister and M. Zuegel, "Determination of the Argon Content of Sputtered SiO_2 Films by X-Ray Fluorescence" Thin Solid Films 3: 35-40 (1969).

32. J.L. Vossen, J.J. O'Neill Jr., K.M. Finlayson and L.J. Royer, "Backscattering of Material Emitted from RF-Sputtering Targets" RCA Review 31: 293-305 (1970).

33. H.J. Bauer, "In-situ Sputter Cleaning of Contacts for Multilayer Chip Metallization" Proc. of Eighth Int. Vacuum Congress 1: 649 (1980).

34. "Periodic Table of the Elements with Ion Beam Etch and Sputter Rates" Commonwealth Scientific Corp., Alexandria, Virginia (1985).

6

Magnetron Plasma Deposition Processes

Stephen M. Rossnagel

6.1 INTRODUCTION

Magnetron sputtering devices have become very widely used and accepted in the past decade. Magnetrons are routinely used to rapidly deposit thin metal films in a broad range of applications, from architectural glass and food packaging to thin film microelectronics. Magnetron-like effects are also used in high-rate sputter and reactive etching devices. Magnetrons, as they are currently used for plasma-based sputtering applications, were developed approximately 20 years ago. Perhaps the most useful description available has been the work of Thornton and Penfold (1), in Vossen and Kern's book dating from the late '70s.

Magnetrons are a class of cold cathode discharge devices used in generally a diode mode. The plasma is initiated between the cathode and the anode at pressures in the mTorr range by the application of a high voltage, which can be either dc or rf. The plasma is sustained by the ionization caused by secondary electrons emitted from the cathode due to ion bombardment which are accelerated into the plasma across the cathode sheath. What differentiates a magnetron cathode from a conventional diode cathode is the presence of a magnetic field. The magnetic field in the magnetron is oriented parallel to the cathode surface. The local polarity of the magnetic field is oriented such that the ExB drift paths of the emitted secondary electrons form a closed loop (Fig. 1). Due to the increased confinement of the secondary electrons in this ExB drift loop compared to a dc or rf diode device, the plasma density will be much higher, often by an order of magnitude or more, than a conventional rf or dc diode plasma. The result of the high plasma density and its proximity to the cathode is a high current, relatively low voltage discharge. Typical discharge parameters for a magnetron might be a voltage of 500V and a current of 5 Amperes, whereas a non-magnetized diode might operate at 2500V and 0.5 amperes.

Due to the effective trapping of the energetic secondaries close to the cathode, a high plasma density can be sustained at significantly lower chamber pressures than a similar power rf or dc diode plasma. A magnetron operates at a pressure ranging from about 1-2 mTorr (0.3 Pa) to 30-40 mTorr (4-5.5 Pa), whereas a typical rf diode might operate at 15-200 mTorr (2 to 25 Pa). The low operating pressure results in a significant reduction in gas scattering between the sputtered atoms and the background gas. The result of this reduction is an effective increase in the average kinetic energy of the sputtered atom (less thermalization) and an increase in the probability of atom transport from the cathode to the substrate.

The result of the high discharge currents is the ability to sputter the cathode at a high rate. Deposition rates on surfaces within 5-10 cm. from the cathode may be as high as several microns/minute for high sputter yield materials. Usually, the typical limiting factor to the maximum deposition rate in a magnetron device is the ability to cool the cathode.

Magnetrons have been developed in a wide range of geometries; each of which satisfies the requirement that the ExB drift path forms a closed loop. Three basic classes of geometries exist: the planar, the cylindrical and the conical designs. The planar design (Fig. 1(a)) is available in a circular geometry at diameters of from 5 to a few 10's of cm. The rectangular or "racetrack" magnetron (Fig. 1(b)) has been developed at lengths exceeding the meter range. The cylindrical geometry is characterized by a central, cylindrical cathode with an axial magnetic field. (Fig. 1(c)). The electric field in this case is radial, and the resultant ExB drift path forms a band around the cathode. These devices need not have a circular cross-section, but have been designed in a flattened mode, where the original circular cross-section is replaced by an almost rectangular cross-section with rounded ends. The third geometry is the conical design (Fig. 1 (d)), which is somewhat similar to the circular planar device. These devices have a cathode surface which is tilted slightly and typically have an opening on the central axis. Often an anode of some sort is placed in this central opening, which helps eliminate the bombardment of the sample with energetic electrons.

While new magnetron designs and applications have been continuously developed over the past 15 years, relatively little work has been published on the fundamental aspects of magnetron operation. This may be due in part to the high level of some of the earlier publications (see ref. 1, for example). It may also be due to the sophisticated engineering work that has gone into the design of magnetron cathodes: i.e., the cathodes function very well, and little effort has gone into process diagnostics. It becomes apparent, after closer examination, that aspects of how magnetrons operate can be exceedingly complex. The various processes of plasma formation, energetic bombardment of the cathode, transport of the sputtered atoms and film deposition are often inter-related in non-trivial ways. One of the goals of this chapter is to identify some of these interactions.

Magnetrons are also routinely used to reactively deposit compound films, such as nitrides and oxides. This topic will be treated at great length in Chap. 9, and will not be included here.

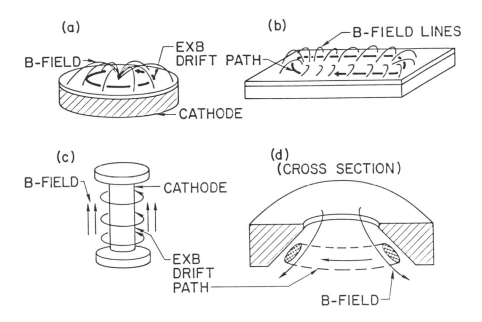

Figure 1: (a) circular planar magnetron, (b) rectangular planar magnetron, (c) cylindrical post magnetron, and (d) conical magnetron.

To define more closely some of the basic physical effects present in magnetron sputtering devices, numerous diagnostic experiments have been reported. Among the techniques used are optical emission spectrometry (2,3) mass spectrometry, the use of electrostatic (Langmuir) (4-6) and magnetic probes (7), gas pressure probes (8,9) energetic neutral and negative ion detectors (10,11), current collection techniques both at the cathode and the film surfaces (12), measurements of the deposition and composition of films around the chamber (13,14), electrical measurements of the current and voltage of the discharge itself (1,15,16) , measurement of the energy distribution of the incident, bombarding ions (17), measurement of the kinetic energy or effective heating energy of the depositing atoms (18,19), as well as other less direct techniques. The combination of results from each of these experiments will be useful in discussing the inter-relations among the various phenomena in the magnetron device.

It has been popular in the past to break up the sputter deposition of films into the sputtering process at the cathode, transport from the cathode to the substrate, and the deposition process at the substrate. Indeed, this book is partitioned along these same lines. These topics are then treated individually and independently. The results of some of these diagnostic measurements suggest that this type of delineation may not be appropriate, at least under some conditions, and that significant inter-relationships are present between these three general categories.

6.2. EXPERIMENTS

For the purposes of this discussion, the general experiment to be described is a conventional, circular, planar magnetron cathode. Some of the reported experiments, however, have used other cathode arrangements, such as the cylindrical post cathodes or conical (S-Gun-type) of cathode. In general, the results should be fairly consistent from one type of cathode to another. A metal target is mounted on the cathode (typically Cu, Al, W, Mo, etc.) which is sputtered in a dc mode from an inert gas plasma of typically Ar, Ne or Kr. The cathode dimensions range from 5 to 50 cm. diameter. The background pressure of the gas is generally a few to a few tens of mTorr (.3 to 4 Pa) and is supplied through mass-flow controllers. For many of these experiments, the chamber has been stripped of additional fixtures, such as shutters, ground shields and other shielding. In addition, in many cases a separate anode has not been used, effectively causing the chamber walls to function as the anode. The cathode is supplied by a highly regulated DC supply, operated in constant voltage, current or power modes. The chamber in which the magnetron is located is large compared to the dimensions of the magnetron.

In normal operation, the chamber is evacuated to 10^{-7} Torr or so, and backfilled to the desired mTorr pressure. A negative voltage on the order of a few hundred volts is applied to the cathode. This leads rapidly to the formation of a plasma, from which several amperes of ions (for the larger cathodes) are accelerated to the cathode, causing physical sputtering. The sputtered atoms then transit the plasma, and may eventually form films on nearby surfaces.

6.2.1 Sputtering at the Cathode Surface

Physical sputtering by energetic ions has been the subject of an earlier chapter (Chap. 3). Magnetrons typically operate with either an applied dc or an effective dc bias (rf mode) of a few hundred volts. Using an inert gas, such as Ar, which will typically be singly ionized, the ions bombarding the cathode are then at energies equivalent to the discharge voltage (in eV). At these energies, the sputtering process is primarily by means of direct knock-on collisions. Sputter yields for most gas-cathode combinations range from 0.1 to 3. This is indicative or a relatively inefficient process: for each incident ion of, let's say, 500 eV, one or two atoms with an average energy of 6-10 eV are ejected. A large fraction of the incident energy is lost to cathode heating. In general, the functional limit to high power, high rate magnetron sputtering is almost always the ability to cool the cathode. Given a maximum water flow-rate and a few simple approximations, the maximum deposition rate in a system can be estimated simply from the consideration of cathode cooling and the melting or damage point of the cathode.

There are several other significant effects that may be observed at the cathode. The first is due to the contamination or poisoning of the cathode when used in a reactive gas. If the gas reacts with the cathode to form a stable, or low sputter yield compound (such as an oxide), the sputtering and electrical characteristics of the discharge will be changed dramatically. This topic will be discussed more fully in Chap. 9. The second major effect is often observed when sputtering from alloy or compound targets. Due, not only to the difference in the sputtering yield of the constituents, but also to thermodynamic considerations, the composition of the target can change dramatically from bulk. This effect has been discussed at length in Chap. 4.

A third, more subtle modification of the cathode may occur due to gas-scattering induced redeposition of the sputtered atoms back onto the cathode surface. In an alloy, depending on the relative masses of the sputtered atoms, as well as the chamber pressure, gas composition and discharge power, a non-stochiometric redeposition of sputtered atoms may over time subtly alter the target composition. This is likely to be most significant is cases where one component of the alloy has a much different mass than the other component, such as AlCu or TiW.

6.2.2 Gas Rarefaction Effects

One effect of the rather large sputtered particle fluxes present near a magnetron cathode is to perturb the local background gas. Hoffman first systematically studied this effect with observations on the non-uniformity of the particle density and direction, designated as the sputtering wind (8). In that study, the pressure increase observed in the static (non-pumped) mode was indicative of gas heating within the chamber. In the dynamic, pumped mode, a decrease in chamber pressure was noted, also indicative of increases in gas temperature (and hence effective pumping speed). Earlier indications also pointed to an effect of the discharge on the effective gas density in the cathode region (20). A systematic study of the effect of the energetic particle species in the magnetron on the gas density and temperature has shown large changes in the gas density as a function of the power (or current) of the magnetron discharge (9). The gas density was sampled by a tube placed parallel to the magnetron cathode, located a distance of a few centimeters from the cathode. The apparent pressure observed in the tube can be converted to a gas density using the thermal transpiration model of Takaishi and Sensui (21). As a function of increasing magnetron discharge current, the gas density in the near cathode region falls drastically (Fig 2.) although the chamber density is unperturbed. (The chamber is large compared to the size of the cathode.)

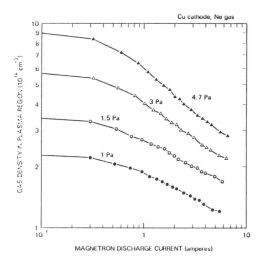

Figure 2: Gas density in the plasma region calculated from measured pressure and model of Takaishi and Sensui (21) for a Cu cathode and Ne gas.

The reduction in gas density is consistent with an increase in the gas temperature, caused by the various energetic processes occurring in the magnetron plasma. The two most likely sources for the energy are the energetic sputtered flux from the cathode and incident, bombarding ions which are reflected and neutralized at the cathode surface. The magnitude of the density reduction is dependent on the background gas species, and also on the cathode material, and tends to be largest for high mass gas atoms and high sputter yield targets. The momentum-transfer cross section for the sputtered atoms with kinetic energy of a few eV is a factor of 5-10X larger than for the energetic reflected neutrals from the cathode, whose energy is in the several hundred eV range (22). The mean free path for the sputtered atoms is in the 1-5 cm range at chamber pressures of 30 to 5 mTorr, which is generally smaller than the cathode-to-sample distances in many systems. This suggests that the energetic sputtered flux is the dominant source for the gas heating and that the reflected neutrals from the cathode are more likely to travel to the sample surface or chamber walls.

A model was suggested for the gas heating induced by the thermalization of the energetic, sputtered atom flux (9). The model calculated the effective gas temperature in the cathode region for a known sputtering flux (as a function of discharge current), allowing the energy to be thermally conducted away by the gas to the chamber walls. The model reduced at large discharge currents to:

$$n_H = (\frac{2n_oT_o\pi fK}{E_aY_v\sigma})^{0.5} \times I^{-0.5} \qquad (1)$$

where n_H is the gas density in the plasma region, I is the discharge current, n_o is the original chamber gas density, T_o is the wall temperature, K is the thermal conductivity of the gas, E_a is the average energy per sputtered atom, Y_v is the voltage-dependant sputter yield, σ is the cross-section for momentum transfer of the sputtered atom, and f is a constant indicating how many mean-free-paths were considered as the thermalization distance. A value of f = 3 was used.

This relation suggests that gas species with high thermal conductivities (He and Ne) will show significantly less density reduction as a function of discharge current, as the energy is more efficiently coupled away to the walls. Also, cathode species with large sputter yields or large average kinetic energy for the sputtered atoms will show significantly more density change with increasing current. This was confirmed for a range of materials and gases (9). The model was used to predict the density changes as a function of increased discharge current by simple substitution of values. The results, shown in Fig. 3, are suggestive that the thermalization of the energetic, sputtered flux is indeed the cause of the significant density changes observed.

The thermalization process, or the cooling of the energetic, sputtered atoms by gas collisions, has been treated by means of calculation and experiment. One interesting experiment measured the Doppler broadening of the emission from the sputtered metal atoms as a function of distance from the cathode (19). The results were generally consistent with the 2 theoretical models available at the time. It should be noted, however, that each of the theoretical treatments in the past has not accounted for the major changes observed in gas temperature and density observed more recently.

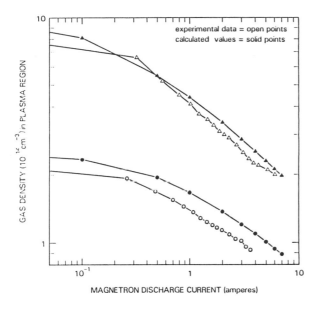

Figure 3: Comparison of experimental data and the thermal conduction model for the case of a Cu cathode and Ar gas. The sampling position was 5.3 cm from the cathode.

6.2.3 Plasma Measurements:

As listed above, a long list of plasma diagnostic measurements have been reported. Rather than exhaustively chronicle each report, a short list or representative studies will be discussed.

Measurements of the electron temperature and density have been made with small Langmuir probes inserted into the plasma (4-6) In one of these studies, the probes were oriented perpendicular to the cathode surface, and scanned up to the sheath edge (Fig. 4) The results showed electron temperatures in the 2-10 eV range, and electron densities in the 10^{10} to 10^{11}cm^{-3} range for low discharge currents. At constant current, these results were strongly dependant on the gas pressure. The electron temperature decreased as pressure was increased, while the electron density increased with increasing pressure. Few measurements were taken at high power, due to thermal damage of the probe. It was not possible to sample a broad range in discharge currents without the use of several probes of varying dimensions. Calculations of the discharge current, using the measured electron temperature and density and the pre-sheath Bohm criteria, were consistent to the experimental results, within experimental error. This suggests that the plasmas are bounded by conventional positive space-charge sheaths.

A magnetron is characterized by an ExB drift current, located near the cathode surface. The magnitude of this drift current has been measured by observing the magnetic field induced by the current loop in a circular, planar device (7). The magnitude of the drift current is typically 3-9 times the total discharge current, and depends on cathode species, gas species and chamber pressure (Fig. 5). This result is consistent with Bohm diffusion, rather than classical collision-dominated electron diffusion across magnetic fields, being the dominant charge-transport mechanism.

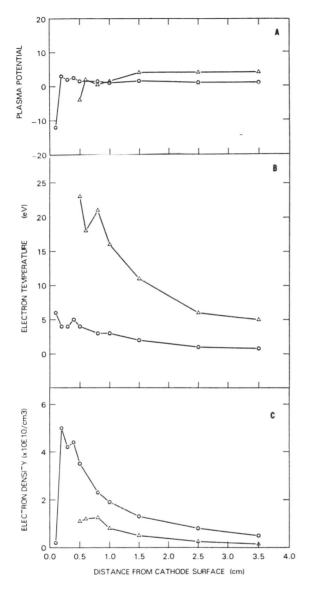

Figure 4: Results of Langmuir probe measurements in a magnetron discharge at 5 and 30 mTorr as a function of distance from the cathode.

The sheath thickness was measured roughly with the Langmuir probe. However, a more accurate measurement has been made using a long-focal length, traveling microscope. This device was focussed to the center of the etch track, oriented parallel to the cathode surface. The apparent dark space thickness could then be measured with the graticle, and calibrated against an object of known size. The dark space thickness was found to decrease rapidly as a function of increasing discharge power (23). In particular, a large, exponential dependance of this thickness on discharge voltage was observed, also dependent on the chamber pressure (Fig. 6).

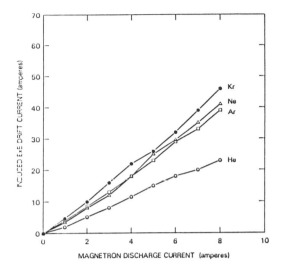

Figure 5: Induced drift current as a function of discharge current for a circular planar magnetron for inert gas species at 20 mTorr with a W cathode.

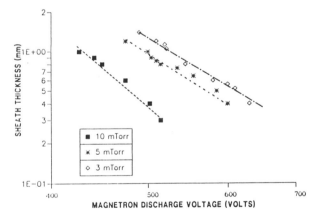

Figure 6: The natural log of the optically measured sheath thickness as a function of the natural log of the discharge voltage for three pressures of Ar.

From this data, the discharge voltage and sheath thickness can be related by: $d = cV^{-m}$, where c is a constant and m is an exponent between -3 and -6. The sheath thickness, current and voltage in a magnetron would be expected to follow Child's Law, which is of the form:

$$I \propto \frac{V^{3/2}}{d^2} \tag{2}$$

When the voltage dependance of the sheath is substituted into Eqn. (2) a relation is found

$$I \propto kV^n \tag{3}$$

where n is on the range of 7.5 to 13.5 for this case. This relation is quite similar to the empirical current-voltage relations observed in magnetrons.

6.2.4 Interactions: Effects on Plasma

The significant modification of the gas density near the cathode due to the energetic sputtered atoms has implications to both the deposition process as well as to the plasma. In particular, it was first suggested by Hoffman that this phenomena should have an effect on the current-voltage relation in the magnetron (8). The probability of ionization of a gas atom, whether by an energetic secondary electron from the cathode or by an electron from the tail of the Maxwellian distribution, will be directly proportional to the local gas density. As that density is reduced due to rarefaction by the thermalization of the hot sputtered atoms, increased discharge currents must require additional energy, as the plasma is becoming effectively more resistive.

In addition, the results of electrical and optical measurements on the plasma described earlier suggest that the plasma is a conventional space-charge limited plasma whose primary electron conduction process is Bohm Diffusion, rather than the classical collision-dominated electron conduction process across field lines. Bohm Diffusion is characterized by collective, turbulent motions of the electrons. The apparent motion of the secondary electrons in a magnetron, therefore, is probably not a simple cycloidal hopping of the electron around the ExB drift path, but more probably a turbulent, buffeted, attenuated drift as the energetic secondary electron rapidly loses its energy sustaining the electron temperature of the plasma. It is then possible that a significant number of the ionizing collisions in the plasma occur between electrons in the tail of the Maxwellian distribution and gas atoms. The probability of this type of collision has been calculated, and can be compared to the discharge current, as recombination at these pressures and plasma densities is low.

The discharge current can then be approximated as: (16)

$$I \propto 2n_e \, n_g \, \sigma \, (m/2\pi kT_e)^{0.5} v_i^2 \exp(-mv_i^2/2kT_e) \tag{4}$$

where v_i is the minimum electron velocity for ionization, n_e is the electron density, kT_e is the electron temperature and m is the electron mass. The current to the cathode can also be approximated by Bohm pre-sheath flow. The current density of ions to the sheath edge is given by: (24)

$$j = 0.6n_e(kT_e/m_i)^{0.5} \tag{5}$$

where m_i is the ion mass. The result of this type of calculation is a relation between the local gas density and the electron temperature and density. Combining these relations leads to an inter-relation between the electron temperature and the gas density of the form:

$$n_g = \frac{G}{\sigma v_i^2 (m_i m)^{0.5}} kT_e \exp\left(\frac{mv_i^2}{2kT_e}\right) \qquad (6)$$

where G is now a geometrical constant related to the cathode size.

The discharge voltage can be described in terms of discharge current and the plasma impedance, which was found to be related to Bohm Diffusion. The voltage is found to increase as a function of the square root of the electron temperature. A comparison of the calculated and experimental discharge voltages is shown in Fig. 7 (16).

The magnetron plasma can be viewed in somewhat dynamic terms, effectively dependant on the interaction of the sputtered atoms on the background gas and the plasma. At a given discharge current (i.e. ion flux to the cathode) there is an emerging flux of energetic, several eV sputtered atoms which enters the plasma region near the cathode. As a result of collisions between these sputtered atoms and the background gas, the net, local gas density is rarefied from its original, pre-plasma value. Therefore, the electron temperature of the plasma must be sufficiently high (at this current) to cause a level of ionization consistent with the discharge current. To increase the discharge current requires overcoming the additional rarefaction caused by the additional sputtered atoms at higher current. This is done by adding additional energy to the plasma through a higher voltage on the cathode. This relatively simplistic, yet consistent process, allows a number of conclusions and predictions to be made about the operating levels of a magnetron device and the effects of changing pressure, cathode or gas species, system geometry, magnetic field, etc.

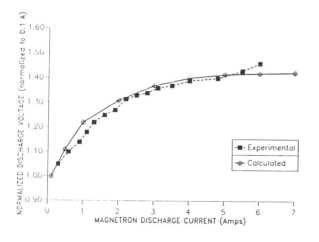

Figure 7: Observed and calculated relative voltage increases as a function of magnetron current for the case of Ar gas and a Cu Cathode at a pressure of 30 mTorr. The curves are normalized to the experimental "turn-on" voltage, which is the minimum stable voltage for operation of the discharge.

The sputter yield is quite dependent on the cathode material. Some materials, such as Cu or Au, have relatively high yields at ion energies of a few hundred eV. Other materials, often the refractory materials or compounds, have relatively low yields. In addition, not only is the yield strongly dependent on the gas species (and mass), but the thermal conductivity of the gas can vary dramatically with gas choice. Combining these effects, the expected flux of sputtered atoms as well as the effect of those atoms on the local gas density near the cathode should be strongly dependent on the choice of gas and cathode species. However, using the model described above (Eq. 1), the magnitude of the gas rarefaction should be easily predicted.

We have suggested that the rate of ionization of the background gas, and hence the discharge impedance and voltage will be strongly perturbed by this effect. In cases where the gas rarefaction effect is strongest (high sputter yields, or low thermal conductivity of the gas), the voltage should rise to a larger degree with increasing current than in equivalent cases with smaller gas rarefaction effects. As a means of comparison, consider the generally accepted empirical current-voltage relation often used with magnetrons (1)

$$I = k V^n \tag{3}$$

where k is a constant and n is an exponent in the range of 5 to 20 or so. In cases where the voltage increases slowly with current, the exponent, n, is large.

Following the discussion of voltage increases related to the magnitude of the gas rarefaction, the exponent, n, should be large in cases of relatively low gas rarefaction, and small in cases of high levels of rarefaction. An example is for the case of sputtering Cu and Al in Ar. Due to the higher sputter yield of Cu, the exponent in the I-V relation should be smaller for Cu than for Al. This is indeed the case, as shown in Fig. 8. Similar arguments can be made for a variation in either gas species or chamber pressure. In each case the general result observed is that large voltage increases (with increasing current) correlate with a high level of gas rarefaction due to the thermalization of the sputtered atoms.

An extreme case of this can be seen for the case of He gas and a W or Mo target. In these cases, the sputter yields are extremely low. In addition, the thermal conductivity of the gas is very high. These two effects together suggest that the voltage will increase exceedingly slowly as a function of current. Indeed, measurements have shown the exponent in the I-V relation to be in the range of 35-70. Often in these plasmas, the current can be increase an order of magnitude or more by increasing the voltage less than 5 volts. It should be noted, however, that in this particular case, the sample undergoes extreme levels of energetic particle bombardment due to the low mass of the gas atoms and the long mean free path of reflected, energetic particles.

6.2.5 Interactions: Effects on Sputtered Material

Usually, the general goal of using magnetron devices in a sputtering mode is for the deposition of films. Atoms sputtered from the cathode may deposit on sample surfaces, forming a thin film of a composition near that of the cathode. The sputtered atoms, however, must transit the region between the cathode and the substrate; a region composed of both the plasma and a large number of neutral gas atoms. The sputtered atoms, depending on the pressure and the distance between the cathode and the substrate, may undergo from zero to many hundreds of collisions. Each collision changes the velocity and direction of the sputtered atom, and usually results in a general cooling (thermalization) of the sputtered atom, while at the same time increasing the average temperature of the background gas.

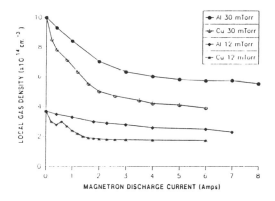

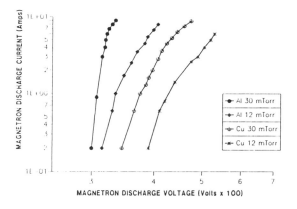

Figure 8: (a) Observed gas density reductions for Cu and Al cathodes in Ar at 30 mTorr as a function of discharge current. (b) Experimental current-voltage traces for the same case as (a) plotted logarithmically.

Several authors have treated the transport of atoms from a sputtering source by computational means. The deposition profiles for simple annular targets have been calculated by Gnaedinger (25) and further modified by Este and Westwood (26) for rectangular targets. Gras-Marti et al (27) has analytically treated some of the scattering processes occurring during transport, and a papers by Motohiro and Taga (28) 8nd Somekh (29) has treated the topic with Monti-Carlo-like techniques. In addition, the so-called "throwing power", or the ability to coat the sides of objects has been treated qualitatively (30).

Experimentally, a study was undertaken to measure the probability of atom transport by measuring the resulting deposition profiles for a fixed number of sputtered atoms

(13,14). The atoms sputtered from a magnetron cathode may deposit on the substrate plane, the side areas of the chamber, the fixtures and shutters in the chamber, or even back onto the magnetron cathode. Atoms deposited onto the etch track of the cathode will most likely be resputtered rapidly. However, atoms deposited in areas on the cathode but not in the etch track have a lower probability of being resputtered due to the lower bombardment rates. In general, thick deposits can be formed in the central, "dead" regions of the cathode and also near the cathode edge.

The results of this study for the case of Cu and Al cathodes can be given in tabular form, in Tables 1 and 2. The probabilities are found by dividing the total number of deposited atoms on a surface by the total estimated number of sputtered atoms. There are certain systematic sources of error (14), but these are usually less than 20%. The redeposition of atoms to the cathode may cause a slow change in the composition of films sputtered from alloy targets. It will also be sensitive to the local gas density and the target-to-sample distance. In addition, as the local gas density is strongly perturbed by the rate of emission of energetic sputtered atoms, the redeposition on the cathode will also be dependant on the operating power of the magnetron. This can be seen in Fig. 9, in which the redeposition on the cathode drops off significantly at higher discharge powers, as the local gas density which causes the scattering and redeposition is reduced. Thus, one would expect compositional changes when sputtering from alloy targets as a function of chamber pressure, throw distance as well as power. These are indeed observed, and are the subject of a related work (31).

Table 1: Deposition probabilities for various surfaces within the chamber for a Cu cathode in Ar as a function of chamber pressure and throw distance.

1000 Watts				
Gas	P (Pa)	Sample	Magnetron	Side areas·
5 cm	0.7	.63	.031	.16
	2.6	.49	.11	.20
	4	.53	.14	.22
9.5 cm	0.7	.48	.031	.24
	2.6	.47	.13	.24
	4	.45	.18	.18
14.5 cm	0.7	.39	.045	.25
	2.6	.35	.16	.30
	4	.31	.18	.35
200 Watts				
5 cm	4	.53	.23	.13
3000 Watts				
5 cm	4	.48	.09	.24

× The side areas include only those areas adjacent to
the magnetron cathode, parallel to the cathode surface. It does
not include all wall areas.

Table 2: Deposition probabilities for various surfaces within the chamber for an Al cathode in Kr, Ar and Ne as a function of pressure and throw distance.

	Throw	P (Pa)	Sample	Magnetron	Side Areas˙
5 cm Throw					
Kr		0.7	.52	.10	.16
		2.6	.45	.18	.17
		4	.38	.34	.13
Ar		0.7	.60	.12	.10
		2.6	.46	.26	.12
		4	.42	.32	.09
Ne		0.7	.80	.08	.05
		2.6	.56	.16	.10
		4	.52	.27	.11
9.5 cm Throw					
Kr		0.7	.35	.18	.20
		2.6	.27	.35	.24
		4	.22	.39	.20
Ar		0.7	.44	.13	.10
		2.6	.45	.35	.15
		4	.36	.40	.17
Ne		0.7	.40	.10	.20
		2.6	.42	.36	.18
		4	.40	.34	.09

˟ This is the area adjacent to the cathode, parallel to the cathode surface. It does not include all of the chamber walls.

Various optical techniques have been used to monitor the magnitude and energy of the atoms during transit from the cathode to the anode. Laser Induced Florescence (LIF) has been used for ion beam sputtering experiments (32) and also for selected plasma-based studies (33). Observations of the optical emission from the plasma region are also reported. In one particular case, the temperature of the sputtered atoms could be deduced from the Doppler broadening of the observed emission (19). Conventional optical emission spectroscopy (OES) has also been used to monitor the relative levels of sputtered atoms in the plasma. The emission intensity is generally proportional to the electron density, n_e, the species density, n_s, and some function of the electron temperature, cross section for excitation, and de-excitation probability (3):

$$I_{emis}^s = n_e n_s A \int \rho_e(E) v \sigma_s(E) dE = A n_s n_e f(T_e, \sigma_s)$$

(6)

where A is a geometry-dependent constant, and $f(T_e, \sigma_s)$ is defined as the excitation rate of the species, which is dependent on the the electron energy (E) distribution, $\rho_e(E)$, or temperature kT_e, electron velocity v, and cross section for excitation, $\sigma_s(E)$. The last term is usually assumed, for convenience, to be constant over the range of interest in plasmas of this type.

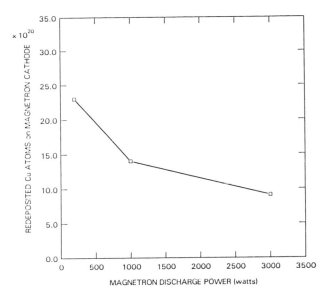

Figure 9: The probability of redeposition (in percent) for Cu atoms back onto the magnetron cathode for Ar gas as a function of discharge power.

The emission intensity of various species present in the discharge can be measured as a function of discharge current (2,3). It is reasonable to assume that the electron density is roughly proportional to the discharge current. From this assumption, the emission levels from the background gas species would be expected to scale with the discharge current to approximately the first power (3). This is observed at low discharge powers (Fig. 10), but as power is increased, the intensity becomes proportional to the discharge current to the 1/2 power. This change can be attributed to the rarefaction effect described earlier, in which the energetic, sputtered atoms cause a reduction in the local gas density due to the thermalization process. As found in Eq. 1, the gas density is proportional at high power to the discharge current to the -1/2 power. When combined with Eq. 4, the observed slope at high power can be predicted.

The density of the sputtered atoms should be directly proportional to the discharge power, or approximately proportional to the discharge current. Again making the assumption that the electron density is proportional to the discharge current, the intensity of the sputtered atoms would be expected to be proportional to the discharge current to the 2nd power (using Eq. 6). The observed values (Fig. 10) appear to approach the second power at low powers, and fall to approximately the 1.3 power at high discharge powers. This may be indicative of gas rarefaction effects, but may also be due to a lack of a direct proportionality between the electron density and discharge current. (Note: if the electron density scales with the discharge current to less than the first power, as might be expected, the difference is exaggerated in the case of sputtered or ionized, sputtered atoms.) The density of ionized, sputtered atoms should be proportional to the discharge power (number of sputtered atoms) times the electron density (probability for ionization). Thus, one might expect that the intensity of ionized, sputtered atoms would scale with discharge current to approximately the third power. The results (Fig. 10(c)) show an exponent of approximately 2.5. The intensities for these particular species are quite low, however, due to the high excitation energies required.

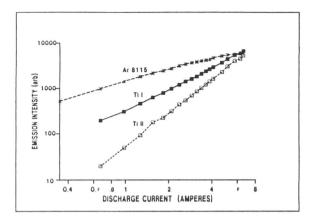

Figure 10: Experimentally observed optical emission intensity for lines from (A) Ar ground state, (B) Ti ground state, (C) Ti⁺ for magnetron sputtering of Ti in Ar at 7 mTorr. Data are plotted as a function of discharge current.

The general result, however, is that the source of individual emission lines in a plasma may be identified by their dependance on the discharge current. In addition, using this type of diagnostic technique to monitor a deposition process must be done very carefully, and generally only over a small range of discharge parameters.

6.2.6 Interactions at the Sample Surface

It has routinely observed that the various physical and electrical characteristics of the deposited films are strongly sensitive to the gas pressure in the chamber, the rate of deposition, and the substrate temperature. An example of this interrelationship is Thornton's version of Movchan and Demichishin's structure zone diagram (34,35). (See, for example, Fig. 1 of Chap 22.) In general, it has been postulated that low pressures correlate with increased energetic particle bombardment of the growing film, causing changes in the grain size, stress and impurity incorporation levels (36). This has been the subject of numerous studies, and will not be redescribed here. Many of the explained effects, however, rely on the bombardment of the film with energetic, neutral particles that originate at the cathode surface during the sputtering process. These energetic neutrals are elastically reflected, Auger neutralized ions that have been accelerated to high energy to the cathode or target surface and may reflect with up to several hundred eV of kinetic energy. In addition, a significant component of energetic neutral bombarding species may be attributable to the formation of negative ions at the cathode surface, with the subsequent acceleration across the cathode sheath and charge neutralization in the plasma. This second species is often observed when sputtering in the presence of oxygen, as well as in the case of materials from the far left side of the periodic table. The negative ion species are usually well collimated in a plasma-sputtering device, whereas the reflected neutrals may have a more isotopic distribution.

Substrate heating during sputter deposition with a magnetron is a combination of many factors. As is the case with all vapor phase depositions, the heat of condensation (3-8 eV/atom) must be considered. Due to the low operating pressure of the magnetron, a significant fraction of the initial kinetic energy of the sputtered atom may still be present for the depositing atoms. This contribution can range up to 20 eV/atom for refractory materials, but is typically closer to 4-8 eV/atom for other metals. The reflection of ions as neutrals from the cathode may also contribute significantly to the energy deposited at the film. This is particularly significant for low mass gas species in combination with high mass cathode species, where the reflection coefficients can be quite large and the sputter yields quite low. Finally, there can also be heating contributions from optical emission from the plasma as well as bombardment with hot gas atoms.

Thornton built a small detector to measure the net energy arriving during film deposition. The detector is based on a thin foil substrate which is thermally isolated from its mount. A thermocouple monitors changes in the foil temperature, which in conjunction with the deposition rate, can be converted into an energy arrival rate per depositing atom. A summary of the results is shown in Table 3, which has been collected from published data (18).

Table 3: Measured and calculated energy arrival rates for Ar sputtering (18).

Metal	Atomic Weight	Planar Mag. eV/atom	Cylindrical eV/atom	Theoretical est. eV/atom
Al	27.0	11	13	13
Cr	52.0	16	20	16
Ni	58.7	15	15	19
Cu	63.5	12	17	12
Mo	95.9	42	47	26
In	1158	15	20	9
Ta	181	96	107	38
W	184	98	100	40
Pt	195	48		30

A second detector has been developed to measure the presence of only the energetic species during a sputter deposition. The device is similar to the work of Brodie, Lamont and Jepson (37) and others (38), and is shown in Fig. 11. The device shields out energetic electrons by means of a magnetic field and a collector biased more negative than the cathode (10). A grid (G-1) allows the introduction of ions from the plasma when biased negatively, or repels the ions when biased more positive than plasma potential. A second grid (G-2) near the collector allows for the emission or suppression of secondary electrons caused by energetic bombardment of the collector. The current to (or from) the collector is then indicative of the magnitude of energetic particle bombardment and the secondary electron yield. By reversing the potential on G-2 with respect to the collector, the secondary electron coefficient can be deduced. Observed currents at the collector with a positive potential on G-2 are then due to the emission of electrons caused by energetic neutral bombardment or photons. The secondary electron yield due to 'neutral' bombardment has been rarely measured in the past, and may or may not be related to an Auger process (24). For the purpose of this study, however, the yields have been routinely measured, and appear to be similar to the yields for ions at comparable energies.

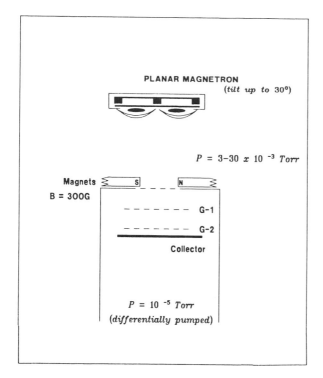

Figure 11: Schematic of energetic neutral detector used for magnetron studies (10,11).

Assuming the secondary electron yield does not depend on kinetic energy in the 20-600 eV range, the flux of energetic neutral particles can be determined in a quantitative manner with this device, as can the average secondary electron yield. In addition, a quartz crystal rate monitor has been positioned immediately adjacent to the energetic neutral detector to measure the net arrival rate of depositing atoms. By comparison of these two signals, the arrival rate ratio of energetic-to-depositing atoms can be determined, although the actual energy of the energetic species cannot be measured (10).

Both the deposition rate of condensing atoms and the arrival rate of the energetic species depends on the chamber pressure. An increase in chamber pressure results in a reduction of both signals due to gas scattering. (Fig. 12). In addition, as might be expected following the earlier discussions of gas rarefaction effects, the arrival rates of both species are dependant on the discharge power, which alters the local gas density due to the thermalization process. (Fig. 13). The ratio of energetic-to-depositing atoms has been found, however, to vary slowly, if at all, with chamber pressure. In many cases, the energetic-to-depositing atom ratio has been found to <u>decrease</u> as the chamber pressure is reduced, rather than increase as might be expected from the effects on the film properties. Upon consideration of the cross sections for collisions (22), however, this result is not too surprising. The sputtered atoms have an average kinetic energy of a few eV and a mean free path on the order of a few centimeters at the operating pressures used. The reflected, neutrals often have energies exceeding 100 or more eV, and thus have a significantly smaller cross section and longer mean free path. Therefore, changes in chamber pressure in the mTorr range will be much more significant to the mean free paths of the low energy sputtered atoms, rather than the reflected, higher energy neutrals.

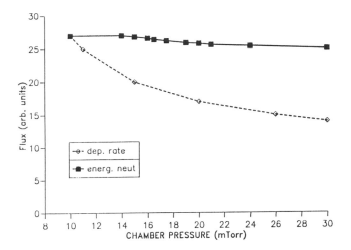

Figure 12: Arrival rates of energetic neutral particles and depositing atoms in arbitrary units as a function of chamber pressure for the case of a Al cathode in Ne gas at a constant discharge current.

The relative arrival rates of energetic neutrals to depositing atoms are strongly dependent on the cathode and gas species. The probability of reflection for a primary ion bombarding the cathode surface has been calculated by Eckstein and Biersak (39), and is greatest for the case of light ions bombarding heavy cathodes. The sputter yield of the cathode is also dependent on the choice of species, and tabulations are available (40). The results of measurements with the energetic neutral detector should scale with predictions made from a comparison of the sputter yield and the reflection coefficient, although the effect of gas scattering as well as emission profiles for the various species must also be considered.

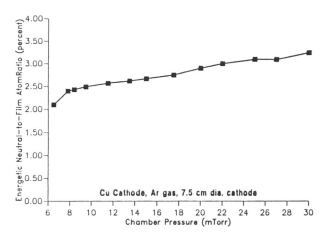

Figure 13: Relative arrival rate ratio of energetic-to-depositing atoms at the sample as a function of chamber pressure for the case of Cu cathode in Ar at 14 mTorr.

6.3 SUMMARY

An extended series of diagnostic measurements on magnetron sputtering devices has pointed out some of the complexities in understanding the various inter-relations between the sputtering process, the plasma formation, the sample and the background gas. The interaction between the sputtered atoms and the background gas, routinely described as a thermalization process, might more aptly be described as a gas heating process. This heating and rarefaction has numerous implications as to how the plasma is formed and its impedance, as well as the transport and deposition of sputtered atoms on surfaces around the chamber. The bombardment of the sample with energetic species is also a critical effect, which strongly affects the properties of the depositing films. While the bombardment rates can vary extensively as a function of cathode and gas species, little significant pressure dependance has been observed in the bombardment rate, suggesting the need to modify currently accepted explanations for changes in the properties of the sputtered materials as a function of discharge pressure. In addition, the presence of negative ions formed at the cathode surface and possibly due to residual gas impurities has been observed. Previous studies have neglected this effect, which will have strong implications not only on film properties, but on the transfer of a process from one chamber to another. This result also suggests that it is desirable to have a low base pressure and a high pumping speed to reduce the effects of impurities.

Other results of these studies are more conventional. The plasma in a magnetron is characterized by Bohm Diffusion, and is surrounded by positive space charge sheaths. The ExB drift currents are not substantial, and the resulting effects on the magnetic field are extremely low. The optical emission from the plasma is reasonable described by a simply model relating the electron density to the discharge current.

6.4 REFERENCES

1. J.A. Thornton and A. Penfold, in Thin Film Processes ed. by J.L. Vossen and W. Kern, (Academic, New York, 1987) p76.

2. S. Schiller, U. Heisig, K. Steinfelder, J. Strümpfel, R. Voight, R. Femdler and G. Teschner, On the investigation of DC plasmetron discharges by optical emission spectrometry, Thin Solid Films, 96: 235 (1982).

3. S.M. Rossnagel and K.L Saenger, Optical emission in magnetrons, J. Vac. Sci. Technol. A7: (1989, in press).

4. S.M. Rossnagel and H.R. Kaufman, Langmuir probe characterization of magnetron operation, J. Vac. Sci. & Technol. A4: 1822 (1986).

5. J.A. Thornton, Magnetron sputtering: basic physics and application to cylindrical magnetrons. J. Vac. Sci. Technol. 15: 171 (1978).

6. B. Singh, presented at AVS National Symposium, Reno, Nevada, (1984) unpublished.

7. S.M. Rossnagel and H.R. Kaufman, Induced drift currents in magnetrons, J. Vac. Sci. Technol., A5: 88 (1988).

8. D.W. Hoffman, A sputtering wind, J. Vac. Sci. Technol. A3: 561 (1985).

9. S.M. Rossnagel, Gas density reduction effects in magnetrons, J. Vac. Sci. Technol. A6:19 (1988).

10. S.M. Rossnagel, Energetic particle bombardment of films during magnetron sputter deposition, J. Vac. Sci. Technol., A7: (1989, in press).

11. S.M. Rossnagel and J.J. Cuomo, Negative ion effects during magnetron and ion beam sputtering of $YBa_2Cu_3O_x$, AIP Conf. Proc 165: (1988) 106.

12. B. Window and N. Savvides, Unbalanced magnetrons as sources of high ion fluxes. J. Vac. Sci. Technol. A4: 453 (1986).

13. S.M. Rossnagel, Magnetron plasma diagnostics and processing implications, J. Vac. Sci. Technol., A6: 1821 (1988).

14. S.M. Rossnagel, Deposition and redeposition in magnetrons, J. Vac. Sci. Technol., A6: 3049 (1988).

15. W.D. Westwood, S. Maniv and P.J. Scanlon, The current-voltage characteristic of magnetron sputtering systems, J. Appl. Phys., 54: 6841 (1983).

16. S.M. Rossnagel, Current-voltage relations in magnetrons, J. Vac. Sci. Technol., A6: 223 (1988).

17. N. Howosokawa, T. Tsudaka and M. Kitahara, in Vide Suppl. 201: 11 (1980).

18. J.A. Thornton and J.L. Lamb, Substrate Heating rates for planar and cylindrical post magnetron sputtering sources, Thin Solid Films 119: 87 (1984).

19. L.T. Ball, I.S. Falconer, D.R. McKenzie and J.M. Smelt, An interferometric investigation of the thermalization of copper atoms in a magnetron sputter discharge, J. Appl. Phys. 59: 720 (1986).

20. D.W. Hoffman, Thin Solid Films 107: 353 (1983).

21. T. Takaishi and Y. Sensui, Trans. Faraday Soc. 59: 2509 (1963).

22. R.S. Robinson, Energetic binary collisions in rare gases, J. Vac. Sci. and Technol. 16: 185 (1979).

23. S.M. Rossnagel and H.R. Kaufman, Charge transport in magnetrons, J.Vac. Sci. & Technol. A5: 2276 (1987).

24. B. Chapman, in Glow Discharge Processes, (J. Wiley and Sons, New York, 1980).

25. R.J. Gnaedinger, Jr., Some calculations of the thickness distribution of films deposited from large area sputtering sources, J. Vac. Sci. Technol. 6: 355 (1969).

26. G.Este and W.D. Westwood, J. Vac. Sci Technol. A2: 1238 (1984).

27. A. Gras-Marti and J.A. Valles-Abarca, Evolution towards thermalization and diffusion of sputtered particle fluxes: spatial profiles, J. Appl. Phys. 55: 1370 (1984).

28. T. Motohiro and Y. Taga, Monte Carlo simulation of the particle transport process in sputter deposition, Thin Solid Films 112: 161 (1984).

29. R.E. Somekh, The thermalization of energetic atoms during the sputtering process, J. Vac. Sci. Technol., A3: 1285 (1983).

30. W. Stowell, J. Foster, W. Berner, C. Wan, D. Chambers and H.Hanes, Throwing power and shadowing effect in planar magnetron sputtering process, J. Vac. Sci. Technol. A3: 572 (1985).

31. S.M. Rossnagel, I. Yang and J.J. Cuomo (submitted to Thin Solid Films)

32. D.M. Gruen, M.J. Pellin, C.E Young and W.F. Calaway, Laser spectroscopy of sputtered atoms, J. Vac. Sci. Technol. A4: 1779 (1986).

33. G.S. Selwyn, J. Vac. Sci. Technol., A6: (1988) 2041.

34. J.A. Thornton, J. Vac. Sci. Technol. 11: 666 (1974).

35. B.A. Movchan and A.V. Demichishin, Study of the structure and properties of thick vacuum condensates of nickel, titanium, aluminum oxide and zirconium oxide. Fiz. Metal. Metalloved. 28: 653 (1969).

36. J.A. Thornton and D.W. Hoffman, J.Vac. Sci. Technol. A3: 576 (1985).

37. I. Brodie, L.T. Lamont, Jr. and R.L. Jepson, Phys. Rev. Lett. 21: (1968) 1224.

38. Y. Shintani, K. Nakanishi, T. Takawaki and O. Tada, Jap. J. Appl. Phys. 14: (1975) 1875.

39. W. Eckstein and J.P. Biersak, Z. Phys. B - Condensed Matter 63: (1986) 471.

40. H.R. Kaufman and R.S. Robinson Operation of Broad Beam Ion Sources (Commonwealth Scientific, Alexandria VA 1988).

7

Broad-Beam Ion Sources

Harold R. Kaufman and Raymond S. Robinson

7.1 INTRODUCTION

Broad ion beams have transverse dimensions that are much larger than the Debye shielding length. The origins of most broad beam ion sources can be traced back to the late 1950's, when electric space propulsion programs were started in several countries. These programs included a wide range of ion source concepts (1).

The broad-beam ion sources presently of most interest use electron-bombardment to generate ions and dc electrostatic acceleration to accelerate the ions into a beam. The electron bombardment is provided with either a dc or rf discharge. The electrostatic acceleration is provided most often by electric fields between closely spaced grids. For a broad beam of ions to be generated in this manner, multiple grid apertures must be operated in parallel. Gridless ion sources have become available in the last several years. The electric field to accelerate ions in these sources is generated by an electron current, of roughly the same magnitude as the ion beam current, interacting with a magnetic field. The ion beam current densities possible with this acceleration process are much greater than those possible with gridded sources, particularly at low ion energies.

The primary use of gridded, broad-beam sources has been in thin film research applications, which started about 1970, and increased rapidly thereafter (2,3). This rapid growth resulted from the advantages of these ion sources compared to competitive processes. These advantages include ions that are accelerated into a beam with a well-defined and controlled direction, density, and energy. Further, the ion generation is removed from, and independent of, target processes. Both control and process definition are more difficult with competitive plasma processes.

The early thin-film applications of gridded ion sources were limited to etching and deposition. In many recent applications the objective can be better described as property modification or enhancement, rather than simply etching or deposition (4).

Until recently, the few successful production applications have usually involved products of very high unit cost, so that the use of highly skilled operators could be justified

(5). The shift to conventional production applications was delayed by the complicated operation and maintenance of early gridded ion sources, which frequently resulted from inappropriate designs derived from the space-propulsion program. Ion sources suited to a production environment, both gridded and gridless, have been available for several years and have resulted in substantial increases in production applications (6,7). The review of technology presented herein will emphasize recent developments.

7.2 GRIDDED ION SOURCES

7.2.1 General Description

The schematic diagram of a gridded broad-beam ion source and its controller (power supplies) is shown in Fig. 1. The working gas is introduced into the discharge chamber, where energetic electrons from the cathode strike and ionize atoms or molecules of the working gas. The ions that approach the ion optics (the screen and accelerator grids) are extracted from the discharge chamber and accelerated into the ion beam. The apertures in the grids are aligned so that the screen grid protects the accelerator grid from direct impingement during normal operation. Electrons from the neutralizer both charge and current neutralize the ion beam. The actual recombination of these electrons with ions is normally a negligible process.

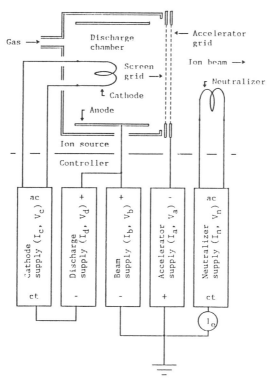

Figure 1: Schematic diagram of gridded, broad-beam ion source and controller.

The function of the discharge chamber is to generate ions efficiently, controllably, and with little need for maintenance. A variety of discharge chamber configurations have been used, and all use a magnetic field to contain the energetic electrons emitted from the cathode and thereby improve the efficiency. Both permanent magnets and electromagnets are used to provide the magnetic field. If an electromagnet is used, an additional power supply is required to energize the electromagnet.

The maximum ion beam current, I_b, that can be accelerated by the ion optics is given approximately by

$$I_b \simeq (\varepsilon_o/9)A_b(e/m)^{1/2}V_t^{3/2}/l_g^2 \tag{1}$$

where ε_o is the permittivity of space, A_b is the beam area, e/m is the charge-to-mass ratio of the accelerated ions, V_t is the total voltage ($V_b + V_a$), and l_g is the gap between the screen and accelerator grids. This equation is derived from Child's law (8), but is only approximate because the effective area for ion extraction is less than the total beam area and the effective acceleration distance is greater than the gap between the grids. The actual beam current is usually only 20-50% of the approximate value given by Eq. (1).

Because the ion-beam current varies as $V_t^{3/2}$, the maximum beam current that can be extracted without direct impingement of energetic ions on the accelerator grid depends strongly on the beam voltage, V_b.

The cathode and neutralizer in Fig. 1 are of the hot-filament type. The electron emission for either of these functions can be supplied instead by a hollow cathode (9), which requires a separate gas flow, usually argon, krypton, or xenon.

7.2.2 Present Technology

The most common working gas for gridded sources is argon. Reactive gases such as nitrogen and oxygen are frequently used, and even more reactive gases incorporating chlorine or fluorine are sometimes used.

The discharge chamber and the ion optics are two major components of the ion source that have been involved in recent technology developments. Most recent improvements in discharge chamber configurations have resulted in reduced maintenance requirements. These improvements have typically used anodes that contain sputtered material and are easily removed for cleaning.

RF discharges for the generation of ions have been the subject of increased interest for thin-film applications. The types presently being investigated include inductively coupled (10), capacitively coupled (11), and microwave (12). (The inductively coupled type has been used previously in the electric space propulsion field.)

The primary advantage of an rf discharge in thin-film applications should be decreased maintenance when the ion source is operated with reactive gases. If rf discharges are to be used in a significant number of thin film applications, this decreased maintenance must be obtained without excessive contamination from the ion source during normal operation and without excessive sensitivity to the normal industrial operating environment.

Over the past decade, improvements in ion optics have permitted increased beam current capacity at moderate beam voltages, often with increased reliability and decreased maintenance. Assuming circular ion optics, the ion-beam current can be shown to be proportional to the square of the ratio of beam diameter to grid gap, $(d_b/l_g)^2$. Assuming the same voltages are used, if one set of ion optics is to have a larger ion-current capacity than another set, the ratio d_b/l_g must be larger for that set. If this ratio is the same, the beam current capacities of the two ion optics sets will be approximately the same, regardless of any difference in physical size.

The ion current densities that are obtainable depend on the grid spacing (l_g in Eq. (1)) and the voltages used. Note that the ion-beam current is very sensitive to total voltage. A quoted ion-beam current or current density therefore has little meaning without the corresponding ion energy. For example, higher beam currents can always be obtained at high beam voltages, V_b, of 1500-2000 V. Such high voltages and ion energies can, however, cause excessive damage to substrates and photoresist in etching applications and are relatively inefficient in terms of material removed per unit beam energy in either etching or deposition applications.

To fully utilize a small grid spacing, small grid apertures and grid thicknesses should be used. As the grid spacing is reduced, then, the reduced aperture diameters and reduced grid thicknesses result in an increasingly fragile grid structure. The limit is not a clearcut one, but the increasing difficulty in handling and maintaining fragile grids does result in a practical limit on the minimum grid spacing. Graphite grids tend to present more handling and maintenance problems than molybdenum grids in a production environment.

The trend is toward larger ion sources for larger production capability. To maintain a small grid gap, l_g, over a large beam diameter, d_b, requires careful thermo-mechanical design. The largest value of d_b/l_g, hence the largest beam current capability at moderate beam voltages, is presently obtained with dished molybdenum grids (7).

An example of present production capability is an ion source with a beam diameter of about 0.4 m (7). Ion-beam currents of 4-5 A are possible - up to 4 A without exceeding 1000 eV (a beam voltage, V_b, of 1000 V). These large ion-beam currents permit a substantial increase in processing capability. A cutaway sketch of a large ion source is shown in Fig. 2. Ease of maintenance and reliable operation are crucial for a production environment. The discharge chamber anode covers and protects the magnet and pole-piece structure, so that this structure does not accumulate debris and require cleaning. The anode is also readily removable for cleaning.

The ion optics are dished molybdenum. As described previously (5), alignment of the ion optics for broad beam sources has been a major maintenance and reliability problem. A large number of ion optics that require a manual alignment procedure have been used in the past. The serious nature of the alignment problem is indicated by the fact that most of these ion optics have, after extended service, accelerator-grid apertures that have been worn into noncircular shapes by operation while misaligned. Ion optics can be designed designed to obtain precise alignment from a straightforward assembly procedure;(13) thus bypassing manual alignment altogether.

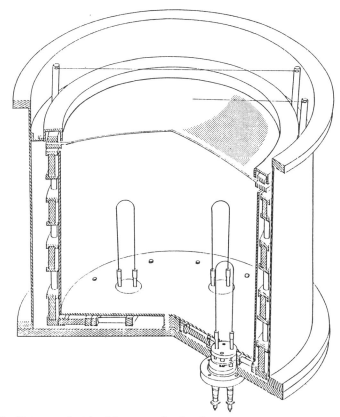

Figure 2: Cutaway sketch of large production ion source.

7.3 GRIDLESS ION SOURCES

7.3.1 General Description

The schematic diagram of a gridless broad-beam ion source and its controller is shown in Fig. 3. The electron emission from the cathode is controlled with the cathode supply. The anode potential is determined by the anode current, the strength of the magnetic field, and the gas flow. An electromagnet is shown in Fig. 3, but a permanent magnet can also be used, thereby eliminating one of the power supplies shown. A gas flowmeter is included because the voltage of the anode supply is normally controlled by the gas flow at a particular beam current. The cathode supply is customarily an ac supply when filament cathodes are used; however, hollow cathodes are also used as electron sources. As mentioned above, the gases used for hollow cathodes in industrial applications have been inert gases.

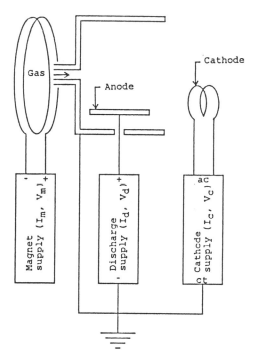

Figure 3: Schematic diagram of a gridless, broad-beam ion source and controller.

A gridless ion source can be described as a plasma device operating in approximately the glow-discharge regime. The ions are electrostatically accelerated into a beam with the accelerating electric field established by an electron current of comparable magnitude to the ion beam current, interacting with a magnetic field. One component of the electron motion is counter to the ion flow. Another component is normal to that direction. The current associated with this normal component is called the Hall current. In gridless ion sources there is a complete, or closed, path for the Hall current. In addition, for the ions to be accelerated into a beam, rather than much more diffusely, the ion cyclotron radius must be much larger than the total acceleration length.

Even when operating properly, though, the ions in a gridless ion source are generated over an extended region with varying potentials, resulting in beam ions with a range of energy, typically ± 30% of the mean ion energy. This is much more than the several Volt variation of potential in the discharge chamber of a correctly operating gridded ion source.

The positive space charge and current due to the ions in this beam are neutralized by some of the electrons that leave the cathode. Most of the electrons from the cathode flow back toward the anode and both generate ions and establish the potential difference that accelerates these ions. The excess electron emission from the cathode is approximately sufficient to current-neutralize the ion beam when the electron emission equals the anode current. The cathode is operated in excess of this current in many thin film applications.

There are several types of gridless ion sources. Two basic geometries are described herein. The end-Hall type, named because the beam exits the acceleration region at the end (axis) of the magnetic field, and the closed-drift type, in which the ion-acceleration channel is annular, rather than circular as it is in the end-Hall. There can be a number of variations within these two general categories that emphasize particular operating or performance characteristics. Usually, but not always, closed paths for the circulating Hall current are provided with axially symmetric electrodes and magnetic pole pieces.

The cross section of a closed-drift ion source is shown in Fig. 4 along with a schematic electrical diagram. The magnetic field direction is generally radial. The electrons from the cathode flow back through the annular channel to the anode. In passing through the radial magnetic field, a circulating Hall current is generated in the annular channel.

Most closed-drift ion sources have had dielectric channel walls and a channel length at least equal to the channel width, as indicated in Fig. 4 (1,15-17). In addition, the electron cyclotron orbit is small compared to the acceleration length.

The electric field that accelerates the ions is generated in the radial magnetic field of a closed drift ion source, and is the result of the reduced plasma conductivity across magnetic-field lines. The strong-field approximation is appropriate for the field strengths used in the closed drift source. The ratio of conductivities parallel and transverse to the magnetic field is then

$$\sigma_{\parallel}/\sigma_{\perp} = (\omega_c/\nu_e)^2 \tag{2}$$

where ω_c is the electron-cyclotron (angular) frequency and ν_e is the electron collision frequency. The electron collision frequency is determined by the plasma fluctuations associated with anomalous diffusion when conduction is across a strong magnetic field. Using Bohm diffusion to estimate this frequency,

$$\sigma_{\parallel}/\sigma_{\perp} = 256 \tag{3}$$

Because Bohm diffusion is typically accurate only within a factor of several, the ratio of Eq. (2) should be treated as correct within an order of magnitude. It should still be expected that

$$\sigma_{\parallel} >> \sigma_{\perp} \tag{4}$$

Analysis of the closed-drift acceleration process shows that two distinctly different acceleration processes can take place. In one case the electrons in the acceleration region were assumed to be at a negligible temperature (zero). The potential variation throughout the acceleration region then was found to be smooth and continuous. As a result of the continuous and extended acceleration process, this type has been called a closed-drift extended-acceleration (CDEA) source (18). If, however, the electrons were assumed to heat up as they flowed from the ion exit to the ion formation region, then a near-discontinuous potential jump occurred at the positive end of the acceleration channel. The remainder of the acceleration was assumed to take place in an axial length of the order of the local electron-cyclotron orbit. Accelerators that operate with this type of acceleration are called anode-layer accelerators (19).

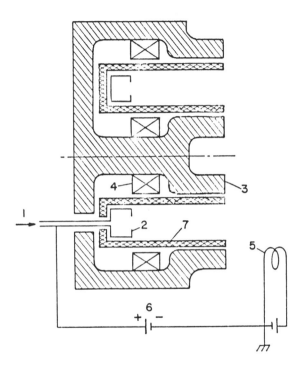

Figure 4: Closed-drift extended-acceleration (CDEA), thruster (single stage). (1) Gas feed; (2) anode distributor; (3) magnetic circuit, pole pieces; (4) magnetic winding; (5) cathode neutralizer; (6) discharge power supply; (7) insulator (Ref. 14).

Except for certain geometrical considerations the operation of the end-Hall source can be described in the same general manner as the closed-drift ion source. The cross section of an end-Hall ion source is indicated in Fig. 5. The neutral atoms or molecules of the working gas are introduced to the ion source through a port. Electrons from the cathode approximately follow magnetic field lines back to the discharge region enclosed by the anode and strike atoms or molecules therein. Some of these collisions produce ions. The mixture of electrons and ions in the discharge region forms a plasma. Because the density of the neutral atoms or molecules decreases rapidly downstream of the anode (toward the cathode) most of the ionizing collisions with neutrals occur in the region surrounded by the anode.

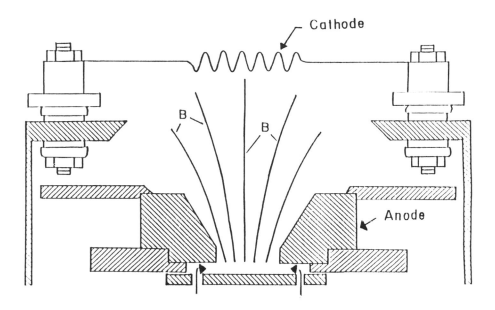

Figure 5: Cross section of an end-Hall ion source.

From the difference in conductivity parallel and normal to the magnetic field (Eq. (4)), it would be expected that the magnetic field lines in Fig. 5 would approximately determine the equipotential contours in the plasma. Further, the field lines closer to the anode would be more positive in potential. Radial surveys of plasma potential made using a Langmuir probe show some potential increase when moving from the axis to a magnetic field line close to the anode, but the increase is only a fraction of the total anode-cathode potential difference. The bulk of this difference appears in the axial direction . That is, parallel to the magnetic field, where, from Eq. (4), the potential difference would be expected to be small.

The time-averaged force of a nonuniform magnetic field on an electron moving in a circular orbit can be calculated. For a variation of field strength in only the direction of the magnetic field, this force is parallel to the magnetic field and toward decreased field strength (opposite the field gradient). Assuming an isotropic distribution of electron velocities, two-thirds of the electron energy is associated with motion normal to the magnetic field, and therefore interacts with this field. For a uniform plasma density, the potential difference in the plasma can then be obtained by integrating the electric field required to balance the magnetic-field force on the electron, which gives

$$\Delta V_p = (kT_e/e)\ln(B/B_o) \qquad\qquad (5)$$

where k is the Boltzmann constant, T_e is the electron temperature in K, e is the electronic charge, and B and B_o are the magnetic-field strengths in two locations. With $B > B_o$, the plasma potential, V_p, at B is greater than that at B_o.

Axial surveys (6) of plasma potential in the end-Hall source are found to be in approximate agreement with Eq. (5). There is an additional effect of plasma density on potential, and a more complete description of the variation of plasma potential with magnetic-field strength must also include this effect.

7.3.2 Present Technology

The only gridless ion sources that are commercially available for thin film applications are the end-Hall type. These gridless ion sources can be used for beam currents up to about one Ampere, and can readily be developed for larger currents. Typical ion energies range from about 30 eV to a little over 100 eV.

End-Hall ion sources have been used in thin-film and surface processing applications for a comparatively short time (6). The high-current, low-energy capabilities of these sources make them particularly suited to thin film property modification or enhancement, such as increasing hardness, passivating surfaces, producing a preferred crystal orientation, activating surface chemical reactions or improving step coverage. They are also suited to a production environment because they are simple to operate, mechanically rugged, and reliable. Oxygen and nitrogen are probably the most frequently used gases in these ion sources.

7.4 CONCLUDING REMARKS

Gridded ion sources with the reliability, ease of maintenance, and large processing capability should find greatly increased use in production applications.

Hall-effect ion sources generate ion beams with fairly well-controlled direction, a controllable energy range and current density. The major advantage of these sources is the ability to generate large ion currents at low energy. These sources should find increased application in thin film and surface processing, especially in production, where a simple, reliable source of large ion currents can have a significant impact.

7.5 REFERENCES

1.   G.R. Seikel, Generation of Thrust - Electromagnetic Thrusters, in NASA-University Conference on the Science and Technology of Space Exploration, Vol. 2: NASA SP-11, Nov. 1962, pp. 171-176; W. D. Rayle, Generation of Thrust - Electrostatic Thrusters, ibid., pp. 177-182; M. C. Ellis, Jr., Survey of Plasma Accelerator Research, ibid., pp.361-381.

2.   D. T. Hawkins, Ion Milling (Ion-Beam Etching), 1954-1975: A Bibliography, J. Vac. Sci. Technol. 12: pp. 1389-1398 (1975).

3.   D. T. Hawkins, Ion Milling (Ion-Beam Etching), 1975-1978: A Bibliography, J. Vac. Sci. Technol. 16: pp. 1051-1071 (1979).

4.   J. M. E. Harper, J. J. Cuomo, R. J. Gambino, and H. R. Kaufman, Modification of Thin Film Properties by Ion Bombardment During Deposition, in Ion Bombardment Modification of Surfaces: Fundamentals and Applications ed. by O. Auciello and R. Kelly, Elsevier Science Publishers B. V., Amsterdam, pp. 127-162 (1984).

5.   H. R. Kaufman, Broad-Beam Ion Sources: Present Status and Future Directions, J. Vac. Sci. Technol. A4: pp. 764-771 (1986).

6.   H. R. Kaufman, R. S. Robinson, and R. I. Seddo , End-Hall Ion Source, J. Vac. Sci. Technol. A5: pp. 2081-2084 (1987); J.J. Cuomo and H.R. Kaufman, US Patent 4,541,890, Oct. 3, 1985.

7.   H. R. Kaufman, W. E. Hughes, R. S. Robinson, and G. R.Thompson, Thirty-Eight Centimeter Ion Source, presented at the 7th International Conference on Ion Implantation Technology, June 7-10, 1988, Kyoto, Japan.

8.   C. D. Child, Discharge from Hot CaO, Phys. Rev. 32: pp. 492-511 (1911).

9.   H. R. Kaufman, Technology of Electron-Bombardment Thrusters, in Advances in Electronics and Electron Physics 36: ed. by L. Marton, pp. 265-373, Academic Press, New York (1974).

10. J. Freisinger, J. Krempel-Hesse, J. Krumeich, H. W. Loeb, and A. Scharmann, Rf-Ion Source RIM 10 for Material Processing with Reactive Gases, presented at International Conference on Gas Discharges and Their Applications, Venice, 19-23 September 1988.

11. R. Lossy and J. Engemann, Characterization of a Reactive Broad Beam Radio-Frequency Ion Source, J. Vac. Sci. Technol. B6: pp. 284-287, (1988).

12. L. Mahoney, M. Dahimene, and J. Asmussen, Low Power, 3.2 cm, Efficient Microwave Electron Cyclotron Resonant Ion Source, Rev. Sci. Instrum. 59: pp. 448-452 (1988).

13. H. R. Kaufman and R. S. Robinson, patent pending.

14. H.R. Kaufman, Technology of Closed Drift Thrusters, AIAA J. 23: pp. 78-87 (1985).

15. G. R. Seikel, and E. Reshotko, Hall Current Ion Accelerator, Bull. Amer. Phys. Soc. Ser. II, 7: p. 414 (1962); E.C. Lary, E. C., R. C. Meyerand, Jr., and F. Salz, Ion Acceleration in Gyro-Dominated Neutral Plasma-Theory, ibid., p. 441; Salz, F., Meyerand, R. G. Jr., and Lary, E. C., Ion Acceleration in a Gyro-Dominated Neutral Plasma-Experiment, ibid., p. 441.

16. E.A. Pinsley, C. O. Brown, and C.M. Banas, Hall-Current Accelerator Utilizing Surface Contact Ionization, J. of Spacecraft and Rockets 1: pp. 525-531 (1964).

17. C. O. Brown and E. A. Pinsley, Further Experimental Investigations of a Cesium Hall-Current Accelerator, AIAA J. 3: pp. 853-859 (1965).

18. I. A. Morozov, Yu. V. Esipchuk, G. N. Tilinin, A. V. Trofimov, Yu. A. Sharov, and G. Ya. Shchepkin, G. Ya., Plasma Accelerator with Closed Electron Drift and Extended Acceleration Zone, Sov. Phys. Tech. Phys. 17: pp. 38-45 (1972).

19. N. A. Bardadymov, A. B. Ivashkin, L. V. Leskov, and A. V. Trofimov, Hybrid Closed Electron Drift Accelerator,   Abstracts for IV All-Union Conference on Plasma Accelerators and Ion Injectors, Moscow, pp. 68-69 (1978).

Part IV
Reactive Plasma Processes

8

Reactive Ion Etching

Gottlieb S. Oehrlein

8.1 INTRODUCTION

Wet etching processes in many semiconductor manufacturing steps have been replaced by plasma assisted etching procedures. The most important driving force behind the rapid introduction of plasma-based etching technology into current semiconductor manufacturing has been the achievement of etch directionality and the ability to faithfully transfer lithographically defined photoresist patterns into underlying layers. In addition, plasma based <u>dry</u> etching processes are superior to wet etching because of cleanliness, compatibility with automation and vacuum processing technologies, such as molecular beam epitaxy. Plasma-based etching techniques include ion milling, sputter etching, reactive ion beam etching, plasma etching, and reactive ion etching, several of which have been reviewed in this book. This chapter is devoted to a survey of reactive ion etching [1].

Reactive ion etching (RIE) is a plasma-based dry etching technique characterized by a combination of physical sputtering with the chemical activity of reactive species. This enables the achievement of material selective etch anisotropy.

8.1.1 Basic RIE Apparatus and Reaction Steps

A basic reactive ion etch system is schematically illustrated in Fig. 1. The following processes take place in the system during ion enhanced etching:

a.   Active species generation: In RIE a glow discharge is used to generate from a suitable feed gas (e.g., carbontetrafluoride - CF_4 - in the case of silicon and silicon dioxide) by electron-impact dissociation/ionization the gas phase etching environment which consists of radicals, positive and negative ions, electrons, and neutrals.

b.   Formation of a dc bias for ion acceleration: The material to be etched is placed on a high-frequency-driven (commonly 13.56MHz) capacitatively coupled electrode. Since the electron mobility is much greater than the ion mobility,

after ignition of the plasma the electrode acquires a negative charge (the corresponding voltage is called self-bias voltage). Therefore, the electrode and
material placed on the electrode will be exposed to energetic, positive ion
bombardment.

c.   Transport of plasma-generated reactive intermediates from the bulk of the
      plasma to the surface of the material being etched: This occurs by diffusion
      which, for particular structures such as narrow deep trenches, can limit the etch
      rate.

d.   Adsorption step: Reactive radicals (F atoms) adsorb on the surface of the
      material (Si) to be etched. This step can be strongly enhanced by concurrent
      ion bombardment which serves to produce "active sites" since it aids in the re-
      moval of the fluorinated surface layer which otherwise passivates the Si surface.

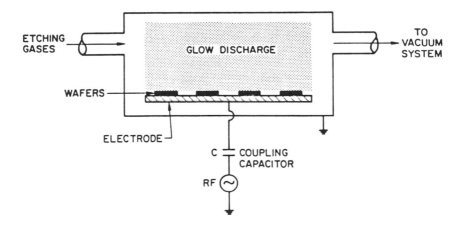

Figure 1: Schematic diagram of apparatus used for reactive ion etching in
semiconductor processing.

e.   Reaction step: A reaction between the adsorbed species and the material to
      be etched must take place. In the case of fluorine-based etching of silicon
      chemical reactions between the fluorine atoms and the surface produces either
      volatile species (SiF_4) or their precursors (SiF, SiF_2, SiF_3). Because of the
      plasma-induced formation of reactive radicals, e.g., fluorine atoms, etc., the
      reaction rate is very large relative to reaction rates in non-plasma environments.
      The reaction step can be greatly enhanced by ion bombardment. For instance,
      chlorine atoms are known to adsorb readily on silicon surfaces but the sponta-
      neous etch rate in a glow discharge without ion bombardment is very slow. Ion
      bombardment makes it possible for adsorbed chlorine atoms to attack more
      efficiently the backbonds of silicon and form a volatile $SiCl_4$ molecule.

f.   Desorption of volatile reaction product: The desorption of the reaction product
      into the gas phase is one of the most critical steps in the overall etching reaction.
      This requires that the reaction product has a high vapor pressure at the
      substrate temperature which, in RIE, is typically below $100°C$. The removal

of reaction product from the surface can be greatly accelerated by ion bombardment via sputtering.

g. Pumpout of volatile reaction product: This requires that the desorbed species diffuse from the etching surface into the bulk of the plasma and are pumped out. Otherwise plasma induced dissociation of product molecules will occur and redeposition can take place.

Table 1 is a (non-critical) collection of typical RIE parameters reported in the literature [1] and is primarily intended to provide the reader with a rough idea of the magnitude of these quantities.

Table 1: Typical characteristics of low pressure plasmas used for reactive ion etching.

Quantity	Typical Values
rf Power Density	0.05-1.0 W/cm^2
rf Frequency	10 kHz - 27 MHz (commonly 13.56 MHz)
Pressure	0.01-0.2 Torr
Gas Flow	10-200 sccm
Wafer Temperature	-120°C up to 300°C
Gas Temperature	300-600 K
Electron Temperature	3-30 eV (bulk of plasma)
Ion Energies	$\simeq$.05 e V (bulk of plasma)
	10-500 eV (after traversing cathode sheath)
Gas Number Density	$3.5 \times 10^{14} - 7 \times 10^{15} cm^{-3}$
Ion Density	$10^9 - 10^{10} cm^{-3}$
Electron Density	Similar to ion density
Ion Flux	$10^{14} - 10^{15} cm^{-2} sec^{-2}$
Radical Flux	$10^{16} cm^{-2} sec^{-1}$
Neutral Flux	$3.6 \times 10^{18} - 7.2 \times 10^{19} cm^{-2} sec^{-1}$

8.1.2 RIE PROCESSES IN SEMICONDUCTOR TECHNOLOGY

Although the physical and chemical processes underlying reactive ion etching are still only incompletely understood, RIE has been very successful in meeting the etching requirements of todays semiconductor technology in regard to etch directionality and etch selectivity [2]. With etch directionality (or etch anisotropy) the ratio of vertical to horizontal etch rate of a material immersed in a plasma is conventionally denoted. The etch selectivity between two materials is the ratio between their etch rates under the same conditions. Etch selectivity is much more difficult to achieve in reactive ion etching than in wet etching, since the substantial ion bombardment involved in RIE makes chemical differences between different materials less important in the etching process.

In Table 2 etching steps in silicon device processing which are currently performed using reactive ion etching or plasma etching are listed. Many of the processes listed are non-critical etches and the desired objectives are relatively easy to achieve. The demands on etch directionality are highest in the formation of deep ($\simeq$ 6 μm and greater) trenches for storage capacitors in the silicon substrate. The most challenging applications from the point of view of etch selectivity are (a) the formation of contact holes though oxide to silicon and silicided junctions and (b) polysilicon/polycide gate definition and stopping on a thin ($\leq$10nm) oxide. Other etching steps are associated with different challenges, e.g. the patterning of Al(Cu) in chlorine discharges [3]. Copper is added at the percent level to Al in order to increase the electromigration resistance of Al lines. $AlCl_3$ has high volatility at room temperature and aluminum etches easily in chlorine; CuCl has low volatility and Cu related residues can form. In order to remove the CuCl effectively both a higher temperature and significant ion bombardment are needed. These critical applications have been well researched and a great deal of understanding has been obtained. In this article we will use these prototypical applications to highlight our current understanding of etch selectivity and etch directionality mechanisms in RIE. The considerations presented in this article apply to etching applications characterized by similar requirements but not covered because of space limitations, e.g. RIE of compound semiconductors, polymers, etc.

Table 2: Common applications of plasma/reactive ion etching in silicon technology.

Application	Etch Step
Device Formation	Polysilicon/polycide gate; sidewall; storage node; emitter contact.
Isolation	Deep trench; shallow trench or recessed oxide.
Interconnections	Contacts; metal; interlevel vias.
Other	Multilayer resist definition; resist strip; backside strip; planarization.

This chapter is a brief review of reactive ion etching as applied to pattern transfer, primarily in silicon technology. Most of the past (and present) efforts to understand plasma-based dry etching processes have been directed to the investigation of halogen-based etching of silicon and silicon related materials and our knowledge of those systems has reached a level of maturity which is far greater than of other etchant-substrate systems. Several of the topics covered also are of particular interest to this author and, for the sake of convenience, I have disproportionately drawn on experimental results of my collaborators in the description of these topics. Rapid progress is being made in all aspects of plasma based etching; therefore this review focuses on concepts, rather than listing data obtained on all different systems. Although the detailed plasma chemistry of rf discharges used for etching materials of interest to compound semiconductor technology, packaging, etc., is different from the one described here, many of the basic processes are similar. Many of the considerations presented in this article can therefore be cautiously adapted to plasmas utilized for the patterning of different materials.

8.2. ETCH DIRECTIONALITY

8.2.1 General Considerations

Etch directionality is due to directed energy input into an etching reaction at a surface and can be accomplished by ion, electron or photon bombardment of a surface exposed to a chemical etchant. The achievement of etch directionality in the case of RIE is due to energetic ion bombardment. An important clarifying experiment was performed by Coburn and Winters [4]. They exposed a silicon surface to a well-defined dosage of chemical etchant, XeF_2, and simultaneous energetic Ar ion bombardment. A key result of their studies has been that the silicon erosion rate obtained for a silicon surface simultaneously exposed to the XeF_2 chemical etchant and to the Ar ion beam is much greater than the sum of the etch rates for exposure to the ion beam and chemical etchant separately. This synergism can explain the etch anisotropy obtained under these conditions. Recent photoemission work by McFeely et al. [5] has shed some light on the mechanism of ion enhanced etching for the XeF_2/Si system: It was observed that a silicon-fluorine reaction layer much thicker than a monolayer was formed. Volatile SiF_4 was seen trapped in the reaction layer. A preponderance of SiF_3 was observed which suggested that the reaction to form SiF_4 from SiF_3 was the rate limiting step of the etching reaction. It was observed that when the reaction layer was bombarded with Ar ions the Ar ion beam tended to drive a disproportionate reaction in which involatile SiF_3 molecules on the Si surface were converted into SiF_2 and volatile SiF_4 etch product.

Several mechanisms have been proposed for ion-induced reactions resulting in enhanced etching [6,7]. Some of the primary models are:

a. Chemically enhanced physical sputtering [8]
    In this model the modified surface layer has a larger sputtering yield than the unmodified surface, e.g. SiF_x − species are less tightly bound than Si and have a greater sputtering yield.

b. Damage model [9]
    Lattice damage produced by ion bombardment increases the reaction rate of etchant species with the substrate relative to undamaged material.

c. Chemical sputtering model [10]
    In this model ion bombardment induced collision cascades supply energy to the reaction layer which is used to increase the mobility of molecules which will form volatile products and desorb into the gas phase.

There are other models or variants of above models. Depending on the particular etchant-substrate under consideration a different ion-enhancement mechanism may be dominant. For instance, it appears that the lattice damage model is not important for the fluorine-silicon system [11], while there is evidence of its importance for the fluorine-tungsten system [11,12].

8.2.2 Fluorine- vs. Chlorine- vs. Bromine-Based Plasmas

Etching of Si can be accomplished using F-, Cl-, and Br-based chemistries and the etch products are volatile SiF_4, $SiCl_4$ and $SiBr_4$, respectively. Most studies have focused on halocarbon chemistries, specifically CF_4. Mogab studied the etching of Si in a CF_4 plasma with negligible ion bombardment of the Si substrate [13]. He measured the intensity of the 704nm atomic fluorine related optical emission. A one-to-one correspondence of Si etch rate and atomic fluorine emission as the rf power was varied was observed, showing that F atoms are directly involved and their gas phase density controls the rate of the Si etching process for simple CF_4 plasmas. Etching of silicon in fluorine-based plasmas results normally in a large undercut of the masking layer, indicating a large chemical etch rate. Because of this fluorine-based plasmas have not commonly been used for anisotropic etching of silicon. However, Tachi and his coworkers showed recently that the horizontal silicon etch rate using an SF_6 plasma can be dramatically reduced by cooling the substrate to a temperature of $-120°C$ and near-ideal etch profiles can be obtained [14]. The low substrate temperature was thought to suppress spontaneous chemical etching reactions occurring on the sidewalls of the trench. Ion assisted etching reactions which dominate at the bottom of the trench were not affected by the low substrate temperature and the vertical silicon etch rate increased as the temperature was decreased, possibly due to condensation of etchant.

Chlorine and bromine based chemistries are primarily used to achieve anisotropic etch profiles in single crystal silicon. Etch directionality for these etchants may be explained by the observation that crystalline silicon and silicon dioxide are not spontaneously etched by chlorine and bromine atoms [15]. Chlorine molecules dissociatively chemisorb on single crystal silicon at room temperature and form an ordered chlorine overlayer. Cluster calculations have shown that chlorine atoms on a silicon surface have to overcome an energy barrier of $\simeq 10eV$ in order to attack the backbonds of silicon surface atoms in order to form $SiCl_4$ [16]. No energy barrier for fluorine to penetration of the silicon surface was found, indicating that sub-surface SiF_x species will form spontaneously. The size of the halogen relative to the silicon atom plays an important role. The results of the calculations are consistent with the absence of spontaneous etching of silicon exposed to chlorine atoms. Chlorine based etching of undoped silicon and equivalent etching conditions have been described as ion-initiated etching in contrast to fluorine-based etching which is ion-assisted [9]. Etching of silicon using Cl_2/Ar RIE results in very directional profiles [17]. It is possible that sidewall passivation is absent under these conditions, although it is not possible to rule out a sidewall passivation layer formed by redeposition of masking material.

In contrast to undoped silicon, highly doped silicon (dopant concentration $\simeq 10^{20}cm^{-3}$) etches spontaneously in a Cl_2 discharge. Schwartz et al. [17] observed horizontal etching of a buried highly As-doped silicon layer in a low pressure (10 mTorr) Cl_2 discharge (see Fig. 2). However, for a CCl_4 discharge or undoped silicon the etching was perfectly directional. Mogab et al. observed that etching of doped polycrystalline silicon in a 300mTorr Cl_2 plasma resulted in an isotropic profile [18]. Directional etching could be achieved by adding C_2F_6 to Cl_2 and forming a sidewall passivation layer. The doping effect and the concept of sidewall passivation will be discussed in the following sections.

Mixed halocarbon etching gases containing chlorine and bromine are often used for anisotropic etching, e.g. $CClF_3$, CCl_2F_2, CCl_3F, CF_3Br. The fluorine-carbon bond is stronger than the chlorine-carbon or bromine-carbon bond. Electron-impact dissociation of the mixed halocarbons produces primarily chlorine or bromine atoms and the etching characteristics using these discharges are chlorine- or bromine-like. For example, Matsuo [19] used a 30mTorr CF_3Br plasma to directionally etch silicon using an oxide mask, whereas a CF_4 plasma using similar conditions resulted in nearly isotropic etching characteristics. The concentration of chlorine and bromine can be increased by adding oxygen to the mixed halocarbon gases [9]. However, this will also result in oxidation of the fluorocarbon recombinant (CF_3) and reduce the tendency for polymer formation and sidewall passivation.

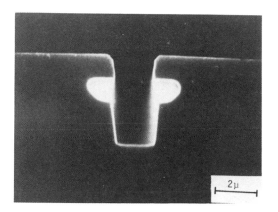

Figure 2: Scanning electron micrograph illustrating the lateral etching of a highly As doped Si layer in a Cl_2/As plasma. The etching parameters were: 2mTorr Cl_2/8mTorr Ar, 11sccm Cl_2, 27.12 MHz, 0.67W/cm² (From Ref. 17).

8.2.3 Doping Effect

The Si etch rate depends on the electronic properties of the Si substrate (doping effect). N-type silicon (e.g. P, As, etc. doped) etches faster than intrinsic silicon which etches faster than p-type silicon (B, Ga, etc. doped). The dopant concentration of silicon needs to be greater than $\simeq 10^{19}cm^{-3}$ in order to observe a doping dependence of the etch rate. Figure 3 is from the work by Lee et al. [20] who measured the chemical etch rate of silicon per gas phase fluorine atom as a function of rf power. Heavily As-doped silicon (n-type) etched faster than intrinsic silicon which etched faster than heavily B-doped silicon (p-type). The increase in the silicon etch rate per gas phase fluorine atom with rf power was thought to be due to heating of the silicon substrates. The doping effect is not chemical in nature since it is absent if the dopants are not electrically activated [18]. The doping effect depends on the electronic structure of the surface and has been explained by band bending effects at the semiconductor surface [20]. Coulomb attraction between uncompensated donors, such as As^+, and chemisorbed halogens, e.g. F^-, enhances the Si etch rate for n-type Si. On the other hand, Coulomb repulsion between uncompensated acceptors, e.g. B^-, and chemisorbed halogens, such as F^-, inhibits the Si etch rate for p-type Si. A detailed study of the doping effect for silicon has recently been completed by Winters et al. [21].

The doping effect decreases with ion-bombardment and is difficult to observe for reactive ion etching conditions as a doping dependence of the vertical etch rate [22]. Its technological significance lies in the fact that it makes the control of profile shapes in trench etching difficult. Trench formation in silicon technology, e.g., for capacitor and device isolation applications, commonly involves etching through Si layers of different doping levels. Since the lateral etch rates (chemical etching only) of the differently doped Si layers are not the same, non-ideal trench profiles due to different, doping-level dependent amounts of mask undercutting would result (see Fig. 2). The solution to this problem has been sidewall passivation.

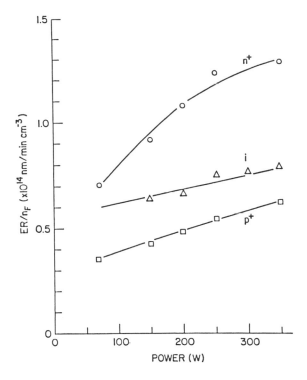

Figure 3: Doping effect in plasma etching. The chemical etch rate per fluorine gas phase atom for n-type, p-type and undoped silicon is shown as a function of rf power. The experimental conditions were: 13.56MHz rf, Al cathode, 76.8%CF_4/19.2%O_2/4%Ar, 50sccm total flow, 25mTorr (from Ref. 20).

8.2.4 Etch Directionality Through Sidewall Passivation

Sidewall passivation layers (see Fig. 4) are key to achieving etch directionality in many dry etching processes [9,23]. The glow discharge chemistry is chosen so that etch inhibiting films can form as long as they are not exposed to ion bombardment, which leads to the dissolution of these films. Sidewalls of trenches are not exposed to ion bombardment and will be covered by the etch-inhibiting films and prevent mask undercutting. The bottom of the trench which is exposed to ion bombardment is free from passivating film and etching reactions can proceed.

Sidewall passivation makes it possible to achieve etch directionality for etchant/substrate systems which normally exhibit isotropic etching characteristics, e.g. fluorine-based etching of silicon using a SF_6 discharge. In Fig. 5 secondary electron micrographs of silicon trenches formed by SF_6/O_2 RIE using various percentages of O_2 are displayed [24,25]. Reactive ion etching of silicon using pure SF_6 results in a large undercut of the oxide mask and nearly isotropic etch profiles (see Fig. 5(a)). As SF_6 is diluted with oxygen the etch profiles become more and more directional and the undercut of the oxide mask is reduced (Figs. 5(b) through 5(f)). The simplest explanation for the observed etching behavior is that in the absence of ion bombardment, i.e. at the trench sidewall, oxidation of silicon takes place rather than fluorine attack and concomitant

(a)

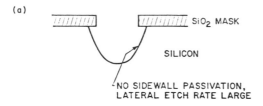

SiO₂ MASK

SILICON

NO SIDEWALL PASSIVATION,
LATERAL ETCH RATE LARGE

(b)

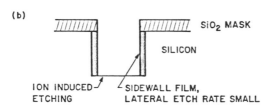

SiO₂ MASK

SILICON

ION INDUCED
ETCHING

SIDEWALL FILM,
LATERAL ETCH RATE SMALL

Figure 4: Schematic of the concept of sidewall passivation enabling directional etching without undercut of etch mask.

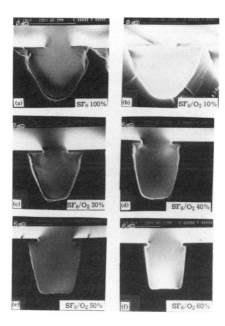

Figure 5: Secondary electron micrographs of Si trenches formed by reactive ion etching at 25mTorr using SF_6/O_2 gas mixtures illustrating the reduction in mask undercut and improvement in etch directionality with increasing oxygen content. The etching was performed using 200W 13.56MHz rf power, a pressure of 25mT and a gas flow of 100sccm and a quartz covered cathode was used. The opening in the oxide mask is 3 μm wide; the etch time was 10 min for all trenches (from Ref. 24).

etching. The sidewall of the trench is protected from etching by the resulting "sidewall film". For bombarded surfaces (bottom of the trench) the fluorine attack of silicon is enhanced, oxidation of silicon is reduced and etching can proceed. Without oxygen in the feed gas the protective sidewall film can not be formed and the trench etch profile is nearly isotropic. The composition of the sidewall film formed in SF_6/O_2 RIE has recently been determined using in-situ angle resolved X-ray photoemission [24]. Regular arrays of trenches were illuminated with X-rays at grazing incidence which caused shadowing of the trench bottoms and no X-ray induced photoelectron emission from those areas. The contribution of the sidewall film was differentiated from the oxide mask by exploiting electrostatic charging differences due to the photoemission process. The composition of the sidewall passivation layer could thus be determined in-situ. For the SF_6/O_2 trench etching process it was found to be a fluorinated oxide-like layer with an oxygen/silicon ratio of 1.7 and a fluorine/silicon ratio of 1.0. The sidewall passivation layer could be dissolved in buffered hydrofluoric acid and was removed with the oxide mask.

Passivation of sidewall features is observed for most reactive chemistries. The sources of sidewall passivation material can be suitable precursors formed in the plasma gas phase, erosion and redeposition of masking material or formation of etch products with low volatility and redeposition. Conceptually it appears simplest to add the sidewall passivation forming gas directly to the primary etching gas, e.g. adding O_2 to SF_6, C_2F_6 to Cl_2 [18], etc. and control the amount of sidewall passivation by the mixing ratio. However, addition of the sidewall forming gases changes the etch rate, mask selectivity, etc. of the process and requires process modifications, e.g. the formation of very thick masking layers for trench etching. For example, addition of 50% O_2 to SF_6/O_2 decreases the silicon etch rate and the etch selectivity to the oxide mask by a factor of ≈ 5. Often too little sidewall passivation is formed using the gas mixing method and horizontal etching still occurs (see Fig. 5 (f)). In many etching processes the supply of sidewall passivation material is therefore enhanced (or sometimes solely controlled) by indirect processes where passivation material is provided by eroding the etch mask, e.g. argon and xenon have been added to the etching gases in order to cause enhanced sputtering of the photoresist or oxide masking layer and subsequent redeposition.

In order to improve control of the etch profile, methods to decouple the etching process from the formation of sidewall passivation have been suggested. Tsujimoto et al. [26] have used a gas and bias voltage chopping method to enable anisotropic etching of silicon and tungsten. They sequentially generated SF_6 etching and NH_3 sidewall film formation plasmas, respectively. At the beginning of each etching cycle the dc bias was increased to enable etching of the passivation film deposited onto the bottom of the feature. The advantage of this method is thought to be that the NH_3 sidewall film formation processes are independent of and do not disturb the SF_6 etching plasma.

8.2.5 Aspect Ratio Dependence of Etch Rate

As lithographic capabilities improve feature sizes in semiconductor technology will continue to shrink. In trench etching the trench width (or opening) will therefore decrease while the etch depth of the trench will remain the same or become even greater. The aspect ratio (depth/width) therefore increases. Reactive ion etching of trenches with submicron openings and high aspect ratio is more difficult than formation of trenches with smaller aspect ratio. For a given (sub-micron) opening width the etch rate decreases as a function of the aspect ratio (or depth of the trench) which increases the demands on etch selectivity with respect to the mask. This effect has been examined by Chin et al. [27] and their results are displayed in Fig. 6. The etch rate decreases almost linearly as the aspect ratio increases and is determined by the aspect ratio, regardless of the opening size (for opening widths less than 1 micron). This phenomenon has been attributed to a diverging electric field in the trench [27], diffusion effects on the supply of reactant to the bottom of the trench and consumption of reactant at the trench sidewalls. At this time the dominant mechanism which causes this effect has not been established.

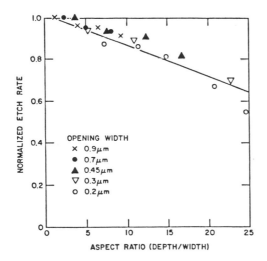

Figure 6: Aspect ratio dependence of the silicon etch rate in submicron trench etching (CCl_2F_2/O_2 gas mixture, oxide mask, from Ref. 27).

8.3 PLASMA CHEMICAL CONSIDERATIONS

A large variety of fluorine, chlorine, bromine and oxygen based etching plasmas with a profusion of gas additives are used in the semiconductor industry (see Table 3). In most cases a specific etching gas mixture (or "recipe") is based on a great deal of empirical evidence obtained for a particular etching application rather than real fundamental understanding of the relevant plasma chemistry. However, certain basic insights have proven to be helpful in formulating etching gas mixtures [28]. The most studied and best understood etching gas mixtures are CF_4/O_2 and CF_4/H_2 plasmas.

8.3.1 Effect of Oxygen Addition

The addition of small amounts of O_2 to a CF_4 plasma is known to increase the fluorine atom concentration in the discharge dramatically [29-31]. This is due to reaction of oxygen with CF_x radicals to form CO, CO_2, and COF_2 and produce more free fluorine. This effect, in combination with the lowering of the concentration of CF_x radicals by oxygen reaction (e.g. CF_3), reduces the recombination of F atoms with CF_3 and increases the steady-state F atom density. The consumption of unsaturated CF_x species by oxygen has the additional effect of suppressing polymer formation on surfaces which proceeds from unsaturated intermediates, such as CF_2. As oxygen is added to CF_4 the fluorine atom

Table 3: Materials and reactive gases used for reactive ion etching in silicon technology.

Material	Reactive Chemistries	Remarks
Silicon	CF_4/O_2, SF_6, NF_3,	Anisotropy difficult
	Cl_2, BCl_3, CCl_4,	Directional, good SiO_2 selectivity.
	HBr, CF_3Br,	Directional.
Oxide	F_4/H_2, CHF_3/C_2F_6, CHF_3/CO_2	Etch selectivity to Si.
Nitride	CF_4, CHF_3, SF_6, NF_3,	Characteristics intermediate
		to Si; SiO_2.
$TiSi_2$	CCl_2F_2, CCl_4	Control of oxygen impurities.
WSi_2	CF_4/O_2, SF_6	
W	CF_4/O_2, SF_6	
Al	Cl_2, BCl_3, CCl_4, $SiCl_4$	Removal of native oxide.
Al(Cu)	Cl_2, BCl_3, CCl_4, $SiCl_4$,	Cu removal, removal of native oxide.
Polymers	O_2, O_2/CF_4	

concentration increases at first (up to $\simeq 20\%$ O_2 addition) and subsequently decreases again due to dilution. These fluorine-rich plasmas are used for isotropic etching of silicon. The etching of silicon in CF_4/O_2 glow discharges is also of interest scientifically since it displays nicely how gas phase processes can control the etching behavior for certain conditions whereas surface processes will limit the etch rate for slightly different experimental conditions. Figure 7, from the work of Mogab et al. [29], shows the etch rate of silicon as a function of the fluorine concentration in the gas phase measured by optical emission. The fluorine concentration in the gas phase was varied by adding oxygen to the CF_4 plasma. Depending on the amount of oxygen added to the plasma two different Si etch rates can be observed for the same fluorine concentration. The Si etch rate is determined by the concentrations of both fluorine and oxygen atoms in the gas phase because they compete for active Si surface sites. Mogab et al. [29] proposed that increased oxidation of the Si surface for increasing oxygen percentages in the feed gas is responsible for the lower Si etch rates observed for high fluorine concentrations if simultaneously the oxygen concentration is large. Recently the etching behavior of silicon in CF_4/O_2 was reexamined and in-situ X-ray photoelectron spectroscopy was used to characterize the silicon surfaces after etching [32]. Photoelectron spectroscopy showed that a SiF_xO_y reaction layer was formed on the Si surface and that the composition of the layer changed from primarily SiF-bonding to SiO-bonding as the percentage of O_2 in CF_4/O_2 was increased. Simultaneously the layer grew in thickness. The silicon etch rate is plotted versus the SiF_xO_y layer thickness in Fig. 8 [32]. The percentage of O_2 in CF_4/O_2 for which a particular etch rate and film thickness value was obtained is also indicated. As oxygen is added to pure CF_4, the etch rate increases and the film thickness decreases. Both of these effects should be a result of the rise in fluorine atom gas phase concentration (see Fig. 7) which was also observed in this study [32]. For O_2 percentages greater than 5% O_2 the film thickness increases, the Si etch rate reaches a maximum near 7.5% O_2 and subsequently decreases. The Si etch rate for oxygen concentrations greater than 7.5% correlates to and appears to be controlled primarily by the thickness of the SiF_xO_y layer, rather than by the F atom concentration in the gas phase which increases up to 15%O$_2$ addition. Progressively thicker films on Si are formed as a result of increased oxidation and decreased fluorination of the Si surface as the percentage of O$_2$ in CF$_4$/O$_2$ is increased. For the same SiF$_x$O$_y$ layer thickness different Si etch rates can be observed. These results show that for low oxygen concentrations the etch rate is controlled by the arrival rate of fluorine to the surface and responds to increases of the <u>gas phase</u> fluorine concentration. For high oxygen concentrations the etch rate is limited by oxidation of the silicon surface and correlates well to the thickness increase of the <u>surface reaction layer</u>.

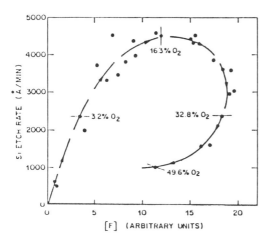

Figure 7: Etch rate of silicon versus fluorine concentration in gas phase determined by optical emission spectroscopy. Percentages of O$_2$ in CF$_4$/O$_2$ are indicated. The experimental conditions were: 350mTorr, 200sccm total flow, 200W rf, 100°C sample temperature, samples grounded (from Ref. 29).

Similar effects of oxygen addition may occur for chloro- and bromocarbon plasmas (e.g., CF$_3$Cl, CF$_2$Cl$_2$, CCl$_4$, CF$_3$Br) where an increase in the Cl or Br concentration and a decrease in the formation of polymer may result [9].

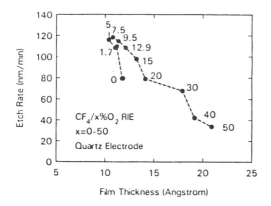

Figure 8: Silicon etch rate as a function of the SiF$_x$O$_y$ layer thickness. The numbers next to the data denote the percentage x of O$_2$ used in CF$_4$/O$_2$ RIE. The fluorine atom gas phase concentration is at a maximum at 15% oxygen addition. Experimental conditions: 200W 13.56MHz RIE, 25mTorr, 100sccm total flow, quartz cathode (from Ref. 32).

8.3.2 Effect of Hydrogen Addition

The addition of small amounts of hydrogen to CF_4 plasmas reduces the concentration of free fluorine because of HF formation. A lower fluorine atom concentration decreases the importance of recombination of fluorine with CF_3 radicals and a discharge rich in unsaturated fluorocarbons, such as CF_2, is produced. These species are precursors of polymeric fluorocarbon films which deposit on the inner surfaces of the plasma chamber. If the hydrogen concentration is too high polymerization occurs on all surfaces and etching stops. Similar effects can be achieved by adding CH_4, C_2H_4, CHF_3, etc. or alternatively C_2F_6, C_3F_8, etc. to CF_4 discharges. These fluorine deficient discharges are important since they enable selective etching of SiO_2 (see section on selective etching).

A useful indicator of the predominance of etching over deposition (polymerization) is the fluorine/carbon ratio of the discharge [33]. In this model the theoretical F/C ratio for the discharge is calculated, i.e. the F/C ratio is 4 for CF_4, 3 for C_2F_6, etc.. Hydrogen addition lowers the F/C ratio by reacting with fluorine atoms to form HF, oxygen addition increases the F/C ratio by CO, CO_2 formation, mixing of CF_4 with CH_4 lowers the F/C ratio, loading with an etchable material which consumes fluorine lowers the F/C ratio, and so forth. For a silicon substrate, etching is observed for F/C ratios greater than 3 whereas fluorocarbon film deposition is observed for F/C ratios of less than 2. At intermediate F/C ratios the changeover from deposition to etching depends on the degree of ion bombardment possible under the particular etching conditions, with greater ion bombardment inducing etching.

It appears that the effect of hydrogen addition on mixed halocarbon based plasmas (such as $CClF_3$) is similar to effects observed with CF_4 plasmas. For $CClF_3$ it has been shown that hydrogen addition results in a discharge with very similar characteristics to a CF_4/H_2 discharge, e.g. for silicon the deposition of a chlorofluorocarbon film is observed [34] and SiO_2/Si etch selectivity is achieved [35].

8.3.3 Other Gas Additives

Noble gases such as argon and helium are often added to stabilize plasmas or for cooling purposes (He for high pressure plasmas). Argon addition can also cause inert ion bombardment of a surface and result in anisotropic etching (e.g., Ar/Cl_2 RIE of Si). The consequences of diluting a reactive gas with a noble gas are not easily understood. The addition of a chemically inert gas may significantly change the electron energy distribution in a plasma and alter the reactive species population in the discharge. This effect is observed when the ionization potential of the chemically inert additive is very different from the ionization potentials of the plasma species of the primary gas. An altered reactive species make-up of the discharge, e.g. enhanced dissociation, can also be due to more complex effects. For example, Gottscho et al. [36] examined the mixing of BCl_3 with He, Ar and Kr using laser induced fluorescence. They found that energy transfer from noble gas metastable states to BCl_3 states to cause enhanced dissociation of BCl_3.

8.3.4 Loading Effect

The "loading" effect refers to a significant depletion of the etchant species in the gas phase due to consumption in the etching process. Depending on the gas phase mean free path, the number and structure of specimens being etched the loading effect may be both global, i.e. the reactant concentration in the reactor is uniformly lowered, and local. Mogab analyzed the relationship between etch rate ER and area A of wafer load and found this expression [13]:

$$ER(A) = \frac{(k_{etch}/k_{loss})G}{1 + (k_{etch}\rho A/k_{loss}V)}$$

(1)

where k_{etch} and k_{loss} are the first order rate constants for etching and etchant loss in an empty reactor, respectively, G is the rate of production of etchant species, ρ the number density of substrate molecules, and V the volume of the reactor. For a large wafer load area A equation (1) becomes $ER(A) = GV/\rho A$ and the etch rate varies inversely with the wafer load area A. The importance of the loading effect is decreased by making k_{loss} large relative to k_{etch}, i.e. by consuming etchant species through processes other than reaction with the wafer load, e.g. rapid pumping.

The local loading effect is important for patterned wafers (pattern sensitivity) and is difficult to minimize. In this case the reactant concentration varies locally due to consumption by a reactive material and non-consumption by a non-reactive material. Figure 9 shows results of the work by Selwyn [37] who measured the spatially resolved oxygen

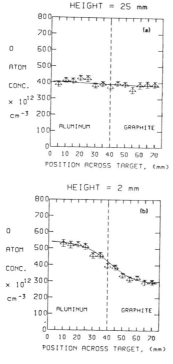

Figure 9: Spatial variation of the oxygen atom density (as determined by two-photon laser-induced fluorescence) as a function of horizontal sample position in the O_2/Ar plasma (27 mTorr O_2 and 80 mTorr Ar). The aluminum cathode was partially covered with graphite and the interface between the two halves is shown by the dashed line. In (a) data obtained at a height of 25mm above the substrate are shown, whereas the data in (b) were obtained 2mm above the substrate. In (a) the O atom concentration is rather uniform. In (b) an O atom gradient exists which is thought to arise from the consumption of O atoms by the etching of graphite (from Ref. 37).

atom concentration in an oxygen plasma over graphite and aluminum surfaces using laser induced fluorescence. At 25mm above the target only a minor variation is observed between the graphite (loaded) and the aluminum (unloaded) portions of the electrode. At a height of 2mm above the samples a strong gradient in oxygen atom concentration can be observed above the two sections of the electrode, which is apparently due to the consumption of oxygen atoms by the etching of graphite. The gradual decrease in oxygen atom concentration observed between the Al and graphite sections of the cathode is indicative of diffusional processes in the plasma. At a height of 25mm above the electrode diffusion/mixing processes have eliminated the O atom concentration gradient.

8.4 ETCH SELECTIVITY

8.4.1 General Considerations

Etch selectivity of a film being etched is required with respect to the etch mask and - if present - to the underlayer. Etch selectivity to the underlayer is more critical since in most cases the mask will be removed after the etching step whereas the underlayer becomes part of the completed device. Commonly a certain amount of overetching (i.e. etching beyond the time when complete removal of the film being patterned is first signalled by endpoint detection - see section 7) needs to occur in order to account for nonuniform etch rates throughout the reactor and ensure complete removal of the film everywhere on the wafer.

Etch selectivity of a material A over a material B in reactive ion etching is due to rate differences of the elementary steps taking place at the surfaces of these materials. These are a) the adsorption step, b) the reaction step, and c) the desorption step. The following mechanisms can be responsible for the achievement of etch selectivity:

a. Selective formation of an etch inhibiting layer on one material. Due to the simultaneous presence of different plasma gas phase species several processes occur in parallel at surfaces immersed in a processing plasma. For example, in fluorocarbon-based plasma etching of silicon and silicon dioxide it is known that fluorine induced etching occurs in parallel with, and competes with, fluorocarbon film deposition. If the processing conditions are chosen such that etching and deposition are nearly balanced for a material A (i.e. SiO_2), this balance may be tilted to deposition for a different material B (i.e. Si) because of a different net adsorption rate for the gas phase precursor of the passivating film (due to higher sticking coefficients, different reactivity, etc. with the surface of B). This is the basis for selective etching of silicon dioxide over silicon in a fluorocarbon plasma, such as CHF_3, and will be discussed in more detail later.

b. Non-reactivity of material B in plasma environment, e.g. ashing of photoresist on a silicon dioxide film in an oxygen discharge. The photoresist layer will volatilize by forming C-O, H-O, etc. related species, but the SiO_2 layer is not attacked by the oxygen plasma.

c. Non-volatility of reaction product, e.g. ashing of photoresist on silicon in an oxygen discharge and formation of involatile silicon dioxide. The photoresist reacts with oxygen to form volatile species whereas silicon reaction with the oxygen plasma causes the formation of an involatile reaction product.

In many practical situations a combination of these factors may determine the achieved etch rate ratio. A very useful indicator of the possible plasma etch selectivity is the volatilization ratio of two materials exposed to controlled atom or molecular beams. Experimentally it has been found that these non-plasma etch rate ratios are relevant to plasma etching environments without ion bombardment. For instance, Flamm and his coworkers have determined an etch rate ratio of silicon to silicon dioxide exposed to fluorine atoms of 41:1 [38]. A similar Si/SiO_2 etch rate ratio can be achieved in a glow discharge of SF_6 which provides a fluorine-rich plasma with a low dc self-bias voltage [24,25].

The effect of ion bombardment is to accelerate the same elementary surface processes that are responsible for the achievement of etch selectivity, i.e. the adsorption, reaction and desorption steps (see section 1). This reduces the importance of "bottlenecks" in the overall etching reaction. It is not surprising therefore that ion bombardment nearly always decreases the possible etch rate ratio of chemically different materials exposed to a reactive plasma from the "intrinsic" value.

8.4.2 Silicon Dioxide to Silicon Etch Selectivity

The important case of etching selectively silicon dioxide over silicon in a fluorocarbon plasma is discussed now in some detail. For SiO_2 and Si no acceptable etch selectivity can normally be obtained in a CF_4 discharge. Heinecke discovered that addition of H_2 to CF_4 makes it possible to minimize the etching of Si as compared to the etching of SiO_2 [39]. This approach was subsequently investigated further and optimized by Ephrath et al. [40] for RIE applications. Lehmann et al. [41] used CHF_3 and obtained similar results. As hydrogen is added to a CF_4 plasma the Si etch rate decreases monotonically as the percentage of H_2 is raised and eventually stops. The percentage of hydrogen where Si etching stops depends on the plasma etching process parameters, e.g. the total gas flow, pressure, etc., but is typically $\simeq 30\text{-}60\%H_2$ in $CF_4/x\%H_2$. For a CF_4/H_2 composition sufficient to stop the etching of Si only a small decrease of the silicon dioxide etch rate ($\simeq 20\%$ of maximum etch rate) is observed [40]. The role of hydrogen in controlling the Si etch rate is twofold. (i) Atomic H scavenges atomic F in the gas phase to form HF molecules and the Si etch rate which depends on the F concentration is consequently reduced. (ii) More important in slowing down the Si etch rate and achieving SiO_2/Si etch selectivity is the selective formation of a fluorocarbon film on the Si surface as a result of hydrogen addition to a CF_4 plasma. For suitably chosen RIE processing conditions the fluorocarbon film is not formed on SiO_2, allowing etching of SiO_2 to proceed [42,43]. This is shown in Fig. 10. Carbon 1s X-ray photoemission spectra are displayed for SiO_2 and Si surfaces after reactive ion etching in $CF_4/40\%H_2$ plasmas, a gas mixture used to selectively etch SiO_2 over Si (etch rate ratio $\simeq 20:1$) [40]. The photoemission peaks are due to the fluorocarbon film which covers the silicon substrate after reactive ion etching. The chemical groups giving rise to the photoemission peaks are $C - CF_x$, CF, CF_2 and CF_3 (in order of increasing binding energy). An additional shoulder centered at a binding energy of 284eV is apparent also in the carbon 1s spectrum for silicon. The chemical origin of the 284eV component is silicon-carbon bonding and arises from bonds localized at the fluorocarbon film/silicon interface [42,44]. The formation of a silicon-carbon bond is a critical step in the formation of a fluorocarbon film on silicon since the silicon-carbon bond is the "bridging bond" between the silicon substrate and the fluorocarbon layer. The importance of surface carbon contamination of silicon in the achievement of SiO_2/Si etch selectivity was first observed by Coburn in Auger studies [45].

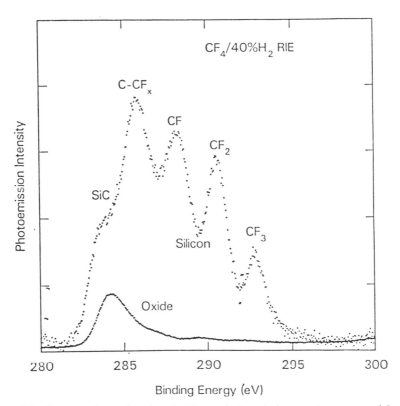

Figure 10: A comparison of carbon 1s X-ray photoemission spectra measured for Si and SiO$_2$ after CF$_4$/40%H$_2$ reactive ion etching. The etching was performed using 200W rf power, a pressure of 25mTorr and a gas flow of 40sccm. The samples were transferred in vacuum from the RIE chamber to the surface analysis chamber. The peaks observed for silicon are due to a fluorocarbon film which is absent for reactive ion etched SiO$_2$ (from Ref. 51).

In the lower panel of Fig. 11, the fluorocarbon steady-state film thickness is shown as a function of the hydrogen percentage in the CF$_4$/H$_2$ discharge for silicon and oxide. Whereas the fluorocarbon film thickness on silicon increases roughly linearly with hydrogen addition to CF$_4$, little fluorocarbon is formed on SiO$_2$ for all hydrogen concentrations. In the upper panel of Fig. 11 inverse Si and SiO$_2$ etch rates are shown. The SiO$_2$ etch rate remains nearly unaffected by the addition of H$_2$ to CF$_4$ and the Si etch rate drops off significantly. Silicon etch rate suppression relative to SiO$_2$ and fluorocarbon film thickness increase on Si relative to SiO$_2$ show a very similar behavior as a function of H$_2$ addition to CF$_4$, showing that the Si etch rate and the achieved SiO$_2$/Si etch selectivity is controlled by the fluorocarbon film thickness. The fluorocarbon film interrupts the chain of elementary surface processes necessary for Si etching to proceed. The film decreases, and eventually completely prevents, the supply of fluorine to the silicon/fluorocarbon film interface [42,43]. Silicon etching stops because the fluorocarbon film limits the fluorine attack necessary to sustain silicon etching.

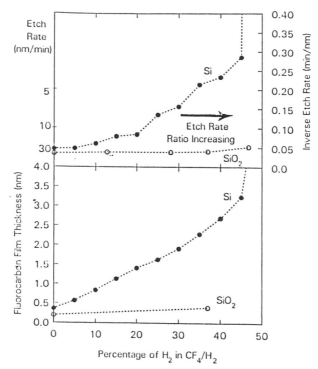

Figure 11: Upper panel: Inverse Si and SiO_2 reactive ion etch rates in a CF_4/H_2 plasma as a function of percentage of hydrogen. A total gas flow of 40sccm was used, the pressure 25mTorr, and 200W rf power supplied to the teflon covered cathode. The cathode diameter was 12 inches. As hydrogen is added the SiO_2/Si etch rate ratio is seen to increase. Lower panel: Fluorocarbon film thickness on Si and SiO_2 measured after 5 min of reactive ion etching using identical conditions. The similarity of the two plots is strongly suggestive that the suppression of the silicon etch rate (and the achievement of SiO_2/Si etch selectivity) is due to the selective formation of the relatively thick fluorocarbon film on silicon (from Ref. 51).

Hydrogen addition to CF_4 plasmas is required since laser induced fluorescence/optical emission studies have shown that atomic hydrogen reacts with CF_3 to form HF and CF_2 [46,47]. The increase in the density of CF_2 radicals, the fluorocarbon film precursor [48], enhances the formation rate of the fluorocarbon film. Since hydrogen also lowers the atomic fluorine concentration via HF formation, the revolatilization of the fluorocarbon film by fluorine-based etching is reduced as the hydrogen percentage in the CF_4/H_2 gas mixture is increased.

Etch selectivity is a consequence of the presence of oxygen in SiO_2 which minimizes fluorocarbon film growth on the oxide (see Fig. 10). The absence of the fluorocarbon film on oxide makes etching of silicon dioxide possible. Qualitatively, the absence of fluorocarbon film on SiO_2 is rather plausible. During etching of silicon dioxide, oxygen is continuously present on the etching surface which can react with the fluorocarbon film precursor(s) to form volatile CO, CO_2 and COF_2. However, the microscopic processes which lead to the fluorocarbon film absence on SiO_2 are likely to be complex and are very difficult to study experimentally. Virtually no experimental data which shed light on the mechanistic details of these processes in realistic etching plasmas are available at this time.

Etch selectivity of SiO_2 with respect to other substrates using the same discharge chemistry (25mTorr RIE conditions) has been shown to be due to the same selective fluorocarbon film formation mechanism. For example, the photoresist etch rate decreases in a fashion similar to that of silicon as H_2 is added to CF_4 [40]. Using photoresist patterned SiO_2/Si specimens it has been shown that the photoresist mask and the Si contact hole are covered by the same fluorocarbon film following RIE [49]. The same conclusion was reached for $TiSi_2$ and Ti substrates using the CF_4/H_2 gas mixture [50,51]. The latter case is significant since TiF_x species have very low volatility (TiF_3 has a boiling point of $1400°C$) and a TiF_x surface passivation layer may have been expected as responsible for SiO_2/Ti etch selectivity.

8.4.3 Silicon to Silicon Dioxide Etch Selectivity

High etch selectivity of silicon over silicon dioxide is required in the formation of silicon trenches using oxide masks, the patterning of poly-Si gate contacts over the gate oxide and a great number of other steps. In the definition of the poly-Si gate the requirement is to stop on a thin ($\leq 10nm$) gate oxide since otherwise the underlying shallow source-drain junctions in the Si substrate would be rapidly etched. As indicated by the "intrinsic" Si/SiO_2 etch rate ratio for fluorine atoms of 41 [38], high Si/SiO_2 etch selectivities of 30 and greater are possible using fluorine- and also chlorine-based plasmas, e.g. SF_6 and Cl_2 discharges enable the achievement of excellent Si/SiO_2 etch selectivity. In fact, thin oxide layers, e.g. the native oxide on silicon, can completely prevent etching of the silicon [18] or, if non-uniformly etched, cause the formation of surface roughness in the silicon layer ("black" silicon or sometimes called "grass"). The native oxide has to be removed initially using a short oxide etch, e.g. a CF_4 plasma. The primary difficulty in etching poly-Si and crystalline Si is control of the etch profile (see section on etch anisotropy). Chlorine-based chemistries have been used for directional silicon etching, e.g. Cl_2, CCl_4 [17] (which is not recommended since it has $\simeq 5$ times worse selectivity to the oxide than a Cl_2 plasma and is a carcinogen), CCl_2F_2, CCl_2F_3, Cl_2/SF_6 mixtures, and so forth which provide good etch directionality. Silicon etching processes using only chlorine, e.g. Cl_2, are characterized by a slow etch rate. The addition of a small percentage of SF_6 to Cl_2 increases the etch rate without loss of directionality, presumably because of sidewall passivation by chlorine [52]. For critical applications "mixed" processes are used where certain characteristics, e.g. high etch rate, directionality and selectivity relative to the photoresist mask, are optimized in the first part of the etching process and other characteristics, e.g. etch selectivity to the SiO_2 substrate, low damage, etc., are achieved in the final part of the process.

8.5 CONTAMINATION & DAMAGE ISSUES

8.5.1 Survey of RIE Damage Effects

The detrimental impact of reactive ion etching on the electrical properties of devices has been an area of considerable concern and is thought to be due to RIE related surface contamination and substrate displacement damage [53]. Etch-selectivity is often due to the deposition of etch inhibitors, which will remain on the exposed material after completion of the dry etching step (see the section on SiO_2/Si etch selectivity) and interfere with device processing following RIE. Bombardment damage is a concern since, although ion energies are typically below 500eV in RIE, the fluence is high ($\simeq 10^{15}$ions/cm^{2}sec) and lattice damage may be introduced. Displacement damage will alter the near-surface region of the material which is exposed to the plasma and change its electrical properties.

The term "RIE damage" has been used for a variety of undesirable RIE effects such as:

a. Surface residues
    These can be intrinsic to the etch process, i.e. related to the chemistry of discharge such as the fluorocarbon film, or due to the formation of involatile products with film impurities, e.g. CaF_2 from Ca in quartz etching. They can be extrinsic to the etch process, e.g. depend on the particular etching chamber configuration (aluminum electrode vs. teflon electrode).

b. Impurity penetration (implantation, diffusion)
    Plasma related impurities can penetrate the substrate during RIE, either as a result of direct implantation or diffusion. Hydrogen is of particular concern [54]. Substrate temperature control during RIE is also of great importance.

c. Lattice damage
    Point defects or extended defects can be introduced into the substrate by RIE. For silicon exposed to CF_4 plasmas, point defects known from radiation damage studies have been observed, e.g. carbon-carbon-silicon self-interstitial complexes [55,56].

d. Dopant loss or loss of dopant activity
    After CHF_3- and CF_4/H_2-based oxide RIE, loss of the electrical activity of dopants in the near-surface region of the Si substrate has been observed [57]. This is in part due to hydrogen-boron interaction in which a hydrogen atom which penetrated the silicon during RIE bonds to the dangling Si bond at the substitutional B site and renders the dopant electrically inactive [57].

e. Heavy metal contamination
    Transition metal contamination (nickel, iron and chromium) of semiconductors is caused primarily by sputtering of stainless steel parts of the chamber and subsequent contamination of the semiconductor [58]. These impurities diffuse very readily into the semiconductor and introduce energy levels near the middle of the energy gap which act as recombination centers and reduce the minority carrier lifetime. Heavy metal contamination is reduced by increasing the grounded/powered electrode area ratio which lowers the plasma potential.

f. Surface roughness
    This effect can be extrinsic, e.g. micromasking due to Al sputtering and redeposition in fluorine containing plasmas [59] or possibly intrinsic, e.g. etching of rough overlayer and replication of roughness in the underlayer.

g. Gate oxide breakdown or introduction of traps [60,61].
    Gate oxide breakdown has been observed as a result of RIE and the origin of the effect is not well understood. In one model oxide breakdown is thought to

be caused by the transient surge current as the rf power is turned off and the coupling capacitor discharges [60].

h. Mobile ion contamination [62].
Etching of the electrode material, e.g. teflon which often contains significant concentrations of sodium, exposes sodium at the surface of the electrode. In a fluorine-based discharge sodium does not form a volatile product and can contaminate the wafer being etched.

i. Post-RIE Corrosion [63]
In chlorine-based etching of aluminum, residues containing chlorine will remain after RIE. Upon exposure to atmosphere HCl is formed and corrosion of the Al lines takes place. The chlorine-containing residues are removed by post-RIE plasma/wet cleaning treatments.

These material modifications impact the performance of electronic devices built from RIE damaged materials. For example, surface residues and lattice damage have been shown to change the Schottky barrier height and reduce the forward leakage current of Schottky barriers formed on dry etched silicon [64]. Surface residues and dopant deactivation caused by contact hole etching through SiO_2 to the Si substrate have resulted in a high contact resistance of ohmic contacts fabricated on the exposed Si surface [57]. Surface roughness, gate oxide breakdown and mobile ion contamination reduce the quality of silicon dioxide layers which were either present during the RIE step or subsequently thermally grown on dry etched Si. In the latter case the interface state density was increased and the breakdown strength of the oxides was reduced as compared to controls. The amount of change depended on the voltage applied during etching [65]. Silicon lattice damage and heavy metal contamination reduce the minority carrier lifetime of silicon.

8.5.2 Silicon Surface Modifications Due to Selective SiO_2;Si RIE

It is important to differentiate between surface modifications which are essential to meeting the objectives of the RIE process and those which occur coincidentally, without any obvious function in the etching process. In the latter case it will be possible to eliminate these material modifications by improved RIE process/chamber design. In this section surface and near-surface substrate modifications caused by a prototypical RIE process, namely CF_4/H_2-based (or CHF_3-based) selective etching of SiO_2 over Si, are described [66,67]. This etching situation encompasses essential possible concerns with RIE, since a critical, active surface region of a Si device is exposed to the plasma.

The changes in the silicon near-surface region incurred as a result of selective oxide removal by CF_4/H_2 RIE are schematically depicted in Fig. 12 [54]. This picture is based on these measurements: i) In ion channeling and X-ray photoemission studies a fluorocarbon film was detected on the silicon substrate. The thickness of the film is limited to less than $\simeq 5nm$. ii) A thin SiO_2 layer is present underneath the C,F-film which is formed after air exposure of the etched specimens. iii) A heavily damaged Si layer ($\simeq 3$-$5nm$ thick) is formed near the Si surface. In ion channeling, this layer causes a more intense and wider Si surface peak. Raman scattering due to the destruction of crystalline long range order has also been observed for dry-etched Si, demonstrating the existence of a disordered, amorphous-like region near the surface. iv) The existence of sub-surface silicon carbon bonding was established by X-ray photoemission spectroscopy. v) Hydrogen at depths in excess of $\simeq 30nm$ was detected in dry etched specimens by nuclear reaction profiling. By Raman scattering the stretching modes of Si-H centers were observed. By substituting deuterium for hydrogen in reactive ion etching and using secondary ion mass spectrometry, deuterium at concentrations of 10^{17}atoms/cm^3 has been detected at a Si depth of more than 200nm from the surface after 1min of plasma exposure. vi) Transmission electron microscopy studies revealed no extended Si defects for pure CF$_4$ or CF$_4$/20%H$_2$ RIE. For CF$_4$/40%H$_2$ or pure H$_2$ RIE extended lattice defects were observed after overetching [68]. The extended defects consisted of {111} planar defects distributing to a depth of 30nm from the Si surface. Hydrogen was shown to play a critical role in the formation of extended Si defects as a result of RIE [69].

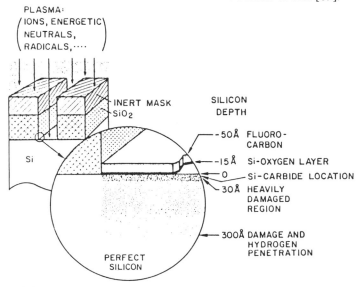

Figure 12: Schematic view of changes of the near-surface properties of the silicon substrate resulting from a SiO$_2$ to Si selective reactive ion etch process using CF$_4$/40%H$_2$. The etching was performed using 200W rf power, a pressure of 25mTorr and a gas flow of 40sccm. The Si substrate was exposed for 1min to the plasma. After RIE and prior to surface analysis the Si sample was exposed to air which caused the growth of the thin oxide layer underneath the fluorocarbon film (from Ref. 54).

The performance of electronic devices formed on CF$_4$/H$_2$ RIE modified silicon (as shown in Fig. 12) is dramatically different from control samples. Data obtained with Schottky barriers demonstrated the following: (i) The leakage current measured was severely reduced for reactive ion etched silicon relative to control specimens. The reduction of the leakage current correlated with the thickness of the C,F-film overlayer [70]. (ii) The ideality factor n was 3.7 for the Si samples exposed for 15 seconds to the plasma, largely due to an increase in the density of surface states by more than an order of magnitude as compared to controls [70]. (iii) In DLTS measurements performed with CF$_4$/H$_2$ dry etched p-type silicon, five hole traps located at 0.18, 0.21, 0.33, 0.43 and 0.48eV above the valence band were observed [71]. None of the observed hole traps could conclusively be related to a known defect structure, although it appeared that the 0.33eV level was due to a defect consisting of two carbon atoms. For n-type Si four electron traps located at 0.14, 0.17, 0.27 and 0.35eV below the conduction band edge were observed as a result of CF$_4$/H$_2$ RIE [72]. The 0.17 and 0.27eV traps appeared to be hydrogen related. Complementary information was obtained by minority carrier life-time measurements using MOS-structures formed with CF_4/H_2 dry etched Si [73]. These showed a severely reduced Si minority carrier lifetime due to defects in the substrate. Both hydrogen and accumulation of carbon in the vicinity of the surface [73] were thought to be responsible for the electrical degradation. The published electrical measurement data are consistent with the picture of RIE induced surface modifications of Fig. 12 as regards both the C,F-overlayer (reduction in diode leakage) and subsurface damage (reduced Si minority carrier lifetime, increased surface state density and deep level traps).

8.5.3 Etch Rate Dependence of Lattice Damage

The residual lattice damage level in a substrate is a strong function of the maximum ion energy as determined by the sheath potential and pressure, the ion flux, the types of species present in the discharge (e.g., hydrogen), the presence/absence of passivation layers, and so forth. However, the primary variable which controls the amount of residual damage in a substrate after RIE is the substrate etch rate. Upon exposure of a substrate to the reactive ion plasma, damage will be introduced into the substrate and accumulate. At the same time, reactive ion etching of the substrate occurs which consumes the damaged layer. Initially the degree of disorder in the near-surface substrate region will increase with etching time. The time necessary to reach a steady-state and a constant damage level will vary with the etch rate. These competitive effects were considered in reference [66] and it was shown that for a location x_1 fixed with respect to the substrate surface, the impurity (or damage) concentration will have reached its maximum possible value to within 1% after a time t_{max}:

$$t_{max} \geq \frac{2.69\Delta R_p + R_p - x_1}{ER} \qquad (2)$$

with ΔR_p being the straggle and R_p the projected range of the impinging ions. The etch rate is denoted by ER. A good approximation for the low ion energies of interest in RIE is the assumption that the range straggling equals the numerical value of the projected range. For the present example they are set equal to 2.3nm. The location x_1 within the substrate for which the time evolution of residual damage is examined is set equal to the projected ion range R_p. Equation (2) becomes

$$t_{max} \simeq \frac{6nm}{ER} \qquad (3)$$

This expression is used to evaluate the maximum RIE related impurity concentration as a result of ion implantation for different typical RIE applications. Table 4 shows that for rapid etching conditions of 600nm/min, representative of silicon etching in a SF_6 discharge, steady-state is reached within 0.6sec. If a dose rate of 10^{15} ions/cm^{2}sec which is typical of RIE plasmas is assumed, that all ions are retained by the sample and that the residual damage profile coincides with the impurity profile, we find that the maximum retained dose is 6×10^{14}ions/cm^2. For a slower etch rate of 60nm/min, which is more typical of a CF_4 discharge, the time to steady-state is 6sec and the maximum possible retained dose is 6×10^{15}ions/cm^2. For a very slow etch rate of 0.6nm/min, which is characteristic of selective etching conditions, the time to reach steady-state is 600sec and the maximum possible retained dose is 6×10^{17}ions/cm^2. These considerations indicate that, depending on the substrate etch rate, the importance of RIE induced damage will vary for different etching applications. For high etch rates little residual damage should be observed. Indeed little Si substrate damage is observed after SF_6 based RIE (rapid Si etch rate). Residual damage will be important primarily for conditions of slow or negligible etching, such as for selective etching conditions. As seen in section 5.2, major Si near-surface modifications can occur during a selective etching process with negligible etching of the Si substrate.

Table 4: Example of the etch rate dependence of the concentration of residual RIE induced substrate impurities (or substrate lattice damage).

Etch Rate (nm/min)	Time to Reach Steady-State (sec)	Maximum Dose Retained (cm^{-2})	Remark
600	0.6	6×10^{14}	SF_6 based RIE of silicon.
60	6	6×10^{15}	CF_4 based RIE of silicon.
0.6	600	6×10^{17}	CHF_3 based RIE of silicon.

8.5.4 Post-RIE Surface Recovery Treatments

The example of the contact hole etching process described in section 8.5.2 indicates that in many cases a reactive ion etching step has to be followed by a surface cleaning step. In general the goal is the removal of etch passivation layers, such as the fluorocarbon film in silicon dioxide etching, chlorine-containing residues for aluminum etching to prevent long-term corrosion, sidewall passivation films in silicon trench etching, the annealing of lattice damage (if introduced), and so forth. Typically RIE induced lattice damage is not dealt with explicitly since device processing invariably involves heat treatments which will anneal out any lattice damage (e.g., thermal oxidation, ion implantation anneal, etc.). On the other hand RIE passivation films have to be removed explicitly as part of the RIE process. In the simplest case the passivation film is removed with the masking layer, e.g. sidewall passivation layers are often due to erosion and redeposition of masking material and the same treatment, such as an acid dip for an oxide mask, which removes the masking layer removes the sidewall passivation film. In other instances a special surface cleaning process has to be introduced, such as a plasma clean in a different plasma etching system. For example, the fluorocarbon film, which is crucial to the achievement of SiO_2/Si etch selectivity, is difficult to remove using solvents. It is commonly removed by volatilization in an oxygen discharge which also causes the formation of a thin silicon-dioxide layer on the silicon surface. It would be desirable to conduct the fluorocarbon removal treatment in the same chamber as used for the oxide etching process in order to minimize sample handling, e.g. an in-situ O_2 clean. Unfortunately, as the oxygen discharge cleans the wafer surface it volatilizes simultaneously fluorocarbon films from the walls of the etching chamber (deposited during the oxide etching step). This produces an oxygen discharge containing a significant density of atomic fluorine and causes etching of the exposed contact hole silicon surface. This is not acceptable for critical applications. In those circumstances the fluorocarbon layer removal treatment has to be undertaken in a different plasma etching chamber not used for fluorine-based etching.

8.6 REACTOR, EQUIPMENT CONSIDERATIONS

8.6.1 Reactor Types

A great number of different reactor types are used for plasma etching. These include the barrel etchers (the name derives from the shape) and downstream plasma etchers in which the plasma is excited using microwaves and which are characterized by minimal ion bombardment and purely chemical etching. Such systems are often used for photoresist stripping and other applications where high selectivity and low radiation damage are key requirements and the isotropic nature of the etch is not a problem. In applications where ion bombardment is required, parallel plate reactors can be employed. In symmetrical parallel plate systems, where the rf driven and grounded electrodes are of equal size and the plasma is truly confined between the electrodes, the plasma potential is high and both electrodes are bombarded by energetic ions. The wafer is placed on the grounded electrode (anode coupled system) and is bombarded by energetic ions because of the high plasma potential. A disadvantage of this system is that the wafer can easily be contaminated by material sputtered off the counter-electrode. Asymmetrical systems, in which the rf powered electrode is small relative to the grounded surface area, are called reactive ion etchers (or reactive sputter etchers) and are more commonly used. These systems are characterized by a low plasma potential ($\simeq$30V) and a large self-bias voltage on the rf driven electrode ($\simeq$300-500eV). Because of the low plasma potential relatively little sputter contamination from grounded surfaces occurs. The two most popular types of reactors used for reactive ion etching have these geometries: (i) The cathode is a horizontal plate and the walls of the chamber act as the anode of the system (see Fig. 1). These reactors can be either batch or single wafer etchers. (ii) The cathode has the shape of a hexagon which is surrounded by the cylindrical chamber walls which form the anode ("hexode" reactor). Hexode reactors are designed for high throughput batch processing.

Most industrial RIE reactors use 13.56 MHz rf power. This frequency is greater than the ion plasma frequency $\omega_I = \sqrt{e^2 n_I/\varepsilon m_I}$ where e is the electronic charge, n_I and m_I the ion density and ion mass, respectively, and ε the permittivity of vacuum [74]. Consequently ions can not follow the applied rf field and respond only to the time average of the voltage at the cathode, i.e. the self-bias voltage. At a frequency of 100 kHz ions can follow the applied rf field and the ion bombardment of the cathode increases relative to high frequency excitation. This effect has been exploited in the triode configuration where 100kHz excitation is supplied to the cathode to maximize ion bombardment and 13.56Mhz is supplied to an annular electrode surrounding the chamber to produce reactive ions.

8.6.2 Reactor Materials

Since both the electrodes and the walls of the reactor can become sources of sputtered material which may deposit on the wafer being etched, the choice of the wall/electrode materials is of critical importance. For example, in RIE batch reactors using fluorine chemistries the choice of an aluminum electrode results in very undesirable etch characteristics. Since AlF_3 is involatile, Al sputtered from the cathode is deposited onto the wafer surface during processing. The deposition of Al results in micromasking and surface roughening of the wafer surface as a result of etching [59]. Micromasking and surface roughening can be avoided by using electrode materials which form volatile products with the etching gas, e.g. silicon, quartz, graphite, teflon, etc. for use with fluorine based chemistries. These electrode materials give rise to different problems: Since fluorine will etch these materials and thus is consumed, the atomic fluorine density in the gas phase will be lowered. The etching of quartz or graphite will change the oxygen or carbon content of the gas phase. These electrode effects can significantly alter the plasma chemistry. For example the few percent of oxygen added to the gas phase by the etching of a quartz electrode in a fluorocarbon plasma prevents the formation of fluorocarbon films on bombarded surfaces and makes it impossible to achieve etch selectivity of silicon dioxide over an underlayer based on fluorocarbon film passivation of the underlayer. In this application an electrode made of graphite, teflon or equivalent is needed instead. The secondary electron emission coefficient of electrode surfaces may also influence the nature of the discharge. These problems are minimized for single wafer reactors where primarily the wafer being etched faces the glow discharge.

In reactive ion etching the plasma potential is low, so ions striking the walls of the reactor have much reduced energies compared with those striking the cathode and little material will be sputtered. However, for stainless steel walls any sputtering will free Fe, Cr and Ni and these impurities introduce deep levels into silicon which degrade the minority carrier lifetime. Even very low concentrations of these heavy metals can make the semiconductor unusable and therefore no stainless steel parts should be in direct contact with the plasma.

8.6.3 Chamber Cleanliness, Process Reproducibility Issues

The addition of small amounts of contaminants to a plasma can significantly change the etching characteristics of a given process. The best studied case is the effect of small amounts of water to the etching of Al in chlorine plasmas [63]. Aluminum films are covered by their native oxide and etching of Al_2O_3 is very difficult as compared to Al; the etching of Al lines proceeds therefore in a two-step process. First the native oxide is removed using considerable ion bombardment and oxygen scavengers, such as BCl_3. Subsequently the etching of Al takes place. The etching of the native oxide is greatly retarded or made irreproducible if small amounts of water are present in the chamber; the water will react with the oxygen scavengers. Since the presence of water is primarily due to exposure of the chamber to room ambient between runs and the adsorption of moisture by the chamber walls, many dry etching chambers used in manufacturing employ load locks which eliminate this problem.

The etching process itself can lead to chamber contamination and process irreproducibility. For example, if fluorocarbon gases are used to selectively etch SiO_2 the same insulating fluorocarbon film which serves as an etch stop layer is deposited at a much greater thickness on the grounded inner surfaces of the reactor. The presence of this film changes the etching characteristics of the plasma since it has an effect on both the electrical properties (by changing the powered/grounded electrode area ratio via insulation of the chamber walls) and chemical characteristics (due to fluorine consumption/recycling by interaction of the film with reactive plasma species) of the discharge. The best procedure appears to be to "condition" the chamber after each clean-up by running the process plasma for some time and depositing a film onto the walls of the system. The oxide etching characteristics will then be stable in subsequent runs. After a certain number of runs the fluorocarbon film on the chamber walls has grown thick enough to loose adhesion and cause particulates. In order to prevent this, the chamber needs to be cleaned by volatilizing the fluorocarbon film using an oxygen discharge. The cycle is then repeated. Similar tool cleaning schedules need to be observed for other etching processes.

8.6.4 Single Wafer vs. Batch Reactors

Batch reactors commonly work at lower pressure and lower power densities than single wafer reactors and the etch rates are smaller. High throughput is achieved with large batch sizes, e.g. up to 24 6-inch Si wafers for commercial systems. Directional etching of materials requiring significant ion bombardment to induce etching, e.g. silicon dioxide, is possible because of etching at low pressure (10-100 mTorr). Increases in semiconductor wafer size to 6-inch and greater and the demand for greater process automation, for instance microprocessor controlled cassette-to-cassette loading/unloading, and improved process control, such as individual end point detection, have made single wafer etching reactors more desirable for many etching applications than batch reactors. In order to achieve adequate throughput, high etch rates ($\simeq 1\mu m/min$) are required for single wafer reactors. Since the arrival rate of reactive species at the wafer surface controls the etch rate, a high reactive species generation rate is a prerequisite. The generation rate R of a reactive specie in a glow discharge by electron impact is given by [75]

$$R = kn_e N \tag{4}$$

where k is the reaction rate constant for ionization (or dissociation), n_e the electron number density and N the neutral gas number density. The reaction rate constant depends on the electron energy distribution $f(\varepsilon)$

$$k = \int_0^\infty \sqrt{\frac{\varepsilon}{2m}}\, \sigma(\varepsilon) f(\varepsilon) d\varepsilon \tag{5}$$

where ε is the electron energy, m the electron mass, $\sigma(\varepsilon)$ the cross section as a function of energy. Increases in either the rate coefficient k, the number density n_e of electrons or the gas number density cause a larger generation rate of reactive species. Different reactor designs optimize different factors.

The approach used in the past for single wafer reactors was to operate at a high gas pressure ($\simeq 1$ Torr and greater) using a small interelectrode gap (less than 1 cm) and high rf input power to achieve high generation rates of reactive species and the required etch rates. High pressure single wafer reactors are characterized by a) a high neutral flux to ion flux ratio and b) little energetic ion bombardment because of ion-neutral collisions in the sheath region. Anisotropic etching in those systems is due to sidewall passivation.

Directional etching of materials where sidewall passivation is difficult to achieve or etching of materials requiring a significant sputtering component (e.g., involatile CuCl removal for Al etching, etching of silicon dioxide) cannot be accomplished in high pressure single wafer reactors and low pressure RIE batch reactors have been used for those applications. However, with the current trend to single wafer reactors a great deal of development effort has gone into producing low pressure single wafer etchers (p<10mTorr) with adequate throughput which would perform tasks currently accomplished in RIE batch reactors. High etchant specie(s) production rates can be achieved at low gas pressure by increasing the electron concentration n_e in equation 4 using magnetic confinement to reduce the loss of electrons to the walls of the system. Two primary technologies of low pressure single wafer reactors are currently available commercially; magnetrons (closely related to conventional RIE reactors) and electron cyclotron resonance systems.

In magnetron ion etching (MIE) magnetic field lines parallel to the cathode surface (produced either by permanent magnets inside the cathode or external electromagnets) and electric field lines normal to the cathode surface (due to the cathode dc bias) confine electrons on cycloidal trajectories near the cathode [76]. The probability of an electron undergoing dissociative/ionizing collisions with gas phase species is thus enhanced and, e.g. the ion/neutral ratio can be ≃50 times greater in MIE than in RIE. The mobility of electrons towards the cathode is decreased because of this confinement, causing the self-bias voltage to be lower than in conventional RIE. A large flux of low energy ions is thus produced in magnetrons at low pressure whereas in RIE a small flux of high energy ions is produced for the same input power. Anisotropic etching is easier to achieve in low pressure single wafer reactors than in high pressure single wafer reactors because of a) a high ion-to-neutral flux ratio and b) the reduced probability of ion-neutral collisions in the sheath region at low pressure.

In electron cyclotron resonance (ECR) systems a discharge is produced by microwave excitation (commonly 2.45 GHz) [77] (see also Chap. 11). A magnetic field of ≃1 kGauss is applied which decreases as a function of distance from the location of the electromagnets. At certain locations the field is 875 Gauss and a resonance between the cyclotron motion of the electrons in the magnetic and microwave field occurs. At resonance the electron cyclotron resonance frequency $\omega_{ce} = eB/2\pi m$ is equal to the microwave frequency (where e is the electronic charge, B the magnetic flux and m the electron mass). Electrons at resonance convert efficiently microwave energy into ionization and dissociation of gas species. The wafer is placed below the discharge chamber and can be rf or dc biased to control the energy of impinging ions. In electron cyclotron resonance reactors the generation of ions and radicals is effectively decoupled from their acceleration and energy gain which potentially enables far greater control of the etching process than possible in RIE.

Low pressure single wafer reactors are much more demanding in terms of pumping equipment and wafer cooling than RIE systems or high pressure single wafer reactors. For high pressure single wafer reactors a mechanical pump is typically sufficient and wafer cooling is not an issue because of the high working pressure. For RIE an additional Roots blower and a turbopump is required to maintain pressures down to 10mTorr at adequate gas flows. Because of the relatively low etch rates the temperature rise of the wafers during etching is in most cases limited to ≃100°C. The pressure for MIE processing is near 1mTorr and for ECR etching it can be even lower. Moderate gas flows at these low pressures demand very high pumping speeds, e.g. for a flow of 30sccm a 1500 liter/sec turbopump may need to be employed. Wafer cooling is a critical issue both because of the achievement of high etch rates, significant ion bombardment and low pressure operation. Backside helium cooling using either a wafer clamp or an electrostatic chuck is necessary in order to control the etching process and prevent damage to the wafer such as resist reticulation.

8.7 END POINT DETECTION and PLASMA DIAGNOSTICS

8.7.1 General Considerations

The most direct need for plasma diagnostic techniques [78-80] arises in the determination of the etch end point for a given process. In addition plasma diagnostic techniques are used for process monitoring and provide information on the types of species present in a reactive ion etching plasma, their concentration, their energy content, and so forth. For etch endpoint detection and plasma diagnostic measurements laser interferometry, optical emission spectroscopy and mass spectrometry are the most commonly used techniques. The first two techniques require only a suitably located optical window on the chamber, are easily implemented and enable the obtaining of a great deal of information about etching plasmas. Langmuir probe measurements, laser induced fluorescence (LIF), coherent anti-stokes spectroscopy (CARS), ellipsometry and infrared/visible region absorption spectroscopy have been used to obtain important insights into reactive ion plasmas but are experimentally more demanding than the former techniques and they have primarily been used for plasma research. These latter techniques will not be covered in this article. In the future some of these techniques may be used for endpoint detection for systems where laser interometry and optical emission methods fail. Selwyn [81] was able to detect the presence of As in the gas phase during etching of GaAs and Si using laser induced fluoresence. He suggested the use of LIF for detecting the etch endpoint in the removal of a boron-doped silicon layer on top of arsenic-doped silicon or vice versa.

8.7.2 Laser Interferometry, Reflectance

In this technique the laser light reflected from the surface of a wafer being etched is measured. For transparent films, e.g. SiO_2, an oscillating signal is observed for the reflected laser light intensity which is due to interference of the reflected light from the film surface and the substrate surface. The spacing between adjacent maxima (or minima) is $\delta d = \lambda/2n$, where λ is the wavelength of the laser light and n the refractive index of the transparent layer. Etch rates can be determined in real time. For nontransparent films, e.g. metals, a change in reflectivity is observed upon complete removal of the metallic film. For patterned wafers without an etch stop layer the pattern can be used as a diffraction grating and the depth of the etched pattern can be determined in-situ. There are two principal drawbacks to these techniques. Firstly, they usually require the presence of a special test site since the features being etched, e.g. contact holes into an SiO_2 film, are too small for measurements. Secondly, information about the etch endpoint is obtained only for one specific area on the wafer, which can cause difficulties in batch processing.

8.7.3 Optical Emission Spectroscopy

Optical emission spectroscopy is the most widely used technique for etch end point detection [78,79,80,82]. The change in emission from a characteristic species is observed as etching of a film is completed. Either the decrease in emission of a suitable etch product specie or the increase in etchant specie at the end of the etching process is monitored. Table 5 lists for some important electronic materials and commonly used etching gases emission lines employed for etch end point detection. The sensitivity of this technique depends on how much etchant is consumed or how much film material is etched per unit time. If the etch rate is too slow or the size of the etched pattern too small, e.g. contact hole etching into SiO$_2$ layers, this technique may not be suitable for end point detection.

Table 5: Table 5: Common optical emission lines used for end-point detection. This table was compiled from data provided in references [78, 82].

Material	Etchant Gas	Emitting Species	Wavelength (nm)
Silicon	CF$_4$/O$_2$;SF$_6$	F (Etchant)	704
	CF$_4$/O$_2$;SF$_6$	SiF (Product)	440;777
	Cl$_2$;CCl$_4$	SiCl (Product)	287
SiO$_2$	CHF$_3$	CO (Product)	484
Si$_3$N$_4$	CF$_4$/O$_2$	N$_2$ (Product)	337
	CF$_4$/O$_2$	CN (Product)	387
	CF$_4$/O$_2$	N (Product)	674
W	CF$_4$/O$_2$	F (Etchant)	704
Al	CCl$_4$;Cl$_2$;BCl$_3$	Al (Product)	391;394;396
	CCl$_4$;Cl$_2$;BCl$_3$	AlCl (Product)	261
Resist	O$_2$	O (Etchant)	777;843
	O$_2$	CO (Product)	484
	O$_2$	OH (Product)	309
	O$_2$	H (Product)	656

8.8. CURRENT TRENDS

A decade ago the primary focus of the RIE research and development efforts was the empirical search for plasma etching processes which would satisfy the etch directionality and etch selectivity requirements of semiconductor device and circuit fabrication. Within the last few years, research and development efforts on reactive ion etching have evolved to address the following topics:

a. Enhanced plasma generation schemes for high rate low pressure etching. Magnetron ion etchers and electron cyclotron resonance single wafer etchers are results of this research and development activity and were discussed in section 8.6. Microwave multipolar plasma reactors equipped with confinement magnets which surround the etching chamber and use ECR sources [83], and the rf driven double cathode etcher [84] are different developments with the promise of high-rate etching at low pressure.

b. RIE process-integration (process clustering). The goal is to effectively integrate RIE into the overall fabrication sequence, e.g. by connecting deposition and etching chambers by clean, evacuated transport chambers. Process clustering requires clean, damage-free etching processes (see section 5) and dry surface cleaning methods.

c.   Real-time control of RIE processes.
Because of the use of large silicon wafers and increasing process complexity the value of partially processed wafers is going up rapidly. This justifies considerable investment in real-time process monitoring equipment (beyond endpoint detection) which will detect equipment/process malfunctioning in real-time and "save" wafers. Better process diagnostics and understanding will enable the design of feedback loops and real-time process control.

d.   Improved fundamental understanding and computer models of RIE processes.
The "output" of a RIE process depends in a non-linear way on a great number of "input" parameters (rf power, frequency, reactant gas composition, pressure, chamber residence time, etc.). We also lack a valid model for the processes occurring in glow discharge etching plasmas. This situation requires extensive experimentation in the development of suitable etching processes. It is expected that accurate computer models of plasma etching processes based on an improved understanding of the science of rf discharges will aid significantly in optimizing their use for electronic materials processing or other applications. A three-fold approach is being pursued in order to reach this goal.

First, measurements are being performed on real rf plasma systems in order to address the question as to what kind of phenomena are occurring. Although there is a great need for new diagnostic techniques, in particular for the study of plasma-surface interactions, certain important glow discharge parameters have been determined for particular plasma-substrate systems. Significant progress has been made in determining atom, radical and ion concentrations and their energies, the electron density and its energy distribution, processes occurring selectively on certain surfaces and not on others, e.g. a material A versus a material B, bottom of a trench versus the sidewall, and so forth. There is an increased emphasis on performing the measurements non-intrusively and in-situ. Multiple techniques are being used to measure the same quantities, e.g. microwave interferometry and Langmuir probes are being used to measure electron densities. New diagnostic techniques are being developed in order to measure the desired glow discharge parameters. For example, two groups independently developed a photoemission optogalvanic method which can be used to characterize in real-time, in-situ the surfaces of semiconductors and metals exposed to a plasma [85].

The second required research component are model system studies, since real glow discharges make well-controlled experiments difficult. Due to the coupling of most parameters in a plasma, a controlled change in one quantity invariably changes other quantities and it is difficult to assess the relative importance of the change of a specific quantity in producing a new result. The goal of the model system studies is to investigate the interaction of fluxes of atoms and radicals with well-specified surfaces, alone or in combination with ion (mass/energy analyzed), electron and photon bombardment, measure the energy dependence of the cross sections for the production of important species found in glow discharges, perform controlled experiments to establish the rate and importance of plasma and surface chemical reactions, and so forth.

The third component needed is <u>numerical modelling [86]</u>. Values of the controllable plasma operating parameters such as rf power and frequency, type of gas, gas pressure, and so forth and the results of the model system approach on cross sections, sticking coefficients, reaction rates etc. are used as inputs of a computer model of a glow discharge for a specific application. A model of the plasma etching process requires treatment of both the discharge physics and chemistry (gas phase and surface) which are coupled [86]. The output of the numerical model can be compared to the results of measurements performed on real systems. For prototypical plasma processes, such as Si etching using SF_6, numerical models are already quite advanced and increasingly accurate [87].

The near future may see the utilization of computer models of RIE discharges in the design of etching processes for new materials. Two-dimensional modelling may be used instead of the demanding experimental approach to optimize etch uniformity. Accurate computer models should also contribute to the scale-up of plasma reactors, e.g. ECR-based systems, and the control of the etching process.

Acknowledgement: I would like to thank T. D. Bestwick for a critical reading of this article and many helpful suggestions.

8.9 REFERENCES

1. Reactive ion etching is covered in these books:
    J. W. Coburn, <u>Plasma Etching and Reactive Ion Etching,</u> (American Vacuum Society Monograph Series, New York, 1982);
    B. Chapman, <u>Glow Discharge Processes,</u> John Wiley & Sons, New York (1980);
    T. Sugano, "Applications of Plasma Processes to VLSI Technology", John Wiley & Sons, New York (1985);
    <u>VLSI Electronics Microstructure Science, Vol. 8, Plasma Processing for VLSI,</u> eds. N. G. Einspruch and D. M. Brown, (Academic Press, New York, 1984);
    The Electrochemical Society (Pennington, NJ) and the Materials Research Society (Pittsburgh, PA) organize regularly symposia on Plasma Processing and publish proceedings. Recent volumes are: Proceedings of the Sixth Symposium on Plasma Processing, <u>edited by G. S. Mathad, G. C. Schwartz and R. A. Gottscho</u> (The Electrochem. Soc., Pennington, 1987) and <u>Plasma Processing,</u> eds. J. W. Coburn, R. A. Gottscho, and D. W. Hess, (Materials Research Society, Vol. 68 of the Symposia Proceedings Series, Pittsburgh, 1986).
    Of great interest is also the series of international symposia on plasma chemistry, e.g. the most recent proceedings volume is: <u>Proceedings 8th Int. Symposium Plasma Chemistry/Tokyo 1987,</u> eds. K. Akashi and A. Kinbara, (Int. Union of Pure and Appl. Chemistry, 1987).

2. See e.g., S. Wolf and R. N. Tauber, <u>Silicon Processing for the VLSI Era</u> (Lattice Press, Sunset Beach, 1986).

3. G. C. Schwartz, in <u>Proceedings of the Fifth Symposium on Plasma Processing</u> (Electrochem. Soc., Pennington, 1985), pp. 26.

4. J. W. Coburn and H. F. Winters, <u>J. Appl. Phys.</u> 50: 3189 (1979).

5. F. R. McFeely, J. F. Morar, and J. A. Yarmoff, in <u>Proceedings of the Sixth Symposium on Plasma Processing,</u> edited by G. S. Mathad, G. C. Schwartz and R. A.

Gottscho (The Electrochem. Soc., Pennington, 1987), pp. 619; F. R. McFeely, J. F. Morar, N. D. Shinn, G. Landgren, and F. J. Himpsel, Phys. Rev. B30: 674 (1984).

6. J. W. Coburn, H. F. Winters, and T. J. Chuang, J. Appl. Phys. 48: 3532 (1977).

7. H. F. Winters, J. W. Coburn, and T. J. Chuang, J. Vac. Sci. & Technol. B1: 469 (1983).

8. J. L. Mauer, J. S. Logan, L. B. Zielinski, and G. C. Schwartz, J. Vac. Sci. & Technol. 15: 1734 (1978).

9. D. L. Flamm and V. M. Donnelly, Plasma Chem. Plasma Process. 1: 317 (1981).

10. Y.-Y. Tu, T. J. Chuang, and H. F. Winters, Phys. Rev. B23: 823 (1981).

11. H. F. Winters and J. W. Coburn, in Plasma Synthesis and Etching of Electronic Materials, eds. R. P. H. Chang and B. Abeles, (Materials Research Society, Vol. 38 of the Symposia Proceedings Series, Pittsburgh, 1985), pp. 189.

12. A. Bensaoula, J. Stozier, A. Ignatiev and J. Wolfe, Plasma Processing, eds. J. W. Coburn, R. A. Gottscho, and D. W. Hess, (Materials Research Society, Vol. 68 of the Symposia Proceedings Series, Pittsburgh, 1986), pp. 429.

13. C. J. Mogab, J. Electrochem. Soc. 124: 1262 (1977).

14. S. Tachi, K. Tsujimoto, and S. Okudaira, Appl. Phys. Lett. 52: 616 (1988).

15. R. A. Haring, A. Haring, F. W. Saris, and A. E. de Vries, Appl. Phys. Lett. 41: 174 (1982); A. W. Kolfschoten, R. A. Haring, A. Haring, and A. E. de Vries, J. Appl. Phys. 55: 3813 (1984).

16. M. Seel and P. S. Bagus, Phys. Rev. B23: 5464 (1981); ibid B28: 2023 (1983); ibid B29: 1070 (1984).

17. G. C. Schwartz and P. M. Schaible, J. Vac. Sci. & Tech. 16: 410 (1979).

18. C. J. Mogab and H. J. Levinstein, J. Vac. Sci. & Technol. 17: 721 (1980).

19. S. Matsuo, Appl. Phys. Lett. 36: 768 (1980).

20. Y. H. Lee and M.-M. Chen, J. Vac. Sci. Technol. B4: 468 (1986).

21. H. F. Winters and D. Haarer, Phys. Rev. B36: 6613 (1987).

22. Y. H. Lee, M. M. Chen, and A. A. Bright, Appl. Phys. Lett. 46: 260 (1985).

23. See e.g., M. Sekine, T. Arikado, H. Okano, and Y. Horiike, in Proceedings of the 8th Symposium on Dry Process, (Inst. Electr. Eng., Tokyo, 1986), pp. 42.

24. G. S. Oehrlein, K. K. Chan, M. A. Jaso, and G. W. Rubloff, J. Vac. Sci. & Technol. (to be published, 1989).

25. For a study of the etching characteristics of SF_6/O_2 plasmas see: M. Pons, A. Inard, and D. Henry, Supplement a la Revue Le Vide, Les Couches Minces 237: 264 (1987).

26. K. Tsujimoto, S. Tachi, K. Ninomiya, K. Suzuki, S. Okudaira and S. Nishimatsu, in Ext. Abstracts of the 18th Int. Conf. Solid State Devices and Materials, (Tokyo, 1986), pp. 229.

27. D. Chin, S. H. Dhong, and G. J. Long, J. Electrochem. Soc. 132: 1705 (1985).

28. For an excellent discussion see reference 9.

29. C. J. Mogab, A. C. Adams, and D. L. Flamm, J. Appl. Phys. 49: 3796 (1978).

30. R. D'Agostino, F. Cramarossa, S. De Benedictis and G. Ferraro, J. Appl. Phys. 52: 1259 (1981).

31. V. M. Donnelly, D. L. Flamm, W. C. Dautrcmont-Smith, and D. J. Werder, J. Appl. Phys. 55: 242 (1984).

32. G. S. Oehrlein, S. W. Robey, and J. L. Lindström, Appl. Phys. Lett. 52: 1170 (1988).

33. J. W. Coburn, and H. F. Winters, J. Vac. Sci. & Technol. 16: 391 (1979).

34. G. S. Oehrlein, C. M. Ransom, S. N. Chakravarti, and Y. H. Lee, Appl. Phys. Lett. 46: 686 (1985).

35. R. S. Bennett, Electrochem. Soc. Extended Abstracts 82-2: 283 (1982).

36. R. A. Gottscho and G. R. Scheller, in Proceedings of the Sixth Symposium on Plasma Processing, edited by G. S. Mathad, G. C. Schwartz and R. A. Gottscho (The Electrochem. Soc., Pennington, 1987), pp. 201.

37. G. S. Selwyn, J. Appl. Phys. 60: 2771 (1986).

38. D. L. Flamm, V. M. Donnelly, and J. A. Mucha, J. Appl. Phys. 52: 3833 (1981).

39. R. A. H. Heinecke, Solid State Electronics 18: 1146 (1975).

40. L. M. Ephrath, J. Electrochem. Soc. 126: 1419 (1979); L. M. Ephrath, and E. J. Petrillo, J. Electrochem. Soc. 129: 2282 (1982).

41. H. W. Lehmann and R. Widmer, J. Vac. Sci. & Technol. 15: 319 (1978).

42. G. S. Oehrlein, and H. L. Williams, J. Appl. Phys. 62: 662 (1987).

43. G. S. Oehrlein, S. W. Robey, and M. A. Jaso, in Plasma Processing, D. Apelian and J. Szekely, eds., (Materials Research Society Symposia Proceedings, Vol. 98, Pittsburgh, 1987), pp. 229.

44. G. J. Coyle, Jr. and G. S. Oehrlein, Appl. Phys. Lett. 47: 604 (1985).

45. J. W. Coburn, J. Appl. Phys. 50: 5210 (1979).

46. P. J. Hargis and M. J. Kushner, Appl. Phys. Lett. 40: 779 (1982).

47. Eric Kay, in Methods and Materials in Microelectronic Technology, ed. J. Bargon, (Plenum Publish. Corp., New York, 1984), pp. 243.

48. M. M. Millard and E. Kay. J. Electrochem. Soc. 129: 160 (1982).

49. G. S. Oehrlein, K. K. Chan, and M. A. Jaso, J. Appl. Phys. 64: 2399 (1988).

50. S. W. Robey, M. A. Jaso, G. S. Oehrlein, J. Appl. Phys. (to be published 1989).

51. G. S. Oehrlein, S. W. Robey, J. L. Lindström, K. K. Chan, M. A. Jaso, and G. J. Scilla, J. Electrochem. Soc. (to be published 1989).

52. M. Mieth, Semiconductor International (May 1984 Issue), pp. 222.

53. For reviews see e.g., S. W. Pang, Solid State Technolog. 27: 249 (1984); S. J. Fonash, Solid State Technolog. 28: 201 (1985).

54. G. S. Oehrlein and Y. H. Lee, J. Vac. Sci. & Technol. A5: 1585 (1987).

55. G. A. Northrop and G. S. Oehrlein, Materials Science Forum 10-12: 1253 (1986).

56. J. Weber and M. Singh, Appl. Phys. Lett. 49: 1617 (1986).

57. J. C. Mikkelsen, Jr. and I.-W. Wu, Appl. Phys. Lett. 49: 103 (1986); X. C. Mu, S. J. Fonash, and R. Singh, Appl. Phys. Lett. 49: 67 (1986).

58. L. M. Ephrath and R. S. Bennett, J. Electrochem. Soc. 129: 1822 (1982).

59. G. S. Oehrlein, R. G. Schad, and M. A. Jaso, Surf. Interf. Analysis 8: 243 (1986).

60. T. Watanabe and Y. Yoshida, Solid State Technol. 27: 213 (1984).

61. D. J. DiMaria, L. M. Ephrath, D. R. Young, J. Appl. Phys. 50: 4015 (1979).

62. S. P. Murarka and C. J. Mogab, J. Electron. Materials 8: 763 (1979).

63. D. W. Hess and R. H. Bruce, in Dry Etching for Microelectronics, ed. R. A. Powell, (Elsevier, New York, 1984), pp. 1.

64. S. J. Fonash, S. Ashok, and R. Singh, Appl. Phys. Lett. 39: 423 (1981); C. M. Ransom, T. I. Chappell, L. M. Ephrath, and R. S. Bennett, Electrochem. Soc. Extended Abstracts 83-1: 282 (1983).

65. S. W. Pang, D. D. Rathman, D. J. Silversmith, R. W. Mountain, and P. D. DeGraff, J. Appl. Phys. 54: 3272 (1983).

66. G. S. Oehrlein, R. M. Tromp, J. C. Tsang, Y. H. Lee, and E. J. Petrillo, J. Electrochem. Soc., 132: 1441 (1985).

67. G. S. Oehrlein, G. J. Coyle, J. C. Tsang, R. M. Tromp, and Y. H. Lee, in Plasma Processing, eds. J. W. Coburn, R. A. Gottscho, and D. W. Hess, (Materials Research Society, Vol. 68 of the Symposia Proceedings Series, Pittsburgh, 1986), pp. 367; G. S. Oehrlein, R. M. Tromp, Y. H. Lee, and E. J. Petrillo, Appl. Phys. Lett., 45: 420 (1984).

68. S. J. Jeng and G. S. Oehrlein, Appl. Phys. Lett. 50: 1912 (1987).

69. S.J. Jeng, G. S. Oehrlein, G. J. Scilla, Appl. Phys. Lett. 53: 1735 (1988).

70. P. Spirito, C. M. Ransom, and G. S. Oehrlein, Solid State Electronics 29: 607 (1986).

71. C. M. Ransom, in "Tegal Eleventh Annual Plasma Seminar", (Tegal Corp., Novato, 1985), pp. 31.

72. Y. Kawamoto, and N. Hashimoto, in Proceedings Second Symposium Dry Process, (Inst. Elect. Eng. Japan, Tokyo, 1980), pp. 63.

73. Y. Ozaki, and K. Ikuta, Jap. J. Appl. Phys. 23: 1526 (1984).

74. D. L. Flamm, J. Vac. Sci. & Technol. A4: 729 (1986).

75. A. T. Bell, J. Macromol. Sci. Chem. A10: 369 (1976).

76. Y. Horiike, H. Okano, T. Yamazaki, and H. Horie, Jap. J. Appl. Phys. 20: L817 (1981); H. Okano and Y. Horiike, in Plasma Processing, eds. J. Dieleman, R. G. Frieser, and G. S. Mathad (Electrochem. Soc., Pennington, 1982), PV 82-6, pp. 206; I. Lin, J. Appl. Phys. 58: 1638 (1985); A. A. Bright, S. Kaushik, G. S. Oehrlein, J. Appl. Phys. 62: 2518 (1987).

77. K. Suzuki, S. Okudaira, N. Sakudo, and I. Kanomata, Japan. J. Appl. Phys 16: 1979 (1977); K. Suzuki, K. Ninomiya, and S. Nishimatsu, Vacuum 34: 953 (1984).

78. W. R. Harshbarger, in VLSI Electronics Microstructure Science", Vol. 8, Plasma Processing for VLSI, eds. N. G. Einspruch and D. M. Brown, (Academic Press, New York, 1984), 411.

79. R. A. Gottscho, and T. A. Miller, Pure Appl. Chem. 56: 189 (1984).

80. G. S. Selwyn, in <u>Proceedings of the Sixth Symposium on Plasma Processing,</u> edited by G. S. Mathad, G. C. Schwartz and R. A. Gottscho (The Electrochem. Soc., Pennington, 1987), pp. 220.

81. G. S. Selwyn, <u>Appl. Phys. Lett.</u> 51: 167 (1987).

82. P. J. Marcoux and P. D. Foo, <u>Solid State Technol.</u> 24: 115 (1981).

83. Y. Arnal, A. Durandet, J. Pelletier, M. Pichot, and L. Vallier, in Supplement a la Revue <u>Le Vide, les Couches Minces</u> 237: 73 (1987).

84. R. W. Boswell, R. K. Porteous, A. Bouchoule, and P. Ranson, in Supplement a la Revue <u>Le Vide, les Couches Minces</u> 237: 78 (1987).

85. G. S. Selwyn, B. D. Ai, and J. Singh, <u>Appl. Phys. Lett.</u> 52: 1953, (1988); S. W. Downey, A. Mitchell, and R. A. Gottscho, <u>J. Appl. Phys.</u> 63: 5280 (1988).

86. D. B. Graves and K. F. Jensen, <u>IEEE Transactions on Plasma Science</u> PS-14: 78 (1986); J. P. Boeuf, <u>Phys. Rev.</u> A36: 2782 (1987); A. D. Richards, B. E. Thompson, and H. H. Sawin, <u>Appl. Phys. Lett.</u> 50: 492 (1988).

87. H. H. Sawin (private communication) and E. Gogolides, J.-P. Nicolai, and H. H. Sawin (to be published).

9

Reactive Sputter Deposition

William D. Westwood

9.1 INTRODUCTION

Reactive sputter deposition involves the sputtering of a metal, alloy or compound in a reactive gas mixture in order to deposit a compound thin film composed of the sputtered material and the reactive species. A wide variety of compounds have been formed in this way, with a wide range of properties. In some cases, these compounds are difficult or impossible to form by other means, particularly at low substrate temperature. The process of reactive sputter deposition can be very complex, and involves the sputtering process, the physics of the plasma discharge, transport of the sputtered and gas species, the kinetics of film growth and chemical interactions at the target and film surfaces. These all interact in some way and therefore can affect the properties of the film.

Films can be reactively sputter deposited in a number of ways, using rf-diodes, triodes, ion beam and dual ion beam systems, magnetrons and modified magnetrons. Of particular interest in this chapter will be the magnetron techniques.

There are many applications for reactively sputter deposited films. Perhaps the most common example is TiN coatings for wear resistance, and also diffusion barriers. Other examples include SiO_2 dielectric coatings, Si-H solar cells, In-Sn-oxide transparent conductors and the new high T_c superconductors. While there is a large volume of literature on reactive sputtering, there are only a few reviews of the topic (1-3).

9.2 PLASMA-BASED SPUTTERING TECHNIQUES: HYSTERESIS EFFECTS

A typical reactive sputter deposition system might be composed of a metallic sputtering target, such as Al or Ti, sputtered in a predominantly inert gas plasma at a pressure between 0.1 and 10 Pa (1 Pa = 7.5 mTorr). Without the introduction of a reactive species, oxygen or nitrogen, for example, the films deposited by the sputtering process would be metallic. Upon introduction of a reactive gas species, those atoms will combine with the sputtered atoms from the target to form a compound thin film. At low levels of the reactive species, the films will be only partially reacted. At sufficiently high flow levels of the reactive species, the films will be fully reacted. However, even higher levels of the reactive species will cause compound formation on the target or cathode surface. This compound formation on the cathode will persist as the flow of reactive gas is reduced, until at a significantly lower flow level the metal cathode is exposed by physical sputtering. This general phenomena is qualitatively known as a hysteresis effect.

The two regimes of operation, i.e. metallic cathode sputtering and compound-coated cathode sputtering, can be described by the plotting of the hysteresis effect between the flow rate, f_r of the reactive species and the chamber pressure, P. A generic example is shown in Fig. 1, which would apply, for example, to the case of the sputtering of an Al cathode in Ar with the addition of O_2 to the chamber. A constant pressure, P_a is maintained by the flow f_a of the non-reactive gas (Ar in this case) into the continuously pumped chamber. The sputtering of the Al target in the Ar alone would result in the deposition of a pure Al film. The dashed line in Fig. 1 shows the linear increase in P which would result simply from increasing the argon flow f_a This follows the relation $Q = S \times P$, where Q is the total flow rate of gas and S is the pumping speed.

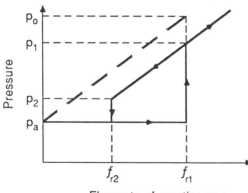

Figure 1: Generic hysteresis curve for system pressure, P, as a function of reactive gas flow rate, f_r.

Flow rate of reactive gas

The hysteresis curve represents two stable states of a system with rapid transitions between the two states. In state A, there is negligible change in the total pressure as the reactive gas flow, f_r, is varied; in state B, the pressure rises linearly with reactive flow rate, but is lower by ΔP that the total pressure in the absence of sputtering. In state A, essentially all of the reactive gas is being incorporated in the deposited film and the atomic ratio of the reactive gas to sputtered metal in the film increases with f_r. Thus, state A can be considered as a regime in which the sputtered metal is doped with reactive gas. In state B, a constant volume of reactive gas is consumed, independent of f_r, and there is an excess of reactive gas so the formation of a stable compound is favored.

The transition from state A to state B is due to the formation of a compound on the surface of the sputtering target. In most cases the sputtering yield for metal atoms from the target will decrease once a compound forms on the target surface. Some of the energy of the incident ion on the target must go to sputtering the other component of the compound. For example, if an Al_2O_3 film is formed on the cathode surface, only 40% of the atoms sputtered from the surface would be Al atoms. Thus, if the discharge power is kept constant as the transition from state A to state B occurs, the sputtering rate of Al would decrease by a minimum of 60%. The greater the ratio of the sputter yields of the metal atoms from the element and compound, the smaller will be the value of ΔP in Fig. 1, and the more rapid the transition from state A to state B. In addition, the deposition rate in state B will be significantly below the deposition rate in state A.

The hysteresis effect is strongly dependent on the pumping speed of the vacuum system. In a series of experiments, Okamoto and Serikawa (5) varied the pumping speed, S, by a factor of 20 to change the flow of Ar from 5 to 100 SCCM for the reactive sputtering of Si in Ar/N_2. At an Ar flow of 5 SCCM, a well defined hysteresis curve was obtained (Fig. 2) with $f_{r1} = 8$ SCCM and $f_{r2} = 5.5$ SCCM with a reduction in the deposition rate from 15 to 3 nm/min. At successively higher Ar flows, the hysteresis effect was diminished until at 100 SCCM Ar flow, there was no effect. However, the deposition rate decreased continuously to approximately 6 nm/min. The Si_3N_4 films had reached their desired composition as $f_r = 25$ SCCM. Although S was increased by a factor of 20, the value of f_r required to make Si_3N_4 only increased by a factor of 3. They also showed that the deposition rate depended only on $P - P_o$ and not on the argon flow.

The effect of pumping speed on the shape of the pressure hysteresis curve was also explored by Kadlec et al (6) for the reactive sputtering of TiN. In their diode system, the critical pumping speed for N_2 was about 200 l/s: for higher values no hysteresis was observed. Danroc et al (7) reported the change in shape of the hysteresis curve during the reactive sputtering of TiN, as a function of both the pumping speed and the location of the N_2 inlet. The width of the hysteresis curve decreased as the nitrogen inlet was moved closer to the pump throat. Since much of the N_2 passes directly to the pump, this is equivalent to either reducing the effective flow of nitrogen or else reducing the gettering rate by the sputtered Ti.

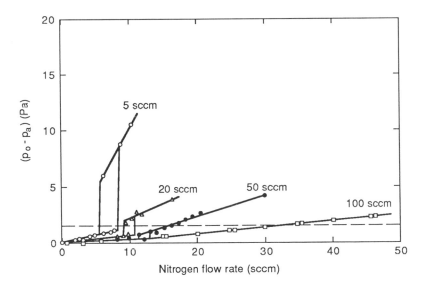

Figure 2: Variation of pressure with N_2 flow rate for different flow rates of Ar during rf planar magnetron sputtering of Si (5). The dashed line shows the value of $(P_o - P_a)$ at which the films were Si_3N_4.

As might be expected, the film deposition rate also shows a hysteresis-like effect as a function of the flow of the reactive gas. The pressure-flow hysteresis curve is shown in Fig. 3(a) for the case of reactive sputtering of Ti in Ar/O_2 mixtures. The effect on the sputtering yield is shown in Fig. 3(c), and the effect on the net deposition rate in Fig. 3(b). This type of behavior is characteristic of most reactive sputter deposition systems.

In addition, due to the change in the surface composition of the target in states A and B, there may often be a change in the discharge voltage and current at constant discharge power. In many cases, such as reactively sputtering Al in Ar/O_2, the voltage drops significantly going from state A to state B. This may be due to changes in the secondary electron coefficient of the cathode. For example, a thin aluminum-oxide layer on the cathode may have a significantly larger secondary electronic coefficient than pure Al. The additional electrons can cause additional ionization in the plasma, resulting in a higher ion flux to the cathode, and hence a lower discharge voltage at constant power. For the $Al - O_2$ system, the voltage changes can be as high as several hundred volts. However, other systems have mush smaller voltage shifts, and some systems, such as $Ti - O_2$ have been reported to increase, rather than decrease the discharge voltage upon transition from state A to state B. This may be indicative of negative ion effects, which will be discussed below.

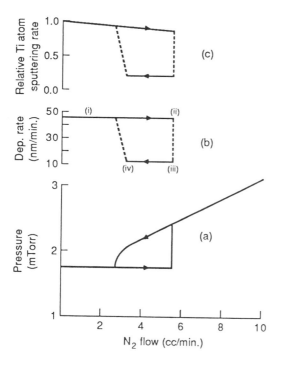

Figure 3: Changes in (a) total pressure, (b) deposition rate and (c) relative Ti sputtering rate for a 5x8 inch planar magnetron Ti target sputtered in Ar/N_2 mixtures at a constant power of 800W.

9.3 REACTION KINETICS: MODELS

The main cause of the hysteresis effect has been attributed to the formation of a compound layer on the surface of the sputtering target or cathode. The getter-pumping effect of the freshly-deposited metal films is reduced by the reduction in metal atom sputtering rate, causing the partial pressure of the reactive species (and the total pressure of the chamber) to increase. Conversion back to the metal mode (state A) occurs only when the flow of reactive gas is reduced to the point where it can no longer maintain the compound layer, which is being continuously sputtered. However, a detailed model of the reaction kinetics is more difficult because all the parameters interact and their behavior in the sputtering environment is not well known.

The first attempt at a model describing this basic phenomena was proposed by Heller (8), addressing the case of rf etching in oxygen. In this model, an equilibrium oxide thickness resulted from a balance between the sputtering rate and the target oxidation rate, assumed to be logarithmic. The basic premise was that these two rates were independent, which is not generally true. Goranchev, et al.(9) introduced the concept of a partial surface coverage, Θ, of the target by oxide and pointed out that Θ depended on both the gas flow and the sputtering power. However, this dependence is even more complex, as the sticking coefficient, η for the reactive gas can vary rapidly with Θ. Harra and Haywood (10) reported changes in the sticking coefficient η of two orders of magnitude for the case of reactive sputtering of Ti in N_2 as a function of N_2/Ti flux ratio. Such rapid changes mean there may be a substantial gradient in η and Θ over a sputtering target, as was shown by Schiller et at (11) for the case of magnetron sputtering.

A number of models describing aspects of the transition from state A to state B have been introduced (8-17). More recent models have been developed by Berg at al. (18), by Larsson et al (19) and by Penfold (20). These models use the consumption rate due to the gettering effect as well as exhaustion by the pump. In the first case, the system-wide balance of atoms can be explicitly solved by 8 coupled equations, and complex hysteresis phenomena modeled. However, each of these models require assumptions about variations in sputter yields under different conditions and variations in Θ on different surfaces. By making suitable assumptions, the hysteresis curve behavior is predicted for reactive sputtering of Ti in N_2. These are steady-state models, so that a series of operating characteristics are developed and the path between them developed as a function of the N_2 flow rate. Although this type of approach should apply to any reactive sputtering system, evaluation of the operating characteristics still requires assumptions about the values of the parameters in the models. In the N_2 reactive sputtering case, these appear to change fairly slowly with increased nitrogen levels. This does not appear to be the case for O_2. This means that various feedback-control systems (to be discussed below) may be more successful in nitrogen-based systems than in oxygen-based systems.

9.4 SPUTTERED SPECIES

9.4.1 Cluster Emission

In the metallic cathode mode (state A), the sputtered atoms consist mainly of individual, neutral atoms. However, some clusters may be ejected, both as neutral and charged species (21). The bonding between the metal atoms is sufficiently strong that some fraction of the bonds may hold together (i.e. form a cluster) during the sputtering process. The bonding between a metal atom and a reactive gas atom, however, can be stronger that the bonds between the metal atoms, and as a result a cluster of metal and reactive gas atoms may result from the sputtering process. Of course, individual metal and reactive gas atoms will also be sputtered and a variety of charge states may occur.

By combining quartz micro-balance measurements of the deposition rate and atomic absorption and emission analysis of Al, Stirling and Westwood (22) showed that clusters must be responsible for the majority of the depositing flux for the reactive sputtering of Al in O_2. This conclusion was reached by the observation that the spectroscopic signal for Al became undetectable upon the transition from state A to state B. Later studies (23,24) found a similar effect when a $NiFe_2O_4$ target was sputtered in Ar/O_2. While Ni and Fe atoms were still sputtered, they accounted for less than 10% of the depositing atoms.

A similar conclusion was reached by Betz and Husinsky (25) using Laser Induced Florescence (LIF) during the sputtering of Cr by Ar^+ in a background pressure of oxygen. Upon undergoing the transition from the metallic to the compound cathode form, the deposition rate decreased by a factor of 4, while the Cr atom LIF signal decreased by a factor of 130. Since less than 25% of the deposited film could be accounted for by Cr atoms alone, they concluded that Cr_xO_y clusters were being formed.

To obtain stoichiometric or fully reacted films by sputtering a bulk compound target, it is usually necessary to add additional reactive gas to the chamber. In the case of oxides, there can be sufficient oxygen present in the background water vapor in the chamber, but this is likely to cause non-reproducible results. Since a reactive gas must usually be added in these cases, either a compound, bulk target or a metallic target may be used. Control of the gas supply for the reactive species will be required in either case, although the flow rates in the metallic case will he significantly higher. There are, of course, advantages to operating in the metallic mode. For example, by controlling the gas species and flow, the same Al target may be used to deposit Al, Al_2O_3 and AlN films. Metal targets are generally easier to fabricate at high purity, and they usually have better thermal conductivity than the compound. They are thus easier to cool, allowing higher power levels, and hence higher deposition rates. Finally, metallic targets can be operated in either a dc or rf mode, whereas the compound targets often require rf.

9.4.2 Negative Ion Emission

During the sputtering process at the cathode surface, there is a probability that some of the sputtered species will be emitted as ions. Due to the high positive potential of the sheath, positive ions formed at the cathode surface will most likely remain on the surface. Negative ions, however, will be accelerated by the high field ($\simeq 5000V/cm$) and enter the plasma. In ion beam sputtering systems, to be discussed later, the electric field is very weak ($\simeq 5V/cm$) and the negative ions do not gain more than a few eV of energy. Harper et al (26) showed that in a plasma sputtering case, the negative ions would gain the full discharge voltage crossing the sheath, and hence have long mean free paths. (The cross section for collision decreases as the particle energy increases.) It was also suggested that due to the low electron affinity (1-2 eV), the extra electron on the negative ion may be quickly stripped upon entering the plasma, which typically has an electron temperature of several eV.

A result of the formation of negative ions during sputtering is sputtering of substrate. This was observed by Hanak (27) for F^- ions from a MgF_2 target, and also by Cuomo et al. (28) for the sputtering of alloy targets of Au and rare earth metals. In the latter case, a model was proposed that treats the target like an ionic solid. To remove an electron from the first target, A, requires an energy equal to the ionization potential, E_i. To form a negative ion, B^-, energy is gained equal to the electron affinity of B, χ. Thus, the total energy required, $E_i - \chi$, is a measure of the difficulty of transferring an electron from A to B. If this value was less than 3.4 eV, Au^- ion were observed in sufficient quantities to etch the substrate.

Later work by Kester and Messier (29) characterized a large number of oxide targets (Table 1), and found negative ion emission even though the energy difference was greater than the empirical 3.4 eV described above. Other studies have shown that the negative ions formed have energies equal to the target potential (30).

Two principle effects can be present due to the formation of large numbers of negative ions during sputtering. The first is a significant change in the net deposition rate. The sputtering caused by the negative, (now neutralized) ions causes an effective reduction in the film deposition rate, as compared to the case without negative ion formation. Secondly, the composition of the deposited film may be dramatically altered as the lower sputter yield components are preferentially sputtered from the depositing film.

Significant changes in composition have been observed in the high T_c oxide films when deposited by sputtering. Films deposited using $MBa_2Cu_3O_{6-7}$ where M is a rare earth such as Y, Yb Er, etc., tend to be deficient in both Cu and often in the rare earth component due to negative ion sputtering (31,32). This is not surprising, upon viewing Table 1, as the yield of O^- ions can be quite large. A variety of solutions have been identified to avoid this problem. Lee et al. (33) mounted two planar magnetron targets opposite to each other and mounted the samples off to one side. This solution has been used in various geometrical forms by others. It was first used to improve ZnO films (34). Clarke (35) has used an S-gun composed of elemental tile segments oriented in conical array. The separation of the compounds, as well as the geometrical dispersion of the negative ions has allowed the deposition of good films. Other approaches forgo the use of oxide targets completely, sputtering from multiple targets of elemental, or simple alloy composition (36).

The occurrence of negative ions during sputtering must be considered when any electronegative species, such as O or F, is present either in the target or the reactive gas. In addition, the presence of O in the residual gas of the chamber, perhaps in the form of OH, can lead to negative ion formation which can change over time as the system is conditioned. Tominaga et al (37) documented the effects of energetic particle bombardment during the sputtering of Al in Ar/N_2 mixtures to form AlN. The film structure was different in regions opposite the magnetron plasma ring in front of the target. Using a time-of-flight method, they concluded that the energetic species were NO and OH, due to residual water vapor in the chamber. A similar conclusion was reached during the sputtering of AlCu in Ar, where significant changes in the morphology of the films opposite the etch track were traced to negative ion formation due to background gases (38).

Table 1: Observed effects of energetic particle bombardment resulting from sputtered negative ions (O^- in all cases except for NO^- and OH^- in ref (d); s = strong effect; w = weak effect, p = possible effect. The lowest values of $E_i - \chi$ are given.

Material	$E_i - \chi$(eV)	Effects	Ref.
$BaTiO_3$	3.74	s	29,30
$LiNbO_3$	3.92	s	29,30
$SrTiO_3$	4.23	s	29,30
$SrZrO_3$	4.23	s	29,30
$Sr_2Nb_2O_7$	4.23	s	29,30
$CaTiO_3$	4.65	s	29,30
$Bi_4Ti_3O_{12}$	5.35	s	29,30
TiO_2	5.35	w	29,30
ZrO_2	5.37	w	29,30
SnO_2	5.88	p	29,30
PbO	5.94	p	29,30
$PbTiO_3$	5.94	s	29,30
$PbZrO_3$	5.94	p	29,30
Ta_2O_5	6.41	s	29,30
WO_3	6.51	w	29,30
ZnO		s	30
$YBa_2Cu_3O_6$		s	32,33
$AlN(+H_2O)$		s	37

Clearly, the types and energies of the species reaching the substrate during reactive sputter deposition in a plasma may differ from the simple sputtering model. In that case, individual atoms leave the target with a few eV of kinetic energy and lose much of this energy through gas phase collisions prior to deposition. Highly energetic atoms and molecules may be present due to both negative ion formation or the reflection and neutralization of incident ions at the cathode surface. Clusters of atoms may arrive at the substrate, and these clusters may be positively charged by Penning ionization. In diode and triode systems, energetic electrons will also be present. This will generally not be the case with magnetrons due to the magnetic fields. However, the so-called "unbalanced" magnetrons (39), as well as small, poorly confined targets, will have a loss path for energetic secondary electrons from the cathode surface.

9.5 PLASMA-BASED SPUTTERING SYSTEMS

9.5.1 Diode Systems

In a diode sputtering system, both the target and the substrate are immersed in the plasma. Ions are extracted from the plasma for sputtering of the target and the pressure is usually high enough (several Pa) that the sputtered atoms are effectively thermalized before reaching the substrate. However, discharge voltages are typically high, 1-3 keV, so that energetic, reflected neutrals, negative ions, and especially secondary electrons may bombard the substrate. The electron current density at the substrate may be as high as

10% of the ion current density at the target. The ion current density is limited by space-charge effects to about $1mA/cm^2$. The power density at the substrate may be as high as $1 W/cm^2$ and may produce substrate temperatures of several hundred degrees C.

Both rf and dc diodes are used for sputtering, but dc is restricted to sufficiently conducting targets. As pointed out by Maissel (40), the diode discharge provides a very reactive environment. Although the percentage of ionization is low ($\approx 0.1\%$), the flux of excited species to the surface may be quite high relative to the sputtered flux. This is due to the generally low sputtering rates caused by the low ion currents.

The basic diode sputtering arrangement is shown in Fig. 4(a). The two electrodes of approximately equal area are separated by 5 to 10 cm. A minimum pressure is required to maintain a glow discharge in the space between them. This is typically 1 Pa, but much higher pressures may be necessary to attain a current density of $1mA/cm^2$. The substrate is usually placed on one of the electrodes, but other positions have also been used to avoid the effects of negative ion bombardment.

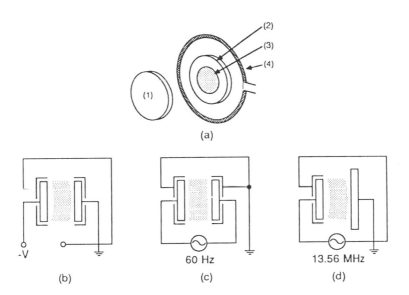

Figure 4: General schematic of (a) diode target-substrate orientation, (b) dc-diode electrical circuit, (c) ac sputtering, and (d) rf-diode sputtering at 13.56 MHz.

There are generally three modes of powering a diode discharge. In dc sputtering (Fig. 4(b)), the target is connected to a negative potential and the other electrode is grounded. In this case, the other electrode also functions as the anode. The discharge is established with the applied potential dropped across the dark space in front of the target, which has a thickness of 1-2 cm. Ions accelerated across the dark space sputter the target. However, due to charge exchange collisions, the average ion energy is typically about 800 eV, even though the target potential may be as high as 5 keV.

In ac sputtering (Fig. 4(c)), a 60 Hz supply is connected between the two electrodes and both are effectively used as targets. Either the same or different materials may be used for the two targets. However, in general this type of system has been used infrequently.

In rf sputtering (Fig. 4(d)), a high frequency generator (usually 13.56 MHz) is connected between the electrodes. The rf voltage is $V_o \cos \omega t$ and an average negative potential is developed on the electrodes because of a difference on ion and electron mobilities (40). If the system is symmetric, as in Fig. 4(c), a potential $-V_o$ is developed on both electrodes. By increasing the effective capacitance of the non-powered electrode (substrate), its potential can be reduced to much lower values, typically -10 to -20 V. Thus, the substrate is usually subjected to ion bombardment. The energy of the ion bombardment is typically the difference between the plasma potential and the floating potential of the substrate electrode. In cases with symmetric electrodes, the plasma potential can be quite high. If the substrate electrode is grounded, along with the chamber walls, the plasma potential can be quite low. Although a net potential of $-V_o$ is developed on the target, there is no net current flow. Therefore, the target may be either conducting or insulating. This allows a great flexibility in target choice, and has greatly expanded the potential of reactive sputter deposition.

In diode sputtering, the substrate is immersed in the plasma, and is thus exposed to all the species listed in Table 2. Since electrons are accelerated across the dark space, they reach the substrate with high energies. Since ions (eg. N_2^+ will reach the substrate with several eV), and excited neutral species may also be present, it is not surprising that the chemical reactivity is high in diode systems.

This reactivity, of course, is desirable in depositing compounds but may be responsible for non-uniform composition of the films across the substrate electrode. For uniform film thickness, the sample is typically located directly in the center of the substrate electrode. However, the reactive gas is usually introduced from the perimeter through some sort of manifold. At a pressure greater than 1 Pa, the mean free path of the reactive gas atoms is less than 1 cm and the reactive gas will then have a high probability of hitting one of the electrode surfaces before it reaches the sample locations. If the sticking coefficient is near unity, due perhaps to the high reactivity of the deposited film and the environment, the gas will be trapped prior to reaching the sample location. For example, if N_2 is added while a Ta target is being sputtered in Ar (41,42), a Ta-N film is deposited. Gettering of the nitrogen reduces the flux towards the center of the substrate, resulting in a radial composition gradient. This gradient will be greatest for the more reactive gases and will also depend strongly on target size and orientation.

In nearly all cases of compound formation by reactive diode sputtering, the target is in state B, the compound state. For most materials, both metallic and compound targets have been used. For some materials, such as $BaTiO_3$ (43), $LiNbO_3$ (44) and lead titanate (45), as well as the superconducting oxides, compound targets have generally been used.

Table 2: Approximate flux and energy of particles reaching the substrate during sputtering of an oxidized layer on a Zn target in Ar/O_2 discharge (i.e. state B). Magnetron sputtering at 1 Pa is assumed. For diode sputtering, electrons have energy equal to the target voltage and the value for the relative flux is 0.1.

Species	Source	Approximate Relative flux	Energy(eV)	Effect of Pressure increase on flux	energy
Zn	sp	1	1	↓	↓
O	sp	1	1	↓	↓
O	sp O^-	0.1	500	↓	↓
ZnO	sp	0.3	1	↓	↓
ZnO^+	sp+Penning	0.05	1	↓	-
O^-	sp	0.05	500	↓	↓
Ar	gas	1000	0.03	↑	-
Ar	refl	0.01	100	↓	↓
O_2	gas	1000	0.03	↑	-
O	refl	0.01	100	↓	↓
Ar^+	plasma	10	1	↑	-
O_2^+	plasma	10	1	↑	-
e	plasma	10	3	↑	-
e	sp	?	500	↓	↓

9.5.2 Magnetron Systems

The use of magnetron sputtering systems has expanded greatly since about 1970. The flexible geometry inherent in the design has distinct advantages for reactive sputtering and special modifications have made it possible to reactively deposit thin films at high rates. The basic physical principles of magnetron operation have been discussed in an earlier chapter (Chap. 6) and also have been the subject of numerous papers (46-51). The planar magnetron, both in circular and rectangular geometry, has been the most widely used design for reactive sputtering.

A simple schematic of a planar magnetron is shown in Fig. 5. Although it appears similar to a diode (Fig. 4), the arrangement of the magnetic field makes the discharge operation quite different. In general, a magnetron is arranged with a magnetic field oriented parallel to the cathode surface, such that the path of electrons undergoing ExB drifts is a closed loop. The plasma density is highest in this drift loop due to the trapping of energetic secondary electrons and the subsequent ionization of the background gas atoms. The proximity of the dense plasma to the target electrode allows large ion currents (many amperes) at relatively modest voltages (200-800V) and pressures of 1 Pa and below.

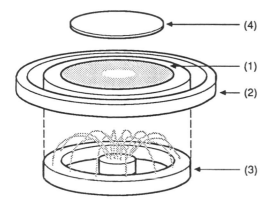

Figure 5: Schematic of circular planar magnetron. (1) target, (2) anode (3) magnet providing a field of ≃ 0.03 T in front of the target with field lines parallel to the target surface. In operation, the magnetic array is typically paced immediately behind the target. (4) substrate.

As is evident in Fig. 5, the magnetic field on some magnetrons is not strictly parallel to the cathode surface at all locations. In particular, areas near the cathode center and perimeter have a field component perpendicular to the cathode surface. This allows secondary electrons emitted from the cathode surface to intercept the substrate plane in some locations. However, these same regions that have a perpendicular magnetic field component also are characterized by significantly lower plasma density, which results in a reduction in the electron bombardment, as compared to the conventional diode case. The highest ion density occurs at the region of the cathode where the magnetic field is parallel to the surface. These areas are also subject to the most ion bombardments, and the sputtering rate, therefore, is non-uniform across the target surface. The rate is greatest just under the ExB drift path, and is lowest in the edge and central regions of the cathode. In many cases, these regions can experience a net <u>deposition</u> during the sputtering of the cathode (Chap 6).

When a reactive gas (eg. N_2) is introduced to the chamber during inert gas sputtering of the cathode, the gettering effects discussed earlier occur and reactive gas (N) atoms must also be sputtered from the cathode surface. The sputter yield of the compound (i.e. reacted) surface is lower that that of the pure metal surface. Where the rate is low, the coverage of N atoms will increase, further decreasing the sputter rate of the target. In the case of a Ti target sputtered in Ar/O_2, Schiller et al (52) found that the width of the eroded annulus on the target decreases from 30m to 18 mm as the fraction of oxygen was increased to the values where full oxidation of the target occurred (state B). (Fig. 7). The very low sputter yield of TiO_2 accentuates the non-uniform sputtering rate intrinsic to magnetron sputtering. In the region of lowest rate, the O coverage becomes sufficient to form TiO_2 and the sputtering rate decreases there. However, the rate is high enough in the region of highest current density to maintain a Ti surface. Thus part of the surface is in state A, while other parts have made the transition to state B. As the flow of reactive gas increases, the whole surface will eventually change to state B, and the total deposition rate falls to a value typical of a TiO_2 surface layer.

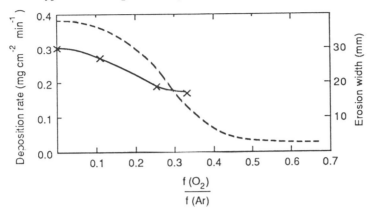

Figure 6: Variation of target erosion width (solid line) and mass deposition rate (dashed line) as a function of O_2 to Ar flow ratio during sputtering of a Ti target (130 mm dia.) at 5 kW. The substrate to target distance was 50 mm. (52).

This transition often results in large changes in the discharge characteristics, as note earlier. Schiller et al (52) observed a maximum in the voltage as the transition to state B occurred. The result shown in Fig. 7 appears to be more typical: the target voltage required to maintain a constant dc current of 2A decreased from 380 to 260V when the Al_2O_3 layer formed on the Al target (53). The decrease is due to the higher secondary electron coefficient, γ_i for Al_2O_3 than Al. Only when the Al_2O_3 is removed from the target, by reducing the oxygen flow, does the voltage again increase.

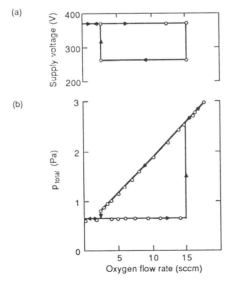

Figure 7: (a) voltage required to maintain a dc current of 2A on a 5x8 inch Al planar magnetron target as a function of O_2 flow rate; f(Ar) = 5 SCCM. (b) Total pressure change for a constant dc power of 560W. (from ref. 53).

If the compound which forms on the target surface is a conductor, rather than an insulator, the value of γ_i may not change significantly. However, there may still be a change in the discharge characteristics due to the change in both pressure, gas composition and gas rarefaction. Noel et al (54) observed an increase in target voltage for a Ti target as the flow of n_2 increased: V_T was 40 V higher for the TiN layer than for the Ti target for a constant discharge current of 2 A.

The large, uniform sputtering source in a cylindrical magnetron (see Chap. 6) is not appropriate for doping by reactive sputtering unless the gas can be introduced fairly uniformly over the deposition area. Otherwise, non-unformity in the film composition must result, especially at high sputtering rates. This is similar to the case of diode sputtering discussed earlier, where substantial doping gradients can result from the strong gettering effects. The magnitude of the effect is enhanced at high discharge current values. The planar magnetron is actually better suited to this type of reactive sputtering (i.e. state A) because the gas can be introduced around the periphery of the target, near the anode or substrate, and the sputtering annulus (etch track) can be quite narrow (Fig. 6). Of course, the gas could also be introduced through the center of the target, where no sputtering takes place.In the sputter-gun arrangement, the anode is located in the center of the target, making the introduction of gas there much easier.

The high values of discharge current possible in magnetrons may not be useful in depositing high resistivity, compound films by reactive sputtering. Arcing is often observed in these cases and this can cause defects in the films and make process control almost impossible. Thornton noted (55) that serious arcing occurred when a Cd cylindrical target was sputtering in Ar/H_2S even at very low discharge currents (0.2 mA/cm^2). The arcs contain high electron currents and propagate under the influence of the magnetic field. Este and Westwood (56) observed both pits and Al particles, approximately 1 μm in size in Al_2O_3 films deposited under arcing conditions. A possible cause of these arcs is the rapid accumulation of charge on a small area of dielectric on the target surface. The subsequent breakdown, somewhat like the discharge of a capacitor, dissipates the energy on the ejection of a particle. At a discharge current density of 0.1A/cm^2, the 1μm diameter area could receive a charge sufficient to cause the breakdown of the dielectric layer in less than 10 ns.

To avoid, or at least minimize arcing, it is common to use rf, commonly at 13.56 MHz, to power the sputtering cathode, particularly for cathodes which have a high resistivity, such as dielectrics. Thornton (55) argued that the magnetron principle is basically a dc concept and should be much less effective in rf operation. Much like diode sputtering, when powered at rf frequencies, the magnetron cathode develops a negative bias potential on the order of 1/2 the applied peak-to-peak voltage. This is slightly inconsistent with calculations (57) which suggest that the mobility of the electron across field lines should be smaller than the ion mobility. This would result in a positive bias at the cathode. The presence of a negative bias may be indicative of turbulent, Bohm-like transport of the electrons (58), which results in effectively higher mobilities for the electrons than the classical predictions.

Thornton operated both cylindrical and planar magnetrons with Al_2O_3 targets at 1.8 MHz in Ar and measured the self bias voltage, V_{sb}, as a function of the rf voltage amplitude V_o, for different configurations (55). He also measured the discharge current, I and derived values of n in the expression $I = k V_o^n$. The values of V_{sb}/V_o and n are given in Table 3, and the configurations are shown in Fig. 8. For the usual single-ended operation (Figs. 8(a), (c)), the rf is connected between the target and the chamber, which is itself grounded. This is equivalent to the diode case in Fig. 4(d). The values of n were low in both cases but V_{sb}/V_o was 1 in the planar magnetron case whereas it was 0.1 in the cylindrical case. The double ended arrangement (Fig. 8(b)) gave the highest value of n, provided that the magnetic traps for the two targets were not common. This is the only report in the literature where the current was measured in an rf system. Usually only the power and the various voltages are reported.

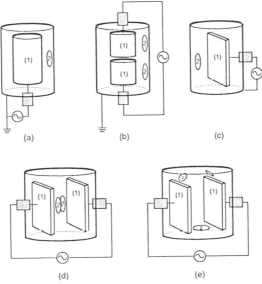

(a)   (b)   (c)

(d)   (e)

Figure 8: Configurations of magnetrons using rf power for sputtering. (1) targets, (2) substrates.

Table 3: Values of self bias, V_{sb} and n in the expression for the discharge current $I_{rms} = kV^n$ for the magnetron configurations in Fig. 8 at 1.8 MHz. (from ref. 55)

Configuration	V_o (volts)	I_{rms} (Amps)	V_{sb}/V_o	n
(a)	300	1	0.1-0.7*	2.2
	600	5		
(b)	400	2		4.5
	550	10		
(c)	1200	1	1	2
	1800	2		

* B decreased from 0.02 to 0.001

Maniv and Westwood (59) also found V_{sb}/V_o to be 1 in a planar magnetron. The difference between the cylindrical and planar magnetrons may be due to the magnetic traps. In the cylindrical case, the B field is parallel to the target surface at all points on the surface. In the planar case, the B field intercepts the cathode at the inner and outer edges of the etch track. Here, the electron velocity normal to the surface is not reduced by the B field so that electrons can rapidly follow the rf field, just as in the diode case.

It has been reported that in the rf case, only 50% of the power output from the rf generator resulted in sputtering of the target (59). Este and Westwood (60) measured both the deposition rate and the target power dissipation in a system with two planar magnetrons run in a double ended mode (Fig. 8(d)) with the substrate holder placed between them. The total deposition rate was the sum of the rates on the substrates placed in front of the two targets. For Al targets in noble gases, they found that the deposition rate, R_f normalized to the rate, R_o for dc sputtering decreased as the frequency increased beyond approximately 30 kHz (Fig. 9). The same frequency dependance was obtained for the deposition of AlN in a N_2 ambient. Due to arcing, no value could be obtained for R_o when the high resistivity AlN formed on the target surface. For all frequencies, R_f was proportional to the total power dissipated in the targets, as measured calorimetrically. Thus, the decrease in R_f was a result of a decrease in the power actually utilized for sputtering. However, they were unable to determine how the rest of the applied power was dissipated in the system. Heating of the matching networks did not appear to account for more than 20% of the discrepancy.

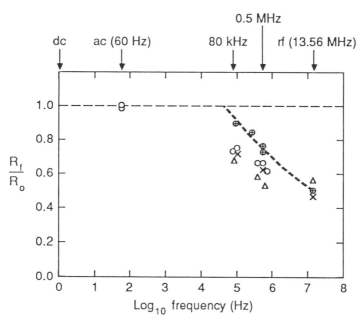

Figure 9: Variation with power supply frequency of the relative sputtering rates from the Al targets in Ar (O), Kr($\times$) and N_2($\oplus$) discharges at 0.3 Pa and in Ne (Δ) at 0.6 Pa. The N_2 values are plotted on the assumption that the 13.56 MHz value is 0.5. From ref. 60).

9.5.3 Modified Magnetron Systems

If reactive sputter deposition of compounds can be carried out without the formations of an insulating layer on the target surface, it would not be necessary to use rf power supplies and the effective deposition rate would also be greatly increased. To do this, the target must remain in state A, while the reaction which would convert it to state B occurs at the substrate to form the desired compound. There are basically two means of doing this: in the first case, the flux of reactant gas to the target must be decreased relative to the flux to the substrate, while still maintaining a similar reaction rate. In the second case, the flux of sputtered metal atoms to the substrate must be much lower than the total sputtered flux; i.e., the deposition area must be much greater that the area of the target which is sputtered. Various methods for meeting these conditions were discussed by Schiller et al (11).

In one of these methods, a baffle in introduced between the target and the substrate, with the reactive gas only entering the chamber on the substrate side (61), as shown in Fig. 10. The O_2 flux to the target is reduced by the baffle, and oxygen reacts with the metal deposited on the walls of the apertures in the baffle. They were able to deposit transparent, conducting films by sputtering a Cd_2Sn alloy target. They also observed the maximum in target voltage reported by Schiller (11). By coupling an rf power of 100W to the substrate holder, they obtained films with a 95% transmittance and a resistivity of $4.5x10^{-4}\Omega cm$. Both the power density and self bias voltage were very low for resputtering of the film, but the oxygen discharge around the substrate increased the reaction rate and thus increased the process window.

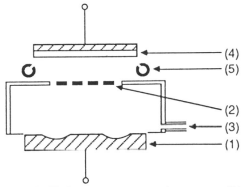

Figure 10: Schematic of baffled magnetron sputtering system. (1) target, (2) baffle, (3) Ar inlet, (4) substrate, (5) reactive gas manifold.

Este and Westwood used the baffled magnetron to deposit Al_2O_3 for optical waveguides (56). They investigated the effect of different aperture sizes in the baffle on the value of f_{r1}, the critical flow rate at which the target converted to state B, and on the deposition rate and uniformity. The results are summarized in Table 4. The critical flow increased only slightly when the apertures in the baffle had a diameter of 4 mm, but it increased 11% when 100W of rf power was coupled to the substrate. Apertures of 2mm diameter increased the critical flow rate by 26%, but then the rf discharge did not make a significant difference. Thus, the smaller apertures gave a larger operating window because the O_2 conductance was lower and more of the sputtered Al flux was deposited on the aperture walls. However, this was coupled with a 40% decrease in the deposition rate, compared to the large apertures. Al_2O_3 films with optical waveguide losses of 1 dB/cm were obtained in all cases, but the flow of oxygen had to be closely monitored.

Table 4: Values for f_{r1} for conversion of the Al target to state B at a dc power level of 1 kW for baffles consisting of apertures in a 5 mm thick plate, with and without rf power coupled to the substrate. The Al_2O_3 deposition rate is normalized to the unbaffled rate obtained by rf sputtering the Al target (56).

Aperture dia (mm)	Conductance l/s	rf power (W)	$f(O_2)$ sccm	Relative Dep. rate	%flux on aperture walls
none	2	-	8.4	1	-
2	0.15	-	10.6	1.2	58
2	0.15	100	10.7	1.2	58
4	0.3	-	8.5	3	49
4	0.3	100	9.3	3	49

As shown in Table 4, the Al_2O_3 deposition rate for the larger apertures was three times the rate obtained for the same total power in an unbaffled magnetron. The higher rate in the baffled case is due, in part, to the 50% efficiency in utilizing the applied rf power discussed above. The optimum arrangement of a baffle will, of course, depend on the reactivity of the system, the specific geometry and the process window required for a particular application. It might seem that an increase in the deposition rate (at constant power) of a factor of 3 would not justify the extra complexity of the baffled magnetrons. However, the use of dc, rather than the rf required in the unbaffled case has a significant advantage: a 20 kW dc power supply and a 2 kW rf power supply are approximately the same size and cost. Jones (62) has recently demonstrated high rate deposition of ZrO_2.

Chang and McGarr obtained silicon nitride films using a Si target in a sputter gun configuration (63). As shown in Fig. 11, the Ar enters the system between the central anode and the target face, while the nitrogen is introduced in a manifold in front of the target, directed at the sample surface. For a discharge current of 3A, the target voltage decreased from 800 to 640 V as the nitrogen flow increases from 5 to 9 SCCM, and then remained constant at higher flows. Silicon nitride films were deposited at flows exceeding 9 SCCM with good thickness and refractive index uniformity. The normalized deposition rate for Si_3N_4 was 40 nm $min^{-1}kW^{-1}$. They noted, however, that the placement of the nitrogen manifold was critical.

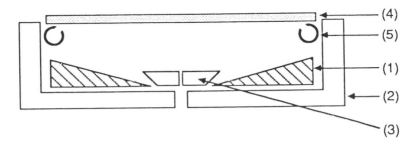

Figure 11: Schematic of sputter gun arrangement for reactive sputtering of Si_3N_4 (1) Si target, dc powered, (2) magnetic field system for magnetron, (3) anode), (4) close-coupled substrate, and (5) N_2 dispenser ring (from ref. 63).

In principle, it should be possible to decrease the flux of sputtered atoms to the substrate while maintaining a constant total sputtering flux by increasing the substrate area. Typically, the deposition area is 1-3 times the area of the erosion ring in the magnetrons. Of course, the sputtered atom flux at the substrate could be reduced by increasing the target to substrate separation. However, the deposition rate is decreased and the environment in which the film grows (eg. atom energy) also changes. Moreover, the effective substrate area must be increased to use the sputtered atoms efficiently. For a given substrate size, a number of substrates may be coated in parallel. Generally, the substrate holder must be moved to obtain uniform deposition on each substrate. As shown in Fig. 12(a), a number of substrates can be moved continuously past the target. However, while deposition at substrate position S_1 is due to sputtered atoms travelling almost normal to the target, any deposition at S_2 is due to atoms which have travelled a considerable distance from the target and will, therefore, have much lower energies and a lower flux. Deposition is usually limited to position S_1 by a shield (Fig. 12(b)) to eliminate the low energy flux. The substrates move sequentially past the opening in the shield.

Suppose that this arrangement is used to sputter an Al target in an Ar/O_2 mixture with the target in state B (oxidized). If the sputtering rate of Al is $1\mu m/$ min and the rotation rate of the substrate holder is $1/6$ rpm, a 300 nm thick Al/Al_2O_3 film will be deposition on each substrate in one rotation. If the rotation speed is 50 rpm, only a 1 nm thick layer will be deposited per rotation. During the $5/6$ of the rotation time when no film is being deposited, the layer may react with the O_2 in the chamber: if there is sufficient O_2, the layer may be completely oxidized. Thus the result will be a film consisting of perhaps hundreds of thin layers. This effect is often seen in metal deposition systems, where the oxidation may be due to background water vapor in the system, and the resulting thin film is really a stack of metallic and partially reacted films (64). In general, only the more reactive compounds can be formed with this process. This is usually limited to oxides with heats of formation greater than 9 eV (65), including oxides of Cr, Al, W, Ta and Ti. For nitride formation, bombardment of the growing film by energetic species is required to form compound films. This can be arranged by the addition of an ion beam or a subsidiary discharge.

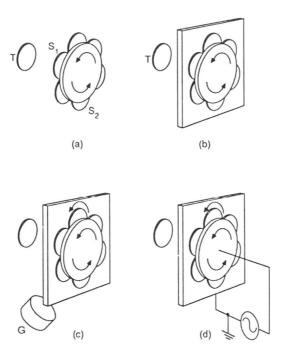

Figure 12: Schematic arrangements for deposition on multiple substrates. (a) substrate rotation through whole sputtering flux, (b) deposition limited by shield, (c) increased reactivity on position S_2 by ion bombardment from gun G, (d) increased reactivity produced by discharge between shield and substrate holder.

9.5.4 Monitoring Systems

The control of the reactive gas flow relative to the sputtering rate is clearly very important in determining the operating point for reactive sputtering. In general, it is desirable to operate the target in state A, but as close as possible to the critical flow for transition to state B. If the ratio of the reactive gas flow to discharge power, f_r/P, increases, the target will convert to state B and the deposition rate may dramatically decrease. If f_r/P decreases, the film composition could change to a more metal rich mixture, with a consequent change in film properties. As discussed earlier, in many target-gas systems, the response of the magnetron in the reactive gas is not a simple linear function of f_r/P, and hence the conversion from state A to state B may be rapid and difficult to control. In addition, as the target conditions change, for example due to the erosion of a deeper etch track in the target, the sputtering rate and the sputtered flux distributions for a given power will change, so that the exact nature of the critical reactive gas flow will also change.

In an experimental system, it is relatively easy to do an initial experiment to determine the value of the critical flow at a given sputtering power, P, and system pressure. The reactive gas flow can then be stopped, and the target will recover to state A. The reactive gas flow can then be adjusted to just below the critical flow level, and monitored carefully. In manufacturing systems, however, a method of continuously adjusting the operating point to maintain constant deposition rate and film properties is necessary. This involves some means of monitoring any change in the operating point and providing a feedback control to change either the reactive gas flow or the discharge power accordingly. In general, the time response of the power supply is faster than the response of the gas flow controllers.

To monitor the operating point in such a non-linear system requires a sensitive method. If the pressure increases significantly, it will be impossible to recover the operating point without essentially tracing out the hysteresis curves in Fig. 1. This is also clearly unacceptable for the deposition of homogeneous films. The parameters which change rapidly near the critical flow transition are the system pressure and the partial pressure of the reactive gas species, the discharge parameters such as the voltage or current in a dc system or the self-bias voltage in an rf system, and the resultant film properties. An additional, observable change is the emission of light from the plasma, which is indicative of both particle density as well as discharge parameters. All of these parameters have been used as monitors, but their application depends on the particular reaction which is being controlled as well as aspects of the sputtering system.

Affinito and Parsons described the detailed operation of a microprocessor-based control tool for the reactive sputtering of Al in Ar/N_2 (13). The values of chamber pressure, P, and nitrogen partial pressure, $p(N_2)$, the gas flows, the discharge current and voltage and the optical emission from the Al were all measured. Using the discharge voltage, V_T, as the experimental variable, they obtained data for several of these parameters (Fig. 13). At low values of V_T, $p(N_2)$ was 2 Pa, the discharge current was low and no Al emission was observed. This suggested the target was in state B. When V_T was increased to 270V, the target converted to state A with a large increase in discharge current, coupled with a strong increase in Al emission and a decrease in $p(N_2)$. As V_T increased to 330 V, the current decreased. All points along this apparently negative resistance region were reached through positive resistance steps away from the equilibrium point and back again. These steps had to be much smaller than the width or height of the negative resistance region; otherwise, oscillations developed from which recovery was not possible.

Affinito and Parsons found that they could control the transition from State A to state B in the Al − N_2 case by this feedback control method, but that the same method was not successful when the nitrogen was replaced by oxygen. They developed a model for the change in rate of target coverage caused by a fluctuation in the current (ΔI)

$$\Delta(\frac{dn_s}{dt}) = -[\frac{\eta p_r}{I} + \frac{\eta + \eta I}{(1 + \gamma_i)e} \frac{\delta F_i}{\delta p} \frac{\delta p_r}{\delta I}]\Delta I \qquad (1)$$

where n_s is the number of reactive gas molecules adsorbed on the target surface, p_r is the relative gas pressure, η/p_r is a sticking coefficient for chemisorption, F_i is the fraction of reactive gas ions bombarding the target (eg. $I(N_2^+)/I$) and η is the sticking coefficient for reactive ion species at the target. As discussed above, the meaning of p_r when the target is in state A is questionable and many of the values of the other parameters are unknown. They proposed that the different behavior of O_2 and N_2 was due to the first term, $\eta p_r \Delta I/I$: for molecular N_2 there is no chemisorption ($\eta = 0$), whereas η is definitely greater than 0 for the case of oxygen. This results in a much faster change in surface coverage for O_2 than N_2, such that their control system could not respond. The monolayer coverage time for the formation of Al-O compounds at their operating condition was estimated to be 1 ms. The control system in this case would allow only a 10% change in discharge current in that time.

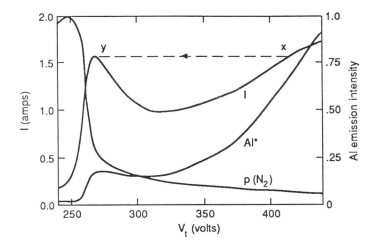

Figure 13: Variation of I, $p(N_2)$ and optical emission intensity from excited Al as a function of the voltage on the planar magnetron cathode in Ar/N_2 The ar flow rate was 1 SCCM and the resulting pressure was 0.93 Pa. The nitrogen flow was 1.5 SCCM. The dashed line from X to Y shows the transition which would occur if I is the experimental variable (from ref. 13).

Sproul used a residual gas analyzer to monitor $p(N_2)$ in the production of wear-resistant coatings of TiN, ZrN and HfN (66). Using feedback control from the RGA, he operated continuously at deposition rates within 15% of those for metals in Ar. Because the chamber pressure for sputtering is much higher than for the operation of the RGA, the RGA must be differentially pumped. He later described the advantages of automatic control using a fast feedback loop (<0.2 s) for the deposition of TiN. Hmiel also described an automated system for the deposition of TiN (67). He pointed out that the response time of the control loop depended of the distances between the target, the N_2 inlet and the RGA. When the RGA was too far from the chamber (1 m), the response time was 1.5 s, and stable operation was not obtainable.

Optical emission from the plasma has been successfully used to drive the feedback loop in several cases. In general, these techniques monitor either a reduction in the emission of the metal species or an increase in the emission of the reactive gas species near the critical flow point. The advantage of an optical emission monitor is that it samples from regions where the reaction is actually taking place: there is no need for differentially pumping as in the case of the RGA. This means that the response time can be much faster. A number of authors have reported results with this technique (68-71), and the control hardware is becoming commercially available.

Finally, for transparent conducting films, both the transmittance and the resistivity depend on the operating conditions for the reactive sputtering. Ridge and Howson (72) have reported measurements of indium-tin-oxide on polyester film sheet resistance used as a feedback loop for controlling the discharge. They used a baffled-magnetron device discussed earlier and found an increase in the sheet resistance of a factor of 10x for only a 10% increase in the oxygen flow.

9.6 REACTIVE SPUTTER DEPOSITION WITH ION BEAMS

Ion beam systems are, at least conceptually, less complex than plasma-based sputtering systems. Ions are generated in a plasma source located away from the target and are extracted from the source with a given energy and directed at the target with a current density J_i. Electrons may be mixed with the ions so that no net charge is delivered to the target. This prevents charge build-up, and as such, the insulating targets can be sputtered as easily as conducting targets.

A schematic of an ion beam system is shown in Fig. 14. Kaufman multiple aperture ion sources (see Chap. 7) have been the most widely used for the past 15 years. They can provide a monoenergetic ion beam with diameters up to 40 cm and energies of up to 2000 eV. Other types of sources, the "End-Hall" or closed-drift source (73), the ECR source (74), the saddle-field ion source (75) and the cold-cathode-type source (76) can be used, depending on the application and the gas choice. Often for reactive gases, the hot filaments present in the Kaufman source can be troublesome and other sources may be preferred.

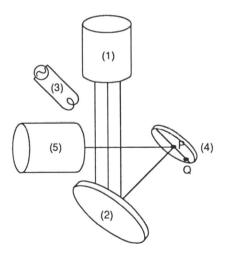

Figure 14: Schematic of dual ion beam sputter deposition system.

The use of ion sources for reactive sputter deposition differs from the plasma-based techniques due to the lower pressure of operation of the ion sources. Typical pressures for the plasma systems are a few Pa (5-100 mTorr) and for the ion beam sources are 0.01 to 0.1 Pa ($7x10^{-5}$ to $7x10^{-4}$). The reduction in pressure means that the sputtered species are not scattered by gas atom collisions following sputtering, and retain their full kinetic energy. Another significant difference from plasma-based techniques is that there is no potential on the target and therefore negative ions or secondary electrons are not accelerated to the depositing film at high energies. Energetic, reflected neutrals from the target surface, however, will not be scattered in an ion beam system, and thus may have a more significant effect on film properties that in the plasma-based techniques.

The ions from the ion source may be either an inert species, such as Ar^+, Kr^+, etc, or mixtures of inert gas and reactive gas species, such as O_2^+ or N_2^+. The ions are usually incident on the target at approximately $45°$ both for geometric reasons and to maximize the sputter yield. To obtain a symmetric deposition with optimum uniformity, the substrate should lie on the axis of the target and be parallel to it.

For many reactive deposition cases with ion beam sputtering, it is not necessary to add the reactive gas to the primary ion source, but simply to the discharge chamber. The ion source is then operated in a pure inert gas environment, and is less susceptible to internal damage caused by the reactive species. For nitride deposition, however, it was observed to be very difficult to deposit Si_3N_4 films by simply bombarding a Si target with N_2^+ ions, and only for very low deposition rates were the films stoichiometric (77) A second source was introduced, as shown in Fig. 14 which delivered 680 eV N_2^+ ions to the substrate while the primary ion source sputtered the Si target with Ar^+ Provided the N_2^+ flux was sufficient, the films produced were of the desired Si_3N_4 composition.

In a similar experiment, Harper et al (78) investigated the sputter deposition of AlN from an Al target using a dual ion beam approach. The Al target was sputtered with 1.5 keV Ar^+, while the second ion source directed N_2^+ ions from 100 to 500 eV to the sample. Due to a gradient in the current density of the second ion source, it was possible to examine regimes where the N_2^+ ion flux both exceeded or was smaller than the Al flux. With excess nitrogen ion bombardment, the films formed were AlN, with the excess nitrogen being desorbed. Where the Al flux was larger, the films formed were a mixture of Al and AlN. However, when the same amount of nitrogen was admitted to the chamber without the operation of the second ion source, there was essentially no reaction with the sputtered Al. A similar effect can be inferred from the work of Kitabatake and Wasa (79), who obtained Si_3N_4 films using a single source operating in Ar and N_2 In this case, the sample was located close to the target such that the ion beam also hit the sample at grazing incidence.

One of the most successful applications of reactive sputter deposition with ion beams has been the deposition of high quality optical films. This is done either in the arrangement of Fig. 14 or with an evaporation source replacing the sputtering target as a source of metal atoms. The films produces with these techniques are superior to films deposited without concurrent bombardment.

9.7 CONCLUSIONS

Reactive sputter deposition continues to be an area of intense interest for the production of compound films. While the ion beam experiments have shown excellent results, particularly for the deposition of optical and nitride films, much of the interest has remained in the use of the magnetron-based reactive deposition technique. Numerous studies have reported techniques or models which deal with the basic problem of target poisoning. Some of these techniques, particularly with the deposition of nitrides, have been very successful. This can probably be traced to the energy requirements to form the nitride. The same cannot generally be said for the reactive deposition of oxides. Generally in this case, process control by feedback techniques has not been successful, at least on a large scale. Individual experiments, using either very large pumping speeds, baffles or some means of optical feedback control have been successful in some cases, but a general solution to this problem still remains elusive.

9.8 REFERENCES

1. N. Schwartz and R.W. Berry, Physics of Thin Films ed. by G. Hass and R.E. Thuns, Vol 2, p.363 (Academic, New York, 1964).

2. W.D. Westwood, Prog. in Surf. Sci. 7: 71 (1976).

3. J.A. Thornton, Surface Eng. 2: 283 (1986).

4. W.D. Westwood, Physics of Thin Films vol. 14 (Academic, New York, 198?).

5. A. Okamota and T. Serikawa, Thin Solid Films 137: 143 (1986).

6. S. Kadlec, J. Musil and J. Vyskocil, Vacuum 37: 729 (1987).

7. J. Danroc, A. Aubert and R. Gillet, Surf. and Coatings Tech. 33: 83 (1987).

8. J. Heller, Thin Solid Films 17: 163 (1973).

9. B. Goranchev, V. Orlinov and V. Popova, Thin Solid Films 33: 173 (1976).

10. D.J. Harra and W.H. Haywood, Supplemento al Nuova Cimento 10: 381 (1967).

11. S. Schiller, U. Heisig, K. Steinfelder and J. Strumpfel, Proc. Int. Conf. on Ion Plating and Allied Techniques, London, p. 211 (1979).

12. K. Steenbeck, E. Steinbeiss, K-D. Ufert, Thin Solid Films, 92: 371 (1982).

13. J. Affinito and R.R. Parsons J. Vac. Sci. Technol. A2: 1275 (1984).

14. C.R. Aita and M.E. Marhic, J. Appl. Phys. 52: 6584 (1981).

15. F. Shinoki and A. Itoh, J. Appl. Phys. 46: 3381 (1975).

16. G. Lemperiere and J.M. Poitevin, Thin Solid Films 111: 339 (1984).

17. D.K. Hohnke, D.J. Schmatz and M.D. Hurley, Thin Solid Films, 118: 301 (1984).

18. G. Lemperiere, Le Vide, Les Couches Minces, 235: 3 (1987).

19. S. Berg, H-O. Blom, T. Larrson and C. Nender, J. Vac. Sci. Technol. A5: 202 (1987).

20. T. Larsson, H-O. Blom, C. Nender and S. Berg, J. Vac. Sci. Technol. A6: (1988).

21. A. Penfold, unpublished (1986).

22. D.E. Harrison, Rad. Eff. 70: 1 (1983).

23. A.J. Stirling and W.D. Westwood, J. Appl. Phys. 41: 742 (1970).

24. A.J. Stirling and W.D. Westwood, Thin Solid Films 7: 1 (1971).

25. A.J. Stirling and W.D. Westwood, . Thin Solid Films 8: 199 (1971).

26. G. Betz and W. Husinsky, Nucl. Instrum. Meth. B13: 343 (1986).

27. J.M.E. Harper, J.J. Cuomo, R.J. Gambino, H.R. Kaufman and R.S. Robinson, J. Vac. Sci. Technol. 15: 1597 (1978).

28. J.J. Hanak, Le Vide 175: 11 (1975).

29. J.J. Cuomo, R.J. Gambino, J.M.E. Harper, J.D. Kuptsis and J.C. Webber, J. Vac. Sci. Technol. 15: 281 (1978).

30. D. Kester and R. Messier, J. Vac. Sci. Technol. A4: 496 (1986).

31. K. Tominaga, S. Iwamura, Y. Shintani and O. Tada, Jpn. J. Appl. Phys. 21: 688 (1982).

32. K. Wasa, M. Kitabatake, H. Adachi, K. Setsune and K. Hirochi, AIP Conf. Proc. 165: 38 (1988).

33. S.M. Rossnagel and J.J. Cuomo, AIP Conf. Proc. 165: 108 (1988).

34. W.Y. Less, J. Salem, V. Lee, C. Rettner, G. Lim, and R. Savoy, AIP Conf. Proc. 165:   (1988).

35. P.J. Clarke AIP Conf. Proc. (Proceedings of 1988 AVS Topical Symposium on High Temperature Superconductors, in-press, 1989).

36. M.R. Scheuermann, Appl. Phys. Lett. 1987.

37. K. Tominaga, S. Iwamura, Y. Shintani and O. Tada, Jpn. J. Appl. Phys. 22: 418 (1983).

38. S.M. Rossnagel, I. Yang and J.J. Cuomo, Int. Conf. Metallurgical Coatings, San Diego, CA, April, 1989.

39. B. Window and N. Savvides, J. Vac. Sci. Technol. A4: 453 (1986).

40. L. I. Maissel, in Handbook of Thin Film Technology ed. by L.I. Maissel and R.H. Glang, Chap. 4 (McGraw-Hill, New York, 1970).

41. R.W. Berry, US Patent 2,993,266 (1961).

42. W.D. Westwood, N. Waterhouse and P.S. Wilcox, Tantalum Thin Films (Academic, New York, 1975).

43. G.H. Maher and R.J. Diefendorf, IEEE Trans. PHP-8: 11 (1972).

44. S. Fukunishi, A. Kawana, N. Uchida and J. Noda, J. Appl. Phys. Suppl. 2: Pt. I, 749 (1974).

45. Y. Higuma, K. Tanaka, T. Nakagawa, T. Kariya and Y. Hamakawa, Jpn. J. Appl. Phys. 16: 1707 (1977).

46. J.A. Thornton and A.S. Penfold, in Thin Film Processes, ed. by. J. Vossen and W. Kern, Chap. II-2, (Academic, New York, 1978).

47. R.K. Waits, in Thin Film Processes, ed. by J. Vossen and W. Kern, Chap. II-4, (Academic, New York, 1978).

48. J.A. Thornton, J. Vac. Sci. Technol. 15: 171 (1978).

49. R.K. Waits, J. Vac. Sci. Technol. 15: 179 (1978).

50. D.B. Fraser, in Thin Film Processes, ed. by J. Vossen and W. Kern, Chap. II-3 (Academic, New York, 1978).

51. D.B. Fraser, J. Vac. Sci. Technol. 15: 178 (1978).

52. S. Schiller, U. Heisig, K. Gooedicke, K. Schade, G. Teschner and J. Henneberger, Thin Solid Films 64: 455 (1979).

53. S. Maniv and W.D. Westwood, Surf. Sci. 100: 108 (1980).

54. J.P. Noel, D.C. Houghton, G. Este. F.R. Shepherd and H. Plattner, J. Vac. Sci. Technol. A2: 284 (1984).

55. J.A. Thornton, Thin Solid Films 80: 1 (1981).

56. G. Este and W.D. Westwood, J. Vac. Sci. Technol. A2: 1238 (1984).

57. W.D. Westwood, S. Maniv and P.J. Scanlon, J. Appl. Phys. 54: 6481 (1983).

58. S.M. Rossnagel and H.R. Kaufman, J. Vac. Sci. Technol. A5: 88 (1988).

59. S. Maniv and W.D. Westwood, J. Vac. Sci. Technol. 17: 743 (1980).

60. G. Este and W.D. Westwood, J. Vac. Sci. Technol. A6: 1845 (1988).

61. S. Maniv, C. Miner and W.D. Westwood, J. Vac. Sci. Technol. 18: 195 (1981).

62. F. Jones, J. Vac. Sci. Technol. A6: 3088 (1988).

63. P. Chang and D.M. McGarr, Diagnostic Techniques in VLSI Fabrication, p. 189 (Semiconductor Equipment and Materials Inst. Inc, Mountain View, CA, 1987).

64. G.D. Davis and M. Natan, J. Vac. Sci. Technol. A4: 159 (1986).

65. ref 65 = old 166, look up.

66. W.D. Sproul, AIP Conf. Proc. 149: 157 (1986).

67. A.F. Hmiel, J. Vac. Sci. Technol. A3: 592 (1985).

68. M. Bhushan, J. Vac. Sci. Technol. A5: 2829 (1987).

69. S. Sciller, U. Heisig, K. Steinfelder, J. Strumpfel, R. Voight, R. Fendler and G. Teschner, Thin Solid Films 96: 235 (1982).

70. K. Enjouji, K. Murata and S. Nishakawa, Thin Solid Films 108: 1 (1983).

71. S. Schiller, O. Heisig, C. Korndorfer, G. Beister, J. Reschke, K. Steinfelder and J. Strompfel, Surf. and Coatings Tech. 33: 405 (1987)

72. M.I. Ridge and R.P. Howson, Vacuum 34: 327 (1984).

73. R.S. Robinson and H.R. Kaufman, in Handbook of Ion Beam Processing Technology ed. by J.J. Cuomo, S.M. Rossnagel and H.R. Kaufman (Noyes, Park Ridge, NJ 1989), p. 39.

74. W. Holber, in Handbook of Ion Beam Processing Technology, ed. by J.J. Cuomo, S.M. Rossnagel and H.R. Kaufman (Noyes, Park Ridge, NJ 1989) p. 21.

75. R.K. Fitch, T. Mulvey, W.J. Thetcher and A.H. McIlraith, J. Phys. D. Appl. Phys. 3: 1399 (1970).

76. Cold cathode ion source, model cc-100, Denton Vacuum, Inc., Cherry Hill, NJ 08003.

77. C. Weissmantel, Thin Solid Films 32: 11 (1976).

78. J.M. E. Harper, J.J. Cuomo and H.T. G. Hentzell, Appl. Phys. Lett. 43: 547 (1983).

79. M. Kitabatake and K. Wasa, J. Vac. Sci. Technol. A5: 1793 (1987).

10

Plasma Enhanced Chemical Vapor Deposition of Thin Films for Microelectronics

Rafael Reif

10.1 INTRODUCTION

Plasma enhanced chemical vapor deposition (PECVD) is an established commercial technique for the deposition of insulating films such as silicon nitride and silicon oxide (1). The major advantage of PECVD is its lower temperature capability compared to that of thermally driven CVD. For example, deposition temperatures of 700 to 900°C are required to deposit silicon nitride films by thermal CVD, while only 250 to 350°C are sufficient to deposit similar films by PECVD (2,3). This lower temperature capability is made possible by the addition of electrical energy to the CVD environment, and the effective substitution of this electrical energy for thermal energy.

PECVD is also being investigated as a potential technique for the deposition of crystalline films such as polycrystalline silicon (4-6), epitaxial silicon (7-9), epitaxial gallium arsenide (10-12), and refractory metal and silicide (13,14) films. More recently, the PECVD of diamond films has also received a great deal of attention (15,16). The driving force for the PECVD of these materials is the same as that for the insulating films; that is, to lower the deposition temperature while maintaining reasonable growth rates and high quality.

This chapter discusses the plasma enhanced chemical vapor deposition technique, emphasizing the issues important to the deposition of thin films for microelectronics. It begins with a review of the basic physics and chemistry of nonequilibrium glow discharges, followed by a discussion of the effects of adding a glow discharge to a chemical vapor deposition (CVD) environment. The latter sections discuss the most important dielectric, semiconductor, and conductor films that have been deposited by PECVD. References (17-24) correspond to other reviews of PECVD.

10.2 NONEQUILIBRIUM GLOW DISCHARGES

A glow discharge can be defined as a partially ionized gas containing equal volume concentrations of positive and negative charged species (mostly ions and electrons, respectively) and different concentrations of ground-state and excited species (25,26). This partially ionized gas can be generated by subjecting the gas to very high temperatures or to strong electric or magnetic fields. In thermal plasmas, the electrons, ions, and neutral species are in local thermodynamic equilibrium. In nonequilibrium or "cold" plasmas, the electrons and ions are more energetic than the neutral species.

Most of the glow discharges used in microelectronics are generated by subjecting the gas to a radio frequency (rf) electric field, and they are nonequilibrium glow discharges (i.e., "cold" plasmas). The electric field initially accelerates a few free electrons present in the gas. Although the electric field also acts on the ions, they remain relatively unaffected because of their much heavier mass. The accelerated electrons do not lose much energy in elastic collisions with gas species because of the large mass difference. Furthermore, these electrons do not lose much energy in inelastic collisions (e.g., excitation and ionization), until their energies reach the necessary threshold energies (e.g., 11.56 eV for excitation and 15.8 eV for ionization of argon (25)). Consequently, these accelerated electrons gain energy quickly from the electric field.

Once these electrons acquire sufficiently high energies, their collisions with gas species result in excitations and ionizations, the latter generating additional electrons that are, in turn, accelerated by the electric field. This transient process avalanches quickly, creating the steady state glow discharge. In steady state, the glow continuously loses charged species (i.e., electrons and ions) to the electrodes and other surfaces within the chamber, and gains a numerically equal number of electrons and ions from ionizations. Other mechanisms that produce additional electrons, such as secondary electron emission from positive ion bombardment on the electrodes and walls, are known to play a major role in sustaining the glow discharge.

The inelastic collisions between high-energy electrons and gas species give rise to highly reactive species, such as excited neutrals and free radicals, as well as ions and more electrons. In this manner, the energy of the electrons is used to create reactive and charged species without significantly raising the gas temperature. The reactive species produced in the plasma have lower energy barriers to physical and chemical reactions than the parent species and, consequently, can react at lower temperatures. PECVD uses these reactive species to deposit thin films at temperatures lower than those possible with thermally driven CVD. The charged species in the glow discharge may also affect the properties of the deposited films (27,28).

There are many possible inelastic collisions between electrons and gas species in a glow discharge. Examples of those believed to be important in PECVD are listed below:

Excitation:	$A + e^- \rightarrow A^* + e^-$	(1)
Ionization:	$A + e^- \rightarrow A^+ + 2e^-$	(2)
Dissociation:	$A_2 + e^- \rightarrow 2A + e^-$	(3)
Electron attachment:	$A + e^- \rightarrow A^-$	(4)
Dissociative attachment:	$A_2 + e^- \rightarrow A + A^-$	(5)
Photoemission:	$A^* \rightarrow A + h\nu$	(6)
Charge transfer:	$A^+ + B \rightarrow A + B^+$	(7)

where A, A$_2$, and B are reactants, e$^-$ is an electron, A* is reactant A in an excited state, and A$^+$, A$^-$, and B$^+$ are ions of A and B.

The rate at which these inelastic collisions create excited species, ions, free radicals, etc., can be estimated by using a reaction rate equation (29). For example, the rate at which A* is created from reaction (1) can be given by:

$$\frac{d[A^*]}{dt} = k_1[A][e^-] \tag{8}$$

where $d[A^*]/dt$ is the rate of formation of A*, k_1 is the reaction rate coefficient, [A] is the concentration of species A, and [e$^-$] is the electron concentration (30). Similar equations can be used to describe the reaction rates corresponding to reactions in Eqns. (2) through (7).

As discussed above, only high energy electrons can take part in inelastic collisions. In order to take this into account, k_1 in Eqn. (8) needs to be defined in terms of the electron velocity and the inelastic collision cross-section. The cross section of an electron-reactant inelastic collision is proportional to the probability that this inelastic collision will occur and is a function of the electron energy. For example, if the energy of the electron is lower than the required threshold energy, the collision cross section is zero. The rate coefficient k_i can be calculated by using the following equation (29):

$$k_i = \int_0^\infty [\frac{2E}{m_e}]^{1/2} \sigma_i(E)f(E)dE \tag{9}$$

where E is the electron energy, m_e is the electron mass, σ_i is the collision cross section of reaction i and is a function of E, and f(E) is the electron energy distribution function and gives the fraction of free electrons having a given energy. The integration is carried out over all possible electron energies. The square root term in Eqn. (9) is the electron velocity.

Some collision cross section data can be found in the literature (31). However, most of the cross sections of interest in microelectronics are not known. A similar situation exists with the electron energy distribution function f(E). It is typical to assume a Maxwell-Boltzmann distribution for f(E), that is, a distribution in which a large fraction of the electrons have energies lower than or equal to the average electron energy, and the fraction of electrons having higher energies decays exponentially with increasing energy. However, the actual electron energy distribution function is not known, and non-Maxwellian distributions have been proposed. Moreover, it is possible that the reactant composition of the gas influences f(E) because the higher-energy electrons lose a significant fraction of their energies in inelastic collisions with these reactants. Consequently, it is difficult to calculate reaction rate coefficients and reaction rates theoretically (32).

The rf glow discharges commercially used in microelectronics operate at frequencies between 50 kHz and 13.56 MHz, and pressures of 0.1-2.0 Torr. The plasma density (i.e. the density of ions and free electrons) is in the range of 10^8 to 10^{12} cm^{-3}. The degree of ionization is typically $\leq 10^{-4}$, i.e., the principle species in the glow is primarily neutrals. A Maxwell-Boltzmann distribution is usually used to approximate the energy distribution of free electrons. Typical average electron energies are 1-3 eV, but the fastest electrons may reach energies as high as 10-30 eV (33). These high energy electrons make possible the creation, at relatively low temperatures, of the reactive species responsible for film formation. Because the average electron energies are much higher than the ion energies, these are known as non-equilibrium glow discharges; i.e. the PECVD environment is not in thermal equilibrium. Consequently, thermodynamics is of little help in predicting the product of a PECVD reaction.

10.3 POTENTIALS IN RF GLOW DISCHARGES

Several potentials are important in the glow discharges used in microelectronics: the plasma potential, the floating potential, and the sheath potential.

The plasma potential (V_p) is the potential of the glow region of the plasma, which is normally considered nearly equipotential. It is the most positive potential in the chamber and is the reference potential for the glow discharge.

The floating potential (V_f) is the potential at which equal fluxes of negative and positive charged species arrive at an electrically floating surface in contact with the plasma. It is approximately given by:

$$V_p - V_f = \frac{kT_e}{2e} \ln(\frac{m_i}{2.3m_e})$$

(10)

where T_e is the electron temperature, e is the unit electron charge, and m_i and m_e are the ion and electron mass, respectively (25,34). Equation (10) can be used to estimate the maximum energy with which positive ions may bombard electrically insulated chamber walls. Most sputtering threshold energies are 20 to 30 eV (25). Therefore, a $V_p - V_f \leq 20$ to 30V would avoid sputtering off the walls, which may lead to film contamination.

The plasma potential is always positive with respect to any surface in contact with the plasma. This is because the mobility of free electrons in the plasma is much greater than that of ions and, consequently, the initial electron flux to all surfaces is greater than the ion flux. Therefore, the surfaces in contact with the plasma become negatively charged, and a positive space charge layer develops in front of these surfaces. Because there are fewer electrons in the space charge layer, or sheath, fewer gas species are excited by electron collisions. Consequently, fewer species relax and give off radiation, and the sheath region is dark relative to the glow discharge. Positive ions that enter the sheaths from the glow region by random thermal motion accelerate into the electrodes and other surfaces in contact with the plasma. Similarly, secondary electrons emitted from the surfaces (e.g., due to positive ion bombardment) accelerate through the sheaths into the glow region. The maximum energy with which positive ions bombard a surface, and the maximum energy with which secondary electrons enter the glow region, is determined by the difference between the potential of the surface and the plasma potential. Because this is the potential across the sheath, it is usually referred to as the sheath potential.

Figure 1(a) shows schematically an rf generator connected to the electrodes of a plasma system (35). A_1, A_2 are the areas of the electrodes and V_1, V_2 are the voltages across the sheaths in front of the electrodes. An rf generator signal of $V_{peak} \sin \omega t$ is assumed in this discussion. As indicated in Fig. 1(b), the average sheath voltages are the same, i.e. $\overline{V}_1 = \overline{V}_2$, because the generator is dc coupled to the reactor. Moreover, the average plasma potential is equal to the average sheath potential, i.e. $\overline{V}_1 = \overline{V}_2 = \overline{V}_p$. The value of $\overline{V}_1 = \overline{V}_2 = \overline{V}_p$ varies from about $0.5V_{peak}$ in symmetric reactors (i.e. where $A_1 = A_2$), to higher values in asymmetric systems (36). If a "blocking" capacitor is added between the generator and the powered electrode (Fig. 2(a)), no dc current is allowed in the circuit in steady-state. Consequently, the capacitor charges up to a sufficient "self bias" voltage until there is no dc current in the circuit. This average self bias potential is indicated as $\overline{V}_T$ in Fig. 2(b). It is negative when the smaller electrode is powered (Fig. 2(b)), but positive when the larger electrode is powered (36). The values of $\overline{V}_1$, $\overline{V}_2$ and $\overline{V}_T$ are determined by the ratio of the electrode areas, i.e. $\overline{V}_1/\overline{V}_2 = (A_2/A_1)^n$ (37, 38).

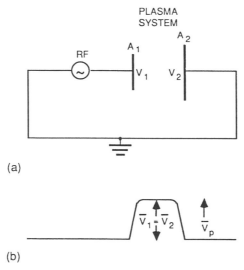

(a)

(b)

Figure 1: Potential distribution in rf plasma systems without blocking capacitor (35). (a) Electric circuit with rf generator connected to the electrodes of the plasma system. (b) Potential distribution: $|\overline{V}_1| = |\overline{V}_2| = \overline{V}_p$ is the average plasma potential.

Koenig and Maissel (37) derived this area ratio expression assuming very low pressure operation and theoretically found $n = 3$ or 4. Experimental data suggest that the ratio $\overline{V}_1/\overline{V}_2$ is also a function of the gas in the discharge and the peak-to-peak rf voltage applied (39). Moreover, for $A_2/A_1 \approx 1 - 1.7$, the value of n was found to be close to 4 (39), but for larger area ratios n has been found to be closer to 1 (34,38,39). In very asymmetric reactors (i.e. $A_2 >> A_1$), $|\overline{V}_1| \simeq |\overline{V}_T| \simeq V_{peak}$, while $\overline{V}_2 = \overline{V}_p \approx 0$. On the other hand, in symmetric reactors $|\overline{V}_1| = |\overline{V}_2| = \overline{V}_p = V_{peak}/2$. Notice that the sheath potentials and the plasma potential are equal to $0.5V_{peak}$ in symmetric systems with or without a blocking capacitor. Tables 1 and 2 summarize the sheath, plasma, and self-bias voltages discussed here.

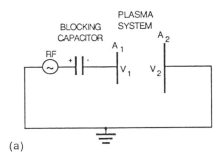

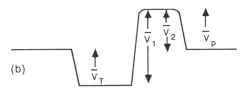

Figure 2: Potential distribution in rf plasma systems with blocking capacitor (35). (a) Electric circuit with rf generator connected to the electrodes of the plasma system through a blocking capacitor. (b) Potential distribution: $\overline{V}_T$ is the self-bias voltage.

dc coupled		
	symmetric $(A_1 = A_2)$	asymmetric $(A_1 \ll A_2)$
$\overline{V}_1$	$V_{peak}/2$	$V_{peak}/2 < \overline{V}_1 < V_{peak}$
$\overline{V}_2$	$V_{peak}/2$	$V_{peak}/2 < \overline{V}_2 < V_{peak}$
$\overline{V}_p$	$V_{peak}/2$	$V_{peak}/2 < \overline{V}_p < V_{peak}$
$|\overline{V}_T|$	0	0

Table 1: Average sheath ($\overline{V}_1$, $\overline{V}_2$), plasma ($\overline{V}_p$), and self bias ($\overline{V}_T$) voltages in dc-coupled reactor. The applied voltage is $V_{peak} \sin \omega t$. Notice that $\overline{V}_1 = \overline{V}_2 = \overline{V}_p$ and that $\overline{V}_T = 0$ as there is no blocking capacitor. (see Fig. 1.)

dc coupled		
	symmetric $(A_1 = A_2)$	**asymmetric** $(A_1 \ll A_2)$
$\bar{V}_1$	$V_{peak}/2$	$V_{peak}/2 < \bar{V}_1 < V_{peak}$
$\bar{V}_2$	$V_{peak}/2$	$V_{peak}/2 < \bar{V}_2 < V_{peak}$
$\bar{V}_p$	$V_{peak}/2$	$V_{peak}/2 < \bar{V}_p < V_{peak}$
$|\bar{V}_T|$	0	0

Table 2: Average sheath $(\bar{V}_1, \bar{V}_2)$, plasma $(\bar{V}_p)$, and self bias $(\bar{V}_T)$ voltages in capacitively coupled reactor. The applied voltage is $V_{peak} \sin \omega t$. Under these conditions, $\bar{V}_1/\bar{V}_2 = (A_2/A_1)^n$, $|\bar{V}_T| = \bar{V}_1 - \bar{V}_2$, and $\bar{V}_2 = \bar{V}_p$. (See Fig. 2.)

10.4 QUALITATIVE MODEL FOR PECVD

In thermally-driven CVD, ground state species containing the elements to be deposited (e.g. silane (SiH_4) and ammonia (NH_3) as parent species for Si and N, respectively, in Si_3N_4 depositions) are transported to the vicinity of the wafer surface where they diffuse to the surface, adsorb on the surface, undergo chemical reactions and surface migration, and eventually yield a solid film. Reaction byproducts also form, and they desorb, diffuse away into the main gas stream, and are transported out of the chamber. This sequence of steps is summarized below:

1. Transport of reactants to the growth region

2. Mass transport of reactants to the wafer surface

3. Adsorption of reactants

4. Physical-chemical reactions yielding the solid film and reaction byproducts

5. Desorption of byproducts

6. Mass transport of byproducts to the main gas stream

7. Transport of byproducts away from the growth region

An equivalent circuit representation of this sequence of steps is shown in Fig. 3 (40).

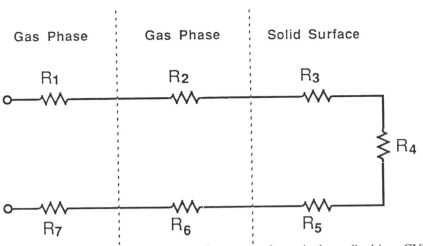

Figure 3: Equivalent circuit representation of sequence of steps in thermally-driven CVD (40). The R_i's (with i = 1 - 7) represent the seven steps described in text.

When a plasma is generated in a CVD environment, a fraction of the ground-state parent species in the gas phase undergoes electron impact dissociation and excitation, and highly reactive species are consequently generated. As a result, in addition to the ground state species, these highly reactive species also diffuse to the surface, and undergo similar processes of adsorption, chemical reactions, surface migration, etc. In other words, these highly reactive species follow an alternative deposition pathway which operates in parallel to the existing thermal deposition pathway. An equivalent circuit representation of this situation is shown in Fig. 4. The plasma kinetic pathway often bypasses that of the ground state species because the sticking coefficients of the highly reactive species are closer to unity (26), and the activation energies for chemical dissociation are typically lower. The latter is illustrated in Fig. 5, which compares the activation energy diagram of a ground-state reaction:

$$A \; \rightarrow \; B$$

which has an activation energy ΔE, with that of

$$A + e^-_{fast} \; \rightarrow \; A^* + e^-_{slow}$$

$$A^* \; \rightarrow \; B^*$$

which has an activation energy ΔE^*. (Strictly speaking, the reaction product B^* is not the same as B. For example, the thermal reaction

$$3SiH_4 + 4NH_3 \; \rightarrow \; Si_3N_4 + 12H_2$$

yields a Si_3N_4 film, while the plasma enhanced reaction

$$SiH_4 + NH_3 \; \rightarrow \; SiNH + 3H_2$$

yields a SiNH film.)

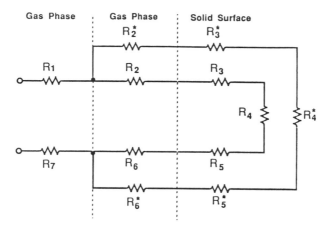

Figure 4: Equivalent circuit representation showing the thermal CVD path, and the parallel plasma-enhanced path represented by the R_i *'s.

Consequently, the plasma kinetic pathway makes possible a higher deposition rate. Moreover, the ions present in the plasma may bombard the substrate surface, further modifying the kinetic pathway by effecting the breaking down of weakly bonded reactive species, the surface migration of adatoms, and/or removing undesired contaminants. (However, if ion energies, fluxes, and/or doses are too high, they may also affect the film quality.) Temperature is still needed to drive the reaction over ΔE^* (Fig. 5), i.e. to provide the energy required to promote surface reactions and desorb byproducts, as well as to lower film contamination.

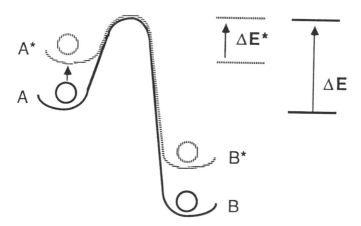

Figure 5: Activation energy diagram for a thermally-driven (solid line) and for a plasma-enhanced (dashed line) reaction.

10.5 COMMERCIAL PECVD SYSTEMS

The commercial PECVD systems discussed here have been used successfully to deposit silicon nitride, silicon oxynitride, silicon oxide, and hydrogenated amorphous silicon films. Some of these systems are also being used to investigate the deposition of polycrystalline (Si, refractory metal, refractory metal silicide, diamond) and epitaxial (Si, compound semiconductor) films.

The first commercially important PECVD reactor was introduced by Reinberg in 1974 (see Fig. 6) (41). The plasma is generated between the two parallel, circular electrodes. The wafers are loaded onto the lower, electrically grounded, electrode. The upper electrode is connected to the rf generator through an impedance matching network. The reactants are fed in from the gas ring, enter the plasma region (i.e., the region between the electrodes) at its outer edge, and flow radially in toward a pumping port at the center of the lower electrode (42, 43). These reactors are also known as "radial flow" reactors.

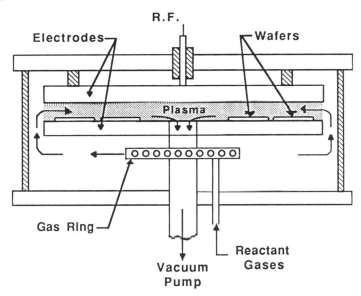

Figure 6: Schematic of radial flow reactor designed by Reinberg (41). (Courtesy of the Electrochemical Society, Inc.)

An "inverse" radial flow reactor was introduced by Applied Materials in 1976 (see Fig. 7) (44). The gas inlet is at the center of the lower electrode, with the gas flow directed radially outward. A magnetic drive assembly permits rotation of the lower electrode, thus randomizing the substrate position and optimizing deposition uniformity. An improvement to this design, also introduced by Applied Materials, is shown in Fig. 8 (43). The perforated electrode in this newer design further improves deposition uniformity.

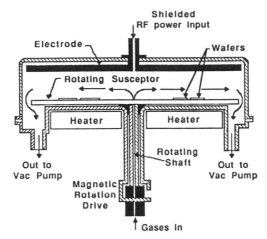

Figure 7: Schematic of inverse radial flow reactor (44). (Courtesy of Applied Materials, Inc.)

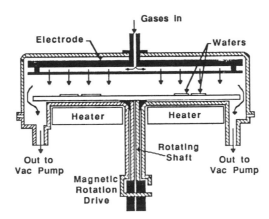

Figure 8: Schematic of inverse radial flow reactor with perforated electrode (43). (Courtesy of Applied Materials, Inc.)

A hot-wall, batch PECVD system (see Fig. 9) was introduced simultaneously by ASM America and Pacific Western Systems in the late 1970s (45,46). The deposition chamber consists of a quartz tube placed within a resistively heated furnace. Vertically oriented graphite slabs carry the wafers in slots. Every other slab is connected to the same rf power terminal, as shown in Fig. 9. The glow discharge is generated between adjacent electrodes. The reactants are directed along the axis of the chamber tube and between the electrodes. The vertical position of the wafers in this "tubular" design makes possible a reduction in the collection of particulates (from wafer handling and flaking off the walls) on the wafer surface. In addition, good ($\pm 5\%$) film uniformity can be achieved over a large batch of wafers (e.g., $\simeq$ 90 125-mm wafers), and the furnace-type heating aids temperature control. Moreover, the plasma excitation technique for these systems makes it possible to pulse the rf power to the electrodes. (The rf power is applied continuously in all other systems.) Pulsing of the rf power improves deposition uniformity in this reactor.

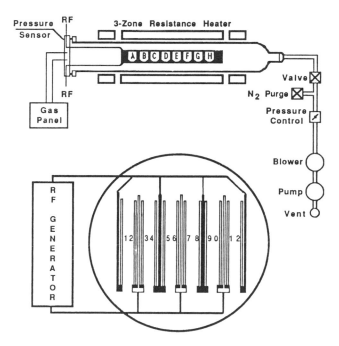

Figure 9: Schematic of hot-wall, batch PECVD system (45). (Courtesy of ASM America, Inc.).

Increasing performance demands and larger wafer sizes are driving the equipment technology away from the batch machines described here and into single-wafer processing. Consequently, next-generation PECVD equipment will probably be single-wafer machines.

10.6 PECVD OF DIELECTRIC FILMS

The most important PECVD dielectric films in microelectronics today are silicon nitride, silicon oxide, silicon oxynitride, and silicate glasses. Silicon nitride was the first material deposited by the PECVD technique on a large production scale. It is used extensively as a final protective passivation and coating layer for integrated circuits because it is an excellent diffusion barrier against moisture and alkali ions. The PECVD technique makes possible the low deposition temperature (250 – 400°C) required to deposit a silicon nitride film over wafers containing an aluminum metallization layer. Furthermore, PECVD nitride films with compressive stress can be obtained, and this permits the deposition of relatively thick films. Silane (SiH_4) and ammonia (NH_3) are typically used as sources of silicon and nitrogen, respectively. Silane and nitrogen (N_2) can also be used, but these reactants typically yield silicon-rich films (probably due to the relatively high bond energy of N_2 (21)), as well as films with low breakdown strengths (47,48). Depositions are normally carried out at pressures of 0.2 to 3 Torr, which yield growth rates of 200 to 500 Å/min. PECVD silicon nitride films contain 15 to 30 at % of hydrogen bonded to either silicon or nitrogen (34,38). Film properties such as refractive index, stress, and optical absorption edge are greatly affected by the concentration and chemical distribution of hydrogen in the film.

The following general trends relating the properties of PECVD silicon nitride films with process parameters and film composition have been observed. These trends are sensitive to reactor geometry and deposition conditions, and are included here only as a guide.

1.   The refractive index (1.9-2.2) increases as the Si-H/N-H bond ratio and/or Si/N ratio in the film increases (47, 49).

2.   The optical gap is 3-4 eV (compared to 5 eV for stoichiometric Si_3N_4), and is a function of the silicon content in the film. It decreases with increasing Si/N ratio (47, 49).

3.   The resistivity ranges from 10^5 to 10^{19} ohm-cm, and decreases with increasing Si/N ratio (47, 50).

4.   Breakdown strengths are $1 - 6x10^6$ V/cm, and are sensitive to film composition, with the silicon-rich films exhibiting the lower breakdown fields (47, 50).

5.   Film etch rates are typically used to determine film quality. Plasma silicon nitride etch rates in aqueous HF acid solutions increase with decreasing Si/N ratios down to 0.75, and with increasing H content (47, 51).

6.   Stress varies from 10^{10}dyn/cm^2, compressive, to 10^{10}dyn/cm^2, tensile, and is a function of substrate temperature, gas composition, operating pressure, rf power, and rf frequency (47,49,52,53). For example, low excitation frequencies (e.g. 50 kHz) usually yield films with small compressive stress ($\simeq$2x10^{9}dyn/cm^2) (54), while higher frequencies (e.g. 13.56 MHz) may yield films with tensile stress ($\simeq$2x10^{9}dyn/cm^2) (52). The optimum stress for silicon nitride films used as final passivation layers is $2 - 5x10^9$dyn/cm^2, compressive (54).

More complete reviews of the PECVD of silicon nitride can be found in references (21,42,47,55,56,57).

PECVD silicon oxide films have been proposed as an interconductor dielectric material because of their low deposition temperature (200-400°C) and relatively low dielectric constant (4-6 vs. 6-9 for PECVD silicon nitride (47)). Silane is typically used as the silicon source, while nitrous oxide (N_2O), nitric oxide (NO), carbon dioxide (CO_2), and oxygen have been used as oxygen sources. Nitrous oxide has been the preferred oxidizer because of the relatively low (1.7 eV) bond dissociative energy of N-O in this molecule (17,18). PECVD silicon oxide films are compressive (0.07 – 2.4x10^{9}dynes/cm^2) independent of rf frequency, and contain 2 to 9 wt % of hydrogen and less than 5 wt % of nitrogen (54,58). Other properties of PECVD silicon oxide films are refractive index (1.45-1.50), breakdown strength $(2 - 6 \times 10^6 V/cm)$, and resistivity $(10^{13} - 10^{17}$ ohm-cm). A more complete review on the PECVD of silicon oxide films can be found in references (2,21,47,59).

PECVD silicon oxynitride films combine some of the best properties of PECVD silicon nitride and oxide films. The presence of oxygen lowers the dielectric constant of silicon nitride films, while that of nitrogen increases the resistance to sodium ions and moisture of silicon oxide films. Consequently, these films have found applications as interconductor dielectric layers and as surface passivation coating for integrated circuits. The deposition conditions for these films are a combination of those used for silicon nitrides and oxides (60).

Phosphosilicate glass (PSG) and boro-phosphosilicate glass (BPSG) can be readily deposited by PECVD (54). PSG is frequently used as the interconductor layer between polycrystalline silicon and aluminum, and it provides conformal step coverage after heating the wafer until the glass softens and flows. This "reflow" process requires phosphorus concentrations of 6 to 8 wt % and temperatures of 1000 to 1100°C. BPSG is sometimes preferred because it softens and flows at temperatures below 1000°C(61,62).

10.7 PECVD OF POLYCRYSTALLINE SILICON FILMS

Polycrystalline silicon (polysilicon) films can be deposited by atmospheric pressure chemical vapor deposition (CVD) (63), low pressure CVD (LPCVD) (64), and molecular beam deposition (MBD) (65) at temperatures over 600°C. Polysilicon is commercially used as the gate electrode and interconnect material in MOS integrated circuits (66), and is being investigated as the active material for thin film transistors (TFTs) (67) and as solar-energy conversion devices (68). The most commonly used deposition technique for integrated circuit applications is LPCVD. This technique has two basic problems: (1) the deposition rate and film structure are a strong function of the deposition temperature, and (2) the thickness uniformity and deposition rate are affected when large quantities of dopant species are introduced in the reactor during growth (4). TFTs are attractive for flat panel displays but require fabrication temperatures much lower than those possible with either CVD, LPCVD, or MBD. PECVD is being studied as an alternative to LPCVD for the fabrication of polysilicon gate electrodes, and as a low temperature fabrication technique for TFTs (67). The potential advantages of PECVD are: (1) less sensitivity to deposition temperature, (2) capability of introducing large quantities of dopant species without affecting the deposition rate, and (3) lower deposition temperature.

Figure 10 shows growth-rate data as a function of deposition temperature for LPCVD and PECVD films deposited in the same reactor (6). As indicated earlier, LPCVD depositions are very sensitive to the substrate temperature. At temperatures below 700°C, the LPCVD process has an apparent activation energy of 48 kcal/mole, which corresponds to the energy required to thermally dissociate the silicon source, silane. At temperatures above 700°C, the growth rate is essentially constant, probably because of mass transport and/or silane depletion limitations in the reactor used (6). PECVD depositions, on the other hand, yield growth rates which are higher and only weakly dependent (7 kcal/mole) on substrate temperature.

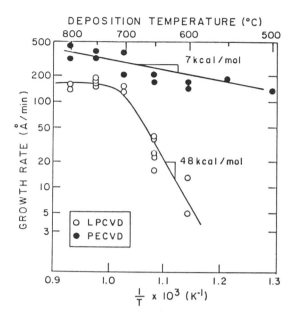

Figure 10: Plots of $\log_{10}$ (growth rate) vs reciprocal temperature for polycrystalline silicon thin films grown on oxidized silicon substrates with and without plasma assistance (PECVD and LPCVD, respectively) (6).

The amorphous-to-polycrystalline transition temperature and the polysilicon structure vary with reactor design and deposition conditions. Polysilicon films have been deposited at 450°C in a silane/argon plasma (69), at 600°C in a silane/hydrogen plasma (70), at 700°C in a silane plasma (6), and at 625°C in a dichlorosilane/argon plasma (4). Grain sizes ranging from 30 Å (71) to 500 Å (72) and deposition rates ranging from 30 Å/min (73) to 3000 Å/min (74) have been reported. Kamins and Chiang (4) found their PECVD polysilicon films to be compressive. They introduced up to 5×10^{20} phosphorous atoms/cm³ in the films by adding phosphine (PH_3) to the gas ambient. However, they also introduced in the film up to 3×10^{20} chlorine atoms/cm³, which were supplied by the dichlorosilane (SiH_2Cl_2) used as the silicon source.

10.8 PECVD OF EPITAXIAL FILMS

10.8.1 Silicon

Silicon epitaxial layers are commercially deposited by atmospheric or reduced (40-100 Torr) pressure CVD at temperatures of 1050 to 1200°C (75). The relatively high deposition temperature imposes limits on the minimum thickness and conductivity of films deposited on heavily doped substrates because of dopant redistribution during growth. These limitations restrict the levels of integration available for VLSI applications, and evidence the need for a lower temperature technique capable of depositing high quality silicon epitaxial layers. Molecular beam epitaxy (76), ion beam epitaxy (77), ion cluster beam deposition (78), solid phase epitaxy (79), ultra high vacuum/CVD (80), and photoenhanced CVD (81) have been proposed as possible low temperature alternatives. Another interesting alternative is PECVD.

Silicon epitaxial layers have been deposited by PECVD at a temperature as low as 800°C using a horizontal water-cooled reactor (82). A SiH_4/H_2 (27 MHz) discharge produced deposition rates of 200Å/min at 800°C, silane partial pressures of about 1 mTorr, and operating pressures of 0.2 to 0.6 Torr. The substrate surface was in-situ cleaned by a hydrogen plasma for a few minutes at the deposition temperature immediately before the start of the deposition. The success of these experiments was attributed to this predeposition plasma cleaning step.

Silicon epitaxial layers have also been deposited at a temperature of 750°C using a vertically aligned PECVD system with rf (13.56 MHz) excitation (7,83). The glow discharge was confined between two mesh electrodes perpendicular to the gas flow, and the wafer was located downstream, parallel to the electrodes, and 150 mm below the lowest electrode. These experiments were carried out at much lower operating pressures, 1×10^{-2} and 3×10^{-3} Torr, but yielded higher deposition rates, 1980 and 840 Å/min, respectively. The power level supplied to the discharge was 200 watts. The gas ambient consisted of silane, but germanium was added to the plasma at the beginning of the deposition. The addition of germanium was found to be essential, and it was proposed that it cleaned the wafer surface by removing the native silicon dioxide layer coating the substrate. The addition of germanium, moreover, resulted in the formation of a Si-Ge alloy in the first 1000 Å of the epitaxial film. Predeposition cleaning consisting of HCl gas (850°C , 10 min) was found unsuitable because it produced epitaxial films with hazy surfaces. The films were in-situ doped by adding phosphine diluted in helium to the plasma, but they had to be annealed (1000°C, 60 min) to electrically activate most of the phosphorus in the film.

Silicon epitaxial films have been deposited at temperatures as low as 650°C using a low pressure CVD system both with and without plasma enhancement using silane (84-87). The reaction chamber consists of a quartz tube fitted with a polished flange and sealed to water-cooled stainless-steel flanges using silicone or Kalrez gaskets (see Fig. 11) (87). A graphite susceptor is suspended from the upper flange and it holds a single wafer (50 or 100 mm) in a vertical position facing an infrared lamp array. A 510 l/s turbomolecular pump system permits total flow rates up to 100 sccm while achieving a hydrocarbon free base pressure in the 10^{-8} Torr range. Operating pressures are 1-100 mTorr. The rf power supply is a 1 kW, 13.56-MHz generator coupled to the reactor through an automatic matching network. Plasma powers from 2.5 to 100 W may be used. A dc power supply is additionally used to bias the susceptor relative to ground. This arrangement decouples substrate biasing from rf plasma power or electrode self-bias.

Figure 12 shows Arrhenius plots of <100> growth rates with (PECVD) and without (CVD) plasma enhancement for temperatures from 750 to 800°C and a silane total pressure of 6 mTorr (88). The thermal CVD deposition rates range from 500 to 600 Å/min and exhibit an apparent activation energy of about 8 kcal/mole. Low rf power (2.5 W) plasma enhanced depositions are 20% faster in this temperature range. By increasing the plasma power to 20 W, an additional 10% growth rate increase is obtained.

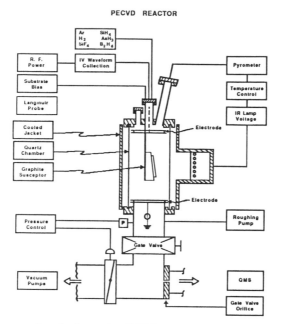

Figure 11: Cross-sectional schematic of PECVD epitaxial silicon reaction chamber (87).

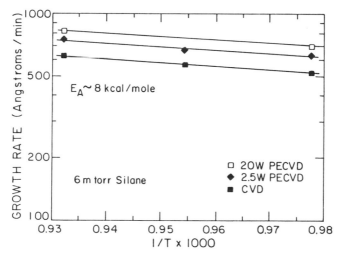

Figure 12: Arrhenius plots of <100> growth rates with and without plasma enhancement (PECVD and CVD, respectively) (88).

A predeposition in-situ cleaning of the substrate surface to remove the native silicon dioxide was found essential for achieving epitaxial growth. Surface cleaning was done by sputtering the wafer in a 5-W argon plasma at deposition temperature for 8-16 min with a negative dc bias of 100 V applied to the susceptor (87,89). Lightly doped epitaxial layers deposited on heavily doped silicon substrates by this technique exhibit extremely abrupt dopant concentration profiles (85). PECVD also makes possible the in-situ incorporation of large quantities of arsenic ($> 10^{19} cm^{-3}$) in the epitaxial layer without degrading film growth rate and morphology (90).

10.8.2 Gallium Arsenide

Several groups have also reported the plasma-enhanced, metal organic CVD (PE-MOCVD) of epitaxial GaAs films (11,12,91-94). Remote plasma configurations are typically used, in which the plasma is confined to a region and separated some distance from the substrate downstream. In these remote plasmas, the growth rate is very sensitive to the distance separating the plasma and the substrate, decreasing as the distance increases. The epitaxial growth rate has also been found to increase with rf power and with substrate temperature. The apparent activation energy from Arrhenius plots is about 13-14 kcal/mole.

10.9 PECVD OF REFRACTORY METALS AND THEIR SILICIDES

Refractory metals and their silicides are compatible with high temperature IC processing and have relatively high conductivities (metals: $\simeq 5\mu\Omega$ −cm, silicides: 16-40 $\mu\Omega$ −cm(95,96)). Consequently, they are attractive as gate, interconnection, and contact metallization materials in VLSI circuits. These materials can be deposited by physical vapor deposition (PVD) methods such as evaporation (97) and sputtering (98), by chemical vapor deposition (CVD) (99), and by PECVD.

10.9.1 Refractory Metals

Tungsten (W) films have been deposited in a radial-flow, parallel plate reactor with rf (4.5 MHz) excitation using tungsten hexafluoride (WF_6) and H_2 (100,101). Hydrogen was used to scavenge fluorine species, which otherwise etch the tungsten film being deposited. Deposition rates of about $40 \text{Å}/min$ were obtained at a substrate temperature of 350°C, operating pressure of 0.2 Torr, and rf power density of 0.06 W/cm^2. Auger studies indicated that silicon and oxygen were present in the films. The silicon contamination may have come from silicon tetrafluoride (SiF_4) in the WF_6 source gas. XPS measurements indicated that the as-deposited (350°C) films have $\simeq 1.1 − 1.5$ at. % flourine, which drops to $\simeq 0.5$ at. % after heat treatments ($\geq 650°C$) in forming gas (23). Film resistivity was sensitive to the H_2/WF_6 ratio in the ambient, with higher ratios yielding lower resistivities. This is probably because the scavenging of fluorine becomes more effective at higher hydrogen concentrations, and lowers the fluorine contamination in the deposited film. The resistivity of as-deposited films decreased with increasing deposition temperature (probably because of larger grains and/or lower defect concentrations), increasing rf power, and decreasing rf frequency and pressure (23). The resistivity also decreased with post-deposition heat treatments, presumably because of outdiffusion of contaminants (e.g., fluorine), annealing of radiation-induced defects created during deposition, or increases in the size of the grains. Films deposited at 400°C and subsequently annealed at 1100°C for 30 min had their resistivities lowered from 40 $\mu\Omega$ − cm to $7\mu\Omega$ −cm.

PECVD molybdenum (Mo) films have been deposited from molybdenum hexafluoride (MoF_6) and H_2 (100,101). These films were heavily contaminated with fluorine ($\simeq 15$ at. %) and had high resistivities ($> 10^{-2}\Omega$ −cm for a 0.3- μm-thick film). Molybdenum films have also been deposited from molybdenum hexacarbonyl [Mo(CO)$_6$] in a dc discharge onto the cathode of a parallel plate system, but these films contained 20 to 30 wt % carbon (102). A more successful attempt used molybdenum pentachloride (MoCl$_5$) diluted in H$_2$ at a pressure of 1 Torr and temperatures of 170 to 430°C (13,99). The as-deposited Mo films were amorphous, but crystallized after high temperature annealing. Auger analysis indicated the presence of chlorine and oxygen in the as-deposited films. The chlorine concentration in the films decreased after post-deposition heat treatments. The resistivity of as-deposited films decreased with increasing deposition temperature, probably because the incorporation of unreacted chloride in the film decreased with increasing temperatures. The resistivity of these films decreased significantly after a post-deposition annealing at 800°C for 20 min in nitrogen, presumably because of crystallization of the films and/or outdiffusion of chlorine. The lowest resistivity obtained for Mo films, after annealing, was $\simeq 10\mu\Omega$ −cm.

Although the high conductivities of refractory metals are desirable for gate and interconnection applications, these materials are chemically unstable in oxidizing ambients (95). Consequently, the silicides of these metals have been used, although their resistivities are an order of magnitude higher than those of the refractory metals. PECVD has been used to deposit silicides of molybdenum, tungsten, tantalum, and titanium.

10.9.2 Refractory Metal Silicides

Mo-silicide films were obtained by adding SiH$_4$ diluted in argon to the MoCl$_5$/H$_2$ plasma discussed above (13). The film composition was controlled by adjusting the composition of the gas ambient. The resistivity of as-deposited films increased with increasing SiH$_4$ flow rate, possibly because of a decrease in the Mo content of the film. The resistivity of these films also increased with increasing hydrogen flow rate, presumably because of a higher concentration of unreacted chloride in the film. The as-deposited films were amorphous and crystallized into the hexagonal structure after a post-deposition annealing in nitrogen at 1000°C for 20 min. It was proposed that chlorine atoms segregated in the grain boundaries prevented the hexagonal structure from changing to the tetragonal structure associated with sputtered and CVD MoSi$_2$ (99). As-deposited (400°C) PECVD resistivities are $\simeq 800\mu\Omega$ −cm (13).

Tungsten silicides (W$_x$Si$_{1-x}$) have been deposited in a parallel-plate reactor with rf (13.56 MHz) excitation using WF$_6$ and SiH$_4$ diluted in helium (103). Deposition rates were about 550 to 600 Å/ min at a substrate temperature of 230°C, and an operating pressure between 0.5 and 0.7 Torr. The atomic ratio of W/Si in the film was controlled by the WF$_6$/SiH$_4$ ratio in the gas ambient. The resistivity of the films decreased with post-deposition heat treatments. This is particularly interesting because the W$_x$Si$_{1-x}$ films with $x \leq 0.45$ were amorphous both as deposited and after a post-deposition annealing at 1100°C for 60 min in nitrogen. Therefore, the decrease in resistivity upon annealing was attributed to outdiffusion of F and H, presumably present in the as-deposited films, and not to the crystallization of the films. The lowest resistivity obtained with these films, after annealing, was about 40 $\mu\Omega$ −cm.

Tantalum-silicide films have been deposited by reacting tantalum pentachloride (TaCl$_5$) and SiH$_2$Cl$_2$ in a hydrogen ambient (104). The films were deposited at 1.38 Torr using an inductive-coupled rf (600 kHz or 3.5 MHz) glow discharge. Films deposited at temperatures below 540°C were amorphous, while those deposited at temperatures above 580°C were crystalline and had a resistivity of $70\mu\Omega$ −cm. The film thicknesses were about 2000 to 5000 Å. After annealing at 900°C for 1 hour in an argon ambient, the resistivity decreased to 55 $\mu\Omega$ −cm.

Titanium-silicide films have been obtained by reacting titanium tetrachloride ($TiCl_4$) and SiH_4 in an argon plasma (105). The depositions were carried out in a hot-wall, parallel-plate, 300 kHz plasma reactor at 1 Torr and temperatures of 300 and 350°C. The film composition was very sensitive to gas-phase composition. The as-deposited films were amorphous, but crystallized after a 750°C anneal for 1 hour to yield a resistivity of 20 $\mu\Omega$ −cm.

Titanium-silicide films have also been deposited in a PECVD system similar to that shown in Fig. 9 but with a modified version of the boat assembly to prevent arcing (106). The rf generator operates at 50 kHz. Deposition rates of 60 to 80 Å/min are obtained with an rf power of about 100 watts and deposition temperatures of 300 to 500°C. The reactants are SiH_4 and $TiCl_4$ diluted in argon. The as-deposited films are amorphous, but crystallize upon sintering above 600°C. Resistivities as low as 20 $\mu\Omega$ −cm were obtained after annealing at 650°C for 5 min. In depositions carried out at 450°C and 1.75 Torr, $TiSi_x$ layers with different silicon compositions were obtained (107). The silicon content was varied from x = 1.1 to 2.0 by varying the $TiCl_4/SiH_4$ flow rate ratio from 0.23 to 0.09.

10.10 PECVD OF DIAMOND FILMS

The high thermal conductivity, transparency, hardness, and high-temperature semi-conductor properties of diamond make it an attractive material for many possible applications. Consequently, the low-pressure, low-temperature growth of crystals and thin films of diamond has been the subject of intense research recently (15,16). PECVD techniques are being investigated because a critical issue with this material is the need for lower temperature deposition techniques.

Diamond films have been deposited at pressures of 1-50 Torr, substrate temperatures above 700°C, and relatively high (>500 W) rf powers (15,16). Arc, dc, rf, and micro-wave discharges have been utilized. Methane/hydrogen mixtures are typically used, and growth rates are approximately 1-20 μm/hour. This material technology is in its infancy, and it is growing at a very fast pace.

10.11 OTHER PLASMA DEPOSITION CONFIGURATIONS

Microwave multipolar plasmas (MMP) are 2.45 GHz glow discharges confined by multipolar magnetic fields. The main differences between MMP's and the conventional plasmas discussed here are: (i) in MMP's, plasma excitation and plasma-surface inter-actions are decoupled, and (ii) there is no self-bias in MMPs, and the substrate bias and ion bombardment energies can be controlled independently. The microwave excitation can be applied in three ways: (i) localized electron cyclotron resonance, (ii) surface wave, and (iii) distributed electron cyclotron resonance (DECR). The latter (DECR) appears to be the most technologically promising. Silicon epitaxial layers have been deposited by DECR excitation at temperatures as low as 400°C (108).

Magnetically enhanced plasma deposition is another configuration in which a magnet is added to confine the electrons near the electrode thereby increasing the rate of electron dissociation collisions with molecules. As a result, a glow discharge can be maintained at pressures in the 1-10 mTorr range. Silicon oxide, silicon nitride, and silicon oxynitride films have been deposited by this technique, as well as other inorganic and organic films (109).

Afterglow CVD is a remote plasma technique that provides independent control of the generation of active species and the reaction chemistry. In the afterglow technique, only certain desired species are excited by the glow discharge. These are then transported to the vicinity of the wafer where the desired deposition reactions take place. The afterglow technique does not require the wafer to be exposed to the plasma discharge environment. Furthermore, it allows independent optimization of plasma, afterglow, and wafer parameters. This technology is presently being used to deposit silicon oxide films (110).

10.12 SUMMARY

This chapter discussed the plasma enhanced chemical vapor deposition technique as applied to thin films for microelectronic applications. In particular, fundamental aspects of nonequilibrium glow discharges were reviewed, as well as the voltage distribution in rf plasma systems. A qualitative model for PECVD was presented, and commercial PECVD systems were briefly reviewed. The PECVD of films of present commercial importance, such as silicon nitride and silicon oxide, was discussed. The state-of-the-art in the development of the PECVD of films such as polycrystalline silicon, epitaxial silicon and gallium arsenide, refractory metals and their silicides, and diamond, was also discussed. PECVD will continue to be the preferred commercial technique for the low temperature deposition of silicon nitride and oxide films, and is showing great promise for the deposition of semiconductor and conductor films.

10.13 REFERENCES

1. Gorowitz, B., Gorczyca, T. B., and Saia, R. J., Solid State Technol. 28(6): 197 (1985).

2. Adams, A. C., in VLSI Technology, S. Sze, Editor, Chap. 3, McGraw-Hill, New York, 1983.

3. Adams, A. C., Solid State Technol. 26(4): 135 (1983).

4. Kamins, T. I., and Chiang, K. L., J. Electrochem. Soc. 129: 2326 (1982) and 2331 (1982).

5. Burger, W. R., Donahue, T. J., and Reif, R., in VLSI Science and Technology/1982, C. J. Dell'Oca and W. M. Bullis, Editors, pp. 87-93, The Electrochemical Society, Proc. Vol. 82-7, Pennington, NJ, 1982.

6. Hajjar, J.-J., Reif, R., and Adler, D., J. Electronic Mat. 15: 279 (1986).

7.   Suzuki, S., and Itoh, T., J. Appl. Phys. 54: 1466 (1983).

8.   Shanfield, S. R., and Reif, R., The Electrochem. Soc. Extended Abstracts, Vol. 83-1, Abs. 144, pp. 230-231 (1983).

9.   Comfort, J. H., Garverick, L. M., and Reif, R., J. Appl. Phys. 62: 3388 (1987).

10. Hariu, T., Takenaka, K., Shibuya, S., Komatsu, Y., and Shibata, Y., Thin Solid Films 80: 235 (1981).

11. Pande, K. P., The Electrochem. Soc. Extended Abstracts, Vol. 83-1, Abs. 340, pp. 531-532 (1983).

12. Pande, K. P., and Seabaugh, A. C., J. Electrochem. Soc. 131: 1357 (1984).

13. Tabuchi, A., Inoue, S., Maeda, M., and Takagi, M., Proceedings of the 23rd Symposium on Semiconductors and IC Technology of the Electrochemical Society of Japan, p. 60 (Dec. 1-2, 1982).

14. Hess, D. W., in VLSI Electronics: Microstructure Science, N. G. Einspruch and D. M. Brown, Editors, p. 55, Academic Press, New York, 1984.

15. Chang, C.-P., Flamm, D. L., Ibbotson, D. E., and Mucha, J. A., J. Appl. Phys. 63: 1744 (1988).

16. Meyer, D. E., Ianno, N. J., Woollam, J. A., Swartzlander, A. B., and Nelson, A. J., J. Mater. Res. 3: 1397 (1988).

17. Reinberg, A. R., Ann. Rev. Material Sci. 9: 341 (1979).

18. Reinberg, A. R., J. Electronic Mat. 8: 345 (1979).

19. Ojha, S. M., in Physics of Thin Films, G. Hass, M. H. Francombe, and J. L. Vossen, Editors, Vol. 12, p. 237, Academic Press, New York, 1982.

20. Hess, D. W., in Silicon Processing, D. C. Gupta, Editor, p. 218, American Society for Testing and Materials, 1983.

21. Hess, D. W., J. Vac. Sci. Technol. A2: 244 (1984).

22. Bonifield, T. D., in Deposition Technologies for Films and Coatings, R. F. Bunshah, Editor, p. 365, Noyes Publications, New Jersey, 1982.

23. Hess, D. W., in Reduced Temperature Processing for VLSI, R. Reif, and G. R. Srinivasan, Editors, p. 3, The Electrochemical Society, New Jersey, 1986.

24. Sherman, A., Thin Solid Films 113: 135 (1984).

25. Chapman, B., Glow Discharge Processes, John Wiley, New York, 1980.

26. Rand, M. J., J. Vac. Sci. Technol. 16: 420 (1979).

27. Greene, J. E., and Barnett, S. A., J. Vac. Sci. Technol. 21: 285 (1982).

28. Greene, J. E., Solid State Technology 30(4): 115 (1987).

29. Turban, G., Catherine, Y., and Grolleau, B., Thin Solid Films 60: 147 (1979).

30. Sawin, H. H., Solid State Technol. 28: 211 (1985).

31. Brown, S. C., Basic Data of Plasma Physics, MIT Press, Cambridge, MA, 1966.

32. Kushner, M. J., J. Appl. Phys. 63: 2532 (1988).

33. Hollahan, J. R., and Bell, A. T., Editors, Techniques and Applications of Plasma Chemistry, John Wiley, New York, 1974.

34. Vossen, J. L., J. Electrochem. Soc. 126: 319 (1979).

35. Reif, R., J. Vac. Sci. Technol. A2: 429 (1984).

36. Köhler, K., Coburn, J. W., Horne, D. E., Kay, E., and Keller, J.H., J. Appl. Phys. 57: 59 (1985).

37. Koenig, H. R., and Maissel, L. I., IBM J. Res. Dev., 14: 276 (1970).

38. Coburn, J. W., and Kay, E., J. Appl. Phys., 43: 4965 (1972).

39. Horwitz, C. M., J. Vac. Sci. Technol. A1: 60 (1983).

40. Reif, R., Kamins, T. I., and Saraswat, K. C., J. Electrochem. Soc. 126: 644 (1979).

41. Reinberg, A. R., The Electrochem. Soc. Extended Abstracts, Vol. 74-1, Abs. 6, Spring Meeting (1974).

42. Sinha, A. K., Solid State Technol. 23(4): 133 (1980).

43. Kumagai, H. Y., Proceedings of the Ninth International Conference on Chemical Vapor Deposition, McD. Robinson et al., Editors, pp. 189-204, The Electrochemical Society, Proc. Vol. 84-6, Pennington, NJ (1984).

44. Hollahan, J. R., and Rosler, R. S., in Thin Film Processes, J. L. Vossen and W. Kern, Editors, Academic Press, New York, 1978.

45. Rosler, R. S., and Engle, G. M., Solid State Technol. 24(4): 172 (1981).

46. Weiss, A. D., Semiconductor International 6: 88 (1983).

47. Adams, A. C., in Reduced Temperature Processing for VLSI, R. Reif and G. R. Srinivasan, Editors, p. 111, The Electrochemical Society, New Jersey, 1986.

48. Maeda, M., and Nakamura, H., Thin Solid Films 112: 279 (1984).

49. Samuelson, G. M., and Mar, K. M., J. Electrochem. Soc. 129: 1773 (1982).

50. Sinha, A. K., and Smith, T. E., J. Appl. Phys. 49: 2756 (1978).

51. Chow, R., Lanford, W. A., Ke-Ming, W., and Rosler, R. S., J. Appl. Phys. 53: 5630 (1982).

52. Sinha, A. K., Levinstein, H. J., Smith, T. E., Quintana, G., and Haszko, S. E., J. Electrochem. Soc. 125: 601 (1978).

53. Koyama, K., Takasaki, K., Maeda, M., and Takagi, M., The Electrochem. Soc. Extended Abstracts, Vol. 81-2, Abs. 301, pp. 738-740 (1981). Also in Plasma Processing, J. Dieleman, R. G. Grieser, and G. S. Mathad, Editors, p. 478, The Electrochemical Society, Proc. Vol. 82-7, Pennington, NJ (1984).

54. van den Ven, E. P. G. T., Solid State Technol. 24(4): 167 (1981).

55. Zhou, N. S., Fujita, S., and Sasaki, A., J. Electronic Mat. 14: 55 (1985).

56. Mar, K. M., and Samuelson, G. M., Solid State Technol. 23(4): 137 (1980).

57. Classen, W., et al., J. Electrochem. Soc. 132: 893 (1985).

58. Ritchie, W., and Metz, W., The Electrochem. Soc. Extended Abstracts, Vol. 82-2, Abs. 187, pp. 295-296 (1982).

59. Kaganowicz, G., Ban, V. S., and Robinson, J. W., J. Vac. Sci. Technol. A2: 1233 (1984).

60. Chu, J. K., Sachdev, S., and Gargini, P. A., The Electrochem. Soc. Extended Abstracts, Vol. 83-2, Abs. 321, pp. 510-511 (1983).

61. Avigal, I., Solid State Technol. 26(10): 217 (1983).

62. Tong, J. E., Schertenleib, K., and Carpio, R. A., Solid State Technol. 27(1): 161 (1984).

63. Seto, J. Y. W., J. Appl. Phys. 46: 5247 (1975).

64. Kamins, T. I., J. Electrochem. Soc. 127: 686 (1980).

65. Matsui, M., Shiraki, Y., Katayama, Y., Kobayashi, K. I., Shintani, A., and Maruyama, E., Appl. Phys. Lett. 37: 936 (1980).

66. Mahan, J. E., Newman, D. S., and Gulett, M., IEEE Trans. Electron Dev. ED-30: 45 (1983).

67. Hirai, Y., Osada, Y., Komatsu, T., Omata, S., Aihara, K., and Nakagiri, T., Appl. Phys. Lett. 42: 701 (1983).

68. Seager, C. H., Sharp, D. J., Panitz, J. K. G., and Hanoka, J. I., J. Vac. Sci. Technol. 20: 430 (1982).

69. Morin, F., and Morel, M., Appl. Phys. Lett. 35: 686 (1979).

70. Burger, W. R., Donahue, T. J., and Reif, R., Proceedings of the Fourth European Conference on Chemical Vapor Deposition, J. Bloem et al., Editors, pp. 265-272, Eindhoven Druk B. V. (1983).

71. Hamasaki, T., Kurata, H., Hirose, M., and Osaka, Y., Appl. Phys. Lett. 37: 1084 (1980).

72. Nagata, Y., and Kunioka, A., Appl. Phys. Lett. 38: 142 (1981).

73. Veprek, S., Iqbal, Z., Oswald, H. R., and Webb, A. P., J. Phys. C: Solid State 14: 295 (1981).

74. Usui, S., and Kikuchi, M., J. Non-crystalline Solids 34: 1 (1979).

75. Borland, J. O., and Drowley, C., Solid State Technology 28: 141 (1985).

76. Ota, Y., J. Appl. Phys. 51: 1102 (1980).

77. Zalm, P. C., and Beckers, L. J., Appl. Phys. Lett. 41: 167 (1982).

78. Takagi, T., Yamada, I., and Sasaki, A., Thin Solid Films 39: 207 (1976).

79. Quach, N. T., and Reif, R., Appl. Phys. Lett. 45: 910 (1984).

80. Meyerson, B. S., Appl. Phys. Lett. 48: 797 (1986).

81. Ishitani, A., Ohshita, Y., Tanigaki, K., Takada, K., and Itoh, S., J. Appl. Phys. 61: 2224 (1987).

82. Townsend, W. G., and Uddin, M. E., Solid State Electronics 16: 39 (1973).

83. Suzuki, S., Okuda, H., and Itoh, T., Jap. J. Appl. Phys., 19: Supplement 19-1: 647 (1979).

84. Donahue, T. J., Burger, W. R., and Reif, R., Appl. Phys. Lett. 44: 346 (1984).

85. Donahue, T. J., and Reif, R., J. Appl. Phys. 57: 2757 (1985).

86. Reif, R., J. Electrochem. Soc. 131: 2430 (1984).

87. Comfort, J. H., Garverick, L. M., and Reif, R., J. Appl. Phys. 62: 3388 (1987).

88. Comfort, J. H., and Reif, R., J. Electrochem. Soc. to be published (1989).

89. Yew, T. R., Comfort, J. H., Garverick, L. M., Berger, W. R., and Reif, R., Mat. Res. Soc. Symp. Proc., Vol. 75: p. 705 (1987).

90. Comfort, J. H., and Reif, R., <u>Appl. Phys. Lett.</u> 51: 1536 (1987).

91. Heinecke, H., Brauers, A., Luth, H., and Balk, P., <u>J. Crystal Growth</u> 77: 241 (1986).

92. Pande, K. P., and Aina, O., <u>J. Vac. Sci. Technol.</u> A4: 673 (1986).

93. Huelsman, A. D., Reif, R., and Fonstad, C. G., <u>Appl. Phys. Lett.</u> 50: 206 (1987).

94. Huelsman, A. D., and Reif, R., <u>J. Vac. Sci. Technol.</u> to be published (1989).

95. Murarka, S. P., in <u>Semiconductor Silicon 1981,</u> H. R. Huff et al., Editors, pp. 551-561, The Electrochemical Soc., Proc. Vol. 81-5, Pennington, NJ, 1981.

96. Murarka, S. P., <u>Materials Lett.</u> 38: 142 (1981).

97. Murarka, S. P., <u>J. Vac. Sci. Technol.</u> 17: 775 (1980).

98. Crowder, B. L., and Zirinsky, S., <u>IEEE Trans. Elec. Dev.</u> ED-26: 369 (1979).

99. Inoue, S., Toyokura, N., Nakamura, T., Maeda, M., and Takagi, M., <u>J. Electrochem. Soc.</u> 130: 1603 (1983).

100. Chu, J. K., Tang, C. C., and Hess, D. W., <u>Appl. Phys. Lett.</u> 41: 75 (1982).

101. Tang, C. C., Chu, J. K., and Hess, D. W., <u>Solid State Technol.</u> 26: (3) 125 (1983).

102. Okuyama, F., <u>Appl. Phys. Lett.</u> A28: 125 (1982).

103. Akitmoto, K., and Watanabe, K., <u>Appl. Phys. Lett.</u> 39: 445 (1981).

104. Hieber, K., Stolz, M., and Wieczorik, C., <u>Proceedings of the Ninth International Conference on Chemical Vapor Deposition,</u> pp. 205-212, The Electrochemical Society, Proc. Vol. 84-6, Pennington, NJ (1984).

105. Kemper, M. J. H., Koo, S. W., and Huizinga, F., <u>The Electrochem. Soc. Extended Abstracts,</u> Vol. 84-2: Abs. 377, pp. 533-534 (1984).

106. Rosler, R. S., and Engle, G. M., <u>J. Vac. Sci. Technol.</u> B2: 733 (1984).

107. Hara, T., Ishizawa, Y., Wu, H. M., Hemmes, D. G., and Rosler, R. S., <u>Proceedings of the Tenth International Conference on Chemical Vapor Deposition,</u> G. W. Cullen, Editor, pp. 867-876, The Electrochemical Society, Proc. Vol. 87-8, Pennington, NJ (1987).

108. Burke, R. R., and Pomot, C., <u>Solid State Technology</u> p. 67, February 1988.

109. Leahy, M. F., and Kaganowicz, G., <u>Solid State Technology</u> p. 99, April 1987.

110. Jackson, R. L., Spencer, J. E., McGuire, J. L., and Hoff, A. M., <u>Solid State Technology</u> p. 107, April 1987.

11

Electron Cyclotron Resonance Microwave Discharges For Etching and Thin Film Deposition

Jes Asmussen

A recent, important development in low pressure and low temperature plasma processing is the microwave electron cyclotron resonance (ECR) discharge. Its lack of electrodes and its ability to create high densities of charged and excited species at low pressures ($\leq 10^{-4}$Torr) make it an attractive processing discharge in etching and thin film deposition applications. This paper reviews the basic physics of ECR discharges and reviews the associated microwave system and applicator technologies. Waveguide and cavity ECR applicators are compared and are described in detail. Several ECR plasma processing reactors are also described. Methods of processing large surfaces are outlined and typical experimentally measured ECR discharge characteristics are also presented.

11.1 INTRODUCTION

Microwave discharges have experienced intense interest and use in recent years. Their electrodeless nature together with their ability to create high densities of excited and charged species have made both high pressure and low pressure microwave discharges an attractive technology for many plasma processing applications. By using the appropriate microwave applicators, microwave discharges can be efficiently created and maintained from pressures above several atmospheres (1-3) to sub-mTorr pressures (4-14) resulting in high pressure discharges with high temperatures (≥ 1000K) for thermal processing applications, and low temperature and low pressure discharges for applications such as thin film deposition and etching. Recent and notable experiments which demonstrate diamond thin film growth in a microwave discharge (15) utilize discharge pressures of 1-100 Torr. These discharge applications lie in the transition between a purely thermal and low temperature discharge.

An important development in low pressure and low temperature microwave plasma processing is the electron cyclotron resonance (ECR) discharge. This technology, borrowed from fusion (16) and electric propulsion (17) plasmas and modified for the requirements of plasma processing (4,5,8-13) can create a variety of low pressure (< 0.5 Torr) discharges. As the name ECR suggests, microwave energy is coupled to the natural resonant frequency of the electron gas in the presence of a static magnetic field. This

285

resonant frequency occurs when the electron cyclotron frequency equals the excitation frequency. The cyclotron frequency is found as:

$$\omega_{ce} = \frac{eB}{m_e} \qquad (1)$$

where e is charge on an electron, B is the strength of the static magnetic field, and m_e is the electron mass. In an actual discharge, this condition can be satisfied in a volume or surface layer within the discharge where the static magnetic field strength is adjusted to resonance, i.e. $\omega = \omega_{ce}$ and a component of electric field is perpendicular to the static magnetic field. The electrons are accelerated in this ECR volume and in turn ionize and excite the neutral gas. The result is a low pressure, almost collisionless, plasma which can be varied from a weakly to a highly ionized state by changing discharge pressure, gas flow rates and input microwave power. The electrodeless and noncollisional heating nature of the discharge together with the availability of well established, low cost microwave power supplies make ECR plasma sources attractive for many plasma processing applications.

This chapter reviews the basic principles of ECR microwave discharge formation first by describing the physics of coupling microwave energy into the discharge and then briefly describes microwave system and applicator technology. ECR waveguide and cavity applicators are described and several ECR plasma reactor geometries used in etching and film deposition are reviewed. Finally measured characteristics of ECR discharges are presented.

11.2 ENERGY COUPLING AND POWER BALANCE IN STEADY STATE MICROWAVE DISCHARGES

A diagram of a generic microwave discharge configuration is shown in Fig. 1. The discharge occupies a finite volume, V_L, and is bounded by the discharge container walls . In practice the walls are made from a microwave transparent material such as quartz or are conducting waveguide walls. The discharge enclosure may also have an opening which allows the excited species and charged particles to diffuse out of the active discharge into a processing zone. An arbitrary discharge volume is composed of at least three interpenetrating gases, i.e. electron, ion, and neutral gases. A steady time independent density of neutrals, electrons and ions exists at each point within the discharge volume. In Fig. 1 the steady-state electron density is denoted as $N_{eo}(\vec{r})$ where the $\vec{r}$ dependence emphasizes that the density is a function of position within the discharge.

The time and spatially varying microwave electric field, $\vec{E}(\vec{r})\epsilon^{j\omega t}$, which maintains the discharge of Fig. 1, is represented by a dashed line. In general this electric field penetrates the discharge and may have a nonzero value at each point inside the discharge volume. A static but spatially varying magnetic field is also impressed on the discharge volume and in Fig. 1 is displayed as the solid field lines drawn in the shape of a magnetic mirror. ECR layers, which are the thin volumes in the discharge where $\omega = \omega_{ce}$, are displayed as the solid, curved lines.

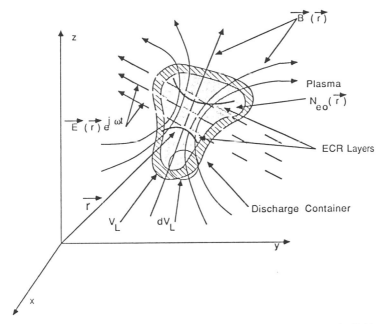

Figure 1: A generic microwave discharge immersed in an electromagnetic field and static magnetic field. The circle encloses an arbitrary differential volume dV_L .

A steady-state microwave discharge is characterized by the equality between the electromagnetic power absorbed by the plasma, P_a and the power losses, P_{loss}, in the plasma volume. Expressed as an equation

$$P_a = P_{loss} \tag{2}$$

The left hand term represents the total power delivered to the plasma by the electromagnetic field. The power absorbed in a unit volume is a function of position, and thus absorbed power per differential volume is expressed as

$$<P>_{abs}(\vec{r}) = 1/2 \, \text{Re} \, [\vec{E}(\vec{r}) \cdot (\tilde{\tilde{\sigma}} \, (\vec{r}) \cdot \vec{E}(\vec{r})^*)] \tag{3}$$

where the discharge complex tensor conductivity $\tilde{\tilde{\sigma}} \, (\vec{r})$ and the electric field $\vec{E}(\vec{r})$ are functions of position $\vec{r}$ in the plasma and $<P>_{abs}(\vec{r})$ has units of power density.

For any differential plasma volume the power input, i.e. equation (3), must equal the power loss, i.e.,

$$<P>_{abs}(\vec{r}) = <P>_{loss}(\vec{r}) \tag{4}$$

where $<P>_{loss}(\vec{r})$ is the power lost per differential volume at position $\vec{r}$. Integrating over the entire plasma volume yields

$$P_a = \int_{V_L} <P>_{abs}(\vec{r})dV_L = \int_{V_L} <P>_{loss}(\vec{r})dV_L = P_{loss} \tag{5}$$

which is, of course, equation (2).

An understanding of the microwave discharge energy absorption and the discharge loss processes can be obtained by investigating the left and right hand sides of equation (5). Considering first the absorption process Eq. (3) includes the microwave energy absorption by both the electron and ion gases. However since the work done on a charged particle by an electric field between collisions varies inversely as the particle mass, the energy imparted to an electron is much greater than the energy imparted to an ion. Therefore direct energy transfer from the field to the ions usually can be neglected (except for ion cyclotron heating) and electromagnetic energy transfer to the discharge takes place through Joule (elastic and inelastic collisional heating) and electron cyclotron heating of the electron gas.

The heating and the energy interchange processes for a small differential volume are shown in Fig. 2. Since direct ion gas heating can be neglected for most plasma processing applications dashed lines are shown between the electric energy source and the ion gas. As shown, the electron gas is heated directly by the electric fields and in turn the heated electron gas transfers its energy to the neutral and ion gases by elastic and inelastic collisions. The neutral and ion gases thus become heated from these electron gas interactions and interchange energy by elastic ion-neutral collisions and transfer energy to the walls by heat conduction and convection.

Referring again to Fig. 2 the power lost per differential volume by the electron gas can be expressed in terms of the removal of energy per unit time from the electron gas by conduction and convection and by elastic and inelastic collisions. That is, per unit volume at position $\vec{r}$ within the discharge

$$<P>_{loss}(\vec{r}) = \text{(elastic collision losses)} + \text{(inelastic collision losses)}$$
$$+ \text{(conduction and convection losses)}$$

In equation form (neglecting electron heat conduction)

$$<P>_{loss}(\vec{r}) = [(\frac{5kT_e}{2})\frac{D_a}{\Lambda^2} + \nu_{men}(\frac{2m_e}{M_n})\frac{3k}{2}(T_e - T_n) +$$

$$eV_i\nu_i + \sum_j eV_{exj}\nu_{exj}] N_{eo}(\vec{r}) \tag{6}$$

where D_a = the ambipolar diffusion coefficients, T_e = the electron temperature, T_n= the neutral gas temperature, k = Boltzman's constant, Λ= discharge diffusion length, M_n = mass of the neutral atoms, ν_i = ionization frequency, ν_{men} = collison frequency for momentum transfer, ν_{exj} = the jth excitation frequency, V_i = the ionization potential and V_{exj} = the excitation potential.

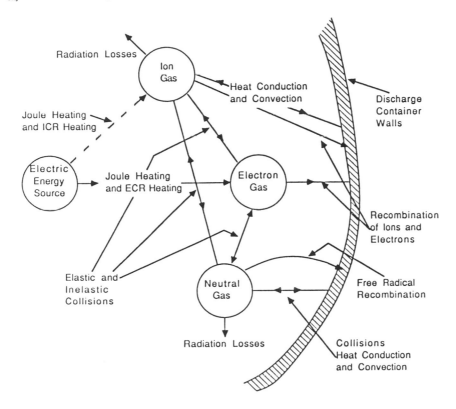

Figure 2: Microwave energy transfer in a weakly ionized gas. Energy coupling is shown for the arbitrary differential volume circled in Figure 1.

Integrating Eq. (6) over the entire discharge volume V_L yields the total power loss in the discharge. Thus it is apparent that discharge losses depend upon discharge geometry, pressure, gas type and the electron density. Since in the steady-state $<P>_{loss}(\bar{r}) = <P>_{abs}(\bar{r})$, the electric field required to sustain a discharge is dependent on many different experimental variables and in practice can vary over several orders of magnitude as pressure, gas type, flow rate, etc. are varied. Thus a versatile microwave discharge system must be be able to adjust the impressed electric field for a wide range of experimental conditions. This has an important impact on the design of microwave power supplies and applicators.

11.3 MICROWAVE ENERGY COUPLING VS PRESSURE IN A UNIFORM MAGNETIC FIELD GRADIENT

Equation (3) can be written entirely in terms of power absorbed by the electron gas (18). Thus in the absence of a static magnetic field the time average absorbed power density is given by

$$<P>_{abs}(\vec{r}) = \frac{N_{eo}(\vec{r})e^2}{2m_e\nu_e}[\frac{\nu_e^2}{\omega^2 + \nu_e^2}]|E(\vec{r})|^2 \tag{7}$$

where $N_{eo}(\vec{r})$ = the time independent electron density, $|E(r)|$ = the magnitude of the electric field, and ν_e = the effective collision frequency for electrons. This expression often is written in terms of an effective electric field, i.e.

$$<P>_{abs}(\vec{r}) = \frac{N_{eo}(\vec{r})e^2}{m_e\nu_e}|E_e|^2 \tag{8}$$

where $|E_e| = \frac{|E(\vec{r})|}{\sqrt{2}}\frac{\nu_e}{\sqrt{\nu_e^2 + \omega^2}}$ = effective electric field .

If a static magnetic field is present the power absorption includes the ECR heating process. Considering only the simple case of when the time varying electric field is perpendicular to the static magnetic field, the time average power density absorbed by the electron gas is

$$<P>_{abs}(\vec{r}) = \frac{N_{eo}(\vec{r})e^2\nu_e}{2m_e}[\frac{1}{\nu_e^2 + (\omega - \omega_{ce})^2} + \frac{1}{\nu_e^2 + (\omega + \omega_{ce})^2}]|E(\vec{r})|^2 \tag{9}$$

The effective electric field is now defined as

$$|E_e|^2 = \frac{\nu_e^2}{2}[\frac{1}{\nu_e^2 + (\omega - \omega_{ce})^2} + \frac{1}{\nu_e^2 + (\omega + \omega_{ce})^2}]|E(\vec{r})|^2 \tag{10}$$

Specifics of the microwave energy absorption can be understood by examining the process in a simple example gas such as helium. The effective collision frequency at 300 K for helium is given by (18) $\nu_e = 2.3x10^9$ p where p = pressure in Torr. Investigating first the zero magnetic field case, when density and electric field are held constant, Eq.(7) has a maximum, when $\omega = \nu_e$. Good microwave energy coupling is directly related to a synchronization between the combined electron-neutral and electron-ion collision processes and the exciting frequency ω . Thus good microwave energy coupling is discharge pressure dependent. For a 2.45 GHz excitation frequency maximum power absorption in helium occurs at approximately seven Torr and discharge pressures of 5-10 Torr provide efficient coupling of microwave energy into a helium discharge. Generalizing this result to other gases with different elastic collision cross sections and accounting for the influence of the discharge walls, the optimum pressure range for efficient discharge breakdown and maintenance with 2.45 GHz microwave energy usually occurs between 0.5-10 Torr (19).

At very low pressure of $\leq$ 100mTorr the mean free path of electron-neutral and electron-ion collision becomes very long, $\nu_e << \omega$ and Eq. (7) becomes

$$<P>_{abs}(\vec{r}) \simeq \frac{N_{eo}(\vec{r})e^2}{2m_e\nu_e} [\frac{\nu_e}{\omega}]^2 |E(\vec{r})|^2 \tag{11}$$

High electric fields are required to sustain the discharge since $<P>_{loss}(\vec{r})$ increases as pressure is reduced. In order to produce the required high electric fields, high incident microwave powers and/or high Q applicators are necessary and therefore it becomes difficult to maintain a discharge at low pressures. However, the presence of an ECR static magnetic field simplifies discharge maintenance (7) below pressures of 20 mTorr.

The influence of an impressed static magnetic field on the energy coupling process can be observed from Eq. (9). At low pressures $\nu_e << \omega$ and Eq. (9) has a pole at $\omega = \omega_{ce}$ indicating high power absorption even for every low impressed electric fields. This can be viewed as an increase in the effective electric field at resonance (20). Physically at electron cyclotron resonance the electron velocity perpendicular to the static magnetic increases, as shown in Fig. 3, resulting in an outward, spiralling motion along a magnetic field line. The electron gains energy proportional to the square of time, and in a typical discharge the radius of the electron orbit is limited by an elastic or inelastic collision, a collision with the walls or the electron moving out of the ECR region. Lax, et al. (20) have shown that in the presence of collisions, but with $\nu_e << \omega$, the energy gain by an ECR accelerated electron between collisions is inversely proportional to ν_e. Thus at low pressures even low electric fields can couple large amounts of energy to the electron gas.

A further examination of Eq. (9) reveals the effect of pressure on ECR coupling. It is observed that as pressure increases $\nu_e \rightarrow \omega = \omega_{ce}$ and the absorbed power density is equal to Eq. (7). Thus at higher pressures the energy absorption process again becomes collisional and the magnetic field has little influence on heating the electron gas. As pressure increases the transition between purely ECR heating and collisional heating is gradual and in helium gas takes place between 0.5 and 3 Torr. ECR heating at 2.45 GHz is not useful above 3 Torr unless the gas temperature is much higher than 300 K. Thus it is clear that ECR is a coupling technique for low pressure discharges where the electrons can orbit many times between elastic and inelastic collisions.

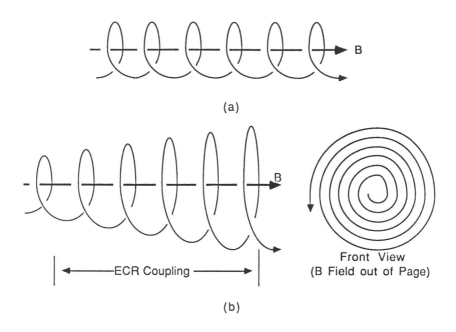

Figure 3: Electron motion in a static magnetic field (a) when the electric field is zero and (b) when $\vec{E} = \vec{E}_o \varepsilon^{j\omega t}$ where $\omega = \omega_{ce}$ and $\vec{E}_o \perp \vec{B}$

11.4   MICROWAVE ENERGY COUPLING IN A NONUNIFORM STATIC MAGNETIC FIELD

In practice ECR discharges make use of a nonuniform static magnetic field. This magnetic field is usually mirror-like or cusp-like and is produced by magnetic coils (4,5) or permanent magnets (7,8). In the absence of an accelerating electric field the motion of an electron in such a magnetic field is well known and is shown as the solid trajectory in Fig. 4(a). When moving into a magnetic mirror a charged particle will spiral with ever decreasing transverse orbits into the converging field until it is reflected. It then reverses direction and spirals out of the mirror with increasing orbits. The radii of these orbiting trajectories are small for a typical electron. For example, a 4 eV electron will have a radius of gyration of 0.05 mm in a 875-G field.

If a transverse, time varying microwave electric field is present in the mirror, ECR acceleration of the electron takes place when the electron passes through a region where $\omega = \omega_{ce}$. This accelerating region is usually very thin (often less than one mm thick) and is referred to as an ECR surface or layer shown as the shaded region of Fig. 4(b). If the electron is outside this region, as Eq. (9) indicates, little microwave energy is coupled to the electron. However, an average electron can experience many oscillations of electric field during the time it spends in the ECR layer. Thus at low pressure considerable energy can be imparted to electrons in this layer with only a small electric field (10-100v/cm). Writing Eq (5) for a low pressure ECR discharge yields:

$$P_a = \int_{V_L} <P>_{abs}(\vec{r})dv = \int_{V_L - V_{ECR}} <P>_{abs}(\vec{r})dv \; +$$

$$\int_{V_{ECR}} <P>_{abs}(\vec{r})dv \; \simeq \int_{V_{ECR}} <P>_{abs}(\vec{r})dv \qquad (12)$$

where V_{ECR} = the volume of the ECR layer. As described by Eq. (12) when $v_e < < \omega$ collisional energy coupling throughout the discharge volume can be ignored and micro-wave energy transfer occurs within the ECR volume. Since the ECR coupling takes place within small, thin volumes, energy coupling occurs with high power densities. This ECR layer, which serves the function of a hot cathode filament in dc discharges, provides the high energy electrons required to sustain the discharge at low pressures.

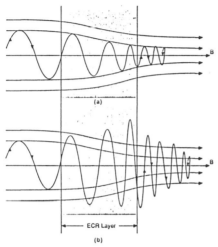

Figure 4: Electron motion in a mirror-like static magnetic field (a) without an accelerating electric field (b) with a perpendicular electric field $\vec{E}_o \varepsilon^{j\omega_{ce}t}$ where the shaded region represents the ECR layer.

Upon leaving the ECR zone the accelerated electrons possess energies usually greater than 10 eV. They move through the discharge volume and excite, dissociate, and ionize neutrals and ions. Because of these high energy electrons and because of an ECR acceleration process that tends to favor higher energy electrons, it is expected the ECR discharges will have a non-Maxawellian electron energy distribution. The shape of the distribution will be dependent upon the intensity of the electric field and the location, shape, thickness, and total volume of the ECR layer in the discharge. Thus it appears that it may be possible to "engineer" the electron distribution in ECR discharges. Knowledge of how electrons are accelerated in the ECR layer is essential to understanding the ECR discharge. However, in most plasma processing applications high energy electrons and multiply charged species are not desired (as they may be in certain ion source applications (14)). Thus a careful management of electron acceleration is important.

11.5 MICROWAVE SYSTEM CONSIDERATIONS

ECR discharges are often required to operate with different gases, variable gas mixtures and flow rates over a wide range of operating (10^{-5} to over 0.1 Torr). Thus the microwave discharge system must be adaptable for many different experimental conditions and should be able to efficiently produce a stable, repeatable and controllable discharge for many experimental situations including discharge start up and adjustment for final processing operation. Further, considering that the ECR system will be placed in an industrial setting, it must be able to be operated as part of a larger production facility. Thus the ECR system must be adaptable to automatic control without the need of a highly trained microwave engineer. These design requirements have an impact upon the entire microwave system and thus some basic considerations of microwave ECR systems are reviewed.

A generic microwave plasma processing system and its equivalent circuit are shown in Fig. 5. It consists of several interconnected components: (1) a power source, usually a constant frequency but variable power microwave oscillator, (2) transmission lines, often waveguide or coaxial cable, (3) a microwave applicator, and (4) the microwave plasma load. An example experimental microwave system is displayed in Fig. 6. It consists of a variable power 2.45 GHz, CW microwave power source, circulator and matched dummy load, directional couplers, attenuators and power meters that measure incident power P_i and reflected power, P_r, and the microwave applicator and plasma load. The microwave power coupled into the plasma loaded applicator is given by $P_t = P_i - P_r$.

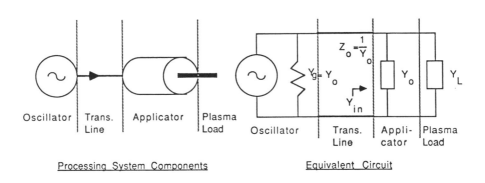

Figure 5: Generic microwave processing system and its equivalent circuit.

An efficient plasma processing system is designed for maximum power transfer between the microwave oscillator and the plasma-loaded applicator. This occurs when the output admittance of the microwave oscillator Y_g (See Fig. 5) and the input admittance of the plasma loaded applicator Y_{in} are equal to the transmission line characteristic admittance Y_o .

The power coupled into the applicator P_t divides itself between the power absorbed in the conducting applicator walls P_b, and the power delivered to the discharge load P_a ; i.e. $P_t = P_b + P_a$. These two quantities can be related to the applicator fields, the intrinsic resistance R of the applicator walls, the discharge volume and the complex conductivity of the discharge. The exact division of the power P_t between the walls and the discharge load depends on the relative losses in the discharge versus the losses in the applicator walls. Applicator design should attempt to minimize P_b, for all operating conditions.

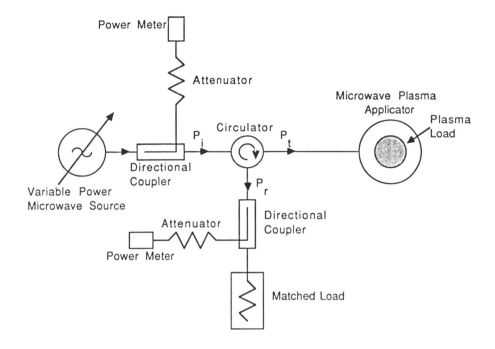

Figure 6: Example experimental microwave system.

A major difficulty in the design of a microwave ECR system is the variable, nonlinear often reactive discharge load. As shown in Sect. 11.2, this load depends on many different experimental conditions such as gas type, mix and flow rate, discharge pressure, etc. At present ECR discharge models can not accurately predict discharge impedance and hence cannot aid in the design process. In addition, similar to lower frequency rf discharges, the applicator/discharge possesses stable and unstable operating conditions (21-24). These must be accounted for and understood (25). Finally from efficiency considerations it is desirable to match (tightly couple) the microwave oscillator to the plasma load. However, under matched conditions the variable plasma load may cause the power oscillator frequency and output power to vary resulting in further system instabilities. Thus it is often desirable to electrically separate the microwave power oscillator and the plasma load with a circulator as shown in Fig. 6.

While ECR processing technology must still be considered in the development stage certain desirable system features are apparent. These are as follows:

1.   a well filtered, variable power but constant frequency microwave power supply;

2.   the use of a circulator to allow the oscillator to work into a matched load independent of discharge variations; this circulator also protects the oscillator from large reflected power conditions that may occur from an unmatched applicator;

3.   the ability to accurately measure incident and reflected power;

4.   a variable, automatic method of matching the applicator/discharge for the numerous discharge conditions that may occur;

5.   a microwave system and applicator/discharge designed to facilitate maintenance.

11.6 FUNDAMENTAL ECR APPLICATOR CONFIGURATIONS

The microwave applicator performs several functions in a specific plasma processing application. These are: (a) to impedance match and focus the microwave energy into the discharge, (b) to efficiently produce high densities of excited and charged species, (c) to produce controllable and uniform densities of excited and charged species over a desired processing area (usually 10 to 30 centimeters in diameter) and (d) to process (etch, deposit, etc.) without producing material damage to the product. Several typical conventional applicator types are displayed in Fig. 7. As shown, they are nonresonant waveguide, single mode and multimode resonant cavities and are specially designed surface-wave applicators.

At low pressures a high Q applicator is required unless an ECR layer exists within the discharge. The ECR layer provides good, stable discharge coupling with low electric fields reducing the required circuit Q and simplifying the coupling and matching of the discharge. Thus even waveguide applicators can sustain a low pressure ECR discharge. However if coupling efficiency and operation over a wide pressure and power range are desired the waveguide applicators are often supplemented by additional external matching (external to the applicator) stubs or screw tuners. These external matching devices produce a standing wave between the discharge and the tuner increasing coupling to the discharge and reducing the reflected power. Thus the applicator and matching network together become a resonant, cavity-like applicator. Under these conditions ECR cavity applicators (7,8,13,26) have advantages over ECR waveguide applicators. Internally tuned resonant cavities excited at 2.45 GHz are able to create well matched ($P_r \approx 0$) discharges with high densities over a wide range of input powers (100-1500W) and can even operate without ECR at higher pressures (1-3).

ECR applicators can be divided into two groups (a) waveguide applicators and (b) cavity applicators and ECR magnetic field configurations can be grouped into mirror and multicusp geometries. Each of these is briefly reviewed below.

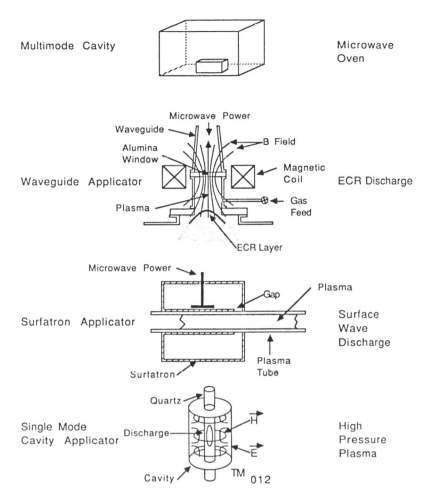

Figure 7: Types of applicators.

11.6.1 Waveguide Applicators

Typical examples of ECR waveguide applicators are displayed as the waveguide applicator (27) shown in Fig. 7 and the two applicators (28,29) shown in Fig. 8. Although often described as distinctly different and unique discharge configurations (and sometimes even described as a cavity), they are the same basic discharge configuration. In each, electromagnetic energy is coupled into the discharge zone from a standard rectangular or circular waveguide excited by an incident, electromagnetic wave. The discharge, which is located at the end of the waveguide, is defined by either a 4-9 cm diameter quartz tube or a waveguide window and surrounding, cylindrical metal enclosure. Process gases are fed radially into the discharge zone, and after microwave excitation the ionized and excited neutral species pass out the open end of the discharge zone into a plasma processing region.

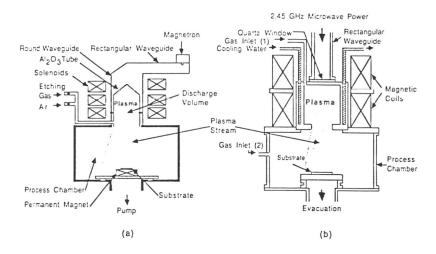

Figure 8: Examples of waveguide, magnetic mirror ECR applicators used in (a) etching (5,28) and (b) low temperature chemical vapor deposition (29).

The applicator discharge zone is surrounded by one or more coils which produce an axial, mirror-like magnetic field. With the proper current bias and coil spacing the magnetic field can be adjusted to produce an axially variable 875-G ECR layer across the discharge cross section. This surface which is clearly displayed in Fig. 7 is a zone of intense electron acceleration. The axial magnetic field strength is adjusted so that the magnitude is the greatest at the microwave input end and decreases vs axial position toward the discharge output. This magnetic field geometry, often called a magnetic beach, positions the intense ECR surface away from waveguide windows or other coupling surfaces. These applicators can be used with external matching networks and a variable ECR surface to provide improved coupling over many pressure and input power conditions.

This type of ECR/magnetic mirror-like waveguide applicator produces a neutralized beam of electrons and ions and was originally investigated as an electric space engine (17). The ECR accelerated electrons immediately experience a longitudinal force due to the diverging magnetic field. Thus electrons are pushed out of the high magnetic field region and as they pass into the low magnetic field regions their transverse kinetic energy is converted into longitudinal kinetic energy. In the steady state ions are attracted to the electrons by Coulomb forces and hence are also accelerated out of the discharge with the electrons. Thus a neutralized beam of electron-ion pairs flows out of the diverging magnetic field and impinges on the substrate. This beam may or may not be useful depending upon the application. Recently (30) it has been shown that the directed ion energy can be influenced by the magnetic field gradient. Apparently ECR discharges with different field gradients will produce ion beams with different energies.

11.6.2. Cavity Applicators

An alternate ECR discharge configuration (6-8,12,13,31-35) called the microwave plasma disk reactor (MPDR), utilizes a tunable microwave cavity and a radially inhomogenous multicusp magnetic field to couple microwave energy into the discharge. It is designed to create a cylindrical disk discharge zone which occupies only a fraction of the cavity volume but provides a large surface for ion extraction or plasma processing (7). The reactor concept can be configured to operate at very low pressures with ECR rare earth magnets or at moderate to high pressures (10 mTorr - 500 Torr) without magnets. It is the low pressure ECR configuration that is described here.

An example of a 10 cm prototype plasma/ion source is displayed in Figs. 9 and 10. It consists of a 17.8 cm i.d. brass cylinder [1] forming the outer conducting shell of the cavity applicator. The sliding short [2], the water-cooled, removable end-plate [3a and 3b] and the cylinder [1] form the cavity excitation zone. A disk-shaped quartz tube [4] confines the working gas to region [5] where the microwave fields produce a disk-shaped plasma adjacent to a screen [8]. The input gas is introduced into the discharge region [5] through eight pin hole openings (not shown) in the annular ring [6] and the gas feed tube [7].

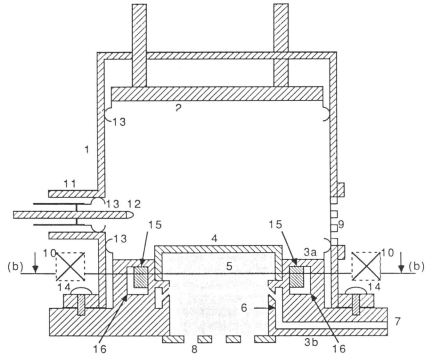

Figure 9: Cross sectional view of cavity ECR applicator.

A screened port [9] is cut in the cavity sidewall for viewing the discharge. Microwave power is coupled into the cavity through a coaxial input port [11] via the length-adjustable coaxial input probe [12]. Four threaded bolts [14] firmly hold the end plate [3b] onto the cylinder [1] during cavity excitation.

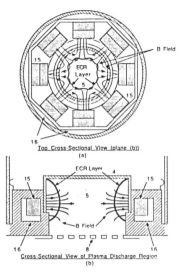

Figure 10: Additional cross sectional views of cavity ECR applicator. (a) cross-sectional view of plane (b) of Fig. 9 and (b) enlarged cross-sectonal view of the discharge region.

The end plate consists of two separate pieces bolted tightly together. The piece [3a] adjacent to the interior of the cavity is made from brass, while the piece [3b], which is exposed to the discharge and the downstream vacuum, is machined from nonmagnetic stainless steel. As shown in Fig. 10 these two cylindrical pieces enclose sixteen 2.54 x 2.54 x 1 cm magnets [15]. Eight pairs of magnets [15] are equally spaced on a circle around and adjacent to the radial gas feed ring [6] and quartz discharge chamber [4]. The magnet pairs are arranged on a soft iron keeper [16] with alternate poles forming a multicusp, octapole, static magnetic field across a radial plane as shown in the cross-sectional view of Fig. 10. The magnetic field strength produced by these magnets is zero at the center and increases in the radial direction. Each magnet pole pair produces a pole-face maximum field strength of approximately 3 kG which is well in excess of the 875-G required for ECR at the cavity excitation frequency of 2.45 GHz. The strength and position of these magnet pairs produces a radial magnetic field surface in excess of 875-G approximately 1 cm inside the discharge zone and thus, as shown in Fig. 10, results in an undulating three-dimensional radial ECR surface inside the quartz chamber. The keeper [16] has an L-shaped cross section and is placed on the outer radius and under the magnet pairs, reducing the fringing static magnetic field in the plasma processing zone.

The cavity excitation region is defined by the brass cylinder [1], the sliding short [2] and the end-plate [3] and during ignition the screen [8] or during operation the discharge which forms in the volume [5]. The cavity can be single mode (TE_{111} or TE_{211}) or controlled multimode excited. External matching stubs are not required since the internal adjustments of sliding short and probe match the plasma loaded applicator to the input transmission line. An important feature of this applicator is its ability to impress a high, tangential, standing wave electric field against the top volume of the discharge without reflecting power from the applicator. Thus even for high density discharges an evanescent electric field is coupled into the discharge. The cavity can be operated either with or without the screen [8] .

The multicusp magnetic field geometry is considerably different than the ECR waveguide magnetic mirror geometry. In this geometry the electrons move through the discharge following magnetic field lines and reflect off adjacent magnetic cusps. As they pass through the ECR layers they are accelerated by the impressed electric fields. Thus the high energy electrons follow this reflection and acceleration process until they elastically or inelastically collide with the larger neutrals or ions and diffuse and recombine on the walls. It is these inelastic collisions that provide the excitation, ionization and dissociation throughout the discharge volume. The high energy electrons are not all pushed out of the discharge by the magnetic field but many are bounced back forth perpendicular to the discharge axis. The low magnetic field region in the center of the discharge allows low energy electrons and ions to diffuse out of the discharge zone. In addition, one or more magnetic coils [10] (shown in Fig. 9 with dashed lines) can be added to this geometry. These coils with just a few hundred gauss will move and modify the ECR surfaces and if desired can be used to accelerate a neutralized beam of charged particles out of the discharge.

11.7 MICROWAVE PLASMA PROCESSING REACTORS

One of the benefits of investigating microwave discharge applications is the potential to evolve new and useful plasma reactor configurations. These new reactors make use of the microwave discharge's ability to create high densities of excited, charged and free radical species without having the disadvantages of large sheath potentials and contamination from electrodes. It is expected that one or more microwave plasma reactor configurations will one day take their place along side barrel and parallel-plate rf plasma reactors as important industrial machines for a variety of plasma processing applications.

Several potentially important microwave plasma reactor processing configurations are shown in Fig. 11. In each, a generic microwave discharge applicator is the source of chemically active species. It is useful to note that, while applicators can be interchanged (i.e. waveguide interchanged with cavity, etc.), the basic plasma processing geometry remains the same. However, the exact processing characteristics and rates will be influenced by the specific applicator.

As shown in Fig. 11 there are three important reactor variations: (a) the substrate (or processed surface) is placed entirely inside the active microwave discharge, (b) the substrate is located downstream from the discharge in a processing chamber and (c) a hybrid reactor where the substrate is again placed downstream in a processing chamber but where rf and/or dc energy creates a new discharge adjacent to the substrate. The screen, shown in reactor (b) and (c) separating the process chamber from the discharge, is optional. Its removal may allow microwave energy and energetic charged particles to impact on the substrate while increasing the density of excited species in the chamber. On the other hand placing a conventional single or double grid in the opening converts this ECR system into a broad beam ion source (7,8,26,36-38).

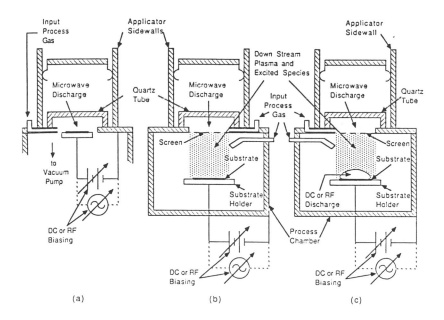

Figure 11: Microwave plasma processing configurations.

Each of these configurations has important similarities and differences. In each, the substrate can be independently biased with dc or rf potentials. In (a) the substrate surface is biased relative to the active microwave discharge while in (b) the bias is applied relative to the chemically active species (ions, radicals, etc.) diffusing into the processing chamber. For example in oxide growth applications the material surface can be biased (12) positive to attract negative ions and electrons. In etching applications the material surface can be biased negative attracting positively charged species (5,13,41). This configuration is essentially an electrodeless, high plasma density version of triode etching. The independent biasing allows more control over the sheath potential and hence etching profile than does conventional parallel plate reactive ion etching.

In reactor (c), rf and dc energy is supplied to create a separate discharge adjacent to the substrate surface. The microwave discharge provides a preionization and excitation of the process gas before the final formation of the process discharge above the substrate. The three reactors allow numerous processing possibilities including the cases where gases are either passed entirely through the discharge, or independently pass through the discharge and directly into the process chamber.

The desirability of using one reactor vs another involves several trade-offs. In reactor (a) the placement of the substrate directly inside the discharge has the advantage of high processing rates due to high densities of excited species with the potential disadvantage of processing damage caused by high energy charged particles and direct microwave interactions with the substrate. In addition, substrate size is limited by the applicator size and discharge nonuniformities. Thus the ability to uniformly process large surfaces in this reactor depends on applicator type.

Reactors (b) and (c) allow chemically active species to diffuse from the applicator into a larger, often lower pressure processing chamber. Thus the specific production non uniformities of the applicator can be smoothed out by diffusion processes (free fall, ambipolar, etc.) in the process chamber. The chamber diffusion can be engineered by controlling pressure and diffusion length or by the use of multipolar plasma confinement (10,11,27,39).

An example of a multipolar processing chamber is shown in Fig. 12. The chamber is lined with closely spaced permanent magnets producing a multicusp magnetic field entirely enclosing the chamber. As shown, one or more plasma applicators can be connected to the chamber as sources of excited species. This multipolar processing chamber produces a well behaved uniform plasma at the expense of reducing excited species densities, usually by a factor of 10 or more, and thus a reduction of process rates. Surrounding the chamber with rare earth magnets and connecting several separate applicators or directly coupling microwave energy into the chamber (11) can improve densities and processing rates but only with the addition of overall system complexity.

In reactor (c) a separate rf or dc discharge is produced above the substrate. The properties of this discharge depend upon both the microwave and rf (dc) inputs. This configuration has the potential advantages of low sheath potentials, improved uniformity and control over the processing surface, and the introduction of new chemistry (40) due to the hybrid excitation of the final process discharge.

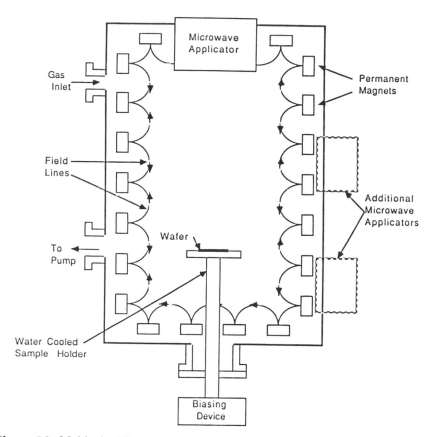

Figure 12: Multipolar Microwave Plasma Processing Chamber

11.8 DISCHARGE CHARACTERISTICS

Conventional wisdom suggests that plasma electron and ion densities within micro-wave discharges are limited to less than a critical density given by

$$n_e = 1.2 \times 10^{-2} \ f^2 \tag{13}$$

where n_e is given in electrons/m³ and f is the excitation frequency. This implies that with 2.45 GHz excitation plasma densities are limited to a maximum of $7.2 \times 10^{10}/cm^3$. In practice waveguide applicators produce slightly higher densities (5,10,11) and cavity applicators are capable of producing densities of 10 to 50 times the critical density at the low ECR operating pressures, and densities above 100 critical densities at high pressures (1-3). The ability to produce high densities no doubt is due to evanescent wave pene-tration in the plasma. This type of coupling is greatly enhanced in cavity applicators be-cause of their ability to impress an intense, standing wave electric field against the discharge without reflecting power from the applicator.

Single (5) and double (13,26,41) Langmuir probe measurements of electron density within and downstream from the discharge have confirmed that ECR discharges are capable of generating high densities of ions and electrons. For example over the 0.1-10 mTorr pressure range in argon gas charge densities increase with pressure (constant input power) and input power (constant pressure), and the degree of ionization increases as the pressure is reduced. Numerous measurements (13,26,41) performed in discharges with different diffusion lengths indicate that electron and ion densities vary between 3×10^{11} and 5×10^{12} cm^{-3} as power and pressure are varied from 0.1-10 mTorr. and the degree of ionization increases to 20-25% at the low pressures. Measured electron temperatures and density profiles obey Schottky ambipolar and free fall diffusion theories (41) inside the discharge and in the processing chamber. This approximate, but preliminary, knowledge of discharge behavior gives the impression that discharge optimization for uniformity, efficiency and control can be engineered by size and type (i.e. multipole, etc.) of the process chamber.

11.9 DISCUSSION

ECR discharges have been demonstrated as a useful, electrodeless, high density source of excited and charged species over $10^{-4} - 10^{-2}$ Torr pressure regimes. ECR/microwave technology allows a number of different design approaches. That is, there are several different processing configurations possible. Both waveguide and cavity applicators have been employed, ECR magnetic fields can be produced with coils or rare-earth magnets, etc. Both low energy plasma or neutralized electron-ion beams can be produced for surface processing. Thus specific applications may have one or more acceptable ECR approaches and/or very specific reactors can be designed for particular applications.

The utility of the ECR discharge has been demonstrated in etching, thin film and broad ion beam applications. Using the configuration of Fig. 11(b), anisotropic etching of Si has been demonstrated without high plasma sheath potentials (5,10,13). Etch rates as high as 0.4 μm /min with an anisotropy of 0.8-0.9 have been achieved over 3-6 inch wafers in SF$_6$/Ar mixtures (11,41). Using ECR discharges as the plasma for a broad beam ion source beam current densities > 5mA/cm^2 have been achieved in argon and oxygen (26,38). Numerous thin film deposition applications including diamond thin film deposition, have also been demonstrated (12,29,42 44).

Considerable work remains on discharge characterization. It is important to determine the number and the energy of ECR accelerated electrons, the shape of the electron energy distribution, the density of doubly ionized species (14), the energy of neutralized electron-ion beams (30) and the relationship between the shape of the ECR zones and the plasma properties such as excitation and ionization efficiency, etc. Such information can be related to reactor design and process chemistry.

Since ECR discharges are a relatively new technology, damage to etched surfaces and thin films either has not been or is in the process of being evaluated. The fact that microwave discharges can be produced without large plasma potentials is a definite advantage over rf parallel plate discharges. Thus surface damage produced by high plasma potentials should not be a problem. However there are other sources of process damage that may occur. These are damage caused by high energy electrons and ions produced and accelerated in magnetic mirror fields, damage caused by direct microwave radiation and damage produced by ultraviolet and other plasma radiation. Thus process damage produced by ECR discharges must be evaluated for each specific application and for each type of applicator.

Finally, it is noted that the technology of producing high density microwave discharges over cross sections of less than $4 - 5 cm^2$ has been well established for many years. The present challenge for microwave discharge technology is to produce high density, uniform microwave discharges over surfaces areas of 300-500 cm^2 without damage to process products. Such discharges would have important applications for processing six to eight inch wafers. An additional important challenge is to design ECR plasma sources to operate in the very low pressure environments of MBE machines. These plasma sources, if retrofitted into existing MBE machines, would advance the scientific investigation of low temperature ion, plasma and free radical chemistry in MBE environments.

11.10 REFERENCES

1.   J. Asmussen, R. Mallavarpu, J. R. Hamman and H. C. Park, Proc. IEEE 62: 109 (1974).

2.   R. Mallavarpu, M. C. Hawley and J. Asmussen, IEEE Trans. Plasma Sci. PS-6: 341 (1978).

3.   S. Whitehair, J. Asmussen and S. Nakanishi, J. of Propulsion and Power 3: 136 (1987).

4.   G. Loncar, J. Musil and L. Bardos, Czech. J. Phys. B30: 688 (1980).

5.   K. Suzuki, S. Okudairo, N. Sadudo and I. Kanomata, Jap. J. Appl. Phys. 16: 1979 (1977).

6.   J. Root and J. Asmussen Rev. Sci. Instrum. 56: 154 (1985).

7.   M. Dahimene and J. Asmussen, J. Vac. Sci. Technol. B4: 126 (1986).

8.   J. Asmussen and M. Dahimene J. Vac. Sci. Technol. B5: 328 (1987).

9.   T. Sugano, Applications of Plasma Processes to VLSI Technology, (J. Wiley, New York, 1985).

10. C. Pomot, B. Mahi, B. Petit, Y. Arnal and J. Pelletier, J. Vac. Sci. Technol. B4: 1 (1986)

11. R.R. Burke and C. Pomot, Solid State Technol. 67 (1988).

12. T. Roppel, D.K. Reinhard and J. Asmussen, J. Vac. Sci. Technol. B4: 295 (1986).

13. J. Hopwood, M. Dahimene, D.K. Reinhard and J. Asmussen, J. Vac. Sci. Technol., B6: 268 (1988).

14. R. Geller, IEEE Trans. NS-26: 2120 (1979).

15. M. Kamo, Y. Sato, S. Matsumoto and N. Setaka, J. Crys. Growth. 62: 642 (1983).

16. W.B. Ard, M.C. Becker, R.A. Dandl, H.O. Eason, A.C. England and J.R. Kerr, Phys. Rev. Lett. 10: 87 (1963).

17. D.B. Miller and G.W. Bethke, AIAA Jour. 4: 835 (1966).

18. B.E. Cherrington, Gaseous Electronics and Gas Lasers, (Pergammon Press, New York, 1979).

19. A.D. MacDonald, Microwave Breakdown in Gases, (J. Wiley and Sons, New York, 1966).

20. B. Lax, W.P. Allis and S.C. Brown, J. Appl. Phys. 21: 1297-1304 (1950).

21. G.I. Babet, J. Inst. Elect. Eng. 94: 27 (1947).

22. T.B. Reed, J. Appl. Phys. 32: 821 (1961).

23. J. Taillet, Am. J. Phys. 37: 423 (1960).

24. A.J. Hatch and L.E. Heuckroth, J. Appl. Phys. 41: 1701 (1970).

25. R.M. Fredericks and J. Asmussen, J. Appl. Phys. 42: 3647 (1971).

26. J. Mahoney, M. Dahimene and J. Asmussen, Rev. Sci. Instrum. 59: 448 (1988).

27. L. Pramathoid, R. Debrie, Y. Arnal and J. Pelletier, Phys. Lett. 106A: 301 (1984).

28. K. Ninomiya, K.Susuki and S. Nishimatsu, Jap. J. Appl. Phys. 22: 139 (1983).

29. S. Matsuo and M. Kiuchi, Jap. J. Appl. Phys. 22: L210 (1983).

30. M. Matsuoka and K. Ono, Appl. Phys. Lett. 50: 1864 (1987).

31. J. Asmussen and J. Root, U.S. Patent No. 4,507,588 (26 March 1985).

32. J.Asmussen and D.K. Reinhardt, U.S. Patent No. 4,585,668 (29 April 1986).

33. J. Asmussen and D.K. Reinhardt, U.S. Patent No. 4,630,566 (23 December 1986).

34. T. Roppel, D.K. Reinhard and J. Asmussen, U.S. Patent No. 4,691,662 (8 September 1987).

35. J. Asmussen, D.K. Reinhard and M. Dahimene, U.S. Patent No. 4,727,293 (23 February 1988).

36. N. Sakudo, K. Tokiguchi, H. Koike and I. Kanomata, Rev. Sci. Instrum. 48: 762 (1977).

37. M. Miyamura, O. Tsukakoshi and S. Komiya, J. Vac. Sci. Technol. 20: 986 (1982).

38. K. Tokiguchi, N. Sakudo and H. Koike, Rev. Sci. Instrum. 57: 1526 (1986).

39. R. Limpaecher and K.R. Mackenzie, Rev. Sci. Instrum. 44: 726 (1973).

40. J.E. Heidenreich and J.R. Paraszczak, J. Vac. Sci. Technol. B5: 347 (1987).

41. J. Hopwood, D.K. Reinhard and J. Asmussen, J. Vac. Sci. Technol. (to be published).

42. T. Ono, C. Takahashi and S. Matsuo, Jap. J. Appl. Phys. 23: L534 (1984).

43. K. Wakita and S. Matsuo, Jap. J. Appl. Phys. 23: L556 (1984).

44. H. Kawarada, K.S. Mar and A. Hiraki, Jap. J. Appl. Phys. 26: L1032 (1987).

12

Hollow Cathode Etching and Deposition

Chris M. Horwitz

12.1 INTRODUCTION

The hollow cathode is an enhanced-discharge configuration which permits high intensity, low voltage discharges to be obtained at low pressures. In this, it is similar to other configurations such as the magnetron and microwave ECR in providing enhanced operation in comparison with the standard radio-frequency sputtering diode. We will see that the hollow cathode can also yield a very high power efficiency, and that its symmetric construction can minimize high-energy electron bombardment of the substrates as well as minimizing particulate contamination. All of the above factors are important in modern semiconductor device processing: low operating pressures permit accurate pattern transfer (1,2); low voltages minimize surface contamination "damage" (3,4,5); high power efficiency minimizes heatsinking requirements (6,7); the absence of high-energy electrons improves dielectric layer properties (8,9); and low particle generation improves overall system performance (10,11).

It must be pointed out that the "hollow cathode" described in this chapter differs from hollow cathodes which are used as electron sources; such sources are often formed from small tubes of refractory metal and are operated in inert gas discharges at red heat (12,13). Here the hollow cathode is formed partly from the semiconductor wafers being processed, and it is thankfully not necessary to operate them at red heat to obtain the performance described here.

This chapter provides an overview of hollow cathode operation, starting with the fundamentals of discharge confinement and basic machine design. Some more complex applications of these principles, related to semiconductor processing, are then described.

12.2 DISCHARGE CONFINEMENT EFFECTS

12.2.1 Diode

Reactive sputtering rates depend on rates of reactant arrival at target surfaces; i.e., upon reactant pressures. Such reactants, formed by discharge dissociation of the input gas, are active chemical species capable of etching or depositing in the presence of energetic discharge processes such as ion bombardment. Low reactant partial pressure, whether due to low gas flow, or to inefficient breakup of the input gas into active constituents, results in low etch and deposition rates. Discharge confinement improves this availability in two ways; firstly, by simply constraining reactants, forcing them to spend their (often short) lifetimes close to the active target area. Secondly, discharge confinement could increase the discharge ionization level. Discharge ionization can be enhanced if the energetic particles produced by discharge heating (e.g., see Ch.6) are retained in the discharge region, again by simple mechanical confinement. In addition the correct choice of confining electrode polarity can result in trapping of energetic electrons. Such increases in discharge ionization would yield increased rates due both to increased reactant supply, and to increased ion bombardment of the target.

Examples of unconfined and confined diode systems are shown in Fig. 1. The upper unconfined diode corresponds to those described in earlier chapters. The central "guard-confined" diode has a target surrounded by material at the guard (i.e., chamber) potential

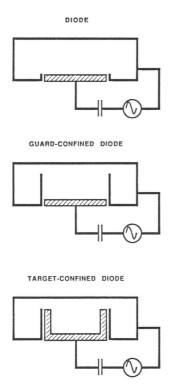

DIODE

GUARD-CONFINED DIODE

TARGET-CONFINED DIODE

Figure 1: Diode configurations. Top: standard system. Center: Confinement at the chamber (guard) potential. Bottom: Confinement at the target potential and guarded on the outside.

and often exhibits increased rates. For instance, etch rate increases of a factor of 2, at constant target voltage and power input have been obtained in CF_4 gas (2, 14). Such rate increases can be attributed to reactant trapping; the fairly constant input power indicates that discharge ionization is not affected by such guard-confinement of a diode.

The lower diagram in Fig. 1 shows a diode target which is confined by material at the target potential. Surrounding this is a guard at chamber potential, limiting the discharge to the central target area. Not only are neutral reactants confined by the arrangement; the extended target area is bombarded by more of the available ions in the glow region, while repelling electrons from its surface for most of the radio-frequency cycle. This "target-confinement" of a diode results in substantial improvements in deposition rate and in power efficiency of the discharge, but instability has made this discharge type hard to use in practice (15).

Common to all diode-confinement schemes is the area ratio problem illustrated in Fig. 2. The upper part of the diagram shows a 50 mm dia. target confined by a 15 mm high, 90 mm dia. chamber. This small chamber has a (chamber:target) area ratio of $A_2/A_1 = 7.6$, implying that ion bombardment of the target is significantly more energetic than that of the chamber walls (16). Thus, in this case the chamber walls are not heavily attacked by sputter-etch processes. Scale-up of the target area to a more practical 200 mm diameter, with all other diameters similarly scaled, results in the geometry illustrated in the lower part of Fig. 2. The nominal chamber:target area ratio is 6, again high. However, the intense glow region delineates the areas to be included in this area calculation (16) resulting in the effective area ratio tending towards unity in the scaled up diode. An area ratio of exactly one results in equal bombardment of the two "electrodes", chamber and target; hence often in the use of sacrificial materials opposing a diode target.

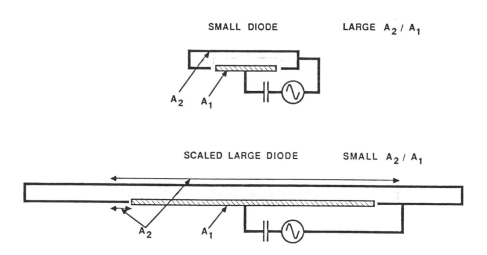

Figure 2: Effective area ratios in small and large diodes. The lower diode has all radii increased by a factor of 4. The intense glow region does not fill the entire volume of the larger chamber.

12.2.2 Hollow Cathode

A simple hollow cathode is formed by confining a diode target with a similar opposing diode target (Fig. 3 and top, Fig. 4). This confinement allows an increase in utilization of the available ions in the glow region, as did the target-confined diode. In addition, the hollow cathode so formed allows each target to repel secondary electrons ejected from the opposing target, forming an "electron mirror" (17). Such secondary electrons, formed by ion impact on a target and then accelerated by the sheath into the discharge glow region, would otherwise be lost at low pressures (2). Application of this electron mirror concept to the hollow cathode indicates that while guard-confinement of a hollow cathode (center, Fig. 4) may increase rates due to retention of reactants and other active neutral discharge components, target-confinement (bottom, Fig. 4) should give the larger improvement due to its more efficient trapping of electrons by the negatively biased targets.

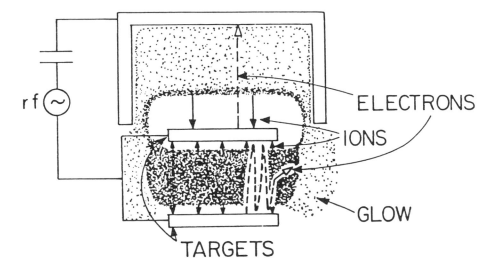

Figure 3:   Secondary electrons, liberated from hollow cathode targets by ion bombardment, can be trapped in an electron mirror.

These general conclusions are borne out by the experimental data. As an example, Si deposition rates from SiH_4 gas are given for various confinement methods in Fig. 5 as a function of target voltage and in Fig. 6 as a function of power input (15). In both cases, the least-confined system (the diode) exhibits the lowest rate, while the most-confined system (the target-confined hollow cathode) exhibits the highest rate. All other systems, including the unstable target-confined diode, have intermediate performance. The impact of confinement is greatest at low pressures; Fig. 7 shows that while the etch efficiency of a guard-confined hollow cathode is about three times that of a diode at 1 Pa CF_4 pressure, the two systems' efficiencies become similar at 10 Pa CF_4 pressure (14).

Figure 4: Hollow cathode configurations: Top: standard system. Center: Confinement at the chamber (guard) potential. Bottom: Confinement at the target potential, guarded on the outside.

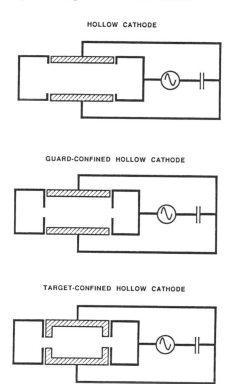

HOLLOW CATHODE

GUARD-CONFINED HOLLOW CATHODE

TARGET-CONFINED HOLLOW CATHODE

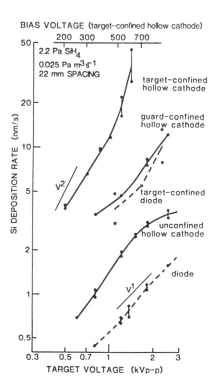

Figure 5: Voltage dependence of deposition rate from silane in diodes (dashed lines) and hollow cathodes (solid lines), with various degrees of confinement. The target confined diode results are sketchy due to discharge instability.

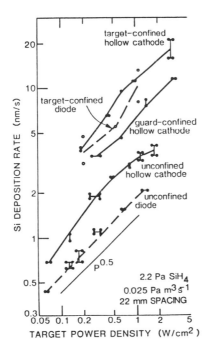

Figure 6: Power dependence of deposition rate from silane for diodes (dashed lines) and hollow cathodes (solid lines), with various degrees of confinement.

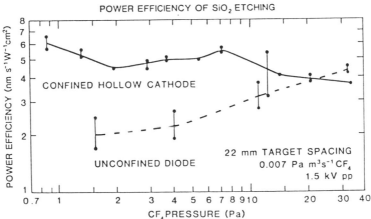

Figure 7: Power efficiency of CF_4 etching as a function of pressure for a diode and hollow cathode. Power efficiency is given here as (SiO_2 etch rate) / (surface power density).

There are minor differences in the confined behaviors of CF_4 and SiH_4 discharges; while guard-confinement of a diode has no effect on SiH_4 discharges, it has a slight power-reducing, rate-increasing effect on CF_4 discharges. In addition, guard-confined

CF_4 diode discharges were unstable at pressures lower than 6 Pa, whereas only the target-confined diode was unstable in SiH_4.

The experimental data shows that confinement of a diode, while conferring some benefits, is not as effective as hollow cathode configurations in obtaining higher rates for a given target voltage and input power density. In particular, hollow cathode guard confinement improves both reactant trapping and discharge ionization by providing a mechanical barrier to the escape of energetic particles. The opposing grounded surface in a diode discharge is probably serving both as a heatsink and as a center for recombination and polymerization of reactants, on balance extracting energy from the diode discharge region and preventing guard confinement from conferring substantial benefits. This energy loss mechanism may also explain the observed instability of confined diode discharges.

Target confinement of the hollow cathode can result in a different type of instability from that seen in diodes; the discharge may exit from the central region in a "plume" at low pressure and/or at high input power. This plume can be suppressed with a small axial magnetic field of 10-50 Gauss, as shown in the "Super-confined Hollow Cathode" of Fig. 8, permitting stable high-efficiency operation at low pressures and at high input power densities.

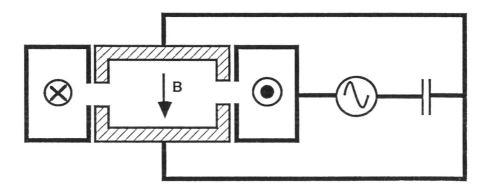

Figure 8: "Super-confined" hollow cathode using a magnetic field and target confinement to obtain a high efficiency low-pressure discharge.

The hollow cathode, like the diode, cannot be scaled in target area indefinitely without regard to the effective area of exposed chamber wall. However very little work has been done on the nature of this effective chamber area, and on the significance of area ratios in the hollow cathode case. Our work to date indicates that scaling of the hollow cathode to large target sizes is easier than in the diode.

12.3 ETCHED SIDEWALL ANGLE CONTROL

12.3.1 Mechanism

The angle of an etched sidewall on a surface structure must be controlled in many applications. One example is in via and contact hole etching, where angles of $10° - 20°$ from the vertical permit good metal coverage (18). Here we discuss a method of sidewall angle control employing a metal compound of low volatility (e.g. MgF_2) which is coated onto surfaces while they are etched. This metal compound is normally present in monolayer quantities, and as will be shown in section 14.4.2, is compatible with standard device processing. As will be seen the process is applicable to a wide variety of etcher configurations, although it has mostly been used with the hollow cathode.

If a conformal uniform-thickness layer is being continuously applied over a surface which is also subject to directional ion-assisted etching, horizontal areas will be etched to completion faster than angled areas, where the effective layer thickness is greater (Fig.9, Ref.19). Defining the angle between the substrate and the incident ion direction as Θ, the effective layer thickness is proportional to $\sin \Theta^{-1}$, hence rises as the angle Θ falls. At large angles Θ (i.e. for horizontal surfaces, normal to the ion direction), this coating typically etches rapidly and so does not greatly subtract from the substrate etch rate. However, at a sufficiently small angle Θ to the ion direction, the effective layer thickness will be so large that the substrate etch rate is reduced to zero. At this angle the conformal deposition rate of this layer is precisely equal to its directional etch rate, resulting in the formation of a stable, very thin equilibrium layer. At this equilibrium angle no further etching of the substrate can take place.

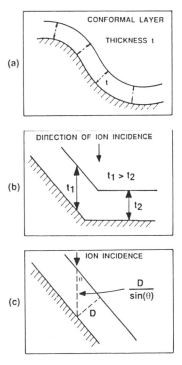

Figure 9: Mechanism of angle control using a surface coating. (a) Conformal surface coating: (b), (c) Effective coating thickness along ion etch direction is larger on angled surfaces. At the angle where effective etched thickness equals deposited thickness in any given time period, an equilibrium state is reached.

The above mechanism implies that the etched angle is dependent on the nature of the coating material and on its deposition rate, but not on the material being etched. This surprising result is borne out by experiment, where both Si and SiO_2 layers are etched to very nearly identical angles in the presence of metallic compound deposition (19-21). Another useful attribute of this angle-control mechanism is its independence of other discharge parameters, allowing independent control of etch selectivity and etched angles (22). We have found that a wide variety of metal and gas combinations result in useful angle control properties, as illustrated in Figs. 10 and 11; in general the metal compound must have a low vapor pressure to have a significant angle-control effect, but not so low that its effect is too localized.

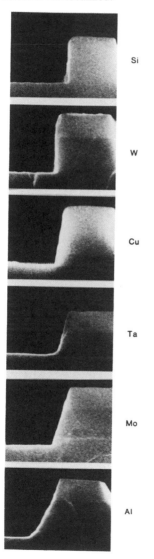

Si

W

Cu

Ta

Mo

Al

CF$_4$ GAS

Figure 10: Effect of upper target material on etched angles in SiO_2 and Si at 1.7 kV_{p-p} in a 2.2 Pa, 0.006 Pa m^{3}s^{-1}CF$_4$ hollow cathode discharge. Heatsunk samples; MgF_2 mask removed. Top layer is 0.6μm thermal SiO_2.

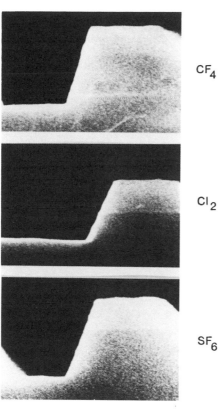

CF$_4$

Cl$_2$

SF$_6$

Mo METAL

Figure 11: Effect of etch gas on etched angles at 1.7 kV$_{p-p}$ with a Mo upper hollow cathode target. Heatsunk samples; MgF$_2$ mask removed. Top layer is 0.6μm thermal SiO$_2$. CF$_4$ and Cl$_2$ at 2.2 Pa, SF$_6$ at 1.1 Pa pressure.

12.3.2 Special Machine Designs

Metal compounds may be added to the discharge gas in a variety of ways. If the operating pressure is high, or the compounds in use have a moderately low vapor pressure (as with Mo-F combinations), a source of metal from a subsidiary discharge at the side of the etching chamber will result in good angle uniformity (Fig.12(a)). Sources of metal closer to the etched substrates permit a wider choice of materials and operating pressures; Figure 12(b) shows that an opposing hollow cathode target may be partly metallic. However this permits etched angle control only through target changes. Another relatively inflexible method relies on a small (chamber:target) area ratio, causing ion bombardment of the chamber to a lesser extent than the target, but nevertheless sufficient to sputter a controlled amount of chamber metal material into the discharge (Fig. 12(c)).

The "trielectrode" hollow cathode (Fig.12(d)) has three main electrodes; central targets, metallic ring targets, and the chamber walls. This configuration provides a source of metal close to the targets, while permitting etched angle control by adjustment of the metal ring target discharge current. These ring targets also contribute to discharge confinement and hence to discharge power efficiency (ref. 21). Although the rf generator is shown connected only to the central targets, and only the dc supply to the ring targets, in fact a fraction of the central target rf voltage appears on the ring targets. External capacitors can be connected between the ring targets and the chamber or central electrodes to adjust the value of this ring rf voltage; a high ring voltage results in low input power density for a given etch rate, but also in a high rate of metal supply to the discharge.

METAL SOURCE AT CHAMBER SIDE

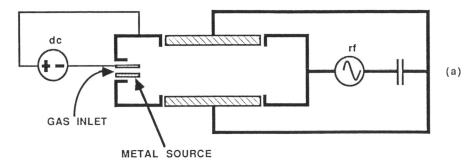

Figure 12: Methods of incorporating a metal source in hollow cathode discharges.

12.4 ETCHING PERFORMANCE

12.4.1 SiO₂ Selectivity and Etching

As in diode reactors, the hollow cathode allows SiO_2 to be selectively etched using controlled polymer deposition during the etch process. Addition of hydrogen to CF_4 etch gas encourages formation of this polymer on photoresist and on silicon, thereby retarding the etch rates of these materials relative to that of SiO_2 (22,23,24). Thus SiO_2 films formed on Si and masked by patterned photoresist can be etched, without excessive erosion of the mask or of the underlying silicon, in a high selectivity process. One limit to the attainable material selectivity is gas flow reproducibility; excessive hydrogen flow, beyond the so-called "polymer point", results in the deposition of a thick continuous polymer film. This is to be avoided as much as the lower selectivity obtained at low hydrogen flow. The precision to which gas flow must be controlled can be derived from the rate of change of selectivity with hydrogen flow; a small rate of change indicates a small (and desirable) sensitivity to hydrogen flow. Figure 13 shows how the etch selectivity of SiO_2 relative to Si varies with hydrogen flow in the hollow cathode. Figure 13(b) also shows the performance of a diode etcher (23,24). In these graphs the hydrogen flow is shown on a logarithmic scale and in arbitrary units to allow comparisons of curve shapes to be made; the relative positions of the curves on this axis have no significance.

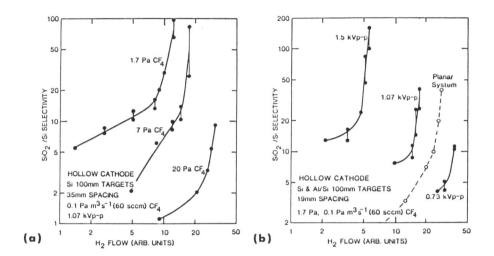

Figure 13: The effect of hydrogen on the SiO_2/SiO selectivity for the hollow cathode. Curve positions on the H_2 flow axis have been shifted for clarity. (a) non heatsunk samples; CF_4 pressure as parameter. (b) Heatsunk samples; target voltage as parameter. The Planar System (diode) curve is replotted from refs. 23, 24.

All the curves in Fig. 13 exhibit regions of low slope, hence of a desirable low sensitivity to hydrogen flow. Beyond a "knee" region the slope increases, making accurate process control more difficult. The value of selectivity at that knee position can be used to compare different operating conditions; for instance at 20 Pa operating pressure, a knee selectivity of roughly 2 is obtained, whereas at 1.7 Pa pressure the knee selectivity is 15, demonstrating one benefit of low-pressure operation (Fig. 13(a)). The knee selectivity varies even more rapidly with target voltage; a doubling from 0.73 kV_{p-p} to 1.5 kV_{p-p} increases knee selectivity from about 4 to 18, at low operating pressure (Fig. 13(b)).

Selectivity at the curve knees in Fig. 13 is clearly related to the etch selectivity of CF_4 in the absence of hydrogen. Although high inherent CF_4 selectivity can be obtained in both diode and hollow cathode reactors (25,26), Figure 14 shows that hollow cathode selectivities are greater than those of diodes over a wide pressure range, for a fixed 50 mm dia. target geometry and operating voltage. Rates and input powers are shown in Fig.14(a) for unconfined and in Fig. 14(b) for glass-ring-confined targets (14). Both figures demonstrate a large SiO_2/Si etch rate ratio for hollow cathode configurations. This behavior enables the larger hollow cathode system used for Fig. 13 to yield selectivities in pure CF_4 of the order of 10 at high target voltage and low pressure. This is high enough for many integrated circuit applications and is also well above the selectivity of 1.3 reported for a diode system in 4.7 Pa CF_4 and at 800 V_{p-p} (Fig. 13(b)) (23,24). Clearly high target voltage by itself does not make CF_4 gas selective. It is the combination of low operating pressure and high input volume power density (i.e., high energy input per input gas molecule) that seems to result in a desirable polymer deposition process.

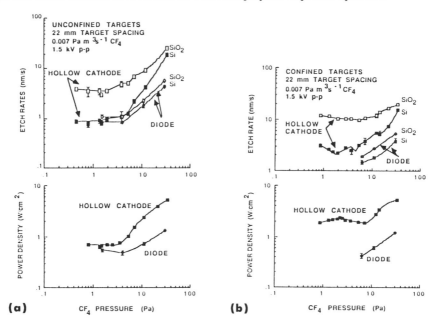

Figure 14: SiO_2 and Si etch rates and power densities in CF_4 discharges. (a) Unconfined targets; SiO_2/Si selectivity is higher in the hollow cathode than in the diode, even at similar target voltage and surface power density. (b) Guard-confined targets; the hollow cathode again exhibits higher selectivity than the diode.

High selectivities are limited not only by gas flow repeatability but also by pattern sensitivity of etching rates. The centers of large apertures etch slowly, probably because of their large polymer acceptance angle (Fig. 15). Another possible explanation may be a local chemical interaction between the plasma and the resist, but the low resist etch rate makes this unlikely. This behavior appears to be the reverse of high-pressure reactor performance, where small opening sizes etch more slowly. The effect can be observed after overetch of an oxide film with large pattern openings; close to the pattern edges silicon is etched deeper than at the pattern center. For instance, with 1.6 μm resist and 1 μm oxide thicknesses, an overetch of 300% at a selectivity of 150 to 300 results in silicon etch depths of 3 to 10 nm within 10 μm of the pattern edges. However, in the remaining areas of the pattern an etch depth of 1 nm is obtained. This pattern sensitivity can be minimized by (a) requiring uniform pattern hole sizes; or (b) operating at selectivities of 100 or below, where this effect has not been observed in patterns as wide as 70 μm.

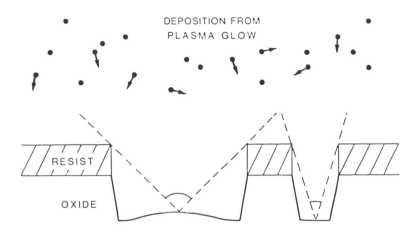

Figure 15: Preferential etching of small apertures at high selectivity. Wide structures have large polymer acceptance angles and have low central etch rates.

Another practical limit to selectivity is the tolerable level of polymer deposition. In the trielectrode chamber (Fig. 12(d)), the rf voltage on the ring can be set at the level where ring etching begins to dominate over polymer deposition, without dc supply current flow. Application of dc current to the rings then permits adjustment of the metal ring sputtering rate. In this case, polymer deposition is inhibited on all central target and ring areas, resulting in polymer film buildup only on chamber surfaces remote from the etched substrate wafer. This "clean" environment for the etched wafer compares with standard unconfined and guard-confined systems, which permit polymer buildup opposite the etched wafer (Fig. 1), and on the periphery of the etched wafers (Fig. 4). Thick polymer deposits can flake on exposure to air, resulting in undesirable particle deposition on etched wafers (10, 11). Only three chamber types discussed here are capable of inhibiting polymer buildup around the etched wafers; symmetric diodes with large etched target areas surrounding the wafers, the trielectrode hollow cathode (Fig. 12(d)), and the hollow cathode surrounded by a reduced-area chamber (Fig. 12(c)). These chamber types offer longer periods between cleanup cycles than the other hollow cathode and diode systems, and the possibility of more prolonged operation at high selectivity levels.

Etch uniformity is of greatest importance in cases where the SiO_2 layer thickness is identical in all etched apertures on a wafer. Then even a low-selectivity process could in principle be stopped exactly at the point where all SiO_2 had been cleared from those apertures, provided that this low selectivity process exhibited uniform etching over the wafer surface. In practice the SiO_2 layer thickness often varies from aperture to aperture because contacts must be made to different layers in a chip, at differing levels. Thus etch uniformity cannot be exactly traded off against selectivity; in chips with varying oxide thicknesses uniformity must be less important than selectivity. Hollow cathode uniformity can be adjusted with gas pressure and target spacing; the trielectrode hollow cathode uniformity can also be varied with the level of ring electrode excitation. In general wide electrode spacing results in low etch rates at the substrate edge in comparison with the central etch rate, probably because energetic particle loss at the discharge edge results in lower discharge intensity there. Closer electrode spacing aids confinement processes and results in lower losses and in higher edge etch rates. These trends are illustrated in Fig. 16, which shows etch rates across a 100mm dia. wafer (clamped by a 90 mm I.D. polyimide-coated metal ring) in a trielectrode hollow cathode. Target spacings were varied by changing the height of the surrounding chamber walls; at a wide target spacing of 34 mm the edge etch rate is lower than that in the center, as expected. Closer spacings, to a minimum target separation of 14mm, demonstrate a general trend towards higher edge etch rates, resulting in ± 1 % etch rate uniformity being obtained between 21 and 24 mm target spacing.

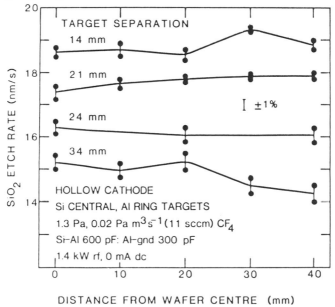

DISTANCE FROM WAFER CENTRE (mm)

Figure 16: Etch uniformity across a 100-mm wafer for various target separations using a trielectrode chamber. The input rf power was kept constant; the rf voltage falls sharply at small separations. The wafer was clamped by a ring of 45-mm radius.

Silicon etch uniformity is of interest because of its impact on etch selectivity. Often the silicon etch rate variation across a wafer is far greater than that of SiO_2. Silicon etch rates are affected not only by ion bombardment (which is the dominat etch mechanism for SiO_2), but by neutral fluorine concentration and by polymer deposition rate. At low polymer generation rates (i.e. with only CF_4 etch gas) the electrode spacing for best silicon etch uniformity is typically a little larger than that for SiO_2; and uniformities to within a few percent are normal at the optimum spacing. However with H_2 added, silicon etch uniformity is controlled by polymer deposition which, in the trielectrode system, depends on metal ring target voltage more than on target spacing. Thus the best silicon etch uniformity, hence the best selectivity uniformity, is obtained when the metal ring voltage is close to that of the target. This would be achieved by ensuring close capacitive coupling between the central targets and the ring targets, and can result in very high input power levels for a given SiO_2 etch rate. High SiO_2 etch rates are more easily obtained under the looser coupling between ring and central targets indicated in Fig. 16, which results in higher silicon etch rates at the edge than in the center. The resultant difference in edge and center selectivities is plotted in Fig. 17, which shows a highest central selectivity of 150-300, and an edge value of 50. The lowest selectivities are obtained in pure CF_4; 15 at the center, falling to 10 at the edge. At the highest selectivities in this system the SiO_2 etch rate remains high at 15nm/s (0.9 μm/ min), and uniform to within $\pm$ 1 % from center to edge.

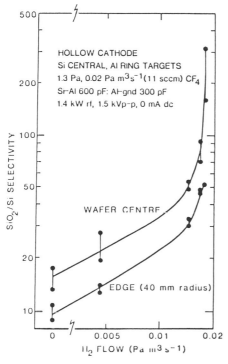

Figure 17: Etch selectivity at center and edge of trielectrode hollow cathode with 21-mm target separation.

The etched SiO_2 angle depends on metal ring target etch rates; with 200 mA ring dc applied current and Al metal electrodes a $75° \pm 5°$ angle is obtained between 0 and 40mm radius (i.e., to within 5mm of the wafer clamp edge). Thus our Al-containing angle control compounds appear to have adequate range with this operating pressure and target geometry.

12.4.2 Device Processing; SiO₂ Etch

The previous sections have shown that low CF_4 pressures and high target voltages allow a highly selective SiO_2 etch to be obtained with added hydrogen, and that angle control can be obtained with added metal. As an example of such conditions, Fig. 18 shows the performance of a guard-confined hollow cathode as a function of hydrogen gas partial pressure. SiO_2 etch rates of 1 - 1.5 μm/ min were obtained at selectivities of 15 - 20, while the amount of Al metal on the target opposing the patterned wafer resulted in a 70° etched angle from the horizontal. The compatibility of this high-rate, high-voltage, angle-controlled etch with CMOS device processing was demonstrated as follows:

(a) Etched contact holes in SiO_2 must yield low contact resistances to the underlying Si or poly-Si substrate. The quality of the etched Si surface can be inferred from previous studies, which have shown that the quality of thermal oxide grown on a previously etched Si wafer falls as CF_4 etch voltage rises. This indicates that high voltage CF_4 discharges cause surface roughness and/or leave chemical residues on Si surfaces (4). Surprisingly, the addition of hydrogen to these discharges resulted in higher surface quality (27). It is worth noting the effect of discharge chemistry on these "damage" levels; a gas without carbon such as SiF_4 resulted in very low damage levels at the highest voltages tested.

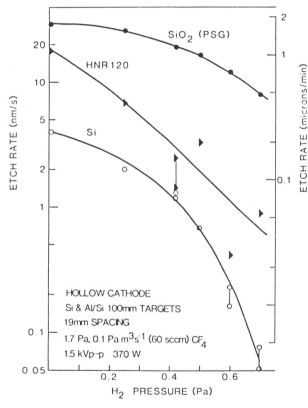

Figure 18: Selective etching of heatsunk substrates in a guard-confined hollow cathode chamber. HNR 120 is a negative photoresist, and PSG is phosphosilicate glass (similar to SiO_2 in our apparatus). CMOS device wafers were processed between 0.4 and 0.6 Pa hydrogen pressure.

Our measured contact resistances correlate well with the above data on damage levels in grown oxides. Intermediate contact resistances to p+ doped Si and to n+ poly-Si, counterdoped with p+ dopant were obtained at completion of the selective CF_4/H_2 etch (Fig. 19, "no final etch" points on left-hand side). Although such resistances may be tolerable in low-current CMOS circuits, they are not as low as can be obtained with wet oxide etching in HF, indicating the presence of residues and/or surface roughness. This "damage" may be removed by etching off a thin Si surface layer in several ways (28-30). In the present case pure CF_4 was used to remove about 10 nm of silicon in a non-selective final etch step, resulting in poor resistances at high applied voltages, but in excellent contact resistances at low applied voltages (Fig. 19). This is again in agreement with the oxide damage studies.

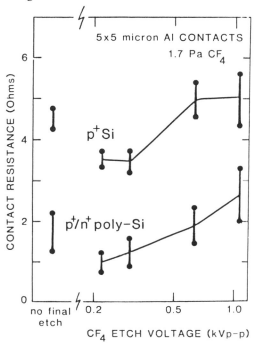

Figure 19: Contact resistances after various CF_4 etch treatments following a selective CF_4/H_2 etch. Errors shown are one σ over ten readings. Silicon etch depths were $\approx 10nm(100\text{Å})$

The above data relates to contact resistances between Al and the relatively lightly doped materials with p-type (boron) doping. In silicon this doping level gave a sheet resistivity of 100 Ω/square. The n+ - type polysilicon, and n+ -type silicon doped to a 10 Ω/square level gave contact resistances between 0.8 and 1.1 Ω in 5 x 5 μm (nominal) contact holes, independent of post processing etch treatment and roughly equal to the value obtained with wet HF etching.

(b) Field-effect devices, such as those used in CMOS logic, can be damaged by changes in the properties of gate oxides. Rapid target potential changes can result in high-voltage gate oxide stress, and in device breakdown (31); in the present study target voltages were ramped and controlled by computer, with no sudden changes permitted. The device yield figures which are listed below indicate that our process has not induced gate breakdown.

Gate oxides can also be modified by injected charges arising either from charged particle bombardment or from discharge UV/Xray irradiation (32); these charges could induce a shift in device threshold voltages. Threshold voltages of n-channel devices with 100 nm oxide thickness showed no detectable deviation (within the $\pm$ 20 mV scatter) between our high-rate hollow cathode process and the control wafers. p-channel thresholds also showed no detectable deviation from the control wafers, within their larger scatter of $\pm$ 50mV.

(c) The sidewall angle etch process relies on novel chemistry and leaves a thin layer, of the order of one monolayer thickness, on etched sidewalls. To test whether this layer causes any yield or long-term reliability problems, CMOS clock generator chips, using

devices with 100 nm oxide thickness and 5 μm minimum gate length, were fabricated using the high-rate hollow cathode process for the final contact hole etch. Control wafers
were etched in a commercial planar etch system, then given a phosphosilicate glass reflow
to obtain sloped sidewalls. All wafers were then metallized, sintered, and overcoated. The
control wafer yields were in the normal range for this device of 52% to 69%; hollow
cathode wafer yields were between 67% and 82% even after over-etching by up to
200%, indicating adequate etch selectivity for these devices, and showing a 15% yield
improvement over the control wafers. When placed on life test for 1000 hours with 5V
supply and at 125°C, no failures occurred in the 89 chips tested.

The above data demonstrates the viability of high-rate, controlled-angle and selective
hollow cathode etching in standard CMOS processing. Lately the angled hollow cathode
etch has been applied to front-surface texturing of solar cells (33). A hollow cathode
silicon trench process (see following section) has also been used to form high-efficiency
solar cell diode structures. Our processes have been compatible with all of these devices,
without special post-etch treatments.

12.4.3 Si Etching

Limited work on silicon etching has been performed in the hollow cathode to date, in
comparison with oxide etching and with silicon deposition. The results reported here relate to process selectivity and to isolated Si beam formation, and have been obtained
during the fabrication of small isolated bipolar devices (34). Throughout this discussion
the mask material is patterned SiO_2.

Silicon may be etched selectively relative to SiO_2 in gases with greater fluorine content
than CF_4. An example is SF_6, where selectivities of around 5 can be obtained at high
pressure and at high etch rate (Fig. 20). Here the observed selectivity is a result of the
high reactivity of Si with free F atoms, and non-directional (isotropic) etching is obtained
under these conditions. At a lower target voltage of 200 V_{p-p}, a selectivity of 200 can
be obtained, again with isotropic Si etching. Such behavior is similar to that of SF_6 in diode systems (35). High selectivity in a directional etch requires gases containing Cl, in
which ion bombardment is required to induce Cl-Si reactions. One example is shown in
Fig. 21, where a selectivity of almost 10 is obtained at a relatively high Cl_2 operating
pressure and etch rate. As with SF_6, selectivities against oxide rise as target voltage is
lowered; in 10 Pa Cl_2 we have measured a selectivity of 15 at 1.4 kV_{p-p}, rising to 32 at 1
kV_{p-p}.

The above etch results relate to "simple" discharge etch processes, without competitive deposition. As in silicon dioxide etching where polymer deposition enables high selectivity to be obtained without etch rate and target voltage tradeoffs, silicon etch
processes can benefit from controlled deposition of a layer containing silicon dioxide. The
silicon for this layer can be sourced from the etched target or from the etch gas (36), and
the rate of oxide layer growth controlled by the oxygen content of the discharge gas. Because the deposition of this layer is from an approximately isotropic source in the discharge it deposits easier on tall masked structures than in deep trenches. This enables etch
selectivity to be increased during trench etching, protecting mask layers from erosion

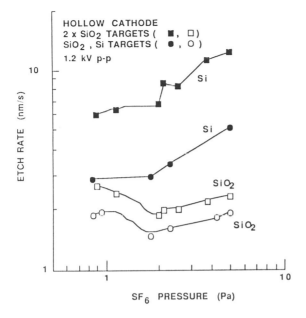

Figure 20: Silicon and SiO$_2$ hollow cathode etch rates in SF$_6$ discharges. High Si etch rates and Si/SiO$_2$ selectivities are obtained in an "unloaded" system with two SiO$_2$ targets.

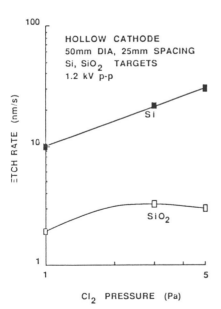

Figure 21: Silicon and SiO$_2$ hollow cathode etch rates in Cl$_2$ discharges, as a function of Cl$_2$ pressure. Note the high Si etch rates; 16.7 nm/s is one micron/minute.

during the final etch stages but allowing the native Si oxide layer to be broken through cleanly in the initial etch phase. The results shown in Fig. 22 for an SiCl$_4$/H$_2$/O$_2$ gas mixture show that selectivities of 10-20 are obtained up to the high- O$_2$ flow point where an oxide coating would form on all exposed flat surfaces. Deep trench etching would commence at such selectivity levels, then operate at increased O_2 flow to permit accurate control of the trench bottom shape while protecting the top mask (Fig. 23). As in diode etching (37-38), low O_2 gas flow allows mask faceting and etch-back; intermediate O_2 flow protects the mask, but results in straight trench walls which increase ion bombardment and etching at the trench sides; and high O_2 flow gradually narrows the top mask aperture, resulting in sloped trench sides and a smooth trench profile.

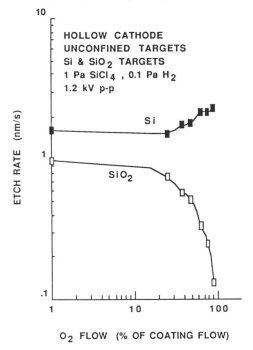

Figure 22: Silicon and SiO_2 hollow cathode etch rates in a $SiCl_4/H_2/O_2$ gas mixture, as a function of O_2 gas flow. "100%" O_2 flow is just sufficient to cause deposition of a SiO_x film on flat exposed target surfaces. Trench bottoms are shadowed from this deposition, and are not coated until higher O_2 flows are reached. Typical etches begin at low flow, rising to above "100%" during the etch.

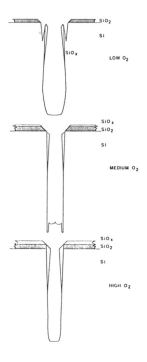

Figure 23: Silicon trench etch profiles. Top: low O_2 levels result in mask faceting and Si edge erosion. Center: medium O_2 levels facet the mask and form bottom trenches. Bottom: high O_2 levels form rounded trench bottom profiles.

The deposited oxide may be removed in a selective wet etch. For instance, 100:1 diluted HF etches the deposited oxide 70 times faster than thermal oxide, allowing thermal oxide masks to be retained if needed (Fig. 24). The deposited oxide may however be retained if isolated silicon beams are required; it acts as a good etch mask against isotropic SF_6 etching. A cantilever structure so formed is shown in Fig. 25, before insulator refill around the Si beam.

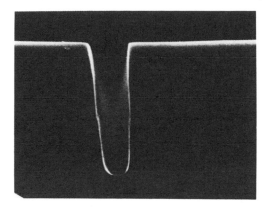

Figure 24: Silicon trench etched in the hollow cathode using low initial O_2 gas flow, rising to high levels later in the etch. Cl_2 etch gas; deposited oxide removed, 0.5-micron thermal oxide mask remaining; 20 μm deep trench.

——————— **10 microns**

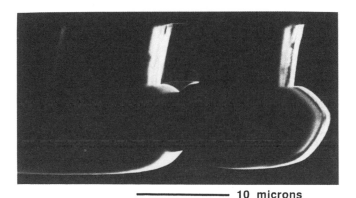

——————— 10 microns

Figure 25: Single-crystal Si cantilever beam after trench etch, SF_6 "cutoff" etch, and oxide removal; before insulator refill.

12.5 Si DEPOSITION PERFORMANCE

12.5.1 Substrate Processes

Previous sections have shown how controlled deposition can benefit etch processes. In this section the benefits of controlled etching during film deposition will be investigated, using silicon deposition from silane as a model. In our discharges the film deposition of interest occurs on ion-bombarded targets, resulting in many film-forming and film-modifying processes:

(a) The discharge glow region can form Si nuclei, resulting in particles which fall or diffuse to the wafer surface. Such "homogeneous nucleation" in the gas results in a rough film if the particles are large in comparison with the scale of redistribution processes on the substrate.

(b) The input SiH_4 gas, or a fragment of it such as SiH_2, may adsorb on the target surface. Thermally activated processes could further break this adsorbate down, depositing Si. Such thermally activated "heterogeneous nucleation" is often the primary mechanism of chemical vapor deposition, but on our room-temperature substrates is negligible.

(c) The surface adsorbates in (b) may be broken down by the energy liberated during ion impact, resulting in Si film formation. In the present case this growth process dominates over (a) (homogeneous nucleation) at low silane pressures.

(d) Ion impact during film deposition redistributes film atoms, removing voids and densifying the film (39). However, interstitials are created which result in a compressive film stress (40), which in some cases has been observed to increase with the square root of the ion energy (41). Films under high compressive stress can fail even during deposition, through loss of adhesion to the substrate and subsequent peeling. High stress can also lead to peeling of the film during high temperature ($1000°C$) doping operations. Film stress can be lowered by deposition above room temperature or by annealing, both of which permit relaxation of strain by thermal diffusion of atoms to low energy sites. The Si films in this study tolerate $1000°C$ thermal treatments after a $600°C$ anneal cycle.

(e) Ion impact also results in sputter etching and redeposition, which "facets" sharp edges and fills in deep holes, resulting in planarization of the growing film (8,9,42).

(f) High-energy ion impact (above 2000 eV) forms interstitials at depths of 10 nm and deeper, below the target surface. Such "ion implantation" in the present case should result in little alteration of film chemistry. However, it should be noted that the hydrogen derived from our silane input gas may have a greater range than the larger ions (43).

(g) Electron bombardment of a growing insulator film results in inferior electronic performance due to trap formation (8,9,32). Although these can be annealed out, the hollow cathode electron mirror phenomena should minimize such trap formation.

(h) Traps may also be formed in insulators by UV and Xray irradiation (32). It is possible that systems with high power efficiency (such as the confined hollow cathodes) have advantages over reactors with lower power efficiency in this regard.

12.5.2 Experimental Results

In our experiments with hollow cathode discharges the dominant deposition mechanism can be deduced by comparing deposition rates on adjacent substrates. Target substrates are exposed to deposition from the glow as well as to ion bombardment, whereas surrounding guard surfaces are only exposed to glow deposition processes. A comparison of target and guard deposition rates at two pressures (Fig. 26) shows that at 20 Pa the guard rate is 27% higher than the average target rate, implying that deposition of silicon is primarily from the discharge glow. High pressure ion bombardment appears to serve more as an agent of etching than of deposition. At a low 1.34 Pa pressure the situation is reversed with a guard rate equal to 55% of the average target rate. Hence at low pressure, ion-induced deposition coupled with ion-induced etching become the dominant film forming mechanisms. Films deposited at low pressures should thus be somewhat smoother than those deposited at high pressures, due to a greater "heterogeneous nucleation" contribution.

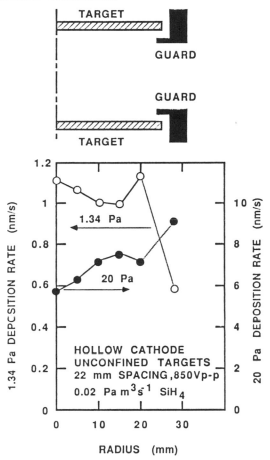

Figure 26: Deposition rate as a function of substrate position at two silane pressures. The upper drawing of (half of) the targets shows the 27mm samples to be on the guard. Uniformity between 0 and 21 mm radius is ± 6 % (1σ) in both cases.

Independent of the deposition mechanism, the step coverage of a growing film is controlled by its (deposition/etching) rate ratio. Large ratios imply that etching due to ion bombardment is swamped by deposition processes, resulting in little film redistribution after initial deposition, and so in poor coverage over steps in the substrate. An example of the resulting re-entrant film profiles, and of void formation, is given in Fig. 27 for a relatively thick (2 micron) film. Such poor deposition conditions are generally obtained at high pressures and at high gas flow rates, where copious chemical reactants are available for film deposition processes. · At low pressures (Fig. 28), or at low input gas flow rates (Fig. 29), etching processes become more effective (15). The results of this etching, and subsequent redeposition of etched material on other parts of the substrate, are better filling of hollows in the substrate and of voids in the growing film; and formation of etched facets on upper exposed portions of the growing film. Sufficiently thick films become planarized by this faceting process (21).

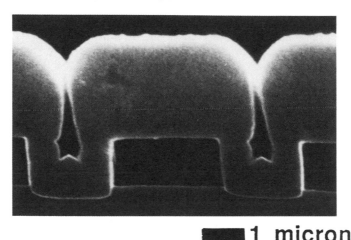

1 micron

Figure 27: Voids and re-entrant profiles in a directionally-deposited film. Si film deposited over SiO_2 grating steps (SiO_2 removed in HF). Unconfined hollow cathode; 3.5 kV_{p-p}, 10 Pa SiH_4, 2 micron nominal Si film thickness.

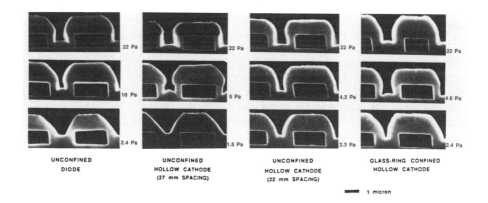

Figure 28: Deposited silicon profiles over SiO_2 grating steps with SiO_2 etched away. Left; diode: Center; unconfined hollow cathodes: Right; glass-ring-confined hollow cathode. This latter is similar to a guard-confined hollow cathode. Silane pressures shown to the right of each picture. For these studies, a high silane flow (about 0.04 Pa m^{3}s^{-1}), and 3.5 kV_{p-p} was used.

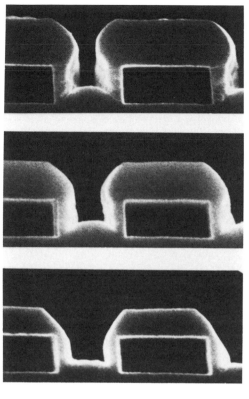

INCREASING SiH$_4$ FLOW RATE ▶→

Figure 29: Flow rate dependence of deposited silicon profiles at 22 Pa silane fill pressure, in an unconfined hollow cathode with remote gas injection. Deposition rates increase by about a factor of 5 from bottom to top of the figure. Flow rates (from bottom): 0.004, 0.016, 0.085 Pa m^{3}s^{-1} of SiH$_4$, with 3.5 kV$_{p-p}$ target voltage.

━━━1 micron

12.6 CONCLUSIONS

Our understanding of discharge behavior and of confinement effects is by no means complete. We do not understand why oxide etching is inherently more selective in hollow cathodes than in diode reactors. In addition the relationship between ion bombardment and target areas, familiar in the diode situation, is not yet clarified for hollow cathodes. Further work in these areas will doubtless clarify the interrelationships between these enhanced discharge systems, and their simple diode precursor. However, confined rf discharges, and especially those incorporating hollow cathodes, permit high deposition rates to be maintained at low pressures, with low target voltages and low rf input power densities. This capability, combined with competitive deposition as in the case of an etch process, or competitive etching as in the case of a deposition process, gives a wide degree of control over the shapes that can be formed in electronic substrate materials.

12.7 REFERENCES

1. G. C. Schwartz, L. B. Rothman, and T. J. Schopen, J. Electrochem Soc.. 126: 464 (1979).

2. C. M. Horwitz, J. Vac. Sci. Technol. A1: 1795 (1983).

3. L. M. Ephrath and D. J. Di Maria, Solid State Technol. 24: 184 (April 1981).

4. S. W. Pang, C. M. Horwitz, D. D. Rathman, S.M. Cabral, D. J. Silversmith and R. W. Mountain, in Proc. 4th ECS symp. on Plasma Processing, (Electrochemical Society, Pennington, NJ, 1983) 83-10: pp.84 - 92.

5. F.H.M. Sanderson and J. Dielman, 3rd Int'l. Symp. on Dry Etching and Plasma Deposition, 26-29 Nov. 1985; Le Vide - Les Couches Minces 229: 45, (1985).

6. E. J. Egerton, A. Nef, W. Millikin, W. Cook, and D. Baril, Solid State Technol. 25: 84, (1982).

7. I.Hussla, K.Enke, H.Grunwald, G.Lorenz and H.Stoll, J. Phys.D: Appl. Phys. 20: 889 (1987).

8. Y. Hazuki and T. Moriya, in Proc. 1985 Symp. on VLSI Technol Kobe, Japan, IEEE Cat. No. 85 CH2125-3 (IEEE, NJ, 1985) pp. 20-23.

9. H. Okabayashi, in Proc.1984 Symp.on VLSI Technol, San Diego, USA, IEEE Cat.No.84 CH2061-0 (IEEE, NJ, 1984) pp 20-23.

10. C.J. Mullins, Microelectron. Manufact. Test. 9: 1, (1986).

11. G. O. Fior, L. N. Giffen, and W. W. Palmer, Solid State Technol. 31: 109 (1988).

12. J. J. Cuomo and S. M. Rossnagel, J. Vac. Sci. Technol. A4: 393 (1986).

13. Y. S. Kuo, R. F. Bunshah, and D. Okrent, J. Vac. Sci. Technol., A4: 397 (1986).

14. K. E. Davies and C. M. Horwitz, "Diode and Hollow Cathode Etching in CF_4 ", submitted to J. Vac. Sci. Technol. (1988).

15. C. M. Horwitz, "Silicon Deposition in Diode and Hollow-Cathode Systems", submitted to J. Vac. Sci. Technol. (1988).

16. C. M. Horwitz, J. Vac. Sci. Technol. A1: 60 (1983).

17. M. E. Pillow, Spectrochim. Acta 36: 821 (1981).

18. J. S. Chang, Solid State Technol. 27: 214 (1984).

19. M. Gross and C. M. Horwitz, "Modelling of Sloped Sidewalls Formed by Simultaneous Etching and Deposition", (1988).

20. C. M. Horwitz, Appl. Phys. Lett, 44: 1041, (1984).

21. C. M. Horwitz, S. Boronkay, M. Gross and K. E. Davies, J. Vac. Sci. Technol. A6: 1837 (1988).

22. C. M. Horwitz, J. Vac. Sci. Technol. B3: 419 (1985).

23. L.M. Ephrath, J.Electrochem. Soc. 126: 1419 (1979).

24. L. M. Ephrath and E. J. Petrillo, in Proc. 3rd. ECS Symp. on Plasma Processing, (Electrochemical Society, Pennington, NJ,. 1982) 82-6: pp. 217-233.

25. C. M. Horwitz, Appl. Phys. Lett. 43: 977 (1983).

26. C. M. Horwitz and J. Melngailis, J. Vac. Sci. Technol. B1: 1408 (1981)

27. S. W. Pang, Solid State Technol. 27: 249, (1984); S. W. Pang, D. D. Rathman, D. J. Silversmith, R. W. Mountain, and P. D. De Graff, J. Appl. Phys. 54: 3272, (1983).

28. H. -O. Blom, H. Norstrom, M. Ostling, P. Wiklund, R.Buchta, and C. S. Peterson, J. Vac. Sci. Technol. A4: 752, (1986).

29. S. J. Fonash, Solid State Technol, 28: 201, (1985).

30. G. S. Oehrlein, J. G. Clabes, and P. Spirito, J. Electrochem. Soc. 133: 1022 (1986).

31. T. Watanabe and Y. Yoshida, Solid State Technol. 27: 263 (1984).

32. D. J. DiMaria, L.M. Ephrath, and D. R. Young, J. Appl. Phys. 50: 4015, (1979).

33. S. Narayanan, M. Gross, C. M. Horwitz, and M. A. Green, "High Efficiency Processing/Texturing of Polycrystalline Solar Cells", B-Ip-9 in 3rd.   Int'l. Photovoltaic Science and Eng. Conf (PVSEC-3), Tokyo, Nov. 3-6, 1987.

34. M. Gross, private communication, 1986.

35. R. A. Gdula, Ext. Abstr. 608, Fall Mtg.of Electrochem. Soc., Los Angeles, October 14-19, 1979, pp.1524-1526.

36. C. M. Horwitz, IEEE Trans. on Electron Devices, ED-28: 1320 (1981).

37. K.Hirobe, K.Kawamura, and K. Nojiri, J. Vac. Sci. Technol. B5: 594 (1987).

38. G. K. Herb, D. J. Reiger, K. Shields, Solid State Technol. 30: 109 (1987).

39. J. E. Yehoda, B. Yang, K. Vedam, and R. Messier, J. Vac. Sci. Technol., A6: 1631 (1988); K.-H. Müller, Phys. Rev. B35: 7906 (1987).

40. K.-H. Müller, J. Vac. Sci. Technol. A3: 2089 (1985); J. Appl. Phys. 59: 2803 (1986); J. Appl. Phys. 62: 1796 (1987).

41. H. Windischmann, J. Appl. Phys. 62: 1800 (1987).

42. C. Y. Ting, V. J. Vivalda, and H. G. Schaefer, J. Vac. Sci. Technol. 15: 1105 (1978).

43. J. M. Heddleson, M. W. Horn, S. J. Fonash, and D. C. Nguyen, J. Vac. Sci. Technol. B6: 280, 1988.

Part V
Related Plasma Processes

13

Ion Plating

Donald M. Mattox

13.1 INTRODUCTION

"Ion Plating" is a generic term applied to atomistic film deposition processes in which the substrate surface and the growing film are subjected to a flux of energetic bombarding particles sufficient to cause changes in the film formation process and the properties of the deposited film. This broad definition does not specify the source of the depositing film particles, the source of bombarding particles nor the environment in which the deposition takes place. The principal criterion is that energetic particle bombardment is used to modify the film formation process and film properties (1-4).

Most recently the term ion plating has been applied to processes where the surface to be coated is in contact with a plasma and the term "Ion Assisted Deposition" (IAD) or Ion Beam Enhanced Deposition (IBED) is used where the substrate is bombarded by an energetic ion beam in a vacuum environment during deposition (e.g. 5,6). There are several other modifying terms which are sometimes used with ion plating such as: "sputter ion plating" and "chemical ion plating" which specify the origin of the depositing species (sputtered material or chemical vapor precursor gases respectively) and "reactive ion plating" used for the deposition of films of compound materials.

Generally, the energetic particles used for bombarding surfaces and growing films are gaseous ions and arise from: i) biasing (dc or rf) a surface in contact with a plasma so that it is bombarded by ions from the plasma, ii) extraction of ions from a confined plasma and accelerating them to a high energy through a grid system into a vacuum environment (ion beam) (7) or iii) reflected high energy neutrals which arise from ion bombarding a surface in a low pressure environment (8,9) such that the reflected neutrals are not thermalized by collisions in the gas phase.

The energetic particles may also be of a condensible species and arise from: i) sources such as are used for isotope separation (10-13), i) acceleration of negative ions from a negatively biased compound or alloy sputtering target (14), i) ions from vacuum or plasma arcs (15) or i) special ion sources (16). In this chapter we will be primarily concerned with the coating of a substrate surface in contact with a plasma where the ion are extracted from the plasma using a DC or RF bias on the substrate or substrate fixturing. However energetic particle bombardment from any source will have the same effects.

13.2 PROCESSING PLASMA ENVIRONMENT

Plasmas are gaseous media which contain enough ions and electrons to be electrically conductive (e.g. 17). Energy is introduced into the plasma by the acceleration of electrons in a DC, RF or microwave electric field. These energetic electrons then fragment, excite and ionize atoms or molecules by collisions. A processing plasma is a plasma that is used in materials processing (18). In many if not most cases the processing plasma is a weakly ionized plasma such that there are many more neutral particles than ions in the gas phase and there is a large number of radical species compared to ions when a molecular gas is used. In a processing system the local plasma densities and properties may vary significantly due to electrode configurations, presence of fixturing and other geometrical factors.

In film processing utilizing plasmas the depositing (condensible) species usually traverse the plasma before condensing on the substrate. In doing so some of the species may be fragmented and/or ionized in the plasma. In addition to ionization and excitation by electron-atom collisions the atoms/molecules may be excited or ionized by collision with an excited metastable species in the plasma (Penning ionization) (i.e. Cu by Ar*). However in the usual ion plating configuration (low density - weakly ionized plasma) little ionization of the condensible species is to be expected (19).

For reactive deposition processes the gaseous reactive species may be "activated" in the plasma to become more chemically reactive. This activation may be in the form of fragmentation (formation of radicals), ionization, atomic excitation and/or increased kinetic energy ("temperature"). Plasma activation of a reactive species is also used in the "Activated Reactive Evaporation" deposition process (20) and Plasma Enhanced Chemical Vapor Deposition (PECVD) (21). A plasma may also be used to form radical species which polymerize to form polymer films of organic and inorganic materials.

In film deposition processes the substrate may be in contact with the plasma in the region of plasma generation (plasma chamber) or may be exposed to the plasma in a "downstream" location. Figure 1 shows some configurations that allow a substrate to be bombarded from a plasma. Figure 2 shows a simple ion plating system using a DC diode gas discharge and a thermal vaporization source (3). Figure 3 shows an ion plating system utilizing a dc diode discharge and a sputtering source (Sputter Ion Plating - SIP) (22). This system allows almost complete coverage of the part except for the point of suspension and high voltage contact.

Plasma enhancement techniques may also be used to locally increase the plasma density. This plasma enhancement may be accomplished by using local RF fields (23), thermo-electron emitting surfaces (24), hollow cathode electron emitters (25-27), deflection of secondary electrons in e-beam evaporation, localized higher gas pressure, etc.

The plasma density may also be increased by the use of magnetic fields which cause the electrons to spiral around the magnetic field lines thus increasing their path length (as in, for example, magnetron configurations) (28). Some of the most dense plasma sources have been developed for the magnetic fusion community (29). Many of these sources use RF power input or thermo-electron emitting surfaces (30) along with confining magnetic fields.

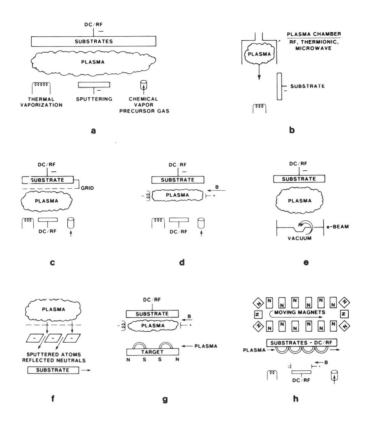

Figure 1: Some configurations for bombarding a surface from a plasma by using accelerated or reflected high energy particles. a) diode, b) "downstream configuration", c) grid to allow bombardment of complex surfaces or insulators, d) thermo-electron sustained plasma with magnetic enhancement/confinement, e) e-beam evaporation with a differentially pumped vacuum chamber, f) utilizing reflected high energy neutrals and sputtering, g) magnetron sputtering source and h) moving magnetron plasma to allow uniform bombardment of substrate surface.

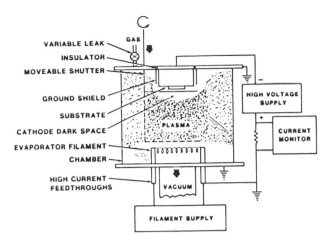

Figure 2: An ion plating configuration using a DC diode discharge and a thermal vaporization source (3)

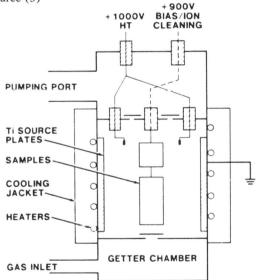

Figure 3: An ion plating configuration using a DC diode discharge and a sputtering vapor source at ground potential (SIP)(22).

13.3 BOMBARDMENT EFFECTS ON SURFACES AND FILM GROWTH

The physical effects of energetic particle bombardment on surfaces and depositing film material are very dependent on the mass, flux, angle of incidence, and energy of the bombarding particles and the atomic mass of the target material. Also of importance is the flux of non-energetic particles i.e. depositing or adsorbing species. In many cases these fluxes are not determined or controlled except by the deposition parameters.

Figure 4 depicts the effects on the surface and the subsurface region of bombardment by energetic species. Surface effects include: 1) desorption of weakly bonded surface species, 2) ejection of secondary electrons, 3) reflection of the energetic species as high energy neutrals, 4) sputter ejection (physical sputtering) of surface atoms by momentum transfer through collision cascades, 5) redeposition of sputtered species by collisions in the gas phase or by ionization and acceleration back to the surface and by "forward sputter deposition" due to the ejection angle on a rough surface, 6) enhanced surface mobilities of atoms on the surface and 7) enhanced chemical reaction of adsorbed species on the surface to produce a modified surface (e.g. plasma anodization) or volatile species ("reactive ion etching" {RIE} or "reactive plasma cleaning") or, in the case of depositing species, "reactive deposition" .

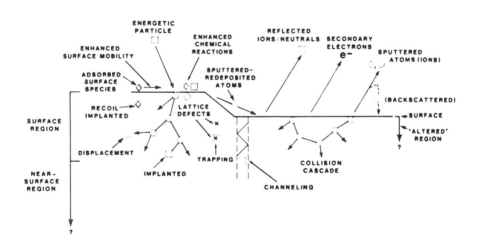

Figure 4: Schematic depiction of the energetic particle bombardment effects on surfaces and growing films. See text for discussion.

In the subsurface region: 1) the impinging particles may be physically implanted, 2) the collision cascades cause displacement of lattice atoms and the creation of lattice defects, 3) surface species may be "recoil implanted" into the subsurface lattice, 4) mobile species may be trapped at lattice defects and 5) much of the particle kinetic energy is converted into heat (31,32). Lattice channeling processes can carry these effects deeply into the surface.

The desorption of weakly bound surface species by bombardment is important to plasma cleaning and may be used to reduce the incorporated contaminants in deposited films (33). The desorption may also be useful in desorbing unreacted species in reactive deposition processes giving rise to more stoichiometric and chemically stable deposits (34).

In the case of dc diode discharges, secondary electrons are accelerated away from the cathode and give rise to ionization in the plasma and to electron bombardment of surfaces in the system. This electron heating may be detrimental to thin film processing and may be reduced or eliminated using magnetron configurations. In addition to being necessary for sustaining the discharge in dc diode discharges, secondary electrons may also assist in the chemical reaction of reactive species on the bombarded surface.

When surfaces are subjected to bombardment by high energy ions a portion of the particles are reflected as high energy neutrals (8,9). If these high energy particles are not thermalized by collisions in the gas phase (35,36) they bombard the growing surface of a depositing material giving rise to such film properties as residual compressive stress (e.g. 37,38).

The physical sputtering of a surface may lead to surface texturing which give a roughened surface (e.g. 39-41). Preferential crystallographic sputtering will result in some crystalline orientations being etched at a faster rate than are others giving rise to "sputter etching". Preferential atomic sputtering can cause changes in the chemical composition of alloy and compound surfaces (42,43).

Energetic particle bombardment of surfaces can also introduce lattice defects into surfaces (44-48). Defect densities of 10-20 atomic percent have been measured using desorption techniques. On semiconductor surfaces these defects may act as electron traps when an interface is formed (49). In semiconductor device fabrication these types of defects must be avoided during surface cleaning and film formation (50).

The heating and formation of lattice defects in the near-surface region increases diffusion and chemical reaction in that region. The implantation of a mobile bombarding species into a surface increases the chemical potential between the surface and the bulk thereby increasing the diffusion rate of mobile species (e.g. hydrogen) into the bulk of the material.

When a reactive species is present, concurrent energetic particle bombardment enhances chemical reactions with the surface. The nature of this enhancement is poorly understood since heating, physical collisions, molecular fragmentation of adsorbed species and the presence of energetic electrons (secondary electrons) may each play a role. The existence of bombardment enhanced chemical reactions is well established in etching studies where the reaction products are volatile (51-53), in reactive plasma cleaning (54) and the same effects are found in reactive film deposition processes where the reaction products are non-volatile (55).

13.4 VAPORIZATION SOURCES FOR ION PLATING

Vaporization sources for ion plating can be of any form including: 1) thermal evaporation/sublimation, 2) physical sputtering, 3) molecular dissociation of a chemical precursor gas or 4) vacuum and plasma arcs.

Thermal vaporization (evaporation or sublimation) can be from resistively heated sources for materials which have a high vapor pressure at temperatures of about 1400°C and below. High current - low voltage electron bombardment may also be used to vaporize these materials (56) and has the added advantage that the dense electron cloud can ionize a portion of the vaporized material which can then be accelerated ("film ions")(57-62). High energy focussed electron beams can be used to vaporize refractory materials into a plasma; however, these sources generally require a differentially pumped vacuum system so that the high voltage (cathodic) thermo-electron emitter can be isolated from the plasma (3).

Sputtering sources can be fabricated from all of the conventional sputtering configurations (63). In the magnetron sputtering configurations it may be desirable to have an auxiliary plasma near the substrate to provide ions for bombardment in that region.

Chemical precursor gases may be introduced through a plasma chamber (64,65) or directly into the plasma (66-68). Ionization of the fragments allow them to be accelerated to the substrate where their properties are dependent on the ionization and acceleration conditions. This is a means for making "i-C" and "i-BN" materials (69).

Vacuum arcs utilize material arc-vaporized from a solid cathode or from a molten anode to supply the ions for sustaining the plasma (no supporting gas). In these types of arcs there is a high ionization efficiencies (15, 70-72). The addition of a gas to the plasma environment allows reactive deposition (73).

13.5 BOMBARDMENT EFFECTS ON FILM PROPERTIES

Concurrent energetic particle bombardment during atomistic film deposition may modify many film properties (e.g. 74-77). The amount of modification will depend on both the mass, energy and flux of the bombarding species and the mass and flux of depositing species. In the case of reactive deposition the availability of "activated" species and the effect of adsorbed surface species may also be important. The following are some of the film properties that can be modified by controlled concurrent bombardment during deposition.

13.5.1 Film Adhesion

The adhesion of a deposited film to a surface depends on the deformation and fracture modes associated with the failure (78,79). Energetic particle bombardment prior to and during the initial stages of film formation may enhance adhesion by: removing contaminant layers, changing the surface chemistry, generating a microscopically rough surface, increasing the nucleation density by forming nucleation sites (defects, implanted and recoil implanted species), increasing the surface mobility of adatoms and by creating lattice defects. Introducing thermal energy directly into the surface region promotes reaction and diffusion. These effects will also improve surface coverage and thus decrease the number of interfacial voids which result in easy fracture and poor adhesion. Film adhesion may be degraded by the diffusion and precipitation of gaseous species at the interface. The adhesion may also be degraded by the residual film stress due either to differences in the coefficient of thermal expansion of the film and substrate material in high temperature processing or the residual film growth stresses developed in low temperature processing.

13.5.2 Film Morphology, Density

Physical sputtering and redeposition, increased nucleation density and increased surface mobilities of adatoms on the surface under bombardment conditions may be important in disrupting the columnar microstructure that develops during low temperature atomistic deposition processes (80-85, also Chap. 22). Figure 5 shows the fracture cross-section and surface morphology of RF sputter deposited chromium films at zero bias and with a -500 volt bias during deposition. Note that the bombardment completely disrupted the columnar microstructure. Bombardment-related effects may also improve the surface coverage and decrease the pinhole porosity in a deposited film. This increased film density is reflected in film properties such as: better corrosion resistance, lower chemical etch rate, higher hardness, lower electrical resistivity (metals) and the increased index of refraction (optical coatings). However it has been found that if the bombarding species is too energetic and the substrate temperature is low, high gas incorporation gives rise to voids (e.g. 86). Some investigators have used the parameter "resputtering rate" (deposition rate with and without an applied bias) as the parameter for disruption of the columnar morphology: however this parameter does not take into consideration the backscattering from the gas phase which will be greater the higher the gas pressure and so must be used with caution.

Figure 5: Fracture cross-section (bottom) and surface morphology (top) of a thick RF sputter deposited chromium deposit (80). A) without bias (no bombardment) and B) with concurrent bombardment (-500 v bias on the substrate).

13.5.3 Residual Film Stress

Invariably atomistically deposited films have residual growth stresses which may be tensile or compressive in nature and may approach the yield or fracture strength of the materials involved. The origin of these stresses is poorly understood although several phenomenological models have been proposed (87). Generally, vacuum deposited films and sputter-deposited films prepared at high pressures have tensile stresses which may be anisotropic with off-normal angle of incidence depositions (88). In low pressure sputter deposition and ion plating, energetic particle bombardment may give rise to high compressive film stresses due to the recoil implantation of surface atoms (38, 89-92). Studies of deposited films with concurrent bombardment have shown that the conversion of tensile to compressive stress is very dependent on the ratio of bombarding species to depositing species (93,94). In plasma processing the residual film stress may be very sensitive to the substrate bias (80) and gas pressure (38) during deposition in a plasma environment.

Figure 6 shows the residual stress and gas content in sputter deposited chromium films as a function of substrate bias. Where rather thick films of high modulus materials are involved these stresses must be controlled or spontaneous failure (adhesion, cracking, blistering) will occur (79).

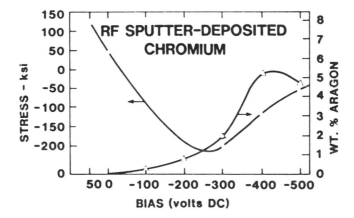

Figure 6: Residual stress and gas content of an RF sputter deposited chromium deposit as a function of substrate bias during RF sputter deposition (80)

The lattice strain associated with the film stress represents stored energy and this energy along with a high concentration of lattice defects may lead to: 1) lowering of the recrystallization temperature in crystalline materials, 2) a lowered strain point in glassy materials, 3) a high chemical etch rate, 4) electromigration problems, 5) void growth in metallization lines by creep and 6) other such mass transport effects.

13.5.4 Crystallographic Orientation

Under proper bombardment conditions the crystallographic orientation of the deposited material is developed such that the more dense crystallographic planes are parallel to the bombarding direction (95,96). This effect is attributed to the channeling of the bombarding species into the film thus decreasing the sputtering rate under this orientation. Under more energetic bombardment condition however the crystallographic orientation is disrupted due to the formation and consolidation of defects.

13.5.5 Gas Incorporation

When a depositing film is bombarded during deposition by energetic gaseous particles the incorporated gas content is dependent on the particle energy, substrate temperature, film material and bombarding species. Generally low mass bombarding particles are more easily incorporated than are large mass particles. The gas incorporation increases with energy of the bombarding species to the point which eating causes gas desorption. Under some conditions very high concentrations of normally insoluble gas may be incorporated into the depositing film by concurrent bombardment during deposition. An example is the incorporation of 20-40 atomic percent hydrogen and helium in gold (97,98) and the incorporation of krypton in amorphous metals films (99). This incorporation is probably due, in part, to the high lattice defect concentration in the bombarded material which traps mobile species (45-48). At very high gas contents the gas may precipitate into voids. Gas incorporation can be minimized by using low energy bombarding species (i.e. less than 100 ev), an elevated substrate temperature during deposition (300-400 0C) and/or using higher atomic mass bombarding species (Kr, Xe).

13.5.6 Surface Coverage

The macroscopic and microscopic surface coverage of a deposited film on a substrate surface may be improved by the use of concurrent bombardment during film deposition. The ability to cover complex geometries depends mostly on scattering of the depositing material in the gas phase (36, 101, 102). If gas scattering is extensive then gas phase nucleation will occur and the resulting deposit will be poorly consolidated. If a plasma is present and the substrate is at a negative potential the gas phase nucleated materials will become negatively charged and repelled from the substrate. In addition, bombardment will heat, densify and consolidate the deposited material into a high quality film over the whole surface. On a more microscopic scale, sputtering and redeposition of the depositing film material will lead to better coverage on micron and submicron sized features (86, 103-105) and reduced pinhole formation. On the atomic scale the increased surface mobility, increased nucleation density and erosion/redeposition of the depositing adatoms will disrupt the columnar microstructure and eliminate the porosity along the column boundaries. In total, the use of gas scattering, along with concurrent bombardment, increases the surface covering ability and decreases the microscopic porosity of the deposited film material as long as gas incorporation does not generate voids.

13.5.7 Other Properties

Many other properties of the film material may be changed and improved by bombardment during deposition. They include: 1) electrical resistivity of metal films, 2) hardness of hard-coatings, 3) chemical etch rate, 4) corrosion resistance, 5) pinhole density, 6) index of refraction of dielectric coatings, 7) color of TiN films, etc.

13.6 PROBLEM AREAS

A major problem area in using plasmas for thin film deposition is how to obtain a uniform plasma density over a surface so that uniform bombardment and reactive gas availability can be attained. Plasma non-uniformity can arise from a number of sources including: 1) geometrical arrangement of power input electrodes and substrate fixturing, 2) substrate geometry, 3) the presence of surfaces that allow recombination and loss of species in the nearby plasma and 4) in the case of reactive deposition, reactive surfaces that deplete the supply of reactive gas at the growing film surface.

As a general rule the best plasma system design is one that is geometrically symmetric. The SIP system shown in Fig. 3 is a good example of this approach. However, in many instances a symmetric geometry is difficult to attain. The use of magnetron configurations is an example. The use of a magnetic field to confine electrons and increase the local plasma density in one region leads to a decrease in plasma density in other regions. Figure 7 shows an example of how two independently sustained plasmas may be used to allow magnetron sputtering of a source and the use of a hot filament sustained plasma in the vicinity of the substrate to provide a plasma from which ions can be extracted to bombard the substrate and film.

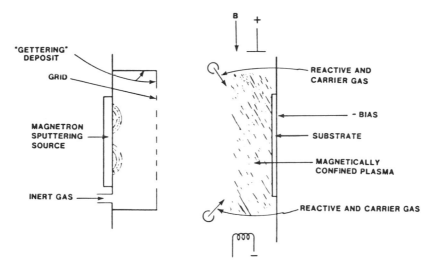

Figure 7: Ion Plating system utilizing a magnetron sputtering source and an auxiliary plasma for supplying the ions for bombarding the substrate and depositing film.

If the part has a very complex configuration the electric field around points and corners focus the bombardment giving high erosion rates and heating in these areas. A thin region gives poor thermal conductance and results in heating. Holes and reentrant features give low field gradients. In these regions heating will be high and erosion will be low giving poor cleaning and allowing reaction with contamination. Excessive heating can sometimes be alleviated by "pulse processing' where the substrate bias is periodically turned on and off.

In some cases high transparency grids at the substrate potential may be used to surround the substrate to give a more uniform bombardment over a complex surface. This is the basis of the equipment used in the "Ion Vapor Deposition (IVD)" process (106) and in the "barrel-plating" ion plating configuration (107). Figure 8 shows a barrel-plating configuration used to coat small parts which are tumbled in the rotating cage. A grid configuration may also be useful in coating dielectric materials where charge buildup may be a problem or in coating moving substrates where electrical contact may be a problem.

ION PLATING

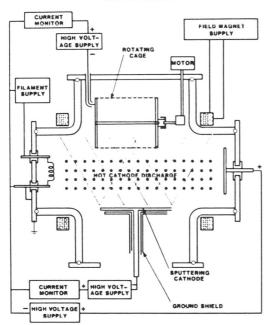

Figure 8: Ion plating "barrel plating" configuration using a rotating cage to contain the parts (106).

"BARREL PLATING" CONFIGURATION

Generally the equipment used for ion plating is the same as that used for sputter deposition except that the substrate is the sputtering target and another vaporization (deposition) source has been added. Because of the high "throwing power" conditions often used in ion plating systems the insulators of electrical feedthroughs must be carefully shielded from deposition or else they will become shorted. These conditions may also lead to gas phase nucleation of particles which will deposit on the system walls (called "black sooty crap" - BSC by the operators). This material has a very low density and if the material is pyrophoric (Ti, Zr etc) the BSC may ignite if disturbed in air. In such a case system cleanup should be done wet.

As with any plasma process, wall effects enhance the desorption of contaminats. This contamination, when introduced into the plasma, is "activated" and can be an important source of contamination which must be controlled.

When using plasmas and bombardment effects there are many processing variables that are unknown. Processing unknowns include: 1) the portion of the substrate current that is due to secondary electron emission , 2) the flux and energy spectrum of the ions and electrons and 3) the flux, adsorption and surface coverage of the neutral gaseous species. Generally no attempt is made to determine these process variables during the processing but rather they are controlled by controlling other processing variables such as: 1) system geometry, 2) deposition rate, 3) gas pressure, 4) gas composition, 5) gas flow rate(s), 6) substrate and system temperatures, 7) contaminants in the plasma and 8) substrate power input per unit area (voltage and current).

13.7 APPLICATIONS

There are many applications of the ion plating process some of which are:

- Obtaining good adhesion - Ag on steel for mirrors, soft metals on surfaces for space lubrication, Ag on Be for diffusion bonding, Cu & Au on Ta and Mo for subsequent brazing, Cu-on- ceramic metallization

- Metallization - Al, Ag, Au on plastics and semiconductors

- Good surface coverage on complex surfaces - TiN on tool bits, injection molds and jewelry items; semiconductor metallization

- Good reaction and stoichiometry - TiN on tool bits, injection molds (hardness, wear); jewelry items (TiN - color)

- Corrosion protection - Al on U, steel & Ti (galvanic); C and Ta on biological implants

- Abrasion resistance - MgF_2 coatings on plastics, i-c

- Deposition of diffusion barriers - HfN & TiN on semiconductor devices

13.8 SUMMARY

Like any deposition technique the ion plating process has its advantages and disadvantages. They include:

- Advantages:
  - Excellent surface covering ability (throwing power) under the proper conditions
  - Ability to have an in-situ cleaning of the substrate surface
  - Ability to obtain good adhesion in many otherwise difficult systems
  - A great deal of flexibility in tailoring film properties by controlling bombardment conditions
  - Equipment requirements are roughly equivalent to those of sputter deposition
- Disadvantages:
  - Many processing parameter that must be controlled
  - Processing may be very dependent on substrate geometry and fixturing

- Obtaining uniform bombardment and reactive species availability over a complex surface may be difficult

- Gas incorporation may be excessive

- High compressive stresses may be generated in the bombarded film

- Substrate heating may be excessive

- Contaminats are desorbed from surfaces and "activated" in the discharge and can contaminate deposited material

In order to achieve the desired film property modification there must be an appreciable ratio of bombarding particles to depositing species. This ratio must be much higher to disrupt the columnar morphology than is necessary to change the film stress. The necessary bombardment conditions for each application are usually determined empirically and controlled by controlling the processing geometry and parameters. A typical condition to control film stress might be a substrate bias of -50 to -100 volts DC, a current density of $1mA/cm^2$ and a deposition rate of 10 nanometers per second. For columnar structure disruption and maximum covering ability a "resputtering rate" might be as high as 30%.

High voltage pulsing of substrates immersed in plasmas is being studied as a way to modify surfaces by ion bombardment (108). This technique could be used in ion plating to allow periodic bombardment of the depositing film material. The ion plating process provides an alternative film deposition technique which should be evaluated for specific applications.

13.9 REFERENCES

1. D.M. Mattox US Patent 3,329,601 (1974).

2. D.M. Mattox, J. Electrochemical Technol. 2: 295 (1964).

3. D.M. Mattox J. Vac. Sci. Technol. 10: 47 (1973).

4. N.A.G. Ahmed, Ion Plating Technology - Developments and Applications, John Wiley (1987).

5. P.J. Martin, R.P. Netterfield, W.G. Sainty and C.G. Pacey, J. Vac. Sci. Technol. A2: 341 (1984).

6. J.M.E. Harper, J.J. Cuomo and H.R. Kaufman, J. Vac. Sci. Technol. 21: 737 (1982).

7. H.R. Kaufman, J. Vac. Sci. Technol. 15: 272 (1978).

8. W.W.Y. Lee and D. Oblas, J. Appl. Phys. 46: 1728 (1975).

9. H.D. Hagstrum, in Inelastic Ion Surface Collisions edited by N.H. Tolk, J.C. Tully, W. Heiland and C.W. White, Academic Press, pp. 1-25 (1977).

10. L. Valyi, Atom and Ion Sources, John Wiley (1977).

11. M.R. Shubaly, Nucl. Instrum. Meth. Phys. Res. B26: 195 (1987).

12. T.E. Romesser, V. Vanek, J.Tang, D. Dixon, J. Bayless, M. Musetto, C. Strawitch and L. Higgins "A Large Area Plasma Source" IEEE Conf Record 1983 IEEE International Conference of Plasma Science 83CH1847-3, US Doe Contract No. DE-ACO3-77ET33006.

13. V.S. Letokhov, Sov. At. Energy. (Translation) 62:(4) 297 (1987).

14. J.J. Cuomo, R.J. Gambino, J.M.E. Harper, J.D. Kuptsis and J.C. Webber, J. Vac. Sci. Technol. 15: 281 (1978).

15. R.L. Boxman and S. Goldsmith, Surf. Coat. Technol. 33: 153 (1987).

16. John Melngailis, "Focussed Ion Beam Technology and Applications" J. Vac. Sci. Technol. B5: 469 (1987).

17. Brian Chapman Glow Discharge Processes, John Wiley (1980).

18. John A Thornton, Thin Solid Films 107: 3 (1983).

19. F. Plas, J. Guille and J. Machet, Le Vide, Suppl. 196: 45 (1979)

20. R.F.Bunshah: please see Chap. 18, this volume.

21. S. Veprek, Thin Solid Films 130: 135 (1985).

22. M.H. Jacobs, Surf. Coat. Technol. 29: 221 (1986).

23. Yoichi Murayama and Toshihiro Takao, Thin Solid Films 40: 309 (1977).

24. D.M. Goebel, Y. Hirooka and T.A. Sketchley, Rev. Sci. Instrum. 56: 1717 (1985).

25. Harold R. Kaufman and Raymond S. Robinson, J. Vac. Sci. Technol. A3: 1774 (1985).

26. Yu Shen Kuo, R.F. Bunshah and D. Okrent, J. Vac. Sci. Technol. A4: 397 (1986).

27. S. Komiya and K. Tsuruoka, J. Vac. Sci. Technol. 12: 589 (1975).

28. J.A. Thornton, Surf. Eng. 2: 283 (1986).

29. A. Theodore Forrester, Large Area Ion Beams: Fundamentals of Generation and Propagation, John Wiley, (1988).

30. D.M. Goebel, G. Campbell and R.W. Conn, J. Nucl. Mat. 121: 277 (1984).

31. A. Mathews and D.T. Gethin, Thin Solid Films 117: 261 (1987).

32. A. Mathews, Vacuum 32: 311 (1982).

33. L.I. Maissel and P.M. Schaible, J. Appl. Phys. 36: 237 (1965).

34. Michael H. Jacobs "Process and Engineering Benefits of Sputter Ion Plated Titanium Nitride Coatings" in Surface Modification and Coatings, edited by Richard D. Sisson, Jr. ASM Conference Proceedings, 291 (1986).

35. R.E. Somekh, J. Vac. Sci. Technol. A2: 1285 (1984).

36. A. Bessaudou, J. Machet and C. Weissmantel, Thin Solid Films 149: 225 (1987).

37. J.A. Thornton and D.W. Hoffman, J. Vac. Sci. Technol. A3: 576 (1985).

38. R.E. Cuthrell, D.M. Mattox, C.R. Peeples, P.L. Dreike and K.P. Lamppa, J. Vac. Sci. Technol. A6: 2914 (1988).

39. R.S. Berg and G.J. Kominiak, J. Vac. Sci. Technol. 13: 403 (1976).

40. Zbigniew W. Kowalski, J. Mat. Sci. Lett. 6: 69 (1987).

41. G.K. Wehner, J. Vac. Sci. Technol. A3: 1821 (1985).

42. G. Betz, <u>Surf. Sci.</u> 92: 283 (1980).

43. J.B. Malherbe, S. Hofmann and J.M. Sanz, <u>Appl. Surf. Sci.</u> 27: 355 (1986).

44. R. Miranda and J.M. Rojo, <u>Vacuum</u> 34: 1069 (1984).,

45. D. Edwards, Jr and E.V. Kornelsen, <u>Rad. Effects</u> 26: 155 (1975).

46. E.V. Kornelsen, <u>Rad. Effects</u> 13: 227 (1972).

47. E.V. Kornelsen and A.A. Van Gorkum, <u>Rad. Effects</u> 42: 93 (1979).

48. A.A. Van Gorkum and E.V. Kornelsen, <u>Rad, Effects</u> 42: 113 (1979).

49. L.J. Brillson, <u>Thin Solid Films</u> 89: 461 (1982).

50. J.L. Vossen, J.H. Thomas III, J.-S. Maa and J.J. O'Neill, <u>J. Vac. Sci. Technol.</u> A2: 212 (1984).

51. M.W. Geis, G.A. Lincoln, N. Efremow and W.J. Piacentini, <u>J. Vac. Sci. Technol.</u> 19: 1390 (1981).

52. Harold F. Winters, J.W. Coburn and T.J. Chuang, <u>J. Vac. Sci. Technol.</u> B1: 469 (1983).

53. J.W. Coburn and H.F. Winters, <u>Nucl. Instrum. Met. Phys. Res.</u> B27: 243 (1987).

54. G.J. Kominiak and D.M. Mattox, <u>Thin Solid Films</u> 40: 141 (1977).

55. J.M.E. Harper, J.J. Cuomo and H.T.G. Henzell, <u>Appl. Phys. Lett.</u> 36: 56 (1980) also <u>Appl. Phys. Lett.</u> 37: 540 (1980).

56. S. Komiya and K. Tsuruoka, <u>J. Vac. Sci. Technol.</u> 12: 589 (1975).

57. D.T. Larson and H.L. Draper, <u>Thin Solid Films</u> 107: 327 (1983).

58. G. Mah, P.S. Mcleod and D.G. Williams, <u>J. Vac. Sci. Technol.</u> 11: 663 (1974).

59. P.S. Mcleod and G. Mah, <u>J. Vac. Sci. Technol.</u> 11: 119 (1974).

60. Carl Schalansky, Z.A. Munir and D.L. Walmsley, <u>J. Mat. Sci.</u> 22: 745 (1987).

61. Hans K. Pulker, US Patent 4,254,159 (Mar 3, 1981)

62. Helmut Kaufmann, US Patent 4,346,123 (Aug 24, 1982)

63. Please see Chaps 3 and 4.

64. Toshio Mori and Yoshikatsu Namba, <u>J. Vac. Sci. Technol.</u> A1: 23 (1983).

65. S. Shanfield and R. Wolfson, <u>J. Vac. Sci. Technol.</u> A1: 323 (1983).

66. D.M. Mattox, US Patent 3,329,601 (July 1974)

67. Robert Culbertson, US Patent 3,604,970 (1971)

68. K.P. Paude and A.C. Seabaugh, <u>J. Electrochem. Soc.</u> 131: 1357 (1984).

69. C. Weissmantel, "Preparation, Structure and Properties of Hard Coatings on the Basis of i-C and i-BN" Ch 4 in <u>Thin Films from Free Atoms and Particles,</u> edited by Kenneth J. Klabunde, Academic Press 1985

70. J.E. Daalder, <u>J. Phys. D: Appl. Phys.</u> 9: 2379 (1976).

71. R.L. Williamson, F.J. Zanner and W.A. Hareland " Monochromatic Imaging Studies of Low Pressure Arcs Burning on Molten Inconel 718 Alloy Electrodes During Vacuum Arc Remelting" Presented to the 9th International Vacuum Metallurgy Conference, San Diego CA April 11-15, 1988 and to be published in the proceedings.

72. F.J. Zanner and L.A. Bertrum, IEEE Trans on Plasma Science Vol PS-11: 223 (1983).

73. S. Boelens and H. Veltrop, Surf. Coat. Technol. 33: 63 (1987).

74. D.M. Mattox and G.J. Kominiak, J. Vac. Sci. Technol. 9: 528 (1972).

75. R.D. Bland, G.J. Kominiak and D.M. Mattox J. Vac. Sci. Technol. 11: 671 (1974).

76. G.J. Kominiak and D.M. Mattox, J. Electrochem. Soc. 120: 1535 (1973).

77. J.E. Harper, J.J. Cuomo, R.J. Gambino and H.R. Kaufman "Modification of thin film properties by ion bombardment during deposition" Ch. 4 in Ion Bombardment Modification of Surfaces - Fundamentals and Applications ed. by Orlando Aucello and Roger Kelly, Elsevier (1984).

78. D.M. Mattox, "Thin film adhesion and adhesive failure - A perspective" in Adhesion Measurement of Thin Films, Thick Films and Bulk Coatings ed. by K.L. Mittal ASTM STP 640, American Society for Testing and Materials, 54 (1978).

79. D.M. Mattox and R.E. Cuthrell, MRS Symposium Proceedings, Adhesion in Solids, Vol 119: ed. by D.M. Mattox, J.E.E. Baglin, R.E. Gottschall and C.D. Batich, 141 (1988).

80. R.D. Bland, G.J. Kominiak and D.M. Mattox, J. Vac. Sci. Technol. 11: 671 (1974).

81. J.A. Thornton, Thin Solid Films 40: 335 (1977).

82. J.A. Thornton, Annual Rev. Mat. Sci. 7: 239 (1977).

83. J.A. Thornton, J. Vac. Sci. Technol. A4: 3059 (1986).

84. R. Messier, A.P. Giri and R.A. Roy, J. Vac. Sci. Technol. A2: 500 (1984).

85. R. Meissier and J.E. Yehoda, J. Appl. Phys. 58: 3739 (1985).

86. J.K.G. Panitz, B.L. Draper and R.M. Curlee "Comparison of the Step Coverage of Aluminum Coatings Produced by Two sputter Magnetron Systems and a Dual Beam In System" Presented to the 1988 ICMC Conference and to be published in Thin Solid Films.

87. E. Klokholm and B.S. Berry, J. Electrochem. Soc. 115: 823 (1968).

88. J.D. Finnegan and R.W. Hoffman, Trans. 8th Nat. Vac. Symp. Pergamon Press, 935 (1961).

89. D.W. Hoffman and J.A. Thornton, J. Vac. Sci. Technol. 16: 134 (1979).

90. A.G. Blachman, J. Vac. Sci. Technol. 10: 299 (1973).

91. J.A. Thornton, J. Tabcock and D.W. Hoffman, Thin Solid Films 64: 111 (1979).

92. J.A. Thornton and D.W. Hoffman, J. Vac. Sci. Technol. 18: 203 (1981).

93. J.A. Thornton and D.W. Hoffman, J. Vac. Sci. Technol. A3: 576 (1985).

94. D.W. Hoffman and M.R. Gaerttner, J. Vac. Sci. Technol. 17: 425 (1980).

95. D.R. Brighton and G.K. Hubler, Nucl. Instrum. Meth. Phys. Res. B28: 527 (1987).

96. D. Dobrev, Thin Solid Films 92: 41 (1982).

97. E. Kay, F. Parmigiani and W. Parrish, J. Vac. Sci. Technol. A5: 44 (1987).

98. D.M. Mattox and G.J. Kominiak, J. Vac. Sci. Technol. 8: 194 (1971).

99. H.T. Weaver, J. Appl. Phys. 42: 2356 (1971).

100. J.J. Cuomo and R.J. Gambino, <u>J. Vac. Sci. Technol.</u> 14: 152 (1977).

101. K.S. Fancey and J. Beynon, <u>Vacuum</u> 34: 591 (1984).

102. K.S. Fancey and A. Mathews "Ion Plating Processes: Design Criteria and System Optimization" Presented to the 1988 ICMC and to be published in <u>Thin Solid Films.</u>

103. Y. Homma and S. Tsunekawa, <u>J. Electrochem. Soc.</u> 132: 1466 (1985).

104. David W. Skelly and Lothar A. Gruenke, <u>J. Vac. Sci. Technol.</u> A4: 457 (1986).

105. H.P. Bader and M.A. Lardon, <u>J. Vac. Sci. Technol.</u> A3: 2167 (1985).

106. D.E. Muehlberger "Application of Ion Vapor Deposited Aluminum Coatings" in <u>Ion Plating and Ion Implantation: Application to Materials,</u> ed. by R.F. Hochman, Conference Proceedings American Society for Metals, 75 (1986).

107. D.M. Mattox and F.N. Rebarchik <u>J. Electrochem. Technol.</u> 6: 374 (1968). saveJ.R. Conrad, J.L. Radtke, R.A. Dodd, F.J. Worzala and N.C. Tran, <u>J. Appl. Phys.</u> 62: 4591 (1987).

14

Ionized Cluster Beam (ICB) Deposition Techniques

Isao Yamada

14.1 INTRODUCTION

Ionized Cluster Beam (ICB) techniques utilize small clusters of atoms, rather than individual atoms, to form thin films on substrates. Clusters of atoms can have unique physical and chemical properties, quite unlike the atomic fluxes and unlike the liquid or bulk states of the film. As a result of the unique properties of small clusters, numerous new applications in plasma physics, atomic and molecular physics, surface science, and thin film formation become available. The clusters used in this work number from a few hundred to a few thousand atoms. In a cluster this size, a large percentage of the atoms are located at or within a few layers of the cluster surface. Therefore, the overall structure of the cluster is dominated by the surface atoms, and we should consequently expect that the physical and chemical properties of the cluster are much different from those of bulk and liquid (1).

The ICB deposition technique has several features which can be attributed both to the unique properties of small clusters and to aspects of the cluster acceleration process (2,3). One of the most significant properties of the ICB deposition technique is an apparent enhancement of the surface adatom migration or diffusion in the depositing film. The ICB deposition process also allows the gradual increase in cluster (or atom) energy. The effective kinetic energy for each depositing atom can be increased easily from thermal energies up into a range similar to sputtering. This great sensitivity will be quite important to modifying or tailoring the properties of thin films.

The importance of low energy ion beams for film formation can be easily understood when we recognize that the binding energies of the atoms in a solid are in the range of a few eV per atom. For atoms evaporated from thermal sources, the kinetic energies correspond roughly to the temperature of the source and are approximately 0.01-0.1 eV, or much less than binding energies of the film atoms. A strong effect can be expected, however, as the result of bombarding by accelerated ion or neutral atom beams, even at energies of only a few eV which correspond to binding energies. The clusters in the ICB technique initially have thermal energies on the order of 0.1 eV per atom. For a cluster of a few hundred to a thousand atoms, this corresponds to less than 100 eV per cluster. If the cluster is ionized and accelerated by a few hundred to many thousands of volts, the average energy for each atom can be increased from the initial thermal energies up to the binding energy of the film atoms and beyond. By working with these high acceleration potentials, space charge problems are strongly reduced, and high fluxes can be achieved.

14.2 EXPERIMENTAL TECHNIQUES

In the Ionized Cluster Beam technique, small clusters of a few hundred atoms each are formed in a source, using techniques somewhat similar to evaporation. As the clusters leave the source, they drift through the vacuum chamber under conditions of pressure low enough that there are no collisions with gas atoms or other clusters. Upon reaching a surface, the clusters condense to form a film. Often the clusters are intentionally ionized in the drift region and accelerated by electric fields to the sample. This acceleration increases the net kinetic energy of the cluster, and can have an effect on the properties of the depositing film.

The design of an ICB system is broken up into four regions. These are the source region, where the clusters are formed; the ionization and acceleration region; a drift region; and finally the substrate. A typical schematic of the ICB system is shown in Fig. 1. These systems operate typically in the 10^{-5} to 10^{-7} Torr region (10^{-3} to 10^{-5} Pascals).

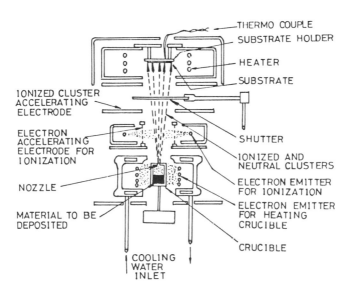

Figure 1: A typical Ionized Cluster Beam (ICB) system. The vacuum system and chamber, as well as the power supplies are omitted for clarity.

In the source region, the clusters are formed by an adiabatic expansion and condensation process (4,5). The nozzle diameter D of the crucible has to be larger than the mean free path λ between vapor atoms in the crucible (Fig. 2). This causes a viscous flow in the nozzle region. In the case where the nozzle diameter is smaller than the mean free path of the vapor atoms (molecular flow), there are few, if any, collisions between atoms in the nozzle region and agglomeration or clustering of the vapor atoms will not occur. The ratio of the vapor pressure P_o in the crucible to the vapor pressure P outside the crucible (in the chamber) must be larger than $10^2 - 10^5$. Therefore, if film deposition in the 10^{-7} to 10^{-5} Torr range is desired, it is necessary to operate the inner pressure in the crucible in the range of 10^{-2} to 1 Torr. To cause a sufficient number of collisions in the nozzle to form clusters, it is necessary to make the nozzle thickness-to-diameter ratio (L/D) in the range of 0.5 to 2.0. This serves to keep the ratio of the chamber pressure P to the crucible pressure P_o high, allowing for low pressure depositions. A simple nozzle shape is cylindrical, with a diameter D and length of 1-2 mm, which is sufficient to form a beam of clusters with a high drift velocity. Multiple nozzle sources may also be used for uniformity and throughput considerations. The range of the source temperature is determined in order to produce the vapor pressure P_o of the order of 10^{-2} to a few Torr. The crucible can be heated by either resistive heating, electron bombardment heating or by hybrid methods according to the application purposes.

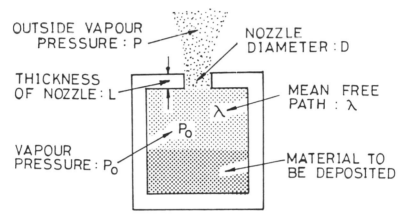

Figure 2: A schematic of the nozzle region for an ICB source. Typical parameters are a nozzle diameter, D, of 2 mm, the nozzle thickness, L, of 0.5 mm. the internal vapor pressure, P_o of a few Torr, the mean free path for the vapor atoms, $\lambda = 0.2$mm and a chamber pressure of 10^{-5} Torr. The crucible can be heated by a number of means, and is generally constructed of graphite and refractory metals.

The kinetic energy of the clusters upon leaving the source region can be considerably higher than for either single atoms or simple groups of atoms evaporated from an open hearth at the same temperature. The kinetic energy is also dependent on the nozzle dimensions. An example of this is shown in Fig. 3 for the case of Ag clusters. For the top curve, the nozzle was opened to 8 mm, which is effectively equivalent to an open hearth.

The clusters are ionized by an electron impact in an ionization electrode region located just above the expansion nozzle. The ratio of number of ionized clusters to the total number of clusters can be adjusted by changing the electron emission current I_e in the ionization region. In general, the clusters only become singly ionized by this technique due to the low currents. The degree of ionization is defined as the percent of the total cluster flux which is ionized. In a typical system, (6) the degree of ionization obtained for a single nozzle is 5-7% at $I_e = 100$mA, 7-15% at $I_e = 150$mA and and 30-35% at $I_e = 300$mA. The ionized clusters are accelerated by the electric field caused by the potential V_a on the accelerating electrode located just outside the ionization region. Typically this electrode would operate at a potential of a few hundred to several thousand volts negative w.r.t. the system ground. The accelerated ionized clusters bombard the substrate together with neutral clusters which are not ionized in the ionization electrode system. The ionized clusters have a kinetic energy corresponding to the acceleration voltage, whereas the neutral clusters have a kinetic energy corresponding to the ejection velocity. The trajectory of the ionized clusters is controlled to obtain a wide and uniform bombardment on the substrate by optimizing the aspect ratio (L/D) of the nozzle or by adjusting the acceleration voltage applied to the acceleration electrode. The uniform radiation by cluster ions of the depositing film is critical in cases where the film properties are dependent on the bombardment by the ions.

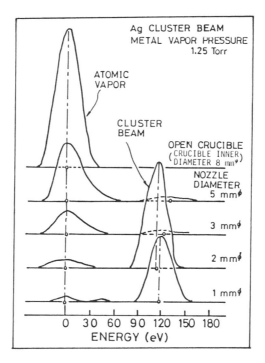

Figure 3: The energy distribution measured using an electrostatic, 90° energy analyzer for Ag clusters for various nozzle diameters. The internal vapor pressure in the crucible was held constant at 1.25 Torr.

The shape and spacing of the acceleration electrodes can be optimized by modeling the ion trajectories through the acceleration region to give the best beam uniformity. One acceleration design is shown in Fig. 4, consisting of a grid, an ionization electrode (part of the electron source for ionization of the clusters), an intermediate electrode and the acceleration electrode. It should be noted that the optimum voltage on each electrode is interrelated. The best or optimum focussing conditions result in a broad, uniform beam at the sample.

Typically these substrate mounts are radiation-heated, and contain a thermocouple for the measurement of sample temperature. It is also usually desirable to measure the current to the sample as a means of monitoring the deposition process. There can also be rate monitors of various designs in the sample region.

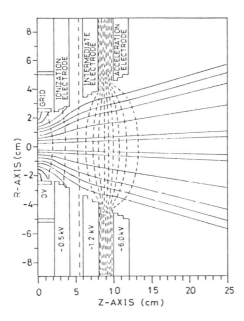

Figure 4: Trajectories for Ag clusters in a multiple-aperture acceleration system. In this case, the optimum voltage is applied to the intermediate electrode.

By introducing a reactive species during ICB operation, it is possible to reactively deposit compound thin films. This allows the deposition of oxide, nitride, hydride or carbide films, for example, while still using relatively simple elemental sources. During a reactive ICB deposition (RICB), an appropriate reactive gas is introduced into the chamber at a pressure of 10^{-5} to 10^{-4} Torr (7). In this low pressure region, no plasma is produced in the acceleration or drift regions, as is the case with Activated Reactive Evaporation (ARE) (8) or ion plating techniques. At higher pressures where a plasma is formed, the clusters are rapidly destroyed by collisions with energetic particles. This eliminates the advantages of using the cluster technology. The chemical reactions at these pressures all take place at the depositing film surface on the sample. The deposition rate of clusters must be carefully controlled along with the partial pressure of the reactive gas to control the film stoichiometry.

Multiple ICB source operation is possible due to the low chamber pressure during operation. (Fig. 5) (9). Multiple source operation is applicable for the deposition of alloys, and in particular those alloys whose components have radically different melting points and vapor pressures. A good example of a relevant compound is GaAs. In a multiple-source system, the sources operate completely independently, and can be used simultaneously to form compounds, or in sequence to form multilayer or superlattice films.

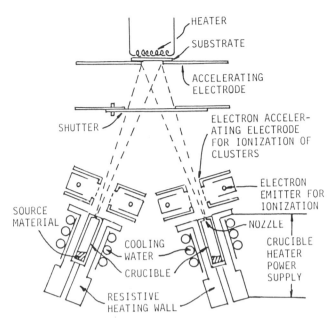

Figure 5: A typical arrangement for a ICB deposition with two sources. Each of the sources is completely independent during operation.

14.3 FILM DEPOSITION WITH ICB

Films deposited by conventional evaporation often differ radically from films of the identical material deposited by physical sputtering, even though in both cases the depositing atoms are arriving at the surface singly or in very small groups. It is therefore not too surprising that films deposited by the ICB technique can have very different qualities than either evaporated or sputtered films. In addition, it should be obvious that by changing the kinetic energy of the cluster from effectively a hundred eV or so to many thousands of eV, the physical properties of the deposited films can also be drastically altered.

The surface binding energy of the adsorbed atom, the nucleation density or critical size for surface nucleation and the level of surface mobility of the adsorbed atom are all critical to the film formation process. The sticking coefficient is a term describing the effective probability of the arriving, condensing atom to be adsorbed on the substrate surface. Such factors as the substrate temperature, the arrival rates of condensing atoms and energetic ions, the presence of impurities and the crystalline orientation of the suface, and even the presence of electric charge on the arriving species will influence the film growth process.

In the case of ICB, a number of features are quite different from conventional evaporation, and these features must be included in discussions of the basic film deposition and modification mechanisms. Clearly there is a significant difference compared to evaporation in the arrival of atoms in the form of large clusters to the film surface. In addition, the additional kinetic energy of the clusters, when ionized and accelerated, must be considered, as must the possible effects of the electronic charge those clusters carry. Some of the effects that can be attributed to the ICB technique include: (a) creation of activated centers for nuclear formation, (b) sputtering or in-situ cleaning, (c) substrate surface heating (higher effective surface temperature), (d) very shallow ion implantation, and (e) enhancement of adatom migration.

The use of ionized clusters in the ICB technique has certain advantages over both conventional evaporation and sputter deposition as well as low energy ion beam deposition. One fundamental difference is the low effective charge-to-mass ratio. Generally only one atom in a cluster of many hundred atoms is ionized. Therefore, space charge effect-based problems that can occur with low energy ion beam deposition techniques are significantly reduced. In addition, the charging problems that can occur with highly ionized ion beams can be reduced or eliminated. The other basic phenomena of critical value to the ICB technique is the reduced internal binding of the cluster atoms. Due to this lower level of interatomic binding, upon collision of the cluster with the sample the cluster atoms are more easily dislodged from the cluster for the purpose of surface diffusion. One result of this effect is the ability to deposit epitaxial thin films at substrate temperatures significantly below those of conventional evaporation techniques.

The initial kinetic energy of the ionized cluster upon impact with the surface can result in several phenomena, including: (a) an increase in the local temperature at the point of impact, (b) a possible implantation of cluster atoms into the bulk of the film, (c) at high enough energies, physical sputtering or desorption from the surface, (d) increased surface diffusion of the surface and cluster atoms, and (e) the creation of activated sites or defects to be nucleation points for film growth. The presence of ions in the arriving particle flux to the surface can have a great influence on critical parameters in the condensation process, such as coalescence and nucleation, and chemical reactions of the condensing atoms with bulk or gas phase atoms.

The magnitude of these effects can be modified by adjusting the acceleration voltage and the content of the ionized clusters in the total flux. An optimum value of the kinetic energy of ionized and accelerated particles in film formation is estimated to be in the range of a few to a hundred eV/atom under the good quality film deposition conditions. However, some amount of defects and displacements of atoms are often effective at the initial stage of film formation. Therefore energies above the damage threshold can often be of great value to film formation. In addition, the optimum energy may vary according to the required characteristics characteristics of the film, such as mechanical properties, optical properties, or morphology and the combination of deposit and substrate materials.

14.3.1 Kinetic Energy Range of ICB and Effects of the Kinetic Energy

The clusters have been analyzed in-flight by electron diffraction techniques and found to have an amorphous structure. The constituent atoms are considered to be loosely coupled to one another compared to those in the crystalline state. An ionized cluster accelerated to an appropriate energy will break up upon striking the sample surface with the kinetic energy distributed for the most part evenly to the individual atoms. The migration of the atoms on the substrate surface has an important role in the film formation kinetics. Moreover, the ICB deposition process allows the production of equivalently low energy and high intensity ion beams without space charge problems.

The degree of surface disorder during the deposition process can have a significant effect on the film nucleation process. The surface crystallinity of Si substrates bombarded by Al clusters was measured by ion channeling after the Al film was removed by chemical etching. A Si substrate bombarded by a 500 eV Ar ion beam to a dose of 2×10^{15}ions/cm^2 was also examined for comparison. Figure 6 compares the number of displaced atoms for the same cases (10). The results show that the displacement of surface atoms induced by the Al ICB bombardment is much smaller than that caused by the Ar ion bombardment. Actually, the disorder caused by ICB bombardment is much smaller than that produced by the naturally occurring oxidized layer. It can be concluded that the kinetic energy of the individual atoms in an accelerated cluster as it impacts the surface appear no larger than the order of a few 10's of eV per atom.

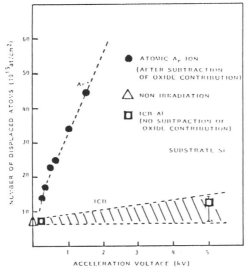

Figure 6: Comparison of the number of displaced Si surface atoms for Si surfaces bombarded by Ar ions at 500 eV and Al ICB clusters.

For an actual film deposition by using the ICB technique, the kinetic energy of the accelerated clusters produces effects such as the following: (1) formation of preferential nucleation sites, (2) surface cleaning by desorption or sputtering, (3) very shallow ion implantation, (4) surface heating at equivalently high temperature, and (5) adatom migration. These effects have been confirmed experimentally.

The spatial density of the nuclei at early stages of film growth has been observed to be dependant on the kinetic energy of the incoming clusters with ICB. By increasing the kinetic energy of the ionized clusters, the density of nuclei is increased monotonically at first and then becomes constant. Fig. 7 shows a plot of the number of nuclei as a function of the acceleration voltage on the cluster. The increase in the density of nuclei at higher acceleration voltages is attributed to the effect of ion bombardment. At a high deceleration voltage (on the sample) greater than 300 V, the increase of nuclei density is considered to be due to electron bombardment. The spatial density of nuclei on the surface is considered to be determined mainly by such factors as the deposition rate, the presence of charges, structural defects, ion bombardment, and statistical fluctuations in the supersaturation conditions. In these experiments the deposition rate and the ionization ratio were kept constant. Therefore it is reasonably assumed that ion bombardment and the resulting creation of surface defects produced the increased number of nuclei (11).

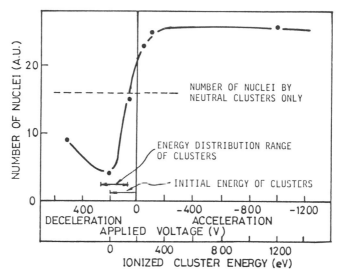

Figure 7: A plot of the number of nuclei (per unit area) as a function of acceleration voltage for the clusters. The initial energy of the clusters is approximately 100 eV.

Surface cleaning or sputtering effects can also be clearly seen by comparing the Si epitaxial growth in an ultra high vacuum (UHV) and a high vacuum chambers. In the epitaxial growth of Si on an atomically clean and well-ordered silicon surface in the UHV chamber, only a 200 V acceleration voltage was sufficient to deposit partially epitaxial films at a substrate temperature (T_s) of 500°C. By increasing the acceleration voltage, an improvement of the crystalline quality could be obtained. For the identical deposition case in the high vacuum chamber, the results were quite different. The chamber was evacuated by an oil diffusion pump to a base pressure of $10^{-7} - 10^{-6}$ Torr. In this system, an acceleration voltage of at least 6 kV was necessary before the deposited films attained a degree of epitaxy. An amorphous or polycrystalline structure is formed in a range of 0 - 4 kV. In this deposition, no special cleaning process except for chemical cleaning was used prior to the deposition. In this case, higher acceleration voltage is required in order to sputter the native oxide and to remove adsorbed residual gas atoms on the substrate surface during the deposition. From the Rutherford backscattering spectra using 185 keV H^+, it was found that the film prepared with clusters accelerated to 6 keV has no oxygen at the interface between the film and the substrate (12).

To measure the enhancement of the surface mobility for a condensing atom, the very early stages of film deposition were examined. In this experiment, Au was deposited onto a silicon oxide (SiO) film which had been deposited on an NaCl substrate. The substrate surface was partially covered with a cleaved NaCl plate to study shadowing at the cleaved edge. The average spacing between the SiO and the NaCl cover was about 80μm. The gold was deposited both by the ionized-cluster beam technique and by conventional vacuum deposition. Fig. 8 shows electron micrographs of the deposited Au film near the edge of the penumbra. In the case of ionized-cluster beam deposition, the deposited gold particles were observed to have migrated under the cleaved NaCl cover.

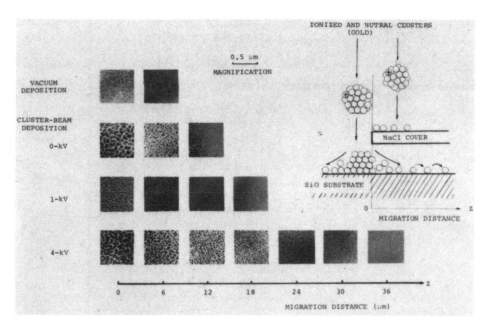

Figure 8: Electron micrographs of the deposited film clusters under an overhanging edge as a function of cluster acceleration voltage.

Even when the acceleration voltage was zero, the migration distance of the deposited particles was greater than in conventional evaporation technique. The increased migration distance could be the result of the breaking up of deposited clusters into atoms upon impact with the film surface.

These and related results strongly suggest that the acceleration of the clusters during ICB influences the dynamic processes in the film formation. These dynamic processes include the breaking of clusters into atoms upon bombarding the substrate surface, sputtering of impurities from the substrate surface, formation of activation centers for nuclear formation, adatom migration, and shallow implantation. In ICB deposition these processes can be controlled by changing the acceleration of ionized clusters and the content of ionized clusters in the total flux, and consequently the physical properties of the deposited films can be controlled.

14.3.2 Film Deposition by Reactive ICB Techniques

Compound films, such as oxides, nitrides or hydrides, can be deposited by introducing the appropriate reactive gas species into the vacuum chamber during the ICB deposition process. The partial pressure of the reactive gas is typically on the order of $10^{-5} - 10^{-4}$ Torr. A fraction of the reactive gas introduced into the chamber is ionized and dissociated in the ionization region of the ICB source. These species can become active and may contribute to the reaction at the film surface.

Reactive ICB (RICB) deposition mechanisms have been studied (13) by examining the deposition of amorphous, hydrogenated silicon (a-Si:H). In this case, silicon clusters were deposited in a hydrogen ambient at 10^{-5} Torr. At this pressure range, there are few gas phase collisions of the hydrogen molecules with the Si clusters, and the reactions take place predominantly at the film surface. The reaction rate appeared to increase with the acceleration voltage on the clusters. Since the background gas pressure before introducing the hydrogen gas was 5×10^{-7} Torr, the main particles impinging on the substrate surface are ionized and neutral silicon clusters from the ion source, and the mixed hydrogen gas and doping gases that are introduced into the chamber through the leak valves. Some fraction of the hydrogen molecules are ionized and dissociated in the ionization section of the cluster beam. Therefore, the flux of hydrogen to the sample surface consists of a range of atoms, molecules and ions. Under typical deposition conditions, the arrival rate of Si atoms (within the clusters) was on the order of $10^{15} - 10^{16}$ atoms cm^{-2} sec^{-1}, as calculated from the measured silicon ion-current to the substrate. The ratio of the hydrogen atoms to the hydrogen molecules was estimated from the change of H and H_2 peaks in a mass spectrum when the electrical input power into the source was varied. From these measurements, the bombardment rate of H_2 molecules to the sample was approximately 10^{16} molecules cm^{-2} sec^{-1} and the bombardment rate of dissociated hydrogen atoms was estimated to be 10^{15} atoms cm^2 sec^{-1}. The rate of impinging hydrogen ions is three orders of magnitude smaller than that of molecular hydrogen. It is not clear yet which state of hydrogen is dominantly involved in the hydrogenation process, but it seems reasonable to consider that hydrogen atoms could have a considerable influence in providing uniform hydrogenation. For doped film formation, the hydrogen gas was mixed with phosphine or diborane on the order of 5000 ppm sequentially in the same chamber. No problems arose as a result of the residual reactive gas used in previous processes. Doped films of either p or n type could be reproducibly deposited at practical deposition rates. Subsequent structural analysis showed that the films mainly consisted of monohydrides. The density of monohydrides can be increased by accelerating the Si clusters to a higher acceleration voltage. For both this case and the parallel case of oxide and nitride RICB deposition, operation at a gas pressure of less than $10^{-5} - 10^{-4}$ Torr was sufficient to cause sufficient surface chemical reactions to form the compound films without forming a plasma within the chamber.

14.3.3 Film Deposition by Simultaneous Use of ICB and Microwave Ion Sources

Concurrent ion bombardment by means of an ion source during the deposition with ICB techniques was first proposed in 1973 (14). Along these lines, the simultaneous use of a microwave ion source and an ICB source has been developed. This technique is attractive because the reactive gas ion energy and the current can be controlled independently from the ICB source operation. Therefore, the reactivities of the gases can potentially be enhanced by this method.

Fig. 9 shows a schematic diagram of the simultaneous system consisting of the microwave ion source and the ICB source. The details of the microwave ion source are not important to this discussion and have been described elsewhere (15). The microwave source requires permanent magnets around the discharge chamber. The source operation can be set to the Electron Cyclotron Resonance (ECR) condition which results in a very high density plasma. The gas ions are extracted by the extraction electrode applied at $V_{ex} = 3 - 15$ kV and the extracted ions are then subsequently decelerated down to 500 eV by the retarding field produced between the source and the substrate holder.

This system was used for the deposition of AlN films. High purity Al metal and N_2 gas were used as source materials. Sapphire (0001) and p-type Si (111) were used as substrates. The substrate temperature (T_s) was 100°C. The films deposited with neutral N_2 (rather than accelerated ions) were opaque and not characteristic of reacted AlN. Films deposited with concurrent N_2^+ were clear and had high optical transmittance. Measurements by Rutherford Backscattering Spectroscopy (RBS). suggested a composition ratio in these cases of AlN.

As an example of oxide film formation using this same technique, Al_2O_3 films have been deposited. For the case of neutral Al-clusters and O_2 gas, the transmittance of the film is low particularly at small wavelengths, suggesting that pure Al_2O_3 has not been formed.

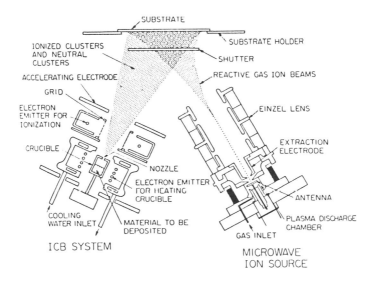

Figure 9: Schematic of the ICB deposition system with simultaneous ion bombardment from a microwave ion source.

On the other hand, the films deposited with neutral Al clusters and O_2 ions had significantly higher transmittances. Also, in the case of the film deposited with both O_2 ions and ionized Al-clusters the film was transparent and its transmittance approached that of the sapphire substrate. It was found from RBS measurements that the composition ratio of oxygen to Al in these last films was 0.67, and that stoichiometric Al_2O_3 films were formed. The film prepared at an incident energy of 500 eV for O_2 ions and an acceleration voltage of 0.5 kV for Al clusters was found to be thermally stable even after annealing at 1000°C. The refractive index (n) is found to increase with increasing ion energy. In addition, the same increase in refractive index for ionized, accelerated clusters compared to neutral clusters was found in this case as was found in the case of AlN (above). The etching rate of these films in 5% HF solutions is found to decrease as a function of increased cluster acceleration voltage. In particular, in the case of using both O_2 ions and ionized Al-clusters, the film prepared at an incident energy of 500 eV was not etched at all in the 5% HF solution. This indicates that the higher incident energy such as 500 eV may increase the packing density of the film.

14.4 SUMMARY

The deposition of thin films by means of beams of large clusters of atoms rather than individual atoms has been shown to have numerous advantages over other deposition techniques. The clusters are generally formed by condensation during the expansion of a vapor through an aperture into high vacuum. Ionization of the clusters in flight and subsequent acceleration of the clusters to the film surface has also been found to be a sensitive technique for the modification of the properties of the deposited film. These techniques are equally applicable to reactive deposition of compound materials, in which clusters of one species are deposited in the presence of background gas atoms and ions of a reactive species.

The critical features of the ICB technique are the control of the cluster kinetic energy through ionization and acceleration, and the subtle characteristics of the clusters themselves. The clusters are characterized by lower levels of inter-atomic bonding than the solid phase. This reduced bonding apparently allows increased surface mobility of the atoms upon arrival at the film surface, compared to conventionally evaporated films. One result of these effects is a greatly lowered temperature for the deposition of epitaxial films, compared to evaporative of MBE techniques.

The control of the cluster kinetic energy, through partial ionization of the clusters and subsequent acceleration by an electric field, results in a broad degree of control in the effective kinetic energy of each of the atoms that arrives at the film surface. In addition, due to the high mass-to-charge ratio of the clusters, such aspects as space charge limited current flow are avoided in most cases and charging effects are reduced significantly. The broad range of energy control is not possible in other techniques such as evaporation or sputtering.

The Ionized Cluster Beam techniques have been shown to be valuable additions to the realm of thin film deposition techniques. The processes are well characterized and reliable equipment is available from a number of sources. The films deposited by these techniques are often superior to those deposited by either evaporation or sputtering, and the range of control of the process exceeds other techniques by a great margin. It is hoped that the technique will find greater acceptance and recognition in the future as its features become even more advanced and more and more of the thin film community becomes familiar with the technology.

14.5 REFERENCES

1.   J. Borel and J. Buttet (ed.), Small Particles and Inorganic Clusters. Surf. Sci. 106: (1981).

2.   P.P. Kulik, G.E. Norman and L.S. Polak, Khimiya Vysokikh Energii 10: p. 203 (1976).

3.   T. Takagi, Thin Solid Films 92: p. 1 (1982).

4. T. Takagi, I. Yamada, M. Kumnori and S. Kobiyama. Proc. 2nd Int. Conf. Ion Sources, Vienna (Osterreichiche Studiengeselshaft fur Atomenrgie, Vienna, 1972)) p. 790.

5. T. Takagi, I. Yamada and A. Sasaki, J. Vac. Sci. Technol. 12: p. 1128 (1975).

6. T. Takagi, I. Yamada and A. Sasaki, Inst. Phys. Conf. Ser. 38: p. 142 (1978).

7. T. Takagi, I. Yamada, K. Matsubara and H. Takaoka, J. Cryst. Growth 45: p. 326 (1978).

8. R.F. Bunshah in Deposition Technologies for Films and Coatings ed. by R.F. Bunshah (Noyes, N.J. 1982) 5.

9. T. Takagi, K. Matsubara, N. Kondo, K. Fujii and H. Tokaoka, Jpn. J. Appl. Phys. 19: Supple. 19-1, p.507 (1980).

10. I. Yamada and T. Takagi, Nucl. Instrum. Methods Phys. Res. B21: p. 120 (1987).

11. I. Yamada, H. Takaoka, H. Inokawa, H. Usui, S.C. Cheng and T. Takagi, Thin Solid Films 92: p. 137 (1982).

12. I. Yamada, F.W. Saris, T. Takagi, K. Matsubara, H. Takaoka and S. Ishiyama, Jpn. J. Appl. Phys. 19: p. 181 (1980).

13. I. Yamada, I. Nagai, H. Horie and T. Takagi, J. Appl. Phys. 54: p. 1583 (1983).

14. K. Fujime, T. Ueda, H. Takaoka, J. Ishikawa and T. Takagi, Proc. Int. Workshop on Ionized Cluster Beam Technique, Tokyo and Kyoto, Japan, p. 195 (1986).

15. J. Ishikawa, Y. Takeiri and T. Takagi, Rev. Sci. Instrum. 55: p. 449 (1984).

15

The Activated Reactive Evaporation (ARE) Process

Chandra V. Deshpandey and Rointan F. Bunshah

15.1 INTRODUCTION

A major advance in the technology for the deposition of refractory compounds such as carbides, oxides, nitrides and sulfides has been the development of and advances in plasma-assisted deposition processes (1). The plasma-assisted chemical vapor deposition (PACVD) or plasma-enhanced chemical vapor deposition (PECVD) process has found extensive applications in the microelectronics industry (see Chap. 10). Remarkable advances have also been made in the plasma-assisted physical vapor deposition (PAPVD) processes and applications have been developing in such areas as microelectronics, tribology, and superconducting films.

Evaporative deposition and sputter deposition are the two basic physical vapor deposition (PVD) processes. The vapor species are produced by thermal means in evaporation; and by momentum transfer in sputtering. Ion plating, in which ions are created from the background gas during evaporation and accelerated to the sample, is a hybrid process where the primary emphasis is on the changes in the microstructure, the surface coverage, the composition and the residual stresses of the deposited film produce by ion bombardment during growth. (Please see Chap. 13 for an extensive discussion of ion plating processes.) The substrate-film interface can also be significantly affected by the ion bombardment in the initial stages of deposition.

The increasing use of plasmas in deposition technology in the past few years has stemmed from the stringent requirements of low temperature processing in modern microelectronics and optoelectronic industries. The plasma is a convenient *insitu* source of activated gas atoms and molecules, and energetic neutrals and ions, which can be used to overcome the activation energy barrier for a particular chemical reaction. It thus becomes possible to synthesize a given compound in a plasma environment at a relatively low substrate temperatures, compared to a non-plasma, thermal process. A variety of plasma assisted techniques and modification have therefore been developed to deposit required films under the given processing constraints (1, and Chap. 13).

Evaporation-based plasma assisted techniques offer the control and flexibility necessary to deposit thin and thick films of alloys, compounds, and novel metastable materials (2). In this chapter, we shall examine the development and current status of the activated reactive evaporation (ARE) process for the deposition of a variety of compound films.

15.1.1 Historical Developments

The need for good quality compound films was felt early during the development of optical interference filters. This provided the stimulus for research and development of suitable techniques to synthesize these films with controlled optical properties. Consequently reactive evaporation, flash evaporation of compounds and reactive, as well as plasma enhanced reactive evaporation processes were developed. A brief review of the development of the these processes is given below.

The historical origins of the reactive evaporation processes go back to 1907 when Soddy (3) found that calcium vapor reacted with gases other than inert gases. The use of reactive evaporation processes in the deposition of oxide films dates to the pioneering work of Brismaid et al (4) in 1957 and Auwarter (5) in 1960 who studied the deposition of oxide films by the reaction between metal or suboxide vapors and oxygen gas. Auwarter (5) also suggested that the reactivity can be enhanced by separate ionization of the oxygen gas molecules using an electrical discharge, prior to interaction with the metal atoms.

Other work on reactive evaporation processes without ionization of the reactive gas is:

(a) Herrick and Tevebaugh (6) deposited copper oxide films by vaporization of copper from resistance heated sources in an oxygen atmosphere (1963).

(b) Novice et al (7) and Schilling (8) deposited Al_2O_3 films by reactive evaporation from a resistance heated aluminum sources in the presence of oxygen (1964).

(c) Ritter (9) produced thin films of SiO_2 and TiO_2 by reactive evaporation of Si, Ti, SiO and TiO from resistance heated sources in the presence of 10^{-4} to 10^{-3} Torr partial pressure of oxygen (1966).

(d) Ferrieu and Pruniaux (10) produced Al_2O_3 by reactive evaporation of Al in an atmosphere of water vapor at 10^{-1} Torr in the reaction zone (1969).

(e) Rairden (11) prepared thin films of NbN and TaN by evaporation of Nb and Ta from an electron beam heated source in an N_2 partial pressure of 10^{-4} to 10^{-3} Torr, and AlN by evaporation of Al in NH_3 atmosphere (12) (1969).

(f) deKlerk and Kelly (13) produced CdS and ZnS films by co-evaporation from two independent sources of Cd and S and condensation on a substrate at temperatures between 50 and 200°C(1965).

(g) Learn and Haq (14) produced β-SiC by reactive evaporation of Si in a C_2H_2 atmosphere (1970).

(h) Itoh and Misawa (15) produced TiC by evaporation of titanium from an electron-beam-heated source in CH_4 or C_3H_8 as the reactive gas. They also deposited AlN films by reaction between aluminum atoms and NH_3 gas (1974).

(i) Abe et al (16) deposited TiC films by reaction between titanium atoms evaporated from a resistance-heated filament and C_2H_2 or C_2H_4 as the reactive gases (1982).

Examples of reactive evaporation processes where the reactive gas was ionized in a separate chamber (located inside or outside the vacuum system) are:

(a) Auwarter (5) studied the deposition of thin films oxides of Si, Zr, Ti, Al, Zn, Sn by reactive evaporation of the metal from resistance heated sources in a partial pressure of oxygen gas. Ionization of the oxygen gas outside the reaction zone by glow discharge between two electrodes is claimed to increase the "affinity" between the gas ion and the metal compound, i.e., enhance the probability of formation of metal compounds. Deposition rates of about $0.2\mu m$ min^{-1} were obtained.

(b) Wank and Winslow (17) deposited films of AlN by evaporating films of Al from an rf heated BN crucible and reacting the Al deposited on the substrate with N_2 gas which has been dissociated by 60 Hz a.c. discharge at the end of the gas feed tube. Deposition rates of 0.1 to $0.2\mu m$ min^{-1} were obtained (1968).

(c) Kosicki and Khang (18) produced GaN thin-films by depositing pure Ga from a resistance heated source onto a substrate in the presence of activated N_2 gas. The N_2 gas was made chemically active by partial dissociation in a microwave discharge located away from the source and the substrate. Deposition rates of 0.2 and 0.3 μm min^{-1} were obtained (1969).

(d) Heitmann (19,20) used a hollow cathode discharge in a glass chamber to ionize oxygen gas and deposit films of SiO_2, SiO_xN_y and TiO_2 (1971).

(e) More recently, Kuster and Ebert (21) have used a modification of the method by Heitmann to deposit TiO_2 layers and study their optical properties. These researchers refer to this process as the Activated Reactive Evaporation Process (1980).

(f) In an excellent and detailed paper by Ebert (22), the deposition of TiO_2, BeO, In_2O_3, SnO_2, and SiO_2 coatings using ionized oxygen gas is described (1982).

At this time it should be pointed out that there is an important distinction between the Reactive Evaporation processes using an ionized gas stream (as detailed above) and the Activated Reactive Evaporation (ARE) process. In the ARE process, ionization of both the metal vapor and the reactive gas or gas mixture occurs in the Reaction Zone which is defined as the space between the metal vapor source and the substrate, unlike the other plasma enhanced evaporation processes discussed above where only the reactive gas is separately ionized. This characteristic of the ARE process and its significance in film growth by this techniques will be discussed in depth in a later section.

15.2 EVAPORATION PROCESSES FOR THE DEPOSITION OF COMPOUND FILMS

Evaporation processes for the deposition of compounds can be subdivided into two types: (a) direct evaporation where the evaporant is the compound itself and (b) reactive evaporation where metal or compounds of a metal in a low valance state is evaporated in the presence of a reactive gas to form a compound, e.g., Si or SiO evaporated in the presence of O_2 to form SiO_2, or Ti evaporated in the presence of N_2 to form TiN.

15.2.1 Direct Evaporation

Evaporation can occur with or without dissociation of the compound into fragments. The observed vapor specie show that a few compounds evaporate without dissociation. Examples are SiO, MgF_2, B_2O_3, CaF_2, and other Group IV divalent oxides (SiO homologs like GeO and SnO).

In the more general case, when a compound is evaporated or sputtered, the material is not transformed to the vapor state as compound molecules but as fragments thereof. This compound fragmentation step is very difficult to characterize and control. Subsequently, the fragments have to recombine most probably on the substrate to reconstitute the compound. Therefore, the stoichiometry of the film depends on several factors including the deposition rate and the ratios of the various molecular fragments, the impingement rate of other gases present in the environment, the surface mobility of the fragments (which in turn depends on their kinetic energy and substrate temperature), the mean residence time of the fragments on the substrate, the reaction rate of the fragments on the substrate to reconstitute the compound and the impurities present on the substrate. For example, it was found that direct evaporation of Al_2O_3 resulted in a deposit which was deficient in oxygen, i.e., which had the composition Al_2O_{3-x}. This O_2 deficiency could be made up by introducing O_2 at a low partial pressure into the environment (23).

In other cases, the situation is more complex (24). ZrB_2 films produced by direct evaporation of ZrB_2 billets from an electron beam heated source either at high or low deposition rates (2.14 and 0.11μm min^{-1} thickness per minute respectively) consisted entirely of the ZrB_2 phase. In contrast, in similar experiments with high rate evaporation of TiB_2, the deposits consisted of a mixture of TiB_2 and TiB phases with the amount of the TiB phase increasing with higher deposition temperatures. Low rate evaporation of TiB_2 produced TiB_2 deposits exclusively.

15.2.2 Reactive Evaporation Processes

15.2.2.1 Using a Compound Evaporant. The above problem related to stoichiometry of the films when deposited by direct evaporation process can be to a certain extent circumvented by introducing the reactive gas at a controlled rate during evaporation to raise the partial pressure to about $10^{-3} - 10^{-4}$Torr. The film stoichiometry is improved due to gas absorption by growing film. The stoichiometry of the films is also enhanced due to: (25) (i) the possibility of collisions between oxygen and evaporating vapor molecules in transit, and (ii) reaction between the vapor and oxygen molecule at the surface. Although composition is improved, it is difficult to ensure exact stoichiometry of the film by this process.

15.2.2.2   Using a Metal Evaporant.   Another variant of the reactive evaporation process involves evaporating the metal in a partial pressure of the reactive gas. However, high substrate temperature and low deposition rates are some of the constraints associated with the process of reactive evaporation with metals (26). These limitations can be addressed in terms of thermodynamic and kinetic considerations.

15.3   THERMODYNAMIC AND KINETIC FACTORS IN REACTIVE EVAPORATION PROCESS

The chemical reaction forming a compound by reactive evaporation process can, in general, be represented as:

$$M \text{ (Metal)} \ + \ X \text{ (ReactiveGas)} \ \rightarrow \ MX \text{ (film)}$$

As with all chemical reactions, thermodynamic and kinetic constraints apply to deposition of compounds by the above type of reaction. Let us analyze these constraints and how they impose limitations on compound growth by reactive evaporation process.

15.3.1   Thermodynamic Factors

Reactions between metal and gas to form a given compound must have negative free energy of formation. Let us consider the reaction involved in the synthesis of some oxides, carbides and nitrides by reactive evaporation process in view of the thermodynamic criteria given above. Given below (27) are the reactions forming Al_2O_3, TiC and TiN, all at 298 K:

$$2Al + \frac{3}{2}O_2 \rightarrow Al_2O_3 \qquad \Delta G^\circ = -250 \text{Kcal } (\text{mol } O_2)^{-1} \tag{1}$$

$$Ti + C_2H_2 \rightarrow 2TiC + H_2 \qquad \Delta G^\circ = -76.5 \text{Kcal } (\text{mol } C_2H_2)^{-1} \tag{2}$$

$$2Ti + N_2 \rightarrow 2TiN \qquad \Delta G^\circ = -73.5 \text{Kcal } (\text{mol } N_2)^{-1} \tag{3}$$

As can be seen from the above reactions, the thermodynamic criterion of negative free energy of formation is satisfied for the respective compounds.

Although formation of these compounds is thermodynamically favored, the observed rate at which the respective films are formed in reactive evaporation is extremely low. This process limitation can be addressed in terms of reaction kinetics in a reactive evaporation process.

15.3.2   Kinetic Factors

The question of reaction kinetics in reactive evaporation processes can be treated in exactly the same manner as for reactions occurring in heterogeneous systems of condensed phases (26). The model for heterogeneous metallurgical reactions involves the following: (i) transport of the reactants to the reaction interface; (ii) transport of reaction products away from the reaction interface; (iii) the chemical reaction at the reaction interface; (iv) the nucleation of new phases; (v) heat transfer to or away from the reaction interface. Any of these can be rate-limiting steps and can control the overall rate of the reaction.

The possible rate-controlling steps in a reactive evaporation process are: (a) the supply of reactants, (b) the collision frequency between reactants, (c) the rate of the chemical reaction at the reaction interface and (d) the rate of removal of products from the interface. It may be noted that the physical location of the reaction interface may be the substrate surface, the surface of the evaporation billet, the gas phase or a combination of these.

It is easy to satisfy conditions (a), (b) and (d) above in reactive evaporation processes. However, condition (c), i.e. the rate of reaction, often becomes the rate-governing step. In reactive deposition processes, another important factor is the deposition rate, which in turn is dependent on the arrival rate of metal atoms or complex species as well as gas atoms on the substrate surface. Thus, Abe et al (16) found that titanium carbide with carbon-to-titanium ratio of 1.0 could be formed by reaction between titanium atoms and C_2H_2 and C_2H_4 molecules on the substrate at $300 - 500°C$ only if the deposition rate was $.3 - 1.5 Å/s$ At higher rates, from $2 - 4 Å/s$, the ratio of carbon to titanium decreased from 1 to 0.2.

However, the reaction between titanium vapor atoms and C_2H_2 gas did not occur readily, i.e. condition (c) was the rate-controlling step due to the inability of the reactants to overcome the activation energy barrier. The problem was solved by imparting sufficient energy to the reactants, i.e. titanium vapor atoms and C_2H_2 gas molecules, to overcome the activation energy barrier by exciting them to high energy levels through the creation of a plasma in the reaction zone between the source and the substrate (28,29). Thus condition (c), i.e. the rate of reaction, was no longer the rate-governing step.

15.4 ROLE OF PLASMA IN EVAPORATION BASED PROCESSES

As illustrated in the previous section, the presence of a plasma can enhance the reaction rate. The second major role of the plasma in this process is to modify the growth kinetics and hence the structure/morphology of the deposits.

15.4.1 Influence of Plasma on Growth Kinetics of the Deposits

In order to understand the role of plasma on overall growth kinetics of the depositing film, one has to consider its influence on the three characteristic steps involved in the formation of the deposit: i) creation of the vapor phase, ii) transport of vapor phase, and iii) film growth on the substrate (30).

15.4.1.1 Plasma–Source Reactions in ARE Processes. In the ARE process, the vapor species are generated by thermal energy imparted to the source. The evaporation rate varies directly as the vapor pressure of the target element which in turn is dependent on the temperature of the target surface. The plasma has little or no influence on the evaporation rate. Therefore the vapor generation rate in the ARE process is plasma independent.

15.4.1.2 Plasma Volume Reactions. Collision of vapor/gas molecules with electrons during transport from source to substrate gives rise to a variety of chemical reactions in that region. These reactions play a dominant role in producing various molecular precursors which in turn govern the growth and properties of the depositing film (31). The important factors affecting the plasma volume chemistry are the electron density, electron energy and distribution function. To obtain the desired control of the plasma volume chemistry, film growth and properties, it is therefore imperative that one should be able to control properties of the plasma independently of the deposition parameters. It is in this respect that the ARE type of processes derives its advantage over the other plasma assisted processes (32). For example, the electron number density can be controlled as a separate variable by use of a thermionic emitter. In addition, the electron energy can be adjusted by selecting the appropriate accelerating voltage.

15.4.1.3 Plasma Substrate Reactions.   Substrates exposed to a plasma (glow discharge) are bombarded by energetic neutrals, ions and electrons. The nature and energy of the bombarding species are primarily dependent on the process parameters and geometrical location of the substrate within or outside the plasma zone (33,34). Such bombardment can initiate a variety of reactions which may lead to substrate heating, substrate surface chemistry changes, gas incorporation in the growing film, as well as modification of the film morphology, crystallite size and orientation and defect level. At significantly higher energies, as may be present with intentional substrate bias, removal of the deposited atoms by sputtering may become important.

In a plasma-based physical sputter deposition process, ion bombardment of the deposited films occurs due to the difference between the sample potential (floating, grounded or biased) and the plasma potential. The plasma potential depends on a number of parameters, including the energy distribution and density of the electrons as well as the geometrical orientation of the chamber and electrodes (35,36). The effect of the plasma on the three general deposition steps outlined above can vary significantly between plasma deposition processes (37). Such differences are manifest in terms of the types and concentration of the metastable species, ionized species, and energetic neutrals which in turn influence the reaction paths or steps involved in the overall reaction for film formation and the physical location of these reactions sites. The advantages and limitations of various plasma assisted deposition techniques can be addressed in terms of the differences in plasma interaction at the source., during transport and at the substrate in the respective processes. The advantages and limitations of the various plasma assisted processes are due to: i) interdependency of the above three plasma interactions and ii) the coupling of the plasma parameters and processes parameters. For an ideal plasma assisted process, one should be able to control each of the above reactions independently of each other.

A summary of the plasma interactions, the parameters controlling these interactions and their effect on structure properties of films by ARE process is given in Table 1.

15.5 IMPLEMENTATION OF THE ACTIVATED REACTIVE EVAPORATION PROCESS

15.5.1 Basic ARE Processes

The two variants of the basic ARE process are (a) the Activated Reactive Evaporation (ARE) process with electron beam evaporation source, (b) the ARE process with resistance heated source. Both of these processes are schematically shown in Fig. 1.

Table 1:   Influence of plasma on three steps of film deposition by ARE process.

GROWTH STEP	PLASMA INTERACTION	ADVANTAGE
Source reactions	no effect on source	absence of source poisoning allows high rate deposition
Transport reactions	Independent control of electron density, energy	1. Better control of film composition 2.Low substrate temperature 3.Synthesize new structures
Substrate reactions	Substrate bombardment controlled independently of source.	Substrate can be located out of plasma region

In ARE using an e-beam source, the metal is evaporated by an electron beam in presence of a reactive gas. The plasma is generated by accelerating the secondary electrons from the plasma sheath above the molten pool towards a probe biased to a small a.c. or positive d.c. potential. This technique has been successfully used to deposit carbides, (28) nitrides, (38,39) oxides, (40,41) sulphides, (42,43) as well as carbonitrides of titanium, (44).

Nath and Bunshah modified the ARE process for use with resistance heated sources. The metal is evaporated from a resistance heated source in the presence of the reactive gas (45). The plasma is generated by accelerating the thermionically emitted electrons from a heated filament towards a positively biased anode. A transverse magnetic field is applied to cause the electrons to travel in spiral paths thereby increasing the probability of ionization. This technique has been successfully used to deposit transparent conducting coatings of indium oxide, indium tin oxide, zinc oxide, etc.

15.5.2 Modification of the Basic ARE Process

There are several modifications of the basic ARE process as illustrated in Fig. 2 (26).

15.5.3 Low Pressure Plasma Deposition (LPPD) Process

Using electron beam evaporation sources, the electric field may be generated for a conducting substrate by biasing the substrate positively instead of using a positively biased interspace electrode. In this case, it is called Low Pressure Plasma Deposition (LPPD) by Nakamura et al (46). However, this version has a disadvantage over the basic ARE process since one does not have the freedom of choice to ground the substrate, let it float or bias it negatively.

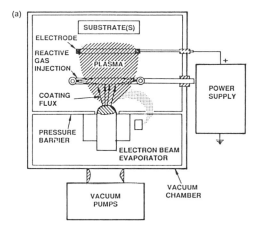

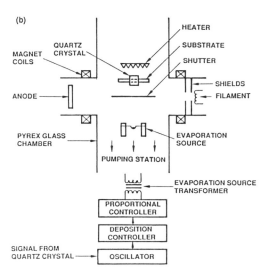

Figure 1: Schematic of the activated reactive evaporation system: (a) using an electron beam evaporation source, and (b) using a resistance heated evaporation source.

If the substrate is biased in the ARE process, it is called biased ARE, or BARE (47). This bias is usually negative to attract the positive ions in the plasma. Kobayashi and Doi (48) reported the same process in 1978 and called it reactive ion plating.

Murayama (49) used an electron beam heated source with a negatively biased substrate and rf activation of the reactants by means of a coil electrode of aluminum wire in the reaction zone to deposit oxide and nitride films.

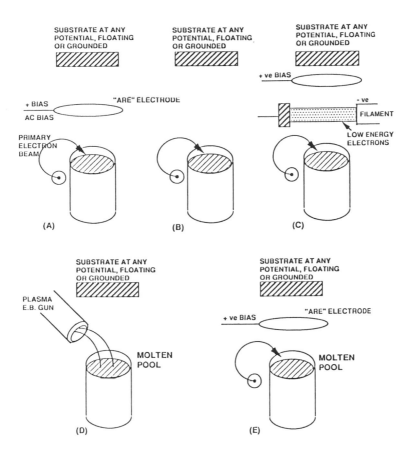

Figure 2: (a) The basic ARE process and (b)-(e) later variations: (b) low pressure plasma deposition process; (c) enhanced ARE process; (d) ARE process with hot hollow cathode electron beam gun or cold cathode discharge electron beam gun; and (e) biased ARE or reactive ion plating process.

15.5.4 Processing Using Plasma Electron Beam Guns

A plasma electron beam gun can be used in place of of the thermionic electron source to increase the level of ionization in the ARE process. The advantage of these guns is that they provide an abundant supply of low energy electrons and are relatively rugged and long-lived. These are two types of plasma-based electron sources that could be used (50). They are:

● The Cold Cathode Plasma Electron Beam - This plasma electron beam gun has a cylindrical cathode cavity made from a metal mesh or sheet containing the ionized plasma from which electrons are extracted through a small aperture in one end. The cathode is maintained at a negative potential, e.g., -5 to -20 kV, relative to the workpiece and remainder of the system, which are at ground potential (50). Zega et al (51) used a cold cathode discharge electron beam gun to deposit titanium nitride films.

● The Hot Hollow Cathode Discharge - The hollow cathode discharge applied to vacuum processing has been reported by Morley (52). Here the cathode operates at an elevated temperature and must be constructed of refractory materials. A gas, often argon or krypton, is introduced into the system through the tubular-shaped cathode. The internal walls of the hollow cathode are heated to thermionic emission temperatures (2000K) by the ion bombardment. A low voltage, high amperage d.c. power source is utilized. Often rf power from a commercial welding starter is coupled to the gas to initiate the discharge. The high current glow discharge that occurs is analogous to that experienced in vacuum arc melting at higher pressures. When a axial magnetic field is imposed on the emitted plasma, it then forms a high power density, well-collimated beam. The hollow cathode discharge beam is operationally stable and efficient over the pressure range from 10^{-4} to 10^{-1}Torr. A more detailed description of physical aspects, operational characteristics, and cathode design has been given by Morley (52). The hot hollow cathode has been used by Komiya et al (53), for example, to deposit TiC films.

15.5.5 Activated Reactive Evaporation Process Using an Arc Evaporation Source

The evaporation of metals using a low voltage arc in the presence of a plasma and a negatively biased substrate is used by Snaper (54) and Dorodnov (55) to deposit nitride and carbide films, with N_2 and hydrocarbon reactive gases respectively. (For a discussion of vacuum arc technology, please see Chap. 18). Since arcs naturally operate at low voltages, ionization processes are very efficient and a reaction plasma is very easily created.

15.6 RECENT DEVELOPMENTS IN THE ARE PROCESS

In the last few years new techniques based on ARE are being developed for the synthesis of novel and unique materials. The emphasis of such developments is generally on two aspects: i) new approaches to produce the vapor species and ii) new plasma excitation techniques and development of modified plasma excitation geometries.

15.6.1 New Approaches to Produce the Various Species

The basic process involves evaporation of the constituent metal alloy, or compound using e-beam or resistance/induction heated sources. However, it is difficult to use this approach with certain materials such as boron and carbon. Two possible solutions can be used to overcome these difficulties: 1) use of a low melting point compound of the respective element, and 2) use of a pulsed laser beam where the pulse rate and pulse width can be appropriately adjusted to control the rate of material generation and fragmentation. Moreover, in many cases, the energy of the laser beam can also be used as a source for plasma excitation.

Both these approaches have been explored. A process developed by Bunshah et al (56) for the synthesis of cubic boron nitride involve boric acid as an evaporant, which can be easily evaporated from a resistance heated tungsten boat. In addition to the ease of evaporation, this process also excludes the toxicity problems associated with fine boron particles which can be produced during e-beam evaporation of boron. A similar approach can be extended to evaporation of carbon using a low melting point carbon compound such as admantine. It is likely that many new materials hitherto difficult to synthesize may possibly be deposited using this route. Moreover, this novel approach may contribute to further development in reactive MBE processes and processes involving organometallic compound reactants.

The use of pulsed laser beams in an ARE type of process has been demonstrated in recent literature on high T_c superconducting films (57). Films with high T_c (90 K) and high critical current density ($0.7 \times 10^6 A/cm^2$ at 77K) have been produced (58). It is claimed that pulsing of the laser beam avoids fractionation of the compound and hence good control of film stoichiometry is achieved. It is also suggested that the photon energy is sufficient to activate the reactive gas/metal species thereby increasing their reactivity leading to increase in oxygen concentration in the deposited films.

15.6.2 New Plasma Excitation Modes and Geometries

As discussed earlier the attributes of the ARE processes are due to the possibility to control the plasma parameters independently of the deposition process. However, improvement in excitation and confinement of the plasma as well as control and optimization of plasma parameters in the ARE processes are likely to enhance the process capabilities. Recent developments include i) the use of inductively coupled rf with parallel plate rf geometries, and ii) the use of multiple filaments and anodes with magnetic confinement. These enhancements have led to substantial improvements in film properties as well as process control. Examples are high rate deposition of a-Si-H films (59), transparent conducting films on polymeric substrates (60) and TiS_x and MoS_x (61,62) films with variable x values.

Two additional modes of ionization are being explored. Currently an auxiliary rf excitation source similar to that reported by Oeschner (63) is being developed for use in ARE. It is believed that the high electron density and energy selectivity offered by this source is likely to enhance advantages of the ARE processes for compound synthesis. Also, work is underway to integrate Electron Cyclotron Resonance excitation at microwave frequencies with the ARE process. ECR plasmas are characterized by a very high level of ionization and excitation, and may greatly enhance the uses of ARE for the deposition and synthesis of films.

15.7 STRUCTURE AND PROPERTIES OF THE FILMS

The physical and chemical properties of films critically depend on structure and morphology, defects, and the impurity content.

The influence of process parameters on the film growth can be understood in terms of their effects on sticking coefficient, surface mobility of adatoms, nucleation density as well as the thermodynamic and kinetic factors determining the various chemical reactions occurring at the substrate, especially in the case of deposition of compound films. Plasma parameters influence film growth and properties in two ways:

1. By controlling the plasma volume chemistry thereby producing molecular precursors which determining the reaction path leading to the formation of one compound on the substrate;

2. By enhancing the energy of the condensing species thereby modifying the nucleation and growth of the films.

The interaction between deposition parameters and plasma or ion bombardment on film properties is indeed complex. This topic will be covered in more detail in Chaps. 19-21.

15.8 MATERIALS SYNTHESIZED USING THE ACTIVATED REACTIVE EVAPORATION PROCESS

A variety of compounds such as carbides, nitrides and oxides of refractory metals, sulphides, alloyed carbides, carbonitrides, superconducting coatings such as Nb_3Ge have been deposited using this technique. A representative list of the compounds synthesized using the ARE technique is given in Table 2.

In recent years, ARE and related processes have been successfully used to synthesize novel materials (64). Of particular industrial interest are cubic boron nitride, (65) diamond and high temperature superconducting films (66). The principal attributes of the process are related to its ability to control stoichiometry, structure and properties of the films as well as its ability to provide high deposition rates as low substrate temperatures.

15.9 FUTURE OUTLOOK AND PERSPECTIVE

With increasing demand for low temperature processing and requirements for new materials, plasma assisted processing is likely to remain a major research area. Modified and novel plasma excitation techniques such as auxiliary rf ion/plasma source/microwave excitation in conjunction with the basic ARE set-up is likely to further enhance its processing capability.

Apart from process development research, interest needs to be directed towards understanding the plasma chemistry and its role in film growth and properties. *Insitu* diagnostic studies using optical emission spectroscopy, mass spectroscopy and plasma mass spectroscopy, and other sophisticated tools such as coherent anti-Stokes Raman spectroscopy and laser induced fluorescence spectroscopy are necessary to develop quantitative models of film growth by the ARE and related processes. Such studies are not only important in understanding the basic film chemistry, growth and properties but also in developing appropriate modifications of the process to optimize the properties of deposited coatings.

15.10 CONCLUSIONS

The ARE process has demonstrated its versatility in the synthesis and deposition of thin films of simple and complex refractory compounds and at low temperatures which makes it compatible with many of the operations in microelectronics, optoelectronics and optical coatings. Further areas of application may be magnetic and ferroelectric films.

This process is used currently in industry in one or more of its variants to deposit TiN coatings on cutting tools. With the advent of reliable rate monitors, gas flow control systems, feed back loops and computer controlled processing, the ARE process should find its way into many other areas, including the synthesis of new and novel materials.

Table 2: Examples if some compounds synthesized and deposition rates obtained using ARE, reactive sputtering, and PACVD.

Compound	ARE $\overset{\circ}{A}$ min^{-1}	Reactive $\overset{\circ}{A}$ min^{-1}	PACVD $\overset{\circ}{A}$ min^{-1}
Carbides TiC, HfC, ZrC, VC	2000-3000	400-500	150-400
Nitrides TiN, HfN, ZrN	2000-3000	300-400	60-150
Oxides TiO$_2$, ZrO$_2$ Al$_2$O$_3$, SiO$_2$	1000-2000	200-800	200-300
Sulphides TiS$_2$, MoS$_2$ MoS$_3$	1000-2000		
Novel Materials			
Superconducting materials Nb$_3$Ge, CuMO$_{6S8}$	1000-1500		
Photovoltaic materials a-SiH, CuInS$_2$	1500-2000	50-200	
Optoelectronic materials Indium-tin-oxide, zinc oxide	500-1000		
Cubic BN	1000-1500		
Diamond			1000$\overset{\circ}{A}$hr^{-1}
carbon	300	200	

15.11 REFERENCES

1.   C. Deshpandey and R. F. Bunshah, Thin Solid Films 163: 131 (1988).

2.   B. Chapman, Glow Discharge Processes (Wiley and Sons Inc., N.Y., 1980).

3.   V. Soddy, Proc. R. Soc. London 78: 429 (1907).

4. S. Brinsmaid, W. J. Keenan, G. E. Koch, and W. F. Parsons, US Patent 2,784,115, March 5, (1957).

5. M. Auwarter, U. S. Patent 2,920,002 (1960).

6. C. S. Herrick and A. D. Tevebaugh, J. Electrochem. Soc. 110: 199 (1963).

7. M. A. Novice, J. A. Bennett, and K. B. Cross, J. Vac. Sci. Technol. 1: 73A, (1964).

8. R. B. Schilling, Proc. IEEE 52: 1350 (1964).

9. E. Ritter, J. Vac. Sci. Technol. 3: 225 (1966).

10. E. Ferrieu and B. Pruniaux, J. Electrochem. Soc. 116: 1008 (1969).

11. J. R. Rairden, Electrochem. Technol. 6: 269 (1968).

12. J. R. Rairden, in Thin Film Dielectrics ed. by F. Vratny (Electrochem. Soc. , New York, 1969) p. 279.

13. J. DeKlerk and E. F. Kelley, Rev. Sci. Instrum. 36: 506 (1965).

14. A. J. Learn and K. E. Haq, Appl. Phys. Lett. 17: 26 (1970).

15. A. Itoh and S. Misawa, Proc. 6th Intl. Vacuum Congress, Kyoto, in Jpn. J. Appl. Phys. Suppl. 2, Part 1: 467 (1974).

16. T. Abe, K. Inagawa, K. Obara, Y. Murakami, Proc. 12th Symp. on Fusion Technology, Zurich, September 13-17 (1982).

17. M. T. Wank and D. K. Winslow, Appl. Phys. Letts. 13: 286 (1968).

18. B. B. Kosicki and D. Khang, J. Vac. Sci. Technol. 6: 592 (1969).

19. W. Heitmann, Appl. Opt. 10: 2414 (1971).

20. W. Heitmann, Appl. Opt. 10: 2685 (1971).

21. H. Kuster and J. Ebert, Thin Solid Films 70: 43 (1980).

22. J. Ebert, SPIE 325: 29 (1982).

23. D. Hoffman and D. Liebowitz, J. Vac. Sci. Technol. 9: 326 (1972).

24. R. F. Bunshah, R. J. Schramm, R. Nimmagadda, B. A. Movchan and V. P. Borodin, Thin Solid Films 40: 169 (1977).

25. L. Holland, Vacuum Deposition of Thin Films (Chapman and Hall, London, 1956).

26. R. F. Bunshah, Thin Solid Films 107: 21 (1983).

27. L. I. Quill in The Chemistry and Metallurgy of Miscellaneous Materials and Thermodynamics (McGraw Hill Inc., New York, 1950).

28. R. F. Bunshah and A. C. Raghuram, J. Vac. Sci. Technol. 9: 1385 (1972).

29. R. F. Bunshah, US Patent 3,791,852, Feb. 2 (1974).

30. C. Deshpandey and R. F. Bunshah, J. Vac. Sci. Technol. A3: 553 (1985).

31. C. Deshpandey, B. P. O'Brien, H. J. Doerr, R. F. Bunshah and D. Hofmann, Surf. Coat. Technol. 33 (1987).

32. C. Deshpandey and R. F. Bunshah in Physics of Thin Films ed. by M. H. Fromcombe and J. L. Vossen (Academic Press, New York, 1987).

33. L. Holland, J. Vac. Sci. Technol. 14:5 (1977).

34. L. Holland, Surface Technology, 11: 145 (1980).

35. J. A. Thornton in <u>Deposition Technologies for Films and Coatings</u> ed. by R. F. Bunshah et al (Noyes, Park Ridge, N.J. 1982).

36. J. A. Thornton, <u>Thin Solid Films</u> 107: 3 (1983).

37. C. Deshpandey and R. F. Bunshah, to be published in Jour. of Materials Education.

38. A. K. Suri, R. Nimagadda and R. F. Bunshah, <u>Thin Solid Films</u> 72: 529, (1980).

39. P. Lin, C. Deshpandey, H. J. Doerr and R. F. Bunshah in <u>Quarterly Progress Report</u> ed. by F. A. Nichols and A. R. Michaels, TRIB-ECUT, 86-1 and 86-2, Argonne National Laboratory, Argonne, Illinois, U. S.

40. R. F. Bunshah and R. J. Schram, <u>Thin Solid Films</u> 40: 211 (1977).

41. M. Colen and R. F. Bunshah, <u>J. Vac. Sci. Technol</u> 13: 536 (1976).

42. K. C. Chi, R. O. Dillan, R. F. Bunshah, S. Alterovitz and J. A. Wollam, <u>Thin Solid Films</u> 54: 259 (1978).

43. H. S. Randhawa, D. Brock, R. F. Bunshah, B. Basol and O. M. Stafsudd, <u>Sol. Energy Materials</u> 6: 4456 (1982).

44. B. E. Jacobson, C. Deshpandey, A. A. Karim, H. J. Doerr and R. F. Bunshah, <u>Thin Solid Films</u> 118: 293 (1984).

45. P. Nath and R. F. Bunshah, US Patent 4,336,277, June (1982).

46. K. Nakumara, K. Inagawa, K. Tsusoka, and S. Komiya, <u>Thin Solid Films 40, 155 (1977).</u>

47. R. F. Bunshah, <u>Physical Vapor Deposition of Metals and Alloys and Compounds,</u> New Trends in Materials Processing, American Society of Metals, Metals Park Ohio (1976) p. 200.

48. M. Kobayashi and Y. Doi, <u>Thin Solid Films</u> 54: 67 (1978).

49. Y. Murayami, <u>J. Vac. Sci. Technol.</u> 12: 818 (1975).

50. R. F. Bunshah in <u>Deposition Technologies for Films and Coatings</u> ed. by R.F. Bunshah et al (Noyes, Park Ridge, NJ 1982).

51. S. Zega, M. Kornmann and J. Amiquet, <u>Thin Solid Films</u> 54: 51 (1978).

52. J. R. Morley, <u>Trans. Vac. Met. Conf.,</u> American Vacuum Society (1966) pg. 166, 186.

53. S. Komiya, N. Umezu and T. Narusawa, <u>Thin Solid Films</u> 54: 51 (1978).

54. A. Snaper, US Patent: 3,125,848, Dec. 7, 1971 and US Patent: 3,836,451, Sept. 17 (1974).

55. A. M. Dorodnov, <u>Sov. Phys.</u> 23: 1058 (1978).

56. R. F. Bunshah, K. L. Chopra, C. Deshpandey and R. F. Vankar, US Patent: 4,714,625, (1987).

57. D. Wu, D. Dijkkamp, S. B. Ogale, A. Inain, E. W. Chase, P. F. Miceli, C. C. Chang, J. M. Tarascon and T. Venkalesan, <u>Appl. Phys. Letts.</u> 51(11): 861 (1987).

58. A. Inam, M. S. Hedge, X. D. Wu, T. Venkatesan, D. England, P. F. Miceli, E. W. Chase, C. C. Chang, J. M. Taraskan and Y. B. Watchman, <u>Appl. Phys. Letts.</u> 53: (10), 908 (1988).

59. C. Y. Chen, M. S. Thesis, Dept. Mat. Sci. & Eng. University of California, Los Angeles, CA (1987).

60. B. P. O'Brien, M. S. Thesis, Dept. Mat. Sci. & Eng. University of California, Los Angeles (1987).

61. D. Zender, C. Deshpandey, B. Dunn and R. F. Bunshah in Proc. 5th Intl. Conf. on Solid State Ionics Part I, ed. by J. B. Boyle, L. C. Dejognhe and R. A. Huggins, (North Holland, Amsterdam, 1986) p. 813.

62. H. Shin, H. J. Doerr, C. Deshpandey, B. Dunn and R. F. Bunshah, to be published in Thin Solid Films.

63. Prof. H. Oeschner, University of Kaiserslauten, FRG, Private Communication, to be published.

64. C. Deshpandey and R. F. Bunshah, Thin Solid Films, 163: 131 (1988).

65. P. Lin, C. Deshpandey, H. J. Doerr, R. F. Bunshah, K. L. Chopra and V. D. Vankar, Thin Solid Films 153: 487 (1987).

66. S. Prakash, C. Deshpandey, R. F. Bunshah, to be published.

16

Formation of Thin Films by Remote Plasma Enhanced Chemical Vapor Deposition (Remote PECVD)

Gerold Lucovsky, David V. Tsu and Robert J. Markunas

16.1 INTRODUCTION

Much of the stimulation for research in the area of Plasma Enhanced Chemical Vapor Deposition, PECVD, comes from a more general interest in the low temperature processing of electronic materials, where low temperature usually means temperatures below about 500°C. In this chapter we emphasize the deposition of silicon containing dielectric materials, i.e., silicon oxide, nitride and oxynitride alloys, as well as hydrogenated amorphous silicon. These materials are currently utilized in several different types of device structures, but also have the potential for additional applications in more advanced and emerging microelectronic structures that require, for example, low temperature dielectrics. The limited use of the PECVD dielectric materials can, in part, be related to the nature of the deposition process reaction pathways in the conventional (and commercialized) Direct PECVD process that promote: (a) deviations from oxide or nitride compound stoichiometry, i.e., Si-Si bonds in addition to the Si-O and/or Si-N bonds; and (b) significant incorporation of bonded hydrogen, 2-10 at.% in the oxides, and as high as 20 to 40 at.% in the nitrides (1,2). The Direct PECVD dielectrics have nevertheless been used in applications such as in passivation and in field oxides, where deviations from compound stoichiometry and hydrogen incorporation are not deleterious to device operation. In contrast, Direct PECVD of a-Si:H (also called Glow Discharge decomposition or simply GD in the amorphous silicon literature) is the preferred method (3) for the a-Si:H films used in photovoltaic cells (4), xerographic photoreceptors and thin film transistors (TFT's) (5). In these applications, controlled incorporation of hydrogen at the 10-15 at.% level is essential for reducing the densities of intrinsic bonding defects, e.g., dangling bonds (3), to the low levels required for satisfactory device operation (3-5).

The deposition of oxide and nitride films on a substrate separated from the existing plasma was apparently first used by Alt et al (6) in 1963, although the description of the method was not reported until 1965 (7). A 500 kHz power supply was used to dissociate O_2 flowing into a reaction chamber into which tetraethoxysilane was introduced. In 1966, Secrist and MacKenzie (8) described the use of a 2.45 GHz discharge to activate O_2 and deposited a variety of films, including SiO_2.

In 1977, Shiloh et al (9) deposited Si_3N_4 by exciting N_2 in a 2.45 GHz microwave cavity from where it flowed into a heated tube into which SiI_4 was introduced; I_2 vapor was used to provide a gaseous source of Si from Si powder.

However, a much greater interest in the Remote PECVD (RPECVD) technique is marked by the publication in 1982 of several reports. The common intent was to deposit films at low substrate temperatures and with minimum introduction of damage, either structural or electrical, to the substrate. Kato et al (10) introduced an Ar/SiH_4 mixture into a 2.45 GHz discharge to deposit a-Si at a distance of 15 cm from the cavity center. Clark and Anderson (11) deposited Si_3N_4 on GaAs substrates using an rf (13.56 MHz) discharge to excite a N_2/H_2 mixture which flowed into the substrate chamber with an Ar/SiH_4 mixture introduced into a gas dispersal ring above the substrate. Meiners (12) deposited SiO_2 films on InP substrates using a 13.56 MHz discharge; he added N_2 to the O_2 in the discharge to increase deposition rates. The excited gas was mixed with a SiH_4/N_4 mixture in a heated tube and gases flowed over the heated substrate to the pump. Bardos, et al (13) compared the efficiency of microwave (2.45 GHz) and rf (13.56 MHz) discharges for the production of excited molecular N_2 for Si_3N_4 deposition by RPECVD.

Since 1982, many papers have been published on the deposition of a-Si, SiO_2 and Si_3N_4 films by RPECVD. It is not the intention here to review this literature in detail, but to discuss the possible reaction paths for film deposition. To provide an explanation of these processes and their consequences, we will use results obtained over several years in our laboratories as examples. This should make it easier for the reader to follow the discussion of the processes without having to consider possible effects of the many experimental arrangements which have been investigated in different laboratories.

This chapter begins with a discussion of the CVD process, focusing on the plasma enhanced procedures that have been applied for the deposition of the electronic materials discussed above. We identify the differences between the conventional Direct PECVD process and the Remote PECVD process, that is the subject of this chapter. We then discuss the Remote PECVD process in greater detail, emphasizing: (a) the deposition processes relative to selective excitation of the different gas reactants and/or diluents; (b) the design of deposition chambers used to implement these procedures or protocols; (c) the reaction pathways for deposition of hydrogenated amorphous silicon, and the silicon dielectrics; (d) selected vibrational, optical and electronic properties of the deposited films; (e) applications of these Remote PECVD films in device structures; and finally (f) new directions in Remote PECVD research, including the extension of the approach to additional electronic materials.

16.2 BACKGROUND - CVD PROCESSES

The CVD process is defined as the deposition of a thin solid film from a chemical reaction involving gas species at a heated substrate (14). For all CVD processes, the determinant factors in film formation are: (a) the rate of delivery of the process gases to the substrate; (b) the chemical reaction rates for film formation at the substrate surface; and

(c) the rate of removal of reaction by-products (14). In general, the transport of the gases is determined by the process pressure and the gas flow rates. Diffusion of source gases to, and by- product gases away from the deposition surface is enhanced at low pressures (below about 1 Torr). In hot wall CVD reactors, the temperature of the gas, T_g, is the same as that of the substrate, T_s. The operation of hot wall reactors at high pressures, e.g., at one atmosphere, can result in homogeneous gas phase reactions, sometimes resulting in the production of unwanted powder species. Powder formation can be eliminated by minimizing homogeneous gas phase reactions either by: (a) diluting the reactant gases with inert gases, thereby reducing the partial pressures, and the collision rates necessary for these reactions; or (b) using cold wall reactors in which only the substrate is heated. In cold wall reactors, the reactant gases generally do not react homogeneously in the gas phase to form the thin film material, but require either: (a) an additional energy input to increase their reactivity (14): or (b) a pre-activated nucleation surface site in order to be able to take part in heterogeneous surface reactions leading to film deposition (15-16). The basic or elementary CVD process is one in which all the additional energy is supplied at the heated substrate, and where the rate of reaction is then determined by the temperature of that substrate; i.e., T_s. There are no inherent restrictions on the nature of the heterogeneous chemical reactions that are used in CVD processes (14); they can be oxidation, pyrolysis, etc. We designate this type of process as thermal CVD. This definition is used to differentiate the thermal CVD processes from other CVD processes in which different source of energy, such as rf or microwave plasmas, are employed to activate the chemical reaction pathways leading to film deposition.

In general and depending on the particular reactants employed, thermal CVD processes for stoichiometric, hydrogen-free silicon oxides and nitrides, and for poly- or single crystal silicon, require relatively high substrate temperatures, in excess of 500°C, and generally in the range of 600 – 900°C (14). These temperatures are too high for many projected VLSI and ULSI devices because of thermal budget limitations (17,18). One approach to reducing substrate temperatures is to increase the reactivity of the process gases before their arrival at the deposition substrate. This can be accomplished by supplying energy to the reactants through excitation in the gas phase, e.g., using energetic electrons produced in either radio-frequency (rf) or microwave discharges, or using photons.

Our discussion of the enhancement mechanisms for CVD, will be limited to the plasma enhanced techniques, and in particular to plasmas generated by rf power. We note that the one important difference between rf and microwave discharges is in the energy distribution of the plasma-generated electrons (19), which results in significant differences in the specific nature of the plasma-activated species that take part in film deposition. We will not focus on this aspect of PECVD process. What concerns us instead is not exactly how the activated species are generated, but where they are generated with respect to the substrate, and which of the reactant gases are directly subjected to plasma excitation. The "where" and "which" represent the differences between two different plasma enhanced processes, Direct and Remote PECVD, which involve respectively either direct or remote plasma excitation of the process gases.

The distinction between Direct and Remote PECVD is made primarily on the basis of which of the gas reactants and diluents are directly plasma excited (2). In the Direct process, all process gases are exposed to a common rf plasma. In diode type rf reactors, the substrate is attached to one of the rf electrodes, usually the grounded electrode, and is immersed in the plasma glow. Silicon oxide and nitride films produced in this way usually display significant departures from compound stoichiometry, and also contain large amounts of bonded hydrogen, 5-30 at.% (1). In contrast, in the Remote PECVD process, not all of the reactant gases are plasma excited and the substrate is removed from the glow region of the plasma. These restrictions on which of the gases are plasma excited, and on the placement of the substrate outside the plasma glow region tend to limit the number of possible reaction pathways and thereby lead to increased control over stoichiometry and hydrogen incorporation (or elimination) in the deposited films. There is another and non-conventional Direct PECVD process technique where very high levels of dilution of the reactant gases by noble gases, approaching 10,000:1 in some cases, can also restrict the process of plasma excitation to a specific subset of the process gases, and therefore also limit the number of reaction pathways. We will not discuss this process in any detail, but instead refer the reader to the literature (20).

Finally, we note that there are several hydrid PECVD processes that combine some of the properties of the Direct and Remote processes. For example, in reactors of the triode design, the substrate sits below a grid which replaces one of the rf electrodes so that the substrate is not exposed directly to the plasma glow. This technique has been used primarily in the deposition of a-Si:H (21). Another technique uses microwave power, and also accomplished deposition outside the plasma. In this process, designated electron cyclotron resonance (ECR) microwave PECVD, the plasma is magnetically contained so that deposition occurs outside the glow region (22). In both these techniques, all the process gases are subjected to the plasma excitation. We refer the reader to another chapter in this volume for a discussion of the ECR PECVD process (23).

The initial attempts at rf excited Remote PECVD are described in Refs. 6-12,24,25. These papers provide the basis for the more recent and extensive studies pursued jointly in the Department of Physics at North Carolina State University and the Semiconductor Research Group at the Research Triangle Institute (2,26-28). These results form the body of this paper are discussed in detail in the sections that follow. Our emphasis is on the deposition process, rather than the film properties. However, we include short discussions of both film properties and device applications to complement the discussions of the deposition processes.

16.3 THE REMOTE CVD DEPOSITION PROCESS

16.3.1 Overall Deposition Reactions

Consider first a symbolic representation of an elementary CVD process that: (i) uses two different reactant gases, A(g) and B(g); (ii) has a gaseous reaction by-product, C(g); and (iii) generates a thin film solid material, F(s). The reaction leading to thin film formation is given by:

$$A(g) \; + \; B(g) \; + \; X(g) \; \rightarrow \; C(g) \; + \; X(g) \; + \; F(s) \tag{1}$$

where X(g) is an inert diluent; e.g., one of the noble gases. It should be noted that throughout this chapter, reaction pathways are designated by an arrow ($\rightarrow$). The pathways listed here have been simplified in that the specific quantities of each of the species have been omitted. To distinguish between the Remote and Direct PECVD processes, we use a starred bracket { }* to indicate those gases that are directly plasma excited. For the same reaction as in Eqn. (1), the Direct PECVD process is defined by

$$\{A(g) + B(g) + X(g)\}^* \to C(g) + X(g) + F(s) \tag{2}$$

and the Remote PECVD process by

$$\{A(g) + X(g)\}^* + B(g) \to C(g) + X(g) + F(s) \tag{3}$$

We also consider a second class of Remote PECVD processes where neither of the two reactant gases is directly plasma excited, but where at least one of the molecular species, e.g., A(g), is activated by electrons, ions, or metastable atoms extracted from a remote noble gas plasma. An illustration of this type of process reaction is given in Eqns. (4a), (4b) and (4c):

$$\{X\}^* \to X', e^*, X^+, \tag{4a}$$

where X is a noble gas, e.g., He, Ar, etc., and X^+ and X' are respectively, noble gas ions and metastables, and e^* are defined as energetic electrons generated in the remote plasma as opposed to those electrons formed as a result of a reaction (29). For a deposition process reaction that is driven by electron and/or ion excitation, we invoke the following two symbolic reaction equations:

$$(X^+, e^*) + A(g) \to A^*(g) + X + e \tag{4b}$$

$$A^*(g) + B(g) \to C(g) + F(s) \tag{4c}$$

where $A^*(g)$ is a reactive species activated: (a) through an inelastic collision with a plasma generated electron or ion (30); or (b) at an active surface site created by one of the plasma extracted species (15,16).

We now list the overall Remote PECVD process reactions that have been used to produce silicon dielectric films (2,26,28,31-33). We first indicate the films grown by the process described by Eqn. (3) that utilizes plasma excitation of noble gas/nitrogen containing molecule and/or noble gas/oxygen containing molecule mixtures:

$$\{O_2 + He\}^* + SiH_4 \to SiO_2 \tag{5}$$

$$\{N_2O + He\}^* + SiH_4 \to SiO_2 \tag{6}$$

$$\{N_2 + He \text{ or } Ar\}^* + SiH_4 \to Si_3N_4 \tag{7}$$

$$\{NH_3 + He \text{ or } Ar\}^* + SiH_4 \to Si_3N_4 \tag{8}$$

$$\{NH_3 + O_2 + He\}^* + SiH_4 \rightarrow \{SiO_2\}_x \{Si_3N_4\}_{1-x} \tag{9}$$

Thin film dielectrics have also been grown by the process described by Eqns. (4a-4c) (33-35), where the deposition process is initiated by extraction of excited species from a He or Ar plasma (30,33-35). For reaction processes involving remote He plasmas, the most probable activating species based on reported cross-sections for excitation are low energy electrons (30) and/or He ions which can result from both direct electron impact ionization as well as by the Penning ionization of He metastables as defined by:

$$\{He\}^* \rightarrow He' + He' \rightarrow He + e + He^+ \tag{10}$$

Although there are many channels operative in the production of He' metastables, e.g., by the direct electron impact, by the cascading of excited He atoms into the metastable state by photon emission, etc., the mechanism represented by Eqn. (10) is an effective way to consume the He metastable species (29). Using electrons and/or positive He ions as activators, the overall reactions for this second class of remote PECVD processes are given by:

$$He^+ + e^* + O_2 + SiH_4 \rightarrow SiO_2 + ... \tag{11}$$

$$He^+ + e^* + N_2O + SiH_4 \rightarrow SiO_2 + ... \tag{12}$$

$$He^+ + e^* + N_2 + SiH_4 \rightarrow Si_3N_4 + ... \tag{13}$$

$$He^+ + e^* + NH_3 + SiH_4 \rightarrow Si_3N_4 + ... \tag{14}$$

Films of intrinsic and doped hydrogenated amorphous silicon have also been grown by this type of process (36-39). The overall reactions here are: (a) for intrinsic a-Si:H thin films,

$$He^+ + e^* + SiH_4 \rightarrow a - Si:H \tag{15}$$

(b) for n-doped a-Si:H films,

$$He^+, e^* + SiH_4 + PH_3 \,[0.01 \text{ percent in } SiH_4] \rightarrow a - Si:H_{(n),} P \tag{16}$$

The Remote PECVD process has also been used to grow expitaxial films of Si and Ge (27), as well as carbon films, including diamond and diamond-like materials (40). The process protocols are essentially the same as that given in Eqn. (15), and the noble gases that have been used for the formation of epitaxial Si and Ge layers include Ar and He (27). For the discussion of these processes and the results obtained, we refer the reader to the literature (27,40).

16.3.2 Deposition Chamber Design and Process Variables

To produce films by Remote PECVD, the reaction chamber design must make provision for the special requirements of this process, specifically for: (a) selective excitation of the process gases; and (b) film deposition on a substrate outside the plasma glow region. We discuss the deposition chamber designs that have been employed in the Remote PECVD studies (26,41). The chamber designs, along with the operating pressures and relative gas flow rates, are designed to promote the reaction pathways indicated above, Eqns. (5-16), and in addition to eliminate, or minimize any direct plasma excitation of the SiH_4 reactant. Figure 1 shows a recent experimental chamber design with a second down-stream gas dispersal ring (41). The range of processing conditions used in the majority of the reported Remote PECVD studies is indicated below (26-28,31-33, 35-39,41,42):

- Chamber pressure prior to deposition: $< 5 \times 10^{-9}$ Torr

- Operating pressure for depositions: 100-300 mTorr

- Substrate temperatures: $100 - 500°C$

- Gas Flow rates: [X = O_2, N_2O, N_2, NH_3] :

  - X/He or Ar Mixtures: 100-200 sccm

  - He: 100-200 sccm

  - X: 100-200 sccm

  - SiH_4 [10% in Ar] : 1 sccm [10 sccm of Ar/SiH_4 mixture]

The low initial base pressure is required to insure the chemical cleanliness of the chamber; it is achieved after a thermal bakeout at $150 - 200°C$ that is designed to remove residual gas contaminants, primarily water vapor, from the chamber walls and fixtures. Water vapor can combine with silane via a homogeneous gas phase reaction to produce a silicon dioxide powder, which is detrimental to the thin film depositions. The operating pressure of 100-300 mTorr promotes the collision that are required for thin film deposition at rates between about 0.05-0.1 and 2-5.0 Å/s (2). The relative flow rates of reactant and diluent gases provide a range in which stoichiometric compound and alloy films have been grown, and in which bonded hydrogen incorporation can be controlled. The range of substrate temperatures does not vary deposition rates significantly, but has a profound effect on the amount of bonded hydrogen retained in some of the deposited films, primarily in the oxides, nitrides and a-Si:H alloys (31,37-39,42). More detailed discussions of the effects of processing variables on the film properties are given in the references cited above.

We now describe the way the chamber design in Fig. 1 is designed to implement the sequential steps of the Remote PECVD process. The Remote PECVD process can be described in terms of four discrete and separate process steps (2): (a) remote plasma excitation of a subset of the reactants and diluents; (b) transport of plasma generated reactive species from the glow region into the reaction chamber; (c) mixing of the plasma extracted reactive species with the remaining process gases; and (d) deposition of a thin film on a heated substrate remote from the plasma glow. The chamber designs provide:

(i) a fused silica tube in which process gases can be inductively rf plasma excited; (ii) one or more gas dispersal rings by which the remaining process gases can be introduced into the reaction chamber; (iii) a heated substrate for film deposition that is outside the plasma glow region. Backstreaming of gases, introduced through the dispersal rings, into the plasma region is minimized by the high flow velocity of the gases travelling through the rf excitation tube (43) and the small diffusion length for molecular migration established by the relatively high operating pressure (43).

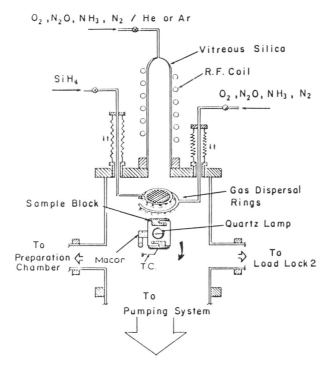

Figure 1: Deposition chamber for Remote PECVD with two downstream gas dispersal rings (41).

16.4. CHEMICAL REACTION PATHWAYS IN THE REMOTE PECVD PROCESS

16.4.1 The Deposition Analysis System

Figure 2 is a schematic representation of a system that has been used to study deposition reaction pathways (43). This system contains the gas feed and processing features of the chamber shown in Fig. 1, plus two additional tools for monitoring the process reaction pathways, optical emission spectroscopy (OES) and mass spectrometry (MS). The system consists of the following: (a) a fused silica feed gas tube with provision for remote plasma excitation by an inductively coupled rf field; (b) two downstream gas dispersal rings to introduce additional process gases; (c) provision to perform optical studies (e.g., OES) in the plasma, or downstream regions; (d) provision to sample process and by-product gases at different positions in the chamber using MS; (e) a movable, heated substrate for film deposition; and (f) a load lock substrate introduction chamber. In addition, studies have been performed in a mode where metallic screens with different bias potentials could be interposed in the gas stream in order to determine the extent to which ions and/or electrons play a role in particular deposition process reactions. Reaction pathways have been studied for the deposition of hydrogenated amorphous silicon, silicon dioxide and silicon nitride.

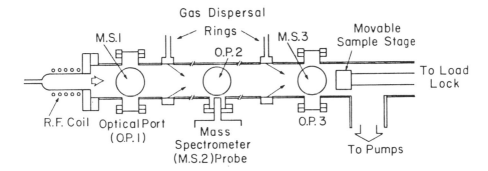

Figure 2: Schematic representation of the deposition/analysis system used to study reaction pathways in the Remote PECVD process (38,42,53).

16.4.2 Deposition of Hydrogenated Amorphous Silicon

We have deposited a-Si:H films using two different excitation mechanisms (36-39); these are described by the reactions given below:

$${Ar}^* \rightarrow Ar^+ + Ar' + e^* \tag{17a}$$

$${Ar}^* + SiH_4 \rightarrow a - Si:H \tag{17b}$$

$${Ar}^* + SiH_4 \rightarrow [SiH_x], \text{ polysilane powders} \tag{17c}$$

$${He}^* \rightarrow He^+ + He' + e \tag{18a}$$

$${He}^* + SiH_4 \rightarrow a - Si:H \tag{18b}$$

We have studied the He driven deposition more extensively because it generates a thin film of device grade a-Si:H with no other solid or powder reaction by-products (45). The Ar process generates polysilane powder via a homogeneous gas phase reaction in addition to thin films of a-Si:H via a heterogeneous surface reaction similar to the one present in the He process (37-39). The studies of the He-driven process include (45): (a) OES studies of the spectral emission from He plasmas; (b) MS studies of the species extracted from the He plasmas; and (c) MS studies of silane under three different conditions: (i) when it is the only gas flowing; (ii) when it is mixed with neutral He; and (iii) when it is mixed with the species extracted from a He plasma. The results of these studies indicate the following (45): (a) OES identifies the formation of metasable He' species by rf plasma excitation; (b) MS and biased grid studies demonstrate that the primary species transported from the plasma are He^+ ions, He neutrals and electrons, and that the He^+ ions and electrons are the SiH_4 activators; (c) MS studies do not show either a fragmentation of silane or the creation of higher silane species, such as disilane, etc., by mixing the silane with either neutral He, or the species extracted from the He plasma. The conclusion drawn from these observations is that the precursor for film deposition of a- Si:H is an excited SiH_4 molecular species, and that this is produced by an interaction with electrons, and/or He^+ ions (30). Additional insight into this process is gained by studying the substrate temperature dependence of the deposition rate as shown in Fig. 3, and the substrate temperature dependence of the bonded hydrogen incorporation as shown in Fig. 4.

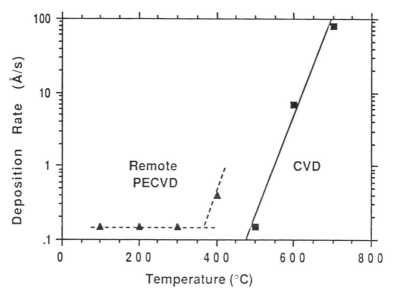

Figure 3: Deposition rate versus substrate temperature for: (a) deposition of a-Si:H alloys by Remote PECVD (3,49); and (b) silicon thin films by CVD (46,47).

Figure 3 shows the deposition rate for a-Si:H is independent of T_s for temperatures between about $100°C$ and $300°C$, but that is rises significantly for $T_s > 400°C$. We have made several observations: (a) the temperature dependence of the deposition rates for "homogoneous" chemical vapor deposition (HOMOCVD) (46,47) and for Remote PECVD (48) display similar behavior; (b) in addition to this similarity, the absolute values of the deposition rates are also about the same; and (c) for $T_s > 350°C$, the Remote PECVD deposition rate increases with about the same activation energy as the

HOMOCVD and thermal CVD processes; however, the deposition rate for the Remote PECVD process is about two orders of magnitude greater than the thermal CVD rates (46-48) at a given temperature.

Figure 4 compares the total bonded hydrogen concentrations, associated with the spectral features characteristic of monohydride and polyhydride bonding environments; e.g., SiH, SiH_2 and $[SiH_2]_n$, for films grown by Glow Discharge (GD) (3,49) and Remote PECVD (36). For T_s greater than about 70°C, the amount of incorporated hydrogen is always less in the Remote PECVD films. Studies of the distribution of the hydrogen between mono- and polyhydride bonding groups also indicate qualitative differences between the Remote PECVD films and the films grown by GD or HOMOCVD (3,37-39,46,47,50). The most notable difference is in the temperature at which polyhydride groups become the dominant bonding configurations. This occurs for T_s below about 200°C in the GD and CVD films (3,46,47,50), whereas in the Remote PECVD films, monohydride bonding dominates for temperatures down to about $50 - 100$°C (36-39).

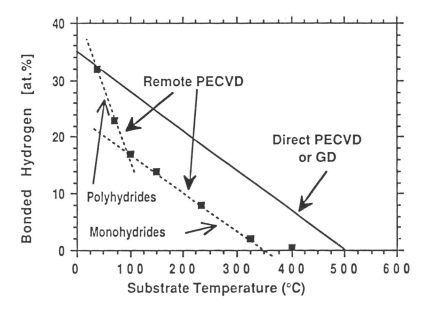

Figure 4: Bonded hydrogen incorporation in Remote PECVD and GD a-Si:H alloys as a function of substrate temperature (3,46,47,49).

The conclusion that is drawn from the comparisons displayed in Figs. 3 and 4 is that in the Remote PECVD process, the precursor species for film growth is different than in HOMOCVD, ordinary thermal CVD and GD with silane. It has been established that the silane molecule undergoes fragmentation into radicals, molecular fragments, ions, etc., in the CVD, HOMOCVD and GD processes (3,46,47,49), whereas in Remote PECVD, there is no evidence from MS for silane fragmentation (45). We believe that the active precursor species for film deposition in Remote PECVD is an excited molecule, SiH_4 *

(45). This is also supported by the very large cross section reported for excitation of SiH_4 by low energy electrons (E < 15eV) (30).

In addition, it is has been shown that the incorporation of hydrogen in a-Si:H deposited by GD (49) and reactive magnetron sputtering (51) derives from a surface that is saturated with hydrogen where the amount of hydrogen retained in the film is determined by substrate temperature (3,51). The comparisons in Fig. 4 lead the to the conclusion that the starting point for film growth in Remote PECVD is different from the GD process, specifically, below 350°C the surface is not saturated with hydrogen, but has a smaller hydrogen coverage determined by the exothermic CVD reaction of the excited silane molecules at the growth surface.

The situation is qualitatively different when species extracted from an argon plasma are used. In this instance, it has been reported that in addition to thin film formation with similar bonded hydrogen incorporation, there is also a homogeneous gas phase reaction that produces polysilane powders of the general composition SiH_x , with x < 2 (36-39). The formation of the solid films of a-Si:H is accomplished via a deposition reaction pathway similar to the remote He excitation pathway described above, but the concurrent powder formation implies a parallel reaction pathway in which there is also gas phase dissociation of the silane, presumably by Ar^+ ions. The reactions for the powder formation process are given by a sequence of attachment reactions of the general form (52):

$$\{Ar\}^* + SiH_4 \rightarrow SiH_2 + H_2 \tag{19}$$

$$SiH_2 + SiH_4 \rightarrow Si_2H_6 + SiH_2 \rightarrow Si_3H_8 \text{ to } \rightarrow SiH_x \tag{20}$$

The differences between the He and Ar processes then derive from differences in cross sections for the fragmentation process that generates the polymerization initiator, SiH_2.

16.4.3 Deposition of Silicon Based Dielectrics

16.4.3.1 Silicon Dioxide (SiO_2): It has been reported that the deposition rate for SiO_2 does not correlate with the plasma generation of atomic oxygen or molecular oxygen ions, O_2^+ , and that the most probable active oxygen species is then a molecular metastable, O_2' (53). It has also been established that atomic oxygen metastables, O', are not generated in rf plasmas (54), so that even though these species are known to be long lived, they are not generated in sufficient number to be important in the deposition of SiO_2 by Remote PECVD. The assumption that O_2' metastables are the active species is consistent with earlier experimental observations in Ref. 12. Combining the use of MS and OES, the following reaction pathway has been found (53):

$$O_2' + SiH_4 \rightarrow SiO_2 + H_2O + H_2 \tag{21}$$

It is also reported that departures from oxide stoichiometry, as Si-Si and Si-H bonds, are correlated with high He dilution ratios, He/O_2 of about 100 or greater (42,53). At these high dilutions, OES indicates that He metastable production in the plasma phase has increased significantly and dominates the plasma glow. Under these conditions, He^+ ions and energetic electrons generated via Penning ionization can excite the silane and open up an additional parallel reaction pathway for an amorphous silicon alloy constituent. The composition of the resulting film will be determined by the relative reaction rates for the two processes; deposition of SiO_2 which requires both SiH_4^* and O_2' and deposition of a-Si:H that simply requires SiH_4^*. This explanation is suggested by the data in Fig. 5, where the deposition rate for SiO_2 is displayed as a function of the He dilution of the O_2 source gas.

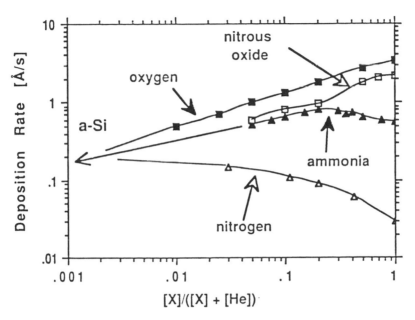

Figure 5: Deposition rate versus gas dilution for silicon oxide films grown from O_2 and N_2O (33,42,55) source gases, and for silicon nitride films grown from NH_3 and N_2 source gases (31,57). The source gases in each case are labelled **X** on the figure.

It has also been shown that an important source of OH contamination in oxide films derives from the purity of the oxygen feed gas   [the likely contaminants are H_2O and CH_4] (42). This has been established by comparing the OH and OD infrared absorption bands in SiO_2 :(OH) films grown from SiH_4 and SiD_4 process gases. In addition, SiOD groups are also found in the films grown from the SiD_4 process gas, indicating that OD groups are also generated in the heterogeneous reaction between the SiD_4 and the O_2. The generation of OH groups by the intrinsic mechanism appears to be correlated with the deposition rate, the higher the deposition rate the greater the SiOH incorporation. The incorporation of OH groups has been minimized by using: (a) down stream excitation of the oxygen as opposed to plasma excitation of oxygen along with the He (53); and (b) N_2O gas, rather than O_2, as the source of the oxygen atoms (55). There are also reported studies of the reaction pathways in the completely downstream excitation process in which active species extracted from a He plasma are mixed with both the reactant gases, SiH_4 and O_2, or SiH_4 and N_2O (55). The reaction pathways in these processes appear to be essentially the same as in the processes discussed above, i.e., they involve a surface reaction between excited SiH_4 molecules and O_2' metastables.

16.4.3.2 Silicon Nitride: Si_3N_4

(a) The Ammonia Process: Studies of the reaction pathways using the NH_3 reactions as described by Eqns. (8 and 14), have indicated the following (56): (i) for pure NH_3 plasmas, the films contain Si-NH bonds, and the OES studies indicate NH and H species in the plasma; (ii) for intermediate and high dilutions of NH_3 with He, to about 95% He, the films contain decreasing amounts of Si-NH, and the OES studies show the same NH and H species; (iii) for still higher dilutions >95 % He, stoichiometric nitride films can be grown. This corresponds to a narrow window, wherein the OES indicates significant decreases in NH emission, the presence of increasing N emission, and strong He emission. Finally, (iv) at the highest He dilutions >98 % He, He emission dominates and the films display significant departures from stoichiometry, containing both Si-Si and SiH bonding configurations. These observations establish that: (a) plasma generated NH species are the precursors for Si-NH bonds in the deposited films; (b) plasma generated N species are the precursors for "Si-N-Si" bonding arrangements; and (c), paralleling the reactions pathways for a-Si:H, silicon suboxides with SiH bonds, He' metastables are the precursors for departures from nitride stoichiometry and SiH incorporation in the resulting subnitrides.

Additional support for this model of two parallel deposition pathways, one for SiN or SiNH groups and a second for Si-Si and SiH groups, is derived from comparisons between films grown from NH_3 /He and NH_3/Ar mixtures (31,57). In both instances the deposition rate drops with increasing dilution. For the films grown from NH_3/Ar mixtures, the decrease in deposition rate is also correlated with the occurrence of SiH bonding in the deposited thin films. The limiting deposition rates for $T_s = 250°C$ are only a small range from about 0.56 Å/s for the deposition of silicon diimide films using pure NH_3, with a saturation of SiNH bonding groups, $Si(NH)_2$, to about 0.81 Å/s for mixed nitride/diimide alloys deposited with NH_3 fractions of about 0.20, and finally to about 0.5 Å/s for nitrides films with small amounts of bonded hydrogen (less than 5 at.%) and deposited with NH_3 fractions of about 0.05. There is a qualitatively different result for the deposition rate versus dilution for films grown from N_2/He gas mixtures; this is discussed below.

(b) The Nitrogen Process: The deposition rate for films grown from N_2/He gas mixtures for $T_s = 400°C$ increases with He dilution (31,57). This again is a manifestation of two different reaction pathways. In this instance the deposition rate for the silicon nitride material is smaller than the deposition rate for hydrogenated amorphous silicon material. As the He dilution increases, the deposition rate montonically increases from about 0.02 Å/s at the nitride end point to about 0.25 Å/s at the a-Si :H end point. If the film deposition depended solely on the presence of activated nitrogen species, we would expect the deposition rate to fall to zero as the source gas is depleted of N_2. Because this behavior is not observed, it shows that there is a smooth transition between the nitride deposition channel, which depends on the presence of nitrogen, and the a-Si:H deposition channel, which, as discussed above, is heralded by the presence of strong He emission lines. This explanation is supported by Infrared (IR) and Auger electron Spectrometry (AES) measurements which indicate the incorporation of both Si-Si and SiH bonds dilution levels greater than about 0.1. Films of silicon nitride have also been deposited with downstream injection of nitrogen; in this case the formation of stoichiometric nitrides required very high N_2 flow rates that correspond to N/Si ratios in the gas phase of greater than 100 (57).

16.4.3.3 Silicon Oxynitrides $[(SiO_2)_x(Si_3N_4)_{1-x}]$. The deposition rate for the silicon-oxynitride films grown from $O_2/NH_3/He$ gas mixtures also reflects a two channel mechanism in the deposition process (32). This is based on the absence of a linear correlation between the relative oxide and nitride bonding groups, and the fraction of O_2 or NH_3 in the feed gas mixture (32). The deposition rate for the "oxide-bonding" component is higher than that of the "nitride-bonding" component, and as a result of this the cross over point between oxide and nitride rich alloys occurs when the relative oxygen concentration in the feed gas is about 10% of its maximum value rather than 50% as would occur for equal deposition rates. We have just developed a second process for silicon oxide deposition based on N_2O as a reactant gas (55). This process is characterized by lower deposition rates than the O_2 process, and therefore offers the potential of being combined with NH_3 in a way in which the relative concentrations of oxygen and nitrogen in the deposited oxynitride films are closer to the relative concentrations of the respective oxygen and nitrogen containing feed gases.

16.5 SELECTED BULK PROPERTIES OF DEPOSITED THIN FILMS

We will present a short discussion of selected bulk properties of the a-Si:H and the silicon based dielectrics. Details are found in the references cited above. For a-Si:H, the studies have included chemical, optical and electronic properties (36-39), whereas for the silicon dielectrics the major emphasis has been on properties that yield information relative to the chemical bonding and composition (31,32,42).

16.5.1 Hydrogenated Amorphous Silicon

The primary tool for determining the chemical bonding in the films has been IR spectroscopy. Once a calibration scheme has been established (3). this turns out to be the most convenient way to determine the bonded hydrogen concentrations. The results of our IR studies are included in Refs. 36-39. There are two important observations relative to the differences between bonded hydrogen incorporation in a-Si:H alloys grown by Remote PECVD and Direct PECVD (or GD): (a) the amount of bonded hydrogen is lower in the Remote PECVD a-Si:H alloys by about a factor of at least two over the transition temperature range between 100°C and 400°C ; and (b) the way the bonded hydrogen is incorporated in the structure in the Remote PECVD films is very different. For example, for the temperature range between 100°C and 325°C , the dominant hydrogen bonding group in the Remote PECVD films is the monohydride (SiH) group, whereas in the Direct PECVD (or GD) films, polyhydride bonding groups such as SiH_2 and $[SiH_2]_n$ dominate for deposition temperatures less than about 200°C (3,36-39,50).

There have been other studies of electronic, optical and photoelectronic properties (36-39). The main differences between the Remote PECVD and GD materials are in the electronic properties of films deposited below about 200°C , and in excess of 300°C. The electronic properties of the GD films degrade significantly for T_s below 200°C (3), and in addition these low T_s films cannot be doped, whereas the Remote PECVD films show only very small degradations in electronic properties and doping efficiencies at T_s as low as 100°C to 125°C (30-32). These differences are correlated with the differences in bonded hydrogen incorporation as mentioned above, and are consistent with other studies which have attributed defect generation to changes in the film morphology due to polyhydride incorporation (3). In a complementary way the GD films grown with T_s between about 300°C and 400°C display much better electrical properties than a-Si:H grown by Remote PECVD for the same T_s range.

16.5.2 Silicon Dielectrics

The silicon dielectric thin films have been studied for the most part by techniques which elucidate various aspects of the chemical bonding: (a) by IR absorption to detect the presence of bonding groups containing hydrogen, i.e., SiH, SiOH and SiNH, and to detect departures from oxide stoichiometry; (b) by ellipsometry to measure the index and to estimate density; and (c) by Auger Electron Spectroscopy and X-ray Photoelectron Spectroscopy (AES and XPS, respectively) to determine stoichiometry, and in the case of the oxynitride alloys to determine the oxygen to nitrogen atom ratio. The details of these measurements and the results are included in Refs. 31, 32 and 42. In summary, the major advantages of the Remote PECVD process over the Direct PECVD of dielectrics identified in these studies are: (i) increased control of bonded hydrogen incorporation and stoichiometry by processing variables including relative dilution of gas mixtures and T_s; and (ii) the resulting ability to produce hydrogen free (defined by the limit of IR detection of about 0.5 to 1.0 at.%) dielectric films at substrate temperatures in the range of 100°C to 550°C. In addition there have been interesting and informative comparisons made between the properties of SiO_2 films deposited by Remote PECVD, and grown via high temperature thermal oxidation of silicon (700 − 1150°C); the results of these comparisons indicate that the local atomic structure and its relationship to the film density are different in the thermal and Remote PECVD oxides, but that these differences do not reflect on the electrical behavior of the films. Details of these comparisons are in Ref. 56 and 57.

16.6 REMOTE PECVD DIELECTRIC FILMS IN DEVICE STRUCTURES

16.6.1 Silicon Dielectrics in MOS Capacitors and FETs

There have been only a limited number of studies in which Remote PECVD dielectrics have been used in device structures. The two most notable examples are the use of a tri-layer oxide/nitride/oxide dielectric that was used for gate electrodes for a field effect transistor device based on (In,Ga)As (26). Three layers were used in the following way: (a) the oxide layers formed a barrier to prevent electron injection into the nitride layer; and (b) the nitride layer acted as a diffusion barrier to any transport of positive ions through the structure. Devices formed in this way displayed a transconductance of about 75 mS/mm, and showed less than a 5% drift during 24 hours stress bias testing.

In addition, there have been several studies using SiO_2 and silicon oxynitride layers in MOS and MIS capacitor studies (2,59). For structures using Remote PECVD oxide layers deposited for T_s between 250°C and 400°C onto crystalline silicon substrates, the following results were obtained: (a) breakdown fields were in excess of about $8x10^6$ V/cm; (b) densities of interfacial traps were generally less than $5x10^{10}cm^{-2}eV^{-1}$, with some devices displaying levels less than $10^{10}cm^{-2}eV^{-1}$ (59). Using silicon oxynitrides, in place of the oxides has the effect of reducing the break-down field by about 25% to about $6x10^6$ V/cm. The achievement of the low interfacial trapping state densities depends critically on the processing of the silicon surface; details are discussed in Ref. 59.

16.6.2 Amorphous Silicon Devices

The electronic and optical properties of Remote PECVD intrinsic and n-doped a-Si:H alloys deposited at temperatures between about $125\,^{\circ}C$ and $275\,^{\circ}C$ are similar to the properties of the so-called device or PV (photovoltaic) grade GD material (3,36-39). However, these films have not been used in device structures, e.g., p-i-n solar cells or TFT's.

16.7 RECENT DEVELOPMENTS IN REMOTE PECVD

16.7.1 Integrated Processing with in situ Process Diagnostics and in-situ Surface Analysis

In-situ analysis and *in-situ* diagnostics have been on going themes of the research activities at both North Carolina State University (NCSU) (41,44) and at the Research Triangle Institute (RTI) (59). The rationale behind the use of *in-situ* techniques is fairly straightforward. In some instances there are narrow windows in processing variables whereby some type of spectroscopic feedback can by used to maintain film composition and purity. One example is the use of OES to monitor the emission spectrum from He/NH_3 discharges to define the regime wherein atomic N spectral features are present, and thereby indicate that hydrogen free films with nitride stoichiometry can be deposited. With regard to *in-situ* surface analysis, this has been used in two ways: (a) to determine the character of silicon surfaces prior to dielectric film deposition for MOS structures (41,59); and (b) to determine oxide and nitride stoichiometry in deposited dielectrics (41).

The research performed at NCSU has used multi-chamber systems with in situ diagnostics and/or analysis (34), while the RTI approach has been with both in situ and free standing analysis, and with UHV transfer accessibility to the free standing instrumentation.

16.7.2 Other Material Systems

In addition to the materials described above, the Remote PECVD process has been used to deposit Group IV crystalline semiconducting films. This was done primarily at the RTI. Materials so far deposited include Si, Ge and Diamond (27,41). Preliminary studies indicate that films of compound semiconductors, e.g., GaN and BN (60) can also be grown by this approach.

There are also plans to extend the approach to other deposition chemistries employing different types of feed gases, e.g., halogenated silanes, SiH_2Cl_2 , and organometallics, $Si(CH_3)_4$ as sources of silicon atoms, and thereby extending the technique to additional materials such as multicomponent or mixed oxides, and metals and metal alloys.

16.7.3 Subcutaneous Oxidation Processes During Remote PECVD

We have have recently discovered that there can be oxidation reactions occurring at a semiconductor substrate during the Remote PECVD process, particularly during the deposition of SiO$_2$ thin films (61). We have found evidence for this process occurring for both Si and GaAs substrates. In the case of deposition of silicon oxides and oxynitrides on to silicon, the oxide that forms on the silicon substrate is self-limiting and grows to a thickness between 25 and 30Å . We have not as yet determined the thickness or composition of the native oxide formed on GaAs, although preliminary studies of the oxide character by AES indicate it has more Ga$_2$O$_3$ character than arsenic oxide character. These subcutaneous oxidation processes have important implications for the fabrication of device structures. In the case of Si/silicon oxide or oxynitride interfaces, the subcutaneous oxide does not prevent the formation of electronic grade device structures with low densities of interface traps, high breakdown fields, etc.. In fact, the subcutaneous oxide could possibly be the factor that promotes the excellent interfacial properties. In contrast, the subcutaneous oxidation of GaAs clearly degrades MOS/MIS device characteristics. We cannot form good GaAs MOS/MIS structures unless there is a 20-50 Å pseudomorphic silicon layer grown on the GaAs substrate prior to oxide deposition. This silicon layer must be thick enough so that it is not fully consumed in a subcutaneous oxidation process during the deposition. Similar considerations apply to the formation of germanium MOS/MIS structures. On the other hand, we have observed that oxide films could be directly deposition on (In,Ga)As substrates, with the resulting semiconductor/dielectric interface displaying excellent device characteristics (26). This means that subcutaneous oxidation of the (In,Ga)As is qualitatively different from the subcutaneous oxidation of GaAs.

The subcutaneous process proceeds in much the same way as a thermal oxidation or anodization process, i.e., active oxygen species (presumed to be atomic) are transported through the depositing oxide layer to the semiconductor surface and promote the oxidation process reactions at that surface. This means that the boundary between the semiconductor and the dielectric material is not the starting semiconductor surface, but rather is buried beneath that surface. This phenomenon clearly needs additional study, since it is one of the important considerations for device fabrication.

16.8 SUMMARY

We have described the important differences between conventional or Direct PECVD and rf-excited Remote PECVD for the deposition of a-Si:H alloys and for silicon dielectrics. We have shown that the two PECVD processes are fundamentally different with regard to the multiplicity of deposition pathways, which in turn has a significant effect on the ability to use process variables to control film composition and purity. In the direct process the simultaneous plasma excitation of all reactant gases and diluents opens many possible reaction pathways and thereby makes it virtually impossible to restrict deposition reactions to those which promote only the desired thin film bonding chemistry. There is one counter-example of a direct process for SiO$_2$ deposition where very high levels of silane dilution (up to 104:1 of He:silane) suppress plasma excitation of the silane gas and thereby restrict deposition pathways according (20).

ACKNOWLEDGEMENTS

The authors acknowledge support for their contributions to this research from The Office of Naval Research, The National Science Foundation, The Semiconductor Research Corporation, and The Solar Energy Research Institute. In addition one of us

(DVT) acknowledges additional support from The Standard Oil Company of OHIO (now British Petrolium/North America) and the Microelectronics Center of North Carolina.

16.9 REFERENCES

1. A.C. Adams, Plasma deposition of inorganic films. Solid State Technology 26: 135 (1983).

2. G. Lucovsky and D.V. Tsu, Plasma enhanced chemical vapor deposition: Differences between direct and remote plasma excitation. J. Vac. Sci. Technol. A5: 2231 (1987).

3. J.C. Knights and G. Lucovsky, Hydrogen in amorphous semiconductors. in CRC Critical Reviews in Solid State and Materials Sciences 9: 211 (1980).

4. D.E. Carlson, Solar energy conversion. in The Physics of Hydrogenated Amorphous Silicon I, ed. by J.D. Joannopolous and G. Lucovsky (Spring-Verlag, Berlin, 1984), p. 203.

5. W.E. Spear and P.G.LeComber, Fundamental and applied work on glow discharge material. in The Physics of Hydrogenated Amorphous Silicon I ed. by J.D. Joannopolous and G. Lucovsky (Spring-Verlag, Berlin, 1984), p. 63.

6. L.L. Alt, S.W. Ing and K.W. Laendle, J. Electrochem. Soc. 110: 465 (1963).

7. S.W. Ing and W. Davern, J. Electrochem. Soc. 112: 285 (1965).

8. D.R. Secrist and J.D. MacKenzie Ceram. Bull. 45: 784 (1966).

9. M. Shiloh, B. Gayer and F.E. Brinchman, J. Electrochem. Soc. 124: 295 (1977).

10. I. Kato, S. Wakana, S. Hara amd H. Kezuka, Jpn. J. Appl. Phys. 21: L470 (1982).

11. M.D. Clark and C.L. Anderson, J. Vac. Sci. Technol. 21: 453 (1982).

12. L.G. Meiners, Indirect plasma deposition of silicon dioxide. J. Vac. Sci. Technol. 21: 655 (1982).

13. L. Bardos, J. Musil and P. Taras, J. Phys. D: Appl. Phys. 15: L79 (1982).

14. W. Kern and V.S. Ban, Chemical vapor deposition of inorganic thin films. in Thin Film Processes, ed. by J.L. Vossen and W. Kern (Academic Press, New York, 1978), p. 258.

15. R.J. Buss, Pauline Ho, W.G. Breiland and M.E. Coltrin, Reactive sticking coefficients for silane and disilane on polycrystalline silicon. J. Appl. Phys. 63: 2808 (1988).

16. S.G. Brass and Gert Ehrlich, Activation Chemisorption: Internal degrees of freedom and measured activation energies. Phys. Rev. Lett. 57: 2532 (1986).

17. R. Rosenberg, Materials and processing science: Limits for microelectronics. AIP Conference Proc. 167: AVS Series, ed. by G.W. Rubloff (in Press).

18. J.F. Gibbons S. Reynolds, C. Gronet, D. Vook, C. King and W. Opyd, Limited reaction processing: Flexible thermal budgeting. AIP Conference Proc. 167: AVS Series, ed. by G.W. Rubloff (in Press).

19. M.R. Wertheimer and M. Moisan, Comparison of microwave and lower frequency plasmas for thin film deposition and etching. J. Vac. Sci. Technol. A3: 2643 (1983).

20. J. Batey and E. Tierney, Low-temperature deposition of high quality silicon dioxide by plasma enhanced chemical vapor deposition. J. Appl. Phys. 60: 3136 (1986).

21. A. Matsuda and K. Tanaka, Investigation of the growth kinetics of glow-discharge hydrogenated amorphous silicon using a radial separation technique. J. Appl. Phys. 60: 2351 (1986)

22. S.R. Mejia, R.D. McLeod, W. Pries, P. Shuffelebotham, D.J. Thomas, J. White, J. Shellenberg, K.C. Kao and H.C. Card, Fabrication of a-Si:H films by microwave plasmas under electron cyclotron resonance conditions. J. Non-Cryst. Solids 77&78: 765 (1985)

23. J. Asmussen, Chapter 11, this volume.

24. M.J. Helix, K.V. Vaidyanathan, B.G. Streetman, H.B. Dietrich and P.K. Chatterjee, RF plasma deposition of silicon nitride layers. Thin Solid Films 55: 143 (1978).

25. R.P.H. Chang, S. Darack, E. Lane, C.C. Chang, D. Allara and E. Ong, Plasma enhanced beam deposition of thin films at low temperatures. J. Vac. Sci. Technol. B1: 935 (1983).

26. P.D. Richard, R.J. Markunas, G. Lucovsky, G.G. Fountain, A.N.Mansour and D.V. Tsu, Remote plasma enhanced CVD deposition of silicon nitride and oxide for gate insulators in (In,Ga)As FET devices. J. Vac. Sci. Technol. A3: 867 (1985).

27. R.A. Rudder, G.G. Fountain and R.J. Markunas, Remote plasma- enhanced chemical-vapor deposition of expitaxial Ge films. J. Appl. Phys. 60: 3519 (1986).

28. G. Lucovsky and D.V. Tsu, Deposition of silicon based dielectrics by remote plasma enhanced chemical vapor deposition. J. Cryst. Growth 86: 804 (1988).

29. R. Deloche, P. Monchicourt, M. Eheret and F. Lambert, High-pressure helium afterglow at room temperature. Phys. Rev. A13: 1140 (1976)

30. A. Garscadden, G.L. Duke and W.F. Bailey, Electron kinetics of silane discharges, Appl. Phys. Lett. 43: 1012 (1983)

31. D.V. Tsu and G. Lucovsky, Silicon nitride and silicon diimide grown by remote plasma enhanced chemical vapor deposition. J. Vac. Sci. Technol. A4: 480 (1986).

32. D.V. Tsu, G. Lucovsky, M. Mantini and S.S. Chao, Deposition of silicon oxynitride thin films by remote plasma enhanced chemical vapor deposition. J. Vac. Sci. Technol. A5: 1998 (1987).

33. S.S. Kim, D.V. Tsu, G.N. Parsons, and G. Lucovsky, unpublished data.

34. S.V. Hattangady, G.G. Fountain, R.A. Rudder and R.J. Markunas, High density, low hydrogen content silicon nitride deposited at low temperature by novel remote plasma technique. J. Vac. Sci. Tech. A7: (1989), in press.

35. S.S. Kim, G.N. Parsons, D.V. Tsu and G. Lucovsky, Deposition of silicon oxide and nitride thin films by remote plasma enhanced chemical vapor deposition. IEEE Trans. Electron Devices (1989) in press.

36. D.V. Tsu and G. Lucovsky, Properties of the Si-H bond-stretching absorption band in a-Si:H grown by remote plasma enhanced CVD (RPECVD). J. Non-Cryst. Solids 97&98: 839 (1987).

37. G.N. Parsons, D.V. Tsu and G. Lucovsky, Optical and electrical properties of a-Si:H films grown by remote plasma enhanced chemical vapor deposition (RPECVD). J. Non-Cryst. Solids 97&98: 1375 (1987).

38. G. Lucovsky and D.V. Tsu, Differences between direct and remote plasma enhanced CVD. J. Non-Cryst. Solids 97&98: 265 (1987).

39. G.N. Parsons, D.V. Tsu and G. Lucovsky, Properties of intrinsic and doped a-Si:H deposited by remote plasma enhanced chemical vapor deposition. J. Vac. Sci. Technol. A6: 1912 (1988).

40. D.J. Vitkavage, R.A. Rudder, G.G. Fountain and R.J. Markunas, Plasma enhanced chemical vapor deposition of polycrystalline diamond and diamondlike films. J. Vac. Sci. Technol. A6: 1812 (1988).

41. S.S. Kim, D.V. Tsu and G. Lucovsky, Deposition of device quality silicon dioxide thin films by remote plasma enhanced chemical vapor deposition. J. Vac. Sci. Technol. A6: 1740 (1988).

42. D.V. Tsu and G. Lucovsky, The growth of silicon oxide thin films by remote plasma enhanced CVD. Mat. Res. Soc. Symp. 77: 595 (1987)

43. B. Chapman, Glow Discharge Processes (John Wiley and Sons, New York, 1980)

44. D.V. Tsu, G.N. Parsons and G. Lucovsky, Spectroscopic emission studies of O2/He and N2/He plasmas in remote plasma enhanced chemical vapor deposition. J. Vac. Sci. Technol. A6: 1849 (1988).

45. G.N. Parsons, D.V. Tsu and G Lucovsky, Deposition mechanisms for remote plasma enhanced deposition (RPECVD) of amorphous silicon hydrogen alloys. J. Vac. Sci. Technol. A7: (1989) in press.

46. B.A. Scott, R.M. Plecenik and E.E. Simonyi, Kinetics and mechanism of amorphous hydrogenated silicon growth by homogeneous chemical vapor deposition. Appl. Phys. Lett. 39: 73 (1981).

47. B.A. Scott, J.A. Reimer, R.M. Plecenik, E.E. Simonyi and W.Reuter, Low defect density amorphous hydrogenated silicon prepared by homogeneous chemical vapor deposition. Appl. Phys. Lett. 40: 973 (1982).

48. G.N. Parsons, D.V. Tsu and G. Lucovsky, Chemical reaction pathways in the formation of amorphous silicon thin films by remote plasma enhanced chemical vapor deposition (RPECVD). Presented at MRS Conf, Boston (1988).

49. K. Tanaka and A. Matsuda, Glow-discharge amorphous silicon: Growth process and structure. Mat. Sci. Reports 2: 139 (1987).

50. G. Lucovsky, R.J. Nemanich and J.C. Knights, Structural interpretation of the vibrational spectra of a-Si:H alloys. Phys. Rev. B19: 2064 (1979).

51. R.A. Rudder, J.W. Cook, Jr., J.F. Schetzina and G. Lucovsky, Planar magnetron sputtering of a-Si:H and a-Ge:H thin films. J. Vac. Sci. Technol. A2: 326 (1984).

52. P.A. Longeway, R.D. Estes and H.A. Weakliem, Decomposition kinetics of a static direct current silane glow discharge. J. Phys. Chem. 88: 73 (1984).

53. D.V. Tsu, G.N. Parsons and G. Lucovsky, Studies of the reaction process in the remote plasma enhanced CVD of SiO$_2$. J. Vac. Sci. Technol. A7: (1989) in press.

54. J.H. Kolts and D.W. Setser, Electronically excited long-lived states of atomic and diatomic molecules in flow systems. in Reactive Intermediates in the Gas Phase, ed. by D.W. Setser (Academic Press, New York, 1979), p.195.

55. S.S. Kim, D.V. Tsu and G. Lucovsky, unpublished.

56. D.V. Tsu, S.S. Kim and G. Lucovsky, Deposition of SiO_2 thin films by remote plasma enhanced chemical vapor deposition (Remote RECVD). <u>Proceedings of Electrochemical Society Meeting,</u> Spring 1988, Atlanta, GA (in press).

57. D.V. Tsu, G. Lucovsky and M. Mantini, "Local atomic structure in thin films of silicon nitride and silicon diimide produced by remote plasma enhanced chemical vapor deposition", Phys. Rev. B 33, 7069 (1986).

58. G. Lucovsky, J.T. Fitch, E. Kobdea and E.A. Irene, Local atomic structure of thermally grown SiO_2 films. <u>Proceedings of Electrochemical Society Meeting,</u> Spring 1988, Atlanta, GA (in press).

59. G.G. Fountain, R.A. Rudder, S.V. Hattangady, R.J. Markunas and P.S. Lindorme, Low interface state density SiO_2 deposited at 300°C by remote plasma-enhanced chemical-vapor deposition on reconstructed Si surfaces. <u>J. Appl. Phys.</u> 63: 4744 (1988).

60. R.A. Rudder, unpublished.

61. G.G. Fountain, S.V. Hattangady, R.A. Rudder, R.J. Markunas, S.S. Kim, D.V. Tsu and G. Lucovsky. Evidence for the occurrence of subcutaneous oxidation during low temperature remote plasma enhanced deposition of silicon dioxide films. <u>J. Vac. Sci. Technol.</u> A7: (1989) in press.

17

Selective Bias Sputter Deposition

Soren Berg and Claes Nender

17.1 INTRODUCTION

It is quite common, during sputter deposition, to introduce some bias to the substrate. This normally improves the quality of the deposited film, due partly to a low energy ion bombardment of the growing film that may preferentially remove loosely bonded atoms or molecules from the surface. The energy released by low energy ions to the surface may also increase the surface mobility of the incoming atoms. Thus more of these atoms will find stable sites before nucleation. The normal energy of the substrate bombarding ions in bias sputtering is in the range of 50-150 eV. In this energy interval the sputtering yield values for most materials are very low. However, the situation may drastically change if the bias is increased to a somewhat higher level. In this case a competition will take place between deposition of material from the target to the substrate and sputter removal of this material from the substrate by the high energy ions. In Fig.1 a schematic drawing of a typical bias sputtering system is shown. In this system the substrates are resting on the substrate table.The target and the substrate table may be excited individually. In such a system the sputtering of material from the target may be kept almost constant by keeping the target voltage fixed at a certain value, V_T . The voltage applied to the substrate table, V_S, may then be varied independently. By increasing the substrate bias V_S and keeping V_T constant one can expect the net deposition rate to decrease. This is due to an increasing fraction of the deposited material that will be removed by physical sputtering. At a certain bias value, V_S, one will find that the sputter removal rate equals the material deposition rate. The net deposition rate at the substrate will then be zero. If the substrate bias is further increased a net substrate etching will occur. The above described effect has been observed and is well known since the time of the introduction of the bias sputtering technique.

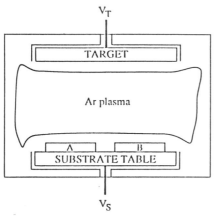

Figure 1: Schematic drawing of a bias sputtering system used for selective bias sputter deposition. V_T and V_S represent the voltages exciting the target and the substrate respectively.

17.2 SUBSTRATE DEPENDENT BIAS SPUTTER DEPOSITION

The region, close to zero net deposition rate in bias sputtering, has not been studied earlier in any greater detail. It has recently been observed that this processing region exhibits substrate dependent properties (1-4). It is thus possible to obtain different effects on different substrate materials during identical processing conditions. Fig. 2 illustrates schematically what can be observed during bias sputter deposition of target material onto two different substrates during identical processing. The result is usually that the bias values for zero net deposition rates V_{SA} and V_{SB}, as described in the figure, are not identical for different substrate materials. In the substrate bias region, where $V_{SA} < V_S < V_{SB}$, a net target film deposition will occur on substrate material B while no material will be deposited onto substrate material A. In fact the substrate surface of material A will be slightly sputter etched (negative "deposition" rate). In the processing region $V_{SA} < V_S < V_{SB}$ a selective bias sputter deposition region is found. A patterned substrate wafer may thus be selectively coated with one of the materials in this processing region. A schematic drawing of such a substrate structure before and after selective bias sputter deposition is shown in Fig 3. As indicated in this figure, it is possible to fill a hole selectively on a patterned substrate structure without using any masking technique.

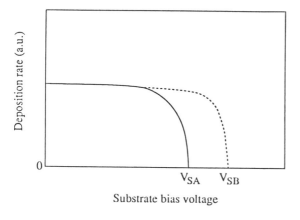

Figure 2: Schematic drawing of the deposition rate as a function of bias voltage V_S for the system shown in Fig. 1. V_T is assumed to be kept constant . The two curves represent deposition on two different substrates (A and B).

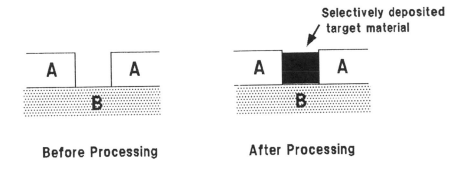

Before Processing   After Processing

Figure 3: Schematic drawing of a patterned substrate consisting of the two materials A and B exposed to the bias sputtering process operating in the region $V_{SA} < V_S < V_{SB}$ as defined in Fig. 2.

17.3 DEPOSITION-ETCHING BALANCE IN BIAS SPUTTERING

The fact that the deposited target material is more easily removed from substrate A than from substrate B in Fig.2 is due to differences in the surface phenomena at the interface between the substrate and the ion-assisted growing film.This interface formation may at a first approximation be described as a balance between deposition of target material and sputter removal of this material from the substrate surface. The situation, at the substrate surface, is shown in Fig. 4. The substrate surface is, at a certain time t, partially covered by the deposited target material. The fraction of the surface covered by a film is denoted Θ. The arrow F_T represents the flux of sputtered target atoms arriving at the substrate. Those atoms that arrive at the fraction $(1 - \Theta)$ of the substrate will have a certain sticking probability α_S to the original substrate material. Atoms from the target arriving at the Θ fraction of the substrate surface will face a film consisting of target material. The sticking probability for atoms arriving on this area may be different from others and will be denoted α_T. The number N_r of sputter deposited target atoms on the substrate will be

$$N_r = F_T[(1 - \Theta)\alpha_S + \Theta\alpha_T] \tag{1}$$

Due to the biasing conditions, the substrate is bombarded by an argon ion flux J that causes sputter removal of some of the deposited film. The sputtering yield of the deposited film is denoted S. The bias sputtering will erode some of this deposited material. The number N_s of target atoms sputtered away from the deposited substrate surface will be

$$N_s = J \Theta S \tag{2}$$

By definition there is no film of target material on the $(1 - \Theta)$ fraction of the substrate surface. When Θ approaches 1, the original substrate is completely covered by a film of the target material. Therefore the conditions during further deposition will not depend on the original substrate material. To understand the selective deposition shown in Fig. 2, we have to investigate in some detail the deposition/etching balance on the surface in the region $0 < \Theta < 1$. This can easily be done by plotting the N_r and N_s from Eqs. (1) and (2) in the nomogram, shown in Fig. 5. The two solid lines represent the deposition fluxes onto two different substrate materials, Eqs. (1). The two dotted lines represent two different sputter removal fluxes from these substrates due to the bias applied to the substrate table, Eqs. (2).

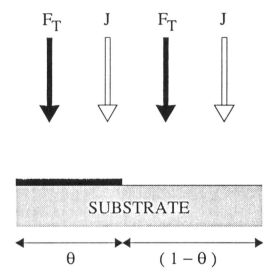

Figure 4: Schematic of particle fluxes on a substrate surface during the bias sputter deposition process. Θ represents the fraction of the substrate surface covered by target atoms. F_T represents the incoming flux of sputtered target atoms and J is the Ar ion flux that causes sputter erosion from the substrate surface.

When the surface is completely covered by a thin film of the target material ($\Theta = 1$), the sticking coefficient is α_T in both cases. That is why the two solid lines coincide at this point for $\Theta = 1$. However, at the initial stage of the deposition process ($\Theta = 0$), the incoming flux of sputtered target atoms will face an uncoated original substrate surface. The two substrate surfaces may differ in the sticking probabilities α_A and α_B to the incoming flux of sputtered target atoms. This is the reason why the deposition fluxes start at different values at $\Theta = 0$. Two levels of sputter erosion, J_1 and J_2, are shown in the nomogram. J_1 is selected so that $J_1 S > F_T \alpha_T$. The dotted line that represents this sputter erosion level in Fig. 5 crosses both solid lines. Before these crosspoints the deposition rate is larger than the sputter removal rate and a net deposition of target material occurs at the substrate surface. However, at the crosspoints the net deposition will be zero. At these points the deposition saturates and no further net deposition will take place. The substrates will thus only partly become covered by the target material. This fractional coverage Θ will be slightly different for the two substrates. J_2 may be selected in a way so that $J_2 S < F_T \alpha_T$. In this case the deposition rate always exceed the sputter erosion rate. A net deposition will therefore, in this case, always occur onto both substrates. The net deposition rate will be different for the two substrate materials as long as $\Theta < 1$. However, as $\Theta > 1$ the deposition rates will be equal and constant onto both substrates. The flux N_a of deposited atoms will simply be

$$N_a = F_T \alpha_T - J_2 S \tag{3}$$

This simple description indicates that the deposition conditions depend on the original substrate before the substrate is completely covered by target material during bias sputtering. However, it did not enable us to explain the possibility of depositing a thick film on one substrate while obtaining an almost uncovered surface on the other substrate surface.

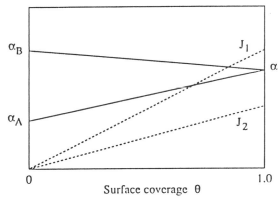

Figure 5: Nomogram representing, in the region $0 < \Theta < 1$, the rate of deposition on to two different substrates, A and B (solid lines). The etching of the deposited material is represented by the dashed lines. Two different etching intensities J_1 and J_2 are shown. The sputtering yield value was assumed to be constant during processing according to expression (2) in the text.

17.4 SPUTTERING YIELD VALUES AT THE FILM-SUBSTRATE INTERFACE

Expression (2) above neglects that the deposited atoms that arrive from the target to the substrate surface, at the initial stage, will bind to the partly covered substrate surface with a binding energy that depends on the composition of this surface. According to the sputtering theory (5) the sputtering yield value S is determined by

$$S = \frac{3\sigma M_{Ar} M_T E}{4\pi^2 (M_{Ar} + M_T)^2 E_{Bi}} \tag{4}$$

where E is the energy of the incoming argon ion, M_{Ar} is the mass of the argon ion, M_T is the mass of the target (film) atom, E_{Bi} is the binding energy of the atom to be sputter removed and σ is a constant. At the initial stage of deposition ($\Theta = 0$), the incoming target atoms will stick to a surface purely consisting of original substrate atoms. The binding energy of a target atom on this surface may be denoted E_{TS}. When this atom is removed by sputtering it will have a sputtering yield value $S(E_{TS})$ given by Eq.(4) using $E_{Bi} = E_{TS}$. When the substrate is completely covered by a film of target material ($\Theta > 1$) further incoming target atoms will bind to the deposited film with a binding energy

E_{TT}. The corresponding sputtering yield value will be $S(E_{TT})$ where $E_{Bi} = E_{TT}$ in Eq.(4). The binding energy E_{Bi} will gradually change from E_{TS} to E_{TT} as Θ increases from 0 to 1. One may therefore conclude from Eq.(4) that the sputtering yield of the deposited target material gradually changes from S_{TS} to S_{TT} in the fractional surface coverage interval $0 < \Theta < 1$. To describe the bias sputter deposition process more correctly the sputtering yield value in Eq. (2) has to be replaced by a yield value that depends on the surface fractional coverage Θ. At a first approximation the sputtering yield may be written as a linear function

$$S(\Theta) = S_{TT}[1 - \mu(1 - \Theta)] \qquad (5)$$

where μ is a constant that may be positive or negative depending on which of S_{TT} or S_{TS} has the largest value. Inserting Eq.(5) into the Eq. (2) will give a new expression for the flux N_s of material sputtered away from the surface

$$N_s = J \Theta S_{TT}[1 - \mu(1 - \Theta)] \qquad (6)$$

This expression is no longer linearly dependent on Θ.

17.5 SELECTIVE BIAS SPUTTER DEPOSITION

Figure 5 may be replaced by a new nomogram using Eq. (6) as a measure of the sputter removal effect. This is shown in Fig. 6. In this figure the solid lines represent the deposition process identical to those in Fig. 5. The dotted curves represent the sputter removal effect according to Eq. (6). If $J = J_1$ is made high the sputtering curve will cross the deposition lines for both substrate surfaces somewhere in the interval of $0 < \Theta < 1$.

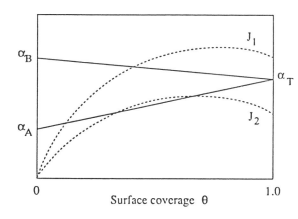

Figure 6: Nomogram identical to Fig. 5, but using a sputtering yield value that depends on the fractional coverage Θ as in Eq. (6).

The net deposition rate at these points then will be zero and the surface coverage saturates at a value of $\Theta < 1$. This processing condition does not give rise to any selective bias sputter deposition. However, if the sputter intensity is somewhat reduced to $J = J_2$ a very interesting situation may occur. The sputtering curve will now cross only one of the substrate deposition lines. This indicates that we have a situation where we will obtain film deposition on the substrate surface B but not on substrate A. The film thickness on substrate material A will saturate at a fraction of a monolayer. The film thickness on substrate B may be grown to any desired thickness. A selective bias sputter deposition processing region may thus be theoretically predicted from this nomogram.

In Fig. 7 the general shapes of the time dependent growth in film thickness on the above described substrates are shown. At $\Theta = 1$ the substrate is completely covered by a film of target material. The film thickness on substrate A will never reach this level. This substrate will thus never be completely covered by a film irrespective of the processing time. The deposition thickness on substrate B will exceed $\Theta = 1$ and continue to grow as long as the process continues.

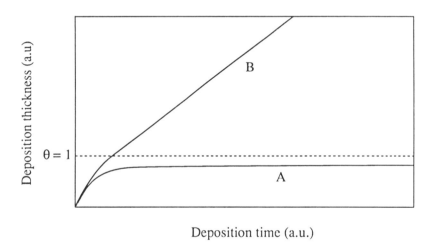

Deposition time (a.u.)

Figure 7: Time dependent growth in film thickness on the two substrates described in Fig. 6 for the conditions that $J = J_2$. On substrate B the deposition rate always exceeds the etching rate. Film growth will proceed during the whole processing time. On substrate A deposition rate will be identical to the etching rate at a certain value of $\Theta, 0 < \Theta < 1$. The film thickness will saturate at this coverage value.

Selective bias sputter deposition has been observed experimentally (2). In Fig. 8 the results from rf bias sputter deposition of Ti in argon onto substrates of Si, Au and Pt are shown. During this experiment the bias voltage V_S was kept constant. These results clearly demonstrate that selective bias sputter deposition can be obtained. At $V_T = 1.75kV$, Ti will be deposited onto Si and Au substrates but not on the Pt substrate (The substrates were made up by thin films of Si, Au and Pt deposited onto silicon wafers).

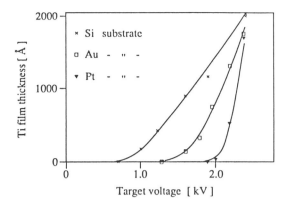

Figure 8: Experimentally observed Ti film thicknesses on three different substrates after selective bias sputter deposition in 15 minutes. The substrate bias was kept constant 0.8 kV. From ref. (2).

17.6 SELECTIVE BIAS SPUTTER ETCHING

A fundamental feature should be pointed out of the selective bias sputtering process. No substrate can be deposited on by this technique without undergoing a certain amount of sputter erosion of the original substrate surface (4). Before the surface is completely covered by a thin film ($\Theta < 1$), the fraction $(1 - \Theta)$ of the original substrate surface is exposed to argon sputter erosion. This sputter erosion will decrease as the value of Θ increases. Finally, when Θ approaches unity, $(1 - \Theta) = 0$, and further erosion is now prevented by the film that has been formed on top of the substrate surface. A schematic drawing of this substrate etching effect during bias sputtering is shown in Fig 9. In this figure the substrate is shown before and after bias sputter deposition of a thin film. It is important to realize that some part of the upper layers of the original substrate has been etched away during the period when $\Theta < 1$. Therefore the value of the film thickness d_o is different from the value of the step height d.

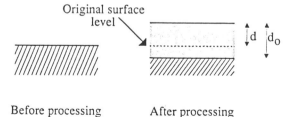

Original surface level

Before processing   After processing

Figure 9: Schematic of unavoidable substrate etching during high bias sputter deposition. The original substrate is etched $(d_o - d)$ before the substrate surface is completely covered by a film of target atoms.

In normal bias sputtering ($V_S < 100$ Volts) the difference ($d_o - d$) is negligible. However, at high bias sputter deposition this difference may be as large as several thousand Ångströms. A mechanical stylus or multiple interference microscope thickness measurement will not produce a proper measurement under these biasing conditions. These techniques normally measure the stepheight d instead of the actual film thickness d_o.

The selective bias sputtering deposition technique may also be used as a mask-less selective etching process. In Fig. 2 it was pointed out that in the region $V_{SA} < V_S < V_{SB}$ deposition took place onto substrate B while etching occurred at substrate A. Selective etching of material A takes place in this processing region. By using e.g. carbon as the target material, substrate areas of material B will be covered by a carbon film while substrate areas of material A will be etched to the desired depth. After processing, this carbon layer can easily be removed by stripping in an oxygen plasma. A simplified drawing of the three steps involved are shown in Fig. 10.

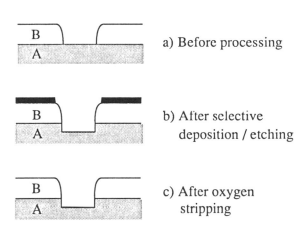

a) Before processing

b) After selective deposition / etching

c) After oxygen stripping

Figure 10: Principle of maskless selective bias sputter etching. (a) Patterned structure before processing. (b) Target material (e.g. carbon) is selectively bias sputter deposited onto substrate areas of material B. Substrate areas of material A will be exposed to a net etching effect assuming that A and B behave like in Fig. 7. (c) The deposited carbon can easily be removed by conventional oxygen plasma stripping, leaving a selectively etched patterned substrate.

17.7 THE SELF LIMITING ETCH DEPTH TECHNIQUE

A further unique property of this bias sputter deposition process is that it enables etching to a predetermined depth without using the etching time as a parameter to determine the etch-depth. In Fig. 9 is shown that it is unavoidable to etch away some substrate material before the substrate is completely covered by a film of the target material. This etch depth is determined by the processing parameters and the properties of the substrate material. However, once the substrate has been covered by some monolayers of the target atoms no further etching of the original substrate surface will take place. This effect is called the Self Limiting Etch Depth effect (1). Without going into the mathematical details, Fig. 11 shows a schematic drawing of the etch-depth penetrations into two different substrates (called X & Y) as a function of bias sputter etching/deposition time. The processing conditions have been assumed to satisfy the requirements that the substrates will be completely covered by a film of target atoms. From Fig. 11 it is seen that the etch depths saturate (d_X and d_Y) after certain times (t_X and t_Y). These length of times are the times needed to deposit some monolayers of film onto the substrate surface. This film will then prevent further etching of the underlaying original substrate surface. If the processing continues further, the film deposition will continue also, but no more etching of the underlaying substrate will be possible. Thus, as long as the processing time t_P is made long enough ($t_P > t_X, t_Y$) the etch depth into the original substrate will depend only on the plasma/substrate conditions and not by the processing time. Neither conventional argon sputter etching, nor plasma etching have this property of etch depth saturation.

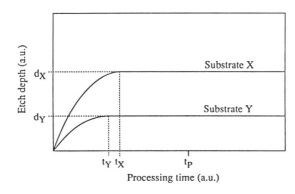

Figure 11: Principle of etch depth penetration into original substrate surface during selective bias sputter deposition onto two materials X and Y. The substrates are covered by a film of target atoms after the times t_X and t_Y respectively. Etch depths saturate at d_X and d_Y in the two substrates.

17.8 CONCLUSIONS

High bias sputter deposition may introduce substrate dependent film thickness formation. The reason for this effect is that sputter etching of the substrate takes place simultaneously with film deposition. This causes the substrate/film interface to be exposed to ion bombardment for a prolonged time. During this ion bombardment of the interface, the sputter erosion rate is substrate dependent. As soon as the interface is completely covered by the deposited film, the substrate dependence of the film growth-rate disappears. Utilizing this property of the plasma exposed interface, makes it possible to design bias sputter processing conditions that enables selective deposition or selective etching of patterned substrates. Thus it is possible to obtain maskless deposition or etching of patterned substrates with this technique.

17.9 REFERENCES

1. S.Berg, B.Gelin, M. Östling and S.M.Babulanam, J. Vac. Sci. Technol. A2(2): 470 (1984).

2. S.Berg, C. Nender, B. Gelin and M. Östling, J. Vac. Sci. Technol. A4: 448 (1986).

3. C.Nender, S.Berg, B.Gelin and B.Stridh, J. Vac. Sci. Technol. A5(4): 1703 (1987).

4. L.P.Andersson and S.Berg, Vacuum, 28: 449 (1978).

5. P. Sigmund, Phys. Rev. 184: 383 (1969).

18

Vacuum Arc-Based Processing

David Sanders

18.1 INTRODUCTION

Vacuum arcs have been employed for current interruption in commercial power systems since the early 1960's. While they were first suggested as a source for making vacuum coatings by Wroe (1) in 1958 and Gilmour (2) in 1972, it was only with the appearance of American and Russian patents by Snaper (3-4) in 1971 and Sablev (5-6) in 1974, respectively, that the use of arcs for the production of coatings achieved any commercial significance, and then only in the USSR in the late 1970's. In the United States, vacuum arcs have been employed since the mid-1980's for the application of titanium nitride to prolong the lifetime of cutting tools used to machine metals. The technology involved has been based either on the Snaper patent coupled with more recent patents by Mularie (7-8) or on that originating with Sablev. The chief advantages touted in using arc technology for this application are its intrinsic high coating rate and the ability to produce adherent stoichiometric nitrides having relative insensitivity to nitrogen partial pressure.

In the last five years, there has been an increasing body of experimental (9-10) and theoretical (11-12) evidence that energetic physical vapor deposition techniques can enable the production of coatings having improved physical and chemical properties (e.g., improved density, enhanced adhesion, improved stoichiometry, and a more bulk-like index of refraction). Since the highly ionized coating atoms produced by arc technology can be used to supply such energy at exactly the location where it can do the most good, (i.e., the interface where the coating is being formed) it would seem beneficial to explore arc coating technology for additional application opportunities.

In Russian literature there are many examples where the high degree of ionization of arc-produced vapor makes it possible to achieve combinations of coating properties and structure with processing conditions which cannot be achieved using competitive techniques such as electron beam evaporation or magnetron sputtering. This is due to the opportunity to control the ionized coating atoms using the combination of magnetic and electric fields. One example of such a combination is the ability to produce dense coatings at high rates and low substrate temperatures. Another is the possibility of achieving good adhesion with a wider variety of coating - substrate combinations. In addition, the ionized plasmas available from the cathodic arc show an enhanced reactivity during reactive coating. This leads to excellent composition control during the fabrication of compound coatings such as oxides and nitrides. Finally, the increased energy available makes possible unusual coating structures such as carbon coatings having hardnesses reported to exceed that of natural diamond.

The purpose of the present chapter is to review some of these opportunities as well as to identify deficiencies in current understanding in order to stimulate further investigation. To achieve this purpose, vacuum arc technology will be discussed in general terms to show how it is related to other vacuum processing, particularly with respect to the production of coatings. Emphasis will be devoted to source design considerations because, as will be stated, the design of suitable sources is a critical aspect in the further development of arc technology for exciting new applications. Representative examples of superior physical properties of coatings produced by vacuum arcs will be presented, followed by a description of some of the applications which could be addressed using those coatings. Finally, some of the areas requiring further investigation will be identified.

18.2 CATEGORIES OF VACUUM ARCS

Karl T. Compton of Princeton University defines an arc as "a discharge in a gas or vapor, that has a voltage drop at the cathode of the order of the minimum ionizing or minimum exciting potential of the gas or vapor". J.M. Lafferty adds that "the arc is a self-sustained discharge capable of supporting large currents by providing its own mechanism of electron emission from the negative electrode" (13). The "arcs" discussed in this chapter will be those which are sustained at least in part on the plasma produced by the erosion of one or both electrodes. These are the arcs which can provide high current densities (>10 As/cm^2) of metal plasma for subsequent vacuum processing.

Figure 1, based on Refs. 13 and 14, illustrates the relationship between the vacuum arcs and other discharges. At high voltages and low currents, one sees a "normal glow" discharge when there is an appropriate pressure of gas in the vacuum chamber to sustain it. In this region, increases in current do not increase voltage appreciably and there is insignificant erosion of the electrodes. As the current is increased further, the voltage also increases, indicating the transition into the "abnormal glow" region. It is in this regime where removal of material from the negatively charged electrode (cathode) occurs by sputtering (15). The behavior of the discharge within the abnormal glow region depends on the extent of electron emission of the cathode. With a cold cathode having a low value of electron emission, an abrupt change in the voltage/current behavior will sometimes occur where the voltage drops by more than an order of magnitude and then increases only slightly as the current is further increased. This occurs only in the discrete cathode spot case. With a sufficiently hot cathode yielding increased electron emission, there is a more gradual transition to a different arc mode where the current density of the electron emission site is many orders of magnitude lower than in the discrete spot case. This is the distributed discharge vacuum arc. With appropriate power supplies and electrode configurations it is possible to limit the current so that the arcing occurs at a higher voltage to produce still another type of vacuum arc, designated the "high voltage arc" in this chapter. Examples will be presented where each of these modes of arc behavior is employed.

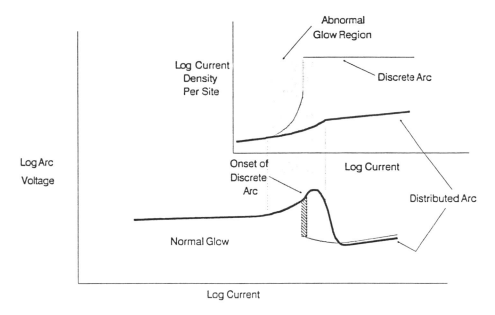

Figure 1: Voltage/current behavior of various types of vacuum discharges.

18.2.1 The Discrete Cathodic Arc

Figure 2 illustrates the emission site from a localized cathodic arc. This site or arc spot can sustain between 10 and 150 A depending on the cathode material. The uncertainty in the current density passing through these arc spots results from the uncertainty in the size of the spots themselves. This current density, as reported by various investigators, ranges widely from 10^4 to $10^8 A/cm^2$ (16-21). The arc spot is active for a short period of time, extinguishes and then re-forms in a new location adjacent to the previous arc crater. This gives rise to the appearance of motion of the arc. The apparent rate of motion is a function of the cathode material, the temperature, the magnetic fields, and the presence of gas molecules as will be discussed shortly.

As illustrated in Fig. 2, electrons, ions, macroparticles and neutral vapor species are emitted from the cathode spot. Electrons flow through the arc spot to surfaces in the chamber having a positive potential with respect to the cathode. For a wide variety of materials, the positive ion current is of the order of 10% of the arc current (22).

Table 1 gives the characteristics of ions emitted by the discrete cathode arc for a number of compositions. As can be seen, the energy of the ions exceeds the arc potential in all cases. This is thought to be due to positive space charge which is built up in front of the cathode caused by the plasma jet formed in front of the arc spot (17,20). The charge state of ions from the arc spot also varies according to composition (22). Metals that are more refractory tend to have a greater proportion of higher charge states.

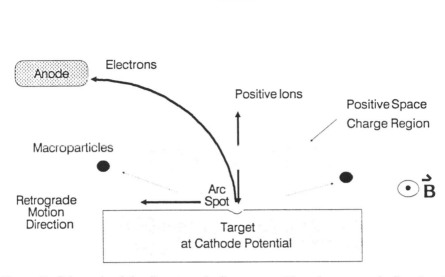

Figure 2: Schematic of the discrete cathodic arc spot. Note the retrograde direction defined by the magnetic field and the plasma flux.

The greatest drawback of the localized cathodic arc process involves the emission of macroparticles. These chunks of material vary in size depending on the cathode composition and temperature. They are thought to result from spattering of molten material from the edges of the arc crater. As illustrated in Fig. 2, the vast majority of these macroparticles is emitted at an angle of roughly 10-20 degrees from the cathode plane (23). The reduction of macroparticle formation and/or the subsequent filtering to remove macroparticles has been an active area of investigation since arcs were first considered for coating sources.

The neutral species emitted from the cathode arc spot are thought to be due the vaporization of small macroparticles by the interaction with the plasma (24). The fraction of ions to neutrals depends on the cathode material, this ratio being greatest for refractory metals such as molybdenum and tungsten.

As stated earlier, there are three major external influences on the cathode arc spot behavior. One is the presence of a magnetic field. Magnetic fields affect the arcing voltage as well as the rate and direction of motion of the arc spot (25-28). Fig. 2 illustrates the so-called retrograde motion which is observed as a result of magnetic fields which are parallel to the cathode surface. The retrograde velocity increases with magnetic field strength to a saturation point. The motion of the arc in an inhomogeneous magnetic field oriented at an angle with the cathode surface is described in the section on arc control using magnetic fields.

Table 1: Comparison of characteristics of some vacuum deposition processes.

Process	Macros?	Source of Discharge Material	Emission Type	Overall Source Temp.	Current Density A/Cm^2	% Ionization of Vapor	Energy of Particles (ev)	Ref. #
Discrete Cathodic Arc	Yes	Cathode	Thermionic Field Emission	Low	$10^4 - 10^8$	10 - 90	10 - 100	14
Distributed Discharge Cathodic	No	Cathode	Anomalous Emission	High	5 - 100	100	1 - 2	14
Anodic Arc	No	Anode	Anomalous Emission	High	1 - 10	5 - 100	0.1 - 1	14
High Voltage Arc	Possible	Both Electrodes	Thermionic Emission	High	5 - 100	?	?	39
Magnetron Sputtering	No	Process Gas	Ion Induced Secondary Emission	Generally Low	0.03 - 0.3	< 1%	~ 10	81
E-Beam Evaporation	No	n/a	Thermionic Emission	High	n/a	0.1 - 0.3	~ 1	81

Gas molecules also have an effect on arc behavior (29). There is a profound difference, for instance, between the arcing behavior of a pristine surface and one which has adsorbed gas molecules. Arcs occurring in the presence of reactive gas tend to move faster and produce smaller macroparticles which are fewer in number (30,31). At still higher pressures the discharge changes in character and the electrodes are no longer eroded by the arc (13).

The final influence on arc behavior is the cathode temperature. At low temperatures, the arc tends to move more rapidly, producing smaller macroparticles. At higher temperatures, the arc spots move in concert at slower rates (32-33). This change in behavior coincides with an increase in size and quantity of emitted macroparticles. As described earlier, at still higher temperatures the nature of the discharge changes completely so that the discharge no longer occurs through discrete arc spots, but rather is distributed over the cathode. More will be said about this shortly.

Table 2 shows the influence of cathode composition on current carried by an arc spot as well as the voltage required to sustain that arc spot. As the arcing current increases, the current passing through a particular spot is able to remain constant because the increased current is carried by the formation of additional spots which exist simultaneously on the cathode surface. This simultaneous existence of multiple cathode spots gives rise to one of the names assigned to this particular type of discharge, i.e., "the multiple cathodic arc".

The localized cathodic arc is characterized by high frequency fluctuations in both voltage and current. These variations are due to the extinguishing of old arc spots and the formation of new ones (33).

Table 2: Characteristics of the discrete cathodic arcs of some selected elements.

Element		Mo	Ta	Zr	Ti	Cu	Ni	Ag	Ref #
Arc Voltage		26.5	24.0	21.5		20.0	18.0	17.5	22
Ion K.E. (ev)		153	177	98		87.5	54	60	22
% in Charge State	1	3	13	14	65	38	48	16.5	
	2	33	35	60	39	55	48	65	
	3	42	28	21	34	7	3	34	80
	4	19	13	5		15		1	
	5	3	10						

18.2.2 The Diffuse Arcs:

At high temperatures where there is substantial electrode emission, so-called distributed or diffuse arcs are formed. These diffuse arcs have the potential for producing extremely high ion currents without the presence of macroparticles (14)(34). Anodic arcs are formed when the anode presented to the cathodic arc plasma is permitted to heat up and emit ions (35-37). Once erosion of the anode starts to occur, plasma from the anode forms the basis for the discharge and the erosion of the cathode stops. The distributed discharge cathodic arc is formed when the cathode is allowed to increase in temperature to the point where the cathode material has sufficient vapor pressure to lead to this type of arc. Little is understood concerning the exact nature of either of the diffuse discharge arcs, particularly with respect to the mechanisms of electron emission (37). Nevertheless, as is illustrated in the section on source design, both show promise as sources for new ion beams where the presence of macroparticles is of concern.

The least understood of the discharges, from a coating-source point of view, are the high voltage arcs described in Refs. 38-41. These arcs are apparently operated near the maximum in the voltage/current curve in Fig. 1. As one might expect, the current must be limited by some means to prevent the natural tendency of the system to go to higher currents and lower voltages characteristic of the arcs just discussed. The current limiting is accomplished with the power supply and/or by disruption of the discharge. The characterization of the plasmas produced by these discharges is not discussed in the references cited as these investigations were restricted to the analysis of the coatings produced. The encouraging results which were discussed suggest that measurements of the plasma characteristics are justified to fully make use of this type of arc for the production of coatings.

18.2.3 Summary of Arc Types

Table 1 summarizes the categories of arcs which have been described in this section emphasizing their characteristics for coating sources. Some other types of coating sources are also listed for comparison. The cathodic arc offers the highest energy vapors because it produces multi-charged ions with potentials which are greater than the arcing voltage. The cathode is cooled, making it possible to operate it in any orientation. The disadvantage of the cathodic arc is the production of macroparticles. While the negative effects of these macroparticles can be minimized or eliminated using concepts to be discussed shortly, such efforts complicate source design. The distributed discharge cathodic arc and the anodic arc both operate with hot eroding electrodes. They provide a means of producing ionized vapor without macroparticles. The energy of the ions is not as high as in the cathodic arc case and the ions are singly charged. Nevertheless, the fraction of vapor which is ionized can approach 100% and these ions can be accelerated using electric fields to achieve enhanced coating properties. The most poorly characterized plasmas are those from high voltage arcs. While interesting coating properties are reported (e.g., epitaxy at lower substrate temperatures), at this point the degree of ionization of the vapor flux is an unknown. Certainly, further investigation in this area will be required if high voltage arcs are to be exploited for making coatings.

18.3 SOURCE DESIGN CONSIDERATIONS

The purpose of this section is to provide a picture of the wide diversity that is possible in vacuum arc and coating technology. To accomplish this, the section will be divided into two parts. One section will discuss general considerations related to vacuum arc source design, while the other will provide specific examples to illustrate the results of those considerations.

18.3.1 General Considerations

In general, some means must be provided to initiate the arc. Once initiated, the arc must be controlled with respect to its position on the cathode surface. Then, to take advantage of the benefits provided by the high degree of ionization of the arc-produced vapor, the plasma must be controlled in some manner. Therefore, arc initiation, arc control, and plasma control comprise the three general considerations which need to be taken into account in designing cathodic arc coating sources.

18.3.1.1 Arc Initiation

There are at least four techniques successfully employed to initiate vacuum arcs. One of the simplest and earliest, depicted in Fig. 3, was the mechanical touching and removal of an electrode from the cathode, drawing an arc. This technique is still used in some commercial arc services for the production of titanium nitride coatings on cutting tools. Its main advantage is its simplicity. One disadvantage is the possibility of the electrode becoming welded to the cathode surface. This can be minimized by the insertion of a resistor between the electrode and the ground. The resistor limits the amount of current which can flow during the arc initiation process. A further drawback is the inability of this approach to achieve high repetition rates which are required for operation of arc sources in a pulsed mode.

An arc initiation technique which does allow for high repetition rates employs the sudden vaporization and subsequent ionization of a thin film metal coating connecting the cathode surface and an auxiliary electrode (42-43). This is accomplished through the discharge of a capacitor. The technique is simple and can be extremely reliable, if geometries are chosen correctly. Once started, the arc continually replenishes the thin film required for its next initiation. A means, however, must be provided for starting the arc for the first time with a fresh target.

The third method involves the discharge of a capacitor which has been charged to several thousand volts by passing an impulse of gas through a tube which is connected to that capacitor. The gas pulse is ionized to form a plasma which carries the current from the capacitor to the cathode until sufficient plasma density has been achieved to initiate the arc. While this is a reliable means for arc initiation without the necessity of touching the cathode, it does introduce a small amount of inert gas into the system and thus would not be appropriate for highly repetitive arc initiation requirements.

The final means of starting an arc involves the use of a laser pulse (44). Such a pulse produces a plasma on the cathode surface. The plasma serves to form the basis of the first cathode spot. If the laser pulse is directed at the cathode surface and local melting occurs, smoothing of the surface may inhibit further initiation. One way to overcome this is to start the arc on an auxiliary electrode made of a material such as carbon which remains unreflective. In using the laser technique, care must be taken to avoid coating the window through which the laser beam is introduced.

18.3.1.2 Arc Control

In order to be useful, the cathodic arc must be controlled. This is critical because the loss of such control can result in the rapid destruction of the arc coating equipment. Arc control can also serve to reduce the presence of macroparticles.

Both electrostatic and magnetic means have been employed to control the location of the cathodic arc. Electrostatic constraints make use of the requirement for the cathodic arc to have access to an anode to complete its electrical circuit. While this anode may be a discrete component in the vacuum chamber, it may also be a combination of components including the vacuum chamber walls. These concepts are illustrated in Fig. 3 where two forms of passive cathodic arc control are shown. On the left side, a screen is employed which is floating electrically and prevents electrons from flowing from the cathode to the chamber, which in this case is the anode (5). On the right hand side, ceramic material with low electron emissivity such as boron nitride is employed (7,8,45,46). In the case of the screen, the arc extinguishes when it reaches the edge of the water cooled target. If additional arcs simultaneously exist on the target surface, or if there is sufficient inductance in the circuit to provide the necessary restarting voltage, then the arc will reform and the process will continue. If not, the arc will remain extinguished and will need to be re-ignited. In the case of the boron nitride restraint, arcs reaching the target-restraint interface are thrown back onto the target, making re-ignition unnecessary.

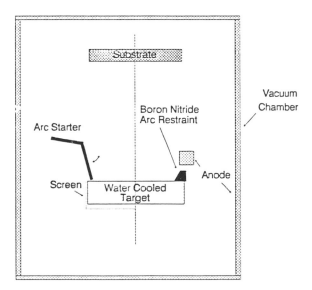

Figure 3: A typical passive cathodic arc configuration. (The shaded pattern codes are used consistently throughout the figures in this chapter for components having similar function).

The advantages of electrostatic arc confinement are its simplicity and good target utilization. One disadvantage, already cited, is the possibility of the arc remaining extinguished and requiring re-ignition. The second disadvantage, involving the boron nitride approach, relates to a tendency for the arc to burn selectively at the insulator metal interface. If this process continues for any length of time, the insulator is destroyed and must be replaced.

The other approach for arc control involves the use of magnetic fields. As already discussed, the arc normally undergoes the so called retrograde motion occurring in response to the component of the magnetic field which is parallel to the cathode surface. The direction of this motion is shown in Fig. 2. The rate of retrograde motion increases with magnetic field (28). One might expect a reduction in macroparticle formation to accompany the more rapid arc motion. While such a reduction appears during reactive arcing of refractory metals (31), it was not observed in the case of titanium metal (10).

The effect of the perpendicular component of magnetic field and arc motion is illustrated in two cases of Fig. 4. In Fig. 4(a) the magnetic field produced by the solenoid is imposed such that the field lines intersect the target at an angle other than 90 degrees. Under these conditions the arc circulates around the perimeter of the cylindrical target, but drifts in the direction of the acute angle between the magnetic field and the target surface. This behavior was first observed by Wroe (1,48) in early work and utilized over the years by a number of investigators (18,27,42,49). Wroe worked with magnetic fields in excess of 500 gauss and provided an anode in close proximity to the cathode; the other investigators used smaller fields ($\simeq 40 - 50$ gauss) with remote anodes.

Figure 4(b) illustrates the second principle, first discussed by Kesaev (50) in his extensive studies in the motion of arcs on mercury surfaces in the presence of an "arched" magnetic field. Under these circumstances, the arc moves in a circular pattern in a position where the normal component of the magnetic field is minimal as indicated in the figure. The rate of circulation is determined by the parallel component of the magnetic field with the target surface (28).

18.3.1.3 Plasma Control

One advantage of using the magnetic fields to control the arc position is that they are well suited for integration into sources where plasma from the arc source must also be controlled. For example, a plasma emitted from the source pictured in Fig. 4(a) is naturally accelerated towards the substrate due to the Hall effect (18). Hall acceleration of the cathodic arc plasma has been found to increase the energy of the ions to values as high as 300 electron volts (10,18). This effect may account for observed improvements in coating properties such as the hundred-fold improvement in the adhesion of copper to glass reported in Ref. 51.

Besides the benefits of Hall acceleration, a substantial reduction in the number of macroparticles can be achieved by passing the plasma emanating from a cathodic arc through the proper magnetic field (10,51,52). In addition, concentration of the arc plasma can lead to a five-fold improvement in condensation rate with an associated reduction in wasted coating material. The introduction of arc plasma into the magnetic field of the solenoid has also been observed to enhance the already high degree of ionization of this plasma (52).

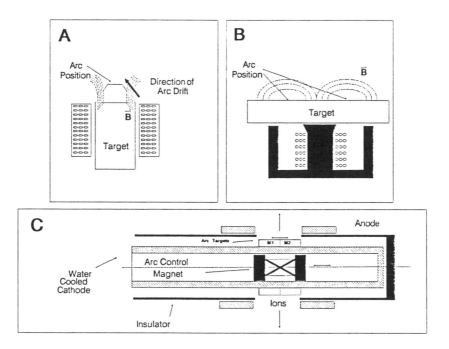

Figure 4: Cathodic arc devices featuring active magnetic control of the arc. (a) Arc source described in Ref. 42. The arc position rotates rapidly around the target in the retrograde direction and drifts in the direction of the reduced normal component of the magnetic field (in this case the acute angle). The coils represent an electromagnet. (b) Another example of magnetic control of the cathodic arc. Again the direction of circulation is defined by the parallel component of the magnetic field and the resulting arc circle resides at the position where the normal component of the magnetic field is minimal. (c) This schematic shows a cylindrical arc geometry. The arc targets are thick walled tubes. This geometry can be used directly where macroparticles can be tolerated in small quantities for coating the inside of tubes. This schematic illustrates how the arc ring can be oscillated over two different target compositions to produce either multilayered coatings or alloy coatings - depending on the rate of oscillation. The "X" represents a permanent magnet.

The final use of plasma control is illustrated in Fig. 5(a). In this case, an electromagnetic filter is employed to separate the macroparticles, produced at the target, from the plasma. This separation is accomplished by causing the plasma to flow through the curved passage indicated toward the substrate surface. Any macroparticles emanating from the target have essentially straight trajectories causing them to be collected on the walls of the plasma filter (53).

The physical basis for the control of the cathodic arc plasma has been understood for some time (53-55). Since the Larmor radius for heavy metal ions is large with respect to the dimensions of the components being discussed here, the magnetic field has little direct effect on the motion of these ions (15). On the other hand, much lighter electrons are easily constrained to rotate around the magnetic field lines and can drift along these lines quite freely as long as these lines do not converge too rapidly. There is a natural resistance of electrons to pass across magnetic field lines, thereby, allowing the building of electrical fields perpendicular to the magnetic field surfaces. These electric fields have a profound influence on the motion of the ions from the cathodic arc and can be used to an advantage in controlling the path of those ions. One of the benefits of using this strategy for plasma control is the possibility for positive ions having different charges and masses to follow similar paths.

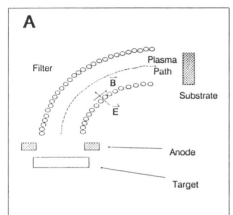
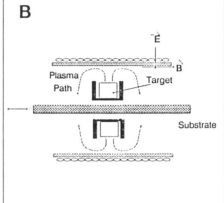

Figure 5: Two schemes for removal of macroparticles. In both cases, the electric field is thought to repel the positive ions and direct them toward the target surface. The macroparticles have no line-of-sight between the target surface and the substrate to be coated.

Quasineutral plasma behavior (such as that from cathodic arcs) in magnetic and electric fields has recently been modeled quantitatively by several investigators (54,56,57). One reason for this interest lies in the potential for developing arc-based ion beams for making coatings. Additional uses for quasineutral beams are for drivers in inertially confined fusion and as supplementary heating for magnetically confined plasmas. In the current context, it is hoped that the development of suitable computer models will make it possible to design sources which make the most effective use of the plasma produced by the vacuum arc.

18.3.2 Specific Examples:

One of the most difficult aspects of discussing specific examples of cathodic arc-based devices is the selection which must be made from such a diverse variety of possible choices. Arc sources can be continuous in operation or pulsed. They can be based on a random arc or one which is tightly controlled. They can employ some method of macroparticle filtration, or can be based on a type of discharge which requires no such filtration, such as the distributed cathodic or anodic arcs. All of these arc sources can form the basis for extremely high current density ion beams. These ion beams can be used by themselves or serve as the starting point for a more complex process or piece of equipment such as an ion implanter. This section will discuss these major categories in general terms only, referring the reader to the references cited for more specific details.

From earliest times, cathodic arc devices for producing coatings could be divided into pulsed and continuous types. The pulsed devices will be described first. In the pulsed mode, the arc is repeatedly ignited and extinguished using a capacitor bank to supply the arc power (2,43,58). Pulsed arcs have the advantage of allowing the target material to cool between arc events. This makes it possible to arc an extremely wide variety of materials with less concern for the overheating of the target. Pulsed arcs, on the other hand, have a dead time in between arc events which limits the steady state coating rate. Since the arc initiates from the same point each time, it is possible to design the length of the discharge such that the arc does not have sufficient time to leave the preferred arcing position before the capacitor is discharged. In other words, the arc constraint requirement in pulsed arc devices tends to be less stringent than for the continuous variety. Pulsed arcs have been employed in conjunction with subsequent macroparticle filtration (59), and have formed the basis for ion beams for ion implanters (43).

The continuous cathodic arc can either be random in nature or controlled. Fig. 3 shows several examples of a random arc source where the arc is constrained at the edge of the target, but allowed random motion within that constraint. Random arc sources have the advantage of simplicity and excellent target utilization because the entire target (except near the very edge) is utilized in the arc process. These sources can be scaled in a straightforward manner to provide for uniform coating of very large parts. The main disadvantage of random arcing is the formation of macroparticles which may cause the resulting coating to be unsuitable in some applications. As pointed out in the discussion of Fig. 2, the macroparticles are ejected at small angles with respect to the target surface, and can therefore be minimized using appropriate shielding. Such a strategy has made possible arc-produced decorative coatings where surface finish and optical specularity are of concern (31).

As discussed earlier, magnetic fields can be used to control the trajectories of the arcs. These fields can be used to discourage the arc from leaving the desired portion of the target surface (as illustrated in Fig. 4) or can actually be used to define a well controlled path for the arc to follow in the so called "steered arc" devices (50,61,62). While the mechanism is still the subject of some debate, it is clear, at least in the case of ceramic coatings based on refractory metals, that steered arcs can produce coatings having extremely low or no measurable macroparticle component (61).

One of the difficulties of tightly controlling the path of the arc, is the tendency to cut a narrow slot into the target surface resulting in extremely poor target utilization. This has been overcome by the strategy of moving the arc controlled magnets with respect to the target so as to make full use of the target surface (60,61). A second advantage of this control of the arc position is the potential for production of coatings having variable composition through suitable programming of the arc motion over segmented targets of multiple composition (62). The target configuration pictured in Fig. 4(c) illustrates one technique for achieving such composition control; the figures in Ref. 61 illustrate another.

Where macroparticles present a problem in the final application, they can be removed through the use of a suitable filter. Figure 5 shows two examples of such filters, both of which are based on the same principle discussed earlier. In Fig. 5(a), a quarter segment of a torus is used to cause the plasma to follow a curved path leaving the macroparticles to collide on the inside of the filter (53). For effective removal of the macroparticles, it is necessary for the filters to be designed to require multiple bounces. In the case shown in Fig. 5(b), a ring target is employed (62), with the arc surface on the outside circumference. In this case, the arc plasma is reflected by the electric field set up due to the insulating property of the magnetic lines running parallel to the surface of the coil (as illustrated). The part being coated is moved, as indicated, to achieve coating uniformity. This particular scheme is most effective in cases where it is desired to obtain a radially symmetric coating.

As described in the section on general considerations, one strategy for dealing with the problem of macroparticles is to employ an arc which does not produce them. Figure 6 shows two categories of diffused arc which do not produce macroparticles. The first is called the cathodic arc distributed discharge. In this case, the cathode is designed in the form of a crucible to contain the target material (34). This crucible is allowed to heat up until the target material reaches a temperature where it has a substantial vapor pressure. At this point the arc voltage decreases. In the case of chrome, for instance, the random arc voltage of 18-20 volts decreases to a voltage of 12-14 volts. As shown in Fig. 1, the current density decreases drastically and, in addition, the plasma becomes brighter due to increased electron emission from the target surface. Macroparticles are no longer formed, and the ions now become singly charged rather than having the multiple charges of the random cathodic arc. The degree of ionization in this process can achieve 100% and the conversion efficiency of arc power to these ions can be extremely high since little energy in the form of heat is conducted to the electrode. A shutter is absolutely necessary with this type of source because, during the heating process, the target actually emits more macroparticles as the target heats to the point where it converts over to the distributed discharge mode. The design of a distributed discharge cathodic arc for practical coating systems becomes quite a challenge due to the necessity of bringing the surface of the target to the appropriate temperature without having spattering from the arc process.

A more straightforward approach for obtaining ionized evaporation material involves the so called anodic arc (36). One version is pictured in Fig. 6(b). In this process, the cathode initially supplies both electrons and ions until the anode target material heats up. Once sufficient electron emission occurs, a diffuse arc forms on the hot anode target material which supplies the ions necessary to sustain the discharge. At this point the cathode material is not expended, but rather becomes coated with some of the vapor emanating from the anode. This process produces no macroparticles and achieves some degree of ionization of the plasma. High rates of condensation have been demonstrated with the process. For instance, adherent and pinhole-free aluminum was deposited at a rate of 10 nm/sec at 30 cm distance from the target. This technique has been used for a wide variety of materials including Al, Ti, V, Cr, Mn, Fe, Ni, Cu, Pd, Ag, Au, Pt, and Pb (35). The process leaves the substrate relatively cool, making it possible to produce adherent coatings on plastics at temperatures less than $70°C$.

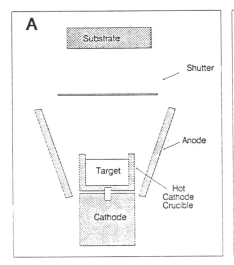

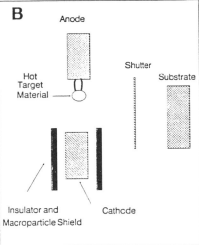

Figure 6: Two configurations for diffuse arcs which do not produce macroparticles. (a) With the polarity shown, this is a schematic of the diffuse cathodic arc. With the polarity reversed, it would be a type of anodic arc. (b) One form of anodic arc.

Alternative configurations exist for the anodic arc. One can be pictured by reversing the electrode polarity of the elements in Fig. 6(a) (36). Another, described in Ref. 63, involves a separate low voltage/high current electron beam originating from a filament source. The hot hollow cathode deposition process (described in another chapter in this book) can also be viewed as a type of anodic arc. It is not clear to this author that each of these configurations produces the same degree of ionization. In fact, it is likely that the basic electron emission mechanisms are different. Some require the addition of a process gas, while others exist solely on the plasma produced from evaporating electrode material. A systematic comparison would seem to be in order, particularly with respect to the degree of ionization of the plasmas produced.

One disadvantage of the process pictured in Fig. 6(a) is the necessity of containing the hot evaporating material. This containment of hot material may lead to contamination if a totally inert crucible material is unavailable. A disadvantage involving the process illustrated in Fig. 6(b), is that the anode surface must be relatively small in order to obtain the proper anodic discharge. Such a small area for the evaporating metal requires some means such as a wire feed device for frequent replenishment of the evaporation material. As discussed earlier, the extent of ionization as well as the energy of those ions, may be lower than the competing cathodic arc process. This last point is still subject to debate due to conflicting claims concerning the degree of ionization from a particular anodic arc source configuration.

Using the same strategy which is employed for controlling the plasma to remove macroparticles, it is possible to generate intense ion beams from an arc source. Figure 7(a) contains an example of one such ion beam described in more detail in Ref. 64. These beams do not suffer the same constraints and current density limitations that are found with multi-aperture sources. In addition, they can operate using any ion for which a suitable cathode can be obtained. As the design of such arc-based ion beams becomes more common, more applications are likely. One recent application was the use of such an ion beam to study a new process called arc ion beam self-sputtering for the development of a sputtering source not requiring process gas for possible operation in UHV conditions (64).

Figure 7(a) illustrates the arc ion beam self-sputtering process also described in Ref. 64 in more detail. The ion beam provides the source of positive ions which are accelerated to the negatively biased sputtering target. If the voltage of the target is appropriate, it will become coated with ions from the arc source. As the target voltage is raised and the sputtering rate increases, the ions from the arc source are converted to neutrals of the same composition. This entire process can be carried out without the presence of a process gas. In addition, one can design a sputtering angle to optimize the efficiency of the sputtering process since the sputtering efficiency tends to be angularly dependent. Also, having the ions of the same composition as the atoms to be sputtered leads to very effective interaction for an efficient process.

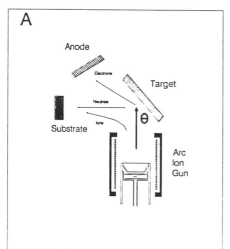
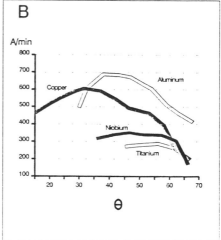

Figure 7: Schematic of arc ion-beam sputtering process. (a) Drawing showing an arc-ion-gun and a setup to determine optimal target angle for an arc sputtering process. (b) Rate dependence on target angle for four elements.

Figure 7(b) shows the effect of the target angle as defined in the schematic on the rate of condensation at the target. In the case of copper, the rate varies with target angle by a factor of two over the range shown. In the case of titanium, there was surprisingly little effect of target angle on rate. Further studies will be required to fully understand the observed effects.

Figure 8 shows a possible source based on the principles of arc based self-sputtering. In this case, the arc target has a cylindrical geometry. The sputtering target is cone shaped. The surface of the cone has a shallow angle with respect to the incoming ions. This angle can be optimized for a particular material, if desired, but this may not be necessary for materials whose self-sputtering rate is insensitive to angle . In addition to allowing sputtering without the need for process gas (true UHV sputtering), this process can present an extremely large effective deposition target area for coating large parts uniformly without the associated requirement for a large arc target. This is desirable because there are many examples of materials (such as the refractory metals) where dense and pure targets are not available in large sizes.

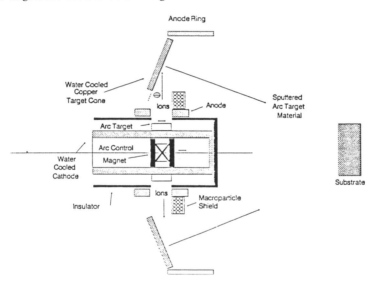

Figure 8: Design of a possible UHV sputtering source based on a vacuum arc. The arc target material condenses on the conical sputtering target and self-sputters toward the substrate. The macroparticles produced by the arc are collected at the anode.

While most of the arcs discussed thus far operate in the low voltage regime shown in Fig. 1, there are examples of studies making use of arcs operating near the maximum voltage of the anomalous glow region (38-41,65). As discussed earlier, these arcs appear to provide some improvements in coating properties, but insufficient understanding exists to define the cause for such improvements. As in the other cases requiring small electrode surface areas to obtain sufficient electron emission, these arc sources are likely to have very specialized applications.

In addition to the arc-based plasma sources described so far, the attention of the reader is directed to Refs. 66 and 67 for reviews of thermionic discharge and hollow cathode discharge sources. The hollow cathode is also treated in another chapter of this book.

18.4 COATINGS FROM ARCS (STRUCTURES AND PROPERTIES)

As mentioned earlier, arc technology shows promise for producing coatings with superior properties because it allows control over the depositing coating atoms by virtue of their charge. This improvement is predicted by theoretical molecular dynamic calculations (10-12). In addition, it has been substantiated by experiments. Such improvements include finer coating morphologies, improved coating density, and reduced intrinsic coating stress (68). All these property improvements occur at lower substrate temperatures than would occur with less energetic techniques. Other considerations suggest an improved adhesion. In the production of ceramic coatings by reactive deposition, the ionized nature of the coating atoms enhances reactivity and leads to coatings with excellent stoichiometry (69). Arc technology can also be employed to produce coatings having tailored compositions, particularly with respect to the interface region (61). Finally, the energetic nature of the arc plasma gives rise, in some cases, to unusual bonding such as the diamond-like bonds found in carbon coatings produced by the arc process (70). This section will present some examples of each of these to provide a motivation for further investigation into the production of coatings using arc technology.

Figure 9 illustrates, on a molecular scale, the case for energetic arc technology. In the case of low energy deposition such as electron beam evaporation, neutral atoms of the coating material arrive at the substrate surface and deposit on top of that surface. Since there is little energy available for coating mobility, particularly during room temperature deposition, the atoms stick at the point where they arrive. If the surface has adsorbed contamination atoms between the substrate and coating, the resulting coating may have poor adhesion. The result of the lack of atomic mobility is predicted to be a coating of poor density, filled with voids and impurity atoms as pictured.

In contrast, as shown in Fig. 9(b), positive ions arrive at the surface with increased kinetic energy due to the acceleration they undergo as they are attracted to the negatively charged substrate. (Alternatively, they may have benefitted from the Hall acceleration discussed earlier.) In either case, they have sufficient energy to clean off the surface atoms prior to forming the coating. In addition they have sufficient mobility to diffuse to low free energy sites, a factor which results in denser coatings. When the substrate has adequate negative bias to accelerate the coating ions sufficiently, implanting these ions into the interfacial region can further strengthen the adhesive bond. To be thorough, it is necessary to point out that such implantation may also lead the introduction of impurity atoms into the substrate (as illustrated in Fig. 9(b)) unless care is taken. Fig. 10 shows the results of an actual molecular dynamic calculation predicting the densification of a model coating structure due to the energetic deposition based on a cathodic arc process (10).

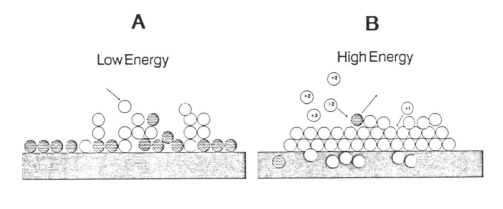

A
Low Energy

B
High Energy

○   Coating Atom

◉   Impurtity Atom

Figure 9: Conceptual diagram showing the case for the energetic cathodic arc process. (a) Sputtering and electron beam evaporation coating atoms are neutral and have limited energy to contribute to atomic mobility after condensation. (b) The arc processes produce positive ions which can be accelerated into the part to be coated. Increased atomic mobility can result in improved properties as discussed in the text.

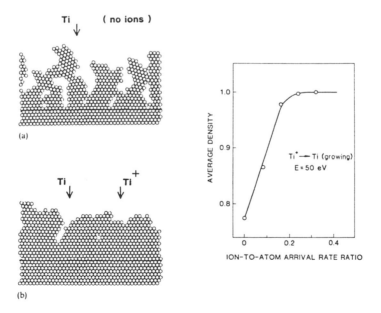

Figure 10: Results of a molecular dynamic modeling calculation carried out by P.J. Martin, et.al., in Ref. 10. Used with permission.

In addition to improvements in coating density, several investigators (38)-(41) have found that high voltage arcs produce epitaxial coatings of refractory metals at lower temperatures than would be expected by other techniques. Since the plasmas produced by such arcs have not been well characterized, the exact mechanism for the creation of such structures is not yet understood. One speculation has been that such arcs produce clusters which may enhance such epitaxy. In contrast to the behavior of low voltage arcs where the morphology is strongly dependent on the substrate bias, coatings produced by high voltage arcs show no such dependence. This observation tends to suggest that the evaporation product from the high voltage arc may not be strongly ionized, as in the low voltage case.

Examples of improved adhesion due to the proper use of arc technology abound. As will be described in the application section, the most important commercial application for the use of arc technology in coatings has been the production of hard coatings of titanium nitride for cutting tools. In this application, it is clear that the coating must be extremely adherent during the violent mechanical abuse to which the cutting tool is subjected for such a coating to have any beneficial effect. As found by a number of investigators (51,52), coating adhesion can be further enhanced by the use of magnetic fields to accelerate the ions of the arc plasma to higher energies. A hundred- fold improvement of the adhesion of copper to glass for instance, has been achieved with such a strategy (51).

Surprisingly little experimental information exists on the stresses produced in the coatings produced by arc technology. Such stresses can be highly compressive in some instances or extremely low in others depending on the details of the process during which the coating is being produced. This area will require much additional investigation if molecular dynamic modeling predictions concerning reductions in stress are to be realized.

Another area which will require substantial further investigation concerns the extent of heating of the substrates by the various arc technology techniques. While it is possible to supply sufficient energy to large substrates to cause them to rise in temperature to values in excess of 500°C, it is also possible to produce dense adherent coatings on plastics at room temperature (35). Part of this difference in behavior involves the separation of the electrons from the ions to minimize heating effects when cold substrate temperatures are necessary. Pulsed arcs offer another approach for maintaining a low substrate temperature; the dead time between pulses can be adjusted to allow for cooling.

Examples of the enhanced chemical reactivity of the plasmas produced by the arc process are also available (10,44,55,71,72). These are particularly evident in the case of the discrete cathodic arc which produces multi-ionized coating material. Such multi-charged ions undergo charge exchange reactions with the reactive gas leading to ionization of the latter. The coatings which are produced tend to be stoichiometric in composition over a broader range of reactive gas partial pressure than is the case with competing magnetron technology (69).

While carbon coatings with the diamond structure are receiving considerable attention currently, it is interesting to note that one of the earliest methods for producing such coatings made use of the vacuum arc (73). Once again, Russian investigators are well represented in early work in this area (74-76). More recent structural studies by other workers (70) have verified that arc technology is capable of producing diamond-type sp3 bonds without appreciable sp2 graphitic bonds and without the need for hydrogen to be present as is the case in competing glow discharge techniques.

18.5. APPLICATIONS AND OPPORTUNITIES

The most widely implemented application of arc deposited coatings has been for improving the lifetime and operational characteristics of cutting tools used in machining of metals. Cutting tools such as drills, endmills, taps, hobs and broaches coated with TiN not only show improvements in service lifetimes due to reduced wear, but operate more efficiently. Due to their improved lubricity and reduced chemical reactivity, it is possible to operate coated tools at higher rates and the parts produced have improved surface finishes (77).

While the variety of current applications is small, this is likely to increase quite quickly as practical sources are developed which reduce or eliminate the macroparticles which are produced by the conventional cathodic arc process. One market which is likely to be impacted is the one for gold-colored decorative coatings. Many consumer products such as watch cases, pens, and the like make use of titanium nitride produced by reactive deposition of the metal. Titanium nitride produced using low macroparticle sources is likely to gain market share in this arena in the near term due to characteristics of the process such as high adhesion, high rates, and ability to achieve excellent stoichiometry in compound coatings over a broad range of processing conditions (31).

Another group of manufacturers which will likely be impacted is the printed circuit board producers. In this case, there is pressure to improve performance and quality due to demands for reducing the size of electronic equipment. The cathodic arc process offers the possibility of producing adherent conductive coatings at high rates. In addition, the process has excellent "throwing power" which allows for coating through holes (31).

The longer term applications are harder to predict because they rely on improved coating properties which are only now being realized. Because the cathodic arc process is well suited for depositing adherent refractory metals on virtually any substrate at high rates, one can speculate on the possibility of coating copper structures with materials such as tungsten and molybdenum for fusion devices, for instance.

Macroparticle-free magnetic coatings would quickly find application in the recording industry for the optical and magnetic storage of data. In this case the ability to produce dense adherent magnetic coatings at high rates is of great interest. In addition to these excellent physical properties, the arc process offers a straightforward means to tailor alloys and to vary the composition during the coating process (as discussed earlier).

With the recently developed capability to produce ceramic coatings which have extremely low or no macroparticle content (61), broad new opportunities are opened up in a variety of industries. While macroparticle-laden arc-produced ceramic coatings have been available for some time for corrosion protection and wear resistance, the reduction in size and numbers of macroparticles makes it possible to use such coatings at high temperature with less concern for macroparticle-induced failure. One mechanism for such failure in coatings containing macroparticles is the localized reduction of the oxide or nitride to sub-stoichiometric levels during heating. Such metal-rich regions might be more reactive to the hostile environments. Even at low temperatures these metallic macroparticles are of concern because of their inferior chemical and tribological behavior. Potential uses for low macroparticle content ceramic coatings as barrier coatings include corrosion protection for turbine blades and chemical reaction vessels.

If the presence of macroparticles can be completely eliminated, it may become possible to employ arc technology for the production of coatings for integrated circuits. Once again the advantages of being able to produce stoichiometric ceramic coatings having excellent adhesion and density at low process substrate temperature make such an approach highly desirable for insulating structures. Dense and adherent refractory metal coatings for conductive elements in integrated circuits are another potential application.

Coatings that are denser than currently produced for optical components would have increased stability in the value of the refractive index of each layer. (Refractive index instabilities result from adsorption of moisture into open coating structures). The improvements in adhesion and stoichiometry might improve the resistance of coatings to laser damage in applications as diverse as laser diodes for telecommunications and large inertial confinement laser systems envisioned for the production of power in the next centuries.

Another far reaching potential application is the possible production of high T_c superconducting thin films which do not require subsequent heat treatment to produce superconducting structures; the energy supplied by the ions might be sufficient. Such coatings might be produced on low temperature substrates which would increase the possibilities for unusual applications.

A final class of applications makes use of the possibility of producing non-equilibrium structures due to the energetic nature of the ions produced by the arc process. Diamond coatings produced using plasma from a cathodic arc might be used for protecting recording disks, optical lenses and fiber optic transmission lines from reactions and mechanical abrasion. If defect-free single crystal diamond coatings could be produced using this approach, they could be employed as active semiconductors for high frequency applications.

18.5.1 Non-Coating Applications

In addition to applications discussed thus far, several suggestions have been made concerning uses for the ions potentially available using arc technology. Arcs can be used as the basis for a sublimation-ion vacuum pump (78). Since the vacuum arc can be operated without the presence of process gas, it is possible to consider a "poor man's" ion implanter in which the part to be implanted is pulsed to a high negative potential for a very short time, having the effect of accelerating the positive ions into the surface of the part. Rather large parts might be treated in this manner without the necessity for expensive and complicated ion-optical systems. Where such ion implantation systems are indicated, the vacuum arc can serve as the source of ions (43). Still another application of arc-generated ion beams is the smoothing of surfaces through the combination of deposition and sputtering (79). In this case, the energy of the cathodic arc plasma-based accelerator is claimed to be ideal for the process. All of these ideas, while exciting in principle, need to be verified experimentally.

18.6 GAPS IN UNDERSTANDING

These suggestions for possible applications are not intended to be an exhaustive list, but rather to serve to suggest the diverse and potentially significant opportunities which may exist with the proper utilization of arc technology. The reason that these opportunities have not been realized is that there still exist serious gaps in the understanding of the technology.

The most obvious is the lack of commercially available macroparticle-free arc sources. While several approaches have been suggested in this chapter which may lead to this objective, the goal has not yet been achieved outside the laboratory. (In fact many of the ideas and claims made by various workers need to be substantiated by independent investigators). Such investigations will naturally lead to improvements in understanding of techniques for control of the arc and its plasma.

In addition, improvements in the quantitative understanding of the condensation behavior of energetic particles will allow for the determination of the limits which may be possible in terms of producing dense coatings at high rates, for instance. As mentioned before, there is surprisingly little information concerning the intrinsic stress in arc coatings and the mechanism for its origin. While workers in the area are aware of the possibility for large compressive stresses, it is not clear which process conditions result in such stresses. On some occasions, coatings having very low stress are observed. Once again computer modeling may offer the necessary understanding.

While other types of ion bombardment, (such as argon bombardment from a multi-aperture ion source), for instance, do not involve the coating atoms themselves directly, the plasma produced by the arc process can be composed of only coating ions. This may lead to some opportunities which may be exploited if there is a quantitative understanding of the events which occur during the condensation of these ions. Currently, for instance, there is virtually no quantitative understanding concerning the details of the chemical interactions of these ions with surfaces.

Finally a detailed understanding of the chemical reactions which occur as a result of coating ions interacting with reactive gas ions and electrons in a magnetic and electric field may lead to the invention of new compound coating structures such as the high T_c superconductors mentioned earlier.

18.7 CONCLUSION

While vacuum arc technology has come a long way since its inception, it still has a long way to go to fully utilize what appear to be some exciting opportunities. This advancement will occur if systematic efforts are made to understand the coating properties which are possible with such technology and if simultaneous efforts are made to understand quantitatively the arc, the plasma from the arc, and the condensation behavior of that plasma to form coatings or to interact with surfaces in the presence of electric and magnetic fields.

18.8 REFERENCES

1. Wroe, H. The Magnetic Stabilization of Low Pressure D.C. Arcs. Br. J. Appl. Phys. 9: 488-491 (1958).

2. Gilmour, A.S., Jr., Lockwood, D. L., Pulsed Metallic Plasma Generators Proc. IEEE 60: No. 8, 977-991 (1972).

3. Snaper, A.A. Arc Deposition and Apparatus, U.S. Patent No. 3,625,848 (1971).

4. Snaper, A.A. Arc Deposition and Apparatus, U.S. Patent No. 3,836,451 (1974).

5. Sablev, L.P. Apparatus for Vacuum Evaporation of Metals under the Action of an Electric Arc, U.S. Patent No. 3,783,231 (1974).

6. Sablev, L.P. Apparatus for Metal Evaporation Coating, U.S. Patent No. 3,793,179 (1974).

7. Mularie, W.M. Evaporation Arc Stabilization, U.S. Patent No. 4,430,184 (1984).

8. Mularie, W.M. Apparatus for Evaporation Arc Stabilization During the Initial Clean-up of an Arc Target, U.S. Patent No. 4,559,121 (1984).

9. Martin, P.J., Netterfield, R.P., et al., Ion-Assisted Deposition of Bulk-Like ZrO_2 Films. Appl. Phys. Lett. 43: 711-713 (1983).

10. Martin, P.J., McKenzie, D.R., et al., Characteristics of Titanium Arc Evaporation Processes Thin Solid Films 153: 91-102 (1987).

11. Müller, K.H., Model for Ion-Assisted Thin Film Densification. J. Appl. Phys. 59: 2803-2807 (1986).

12. Müller, K.H., Modeling Ion-Assisted Deposition of CeO_2 Films. Appl. Phys. A 40: 209-213 (1986).

13. Cobine, J.D., Introduction to Vacuum Arcs. in Vacuum Arcs: Theory and Application ed. by J.M. Lafferty John Wiley, New York 1-18 (1980).

14. Dorodnov, A.M. and Petrosov, B.A., Physical Principles and Types of Technological Vacuum Plasma Devices. Sov. Phys. Tech. Phys. (Engl. Transl. of Zh. Tekh. Fiz.) 26: 304-315 (1981).

15. Thornton, J.A. Plasma-Assisted Deposition Processes: Theory, Mechanisms, and Applications. Thin Solid Films 107: 3-19 (1983).

16. Daalder, J.E. Erosion Structures on Cathodes Arced in Vacuum J. Phys. D: Appl. Phys. 16: 17-27 (1983).

17. Davis, W. D., Miller, H. C., Analysis of the Electrode Products Emitted by DC Arcs in Vacuum Ambient. J. Appl. Phys. 40: 2212-2221 (1969).

18. Dorodnov, A.M., Muboyadzhyan, S.A., et al., A Cold Cathode Hall Plasma Accelerator. J. Appl. Mech. and Tech. Phys. (Engl. Transl. of PMTF) 22: 28-32 (1981).

19. Kimbin, C.W. Erosion and Ionization in the Cathode Spot Regions of Vacuum Arcs. J. Appl. Phys. 44: 3074-3081 (1973).

20. Plyutto, A.A., Ryzhkov, V.N., et al., High Speed Plasma Streams in Vacuum Arcs. Sov. Phys. JETP (Engl. Transl. of Zh. Eksp. Teor. Fiz.) 20: 328 (1965).

21. Rakhovsky, V.I. Current Density Per Cathode Spot In Vacuum Arcs. IEEE Trans. Plasma Sci. PS12: 199-203 (1984).

22. Daalder, J. E. Cathode Erosion of Metal Vapor Arcs in Vacuum, Ph.D Thesis (Eindhoven, Netherlands) (1978).

23. Arksenov, I.I., Konovalov, I.I., et al., Droplet Phase of Cathode Erosion in a Steady Vacuum Arc. Sov. Phys. Tech. Phys. (Engl. Transl. of Zh. Tekh. Fiz.) 29: 893-894 (1984).

24. Boxman, R.L., Goldsmith, S., The Interaction Between Plasma and Macroparticles in Multi-Cathode Spot Vacuum Arc. J. Appl. Phys. 52: 252-161 (1981).

25. Argarwal, M.S., Holmes, R., Arcing Voltage of the Metal Vapor Vacuum Arc. J. Appl. Phys. 16: 757-767 (1984).

26. Agarwal, M.S., Holmes, R., Cathode Spot Motion in High-Current Vacuum Arcs under Self-Generated Azimuthal and Applied Axial Magnetic Fields. J. Phys. D: Appl. Phys. 17: 743-756 (1984).

27. Aksenov, I.I., Andreev, A.A., Motion of the Cathode Spot in a Vacuum Arc in an Inhomogeneous Magnetic Field. Sov. Tech. Phys. Lett. (Engl. Trans. of Pis'ma Zh. Tekh. Fiz.) 3: 525-526 (1977).

28. Fang, D.Y., Cathode Spot Velocity of Vacuum Arcs. J. Appl. Phys. 15: 833-844 (1982).

29. Moizhes, B.Y., Nemchinski, V.A., Influence of External Gas Pressure on Cathode Spot Motion in a Magnetic Field. Sov. Phys. Tech. Phys. (Engl. Transl. of Zh. Tekh. Fiz.) 30: 136 (1985).

30. Guile, A.E., Juttner, B., Basic Erosion Processes of Oxidized and Clean Metal Cathodes by Electric Arcs. IEEE Trans. Plasma Sci. PS8: 259-269 (1980).

31. Randawa, H., Johnson, P. C., Technical Note: A Review of Cathodic Arc Plasma Deposition Processes and Their Applications. Surf. Coat. Technol. 31: 308-318 (1987).

32. Aksenov, I.I., Konovalov, I.I. et al., Plasma in a Stationary Vacuum-Arc Discharge. High Temp. (Engl. Transl. of Teplofiz. Vys. Temp.) 21: 484-488 (1983).

33. Harris, L. P., Arc Cathode Phenomena. in Vacuum Arcs: Theory and Application ed. by J.M. Lafferty, John Wiley, New York 120-168 (1980).

34. Vasin, A.I., Dorodnov, A.M. et al., Vaccum Arc with a Distributed Discharge on an Expendable Cathode. Sov. Tech. Phys. Lett. (Engl. Trans. of Pis'ma Zh. Tekh. Fiz.) 5: No. 23-24, (1979).

35. Ehrich, H., Hasse, B. et al., The Anodic Vacuum Arc. Proc. 8th Intl. Conf. Gas Discharge Appl. (Essen Univ.) 591-592, 596 (1985).

36. Dorodnov, A.M., Kunetsov, A.N. et al., New Anode-Vapor Vacuum Arc with Permanent Hollow Cathode. Sov. Tech. Phys. Lett. (Engl. Trans. of Pis'ma Zh. Tekh. Fiz.) 5: 418-419 (1979).

37. Ehrich, H., The Anodic Vacuum Arc I, Basic Construction and Phenomenology. J. Vac. Sci. Technol. A6: 134-138 (1988).

38. Igarashi, Y., Kanayama, M, High-Quality Single-Crystal Niobium and Tantalum Films Formed by an Ultra-High Vacuum Arc Method. J. Appl. Phys. 57: 849-854 (1985).

39. Igarashi, Y., Kanayama, M, Growth of Tungsten Single-Crystal Films Deposited on MgO (100) Substrate. J. Appl. Phys. 52: 7208-7211 (1981).

40. Igarashi, Y., Kanayama, M, New Evaporation Method of High Melting Temperature Materials, Utilizing A Vacuum Discharge. Appl. Phys. Lett. 28: 481-482 (1976).

41. Krohn, M., Meyer, K.P. et al., Epitaxy by Vacuum Arc Evaporation. J. Cryst. Growth 64: 326-332 (1983).

42. Aksenov, I.I., Belous, V.A., Ignition of a Vacuum Arc in Stationary Sources of a Metal Plasma from an Autonomous Plasma Injector. Instrum. and Exp. Tech. (Engl. Transl. of Prib. Tekh. Eksp.) No. 3, Pt. 2, 785-786 (1979).

43. Brown, I., Washburn, J, MEVVA Ion Source for High Current Metal Ion Implanation, Intl. Conf. on Ion Implantation Technol. (Berkeley CA) NTIS DE87000069: (1986).

44. Shinno, H., Fukutomi, M. et al., In Situ Coating of Low-Z Materials by Reactive Vacuum Arc Deposition with a Stabilized Arc Cathode. J. Nucl. Mater. 133-134: 749-753 (1985).

45. Morrison Jr., C. F. Method and Apparatus for Arc Evaporating Large Area Targets, U.S. Patent No. 4,724,058 (1984).

46. Morrison Jr., C. F. Method and Apparatus for Evaporation Arc Stabilization Including Initial Target Cleaning, U.S. Patent No. 4,448,659 (1984).

47. Mularie, W.M. Method and Apparatus for Evaporation Arc Stabiliztion for Permeale Targets, U.S. Patent No. 4,559,121 (1983).

48. Wroe, H. Stabilization of Low Pressure D.C. Arc Discharges, U.S. Patent: 2,972,695 (1961).

49. Sablev, L.P., Dolotov, Y.I. et al., Electrical-Arc Vaporizer of Metals with Magnetic Confinement of Cathode Spot. Instrum. and Exp. Tech. (Engl. Transl. of Prib. Tekh. Eksp.) 19: 1211-1213 (1976).

50. Kasaev, I.G., Pashkova, V.V., The Electromagnetic Anchoring of the Cathode Spot. Sov. Phys. Tech. Phys. (Engl. Transl. of Zh. Tekh. Fiz.) 4: No. 254-264, (1959).

51. Sanders, D.M., Pyle, E.A., Magnetic Enhancement of Cathodic Arc Deposition. J. Vac. Sci. Technol. A5: 2728-2731 (1987).

52. Aksenov, I.E., Bren', V.G. et al., Mechanism Shaping the Ion Energy Distribution in the Plasma of a Vacuum Arc. Sov. Phys. Tech. Phys. (Engl. Transl. of Zh. Tekh. Fiz.) 7: No. 10, 497-489 (1981).

53. Aksenov, I.I., Belous, V.A. et al., Apparatus to rid the Plasma of a Vacuum Arc of Macroparticles. Instrum. and Exp. Tech. (Engl. Transl. of Prib. Tekh. Eksp.) 21: No. 5, Pt. 2, 1416-1418 (1978).

54. Aksenov, I.I., Belokhvostikov, A.N. et al., Plasma Flux Motion in a Toroidal Plasma Guide. Plasma Phys. Contr. Fusion (GB) 28: No. 5, 761-770 (1986).

55. Aksenov, I.I., Bren', V.G. et al., Chemical Reactions in the Condensation of Metal-Plasma Streams. Sov. Phys. Tech. Phys. (Engl. Transl. of Zh. Tekh. Fiz.) 23: No. 6, 651-653 (1978).

56. Hitchon, W.N.G., A Plasma-Optical System Modeled Using Particles, J. Plasma Phys. (UK) 38: Pt. 1, 87-94 (1987).

57. Robertson, S., Magnetic Guiding, Focusing and Compression of an Intense Charge-Neutral Ion Beam. Phys. Fluids. 26: No. 4, 1129 (1983).

58. Boxman, R.L., Goldsmith, S., et al., Fast Deposition of Metallurgical Coatings and Production of Surface Alloys Using a Pulsed High Current Vacuum Arc" Thin Solid Films 139: No. 1, 41-52 (1986).

59. Chernyaev, V.N., Korze, V.F. et al., The Manufacture of Strip-Line Microwave Devices Using Pulsed Plasma Accelerators. Radioelectron. and Commun. Syst. (Engl. Transl. of Izv. Vyssh. Uchevn. Zaved. Radioelektron.) 25: No. 12, 68-71 (1982).

60. Drodnov, A.M., Miroshkin, S.I. Vacuum Erosion-Type Generators and Plasma Accelerators Working on Alternating High Temp. (Engl. Transl. of Teplofiz. Vys. Temp.) 18: No. 5, 821-830 (1980).

61. Ramalingam,S. Controlled Vacuum Arc Material Deposition, Method and Apparatus, World Patent #85/03954 (1985).

62. Kljuchko, G.V., Padalka, V.G. et al., Plasma Arc Apparatus for Applying Coatings by Means of a Consumable Cathode, U.S. Patent No. 4,492,845 (1982).

63. Buhl, R., Moll, E. et al., Method and Apparatus for Evaporating Material Under Vacuum using both an Arc Discharge and Electron Beam, U.S. Patent No. 4,448,802 (1981).

64. Sanders, D.M. Ion Beam Self-Sputtering Using a Cathodic Arc Ion Source. J. Vac. Sci. Technol. A6: No. 3, 1929-1933 (1988).

65. Kanayama, M., Igarashi, Y. Ultrahigh Vacuum Arc Method to Form Thin Refractory Metal Films. Rev. Sci. Instrum. 54: No. 2, 220-225 (1983).

66. Saenko, V.A., Vladimirov, A.I. et al., Thermionic Deposition Devices" Instrum. and Exp. Tech. (Engl. Transl. of Prib. Tekh. Eksp.) No. 3, 9-21 (1985).

67. Saenko, V.A., Vladimirov, A.I. et al., Hollow Cathode Evaporators. Instrum. and Exp. Tech. (Engl. Transl. of Prib. Tekh. Eksp.) 28: No. 1 Pt. 2, 131-264 (1985).

68. Muller, K. H. Stress and Microstructure of Sputter-Deposited Thin Films: Molecular Dynamics Investigations. J. Appl. Phys. 62: No. 5, 1796-1799 (1987).

69. Poppov, D.N., Uzunov, T.D. et al., Influence of the Nitrogen Partial Pressure on the Composition and Color of Titanium Nitride Coatings, Obtained by Reactive Magnetron Sputtering and Reactive Arc Deposition. Bulg. J. Phys. 13: No. 5, 470-476 (1986).

70. Martin, P.J., Filipczuk, S.W. et al., Structure and Hardness of Diamond-Like Carbon Films Prepared by Arc Evaporation. To be published in J. Mater. Sci. Lett..

71. Freller, H., Haessler, H. $Ti_xAl_{1-x}N$ Films Deposited by Ion Plating with an Arc Evaporator. Proc. Intl. Conf. on Metal. Coatings (1987).

72. Randhawa, H. Cathodic Arc Plasma Deposition of TiC and TiC_xN_{1-x} Films Thin Solid Films 153: 209-218 (198?).

73. Aisenberg, S., Chabot, R. Technol. 8: No. 1, (1971).

74. Aksenov, I.I., Vakula, S.I. et al., High-Efficiency Source of Pure Carbon Plasma. Sov. Phys. Tech. Phys. (Engl. Transl. of Zh. Tekh. Fiz.) 25: No. 9, 1164-1166 (1980).

75. Stel'nitskii, V.E., Padalka, V.G. et al., Properties of Diamond-Like Carbon Film Produced by the Condensation of Plasma Stream with a RF Potential. Sov. Phys. Tech. Phys. (Engl. Transl. of Zh. Tekh. Fiz.) 23: No. 2, 222-224 (1978).

76. Strel'nitskii, V.E., Arksenov, I.I. et al.,   Properties of Diamond-Like Carbon Coatings Produced by Plasma Condensation. Sov. Phys. Tech. Phys. (Engl. Transl. of Zh. Tekh. Fiz.) 4: No. 11, 546-547 (1978).

77. Randhawa, H. TiN - Coated High-Speed Steel Cutting Tools. J. Vac. Sci. Technol. A4: 2755-2758 (1986).

78. Dorodnov, A. M., Minaichev, V. E. et al., High-Vacuum Plasma Pump. Instrum. and Exp. Tech. (Engl. Transl. of Prib. Tekh. Eksp.) 23: No. 6, 1449-1452 (1980).

79. Dorodnov, A. M., Miroshkin, S. I. et al., Surface Machining by Ion Sputtering. Sov. Tech. Phys. Lett. (Engl. Trans. of Pis'ma Zh. Tekh. Fiz.) 5: No. 4, 172-173 (1979). 80. Lunev, V. M., Ovcharenko, V. D. et al., Plasma Properties of a Metal Vacuum Arc. Sov. Phys. Tech. Phys. (Engl. Transl. of Zh. Tekh. Fiz.) 22: No. 7, 856-861 (1977).

Part VI
Plasma
Surface Interactions

19

Ion-Surface Interactions: General Understandings

Russell Messier, Joseph E. Yehoda and Lawrence J. Pilione

19.1 INTRODUCTION

Ion-surface interactions are present and play a significant role in many plasma-based thin film deposition techniques (1). The term ion has often referred to both ionized and neutral energetic particles in the literature. It has been shown in previous chapters that plasmas are sources of both non-equilibrium gas phase/surface chemistry and particle bombardment. The net effect is that very often specific materials can be obtained at lower deposition temperatures, and as a result a wide and controllable range of film properties can be attained, in addition to new metastable structures or compositions. In this chapter we will restrict our discussions to the physical effects of ion-surface interactions on relatively low temperature surfaces, and thus, mainly inert gas ion bombardment will be considered. Furthermore, we will focus attention on the atomistic aspects of ion-surface interactions especially at low ion energies and ion-to-atom arrival rate ratios.

Thin films are generally not the same as bulk materials since, in most cases, they contain impurities, internal and external surfaces/interfaces, density variations with thickness, short range density fluctuations, etc., which are highly dependent upon the particular deposition technique parameters and fundamental processes such as energetic particle bombardment. The result is a virtual infinity of thin film materials covering a broad continuum of free energy states and macroscopic and microscopic structures. It is this variability which leads to the wide range of possible characteristics and resulting properties that make thin films such extensively used materials both scientifically and technologically. At the same time, quantitative preparation-characterization-property relations remain an elusive goal, in large part due to the seeming simplicity - and yet actual complexity - of vapor-deposited films (2,3).

19.2 PREPARATION-ION BOMBARDMENT RELATIONS

It has only been since the mid-1960's that a number of new deposition processes based upon plasma generation and activation of species have been developed. Although dc-sputtering was invented over a hundred years before, it was not until the advent of commercial rf-diode sputtering systems that plasma-based processes became extensively used. Since then such deposition techniques as triode sputtering, rf- and dc-magnetron sputtering, ion plating, activated reactive evaporation (ARE), dc-, rf-, and microwave-plasma assisted chemical vapor deposition (PACVD), remote PACVD, ion-beam assisted evaporation, ion beam sputtering, dual ion beam sputtering, and direct ion beam deposition have become commonly used both scientifically and technologically (1). In addition, many variations on these techniques have been developed. Except for the ion beam-assisted processes, where ion energy and flux can be independently and precisely controlled, the ion energy and flux of species bombarding the growing film can be highly dependent upon the various deposition parameters. For instance, both the plasma current density and the floating self-bias potential (V_{sb}) of surfaces in contact with a diode sputtering plasma increase, with different functional relationships, with an increase in the plasma power density. Besides floating potential induced bombardment processes, sputtering gas ions can also be reflected, and neutralized, at the target. In both cases the energy, energy distribution, and energetic particle flux are not easy to measure or predict.

The bombarding flux of particles (energy and angle) from a sputtering target due to sputtered atoms ($E_o \cong 5$ to $10eV$) and reflected neutrals ($E_o > 100eV$) can be modified as a function of: total gas pressure, target-substrate distance, target voltage and power, substrate self-bias, plasma temperature, collision and charge exchange cross-sections, collision mean free path, scattering angle, and the masses of the target and gas atoms. The interdependence of some of these parameters makes it extremely difficult, if not impossible, to control any one of them independent of the others. Such is the case in magnetron (dc and rf), triode, and diode sputtering where the operating pressures and/or lack of plasma confinement near the target surface dictates an "averaging approach" to selecting deposition parameters. That is, one selects the deposition conditions to produce final film properties that are the result of a number of intertwined sputtering parameters.

A number of studies (4-13) have been reported that investigate the interaction of atoms/ions with the plasma and the subsequent effects at the target (sputtering process) and the substrate (film evolution). Important parameters in these analyses are the collision and charge exchange cross-sections, both of which are energy dependent (7). The careful use of these cross-sections allows one to predict the energy exchange and post-collision scattering angle between colliding atoms. This information, coupled with the make-up of the plasma (mass of sputtering gas, total gas pressure and target-to-substrate distance), can be used to calculate the effects of multiple collisions. The averaged energy loss per collision is normally used to calculate the mean free path and the final angular and energy distributions of the particles (4,5,10,12). However, recently Monte Carlo calculation methods have been introduced by Motohiro and Taga (8) and Somekh (7) to study what occurs along the trajectory of an atom/ion, and give insights into the particle transport process. These studies show in more detail than in previous ones (4,5,12) that the reduction in initial energy of sputtered atoms and reflected neutrals is a function of the product of gas pressure and target-substrate distance (7), i.e., pressure-distance product. Figure 1 illustrates the trajectories of sputtered Ag particles as a function of gas pressure and target-substrate distance. It is evident from this modeling that significant modification of the initial angular and energy distributions of sputtered and reflected neutrals occurs in the plasma as the deposition parameters are changed. Major changes can also occur in final particle distributions by varying the type of gas used in the plasma, the target-substrate distance, and the target material. In addition to these effects, it has been found that the return rate to the target of the sputtered particles depends on gas pressure and target-substrate distance. Also, the ratio of the atomic numbers between the target and sputtered gas atoms can control the arrival rate at the substrate and the return rate to the target of the sputtered atoms (8). Such dependencies can affect the composition and/or structure of the final film as can different atomic masses having different angular distributions at the substrate. Rarefaction of the gas density in front of a magnetron target as a function of the magnetron current has also been reported (13). This reduction in gas density is due to collisional heating of the gas by sputtered atoms, and results in changes in film bombardment. These changes, in turn, can produce variations in composition as well as film stress and grain size.

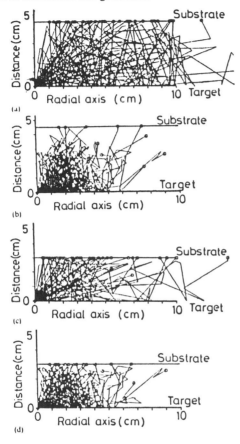

Figure 1: Computer generated trajectories of 50 silver atoms ejected into an argon gas at a pressure, P, and target-substrate distance, D. (a) P = 5mTorr, D = 45mm; (b) P = 15mTorr, D = 45mm; (c) P = 5mTorr, D = 30mm; (d) P = 15mTorr, D = 30mm. (data from ref. 8).

Ion beam sources have become essential tools in fundamental studies of ion-surface interactions because they allow for the independent control of energetic particle bombardment processes. With the development of efficient Kaufman type broad beam ion sources capable of both low energy and high ion flux (14), it is possible to controllably bombard a growing film with an energy input ranging from 1 to 1000eV per depositing atom. These sources typically operate at low gas pressures ($< 10^{-4}$ Torr) and as such do not have the added complication of gas scattering events. Generally the ion energy (E_i) can be varied from 10 to more than 1000eV with the ion flux ranging from 0.02 to 2 mA/cm^2 , with independent control over both bombardment parameters. Together with the mass of the bombarding ions and the depositing atoms, the ion-surface interaction is defined in a quantitative and reproducible manner. For typical deposition rates (1 to 30 Å/ sec) this allows for either low ion energy or low ion flux while still maintaining the range of energy per depositing atom indicated above. This can be important when the particular property being controlled requires a limited range of acceptable parameters: for example, low ion energy to minimize bombardment induced short range disorder.

19.3 ION BOMBARDMENT-PROPERTY RELATIONS

The modification of thin film properties by simultaneous ion bombardment during deposition has been the topic of a number of papers over the years. Harper et al.(15) have summarized 16 examples where sufficient data was obtainable (Table 1) to compare structure related property modification using a "universal plot" which is shown in Fig. 2. As seen in this figure and table, most of the data are for ion energies greater than 100eV. This is representative of the available literature. Only within the last several years have an increasing number of such studies explored the lower energy regime (<100eV). Since most of these property changes have only been phenomenologically related to the ion bombardment conditions, no fundamental understandings have been developed in large part. Several recent studies have gone beyond the simple empirical preparation-property relations and are providing insights into the atomic level connections between controlled ion-surface interactions and resulting lattice distortion and, in turn, the compressive stress in polycrystalline thin films.

Table 1: Examples plotted in Fig. 2 of thin film property modification by ion bombardment during deposition (from Ref. 15)

Num.	Film material	Ion species	Property modified	Ion energy (eV)	Ion/atom arrival rate ratio
1	Ge	Ar^+	stress, adhn.	65-3000	2×10^{-4} to 10^{-1}
2	Nb	Ar^+	stress	100-400	3×10^{-2}
3	Cr	Ar^+, Xe^+	stress	3400-11500	8×10^{-3} to 4×10^{-2}
4	Cr	Ar^+	stress	200-800	$\approx 7 \times 10^{-3}$ to 2×10^{-2}
5	SiO_2	Ar^+	step coverage	500	0.3
6	SiO_2	Ar^+	step coverage	$\approx 1 - 80$	≈ 4
7	AlN	N_2^+	preferred orientation	300-500	0.96 to 1.5
8	Au	Ar^+	coverage at 50 Åthickness	400	0.1
9	GdCoMo	Ar^+	magnetic anisotropy	$\approx 1 - 150$	≈ 0.1
10	Cu	Cu^+	improved epitaxy	$50 \approx 400$	10^{-2}
11	BN	$(B-N-H)^+$	cubic structure	200-1000	≈ 1
12	ZrO_2, TiO_2 SiO_2	Ar^+, O_2^+	refractive index amorph. → crys.	600	2.5×10^{-2} to 0.1
13	SiO_2, TiO_2	O_2^+	refractive index	300	0.12
14	SiO_2, TiO_2	O_2^+	optical transmission	30-500	0.05 to 0.25
15	Cu	N^+, Ar^+	adhesion	50000	10^{-2}
16	Ni on Fe	Ar^+	hardness	10000-20000	≈ 0.25

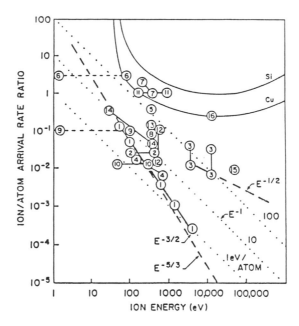

Figure 2: Ion bombardment modification of several different thin film properties as a function of the ion energy and ion to atom arrival rate ratio needed to cause modification. (from Ref 15.)

Windischmann (16) has developed a model based upon the elastic modulus and the molar volume of the film material and the lattice distortion resulting from energetic particle bombardment. An assumption in this model is that the thin film material-specific properties are the same as the bulk properties, which is reasonable in light of the preponderance of evidence reporting dense (low void volume) films for ion bombarded films with associated high compressive stress state when deposited with concurrent ion bombardment. Based upon Sigmund's theory of forward sputtering (17) in a film under energetic particle bombardment, Windischmann derived an expression for stress (S),

$$S = 1.91K\, \Phi_i\, E_i^{1/2}Q/N_o \qquad (1)$$

in which K is a proportionality factor relating relative volumetric strain to the fractional number of atoms displaced from equilibrium sites under the energetic bombardment, Φ_i is the ion flux, E_i is the energetic particle's energy, N_o Avogadro's number, and Q represents the elastic energy per mole [$Q = EM/(1 - \nu)D$] where E is Young's modulus, M is the atomic mass, and ν is Poisson's ratio. Thus the bombardment induced stress is related to the physical properties of the material, the relative atomic number and mass of the bombarding particle and film material, and to the bombarding particle energy and flux.

The ideas of ion-surface interactions leading to both elastic (18,19) and elastic plus plastic (20) lattice distortions are clearly reflected in lattice spacing dilation measurements. These and similar studies are consistent with Windischmann's work. An important further conclusion from his model is that stress is related to the momentum rather than the energy of the incident particle, as indicated by the square-root dependence of E_i. This is supported by previous experimental studies of Hoffman and Gaerttner (21), and Ziemann and Kay (22) for polycrystalline metal films and Nir (23) for amorphous diamond-like films.

Windischmann measured the stress vs. Q relation for 30 samples from both his study (by ion beam sputtering) and others (mainly magnetron sputtering) and found a linear curve fit the data. This is shown in Fig. 3, and Table 2. The samples were all about the same thickness and subjected to sufficient energetic particle bombardment to insure nearly fully-dense films. It is interesting to note that for thermal evaporation without concurrent ion bombardment the stress is tensile and shows no correlation with the S vs. Q linear relation. One possible explanation suggested was that films prepared under low mobility conditions are known to contain a significant percentage of void volume which may invalidate the use of bulk properties in calculating Q.

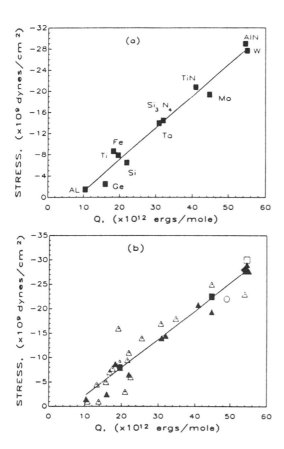

Figure 3: Variation of intrinsic stress with Q, the elastic energy/mole, for films prepared by (a) ion beam sputtering and (b) the present data superimposed on data taken from the literature for other deposition techniques, as shown in Table 2. (data from Ref 16.)

Table 2: Compressive stress data from the literature and calculated Q values for films deposited by various sputtering techniques (from Ref. 16).

Material	Stress ($\times 10^9$ dyne/cm^2)	Q ($\times 10^{12}$ erg/mole)	Deposition technique
Al	1	10.4	MS
Ni	3	21.1	MS
Ti	16	18.3	MS
V	7	16.8	MS
Gd	5	15.8	MS
Cr	12-14	25.5	MS
Rh	18	34.8	MS
Zr	9	21.6	MS
Pt	6	22.5	MS
Si	11	22.0	MS
Nb	9	19.5	MS
Nb	9.5	19.5	MS
Mo	20-25	44.7	IBS
Mo	25-30	44.7	MS
Ta	18-20	30.8	MS
W	23	54.0	MS
W	29	54.0	RFS/triode
ZrO$_2$	22	49.0	RFS/diode
AlN	30	54.5	MS

MS = magnetron sputtering. RFS = rf sputtering. IBS = ion beam sputtering.

A more direct method for examining the bombardment induced lattice distortion during ion-assisted evaporation is to perform a molecular dynamics (MD) calculation of the deposition and concurrent energetic bombardment processes. Müller (24) has carried out 2-dimensional MD calculations using a Lennard-Jones potential for film-atom interatomic potentials, descriptive of close packed metal atomic structures, while the Ar bombarding particle-film atom interaction is described by a Moliere potential. Further assumptions include normal incidence of both the depositing vapor and bombarding particles, an absolute zero temperature substrate, a limited number of atoms considered ($\simeq 500$) and related small simulation cell with periodic boundary conditions, and a purely repulsive Ar-film atom interaction which excludes the possibility of Ar entrapment.

Despite these limitations, imposed in part by the cost and speed of present-day computers, it has been shown that simple stress calculations of the final simulation cell atomic positions for Ar$^+$ bombardment of a Ni growing film lead to a stress vs. bombarding energy curve in qualitative agreement with experimental data such as that described by Windischmann (16) and references therein. Under zero and low bombardment energy the stress is tensile and increases, instead of decreasing, to a maximum value at 3.2eV per deposited film atom before decreasing as Windischmann has shown. At these conditions the voids are still present, though becoming smaller and less connected, and related to the tensile stress. Only at higher Ar bombardment energies (at a fixed ion-to-atom rate ratio (Φ_i/Φ_a) of 0.16) does the tensile stress decrease and at the same time the voids are even smaller and fewer in number. Unfortunately his simulations were not carried out to high enough energies or arrival rate ratios to reach a dense morphology (minimal void content) with a maximum value of compressive stress. Thus, his simulations cannot be directly compared to the Windischmann model (16) calculations.

19.4 ION BOMBARDMENT-STRUCTURE RELATIONS

The present status of models describing thin film morphology is the qualitative representations provided by the structure zone models (SZM's) of Movchan and Demchishin (25), Thornton (26), and Messier et al. (2,27). The salient features of each representation are the effects of: temperature on evaporated films (25); temperature and bombardment from both normal and oblique deposition components and variations with sputtering gas pressure (26) and thickness evolution and the bombardment controlled by the V_{sb} dependence on the sputtering gas pressure (27). These classification schemes are discussed in more detail in another chapter.

The density deficit regions (normally referred to as voids) which are seen in Fig. 4, and have been noted in the SZM's described above, are not uniformly dispersed throughout a thin film but form in a self-organized array, commonly referred to as a void network throughout the film. These are most easily imaged using a defocused phase-contrast technique in a transmission electron microscope (28) and are directly related to the cauliflower-like structures seen in SEM micrographs of thicker films typically used to define the SZM's. These void regions delineate the columns found in thin films, especially those grown under low adatom mobility conditions. It is the competition between these columnar units which is directly affected by ion-surface interactions. In turn, the optical density and properties which are affected by density change, can be influenced to a large extent. It is apparent that understanding the clustering of adatoms and the competition between the resulting columnar structures is imperative if a quantitative connection between these microscopic processes and measured macroscopic properties are to be achieved. Unfortunately, these structural units contain many atoms, and solutions will have to await more powerful computers and computation schemes.

The importance of molecular dynamics calculations in linking our understanding between ion-surface interactions, resulting short- and intermediate-range structure, and film properties are seen in the above example. At the same time it points out the practical difficulties in this approach. If computers were available to carry out the simulations that are clearly needed, then significant progress in our fundamental understanding of ion-surface interactions could be made rapidly. However, that not being the case, limited MD calculations which address only portions of the larger problems, will have to be used. Furthermore, the coordination of such simulation studies with highly defined experimental studies should lead to progress in the ion-surface interaction field.

Early attempts at simulating thin film growth involved simple hard sphere (billiard ball) approach (29), to more sophisticated Monte Carlo (30-32) and molecular dynamics (24,29,33,34) methods. Recent studies, though, have provided the most detailed and realistic modeling efforts to date. For instance, in an extension of the MD simulations described above, Müller (24) has determined the density of his computer generated Ni "films" as a function of both E_i (0 to 100 eV Ar$^+$) and Φ_i/Φ_a (0 to 0.16) and shown that the trends in his simulated experiments are consistent with real deposition experiments.

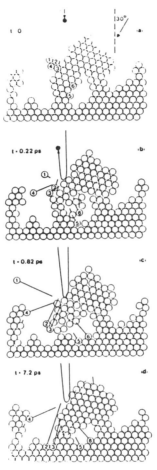

Figure 4: Molecular dynamics simulation of a low energy ion-surface interaction. (from Ref 35.)

Film density is a fundamental factor in any preparation-property relation. Furthermore, it is not expected that the average density will be nearly as crucial as the atomistic details - lattice distortions, interstitials, vacancies, vacancy clusters, and voids, and atomic-level fluctuations in these structural defects which lead to void networks and density fluctuations. The latter structural details are not singular entities but will need to be described by distribution functions if a detailed and realistic understanding of thin film structure (or what is often called microstructure or morphology) is to be developed. At this stage of understanding it is known that such nanometer-level defects are present, but there is no quantitative description of them, and it is not known if such detailed information can be combined into an average quantity, such as average film density, without losing the fundamental aspect of the structure-property relation. Thus, it is suggested that the statistical nature of film microstructure must be addressed if any significant fundamental progress in ion-surface interaction effects is to be made.

In order to demonstrate the complexity of the various processes occurring during ion-surface interactions and their effects on atomic-level structure, a time sequence during an ion-surface collision process is considered. In Fig. 4, Müller (35) simulates an ion-surface interaction event in which a low energy Ar$^+$ ion (100 eV) collides with a porous columnar Ni film at its early stages of formation on a perfect 2-dimensional Ni lattice. The Ni vapor, with energy representative of thermally evaporated atoms (0.1eV), impinges at 30° from the surface normal while the Ar$^+$ bombardment is at normal incidence. These deposition conditions and configurations are typical of the ion-assisted deposition process. Upon impact the Ar ion transfers a part of its kinetic energy to the surface atoms which, in turn, transfer their kinetic energy to other surface and sub-surface atoms. A large number of atoms are displaced (Fig. 4) and are indicated by the straight lines (not trajectories) which indicate only their initial and final (or intermediate) positions. Six atoms which suffered large displacements are numbered and are indicative of the range of different mechanisms of bombardment induced structural rearrangement. Atom 1 is completely sputtered from the film while the other five atoms are driven deeper into the film structure. Atoms 2 and 3 migrate along the surface of the central cluster and end finally at the bottom of the cluster at the original substrate interface. Atom 4 is sputtered from the surface and redeposits on an adjoining column while atoms 5 and 6 are also sputtered/redeposited but within a closed void. In addition to these large displacements, a large number of smaller displacements occur collectively at the latter stages of the lattice relaxation process. It is noted that the loosely bound overhanging atoms (1-4) have been eliminated and many atoms have been driven to lower-lying states as a result of just a single ion-surface interaction event.

19.5 THE INTERACTION OF IONS WITH THE GROWING FILM

The processes occurring when a growing film is bombarded by energetic ions or neutral species must be considered (36). For "non-reactive" bombarding species (not chemically reactive with the depositing species), the situation is simplified somewhat. The main processes which can occur are: (1) momentum transfer (knock-on) displacement; and (2) direct temperature effects (thermal annealing due to temperature rise caused by thermal spikes). These processes can in turn cause various effects as the thin film grows, including enhanced surface mobility, enhanced accretion of nuclei, desorption of surface impurities, redistribution of atoms in the film, and also the implantation of bombarding species into the growing film (37).

The idea of thermal spike generation is not new and has been considered by others as a mechanism for sputter ejection of atoms (38). Weissmantel et al.(39) have used the idea of thermal spike generation and the production of a shock zone front to explain the formation of metastable phases of cubic BN and diamond-like carbon films. Because of the rapid rise and fall of the temperature spike and the higher pressures caused by the shock wave generated by an impacting ion it has been suggested that a high pressure metastable structure can be formed and then frozen in. Hirsch and Varga (40) have also suggested that an annealing affect is present in thin films undergoing simultaneous ion bombardment during growth due to thermal spike generation, and that this has a threshold which is dependent on the "intensity" of ion bombardment. Martin et al. (41) have also suggested that ion impact crystallization, via thermal spikes, may be the mechanism responsible for the appearance of the cubic phase of ZrO_2 undergoing energetic ion bombardment.

Müller (30) has used 2-dimensional Monte Carlo calculations to simulate the effects of thermal spike generation on the structure of vapor deposited films. He has shown that the elongated voids found in thin films due to low adatom mobility are bridged, forming a structure with isolated pockets, but still appearing to have a large fraction of voids left in the films. He also finds a dependence on the energy of the incoming ions and the ion to atom arrival rate ratio; namely for $E_i = 150$ eV Ar^+, as Φ_i/Φ_a is increased, the elongated voids are bridged to a greater extent. If, however, E_i is increased, the arrival rate ratio needed to cause the same degree of bridging is now less. In both cases, however, there still exists a large fraction of voids. From this it can be concluded that, although thermal spike generation can affect the thin film structure, it appears not to be a dominant process. Thus the generation of thermal spikes appears to be a mechanism of inducing a phase change (39,41), but not a dominant mechanism in densification of films due to the filling in of voids.

The momentum transfer process takes into account the displacement of deposited atoms due to bombarding species. This displacement can take on several forms; resputtering of deposited atoms which results in a net loss of film atoms, forward sputtering which leads to a densification and filling in of voids, lattice relaxation, and, of course, the impacting ion may also implant in the growing thin film, acting as an impurity. Several of these effects are shown in Fig. 4. Because of the variation in sputtering yields as a function of incident ion energy, the use of lower energy ions ($\simeq 100$ eV) will result in more forward sputtering and redistribution than the complete resputtering of deposited species. In addition, since the incorporation of bombarding species has been shown to be dependent on incident ion energy, the use of lower energy ions has an advantage of minimizing these incorporated atoms.

It has been shown previously (16) that momentum characterizes the behavior of stress in a series of materials covering the range from metals to semiconductors to insulators, thus showing wide applicability. Targrove et al. (42) have also addressed the question of momentum transfer, and found it to be the dominant mechanism in the densification of LaF_3 thin films, using ion-assisted evaporation. By observing the changes in the index of refraction as a function of the momentum imparted to the film, a good correlation with momentum was observed.

In recent studies (43,44), the role of lower energy ion bombardment on the changes in density (void fraction) and other properties (optical band gap and inert gas incorporation) using ion-assisted evaporation has also pointed to momentum transfer being an important aspect in modifying the density, a fundamental characteristic of a material upon which many properties depend. Amorphous Ge was used as a model system for these studies, and in view of the general applicability of such representations as the structure zone models (2,25-27), the results are believed to be of general applicability to other material systems.

Using spectroscopic ellipsometry for the determination of the density (void fraction), it has been shown that the density exhibits a common behavior when plotted in terms of the energy deposited per arriving atom (E_n) for the energy range of 15 to 600 eV (Fig. 5). Several unique features are observed, with three distinct regions present. At low levels of bombardment, there is a sharp rise in density followed by a leveling off. This can be explained as due to bombardment induced densification and "annealing" of the film as it grows. However, as the energy of the incoming ion increases, another competing effect must be addressed: bombardment-induced damage. This is believed to be the cause of the sudden drop in density seen in Fig. 5. Whether this damage is due to network induced disorder or to an increase in the implantation of Ar is not known. It is apparent, though, that the combined effects of energy and flux are important for the film densification process.

To better understand the nature of this possible effect, the previous literature on bombardment-induced damage is considered. From the literature on sputtering yield measurements and radiation damage (45), the critical energy which is necessary to cause displacements can be taken to first order as 4 times the heat of sublimation, i.e. $4\Delta H_{subl}$. For Ge, $\Delta H_{subl} = 4.08$ eV (46). Using this value, a critical Φ_i/Φ_a for each incident ion energy can be calculated. If an elastic energy transfer is assumed and correction is made for the angle-of-incidence of the ions with respect to the substrate normal, then a $(\Phi_i/\Phi_a)_{critical}$ can be given as follows:

$$(\Phi_i/\Phi_a)_{critical} = \frac{\Delta H_{subl}(m_i + m_a)^2}{m_i m_a E_i \cos \Theta_i} \tag{2}$$

where m_i and m_a are the ion and atom masses, respectively. In Table 3 are the calculated $(\Phi_i/\Phi_a)_{critical}$ values along with the $(E_n)_{critical}$ values obtained by multiplying $(\Phi_i/\Phi_a)_{critical}$ by $E_n \cos \Theta_i$. This represents the critical threshold energy per deposited atom necessary to cause displacement type damage. This value of $E_n = 17.8$ eV/Ge is in good agreement with Fig. 5 ($E_n \simeq 18$ eV/Ge with an uncertainty of a few eV/Ge), thereby lending support for this mechanism.

Table 3: Calculation of the critical Φ_i/Φ_a and E_n for Ar+ bombardment of a-Ge using Eqn. 2, which assumes elastic energy transfer and corrects for the angle-of-incidence of the ion with respect to the substrate normal ($\Delta H_{subl} = 4.08$eV and $\Theta_i = 30°$) (from Ref. 43).

E_i (eV)	$(\frac{\Phi_i}{\Phi_a})_{critical}$	$(E_n)_{critical}$ (eV/Ge)
600	0.034	17.8
400	0.051	"
200	0.103	"
90	0.229	"
70	0.294	"
50	0.412	"
30	0.686	"
15	1.372	"

As mentioned previously, Müller (24) has modeled the effects of momentum transfer using a 2-dimensional MD simulation for evaporated Ni with Ar+ assist; E_i varied from 0 to 100 eV and Φ_i/Φ_a from 0 to 0.16. He found that low energies and small Φ_i/Φ_a are enough to cause substantial modification of the void structure with the packing density increasing from 0.74 (as-deposited Ni with no bombardment) to 0.84 (10 eV Ar) and 0.95 (50 eV Ar), both at $\Phi_i/\Phi_a = 0.16$. This range of energies and arrival rate ratios is similar to that used by Yehoda et al. (43) and Yehoda (44). However, care must be taken when making exact comparisons due to the 2-dimensional nature of the simulations, but general trends should be similar. Although Müller (35) does not show a saturation in the packing density at the higher levels of bombardment, he does indicate that this saturation was observed but was not studied extensively due to the high cost of computation time. If the simple model of Eqn. 2 is applied to his work, it is found that $(\Phi_i/\Phi_a)_{critical} = 0.64$ for 50 eV Ar bombardment, corresponding to $(E_n)_{critical} = 24\mathrm{eV/Ni}$ ($\Delta H_{subl} = 6.72\mathrm{eV}$ for Ni). Since his simulations do not consider flux ratios larger than 0.16, the correspondence with Eqn. 2 could not be checked.

Using a 3-dimensional Monte Carlo collision cascade simulation, Müller (31) has developed a model which attempts to explain the densification which takes place during ion bombardment due to surface sputtering and recoil implantation, followed by constant refilling from the vapor atoms. He was able to generate density profiles of ZrO_2 films bombarded by O^+, in addition to film density changes versus Φ_i/Φ_a for 600 eV O^+. His results are in agreement with similar experimental evidence by Martin et al. (41) for ion assisted ZrO_2 evaporated films. The theory starts to breakdown at higher Φ_i/Φ_a where experiments find that densification saturates while the theory predicts a continual increase. This discrepancy can easily be accounted for, though, since repulsive effects between the film atoms were not taken into account. It would be interesting to perform depth profiling on films of this type to compare an experimental depth distribution of the atoms with those generated by Müller.

Similarly, using experimental results on CeO_2 evaporated with O_2^+ ion assist (47) Müller (32) has formulated a simulation which describes the bulk density changes in an ion assisted film in terms of the sputtering yields of atoms on the surface, their recoil implantation, and the incorporation of ions. What he finds is that there exists a density increase with increasing Φ_i/Φ_a at fixed E_i. Additionally, if Φ_i/Φ_a is held constant with E_i varying, an optimum film density occurring at $E_n \simeq 167\mathrm{eV/CeO_2}$ was found, with the density decreasing at higher E_i. Experimentally this is also observed, but the fall off is at a much slower rate. This behavior was similarly observed for the a-Ge when plotted in terms of E_n (Fig. 5). If Eqn. 2 is applied to O^+ bombarding CeO_2 ($\Theta_v = 30°$), then $(E_n)_{critical} \simeq 78$ eV/CeO_2, since $\Delta H_{subl} = 7$ eV (32). It is apparent that this value of $(E_n)_{critical}$ is approximately half that found by Müller. Four possible explanations for these differences are: (1) Eqn. 2 is only a very simplified representation taking into account damage due to impinging ions, and does not address other important factors such as recoil implantation and ion incorporation, which Müller includes; (2) the value $4\Delta H_{subl}$ used in obtaining Eqn. 2 is only an approximation to the damage threshold in a material, where significant damage may not occur until several times this value is transferred to the structure; (3) since the material is being bombarded with a chemically active ion, its effects on adatom mobility may be such that more energy is necessary to cause rearrangement; (4) the choice of target mass in Eqn. 2 is not all that straightforward for a compound, whereas for a single component film the choice is obvious. At this stage more work is needed to understand the relative importance of these factors.

For films of SiO_2 and TiO_2 deposited by ion-assisted evaporation, with energies of 30 and 500 eV, McNeil et al. (48) observed a change in the optical transmission

$(T_{substrate} - T_{film/substrate})$ of the films with respect to the bare silica substrate at $\lambda = 2500\text{Å}$.   For SiO_2 films, the transmission changed little under 30 eV O_2^+ bombardment while under 500 eV bombardment it decreased by up to 12%.   In TiO_2 the changes at 30 eV were again small, while 500 eV bombardment caused an even greater decrease under low to moderate fluxes. Their explanation for this behavior is the preferential resputtering of oxygen which causes an enrichment in Si or Ti, resulting in increased absorption. Thus, selecting the degree of bombardment is seen to be important in achieving a desired result.

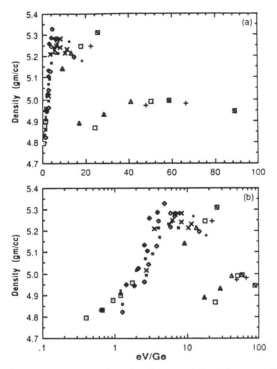

Figure 5: Density versus energy deposited per arriving Ge atom (E_n) for different ion energies. 15 eV (□); 30 ev (◆); 50 eV (■); (b) 70 eV (◇); 90 eV (X); 110 eV (+); 200 eV (▲); 300 eV (△); 400 eV (□); 500 eV (+); and 600 eV (□) Ar. (from ref. 43.)

Hultman et al.(49) have observed a critical substrate bias voltage where the dislocation loop density is a minimum in epitaxial TiN films grown by reactive magnetron sputtering. Above this critical voltage the dislocation loop density is found to increase, a result of lattice damage from excessive ion bombardment. At the low bias voltages, they attribute the increased defect density to the low adatom mobility of the films which results in point defects aggregating to form dislocation loops. Since no values for ion densities bombarding the film are given, Eqn. 2 cannot be used for a comparison.

Whereas most of the previous examples have dealt with compound systems, Huang et al. (18) and Parmigiani et al. (50) looked at the effects of Ar bombardment on Ag films grown by dual ion beam sputtering as a function of the normalized energy E_n (eV/Ag atom). Their results for the dislocation density did not show a minimum as did Hultman et al. (49). This may be a consequence of the minimum energy deposited into the film already being surpassed. If Eqn. 2 is used to calculate the $(E_n)_{critical}$ for Ar on Ag, it gives $E_n = 21.8$ eV/Ag, the value at which we would expect damage to start to occur. In their study, the minimum E_n was approximately 20 eV/Ag, very close to the calculated critical value. Void fractions in these films show a continual decrease with increasing E_n. This may not show the initial increase followed by a plateau and then a decrease as seen in Fig. 5, because of the higher initial starting value of E_n.

These are just a few representative examples which show the importance of ion-surface interactions and how controlling ion flux and energy can have important consequences on thin film characteristics and related properties.

19.6 CONCLUSIONS

The state of knowledge concerning ion-surface interactions with regard to thin film growth and evolution has only recently been addressed in a systematic and quantitative manner. The low energy regime of bombardment (< 100 eV) is found to be necessary and desirable in view of the results concerning densification and inert gas incorporation, and is an area where attention has only recently been given. In addition, the importance of momentum transfer in modifying the thin film structure is apparent. Although not specifically addressed in this chapter, molecular dynamics simulations of epitaxial growth have shown that optimum energies of the depositing atoms are on the order of 5 to 10 eV (51,52), again pointing toward low energy processes. Extension of the molecular dynamics modeling to thicker films and especially to 3-dimensions is necessary to gain a more complete understanding between theory and experiment. Each of these approaches will help lead to a quantitative description of thin film growth and the role that ion-surface interactions play.

19.7 REFERENCES

1.   For instance: Vossen, J.L. and Kern, W. (eds), Thin Film Processes, (New York: Academic Press, Inc., 1978) (1978); Bunshah, R.F., et al. (eds), Deposition Technologies for Films and Coatings: Developments and Applications, (Noyes Publications, New Jersey 1982); Chapman, B., Glow Discharge Processes: Sputtering and Plasma Etching, (John Wiley & Sons, New York, 1980).

2.   Messier, R., Toward quantification of thin film morphology. J. Vac. Sci. Technol. A4: 490-95 (1986).

3.   Yehoda, J.E. and Messier, R., Quantitative analysis of thin film morphology evolution. Proc. SPIE 678: 32-40 (1986).

4.   Wu, C.T., Kampwirth, R.T., and Hafstrom, J., High-rate magnetron sputtering of high T_c Nb$_3$Sn films. J. Vac. Sci. Technol. 14: 134-37 (1977).

5.   Cadieu, F.J. and Chencincki, N., Selective thermalization in sputtering to produce high Tc films. IEEE Trans. Mag. 11: 227-30 (1975).

6.   Robinson, R.S., Energetic binary collisions in rare gas plasmas. J. Vac. Sci. Technol. 16: 185-88 (1979).

7.   Somekh, R.E., Calculations of thermalization during the sputter deposition process. Vacuum 34: 987-90 (1984).

8. Motohiro, T. and Taga, Y., Monte Carlo simulation of the particle transport process in sputter deposition. Thin Solid Films 112: 161-67 (1984).

9. Schuller, I.K., New class of layered materials. Phys. Rev. Lett. 1597-600 (1980)

10. Meyer, K., Schuller, I.K., and Falco, C.M., Thermalization of sputtered atoms. J. Appl. Phys. 52: 5803-08 (1981).

11. Hoffman, D.W. and Thornton, J.A., Internal stresses in sputtered chromium. Thin Solid Films 40: 355-63 (1977).

12. Westwood, W.D., Calculation of deposition rates in diode sputtering systems. J. Vac. Sci. Technol. 15: 1-9 (1978).

13. Rossnagel, S.M., Gas density effects in magnetrons. J. Vac. Sci. Technol. A6: 19-24 (1988).

14. Kaufman, H.R., Cuomo, J.J., and Harper J.M.E., Technology and applications of broad-beam ion sources used in sputtering. Part I. Ion source technology. J. Vac. Sci. Technol. 21: 725-36 (1982); and Harper, J.M.E., Cuomo, J.J., and Kaufman, H.R., Technology and applications of broad-beam ion sources used in sputtering. Part II. Applications. J. Vac. Sci. Technol. 21: 737-56 (1982).

15. Harper, J.M.E., Cuomo, J.J., Gambino, R.J., and Kaufman, H.R., Modification of thin film properties by ion bombardment during deposition. Nucl. Instrum. & Methods Phys. Res. B7/8: 886-92 (1985).

16. Windischmann, H., An intrinsic stress scaling law for polycrystalline thin films prepared by ion beam sputtering. J. Appl. Phys. 62: 1800-1807 (1987).

17. Sigmund, P., in: Sputtering by Particle Bombardment I, ed. by R. Behrisch, Chapter 2 (Springer-Verlag, New York 1981).

18. Huang, T.C., Lim, G., Parmigiani, F., and Kay, E., Effects of ion bombardment during deposition on the x-ray microstructure of thin silver films. J. Vac. Sci. Technol. A3: 2161-66 (1985).

19. Kay, E., Parmigiani, F., and Parrish, W., Effects of energetic neutralized noble gas ions on the structure of ion beam sputtered thin metal films. J. Vac. Sci. Technol. A5: 44-51 (1987).

20. Window, B. Sharples, F., and Savvides, N., Plastic flow in ion-assisted deposition of refractory metals. J. Vac. Sci. Technol. A6: 2333-40 (1988).

21. Hoffman, D.W. and Gaerttner, M.R., Modification of evaporated chromium by concurrent ion bombardment. J. Vac. Sci. Technol. 17: 425-28 (1980).

22. Ziemann, P. and Kay, E., Correlation between the ion bombardment during film growth of Pd films and their structural and electrical properties. J. Vac. Sci. Technol. A1: 512-16 (1983).

23. Nir, D., Energy dependence of the stress in diamond-like carbon films. J. Vac. Sci. Technol. A4: 2954-55 (1986).

24. Müller, K.-H., Ion-beam epitaxial vapor-phase growth: A molecular-dynamics study. Phys. Rev. B35: 7906-13 (1987).

25. Movchan, B.A. and Demchishin, A.V., Study of the structure and properties of thick vacuum condensates of nickel, titanium, tungsten, aluminium oxide and zirconium dioxide. Physics of Metals and Metallography 28: 83-90 (1969).

26. Thornton, J.A., High rate thick film growth. Ann. Rev. Mater. Sci. 7: 239-60 (1977).

27. Messier, R., Giri, A.P., and Roy, R.A., Revised structure zone model for thin film physical structure. J. Vac. Sci. Technol. A2: 500-03 (1984).

28. Staudinger, A. and Nakahara, S., The structure of the crack network in amorphous films. Thin Solid Films 45: 125-33 (1977).

29. Leamy, H.J., Gilmer, G.H., and Dirks, A.G., The microsturcture of vapor deposited thin films. Current Topics in Materials Science Vol. 6, ed. E. Kaldis (North Holland, New York, 1980) 310-344.

30. Müller, K.-H., Monte Carlo calculation for structural modifications in ion-assisted thin film deposition due to thermal spikes. J. Vac. Sci. Technol. A4: 184-88 (1986).

31. Müller, K.-H., Model for ion-assisted thin-film densification. J. Appl. Phys. 59: 2803-07 (1986).

32. Müller, K.-H., Modelling ion-assisted deposition of CeO_2 films. Appl. Phys. A40: 209-13 (1986).

33. Müller, K.-H., Stress and microstructure of sputter-deposited thin films: Molecular dynamics investigations. J. Appl. Phys. 62: 1796-99 (1987).

34. Müller, K.-H., Molecular dynamics and collision cascade studies of ion-assisted thin film deposition. J. Vac. Sci. Technol. A5: 2161-62 (1987).

35. Müller, K.-H., unpublished

36. Kelly, R. and Auciello, O. (eds), Ion bombardment modification of surfaces: Fundamentals and applications, (Elsevier, New York, 1984).

37. Takagi, T., Role of ions in ion-based film formation. Thin Solid Films 92: 1-17 (1982).

38. Webb, R.P. and Harrison, D.E., Evidence for ion-induced hypersonic shock waves for computer simulations of argon ion bombardment of copper. Appl. Phys. Lett. 39: 311-12 (1981).

39. Weissmantel, C., Bewilogua, K., Dietrich, D., Erler, H.-J., Hinneberg, H.-J., Klose, S., Nowick, W., and Reisse, G., Structure and properties of quasi-amorphous films prepared by ion beam techniques. . Thin Solid Films 72: 19-31 (1980).

40. Hirsch, E.H. and Varga, I.K., Thin film annealing by ion bombardment. Thin Solid Films 69: 99-105 (1980).

41. Martin, P.J., Netterfield R.P., and Sainty, W.G., Modification of the optical and structural properties of dielectric ZrO_2 films by ion-assisted deposition. J. Appl. Phys. 55: 235-41 (1984).

42. Targove, J.D., Lingg, L.J., and Macleod, H.A., Verification of momentum transfer as the dominant densifying mechanism in ion-assisted deposition. Optical Interference Coatings 1988 Technical Digest Series (Optical Society of America) 6: 268-71 (1988).

43. Yehoda, J.E., Yang, B., Vedam, K., and Messier, R., Investigation of the void structure in amorphous germanium thin films as a function of low-energy ion bombardment. J. Vac. Sci. Technol. A6: 1631-35 (1988).

44. Yehoda, J.E., Influence of bombardment on the nanostructure and microstructure in amorphous germanium. Ph.D. Thesis, The Pennsylvania State University, (1988).

45. Stuart, R.V. and Wehner, G.K., Sputtering yields at very low bombarding energies. J. Appl. Phys. 33: 2345-52 (1962).

46. Smithells, C.J., Metals Reference Book, Fifth Ed., (Butterworths, London 1976).

47. Netterfield, R.P., Sainty, W.G., Martin, P.J., and Sie, S.H., Properties of CeO_2 thin films prepared by oxygen-ion-assisted deposition. Applied Optics 24: 2267-72 (1985).

48. McNeil, J.R., Barron, A.C., Wilson, W.C., and Herrmann, W.C., Ion-assisted deposition of optical thin films: Low energy vs high energy bombardment. Applied Optics 23: 552-59 (1984).

49. Hultman, L., Helmersson, U., Barnett, S.A., Sundgren, J.-E., and Green, J.E., The role of low-energy ion bombardment during the growth of epitaxial TiN (100) films by reactive magnetron sputtering: Defect formation and annihilation. J. Vac. Sci. Technol. A5: 2162-64 (1987).

50. Parmigiani, F., Kay, E., Huang, T.C., Perrin, J., Jurich, M., and Swalen J.D., Optical and electrical properties of thin silver films grown under ion bombardment. Phys. Rev. B33: 879-88 (1986).

51. Dodson, B.W. and Taylor, P.A., Interaction of a 10 eV silicon beam with the Si (111) surface: A molecular dynamics study. J. Mater. Res. 2: 805-08 (1987).

52. Garrison, B.J., Miller, M.T., and Brenner, D.W., Kinetic energy enhanced molecular beam epitaxial growth of Si {100}. Chem. Phys. Lett. (in press).

20

Ion Assisted Deposition

James J. McNally

20.1 INTRODUCTION

The optical, electrical, mechanical and chemical properties of materials in thin-film form can vary significantly from their bulk properties. These differences in properties are directly related to film microstructure which, for vacuum deposited films, is predominantly columnar, containing voids and material inhomogeneities. Modifications to film properties can occur when the film is subject to ion bombardment during growth. In fact, significant improvements have been realized with controlled ion bombardment of growing films. A detailed review of ion-surface interactions is not the intent of this chapter; nor, is a discussion of the various technique used to achieve film bombardment. Excellent treatment of those topics can be found in Reference 1 and the earlier chapters of this book.

The discussion in this chapter is focused on ion-assisted deposition (IAD). Ion assisted deposition is a plasma-based deposition technique that employs a separate ion source to direct a beam of ions at a growing film during deposition. A key distinction between conventional ion bombardment configurations and IAD is the isolation of the substrates from the ion production and acceleration process. This, in turn, permits separate control of the ion bombardment parameters independent of the material deposition process.

The following material is oriented toward a general overview with an emphasis on the fundamentals of the IAD process. References are given for in-depth treatments of several topics. In this chapter a brief background of the IAD process is given, followed by details on experimental arrangements and procedures. A results section follows that discusses specific effects that IAD has on film properties. The chapter concludes with a discussion of the limitations in applying IAD and some advantages over other energetic deposition techniques.

20.2 BACKGROUND

The fundamental properties of vacuum deposited films vary significantly from their bulk values due to poor film microstructure. Microstructure-related effects on film properties can be observed in low optical refractive index, high optical scatter, low dielectric constant, varying grain size, low density and poor environmental durability and optical stability. A number of novel deposition techniques have been developed to overcome the weaknesses of films relative to bulk materials. In these techniques, energetic processes are employed to supply sufficient activation energies to increase adatom mobility and eliminate the formation of columnar microstructure (see detailed discussions in other chapters of this book). A shortcoming of some of these techniques is the lack of versatility in controlling the energetic/reactive process parameters independent of the film deposition parameters. Ion-assisted deposition uses a separate, well-controlled ion source to direct a beam of ions at the film surface during deposition. A separate ion source allows control of the ion energy, current density, arrival direction and species independent of the material deposition process (e.g. evaporation or sputtering). Note: the discussion in this chapter is restricted to using the Kaufman ion source for bombardment. See Ref. 2 for discussion of other ion sources.

The flexibility provided by a separate ion source allows the tailoring of the optical, electrical, structural and chemical properties through proper selection of ion parameters. It allows an examination of thin film growth processes and the fabrication of unique film properties. Examples of this are found in the low temperature deposition onto sensitive substrates of materials normally requiring elevated substrate temperatures (3). Examples are found in coatings where the film stoichiometry can be varied as a function of thickness (4,5). Other examples are found in the modification of stress in Nb films (6), and in the control of the microstructure of Cu films (7).

To fully understand and model the effects of ion bombardment, one must examine the ion-surface interactions. The energetic ions and ad-molecules arrive at the surface and dissociate resulting in enhanced adatom migration. The high surface diffusion energies, equivalent to elevated substrate temperatures, result in diminished film columnar microstructure. A detailed discussion of ion-surface interactions are given in Chaps. 19 and 21. and results from an experiment to investigate ion-surface reactions are given in Ref. 8. Also, a very good discussion on modeling the IAD film growth process is given by Müller (9).

20.3 EXPERIMENTAL APPARATUS

Two general arrangements are most popular for application of the ion source to thin film coating. Ions from the source are directed to the substrate which is being coated with material generated by thermal or e-beam evaporation. This is termed ion assisted deposition (IAD). Second, ions from one source are directed at a target which is sputtered, and the sputtered material is deposited on a substrate while a second ion source bombards the growing film. This is termed dual ion beam sputter deposition (DIBS).

20.3.1 Ion Source

Broad-beam ion source technology is discussed in detail in an earlier chapter. A brief description is given here only to cite some specific examples of operational characteristics that impact the system design of IAD tasks. Ion sources are like most apparatus, in that when they are optimized for a specific process, they tend to sacrifice performance in other areas. This tendency leads to groupings of types of sources that conform to the process parameters of interest.

Briefly, the ion source operates as follows. Gas is introduced into the discharge chamber; electrons emitted from the cathode impact ionize the gas molecules. The discharge-chamber contains a conducting plasma composed of approximately equal numbers of ions and electrons. The plasma potential is essentially equal to the anode potential, therefore the ions originate at approximately the anode potential ("beam voltage"). The screen grid aligns the ions that are accelerated from the source by the electric field established in the region between the screen and accelerator grids. The ions travel from the source to the substrates which are held at ground potential.

Two collisional processes that could occur for the ions traveling to the substrates are resonant charge exchange and elastic collisions. The mean-free paths, at a standard operating pressure used (10^{-4}Torr) , are greater than 100 cm for resonant charge exchange collisions. Therefore, the ion source-to-substrate or to-target distance should be less than 100 cm. The mean free paths for elastic collisions are about ten times larger than for resonant charge exchange collisions. Therefore, the ions reach the substrate or target with negligible scattering.

An attractive feature of a Kaufman ion source is the monoenergetic ion beam it produces. The energy distribution can be characterized using a retarding grid arrangement in front of a Faraday probe. The energy spread is approximately 10 eV over a range of beam energies from 300-2000 eV for the dual grid extraction arrangement (10). The energy spread from a source with a single grid arrangement is somewhat larger (10).

For the discussion in this chapter one can classify an ion source as a sputtering source or an enhancement source. Sputtering sources are those used to remove the maximum amount of deposition material from a target in the minimum time. In general, beam uniformity is not of great importance; the source operates at 1 to 2 kV (11) and it is desirable to deliver as much ion current to the sputter target as possible. More details on the specific parameters for sputtering sources are given in the section on dual ion beam sputtering. Enhancement sources provide ion bombardment to growing film material produced by another means. Beam uniformity is important; the source typically operates at low beam energies and current densities; and it is frequently required to operate with reactive gases which severely impact filament lifetimes.

The point of this discussion is to make the reader aware of the variety of potential tasks (others, such as ion beam etching, are discussed in an earlier chapter) that can be accomplished using broad-beam ion sources, and that the devices can be optimized for various tasks. Frequently, the optimization from one specialized task to another can be accomplished by something as simple as a grid change. Other optimization can require extensive hardware changes (such as the incorporation of a hollow-cathode emitter in the main chamber and as the neutralizer emitter), and include significant variations in control systems and operating procedures.

20.3.2 Operational Considerations

All ion sources that produce beams using electrostatic acceleration present certain potential problems. The beam is extracted and accelerated by significant dc potentials (200-2000 eV typically). The workchamber contains a moderate current (> 1A) beam and is filled with a dilute, conducting plasma. Care must be taken to electrostatically shield the high potential leads to the source. Electrical breakdown is possible between closely spaced leads, and this is enhanced by the dilute plasma. Some ion sources are designed in which gas flow lines are isolated from ground potential near the ion source; other sources have a conducting gas line at high voltage that passes through an insulator in the vacuum system wall and is electrically isolated outside the chamber. This line is often overlooked as a high voltage electrode source and can also be a significant safety factor.

The pressure inside the gas line goes from a few psi above atmosphere at the gas cylinder to approximately 10^{-3} Torr in the ion source plasma region. Screens of metal wool pads are frequently used to provide large area surfaces on which ions can recombine and this prevents electrical breakdown in the gas feed tubes.

Oxidation can occur if a hot ion source is vented at atmosphere too soon after operation. The oxide films on the various electrodes can become sufficiently insulating to prevent source operation on a subsequent pump down. Similarly, sputtering of materials in a reactive atmosphere can produce insulating coatings. To avoid problems in this situation, regular cleaning of the ion source is important. This can be accomplished mechanically, for example, using bead blasting, or chemically, using acids to remove non-conductive thin film material.

The applications of ion beams to thin film deposition require knowledge of the ion flux at the substrate or target. For ion assisted deposition this measurement is very important; knowing just the total beam current is not sufficient.

When a standard Faraday probe arrangement is used while depositing conducting film materials, no special precautions are necessary. The probe element should remain insulated from the rest of the probe body, and the electrical characteristics of the probe element should remain constant. The probe might be moved into the ion beam just prior to the deposition process in order to check the beam condition. The probe would then be moved out of the beam.

When insulating materials are being deposited, care should be exercised to prevent the probe element from becoming coated. This would change the probe characteristics to provide incorrect indications of ion beam current density. During deposition the probe might be moved to an area where it is shielded from the film material, or the probe might have a shield attached. If the beam is to be monitored during deposition, some accumulation on the probe element is inevitable, and the probe should be later cleaned.

20.3.3 Ion Preclean of Substrates

Substrate condition prior to coating is extremely important for proper film adhesion; in addition, it has an influence on subsequent film growth characteristics. In this section the application of ion beams as the final step of cleaning a surface immediately before film deposition is discussed Results of ion beam cleaning and the improved adhesion of films which this can provide, such as Au on BK-7 glass, are discussed in Ref. 12. Ion beam cleaning obviously represents no added equipment to the deposition system when IAD is employed.

The processes which occur on the substrate due to ion bombardment include a number of things. This includes desorption of adsorbed water vapor, hydrocarbons and other gas atoms. Chemisorbed species and occluded gases are sputtered. If the bombarding ion is an oxygen species, chemical reactions with organic species on the surface can result in compounds which are more volatile and hence more easily removed. For the levels of ion flux (20-100 μA/cm^2) and energy employed, and for the small time required for cleaning, the substrate temperature rise is usually negligible, and this has little effect on substrate outgassing. Relatively low energy (300 eV) ions are preferable to higher energy ions to minimize substrate sputtering, while still being sufficiently energetic to produce the effects mentioned above. Ion bombardment causes substrate defect production which in general is beneficial for subsequent film nucleation and adhesion.

If there is only single-axis rotation of the substrates, the ion source might be placed directly below the center of the substrates; if it is not directly below the substrates, then the beam pattern is simply spread over a larger area. If the fixturing involves planetary rotation, then the beam should be directed to a region that will ultimately provide bombardment of all substrates. In this case, the ion beam is obviously not on a particular substrate continuously; it is "time-shared" between all substrates. This, however, does not present the potential problems that are discussed in connection with IAD of substrates in planetary arrangements.

To estimate the time required for cleaning substrates, one should consider the amount of material which is sputtered. This is determined in part by the sputter yield of the substrate material and that of the unknown species on the substrate. Sputter yields for many materials are well characterized for various incident ions and ion energies; typical values range from 0.1 to 3 atoms/ion for inert gas ions of 0.5 to 2 keV energy (11). If a sputter yield (S) of 0.1 atoms/ion is assumed, the thickness (L) of the layer of material removed in 5 minutes (t) due to a beam of 50μa/cm^2 current density (J) is given by

$$L = S J V t / q \qquad (1)$$

Or equivalently, L = 25Å. Here V is an assumed volume of the sputtered atoms, taken to be 27Å^3, and q is the charge of the ion in Coulombs. This simple calculation illustrates how several atomic layers of material can be quickly removed from the substrate even at relatively low current densities to leave it atomically clean. However, it leaves open to question what the effective sputter yield of the contaminant layer is. If the beam is time-shared as described above in connection with planetary fixturing, then one must estimate the fraction of time F the substrates are in the ion beam; in the expression above, t would become t/F.

There are four considerations one should be aware of in applying ion bombardment to clean substrates. The first is the influence of ion bombardment on the substrate microroughness. If the substrate is polycrystalline and composed of relatively large crystallites, the microroughness of the substrate increases significantly if the substrate is ion bombarded for a long time. For example, Cu substrates have demonstrated an increase in rms roughness from approximately 25 Å to nearly 50 Å when 1200 Å of the substrate was removed using ion beam sputtering (12). (This amount of material removal is somewhat severe in terms of substrate cleaning, but it illustrates the point.) One the other hand, amorphous or very small-grained polycrystalline substrates as well as single crystalline materials are less likely to develop a significant surface topography with this level of sputtering.

The second consideration when applying ion precleaning is that the stoichiometry of the top few atomic layers of substrates composed of compound species can be altered. This is due to the ions preferentially sputtering one atomic species, leaving the surface rich in the other atomic species. The extent of this altered layer production is naturally minimum with minimum ion energy (for energies less than approximately 2 keV) and flux.

A third consideration when applying ion beam precleaning involves the potential damage to a crystalline substrate surface, such as semiconductor materials. It is very difficult to obtain a clean semiconductor surface and maintain the bulk properties at the surface; atoms in the crystal lattice structure are displaced due to the ion bombardment. A general guideline is to reduce the ion energy to the lowest level possible if substrate damage is a concern.

A fourth consideration in applying ion precleaning involves contaminating the surface of the substrate being cleaned with the material from the fixturing holding the substrate. Slight contamination, especially around the periphery of the substrate is usually unavoidable. When possible, the fixturing material should be constructed of material which is similar the the film material.

20.3.4 Ion Assisted Deposition

Ion assisted deposition (IAD) employs an ion source to direct a beam of ions at the substrate during deposition where the vapor source is either thermal or electron-beam evaporation. (Dual ion beam sputter deposition is discussed in the next section.) An obvious advantage to utilizing IAD is that the process can easily be incorporated into an existing vacuum deposition system. In this section we describe the equipment to deposit thin films using IAD.

A schematic of a vacuum deposition system configured for IAD is shown in Fig. 1. The operation of the source to provide the thin film material is totally independent from the ion source, and the configuration provides the ability to accurately measure all critical deposition parameters. The ion source provides a neutralized ion beam directed at the substrates.

As illustrated in the schematic, the gas is introduced through the ion source into the chamber. IAD is inherently a low pressure process (10^{-5} to 10^{-4} Torr) that permits a great deal of flexibility in deposition configurations. Any number of gas species may be introduced through the ion source depending upon the complexity of the gas manifold. Neutral background gas may also be introduced into the vacuum chamber through another inlet if desired. An attractive feature with IAD is that substrate cleaning (Section 20.3.3) may be readily accomplished before deposition by controlling the appropriate gas species through the ion sources. Immediately upon completion of the cleaning process, deposition can commence. The minimal time lag between the two processes is due to the delay, if any, associated with changing the gas species flowing though the ion source.

As described in Sect. 20.3.2, it is essential that ion beam probing be undertaken carefully. For certain materials, film properties are sensitive to bombarding ion flux levels (examples are given later in this chapter). As illustrated in Figure 1, an ion current probe is located just below the substrates. The probe platform is mounted on a rotary feedthrough such that it can be moved through the ion beam immediately below the substrates. After the ion flux value is measured, the probe is rotated away from the substrate area to minimize the coating of the probe. Not shown in the figure is a shield attached to the probe platform which protects the probe from film material during deposition.

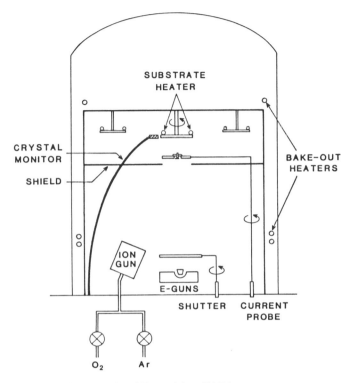

Figure 1: Schematic of Ion Assisted Deposition (IAD) system.

An important parameter in depositing thin films using IAD is the ratio of the ion-to-depositing atom arrival rates. Proper beam probing allows accurate determination of the ion flux. One method to determine the flux of arriving, condensing film atoms is measurement of the film deposition rate using a crystal monitor. As illustrated in Fig. 1, the monitor may be located very close to the substrates. However, it should be shielded from the direct ion beam to minimize sputtering of the monitor material. The monitor must be calibrated to determine an accurate tooling factor for different film materials and for various ion source conditions (i.e. accurately account for sputtering). If the substrate fixturing involves planetary rotation, then the monitor cannot be located immediately adjacent to the substrates. In this arrangement, determination of the flux of depositing atoms is more difficult. Usually the substrates are exposed to the ion beam for only a fraction of time (F). This complicates the procedure to account for sputtering when determining the flux of film atoms. For the fixed geometry illustrated in Fig. 1, the substrates are exposed to the ion beam continuously. Modification to the thin film properties can occur on a continuous basis. When using IAD with a planetary rotation geometry, care must be employed in selecting the ion beam parameters which result in the desired thin film properties.

Another important consideration when applying IAD is the respective arrival directions of the bombarding ions and the film molecules. As illustrated in Fig. 1, when employing a fixed-position substrate geometry with an off-axis ion source, it is important that substrate rotation be employed. The rotation of the substrates is necessary to minimize anisotropic properties in the films due to the different arrival directions of the ions and the molecular species.

For the ion source proper selection of the discharge voltage is important. The value should be high enough to sustain an appropriate discharge in the source (typically 40 V). However, too high a value (70-90 V) will cause increased production of doubly ionized atomic (molecular) ions. The doubly ionized species will be accelerated to twice the beam energy (the energy of the singly ionized ions). This results in increased sputtering of the sample, which may be desirable, but can also lead to increased damage of sensitive samples. Also, high values of discharge voltage can decrease the lifetime of the cathode filament in the source and cause additional sputtering inside the source, leading to contamination of the beam. For a 10 cm source, cathode filament lifetime for average IAD conditions (500 eV, $30\mu a/cm^2$) operating in oxygen is approximately 4-hours for 0.4 mm (0.015 in.) diameter tungsten wire. The lifetime for 0.5 mm diameter (0.020 in.) tantalum wire is only 1-1.5 hours under similar conditions. For this reason, one might consider using thoreated filaments to increase lifetime.

As mentioned earlier, it is necessary to provide a compensating density of electrons to the ion beam, especially when bombarding an insulating target. This is often accomplished using a thermionic neutralizer filament which emits the appropriate electron current into the beam. The value of this neutralizer current is matched to the beam current. Note that the ions are not neutralized in-flight but rather the total beam current is zero due to the intermixing of the electrons into the ion beam. When using this simple arrangement for beam neutralization, consideration must be given to contamination arising due to neutralizer filament sputtering. Another technique for beam neutralization is the use of a plasma bridge neutralizer arrangement.

20.3.4.1 Procedures. It is critical that the ion flux is stable and accurately measured before deposition begins. The film material should be pre-heated and a shutter employed to prevent deposition before the ion source is stable. The gas discharge of the ion source should be established and the desired beam parameters (ion energy, flux and neutralizer current) set at the ion source controller. When the ion flux is measured by the probe, an accurate record of its value and all ion source parameters should be made. When the probe is rotated out of position, deposition may commence. During deposition the beam energy and current must be monitored to ensure stable ion source operation. At the completion of deposition, the ion flux should be checked by rotating the probe back to the original measurement position.

20.3.5 Dual Ion Beam Sputtering (DIBS)

When energetic ions or neutral atoms strike a surface, many processes can occur. One of these is the ejection of atoms of the surface (target) materials, and this is known as sputtering. Of primary concern in sputtering is the sputter yield (S), in atoms/ion, and the relation of S to parameters involved such as ion and target species, ion energy, ion incident angle and target condition. In addition, it is very important to have an idea of the average ejection energy of sputtered atoms, as this has a significant influence on resulting thin film properties. Similarly, the angular distribution of the sputtered atoms is of importance in determining film deposition rate, uniformity, etc. Detailed treatments of sputtering are given in an earlier chapter as well as in Reference 2. In this section experimental aspects of dual IBS will be described.

Figure 2 illustrates the apparatus used in ion beam sputtering. In this case, two ion sources are shown, one for sputtering and one for bombarding the substrate prior to coating or during deposition. Also shown is a probe to characterize the beam in the vicinity of the target, as well as the other shutters typically found in a deposition system.

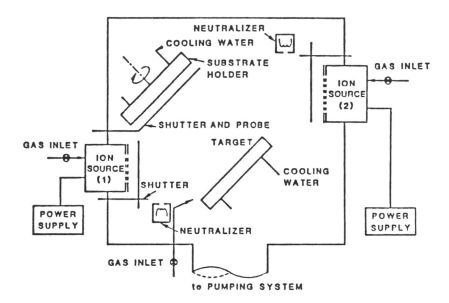

Figure 2: Schematic of Dual Ion Beam Deposition (DIBS) system.

Chamber size requirements are influenced little by addition of a small ion source; more elaborate arrangements such as illustrated in Fig. 2 require a specially designed system. Typical size of the arrangement shown in the figure is roughly 50 cm in diameter. Similarly, vacuum pumping requirements are not influenced greatly with the addition of a small ion source; typical added gas load is 2-4 SCCM (cm^3/ min) for a 2.5 cm diameter ion beam source. A 6-inch diffusion-pumped or cryogenically-pumped system will typically operate in the 10^{-5} to low 10^{-4} Torr region with this gas load. Incorporating large ion sources into a system may require additional pump capability.

The arrangement of the sputter target and the substrates is often as illustrated in Fig. 2. A typical separation between the ion source and the target is 30 cm. The target is arranged at an angle of approximately 45 degrees to the ion beam to increase the sputter yield (2). The energetic neutralized ions which are reflected from the target can, in some situations, be detrimental to the film if they are allowed to bombard the substrate. This is the case, for example, when high quality oxide films are being deposited using Ar ions to sputter a target and an O_2 partial background pressure (13). To minimize this effect, the substrates are arranged as shown in Fig. 2. Although the neutralized ions do not all reflect in a specular sense, it is believed they are predominantly directed in this "direction.

For ion beam sputtering it is usually desirable to deliver as much ion current to the sputter target as possible, and this dictates the use of large ion sources (e.g. 10-15 cm diameter. Wire filament cathodes and neutralizers can be used which are made of W or Ta typically 0.010 to 0.015 inches in diameter. Both have lifetime limits of several (one to over ten) hours. Lifetime of the neutralizer is increased if it is placed near the edge of the ion beam and not through the center. This can be tedious to achieve, as the beam profile and therefor e the position of the neutralizer are somewhat dependent on operating conditions (pressure, beam energy, etc.). Both the cathode and neutralizer lifetime are greatly reduced if a reactive gas is passed through the ion source. In addition, the W or Ta material can contaminate the target and be deposited in the film at a low level. In place of the wire cathode, a hollow cathode discharge device can be used to supply electrons to the main discharge of the ion source. Although this operates very well with inert gas, operation with O_2 has not be satisfactory. Similarly, the wire neutralizer can be replaced with an auxiliary discharge device, a plasma bridge neutralizer, to supply neutralizing electrons to the beam. This must remain outside of the beam to avoid being sputtered and contaminating the target material. Another approach is to construct the housing of the plasma bridge neutralizer of a material which is compatible with the target and film.

When larger loads of substrates need to be coated, larger diameter sources are used and the source - target - substrate distances are increased. This geometric scaling results in inverse square losses, with corresponding reduction in deposition rates.

In general, the angular distribution of sputtered particles is peaked in a forward direction, at an angle roughly comparable to that of the incident ions. A cosine distribution has been used to describe this, although several factors have an influence. In particular, the target condition is very important. The distribution pattern will vary depending on target crystallinity, target age, a target of solid material will provide a distribution pattern different from that of one made of pressed powder and the ion-target incidence angle.

From what has been described, it is apparent that the best approach to characterize the distribution pattern in applications in which it is critical is to simply use trial and error. For example, sample substrates might be coated. Film deposition rate and uniformity could be determined from subsequent examination using a spectraphotometer or other types of interferometry.

Target size should be sufficient to insure that none of the beam passes the target and sputters other material. In optical coating arrangements in which large ion sources are used, target size is typically 20 cm wide and 30 cm long. Placement of the target and the influence of this on the distribution of sputtered atoms has been discussed.

In the case of optical coatings, elemental targets of Si, Ti, Ta, etc., are often preferred because of the higher sputter yields and therefore large deposition rates provided, compared to targets composed of the oxide materials. In this particular situation, Ar ions are often used to sputter the target; the second ion source, possibly with a single-grid arrangement to provide very low-energy ion extraction, is often used with O_2 to improve film stoichiometry. Deposition rates of 1-2 Å/ sec can be achieved (13). Similar techniques have been used in the case of nitride film deposition (8).

In general, there is no restriction placed on a target used in ion beam sputtering; the target can be an insulator since the ion beam can be neutralized. Sputter targets are often water-cooled due to the incident power (e.g., 0.25 A at 1500 V in vacuum).

A technique which has been used to ion beam sputter compounds of materials involves placing pieces of one target material on a second target material (2,14). The film composition depends on the relative sputter yields, the relative areas of the targets which are sputtered and the relative sticking coefficients of the atoms at the substrate.

20.4 PROPERTIES OF IAD FILMS

Early studies utilizing an ion beam to modify the properties of evaporated films were reported by Heitman (15). Another study utilizing a separate ion source to bombard evaporated SiO with 5 keV oxygen ions during deposition was done by Dudonis and Pranevicius (16). They investigated the effects of ion flux on film stoichiometry and found that for increasing flux values, the 0/Si ratio approached two. Cuomo, et al.(6) obtained superconducting NbN films by bombarding evaporated Nb with $N_2{}^+$ during deposition. Netterfield and Martin have studied the effects on the properties of ZrO_2 and CeO_2 films bombarded with $O_2{}^+$ and Ar^+ during deposition (17-19). They reported increased packing densities, reduced permeability to water and changes in film crystal structure. Argon ion bombardment produced changes in film stoichiometry. McNeil et al, (20,21) have examined the effects of 30-500 eV oxygen ion bombardment on the properties of TiO_2 and SiO_2 films deposited using TiO and SiO starting materials. They reported that improvements in optical properties were obtained at 30 eV; in particular, better film stoichiometry. McNally, et al.(22,23) reported the effects of oxygen ion bombardment on the properties of Ta_2O_5, Al_2O_3, TiO_2, and SiO_2 films. Increases in the values of refractive index were reported for 200, 300, 500 and 1000eV bombardment.

The values of n (at $\lambda = 400$nm) for Ta_2O_5 coatings bombarded with 200, 300 and 500 eV oxygen ions are plotted in Fig. 3 as a function of O_2^+ current density. The error bars indicate the uncertainty in the index measurements. The values increase from 2.16 for coating deposited without bombardment to maximum values of 2.25, 2.28 and 2.19 for films bombarded with 500, 300 and 200 eV O_2^+, respectively.

The current density value (for a fixed ion energy) at which the maximum n occurs is termed the critical value. The results in Fig. 3 illustrate that film index values decrease for ion current densities greater than the critical values. The decrease in index may be explained as a result of degradation in film stoichiometry, creation of closed isolated voids or oxygen incorporation into the films. Similar results for which the values of refractive index decrease for current densities greater than the critical values have been reported for ion assisted ZrO_2 films (18) and CeO_2 films (19).

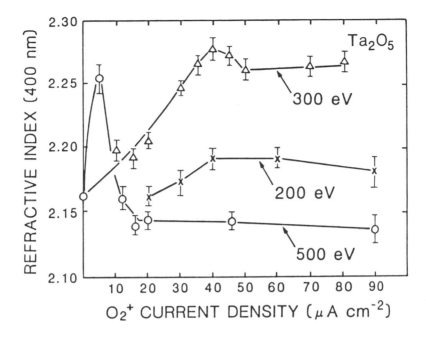

Figure 3: Refractive index as a function of oxygen ion beam current density for Ta_2O_5 films as a function of ion energy during deposition.

The coatings bombarded during deposition at oxygen ion current densities up to approximately the critical values exhibit good optical characteristics. For higher levels of bombardment, the optical absorption of the coatings increase. In Fig. 4, values of extinction coefficient (k) for Ta_2O_5 coatings (300 nm thick) bombarded with 500, 300 and 200 eV oxygen ions are plotted as a function of O_2^+ current density. The values of k were calculated at $\lambda = 400$ nm. The error bars indicate the uncertainty in the measurements. The dashed line across the bottom at $k = 2.0 \times 10^{-4}$ indicates the level below which the values of k were too small to be regarded as reliable because of the minimum sensitivity of the measurement technique.

As illustrated in Fig. 4, film optical absorption increased with higher levels of oxygen bombardment. The most probable mechanism for this is the preferential sputtering of oxygen in the Ta_2O_5 molecule. This damage mechanism has been observed in other IAD films (18). This highlights the requirement for proper beam probing to avoid compositional change by preferential sputtering.

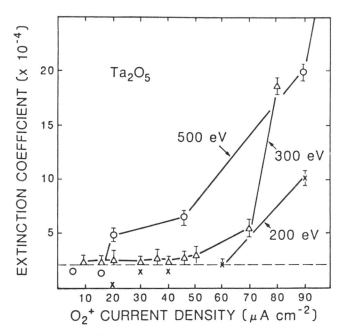

Figure 4: Extinction coefficient as a function of oxygen ion current density and ion energy for Ta_2O_5 films.

The environmental stability of optical coatings is in large part limited by the porosity of the film microstructure. Results have been reported for IAD ZrO_2 and Ta_2O_5 coatings (22) where the refractive index value remained stable to less than 0.3% after exposure to high humidity. IAD can affect intrinsic stress in films. Changes in stress for Ta_2O_5 coatings have been reported (22). Cuomo, et al.(6) reported a change in stress from tensile to compressive for evaporated Nb films bombarded with 100-800 eV Ar^+ during deposition. They attributed the changes in stress to modifications in film microstructure and incorporation of argon. Hirsh and Varga (24) measured stress relief in evaporated Ge films bombarded with 100-300 eV Ar^+ during deposition. The stress changed toward compressive values.

Another example of recent IAD work is the deposition of protective coatings on sensitive substrates at low temperatures (3). MgF_2 films were successfully deposited on heavy metal fluoride glass substrates at 100°C The films were bombarded with 300 eV Ar^+ during deposition. Conventional evaporated MgF_2 films are soft when deposited at substrate temperatures less than 250°C(25). The IAD MgF_2 films were hard and robust. ThF_4 films have also been successfully deposited at ambient temperatures using IAD (26). Film stability to humidity was significantly improved for the IAD films.

IAD has been used to affect the microstructure and properties of metal films (27). An excellent recent report (6) examines the effects of IAD on resistivity, stress, hardness, crystallinity and the surface morphology of evaporated Cu films. Films were bombarded with 600, 125 and 62 eV Ar ions at various ion flux levels. The results illustrated that using a general energy parameter (i.e. eV/atom) to predict film property modifications is incorrect. Thus, the effect of ten 600 eV ions is different than the effect of one hundred 60 eV ions. This work demonstrates the independence of ion energy -and ion flux as they affect film properties.

Control of stoichiometry is important in tailoring the optical and electrical properties of films. The results of N_2^+ and O_2^+ bombardment during the evaporation of Si and Al can be found (4,5,28). Netterfield (28) examined the effects of 60 and 100 eV N_2^+ bombardment on the optical constants of Si_3N_4 films. With 60 eV ion bombardment the films were lossless. At 100 eV bombardment the refractive index value increased but the films became lossy. Donovan (5) investigated the feasibility of designing rugate filters by varying the flux of 500 eV N_2^+ bombarding the substrate during deposition. Al-Jumaily, et al. (4) varied the stoichiometry of silicon and aluminum oxynitrides by varying the gas mixture in the ion beam. They studied the optical properties and the humidity stability of the resulting films.

20.5 PROPERTIES OF DUAL IBS FILMS

A number of references (2,29) are available that describe the properties of thin films deposited by dual IBS. Improvements in the properties of carbon films are presented in Ref. 30. A graphite target is sputtered by argon gas or a mixture of argon/methane gas. The second ion source also uses either argon or argon/methane mixture as its working gas. The films sputter-deposited with no ion assist were amorphous, a dark brown color and soft. The films deposited with low energy ion bombardment of the substrates were insulating, transparent and hard. However, if the ion energy or flux levels were increased too much the films became brittle. In another study, (29) dual IBS was applied to deposit Al-N films. A 1500 eV Ar^+ sputters the Al target while a 100- 500 eV N_2^+ beam bombards the substrate. The properties of the thin films were examined as a function of varying ion flux levels. The films' visual appearance changed as the amount of nitrogen in the films varied: from a shiny metallic appearance for N-Al ratios less than 0.54, to a shiny gray for $0.82 < N/Al < 1.0$, to transparent for stoichiometric AlN. The electrical properties also varied as a function of N-Al ratio.

The optical properties of Cu films deposited under different ion flux levels were found to vary (31). Films deposited with a factor of three variation in the bombarding ion current density were found to have differences in microstructure (voids and grain size) which caused differences in the films optical constants. Recently, dual IBS oxides were found to exhibit optical properties which equal or surpass conventionally deposited films (13,32). In one example, low-scatter optics are critical to the proper operation of ring laser gyroscopes and low-gain laser systems. (Scattering in laser gyroscopes is detrimental because it causes an effect called lock-in which severely decreases output precision.) Demiryont, et al. (32) used dual IBS to study the effects of various Ar/O_2 gas mixtures on TiO_2 and Ta_2O_5 film properties. Holmes (13) has deposited films with total optical losses less then 100 parts per million as measured in a ringdown laser arrangement. These films were highly stable with temperature cycling to 300°C in atmosphere for several hours.

20.6 ADVANTAGES and LIMITATIONS

The two configurations for using ion beams for thin film deposition (Figs. 1 and 2) each contain their distinct advantages. Direct comparison of the two configurations to determine which provides the "best" coatings is difficult. The decision as to which configuration to employ must be made with consideration of the end application, the existing deposition system (if any), total costs and the issues discussed in previous sections. In this section, a discussion summarizing the advantages and disadvantages of dual IBS and IAD is given with the emphasis on listing information to aid the users in deciding which configuration would better serve their needs.

The improvements in the properties of thin films produced using dual IBS and IAD are are given in a previous section. It appears that each technique results in thin films of similar quality. Thus, a decision based on film quality would need to be made on a case-by-case basis However it is clear that films produced using dual IBS or IAD possess properties superior to films deposited by evaporation alone.

A direct advantage of IAD is that the technique is readily implemented with the addition of an ion source apparatus to an existing vacuum deposition system. This offers significant savings in both time and money. On the other hand, dual IBS may require more modifications to an existing deposition system, or the purchase of a totally dedicated one. Either choice requires a major investment. Another advantage of IAD is the ease in which the technique can be scaled to large geometries. Scaling the dual IBS process is more limited than the IAD process by the size of ion sources available. A number of trade-offs among the deposition parameters (deposition rate, uniformity, etc.) exist, and they must be considered before choosing which technique would best achieve the desired results.

In sputter applications, ion beams provide control of ion energy, flux, species and angle of incidence. These parameters are not only controllable over a wide range, they can be controlled nearly independently of each other. This represents significant advantages compared to other forms of sputtering. In addition, the gas discharge of the ion source is contained and separate from the rest of the deposition system. For example, in the case of magnetron sputtering the ion energy cannot be controlled over a wide range, and it is closely coupled to the magnetron discharge current. Being able to arrange the sputter target at an angle to the incident ion beam is advantageous both in terms of sputter yield and sputtered atom energy, as well as allowing flexibility in the experimental arrangement. In the case of magnetron sputtering or other processes in which the sputter target is in contact with the discharge, there is no control of the incident angle. Ion beam sputtering allows greater flexibility in target material and composition than in other forms of sputtering. As another example, the species in the ion beam can be easily and accurately controlled by adjusting the flow of one or more types of gas through the source; reactive (O_2, N_2, etc.) or inert ion species can be present in practically any ratio desired. The low background pressure present during ion beam sputtering might lead to less gas inclusion compared to other processes. However, substrates will be bombarded with energetic neutralized ions which are reflected from the target unless special precautions are taken. In this case the incorporation could increase significantly due to a larger sticking coefficient of the energetic atom.

An obvious disadvantage of application of ion beams in general is the added expense and complexity of the coating process. However, neither of these is severe. It is more difficult to scale the ion beam sputter process compared to magnetron or some other sputter process. Geometries of the ion beam sputter arrangement sometimes must be small in order to avoid prohibitively slow deposition rates, and this might be a problem.

20.7 CONCLUSION

In this chapter, I presented a general overview of two specific ion deposition techniques. The advantages offered by dual IBS and IAD are the degree of flexibility and independence provided, compared to other gas discharge techniques. The capability to tailor and study film properties for varying controlled bombardment conditions is unique. As improvements in ion beam technology continue, a wide variety of "novel" deposition arrangements will appear. Further improvements in film properties and expanded applications to production (electronics, optics, protective) coatings will allow the advantages of dual IBS and IAD to outweigh the disadvantages.

ACKNOWLEDGMENTS

The author thanks J. R. McNeil for many helpful discussions and G. A. Al-Jumaily for making manuscripts available prior to publication.

20.8 REFERENCES

1. J.M.E. Harper, J.J. Cuomo, R.I. Gambino and H.R. Kaufman, Ion Bombardment of Surfaces: Fundamentals and Applications O. Auciello and R.Kelly, eds., pp 127-162, (Elsevier, Amsterdam 1984).

2. J.M.E. Harper, Thin Film Processes, ed. by J.L. Vossen and W.Kerns pp 175-206 (Academic Press, New York (1978).

3. J.J. McNally, G.A. Al-Jumaily, J.R. McNeil and B.Bendow, Appl. Opt. 25: 1973 (1986).

4. G.A. Al-Jumaily, T.A. Mooney, W.A. Spurgeon and H.M. Dauplaise, J. Vac. Sci. Technol. A7: to be published (1989).

5. E.P. Donovan, D. Van Vechten, A. Khan, C.A. Carosella, and G.K. Hubler Optical Interference Coatings, 1988 Technical Digest Series 6: 122 (1988).

6. J.J. Cuomo, J.M.E. Harper, C.R. Guarnieri, D .S. Yee, C.J. Attanasio, J. Angilello, C.T. Wu and R. H. Hammond, J. Vac. Sci. Technol. 20: 349 (1982).

7. R.A. Roy, J.J. Cuomo and D.S. Yee, J. Vac. Sci. Techol. A6: 1621 (1988).

8. C. Weissmantel, Thin Solid Films 32: 11 (1976).

9. K.H. Müller, J. Vac. Sci. Technol. A6: 1690 (1988); Also, J. Appl. Phys., 61: 2516 (1987).

10. H.R. Kaufman and H.R. Robinson, AIAA Journal 20: 745 (1982).

11. J.L. Vossen and J.J. Cuomo, Thin Film Processes ed. by J.L. Vossen and W. Kern, pp 11-73 (Academic Press, New York, 1978)

12. W.C. Herrmann, Jr. and J.R. McNeil, Proc. SPIE 325: 101 (1982).

13. S. Holmes, private communication.

14. S. Masaki and H. Morisaki, Proc. 10th Symp. on ISIAT 86, 427, Tokyo (1986).

15. W. Heitman Appl. Opt. 10: 2414 (1971).

16. J. Dudonis and L. Prannevicius, Thin Solid Films, 36: 117 (1976).

17. P.J. Martin, H.A. Macleod, R.P. Netterfield, C.G. Pacey and W.G. Sainty. Appl. Opt. 22: 178 (1983).

18. P.J.Martin, R.P. Netterfield and W.G. Sainty, J. Appl. Phys. 55: 235 (1984).

19. R.P. Netterfield, W.G. Sainty, P.J. Martin and S.H. Sie, Appl. Opt. 24: 2267 (1985).

20. J.R. McNeil, G.A. Al-Jumaily, K.C. Jungling and A.C. Barron, Appl. Opt. 24: 486 (1985).

21. J.R. McNeil, A.C. Barron, S.R. Wilson and W.C. Herrmann, Jr., Appl. Opt. 23: 552 (1984).

22. J.J. McNally, G.A. Al-Jumaily and J.R. McNeil, J. Vac. Sci Technol., A4: 437 (1986).

23. J.J. McNally, F.L. Williams, K.C. Jungling and J.R. McNeil, J.Vac Sci. Technol., A5: 2145 (1987).

24. E.H. Hirsh and I.K. Varga, Thin Solid Films, 69: 99 (1980).

25. P.J. Martin and R.P. Netterfield, Appl. Opt. 24: 1731 1985.

26. G.A. Al-Jumaily, L.A. Yazlovitsky, T.A. Mooney and A. Smajkiewicz, Appl. Opt. 26: 3752 (1987).

27. G.A. Al-Jumaily, L.A. Yazlovitsky, T.A. Mooney and A. Smajklly, K.C. Jungling and J.R. McNeil, J. Vac. Sci. Technol. A4: 439 (1986); also, G.A. Al-Jumaily, S.R. Wilson, J.J. McNally, J.R. McNeil, J.M. Bennett and H.H Hunt, Appl. Opt. 25: 3631 (1986).

28. R.P. Netterfield, P.J. Martin and W.G. Sainty, Appl. Opt. 25: 3808 (1986).

29. J.M.E. Harper, J.J. Cuomo and H.T.G. Hentzel, Appl. Phys. Lett. 43: 547 (1983).

30. C. Weissmantel, E. Achemann, K. Bewilogua, G. Hecht, H. Kupfer and B. Rau, J. Vac. Sci. Technol. A4: 2892 (1986).

31. F. Parmigiani, E. Kay, T.C. Huang and J.D. Sawlen, Appl. Opt. 24: 35 (1985).

32. H. Demiryont, J.R. Sites and K. Geib, Appl. Opt. 24: 490 (1985).

21

Microstructural Control of Plasma-Sputtered Refractory Coatings

David W. Hoffman and Robert C. McCune

21.1 INTRODUCTION

One of the foremost attractions of sputtering versus thermal evaporation for the vacuum deposition of materials is the relative ease with which refractory elements and compounds can be vaporized. It is well known that the sputtering yields of materials vary less widely than their vapor pressures. Thus, although refractory materials are characterized by high melting temperatures and very low vapor pressures, they sputter almost as readily as other substances. Even when sputtered, however, the sedentary nature of refractories asserts itself at the point of deposition, where their low mobility restricts diffusion from the random points of impingement onto energetically favorable sites. Consequently the very materials for which sputtering is most advantageous at vaporization tend to yield the greatest disorder and anomalous properties in their deposits. This chapter considers the manipulation of the plasma sputtering environment to influence the microstructure and properties of coatings deposited under conditions where the materials in question have low adatom mobilities. Examination of primitive growth structures obtained without modification will be followed by discussions of stimulated bombardment by bias sputtering, and coincidental control by sputtering at low gas pressures. The chapter will conclude with a discussion of selected mechanisms and models relevant to the influence of the plasma environment on resulting film microstructures and properties.

21.1.1 Primitive Microstructures

The tapered grain microstructure consisting of a multitude of competitively growing, domed "grains", which may be touching but not strongly interbonded, is a common feature of materials deposited at low temperatures that has long been associated with degraded appearance and physical properties. The deposition of thermally evaporated metals in the form of tapered grains was determined by Movchan and Demchishin (1) to occur at temperatures below about one third of the respective melting temperatures, as their classic diagram indicates in Fig. 1(a). When deposited above this temperature, evaporated materials exhibit different features such as faceted surfaces and strongly interbonded, columnar microstructures. The temperature regimes below and above the transition have become known as Zone 1 and Zone 2 respectively. Although the transition may be somewhat gradual, the interzone boundary is sufficiently well defined to reveal a secondary dependence on the class of material, e.g., pure metals versus ceramic compounds. The suggestion of Movchan and Demchishin that the location of the transition is determined by a competition between geometric impingement effects, e.g., self-shadowing, that promote the growth of isolated grains and the onset of surface diffusion has been theoretically quantified by Srolovitz, Mazor, and Bukiet (2).

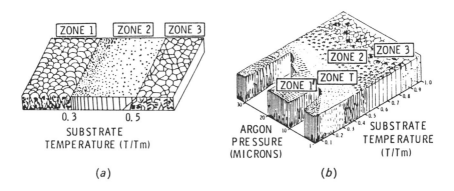

Figure 1: Structural zone models for coating growth. (a) Model proposed by Movchan & Demchishin (1). (b) Model proposed by Thornton for sputtered metal coatings (3). The zone notation " 1′ " is inserted into Thornton's model to distinguish the sputtered microstructure from the Zone 1 microstructure produced by evaporation.

From observations on metal coatings deposited by plasma sputtering Thornton (3) adapted the zone diagram of Movchan and Demchishin by adding a second axis for sputtering gas pressure, as shown in Fig. 1(b). Bearing in mind the qualitative nature of such diagrams, it seems nevertheless evident that the lower limit of Zone 2 microstructures is retracted to higher temperatures for deposition by plasma sputtering, extending no lower than one-half the melting temperature as opposed to one-third T_m by thermal evaporation. In other words, plasma sputtering appears to expand the range below Zone 2 of refractory deposition, implying that self-shadowing effects become relatively more potent in the competition with surface diffusion. Thornton (4) proposed that enhancement of tapered grain deposition (sometimes also confusingly called columnar) results from gas scattering of the sputtered vapor, thereby randomizing the directions of incidence of the coating flux upon the substrate, as sketched by him in Fig. 2. The indicated geometric shadowing favors preferential accumulation toward the tips of the surface protrusions thereby increasing the amount of counteracting diffusion transport required to achieve a Zone 2 microstructure. Since Thornton's original determination it has become clear that the randomized coating flux also alters the internal structure of tapered grains to such an extent that a special nomenclature, Zone 1', may be useful to distinguish the sputtered coatings. Thornton (3) postulated the interpolation of a transitional Zone T between Zones 1' and 2, when sputter deposition was performed at reduced gas pressures.

The empirical zone models derive from observations at the magnifications available in light and scanning electron microscopy having resolutions no finer than 0.1 micrometer, thereby inviting speculation about the internal structures of the grains and columns. Although debate flourished about crystalline defect densities and atomic configurations within tapered grains, evidence for substructure of a different sort was inferred by Westwood (5) from decreasing physical densities measured on platinum films sputter deposited at increasing gas pressures. Since platinum was selected to minimize the possibility of reactive gas pickup, these results suggest the existence of an array of fine internal voids variable over a substantial range of macroscopic densities. Subsequently Nakahara et al. (6) observed copious atomic scale voids in evaporated refractory coatings of a nickel-iron alloy by transmission electron microscopy, where self-shadowing was accentuated by depositing at oblique incidence. Startling images of highly convoluted morphologies that refractory microstructures may incorporate were also generated by computer modelling studies of ballistic aggregation beginning with Henderson et al. (7,8), motivated by the observation of anisotropy in amorphous Gd-Co magnetic bubble films. When deposited at oblique incidence to the substrate, the simulated growth structures incorporated a host of elongated, atomic-scale voids tilted to a degree studied by Meakin et al. (9) toward the direction of the incoming condensate. Notably both the TEM observations and simulated microstructures represent thermally evaporated (not plasma sputtered) coatings with self-aligned vapor streams, and both indicate that oblique incidence accentuates the generation of numerous voids. In fact physical property observations suggest that thermally evaporated metallic coatings grown under Zone 1 conditions, while incorporating tapered grains, may not necessarily develop a voided intragrain substructure when deposited at normal incidence.

Void incorporation in plasma sputtered coatings, however, is exacerbated by the gas scattering mechanism of Fig. 2 when extrapolated to the atomic scale. By transmission electron microscopy of sputtered stainless steel Fabis (10) observed microporosity that may, however, not represent a totally primitive structure, owing to the use of a relatively low argon pressure. An instructive ballistic simulation was carried out by Dirks and Leamy (11,12), using oblique incidence from two opposing angles (an approximation to randomized incidence) as shown in Fig. 3. Near the center of the finite simulated structure appear elongated microvoids oriented normal to the plane of the substrate. Microvoid formation was also promoted by the use of two atom sizes simulating a binary alloy. While the atomic scale substructure of Zone 1' plasma sputtered coatings remains the subject of active investigation, their physical and mechanical properties indicate that it is substantially different from Zone 1 of evaporated coatings, representing a more extreme state of dis-equilibrium. The intragrain microstructure of coatings plasma sputtered in Zone 1' may approach a steady state, as deduced by Ball and Witten (13) and Meakin (14), having an interconnected void network and highly non-bulklike physical properties. Such a sponge-like microstructure would also be consistent with low physical density and the state of near-zero residual stress observed in Zone 1' plasma-sputtered materials (15,16).

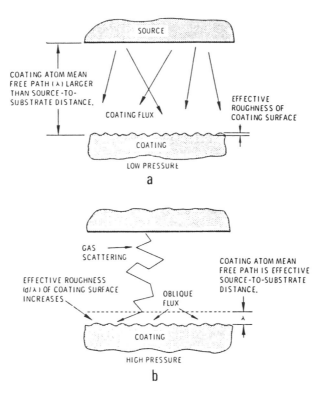

Figure 2: Schematic representation of influence of sputtering gas pressure in producing oblique component in coating flux (4).

Messier et al. (17) have elaborated the evolutionary nature of thin film microstructures noted by Movchan and Demchishin (1) in their reference to tapered grains. Yehoda and Messier (18,19) propose a self-similar fractal model of void coarsening during film growth. Film microstructures were observed to pass through successive stages of increasing scale as a function of thickness. In this context Zone T is regarded as the retention of less-coarsened Zone 1 (or 1′) structures to greater thicknesses owing to the counteracting stimulation of adatom mobility by temperature and/or bombardment. However, this interpretation does not account for the unique properties of Zone T films, in particular the development of compressive residual stress. The accumulated evidence provides a concept of the unmodified or primitive microstructure of materials plasma sputtered and deposited under refractory conditions. The picture is one of competitively growing tapered grains containing a finer structure of atomic-scale elongated voids (20), which impart directional properties to even amorphous materials. Surface roughness may evolve in proportion to a power of film thickness, while incorporated microvoids develop a semi-independent internal distribution. Succeeding sections will examine how this primitive microstructure can be modified and densified during discharge sputter deposition by stimulated bombardment or coincidental control.

Figure 3: Structure formed by oblique-incidence deposition of hard disks from two directions at ± 30° relative to the substrate normal. Disks were allowed to relax to the nearest point of contact with two other disks (12).

21.1.2 Comparative Modification Strategies

Before discussing bias sputtering and coincidental control individually, it is instructive to compare these and other microstructural control schemes from a mechanistic perspective. The gas pressure axis on Thornton's zone diagram for sputtering in Fig. 1 (b) involves the two overlapping mechanisms of directional scattering of the coating flux at higher pressures and coincidental bombardment by backscattered neutrals and sputtered atoms at reduced pressures. To separate these effects it is useful to construct a new vertical axis from the temperature-pressure plane of Fig. 1(b) to represent bombardment of the coating by energetic atomic or ionic particles. Moreover, the old pressure axis can now represent merely the geometrical component of gas scattering in terms of the reciprocal mean-free-path. Fig. 4 illustrates schematically an isothermal section through such a plot at a temperature below Zone 2, where the mean-free-path has been divided into the source-to-substrate distance to generalize the scale.

The general configuration of this specialized zone diagram derives as follows. Along the horizontal scattering axis at zero bombardment is found classical Zone 1 deposition, when the mean-free-path is greater than the distance to the substrate, i.e., $L/\lambda < 1$, so there is little or no scattering of the coating material in transit. Further out the scattering axis, where the mean-free-path is less than about one-half L, the coating flux is well randomized before reaching the substrate leading to Zone 1' microstructures with the incorporation of copious microvoids. Between these limiting cases lies a transition, shaded on the plot, from Zone 1 to Zone 1' microstructures as a function of increasing scattering. The vertical dimensions of the Zone 1, Zone 1', and transition regions schematically indicate the relative amounts of bombardment required to convert the respective deposition to the Zone T microstructure. The postulation of greater densifying bombardment for Zone 1' than for Zone 1 derives from the substantial difference between these primitive microstructures. Supporting evidence is given by Leamy et al. (21) who showed by molecular dynamics simulation that particle energies sufficient to densify normal-incidence deposits were insufficient to densify oblique deposits accumulated under otherwise identical conditions.

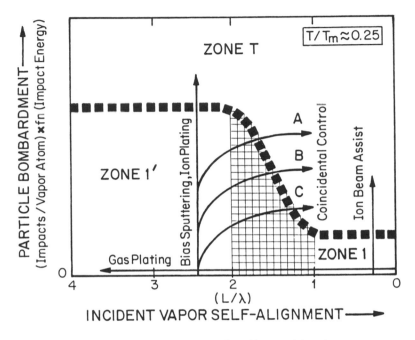

Figure 4: Low temperature zone diagram produced by resolving the gas pressure axis of Thornton's model for sputtered film structures into the mechanistic components of incident vapor self-alignment (opposite to directional scattering) and energetic particle bombardment during growth.

Locus lines superimposed on Fig. 4 indicate the comparative regimes of various treatments such as bias sputtering, coincidental control, pressure plating, ion plating, and ion beam assistance. The vertical locus line near the right edge of the figure indicates ion beam bombardment or "assistance" of metal coatings deposited by thermal evaporation at low background pressures. Only moderate bombardment is required to convert such pure metal coatings to the Zone T microstructure. Biased deposition of arc evaporated coatings and simple ion beam deposition could also fall along this locus. A locus line along the base of the figure indicates the regime of pressure plating, which employs gas scattering to increase the throwing power of evaporated coatings beyond line-of-sight incidence, but which also incurs a microstructural transition from Zone 1 to Zone 1'. In the Zone 1' regime lies a vertical locus line representing the regime of bias sputtering and ion plating. A heavier dose of ion bombardment is required to suppress the Zone 1' microstructure incurred by deposition at the elevated pressures characteristic of these processes. Curved loci illustrate the course of treatment by coincidental control wherein both the scattering and the bombardment change with reduction of the sputtering gas pressure.

As indicated, the reduction of directional scattering allows the Zone T microstructure to be achieved with less coincidental bombardment and consequent damage.

Figure 4 highlights the difference between the techniques of bias sputtering and co-incidental control for improving the microstructures and properties of refractory materials deposited by plasma sputtering. While bias sputtering employs sufficient bombardment to suppress the unmitigated effects of directional scattering, coincidental control felicitously reduces the detrimental gas scattering simultaneous with the administration of mild bombardment to achieve a similar effect. This perspective sets the stage for further discussions of these two control strategies.

21.2 BIAS SPUTTERING

In this, and the following section of the chapter, consideration is given to generic means for harnessing the available energy in rf and dc discharge sputtering processes for control of film structure and consequent physical properties. This section considers bias sputtering while the following section reviews phenomena occurring coincidentally as the sputter gas pressure is reduced through use of magnetron arrangements or supported plasma discharges. The use of impressed substrate biases in dc and rf diode sputter depositions is historically one of the first attempts to control film properties through particle bombardment of the growing film. Reviews of bias sputtering have been previously prepared (22-25) and specific details of its various means of implementation will therefore be minimal. The focus of this section will be instead on the utility of bias sputtering as a means of film property control for a wide variety of materials.

The understanding of structure/property-tailoring by particle bombardment of growing films has perhaps reached its greatest extent in the case of ion beam-assisted depositions. In these processes, it is often possible to reduce the number of variables that exist in plasma-diode type configurations. Thus, models which prescribe a roadmap for property modification in terms of bombarding ion energy and ion/atom arrival rate ratios have been developed for ion assisted depositions (26-29). It is generally recognized that the decoupling of various modes of momentum transfer into growing films (e.g. reflected neutrals, charge-exchange collisions, and negative ion emission) by use of ion beam techniques has allowed this level of sophistication.

Certain specific versions of plasma-based sputtering have also permitted modelling in terms of the bombardment flux/deposition rate domain. In particular, Ziemann and Kay (30,31), using variations of a model for triode bias sputtering developed earlier by Kay and Heim (32), measured film property changes in Pd as a function of the energy deposited per arriving film atom. The triode arrangement lends itself to such an analysis by virtue of its relatively low operating pressure (ca. 1 mTorr), which minimizes the need for consideration of charge exchange collisions and attendant changes in the energies of ions taking part in primary and bias-induced sputtering.

Recognizing the complexity of the plasma/film interaction and its characterization, Thornton (33) proposed using the resputter fraction as a fundamental measure of the deposited energy required to control film morphology and properties. This theme can also be found in a number of studies where control of film features has been promoted through manipulation of variables which affect bias and coincidental bombardment. The use of resputter fraction for growing films as an indicator of the extent of film bombardment during growth provides a parameter which is decoupled from the particulars of the deposition process; requiring neither a measure of the incident particle type, flux or energy distribution. This viewpoint will be revisited in the discussion of the role of bias sputtering in control of film structure and morphology.

21.2.1 Fundamental Aspects of Bias Sputtering

A common feature among various embodiments of bias deposition is the introduction of ion bombardment at the surface of a growing film by imposition of a negative potential at the surface of the growing film relative to the plasma. In this case, positive ions from the plasma are accelerated across the sheath created by the substrate bias and impart sufficient energy to the growing film that atomic rearrangements, including enhanced resputtering and recoil bombardment, are promoted. Such modification of a growing film can substantially alter the Zone 1 or Zone 1' type primitive structures, which would otherwise occur at low deposition temperatures, and promote transformation to Zone T morphologies.

In general, the establishment of a substrate bias condition acts in concert with other features of the plasma and deposition geometry, such that the total collisional energy brought to the surface of the growing film arises from a number of contributions. In a simplified diode sputtering arrangement with biased substrate, these factors include: energetic atoms from the target material, reflected neutrals, negative ions from the target, electrons, and ions from the plasma accelerated across the sheath. This latter group includes charge-exchange ions produced in the vicinity of the substrate sheath, since positive ions produced near the cathode cannot overcome the applied potential. The energy with which particles emanating from the cathode strike the substrate is mitigated by the system pressure. The measured or applied bias voltages represent only upper limits to the energies of bombarding ions from plasma, since the ion energy distribution will be determined by the mean free path for charge exchange collisions and the potential across the sheath developed between the substrate and the plasma (34-37).

Several limiting cases for plasma-based processes exist, where the bombardments of the growing film are largely from a single species. One such limiting case is "ion plating" (38), where the principal introduction of collisional energy deposition into a growing film is from bias-induced ion impact. In this process, the film deposition is often from an evaporative source, which of itself would normally lead to Zone 1 structures in the deposited film at low temperatures and low pressure. By utilizing the substrate as a primary cathode, and with introduction of sufficient gas to sustain a glow discharge, the growing film is bombarded with ions from the plasma so created. With regard to Figure 4, the effect of increasing the system pressure is to promote movement to the left along the "gas plating" locus, promoting a Zone 1' ultrastructure. The bias-induced bombardment now refines this structure, although a greater energy/particle flux is needed to effect the transition to Zone T than would be required for the case of evaporation at low pressures, since the effect of increasing the system gas pressure is to promote the Zone 1' structure.

In ion plating, it has been estimated that only about 1% of the collisional energy deposition is from impact of ionized atoms of the film material itself (37), the remainder being due to the effects of gas ions created by the discharge. While various arrangements of the ion plating process have been developed, nominally high gas pressures and cathode voltages are required to initiate and sustain the plasma discharge. Since the substrate becomes a sputter cathode, overall film deposition rates may be lower than expected in the absence of the plasma-assisted process.

The cathodic arc process (39) is another limiting case wherein the ionized target atom flux is now the dominant contributor to the energy deposition in the growing film. Since the arc plasma is sustained chiefly by vaporized atoms of the target material, the necessity for a gas to sustain the discharge is primarily limited to those embodiments of the process where reactive species are introduced for the formation of compound films. Furthermore, multiple charge states of target ions usually exist, thus greatly increasing the energy input from these ions under bias conditions at the growing film.

In a particularly interesting implementation of "unbalanced magnetron" sputtering, Window and Savvides (40,41) have developed a plasma-based deposition process in which a degree of control exists over both bias voltage and plasma density. This control is made possible by spatially tuning the plasma plume associated with a planar magnetron by adjusting the degree of electron confinement with an electromagnet. In this manner, the flux of impinging ions, acting under the influence of an imposed substrate bias, can be adjusted over several orders of magnitude. Since dc biasing in balanced magnetrons is ineffectual due to the plasma confinement near the cathode, this arrangement allows a compromise in terms of enhanced sputter flux from the cathode and reduced operating pressures, in tandem with an ability to impose a dc sheath at the substrate position.

As had been suggested by Thornton (33), the refinement of Zone 1' primitive micro-structures through bias sputtering may be viewed in terms of resputtering. Historically, the concept of introducing a second level of sputtering at the growing film for adjustment of film properties has been attributed to Frerichs (42) who developed an asymmetric ac deposition system for diode sputtering. Maissel and Schaible (43) described a dc bias system for deposition of tantalum films, wherein a substrate bias of approximately - 200V resulted in films of minimum resistivity. For conductive targets and substrates dc biasing represents a straightforward approach, in which the substrate becomes a secondary cath-ode with respect to the system ground or alternate anode. The limiting energy of im-pinging ions across the substrate sheath will be the difference between the applied potential and that of the plasma. Depending on the extent of inelastic collisions (which will be a function of gas pressure and sheath dimension), the ions impacting the surface will have a distribution of energies with usually only a small fraction of the total flux having the full potential of the sheath (34-37). Sputter deposition configurations which operate at lower pressure regimes (e.g. triodes (33) or magnetrons (44)), will, in general, permit a distribution of ion energies with a greater proportion having the full energy of the sheath. Both triode and magnetron arrangements, however, also permit more non-randomized bombardment by reflected neutral atoms of the sputter gas produced at the cathode surface. Of themselves, these arrangements promote Zone 1/Zone T transitions by coincidental bombardments, and minimization of Zone 1' primitive microstructures. With regard to Fig. 4, these methodologies tend to be on the right-hand side of the dia-gram. Substrate biases induced by rf means (owing to the plasma localization near the cathode and typically low operating pressures), do not therefore need to produce the high degrees of particle impact energy or flux to produce a transformation to Zone T micro-structures.

The ability to deposit both insulating materials as well as metals on insulating substrates has arisen from the practical development of rf sputter deposition and biasing techniques. These methods, and various means of introducing substrate bias under rf conditions have been reviewed by Vossen (24). The upper limit to the energy of an impinging ion in an rf deposition may be as much as twice the sheath potential developed between the substrate and the plasma (45). As surmised from Figure 4, operation in a low pressure regime reduces the flux-energy product requirements permitting more modest bias potentials than those needed in ion plating for achieving the transition to Zone T.

21.2.2 Applications

21.2.2.1 Impurity Atom Resputtering and Ion Implantation Effects: One of the earliest applications of bias sputtering arose from a desire to minimize the gaseous impurity content of thin resistive and superconductor films, whose properties were greatly influenced by the uptake of, and bombardment by, reactive gases (42,43). The mechanism for the beneficial removal of contaminants from the film surface through use of substrate bias has been attributed to the preferential resputtering of the atomically lighter impurity species (e.g. oxygen, nitrogen) from the growing film surface (46). The process may become self-defeating, if the bombarding ions used to "clean" the growing films become implanted under the influence of sufficiently high applied bias. Secondly, reactive ions present in contaminated plasmas may also be implanted, rather than removed from the surface, thus tending to stabilize defects within the coating. Energetic, reflected neutrals may also be implanted in the growing film at sufficiently high cathode voltages and low operating pressures. Ion implantation accompanying bias sputtering has been addressed by various investigators (47-50). Generally, a combination of high bias voltages, low atomic number sputter gases and low atomic number matrices will promote ion implantation in biased deposition.

21.2.2.2 Control of Film Stress and Microstructure: Since Zone 1 or Zone 1' microstructures represent highly defective films in terms of both tapered, unbonded grains as well as atomic scale voids in the Zone 1' case, it may be expected that such structures will be stabilized against post-deposition thermal annealing by the introduction of surface active contaminants either during or after deposition. The typically tensile intrinsic stresses observed in these primitive structures (51) may promote degradation by cracking and an enhanced propensity for chemical reactions relative to the large extent of available surface area. Minimization of film impurity content through bias sputtering is one means of influencing the evolution of film microstructure through elimination of species which retard both bulk and interfacial diffusion as a consequence of their chemical affinities for the host material or segregation tendencies which tend to stabilize interfaces.

While removal of stabilizing impurities is one consequence of bias sputtering which may allow favorable microstructural evolution, there are intrinsic restructuring aspects of the bombardment which promote refinement of the primitive microstructures. These intrinsic atomic rearrangements associated with the bias sputtering process account for its utility in disrupting the Zone 1' primitive microstructures for a wide variety of film materials. Thornton discussed the morphological changes accompanying bias deposition of copper films in a hollow cathode system at various pressures (33). Resputtering in principally forward directions was believed to be primarily responsible for disruption of the primitive growth structure. Increasing the sputter gas pressure in this particular configuration was felt to promote forward resputtering in directions which were effective in suppressing large topographical features associated with a roughened substrate. Increased pressures in this geometry did not, however, reduce the effects of bias in disrupting the

Zone 1 microstructures. Thornton has reviewed a number of developments in the understanding of the evolution of thin-film microstructures which support the resputtering viewpoint (20). Results of molecular dynamics computer simulations by Müller (52) also suggest that forward resputtering of a growing film promotes elimination of Zone 1' type ultrastructures. One of the earliest indications that resputtering associated with biased deposition of film material promoted densification of films was observed for rf-sputtered SiO_2 by Jones, et al. (53) as a noted difference in etch rates for the primary (biased) deposit, and the secondary deposit formed by resputtered material. Further studies of the resputtering phenomena with SiO_2 (54) showed that optimum film quality (e.g. etching behavior, and dielectric strength) was achieved at a resputter fraction of approximately 60%. This degree of resputtering falls within the window of 30-70% suggested by Thornton (33) as being desirable to obtain optimum film properties.

Vossen and O'Neill (55) studied the rf bias deposition of various metals and observed that optimum densification of gold (determined microscopically) coincided with a minimum resistivity approaching the bulk value. Later tabulations by Vossen (24) suggested optimum bias voltages for various materials. In a qualitative sense, more noble fcc metals (e.g. Au, Ag, Cu) required lower degrees of bias than did more refractory metals such as tungsten and tantalum which required the highest levels of bias to obtain optimum physical properties. Vossen and O'Neill (55) also suggested the significance of the bulk recrystallization temperatures of these metals as a guideline in assessing the energy deposition required to effect an approach to bulk-like physical properties by bias deposition.

Blachman (56) also suggested classification of various metals by their refractory nature and nobility with regard to control of stress and the role of bias in impurity resputtering. In light of both high reactivities of the refractory metals for such contaminants as oxygen and nitrogen, as well as generally high activation energies for surface and bulk diffusion, relative to the more noble metals such as gold, the mechanisms which lead to structural refinement during bias sputtering may be difficult to separate when film contamination by reactive species is possible. The elimination of reactive contaminants during bias bombardment should promote both adatom diffusional processes and recoil implantation of adatoms into void regions. In the absence of reactive contaminants, the ease with which atoms of the growing film are forward scattered into void regions would appear to be governed by the extent of momentum transfer from the impinging particle flux and the imparted energy relative to the binding energy of the recoiling atom in its surface or bulk site.

In the development of a model to predict critical ion/atom arrival rate ratios as a function of energy for covalently bonded materials such as germanium, Brighton and Hubler (29) concluded that atomic rearrangements in the bulk were primarily responsible for ion-assisted stress annealing, as had previously been described by Hirsch and Varga (57). They discounted effects of enhanced surface diffusion or thermal spikes associated with the bombardment process.

Direct evidence for microstructural changes occurring with bias sputtering was obtained by Mattox and coworkers (58,59). Since that time, there have been numerous reports in the literature of both film stress and microstructural modification through use of bias deposition techniques. The ability to disrupt the Zone 1 or Zone 1' type morphologies for a variety of material types (including metals, alloys, compounds and amorphous materials) suggests the importance of models involving material redistribution. Table 1 summarizes a number of reported film modification results from the literature, where bias sputtering had been employed to change film properties and structure.

Table 1: Summary of selected applications of bias sputtering for thin film property modification

Material		Bias/configuration	Property change observed	Ref.
Elements	Al	rf-diode	Structure, Resistivity	55
		rf-diode	Planarization	64
		rf-mag.	Morphology, Step coverage	65,66
		dc-mag.	Step Coverage	67-69
		rf-dc-mag.	Resistivity, Resputtering	70
		dc-diode	Resis., Stress, Ar implantation	71
	Ag	rf-diode	Physical prop.	24
	Au	rf-diode	Structure, Resistivity	55
		dc-diode	Stress, Resistivity	56
	Be	rf-dc-mag.	Morphology	72
	C	dc-unbal.mag	C-C bonding	41
	Cr	dc-triode	Microstructure, hardness	73
		rf-dc-diode	Stress, Density	59
	Cu	dc-hol.cath	Microstructure	33
		dc-triode	Recrystallization behavior	74
		rf-diode	Resistivity	55
	Fe	dc-unbal-mag	Stress, Resistivity	75
	Ge		Physical properties	24
		dc-diode	Crystallinity	61
	Mo	dc-diode	Stress, Resistivity	56,76,77
		rf-dc-diode	Purity, Structure	78
		dc-unbal-mag	Resistivity, Stress	75
	Nb	ac-diode	Purity	42
		rf-dc-diode	Resistivity, Resputtering	70
		dc-triode	Purity, Lattice dilation	32
		dc-unbal. mag.	Resistivity, Stress	75
		dc mag.	Stress, Microstructure	79
	Ni	dc-diode	Ar implantation	47
		rf-triode	Density, Resistivity	55
	Pd	dc-triode	Stress, Resistivity	31
	Pt	rf-diode	Adhesion	24,55
		dc-unbal-mag	Resistivity, Stress	75
	Ta	ac-diode	Purity	42
		dc-diode	Resistivity, Structure	43,59
		rf-diode	Resistivity	55
		dc-unbal-mag	Resistivity, Stress	75
	W	rf-diode	Microstructure	59
		dc-unbal-mag	Resistivity, Stress	75

Table 1: continued.

Alloys				
Al-Cu	rf-mag.	Microstructure	80
Co-Cr	rf-diode	Epitaxy, Magnetic anisotropy	81,82
Cu-Cr	rf-dc-diode	Crystallinity	83
Gd-Co	rf-diode	Magnetic anisotropy	84-86
Gd-Co-Fe	dc-diode	Comp., Magnetic anisotropy	87
Ni-Cr	dc-diode	Preferred Orientation	88
Ni-La, Y	dc-triode	Microstructure	89
Ti-W	rf-mag.	Composition, Resistivity	90
WC-Co	rf-dc-diode	Composition, Microstructure	91
304 Stainless	dc-triode	Composition	92
Compounds				
Al_2O_3	rf-diode	Step coverage, Resputtering	62
NbN	dc-diode	Composition, Superconduct.	93
SiC	rf-diode	Morphology	17
Si_3N_4	rf-diode	Step coverage, Resputtering	62
SiO_2	rf-diode	Structure, Step coverage	54,62,63
TiC	rf-dc-diode	Adhesion, Tribology	94
	rf-react.	Composition, Lattice param.	95
TiN	rf-react.	Resistivity, Structure	96
	dc-react.	Purity	97
Ti(OC)	rf-diode	Microstructure	98
Doped ZrO_2	rf-diode	Microstructure	99,100
7120 Glass	rf-diode	Thermal Expansion coef.	101

The acme of ion-assisted modification is no doubt seen in methods of arriving at high states of crystalline perfection for such materials as compound semiconductors. Greene and Barnett have reviewed the role of ion-assisted depositions in such endeavors (60). It is interesting to note that Wehner in a 1962 patent (61) claimed an ability for utilizing the energy available in a glow discharge plasma to arrive at epitaxially grown crystalline deposits, and that the optimum degree of resputtering had been specified at 12.5% for the case of germanium.

21.2.2.3 Control of Film Topography: Two other key applications of bias sputtering have emerged largely from requirements for topographic control of depositions in microelectronics. In the first, resputtering is accentuated through bias deposition for promoting step coverage as would occur where metallizations or other films are required to follow contours over features in integrated circuits. Seeman (22) originally showed the ability of biased deposition to promote coverage of trench sidewalls through the resputtering of material from the floor of the trench. Vossen (24) and later Kennedy (62) have shown the utility of bias sputtering in obtaining suitable topographical coverages in microelectronics. In these cases, redistribution of material during resputtering also tends to "fill in" regions which may normally have been shadowed from the deposition leading to circuit "opens" or points of mechanical weakness due to lack of material.

A somewhat inverse situation exists where it is desirable to apply a film wherein underlying protuberances are minimized at the final surface so that lithography and further metallizations are occurring on a planarized surface. Bland, et al (59) suggested how forward resputtering of geometric features on surfaces could be used to refine surface morphology. In the case of "planarization", where it is both desired to produce a deposit and also minimize existing surface topography, the resputtering in largely a forward direction is exploited. The role of bias-induced resputtering on planarization has been discussed by various authors (20,59,63)

21.3 COINCIDENTAL CONTROL OF COATINGS DEPOSITED BY PLASMA SPUTTERING

Coincidental control harnesses the forces already at play in plasma sputtering to improve the resultant coatings. These forces consist on the one hand of the energetic particles naturally issuing from the target, including both the atoms of coating material having average energies in the range of 10 eV and the neutralized sputtering ions rebounding from the surface with energies frequently in the range of 100 eV or greater. On the other hand are the forces tending to diffuse the alignment of the incident coating flux at the surface being coated. As was discussed with reference to Fig. 4, reduction of the sputtering gas pressure changes both of these effects simultaneously. Although recent attention has tended to focus on the passage of bombarding particles to the substrate, self-alignment of the incident coating material may be of equal importance by minimizing the required concurrent bombardment.

While the emission of energetic neutrals was recognized and studied prior to the development of magnetron plasmas operable at low pressures (see for instance Winters and Kay (47)) coincidental control was not purposely employed for microstructural modification of sputtered coatings. Several instances are seen in retrospect where the effects of coincidental bombardment are evident, when sputter deposition was infrequently carried out by techniques such as ion beam sputtering (Chopra (102)), triode sputtering (Stuart (103)), and others (104) at especially low gas pressures (105) or with massive target elements such as tantalum (106,107), tungsten (108-110), and platinum (111). The development of magnetron sputtering and the consequent ready access to low pressure sputtering capability set the stage for the identification and investigation of coincidental control as a deposition technique (15,16,112,113). Indeed, for low pressure magnetron sputtering with the usual well-confined plasmas (excepting the recent "unbalanced magnetron" (40)), where the absence of ionized species near the substrates precludes bias sputtering, coincidental control becomes, without the introduction of ion beams, the only plasma-based option. All that is required is to reduce the gas pressure sufficiently to decrease the randomization of the sputtered flux and simultaneously allow some of the existing energetic neutrals to penetrate through to the substrates. Motohiro and Taga (114), Graz-Marti and Valles-Abarca (115), and Somekh (116) have theoretically studied the gas scattering of particles issuing from a sputtering target with valuable insights, but the practical application of coincidental control remains empirical.

21.3.1 Internal Stresses and Physical Properties

While the physical properties of sputtered refractory coatings may often be of primary importance in application, the intrinsic (i.e. nonthermal) film stress is a highly structure-dependent property that can serve as a sensitive barometer of deposition conditions and resultant physical properties. For the case of molybdenum sputtered in argon from a cylindrical magnetron Fig. 5 illustrates the wide variations of intrinsic stress typically found in metal films deposited at various gas pressures down to 1 mTorr (0.13 Pa) (117). At high pressures the stress approaches zero. This differs from the fixed tensile stress normally observed in thermally evaporated metals, as indicated for molybdenum on Fig. 5 (118). Consistent with the deduced microporosity of such sputtered films the trend toward zero stress coincides with the diminishing lateral connectivity of the structure and the consequent inability to support appreciable stress. By comparison the evaporated materials are sufficiently strong in the lateral direction to support high tensile stresses. Klokholm and Berry (51) report intrinsic tensile stresses of 1.1 GPa in evaporated molybdenum, which exceeds the 0.6 GPa tensile strength of the bulk pure metal (119), owing to the refined grain size of evaporated films. Clearly there is not much weakness from voids or weak grain boundaries in evaporated molybdenum. These differences are consistent with the hypothesis of Figs. 1(b) and 4 that the Zone 1' structure in sputtered materials is distinct from and less bulklike than the Zone 1 structure of evaporated metal coatings. Physical property measurements supporting this observation are seen in Table II, where more anomalous values of resistivity and reflectivity are reported for Zone 1' sputtered molybdenum.

Table 2: Properties of Bulk, Sputtered and Evaporated Molybdenum

Material Mo	Microstructure Zone	Intrinsic stress (GPa)	Resistivity (Ω −cmx10^6)	Reflectivity (% at 560nm)	Ref.
bulk	3	0	5.6	58	119
evaporated	1	1.1 (tens.)	30	50	120
sputtered*	1'	$\simeq$ 0	100	35	121

*Even higher resistivity and lower reflectivity are observed when film preparation conditions allow the possible incorporation of oxygen from background gas.

From the high pressure extreme of the Zone 1' microporous microstructure Fig. 5 shows that films deposited at successively lower gas pressures support tensile intrinsic stresses increasing to a peak value of substantial magnitude. The evident gain in film integrity indicates that microporosity must be largely suppressed at pressures approaching the tensile maximum. With continued reductions of the pressure the trend in intrinsic stress reverses moving sharply through zero to large compressive stresses. While the tensile stress excursion may result in part from reduced scattering and increased alignment of the coating flux, the reversal of stress toward compression clearly indicates the increasing effects of particle bombardment, sometimes likened to atomic shot peening (122). Moreover, the incorporation of high compressive stresses suggests the accumulation of impact damage and resultant overcrowding of coating atoms in disordered regions such as grain boundaries. The zero intercept at the point of stress reversal has been termed the transition pressure for the sake of reference and may also represent an adjustment by coincidental control that yields coatings with the least structural disorder (81).

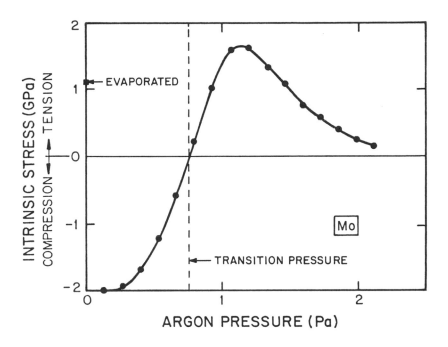

Figure 5: Argon pressure dependence of intrinsic film stress in molybdenum metal films sputtered from a cylindrical magnetron and deposited at 1nm/s onto molybdenum coated substrates at a distance of 0.1 m (121).

Figure 6 shows corresponding changes in physical properties and gas incorporation in coatings deposited at various argon pressures. The reflectance reaches bulklike values at the transition pressure. The resistivity decreases markedly with decreasing pressure and passes through a shallow minimum below the transition pressure. The slight increase at lower pressures correlates with the increasing content of argon embedded in the metal, which again evidences substantial bombardment. The presence of oxygen, which is detected only in films deposited at the higher pressures, is believed to result from oxygen uptake and absorption in the corresponding microporous structure after deposition. Judging from the argon incorporation in the sputtered molybdenum coatings, as well as the relative atomic masses which indicate that argon will backscatter from molybdenum with 41 percent or more of its primary energy, the locus of coincidental control for the depositions of Figs. 5 and 6 is expected to lie on the zone diagram of Fig. 4 along a curve such as that labeled "A". This is an example of the locus to be expected when the coincidental bombardment is relatively vigorous. Consequently the events and the resulting films should resemble those obtained by bias sputtering.

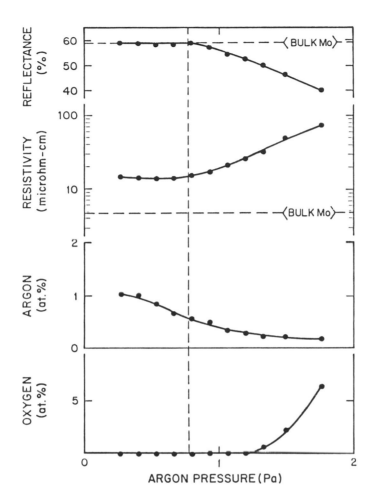

Figure 6: Argon pressure dependence of reflectance (at 560 nm), resistivity, and argon and oxygen concentrations detected by electron microprobe in molybdenum films sputtered from a cylindrical magnetron at 1 nm/s onto molybdenum coated substrates at a distance of 0.1 m.

Observations on a variety of sputter deposited coatings have established that the effects induced in molybdenum by coincidental control are representative of other materials (15,16,112,113). For any given material, however, the salient pressure regime characterized by the transition pressure is strongly dependent on the relative atomic masses of the sputtering target and gas. Figure 7 shows a systematic shift of the transition pressure with target atomic mass for elemental metals sputtered with argon. The two separate data lines for cylindrical and planar magnetrons indicate a further dependence on target geometry. Although the trends are universal, the specific location of the curves will vary with differing apparatus geometries.

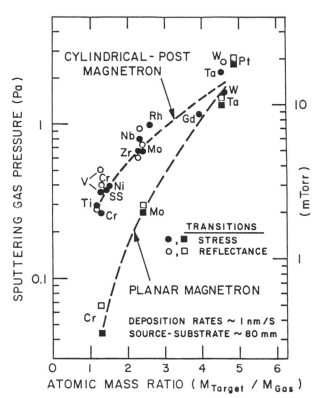

Figure 7: Sputter-deposition map on coordinates of sputtering gas pressure and target-to-gas atomic mass ratio showing the stress/reflectance transition boundaries for metals dc sputtered from cylindrical and planar magnetrons and deposited at 1 nm/s at distances of 0.1 to 0.2 m. Sputtering conditions below and to the right of the transition pressure line yield coatings with compressive stresses, maximum reflectance, and otherwise optimized physical properties (16).

A similar shift occurs when a given target is sputtered with the other inert gasses. Figure 8 shows the results of stress measurements bracketing the transition pressure for molybdenum films deposited with neon, argon, krypton, and xenon (123). A systematic shift with atomic mass is again evident. Of special significance, however, is the presence at sufficiently low pressures of compressive residual stresses even when Mo is sputtered with Xe. Since the atomic mass of xenon exceeds molybdenum, the energy of gas particles rebounding from the target should be quite low, similar to the energies of the sputtered particles themselves. Consequently the potential for bombardment in this case is limited and coincidental control relies more heavily on the directional self-alignment mechanism. The relevant locus on Fig. 4 is indicated by the curve labeled "C". When embedded gas contents of the same four gasses were measured on the compressive molybdenum coatings, the levels varied systematically from 5 percent of neon to undetectable amounts of xenon, i.e., less than 0.01 percent. Again this suggests minimal bombardment in the latter instance.

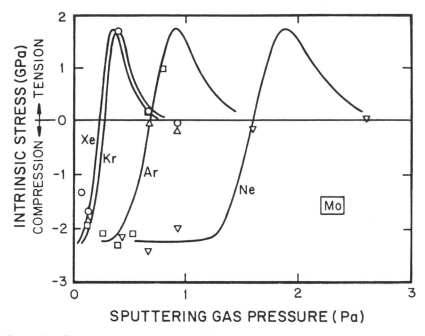

Figure 8: Gas pressure dependence of intrinsic film stress in molybdenum metal films sputtered from a cylindrical magnetron with Ne, Ar, Kr, and Xe noble gasses and deposited at 1 nm/s at a distance of 0.1 m (123).

The preceding discussion indicates that the choice of sputtering target material and sputtering gas with respect to their relative atomic masses is an important if not crucial consideration for the application of coincidental control. In cases where the optimization of physical properties is desired coincidental control enables the Zone T microstructure to be achieved without excessive bombardment through the self-alignment of the coating flux that accompanies reduction of the gas pressure. This can be accomplished either by the selection of lighter target materials where there is a choice, or alternatively by use of the heavier inert gasses. A further instance of this approach has been reported for silicon sputtered with argon (124). The added cost of the heavier inert gasses, Kr or Xe when called for, can be moderated by the practice of static chamber sputtering (125), a viable technique when practiced in conjunction with a load lock to minimize the introduction of contaminating gasses (51).

In addition to the gas pressure and the choice of gas and target material, practically every other plasma sputtering process parameter exerts at least a secondary influence on coincidental control which can sometimes be used to advantage. These include the dynamic gas flow (117), the sputtering rate (121,126), the cathode voltage (127), the target shape (113,128) and the substrate proximity (117), orientation (129), and motion (129). Early recognition of the fundamental role of gas scattering in coincidental control immediately suggested a coupled effect of substrate-target proximity, however preliminary measurements were inconclusive. Then Wu (79), sputtering niobium with argon, demonstrated that close proximity to the target increased the transition pressure in a manner consistent with such coupling. Somekh (116) suggested that the product of pressure and distance could be usefully plotted rather than pressure alone to rationalize results from coatings prepared at various distances from the target. An experimental test, however, did not bear out the quantitative applicability of this approach (117), owing most probably to the additional effect of the self-alignment of coating flux on coating microstructure and properties, beyond the simple bombardment concept. While the cathode voltage is not ordinarily an independent control parameter in magnetron sputtering, Thornton et al.(127) varied the confining magnetic field to enable independent excursions of the voltage, thereby demonstrating a marked dependence.

Perhaps more unexpectedly, increasing the rate of sputtering as determined by the cathode current also moves the deposited microstructure and properties along the locus of coincidental control toward Zone T (121). Since the cathode current is, in addition to pressure, the principal control parameter in magnetron sputtering, this provides another practical stratagem for coincidental control. As demonstrated by Rossnagel (130) and detailed elsewhere in this volume, the rate effect arises from heat dissipation in the sputtering gas with consequent thinning of its density in the vicinity of the target, thereby reducing the associated gas scattering.

An attribute of magnetron sputtering is the relative freedom afforded in the placement and manipulation of a substrate, owing to its de-coupling from the electrodes. Substrates are frequently rotated or moved past the source in order to distribute the coating more uniformly. A consequence, however, is to present the surface being coated at a variety of angles to the arriving flux, thereby simulating the dis-alignment of the flux by gas scattering. It is not surprising, therefore, that substrate inclination and rotation have been reported to move a coincidental control point along its locus away from Zone T toward Zone 1' with more porous, tapered grain microstructures, tensile stress, and anomalous physical properties resulting (129).

21.3.2 Special Investigations and Applications

While the possibility of coincidental control has been established for some time, published reports of its application remain infrequent. This may derive in part from a failure to identify its advantage over bias sputtering in utilizing less bombardment to effect Zone T deposition. Nevertheless some notable examples of coincidental control have appeared. Entenberg et al. (131) studied the residual stress, physical properties, and microstructure of copper sputtered onto polyimide webbing. Although copper is a relatively soft and noble metal in terms of Blachman's classification (56), their results offer a striking demonstration of coincidental control of copper films on flexible substrates of low thermal capacity, confirming in detail the phenomena seen with more refractory materials. Amorphous coatings of a Mo-Ru-B refractory alloy were sputtered by Bieg (132) onto inertial confinement microspheres with stress minimization by coincidental control in order to build up heavier deposits, thereby demonstrating its application to noncrystalline materials. Thakoor et al. (133) also included W-Ru-B alloys in their study of metallic glasses for corrosion and wear applications, minimizing internal stresses by coincidental control to obtain thick, dense, protective coatings. They point out that the observation of coincidental control and associated phenomenology in glassy metals constrains models of intrinsic tensile and compressive stresses not to rely on crystalline mechanisms.

It has been noted that the sharpness of the transition from tensile to compressive stress as a function of sputtering gas pressure poses a difficulty when coincidental control at the zero stress crossover is desired. Bensaoula et al. (126) reported that the stress transition for Mo and W becomes more gradual at higher sputtering rates, thereby easing the margin of error in process control. In addition they employed rf substrate bias to broaden the parameter space for control at zero stress. This can be understood with reference to Fig. 4 where it is apparent that an excursion by biasing from a coincidental control pathway into the direction of pure bombardment will cross into Zone T more gradually, albeit at the possible cost of greater resputtering, impact damage, gas entrapment and heating. A hybrid approach, however, may offer a way to minimize this penalty while improving control stability. An alternative control scheme has been investigated and practiced by Cuthrell et al. (134) in a unique application requiring a coating with high uniformity, low resistivity, and tensile or zero stress having minimal stress anisotropy in the plane of the film. By toggling the argon pressure alternately between settings above and below the stress transition they achieved reproducible control yielding nearly isotropic tensile, compressive, or zero stress as desired, while retaining a suitably low resistivity.

While the study of coincidental control has adhered almost exclusively to metals and alloys, Este and Westwood (135) applied it to the reactive deposition of Al and Ti nitrides, materials often obtained with undesirably high compressive stresses under reactive sputtering conditions. Raising the nitrogen pressure or adding a partial pressure of argon caused a moderation of the compressive stress and a transition into tension, however the correlation of the stress transition with optimum physical properties seems to be different from metals. Full density and bulklike physical properties in the nitrides may be achieved only at elevated values of compressive stress, owing most probably to directional nonmetallic bonding and a resulting propensity to incorporate microporosity even without dis-alignment of the coating flux by gas scattering. In other words, the regime of Zone 1' in Fig. 4 may extend further to the right for this class of materials so that Zone T cannot be entered as readily by a reduction of directional scattering, but requires in addition a greater dose of bombardment.

In metals the correlation of optimum physical properties with the stress transition suggests that the corresponding microstructure may incorporate a minimum of defects, balanced as it were between the onset of microporosity on the one hand and the overcrowding of atoms at the other. In this light, the report of Leu et al. (81) offers the intriguing possibility of epitaxial growth of sputtered Co-Cr magnetic films on MgO single crystals by coincidental control. The best results were obtained at the low argon pressures of 1 to 2 mTorr (0.13-0.27 Pa) on unheated substrates with chromium contents of 21 to 23 percent. By comparison sputter deposition at 5 mTorr (0.68 Pa) or with negative substrate bias of 25 and 50 volts produced polycrystalline films. The atomic masses of cobalt and chromium are sufficiently close to argon that the energies of argon neutrals rebounding from the target will be mild. The locus of coincidental control for this combination should resemble curve "C" on Fig. 4. Apparently the directional alignment plus mild bombardment incurred by coincidental control promotes full density epitaxial growth without the incorporation of excessive defects or impurities leading to renucleation.

Other studies of coincidental control include the combined effects of argon pressure and substrate-to-source proximity on the microstructure of sputter deposited Cu-Ni alloys by Barber and Somekh (136), as detected by changes in thermopower. Hoshi et al. (137)

investigated the effects of pressure on the magnetic properties, surface smoothness, elastic modulus, and corrosion resistance of sputter deposited Co-Pt magnetic recording films, finding the best magnetic response at high pressures where the other properties were degraded. Significantly, microporosity caused by sputtering at 30 mTorr (4 Pa) reduced Young's modulus of the films to a quarter of the bulk value. Nakahara et al. (138) followed the microstructural transition as a function of sputtering pressure in Fe and amorphous Fe-Tb magneto-optic films by transmission electron microscopy. Jankowski et al. (139) utilized coincidental control to fabricate stress-free Al/Ta multilayers with more than a thousand laminations for transmissive X-ray optics. The argon pressure was cycled between 5 and 50 mTorr under computer control in deposition of the aluminum and tantalum layers respectively in order to maintain strict planarity of the laminate.

A final example involves the deposition of highly refractory molybdenum metal coatings onto exceedingly soft plastic substrates. In this case coincidental control was practiced by varying the cathode current and consequent sputtering rate while holding the argon pressure constant. Stresses in coatings deposited at various rates were determined from the associated substrate bending. Elastic strains in the same coatings were deduced from X-ray peak shifts and lattice spacings normal to the plane of the films. Together these results yield the stress-strain plot of Fig. 9, where the central near-linear portion of the curve corresponds to the tensile-to-compressive stress transition and has a slope in good agreement with the appropriate combination of handbook elastic constants (140).

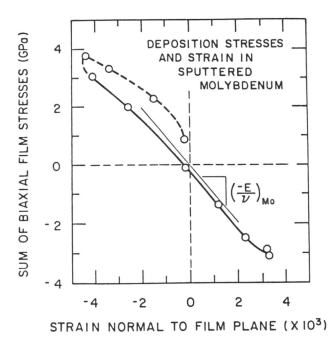

Figure 9: Sum of biaxial film stresses vs X-ray lattice strain in Mo films sputtered at various rates from a cylindrical magnetron with argon at 0.74 Pa pressure and deposited at a distance of 0.1 m (140).

The loop at the top of the curve corresponds to films in Zone 1' where the increasing microporosity gives rise to non-linear behavior. Again by varying only the sputtering rate, molybdenum films with tensile, zero, and compressive stress were deposited onto lacquered ABS plastic substrates of the type frequently used for decorative metallization. The low magnification photographs of Fig. 10 show the resultant cracked, specular, and buckled coatings. For such an application, where the substrate is non-conductive, heat-sensitive, and easily deformed, the technique of coincidental control is eminently suited by not requiring electrical coupling to the substrate and by the use of only a moderate amount of bombardment and consequent heating to achieve a stress-free, bulklike metallization.

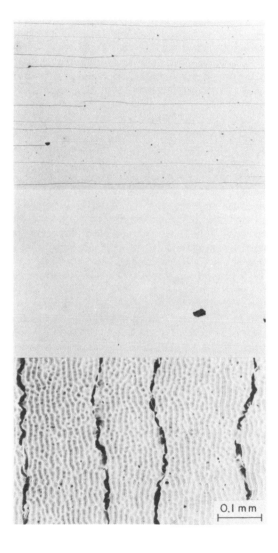

Figure 10: Coating failure modes on ABS plastic substrates observed by optical microscopy on molybdenum films sputter-deposited at rates of a) 0.23 nm/s, b) 1.5 nm/s, and c) 3.5 nm/s at a distance of 0.1 m from a cylindrical magnetron cathode operated in argon at 0.74 Pa pressure (140).

0.1 mm

21.4   MODELLING OF MATTER-ENERGY CO-DEPOSITION IN REFRACTORY COATINGS

The differing positions of the Zone 1-T and Zone 1priem -T boundaries in Fig. 4 are each determined by a balance of competing mechanisms, where the deposition of directionally diffuse coating flux favoring Zone 1' is clearly the more difficult for counteracting bombardment to overcome. The understanding and modelling of these two cases will necessarily also be distinct. A number of modelling approaches have been attempted for various sets of assumptions that throw light on portions of the processes at hand. These include ballistic computer simulations of various sophistication and scope, and parametric analysis based on continuum approximation. Ultimately it should be possible to formulate an analysis that will predict the dissimilar locations of the limiting boundaries and the interconnecting transition.

Brighton and Hubler (29) predict a critical ion-to-atom arrival ratio for relief of tensile intrinsic stress in the Zone 1-T structural transition by positing that the region affected by a collision cascade becomes effectively annealed and consequently stress free. Invoking the criterion that the input of binary collision cascades must be sufficiently dense to affect all deposited atoms, they obtained results agreeing in magnitude and energy dependence with observations on Hirsch and Varga (28) on bombarded germanium. While the mechanism of overlapping collision cascades is appealing, it lacks in this manifestation the capacity to simulate the continuous transition from tensile to compressive stress observed experimentally in a majority of cases.

The computer models of Müller (141,142) simulate the effects of energetic particle bombardment on the structures, densities, and stresses of vapor deposits incident without directional scattering, providing insights into the mechanisms at play in bombardment of both Zone 1 and Zone 1' microstructures. It has been demonstrated that energetic particle bombardment during growth can densify microporous structures by forward sputtering of condensed atoms from the advancing near-surface region into underlying pores in a steady state manner. Density increases have been simulated both by increasing the incident energy of metal vapor atoms above the thermal level (143) and by simultaneously bombarding with a secondary beam of inert or reactive gas. As expected, fewer bombarding gas atoms are required as their energy rises. Müller has found, however that pore bridging is promoted by transient diffusion during the dissipation of thermal spikes associated with energetic particle bombardment (144). Also observed is behavior suggesting the possibility of near-perfect epitaxy as the intensity of bombardment becomes great enough to eliminate microporosity. Müller has computed intrinsic stresses in the simulated films and found tensile stresses that pass through a maximum with increasing bombardment by inert gas or fast vapor atoms in a manner reminiscent of experimental observations (145). However, the experimentally observed continuous transition to compressive stress does not reasonably occur in the model, again raising a cautionary flag concerning the presently remaining deficiencies of the computer as an ultra-microscope.

The interchangeability of bombarding particle energy and flux can be quantitatively examined from Müller's results on Ni growing under Ar and self-bombardment (142,143). In Fig. 11 the reported packing densities have been replotted against the product of relative ion flux and the particle energy scaled to the sputtering threshold energy (21 eV) and raised to the powers of one (Fig. 11 (a)) and one-half (Fig. 11(b)). Four sets of results are included for nickel bombarded with varying fluxes of argon at 10

and 50 eV, at varying voltages with a fixed flux ratio, and with the nickel vapor accelerated in the absence of argon. Straight lines indicate the effect of varying the ion flux from
0 to 0.16 at the constant accelerating voltages of 10, 25, 50, 75, and 100 eV. Intermediate flux points reported by Müller at 10 and 50 eV are also indicated. Figure 11 reveals
that the square-root scaling of energy affords a consolidation of results along a linear
trendline.

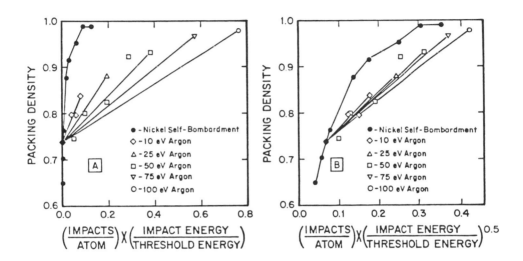

Figure 11: Simulated packing densities of nickel vapor deposits determined by molecular
dynamics computer modelling showing the densifying effects of Ni self-bombardment and
supplementary argon bombardment (142,143). Scaling the bombarding particle energy
to a) the first power and b) the one-half power reveals a linearization of results versus the
square root.

On the other hand, Yehoda et al. (146) find their experimental observations of void
fraction in ion bombarded germanium to scale as the first power of energy, in agreement
with the findings of Ziemann and Kay (30) for bias sputtering. Thus, in general it appears
that changes in density and derivative properties caused by irradiation with particles having energies in range of 10-100 eV or greater can be represented by functionality of the
form

$$X - X_o = \beta \cdot (J_i/J_v) \cdot (E_i/E_o)^p \tag{1}$$

where X is a property of interest for which X_o is a reference value, J_i/J_v is the ion-to-
vapor ratio, and E_i/E_o is the ratio of ion energy to a reference energy such as the sput-

tering threshold energy. The slope β is independent of the ion flux and particle energies but will depend on the relative ion and vapor atomic masses. The findings of 0.5 and 1.0 for the exponent p respectively for Ni and Ge may relate to the different natures of interatomic bonding in these materials (or to the two-dimensional nature of the simulation). Processing to a constant or completion value of $X = X_c$, say 95 percent density, enables a determination of p from the negative slope of $\log(J_i)$ vs $\log(E_i)$ as originated by Hoffman and Gaerttner (26) and developed by Harper et al (27).

Of special significance for plasma sputtered coatings are the results for self-bombardment ($J_i/J_v = 1$) shown in Fig. 11, where the individual particle energies varied from 0 to 2.6 eV. In contrast to gas bombardment it is clear that self-bombardment at low particle energies does not scale linearly with the square-root of energy, and is, moreover, more effective in increasing the packing density than bombardment with fewer but higher energy gas ions. These various observations imply, on the one hand, that a category of displacement mechanism dominates for bombardment with 10-100 eV particles, where the number of impacts and the particle energy are interchangeable in their effect and may be substituted one for the other using an energy scaling exponent that varies among classes of materials with different bonding types. On the other hand, the rather different behavior under low energy self-bombardment implies a fundamental change in the nature of the displacement cascades that more effectively suppresses microporosity. As pointed out by Müller (144), the self-energies required to simulate full density nickel fall well within the range of sputtered particle energies.

It seems evident that an advantageous route to achieving Zone T microstructures and properties in plasma sputtered refractory coatings with the least application of force is to take the greatest possible advantage of the self energies of the sputtered vapor particles. This is the situation represented along locus C in Fig. 4, achieved by sputtering at low pressures with ions heavier than the target atoms, so that vapor particles are the principal energetic species exiting the source. Additional atomic peening by higher energy gas neutrals reflected from the sputtering target should be largely unnecessary, although in many practical cases unavoidable. Where practical or desirable it should be possible to obtain Zone T microstructures with the most bulklike physical properties by judicious choice of gas and/or target material to minimize the energy of backscattered neutrals, thereby minimizing gas entrapment and gratuitous damage to the coating or substrate. Indeed under careful process tuning the possibility of epitaxial growth by coincidental control with a minimum of substrate heating is indicated. Where necessary, Zone T deposition can be attained under increased peening by backscattered neutrals or bias sputtering. Although the point of view adopted herein has been to apply just sufficient bombardment to overcome microporosity as promoted by directional scattering of the vapor flux, situations may arise in practice, say when sputtering heavy metals with argon, where gas scattering of the vapor is purposely increased to balance off excess atomic peening by backscattered neutrals.

In some cases, the excess bombardment and consequent compressive residual stress may be desired. It is commonly observed that the compressive residual stresses appear to reach a saturation level in coatings sputtered with sufficient bias or coincidental bombardment. From a consideration of the linear cascade theory of forward sputtering Windischmann (147) has shown that these saturation stresses correlate remarkably well with the product of elastic Young's modulus and molar volume over a wide selection of elements and nitrides sputtered from both plasma and ion beam sources. Of particular interest are his observations of Zone T properties in ion beam sputtered coatings of aluminum, aluminum nitride, and silicon. The fact that these elements are less massive than the argon sputtering ion implies that backscattered neutrals carried little energy to the coatings and that coincidental self-bombardment by the sputtered vapor was indeed sufficient to densify the structure into the Zone T configuration.

In summary, experimental and simulation studies have provided a fundamental understanding of the porous and evolutionary nature of the primitive Zone 1 growth structures of vapor deposited refractory materials, however the effect of directional diffusion of the vapor by gas scattering in plasma processes adds an additional factor that leads to marked further structural disorder and degradation of properties in Zone 1'. Application of energetic particle bombardment works to counteract these effects leading to densification and Zone T microstructure with bulklike properties and compressive residual stresses, when sufficient doses are administered to counteract low adatom mobility and the preferential accumulation on growth tips caused by oblique components of scattered vapor. The latter effect requires greater offsetting doses by conventional bias sputtering with consequent undesirable side effects such as gas entrapment and substrate damage. An alternative plasma deposition treatment is coincidental control, which effects a reduction of vapor scattering in concert with greater or lesser bombardment, depending on the choice of target and gas constituents, to enter Zone T. It appears that the critical bombardment for densification may follow a power scaling law, when administered by gas ions, but may be most effective requiring the least treatment, when administered by low energy vapor self-bombardment.

21.5 REFERENCES

1.   B.A. Movchan and A.V. Demchishin, Study of the structure and properties of thick vacuum condensates of nickel, titanium, tungsten, aluminum oxide and zirconium oxide. Fiz. Metal. Metalloved. 28: 653 (1969).

2.   D.J. Srolovitz, A. Mazor, and B.G. Bukiet, Analytical and numerical modeling of columnar evolution in thin films. J. Vac. Sci. Technol. A6: 2371 (1988).

3.   J.A. Thornton, Influence of apparatus geometry and deposition conditions on the structure and topography of thick sputtered coatings. J. Vac. Sci. Technol. 11: 666 (1974).

4.   J.A. Thornton and D.W. Hoffman, Stress-related effects in thin films, Thin Solid Films, in press.

5.   W.D. Westwood, Porosity in sputtered platinum films, J. Vac. Sci. Technol. 11: 466 (1974).

6.   S. Nakahara, K. Kuwahara, and A. Nishimura, Microstructure of permalloy and copper films obtained by vapor deposition at various incidence angles. Thin Solid Films 72: 297 (1980).

7.   D. Henderson, M.II. Brodsky, and P. Chaudhari, Simulation of structural anisotropy and void formation in amorphous thin films. Appl. Phys. Lett. 25: 641 (1974).

8.   S. Kim, D. Henderson, and P. Chaudhari, Computer simulation of amorphous thin films of hard spheres. Thin Solid Films 47: 155 (1977).

9. P. Meakin, R. Ramanlal, L.M. Sander, and R.C. Ball, Ballistic deposition on surfaces. Phys. Rev. A 34: 5091 (1986).

10. P.M. Fabis, Microporosity in 304 stainless steel films prepared by vapor quenching. Thin Solid Films 128: 57 (1985).

11. A.G. Dirks and H.J. Leamy, Columnar microstructure in vapor deposited thin films. Thin Solid Films 47: 219 (1977).

12. H.J. Leamy and A.G. Dirks, Microstructure and magnetism in amorphous rare-earth transition-metal thin films. I. Microstructure. J. Appl. Phys. 49: 3430 (1978).

13. R.C. Ball and T.A. Witten, Causality bound on the density of aggregates. Phys Rev. A 29: 2966 (1984).

14. P. Meakin, Effects of particle drift on diffusion-limited aggregation. Phys. Rev. B 28: 5221 (1983).

15. D.W. Hoffman and J.A. Thornton, Internal stresses in sputtered chromium. Thin Solid Films 40: 355 (1977).

16. D.W. Hoffman and J.A. Thornton, Internal stresses in Cr, Mo, Ta, and Pt films deposited by sputtering from a planar magnetron source. J. Vac. Sci. Technol. 20: 355 (1982).

17. R. Messier, A.P. Giri, and R.A. Roy, Revised structure zone model for thin film physical structure. J. Vac. Sci. Technol. A2: 500 (1984).

18. J.E. Yehoda and R. Messier, Are thin films physical structures fractals? Appl. Surf. Sci. 22/23: 590 (1985).

19. R. Messier, Toward a quantification of thin film morphology. J. Vac. Sci. Technol. A4: 490 (1986).

20. J.A. Thornton, The microstructure of sputter-deposited coatings. J. Vac. Sci. Technol. A4: 3059 (1986).

21. H.J. Leamy, G.H. Gilmer and A.G. Dirks, The microstructure of vapor deposited thin films. Current Topics in Materials Science 6: 309 (1980).

22. J. M. Seeman, Bias sputtering: its techniques and applications. Vacuum 17: 129 (1967).

23. O. Christensen, Characteristics and applications of bias sputtering. Solid State Technol. 13: 39 (1970).

24. J. L. Vossen, Control of film properties by rf-sputtering techniques. J. Vac. Sci. Technol. 8: 12 (1971).

25. W. D. Westwood, Glow discharge sputtering. Progr. in Surf. Sci. 7: 71 (1976).

26. D. W. Hoffman and M. R. Gaerttner, Modification of evaporated chromium by concurrent ion bombardment. J. Vac. Sci. Technol. 17:425 (1980).

27. J.M.E. Harper, J.J. Cuomo, R.J. Gambino and H.R. Kaufman, Modification of thin film properties by ion bombardment during deposition. p. 127 in Ion Bombardment Modification of Surfaces, ed. by O. Auciello and R. Kelly (Elsevier, Amsterdam 1984).

28. E. H. Hirsch and I.K. Varga, Thin film annealing by ion bombardment. Thin Solid Films 69: 99 (1980).

29. D. R. Brighton and G. K. Hubler, Binary collision cascade prediction of critical ion-to-atom arrival ratio in the production of thin films with reduced intrinsic stress. Nucl. Instr. and Meth. B28: 527 (1987).

30. P. Ziemann and E. Kay, Model of bias sputtering in a dc-triode configuration applied to the production of Pd films. J. Vac. Sci. Technol. 21: 828 (1982).

31. P. Ziemann and E. Kay, Correlation between the ion bombardment during film growth of Pd films and their structural and electrical properties. J. Vac. Sci. Technol. A1: 512 (1983).

32. E. Kay and G. Heim, Model of bias sputtering applied to the control of Nb film properties. J. Appl. Phys. 49: 4862 (1978).

33. J. A. Thornton, The influence of bias sputter parameters on thick copper coatings deposited using a hollow cathode. Thin Solid Films 40: 335 (1977).

34. W.D. Davis and T. A. Vanderslice, Ion energies at the cathode of a glow discharge. Phys. Rev. 131: 219 (1963).

35. R. T. C. Tsui, Calculation of ion bombarding energy and its distribution in rf sputtering. Phys. Rev. 168: 107 (1968).

36. J.W. Coburn and E. Kay, Positive-ion bombardment of substrates in rf glow discharge sputtering. J. Appl. Phys. 43: 4965 (1972).

37. D.G. Teer, Adhesion of ion plated films and energies of deposition. J. Adhes. 8: 289 (1977).

38. D. M. Mattox, Film deposition using accelerated ions, Electrochem. Tech. 2: 295 (1964).

39. R.L. Boxman and S. Goldsmith, Cathode-spot arc coatings: physics, deposition and heating rates and some examples. Surf. and Coat. Technol. 33: 153 (1987).

40. B. Window and N. Savvides, Charged particle fluxes from planar magnetron sources. J. Vac. Sci. Technol. A4: 196 (1986).

41. N. Savvides and B. Window, Unbalanced magnetron ion-assisted deposition and property modification of thin films. J. Vac. Sci. Technol. A4: 504 (1986).

42. R. Frerichs, Superconductive films made by protected sputtering of tantalum or niobium. J. Appl. Phys. 33: 1898 (1962).

43. L.I. Maissel and P. M. Schaible, Thin films deposited by bias sputtering. J. Appl. Phys. 36: 237 (1965).

44. J. A. Thornton, High rate sputtering techniques. Thin Solid Films 80: 1 (1980).

45. J. L. Vossen and J. J. Cuomo, p. 56 in Thin Film PRocesses ed. by J. L. Vossen and W. Kern (Academic Press, New York 1978).

46. J. J. Cuomo, J.M.E. Harper, C.R. Guarnieri, D.S. Yee, L.J. Attanasio, C.T. Wu and R. H. Hammond, Modification of niobium film stress by low-energy ion bombardment during deposition. J. Vac. Sci. Technol. 20: 349 (1982).

47. H. F. Winters and E. Kay, Gas incorporation into sputtered films. J. Appl. Phys. 38: 3928 (1967).

48. J. Comas and E. A. Wolicki, Argon content in (111) silicon for sputtering energies below 200 eV. J. Electrochem. Soc. 117: 1197 (1970).

49. I. V. Mitchell and R. C. Maddison, Gas incorporation in sputtered and evaporated gold films. Vacuum 21: 591 (1971).

50. G. Heim and E. Kay, Ion implantation during film growth and its effect on the superconducting properties of niobium. J. Appl. Phys. 46: 4006 (1975).

51. E. Klokholm and B.S. Berry, Intrinsic stress in evaporated metal films. J. Electrochem. Soc. 115: 823 (1968).

52. K.-H. Müller, Ion-beam induced epitaxial vapor-phase growth: A molecular-dynamics study. Phys. Rev. B 35: 7906 (1987).

53. R. E. Jones, C. L. Standley and L.I. Maissel, Re-emission coefficients of Si and SiO₂ films deposited through rf and dc sputtering. J. Appl. Phys. 38: 4656 (1967).

54. L. I. Maissel, R.E. Jones and C.L. Standley, Re-emission of sputtered SiO₂ during growth and its relation to film quality. IBM J. Res. and Dev. 14: 76 (1970).

55. J. L. Vossen and J. J. O'Neill, Jr., rf Sputtering processes. RCA Review 29: 149 (1968).

56. A. G. Blachman, Stress and resistivity control in sputtered molybdenum films and comparison with sputtered gold. Met. Trans. 2: 699 (1971).

57. E. H. Hirsch and I.K. Varga, Thin film annealing by ion bombardment. Thin Solid Films 69: 99 (1980).

58. D. M. Mattox and G. J. Kominiak, Structure modification by ion bombardment during deposition. J. Vac. Sci. Technol. 9: 528 (1971).

59. R. D. Bland, G.J. Kominiak and D. M. Mattox, Effect of ion bombardment during deposition on thick metal and ceramic deposits. J. Vac. Sci. Technol. 11: 671 (1974).

60. J. E. Greene and S. A. Barnett, Ion-surface interactions during vapor phase crystal growth by sputtering, MBE and plasma enhanced CVD: Applications to semiconductors. J. Vac. Sci. Technol. 21: 285 (1982).

61. G. K. Wehner, Growth of solid layers on substrates which are kept under ion bombardment before and during deposition, U. S. Patent 3,021,271 Feb. 1962.

62. T. N. Kennedy, Sputtered insulator film contouring over substrate topography. J. Vac. Sci. Technol. 13: 1135 (1976).

63. C. Y. Ting, V. J. Vivalda and H. G. Schaefer, Study of planarized sputter-deposited SiO₂. J. Vac. Sci. Technol. 15: 1105 (1978).

64. H. P. Bader and M. A. Lardon, Planarization by rf bias sputtering of aluminum as studied experimentally and by computer simulation. J. Vac. Sci. Technol. A3: 2167 (1985).

65. N. McIntyre and S.J. Wright, Characterization of bias sputtered metallization for IC technology. Vacuum 34: 963 (1984).

66. Y. Homma and S. Tsunekawa, Planar deposition of aluminum by rf/dc sputtering with rf bias. J. Electrochem. Soc. 132: 1466 (1985).

67. D. W. Skelly and L. A. Gruenke, Significant improvement in step coverage using bias sputtered aluminum. J. Vac. Sci. Technol. A4: 457 (1986).

68. J. F. Smith, Influence of dc bias sputtering during aluminum metallization. Solid State Technology 27: 135 (1984).

69. J. F. Smith, F.T. Zold and W. Class, The influence of bias sputtering and wafer preheating on the step coverage of sputtered aluminum. Thin Solid Films 96: 291 (1982).

70. J. J. Cuomo, R. J. Gambino and R. Rosenberg, The influence of bias on the deposition of metallic films in rf and dc sputtering. J. Vac. Sci. Technol. 11: 34 (1974).

71. A. G. Blachman, dc bias-sputtered aluminum films. J. Vac. Sci. Technol. 10: 299 (1973).

72. C. W. Chen and C. S. Alford, Optimization of the sputter deposition process for preparing smooth coatings of beryllium on microspherical substrates. J. Vac. Sci. Technol. A6: 128 (1988).

73. J.W. Patten and E.D. McClanahan, Effect of substrate bias and deposition temperature on the properties of thick sputtered chromium deposits. J. Appl. Phys. 43: 4811 (1972).

74. J.W.Patten, E.D. McClanahan and J.W. Johnston, Room temperature recrystallization in thick bias-sputtered copper deposits. J. Appl. Phys. 42: 4371 (1971).

75. B. Window, F. Sharples and N. Savvides, Plastic flow in ion-assisted deposition of refractory metals. J. Vac. Sci. Technol. A6: 2333 (1988).

76. R. Glang, R. A. Holmwood and P.C. Furois, Bias sputtering of molybdenum films. Proc. 3rd. Int. Vacuum Congress, Stuttgart, v.2, pt.3, (Pergamon, 1966-67).

77. F. M. d'Heurle, Resistivity and structure of sputtered molybdenum films, Trans. AIME 236: 321 (1966).

78. R. S. Nowicki, W. D. Buckley, W. D. Mackintosh and I.V. Mitchell, Effect of deposition parameters on properties of rf sputtered molybdenum films. J. Vac. Sci. Technol. 11: 675 (1974).

79. C. T. Wu, Intrinsic stress of magnetron-sputtered niobium films. Thin Solid Films 64: 103 (1979).

80. T. Lin, K.Y. Ahn, J.M.E. Harper, P.B. Madakson and P.M. Fryer, Relationship between substrate bias and microstructure in magnetron sputtered Al-Cu films. Thin Solid Films 154: 81 (1987).

81. C. Leu, G. Chen, J. M. Sivertsen and J. H. Judy, Epitaxial growth of Co-Cr films and their characterization. J. Appl. Phys. 57: 4003 (1985).

82. M. Ohkoshi and T. Kusuda, Effect of negative substrate bias on the film structure and magnetic properties in sputter-deposited Co-Cr films. J. Vac. Sci. Technol. A5: 2859 (1987).

83. S. M. Shin, M.A. Ray, J.M. Rigsbee and J.E. Greene, Growth of metastable $Cu_{1-x}Cr_x$ solid solutions by ion mixing. Appl. Phys. Lett. 43: 249 (1983).

84. P. Chaudhari, J.J. Cuomo and R.J. Gambino, Amorphous metallic films for bubble domain applications, IBM J. Res. Dev. 17: 66 (1973).

85. R. J. Gambino and J.J. Cuomo, Selective resputtering-induced anisotropy in amorphous films. J. Vac. Sci. Technol. 15: 296 (1978).

86. T. Kusuda, S. Honda and M. Ohkoshi, Perpendicular anisotropy of bias-sputtered GdCo film. J. Appl. Phys. 53: 2338 (1982).

87. C. T. Chen and W.L. Wilson, Jr., Magnetic properties of bias-sputtered Gd-Co-Fe amorphous films with uniaxial perpendicular anisotropy. J. Appl. Phys. 49: 1756 (1978).

88. E. Stern and T.B. Light, Preferred orientation in bias-sputtered nickel chromium films. Appl. Phys. Lett. 13: 381 (1968).

89. R. W. Knoll, E.D. McClanahan and H. E. Kjarmo, Heterogeneous growth in transition metal-rare earth films during bias sputter deposition. Thin Solid Films 118: 93 (1984).

90. L. D. Hartsough, Resistivity of bias-sputtered Ti-W films. Thin Solid Films 64: 17 (1979).

91. B. Eser, R.E. Ogilvie and K.A. Taylor, The Effect of bias on dc and rf sputtered WC-Co coatings. Thin Solid Films 67: 265 (1980).

92. S. D. Dahlgren and A. G. Graybeal, Reduced nickel concentration in a stainless steel deposit from bias sputtering. J. Appl. Phys. 41: 3181 (1970).

93. T. Goto and P. Anprung, Fabrication of NbN films by dc bias sputtering and their application to superconducting bridges. Jpn. J. Appl. Phys. (Part 1) 22: 955 (1983).

94. L.C. Wu, J.L. Zilko, J.L. Mukherjee, J.E. Greene and H.E. Cook, Tribology, chemistry and structure of bias sputtered TiC films on steel substrates, p. 364. in Wear of Materials ed. by W.A. Glaeser, K.C. Ludema and S.K. Rhee, (ASME, New York 1977).

95. J.-E. Sundgren, B.-O. Johansson and S.-E. Karlsson, Influence of substrate bias on composition and structure of reactively rf-sputtered TiC films. Thin Solid Films 80: 77 (1981).

96. Y. Igasaki and H. Mitsuhashi, The Effects of substrate bias on the structural and electrical properties of TiN films prepared by reactive rf sputtering. Thin Solid Films 70: 17 (1980).

97. J. M. Poitevin, G. Lamperiere and J. Tardy, Influence of substrate bias on the composition, structure and electrical properties of reactively dc sputtered TiN films. Thin Solid Films 97: 69 (1982).

98. W.W. Carson, Sputter gas pressure and dc substrate bias effects on thick rf diode sputtered films of Ti-Oxycarbides. J. Vac. Sci. Technol. 12: 845 (1975).

99. J.E. Greene, R.E. Klinger, L.B. Welsh and F.R. Szofran, Growth and characterization of doped ZrO_2 and CeO_2 films deposited by bias sputtering. J. Vac. Sci. Technol. 14: 177 (1977).

100. R. W. Knoll and E.R. Bradley, Correlation between the stress and microstructure in bias-sputtered $ZrO_2 - Y_2O_3$ films. Thin Solid Films 117: 201 (1984).

101. D. M. Mattox and G.J. Kominiak, Physical properties of thick sputter-deposited glass films, J. Electrochem. Soc. 120: 1535 (1973).

102. K.L. Chopra, Thin Film Phenomena (McGraw-Hill, New York, 1969) p.311.

103. P.R. Stuart, Some measurements of stress in thin films prepared by low pressure triode sputtering. Vacuum 19: 507 (1969).

104. R. Messier, T. Takamori, and R. Roy, Structure-composition variation in rf-sputtered films of Ge caused by process parameter changes. J. Vac. Sci. Technol. 13: 1060 (1976).

105. F. Shoji and S. Nagata, Internal stress in thin metal films prepared by low pressure plasma sputtering. Oyo Butsuri 42: 115 (1973).

106. E. Krikorian and R.J. Sneed, Deposition of tantalum, tantalum oxide, and tantalum nitride with controlled electrical characteristics. J. Appl. Phys. 37: 3674 (1966).

107. S.S. Lau and R.H. Mills, Properties of rf sputtered β –Ta films. Phys. Stat. Sol.(a) 17: 609 (1973).

108. W.W.Y. Lee, High resistivity of dc-sputtered metal films. J. Appl. Phys. 42: 4366 (1971).

109. R.C. Sun, T.C. Tisone, and P.D. Cruzan, Internal stresses and resistivity of low-voltage sputtered tungsten films, J. Appl. Phys. 44: 1009 (1973).

110. R.S. Wagner, A.K. Sinha, T.T. Sheng, H.J. Levinstein, and F.B. Alexander, Tungsten metallization for LSI applications. J. Vac. Sci. Technol. 11: 582 (1974).

111. S.P. Murarka, R.F. diode sputtered platinum films. Thin Solid Films 23: 323 (1974).

112. J.A. Thornton and D.W. Hoffman, Internal stresses in Ti, Ni, Mo and Ta films deposited by cylindrical magnetron sputtering. J. Vac.Sci. Technol. 14: 164 (1977).

113. D.W. Hoffman and J.A. Thornton, The compressive stress transition in Al, V, Zr, Nb, and W metal films sputtered at low working pressures. Thin Solid Films 45: 387 (1977).

114. T. Motohiro and Y. Taga, Monte carlo simulation of thermalization process of sputtered particles. Surf. Sci. 134: L494 (1983).

115. A. Graz-Marti and J.A. Valles-Abarca, Slowing down and thermalization of sputtered particle fluxes: Energy distributions. J. Appl. Phys. 54: 1071 (1983).

116. R. E. Somekh, The thermalization of energetic atoms during the sputtering process. J. Vac. Sci. Technol. A2: 1285 (1984).

117. D.W. Hoffman and C.M. Kukla, Determination of film stresses during sputter deposition using an in situ probe. J. Vac. Sci. Technol. A3: 2600 (1985).

118. R.W. Hoffman, Mechanical properties of thin condensed films. in Physics of Thin Films Vol. 3: G. Hass and R.E. Thun, eds. (Academic Press, New York, 1966).

119. J.Z. Briggs and R.Q. Barr, Molybdenum. in Metals Handbook Ninth Edition, Vol. 2 (American Society for Metals, Metals Park, Ohio, 1979) p. 771.

120. J.E. Nestell,Jr. and R.W. Christy, Reflectance and structure of evaporated chromium and molybdenum films. J. Vac. Sci. Technol. 15: 366 (1978).

121. D.W. Hoffman, Stress and property control in sputtered metal films without substrate bias. Thin Solid Films 107: 353 (1983).

122. F. D'Heurle, Aluminum films deposited by rf sputtering. Metall. Trans. 1: 725 (1970).

123. D.W. Hoffman and J.A. Thornton, Compressive stress and inert gas in Mo films sputtered from a cylindrical-post magnetron with Ne, Ar, Kr, and Xe. J. Vac. Sci. Technol. 17: 380 (1980).

124. J.A. Thornton and D.W. Hoffman, Internal stresses in amorphous silicon films deposited by cylindrical magnetron sputtering using Ne, Ar, Kr, Xe, and Ar + H_2. J. Vac. Sci. Technol. 18: 203 (1981).

125. W.W. Carson, Getter pumping to allow economical sputtering with xenon. Thin Solid Films 40: 385 (1977).

126. A. Bensaoula, J.C. Wolfe, A. Ignatiev, F-O. Fong, and T-S. Leung, Direct-current-magnetron deposition of molybdenum and tungsten with rf-substrate bias. J. Vac. Sci. Technol. A2: 389 (1984).

127. J.A. Thornton and D.W. Hoffman, The influence of discharge current on the intrinsic stress in Mo films deposited using cylindrical and planar magnetron sputtering sources. J. Vac. Sci. Technol. A3: 576 (1985).

128. D.W. Hoffman and P.J. Goodsmith, Decorative metallizing by magnetron sputtering - effects of geometry on film properties. Trans. SAE 88: 808 (1979).

129. D.W. Hoffman and J.A. Thornton, Effects of substrate orientation and rotation on internal stresses in sputtered metal films. J. Vac. Sci. Technol. 16: 134 (1979).

130. S.M. Rossnagel, Gas density reduction effects in magnetrons. J. Vac. Sci. Technol. A6: 19 (1988).

131. A. Entenberg, V. Lindberg, K. Fletcher, A. Gatesman, and R.S. Horwath, Stress measurement in sputtered copper films on flexible polyimide substrates. J. Vac. Sci.Technol. A5: 3373 (1987).

132. K.W. Bieg, Internal stress and mechanical properties of planar-magnetron-sputtered Mo-Ru-B alloys, Thin Solid Films 96: 161 (1982); K.W. Bieg, Characteristics of magnetron-sputtered metallic glass internal confinement fusion target materials. J. Vac. Sci. Technol. 20: 1347 (1982).

133. A.P. Thakoor, J.L. Lamb, R.M. Williams, and S.K. Khanna, Internal stresses in wear and corrosion resistant amorphous metallic coatings of $(W_{0.6}Re_{0.4})_{76}B_{24})$ and $(Mo_{0.6}Ru_{0.4})_{82}B_{18}$. J. Vac. Sci. Technol. A3: 600 (1985).

134. R.E. Cuthrell, D.M. Mattox, C.R. Peeples, P.L. Dreike and K.P. Lamppa, Residual stress anisotropy, stress control and resistivity in post cathode magnetron sputter-deposited molybdenum films, J. Vac. Sci. Technol. A6: (1988).

135. G. Este and W.D. Westwood, Stress control in reactively sputtered AlN and TiN films, J. Vac. Sci. Technol. A5: 1892 (1987).

136. Z.H. Barber and R.E. Somekh, Magnetron sputtering of $Cu_{55}Ni_{45}$, Vacuum 34: 991 (1984).

137. Y. Hoshi, M. Matsuoka and M. Naoe, Dependence of magnetic properties of Co-Pt films on sputtering conditions. J. Appl. Phys. 57: 4022 (1985).

138. S. Nakahara, M. Hong, R.B. van Dover, E.M. Gyorgy, and D.D. Bacon, Micro-structures of thin sputtered amorphous $Tb_{0.26}Fe_{0.74}$ and polycrystalline Fe films. J. Vac. Sci. Technol. A4: 543 (1986).

139. A.F. Jankowski, R.M. Bionta, and P.C. Gabriele, Internal stress minimization in the fabrication of transmissive multilayer X-ray optics. J. Vac. Sci. Technol. A6: in press.

140. D.W. Hoffman and C. Peters, Control of stress and properties in sputtered metal films on nonconductive and heat-sensitive substrates. in Proceedings of the IXth Int. Vac. Cong. and Vth Int. Conf. on Sol. Surf. (Associacion Espanola Del Vacio, Madrid, 1983) p. 415.

141. K.-H. Müller, Model for ion-assisted thin-film densification, <u>J. Appl. Phys.</u> 59: 2803 (1986).

142. K.-H. Müller, Ion-beam-induced epitaxial vapor-phase growth: A molecular-dynamics study. <u>Phys. Rev.</u> B 35: 7906 (1987).

143. K.-H. Müller, Role of incident kinetic energy of adatoms in thin film growth. <u>Surf. Sci.</u> 184: L375 (1987).

144. K.-H. Müller, Monte Carlo calculation for structural modifications in ion-assisted thin film deposition due to thermal spikes. <u>J. Vac. Sci. Technol.</u> A4: 184 (1986).

145. K.-H. Müller, Stress and microstructure of sputter-deposited thin films: Molecular dynamics investigations, <u>J. Appl. Phys.</u> 62: 1796 (1987).

146. J.E. Yehoda, B. Hand, K. Vedam, and R. Messier, Investigation of the void structure in amorphous Germanium thin films as a function of low-energy ion bombardment. <u>J. Vac. Sci. Technol.</u> A6: 1631 (1988).

147. H. Windischmann, An intrinsic stress scaling law for polycrystalline thin films prepared by ion beam sputtering. <u>J. Appl. Phys.</u> 62: 1800 (1987).

INDEX